ENCYCLOPEDIA OF WORLD BIOGRAPHY

16

ENCYCLOPEDIA OF WORLD BIOGRAPHY

SECOND EDITION

Vitoria
Zworykin
16

GALE

DETROIT • NEW YORK • TORONTO • LONDON

Staff

Senior Editor: Paula K. Byers
Project Editor: Suzanne M. Bourgoin
Managing Editor: Neil E. Walker

Editorial Staff: Luann Brennan, Frank V. Castronova, Laura S. Hightower, Karen E. Lemerand, Stacy A. McConnell, Jennifer Mossman, Maria L. Munoz, Katherine H. Nemeh, Terrie M. Rooney, Geri Speace

Permissions Manager: Susan M. Tosky
Permissions Specialist: Maria L. Franklin
Permissions Associate: Michele M. Lonoconus
Image Cataloger: Mary K. Grimes

Production Director: Mary Beth Trimper
Production Manager: Evi Seoud
Production Associate: Shanna Heilveil
Product Design Manager: Cynthia Baldwin
Senior Art Director: Mary Claire Krzewinski

Research Manager: Victoria B. Cariappa
Research Specialists: Michele P. LaMeau, Andrew Guy Malonis, Barbara McNeil, Gary J. Oudersluys
Research Associates: Julia C. Daniel, Tamara C. Nott, Norma Sawaya, Cheryl L. Warnock
Research Assistant: Talitha A. Jean

Graphic Services Supervisor: Barbara Yarrow
Image Database Supervisor: Randy Bassett
Imaging Specialist: Mike Lugosz

Manager of Data Entry Services: Eleanor M. Allison
Data Entry Coordinator: Kenneth D. Benson

Manager of Technology Support Services: Theresa A. Rocklin
Programmers/Analysts: Mira Bossowska, Jeffrey Muhr, Christopher Ward

Copyright © 1998
Gale Research
835 Penobscot Bldg.
Detroit, MI 48226-4094

ISBN 0-7876-2221-4 (Set)
ISBN 0-7876-2556-6 (Volume 16)

Library of Congress Cataloging-in-Publication Data

Encyclopedia of world biography / [edited by Suzanne Michele Bourgoin and Paula Kay Byers].
    p. cm.
    Includes bibliographical references and index.
    Summary: Presents brief biographical sketches which provide vital statistics as well as information on the importance of the person listed.
    ISBN 0-7876-2221-4 (set : alk. paper)
    1. Biography—Dictionaries—Juvenile literature. [1. Biography.]
I. Bourgoin, Suzanne Michele, 1968- . II. Byers, Paula K. (Paula Kay), 1954- .
CT 103.E56   1997
920′ .003—dc21
                              97-42327
                                  CIP
                                  AC

Printed in the United States of America
10 9 8 7 6 5 4 3 2

ENCYCLOPEDIA OF WORLD BIOGRAPHY

16

V

Francisco de Vitoria

The Spanish theologian and political theorist Francisco de Vitoria (ca. 1483-1546) was the first great theorist of modern international law. He provided an updated, if uneasy, justification for Spain's conquests in the New World.

L ittle is known of the early life of Francisco de Vitoria. He studied at Burgos and taught at the universities of Valladolid (1523-1526) and of Salamanca. At the latter institution, in 1539, he delivered his famous lectures on law, war, and the New World, eventually published as *De Indis et de jure belli relectiones* (*On the Indians and the Law of War*).

As a Dominican friar, Vitoria was deeply involved with the teachings on theology and politics of his great predecessor St. Thomas Aquinas. Yet there were worlds of difference between the Mediterranean-centered civilization of the 13th-century Angelic Doctor and the ocean-spanning Hapsburg Empire of Vitoria's day. Vitoria and his colleagues at Salamanca undertook to reconcile these differences with established doctrine. Their success produced a body of theoretical legal principles for the age of European imperialism and the nation-state.

By 1539 Spain (then part of the Hapsburg Empire) was well entrenched in the Americas—but old doubts about its exercise of sovereignty persisted. Vitoria, in effect, revised the medieval doctrines (derived in part from Roman law) on the laws of God, nature, and nations. In brief, these doctrines stated that God's law, known only in full to Him, could be apprehended by humanity, in part, through divine

revelation and through right reason. By means of the latter, men could discover those practices that were universally just. They were then gradually incorporated into customary law or framed by the just ruler as positive law. The law of nations allowed different peoples to live together under the same ruler; it also retained what was left of the spontaneous, natural law relations between individuals after they had passed out of the "state of nature" into political life.

Vitoria adapted the doctrine of the law of nature to the new conditions. The law of nature became a public law that regulated relations between territorial states, which, because of their sovereign status, resembled the sovereign individuals of the prepolitical "state of nature." The law of nature regulated their relations, irrespective of their religious or political convictions; and this law, now called international law, applied to the conduct of and grounds for war as well. Although the pope continued to exercise a spiritual dominion over Christendom, Christendom was no longer the whole world—which was now seen to be divided among legally independent states. With this formula, Vitoria laid to rest the political universalism of the Middle Ages; and he denied the superior right of Christian princes to conquer and rule over remote heathen peoples by virtue of the latters' religious "errors."

Vitoria, however, upheld the pope's authority to entrust one Christian power with the task of converting the heathen. He also included among the rights of nations the right to enter into trade relations and to export missionaries for peaceful evangelical work. Moreover, if the state to which these benign and pacific agents were dispatched forcefully repelled or mistreated them in any way, these measures could constitute grounds for just war, conquest, and subsequent administration of the offending state. Finally, said Vitoria, such administration should take the form of a guard-

1

ianship concerned with the material—and, above all, spiritual—welfare of the conquered peoples.

Initial hostility to Vitoria's views eventually gave way to recognition of their utility and to their partial incorporation into Spanish imperial law. Vitoria died in Salamanca on Aug. 12, 1546.

Further Reading

Vitoria's Latin texts appear as volume 7 of the series *Classics of International Law* (1917). Three books by J. H. Parry provide the intellectual and historical setting: *The Spanish Theory of Empire* (1940), *The Age of Reconnaissance* (1963), and *The Spanish Seaborne Empire* (1966). Vitoria's place in the history of Spanish and European thought is evaluated in Friedrich Heer, *The Intellectual History of Europe,* vol. 2 (1968), and in Frederick Copleston, *A History of Philosophy,* vol. 3, pt. 2 (1963). □

Philippe de Vitry

Philippe de Vitry (1291-1360) was a French poet, composer, and churchman-statesman. His treatise *Ars nova* became the rallying cry for all "modern" composers after about 1320.

Born in Paris, Philippe de Vitry was the son of a royal notary. Philippe served several French kings, carrying out political missions that took him to southern France and a meeting with the Pope at Avignon. As a cleric, he received several money-producing canonates; in 1351 he became bishop of Meaux near Paris. One of his friends, Italy's leading poet, Petrarch, in a letter of 1350, called Vitry the foremost French poet of his time.

Nearly all Vitry's literary works are lost. Especially regrettable is the loss of his French poetry set to music, ballades and rondeaux in which he created a new style in song anticipating Guillaume de Machaut. Surviving are one ballade without music; two longer poems, one written in reference to a crusade planned for 1335 by King Philip VI; and two poems that serve one of his 12 extant motets. Of Vitry's Latin poems only one has reached us outside of those that are incorporated in his motets.

Vitry's earliest musical works, five motets, are preserved in a musical appendix added in 1316 to a moralistic romance, *Le roman de Fauvel,* written in 1314. Seven motets by Vitry, mostly composed between 1320 and 1335, are included in later collections, and the texts of a thirteenth work survive in one of the many additional manuscripts that include these pieces. In his motets Vitry emerges as the first highly individual composer. Each work is a distinctive work of art, expresses personal ideas, and is characteristically shaped.

The new techniques which Vitry embraced in his music he expounded in his famous treatise *Ars nova* (ca. 1320). It is mainly through him that these techniques gained widespread acceptance. They include a new system of propor-

tional tempo changes and meters, including the adoption of the formerly neglected duple meter beside the triple meter; the introduction of the intervals of the third and sixth as consonances, considered as dissonant before him, and therewith of the triad and what we now call its first inversion; a freer use of accidentals; and the employment of new, smaller note values.

In addition to the new ballade style, Vitry created a new technique in motet composition, today called isorhythm. This consists in employing a long and complex rhythmic pattern, which governs one or all voice parts of a motet in one of the following ways: both melody and rhythmic pattern may be repeated, sometimes in a new tempo, usually twice as fast; the rhythmic pattern may be repeated but superimposed on new melodic content; or the pattern may be divided into several subpatterns, which, with ever new melodic content, may be repeated in an arbitrary order and any number of times. This highly complex method has been said to foreshadow some 20th-century approaches.

Further Reading

Vitry's music is available in a modern edition by Leo Schrade. Information on him appears in Gustave Reese, *Music in the Middle Ages* (1940); Paul Henry Lang, *Music in Western Civilization* (1941); and Denis Stevens and Alec Robertson, eds., *The Pelican History of Music,* vol. 1 (1960). □

Elio Vittorini

The Italian novelist, translator, editor, and journalist Elio Vittorini (1908-1966) helped to prepare the ground for the Italian neorealist movement.

Elio Vittorini was born on July 23, 1908, at Siracusa, Sicily, the son of a railroad employee. His formal education was scant and rudimentary; after a few years at a technical school he left Sicily at the age of 17 and worked at road construction near Udine in northern Italy. In the late 1920s he quit road work and moved to Florence, where he settled with his wife, Salvatore Quasimodo's sister. There he held a job as proofreader for the daily *La Nazione* and for some time was editor of the review *Solaria.* During this time he began writing short stories, which appeared in *Solaria.* He learned English from an old printer, who had been abroad, and began translating American fiction; then he was forced to leave the paper, suffering from lead poisoning.

While writing *Conversazione in Sicilia,* which he finished in the winter of 1939, Vittorini moved to Milan. After a first edition in 1941, the book was attacked, then withdrawn. In 1943 he was jailed for a time for political reasons. He joined the Communist party but withdrew again after a public debate in the late 1940s, and in the 1958 elections he was the Radical candidate in Milan. From 1945 to 1947 he edited the Marxist review *Il Politecnico.* Later he edited the review *Il Menabò* together with Italo Calvino. The death of his son Giusto in 1955 caused Vittorini to interrupt for some time, his work on his last novel, *Le città del mondo*. It remained unfinished when he died on Feb. 14, 1966, in Milan.

Most of Vittorini's works are autobiographical in one sense or another. Through his use of narration by implication and a fuguelike technique, he exerted a considerable influence on the postwar generation of Italian writers. Most of the stories contained in *Piccola borghesia* (1931) had been published in *Solaria*. *Viaggio in Sardegna* (1936) is only seemingly a travel book, a report of a trip to Sardinia. In a deeper sense the trip is seen as a "return to the fountains," a retrieval of the golden age of childhood in Sicily, the primeval state of human existence.

Vittorini's first novel, *Il garofano rosso* (1948), was begun about the same time as *Viaggio in Sardegna,* toward the end of 1932, and published in installments in *Solaria*. Vittorini was later dissatisfied with this perfect specimen of a bourgeois psychological novel and rejected the approach he had used. *Conversazione in Sicilia* (1941), Vittorini's major work, had a considerable impact upon the younger generation of writers. Built around key images, the novel on the surface is the story of a young Linotype operator's brief visit to his birthplace, Siracusa, in Sicily. The underlying theme, however, is the spiritual experience of rediscovering the genuine sense of life of his youth and thus regaining the lost meaning of his existence.

Uomini e no (1945) is Vittorini's contribution to the genre of the Resistance novel. *Il Sempione strizza l'occhio al Fréjus* (1947) is a short novel about a worker's family in a suburb of Milan with hardly a plot. *Le donne di Messina* (1949), Vittorini's most involved novel—there exist several versions—deals with the conflict between individualism and socialism. *La Garibaldina* (1950), Vittorini's last piece of fiction, is in a way similar to *Conversazione in Sicilia* as it recasts the "return to the fountains" in almost identical fashion. With the fragment of a novel, *Le città del mondo* (1969), Vittorini returned again to Sicily. *Diario in pubblico* (1957) is a selective collection of Vittorini's critical writing.

Further Reading

Most of the writing on Vittorini is in Italian. In English, an excellent study of his works appears in Donald N. Heiney, *Three Italian Novelists: Moravia, Pavese, Vittorini* (1968). Recommended for general historical background is Sergio Pacifici, *A Guide to Contemporary Italian Literature* (1962).

Additional Sources

Potter, Joy Hambuechen, *Elio Vittorini,* Boston: Twayne Publishers, 1979. □

Antonio Vivaldi

Antonio Vivaldi (1678-1741) was an Italian violinist and composer whose concertos were widely known and influential throughout Europe.

Antonio Vivaldi was born in Venice on March 4, 1678. His first music teacher was his father, Giovanni Battista Vivaldi. The elder Vivaldi was a well-respected violinist, employed at the church of St. Mark's. It is possible, though not proved, that as a boy Antonio also studied with the composer Giovanni Legrenzi.

Antonio was trained for a clerical as well as a musical life. After going through the various preliminary stages, he was ordained a priest in March 1703. (He was later nicknamed "the red priest" because he was redheaded.) His active career, however, was devoted to music. In the autumn of 1703 he was appointed a violin teacher at the Ospitale della Pietà in Venice. A few years later he was made conductor of the orchestra at the same institution. Under Vivaldi's direction, this orchestra gave many brilliant concerts and achieved an international reputation.

Vivaldi remained at the Pietà until 1740. But his long years there were broken by the numerous trips he took, for professional purposes, to Italian and foreign cities. He went, among other places, to Vienna in 1729-1730 and to Amsterdam in 1737-1738. Within Italy he traveled to various cities to direct performances of his operas. He left Venice for the last time in 1740. He died in Vienna on July 26 or 27, 1741.

Vivaldi was prolific in vocal and instrumental music, sacred and secular. According to the latest research, his compositions may be numbered as follows, though not all these compositions are preserved: 48 operas (some in collaboration with other composers); 59 secular cantatas and serenatas; about 100 separate arias (but these are no doubt

from operas); two oratorios; 60 other works of vocal sacred music (motets, hymns, Mass movements); 78 sonatas; 21 sinfonias; one other instrumental work; and 456 concertos.

Today the vocal music of Vivaldi is little known. But in his own day he was famous and successful as an opera composer. Most of his operas were written for Venice, but some were commissioned for performance in Rome, Florence, Verona, Vicenza, Ancona, and Mantua.

Vivaldi was also one of the great violin virtuosos of his time. This virtuosity is reflected in his music, which made new demands on violin technique. In his instrumental works he naturally favored the violin. He wrote the majority of his sonatas for one or two violins and thorough-bass. Of his concertos, 221 are for solo violin and orchestra. Other concertos are for a variety of solo instruments: recorder, flute, piccolo, clarinet, oboe, bassoon, trumpet, viola d'amore, and mandolin. He also wrote concertos for several solo instruments, concerti grossi, and concertos for full orchestra. The concerto grosso features a small group of solo players, set in contrast to the full orchestra. The concerto for orchestra features contrasts of style rather than contrasts of instruments.

Vivaldi's concertos are generally in three movements, arranged in the order of fast, slow, fast. The two outer movements are in the same key; the middle movement is in the same key or in a closely related key. Within movements, the music proceeds on the principle of alternation: passages for the solo instrument(s) alternate with passages for the full orchestra. The solo instrument may elaborate on the material played by the orchestra, or it may play quite different material of its own. In either case, the alternation between soloist and orchestra builds up a tension which can be very dramatic.

The orchestra in Vivaldi's time was different, of course, from a modern one in its size and constitution. Although winds were sometimes called for, strings constituted the main body of players. In a Vivaldi concerto, the orchestra is essentially a string orchestra, with one or two harpsichords or organs to play the thorough-bass.

Some of Vivaldi's concertos are pieces of program music, for they give musical descriptions of events or natural scenes. *The Seasons,* for instance, consists of four concertos representing the four seasons. But in his concertos the "program" does not determine the formal structure of the music. Some musical material may imitate the call of a bird or the rustling of leaves; but the formal plan of the concerto is maintained.

Vivaldi's concertos were widely known during and after his lifetime. They were copied and admired by a colleague no less distinguished than Johann Sebastian Bach. In musical Europe of the 18th century Vivaldi was one of the great names.

Further Reading

There are two books in English on the life and works of Vivaldi: Marc Pincherle, *Vivaldi: Genius of the Baroque* (1955; trans. 1957), and Walter Kolneder, *Antonio Vivaldi: His Life and Work* (1965; trans. 1971). For the historical background, Donald Jay Grout, *A History of Western Music* (1960), is recommended. ☐

Vivekananda

Vivekananda (1863-1902) was an Indian reformer, missionary, and spiritual leader who promulgated Indian religious and philosophical values in Europe, England, and the United States, founding the Vedanta Society and the Ramakrishna mission.

Vivekananda was born in Calcutta of high-caste parents. His family name was Narendranath ("son of the lord of man") Datta. His father was a distinguished lawyer, and his mother a woman of deep religious piety. The influence of both parental figures clearly affected Vivekananda's early life and mature self-conception. He was a fun-loving boy who also showed great intellectual promise in the humanities, music, the sciences, and languages at high school and college. At the age of 15 he had an experience of spiritual ecstasy which served to reinforce his latent sense of religious calling—through he was openly skeptical of traditional religious practices. He joined the liberal Hindu reforming movement, the Brahmo Samaj (Association of God). But his deeper religious aspirations were still unsatisfied.

In 1881 Vivekananda met the great Hindu saint Ramakrishna, who recognized the young man's immense talents and finally persuaded him to join his community of disciples. After Ramakrishna's death in 1885, Vivekananda assumed leadership of the Ramakrishna order. He prepared the disciples for extensive missionary work, which he himself undertook throughout India—preaching both on the spiritual uniqueness of Indian civilization and on the need for massive reforms, especially the alleviation of the poverty of the Indian masses and the dissolution of caste discrimination. In 1893 his fame and brilliance gained him the nomination as Indian representative to the Parliament of Religions in Chicago.

Vivekananda's successes there led to an extended lecture tour. He stressed the mutual relevance of Indian spirituality and Western material progress—both, in his view, were in need of each other. In Boston he found much in common with the philosophy of the transcendentalists—Emerson, Thoreau, and their followers. After touring England and Europe, Vivekananda returned to the United States, founding the Vedanta Society of New York in 1896. His lectures on the Vedanta philosophy and yoga systems deeply impressed William James, Josiah Royce, and other members of the Harvard faculty. Vivekananda then went back to India to promote the Ramakrishna mission and reforming activities.

Seemingly indefatigable, Vivekananda traveled once again to the United States, in 1898, where he established a monastic community, the Shanti Ashrama, on donated land near San Francisco. In 1900 he attended the Paris Congress of the History of Religions, speaking extensively on Indian religious and cultural history. He returned to India in December of that year, his health much undermined by his strenuous activities. His work is still maintained today internationally by the many organizations which he founded.

Further Reading

Vivekananda's writings and speeches are collected in *The Complete Works of Swami Vivekananda* (7 vols., Almora, Advaita Ashrama, 1918-1922). A useful study of Vivekananda is Swami Nikhilananda, *Vivekananda: A Biography* (1953). Other studies include Romain Rolland, *Prophets of the New India* (trans. 1930); Christopher Isherwood's biographical introduction to Vivekananda's *What Religion Is in the Words of Swami Vivekananda* edited by John Yale (1962); and Ramesh Chandra Majumdar, ed., *Swami Vivekananda Centenary Memorial Volume* (Calcutta, 1963).

Additional Sources

Burke, Marie Louise, *Swami Vivekananda in the West: new discoveries,* Calcutta: Advaita Ashrama, [1985]-1987.

Chetanananda, Swami, *Vivekananda: East meets West: a pictorial biography,* St. louis, MO: Vedanta Society of St. Louis, 1994.

The Life of Swami Vivekananda, Calcutta: Advaita Ashrama, 1979. □

Vladimir I

Vladimir I (died 1015), also called Vladimir the Great and St. Vladimir, was grand prince of Kievan Russia from about 980 to 1015. His reign represents the culmination in the development of this first Russian state.

The youngest son of Grand Prince Sviatoslav Igorevich of Kiev and a servant girl, Vladimir distinguished himself first as his father's governor in Novgorod, where he had been appointed in 969. In a civil war that followed Sviatoslav's death (972 or 973), Vladimir fled to Scandinavia, leaving the reign to his oldest brother, Iaropolk (976). But in 978, aided by a large force of the Varangians (Normans), he resumed the struggle and by about 980 became grand prince of Kiev.

Vladimir's first goal seems to have been to recover his father's conquests, lost during the civil war, and add to them conquests of his own. Although Vladimir stayed out of the Balkans, he regained the territory of the Viatichi and Radimichi in the east (981-982, 984) and thus reunited all eastern Slavs under Kiev. In the west he recovered a number of Galician towns from Poland (981) and conquered the territory of the Lithuanian Iatvigs (983). But his campaign against the Volga Bulgars in 985 was indecisive and ended his intentions to recover the Volga Basin. In the south he was similarly barred by the Turkic tribe of the Pechenegs (Patzinaks), who had captured the control of the Black Sea steppes, but he did regain some of the steppelands and secured them by a system of earth walls, forts, and fortified towns. The quest for unity and security was also the goal of Vladimir's domestic policy. He substituted his sons and lieutenants for the too independent tribal chieftains as governors of individual sections of the state and subjected them to a rigid supervision.

Even religion seems to have been employed by Vladimir in the service of this goal. At first he made an attempt to create a pagan creed common to his entire realm by accepting all gods and deities of local tribes and making them an object of general veneration. In the end he turned to Christianity, probably because a faith believing in a single God appeared better suited to the purposes of a prince seeking to entrench the government of a single ruler in his realm. The exact circumstances of this event, however, are not completely known. It seems that in 987 Byzantine emperor Basil II, in return for Russian assistance against uprisings in Bulgaria and Anatolia, agreed to give Vladimir the hand of his sister Anna if he became a Christian. Vladimir was baptized about 988, received the Byzantine bride, and proceeded to make Christianity the official religion of his state. He ordered, and eventually forced, his subjects to accept baptism too, destroyed pagan idols, built Christian churches and schools and libraries, kept peace within and without the realm, and indulged in charities for the benefit of the poor and sick.

The baptism of Russia was not, of course, an immediate success. It took several decades before Christianity struck roots in Russia firmly and definitely. Nor was Vladimir completely successful in checking the danger of feudal disintegration. In fact, he died in 1015 in the midst of a campaign against the revolt of his son Iaroslav. A civil war resulting from it ended only in 1026 in a division of Russia between Iaroslav and his brother Mstislav, and the country was not reunited again until 1036, following the latter's demise.

Vladimir I completed unification of all eastern Slavs in his realm, secured its frontiers against foreign invasions, and—by accepting Christianity—brought Russia into the community of Christian nations and their civilization. He was remembered and celebrated in numerous legends and songs as a great national hero and ruler, a "Sun Prince." Venerated as the baptizer of Russia, "equal to Apostles," he was canonized about the middle of the 13th century.

Further Reading

A concise and popular sketch of Vladimir's life is in Constantin de Grunwald, *Saints of Russia* (trans. 1960). For varying interpretations of the disputed segments of his life and work consult these standard surveys of early Russian history: Vasilii O. Kliuchevskii, *A History of Russia,* vol. 1 (trans. 1911); George Vernadsky and Michael Karpovich, *A History of Russia,* vol. 2: *Kievan Russia* (1948); Boris D. Grekov, *Kiev Rus* (trans. 1959); and Boris A. Rybakov, *Early Centuries of Russian History* (1964; trans. 1965).

Additional Sources

Volkoff, Vladimir, *Vladimir the Russian Viking,* Woodstock, N.Y.: Overlook Press, 1985, 1984. □

Maurice Vlaminck

The French painter Maurice Vlaminck (1876-1958) was one of the great Fauves, artists who stressed the primacy of pure color. In his later work he moved toward a kind of expressive realism.

The son of a Flemish father and a French mother from Lorraine, Maurice Vlaminck was born in Paris on April 4, 1876, and grew up in the suburb of Le Vésinet. Both his parents were musicians, and at the age of 16 Vlaminck moved to Chatou near Paris and earned his living as a violinist and a bicycle racer. In 1894 he married and started a large family. He learned to draw from J. L. Robichon, and at Chatou he worked with Henri Rigal.

Vlaminck was one of the most colorful personalities among French artists. A person of great vitality, he was self-willed, radical, and independent. Very Flemish in temperament, he admired folk art, naive imagery, and African sculpture and was against all schools and academies.

In 1900 the young painter André Derain and Vlaminck shared a studio in Chatou. The decisive event in Vlaminck's artistic development was the large exhibition of Vincent Van Gogh's work in 1901 in Paris. Shortly afterward Vlaminck met Claude Monet and Henri Matisse.

In 1905 Vlaminck, encouraged by Matisse, exhibited at the Salon des Indépendants, at the Berthe Weill gallery, and

in the famous "Fauvist zoo" at the Salon d'Automne. Fauve means wild beast, and nobody was wilder in his brushwork and his palette than Vlaminck. Typical canvases of his Fauve period are the *Gardens of Chatou* (1904), *Picnic in the Country* (1905), and *Circus* (1906).

In 1908 Vlaminck's style changed, and under the influence of Paul Cézanne's work he aimed at well-constructed compositions. This is exemplified in *Barges* (1908-1910) and *The Flood, Ivry* (1910). About 1915 Vlaminck entered his expressionist phase, characterized by earthy colors and simplified forms. He painted landscapes, portraits, and still lifes with impetuous brushwork. In 1919 a large exhibition of his work took place in Paris.

Vlaminck lived in Anvers-sur-Oise from 1920 to 1925, when he moved to Rueil-la-Gadelière, where he died on Oct. 11, 1958. His late work continued to be in the expressive realist manner. The landscapes, such as *Hamlet in the Snow* (1943), have a heavily textured brushstroke and are charged with emotion.

Further Reading

Pierre MacOrlan, *Vlaminck* (1958), has fine color plates defining the artist's stylistic development. Patrick Heron, *Vlaminck: Paintings, 1900-1945* (1948), offers an analysis and assessment by a painter. Jacques Perry, *Maurice Vlaminck* (1957), reproduces personal photographs by Roger Hauert. For background material on the Fauvist movement see Georges Duthuit, *The Fauvist Painters* (1950), and Jean Paul Crespelle, *The Fauves* (1962). □

Eric Voegelin

The German-Austrian political theorist Eric Voegelin (1901-1985), who became an American citizen after exile from Nazi Germany, will probably gain influence as the most subtle rethinker of Augustine's *City of God* and the leading Christian philosopher of history of the 20th century.

Eric Voegelin was born in Cologne, Germany, on January 3, 1901, and moved as a boy to Vienna, Austria. He received his doctorate with a dissertation written under the legal positivist Hans Kelsen in 1922. His American education, under a Rockefeller grant from 1924 to 1927, was most significant. In contrast to the positivism which dominated political philosophy in Europe, what he discovered in the United States was intellectual life still rooted in Christianity and in classical culture. His first book, *On the Form of the American Spirit* (1929, not yet translated into English), although on the interpretation of law, was broadly based on a knowledge of the great American Golden Age of Philosophy (James, Santayana). And he had heard Dewey and Whitehead lecture. He also was familiar with such concrete problems of American life as the Eighteenth Amendment, class conflict, and La Follette's Wisconsin ideal.

Voegelin's career as instructor at the University of Vienna was broad in its international interests, yet coupled with the practical problems of the civil service, such as supervision of schools. He knew what was then the avant garde of English literature and was probably the first non-English-speaking professor to teach James Joyce's *Ulysses*. He also made a specialty of the writings of Paul Valéry. He served as secretary of the Committee for Intellectual Cooperation, set up under the League of Nations (1936-1938).

Political and Philosophical Crises

It remains controversial how sympathetic Voegelin was with the Austrian dictator Engelbert Dollfuss. Voegelin's conservative friends insist that *The Authoritarian State* (1936) is only a study of the Austrian constitution. What is important and very clear is that Voegelin's two other books, also in German, did not satisfy the Nazis who submerged Austria into the Third Reich in 1938. Hitler's idea of eliminating the so-called "inferior and non-Aryan" people was based, according to *Race and State* (1933) and *The Idea of Race in the History of Ideas* (1933), on specious 19th-century sources. Voegelin's contempt for the very idea of a "Master race" led him to the conclusion that no just government can be based on anything but universal humanity. Voegelin was dismissed by the Nazis in 1938, and Voegelin and his wife narrowly escaped apprehension by the Gestapo. They became political refugees in Switzerland.

Exile was the occasion for Voegelin to reflect on what had gone wrong with the modern state. The monarch of the 17th century, particularly Louis XIV of France, who considered himself the sun-king, the source of light, thus tended to replace God. The English ideal state of Hobbes was a Leviathan, headed by an almost absolute supreme head of both church and state. All the symbols of modernity, according to Voegelin's *The Political Religions* (1938), succeeded in "decapitating God" and thus robbed the modern hierarchy of the true source of norms. There is no political legitimacy without transcendent sanction.

Voegelin was fiercely independent in his political science and failed in several noted institutions—Harvard, for example—to get permanent status. Finally, beginning in 1942 he had a long period of 16 years during which he was Boyd Professor at Louisiana State University and wrote and published the first half of the projected six-volume *Order and History*. Voegelin became an American citizen by naturalization in 1944.

Voegelin's Interpretation of History

His interpretation of history is designed, as Augustine's *City of God,* to show the sources of civic order in the divine order proclaimed by the prophets of Israel and reasoned by the Greek philosophers. The point of *Israel and Revelation, The World of the Polis,* and *Plato and Aristotle* is not antiquarian nor is it "scientific historiography," but the historical evidence that the order established in the soul of Western man depends upon transcendence. Only when nature and history are regarded as created by God can man discover the true norms according to which human affairs are to be regulated. But the modern world, in freeing philosophy from theology, freeing the arts from the church, and making state power supreme and independent of traditional prohibited excesses, has plunged man into disorder. This program is best studied in *The New Science of Politics: An Introduction* (1952). Originally the great work *Order and History* was to include *Empire and Christianity, The Protestant Centuries,* and *The Crisis of Western Civilization.* What we now have is *The Ecumenic Age* and *From Enlightenment to Revolution,* and what we will soon have is *In Search of Order.* All the secular ideologies of modernity are departures from what Voegelin believed were established principles of order. No set of abstract principles arrived at by reason, however powerful the deductive and inductive methods, can ever provide the rich symbolic meanings of the classical Christian tradition. Voegelin rather abhorred metaphysics and refused ever to define order or demonstrate his principles of order. Nonetheless, many readers became convinced that there was a 20th-century crisis and that the only answer to modern barbarity, such as Hitler's Nazidom, was the recovery of human order based ultimately in God.

The stature of Voegelin can be measured in two ways: by his astonishing scholarship, which extended from ancient Near and Far East through Biblical, classical, medieval, and modern periods and with respect to which there is little disagreement; and by his achievement of wisdom, with respect to which there is a division between a few loyal followers who count Voegelin a great prophet and the majority who say they cannot comprehend his ideas of mythical symbolism, memory and consciousness (anamnesis), the leap in being, and, most of all, his attack on modernity as the perversion of "gnosticism." Voegelin never professed to know God, but only to deal with the symbols of transcendence found in literature. His Christianity was deeply credal and included a defense of the Incarnation (that God became man) and the Holy Trinity (Father, Son, and Holy Ghost).

Voegelin returned to Germany in 1958 where, at the University of Munich, through the Institute of Political Science, he exercized great influence on the political theory of the Federal Republic. The wide respect he was accorded can be judged from the papers in his honor, presented on his 60th birthday, *Politische Ordnung und Menschliche Existenz, München* (1962).

When Voegelin retired he became associated with the Hoover Institute at Stanford University. He died at the age of 84 on January 19, 1985. Happily, for his 80th birthday, a group of essays, probably the best dealing with his concepts, was published: *The Philosophy of Order* (1981).

Further Reading

Voegelin's philosophy can best be explored in his own works, which include "The German Universities in the Nazi Era," in *The Intercollegiate Review* (Spring/Summer 1985); the series *Order and History* which consists of *Israel and Revelation* (1956), *The World of the Polis* (1957), *Plato and Aristotle* (1957), *The Ecumenic Age* (1974), and *In Search of Order* (1987); *Anaminesis* (translated by Gerhart Niemeyer, 1978); *The New Science of Politics* (1952); and *Science, Politics and Gnosticism* (translated by William J. Fitzpatrick, 1968). Peter

J. Opitz and Gregor Sebba, *The Philosophy of Order: Essays on History, Consciousness and Politics* (Stuttgart, 1981); John H. Hollowell, *From Enlightenment to Revolution* (1975); and Ellis Sandoz, *The Voegelinian Revolution: A Biographical Introduction* (1981) explore his philosophy.

Additional Sources

Sandoz, Ellis, *The Voegelinian revolution: a biographical introduction,* Baton Rouge: Louisiana State University, 1981.

Voegelin, Eric, *Autobiographical reflections,* Baton Rouge: Louisiana State University Press, 1989.

Webb, Eugene, *Eric Voegelin, philosopher of history,* Seattle: University of Washington Press, 1981. □

Hans-Jochen Vogel

After serving as mayor of Munich for 12 years, Hans-Jochen Vogel (born 1926) became a member of the West German government. In 1983 he led the Social Democratic Party ticket, but lost to the Christian Democrats led by Helmut Kohl. He was chairman of the Social Democrats from 1987 to 1991.

Hans-Jochen Vogel was born on February 3, 1926, in the north German city of Göttingen. He came from a middle-class, politically active family. His father was a university lecturer, and his mother inspired excellence in her sons. His brother Bernhard became the Christian Democratic Party prime minister of the state of Rhineland-Palatinate.

During World War II, Vogel served a mandatory term in the Hitler Youth. He served in the German army in 1943 and was wounded in Italy and taken prisoner. After the war, he studied law and became active in politics. Despite his north German origins, Vogel rose to political prominence in the southern state of Bavaria. After studying at the universities of Marburg and Munich and qualifying for the bar in 1951, Vogel became a member of the Bavarian civil service.

Vogel was typical of young men who came to political prominence in the 1950s and 1960s and steered the SPD away from its Marxist ideas toward becoming a pragmatic and reformist party. Throughout his career, he had a reputation as a master of compromise and a man who was willing to listen to a variety of opinions. Vogel disdained emotional and demagogic appeals and relied on logical persuasion both in intimate settings and in addressing large rallies. For Vogel, Democratic Socialism was essentially a belief in human progress and rationality, in equal opportunity for all members of society and affirmative action for the economically and socially disadvantaged.

Mayor of Munich

Soon after his graduation from college, Vogel, like many West German Social Democrats of his generation, became active in municipal politics. In 1958 he was elected to the Munich city council and two years later was elected mayor of the Bavarian capital. Vogel remained the city's chief executive for the next 12 years, becoming one of the most popular and influential of the big city mayors in the Federal Republic of Germany. His administration was noted for its systematic expansion of Munich's system of urban transport. In 1965, he visited Rome and convinced officials of the International Olympic Committee to designate Munich as the site of the 1972 Summer Olympics. The games provided Vogel with the support needed to undertake a vast urban renewal project.

Rise in National Politics

Vogel's popularity gave him national exposure, and in 1970 he became a member of the Social Democratic Party's national executive board. Despite opposition from the left wing of the SPD, Vogel in 1972 was elected state chairman of the SPD in Bavaria, a state dominated by Franz Joseph Strauss' Christian Democratic Union. In November 1972 he was elected to the federal *Bundestag* (legislature), and in December was appointed minister of regional planning, housing and urban development in Chancellor Willy Brandt's coalition cabinet of Social Democrats and Free Democrats.

After Brandt's resignation in 1974, Vogel moved to the more important position of minister of justice in the cabinet of Helmut Schmidt. In his seven years as justice minister, Vogel modernized and liberalized the West German judicial code in such areas as abortion rights, divorce law, and sex discrimination. This work helped him make peace with the left wing of his party. Vogel also won praise for his strong actions curbing resurgent Nazi activity and leftist terrorism. By 1980 Vogel was viewed as Schmidt's likely successor as federal chancellor.

Mayor of West Berlin

In 1981, Vogel was chosen by the SPD's national leadership to clean up an embarrassing scandal in West Berlin. That city's SPD mayor, Dietrich Stobbe, had resigned amid charges of massive graft in his administration. Vogel was elected interim mayor by the SPD-dominated city council, and weeded out many of the corrupt elements in the Berlin SPD organization and in the administration. During his 100 days in office, he tried to make peace with squatters who were protesting the city's severe housing shortage, granting them status as tenants and authorizing $10 million to repair their houses. In June 1981 Vogel and the SPD lost the mayoral and city council elections to the Christian Democrat Union (CDU), but Vogel stayed in West Berlin as opposition leader.

Bid for Chancellor

Schmidt's coalition collapsed in 1982, and the Social Democrats no longer had a majority in the *Bundestag,* which named Christian Democratic leader Helmut Kohl as chancellor. Kohl scheduled federal elections for March 1983. The SPD named Vogel as its candidate for chancellor. Kohl campaigned in support of NATO deployment of Cruise and Pershing II nuclear missiles in West Germany and on a free-market, private-investment platform. Vogel opposed unconditional acceptance of the missiles, took a strong pro-environment stand, and called for higher taxes on the rich and a shorter work week. Vogel lost to Kohl and the CDU, but remained as the party's leader of the opposition in the *Bundestag.*

Vogel's failure to lead the party to victory in 1983 cost him the SPD nomination for chancellor in the 1987 election. Johannes Rau led the party, but he too went down to defeat at the hands of Kohl. That year, Vogel succeeded Willy Brandt as SPD chairman and remained in that post until 1991, and he gained praise for putting a lid on the party's internal bickering. "A notorious early riser with a punctilious lawyer's mind, he demands hard work and discipline and smartly raps the knuckles of those who get out of line," according to an assessment in *The Economist* in 1988. But Vogel never again headed the party's national ticket. He remained a member of the *Bundestag* in the 1990s.

Further Reading

Literature in English on Vogel is scant; no full-scale biography has appeared. Vogel provided an autobiographical account of his Munich years in *Die Amtskette* (The Badge of Office, 1972) and of his political ideas in *Reale Reformen: Beiträge zu einer Gesellschaftspolitik der neuen Mitte* (Real Reforms: Contributions to a Social Policy of the New Center, 1973). Vogel also wrote a book on urban policy, *Städte im Wandel* (Cities in Transition, 1971). The best analysis of Social Democratic politics in English is Gerald Braunthal, *The West German Social Democrats, 1969-1982: Profile of a Party in Power* (1983). Klaus Bölling, *Die letzten 30 Tage des Kanzlers Helmut Schmidt: Ein Tagebuch* (The Last 30 Days of Chancel-

lor Helmut Schmidt: A Diary, 1982) is the best insider account of the dramatic events that brought Vogel to his position of leadership. □

Sir Julius Vogel

Sir Julius Vogel (1835-1899) was a New Zealand journalist, financier, politician, and prime minister. He led the country to economic recovery after the post-gold rush depression.

Julius Vogel was born in London on Feb. 24, 1835. At the age of 17 he joined the gold rush to Australia and became editor of the *Maryborough and Dunolly Advertiser* in Victoria. In 1861 he moved on to Otago, where he helped to start the first daily newspaper in New Zealand. In 1862 he was elected to the provincial house, and the following year he won a seat in the central legislature in Auckland.

Vogel's precise political orientation was difficult to deduce, but he was associated with the conservatives, and in 1869 he became colonial treasurer in the administration headed by William Fox. It was a period of economic depression, following the boom of the gold rush, and Vogel proposed that the government should embark on a policy of heavy borrowing in London for the construction of roads, railways, and other public works, which would create jobs, increase purchasing power, and renew public confidence. It was a philosophy that acquired the label "Vogelism," and although it was widely criticized, it was accepted by Parliament, and the London market responded freely to his appeals.

In 1873 Vogel headed an administration in which he was both prime minister and treasurer. When the provincial governments put obstacles in the path of his policy, they were abolished, and the country thenceforward was governed under a unitary instead of a federal system. Whatever the criticism of the Vogel financial program, the New Zealand economy was buoyant when his prime ministership ended in 1876, and it remained so until the land boom collapsed in 1880.

Apart from his specifically financial measures, Vogel was also instrumental in the establishment of a government life-insurance office and in the creation of a public trust office for supervising the estates of deceased persons who had left no provision for the administration of their wills or had appointed the office to administer them. He was responsible for the arrangement whereby colonial loans were issued in the form of inscribed stock, and the Colonial Stock Act of 1877 was introduced by the British government largely as a result of his representations.

Vogel left for London in September 1876 to serve as the New Zealand agent general. He returned to New Zealand in 1882 and two years later took office for the last time in an administration which he led in collaboration with Sir Robert Stout and which lasted three years, until its defeat in 1887. Vogel finally left New Zealand in 1888, returned to live his last years in England, and died in poverty at East Molesey near London on March 12, 1899.

Further Reading

Randal M. Burdon, *The Life and Times of Sir Julius Vogel* (1948), is the standard political biography. W.P. Morrell, *The Provincial System in New Zealand* (1932; 2d rev. ed. 1964), is a good guide to the politics of the period 1852-1876. □

Walther von der Vogelweide

Walther von der Vogelweide (ca. 1170-1229) was the greatest German poet, composer, and singer of minnesongs and Spruche—gnomic or didactic songs—of the Middle Ages.

The work of Walther von der Vogelweide is distinguished by genuine feeling and meticulous skill in metrics and rhyme patterns; his personality embraced a sterling character and a wide range of interests. As a mentor of society, Vogelweide exhibited unshakable ethical principles, religious faith, and a robust attitude toward life. Although only about 5,000 lines of his poetry are extant, his utterance is so personal and natural that more is known about him than about, for example, William Shakespeare, despite the fact that Vogelweide was restricted by the conventions of courtly culture, which, however, he did not always observe.

Born in Austria to an impoverished knightly family, probably in Bolzano (Bozen) in the South Tirol, and in or near a bird reserve (as his name indicates), Vogelweide went as a youth to the Viennese court of Duke Frederick I of the Babenberg line. There, where his teacher was the famous singer Reinmar von Hagenau, he remained until Frederick died on a crusade in 1198. After visiting the court of Landgrave Hermann of Thuringia several times, Vogelweide joined the retinue of Philip of Swabia, the rival of Otto IV of Brunswick for the crown of the Holy Roman Empire. Walther became disappointed in Philip, especially after his coronation, vainly urging him to adopt a strong imperial policy. After Philip's assassination in 1208, Vogelweide gave Otto IV his allegiance. Though a staunch adherent of the Church, Vogelweide criticized both Innocent III and Gregory IX for their worldly policies. Later he joined Emperor Frederick II, who gave him a fief near Würzburg. Vogelweide was buried in the cloister garth of the Cathedral there.

Vogelweide created verse and music for all his works and sang the songs himself as he moved from place to place. His fame was widespread. He used and refined every known type of song and added new ones: genuine ''lofty'' (conventional) minnesongs addressed to ladies of rank; ''natural'' (unconventional) minnesongs addressed to humble lasses; dancing songs; songs of nature, of summer, of complaint, and of vituperation; fables; riddles; parodies; elegies; prayers; panegyrics; philippics; and a crusading song in which he expressed the doctrine of Christian salvation. He was particularly noted for his bold political songs aimed at secular and temporal authorities from popes and emperors down, attacking them for what he considered malfeasance, duplicity, greed, and other vices. But Vogelweide was just as critical of society. He never compromised his ideals or questioned Christian dogma. In a famous messenger song he expressed cultural nationalism—but without chauvinism—born of pride in his fatherland.

In spite of his fame while alive, Vogelweide is mentioned in only one contemporary document, as having received money for a fur coat in 1203 from the bishop of Passau. Two hundred years after his death he was revered by the Meistersingers as one of their 12 masters. In the 16th century Martin Luther adapted one of his songs.

Until recently there was little interest in, and knowledge of, the music to Vogelweide's songs. Generations of serious scholars puzzled over textual cruxes without giving much thought to the music. This omission is now being corrected despite the scarcity of authentic musical notations. In some cases contrafactures (later songs in identical meters set to melodies apparently borrowed from Walther) have been discovered.

No existing manuscript of Vogelweide's works was written before his death. The most important manuscripts date from the 14th century, and the best of these is the Great

Heidelberg Codex (C), beautifully illustrated with stylized colored pictures of singers and their coats of arms.

Further Reading

George F. Jones, *Walther von der Vogelweide* (1968), is an excellent introduction. Recommended for historical background are August Closs, *The Genius of the German Lyric: An Historic Survey of Its Formal and Metaphysical Values* (1938), and Martin Joos and Frederick R. Whitesell, eds., *Middle High German Courtly Reader* (1951). □

Paul Volcker

As chairman of the Federal Reserve Board during one of the most turbulent periods in U.S. monetary history, Paul Volcker (born 1927) helped lower double-digit inflation rates in the early 1980s and ushered in an era of financial deregulation and innovation.

Paul Adolf Volcker was born in Cape May, NJ, on September 5, 1927. His father was city manager of Teaneck, NJ, and turned the town from bankruptcy to solvency. After graduating *summa cum laude* from Princeton University in 1949, Volcker attended Harvard University's Graduate School of Public Administration, earning a masters degree in political economy and government in 1951. The following year he did postgraduate work at the London School of Economics as a Rotary fellow. During summers Volcker worked at the Federal Reserve Bank of New York, and in 1952 he joined the staff there as a full-time economist.

Volcker left the Federal Reserve Bank of New York in 1957 to become a financial economist with Chase Manhattan Bank. In 1962 he joined the U.S. Treasury Department as director of financial analysis, and in 1963 he became deputy under secretary for monetary affairs. Volcker returned to Chase Manhattan Bank as vice-president and director of planning in 1965. In 1969 he was appointed under secretary of the U.S. Treasury for monetary affairs and remained there until 1974, engaging in international negotiations on the introduction of floating exchange rates. The following year he became a senior fellow in the Woodrow Wilson School of Public and International Affairs at Princeton University. In 1975 Volcker became the president of the Federal Reserve Bank of New York, the most important bank in the Federal Reserve System.

Economic Leader

During the more than 30 years Volcker worked in and out of the federal government he developed an expertise in monetary economics and served under three presidents. The cigar-chomping Volcker, admired for his dedication and commitment by friends and foes alike, appeared implacable and unflappable with his six- foot-seven inch frame. In 1979 he was nominated by President Jimmy Carter to fill

the most powerful economic seat in government—chairman of the Federal Reserve Board (the Fed). An act of Congress in 1913 had established the independent Central Bank to create money, regulate its value, and maintain the stability of the financial system through 12 regional banks. When Volcker took over in August of 1979, inflation was running over 13 percent a year, the value of the dollar was falling, and financial markets were concerned about renewed inflation. Volcker's appointment to a four-year term as chairman calmed those fears and was greeted with acclaim in the financial community. As Volcker recalled in a 1989 *Time* magazine interview: "The [Carter] Administration had got deeply concerned. They said to me they were scared of this exploding inflation and were willing to stand still for stronger measures than would ordinarily be the case. And that is a great advantage. If you can walk into a situation that is felt to be so severely out of kilter, you have greater freedom of action."

The chairman of the Fed also oversees the 12-member Federal Open Market Committee (FOMC), which decides the conduct of U.S. monetary policy. During 1979 and 1980 the FOMC, under Volcker's leadership, sought to reign in double-digit inflation by setting strict money supply growth targets. This direction was in opposition to past policies that sought to control interest rates at the expense of higher money supply growth rates. The result of the switch in policy was a substantial rise in interest rates, with the prime rate peaking at 21.5 percent in December 1980. With higher interest rates, the economy fell into the worst recession in 40 years, causing unemployment to reach 10.7

percent in 1982. During this period, Volcker was widely criticized. The cover of a building trade publication carried a "WANTED" poster of Volcker and his Fed colleagues, accusing them of "premeditated and cold-blooded murder of millions of small businesses." The economic crisis led the FOMC to abandon strict adherence to monetary targets in 1982, but not before the rate of inflation had fallen to below four percent.

The hard-line actions of the FOMC drew criticism from those who felt the price exacted to cure inflation was too high. The crisis raised questions in Congress about whether the "independence" of the Fed should be rescinded. Nevertheless, Volcker was reappointed by President Reagan in August 1983 to a second four-year term as Federal Reserve chairman and was confirmed by the Senate in an 84-16 vote.

From Villain to Hero

Volcker studiously avoided taking rigid ideological positions with regard to monetary policy, preferring a more flexible and discretionary approach. In addition to fighting inflation, Volcker presided over the Central Bank in an era in which control of the money supply was greatly complicated due to the deregulation of the financial industry in 1980. This resulted in large-scale shifts in deposits between different types of accounts, causing unpredictable changes in the rate of growth of money.

Volcker also successfully defended the Fed's oversight powers in banking regulation that were threatened by proposals to streamline the regulatory process. He argued that in order to fulfill the Fed's role of "lender of last resort" to financially troubled banks, the Fed must maintain day-to-day regulation over those banks, along with the U.S. comptroller of the currency. At the end of his second term in 1987 Volcker became a consultant to various financial institutions, including the World Bank.

"For eight years, as chairman of the Federal Reserve Board, Paul Volcker was perhaps the second most powerful man in Washington," noted Lawrence Malkin in *Time* (January 23, 1989). "There were no doubt times, as he squeezed the money supply and cost people jobs in his battle against double-digit inflation, when he was also one of the most unpopular." Volcker's moves had tremendous impact on the nation's economy and were watched worldwide. "He is the most revered economic leader of his era," Stephen Koepp noted in *Time* on June 15, 1987. "He had profound impact on a $4.3 trillion economy but lived in a tiny $500-a-month apartment furnished with castoffs. He ran his agency in a notably serene and straightforward style, and still his mystique grew so potent that his every move sent global financial markets into spasmodic guessing games about what he was thinking." After he had tamed the inflation rate and turned the economy around in the mid-1980s, he became a sort of folk hero.

Volcker, who took a substantial cut in salary to head the Fed, received numerous awards, including One of Ten Outstanding Young Men in Federal Service (1969) and the Alexander Hamilton Award for his efforts at implementation of flexible exchange rates while at the Treasury Department

during the early 1970s. He received honorary degrees from a number of institutions, including Notre Dame, Princeton, Dartmouth, New York University, Fairleigh Dickinson, Bryant College, Adelphi, and Lamar University.

Volcker's first job after leaving government in 1987 was as unpaid chairman of the National Commission on the Public Service, a private group working on behalf of the nation's civil servants. He soon became chairman of the New York investment banking firm James D. Wolfensohn, earning a large salary for the first time in his life, and continued to be a respected commentator on the nation's financial affairs in the 1990s.

Further Reading

Some of Volcker's lectures on the workings of the economy are found in Paul Volcker, *The Rediscovery of the Business Cycle* (1978). For further details on the operation of the Fed, see U.S. Board of Governors, *The Federal Reserve System: Purposes and Functions* (7th edition, 1984); Maxwell Newton, *The Fed* (1983); and Paul De Rosa and Gary H. Stern, *In the Name of Money* (1981). For a good historical look at the Fed's role in the fight against inflation in the early 1980s see Lawrence S. Ritter and William L. Silber, *Principles of Money, Banking, and Financial Markets* (5th edition, 1985) and William Melton, *Inside the Fed Making Monetary Policy* (1985). In 1992, Volcker and Toyoo Gyohten published *Changing Fortunes: The World's Money and the Threat to American Leadership* (1992), based on a series of lectures they gave at Princeton's Woodrow Wilson School. □

Alessandro Volta

The Italian physicist Alessandro Volta (1745-1827) invented the electric battery, or "voltaic pile," thus providing for the first time a sustained source of current electricity.

A lessandro Volta was born on Feb. 18, 1745, in Como. He resisted pressure from his family to enter the priesthood and developed instead an intense curiosity about natural phenomena, in particular, electricity. In 1769 he published his first paper on electricity. It contained no new discoveries but is of some interest as the most speculative of all Volta's papers, his subsequent ones being devoted almost exclusively to the presentation of specific experimental discoveries.

Early Investigations and Inventions

In 1774 Volta was appointed professor of physics at the gymnasium in Como, and that same year he made his first important contribution to the science of electricity, the invention of the electrophorus, a device which provided a source of electric potential utilizing the principle of electrostatic induction. Unlike earlier source of electric potential, such as the Leyden jar, the electrophorus provided a sustained, easily replenishable source of static electricity. In 1782 Volta announced the application of the electrophorus to the detection of minute electrical charges. His invention of the so-called condensing electroscope culminated his efforts to improve the sensitivity of earlier electrometers.

During these same years Volta also conducted researches of a purely chemical nature. He had for some time been experimenting with exploding various gases, such as hydrogen, in closed containers and had observed that when hydrogen and air were exploded there was a diminution in volume greater than the volume of hydrogen burned. In order to measure such changes in volume, he developed a graduated glass container, now known as a eudiometer, in which to explode the gases. Utilizing this eudiometer he studied marsh gas, or methane, and distinguished it from hydrogen by its different-colored flame, its slower rate of combustion, and the greater volume of air and larger electric spark required for detonation.

In 1779 Volta was appointed to the newly created chair of physics at the University of Pavia. In 1782 he became a corresponding member of the French Academy of Sciences. In 1791 he was elected a fellow of the Royal Society of London, and in 1794, in recognition of his contributions to electricity and chemistry, he was awarded the society's coveted Copley Medal. However, his most significant researches—those which were to lead to the discovery of current electricity—were yet to be undertaken.

Discovery of Current Electricity

Until the last decade of the 18th century electrical researchers had been primarily concerned with static electricity, with the electrification produced by friction. Then, in

1786, Luigi Galvani discovered that the muscles in a frog's amputated leg would contract whenever an electrical machine was discharged near the leg. As a result of his initial observations, Galvani undertook a long series of experiments in an effort to more thoroughly examine this startling phenomenon. In the course of these investigations he discovered that a frog's prepared leg could be made to contract if he merely attached a copper hook to the nerve ending and then pressed the hook against an iron plate on which the leg was resting so as to complete an electrical circuit, even though no electrical machines were operating in the vicinity. Galvani concluded the contraction was produced in the organism itself and referred to this new type of electricity as "animal electricity."

Galvani's experiments and interpretation were summarized in a paper published in 1791, a copy of which he sent to Volta. Although, like most others, initially convinced by Galvani's arguments, Volta gradually came to the conclusion that the two metals were not merely conductors but actually generated the electricity themselves. He began by repeating and verifying Galvani's experiments but quickly moved beyond these to experiments of his own, concentrating on the results of bringing into contact two dissimilar metals. By 1794 he had convinced himself that the metals, in his own words, "are in a real sense the exciters of electricity, while the nerves themselves are passive," and he henceforth referred to this new type of electricity as "metallic" or "contact" electricity.

The announcement of Volta's experiments and interpretation touched off one of the great controversies in the history of science. Although other factors were important as well, the physiologists and anatomists tended to support Galvani's view that the electricity was produced by the animal tissue itself whereas the physicists and chemists, like Volta, tended to see it as produced by the external bimetallic contacts. The resulting rivalry not only took on international dimensions but died out only gradually after more than a decade. Although Galvani withdrew from the arena, allowing others to carry his standard, Volta took an active role in the controversy and vigorously pursued his research.

Volta discovered that not only would two dissimilar metals in contact produce a small electrical effect, but metals in contact with certain types of fluids would also produce such effects. In fact, the best results were obtained when two dissimilar metals were held in contact and joined by a moist third body which, in modern terminology, completed the circuit between them. Such observations led directly to the construction in 1800 of the electric battery, or "pile" as Volta called it, the first source of a significant electric current.

Volta announced his discovery in a letter to Sir Joseph Banks, then president of the Royal Society of London. The letter, dated March 20, 1800, created an instant sensation. Here for the first time was an instrument capable of producing a steady, continuous flow of electricity. All previous electrical machines, including Volta's electrophorus, had produced only short bursts of static electricity. The ability to create at will a sustained electrical current opened vast new fields for investigation, and the significance of Volta's discovery was immediately recognized.

Acclaim and Retirement

Volta was summoned to Paris by Napoleon and in 1801 gave a series of lectures on his discoveries before the National Institute of France, as the Academy of Sciences was then called. A special gold medal was struck to honor the occasion, and the following year Volta was distinguished by election as one of the eight foreign associates of the institute.

Although only in his mid-50s when he announced the discovery of the "pile," Volta took no part in applying his discovery to any of the immense new fields it opened up. During the last 25 years of his life he demonstrated none of the intense creativity that had characterized his earlier researches, and he published nothing of scientific significance during these later years. He continued, at the urging of Napoleon, to teach at the University of Pavia and eventually became director of the philosophy faculty there. In 1819 he retired to his family home near Como. He died there on March 5, 1827, little realizing that current electricity would eventually transform a way of life.

Further Reading

Recommended for further details on Volta is the excellent brief treatment in Bern Dibner, *Alessandro Volta and the Electric Battery* (1964). A good historical account of the beginning of the age of electricity is in F. Sherwood Taylor, *A Short History of Science and Scientific Thought* (1949), and Bern Dibner, *Galvani-Volta: A Controversy That Led to the Discovery of Useful Electricity* (1952). □

Voltaire

The French poet dramatist, historian, and philosopher Voltaire (1694-1778) was an outspoken and aggressive enemy of every injustice but especially of religious intolerance. His works are an outstanding embodiment of the principles of the French Enlightenment.

François Marie Arouet rechristened himself Arouet de Voltaire, probably in 1718. A stay in the Bastille had given him time to reflect on his doubts concerning his parentage, on his need for a noble name to befit his growing reputation, and on the coincidence that *Arouet* sounded like both a *rouer* (for beating) and *roué* (a debauchee). In prison Voltaire had access to a book on anagrams, which may have influenced his name choice thus: *arouet, uotare, voltaire* (a winged armchair).

Youth and Early Success, 1694-1728

Voltaire was born, perhaps on Nov. 21, 1694, in Paris. He was ostensibly the youngest of the three surviving children of François Arouet and Marie Marguerite Daumand,

although Voltaire claimed to be the "bastard of Rochebrune," a minor poet and songwriter. Voltaire's mother died when he was seven years old, and he was then drawn to his sister. She bore a daughter who later became Voltaire's mistress.

A clever child, Voltaire was educated by the Jesuits at the Collège Louis-le-Grand from 1704 to 1711. He displayed an astonishing talent for poetry, cultivated a love of the theater, and nourished a keen ambition.

When Voltaire was drawn into the circle of the 72-year-old poet the Abbé de Chaulieu, "one of the most complete hedonists of all times," his father packed him off to Caen. Hoping to squelch his son's literary aspirations and to turn his mind to the law, Arouet placed the youth as secretary to the French ambassador at The Hague. Voltaire fell in with a jilted French refugee, Catherine Olympe Dunoyer, pretty but barely literate. Their elopement was thwarted. Under the threat of a *lettre de cachet* obtained by his father, Voltaire returned to Paris in 1713 and was articled to a lawyer. He continued to write, and he renewed his pleasure-loving acquaintances. In 1717 Voltaire was at first exiled and then imprisoned in the Bastille for verses offensive to powerful personages.

As early as 1711, Voltaire, eager to test himself against Sophocles and Pierre Corneille, had written a first draft of *Oedipe*. On Nov. 18, 1718, the revised play opened in Paris to a sensational success. The *Henriade*, begun in the Bastille and published in 1722, was Voltaire's attempt to rival Virgil and to give France an epic poem. This work

sounded in ringing phrases Voltaire's condemnation of fanaticism and advanced his reputation as the standard-bearer of French literature. However, his growing literary, financial, and social successes only partially reconciled him to his father, who died in 1722.

In 1726 an altercation with the Chevalier de Rohan, an effete but influential aristocrat, darkened Voltaire's outlook and intensified his sense of injustice. Rohan had mocked Voltaire's bourgeois origin and his change of name and in response to Voltaire's witty retort had hired ruffians to beat the poet, as Voltaire's friend and host, the Duc de Sully, looked on approvingly. When Voltaire demanded satisfaction through a duel, he was thrown into the Bastille through Rohan's influence and was released only on condition that he leave the country.

England willingly embraced Voltaire as a victim of France's injustice and infamy. During his stay there (1726-1728) he was feted; Alexander Pope, William Congreve, Horace Walpole, and Henry St. John, Viscount Bolingbroke, praised him; and his works earned Voltaire £1,000. Voltaire learned English by attending the theater daily, script in hand. He also imbibed English thought, especially that of John Locke and Sir Isaac Newton, and he saw the relationship between free government and creative speculation. More importantly, England suggested the relationship of wealth to freedom. The only protection, even for a brilliant poet, was wealth. Henceforth, Voltaire cultivated his Arouet business cunning.

At Cirey and at Court, 1729-1753

Voltaire returned to France in 1729. A tangible product of his English stay was the *Lettres anglaises* (1734), which have been called "the first bomb dropped on the Old Regime." Their explosive potential included such remarks as, "It has taken centuries to do justice to humanity, to feel it was horrible that the many should sow and the few should reap." Written in the style of letters to a friend in France, the 24 "letters" were a witty and seductive call for political, religious, and philosophic freedom; for the betterment of earthly life; for employing the method of Sir Francis Bacon, Locke, and Newton; and generally for exploiting the intellect toward social progress. After their publication in France in 1734, copies were sized from Voltaire's bookseller, and Voltaire was threatened with arrest. He fled to Lorraine and was not permitted to return to Paris until 1735. The work, with an additional letter on Pascal, was circulated as *Letters philosophiques*.

Prior to 1753 Voltaire did not have a home; but for 15 years following 1733 he had a refuge at Cirey, in a château owned by his "divine Émilie," Madame du Châtelet. While still living with her patient husband and son, Émilie made generous room for Voltaire. They were lovers; and they worked together intensely on physics and metaphysics. The lovers quarreled in English about trivia and studied the Old and New Testaments. These biblical labors were important as preparation for the antireligious works that Voltaire published in the 1750s and 1760s. At Cirey, Voltaire also wrote his *Éléments de la philosophie de Newton*.

But joining Émilie in studies in physics did not keep him from drama, poetry, metaphysics, history, and polemics. Similarly, Émilie's affection was not alone enough for Voltaire. From 1739 he required travel and new excitements. Thanks to Émilie's influence, Voltaire was by 1743 less unwelcome at Versailles than in 1733, but still there was great resentment toward the "lowborn intruder" who "noticed things a good courtier must overlook." Honored by a respectful correspondence with Frederick II of Prussia, Voltaire was then sent on diplomatic missions to Frederick. But Voltaire's new diversion was his incipient affair with his widowed niece, Madame Denis. This affair continued its erotic and stormy course to the last years of his life. Émilie too found solace in other lovers. The idyll of Cirey ended with her death in 1749.

Voltaire then accepted Frederick's repeated invitation to live at court. He arrived at Potsdam with Madame Denis in July 1750. First flattered by Frederick's hospitality, Voltaire then gradually became anxious, quarrelsome, and finally disenchanted. He left, angry, in March 1753, having written in December 1752: "I am going to write for my instruction a little dictionary used by Kings. 'My friend' means 'my slave.'" Frederick was embarrassed by Voltaire's vocal lawsuit with a moneylender and angered by his attempts to ridicule P. L. M. de Maupertuis, the imported head of the Berlin Academy. Voltaire's polemic against Maupertuis, the *Diatribe du docteur Akakia,* angered Frederick. Voltaire's angry response was to return the pension and other honorary trinkets bestowed by the King. Frederick retaliated by delaying permission for Voltaire's return to France, by putting him under a week's house arrest at the German border, and by confiscating his money.

Sage of Ferney, 1753-1778

After leaving Prussia, Voltaire visited Strasbourg, Colmar, and Lorraine, for Paris was again forbidden him. Then he went to Geneva. Even Geneva, however, could not tolerate all of Voltaire's activities of theater, pen, and press. Therefore, he left his property "Les Delices" and bought an estate at Ferney, where he lived out his days as a kingly patriarch. His own and Madame Denis's great extravagances were supported by the tremendous and growing fortune he amassed through shrewd money handling. A borrower even as a schoolboy, Voltaire became a shrewd lender as he grew older. Generous loans to persons in high places paid off well in favors and influence. At Ferney, he mixed in local politics, cultivated his lands, became through his intelligent benevolence beloved of the townspeople, and in general practiced a self-appointed and satisfying kingship. He became known as the "innkeeper of Europe" and entertained widely and well in his rather small but elegant household.

Voltaire's literary productivity did not slacken, although his concerns shifted as the years passed at Ferney. He was best known as a poet until in 1751 *Le Siècle de Louis XIV* marked him also as a historian. Other historical works include *Histoire de Charles XII; Histoire de la Russie sous Pierre le Grand;* and the universal history, *Essai sur l'histoire générale et sur les moeurs et l'esprit des nations,* published in 1756 but begun at Cirey. An extremely popular dramatist until 1760, when he began to be eclipsed by competition from the plays of Shakespeare that he had introduced to France, Voltaire wrote—in addition to the early *Oedipe*—*La Mort de César, Ériphyle, Zaïre, Alzire, Mérope, Mahomet, L'Enfant prodigue, Nanine* (a parody of Samuel Richardson's *Pamela*), *L'Orphelin de la Chine, Sémiramis* , and *Tancrède.*

The philosophic *conte* was a Voltaire invention. In addition to his famous *Candide* (1759), others of his stories in this genre include *Micromégas, Vision de Babouc, Memnon, Zadig,* and *Jeannot et Colin* . In addition to the *Lettres Philosophiques* and the work on Newton, others of Voltaire's works considered philosophic are *Philosophie de l'histoire, Le Philosophe ignorant, Tout en Dieu, Dictionnaire philosophique portatif,* and *Traité de la métaphysique.* Voltaire's poetry includes—in addition to the *Henriade*—the philosophic poems *L'Homme, La Loi naturelle,* and *Le Désastre de Lisbonne,* as well as the famous *La Pucelle,* a delightfully naughty poem about Joan of Arc.

Always the champion of liberty, Voltaire in his later years became actively involved in securing justice for victims of persecution. He became the "conscience of Europe." His activity in the Calas affair was typical. An unsuccessful and despondent young man had hanged himself in his Protestant father's home in Roman Catholic Toulouse. For 200 years Toulouse had celebrated the massacre of 4,000 of its Huguenot inhabitants. When the rumor spread that the deceased had been about to renounce Protestantism, the family was seized and tried for murder. The father was broken on the rack while protesting his innocence. A son was exiled, the daughters were confined in a convent, and the mother was left destitute. Investigation assured Voltaire of their innocence, and from 1762 to 1765 he worked unceasingly in their behalf. He employed "his friends, his purse, his pen, his credit" to move public opinion to the support of the Calas family.

Voltaire's ingenuity and zeal against injustice were not exhausted by the Calas affair. Similar was his activity in behalf of the Sirven family (1771) and of the victims of the Abbeville judges (1774). Nor was Voltaire's influence exhausted by his death in Paris on May 30, 1778, where he had gone in search of Madame Denis and the glory of being crowned with laurel at a performance of his drama *Irène.*

Assessment of Voltaire

John Morley, English secretary for Ireland under William Gladstone, wrote of Voltaire's stature: "When the right sense of historical proportion is more fully developed in men's minds, the name of Voltaire will stand out like the names of the great decisive moments in the European advance, like the Revival of Learning, or the Reformation." Gustave Lanson, in 1906, wrote of Voltaire: "He accustomed public common sense to regard itself as competent in all matters, and he turned public opinion into one of the controlling forces in public affairs." Lanson added: "For the public to become conscious of an idea, the idea must be repeated over and over. But the sauce must be varied to please the public palate. Voltaire was a master chef, a superb *saucier.*"

Voltaire was more than a thinker and activist. Style was nearly always nearly all to him-in his abode, in his dress, and particularly in his writings. As poet and man of letters, he was demanding, innovative, and fastidious within regulated patterns of expression. Even as thinker and activist, he believed that form was all-or at least the best part. As he remarked, "Never will twenty folio volumes bring about a revolution. Little books are the ones to fear, the pocket-size, portable ones that sell for thirty sous. If the Gospels had cost 1200 sesterces, the Christian religion could never have been established."

Voltaire's literary focus moved from that of poet to pamphleteer, and his moral sense had as striking a development. In youth a shameless libertine and in middle years a man notorious throughout the literary world, with more discreet but still eccentric attachments-in his later years Voltaire was renowned, whatever his personal habits, as a public defender and as a champion of human liberty. "Time, which alone makes their reputations of men," he observed," in the end makes their faults respectable." In his last days in Paris, he is said to have taken especially to heart a woman's remark: "Do you not know that he is the preserver of the Calas?"

Voltaire's life nearly spanned the 18th century; his writings fill 70 volumes; and his influence is not yet exhausted. He once wrote: "They wanted to bury me. But I outwitted them."

Further Reading

The best introduction in English to Voltaire's life is Gustave Lanson, *Voltaire* (1906; trans. 1966). John Morley's *Voltaire* (1903) also remains a readable and stimulating appreciation. A detailed and scholarly biography, by one of the world's leading authorities on Voltaire, is Theodore Besterman, *Voltaire* (1969). Ira O. Wade, *The Intellectual Development of Voltaire* (1969), in attempting to synthesize the many facets of Voltaire's mind for a unified view of his life, is often more encyclopedic than stimulating, but it provides a full and judicious treatment. Other useful studies include George Brandes. *Voltaire* (trans., 2 vols., 1930), and Henry Noel Brailsford, *Voltaire* (1935).

Interesting works that deal with various aspects of Voltaire's life include Ira O. Wade, *Voltaire and Madame du Châtelet* (1941); Edna Nixon, *Voltaire and the Calas Case* (1961); John N. Pappas, *Voltaire and D'Alembert* (1962); and H. T. Mason, *Pierre Bayle and Voltaire* (1963). Other specialized works worth consulting are Constance Rowe, *Voltaire and the State* (1955); J. H. Brumfitt, *Voltaire: Historian* (1958); Peter J. Gay, *Voltaire's Politics: The Poet as Realist* (1959); Virgil W. Topazio, *Voltaire: A Critical Study of His Major Works* (1967); and, for an excellent anthology of various critical opinions, William F. Bottiglia, ed., *Voltaire: A Collection of Critical Essays* (1968). □

Wernher von Braun

The German-born American space scientist Wernher von Braun (1912-1977), the "father of space travel," developed the first practical space rockets and launch vehicles.

Born March 23, 1912, in Wirsitz, Posen (Germany), his father, Baron Magnus von Braun, was a founder of the German Savings Bank, a member of the Weimar Republic Cabinet and minister of agriculture. His mother, the former Emmy von Quistorp, an excellent musician and outstanding amateur astronomer, exerted a strong influence on her son.

At the French Gymnasium, Wernher excelled in languages but failed physics and mathematics. He then attended the Hermann Lietz School at Ettersburg Castle, a school famous for its advanced teaching methods and emphasis on practical trades. He soon developed an intense interest in astronomy. Fascination with the theories of space flight then prompted him to study mathematics and physics with renewed interest. Before he graduated, he was teaching mathematics and tutoring deficient students.

Von Braun enrolled in the Charlottenburg Institute of Technology in Berlin. He became an active member of the VfR (Verein für Raumschiffahrt, or Society for Space Travel) and an associate of Hermann Oberth, Willy Ley and other leading German rocket enthusiasts.

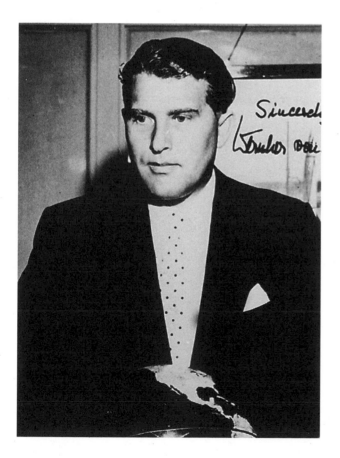

Soon afterward Oberth came to Berlin at the request of the VfR, and von Braun became his student assistant. Together they developed a small rocket engine which was a technical success. Funding for the project, however, ended and Oberth returned to his native Romania. Von Braun and his associates continued their work at an abandoned field outside Berlin and used the old buildings for laboratories and living quarters.

For a time von Braun attended the Institute of Technology in Zurich, Switzerland. There he began the study of the physiological effects of space flight, conducting crude experiments with mice in a centrifuge. The experiments convinced him that man could withstand the rapid acceleration and deceleration of space flight. He then returned to re-enter Charlottenburg Institute and work at the rocket field.

German Army Rocket Program

Adolf Hitler manipulated his way to power during the Weimar Republic and became chancellor of Germany on January 30, 1933. He then maneuvered a parliamentary coup, suspended the constitution and began rule by decree. Still smarting from the restrictions imposed by the Treaty of Versailles that ended World War I, the German army yearned to rebuild. The treaty had forbidden Germany to have any gun, cannon, or weapon with a bore exceeding three inches. But the Nazis saw a loophole. The treaty did not envision rockets and made no mention of them. So German military planners hoped to develop rockets as weapons. German army ordnance experts then began frequent visits to the rocket field and monitored the rocket development work. Impressed with the knowledge and scope of von Braun's imagination, they invited him to continue his research at the army's new Kummersdorf facilities. On Oct. 1, 1932, he officially joined the German Army Ordnance Office rocket program. He subsequently received his doctorate in physics from the University of Berlin in 1934. By that time, he was technical director at Kummersdorf with a staff of 80 scientists and technicians.

Rocket Development at Peenemünde

The Nazis moved the rocket center to Peenemünde, on Germany's Baltic coast, in 1937 and made von Braun technical director. When World War II began, Germany gave rocket development assumed highest priority. Work was well under way on a rocket 46 feet long with a thrust of 55,000 pounds, the largest in the world at that time. (By contrast, Oberth's first rocket had a thrust of 20 pounds; the Saturn V booster stage generated a thrust of 7.5 million pounds.) This rocket, later to be known as the V-2, was an enormous technical challenge. It required significant advances in aerodynamics, propulsion and guidance. Von Braun's team attacked the problems, and despite initial setbacks, persevered. They successfully produced V-2. The Nazis wanted it as a weapon of war. Von Braun had a different vision: space travel.

His interest in space exploration rather than military application led to his arrest and imprisonment by the German secret police. The Nazis released him only after they realized the implication of jailing their lead rocket scientist.

The program lurched backward without his leadership. It disrupted Hitler's timetable for the war.

By 1943 the rocket complex at Peenemünde was a priority Allied target. When Germany was near collapse, von Braun evacuated his staff to an area where they might be captured by the Americans. He reasoned that the United States was the nation most likely to use its resources for space exploration. He led more than 5,000 of his associates and their families to the southwest just before the Russians advanced into the abandoned rocket development center. The rocket team surrendered to U.S. Forces on May 2, 1945.

Early U.S. Rocket Experiments

During interrogation by Allied intelligence officers, von Braun prepared a report on rocket development and applications in which he forecast trips to the moon, orbiting satellites and space stations. Recognizing the scope of von Braun's work, the U.S. Army authorized the transfer of von Braun, 112 of his engineers and scientists, 100 V-2 rockets and the rocket technical data to the United States.

Von Braun and his advance group arrived in the United States as "wards of the Army" on Sept. 29, 1945. They arrived at Ft. Bliss, Tex. with a mandate to re-assemble and further develop A-4 rockets, the German successor to the V-2. There they taught what they knew to what was then a limited audience. The team moved what is now White Sands Proving Grounds in New Mexico in 1946 and then to Redstone Arsenal in Huntsville, Alabama in 1950 where von Braun remained for the next twenty years. He used his free time to write about space travel and to correspond with his family and his cousin, Maria von Quistorp. In early 1947 he obtained permission to return to Germany to marry Maria. They had three children.

Von Braun continued work on V-2 launchings, conducting some of the earliest experiments in recording atmospheric conditions, photographing the earth from high altitudes, perfecting guidance systems, and conducting medical experiments with animals in space. He also completed his book, *The Mars Project,* an account of planetary exploration, but he was unable to interest a publisher until much later.

The U.S. Army gave von Braun the job of developing the Redstone rocket, which was to play a significant role in America's early space program. On April 15, 1955, von Braun and 40 of his associates became naturalized citizens.

The Russian space program outstripped that of the United States in the 1950s. Von Braun warned American officials of this repeatedly, in official communications and in public speeches, but his numerous requests for permission to orbit a satellite were denied. When the Russians successfully orbited *Sputnik I* and the U.S. Navy's Vanguard program failed, the United States finally unleased von Braun's group. Within 90 days, using a modified Redstone rocket (the Jupiter C), and with the cooperation of the Jet Propulsion Laboratory of the California Institute of Technology, the team launched into orbit the free world's first satellite *Explorer I* on January 31, 1958.

U.S. Space Program

After creation of the National Aeronautics and Space Administration, they appointed von Braun director of the George C. Marshall Space Flight Center at Huntsville on July 1, 1960. For the first time, von Braun found his efforts directed to the development of launch vehicles solely to explore space. The space agency sought his advice about techniques later used in the landing on the moon. On Oct. 27, 1961, agency launched the first Saturn I vehicle. It was 162 feet long, weighed 460 tons at lift-off, and rose to a height of 85 miles. On Nov. 9, 1967, the newer Saturn V made its debut. It was more than twice as long as the Saturn I. Just before Christmas, 1968, a Saturn V launch vehicle, developed under von Braun's direction, launched *Apollo 8,* the world's first spacecraft to travel to the moon. In March 1970, the National Aeronautics and Space Administration (NASA) transferred von Braun to its headquarters in Washington, D.C., where he became Deputy Associate Administrator.

Von Braun resigned from NASA in July, 1972, to become vice president for engineering and development with Fairchild Industries of Germantown, Maryland. Besides his work for that aerospace firm, he continued his efforts to promote human space flight, helping to found the National Space Institute in 1975 and serving as its first president. On June 16, 1977, he died of cancer at a hospital in Alexandria, Virginia.

Von Braun was always a firm believer in personal experience as a teacher, and often took part in experiments conducted to determine the physiological aspects of space flight. Long before the acceptance of the feasibility of space flight, he subjected himself to experiments in weightlessness and high acceleration.

Considered one of the world's great scientists, von Braun was a profoundly religious man. On one occasion he remarked: "We should remember that science exists only because there are people, and its concepts exist only in the minds of men. Behind these concepts lies the reality which is being revealed to us, but only by the grace of God."

Further Reading

Erik Bergaust, *Reaching for the Stars* (1960); Helen B. Walters, *Wernher von Braun: Rocket Engineer* (1964); Heather M. David, *Wernher von Braun* (1967); and John Goodrum, *Wernher von Braun: Space Pioneer* (1969). The most detailed accounts of German rocket development under Von Braun and the experiences of the German rocket team are in Walter Dornberger, *V-2* (1952; trans. 1954), and Dieter K. Huzel, *Peenemünde to Canaveral* (1962). An excellent account of the U.S. Army's rocket development efforts under Von Braun and the launching of *Explorer I* is given in John B. Medaris, *Countdown for Decision* (1960). For additional background see Wernher von Braun and Frederick I. Ordway, *History of Rocketry and Space Travel* (1967); Edward O. Buckbee, *Biographical Data: Wernher von Braun* (1983); Hunt, Linda, *Secret Agenda: The United States Government, Nazi Scientists, and Project Paperclip* (1991); and Ernst Stulinger and Frederick Ordway, *Wernher von Braun: Crusader for Space* (1994). □

Joost van den Vondel

The Dutch poet and dramatist Joost van den Vondel (1587-1679) ranks as the greatest of all Dutch writers. He achieved his status of national poet during the period when the Netherlands was emerging as a national state.

Joost van den Vondel was born in Cologne, Germany, on Nov. 17, 1587. His father, a hatter, had been forced to flee from Antwerp because of his Anabaptist convictions. Between 1582 and 1596 his parents, as persecuted members of the Anabaptist sect, were intermittently compelled to flee from the inquisitorial reign of terror instituted in the Lowlands by its Spanish regent and governor general, the Duke of Alba. In 1597, a year after his arrival in Amsterdam, Vondel's father acquired Amsterdam citizenship, enabling the family to settle in the "Venice of the North."

During this period Amsterdam was the commercial and cultural capital of northern Europe. The senior Vondel established a hosiery business and expected his oldest son to follow him in his trade. However, the younger Vondel was introduced early to one of the popular Chambers of Rhetoric, societies of poets; he soon became a member of Het wit Lavendel (White Lavender). The friendships made in this circle with leading artistic and intellectual figures of the day encouraged Vondel's interest in poetry and in study and led to the beginning of his long career as poet and dramatist.

Early Works

After Vondel's father died, the poet married Maria (Maaiken) de Wolff, with whom he lived happily for 25 years and in whose hands he left the management of his affairs. Vondel passed on from his early *rederijker* influences to a close study of French contemporary poets, being much influenced by Guillaume du Bartas's epic poem, *La Sepmaine; ou, Creation du monde* (1578). Vondel then made several translations from the German, soon becoming a member of the literary circle that clustered around Roemer Visscher. With these friends Vondel made a close study of Greek and Roman writers. His first play, *Het Pascha* (*The Passover*), performed in 1610 and published in 1612, dramatized the Jewish Exodus from Egypt and served as an allegorical representation of the plight of the Calvinists who had fled Spanish tyranny in the Lowlands.

Meanwhile, Vondel's hatred of all kinds of tyranny gradually weaned him from Calvinism's theocratic doctrines, and by 1625 he had joined the Remonstrants, whose Arminian opposition to Calvinist dogma appealed to him. After the production in 1625 of *Palamedes, of Vermoorde onnooselheyd* (*Palamedes, or Murdered Innocence*), he suffered political persecution and was forced to go into hiding. This drama, which transposed the judicial murder of Holland's lord advocate Johan van Oldenbarnevelt in 1619—a cause that had inflamed Holland and all of Europe—into a classical setting, struck sharply against Oldenbarnevelt's jury, Calvinism's doctrine of predestination, and Calvinist

divines in Amsterdam. The city's magistrates eventually forgave Vondel and exacted only a small fine.

In the following years Vondel entered into a close friendship with Hugo Grotius, translating his Latin *Sofompaneas* in 1635. That same year Vondel's wife died, and earlier two of his children had died, leaving only his eldest son Joost (died 1660) surviving. These deaths, and his imminent conversion to Roman Catholicism, inspired many of Vondel's best poems. Long attracted by Roman Catholicism's esthetic side, and after national independence seemed virtually assured, he converted to Catholicism about 1640. This revolt against Calvinist tyranny was not well received by many of his friends, but it probably strengthened his ties with Marie Tesselschade Visscher, the Catholic and liberal widow of his friend Roemer Visscher.

Vondel's last years were clouded by the disgraceful behavior of his son Joost. Entrusted with the family hosiery business, his son mismanaged affairs, fleeing in 1657 to the Netherlands Indies and leaving his father to deal with the creditors. After sacrificing his small fortune, Vondel became a government clerk. Pensioned after 10 years' service, he died on Feb. 5, 1679, in Amsterdam.

Plays and Poetry

Vondel wrote 32 plays, as well as a famous series of prefaces to Ahem. He also made numerous translations from German, French, Latin, Italian, and Greek; produced a large body of poetry, including emblems, lyrics, occasional poems, long theological poems, didactic verses, pastorals, and an epic; and wrote essays.

Of his plays, the most important—in addition to the two already mentioned—are *Hierusalem Verwoest* (1620; *Jerusalem Laid Desolate*); *Gijsbrecht van Aemstel* (1637), whose hero was modeled on the Aeneas of book 2 of Virgil's *Aeneid; De Gebroeders* (1640; *The Brothers*), the story of the ruin of Saul's sons, Vondel's first drama on the Greek model; *Joseph in Egypten* (1640), another biblical drama in the Greek style; *Maria Stuart, of gemartelde majesteit* (1646), one of his most famous plays; *De Leeuwendalers* (1648), a pastoral that anticipated the Treaty of Westphalia; *Salomon* (1648), a biblical play in the Greek style; *Lucifer* (1654), generally considered his masterpiece; *Jephtha* (1659), which Vondel believed to be his finest play; *Konig David in Ballingschap* (*King David in Exile*), *Konig David hersteld* (*King David Restored*), and *Samson*, three dramas on biblical themes (all 1660); *Batavische Gebroeders* (1663), a play on the history of Claudius Civilis; and *Adam in Ballingschap* (*Adam in Exile*), an adaptation of a Latin tragedy by Hugo Grotius.

Many of Vondel's plays illuminate a recurring theme: the conflict between man's will to rebel and his desire to find peace in God. Modeled on medieval mystery plays and on classical dramas, they are deeply Christian and tragic, or semi–tragic, in treatment. His style has been termed high baroque, and it is preeminent in dramatic force and in loftiness of language.

Vondel's poetry is notable for its melodiousness, sonorousness, and seemingly effortless and spontaneous production. Vowel elision, which he regularized in Dutch poetry, and rhythmic patterns, brought over from contemporary French poetry, characterize his verse. His epic, *Johannes de Boetgezant,* was published in 1662, as was his long theological poem, *Bespiegelingen van Godt en Godtsdienst.*

Further Reading

Biographical and critical studies of Vondel in English are George Edmundson, *Milton and Vondel: A Curiosity of Literature* (1885), and Adriaan J. Barnouw, *Vondel* (1925). Theodore Weevers, *Poetry of the Netherlands in its European Context, 1170-1930* (1960), contains a useful chapter on Vondel. Recommended for general background is Johan Huizinga, *Dutch Civilization in the Seventeenth Century and Other essays,* selected by Pieter Geyl and F. W. N. Hugenholtz (1968). □

Diane von Furstenberg

Among a handful of successful women fashion designers, Diane von Furstenberg (born 1946) made a name for herself when she devised a simple jersey wrap dress. She became internationally acclaimed for her no-nonsense, affordable clothing that acknowledged the modern woman as both beautiful and career-minded.

Diane von Furstenberg was born Diane Simone Michelle Halfin on December 31, 1946, in Brussels, Belgium. Her well-to-do Jewish parents, Leon, an electronics executive, and Liliane Nahmias Halfin, provided von Furstenberg with a comfortable childhood. Her mother, a Nazi concentration camp survivor, imbued her with the self-confidence and drive that helped her become one of the world's most successful fashion designers.

Von Furstenberg attended finishing schools in Switzerland, Spain, and England, and in 1965 entered the University of Madrid. Transferring a year later to the University of Geneva, she selected economics as a major. She then worked briefly at Investors Overseas Ltd., a mutual fund company in Geneva.

The Princess Designer

While attending the University of Geneva, Diane Halfin met Prince Eduard Egon von Furstenberg, heir to the *Fiat* automobile fortune. The two were married in Paris on July 16, 1969. At her wedding von Furstenberg, now Princess von Furstenberg, wore a white piqué dress of her own design made by the fashion house of Dior.

That same year she apprenticed with Italian textile manufacturer Angelo Ferretti and was soon designing simple dresses using his silk jersey prints. The von Furstenbergs moved to New York City in late 1969, where her husband went to work on Wall Street. In New York Diane attempted to interest garment manufacturers in her sample designs. In

her early months of designing and promoting, she worked out of the dining room of her Park Avenue apartment.

Encouraged by designers Bill Blass and Kenny Lane and by Diana Vreeland, editor of the influential *Vogue* magazine, Diane von Furstenberg put together a collection of her dress designs. In April 1970 von Furstenberg revealed her first collection at the Gotham Hotel in New York City. The price range was moderate, from $25 to $100.

The Wrap Dress

Although her designs were a commercial hit, her marriage failed. Von Furstenberg aimed even more at making herself financially independent and stable. Because she had little experience in producing clothes on a large scale, von Furstenberg at first worked with major women's clothing manufacturers, but in April 1972 she established her own manufacturing business. With the help of friend and entrepreneur Richard Conrad, and with a $30,000 loan from her father, Diane von Furstenberg opened a Seventh Avenue showroom. Although her designs were variations on items in her initial collection, she produced a new, very popular sweater dress named "Angela," after the black activist Angela Davis. Next came von Furstenberg's enormously popular wrap dress. "Fed up with the bell-bottom jeans and sexless pantsuits of the day, she devised a slinky, moderately priced wrap dress that turned millions of mall mothers and working women into saucy sirens virtually overnight," noted J.D. Polosky in *People*. After only a few months of business, her wholesale sales topped $1 million.

In 1973 von Furstenberg bought an old farmhouse in Connecticut, where she retreated from her frenetic business life. In 1975 she separated from the prince, and in 1983 divorced him, retaining custody of their two children, Alexandre and Tatiana.

Expanding Business

With a good grasp of both design and economics, von Furstenberg augmented her fashion line several years after opening her showroom. She added jewelry, furs, shoes, scarves, and sunglasses to the articles bearing her signature. Later she conceived of a cosmetic line, including a fragrance named for her daughter, *Tatiana*. She branched into housewares: sheets, bath towels, and home accessories. Soon her trademark began appearing on fashions for children.

Her dynamic career and elegant looks kept her in the public eye. Diane von Furstenberg, the princess-turned-designer, was featured often in magazine articles and interviews. In 1977 she published *Diane von Furstenberg's Book of Beauty*. She appealed to working women because her practical designs acknowledged the growing number of career women. In 1984 von Furstenberg opened a Fifth Avenue boutique catering to women who desired a more luxurious type of women's apparel.

Von Furstenberg proved herself a financial genius and fashion wizard whose achievement was based on creativity, imagination, and hard work. Her line eventually included eyeglasses and even nurse's uniforms and brought sales of more than $1 billion in the 1980s. "I lived the American dream," she told *People*. "I made money, I made children, I became famous, and I dressed everybody in America."

New Horizons

In 1985, she moved to Paris, and lived with French novelist Alain Elkann. She founded a publishing house. She broke up with Elkann in 1989 and returned to the United States, living at a farm in Connecticut.

Her 1991 book *Beds* displayed the bedrooms of celebrities and royalty. She followed by making a comeback to the dress designing world, releasing a 1990s version of her signature wrap dress. In 1993, another book, *The Bath*, offered a brief history of bathing and a look into celebrity bathrooms.

Seeing new possibilities for commercial success, von Furstenberg, in the mid-1990s, began marketing her dresses, home furnishings and other items on a cable television home shopping network. During her first segment, she sold $1.2 million worth of clothes in two hours. "She's smart and warm, glamorous and earthy, and she know how to seduce her customers," Jane Shapiro explained in a January 1994 article in *Lear's*. Asked to explain why middle-class customers always were her mainstay, von Furstenberg answered: "Because I think women are all the same. And I think that women are wonderful, strong, and beautiful, and if you get two women in the room, they're gonna start winking at each other."

Further Reading

Numerous articles and interviews describing Diane von Furstenberg throughout her career appeared in popular magazines. One of the most informative is J.D. Polosky, "Not Lying on Her Laurels," *People*, December 9, 1991. Diane von Furstenberg's books include *Diane von Furstenberg's Book of Beauty* (1977), *Beds* (1991), and *The Bath* (1993). □

Baron Friedrich von Hügel

Baron Friedrich von Hügel (1852-1925) wrote extensively on issues in the philosophy of religion. He was particularly concerned with questions relating to the importance of the truth—claims of modern science to believing Christians.

Baron Friedrich von Hügel was born in Florence, Italy, on May 5, 1852, the son of an Austrian diplomat and his Scottish wife, recently converted to her husband's Catholic faith. Friedrich's early education was provided by tutors at home; indeed, he never attended school or college and was largely self-taught throughout his life. In 1860 Baron Karl moved his family to Brussels, where he served as ambassador until his retirement in 1867; thereafter the von Hügels resided in Torquay, England, while making frequent visits to the Continent.

Von Hügel's upbringing continued under rather mixed influences. A Quaker tutor introduced him to the study of geology, which became his lifelong avocation. Soon after his father's death in 1870 the young man fell gravely ill with typhus. This left him with impaired hearing, which became worse as he grew older. Deprived of normal social opportunities, Friedrich turned to reading and amateur scholarship, learning some Hebrew, with a nearby rabbi's help, while pursuing his scientific work. On a trip to Paris he met the Abbé Huvelin, a gifted counselor who had a lasting influence on von Hügel's somewhat troubled spiritual development.

In 1873 the baron was married to Lady Mary Herbert who, like his mother, was a recent Catholic convert. Their family consisted of three daughters, for whose religious education the father took personal responsibility. They lived first in Hempstead, then in Kensington, London, where von Hügel died on January 27, 1925.

Von Hügel's books were published only after he was 56 years old, the products of a fully matured, still vigorous mind. The longest and perhaps best-known, *Mystical Element of Religion* (1908), grew out of long study of St. Catherine of Genoa; in it he wrestled with the charges of psychological abnormality in the mystic's experience, insisted on the mystic's right to be heard both inside and outside the Church, and defended his view that direct experience of a divine reality can be attained. In 1912 a second book appeared, *Eternal Life*, interpreting this central theme in the Gospel of John in fresh, robust fashion. A shorter work titled *The German Soul* (1916) sought to counteract the then-current diatribes against everything German.

Two volumes of *Essays and Addresses on the Philosophy of Religion* (1921 and 1926) gathered together some of the baron's papers and lectures on diverse topics dating back to 1904. These books greatly extended their author's influence as a seminal thinker in a field too long dominated by "scholastic and theoretical" rather than "mystical and positive" approaches, to adopt one of von Hügel's favorite contrasts. Although his poor health prevented him from giving the Gifford Lectures for 1924-1925, the unfinished manuscript was published in 1931 as *The Reality of God*.

The slow, strenuous development of von Hügel's thought is better traced in two volumes of correspondence with his wide circle of friends, including thinkers such as Wilfrid Ward, Clement Webb, Ernst Troeltsch, Rudolf Eucken, Maurice Blondel, and Louis Duchesne. This material is contained in *Selected Letters 1896 to 1924* (edited by Bernard Holland); a more intimate glimpse of the baron's thought processes is given in *Letters from Baron von Hügel to a Niece,* Gwendolyn Greene. They make lively reading as they disclose an honest mind at grips with "indefinitely apprehensible truth."

Never thoroughly at home in English, von Hügel's style of writing often seems "uncouth and ponderous," as Dean Inge once remarked. However, it contains sentences and phrases of memorable vibrancy as well, which accurately reflect the rock-like quality of the writer's thinking—in constant dialogue with itself, utterly candid, and without any flourish of finality. The same conversational freshness marks his work intended for publication and engages the reader in a shared search for needed authenticity.

The baron's large capacity for friendship led him naturally into many discussions over issues in the philosophy of religion, especially those raised by the truth claims of modern science for believing Christians like himself. Problems of biblical interpretation interested him always and soon brought him into contact with the Modernist movement through its leading representatives, Alfred Loisy in France and George Tyrrell in England.

Just what part he played in Modernism has been much debated. Never sympathetic toward fundamentalist and absolutist tendencies within his own church, he tried to keep an open mind in matters such as the historical-critical study of Scripture or the claims of papal primacy in defining dogma. So he could, and did, encourage Loisy and Tyrrell, the *enfants terribles* of Modernism, in their researches and hypotheses while refusing to follow them into rebellion against Church authority. When his friends were censured by the Vatican and the papal encyclical *Pascendi* (1907) brought public debate to an end, von Hügel's own writing escaped being placed on the Vatican's index of forbidden books and his influence as an ecumenical thinker was secured.

It is of course impossible to reduce such ruggedly unsystematic, metaphorical ways of thinking to a few generalized propositions, but something like an overview can be attempted. The baron thought habitually in both/and rather than either/or terms; he called his method a "critical realism" that takes first-order experience as evidential but insists upon the need for second-order reflection and qualification. Resisting oversimplification, he studied religious phenomena as a "complex of characteristics" to be approached dialectically, fully aware of the genuine tensions they present, unwilling to presume to solve in theory what may only be resolved in practice. His treatment of the "problem of evil" is a good example of his method, as is also his treatment of "miracle" over against both nature and the supernatural. For von Hügel, mystery and reality are two ways of saying the same thing—or, rather, the whole of things—each of which would be strictly unthinkable without the other.

He thus remained an independent, deeply provocative thinker whose writings will no doubt continue to intrigue and inspire others who concern themselves with the truth of Christian faith. In him, as in his thought, intellectual honesty kept intimate company with a sincerity of spirit; this may well be the source of von Hügel's influence and importance.

Further Reading

There are three useful biographies of von Hügel in English. Michael de la Bedoyère, *The Life of Baron von Hügel* (1951) gives the fullest account of his personal development, family relationships, and influential friendships. L. V. Lester Garland, *The Religious Philosophy of Baron F. von Hügel* (1933) provides the best overview of salient features in his thought, with ample and well-chosen quotations from letters and occasional papers as well as longer works. Maurice Nédoncelle, *Baron Friedrich von Hügel* (1937), with an extensive bibliography of material by and about the baron, is chiefly interested in his struggle with Catholic orthodoxy. □

Max von Laue

The German physicist Max von Laue (1879-1960) was the first to use x-rays to study the arrangement of atoms in crystals. His work in x-ray crystallography earned him the Nobel Prize in physics in 1914.

Max Theodor Felix von Laue was born on October 9, 1879, in Pfaffendorf, Germany. His father was a civilian official in German military administration who in 1913 was raised to the hereditary nobility (hence the *von* in the family name). In the early 1890s the young von Laue gained a passionate interest in physics that lasted until his death some 60 years later.

Von Laue received his scientific training at the universities of Strasbourg, Munich, and Göttingen. He was awarded a doctorate in mathematics and physics by the University of Berlin (1903) where he came under the influence of Max Planck, one of the greatest physicists of the 20th century. In the fall of 1905 Planck offered von Laue a post at the Institute for Theoretical Physics. The four years (1905-1909) during which von Laue worked closely with Planck marked the beginning of his career as a creative scientist. An early and lifelong champion of the physical ideas of Albert Einstein, von Laue began publishing papers on the theory of relativity in 1907.

In 1909 von Laue moved to the University of Munich where he was associated with yet another distinguished physicist, Arnold Sommerfield. Continuing his interest in relativity at Munich, von Laue prepared a 200-page monograph on the subject, the first such book to be published on Einstein's revolutionary theories. At Sommerfield's suggestion von Laue began writing a treatise on wave optics. This undertaking led him to the famous work on x-ray analysis of the atomic structure of crystalline material.

The precise nature of x-radiation, discovered by W. C. Roentgen in 1895, had not yet been determined when von Laue initiated his study of x-rays. If, as some argued, x-rays were not made up of particles but were a form of electromagnetic radiation similar to ordinary light, then it should be possible to repeat well-known optical experiments using x-rays instead of beams of ordinary light. For example, when ordinary light passes through a diffraction grating (a piece of glass covered with a series of fine, parallel, equidistant lines engraved upon its surface) a characteristic diffraction or interference pattern results. Because the wave-length of x-rays was assumed to be much shorter than that of light, an x-ray diffraction experiment required a grating with lines more finely ruled than was physically possible.

Von Laue's contribution was the insight that when using x-radiation the glass diffraction grating can be replaced by crystalline material. The regular spacing of the atoms in the crystal will affect x-rays penetrating it in the same way that the closely engraved lines of the grating affect light passing through. Von Laue, always the theoretician, did not actually make the necessary experiments, but those

who did confirmed his predictions—x-rays diffracted by crystals yielded the expected interference patterns.

Von Laue's discovery, which Einstein hailed as one of the most beautiful in the history of physics, won him the Nobel Prize in 1914. This pioneering work in x-ray crystallography opened the way for two quite different developments in physics, both of them of immense importance. First, it confirmed the electro-magnetic nature of x-radiation and made it possible to determine the wave length of x-rays with great accuracy. Second, it gave physicists and chemists a new tool for investigating the atomic structure of matter. In the 1950s it was x-ray diffraction studies that enabled scientists to reveal the structure of the nucleic acids (DNA and RNA) and to establish the new discipline of molecular biology.

During World War I von Laue helped to improve the electronic vacuum tubes used in the German army's communication system. After the war (1919) he accepted a post at the University of Berlin. Subsequent research led von Laue to refine his study of x-ray interference and to explore the phenomenon of super-conductivity whereby certain metals lose virtually all of their resistance to the flow of an electric current at temperatures approaching absolute zero (-273.16 C).

Between the two world wars, von Laue became a leading statesman of German theoretical physics. He held high positions in academic scientific institutions and used his influence there to defend freedom of thought and expression in science. He battled particularly against Nazi attempts to suppress relativity theory as the degenerate product of an inferior Jewish scientific outlook.

After World War II von Laue labored to revive German physics and bring it back into the world scientific community. In 1951 he was made director of the prestigious Fritz Haber Institute of Physical Chemistry, a post he held until his retirement in 1958. Two years later he lost his life in an automobile accident.

Further Reading

Max von Laue's life and scientific achievements are covered in P.P. Ewald, "Max von Laue," in *Biographical Memoirs of Fellows of the Royal Society,* vol. 6 (1960) and in Armin Hermann, "Laue, Max von," in the *Dictionary of Scientific Biography* , vol. VIII, edited by C.C. Gillispie (1970). For a history of physics in Germany during von Laue's lifetime see Armin Hermann, *The New Physics* (Munich, 1979). □

Robert Brandt von Mehren

The American lawyer Robert Brandt von Mehren (born 1922) was instrumental in creating the legal structure of the International Atomic Energy Agency.

Robert B. von Mehren was born in Albert Lea, MN, on August 10, 1922. His twin brother, Arthur T. von Mehren, was the Story Professor of Law at Harvard University. He also had a younger brother who was killed in World War II. His father, a civil engineer, was born in Denmark, and his mother was American. An educated and cultured man with a keen interest in art, history, and literature, von Mehren's father had a strong influence on him.

Von Mehren attended Sidney Pratt Elementary School and John Marshall High School in Minneapolis, MN. He won a scholarship to Yale University, where he majored in comparative government, with a minor in economics and politics. He graduated *summa cum laude* in December 1942.

In 1943 he was awarded a scholarship to Harvard Law School and entered it in the fall of that year. He decided to study law because, as he believed, it provides "an excellent combination of the active and contemplative" and "unlocks the door to many opportunities." He was a member of the board of editors of the Harvard Law Review from 1943 to 1946 and was elected its president for volume 59. He graduated *magna cum laude* in February 1946.

Von Mehren started his legal career in April 1946 with the New York law firm of Debevoise, Plimpton, Lyons and Gates. He took a leave of absence to serve as law clerk for Judge Learned Hand of the U.S. Circuit Court of Appeal for the Second Circuit during the October 1946 term. During the October 1947 term he served as law clerk for Justice Stanley F. Reed of the Supreme Court of the United States. After 1948 he returned to Debevoise, Plimpton, Lyons and

Gates, and became a member of the firm in April 1957. He remained a partner at the firm until 1993.

In 1954 von Mehren was admitted to practice before the Supreme Court of the United States. He was also admitted to practice before six lesser but important courts—the U.S. Circuit Courts of Appeal for the Second Circuit (1950), the Third Circuit (1953), and the District of Columbia (1974); the U.S. District Courts for the Southern District of New York (1949) and the Eastern District of New York (1971); and the U.S. Tax Court (1972).

A leading expert on international law, von Mehren served as legal counsel to the preparatory commission of the International Atomic Energy Agency from 1956 to 1957. He was closely involved in setting up the legal structure of the agency and in making the preparations for the first conference of the International Atomic Energy Agency, which was held in Vienna, Austria, in the fall of 1957. He was a consultant to the Rand Corporation on disarmament problems from 1960 to 1966 and to the Hudson Institute on international law problems from 1962 to 1966.

From 1961 to 1966 von Mehren was also director of the Legal Aid Society. A hard-working activist, especially in international law, he was president of the American branch of the International Law Association, a member of the executive council of the American Society of International Law, a member of the board of editors of the American Journal of International Law, and a member of the Council on Foreign Relations.

Von Mehren was also an influential member of the Association of the Bar of the City of New York, serving as chairman of its Committee on International Law, of the Committee on Law Reform, and of the Ad Hoc Committee on Foreign Payments. He served as chairman of the Special Committee to Study Defender Systems (a joint committee of the Association of the Bar of the City of New York and the National Legal Aid and Defender Association), which published its report, "Equal Justice for the Accused," in April 1959. In addition, he served as secretary of the Special Committee on Atomic Energy and was a member of the Special Committee to Co-operate with the International Commission of Jurists.

Von Mehren was a trustee of the Practicing Law Institute in New York City starting in 1972 and served as its president (1979-1986) and its board chairman, beginning in 1986. He contributed numerous articles to professional law journals. He married Mary Katharine Kelly on June 26, 1948, and they had five children. After her death in 1985, he married Susan Heller Anderson in 1988.

Further Reading

Von Mehren's many articles include two on atomic energy: "The Atomic Energy Act and The Private Production of Atomic Power," co-authored with Oscar M. Ruebhausen and published in the *Harvard Law Review* (June 1953), and "The International Atomic Energy Agency in World Politics," *Journal of International Affairs* (January 1959). Also useful is his study with P. Nicholas Kourides of "International Arbitrations between States and Foreign Private Parties: The Libyan Nationalization Cases," *American Journal of International Law* (1981). □

Ludwig von Mises

Ludwig von Mises (1881-1973) an Austrian econo-mist and social philosopher, was the leading expo-nent, in the 20th century, of the Austrian school and an extreme conservative in matters of economic and social policy.

Ludwig von Mises was born September 29, 1881, in the city of Lemberg which was located in the former Austria-Hungary. He was born the son of a highly successful and respected engineer. By the time von Mises was 19 he had already entered the prestigious University of Vienna, studying under Eugen von Böhm-Bahwerk and Eugene von Philippovich. Ludwig von Mises earned his doctorate degree in Both (Canon and Roman) Laws by the time he was 27 years of age.

After receiving his advanced degree, von Mises wrote the first of what would be a long list of phenomenal works, *The Theory of Money and Credit* (1912). Von Mises was revolutionary in his thinking. He would successfully argue that money had a price, not unlike any other commodity. The theory was based on the economic notion that all things were priced according to supply and demand. Von Mises theorized that money would have the same effect, therefore, its "price" would rise and fall as well.

Von Mises was privatdozent of economics at Vienna (1913-1934) and professor of international relations at the Graduate Institute of International Studies in Geneva, Swit-zerland (1934-1940). In 1945 he became visiting professor of economics at the Graduate School of Business Adminis-tration of New York University; he retired in 1969. Between the years of 1909 and 1934 he held various economic advisor positions with the Austrian Chamber of Commerce.

Von Mises was known throughout his career as an uncompromising champion of laissez-faire, arguing in *So-cialism: An Economic and Sociological Analysis* (1922) and *Human Action: A Treatise on Economics* (1949) that a so-cialist system cannot function because it lacks a true price system. It has been written that *Socialism* was a prediction of the fall of communism. Von Mises argued that socialism could not sustain an economy, due to the fact that under socialism there is no market for goods or services. Von Mises projected that without an industrial economy, there would be no price system. It is the price system which determines profit and loss. In the same book, von Mises also theorized that mixed economies would fare no better, be-cause of the distortion involved. He also held that lesser types of intervention, such as minimum-wage laws, are equally futile. In his writings on the epistemology of eco-nomics, he maintained that the only approach to economics is a deductive system based on self-evident axioms stressing the individual's purposive choice of means to arrive at preferred ends.

A theory of the business cycle grew out of Von Mises's theory of money and was developed by him in detail by 1928. This theory emphasized the role of the banking sys-tem in the expansion of the money supply, the consequent artificial lowering of the interest rate, and the resulting overinvestment. When the money supply reaches the limits of its ability to expand, a depression inevitably follows. The theory aroused considerable interest among economists in the early 1930s but was lost sight of with the advent of the "Keynesian revolution," which began in 1936. Later in the century, economists reconsidered the role of overinvestment as a factor in business fluctuations.

Von Mises's publications include almost 20 books as well as numerous articles and other, shorter pieces ranging from economic theory and the history of economic thought to methodology and social and political philosophy. In 1969 he was named distinguished fellow of the American Economic Association in recognition of his valuable contri-butions to economics.

Due to von Mises's critical views on socialism he re-mained in exile from the National Socialists in Geneva until his death in 1973. Von Mises's most highly regarded work was his 900-page *Human Action* which was not published until 1949. The book had been written in early 1940; how-ever, amidst the effects of the war, it was placed on hold.

Further Reading

Mary H. Sennholz, ed., *On Freedom and Free Enterprise: Essays in Honor of Ludwig von Mises* (1956), contains considerable information on von Mises and his work. A chapter on him is in the excellent study by Ben B. Seligman, *Main Currents in Modern Economics: Economic Thought since 1870* (1962). Additional material on Von Mises is in Howard S. Ellis, Ger-man *Monetary Theory, 1905-1933* (1934), and Israel M. Kirzner, The *Economic Point of View: An Essay in the History of Economic Thought* (1960). Information regarding Ludwig von Mises is also accessible at http://www.mises.org. □

Kurt Vonnegut Jr.

Kurt Vonnegut Jr. (born 1922) is acknowledged as a major voice in American literature and applauded for his pungent satirical depictions of modern soci-ety. Emphasizing the comic absurdity of the human condition, he frequently depicts characters who search for meaning and order in an inherently mean-ingless and disorderly universe.

Vonnegut was born on November 11, 1922, in India-napolis, Indiana, the son of a successful architect. After attending Cornell University, where he majored in chemistry and biology, he enlisted in the United States Army, serving in the Second World War and eventually being taken prisoner by the German Army. Following the war, Vonnegut studied anthropology at the University of Chicago and subsequently moved to Schenectady, New York, to work as a publicist for the General Electric Corporation. During this period, he also began submitting short stories to various journals, and in 1951, he resigned his position at General Electric to devote his time solely to writing.

Vonnegut published several novels throughout the 1950s and 1960s, beginning with *Player Piano* in 1952. However, his frequent use of elements of fantasy resulted in his classification as a writer of science fiction, a genre not widely accepted as "serious literature," and his work did not attract significant popular or critical interest until the mid-1960s, when increasing disillusionment with American society led to widespread admiration for his forthright, irreverent satires. His reputation was greatly enhanced in 1969 with the publication of *Slaughterhouse-Five,* a vehemently antiwar novel that appeared during the peak of protest against American involvement in Vietnam. During the 1970s and 1980s, Vonnegut continued to serve as an important commentator on American society, publishing a series of novels in which he focused on topics ranging from political corruption to environmental pollution. In recent years, Vonnegut has also become a prominent and vocal critic of censorship and militarism in the United States.

Although many critics attribute Vonnegut's classification as a science-fiction writer to a complete misunderstanding of his aims, the element of fantasy is nevertheless one of the most notable features of his early works. *Player*

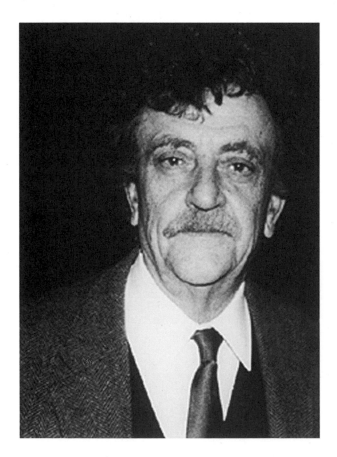

Piano depicts a fictional city called Ilium in which the people have relinquished control of their lives to a computer humorously named EPICAC, after a substance that induces vomiting, while the *The Sirens of Titan* (1959) takes place on several different planets, including a thoroughly militarized Mars, where the inhabitants are electronically controlled. The fantastic settings of these works serve primarily as a metaphor for modern society, which Vonnegut views as absurd to the point of being surreal, and as a backdrop for Vonnegut's central focus: the hapless human beings who inhabit these bizarre worlds who struggle with both their environments and themselves. For example, in *Player Piano,* the protagonist, Dr. Paul Proteus, rebels against the emotional vapidity of his society, wherein, freed from the need to perform any meaningful work, the citizens have lost their sense of dignity and purpose. Proteus joins a subversive organization devoted to toppling the computer-run government and participates in an abortive rebellion. Although he is imprisoned at the end of the novel, Vonnegut suggests that Proteus has triumphed in regaining his humanity.

Vonnegut once again focuses on the role of technology in human society in *Cat's Cradle* (1963), widely considered one of his best works. The novel recounts the discovery of a form of ice, called *ice-nine,* which is solid at a much lower temperature than normal ice and is capable of solidifying all water on Earth. *Ice-nine* serves as a symbol of the enormous destructive potential of technology, particularly when developed or used without regard for the welfare of humanity. In contrast to what he considers the harmful truths represented by scientific discoveries, Vonnegut presents a religion called Bokononism, based on the concept that there are no absolute truths, that human life is ultimately meaningless, and that the most helpful religion would therefore preach benign lies that encourage kindness, give humanity a sense of dignity, and allow people to view their absurd condition with humor. The motif of the cat's cradle, a children's game played by looping string about the hands in a complex pattern, is used by Vonnegut to demonstrate the harm caused by the erroneous paradigms presented by traditional religions: "No wonder kids grow up crazy. A cat's cradle is nothing but a bunch of X's between somebody's hands, and little kids look at all those X's . . . *no damn cat, and no damn cradle.*"

In *God Bless You, Mr. Rosewater; or, Pearls before Swine* (1965), Vonnegut presents one of his most endearing protagonists in the figure of Eliot Rosewater, a philanthropic but ineffectual man who attempts to use his inherited fortune for the betterment of humanity. Rosewater finds that his generosity, his genuine concern for human beings, and his attempts to establish loving relationships are viewed as madness in a society that values only money. The novel includes traditional religions in its denunciation of materialism and greed in the modern world, suggesting that the wealthy and powerful invented the concept of divine ordination to justify and maintain their exploitation of others.

Vonnegut described *Slaughterhouse-Five* as a novel he was compelled to write, since it is based on one of the most extraordinary and significant events of his life. During the time he was a prisoner of the German Army, Vonnegut witnessed the Allied bombing of Dresden, which destroyed the city and killed more than 135,000 people. One of the few to survive, Vonnegut was ordered by his captors to aid in the grisly task of digging bodies from the rubble and destroying them in huge bonfires. Although the attack claimed more lives than the bombing of Hiroshima and was directed at a target of no apparent military importance, it attracted little attention, and *Slaughterhouse-Five* is Vonnegut's attempt to both document and denounce this event. Like Vonnegut, the protagonist of *Slaughterhouse-Five,* named Billy Pilgrim, has been present at the bombing of Dresden and has been profoundly affected by the experience. His feelings manifest themselves in a spiritual malaise that culminates in a nervous breakdown. In addition, he suffers from a peculiar condition, that of being "unstuck in time," meaning that he randomly experiences events from his past, present, and future. The novel is therefore a complex, nonchronological narrative in which images of suffering and loss prevail. Charles B. Harris has noted: "Ultimately, [*Slaughterhouse-Five*] is less about Dresden than it is about the impact of Dresden on one man's sensibilities. More specifically, it is the story of Vonnegut's story of Dresden, how he came to write it and, implicitly, why he wrote it as he did."

In the works written after *Slaughterhouse-Five,* Vonnegut often focuses on the problems of contemporary society in a direct manner. *Breakfast of Champions, or Goodbye Blue Monday* (1973) and *Slapstick, or Lonesome No More* (1976), for example, examine the widespread feelings of despair and loneliness that result from the loss of traditional culture in the United States; *Jailbird* (1979) recounts the story of a fictitious participant in the Watergate scandal of the Nixon administration, creating an indictment of the American political system; *Galapagos* (1985) predicts the dire consequences of environmental pollution; and *Hocus-Pocus; or, What's the Hurry, Son?* (1990) deals with the implications and aftermath of the war in Vietnam. In the 1990s, he also published *Fates Worse Than Death* (1991) and *Timequake* (1997). Although many of these works are highly regarded, critics frequently argue that in his later works Vonnegut tends to reiterate themes presented more compellingly in earlier works. Many also suggest that Vonnegut's narrative style, which includes the frequent repetition of distinctive phrases, the use of colloquialisms, and a digressive manner, becomes formulaic in some of his later works.

Nevertheless, Vonnegut remains one of the most esteemed American satirists. Noted for their frank and insightful social criticism as well as their innovative style, his works present an idiosyncratic yet compelling vision of modern life.

Further Reading

Authors in the News, volume 1, Gale, 1976.
Bellamy, Joe David, editor, *The New Fiction: Interviews with Innovative American Writers,* University of Illinois Press, 1974.
Bryant, Jerry H., *The Open Decision,* Free Press, 1970.
Chernuchin, Michael, editor, *Vonnegut Talks!,* Pylon, 1977.
Clareson, Thomas D., editor, *Voices for the Future: Essays on Major Science Fiction Writers,* volume 1, Bowling Green University Popular Press, 1976.
Concise Dictionary of American Literary Biography: Broadening Views, 1968-1988, Gale, 1989.
Contemporary Literary Criticism, Gale, volume 1, 1973; volume 2, 1974; volume 3, 1975; volume 4, 1975; volume 5, 1976; volume 8, 1978; volume 12, 1980; volume 22, 1982; volume 40, 1986; volume 60, 1991. □

John Von Neumann

The Hungarian-born American mathematician John Von Neumann (1903-1957) was the originator of the theory of games and an important contributor to computer technology.

John Von Neumann was born in Budapest on Dec. 28, 1903. He left Hungary in 1918 and studied at the University of Berlin and the Zurich Institute of Technology. After receiving his doctorate in mathematics from the University of Budapest in 1926, he attended the University of Göttingen for a year. Göttingen enjoyed a tremendous reputation in the mathematical sciences: the great master and inspirer of generations of students, David Hilbert, had not yet retired, the "ex-prodigy" Norbert Wiener was a visiting fellow from the United States, and the university was the meeting ground for many brilliant young scientific intellects. One of Von Neumann's fellow students was the future atomic scientist J. Robert Oppenheimer.

Von Neumann taught mathematics at the University of Berlin (1927-1929) and the University of Hamburg (1929-1930). Then the young Hungarian, like so many others at that time, found refuge in the United States, obtaining a post at Princeton University, where he taught mathematical physics until 1933. He had been working on quantum mechanics for a number of years, and his book on that subject, published in 1932, provided a useful exposition of the mathematical logic of the theory.

However, Von Neumann had already developed a theory which was to be potentially of much greater value but which was not fully developed for nearly 20 years. In 1927 he propounded a mathematical technique for the analysis of conflict, but it was only in 1944 that he and Oskar Morgenstern wrote the celebrated *Theory of Games and Economic Behavior,* which had a profound influence on the development of strategy in widely differing fields of application. The theory of games is a concept which can be applied to the logic of conflict; it is an attempt to provide a quantitative basis for rational behavior in a situation which has conflict potential. This purely mathematical technique has developed as an important subject of study for its economic, social, political, and military applications.

In 1933 Von Neuman became professor of mathematics at the Institute for Advanced Study in Princeton, a position he held until his death. During World War II he played

National Socialism, he helped prepare the way for the Third Reich.

Von Papen came from a landowning Westphalian Catholic family which belonged to the lower nobility. Like many young men of his social class he entered the officer corps, and in 1914 he became the German military attaché in Washington. He was recalled late the following year, however, because of his involvement in secret sabotage activities. He then fought on the Turkish front, but left military service in 1918, unable to accept the new republican regime. Entering politics, he assumed leadership of the conservative, monarchist wing of the Catholic Center Party. The onset of the Depression in 1929 convinced him that the time had come to replace the democratic government with an authoritarian, hierarchical system. Leaving the Center Party, he became one of the leaders of the right-wing politicians who plotted the downfall of the hapless Weimar Republic.

His big chance came in July 1932 when President Hindenburg, whose confidence he enjoyed, made him chancellor. He had hoped that the disastrous state of the economy would produce popular support for his program of elite rule and conservative policy. But he completely misjudged the country's political mood. The chief beneficiaries of the economic crisis were the parties of the radical right and left, the National Socialists and the Communists. Two elections, one in July and the other in November, failed to win any significant support for him in the Reichstag, and

an important role in the field of applied mathematics devoted to military needs and worked on the motion of compressible fluids caused by explosions. He was a consultant at the Los Alamos Scientific Laboratory (1943-1955), where his extraordinary intellectual grasp coupled with common sense were of considerable influence. Having seen the potential of high-speed machine calculation in these problems, he studied the mathematical logic of computers and their complex technology. The first computer at Princeton was built in 1952 under his guidance. The U.S. Atomic Energy Commission placed him on its Central Advisory Committee in 1952 and made him a commissioner 2 years later. His interest in computer technology continued until his death on Feb. 8, 1957, in Washington, D.C.

Further Reading

Biographical information on Von Neumann appears in the National Academy of Sciences, *Biographical Memoirs,* vol. 32 (1958), and Shirley Thomas, *Men of Space,* vol. 1 (1960). ☐

Franz von Papen

Franz von Papen (1879-1969) was one of the conservative German politicians whose fear of social unrest and hostility toward the democratic Weimar Republic led them to support the rise of Hitler. Although never a believer in the more extreme doctrines of

early in December he was replaced as chancellor by Kurt von Schleicher, an ambitious army officer whose tactics may have been different, but whose political principles were essentially the same. Von Papen now decided to work for the appointment of a Hitler cabinet, in which the charismatic Fuhrer would mesmerize the masses, while behind the scenes he himself would make the important decisions. He persuaded Hindenburg of the wisdom of this plan, and on January 30, 1933, a new ministry took power, with Hitler as chancellor and von Papen as vice-chancellor.

The latter soon discovered, however, that it was easier to conspire with the Fuhrer than to control him. At first von Papen worked loyally for the new order, organizing support for it in the elections of March 1933 and negotiating a concordat with the papacy in July. But the growing brutality of the regime and its increasingly reckless policies gradually alienated von Papen. The National Socialists came to regard him as unreliable, and after the "blood purge" of June 1934, when hundreds of critics of Hitler's program were summarily executed, von Papen was forced out of the cabinet. Ultimately that proved a blessing, but at the time he found himself relegated to minor diplomatic posts. He became ambassador to Austria, helping to prepare the way for the absorption of that country by Germany in 1938, and then served as envoy to Turkey, whose neutrality in World War II he managed to secure until 1944. By the time the Third Reich collapsed, he was almost a forgotten man.

The victorious allies did remember him well enough to include him among the defendants tried at Nurenberg in 1945-1946 before the International Military Tribunal. However, the fact that he had not been involved in the formulation of German national policy during the preceding ten years led to his acquittal. Though tried again by a German denazification court and sentenced to eight years imprisonment, he was released in 1949 and spent the last two decades of his life in obscure but comfortable retirement. Von Papen belonged to that influential group of conservative political leaders whose fear of the democratic principles underlying the Weimar Republic blinded them to the danger of totalitarianism. Like the sorcerer's apprentice, he invoked the aid of demonic forces in German national life which he was then unable to exorcise.

Further Reading

After World War II von Papen published his *Memoirs* (translated in 1952), full of rationalizations and excuses which do not shed much light on the crucial events in which he played a part. There is no biography of him in English, but there are several works on German history during the interwar period which examine his public career. See, for example, the older account by S. William Halperin, still readable and perceptive, entitled *Germany Tried Democracy* (1946). Among more recent books two in particular deserve mention: John W. Wheeler-Bennett, *The Nemesis of Power: The German Army in Politics, 1918-1945* (1964), and Gordon A. Craig, *Germany, 1866-1945* (1978). Finally, there is a work by the leading authority on the Third Reich in which von Papen appears prominently: Karl Dietrich Bracher, *The German Dictatorship: The Origins, Structure, and Effects of National Socialism* (translated in 1970). □

Gerhard von Rad

The German theologian Gerhard von Rad (1901-1971) developed the "tradition history" approach to the Old Testament that has dominated the study of the Bible for nearly 40 years.

Gerhard von Rad was born to a patrician medical family in Nürnberg on October 21, 1901. After studying theology at Erlangen and Tübingen, he served briefly as a pastor in a Bavarian church before preparing himself to teach Old Testament. On completing a dissertation on *Das Gottesvolk im Deuteronomium* (*The People of God in Deuteronomy*), he took a teaching position at Erlangen. Here he wrote *Das Geschichtsbild des Chronistischen Werkes* (*The Concept of History in the Work of the Chronicler*) and studied Semitics with Albrecht Alt at Leipzig. In 1930 von Rad moved to Leipzig, where he taught until 1934. During these years he gained competence in archaeology and wrote several important essays, the main one of which dealt with the priestly writing in the Hexateuch, the first six books of the Bible. In 1934 von Rad moved to Jena, where he had few students but considerable time for research. Here he wrote his epoch-making study of the form-critical problem of the Hexateuch and an exquisite literary study of the beginnings of historiography in ancient Israel, as well as such popular books as *Moses* and *The Old Testament—God's Word for the Germans!* At Jena von Rad began his commentary on Genesis, but World War II delayed its appearance.

In the summer of 1944 he was inducted into military service, assuming some responsibility for housing soldiers in barracks until becoming a prisoner of war in mid-March of 1945. From then until the end of June he remained in the camp at Bad Kreusnach, where he endured much hardship. After his release, he taught briefly at Bethel, Bonn, Erlangen, and Göttingen before moving to Heidelberg in 1949. From then until his retirement in 1967 he remained at Heidelberg except for temporary visits abroad. During these years he published his influential theology of the Old Testament in two volumes and his analysis of Israelite wisdom (*Weisheit in Israel*), as well as two brief monographs of great value: *Der heilige Krieg im alten Israel* (*Holy War in Ancient Israel*) and *Das Opfer des Abraham* (*The Sacrifice of Abraham*).

Von Rad died on October 31, 1971. He had received honorary degrees from the Universities of Leipzig, Glasgow, Lund, Wales, and Utrecht. Moreover, he had been elected to membership in the Heidelberg Academy of Sciences and he was the first Protestant after Adolph Harnack to be named to the *Order pour le merité* for science and art. Von Rad's colleagues held him in such esteem that they contributed essays to two *Festschriften* (a collection of tributes by colleagues) and to a memorial volume, *Gerhard von Rad: Seine Bedeutung für die Theologie* (*Gerhard von Rad: His Significance for Theology*).

Reflecting on his career as an interpreter of Scripture, von Rad described himself as a historical "monoman" and emphasized his wish to overcome the atomism of research that was dominant when he entered the discipline. These two ideas imply that he sought to apply the category of *Heilsgeschichte* (salvation history) to the Hebrew Bible and that he endeavored to link the different biblical traditions in a coherent manner. The book of Deuteronomy provided the norm for virtually every discussion; von Rad actually published three books about this central text, which he believed represented early northern traditions arising among levitical priests, traditions that were later presented in the form of a sermon placed in the mouth of Moses and used in connection with King Josiah's reform in 621 B.C.

According to von Rad, the Hexateuch grew out of liturgical recitations (little credos) that the people spoke in connection with the festival of Weeks at Gilgal. The original credos consisted of Joshua 24:2-13 and Deuteronomy 6:20-24 and 26:5-9. These confessions of faith allude to the essential traditions comprising Genesis through Joshua (patriarchs, exodus, wilderness wandering, conquest), with two glaring omissions (Sinai and the primeval history, Genesis 1-12). Von Rad argued that the Sinai narrative about Moses' receipt of the law was a separate tradition from the four complexes in the Hexateuch and that the author known to scholars as the Yahwist wrote the primeval history as a preface to the story about divine promise and its fulfillment, the settlement in Canaan by the people of God.

Von Rad's thesis depended on an understanding of ancient Israelite life prior to a Solomonic "enlightenment" as entirely sacral. Furthermore, the proposed origin of the Hexateuch assumed that the Bible arose out of the actual practice of worship. Generation after generation adapted earlier liturgical traditions to new historical circumstances, dropping some emphases and introducing new ones. Von Rad devoted his efforts to charting the course of living traditions. In his view, Old Testament theology derived its categories from ancient Israelite confessional statements rather than from modern systematic thought. Therefore, he described several theologies, those of the main sources of the Hexateuch (the Yahwist, Elohist, Deuteronomist, and Priestly writer), as well as those represented by the prophetic traditions and wisdom literature (Proverbs, Job, Ecclesiastes, Sirach, and Wisdom of Solomon).

Naturally, this mode of presenting a theology of the Old Testament raised the issue of unity, for the diversity in viewpoint came into focus at every point. Von Rad believed in the unity of the Bible, which he described under the categories of promise and fulfillment. In his view, Israel's God promised land, progeny, and blessing—promises that were constantly being fulfilled. The result was eschatology, a looking to the future for the full measure of divine promise. Such an approach was related to the typology of early church Fathers, but von Rad insisted that the Old Testament contained both promise and fulfillment.

When he turned to the wisdom literature, von Rad discovered that tradition history was not all that useful as an interpretive device. This new interest prompted him to acknowledge that too much emphasis had been put on history, for in wisdom literature the deity's action was identified with creation and humans went on the initiative against God in such works as Job and Ecclesiastes. His last three published works concentrated on the silence of God (the doxology of judgment, Israelite wisdom, the sacrifice of Abraham in Genesis 22). One dimension of his work, the exposition of the Bible in sermons, proved that the most exhaustive study of the Scriptures need not diminish religious commitment to the power of the word.

Von Rad's views were highly controversial, evoking considerable heat. Many of his theories have not stood the test of time, but it would be difficult to find another person who has contributed so much to the understanding of the Old Testament. It may be that in truth he wrote a history of Israelite religion rather than an Old Testament theology, but he insisted that the Hebrew Bible be understood in the context of the religious life of ancient Israel. That is surely a correct insight.

Further Reading

The most comprehensive study of von Rad's life and thought will be found in James L. Crenshaw, *Gerhard von Rad* (1978). Two other sources in English are found in books that discuss von Rad among others. These books are D. G. Spriggs, *Two Old Testament Theologies* (1974) and G. Henton Davies, "Gerhard von Rad, 'Old Testament Theology,'" in *Contemporary Old Testament Theologians,* edited by Robert B. Laurin (1970). One may also consult Crenshaw, "Wisdom in Israel, by Gerhard von Rad," *Religious Studies Review* 2 (1976).

Additional Sources

Crenshaw, James L., *Gerhard von Rad,* Peabody, Mass.: Hendrickson Publishers, 1978, 1991. □

Balthazar Johannes Vorster

Balthazar Johannes Vorster (1915-1983) was a South African political leader who emerged as a major figure in Afrikaner nationalism. Noted as a right-wing figure, he was passionately hostile to liberalism and communism.

Balthazar Vorster was born on April 11, 1915, in the rural area of Jamestown in the Eastern Province. He attended school there and subsequently entered Stellenbosch University as a law student. Stellenbosch University can be called the "cradle of Afrikaner nationalism." Its influence on the development of Afrikaans culture has been profound: no fewer than six out of the seven prime ministers South Africa had between 1910 and 1971 are former Stellenbosch men. Vorster soon involved himself in student politics. In time he became chairman of the debating society, deputy chairman of the student council and leader of the junior National party.

Vorster graduated in 1938 and became registrar (judge's clerk) to the judge president of the Cape Provincial Division of the South African Supreme Court. But he did not remain in this post for long, entering practice as an attorney in Port Elizabeth and then in the Witwatersrand town of Brakpan.

Involvement in Politics

The outbreak of war in September 1939 saw Vorster's first serious involvement in national politics. The decision of the South African Parliament to enter war on the side of the Allied Powers bitterly alienated Afrikaner nationalists, who resented South Africa's alliance with their ancient foe, England. Many nationalists, more out of an anti-English feeling than a positively pro-Nazi spirit, fervently hoped for a German victory.

Vorster channeled his activities into an organization called the Ossewabrandwag (literally, "Ox-wagon Sentinel"), which had been founded in 1938 to perpetuate the spirit engendered by the celebration in that year of the centenary of the Great Trek. Under the führer-type leadership of J. F. van Rensburg, the Ossewabrandwag became an extremist neo-Nazi organization that did its best to hamstring the South African war effort. Although Vorster himself claimed not to have participated, many acts of sabotage and violence committed in the country during the war were attributed to the Ossewabrandwag.

Rising rapidly in the organization, which was run on paramilitary lines, Vorster reached the rank of general. In one statement made in those times he identified himself with "Christian Nationalism," which he described as the South African equivalent to National Socialism. Vorster's brother, J. D. Vorster, a Dutch Reformed Church clergyman,

also leaned heavily to the German side, receiving a prison sentence for conveying information about Allied shipping movements to the enemy.

In September 1942, Vorster was interned in a detention camp at Koffiefontein, Cape, because of his activities. He repeatedly demanded that he be brought before a court of law, and he even led a hunger strike in an attempt to pressure the authorities to charge or release him. He remained an internee until February 1944, when he was released and placed under restrictions. He refused to obey these restrictions, which included confinement to a particular district, but he was not punished or reinterned for doing so.

In later years when Vorster had become an important figure in the National party, his opponents taunted him with his wartime activities. Vorster never tried to disavow anything he did or said at that time. He described his internment in a speech in Parliament in May 1960, saying that one possible reason had been that he was believed by the authorities to have harbored antiwar fugitives. He described also how, on being released, he had called on the minister of justice, Colin Steyn, to plead on behalf of those who were still interned. Steyn, he said, threatened to have him arrested unless he left the building immediately. The experience of internment had an embittering, searing effect on Vorster and increased his extremism.

Running for Parliament

Relations between the Ossewabrandwag and the National party, led by Daniel Malan, reached breaking point by the end of 1941. Having been repudiated by the Nationalists, the Ossewabrandwag subsequently entered into alliance with the Afrikaner party, which was formed in 1941. The next important stage in Vorster's political career came in 1948, when he sought to gain nomination as the Afrikaner party candidate for Brakpan in the elections of that year. Relations between the National and Afrikaner parties had been sufficiently restored to enable them to enter an electoral pact against Jan Smuts's United party, which was then in power. The Nationalists, however, mistrusted the young firebrand Vorster and refused to endorse his candidacy. He stood as an independent only to be defeated by the narrowest of margins—four votes. Vorster had to wait until the 1953 election to enter parliament, which he did as the Nationalist member of the Transvaal constituency of Nigel.

Vorster soon proved himself to be a very able parliamentarian, a good debater, highly skilled at political infighting and popular as a speaker at Nationalist party meetings. His rise in the party hierarchy was rapid. He was made deputy minister of education, arts and science in 1958, and in 1961 he was made a full minister and given the important portfolio of justice, as well as that of social welfare and pensions.

Shaping of a Security System

In 1961 South Africa was still under the pall of Sharpeville (the killing of 83 demonstrating Africans by police fire in March 1960). Both the major African political organizations, the African National Congress and the Pan-

African Congress, had been proscribed, but the possibility of internal insurrection was real as various underground organizations committed to violence were formed. Vorster's response was to arm himself, as minister of justice, with extraordinary powers to deal with extra parliamentary opposition.

Under Vorster's aegis the security police became a formidable machine, penetrating every nook and cranny of society, ferreting out opponents, and exposing underground movements. Draconian security legislation was passed, giving the authorities, in effect, carte blanche to do what they liked, with little or no possibility of being curbed by the courts. Detention without trial, initiated as a temporary measure, became a permanent part of the South African scene and was used extensively against persons suspected of unlawful political activity.

Vorster's vigorous and, from the Nationalists' point of view, highly successful handling of the security situation greatly enhanced his prestige in his party. He could claim to be the "strong man" who had smashed internal resistance movements and made the country secure. Moreover, his controversial activities as minister of justice had ensured him of a constant place in the political limelight. It was little surprise, then, when after the assassination of Hendrik Verwoerd in September 1966, Vorster was unanimously elected leader of the National party and became prime minister.

As prime minister Vorster cultivated a more "moderate" image, going out of his way to attract English-speaking whites and assiduously trying to win the friendship of black African states. Both of these aspects of his policy aroused the ire of the extreme right wing of the party, the Verkramptes, who were grouped around a Cabinet minister, Albert Hertzog. Vorster moved very gingerly in the face of growing Verkrampte criticism: he did not wish to go down in history as the leader who had allowed Afrikaner nationalism to lose its hard-won unity.

For two stormy years, from 1967 until late in 1969, Vorster attempted to hold the party together, but finally his patience and that of his key lieutenants was exhausted, and the Verkramptes (including four Nationalist members of Parliament) were flushed out of the party. In a snap election held in April 1970, the Reconstituted National party (as the Verkramptes called the party they formed) was thoroughly trounced.

Despite this apparent vindication, it was clear that Vorster's control of Nationalist Afrikanerdom was by no means as complete as Verwoerd's had been. For one thing, he was no intellectual, and this was a serious disadvantage for a party whose apartheid policies were manifestly failing. For another, Afrikanerdom has become more diversified, more pluralist, and consequently the sources of internal conflict have become greater.

Vorster served briefly in the largely ceremonial position of president (1978-79) and died Sept. 10, 1983.

Further Reading

There is neither a biography of Vorster nor a work which deals exclusively with his activities as minister of justice or prime minister. His parliamentary speeches may be read in the verbatim reports of the House of Assembly Debates. Recommended for general historical background are Leopold Marquard, *The Peoples and Policies of South Africa* (1952; 4th ed. 1969), and Margaret Livingstone Hodgson Ballinger, *From Union to Apartheid: A Trek to Isolation* (1969). □

Marilyn vos Savant

Writer Marilyn vos Savant (born 1946) has an I.Q. of 228, the highest ever recorded.

Marilyn vos Savant's intelligence quotient (I.Q.) score of 228, the highest ever recorded, brought the St. Louis-born writer instant celebrity and earned her the sobriquet "the smartest person in the world." Although vos Savant's family was aware of her exceptionally high I.Q. scores on the Stanford-Benet test when she was 10 years old (she is also recognized as having the highest I.Q. score ever recorded by a child), her parents decided to withhold the information from the public in order to avoid commercial exploitation and assure her a normal childhood.

Bored with college, vos Savant left Washington University after two years and launched a career in stocks, real estate, and investment. Her real interest had always been in becoming a writer, but she realized that she first needed to establish a financial base with which to support herself. Within five years her personal investments afforded her the financial independence to become a full-time writer. Vos Savant wrote novels, short stories, and magazine and newspaper pieces, mostly political satire, under a pseudonym.

Vos Savant's attempt at anonymity ended in 1985 when *The Guinness Book of World Records* obtained her I.Q. test scores from the Mega Society, a group whose membership is restricted to those with only the highest of the high-I.Q. scores. (As members' I.Q. scores must be higher than 99.999 percent of the general population, membership has been limited to as few as 30.) Most people's intelligence scores fall within a narrow range on either side of the "normal" score of 100; by contrast, vos Savant's I.Q. score is more than double that of a person with normal intellect and 88 points higher than the genius level.

With the publication of her I.Q. scores in *Guinness*, vos Savant became the focus of media attention. Hardly the stereotypical stuffy supergenius, the outgoing, fun-loving vos Savant became a favorite on the talk-show circuit. By the time her two children from her first marriage reached college age, vos Savant decided to move to New York City and enjoy her newfound celebrity. In 1987 she married Robert K. Jarvik, the surgeon who developed the mechanical artificial human heart that bears his name. Together they follow pursuits both intellectual and jovial—the latter of which including ballroom dancing lessons. As vos Savant

And when asked if people with special gifts of intelligence felt an obligation to society, vos Savant replied: "I think it would be totally wrong of me to just reap the benefits of society while other people are out there digging the roads and building the schools and all of that. I wouldn't dream of it. However, I feel that we all have this responsibility and not just those of us who happen to be able to score well on intelligence tests. I think we all bear a great responsibility to give back to society. We can not give as much as we can gain. There's no way. Society is offering us so much. I don't think we could do enough to give it back, but I think we all bear a social responsibility and I think I bear one too. And I rather think that writing is an excellent way to give back to people what they have given to me."

Further Reading

Booklist, May 1, 1994; March 1, 1996.
Chicago Tribune, September 29, 1985.
Detroit News, September 26, 1985, March 1, 1986.
Los Angeles Times, August 27, 1987.
Parade, June 22, 1986.
People, July 27, 1987; March 7, 1994.
Time, April 6, 1987.
USA Today, March 16, 1986. □

admitted in a 1994 *People* article, "My husband's not so hot at the tango, but don't tell him."

In 1994 vos Savant published her book *"I've Forgotten Everything I Learned in School!" A Refresher Course to Help You Reclaim Your Education.* Despite the catchy title, the volume, according to *Booklist* reviewer Denise Perry Donavin, is not a piece of "pop psychology or mnemonics," but a series of exercises designed to help readers strengthen their mental focus. Two years later vos Savant released *The Power of Logical Thinking: Easy Lessons in the Art of Reasoning . . . and Hard Facts about Its Absence in Our Lives.* In this book the author "shows us how even the most well educated can be semiliterate in the arts of reasoning and problem solving," according to Patricia Hassler, also writing in *Booklist.*

"We only use something like 10 percent of our brain, anywhere between 5 and 15 percent—I don't know what the current estimates are," as vos Savant told the reference book *Newsmakers.* In her view, humans are capable of much more. But motivation is the key: "So how much of a role is motivation playing day-to-day, when we are talking about much smaller differences? And is it measuring, perhaps—this is just a wild, out-of-the-blue kind of a guess—does it measure one person using 17.7 percent of their brain versus some one person who uses 17.8 percent? Is that what I.Q. does? I doubt it. But it's one of those things where personality—or whatever you might call it—plays a great role, and I happen to have [it]. "

Hugo de Vries

Hugo de Vries (1848-1935), Dutch botanist and geneticist, is the author of the mutation theory of evolution. His work led to the rediscovery and establishment of Mendel's laws.

Hugo de Vries was born on Feb. 16, 1848, in Haarlem. His father had been prime minister of the Netherlands. After studying at the universities of Leiden, Heidelberg, and Würzburg, De Vries was appointed a lecturer in botany at the University of Amsterdam in 1871. In 1878 he became professor of botany, a position he retained until his retirement in 1918. He was at the same time director of the Botanic Gardens at the University of Amsterdam.

De Vries made his first notable contributions to science in the 1880s in the field of plant physiology. While investigating the movement of fluids in plants, he confirmed Jacobus Hendricus Van't Hoff's theory of osmosis and Svante Arrhenius's theory of ionic diffusion. During the 1870s De Vries had carried out a series of studies for the Prussian Ministry of Agriculture involving the problems of plant breeding and hybridization. The results of this research were published in monographs on clover, the sugarbeet, and the potato. After his appointment as professor, he turned his attention more and more to questions concerned with the theory of evolution and the ways in which new species might evolve.

Evolutionary Theory in the Late 19th Century

To understand the significance of De Vries's research, it is important to place his investigation in the context of the scientific debates of the period. Charles Darwin's theory of evolution by natural selection was published in 1859. He held that species evolved or changed in form from generation to generation because some members of the species lived for a longer time than others and were able to produce more offspring than their less fit fellows. In the long run, this would result in a species becoming more like the favored variation and less like the unfavored variations. In his *Origin of Species* Darwin did not establish how variations occurred or how they were inherited. Subsequently, the area of heredity and variation became a recognized field of research for biologists interested in evolutionary theory.

Darwin had put forward the idea that variations between different individuals in a species were usually of a continuous nature. He believed that because of natural selection certain ranges of this continuous variation would be more favored in the struggle for survival and the species would become changed toward those ranges. However, by the late 1880s and the 1890s some biologists were becoming convinced that evolution depended on the effect of natural selection on discontinuous variations, not on continuous variations. In the period of De Vries's greatest contributions to science, 1880-1910, he participated vigorously in the debate about the respective roles of continuous and discontinuous variations in the evolutionary process.

Biologists were at the same time involved in much debate and research about the nature of heredity. Darwin realized that one of the gaps in his theory of evolution was an adequate explanation of the mechanism of heredity. To fill this gap, he proposed his theory of pangenesis: Each character in a mature organism was determined by a minute particle, or pangene, passed on from the parental organisms via the sex cells. The pangenes passed from all parts of the parental body through the bloodstream to the sex cells and then determined the character of the appropriate parts of the offspring by similar diffusion as the offspring grew.

One aspect of Darwin's theory of pangenesis caused much debate among biologists. How, they asked, could the pangenes, which were discrete particles, give rise to continuous variations? For this to occur, there would probably have to be some blending of the pangenes from different parents into one pangene. Some biologists preferred to believe that if heredity did depend on the passing of discrete units from parents to offspring, these units would remain discrete in the offspring and give rise to discontinuous variations in the mature offspring. De Vries played an important role in the debate about the process of heredity.

Another area of research was of great importance in the overall picture of evolution. This was the question of the structure of the cell and its nucleus and the analysis of the behavior of cell and nucleus during division. During the last quarter of the 19th century cytologists established a fairly detailed picture of what happened to the nuclear material during cell division. The material was chemically identified, and biologists began to speculate on the connection between the nucleic acids of the chromosomes and the mechanism of inheritance. Again De Vries played an important role in pointing out the connection between the nuclear material and the particles which controlled the inheritance of characteristics from generation to generation.

De Vries's Pangenesis Theory

De Vries published his theory of pangenesis in *Intracellular Pangenesis* (1889; trans. 1910). He took the name "pangenesis" from Darwin and, like Darwin, he held that characters were passed from parent to offspring through the medium of small particles or elementary units. These units he called "pangenes." De Vries held that the pangenes were located in the nucleus of each cell and that every nucleus contained a complete set of the pangenes for that particular individual. The complete set of pangenes represented all the potential characters of the mature organism. He further maintained that at the time of cell division the whole set of pangenes also divided so that every daughter cell contained a complete set of pangenes. By placing his pangenes in the nucleus and suggesting that they were present in the chromosomes, he was able to tie his theory of pangenesis much more closely to cytological observations than Darwin was.

Although De Vries was not able to outline in any detail how the pangenes determined the character of an organism, he suggested that a pangene left the nucleus of the cell, entered the surrounding cytoplasm, and thus controlled the activity of the cell. In *Intracellular Pangenesis* he stated that each pangene represented "a special hereditary character . . . The pangenes are not chemical molecules, but morphological structures each built of numerous molecules . . . they assimilate and take nourishment and thereby grow, and then multiply by division; two new pangenes, like the original one, usually originate at each cleavage. Deviations from this rule form a starting point for the origin of variations and species."

De Vries's theory of pangenesis put forward a hereditary mechanism which did not allow for any possibility of environmental or Lamarckian influence on heredity. His theory was also capable of fitting in with the findings of the contemporary cytologists on the nature of cell division and the role of the nucleus. The most important area for further work seemed to him to be the whole question of the source and nature of biological variation.

De Vries's Work on Variation

Darwin's theory of evolution maintained that new species were formed by the action of natural selection on variations which always occurred among the members of a species. In the mid-1880s De Vries did a great deal of work on the inheritance of the different characteristics of marigolds. He was impressed by the constancy of the species over several generations and became convinced that the ordinary or continuous variations were not the source of the new forms needed for new species.

In 1886 De Vries came across some evening primroses (*Oenothera lamarckiana*) growing in a field near Amsterdam and noticed that they showed great variations in height, form of leaves, and pattern of branching. By 1889 he had examined over 53,000 of these primrose plants from eight generations. In that time he found eight completely new types, which he felt were different enough from the original plants to be called new species. These new types bred true, that is, they had offspring similar to themselves, when they were cross-pollinated. He felt that he had at last uncovered the secret of the origin of new species, which he put forward in *The Mutation Theory* (1901-1903; trans. 1909).

De Vries's Mutation Theory

In his theory of mutation De Vries combined his theory of pangenesis, which explained heredity, with his theory that new species could arise only from a very large and completely spontaneous variation, which he called a "mutation." This mutation was the result of a new pangene or several new pangenes. In *The Mutation Theory* he said that the adoption of this new theory "influences our attitude toward the theory of descent [or evolution] by suggesting to us that species have arisen from one another by a discontinuous, as opposed to a continuous, process. Each new unit, forming a fresh step in the process, sharply and completely separates the new form as an independent species from that from which it sprang. The new species appears all at once; it originates from the parent species without any visible preparation and without any obvious series of transitional forms."

De Vries contrasted his mutation theory with the Darwinian theory of selection, emphasizing that he saw the origin of species through mutation whereas Darwin had seen it through the selection of ordinary or fluctuating variation. The mutation theory was widely accepted in the years immediately after it was published. In 1904 he made a lecture tour of the United States, where he expounded his theory. It soon came under attack, particularly by some of the geneticists who had adopted Mendelian principles.

Rediscovery of Mendel's Work

During the 1890s De Vries carried out many experiments in breeding plants. He crossed plants with different characteristics (for example, hairy and smooth stems) and counted the numbers of plants in succeeding generations which had the different parental characteristics. By the end of the 1890s he had gathered much evidence to show that there were definite rations which kept recurring among the offspring (for instance, hairy and smooth stems would occur in the ratio 3 to 1). By late 1899 he had obtained similar results in more than 30 different species and varieties. De Vries reasoned that the obtaining of fixed ratios supported his theories of pangenesis and mutation. The pangenes, which determined the characters of the plants, were seen as units which must separate and recombine according to regular patterns during breeding; these regular patterns would give rise to the fixed ratios he had discovered. Mutations would arise from the loss or great change of some of the pangenes.

Sometime in 1900, before De Vries published his new findings about the fixed ratios of characters among the offspring in cross-breeding experiments, he discovered a paper by Gregor Mendel which included an account of the same laws about the regular patterns of inheritance. Mendel's paper had been published in 1866 and had been ignored by the scientific world. The laws which Mendel had originally discovered and which De Vries had independently rediscovered became the basis of the modern study of genetics. Simultaneously, two other European biologists, Karl Correns and Eric Tschermak, rediscovered Mendel's work.

There has been some controversy about De Vries's role in the rediscovery of Mendel's work, including the suggestion that he did not want to acknowledge Mendel's priority in the discovery of the basic laws of genetics. However, it would seem that De Vries never felt that the Mendelian laws were as significant as his own mutation theory, so that his apparent lack of recognition for Mendel could stem from a feeling that biologists were placing too much emphasis on Mendel's laws and not paying enough attention to De Vries's mutation theory.

From 1900 until he retired in 1918 De Vries spent most of his energy trying to find further evidence for his mutation theory. It drew less support as geneticists found more evidence to support Darwin's original theory that the source of evolutionary change was the normal variations that occurred among all numbers of a species. By the time of De Vries's death in Amsterdam on May 21, 1935, the action of natural selection on ordinary variations had again become the accepted version of evolutionary theory and the term "mutation" was used to apply to any new character of a plant or animal—not only very large and striking variations.

Further Reading

There is no standard biography of De Vries in English. For a general account of his work the best books are L. C. Dunn, *A Short History of Genetics* (1965), and A. H. Sturtevant, *A History of Genetics* (1965). For De Vries's part in the rediscovery of Mendel see Robert C. Olby, *Origins of Mendelism* (1966). □

Jean Édouard Vuillard

Jean Édouard Vuillard (1868-1940) was a member of the group of French painters who called themselves Nabis. His best pictures were inspired by the immediate activity around him, to which he imparted a mysterious, ritualistic character.

Édouard Vuillard was born at Cuiseaux on Nov. 11, 1868. After his father's death in 1883, Vuillard's mother established a dressmaking workshop in their apartment in Paris. She encouraged her son's artistic ambitions from the first. Vuillard never married and, in terms of external incidents, led an uneventful life.

In 1889 Vuillard began to work at the Académie Julian, where he met Maurice Denis, Pierre Bonnard, Paul Ranson, and Paul Sérusier. This was the nucleus of the Nabi (a Hebrew word meaning prophet) group. After the Salon of 1890 rejected Vuillard's work, he never again submitted anything for consideration by official circles. That year he made his first theater programs for the Théâtre Libre, an art he perfected in his collaboration with the symbolist-oriented Théâtre de l'Oeuvre from 1893, when he helped found it, until 1898.

In 1890 Denis had published the famous dictum, "Remember that a painting, before being a battle horse, a nude, or some anecdote, is essentially a flat surface covered with colors arranged in a given order." It was on this flat surface that Vuillard effected his astonishing transformations of ordinary activities into evocative and expressive arrangements. His best works, such as *Mother and Sister of the Artist* and *Dressmaker's Studio,* strike a rare balance between spontaneity and studied structure in the delicate handling of value relationships and textures. Many of his early works are modest in size and were considered "illegible" in their rarefied tints, yet Vuillard demonstrated his skill on a large scale in many decorative panels. Perhaps the most successful are the set for Alexandre Natanson, director of the *Revue blanche,* the magazine to which the Nabis contributed illustrations. Vuillard's early period also includes the influential set of color lithographs *Paysages et intérieurs* (1899). He exhibited with the Nabis between 1891 and 1896.

After the turn of the century, Vuillard's art lost much of its originality and force. He was always a skillful painter, however, and his portraits of members of the upper classes, while no longer searching creations, are extraordinary for their interest in the sitters and the minutiae of their surroundings. In 1937 he designed decorations for the Palais de Chaillot and in 1938 for the League of Nations Palace, Geneva. In 1938 he received a large retrospective exhibition at the Musée des Arts Décoratifs and was elected to the Academy of Fine Arts. He died at La Baule on June 21, 1940.

Further Reading

There are studies of Vuillard available in English: Claude Roger-Marx, *Vuillard: His Life and Work* (1946); Andrew Carnduff Ritchie, *Édouard Vuillard* (1954); John Russell, *Vuillard* (1971); and Stuart Preston, *Vuillard* (1971).

Additional Sources

Makarius, Michel, *Vuillard,* New York: Universe Books, 1989.
Roger-Marx, Claude, *Vuillard, his life and work,* New York: AMS Press, 1977. □

Andrei Vyshinsky

Andrei Vyshinsky (1883-1954) was the state prosecutor in Stalin's purge trials in the 1930s and later served as head of the U.S.S.R.'s foreign ministry and as Soviet ambassador to the United Nations.

Andrei Ianuar'evich Vyshinsky, also spelled Vyshinskii, became one of the Soviet Union's best known political figures in the early 1950s when he served as head of the Soviet mission to the United Nations (UN). A master of inflamatory rhetoric, combative, scornful, and ready in an instant to heap the most undiplomatic abuse on other UN spokesmen, Vyshinsky drew wide attention, none of it favorable. Visitors to the UN hoped to catch him in the act of banging his fist or flailing his arms. Delegates complained that he attacked them like criminals. At his death a few weeks before his 71st birthday on November 22, 1954, the *New York Times* called him a "master of the vitriolic word." Other editorialists, remembering as well the role he had played as state prosecutor in Stalin's purge trials, thought this too kind. A living symbol of the worst of Stalinism, Vyshinsky died unmourned and unmissed in the Soviet Union as well as abroad. His official biographers emphasize the "serious mistakes" and "violations of socialist legality" he made in interpreting and implementing Soviet law.

Vyshinsky was born December 12, 1883, in Odessa, on the Black Sea. Because he joined the Menshevik wing of the Social Democratic Party in 1903, rivalling the Bolsheviks, it is hard to know whether the accounts of his early life are accurate or designed to protect him from an undesirable past. He is said to have come from a relatively wealthy family, to have become active among militant Mensheviks in Baku at the time of the first Russian revolution in 1905, and to have served a year in jail for political activities in 1906. He is also reported to have been wounded in an attack by the right-wing "Black Hundreds" group in 1907. We do know for sure that he found his way to Kiev, entered

Kiev University, and graduated in law in 1913. In all likelihood, he was expelled from graduate study because of renewed political activities. Throughout World War I and the October Revolution he worked in the Ukraine and elsewhere as a political activist, lecturing and writing, and working for a time in the food distribution apparatus. According to one account, he volunteered for the Red Army and served in 1919 and 1920.

Vyshinsky joined the Bolshevik Party only at the end of the civil war in 1920. Whether his Menshevik past affected the strength of his new commitment to Bolshevism is difficult to tell, but he soon became a strident partisan and an ardent supporter of Stalin. In the 1920s he lectured, served as a prosecuting attorney, and held several important educational posts, including the deanship of the Plekhanov Economic Institute (1923-1925) and the post of rector (chancellor) of Moscow State University (1925-1928). His metier, however, was the courtroom. In 1928 Stalin chose Vyshinsky to head a special office attached to the U.S.S.R. supreme court to investigate and prosecute "wrecking" (disloyalties to the state), and he soon became famous as the state's attorney in the first of Stalin's notorious show trials.

Thereafter, Vyshinsky was constantly in the public eye. Writing and lecturing about the principles of socialist legality, and author of the leading Soviet textbook on criminal law, he revealed in practice that Stalinist law meant whatever the prosecutor's office said it meant. Between 1935 and 1939 prosecutor Vyshinsky took each of Stalin's leading victims to the dock, haranguing Nikoli Bukharin and Aleksei Rykov, castigating Sergei Kamenev and Gregori Zinoviev, attacking the old Bolshevik cadre as traitors and "swine." Compulsion and torture became the instruments of investigation and prosecution; false confessions the symbol of the prosecutor's "success." Even those inclined at first to believe in the trials, like the American ambassador Joseph Davies, found Vyshinsky's conduct appalling and demonic.

Had Stalin been consistent in these matters, Vyshinsky himself would have followed NKVD police chiefs Yezhov and Yagoda into prison along with the other leading purgers, but Stalin spared his slavish prosecutor, preferring instead to apply his talents to foreign affairs. In 1940 Vyshinsky became deputy foreign minister, a post which brought him in close contact with Western leaders during World War II, and from 1949 until Stalin's death in 1953 he headed the foreign ministry. In this capacity he represented the U.S.S.R. on various Allied commissions. In 1945 he signed the document of German surrender on behalf of his government. He also led the Soviet delegation to peace talks in Paris and to the initial United Nations meeting in New York, where his oratorical skills helped secure an "independent" status in the UN for the Soviet republics Ukraine and Belorussia.

From 1947 until 1953 Foreign Minister Vyshinsky headed the Soviet UN delegation, and he resumed his post in New York after Stalin's death despite being stripped of his ministerial position. The old Menshevik had, by this time, become an old Stalinist. He must have known when he died that his usefulness to Stalin's successors was limited, but his personal insecurities, if any, remained hidden, as always, behind a constant stream of angry bluster. His ashes are buried in the Kremlin wall.

Further Reading

Vyshinsky's career is best pursued through studies of Soviet law and foreign relations. See especially Harold J. Berman, *Justice in the U.S.S.R.* (1966); Peter Juviler, *Revolutionary Law and Order: Politics and Social Change in the U.S.S.R.* (1976); and Peter H. Solomon, "Soviet Penal Policy, 1917-1934: A Reinterpretation," in *Slavic Review* (June 1980). On Soviet foreign policy under Vyshinsky see Adam B. Ulam, *The Rivals: America and Russia since World War II* (1971) and Walter LaFeber, *America, Russia and the Cold War, 1945-1966* (1967). Vyshinsky's own writings are voluminous. His most important work in English is *The Law of the Soviet State* (1939, 1948).

Additional Sources

Vaksberg, Arkadiei, *The prosecutor and the prey: Vyshinsky and the 1930s' Moscow show trials,* London: Weidenfeld and Nicolson, 1990.

Vaksberg, Arkadiei, *Stalin's prosecutor: the life of Andrei Vyshinsky,* New York: Grove Weidenfeld, 1991. □

W

Benjamin Franklin Wade

Benjamin Franklin Wade (1800-1878), a U.S. senator, was a leading Radical Republican in the Civil War era. He supported a vigorous military effort against the South, emancipation, civil rights for African Americans, and a severe Reconstruction.

Benjamin Franklin Wade was born on Oct. 27, 1800, on a farm in Feeding Hills, Mass. He had some scattered schooling before his family moved to Ohio's Western Reserve in 1821. He worked as a farmer, drover, laborer, and schoolteacher, finally establishing a successful law practice in Jefferson, Ohio. He was elected to the Ohio Senate as a Whig in 1837 and 1841. His career there marked him as a product of the reform spirit so prevalent in the Western Reserve in the first half of the 19th century.

Wade opposed imprisonment for debt and special privileges for corporations, and, most of all, he established himself as a convinced opponent of slavery. He vigorously challenged Ohio's Fugitive Slave Law compelling the return of escaped slaves. He believed that slavery could be restricted only through the concerted action of a major party. When a coalition of Whigs and Free Soilers gained control of the legislature, they elected Wade as a compromise choice to the U.S. Senate in 1851.

Wade was firmly opposed to the Kansas-Nebraska Bill of 1854, took a prominent part in the ensuring debates, and ultimately joined the Republican party as it formed to carry on the abolition fight. He served as a member of the Senate Committee of Thirteen in the secession crisis of 1860-1861, strongly opposing any compromise with the South in the form of Federal guarantees to protect slavery.

At the outbreak of the Civil War, Wade joined other Radical Republicans in advocating total war. He chaired the Joint Congressional Committee on the Conduct of the War, which became the prime Radical instrument to spur on Abraham Lincoln's administration—which preferred more moderate war aims. In 1863 Lincoln announced that he would recognize new Southern state governments formed by 10 percent of the electorate taking a loyalty oath. Wade and the other Radicals were outraged. He and Representative Henry Winter Davis sponsored a bill making restoration of the seceded states much more difficult. When Lincoln pocket-vetoed the measure, Wade again joined Davis in issuing a manifesto (Aug. 5, 1864) violently attacking Lincoln's policies. Nevertheless, Wade worked for Lincoln's reelection in 1864, having no party alternative and fearing a Democratic victory.

After the war's end, Wade also clashed with President Andrew Johnson over Reconstruction. Convinced that Johnson's policies would restore an unrepentant South to power and leave African Americans and unionists without protection, he supported strong measures to control the South and to guarantee civil and political rights for the freedmen. In 1867 he was elected president pro tempore of the Senate and would have succeeded to the presidency had Johnson been convicted on impeachment charges in 1868. Instead Wade was himself defeated for reelection. He retired to Ohio and resumed his law practice. He died in Jefferson, Ohio, on March 2, 1878.

Further Reading

Hans L. Trefousse, *Benjamin Franklin Wade* (1963), is a sympathetic and scholarly modern biography. Trefousse's *The Radical Republicans* (1969) places Wade's advocacy in wider context. T. Harry Williams, *Lincoln and the Radicals* (1941), finds more to criticize in Wade's actions. An authoritative biographical sketch of Wade is in Kenneth W. Wheeler, ed., *For the Union Ohio Leaders in the Civil War* (1967).

Additional Sources

Trefousse, Hans Louis, *Benjamin Franklin Wade, radical Republican from Ohio*, New York, Twayne Publishers 1963. □

Otto Wagner

Otto Wagner (1841-1918), Austrian architect and teacher, advocated a breakaway from historicist architecture and became a founder of modern European architecture.

Otto Wagner was born in Vienna, Austria, on July 13, 1841. First he attended the Technical University there; in 1860 he attended the Bauakademie in Berlin; and in 1861-1863 he studied at the Academy of Fine Arts in Vienna. Up to 1894 Wagner's architectural practice was fully in the prevalent Neo-Renaissance and Neo-Baroque modes. This can be seen in the private dwelling Rennweg 3 in Vienna from 1889, a Baroque, palacelike residence with rather conventional decoration. Wagner's 1897-1898 project for an academy of fine arts combined classical planning principles inspired from the Roman imperial fora with an aggressive monumentality; however, the open metallic crown with floral decoration which topped the main building was a distinctly modern element.

In 1894 Wagner was appointed professor of architecture at the Vienna Academy of Fine Arts, replacing Carl von Hasenauer, and Wagner held that position until 1913. In his remarkable inaugural lecture, Wagner, who was already in his fifties, declared himself absolutely and without reservation in favor of a modern architecture in response to modern needs and condemned all stylistic imitation as false and inappropriate. This inaugural lecture, which epitomized Wagner's philosophy of architecture and design, was published in the following year as a book under the title *Moderne Architektur*. Shortly thereafter this book was made available to the American public by N. Clifford Ricker, who translated it and published it first in serialized form in 1901 in the *Brickbuilder* and in the following year as a book.

The functionalist message that Wagner set forth was that "Modern art must yield for us modern ideas, forms created for us, which represent our abilities, our acts, and our preferences" and that "Objects resulting from modern views . . . harmonize perfectly with our surroundings, but copied and imitated objects never do." Moreover, Wagner repeated *verbatim* the famous functionalist principle advocated by the great German architect Gottfried Semper: "Necessity is the sole mistress of art," to which he subsequently added his own emphasis on structure and materials.

Wagner's outspoken, strongly rationalist functionalism was indeed more revolutionary than his architecture. In 1894 he was commissioned to design the stations of the elevated and underground railroad (*Stadtbahn*) of Vienna. The stations that he designed at the start were in a rather conventional historicist mode. This, however, changed drastically in later stations, presumably under the influence of his pupils Josef Hoffmann and Josef Maria Olbrich, both of whom worked for him for several years. Thus in the later stations, such as the *Hofpavillon* in Schönbrunn and the Karlsplatz Station, Wagner used the historicist formal vocabulary in a freer and more innovative manner. In his blocks of flats in Vienna, such as Linke Wienzeile 38 and 40 of 1898, Wagner adorned the facades, which were essentially inspired from Renaissance palace architecture, with bold flat ornament, purely Art Nouveau in character. In that year Wagner joined the Vienna Secession, remaining a member until 1905.

After the turn of the century, Wagner started throwing off the Art Nouveau influence. His work in the new mode culminated in Sankt Leopold, the church of the Steinhof Asylum in Penzing outside Vienna, built in 1904-1907. This was a large cruciform edifice with a hemispherical dome raised on a cylindrical drum. There was abundant decoration, but this had been submitted to a linear stylization and was kept within rectangles and squares. Although remotely Byzantinesque in character, it appeared nonhistoricist and very much in the spirit of the work of younger architects such as Josef Maria Olbrich and Peter Behrens. Wagner's masterpiece of the time was the Postal Savings Bank in Vienna of 1904-1906, a work characterized by linearity, smoothness, and crispness of design. The external walls were covered by marble revetments held in place by exposed aluminum fastenings. The interior, equally striking in its lightness and in the elegant use of exposed metal and glass, secured Wagner a place among the 20th-century pioneers. Wagner died in Vienna on April 11, 1918.

Through his 1894 lecture, which was published as a book in numerous editions, Wagner facilitated greatly the reform of architectural practice and the establishment of modern design principles, such as honest use of materials, especially steel; rejection of historicist formal vocabulary; and preference for simplicity and clarity of form. His own work remained tied to tradition much longer, although it became increasingly modern after the turn of the century. Among his works, the Vienna railroad with its stations and the Postal Savings Bank provided exemplary solutions to contemporary and relatively new architectural problems. His theories and teachings, on the other hand, exercised a broad and fruitful influence and found their full realization in the work of subsequent generations.

Further Reading

Wagner is discussed in Henry-Russell Hitchcock, *Architecture: Nineteenth and Twentieth Centuries* (4th ed., 1977); Leonardo Benevolo, *History of Modern Architecture,* 2 vols. (1977); and Nikolaus Pevsner, *Pioneers of Modern Design: from William Morris to Walter Gropius* (2d ed., 1975). The best sources on his life and work are in German—Josef A. Lux, *Otto Wagner* (1914) and an exhibition catalogue *Otto Wagner: das Werk des Architeckten 1841-1918* (1964); many of his beautiful drawings and sketches are published in *Die Kunst des Otto Wagner* (1984).

Additional Sources

Geretsegger, Heinz, *Otto Wagner 1841-1918: the expanding city, the beginning of modern architecture,* New York: Rizzoli, 1979. □

Richard Wagner

The German operatic composer Richard Wagner (1813-1883) was undoubtedly the most important seminal figure in 19th-century music, Beethoven notwithstanding. Wagner was also a crucial figure in 19th-century cultural history for both his criticism and polemical writing.

Richard Wagner was born on May 22, 1813, in Leipzig into an unassuming family. His father died shortly after Richard's birth, and within the year his mother married Ludwig Geyer. There is still some controversy as to whether or not Geyer, an itinerant actor, was Wagner's real father. Wagner's musical training was largely left to chance until he was 18, when he studied with Theodor Weinlig in Leipzig for a year. He began his career in 1833 as choral director in Würzburg and composed his early works in imitation of German romantic compositions. Beethoven was his major idol at this time.

Wagner wrote his first opera, *Die Feen* (The Fairies), in 1833, but it was not produced until after the composer's death. He was music director of the theater in Magdeburg from 1834 to 1836, where his next work, *Das Liebesverbot* (Forbidden Love), loosely based on Shakespeare's *Measure for Measure* was performed in 1836. That year he married Minna Planner, a singer-actress active in provincial theatrical life.

In 1837 Wagner became the first music director of the theater in Riga, where he remained until 1839. He then set out for Paris, where he hoped to make his fortune. While in Paris, he developed an intense hatred for French musical culture that lasted the remainder of his life, regardless of how often he attempted to have a Parisian success. It was at this time that Wagner, in financial desperation, sold the scenario for *Der fliegende Holländer* (The Flying Dutchman) to the Paris Opéra for use by another composer. Wagner later set another version of this tale.

Disillusioned by his lack of success, Wagner returned to Germany, settling in Dresden in 1842, where he was in charge of the music for the court chapel. *Rienzi,* a grand opera in imitation of the French style, enjoyed a modest success; the Overture is still popular. In 1845 *Tannhäuser* was premiered in Dresden; this proved the first undoubted success of Wagner's career. In November of the same year he finished the poem for *Lohengrin* and began composition

early in 1846. While at work on *Lohengrin* he also made plans for his tetralogy, *Der Ring des Nibelungen* (The Ring of the Nibelungen), being captivated by Norse sagas. In 1845 he prepared the scenario for the first drama of the tetralogy to be written, *Siegfried's Tod* (Siegfried's Death), which later became *Die Götterdämmerung* (The Twilight of the Gods).

Years of Exile

Wagner had to flee Dresden in 1849 in the aftermath of the Revolution of 1848. He settled in Switzerland, first in Zurich and then near Lucerne. He remained in Switzerland for the most part for the next 15 years without steady employment, banished from Germany and forbidden access to German theatrical life. During this time he worked on the *Ring,* which dominated his creative life over the next 2 decades.

The first production of *Lohengrin* took place in Weimar under Franz Liszt's direction in 1850 (Wagner was not to see *Lohengrin* until 1861). By this time Wagner was moderately notorious as a polemicist, and his most fundamental work of theory, *Opera and Drama,* dates from 1850-1851. In it he discusses the significance of legend for the theater and how to write singable poetry, and he presents his ideas with regard to the realization of the "total work of art" which would effectively change the course of theatrical life in Germany if not the world.

The year 1850 also saw publication of one of Wagner's most scurrilous tracts, *The Jew in Music,* in which he viciously attacked the very existence of the Jewish composer and musician, particularly in German society. Anti-Semitism remained a hallmark of Wagner's philosophy the rest of his life.

Between 1850 and 1865 Wagner fashioned most of the material to which he owes his reputation. He purposefully turned aside from actual composition to plan an epic cycle of such grandeur and proportion as had never been created before. In 1851 he wrote the poem for *Der junge Siegfried* (Young Siegfried), the work now known as *Siegfried,* to prepare the way for *Götterdämmerung.* He realized he would need not only this drama to clarify his other work but two additional dramas as well, and he sketched the remaining poems for the *Ring* by the end of 1851. He completed *Das Rheingold* (The Rhinegold) in 1852 after he had revised the poem for *Die Walküre* (The Valkyrie).

In 1853 Wagner formally commenced composition on the *Rheingold;* he completed the scoring the following year and then began serious work on the *Walküre,* which was finished in 1856. At this time he was toying with the notion of writing the drama *Tristan and Isolde.* In 1857 he finished the composition of Act II of *Siegfried* and gave himself over entirely to *Tristan.* This work was completed in 1859, but it was mounted in Munich only in 1865.

Last Years

In 1860 Wagner received permission to reenter Germany except for Saxony. He was granted full amnesty in 1862. That year he began the music for *Die Meistersinger von Nürnberg* (The Mastersingers of Nuremburg), which he

had first thought of in 1845. He resumed composition on *Siegfried* in 1865 and began sketching what would eventually become *Parsifal,* also a vague possibility since the mid-1840s. He began *Parsifal* at the urging of the Bavarian monarch, Ludwig II, then Wagner's patron. The *Meistersinger* was completed in 1867; the first performance took place in Munich the following year. Only then did he pick up the threads of the *Ring* and resume work on Act III of *Siegfried,* which was finished in September 1869, a month that also saw the first performance of the *Rheingold.* He wrote the music for *Götterdämmerung* from 1869 to 1874.

The first entire *Ring* cycle (*Rheingold, Walküre, Siegfried,* and *Götterdämmerung*) was given at the Festspielhaus, the shrine Wagner built for himself at Bayreuth, in 1876, over 30 years after the idea for it had first come to mind. He finished *Parsifal,* his final drama, in 1882. Wagner died on Feb. 13, 1883, in Venice and was buried at Bayreuth.

Philosophy of the *Ring*

The *Ring* is central to Wagner's career. Here he wished to present new ideas of morality and human activity that would completely alter the course of history. He envisioned a world made entirely free from subservience to supernatural bondage, which he believed had adversely affected Western civilization from ancient Greece to the present. Wagner also held that at the source of all human activity was fear, which must be purged so that man can live the perfect life. In the *Ring* he attempted to set forth the standards for superior humans, those beings who would dominate individuals less fortunate; in turn, such lesser mortals would recognize their own inferior status and yield to the radiance offered by the perfect hero. The implications inherent in a quest for moral and racial purity are vital to Wagner's intentions in the *Ring.*

It is interesting to note that Wagner believed it was only by submitting completely to the sensuous experience that man could be liberated from the restraints imposed by rationality. However valuable the intellect might be, the rational life was regarded as a hindrance to achieving the fullest development of human awareness. Only when perfect man and perfect woman came together could a transcendental heroic image be created. Siegfried and Brünnhilde together are invincible after each has submitted to the other; apart they are imperfect.

There is no charity or idealism present in the Wagnerian myth world. The perfect ones exult only in each other. All men must recognize the superiority of certain creatures and then bow to their will. Man may quest for his destiny, but he must submit to the will of the superior one if the two come into conflict. In the *Ring* Wagner wanted to turn his back upon the civility inherent in the Hellenic-Judeo-Christian world. He preferred a realm dominated by the strength and savagery exemplified in the Norse sagas. The implications for the future of Germany were immense.

Philosophy of Other Operas

In *Tristan* Wagner rejected the affirmative way he developed in the *Ring*. Instead, he explored the dark side of love in order to plunge to the depths of negative experience. Tristan and Isolde, liberated and not doomed by a love potion they drink, willingly destroy a kingdom in order to love and to live; the sensual power of love is seen here as a destructive force, and the musical style of devious chromaticism and overwhelming orchestral pulsation is perfect for the messages of the drama.

Wagner's egomania, never tolerable to anyone save those who could blind themselves totally to his flaws, came to the fore in the *Meistersinger*. The tale of the young hero-singer who conquers the old order and forces a new, sensually more exciting style upon the tradition-bound Nuremburg society is the tale of the *Ring* in a slightly different guise. (Wagner openly claimed *Tristan* to be the *Ring* in microcosm.) It is obvious in the *Meistersinger* that Wagner identifies himself with the messianic figure of a young German poet and singer who wins the prize and is finally accepted as the leader of a new society.

In *Parsifal* Wagner identified himself even more intensely with the hero as the savior, the world's redeemer. The mysteries celebrated in *Parsifal* are those prepared for the glory of Wagner himself and not for any god.

Musical Language

The scope of Wagner's vision is as breathtaking as his ideas and metaphysics are repugnant. Without the music his dramas would still be milestones in the history of Western thought. With the music, however, Wagner's importance is greatly magnified. He conceived a musical language that would most effectively present his philosophies. He intended to batter down the resistant forces of reason by means of the music. Ideally, there would be an unending melody in which the voice and text are but part of the fabric, united with a magnificent orchestral web which becomes the action at a distinctly musical pace. The verbal language, often very obscure and tortured in syntax, is acceptable only through the music.

For Wagner, music was in no sense additive, tacked onto the dramas after completion, anymore than it was an exercise in formal rhetoric, mere "art for art's sake." Music could bind all life, art, reality, and illusion together into one symbiotic union that would then work its own unique magic upon an audience. It is no accident that Wagner's musical language is intended to dethrone reason and to ask for unquestioning acceptance of the composer's beliefs. In Wagner's reading of Schopenhauer, the musical ideal in his dramas would be not a reflection of the world but would be that very world itself.

Personal Characteristics

Such a summary of Wagner's creative life hardly hints at the extraordinary complications of his personal life which, in turn, affected his dramas. Wagner was that rare individual—a truly charismatic figure who overcame all adversities. During the years in Switzerland he managed to live for the most part on charity by means of the most amazing conniving and manipulation of people conceivable. The Wesendonck family in particular contributed to his well-being, and Mathilde Wesendonck, one of Wagner's

many mistresses, was credited with partially inspiring *Tristan*.

Wagner's life after leaving Saxony was a constant series of intrigues, harangues, and struggles to overcome the indifference of the world, to find the ideal woman worthy of his love, and to be the worthy recipient of the benefits offered by the perfect patron. Cosima Liszt von Bülow was the answer to his quest for the ideal female, subservient and fanatically devoted to his well-being. Although Wagner and Minna had lived apart for some time, Wagner did not marry Cosima until 1870, almost a decade after Minna's death. Over 30 years her husband's junior, Cosima was to be the dominating, guiding spirit in the Wagnerian shrine at Bayreuth until her death in 1930.

The perfect patron proved to be Ludwig II, who literally rescued Wagner from debtors' prison and brought the composer to Munich with a near carte blanche for life and creativity. Once salvaged, however, Wagner was so offensive to all save the blindly adoring young monarch that he was forced to flee within 2 years. Ludwig, despite eventually disillusionment, remained a loyal supporter of Wagner. It was his generosity that made possible the first festival performances of the *Ring* in Bayreuth in 1876.

Never one of amenable disposition, Wagner held convictions of his own superiority that developed monomaniacal proportions as he grew older. He was intolerant of any questioning, of any failure to accept him and his creation. His household revolved completely in his orbit, and his demands upon wives, mistresses, friends, musicians, and benefactors were legion. Those who ran afoul of him were pilloried unmercifully, often unscrupulously, such as Eduard Hanslick, the distinguished Viennese music critic who became the model for Beckmesser in the *Meistersinger*.

When the young philosopher Friedrich Nietzsche first met Wagner, he thought he had found his way into the presence of a god, so radiant and powerful did Wagner seem to him. Later Nietzsche realized that the composer was something less than the perfection of the superman incarnate he had imagined him to be and turned away in disgust. Wagner never forgave Nietzsche for his desertion.

Place in History

In retrospect, Wagner's accomplishments outweigh both his personal behavior and his legacy for the 20th century. He has even managed to survive the predictable rejection by later generations of composers. Wagner created such an effective, unique musical language, especially in *Tristan* and *Parsifal,* that the beginnings of modern music are often dated from these scores.

Wagner demonstrated that music was not restricted to being pure formalism and abstract theoretical exploration but was a living, vibrant force capable of changing men's lives. He also proved that the music theater is a proper forum for ideas as opposed to being an arena for only escape and entertainment. And he demonstrated that a composer could rightfully take his place among the great revolutionary thinkers of Western civilization, questioning and attacking what seemed intolerable in traditional modes of behavior, experience, learning, and creation. Together with Karl Marx and Charles Darwin, Wagner must be given his rightful due as one of the greatest forces in 19th-century cultural history.

Further Reading

A representative sampling of Wagner's important prose writings is in *Wagner on Music and Drama,* edited by Albert Goldman and Evert Sprinchorn (1964). The standard biography in English is that of the great English Wagnerian, Ernest Newman, *The Life of Wagner* (4 vols., 1933-1946). See also Newman's other important studies, *The Wagner Operas* (1959) and *Wagner as Man and Artist* (1960). Recommended to bring Newman's work up to date are Robert Gutman, *Richard Wagner: The Man, His Mind, and His Music* (1968), and Chappel White, *An Introduction to the Life and Works of Richard Wagner* (1970). Also valuable are the specific studies, such as Jack Stein, *Richard Wagner and the Synthesis of the Arts* (1960); Robert Donington, *Wagner's Ring and Its Symbols: The Music and the Myth* (1963); and Elliot Zuckerman, *Tristan: The First Hundred Years* (1964). □

Robert Ferdinand Wagner

Robert Ferdinand Wagner (1877-1953) was probably the most effective legislative leader in the history of the U.S. Senate and one of the principal architects of modern American political liberalism.

Robert F. Wagner was born in Nastätten, Germany, on June 8, 1877, into a staunch Lutheran family, the youngest of nine children. In 1886 the family emigrated to New York City. Robert was unable to speak English when he entered school, but he proved a diligent student. He sold newspapers and worked as a grooery boy to supplement the family's income. He graduated from the City College of New York in 1898, a Phi Beta Kappa. Two years later he graduated from the New York Law School and gained admittance to the state bar.

Attracted to politics, Wagner associated himself with the Democratic Tammany Hall machine. In 1904 he won election to the New York Assembly and 4 years later to the Senate, becoming Democratic floor leader. He helped push through legislation pertaining to workmen's compensation and other social welfare measures.

In 1926, after eight years as a member of the New York Supreme Court, Wagner won election to the U.S. Senate. He was reelected three times. He became chairman of the Senate Banking and Currency Committee in 1931; 2 years later, after the election of Franklin Roosevelt and solid Democratic majorities, Wagner moved to the center of the liberal reform movement. He drafted the crucial National Industrial Recovery Act, and in 1933-1934 he chaired the new National Labor Board. During the remainder of the 1930s Wagner authored and sponsored a long list of far-reaching social legislation. In 1935 his career reached its pinnacle with the passage of the National Labor Relations Act—commonly called the Wagner Act—which committed the Federal government to protecting and encouraging unions.

Wagner was a loyal supporter of Roosevelt's policies. During World War II Wagner's main concern was warbred inflation. In the Employment Act of 1946 he helped bring about Federal responsibility for maintaining a healthy economy, and at his urging Congress significantly expanded social security coverage and benefits.

Wagner gave up his Senate seat in 1949. He died in New York City on May 4, 1953. His son, Robert Wagner, Jr., was mayor of New York City from 1954 to 1965.

Further Reading

J. Joseph Huthmacher gives a full account of Wagner's public career in *Senator Robert F. Wagner and the Rise of Urban Liberalism* (1968). Arthur M. Schlesinger, Jr., *The Age of Roosevelt* (3 vols., 1957-1960), shows Wagner to be a central figure in the development of the New Deal, as does William E. Leuchtenburg, *Franklin D. Roosevelt and the New Deal: 1932-1940* (1963). Wagner's work in labor and housing legislation is treated by Harry A. Millis and Emily Clark Brown, *From the Wagner Act to Taft-Hartley* (1950), and by Timothy L. McDonnel, *The Wagner Housing Act* (1957). For Wagner's later employment legislation see Stephen K. Bailey, *Congress Makes a Law: The Story behind the Employment Act of 1946* (1950). □

Robert Ferdinand Wagner Jr.

A lawyer and public official, Robert F. Wagner (1910-1991) was one of New York City's last Tammany Hall mayors, 1954-1965.

A New York City mayor for 12 years, Robert F. Wagner was intimately involved in politics from childhood. His mother died when Robert was nine. His father, a senator, was a powerful figure in the New Deal wing of the Democratic Party and a sponsor of several significant reform acts, including the Wagner Act, which created the National Labor Relations Board. Wagner reaped the benefit of his father's famous name as well as his enormous popularity when he ran for public office.

Early Start in Politics

Young Robert attended a public school in New York and the Taft School in Watertown, CT, and received his law degree from Yale Law School in 1937. In that same year he was elected to the New York State Assembly and remained there until 1941, when he entered the U.S. Air Force. He served for the rest of World War II and was discharged in 1945 as a lieutenant colonel decorated with six battle stars. In 1942 Wagner married Susan Edwards of Greenwich, CT.

After the war, Wagner, with the backing of the Democratic Party and Tammany Hall, the infamous New York City political machine which had controlled city affairs for more than a century, rose rapidly up the political ladder. He won appointments as city tax commissioner and as commissioner of housing and buildings, and then as chairman of the city planning commission. Elected Manhattan borough president in 1949, Wagner made a bid for the 1952 Democratic senatorial nomination but lost. The following year Wagner challenged the Democratic incumbent mayor, Vincent Impellitteri, in the primary and beat him by nearly a two to one margin. With the backing of controversial Tammany Hall boss Carmine De Sapio, he went on to win the mayoralty in 1953, a post he would hold for 12 years. He again ran for the U.S. Senate in 1956 but lost. Wagner and his wife had two sons, Robert F. Wagner, III, who also had a long career in New York City politics, and Duncan Wagner. After his first wife's death in 1964, Wagner married Barbara Joan Cavanagh the following year, and after their divorce in 1971, he married Phyllis Fraser Cerf in 1975.

Mayor of New York City

As mayor, Wagner pushed through the city council measures barring discrimination in the rental and sale of housing, thoroughly revised New York City's zoning ordinances, pushed slum clearance and public housing projects forward, enlarged the police force, and streamlined the budget-making process. During his first two administrations Mayor Wagner encouraged the formation of municipal unions with what was called the "little Wagner Act," giving the city's employees, except the police, the right to form unions and to engage in collective bargaining. He became so powerful nationally that his support of John F. Kennedy in 1960 helped win Kennedy the presidential nomination.

Wagner broke his alliance with Tammany Hall in 1961, when he was at the peak of his popularity. He defeated his Tammany Hall-supported opponent in the Democratic primary and with the support of a growing Manhattan reform movement and the powerful Central Labor Council went on to win a third term by a large margin. Wagner's power as mayor was also enlarged by a new charter approved that same year by the voters. But his last term proved to be a troubled one, as his administration was caught up in the urban unrest of the 1960s. Facing increasingly heavy social obligations and massive increases in welfare spending, Wagner resorted to economic expediences to pay the bills. With the permission of the state legislature he increased the city's borrowing limits and issued "revenue anticipation notes" not only for the current fiscal year but for fees and taxes that were estimated to be available the following year. In 1965 Wagner submitted a record budget of $3.8 billion. Later critics would cite that budget as the beginning of the heavy deficit spending that would get the city into serious financial trouble a decade later.

Wagner was placid and methodical, and critics said he was too slow to act to curb the city's growing urban problems. After rioting broke out in Harlem and Bedford-Stuyvesant, Wagner launched several new programs, including a city jobs program for disadvantaged youth. With the backing of the federal government and the Ford Foundation he initiated a program called Mobilization for Youth (MFY) which aimed at retraining inner-city youth. He also launched another anti-poverty program called Harlem Youth Opportunities Unlimited and Associated Community Teams (HARYOU-ACT). But critics were not satisfied, and Wagner decided not to seek a fourth term. On leaving office, he said: "The days of scandal, the days of political influence, getting contracts and assistance from the city have disappeared, and I believe I hand on to my successor a government that had changed radically in this way."

During his administration, Wagner had helped bring a World's Fair to Flushing Meadow, helped establish the Lincoln Center for the Performing Arts and helped created the Jamaica Bay wildlife preserve. New York lost major league baseball's Giants and Dodgers to California, but gained the Mets.

Later Career

After leaving office, Wagner returned to his private law practice with Finley, Kumble, Wagner, Heine, Underberg, and Casey. Still visible in Democratic Party circles, Wagner entered the New York mayoral primary in 1969 and lost. A deal that would have made him the Republican-Liberal candidate for mayor in 1973 collapsed. He was appointed ambassador to Spain, 1968-1969, and continued to serve as a political adviser on the national scene. President Jimmy Carter appointed him as his unofficial personal envoy to the Vatican, 1978-1981. In 1976 Wagner's law firm merged with another, and he continued in private practice until his death. In the 1980s Wagner was a member of the city's

Charter Revision Commission. In 1989 New York University named its school of public service for him.

Wagner died of cancer on February 12, 1991 at his home in Manhattan. New York Governor Mario Cuomo eulogized him: "A large, living piece of our best political history has fallen away, and there is nothing adequate to replace it. Robert F. Wagner was a superb public person, servant of the people, and adviser to their leaders."

Further Reading

For general information on Wagner see *Political Profiles: The Johnson Years* (1976) and Edward Kenworthy, "The Emergence of Mayor Wagner," *New York Times Magazine* (August 14, 1955). For some of the conflicts and accomplishments of the Wagner years see Warren Moscow, *The Last of the Big-Time Bosses* (1971); Robert Caro, *The Power Broker* (1975); William F. Buckley, Jr., *The Unmaking of a Mayor* (1966), and Edward C. Banfield and James Q. Wilson, *City Politics* (1963).

□

Jonathan Mayhew Wainwright

Jonathan Mayhew Wainwright (1883-1953) commanded the American forces in the Philippines during World War II. He became a world symbol of resistance to the Axis in the siege of Corregidor and during four years in Japanese captivity.

Jonathan Wainwright was born on Aug. 23, 1883, in Walla Walla, Wash., the son of a career Army officer. A solemn young man, Wainwright graduated from the U.S. Military Academy in 1906. He served in the cavalry in Texas and the Philippines. In World War I he was a member of the general staff of the 82d Division and saw action in Europe.

Wainwright attended the Army's postgraduate schools and advanced to the rank of major general. In October 1940 he went to the Philippines to help Gen. Douglas MacArthur prepare the American colony for the expected Japanese invasion. A shortage of funds, however, meant few improvements, and when war came on Dec. 7, 1941, the Americans and the Philippine troops were woefully unprepared. The Japanese caught their B-17 bombers on the ground at Clark Field and destroyed them, making the defense of the islands hopeless. The Japanese landed on the major island of Luzon on December 10 and by early January 1942 had forced Wainwright, commanding the North Luzon Force, to fall back to the Bataan peninsula.

The Navy, badly hurt at Pearl Harbor, dared not sail into Japanese-controlled waters to lift the siege. Wainwright continued to fall back. On March 12 he took command on Luzon. He moved his headquarters to the tiny island of Corregidor, at the mouth of Manila Bay, under constant Japanese artillery bombardment. On April 8 the pitiful remnants on Bataan surrendered, and Wainwright's force of 11,000 men faced the vastly superior Japanese alone.

Manila harbor was a key strategic point in Japanese offensive plans, so they committed major forces to Wainwright's destruction. Except for an occasional submarine, no supplies reached Wainwright. He and his men suffered terribly but held out for nearly a month. Finally, on May 5, 1942, Wainwright wired MacArthur: "As I write this we are being subjected to terrific air and artillery bombardment and it is unreasonable to expect that we can hold out for long. We have done our best, both here and on Bataan, and although we are beaten we are still unashamed." That night the Japanese landed on Corregidor, and at noon the next day Wainwright initiated surrender negotiations.

Wainwright's opponent, Gen. Homma, refused to accept the surrender of the garrison unless Wainwright ordered the remaining American forces on the southern Philippine islands to lay down their arms also. Desperate to avoid the annihilation of his troops on Corregidor, Wainwright complied. MacArthur, in Australia, was furious and ordered Wainwright's subordinates to disregard the surrender order. They did not. MacArthur refused to agree to Gen. George Marshall's recommendation of a Medal of Honor for Wainwright. "His animosity toward Wainwright was tremendous," Marshall recalled later.

Wainwright had become America's first World War II hero. The press gave the siege of Corregidor enormous coverage. In the prisoner-of-war camps Wainwright shared all his men's privations and—often at great personal risk—intervened with his Japanese captors to try to obtain better treatment for the men. He was liberated in early September

1945; always a thin man, he now looked like a walking skeleton.

Congress awarded Wainwright the Medal of Honor in 1945. He retired in 1947, became a successful businessman, and died in San Antonio, Tex., on Sept. 2, 1953.

Further Reading

Wainwright's own account of the Philippine campaign and of his experience in prison are in *General Wainwright's Story* (1946). By far the most competent account of the campaign is Louis Morton, *The Fall of the Philippines* (1953).

Additional Sources

Beck, John Jacob, *MacArthur and Wainwright; sacrifice of the Philippines,* Albuquerque, University of New Mexico Press 1974.

Schultz, Duane P., *Hero of Bataan: the story of General Jonathan M. Wainwright,* New York: St Martin's Press, 1981. □

Morrison Remick Waite

Morrison Remick Waite (1816-1888), seventh chief justice of the U.S. Supreme Court, was a skillful administrator of the nation's highest bench.

Born in Lyme, Conn., on Nov. 29, 1816, Morrison R. Waite graduated from Yale in 1837, read law, and began to practice in Maumee, Ohio, moving later to Toledo. A lawyer rather than a politician, he served in the Ohio Legislature (1849-1850) as a Whig. Later he was a Republican but played no conspicuous role in the politics of the Civil War or the Reconstruction era.

Capable and noncontroversial, Waite was named by President Ulysses S. Grant to join Caleb Cushing and William M. Evarts as counsel before the tribunal hearing the Alabama Claims against England for Civil War damages. Waite helped prevent inflammatory peripheral issues from disrupting negotiations, and the United States was awarded $15,500,000 in a decision of major significance in the history of the settlement of international disputes by arbitration.

A prolonged competition for the chief justiceship of the Supreme Court followed the death of Salmon P. Chase in 1873. Bypassing other strong contenders, Grant in 1874 finally named Waite. Respectability and the need to end the leadership crisis won Waite swift confirmation.

On the Supreme Court, Waite's demeanor foreshadowed the doctrine of judicial restraint. Unlike chief justices John Marshall and Roger B. Taney, he sought less to lead than to follow the thinking of the nation. Tired of the era's racial controversies and convinced that white moderates in the South should establish the racial rules for the region, the Waite Court weakened the concept of national citizenship based on the 14th Amendment. In cases involving violent interruption of a political meeting, refusal to allow a registered black American to vote, and a lynching, the Federal government was not sustained in efforts to protect black citizens. That responsibility was left to state governments. Similarly, the *Civil Rights Cases* (1883) permitted racial segregation in privately owned places of public accommodation. On the other hand, African Americans had been sustained in their right to serve on juries in *Strauder v. West Virginia* (1880).

Waite's most famous decision was *Munn v. Illinois* (1877), which upheld the right of state legislatures to enact granger laws, in this case the regulation of grain storage rates. Retrieving a 17th-century English decision, Waite held that legislators could regulate in a matter "affected with a public interest." Later, however, the countervailing interest of the railroads to avoid such regulation was established when Waite, while avoiding express disavowal of the Munn doctrine, permitted a broad reading of the 14th Amendment that limited the power of government to regulate business.

Waite was married in 1840 to Amelia Champlin Warner; of their five children, four lived beyond childhood. Waite died in Washington, D.C., on March 23, 1888.

Further Reading

An excellent biography of Waite is C. Peter Magrath, *Morrison R. Waite: The Triumph of Character* (1963). □

Terry Waite

Terry Waite (born 1939), an official of the Church of England, made three trips to Lebanon in an effort to free westerners held hostage there. On his third try in 1987, he himself was taken hostage and not freed until almost five years later.

Even after publication of his book *Taken on Trust*, chronicling his 1,763 days of being held by Islamic fundamentalists in Lebanon, Terry Waite remains a controversial figure. For many years he was a hero to the British media and public. When he was captured and throughout the years during which there was no news of his whereabouts, prayers were said in churches all over Britain for his safe return. To some he remained a saintly and courageous figure, the innocent envoy from the archbishop of Canterbury, whose intercession saved the lives of a number of Middle East hostages. But to others, notably including journalists specializing in Middle East affairs, he was a muddle-headed meddler and publicity-seeker who allowed himself to be used by Oliver North and the Central Intelligence Agency (CIA). Waite allegedly took credit for hostage releases that had almost everything to do with arms deals and little to do with his efforts. To those critics he was a man who defied his church's wishes for his own vainglory and who put his family on the rack to feed his own hunger for headlines. When he was united with fellow hostages John McCarthy, Terry Anderson, and Tom Sutherland during the last year of his captivity, they were reported to have found him an awkward companion. And in *Taken on Trust* he is evasive about his knowledge of the Iran-Contra affair.

Although he says of himself in his book: "Inwardly you are a small, frightened child, anxious to impress people," there is certainly no denying the courage of the seventeen stone (238 pounds), 6 foot 7 inches man who spent almost five years in captivity, nearly four years of it in solitary confinement, after he was seized by Islamic Jihad from a go-between's house in Lebanon on January 20, 1987. Before his release in November 1991 he was frequently blindfolded, beaten, and subjected to mock executions. He lived much of the time chained to a radiator, suffered desperately from asthma, and was transported in a giant refrigerator as his captors moved him about. And yet he emerged from his ordeal able to make a witty and eloquent speech to the waiting media before even greeting his family. In his earlier efforts for other hostages he had shown total disregard for his own safety as virtually the only western figure who ever gained direct access to the kidnappers.

Terry Waite, whose entry in *Who's Who* ironically records one of his hobbies as "travel, especially in remote parts of the world," was born on May 31, 1939, the son of a village policeman, and spent his early life in Styal, Cheshire. He left school at 16, having learned the prayer book by heart. He did not last the two-year National Service period in the Grenadier Guards, being discharged after a year because of an allergy to the dye in the uniforms. He then took a degree in theology at the Church Army College in London but decided he did not want to be ordained a priest.

His first job was as an adviser on adult education to the bishop of Bristol from 1964 to 1968. Soon after that, working in Africa for the bishop of Uganda, he was taken hostage for the first time with his wife, Frances, and two children.

In the early 1970s he worked for the Roman Catholic Church as a widely-traveled consultant on missionary work. In 1980 Robert Runcie, the archbishop of Canterbury, appointed him secretary for Anglican Communion Affairs to work with churches abroad and to organize the archbishop's foreign trips. In this role he quickly became a media figure. After a few months he played the key role in securing the release of a missionary, his wife, and the bishop of Iran's secretary, Jean Waddell, when they were held on spy charges in Tehran. At one stage he greeted the arrival of five gunmen in a cell where he was celebrating holy communion by coolly repeating his sermon. After his efforts had led to the release of a fourth detainee, appreciation for Waite's role was shown with the award of a Member of the British Empire (MBE) in the next honors list.

Waite's reputation as an emissary extraordinary was cemented when in 1984 he established contact with Colonel Muammar Gadaffi in Libya, where four Britons had been detained following the murder of a policewoman outside the Libyan Embassy in London. He eventually secured their release after protracted negotiations and his own theological discussions with the Libyan leader on Christmas Day.

Over the next two years there followed a series of efforts on behalf of four American hostages held in Lebanon, including one when he was dropped at dead of night by an American helicopter. In this period some critical articles began to appear suggesting that Waite was obsessed with his own publicity, but he insisted that although he had frequent meetings with Oliver North he was never told about the efforts to trade hostages for arms. When the Irangate storm broke, he said in a statement from his archbishop's Lambeth Palace headquarters: "At no time have I ever had any dealings in arms or money."

His third and final trip to Lebanon in 1987 was made despite a visit from the British ambassador, who urged him not to go because the Amal militia had lost out to the more extreme pro-Iranian Hizbollah faction. Waite himself described the trip that led to his capture and incarceration as "a walk into a minefield." But he insisted he had to go ahead because he was the one person who had met the kidnappers face to face.

Soon after his release in 1991 Terry Waite resigned his position with the archbishop and became fully engaged with writing his book *Taken on Trust,* published in September 1993. He took up a fellowship at Trinity Hall, Cambridge, and said that he hoped to use proceeds of his writing to help the poor and to work for justice and reconciliation. True to his word, in July 1996 Waite, along with fellow former hostage John McCarthy, sent messages urging the release of four people on the first anniversary of their capture in Kashmir. Waite's various honors include the Commander of the Order of the British Empire bestowed upon him by Queen Elizabeth II.

Further Reading

Terry Waite's own account of his earlier life and his nearly five years as a hostage, *Taken on Trust,* was published in London (September 1993). Other books by Lebanon hostages include Brian Keenan's *An Evil Cradling* (1993) and Terry Anderson's *Den of Lions* (1993). Further light is cast on the Lebanon hostages affair in the various histories of the Iran-Contra affair chronicling the doings of Oliver North. Waite's mid-1990s activities have been noted in various news services including Yereth Rosen, "Britain still seeking release of Kashmir hostages," *Reuters* (July 3, 1996); and Patricia Edmonds, "Iran-Contra Charge," *USA Today* (May 5, 1994). □

Edward Gibbon Wakefield

Edward Gibbon Wakefield (1796-1862) was a British colonial reformer, promoter, and advocate of systematic colonization.

Edward Gibbon Wakefield, a London land agent's son, was born on March 20, 1796. He was educated at Westminster and entered the Foreign Service in 1814. Two years later he eloped with a ward in chancery, and Parliament condoned the offense. In 1826, six years after the death of his wife, Wakefield abducted a 15-year-old heiress from school; this time Parliament annulled the mar-

riage, and Wakefield spent three years in Newgate Prison. In prison he became interested in both corrective punishment and colonial development. He advocated the abolition of transportation on the grounds that it had no deterrent effect and attributed the slow development of the Australian colonies to a policy based on free land grants and convict labor.

In *A Letter from Sydney* (1829), *England and America* (1833), and *The Art of Colonisation* (1849), Wakefield propounded a theory of systematic colonization: he wanted to transplant British society without the many social evils evident at home. Colonial land sold at a high, uniform price would produce revenue to pay for the immigration of free settlers. Newcomers unable to afford land would constitute a laboring class. Economic growth would result, and by concentrating settlement, a civilized society capable of self-government would evolve.

The Ripon Regulations (1831) discontinued free land grants in Australia, and a land fund assisted immigrants. But when the price of land was raised from five to 20 shillings an acre, pastoralists began to squat farther afield, and settlement became more dispersed. In 1838 Wakefield accompanied Lord Durham to Canada, and his influence on the *Report on the Affairs of British North America,* recommending local self-government, is evident in the sections on public lands and migration.

Wakefield was intimately involved in many private schemes to promote new colonies. In 1834 the South Australian Company secured a parliamentary act whereby control of a proposed colony was shared by the Colonial Office

and a board of commissioners responsible for land sales, immigration, and public finance. Settlement began in 1836, but Wakefield, disapproving of various details, transferred his interest to New Zealand.

In 1837 the British government refused to charter the New Zealand Association because New Zealand was not then part of the Crown's dominions and because missionaries sought to protect Maori land rights. Nevertheless, before the Treaty of Waitangi in 1840, a reformed New Zealand Land Company had managed to establish settlements, after acquiring land on easy terms and dispatching immigrants without parliamentary sanction. When its land titles were subsequently questioned by the government, Wakefield campaigned for local self-government, a proposal which the governor, Sir George Grey, successfully opposed.

In 1853 Wakefield emigrated to Wellington and was elected to the colony's first General Assembly, following the New Zealand Constitutional Act (1852). After 1854, when his health broke, he lived in retirement until his death on May 16, 1862.

Doctrinaire and uncompromising, Wakefield frequently quarreled with his disciples. Lacking firsthand knowledge, he often had impracticable ideas. Nevertheless, at a time when new colonial policies were being devised, his writings and actions helped to reshape British attitudes toward colonial development.

Further Reading

After a long period of relative neglect, Wakefield has been resurrected as an architect of the British Commonwealth. The best account, by Paul Bloomfield, *Edward Gibbon Wakefield* (1961), attempts to bring into focus the magnitude of Wakefield's achievements as an empire builder and analyzes his extraordinary personality. Older biographies include Richard Garnett, *Edward Gibbon Wakefield* (1898), and Irma O'Connor, *Edward Gibbon Wakefield: The Man Himself* (1928). Two studies which include important discussions of Wakefield's work are Donald Winch, *Classical Political Economy and Colonies* (1965), and Peter Burroughs, *Britain and Australia, 1831-1855: A Study in Imperial Relations and Crown Lands Administration* (1967). □

Selman Abraham Waksman

The American microbiologist Selman Abraham Waksman (1888-1973) received the Nobel Prize in physiology or medicine for his discovery of streptomycin.

Selman Abraham Waksman was born on July 2, 1888 in Novaia-Priluka near Kiev in what is now the Ukraine. In 1908 he went to Odessa to study and garnered a matriculation diploma in 1910 from the Fifth Gymnasium in Odessa. He left almost immediately for the United States where he entered Rutgers College (now University) of Agriculture on a scholarship in 1911 and received

a bachelor's degree in 1915. While completing work for a master's degree, awarded by Rutgers in 1916, he was a research assistant in soil bacteriology at the New Jersey Agricultural Experiment Station.

On August 4, 1916, Waksman married Bertha Deborah Mitnik. That same year he became a citizen of the United States. He received a doctorate in biochemistry from the University of California in 1918. He returned to New Jersey as microbiologist at the experiment station and as lecturer in soil microbiology at the university. In 1922 his *Principles of Soil Microbiology* was published.

Waksman became an associate professor at Rutgers in 1925 and professor in 1930. From 1929 until 1939 his major research was on humus, and he published a volume entitled *Humus* in 1936. From 1931 until 1942 he spent summers at Woods Hole Oceanographic Institution, developing marine bacteriology. In 1940 he was named head of the department of microbiology at Rutgers.

In 1932 Waksman began to direct a project to study tuberculosis germs, particularly what happens to them in the soil. It was known that these microorganisms were somehow destroyed in soil, and Waksman learned that they were destroyed by other microbes. A series of studies on the effect of one kind of microbe on another led him to then begin, in 1939, a systematic search for antibiotics, the substances produced by microorganisms that inhibit or destroy other microorganisms. His search was primarily among the actinomycetes, a group of organisms that he first studied in

1915. This led to the discovery of several antibiotics, the best-known of which is streptomycin.

Waksman discovered streptomycin in 1943 and reported it in the January 1944 *Proceedings of the Society of Experimental Biology and Medicine*. It proved to be the first chemotherapeutic agent able to control tuberculosis and was useful in treating many other diseases, like influenza, meningitis and urinary tract infections.

In 1949 Waksman became director of the Institute of Microbiology founded that year at Rutgers with royalties from the antibiotics discovered by Waksman and his colleagues. He retired in 1958. On August 16, 1973, Waksman died suddenly in Hyannis, Massachusetts, of a cerebral hemorrhage. He was buried near the institute to which he had contributed so much. Waksman's honors over his professional career were many and varied, including the Nobel Prize (1952), recognition by the French Legion of Honor, the Lasker Award, and election as a fellow of the American Association for the Advancement of Science.

Further Reading

Selman A. Waksman, *The Microbes Have Come to Israel,* 1967; Waksman, *The Antibiotic Era: A History of the Antibiotic and of Their Role in the Conquest of Infection in Other Fields of Human Endeavor,* 1975; *American Portrait: Dr. Selman Waksman* (a videocassette), CBS, Inc., 1984. Waksman's autobiography, *My Life with the Microbes* (1954), traces the events leading to the discovery of streptomycin. Other sources of information include Theodore L. Sourkes, editor, *Nobel Prize Winners in Medicine and Physiology, 1901-1965* (rev. ed. 1967); Magill, F. N., editor, *The Nobel Prize Winners: Physiology or Medicine, Volume 2, 1944-1969,* Salem Press (1991); and Nobel Foundation, *Nobel Lectures: Physiology or Medicine, 1942-1962,* Volume 3 (1964). □

Derek Alton Walcott

Nobel Prize winning poet and dramatist from the West Indies, Derek Alton Walcott (born 1930) used a synthesis of Caribbean dialects and English to explore the richness and conflicts of the complex cultural heritage of his homeland.

Derek Alton Walcott was born in Casties, St. Lucia, West Indies, on January 23, 1930. The son of a civil servant and a teacher, he was of mixed African, Dutch, and English heritage. He received a B.A. from St. Mary's College, St. Lucia, in 1953 and attended the University of the West Indies at Kingston, Jamaica. A Rockefeller fellowship brought him to the United States in 1957; he studied under the American stage director Jose Quintero, returned to the islands in 1959 to found the Trinidad Theatre Workshop. He taught in St. Lucia, Grenada, and Jamaica and at many American universities: Boston, Columbia, Harvard, Rutgers, and Yale.

Walcott was married to dancer Norline Metivier and had three children by previous marriages. Unlike fellow West Indian writer V. S. Naipaul, he kept a home in Trinidad and was a familiar and revered figure in his homeland. Walcott received a five-year "genius" grant from the John D. and Catherine T. MacArthur Foundation in 1981.

Central to both Walcott's drama and his poetry is an exhilarating tension between two disparate cultural traditions, the Caribbean and the European. Sometimes the two idioms jostle uncomfortably; yet upon occasion they combine with stunning effect to form a brilliant synthesis.

Walcott observed: "My society loves rhetoric, performance, panache, melodrama, carnival, dressing up, playing roles. Thank God I was born in it. . . ." In his dramatic works, this vivacious island culture, with its historical roots and its political subtexts, takes precedence. *Henri Christophe: A Chronicle* (1950), his first play, explores the popular story of a 19th-century slave who became king of Haiti. Another early play, *The Sea at Dauphin* (1953), experiments with French/English island patois, transforming it into a powerful poetic tool. *Dream on Monkey Mountain* (Obie Award winner, 1971) illustrates the way the dreams of a poor charcoal vendor, however flawed and quixotic, help preserve tribal memories within the sterile colonial world. *O, Babylon* (1974) employs interludes of dance, along with a contemporary score by Galt McDermott, to recount events in a small Rastafarian community during the 1966 visit of Haile Selassie.

In all these dramas, Walcott struggled to be true to his roots without sacrificing literary virtuosity. He was eager to incorporate native elements, "chants, jokes, folk-songs, and

fables," into his dramas;" to write powerfully . . . without writing down . . . so that the large emotions could be taken in by a fisherman or a guy on the street"; "to get something clean and simple into my plays . . . something Caribbean"; and to achieve a balance "between defiance and translation." The central character of *Remembrance* (1979), a retired schoolteacher of Port of Spain who loses one son to a revolution, another to the "slower death" of art, may reflect his powerful, if conflicting, loyalties.

While Walcott's plays were often commended for their colorful performances, they tended to meet resistance from more stringent critics. *Pantomime* (1978), which examines the ambiguous relationship between a Tobagan innkeeper and his servant, is one example. Though Walter Goodman found it "fresh and funny . . . filled with thoughtful insights," Frank Rich downgraded the play for lacking the "esthetic rigor" of Walcott's poetry.

This poetry is, indeed, extraordinary—complex, powerful, almost Elizabethan in its delight in form, its flamboyant eloquence and lush imagery. From the beginning—his first poem was published in a local newspaper when he was 14—Walcott sought inspiration among great poets of the English language; Shakespeare, Marvell, Auden, Eliot, Lowell. Nevertheless, Caribbean rhythms, themes, and idioms inevitably find their way into the verse—through vivid dialect personae like Shabine, the sailor in *The Star-Apple Kingdom* (1979), often regarded as the poet's alter-ego; in the perennially anguished voice of a "divided child," "schizophrenic, wrenched by two styles," that lurks beneath the cosmopolitan surface.

Walcott's range as a poet was remarkably varied and generous. *Another Life* (1973), a sweeping, open-hearted narrative, can be ranked among the best verse autobiographies in the language. The exuberant ten-poem sequence *The Star-Apple Kingdom,* which consolidated Walcott's stature as a major poet, features multiple narrative voices tracing the arc of the Caribbean archipelago through space and time, with near-epic scope.

In *The Fortunate Traveller* (1981) the poet chronicled provocative journeys of self-discovery through New England and the American South to Dachau and other places that illuminate his sense of himself as artist and man. The 54 separate poems in *Midsummer* (1984), a diary in verse, offer a year's worth of meditations on approaching middle age, divided linguistic allegiances and the consolations of art. *The Arkansas Testament* (1987) contains a stunning love sequence, along with the powerful title work, a further exploration of the poet's role as racial and cultural exile. This poignant, accomplished volume shows the poet working at the height of his powers.

Walcott's other popular poems include "A Far Cry from Africa" (1962), "Codicil" (1965), "Sainte Lucie" (1976), "The Schooner Flight" (1979), and "North and South" (1981). *Collected Poems* (*1948-1984*) (1986) provides an excellent selection of his work.

Walcott's epic-length *Omeros,* which echoed the *Iliad* and the *Odyssey* was chosen by *The New York Times* as one of the best books of 1990. *Omeros* took up the classic themes of abandonment and wandering, but it also revealed Walcott's love for his native Caribbean. During an interview, Walcott once described the fondness he had for his native homeland surrounded by the sea: "nobody wishes to escape the geography that forms you. In my case it is the sea, it is islands, I cannot stay too long away from the sea."

In 1992 Walcott received the Nobel Prize in literature. His verse play *The Odyssey* was produced on stage in New York and London in 1993. His love of grand themes continued with the publication of a collection of poems titled *The Bounty* (June 1997). In *Bounty* Walcott used his poetic talents to eulogize the beauty of his native land. Walcott's contributions to West Indian drama and poetry were immense. He created a world-class theater ensemble in a postcolonial environment and used his poetic skills to describe the culture and beauty of his Caribbean.

Further Reading

James Altas' article in the *The New York Times Magazine,* "Derek Walcott: Poet of Two Worlds," (May 23, 1982) gives a lively, balanced picture of the poet. Essays in the *New York Review of Books* by Helen Vendler (March 4, 1982) and Joseph Brodsky (November 10, 1983) are provocative, yet fair. Robert D. Hamner's *Derek Walcott* (1981) and Irma Goldstraw's *Derek Walcott: An Annotated Bibliography of His Works* (1984) are quite useful as well. The poet's revealing essay "What the Twilight Says" appears in *Dream on Monkey Mountain and Other Plays* (1970). Rei Terada's *Derek Walcott's Poetry: American Micicry* (Northeastern University Press, 1992) is recommended. A collection of critical perspecitves on the works of Walcott was edited by lifelong friend Robert Hammer: *Critical Perspectives on Derek Walcot (Critical Perspective No. 26*; Passeggiata Press, 1993). □

George Wald

The American biochemist George Wald (born 1906) discovered the role that vitamin A plays in vision and made many contributions to the knowledge of the biochemistry of vision. He won the Nobel Prize in medicine/physiology in 1967 and was a prominent activist in the movement against the Vietnam War and the nuclear arms race.

George Wald was born in Manhattan, NY, on November 18, 1906, the son of Ernestine Rosenmann, a Bavarian immigrant, and Isaac Wald, a Polish immigrant tailor. He was raised in Brooklyn, NY, and attended Brooklyn High School. He earned a bachelor of science degree in zoology at New York University.

Wald went to Columbia University to do graduate work, receiving a masters degree in 1928 and his Ph.D. in 1932. At Columbia he worked under Selig Hecht, one of the founders of biophysics and an expert in the physiology of vision. Hecht had great influence on Wald. In a memorial written after Hecht's death in 1947, Wald observed that "Hecht had a high sense of the social obligation of science.

He thought it imperative that science be explained to the layman in terms that he could understand and could use in coming to his own decisions." Hecht wanted to abolish the military uses of atomic energy, and Wald came to similar beliefs.

Work on Vision

After completing his Ph.D., Wald was awarded a National Research Council Fellowship in Biology (1932-1934). He worked first in the laboratory of Otto Warburg in Berlin-Dahlem, Germany. There he first identified vitamin A as one of the major components of pigments in the retina and part of the process that turns light into sight. He completed the identification in the laboratory of Paul Karrer at the University of Zurich, Switzerland, the laboratory in which Vitamin A had just been isolated. Wald next worked in the laboratory of Otto Meyerhof at the Kaiser Wilhelm Institute in Heidelberg, Germany. There he discovered retinal (vitamin A aldehyde), a component of the visual cycle, in a batch of frogs imported from Hungary. Wald completed the second year of his fellowship at the University of Chicago (1933-1934).

In 1934 Wald was appointed a tutor in biochemical sciences at Harvard University, where he spent the rest of his academic career. He became instructor and tutor in biology (1935-1944), associate professor (1944-1948); professor (1948-1968), Higgins Professor of Biology (1968-1977), and Higgins Professor of Biology Emeritus (after 1977). He also was visiting professor of biochemistry at the University of California at Berkeley for the summer term in 1956. As his reputation grew, he frequently lectured to packed classrooms and his energetic style aroused students' interest in science.

In the late 1930s Wald discovered that the pigment of rhodopsin is the light-sensitive chemical in the rods, the cells in the retina responsible for night vision. He found rhodopsin was derived from opsin, a protein, and retinene, a modified form of Vitamin A.

For more than 20 years, Wald's research colleague was Paul K. Brown, who started out as his research assistant, then became a full-fledged collaborator. With Brown, Wald studied cones, the retinal cells responsible for color vision, and found that color blindness is caused by the absence of either of the pigments sensitive to red and yellow-green, two different forms of Vitamin A that exist in the same cone.

Wald married Frances Kingsley in 1931 and they had two sons, but they divorced. A former student, Ruth Hubbard, became Wald's second wife in 1958, and they had a son and a daughter. Hubbard joined Brown and Wald and formed a productive research team, "the nucleus of a laboratory that has been extraordinarily fruitful as the world's foremost center of visual-pigment biochemistry," according to John Dowling in *Science* (October 27, 1967).

Many Honors

In 1950 Wald was elected to the National Academy of Science and in 1958 to the American Philosophical Society. He was a fellow of the American Academy of Arts and Sciences in Boston and of the Optical Society of America. As a Guggenheim fellow, he spent a year in 1963-1964 at Cambridge University in England, where he was elected an Overseas fellow of Churchill College. He became an honorary member of the Cambridge Philosophical Society (1969).

Wald received many awards, including the Eli Lilly Award from the American Chemical Society (1939), the Lasker Award of the American Public Health Association (1953), the Proctor Medal of the Association for Research in Ophthalmology (1955), the Rumford Medal of the American Academy of Arts and Sciences (1959), the Ives Medal of the Optical Society of America (1966); and, with Hubbard, the Paul Karrer Medal of the University of Zurich (1967).

In December 1967 Wald was awarded the Nobel Prize in physiology/medicine, sharing the prize with Haldan Keffer Hartline and Ragnar Granit. Dowling noted: "No one has contributed more to our understanding of the visual pigments and their relation to vision than George Wald."

Political Activism

Six days after receiving the Nobel Prize, Wald exploited his new prestige by going before the city council of Cambridge, MA, to support a resolution placing a referendum on the Vietnam War on the city's ballot. A few years earlier, Wald had stunned an audience at New York University by denouncing the war while receiving an honorary degree. He also declared his support for anti-war presidential candidate Eugene McCarthy in 1968.

On March 4, 1969, Wald gave a talk at the Massachusetts Institute of Technology titled "A Generation in Search

of a Future." It was part of a teach-in organized by radical students. The speech became famous and "upended his life and pitched him abruptly into the political world," according to an article by Richard Todd in the *New York Times Magazine* . Rejecting military uses of science and denouncing nuclear weapons, Wald said: "Our business is with life, not death." He called some political leaders "insane" and referred to American "war crimes" in Vietnam. The speech was widely reprinted and distributed.

In ensuing years, Wald poured his efforts into what he called "survival politics." He served as president of international tribunals on human rights issues in El Salvador, the Philippines, Afghanistan, Zaire, and Guatemala. In 1984, Wald was one of four Nobel Prize laureates who went to Nicaragua on a "peace ship" sent by the Norwegian government.

Wald's activism didn't halt the honors bestowed on him for his work in the field of vision. They included the T. Duckett Jones Memorial Award of the Whitney Foundation (1967), the Bradford Washburn Medal from the Boston Museum of Science (1968), the Max Berg Award (1969), the Joseph Priestley Award (1970), and honorary degrees from several universities.

Wald was also a collector of Rembrandt etchings and primitive art, particularly pre-Columbian pottery. Speaking of his interests in science, art and politics, Wald told the *New York Times Magazine* in 1969: "Nature is my religion, and it's enough for me. I stack it up against any man's. For its awesomeness, and for the sense of the sanctity of man that it provides."

Further Reading

A list of 183 publications by George Wald was printed in *The Journal of the Optical Society of America* 57 (November 1967). Wald's books include *General Education in a Free Society* (1945) and *Visual Pigments and Photoreceptors: Review and Outlook* (1974). Among notable articles by Wald are "Fitness in the Universe: Choices and Necessities," *Origins of Life* 5 (1974); and "Life and Mind in the Universe," *International Journal of Quantum Chemistry. Quantum Biology Symposium 11* (1984). See also John E. Dowling, "News And Comment. Nobel Prize: Three Named for Medicine, Physiology Award. George Wald," *Science* (October 27, 1967), and "George Wald: The Man, the Speech," *New York Times Magazine* (August 17, 1969). □

Lillian Wald

Lillian Wald (1867-1940), American social worker, nurse, pacifist, and reformer, founded one of the first great American settlement houses.

Lillian Wald was born on March 10, 1867, in Cincinnati. Her father, a dealer in optical goods, moved often, but she thought of Rochester, N.Y., where she was privately educated, as her hometown. In 1891 she graduated from the School of Nursing at Bellevue Hospital

in New York City. After a year's work in a juvenile asylum, she entered the Women's Medical College. While a medical student she was asked to teach home nursing in New York City's East Side, then the most congested residential area in the world. The need of the immigrants living there was so great and the medical care available to them so slight that Wald abandoned her career and with another student took up residence on the East Side in 1893. Their tenement flat was the place from which both the Henry Street Settlement and the New York public health nursing service grew.

There were no city public health nurses in New York when Wald began her work. A score of agencies—most of them private, sectarian, charitable bodies—provided visiting nurses. Wald early resolved that the Henry Street nurses would be nonsectarian and would charge fees only to those who could pay. The service rapidly expanded, and 100 nurses were working out of what was then called the Nurses' Settlement by 1914. They treated more patients than the three largest city hospitals combined. The Henry Street Settlement also grew into a great neighborhood center. By 1913 it owned nine houses, seven vacation homes in the country, and three stores used as stock rooms, milk stations, clinics, and the like. The settlement enrolled 3,000 people in its clubs and classes and offered many cultural activities.

Wald also helped organize the first public school nursing services in New York City, as well as Lincoln House, one of the first settlements with an African American clientele. She was a founding member of the National Association for the Advancement of Colored People. She helped

create the New York State Bureau of Industries and Immigration and the Federal Children's Bureau.

Like other settlement leaders, Wald was a pacifist, and, also like them, she found World War I to be the gravest challenge of her career. She was chairman of the American Union against Militarism (AUAM), which had helped prevent a war with Mexico in 1916. Regarding American entry into the Great War, some members wished to concentrate chiefly on combating militarism, others to defend civil liberties. A third group, to which she belonged, hoped to devise alternatives to war without pitting themselves directly against the government. The struggle led to her resignation as chairman in 1917, after which the AUAM took a more radical line. Though it later dissolved, it helped father the American Civil Liberties Union and the Foreign Policy Association, a study group interested in promoting a just and durable peace. This was the approach she found most congenial.

In later years Wald became more involved in partisan politics. She supported Governor Al Smith, a good friend of social welfare, and later Franklin Roosevelt, an even better one. She died on Sept. 1, 1940, in Westport, Conn.

Further Reading

Wald wrote two books about her work: *The House on Henry Street* (1915) and *Windows on Henry Street* (1934). Her biographers are Robert L. Duffus, *Lillian Wald: Neighbor and Crusader* (1938), and Beryl Epstein, *Lillian Wald: Angel of Henry Street* (1948). □

Kurt Waldheim

Kurt Waldheim (born 1918) was an Austrian diplomat and politician who served as secretary general of the United Nations from 1972 to 1982. In 1986 he was elected president of Austria despite a controversy over his role as a Nazi intelligence officer in World War II.

Kurt Waldheim was born in St. Andrä-Wördern, a village near Vienna, Austria, on December 21, 1918. His father was a Roman Catholic school inspector and an active Christian Socialist. Waldheim's youth was spent in a country searching for identity amid domestic turmoil. During his years of schooling at the Vienna Consular Academy he was nonpartisan politically.

War Record

After graduation in 1936 Waldheim entered the University of Vienna and studied law and diplomacy. In 1938, three weeks after Adolph Hitler annexed Austria, Waldheim joined the Nazi student union, and later that year he joined the mounted unit of the Nazis' notorious paramilitary force, the *Sturm- Abteilung* (S.A.) or "brown-shirts." It was a membership that Waldheim later concealed. When war broke out, he was drafted into the army, sent to the Eastern front,

wounded in the spring of 1941, and received a medical discharge. According to two autobiographies, *The Challenge of Peace* (1980) and *In the Eye of the Storm* (1986), he then quit active service, returned to Vienna, completed his doctorate in law in 1944, and married his wife Cissy before the end of the war.

But documents uncovered in the mid-1980s showed that Waldheim remained active in the Germany army until 1945, assigned as an intelligence officer on the staff of General Alexander Löhr, an Austrian who was executed in 1947 as a war criminal. Löhr's forces committed atrocities against Yugoslav resistance fighters and deported 40,000 Greek Jews to the concentration camp at Auschwitz. Waldheim told reporters in 1986 that he was only an interpreter and clerk on Löhr's staff and had no part in war crimes, but intelligence reports and eyewitnesses indicated he was aware of the atrocities. After the war, the Allied war crimes commission ruled that Waldheim should be tried as a war criminal, but he was among 40,000 suspects whose files were sealed and given to the United Nations and who were never tried.

Postwar Political Rise

After the war, Austria was considered a victim of a Nazi invasion, and Austrians' complicity in Nazi war crimes was generally overlooked. Talented and ambitious, Waldheim advanced rapidly in politics. Late in 1945, he took a job in the Foreign Ministry and became involved in negotiations for an end to the Allied occupation. He became secretary to the Austrian foreign minister and rose quickly through the

diplomatic ranks, serving for three years in Paris. When Austria regained its sovereignty in 1955, Waldheim was its first delegate to the United Nations. He was Austria's ambassador to Canada (1956-1960), then served four years in high posts in Austria's ministry for foreign affairs (1960-1964), and returned to the United Nations as Austria's representative (1964-1968), where he was chairman of the Committee on Peaceful Uses of Outer Space (1965-1968).

In 1968, Waldheim became Austria's foreign minister. He lost his job in a change of government and returned to the United Nations a third time as Austria's ambassador in 1970. In 1971, he made an unsuccessful bid to become Austrian president as the candidate of the Independent party. Back at the UN, he became chairman of the safeguards committee of the Atomic Energy Agency.

United Nations Head

In 1972, Waldheim took over from U Thant of Burma as secretary general of the United Nations. His polished diplomacy and studied neutrality appealed to both the Soviet Union and the United States. During his eight years as UN leader, he promoted the ideals of world peace, justice, and human rights. With many new Third World nations gaining admission to the UN, Waldheim sought to lead by consensus. He put the United Nations back on a sound financial footing by reducing operating costs and getting dues collected. He led peacekeeping efforts in Cyprus, the Middle East and Vietnam. Waldheim was praised for initiating talks that ended the 1973 Arab-Israeli war, but later drew the wrath of the American Jewish community for condemning Israel's 1976 raid to rescue hostages on a hijacked plane in Uganda. In his second term, Waldheim faced several crises which the United Nations had little power to resolve, including Israel's occupation of southern Lebanon, the war in Afghanistan, the conflict between Iraq and Iran, and the Iranian hostage crisis.

In 1981, Waldheim sought an unprecedented third term, but lost to Javier Perez de Cuellar of Peru despite the backing of the United States and the Soviet Union. He then became special Austrian envoy to international congresses and a visiting professor of diplomacy at Georgetown University in Washington, DC (1982-1984).

Controversial President

In 1986, Waldheim campaigned for president of Austria as the candidate of the conservative People's party, seeking to end 16 years of Socialist rule. During the campaign, the World Jewish Congress and an Austrian news magazine produced documents revealing Waldheim's Nazi past. Waldheim insisted he had joined the Nazi groups only because he wanted to protect his family. Many Austrian voters accepted his explanation that he was the victim of an international smear campaign, and he was elected president to a six-year term amid an angry eruption of anti-semitism. U.S. Senator Daniel Moynihan called Waldheim's victory "a symbolic amnesty for the Holocaust."

Israel boycotted his inauguration and recalled its ambassador to Austria. The United States banned Waldheim as a war criminal. On February 8, 1988, a six-man international commission of prestigious historians found that Waldheim was aware of Nazi atrocities and did nothing to stop them, though he did not personally participate in war crimes. Waldheim resisted calls for his resignation and continued to insist he was innocent. Shunned by almost every world leader, he served out his term but did not run again in 1992. Waldheim's efforts to clear his name resulted in another autobiography, *The Answer,* published in 1996, in which he wrote of his wartime activities: "I did what was necessary to survive the day, the system, the war—no more, no less."

Further Reading

Much autobiographical material is included in Kurt Waldheim, *The Challenge of Peace* (1980), while his *The Austrian Example* (1973) cites the neutral role of his own country as a blueprint for world stability and international exchange. *Building the Future Order* (1981) contains a synthesis of Waldheim's key reports and speeches between 1972 and 1980. In 1986 he published *In the Eye of the Storm: A Memoir* and in 1996 he answered critics of his Nazi war record with *The Answer.* A critical look at Waldheim is contained in "Waldheim and History: Austria Recalls the Anschluss," *The Nation* (March 19, 1988) and in "Waldheim: the Historians' Verdict," *The Economist* (March 12, 1988). □

Peter Waldo

The French religious leader Peter Waldo (active 1170-1184) believed in voluntary poverty and religious simplicity. His followers were considered heretics by the Church.

Some men's personal lives are eclipsed by the movements they start. Peter Waldo was such a man. He appears on the scene of history in 1170 in Lyons as a successful businessman who, touched to his core by a traveling minstrel's religious ballad, gave away his money to live in poverty as a preacher of the Gospel. Having persuaded a sympathetic priest to translate large sections of the New Testament from Latin into the regional language, Provençal, Peter wandered through Lyons, bringing the message of Christ to anyone who would listen to him. He soon had the Gospels memorized. A number of young men, impressed by his intelligence and sincerity, followed him in giving away their possessions and found a new joy and freedom in living according to the spirit of the Gospels.

Some priests of Lyons, disturbed by Peter's popularity, tried to curb his activities. Peter appealed directly to Pope Alexander III in Rome. The Pope responded in 1179 by praising the group's poverty but said that because they had no theological training they could preach only if the archbishop of Lyons gave them permission. The Waldenses, as they had come to be known, felt that their message was too important to be checked by traditional Church discipline, and they rejected the Pope's directive. They were excommunicated at a Church council in Verona by the next pope, Lucius III, in 1184.

The Waldenses continued to live by their understanding of the New Testament rather than by the procedures of the Church. They refused to accept the existence of purgatory because it is not in the Bible. They rejected the practice of venerating the saints for the same reason. Not just priests, they said, but any person can consecrate the sacramental bread and wine. They rejected the authority structure of the Church as unbiblical. Their refusal to take oaths and also to participate in war made them unpopular with the secular as well as the Church authorities. Peter Waldo himself was not heard from after his excommunication in 1184. His followers were harassed by the Inquisition. They escaped when possible to the nearly inaccessible mountain regions of northern Italy, where Waldo's ideas managed to survive over the centuries despite periodic attempts by Church authorities to eliminate them.

Further Reading

Gordon Leff, *Heresy in the Later Middle Ages* (2 vols., 1967), examines the religious ideas in Waldo's movement. Walter L. Wakefield, *Heresies of the High Middle Ages* (1969), contains interesting documents pertaining to Waldo, including a profession of faith he once made. □

Martin Waldseemüller

The German geographer and cartographer Martin Waldseemüller (ca. 1470-ca. 1518) was the first to

suggest that the newly discovered landmass in the New World should be called America.

Martin Waldseemüller was born at Radolfzell on the Bodensee and matriculated at the University of Freiburg in 1490. Much of Waldseemüller's early life is obscure. He first comes to light as a member of the group of humanist scholars and geographers which thrived at the court of Duke René II of Lorraine and influenced later-16th-century German interest in geography. News of the discoveries in the New World traveled quickly to transalpine Europe, and Alsace and Lorraine soon became important centers of interest and study in the discoveries and their consequences.

When copies of the letters of Amerigo Vespucci arrived at the court, they generated even more interest in the New World, and in 1507 Waldseemüller published a volume called *Cosmographiae introductio,* which contained a description of the New World as well as a translation of Vespucci's letters. Seeking a name for the new lands, Waldseemüller (who had not then heard of Christopher Columbus) suggested that they be called America, after Vespucci. Although Waldseemüller later suggested a revision when he became aware of Columbus's role in the discoveries, his original suggestion had become too popular. America remained the common designation for the new continents, and Waldseemüller retained the nickname "the godfather of America."

Also in 1507, Waldseemüller published another work which was to have immense influence on later cartography, his great world map. This woodcut map, engraved on 12 blocks, became one of the earliest examples of humanist interest in New World cartography. In the same year Waldseemüller also constructed a globe. For the next 30 years these were the standard examples of their kind. In 1511 Waldseemüller made a large-scale map of Europe and in 1513 did new maps for the great Strassburg edition of the works of Ptolemy.

J. H. Parry characterized Waldseemüller's work as follows: he was "an important transitional figure in the history of cartography. He was not an original scientist, but an encyclopaedic and intelligent interpreter. His maps, his globe, and his *Cosmographiae introductio* form an impressive body of old and new geography which to some extent anticipated the equally popular and still more fruitful work of Mercator." Waldseemüller was also an example of an intellectual type whose work in the 16th and 17th centuries would contribute to the popularization of the considerable body of knowledge about the world and man which had to be spread, absorbed, and acted upon by an increasingly larger public.

Further Reading

There is no biography of Waldseemüller in English. Good accounts of his era and early cartography are Ronald V. Tooley, *Maps and Map-makers* (1949; rev. ed. 1952), and J. H. Parry, *The Age of Reconnaissance* (1963). □

Lech Walesa

Lech Walesa (born 1943), charismatic leader of Solidarity, the independent trade union movement in Poland, was awarded the 1983 Nobel Peace Prize for his valiant struggle to secure workers' rights through negotiation and peaceful means.

Lech Walesa was born on September 29, 1943, in the village of Popowo, located between Warsaw and Gdansk, the son of a private farmer and carpenter. He attended technical school in nearby Lipno and worked briefly as an electromechanic in Lochocin. After completing military service from 1963 to 1965, he moved to Gdansk where he was employed as an electrical technician at the Lenin Shipyard. While there, Walesa was in the vanguard of trade union activists who sought to redress workers' grievances. To gain objectives, he pursued negotiations and nonviolent resistance when dealing with government authorities.

In December 1970, as food shortages and drastic increases in food prices precipitated violent protest strikes in shipyards along the Baltic coast, Walesa was elected chair of the Strike Committee at the Lenin Shipyard. There, on January 15, 1971, he was among those who negotiated workers' demands with First Secretary of the Communist Party Edward Gierek. After an interim of political inactivity, Walesa was elected delegate to the shipyard Works' Council meeting in February 1976, where he spoke out against the authorities for reneging on concessions agreed to in the 1971 negotiations. Dismissed from his job at the shipyard, he found work in May 1976 at a construction machinery enterprise.

Working To Build True Trade Unionism

During the fall of 1976 Walesa made contact with the Workers' Defense Committee (KOR, Polish initials), renamed Committee for Social Self-Defense, which was founded in September 1976 by dissident intellectuals in Warsaw to provide aid to the brutalized workers of Warsaw and Radom. June strikes against increased food prices. Walesa and union activists in Gdansk drew up a Charter of Workers' Rights on April 29, 1978, and formed the unofficial Baltic Committee of Independent Trade Unions to defend the workers' economic, legal, and human rights.

Although involved in the underground trade union movement, Walesa continued to work with the government-controlled, official trade unions. Elected delegate to the official union's elections, he protested against flagrant election manipulation and in December 1978 was fired from his job. Five months later Walesa began work at the engineering enterprise Elektromontaz, where he earned recognition as an outstanding electrician.

Walesa and union activists arranged unofficial memorial services in December 1978 at Gate Number Two of the Lenin Shipyard for the 45 workers who were killed by military and government security forces in the 1970 food strikes. On the following anniversary, December 16, 1979, Walesa and members of the Baltic Committee organized unauthorized mass demonstrations at the gates. He urged the formation of independent trade unions and social self-defense groups, modeled on KOR, to assist workers. After numerous arrests were made, Walesa defended his coworkers who were to be discharged in January 1980 for taking part in the rally. He, too, lost his job at Elektromontaz. Over a ten-year period, Walesa was held under 48-hour arrest with great regularity.

After the government covertly attempted to increase meat and meat product prices in July 1980, triggering numerous strikes, Walesa, unemployed, scaled the 12-foot-high perimeter fence of the Lenin Shipyard on August 14, 1980, and took charge of the shipyard strike. He demanded his own job reinstatement and that of the recently fired veteran crane operator and union activist Anna Walentynowicz and stipulated that the proceedings be broadcast throughout the yard. At the successful conclusion of three days of negotiations, Walesa abruptly reversed his decision to call off the strike and began a solidarity strike in behalf of sympathy strikers from factories in the Gdansk area who were excluded from the settlement. With 21 demands in hand and his commission of experts, Walesa entered into negotiations with Deputy Prime Minister Mieczyslaw Jagielski on August 23 and, after a week of hard negotiations, won the government's acceptance of independent autonomous trade unions and the right to strike. On August 31, 1980, he signed the final phase of the Gdansk Agreement and ended the strike.

The Founding of "Solidarity"

Walesa issued the official Charter of the Independent Autonomous Trade Union in Gdansk on September 15, 1980 as Party First Secretary Stanislaw Kania extended the Gdansk Accords to the entire country. On September 17, 1980, Walesa was elected chair of the highest decision-making body of the new national union, the National Coordinating Commission of the Independent Autonomous Trade Union "Solidarity" (*NSZZ Solidarność*). Leading a large delegation, Walesa presented Solidarity's statutes to the Warsaw District Court on September 24 for registration as required by law. From September to November 1980 Walesa utilized the "strike" mechanism effectively to counter a series of confrontations designed by the authorities to weaken and destroy Solidarity.

On December 16, 1980, Walesa dedicated the long-promised monument to the martyred workers of December 1970 at the gates of the Lenin Shipyard. With only 27 names of the dead conceded by the government, Walesa commemorated the tenth anniversary together with representatives of Solidarity, the Catholic Church, and the Communist Party in a public display of unity. In mid-January 1981 Walesa led a delegation to Rome where he was received by Pope John Paul II and met with Italian trade union leaders.

During 1981 Walesa was frequently called upon to defuse wildcat strikes. To halt rampant strike activity, Walesa acquiesced to Prime Minister Wojciech Jaruzelski's request of February 10 for a 90-day strike moratorium and promise of dialogue on the reform of labor laws.

The unprovoked, violent police action against representatives of Rural Solidarity in Bydgoszcz on March 19, 1981, required the hospitalization of three Solidarity members. Walesa demanded the arrest and prosecution of those responsible. He began a nationwide four-hour warning strike and prepared for a massive, general strike scheduled for March 31, 1981. When the Warsaw Agreement was reached, Walesa drew severe criticism from Solidarity members for his undemocratic actions and for arbitrarily suspending the planned general strike. He was also castigated by members of Rural Solidarity, who were dissatisfied with the outcome. As a result of Walesa's negotiations, however, the weekly journal "Solidarity" (*Solidarność*) was published a few days later and Rural Solidarity was registered as an independent union on May 12, 1981.

By August 1981 talks between Walesa and government negotiator Mieczyslaw Rakowski collapsed as Solidarity, with ten million members, prepared for its first national congress. Walesa and Solidarity came under fire from fierce propaganda attacks while Soviet military and naval maneuvers increased fears of an invasion. Opening the first session of the national congress in September 1981 in Gdansk, Walesa defended his undemocratic negotiating methods and called for free elections on local and parliamentary levels. Between sessions he pushed through a workers' self-management compromise on worker participation in economic reform at the factory level, which the Sejm (parliament) hastily passed. Walesa was reelected chairman of Solidarity on October 1, 1981.

"Solidarity" Declared Illegal

With strikes and protests continuing unabated, Walesa declared a three-month strike moratorium on November 4, 1981, and met at an unprecedented summit with Archbishop Jozef Glemp and Party First Secretary General Wojciech Jaruzelski, who offered plans for a Council for National Agreement. Recognizing that Solidarity and the Church would play mere consultative and symbolic roles, Walesa rejected the plans. On November 19, due to a severe national economic downturn, he appealed to the West for food aid for a period of five months.

Despite Walesa's conciliatory gestures, riot police forcibly evicted strikers at the Warsaw Fire Service Academy's sit-in on December 2, 1981. Walesa called the presidium and regional chairmen into closed session in Radom, where he issued a statement on the government's refusal to conclude a genuine national agreement. On December 7, 1981, a secretly obtained, edited tape of the meeting was broadcast by Warsaw Radio, implicating Walesa in confrontation with the authorities and the Solidarity militants in the overthrow of the government.

In a massive, predawn, secretive military crackdown, Walesa and nearly all of Solidarity's leadership were arrested and interned on December 13, 1981, and martial law was imposed. Flown to Warsaw for talks with General Wojciech Jaruzelski, he refused to negotiate or televise an appeal for calm and, while in custody in Warsaw, smuggled messages to Solidarity advocating peaceful resistance. Transferred to the Arlamow hunting reserve in southeast Poland, Walesa continued in his refusal to cooperate with the authorities. Solidarity was delegalized in October 1982 by the Party-dominated and controlled Sejm. Walesa was released on November 11, 1982, after 11 months of internment.

Wins Nobel Prize for Peace

In June 1983 during Pope John Paul II's second journey to Poland Walesa was granted leave for a private audience with the pope at a remote retreat in the Tatra Mountains of southern Poland. As a result of the meeting Walesa lessened his overt political activity to ease the internal situation in Poland. After receiving permission to return to the Lenin Shipyard in April 1983, he resumed work at his own request in August 1983, ten days after martial law was lifted.

For his determined and nonviolent fight for human rights, Walesa won the 1983 Nobel Prize for Peace. But, fearing that Polish authorities would block his return to Poland, he designated his wife, Danuta, mother of his seven children, to accept the award in his name in Oslo in December 1983. In his acceptance speech, delivered by his wife, Walesa declared, "We crave for justice, and that is why we are so persistent in the struggle for our rights." He called for dialogue with the authorities, as well as East-West dialogue, and appealed for aid to Poland.

Walesa dedicated the Nobel Prize to the ten million members of the outlawed Solidarity movement and pledged the prize money to a Church-sponsored agricultural foundation for private farmers. He called for the resumption of dialogue with the authorities, with the Church as intermediary, and continued to seek talks during the succeeding years while maintaining a low profile.

On August 30, 1985, the fifth anniversary of the Independent Autonomous Trade Union in Gdansk, Walesa appealed once again to the authorities to resume talks and to seek an agreement. He offered positive proposals in a document, "Poland Five Years after the August," compiled by Solidarity activists, which would serve as a basis for dialogue and which would bring about the hoped-for peaceful solution to workers' problems in Poland.

In 1989, when it was announced that Poland would be able to freely choose its government, Walesa began promoting a new presidential election, and when it was apparent that he had public support, he announced his intention for candidacy. In 1990 he was elected president of Poland. Although the country suffered a deadlocked government and high unemployment rate during Walesa's term, he accomplished much. Walesa pushed hard for reforms, and devoted a great deal of energy to ensuring Poland's entry to the European Union. He was responsible for ending Polish ties to Russia and even received a declaration from Russian president Boris Yeltsin that stated Russia's lack of objection to Poland's entry into the North Atlantic Treaty Organization (NATO). Under Walesa, the Polish economy became sixty percent privatized, with a growth rate of six percent. He is, however, not credited with this achievement, because of both his apparent lack of interest in the plight of workers mired in the transition economy and the Polish people's rather unrealistic desire for immediate change. Many of his critics say that Walesa failed to prepare Poland for the shock of the economy's transformation from Communism to democracy. The Poles' dissatisfaction with the pace of change helped ensure Communist opponent Aleksander Kwasniewski's presidential victory in the elections of 1995.

While he lost the presidency to a former Communist in Poland's 1995 elections, Walesa can nevertheless be credited with helping to unfurl the banner of democracy across Communist Europe. Indeed, the key role he played in liberalizing Eastern Europe has earned him a long list of honors, not least of which was the Nobel Peace Prize in 1983. Walesa is also the author of several books, including *A Way of Hope* (1987) and *The Struggle and the Triumph* (1991). In 1995, he became the vice president of the Lech Walesa Institute Foundation.

Further Reading

The Book of Lech Walesa (1982), a collective portrait by Solidarity members and friends, provides valuable insights, as does Robert Eringer, *Strike for Freedom: The Story of Lech Walesa and Polish Solidarity* (1982). Michael Dobbs presents Lech Walesa as the "Symbol of Polish August" in *Poland, Solidarity and Walesa* (1981). For a personal glimpse, read Walter Brolewicz, *My Brother, Lech Walesa* (1983). Neal Ascherson, *The Polish August: The Self-Limiting Revolution* (1981) and Timothy Garton Ash, *The Polish Revolution: Solidarity* (1983, 1985) are indispensable, definitive historical accounts of Solidarity and Lech Walesa's role in the movement. Other important works include A. Kemp-Welch, *The Birth of Solidarity:*

The Gdansk Negotiations, 1980 (1983) and Alain Touraine, *Solidarity, the Analysis of a Social Movement: Poland 1980-81* (1983). A brief chapter on "Solidarity, 1980-1981" is included in Volume II of Norman Davies, *God's Playground: A History of Poland,* 2 vols. (1982). In 1987 Walesa published his reminiscences in *A Way of Hope*. □

Alice Malsenior Walker

Pulitzer prize novelist Alice Walker (born 1944) was best known for her stories about black women who achieve heroic stature within the confines of their ordinary day-to-day lives.

Alice Walker was born on February 9, 1944, in Eatonton, Georgia, to Willie Lee and Minnie Tallulah (Grant) Walker. Like many of Walker's fictional characters, she was a sharecropper's daughter and the youngest of eight children. At age eight, Walker was accidentally injured by a BB gun shot to her eye by her brother. Her partial blindness caused her to withdraw and begin writing poetry to ease her loneliness. She found that writing demanded peace and quiet, but these were difficult commodities to come by when ten people lived in four rooms, so she spent a great deal of time working outdoors sitting under a tree.

Walker's Education

Walker attended segregated schools which would be described as inferior by current standards, yet she recalled that she had terrific teachers who encouraged her to believe that the world she was reaching for actually existed. Although Walker grew up in what would traditionally be called a deprived environment, she was sustained by her community and by the knowledge that she could choose her own identity. Moreover, Walker insisted that her mother granted her "permission" to be a writer and gave her the social, spiritual, and moral contexts for her stories. These contexts, as critic Mary Helen Washington explained, were built on personal authority, ancestral presence, "generational continuity, historical awareness, street-wise sophistication [and] cultural integrity."

Upon graduating from high school, Walker secured a scholarship to attend Spelman College in Atlanta, where she got involved in the burgeoning Civil Rights movement. In 1963, Walker received another scholarship and transferred to Sarah Lawrence in New York, where she completed her studies and graduated in 1965 with a B.A. While at Sarah Lawrence, she spent her junior year in Africa as an exchange student. After graduation she worked with the voter registration drive in Georgia and with the Head Start program in Jackson, Mississippi. It was there that she met, and in 1967, married, Melvyn Leventhal, a civil rights lawyer. Their marriage produced one child, Rebecca, before ending in divorce in 1976.

Writing and Teaching Careers Begin

In 1968, Walker published her first collection of poetry, *Once.* Walker's teaching and writing careers overlapped during the 1970's. She served as a writer-in-residence and as a teacher in the Black Studies program at Jackson State College (1968-1969) and Tougaloo College (1970-1971). While teaching she was at work on her first novel, *The Third Life of Grange Copeland* (1970), which was assisted by an award from the National Endowment for the Arts (1969). She then moved north and taught at Wellesley College and the University of Massachusetts at Boston (both 1972-1973). In 1973 her collection of short stories, *In Love and Trouble: Stories of Black Women,* and a collection of poetry, *Revolutionary Petunias,* appeared. She received a Radcliffe Institute fellowship (1971-1973), a Rosenthal Foundation award, and an American Academy and Institute of Arts and Letters award (both in 1974) for *In Love and Trouble.*

In 1976 Walker's second novel, *Meridian,* was published, followed by a Guggenheim award in 1977-1978. In 1979 another collection of poetry, *Goodnight, Willie Lee, I'll See You in the Morning,* was published, followed the next year by another collection of short stories, *You Can't Keep a Good Woman Down* (1980). Walker's third novel, *The Color Purple* was published in 1982, and this work won both a Pulitzer Prize and the American Book Award the following year. Walker was also a contributor to several periodicals and in 1983 published many of her essays, a collection titled *In Search of Our Mother's Gardens: A Col-*

lection of Womanist Prose (1983). Walker worked on her fourth novel while living in Mendocino County outside San Francisco.

Walker's Writing Analyzed

At the time of publication of her first novel (1970) Walker said in a *Library Journal* interview that, for her, "family relationships are sacred." Indeed, much of Walker's work depicted the emotional, spiritual, and physical devastation that occurs when family trust is betrayed. Her focus is on black women, who grow to reside in a larger world and struggle to achieve independent identities beyond male dominion. Although her characters are strong, they are, nevertheless, vulnerable. Their strength resides in their acknowledged debt to their mothers, to their sensuality, and to their friendships among women. These strengths are celebrated in Walker's work, along with the problems women encounter in their relationships with men who regard them as less significant than themselves merely because they are women. The by-product of this belief is, of course, violence. Hence, Walker's stories focus not so much on the racial violence that occurs among strangers but the violence among friends and family members, a kind of deliberate cruelty, unexpected but always predictable.

Walker began her exploration of the terrors that beset black women's lives in her first collection of short stories, *In Love and Trouble.* Here, she examined the stereotypes about their lives that misshape them and misguide perceptions about them. Her second short story collection, *You Can't Keep a Good Woman Down,* dramatizes the resiliency of black women to rebound despite racial, sexual, and economic oppression.

Walker's Novels

Walker's first novel, *The Third Life of Grange Copeland,* centers on the life of a young black girl, Ruth Copeland, and her grandfather, Grange. As an old man, Grange learns that he is free to love, but love does not come without painful responsibility. At the climax of the novel, Grange summons his newly found knowledge to rescue his granddaughter, Ruth, from his brutal son, Brownfield. The rescue demands that Grange murder his son in order to stop the cycle of deliberate cruelty.

Her second novel, *Meridian,* recounts the life of a civil rights worker, Meridian Hill. Meridian achieves heroic proportions because she refused to blame others for her own shortcomings, becoming a model for those around her.

Walker's third and most famous novel, *The Color Purple,* is an epistolary novel about Celie, a woman so down and out that she can only tell God her troubles, which she does in the form of letters. Poor, black, female, alone and uneducated, oppressed by caste, class, and gender, Celie learns to lift herself up from sexual exploitation and brutality with the help of the love of another woman, Shug Avery. Against the backdrop of Celie's letters is another story about African customs. This evolves from her sister Nettie's letters which Celie's husband hid from Celie over the course of 20 years. Here, Walker presented problems of women bound within an African context, encountering many of the same problems that Celie faces. Both Celie and Nettie are restored to one another, and, most important, each is restored to herself.

Walker's Works

Walker's other books include *Langston Hughes" American Poet* (1973). *I Love Myself When I'm Laughing . . . and then Again When I Am Looking Mean and Impressive: A Zora Neale Thurston Reader* (1979), which she edited. *Horses Make a Landscape Look More Beautiful* (1986). *Living By the Word: Selected Writings, 1973-1987* (1988). *Finding the Green Stone* (1991) with Catherine Deeter (Illustrator). *Her Blue Body Everything We Know: Earthling Poems 1965-1990 Complete* (1991). *Possessing the Secret of Joy* (1992). *Everyday Use (Women Writers;* 1994) with Barbara T. Christian (Editor).*The Same River Twice: Honoring the Difficult* (1996). *Archbishop Desmond Tutu: An African Prayer Book* (1996) with Desmond Tutu. *Banned* (1996) with an introduction by Patricia Holt. *Anything We Love Can Be Saved: A Writers Activism* (1997).

Further Reading

For biographical information see David Bradley, "Novelist Alice Walker: Telling the Black Woman's Story," *The New York Times Magazine* (January 8, 1984). Gloria Steinem, "Do You Know This Woman? She Knows You: A Profile of Alice Walker," *Ms.* (June 1982). For critical information see Deb Price, "Alice Through the Looking Glass," *The Detroit News* (March 1, 1996). David Templeton, "Difficult Honor," *Sonoma Independent,* (February 15–21, 1996). Barbara Christian, *Black Feminist Criticism* (1985). Mari Evans, *Black Women Writers, 1950-1980* (1983). Claudia Tate, *Black Women Writers at Work* (1983). For information on the World Wide Web (1997) see "Anniina's Alice Walker Page" at http://www.luminarium.org/contemporary/alicew/ and "Alice Walker—Womanist Writer" at http://www.vms.utexas.edu/~melindaj/alice.html □

C. J. Walker

As a manufacturer of hair care products for African American women, Madame C.J. Walker, born Sarah Breedlove (1867-1919), became one of the first American women millionaires.

Madame C.J. Walker, named Sarah Breedlove at birth, was born December 23, 1867, in Delta, Louisiana, to Owen and Minerva Breedlove, both of whom were emancipated slaves. The Breedloves worked as sharecroppers on a cotton plantation. At the age of six Sarah was orphaned, and in 1878, after the cotton crop failed and a yellow fever epidemic struck, the young girl moved to Vicksburg to live with her sister Louvinia and to work as a domestic. She worked hard from the time that she was very young, suffered great poverty, and had little opportunity to get an education. In order to escape the oppressive environment created by Louvinia's husband, Sarah married Moses McWilliams when she was only four-

teen years old. At eighteen she gave birth to a daughter she named Lelia, and at twenty she was widowed.

Sarah then decided to move to St. Louis, where she worked as a laundress and in other domestic positions for eighteen years, joined St. Paul's African Methodist Episcopal Church, and put her daughter through the public schools and Knoxville College. Sarah, who was barely literate, was especially proud of her daughter's educational accomplishments.

By the time she was in her late thirties, Sarah was contending with hair loss because of a combination of stress and damaging hair care products. After experimenting with various methods, she developed a formula of her own that caused her hair to grow again quickly. She often recounted that after praying about her hair, she was given the formula in a dream. When friends and family members noticed how Sarah's hair grew back, they began to ask her to duplicate her product for them. She began to prepare her formula at home, selling it to friends and family and marketing it door to door.

With the help of her family and her second husband, Charles Joseph Walker, a newspaperman whom she had married in 1906 after she moved to Denver, she began to advertise a growing number of hair care products. She also adopted her husband's initials and surname as her professional name, calling herself Madam C.J. Walker for the rest of her life, even after the marriage ended. Her husband helped her develop mail marketing techniques for her products, usually through the medium of African American-

owned newspapers. When their small business was successful, with earnings of about $10 a day, Walker felt that she should continue to expand, but her husband felt that she was too ambitious. Rather than allow her husband's wishes to restrain her, the couple separated.

Walker's business continued to develop, as she not only marketed her hair care products but also tutored African American men and women in their use, recruiting a group called "Walker Agents." Her products were often used in conjunction with a metal comb that was heated on the stove and used to straighten very curly hair. She also began to manufacture a facial skin cream. The hair process was controversial because many felt that African American women should wear their hair in natural styles rather than attempt to change the texture from curly to straight. In spite of critics, Walker's hair care methods gained increasing popularity among African American women, who enjoyed products designed especially for them. This resulted in growing profits for Walker's business and an increasing number of agents who marketed the products for her door to door.

Working closely with her daughter Lelia (who later changed her name to A'Lelia), Walker opened a school for "hair culturists" in Pittsburgh—Lelia College—which operated from 1908 to 1910. In 1910 the Walkers moved to Indianapolis, where they established a modern factory to produce their products. They also began to hire African American professionals who could direct various aspects of their operation. Among the workers were tutors who helped Walker get a basic education.

Walker traveled throughout the nation demonstrating her products, recruiting salespersons and practitioners, and encouraging African American entrepreneurs. Her rounds included conventions of African American organizations, churches, and civic groups. Not content with her domestic achievements, Walker traveled to the Caribbean and Latin America to promote her business and to recruit individuals to teach her hair care methods. Observers estimated that Walker's company had about three thousand agents for whom Walker held annual conventions where they were tutored in product use, hygienic care techniques, and marketing strategies. She also gave cash awards to those who were most successful in promoting sales.

At A'Lelia's urging, Walker purchased property in New York City in 1913, with the belief that a base in that city would be important. In 1916 she moved to a luxurious townhouse she had built in Harlem, and a year later to a posh estate called Villa Lewaro she had constructed at Irvington-on-Hudson, New York.

Although Walker and her daughter lived lavishly, they carefully managed each aspect of their business, whose headquarters remained in Indianapolis, and gave to a number of philanthropic organizations. According to rumor, Walker's first husband was lynched. Perhaps it was partially for this reason that Walker supported anti-lynching legislation and gave generously to the National Association for the Advancement of Colored People, eventually willing that organization her estate in Irvington-on-Hudson. The

Walkers generously supported religious, educational, charitable, and civil rights organizations.

Although cautioned by her doctors that her fast-paced life was impairing her health, Walker did not heed the warnings. On May 25, 1919, when she was 51 years old, she died of hypertension. Her funeral service was held in Mother Zion African Methodist Episcopal Zion Church in New York City. Renowned African American educator Mary McLeod Bethune delivered the eulogy, and Walker was buried at Woodlawn Cemetery in the Bronx. Her daughter, A'Lelia, succeeded her as president of the Madame C.J. Walker Manufacturing Company.

Further Reading

No full-length biography of Walker is available. Many articles, biographical sketches, and juvenile books have been written about Walker (sometimes called madam), including some by her great-great granddaughter, A'Lelia Bundles. Bundles' children's book is entitled *Madam C.J. Walker* (1991). Other books for youths are Penny Colman, *Madam C.J. Walker: Building a Business Empire* (1994); Marian Taylor, *Madam C.J. Walker* (1993); and Pat McKissack, *Madam C.J. Walker: Self-Made Millionaire* (1992). Biographical sketches of Walker appear in reference works such as the *Dictionary of American Biography, Notable American Women, Notable Black American Women, Black Women in America,* and the *Dictionary of American Negro Biography.* □

David Walker

African American abolitionist David Walker (1785-1830) wrote *Walker's Appeal,* urging slaves to resort to violence when necessary to win their freedom.

David Walker was born free, of a free mother and slave father, in Wilmington, N.C., on Sept. 28, 1785. He early learned to read and write, and he read extensively on the subjects of revolution and resistance to oppression. When he was about 30, he left the South, because "If I remain in this bloody land, I will not live long. As true as God reigns, I will be avenged for the sorrows which my people have suffered." In 1826 Walker settled in Boston, Mass., where he became the agent for *Freedom's Journal,* the black abolitionist newspaper, and a leader in the Colored Association. For a living he ran a secondhand clothing store.

Walker published an antislavery article in September 1828; with three others, it became the pamphlet *Walker's Appeal* (1829). The articles were articulate and militant in their bitter denunciation of slavery, those who profited by it, and those who willingly accepted it. Walker called for vengeance against white men, but he also expressed the hope that their cruel behavior toward blacks would change, making vengeance unnecessary. His message to the slaves was direct: if liberty is not given you, rise in bloody rebellion.

Southern slave masters hated Walker and put a price on his head. In 1829, 50 unsolicited copies of *Walker's Appeal* were delivered to a black minister in Savannah, Ga. The frightened minister, understandably concerned for his welfare, informed the police. The police, in turn, informed the governor of Georgia. As a result, the state legislature met in secret session and passed a bill making the circulation of materials that might incite slaves to riot a capital offense. The legislature also offered a reward for Walker's capture, $10,000 alive and $1,000 dead.

Other Southern states took similar measures. Louisiana enacted a bill ordering expulsion of all freed slaves who had settled in the state after 1825. The slaveholding South was frightened by men like Walker, and their harsh reactions to the threat they saw in *Walker's Appeal* seemed justified when black slave Nat Turner led his bloody rebellion in 1831.

Most abolitionists disagreed with Walker's advice to the slaves to resort to violence to obtain freedom. White abolitionist William Lloyd Garrison, who believed in immediate emancipation but thought it could be accomplished through persuasion and argument, did endorse the spirit of the *Appeal,* however, and ran large portions of it, together with a review, in his paper, the *Liberator.* On the other hand, Frederick Douglass accepted a more activist position, probably due to Walker's influence and that of Henry H. Garnet, who also called for massive slave rebellions.

Walker died in Boston on June 28, 1830, under mysterious circumstances. His challenge to the slaves to free themselves was an important contribution to the assault on human slavery.

Further Reading

Walker's Appeal is available in recent editions: *Walker's Appeal, in Four Articles* [by] David Walker; *An Address to the Slaves of the United States of America* [by] Henry Highland Garnet (1948; reprinted 1969 with an introduction by W. L. Katz and a brief sketch of Walker's life); *David Walker's Appeal,* edited by Charles M. Wiltse (1965); and *One Continual Cry: David Walker's Appeal . . . Its Setting and Its Meaning,* edited by Herbert Aptheker (1965). A brief biography of Walker appears in *Historical Negro Biographies,* edited by Wilhelmena S. Robinson (1968). Lerone Bennett, Jr., *Pioneers in Protest* (1968), contains a chapter on Walker. Walker figures in the surveys by John Hope Franklin, *From Slavery to Freedom: A History of American Negroes* (1947; 3d rev. ed. 1968), and Lerone Bennett, Jr., *Before the Mayflower: A History of the Negro in America, 1619-1962* (1962; 4th ed. 1969). □

Joseph Reddeford Walker

Joseph Reddeford Walker (1798–1876) was a fur trapper and was one of the first Americans partaking in open fur trade with the Spanish of Santa Fe.

Joseph Reddeford Walker was born in Virginia shortly before his parents migrated to Roane County in eastern Tennessee. In 1819 he moved to Independence in western Missouri, then the farthest west of all American settlements and the center for the Western fur trade and what was to become the Santa Fe Trail.

Walker became a fur trapper and trader and took part in the first attempt that the Americans made to travel to Santa Fe and open trade with what was then a Spanish colony. For a while Walker was sheriff of Jackson County, Missouri. On May 1, 1832 Walker set out with Benjamin Bonneville on a fur-trading expedition to the West. After a year of trapping, Walker met up with Bonneville in July 1833 at the annual fur rendezvous on the Green River in eastern Utah. Bonneville then sent Walker west to look for furs and/or find a trail to the Pacific Ocean.

Walker and his party traveled for a month over the desert west of the Great Salt Lake before reaching the Humboldt River in northern Nevada that had been found by Peter Skene Ogden in 1828. They followed the river to the Humboldt Sinks, a series of marshy lakes in the desert where the Humboldt River disappears. There, Walker and his group of 60 men were approached by a band of curious Digger tribesmen. The Americans opened fire and killed "several dozen" of them within a few minutes. From there, Walker traveled up the Walker River to Walker Lake and then crossed over the Sierra Nevada Mountains at Mono Pass between the Merced and Tuolumne Rivers. They entered what is now Yosemite National Park and were the first Westerners to see its famous waterfalls.

Traveling through California, Walker and his party were amazed by the redwood forests they saw, experienced a major earthquake, and witnessed a meteor shower. They traveled to San Francisco Bay and then down the coast to Monterey, the capital of Mexican California. The Americans were well received and stayed there from November 1833 until January 13, 1834. On the return east, Walker went down to the southern end of the San Joaquin Valley and traveled through Walker's Pass, which was to be one of the main gateways for Americans moving into California.

The Americans then turned north through the desert where they almost died of thirst before reaching the Humboldt Sinks once again. Again, they fired on defenseless Digger Indians, this time killing 14 of them and wounding many more. From there, the Americans headed north from the Humboldt River to the Snake River in southern Idaho, thereby avoiding the desert west of the Great Salt Lake. Walker and his men met up with Bonneville on the Bear River on July 12, 1834. The route that Walker had found was to become the main trail to California in following years.

Walker continued to trap and trade in the Rocky Mountains for the next nine years, making one trip to Los Angeles to buy horses in 1841. In 1843 he led a group of American settlers to California via Walker's Pass and met up with John Charles Frémont on his return. He then served as guide for Frémont's 1845-1846 expedition to California. In 1849 he joined the flood of Americans heading west during the Gold Rush and went into business selling cattle to the miners as well as leading several prospecting expeditions. He led a group of prospectors to Arizona in 1861 and finally retired and settled down with his nephew in Contra Costa County near San Francisco in 1868, where he died eight years later. □

LeRoy Tashreau Walker

U.S. sports official, university chancellor, educator, and track coach, LeRoy Tashreau Walker (born 1918) became the first African American elected to serve as president and chief executive officer of the United States Olympic Committee in 1992. As such he directed U.S. participation in the 1996 Olympic Centennial Games held in Atlanta, Georgia.

LeRoy Walker was born on June 14, 1918, in Atlanta, Georgia, the grandson of slaves and the youngest of 13 children in a close-knit family. His mother, Mary, always told him not to worry about the difficulties and to just keep pushing and honing his talents; recognition by others would follow. After his father, a fireman on the railroad, died when LeRoy was nine, his older brother, Joe, chose the littlest Walker to live with him in Harlem. But Walker returned to Georgia for his senior year of high school.

As a youth he worked in the family's barbecue restaurant and window cleaning businesses to earn money during the Great Depression. A strong father-figure, Joe taught an iron work ethic and never permitted him to rationalize in spite of prejudice. This attitude of perseverance provided Walker with inner strength to deal with subtle Northern discrimination and Southern racial segregation.

At Benedict College, an historically African American church-related college in Columbia, South Carolina, Walker earned 11 letters in football, basketball, and track and field. He graduated in three and one-half years in 1940, majoring in science and romance languages. Only Meharry and Harvard medical schools were open to African Americans, and because he missed the registration cycle, Walker decided to work with people through a program in health and physical education at Columbia University. He studied under Jesse F. Williams and received an M.S. degree a year later.

After one-year periods as chair of departments of physical education and of recreation and head track coach at Benedict and Bishop Colleges, Walker went to Prairie View University in Texas. While there he also directed the Army Specialized Training Program (ASTP) as a military training officer at night after teaching and coaching by day. Walker then accepted a one-year appointment as a football and basketball coach at North Carolina Central College in Durham in 1945. After gaining valuable professional experience, Walker returned to graduate school at New York University, receiving his Ph.D. in 1957.

Coach and Administrator of Sports

At North Carolina Central, Walker had started a track and field program as an off-season training program for his football and basketball players. This event led to a successful career as a legendary track coach. He coached 11 Olympic medalists and sent track and field athletes to every Olympic Games from 1956 to 1980. His top reputation began when Lee Calhoun won back-to-back gold medals in the 110-meter hurdles in the 1956 and 1960 Summer Games.

Much publicity was received during the 1960 Rome Games. Walker was coaching two teams at the same time. It was dramatic for him when Ethiopia's Abebe Bikila won the first of his back-to-back Olympic gold marathon medals while running without shoes. Later he was an Olympics consultant for the following national teams: Trinidad-Tobago in Tokyo (1964), Jamaica in Mexico City (1968), and Kenya in Munich (1972). In 1976 Walker was selected as the head men's coach for the U.S. track and field team at the Montreal Olympic Games.

Walker became the first African American president of the American Alliance for Health, Physical Education, Recreation, and Dance (AAHPERD) when he was elected at the Seattle convention in 1977. He provided strong leadership during his three-year executive committee term as an advocate to implement quality AAHPERD programs. Another theme was "unity through diversity," and he promoted minority involvement on national, district, and state levels. Earlier, Walker had assisted with efforts to integrate the National Education Association (NEA), which did not allow African American members.

In 1974 Walker was appointed as vice-chancellor for university relations at North Carolina Central University (NCCU). He moved up to become chancellor in 1983, serving as chief executive officer (CEO) for one of the 16 campuses of the University of North Carolina system.

Walker's coaching and administrative skills led to other positions. He chaired the men's track and field committee for the Amateur Athletic Union (1973-1976), served a term as president of the National Association of Intercollegiate Athletics, and was the president of the Athletics Congress (1984-1988), the U.S. governing body for track and field.

As a member of the important Knight Commission on Intercollegiate Athletics (the first major study in 66 years) in 1991-1992, he made strides toward key reforms, using a formula of "one-plus three," recommending to the NCAA: greater presidential control plus financial integrity, academic standards, and the innovative "independent certification" of programs.

Head of the U.S. Olympic Committee

On October 11, 1992, at age 74, Walker became the first African American elected by the United States Olympic Committee to serve as its president and CEO. Walker resigned his paid position as senior vice-president for sports with the Atlanta Committee for the Olympic Games (ACOG) to take the voluntary post.

Called "an inspired choice" by sportswriters, Walker's milestone election was a tribute to his dedication to excellence and ethical standards. Outgoing president William J. Hybl stated that Walker was "uniquely qualified" because of his coaching of Olympians; wealth of leadership experience, including service as a past president of a major national governing body; and esteemed image among the USOC membership.

The Amateur Sports Act of 1978 gave the USOC the authority to promote and coordinate amateur athletic activity in the United States, to recognize certain rights for American amateur athletes, and to provide for the resolution of disputes involving national governing bodies. New challenging trends for the USOC cited by Walker included more sports governing bodies; needs for infrastructure, such as training facilities; demands of high stakes sponsors; fundraising for the U.S. effort for the Summer Olympics in 2000 in Melbourne, Australia; revisions in committee and program structure; and increased public ownership via open disclosure of budget details for 1993-1996.

A critical issue that faced the USOC's executive board and the governing bodies was the mounting pressure for more U.S. Olympic gold medals. Walker opposed the commercialism of "Dream Teams" selected from professionals without college tryouts. He cited the fact that 64 nations won medals in the 1994 Lillehammer Winter Games, including nations in conflict or with few resources. Further, he felt the Olympic Village experience should be shared by all competitors.

The 1996 Olympic mascot, "Izzy" (formerly "Whatizit"), received much press coverage. Designed to create worldwide "Olympic fever," the futuristic Izzy succeeded "Cobi" (Barcelona's dog mascot in 1992) and "Hodori" (Seoul's baby tiger mascot in 1988). The Olympic Motto is "Citius, Altius, Fortius," meaning "Swifter, Higher, Stronger," as related to improving athletic performance.

Walker received many honors and awards in his long career. He was the first African American to receive the James J. Corbett Memorial Award (1993), the top honor granted by the National Association of Collegiate Directors of America. In carrying out his duties as USOC president and CEO, Walker occupied an office on the NCCU campus in Durham, where he was chancellor emeritus. In 1996 Walker was named the first President Emeritus of the United States Olympic Committee. He was widowed with two children, LeRoy Jr. and Carolyn.

Further Reading

Walker wrote the following books: *A Manual in Adapted Physical Education; Physical Education for the Exceptional Student; Championship Techniques in Track and Field;* and *Track and Field for Boys and Girls.* He is also noted in the following; Charles Belle, "Business In The Black: Onward and Upward," *Sun Reporter, The* (November 14, 1996).

His career is profiled in *Who's Who Among Black Americans. A Hard Road to Glory: A History of the African-American Athlete* by Arthur R. Ashe, et al. (1988), contains several citations concerning Walker. For details regarding Walker's career highlights see *AAHPERD Leaders: The First 100 Years,* an oral history project of the National Association for Sport and Phys-

ical Education by Sharon L. Van Oteghen and Allys M. Swanson (1994).

The *Olympian* (November 1992) featured Walker with a cover photograph and a biographical article by Mike Spence focusing on his milestone election as president of the U.S. Olympic Committee. Articles in popular periodicals include "Dr. LeRoy Walker Poised To Take USOC Presidency," *Jet* (June 29, 1992); "An Inspired Choice," *Sports Illustrated* (October 19, 1992); "New USOC Head: Dr. LeRoy Walker Named President of USOC," *Jet* (October 26, 1992); "USOC's Walker Nixes Idea of Baseball Dream Team," *Jet* (November 2, 1992); "LeRoy Walker Receives Top Collegiate Honor," *Jet* (June 14, 1993), and a photo essay in *Ebony* (June 1994). □

Maggie Lena Walker

Maggie Lena Walker (1867-1934) was an African American entrepreneur and civic leader. She and her associates organized a variety of enterprises that advanced the African American community while expanding the public role of women.

Maggie Lena Walker was born in Richmond, Virginia, just after the Civil War. Family tradition says that her father was Eccles Cuthbert, an Irishborn newspaperman. Her mother, Elizabeth Draper, married William Mitchell while they were both working in the home of Elizabeth Van Lew, a famous Union spy. He later became a waiter in one of the fashionable hotels in the city, but after only a few years was found drowned. Elizabeth Mitchell then supported her family by doing laundry. They lived in a small alley house shared with several relatives.

Despite her poverty, she persevered through the city school system and graduated from the Colored Normal School in 1883. Her class of seven protested the fact that African Americans were not allowed to use the city auditorium for their graduations as whites did, but had to use an African American church. Their stand was courageous since it risked their hopes for jobs as teachers in the system they challenged. A compromise permitted the graduation to take place in the school itself.

She taught for three years but, following school system policy, gave up her job when she married Armstead Walker, Jr., who worked in his family's construction and bricklaying business. Later he was also a postal carrier. The Walkers had three sons, one of whom died in infancy.

While she was still in high school Walker joined a fraternal organization, the Independent Order of St. Luke. Such organizations were popular and numerous. Membership gave people a group that helped in times of illness and death and provided sickness and life insurance, often otherwise not available to African Americans. The meetings centered around a ritual with colorful robes, chances to earn advancement, and opportunities to learn new skills. A "fraternal" provided an important way to bring individual contributions of time and money together to run businesses and carry out significant social projects.

The Independent Order of St. Luke was founded in Baltimore in 1867. When the order moved into Richmond, it did not flourish as other societies had. In 1899, when Walker was elected secretary, it was on the verge of bankruptcy. She brought some training in business, 16 years of experience holding minor posts in the order, and energy, enthusiasm, and organizational ability to the job. St. Luke soon created the combined position of secretary-treasurer for her, and she devoted the rest of her life to building membership and resources, expanding activities in business and social service, and keeping the financial base efficient. She liked to describe the order as a woman's organization that gave equal opportunity to men. At its height in the 1920s it claimed 100,000 members in 22 states.

In addition to real estate and the insurance program, the major St. Luke businesses founded under Walker's leadership included the St. Luke Penny Savings Bank, which opened in 1903. It had a woman president and several women board members. By 1931 it had merged with the two remaining African American banks in Richmond, resulting in the Consolidated Bank and Trust Company, which still existed in the mid-1980s. Walker is often described as the first woman bank president in the United States, but her achievement lay in presiding over a successful bank. Another project, the order's newspaper, the *St. Luke Herald*, printed outspoken editorials on the condition of African Americans in bigoted times.

As segregation in the South increased, many African American leaders emphasized entrepreneurship, "buy Black" campaigns, and the employment of African Americans as a primary avenue for community advancement. Walker agreed to that agenda and added a powerful plea for the creation of employment for African American women other than in domestic service.

Walker was a charismatic speaker whose favorite topics were race pride and unity, women's problems and potential, African American business, and oppression. As her importance grew, she became more and more active in civic affairs. She was the founder and lifelong head of the Colored Women's Council of Richmond, which raised money for local projects and maintained a community house.

She served many years on the executive committee of the National Association of Colored Women, whose projects included restoring and opening the Frederick Douglass Home to the public. For over a decade she was a member of the board of the National Association for the Advancement of Colored People and the guiding spirit of the Richmond branch. She was on the board of the Richmond Urban League and a member of the Interracial Commission. She was on the board of two schools for girls—one in Richmond and one in Washington—and served as a trustee of Hartshorn College and Virginia Union University. She was an active contributor to the work of her beloved First African Baptist Church.

Walker became a relatively wealthy woman and a philanthropist. Her home was made a national historic site, administered by the National Park Service. There one can see how the family lived, learn about the Richmond African American community, and appreciate the breadth of her friendships. The library walls are lined with pictures of friends: Booker T. Washington, W. E. B. DuBois, Marcus Garvey, Nannie Helen Burroughs, Mary McLeod Bethune, Langston Hughes, and many others. The shelves are full of books on African American history and life.

Walker achieved what she did despite the heavy social odds against her. She also had personal handicaps and suffering. In 1915 her husband Armstead was shot and killed by their son, Russell, who mistook his father for a burglar. He was indicted for murder, but acquitted. Walker had severe health problems and spent the last seven years of her life in a wheelchair. However, she continued to travel to places as far away as Florida and Chicago. Walker died of diabetic gangrene on December 15, 1934. According to tradition, her last message was "Have hope, have faith, have courage, and carry on."

Further Reading

The standard book on Maggie Walker is still *Maggie L. Walker and the I.O. of St. Luke: The Woman and Her Work* by her lifelong friend and classmate Wendell P. Dabney (1927). Brief biographical sketches include Sadie Daniel St. Clair's in *Notable American Women, 1607-1960* (1971) and Rayford Logan's in the *Dictionary of American Negro Biography*, edited by Rayford W. Logan and Michael R. Winston (1982). Longer accounts are in Lily H. Hammond's *In the Vanguard of the Race* (1922), Mary White Ovington's *Portraits in Color* (1927), and Sadie I. Daniel's *Women Builders* (1931). □

Margaret Walker

Margaret Walker (born 1915), novelist, poet, scholar, and teacher, was best known for her Civil War novel *Jubilee* (1963) and for her powerful collection of poetry about racial affirmation, *For My People* (1942).

Margaret Abigail Walker was born on July 7, 1915, in Birmingham, Alabama, to Sigismund and Marion (Dozier) Walker. In 1943 she married Firnist James Alexander (deceased 1983), and they parented four children: Marion Elizabeth, Firnist James, Sigismund Walker, and Margaret Elvira. Walker received her A.B. from Northwestern University (1935) and an M.A. (1940) and Ph.D. (1965) from the University of Iowa. For more than 30 years Walker taught literature at Livingstone College, Salisbury, North Carolina (1941-1942); West Virginia State College (1944-1945); and Jackson State University, Jackson, Mississippi (1949-1979).

In addition to teaching, Walker was a prolific writer. She wrote six books between 1942 and 1974. *For My People* (1942), a collection of poetry about African American racial pride and heritage, brought her instant recognition. Her Civil War novel *Jubilee* (1966), begun when she was 19, dramatizes actual historical events from American slavery to Reconstruction as the setting for the fictionalized life of her maternal great-grandmother, Margaret Duggans. This novel was translated into five languages and went through 43 printings. Her other book-length works include *Prophets for a New Day* (1970), *How I Wrote Jubilee* (1972), *October Journey* (1973), and *A Poetic Equation: Conversations between Margaret Walker and Nikki Giovanni* (1974). Walker also wrote numerous articles on African American literature and culture. Moreover, she recorded her own poetry, as well as selections from the work of Paul Lawrence Dunbar, James Weldon Johnson, and Langston Hughes, on Folkways Records.

Her literary activities won her many honors. In 1942 she received the Yale Series of Younger Poets Award for *For My People,* followed by the Rosenthal fellowship in 1944, Ford Foundation fellowship in 1954, Houghton Mifflin Literary fellowship in 1966 for *Jubilee,* Fulbright fellowship in 1971, and National Endowment for the Humanities fellowship in 1972. Walker also held honorary degrees from Northwestern University, Rust College, Dennison University, and Morgan State University.

After retiring from teaching at Jackson State University, Walker devoted full-time effort to her writing. She prepared two books for publication in the 1980s—*The Daemonic Genius of Richard Wright,* a definitive, critical biography of Wright; and *This is My Century,* a collection of poetry possessing the power of *For My People.* Walker also worked on five other book-length manuscripts: *Mother Broyer,* a novel about a faith healer and cult leader; *Goose Island,* a collection of short stories; *A New Introduction to the Hum-*

anities, a textbook; *Twentieth Century Afro-American Literature,* an anthology; and *Minna and Jim,* a sequel to *Jubilee.*

Walker continued to reside in Jackson, Mississippi, where she said she must stay and "write for the rest of [her] life, no matter how short or long it is." In addition to working on the *Jubilee* she is also writing an autobiography. When she is not writing she lectures on African American literature.

Further Reading

The following works contain biographical and critical information: Phanuel Egejuru and Robert Elliot Fox, "An Interview with Margaret Walker," in *Callaloo* (1979); Mari Evans, "Margaret Walker," in *Black Women Writers, 1950-1980* (1983); R. Baxter Miller, "The 'Etched Flame' of Margaret Walker: Biblical and Literary Re-Creation in Southern History," in *Tennessee Studies in Literature* (1981); Charles H. Rowell, "An Interview with Margaret Walker," in *Black World* (December 1975); James E. Spears, "Black Folk Elements in Margaret Walker's *Jubilee,*" in *Mississippi Folklore Register* (Spring 1980); Claudia Tate, "Margaret Walker," in *Black Women Writers at Work* (1983); and Margaret Walker, *How I Wrote Jubilee* (1972). □

Robert John Walker

Robert John Walker (1801-1869) was a U.S. Senator and served as secretary of the Treasury. A lifelong

regular Democrat, he fell out with the party leaders over the status of slavery in Kansas.

Robert John Walker was born in Northumberland, Pa., on July 19, 1801, the son of Jonathan Hoge Walker. After graduating from the University of Pennsylvania in 1819, Robert practiced law in Pittsburgh. He married Mary Bache (Benjamin Franklin's grand daughter) in 1825 and moved to Natchez, Miss., to enter his brother's law office. There he prospered as a lawyer and land speculator, acquiring several plantations. In 1836 he entered the Senate as a Jacksonian Democrat. In spite of his slight stature (he was five feet three inches tall and weighed 100 pounds) and his wheezy voice, he was an active and influential speaker. A party regular, he supported the independent treasury system and constantly attacked the protective tariff, the distribution of the surplus, and abolitionists. As a passionate exponent of manifest destiny, he endorsed the annexation of Texas.

It was largely due to Walker's efforts that the Democrats nominated James K. Polk as their presidential candidate in 1844 instead of Martin Van Buren. Polk appointed Walker to his Cabinet as the secretary of the Treasury. In that office Walker sought to secure the adoption of the independent treasury and to implement tariff reductions. His recommendations were largely responsible for the creation of a Department of the Interior in 1849 and the establishment of customs warehouses. He was an extremely able treasury administrator, and his important financial connections enabled him to negotiate loans for the Federal government on favorable terms during the Mexican War.

After Walker left office in 1849, he settled in Washington, D.C., having disposed of his plantations and slaves in Mississippi in 1843. He practiced law before the Supreme Court and promoted the stocks of railroads in which he was interested. In 1857 President James Buchanan appointed him governor of the territory of Kansas. Although Walker held moderate views on slavery, his stand that the citizens of Kansas should be left free to choose to have slavery or not was regarded as a betrayal by Democratic party leaders, who were committed to make Kansas a slave state. When Buchanan refused to approve the free-soil constitution, Walker resigned. During the Civil War, Walker was active in support of the Union cause and went on a successful mission to Europe to sell Federal bonds in 1863-1864. He died on Nov. 11, 1869, in Washington, D.C.

Further Reading

A recent study of Walker is James P. Shenton, *Robert John Walker: A Politician from Jackson to Lincoln* (1961). An early work is George Washington Brown, *Reminiscences of Gov. R. J. Walker: With the True Story of the Rescue of Kansas from Slavery* (1902). □

William Walker

William Walker (1824-1860) was a United States adventurer and filibuster in Central America. His armed intervention in Nicaragua gave liberals temporary advantage in their internal war with conservatives and inflamed the slavery controversy in the United States.

William Walker was born in Nashville, Tenn., on May 8, 1824. He earned a medical degree (1843), spent 2 years in Europe, returned, and began a career in law. In New Orleans and, after 1850, in San Francisco, however, he engaged chiefly in newspaper work. A reputation as a crusading journalist and lawyer gave him political potential; but his restlessness and the example of French adventurers who launched from California a colonizing-filibustering venture in Sonora, Mexico, embarked him on another career.

Walker's filibustering began in Mexico. With a small force he invaded Baja California in 1854 and declared that province and Sonora an independent republic, but he was forced to seek refuge in the United States.

A "colonization" contract granted by a Nicaraguan political faction offered Walker new opportunity. With 58 (tradition says 56) armed men—"the immortals"— recruited to aid the Democrats (liberals) in their attempt to overthrow the Legitimists (conservatives), he sailed from San Francisco in May 1855. In Nicaragua he seized control of the Accessory Transit Company's interoceanic route, his sole source of supplies and recruits from the United States; captured Granada, the Legitimist capital; and mollified the factions and established a provisional government with Patricio Rivas as president and himself as commander in chief of the army. The United States recognized his regime in May 1856.

In July, after systematically disposing of everyone who could challenge his power, Walker broke with Rivas and had himself elected president. He initiated a number of measures to promote development—United States style. The most controversial was reinstitution of slavery, ostensibly to attract United States investors to acquire and develop Nicaraguan land.

Walker now tampered with the Accessory Transit Company. From Cornelius K. Garrison and Charles Morgan, who managed the company, he had accepted cash advances and transport of recruits and supplies against the debt the company owed Nicaragua. When, incident to their maneuver to oust Cornelius Vanderbilt from control of the company, they approached him to revoke the Vanderbilt charter and reissue it to them, he obliged.

The choice was fatal. Vanderbilt diverted company service to Panama, isolated Walker, and aided the Central American coalition operating against him. Defeated, and his cause hopeless, Walker surrendered to a U.S. naval officer in May 1857 and was returned to the United States.

Twice again Walker returned to Central America. In November 1857 he reached Greytown but was arrested by Commodore Hiram Paulding and again returned to the United States. He made his final attempt against Honduras in August 1860 but was taken prisoner by the commander of a British vessel and turned over to the Honduran authorities, who executed him on Sept. 12, 1860.

Further Reading

The old, but still standard, work on Walker is William O. Scroggs, *Filibusters and Financiers: The Story of William Walker and His Associates* (1916). Other biographies are Laurence Greene, *The Filibuster: The Career of William Walker* (1937), and Albert Z. Carr, *The World and William Walker* (1963).

Additional Sources

Bolanos Geyer, Alejandro, *William Walker, the gray-eyed man of destiny,* Lake Saint Louis, Mo.: A. Bolanos-Geyer, 1988-1991.
Gerson, Noel Bertram, *Sad swashbuckler: the life of William Walker,* Nashville: T. Nelson, 1976.
Rosengarten, Frederic, *Freebooters must die!: The life and death of William Walker, the most notorious filibuster of the nineteenth century,* Wayne, Pa.: Haverford House, 1976.
Walker, New York: Perennial Library, 1987. □

Alfred Russel Wallace

The English naturalist and traveler Alfred Russel Wallace (1823-1913), independently of Darwin, dis- cerned the mechanism of evolution by natural selection.

Alfred Russel Wallace, the eighth of nine children, was born on Jan. 8, 1823, at Usk, Monmouthshire. He was educated at Hertford Grammar school and left at the age of 14. He learned surveying and some geology from his brother William.

In 1844 Wallace became a schoolmaster at the Collegiate School in Leicester, where he met the naturalist Henry Bates. Wallace convinced Bates to join him on an expedition to the Amazon to collect specimens. They sailed in April 1848; by March 1850 they separated so as to exploit wider collecting grounds. Wallace sailed for England in 1852; his specimens were lost when the ship was destroyed by fire. He reported on his findings in *Travels on the Amazon and Rio Negro* and *Palm Trees of the Amazon* (both 1853).

In 1854 Wallace was given a government passage to Malaysia, where he spent 8 years and amassed an outstanding collection of specimens. In 1855 he wrote the essay "On the Law Which Has Regulated the Introduction of New Species," demonstrating that "every species has come into existence coincident both in time and space with a preexisting closely-allied species." This attracted the attention of Charles Lyell and Charles Darwin.

By February 1858 Wallace conceived a method of evolution and sent his account, "On the Tendency of Varieties

to Depart Indefinitely from the Original Type," to Darwin. To his amazement, he found Wallace's material to be almost identical with his own 1842 manuscript that had never been published. Anxious considerations of priority were solved by Lyell and J. D. Hooker, who advised Darwin to make a joint presentation of both papers. This took place on July 1, 1858, at a meeting of the Linnean Society of London. Darwin's extended summary of his views became the *Origin of Species* (1859); Wallace's fame as the codiscoverer of the principle of descent with modification through selection was assured.

Wallace continued his studies of the distribution of animals. The sale of his collections of biota yielded an annual income of £300, later lost through unwise speculation. He supported himself thereafter through his publications. His most notable works were *The Malay Archipelago* (1869), which combined sketches of travel and natural history with a discussion of evolutionary biology: *Contributions to the Theory of Natural Selection* (1870), which contained reprints of his earlier papers and indicated his differences with Darwin's views; and *The Geographical Distribution of Animals* (2 vols., 1876), a noteworthy pioneering work that was fundamental for all subsequent investigations in this field. Wallace was elected fellow of the Royal Society in 1893 and was a recipient of the Copley, Royal, and Darwin medals. He received the Order of Merit in 1909. He died at Broadstone, Dorset, on Nov. 7, 1913.

Further Reading

Considerable biographical information can be gleaned from Wallace's own writings, *My Life: A Record of Events and Opinions* (2 vols., 1905) and *A. R. Wallace: Letters and Reminiscences* (2 vols., 1916). Books on his life and work include Lancelot T. Hogben, *A. R. Wallace: The Story of a Great Discoverer* (1918); Wilma George, *Biologist Philosopher: A Study of the Life and Writing of Alfred Russel Wallace* (1964); and Amabel Williams-Ellis, *Darwin's Moon: A Biography of Alfred Russel Wallace* (1966). For background see Lorin C. Eiseley, *Darwin's Century* (1958).

Additional Sources

Brackman, Arnold C., *A delicate arrangement: the strange case of Charles Darwin and Alfred Russel Wallace,* New York: Times Books, 1980.

Brooks, John Langdon, *Just before the origin: Alfred Russel Wallace's theory of evolution,* New York: Columbia University Press, 1984.

Fichman, Martin, *Alfred Russel Wallace,* Boston, MA: Twayne Publishers, 1981.

Wallace, Alfred Russel, *My life; a record of events and opinion,* New York, AMS Press, 1974. □

DeWitt Wallace

DeWitt Wallace (1889-1981), American publisher, was the founder of *Reader's Digest,* one of the world's largest-selling magazines.

DeWitt Wallace was born on November 12, 1889, in St. Paul, Minnesota, where his father was on the faculty (and later president) of Macalester College. DeWitt attended Macalester from 1907 to 1909 but, finding life there too confining, transferred to the University of California at Berkeley. He returned to St. Paul in 1912 and was hired by a publishing firm specializing in farming literature. Much of the company's information was provided without cost by federal and state agencies. Wallace compiled a list of the available public documents, added his own comments, and published the result in 1916 in a pamphlet entitled *Getting the Most Out of Farming.* Acting as his own salesman, Wallace sold nearly 100,000 copies, primarily to rural bankers who offered it to their customers as a promotional device.

When America entered World War I Wallace enlisted in the Army, was sent to France, and in 1918 was seriously wounded in action near Verdun. Wallace passed the hours in a French military hospital editing superfluous words from magazine articles, preparing himself for his next publishing venture—*Reader's Digest.*

For six months in 1919 Wallace was a constant visitor to the periodical room of the Minneapolis Public Library. He pored through a host of magazines, seeking out those articles that still retained general interest even ten years after publication. The chosen few were then carefully condensed. By January 1920 he had prepared a sample issue of the *Reader's Digest,* "31 Articles Each Month From Leading

DeWitt Wallace (left)

Magazines, Each Article of Enduring Value and Interest, In Condensed and Permanent Form.'' The sample contained all of the essential elements that would make the *Reader's Digest* a world-wide success. Unlike most magazines of the day, the *Digest* contained no fiction, for it was envisioned as a service for busy readers who wanted hard facts conveyed quickly, clearly, and concisely. Wallace edited the *Digest* to speak directly to the concerns of the average reader, skillfully blending stories of human interest, down-to-earth advice, and good-natured humor. The *Digest* frankly acknowledged the world's problems but remained ever-confident of their eventual solution.

Wallace's initial plans for the *Reader's Digest* were, in retrospect, quite modest. He offered to give his idea to any publisher who would make him editor of the new magazine. But even on those generous terms no one was interested. So, as a last resort, he decided to publish the *Digest* himself. A small office was rented in New York City's Greenwich Village and hundreds of circulars were sent out to potential subscribers. His sole partner then, and in the years to come, was Lila Bell Acheson, the sister of a Macalester classmate. The couple were married in October 1921. When they returned from their honeymoon some 1,500 orders awaited them.

The first official edition of *Reader's Digest* appeared in February 1922. Most magazine publishers readily granted re-publication rights, for they considered a credit in the *Digest* a form of free advertising for their periodicals. In its early years the *Digest* itself carried no advertising and was sold solely by subscription. On that basis the magazine grew slowly, but steadily. In 1922 Wallace was able to move the company to its permanent headquarters in Pleasantville, New York. Three years later the *Digest* had a circulation of 20,000 copies. The real growth of the *Reader's Digest* did not come until it was sold on the nation's newsstands, but Wallace did not take that step until 1929. He feared that other magazines, sensing new competition, would no longer grant reprint rights. Most of the major periodicals, however, continued with the *Digest* (some for a fee), and by the end of 1929 circulation had climbed over 100,000.

Wallace constantly adjusted his editorial product to meet the needs of his rapidly growing readership. For example, in February 1933 the *Digest* began presenting signed, original articles. In time the magazine would produce over half of its own material. As the *Digest* grew in size and influence it inevitably attracted its share of critics. Some scorned the *Digest's* brand of condensed English; others objected to its alleged conservative political bias.

Yet the *Reader's Digest* did have its crusading moments. It was one of the first major periodicals (in 1954) to link cigarette smoking and cancer, and it frequently attacked unfair business practices. The *Digest's* most famous article, ''. . .And Sudden Death,'' published in August 1935, graphically portrayed the hazards of reckless driving. It became the most widely reprinted article in magazine history, with four million copies in circulation.

By the end of the 1930s *Reader's Digest* was moving into the international market. A British edition was produced in 1938, to be followed by editions in Spanish (1940), Portuguese (1942), Swedish (1943), and, eventually, most of the world's major languages. The foreign editions carried advertising from their inception. The American edition followed suit in 1955, but only after Wallace, in typical fashion, had first surveyed the likely reaction of his readers. Wallace, meanwhile, was reaching out into other areas of publishing, usually successfully. The *Reader's Digest* Book Club, for example, offered its members quarterly volumes of condensed books, primarily current novels. When the club started in 1950 it had 183,000 subscribers; in four years there were two and a half million.

Wallace gradually began to withdraw from the active management of the company in the mid-1960s, although he remained as chairman of the board until 1973. He died on March 30, 1981. At the time of his death over 30 million copies of *Reader's Digest* were being sold every month to readers in 163 countries.

Further Reading

The biography of DeWitt Wallace, a man who long shunned publicity, is inseparable from the story of his great creation, *Reader's Digest*. James Playsted Wood, *Of Lasting Interest: The Story of the* Reader's Digest (1967) was written with the cooperation of the magazine's management. Samuel A. Schreiner, Jr., *The Condensed World of the* Reader's Digest (1977) is a sometimes critical insider's view of Wallace and life at the *Digest*.

Additional Sources

Heidenry, John, *Theirs was the kingdom: Lila and DeWitt Wallace and the story of the Reader's digest,* New York: W.W. Norton, 1993. □

George Corley Wallace

George Corley Wallace (born 1919) was an Alabama governor and a third-party presidential candidate in 1968.

Born on Aug. 25, 1919, at Clio, Ala., he studied at the University of Alabama and received his law degree in 1942. That same year he was admitted to the Alabama bar. In 1943 he married Lurleen Burns. They had four children. Between 1942 and 1945 Wallace served in the U.S. Army Air Force. After the war, he became assistant attorney general of Alabama. In 1947 he entered the Alabama Legislature, representing Barbour County, and remained until 1953. He served as judge of the Third Judicial District of Alabama between 1953 and 1958, after which he returned to private law practice in Clayton.

Wallace's experiences in Alabama politics prepared him for his election to governor in 1962. In 1966, barred by Alabama law from another term, he supported his wife's candidacy. Lurleen Wallace won a landslide victory. As governor, she admitted that her husband would continue to make the policy decisions. She died in May 1968. Meanwhile her husband had emerged as a national political figure.

An outspoken critic of Federal-government interference in southern schools and an ardent segregationist, Wallace entered a number of presidential primary races in 1964, largely to channel opposition to the civil rights bill. His name appeared on the ballots in at least nine states, and in Wisconsin, Indiana, and Maryland he polled 25, 30, and 43 percent of the vote respectively. At the governors' conference in June, he declared that he would run in the national election wherever he could place his name on the ballot. When the republican party nominated a conservative candidate, Senator Barry Goldwater of Arizona, however, Wallace withdrew from the race.

In February 1968 Wallace announced his intention to again challenge the Democratic and Republican parties in the race for the presidency. His appeal, as in 1964, embraced the discontent of conservative citizens, rich and poor, who believed their welfare endangered by high taxes, liberal court decisions, and Federal interference in local and state affairs. Wallace's program, repeated across the country almost without change, revealed his single-minded concern for property rights and freedom of local and individual decision—which, he warned, were threatened by the Federal bureaucracy.

Wallace's program called for an end to crime in the cities. He denied that he favored segregation but insisted that individuals rather than government officials had the right to decide where their children would go to school and

to whom they would sell their houses. Although his campaign lost momentum during its final weeks, his strong states'-rights stand gave him wide support in the Deep South. In the November election he captured Arkansas, Louisiana, Mississippi, Alabama, and Georgia. His popular vote across the country was almost 14 percent.

In 1970 Wallace won a landslide victory for a second term as governor of Alabama. The following year he married Cornelia Ellis Snively in Montgomery. In 1972 he entered the presidential campaign as a Democrat and had victories in Michigan and Maryland. In May, while campaigning in Maryland, he was shot and was partially paralyzed as a result of the assassination attempt.

In 1982 he ran again and won a fourth term as governor of Alabama. His final term saw him sponsor an Alabama constitutional amendment that created an oil and gas trust fund whose interest supported the finances of all non-education segments of state government. He also worked a controversial bill that restructured the state's job-injury laws along with an attempt to promote a $310 million education bond issue. His further attempts, however, to fund education programs by raising property and income taxes met with failure.

In his later years, Wallace apologized for his stance against integration he held early in his political career. At the same time, he insisted that his infamous statements supporting segregation had to do with his fight against federal courts interfering with state issues rather than a being sign of racism against blacks. In a 1992 interview in *Time,* Wallace said he eventually realized that "either we had to do away with segregation or we wouldn't have peace in this country." He added, "I know that I love every citizen of Alabama, black and white." In March of 1995, Wallace was present for a reenactment of the famous Selma to Montgomery civil rights march of 1965.

Further Reading

John Craig Stewart, *The Governors of Alabama,* 1975; James Gregory*The Wallaces of Alabama: My Family by George Wallace, Jr.,* 1975; Marshall Frady, *Wallace* (1968), is a fascinating personality study of Wallace by a journalist. A biting, unsympathetic profile of Wallace is in Robert Sherrill, *Gothic Politics in the Deep South: Stars of the New Confederacy* (1968). Discussions of Wallace's career and impact on the 1968 presidential elections are in Lewis Chester and others, *An American Melodrama: The Presidential Campaign of 1968* (1969); David English and the Staff of the London Daily Express, *Divided They Stand* (1969); and Theodore H. White, *The Making of the President, 1968* (1969). For further information, please see *George C. Wallace, the Politics of Race,* produced by ABC news (1994); *Boston Globe* (December 2, 1993); *Chicago Tribune* (January 30, 1996); *New York Times* (February 11, 1994); and *Time* (March 2, 1992). □

Henry Wallace

Henry Wallace (1836-1916) was an American agricultural publicist and editor of the newspaper *Wallaces' Farmer* from 1895 to 1916.

Henry Wallace was born on a farm outside West Newton, Pa., on March 19, 1836. His parents were hardworking, religious, Scotch-Irish farmers who had come to the United States from Northern Ireland in 1832. Henry graduated from Jefferson College, Pa., in 1859 and then taught for a year at Columbia College in Kentucky. After theological study at Allegheny Seminary in Pennsylvania (1860-1861) and Monmouth College in Illinois (1861-1863), he was ordained. He was a Union chaplain during the Civil War.

Wallace was pastor at various churches in Illinois and Iowa until 1877, when he retired from the ministry for health reasons. But for this forced retirement he might never have developed his later, and historically more important, career as a journalist, which helped to lead his two sons into political life. Wallace had already developed a taste for journalism and had published articles and become mildly interested in the reforms of his day, including temperance and antislavery.

In 1877 Wallace moved to Winterset, Iowa, and took up farming. He had decided against accepting either the presidency of Monmouth College or entering religious jour-

nalism, for he felt the need for an outdoor life. He became involved in editorial work for local farm papers and eventually took part ownership in the *Iowa Homestead*. In 1895, with his two sons, he established his own paper to push "the agricultural interest." The newspaper later became known as *Wallaces' Farmer*.

Wallaces' Farmer was a leading organ and spokesman for the midwestern farmer. It fought for railroad regulation and for agricultural education, while maintaining a strong religious interest. The paper is now an important source for historians, as are Wallace's writings. These include *Doctrines of the Plymouth Brethren* (1878); three works on technical aspects of farming: *Clover Culture* (1892), *Clover Farming* (1898), and *The Skim Milk Calf* (1900); two volumes of popular education: *Uncle Henry's Letters to the Farm Boy* (1897) and *Letters to the Farm Folks* (1915); and a polemic against monopoly: *Trusts and How to Deal with Them* (1899).

In 1908 President Theodore Roosevelt appointed Wallace a member of the Country Life Commission. Two years later he became president of the National Conservation Commission. In 1891 he traveled in Europe for the U.S. Department of Agriculture to investigate flax growing, and in 1913 he was again sent abroad to study farm conditions in Britain. He died on Feb. 22, 1916.

Further Reading

The chief source of information on Wallace is his post-humously published autobiography, *Uncle Henry's Own Story of His Life: Personal Reminiscences* (3 vols., 1917-1919). Russell Lord, *The Wallaces of Iowa* (1947), is a history of the entire family.

Additional Sources

Kirkendall, Richard Stewart, *Uncle Henry: a documentary profile of the First Henry Wallace,* Ames: Iowa State University Press, 1993. □

Henry Agard Wallace

Henry Agard Wallace (1888-1965), a secretary of agriculture and of commerce and vice president of the United States, was one of the most controversial Federal officials for 13 years. Wallace became almost the official ideologist of the New Deal.

Henry A. Wallace was born on a farm in Adair County, Iowa, on Oct. 7, 1888. In 1895 his grandfather founded a weekly agricultural newspaper called *Wallaces' Farmer*. Henry became its editor in 1916. Meanwhile he had earned his bachelor's degree from Iowa State University and had married Ilo Browne. Involved in plant research and agricultural economics, he eventually developed a species of hybrid corn and founded a company to exploit the discovery. Moreover, he worked out detailed studies of weather cycles in the Midwestern farming region and a corn-hog ratio chart that proved effective for predicting market variations.

During the 1920s, while his father served as U.S. secretary of agriculture, Wallace became increasingly prominent among agricultural leaders. The total collapse of American agriculture during the Great Depression convinced him of the necessity for curtailing agricultural production under a federally administered acreage allotment program. Although his family had been traditionally Republican, Wallace fervently embraced the presidential candidacy of Franklin Roosevelt in 1932, and after his election Roosevelt named Wallace secretary of agriculture.

Wallace proved an extraordinarily effective administrator. But also, as the implementer of the New Deal's strategy of paying farmers to cut back on crop production and as an advocate of massive Federal efforts to promote social welfare, he was bitterly criticized. It was only by threatening to refuse renomination himself that Roosevelt secured Wallace's nomination for the vice presidency in 1940. Wallace's strength in the farm states contributed significantly to Roosevelt's reelection.

Roosevelt made Wallace the most active vice president in the nation's history. During World War II he headed the powerful Board of Economic Warfare and other economic coordinating agencies. More importantly, he became the foremost articulator of American ideals and objectives. He called for international cooperation to achieve the "century of the common man" and for "60,000,000 jobs" in the postwar period at home. By 1944, however, anti-Wallace

feeling within the Democratic party was so powerful that Roosevelt dropped Wallace for the vice-presidential nomination. Yet as soon as he was reelected, Roosevelt appointed Wallace secretary of commerce.

After Roosevelt's death Wallace openly attacked Harry Truman's uncompromising stance regarding the Soviet Union; the President asked for and received Wallace's resignation. In 1948 he accepted the presidential nomination of the Progressive party, a broad leftist coalition. Losing the bitter 1948 presidential campaign, Wallace retired from public life. He spent most of his time at his farm at South Salem, N.Y., working on improving egg yields and strawberries and gladiolus. He died in Danbury, Conn., on Nov. 18, 1965.

Further Reading

The best study of Wallace is Russell Lord, *The Wallace of Iowa* (1947), which extends only through the period of World War II. Also helpful are Edward L. and Frederick H. Schapsmeir's *Henry A. Wallace of Iowa: The Agrarian Years, 1910-1940* (1968), which focuses on Wallace's role in the New Deal, and their *Prophet in Politics: Henry A. Wallace and the War Years, 1940-1965* (1971). See also Dwight Macdonald, *Henry Wallace: The Man and the Myth* (1948). Wallace figures centrally in two excellent monographs on New Deal farm policy: Richard S. Kirkendall, *Social Scientists and Farm Politics in the Age of Roosevelt* (1966), and Van L. Perkins, *Crisis in Agriculture: The Agricultural Adjustment Administration and the New Deal, 1933* (1969). A detailed account of the Progressive party and Wallace's presidential candidacy is Curtis D. MacDougall, *Gideon's Army* (3 vols., 1965).

Additional Sources

Macdonald, Dwight, *Henry Wallace, the man and the myth,* New York: Garland Pub., 1979, 1948.

White, Graham J., *Henry A. Wallace: his search for a new world order,* Chapel Hill: University of North Carolina Press, 1995. ☐

Lewis Wallace

Lewis Wallace (1827-1905) was an American military leader and popular author, remembered especially for the novel *Ben-Hur*.

Lew Wallace was born in Brookville, Ind. He became a lawyer but left his practice to serve in the Mexican War in 1846. During the Civil War he served in the Union forces with such distinction that he was promoted to major general. He led the courts of inquiry investigating the conduct of Gen. D.C. Buell and of the commander of the Andersonville prison and was a member of the court trying those charged with conspiring against President Lincoln. In 1865 he resigned from the Army and for the rest of his life practiced law. He served as governor of the new Mexican Territory (1878-1881) and minister to Turkey (1881-1885) and wrote very popular novels and an excellent autobiography.

Wallace's romantic novel *The Fair God; or, The Last of the Tzins* (1873) told about Hernán Cortés's invasion of the Aztec empire in Mexico and his eventual defeat by Prince Guatamozin. The considerable success of this book encouraged him to write *Ben-Hur: A Tale of the Christ* (1880), a colorful story about a young Jewish patrician, Judah Ben-Hur, who as a result of false accusations by Messala is sent to the galleys for life. He escapes, returns as a Roman officer, wins a chariot race against Messala, and exposes him. Meanwhile Ben-Hur's mother and sister have been imprisoned and have contracted leprosy. The hero rescues them and goes with them to seek out Christ. When Christ cures the women, they and Ben-Hur become converts. Wallace's skill as a storyteller, his invention of exciting events, and his vivid representation of the late Roman Empire and the beginnings of Christianity made the novel one of the best-selling books of its period in the United States (more than 2 million copies) and in many foreign countries.

Wallace's stay in Turkey prompted him to write *The Prince of India* (1893), a lengthy novel based upon the legend concerning the Wandering Jew. Wallace also wrote the narrative *The Boyhood of Christ* (1888) and had almost finished *Lew Wallace: An Autobiography* at the time of his death. Completed by his wife, Susan Arnold Wallace, who also was a writer, it was published in 1906.

A dramatization of *Ben-Hur* (1899), featuring spectacular scenes—in which, onstage, the galley was wrecked, the chariot race was presented, and Christ wrought miraculous cures—was one of the most popular American plays for many years. Three motion picture versions, one made in the days of silent pictures, were extraordinarily successful.

Further Reading

Wallace's autobiography contains an excellent account of his military and literary career. Biographies which stress respectively Wallace as soldier and Wallace as author are Floetta Goodwin, *Lew Wallace during the Civil War and Reconstruction* (1927), and Irving McKee, *"Ben-Hur" Wallace: The Life of General Lew Wallace* (1947).

Additional Sources

Morsberger, Robert Eustis, *Lew Wallace, militant romantic,* New York: McGraw-Hill; San Francisco: San Francisco Book Co., 1980. □

Sir William Wallace

The Scottish soldier Sir William Wallace (ca. 1270-1305) led the Rising of 1297, an attempt to reverse the loss of Scottish independence to England. Although he failed, he is remembered as a champion of Scottish nationalism.

Very little is known of the early life of William Wallace. His father is known to have been a member of the lesser nobility in the west of Scotland, and so his origins were decent but undistinguished. Beyond brief references to his schooling, there is not record of Wallace until he is identified as a fugitive from justice, the result of his having slain an English sheriff. He became the leader of a small band and earned the reputation of being a friend to Scots who suffered at the hands of their English conquerors. It is difficult to assess with precision the nature of Wallace's activities since legends about his early life are colored by his later exploits. Whether he was an ordinary brigand or a sort of Robin Hood, he was the leader of but one of many peasant bands. What does set Wallace apart is that he emerged as the leader of guerrilla resistance to English occupation for the Scots at large, and so he became a figure of national significance.

Wallace's support came from the lower classes and the lesser nobility; with few exceptions, the greater nobles were never enthusiastic, loyal, long-term allies. While they may have mistrusted his social origins, the more important fact is that members of that class were favorably disposed toward England, where many of them still had lands and relatives. The failure of the upper nobility to support Wallace, especially on the field of battle, proved to be his undoing.

The Rising of 1297, led by Wallace, caused Edward I of England to send a special force against him. The first meeting of the two armies was at Stirling Bridge on September 11, and here Wallace gained a great victory. The English had superior numbers, but Wallace had a favorable position, a large measure of patience, and a sufficient talent for tactics to rout the impatient and poorly led enemy. Wallace

followed up his triumph by moving swiftly to restore Scottish control over every fortress and castle in Scotland. The victory at Stirling Bridge had made Wallace the liberator of Scotland.

Riding the wave of success, Wallace carried the war into England. In this period he gained a noble title, and he styled himself "guardian of the realm of king John." So devastating was Wallace's work that Edward made truce in his war with France so as to be free to face the threat from the north. Wallace met the English counteroffensive with a calculated retreat and scorched-earth policy, and for a time his strategy worked. In the face of the pinch of scarce supplies and threats of mutiny, Edward was preparing to abandon his pursuit when he learned that Wallace was within striking distance. Edward moved quickly to force an open battle.

The battle of Falkirk (July 22, 1298) is remembered in Scottish history as the occasion on which Scots fought valiantly but vainly in defense of their independence against far greater numbers. The noble cavalry defected from Wallace's army without striking a single blow. The Scottish infantry withstood the onslaughts of English cavalry, but without horsemen Wallace was unable to carry the battle to the enemy. When Edward brought his archers into play, the Scots were doomed. With his army decimated, Wallace resigned his office as guardian of the realm and withdrew from the center of the political stage.

Little is known of Wallace's career in the years between 1298 and 1303 except that he visited France and Rome in

an unsuccessful search for help against Edward. On his return to Scotland, Wallace became the object of relentless pursuit by Edward, and on Aug. 5, 1305, he was betrayed to the English by his one-time subordinate Sir John Menteith.

Transported to London, Wallace was obliged to stand trial for acts of war and treason. The condemned Wallace was dragged by horses to the gallows, hanged, and disemboweled. His head was impaled on London Bridge; his quartered body was distributed for display at four castles in Scotland.

Intended to be advertisements of Edward's victory, those bloody quarters became banners of the cause that Wallace bespoke. Within months Edward was faced with a resurgence of Scottish nationalism that he could not put down.

Further Reading

A eulogistic biography which contains many extracts from early sources and is, therefore, informative about the legends which have grown up around the memory of Wallace is John Carrick, *Life of Sir William Wallace, of Elderslie* (2 vols., 1830). A balanced and reliable narrative of events is provided by Robert Laird Mackie, *A Short History of Scotland,* edited by Gordon Donaldson (rev. ed. 1962). A colorful but dependable account is Eric Linklater, *The Survival of Scotland* (1968).

Additional Sources

Fisher, Andrew, *William Wallace,* Edinburgh: J. Donald Publishers; Atlantic Highlands, N.J.: Distributed in the U.S.A. and Canada by Humanities Press, 1986.

Gray, D. J., *William Wallace: the king's enemy,* London: R. Hale, 1991. □

Isaac Theophilus Akunna Wallace-Johnson

Isaac Theophilus Akunna Wallace-Johnson (1895-1965) was a West African trade union organizer, nationalist political leader, journalist, and pan-Africanist.

I saac Wallace-Johnson was born of Creole parents in Wilberforce, Sierra Leone. Educated mainly in mission schools, he had to abandon secondary school in order to support his family. He worked in various commercial establishments until 1913, when he became a clerk for the colonial government.

Bureaucratic Career

Wallace-Johnson's talents as an organizer and public speaker quickly propelled him to a position of leadership. At the Customs Department, he organized the first trade union in Sierra Leone, among temporary customs officers. When he called for a strike in 1914, he was fired. He entered the British army in 1915 as a clerk in the Carrier Corps. Returning to Sierra Leone in 1920, he worked for the Freetown City

Council but resigned in 1926 to serve on a United States merchant ship. He published *The Seafarer,* an occasional journal of maritime labor news, then joined the staff of the *Lagos Daily Times.*

Wallace-Johnson first came to the attention of the Moscow Comintern in 1930 at an International Conference of Negro Workers in Hamburg, Germany. After organizing the African Workers' Union in Nigeria in 1931, he and other black nationalist leaders were invited to the Soviet Union to attend the International Labor Defense Congress. He may have also enrolled briefly in the People's University of the East in Moscow under his favorite pseudonym, W. Daniels. Eventually, he became an associate editor of the Paris Communist publication *Negro Worker,* contributing articles under several pseudonyms.

Journalist and Organizer

Wallace-Johnson then moved to the Gold Coast to write for the *African Morning Post* of his friend Nnamdi Azikiwe and to organize workers in the mining areas. Identified by the British as an agitator and potential troublemaker, he was arrested, along with Azikiwe, for writing and publishing a seditious editorial. Convicted, he appealed and lost, then appealed to Great Britain's Privy Council.

In England, Wallace-Johnson attracted attention and support from leading British left-wing intellectuals and politicians. He also intensified his contact with George Padmore, Jomo Kenyatta, C. L. R. James, and others affiliated with the newly established International African Service Bureau. Wallace-Johnson became editor of *Africa and the World* and with Padmore, of the *African Sentinel.*

In April 1938 Wallace-Johnson returned to Freetown, intending to make his stay a short one. But customs agents seized 2,000 copies of the *African Sentinel* which he was bringing into Sierra Leone. The resulting publicity drew crowds to his series of public lectures. His oratory was brilliant, his targets well chosen, the population ready for leadership. Less than three weeks after his arrival, bolstered by a mass following, Wallace-Johnson inaugurated the West African Youth League, the first effective, large-scale political movement in Sierra Leone's history.

Supported by wage earners and the unemployed, the Youth League swept two elections in a row: the Freetown Municipal Council elections of 1938 and the Legislative Council elections of 1939. These successes, plus Wallace-Johnson's charismatic effect on the masses, his unrelenting exposure of labor exploitation, and his uncanny ability to discredit the colonial government, further angered British officials.

Fearing that Wallace-Johnson would foment disloyalty among African soldiers and policemen, the government enacted a series of ordinances in the summer of 1939 which severely limited his and other Sierra Leoneans' liberties. At the start of World War II he was interned as an "undesirable."

Upon his release late in 1944, Wallace-Johnson resumed his activities immediately. He was an influential spokesman at several international conferences, particularly the 1945 Manchester Pan African Conference. Within Sierra Leone, however, he entered a political cul-de-sac. The Youth League foundered, never regaining the momentum and following which it had lost during the war. Wallace-Johnson himself lost considerable popular support when he opposed the planned reconstitution of the Legislative Council to give majority representation to the protectorate. Although he was still respected and admired as a witty political critic, his stand on this issue denied him a major role in Sierra Leone's postwar independence movement. On May 10, 1965, at the age of 70, he died in a car crash in Ghana while attending the AfroAsian Solidarity Conference.

Further Reading

There is no study of Wallace-Johnson as yet, but some information can be found in James Hooker, *Black Revolutionary: George Padmore's Path from Communism to Pan-Africanism* (1967). Wallace-Johnson's career is recounted in John R. Cartwright, *Politics in Sierra Leone, 1947-67* (1970). Good background information is in Martin Kilson, *Political Change in a West African State: A Study of the Modernization Process in Sierra Leone* (1966). □

Graham Wallas

Graham Wallas (1858-1932) was a British sociologist, political scientist, antirationalist, and proponent of a psychological approach to the study of politics.

The son of a Sunderland clergyman, Graham Wallas endured a strict puritanical upbringing, and it was not without some relief that he left home to attend Shrewsbury School and Corpus Christi College, Oxford. Following his studies, he pursued a preparatory school teaching career but was constantly in trouble regarding matters of religious conformity.

In 1886 Wallas joined the Fabian Society and became a member of its executive committee. He resigned from the society in 1895 partly because of political disagreement and partly because of boredom. Although he was primarily concerned with the almost universal lack of concern for psychology on the part of political scientists, he dealt also with general problems of epistemology and methodology.

Assuming an antirationalist posture, Wallas believed it dangerous (especially in a democracy) to assume "that every human action is a result of an intellectual process . . . [that] man first thinks of some end which he desires, and then calculates the means by which that end can be accomplished." Furthermore, he did not believe that people, in the light of history, any longer relied upon "enlightened self-interest" or some similar concept. Indeed, he seemed especially intent upon refuting the then popular application of Darwinism to social affairs and to individual human behavior.

Wallas observed that, since the discovery of human evolution, psychologists had made new and important discoveries concerning human nature. Sociology had emerged as a new science which took some cognizance of these discoveries. Political science, however, had neither contributed to these discoveries nor been affected by them. This he considered a tragedy.

For the earlier notions of an "unseen hand" and purely a priori assumptions, Wallas would substitute a more scientifically conceived foundation—"a conscious and systematic effort of thought" based upon cognizance of a sound psychology. "Political acts and impulses," he held, "are the result of the contract between human nature and its environment."

Wallas thought that the introduction of psychological aspects into the examination of the basis of politics would reopen many of the traditional discussions, such as that concerning representative government. Representative government, he held, was earlier "inspired by a purely intellectual conception of human nature," and in the real world these assumptions had not produced the predicted results. Later, the old psychology having been discarded, the question remained as to whether this necessitated discarding concepts of representative government. Wallas thought not. A rule by consent of the governed need not be dependent upon the old psychology's assumptions. The problem does not lie in the concept of representative government but in the fact that there is too limited participation, for whatever reason. The need is for more votes with more knowledge. However, he preferred the short ballot, for voters must not have too much strain put upon them and too hard choices.

In many respects Wallas is at once more democratic and more elitist. His elitism, however, is not based upon "natural selection." His elite should be an ever-expanding one which makes choices on the basis of latest scientific discoveries in both the natural and social sciences (especially psychology). Perhaps this elite could become so numerous as to no longer be an elite.

Wallas's apparent ambivalence about rationalism and intellectualism is best reflected in the preface to the 1914 edition of *The Great Society*. "I may, therefore, say briefly that the earlier book [*Human Nature in Politics,* 1908] was an analysis of representative government, which turned into an argument against nineteenth-century intellectualism; and that this book is an analysis of the general social organization of a large modern state, which has turned, at times, into an argument against certain forms of twentieth-century anti-intellectualism."

Further Reading

For a thorough understanding of Wallas, one should begin with his dissertation, *The Life of Francis Place* (1898; rev. ed. 1918), and follow up with his contributions in *Fabian Essays in Socialism,* with an introduction by Asa Briggs (1962). In his *Great Society: A Psychological Analysis* (1914) Wallas launches his lifelong campaign for the application of psychological analysis to the study of politics. Representative of his mature works in this vein are *Human Nature in Politics* (1908) and *Our Social Heritage* (1921). See also Gilbert Murray's "Preface" to Wallas's *Men and Ideas* (1940) and the remarks by his daughter, May Wallas, in the 1935 edition of Wallas's *Social Judgment,* which she edited. Wallas figures in works on

Fabian socialism: Anne Fremantle, *The Little Band of Prophets: The Story of the Gentle Fabians* (1960); Margaret Cole, *The Story of Fabian Socialism* (1961); and A. M. McBriar, *Fabian Socialism and English Politics, 1884-1918* (1962).

Additional Sources

Qualter, Terence H., *Graham Wallas and the great society,* New York: St. Martin's Press, 1979. □

Raoul Wallenberg

Raoul Wallenberg (1912-?) was one of the great heroes of World War II and one of the first victims of the Cold War. In 1944, as a Swedish diplomat in Budapest, he saved tens of thousands of Hungarian Jews from certain death. Taken into custody by the Russians at the beginning of 1945, he simply disappeared.

Raoul Wallenberg was born on August 4, 1912, into one of Sweden's wealthiest families, three months after his father had died of cancer. His grandfather, a distinguished diplomat, saw to it that the precocious boy traveled and studied widely, acquiring fluency in several languages, international perspective, and savoir-faire.

After graduation in 1935 from the University of Michigan with an honors baccalaureate in architecture, Wallenberg worked in commercial enterprises first in Capetown and then in Haifa, where he learned from German refugees what was happening to the Jewish Germans under Hitler. In 1941 he joined a Stockholm-based export firm whose Jewish owner could no longer safely travel in Hitler-controlled Central Europe. In this position he developed a knowledge of Budapest that made him an ideal volunteer three years later for a desperate rescue mission initiated by the U.S. War Refugee Board.

Until the last year of the war, Hungary, though an Axis ally, had not cooperated in Hitler's program of genocide. Its Jewish community, once Europe's third largest, had even been increased by Jews seeking refuge in Hungary. In 1944, however, German army units moved in, together with a special SS force commanded by SS-Lt. Col. Adolf Eichmann, the engineer of the Holocaust. During the spring and summer of 1944 his men scoured the Hungarian countryside, rounding up and sending 400,000 Jews and others to the death camps.

Determined to do whatever he could to save the 200,000 surviving Jews assembled in Budapest, Wallenberg accepted a diplomatic appointment to the Swedish legation as special attaché for humanitarian questions. Carrying the two knapsacks he had used hitchhiking in America, a sleeping bag, a windbreaker, and a revolver, the soft-spoken, dark-eyed bachelor of 31 arrived in Budapest in July 1944 with a mandate even more unusual for a diplomat than his baggage: he had elicited from the Swedish Foreign Ministry, with American support, formal personal authorization to

appeal directly to Stockholm, to use his unprecedented funding (from U.S. and Jewish sources) even for bribery, and to grant Swedish diplomatic asylum to documented victims of persecution.

He opened a special branch office of the Swedish legation near the Jewish quarter, built up a staff of 400 (mostly Jews, all granted diplomatic immunity), and by January 1945, when the Russians took Budapest, had issued protective passports to perhaps 20,000 Jews placing them under the protection of the Swedish crown until they could emigrate to Sweden. He sheltered over 12,000 in dozens of buildings over which he flew the Swedish colors, making them de facto annexes of the Swedish legation with extraterritorial status.

To the consternation of bureaucratic colleagues, Wallenberg acted on the premise that the conventional rules could not be honored. "When there is suffering without limits, there can be no limits to the methods one should use to alleviate it," he argued and, with desperate ingenuity, acted accordingly. He cajoled, intimidated, and bribed Axis officials, established networks of spies within the Hungarian fascist party and the Budapest police, provided officials with food and amenities from hoards he could afford to lay in before the black market was sold out, and even issued protective passes to key fascists—documents that might greatly facilitate their "disappearance" at the end of the war.

His authority with the Hungarians established, Wallenberg fearlessly challenged the Germans, going so far as to

retrieve intended victims from the trains on which they had been jammed for shipment to Auschwitz and personally to confront Eichmann, who was behind at least one attempt on his life. His approach was vigorously followed by representatives of other neutrals, particularly the Swiss consul Charles Lutz, who not only provided documentation to thousands of Jews but accompanied Wallenberg in the perilous retrieval of Auschwitz-bound victims.

In the final days of his mission, as the Russians closed in on the surrounded city, fanatically anti-Semitic Hungarian fascist death squads sought to finish what Eichmann, who had withdrawn in December 1944, had left undone. Countless Jews saved from Auschwitz were murdered in the streets or drowned in the Danube. But Wallenberg's network of collaborators thwarted the fascist murderers' plans for a last-minute, full-scale massacre of the 100,000 Jews who had survived in Budapest.

When the city fell to the Soviet Army in January 1945, Wallenberg was taken into custody by the Russians—possibly as an American agent or possibly because of his fascist connections (realistically cultivated to fulfill his mission). That spring, he did not return to Sweden with the other members of the Budapest legation staff who were held for six weeks after their "liberation" in a Soviet internment camp. The Swedish government then enquired about Wallenberg.

In 1947 Soviet Deputy Foreign Minister Andrei Vyshinsky finally came up with an answer: Wallenberg was not in the Soviet Union and was assumed to have died during the struggle for Budapest. Not until 1957, after Stockholm had begun to pursue the matter seriously, did Moscow acknowledge responsibility and formally expressed regrets. Deputy Foreign Minister Andrei Gromyko informed the Swedish ambassador that Wallenberg had died of heart failure in prison in 1947 and had been cremated. But numerous reports indicated that Wallenberg was moved with deliberate frequency from one location to another and was alive in captivity, possibly as late as 1981.

By the end of the 1970s an international movement on behalf of Wallenberg, including participation by many he had saved, organized support for his release to the United States, at whose behest he had undertaken his mission to Hungary. In October 1981 Wallenberg was proclaimed an honorary citizen of the United States—a distinction previously accorded only the descendants of the Marquis de Lafayette and Sir Winston Churchill. The law granting him honorary citizenship also provided, belatedly if not posthumously, for "all possible steps [to be taken] . . . to secure his return to freedom."

Russian President Boris Yeltsin created a special commission in 1991 to study the Wallenberg case. The commission was short-lived and failed to shed any new light on the Wallenberg mystery. Through the efforts of a number of Holocaust survivors, now American citizens, a bust honoring Wallenberg was placed in the U.S. Capitol Rotunda in 1995. The U.S. Postal Service issued a stamp (1996) in honor of the Swedish diplomat. Because of the popular belief that Wallenberg may still be alive, the Postal Service did not issue the stamp as a "commemorative," which would have implied that Wallenberg was dead. U.S. government documents released from the Central Intelligence Agency (CIA) in 1996 confirmed that Wallenberg had been a valued agent for the Office of Strategic Services (precursor to the CIA). Why the Soviets would have executed Wallenberg or have held him in captivity for so long remains unknown.

Further Reading

The Wallenberg case was made widely known in the United States by an article in the *New York Times Magazine* of March 30, 1980, "The Lost Hero of the Holocaust: The Search for Sweden's Raoul Wallenberg," by Frederick E. Werbell, a Swedish-born rabbi, and Elenore Lester. Foreign correspondent Kati Marton has provided in *Wallenberg* (1982), with eight pages of photographs, a concise, readable account based on extensive interviews and archival research. A memoir by a Swedish diplomat is Per Anger's *With Raoul Wallenberg in Budapest: Memories of the War Years in Hungary,* translated by David Mel Paul and Margareta Paul (1981). Focusing sharply on the failure of the Swedish government to pursue the case vigorously during the crucial first years after the war is Harvey Rosenfeld's *Raoul Wallenberg: Angel of Rescue—Heroism and Torment in the Gulag* (1982). Two U.S. congressional publications include the War Refugee Board report from 1945 on Wallenberg's activities and information on the U.S. government's efforts on his behalf since 1981: U.S. House Committee on Foreign Affairs, *Proclaiming Raoul Wallenberg To Be an Honorary Citizen of the United States,* hearing before the Committee, June 4 and 9, 1981; and U.S. House Committee on Foreign Affairs, *Update on Raoul Wallenberg,* hearing before the Committee's Subcommittee on Human Rights and International Organizations, August 3, 1983. Charles Fenyvesi and Victoria Pope provide an account of CIA documents identifying Wallenberg as a U.S. spy: *The Angel Was a Spy* (U.S. World News, May 13, 1996). □

Albrecht Wenzel Eusebius von Wallenstein

The Bohemian soldier of fortune Albrecht Wenzel Eusebius von Wallenstein (1583-1634) was one of the major figures in the Thirty Years War. His administrative and financial talents made him one of the richest and most powerful men in Europe.

Albrecht von Wallenstein was born on Sept. 24, 1583, at Hermanitz in Bohemia of noble family. Reared in the Utraquist (Protestant) faith, he converted to Catholicism before 1606 and attached himself to the court of the Hapsburg archduke (later emperor) Matthias, with whom he shared a strong interest in astrology. Marriage with a rich widow in 1609 added large Moravian estates to his possessions.

In 1618, when the Protestant Bohemian nobles rebelled against Matthias's aggressively pro-Catholic successor, Ferdinand II, Wallenstein remained loyal to the Hapsburgs. Although he did not participate in their decisive

victory in 1620 near Prague, wholesale confiscation of rebel property enabled him to purchase the vast estates of Reichenberg and Friedland. By 1622 he was one of the largest landholders in the kingdom, a status Ferdinand II recognized in 1624 by granting him the title Duke of Friedland. Wallenstein's second marriage, in 1623 to Isabella von Harrach, brought him into the Emperor's most intimate circle.

Wallenstein's astonishingly rapid acquisition of enormous wealth and influence resulted from his ability to grasp every possible advantage from a political system dependent on mercenary armies. From the beginning, he organized his own estates to provide recruiting areas and supporting industries for equipping his regiments, whose services he offered at great profit. He was coldly calculating, shrewdly acquisitive, and enormously ambitious. But his talents as a commander in the field were mediocre.

Wallenstein was named imperial commander against the allied Protestant German and Danish forces in 1625. His first campaigns were disappointing in spite of the astonishing speed he had shown in raising and equipping the army. In 1627, with larger forces at his disposal, he swept the Danes out of Silesia and northern Germany, and by 1629 the Emperor could impose peace on Germany. Wallenstein's price for his services included payment of his debts, large new grants of land, and the duchy of Mecklenburg, this last making him a sovereign prince of the empire.

Overestimating the security of his position in Germany, Ferdinand II dismissed Wallenstein from command in 1630. The Swedish invasion of the same year, however, undid the earlier victories, and Ferdinand II again had to call on Wallenstein's services. The Emperor was at his general's mercy, and the price was exorbitant. The terms of their agreement are still a mystery, but they included, in addition to money and new estates, virtual independence from political or religious interference in territories won back from the Protestant forces. Wallenstein began his last campaign in 1632 by driving the Saxons from Bohemia and then forcing Gustavus II (Gustavus Adolphus) to withdraw from Bavaria. On Nov. 16, 1632, the Swedish army struck Wallenstein's forces at Lützen. Wallenstein withdrew from the field, abandoning his artillery, but Gustavus himself was killed, and the Swedish army retired leaderless.

Wallenstein had been incredibly lucky, and at this point he contemplated using his unprecedented powers as commander in chief to impose a peace on Germany with terms which fell far short of fulfilling Ferdinand's own policies. Wallenstein's own intentions are unfathomable, but both sides feared him as both competed for his allegiance. It is quite possible that he hoped to gain the Bohemian crown for himself. Whatever his motives were, he had decided by the end of 1633 to break with Ferdinand II, and he began negotiating with the Protestant princes. The Emperor again ordered Wallenstein's dismissal in January 1634 and, to prevent betrayal, ordered loyal officers to imprison him and bring him to Vienna, or if necessary, to kill him. Worn down by illness and enmeshed in the tangle of his own conspiracies, Wallenstein could not complete his negotiations with his former enemies before he was caught by officers loyal to the Emperor at the fortress of Eger in Bohemia. These officers shot Wallenstein on the night of Feb. 25, 1634.

Further Reading

The two standard works on Wallenstein are in German. The best study in English remains Francis Watson, *Wallenstein: Soldier under Saturn* (1938). Extensive material on Wallenstein is in Cicely Veronica Wedgwood, *The Thirty Years War* (1939).

Additional Sources

Liddell Hart, Basil Henry, Sir, *Great captains unveiled,* New York: Da Capo Press, 1996.

Mann, Golo, *Wallenstein, his life narrated,* New York: Holt, Rinehart and Winston, 1976. □

Thomas Wright Waller

Thomas Wright Fats Waller (1904-1943) was a popular American jazz singer, pianist, organist, bandleader, and composer; on radio and records and in movies. His ebullient personality endeared him to a wide jazz and pop audience.

Thomas Wright Waller was born in New York City on May 21, 1904. His father was a Baptist minister; his mother was a musician who played and taught piano and organ. As a child Waller studied piano, bass, and violin, but after a time devoted himself exclusively to keyboards—chiefly piano (with a bit of organ), which he had begun playing at age six. His father wanted him to be a clergyman and objected emphatically when, at age nine, Waller jazzed up a hymn on the church organ.

Waller worked in a grocery store to pay for music lessons and played in his grade school orchestra, which was led by Edgar Sampson (later a famous arranger for Benny Goodman). Waller then attended DeWitt Clinton High School, but quit after a year, and at 15 was organist in a Harlem movie theater, earning $32 a week. (He was later to earn as much as $72,000 in a single year.) He continued to study with a number of teachers, including ragtime piano great James P. Johnson. He began his recording career in 1922, played in a silent movie house in Washington, D.C., and led his own trio in Philadelphia into the mid-1920s. The first of his nearly four hundred compositions, ''Squeeze Me,'' was published in 1924.

The late 1920s was a watershed period for Waller. Despite a distracting series of court appearances for nonpayment of alimony, he began a highly successful collaboration with lyricist Andy Razaf; and in 1927, reunited with his former mentor James P. Johnson, he led the band and wrote the score for a hit revue, ''Keep Shufflin','' which featured two of Fats' trademark songs, ''Ain't Misbehavin''' and ''Honeysuckle Rose.'' In 1928 he performed at Carne-

gie Hall along with Johnson and W. C. Handy ("The Father of the Blues"); and in 1929 he was the featured organist at New York's Paramount Theater and composed some of the music for another hit revue, "Hot Chocolates."

In the early 1930s Waller did a series of radio broadcasts for WABC and CBS and worked in a variety of bands, usually as leader. His first semi-permanent unit was formed in 1935 and made a classic series of fun-pop-and-jazz recordings; their great appeal for both the jazz audience and the larger commercial market led to many tours for the small band (usually a sextet) and, ultimately, to international fame.

In the late 1930s and early 1940s the group played frequently at New York's Famous Door and the Apollo Theater, at Chicago's Hotel Sherman, and at Boston's Tic-Tac Club. In 1943 Waller's last big show, "Early to Bed," opened in Boston. Also in the year that was to be his last, he toured armed service camps, made some cameo appearances in Hollywood movies—most notably "Stormy Weather"—and played at Los Angeles' Zanzibar Club. It was on the return trip from the West Coast to New York, on December 15, 1943, that Waller, at age 39, died in his train berth of bronchial pneumonia.

Waller's reputation is permanently embedded in jazz and pop lore, and his fame was underscored by the huge late 1970s success of the Broadway musical revue "Ain't Misbehavin'," a funny and loving tribute to the man and his music.

Nowhere in musical history has there been a closer alliance of man and music than in Fats Waller. He was 5 feet 11 inches and his weight wavered between 280 and 300 pounds. He was a jolly, quick-witted man whose compositions were almost always playful (even the sad ones are leavened by a cheerful acceptance of life's difficulties and vagaries). He was generous to a fault, frequently selling a minor compositional masterpiece for a pittance to a needy friend or even a down-and-out barstool acquaintance; money simply didn't matter to him.

For white America Waller seemed to play the self-mocking Negro clown, but attentive listening dispels the notion that his was the persona of a racially accommodating fool: his sense of fun and self-mockery were most often slyly satiric of the culture-at-large.

Fats was well-loved in the music business and his musicianship respected. His digital dexterity, particularly considering the plumpness of his fingers, was astonishing, and jazz critics regard him as one of the very greatest of "stride," or early, pianists. His vocal style—the light, grainy voice, with its sly inflections and defensively argumentative stance—was unique.

Many of Waller's vocal and pianistic performances of his own and others' compositions were reissued in the 1970s on RCA's Vintage series. Included, of course, are his earliest compositions, "Squeeze Me," "Ain't Misbehavin'," and "Honeysuckle Rose," in addition to some unjustly forgotten late 1930s tunes such as "Jitterbug Waltz," "Hold My Hand," "Thief in the Night," "The Girl I Left Behind Me," "What's the Reason I'm Not Pleasin' You," "The Joint

Is Jumpin'" (on which he typically interpolates "Don't give your right name!" as police sirens are heard in the background), and "Spring Cleaning" (Waller interpolates "No, lady, we can't haul your ashes for 25 cents—that's bad business!").

There are also splendid (often humorous) vocal readings of tunes written by others: "Jingle Bells" (a strangled "Jingle Bells!" followed by a concerned "What's the matter with him?" "I don't know—I think the jingle bells got him."); "Two Sleepy People"; "It's a Sin to Tell a Lie" ("If you break my heart/I'll break your jaw/And then I'll die."); Earl Hines' "Rosetta," Harburg & Schwartz's lovely "Then I'll Be Tired of You"; Caesar & Lerner's "(O Susanna) Dust Off That Old Pianna"; and "Your Feet's Too Big" (Gun the gunboats!"). Waller's instrumental skills are in full evidence throughout, especially on the straight instrumental versions of "Ain't Misbehavin'," "Honeysuckle Rose," and "Tea for Two."

Further Reading

Waller is the subject of a great number of periodical articles and book chapters; there are several biographies, the most noteworthy of which are his son Maurice Waller's *Fats Waller* (1979) and Alyn Shipton's *Fats Waller* (1988).

Additional Sources

Kirkeby, W. T. Ed., *Ain't misbehavin': the story of Fats Waller,* New York: Da Capo Press, 1975, 1966.
Vance, Joel, *Fats Waller, his life and times,* Chicago: Contemporary Books, 1977.
Waller, Maurice, *Fats Waller,* New York: Schirmer Books, 1977.
    □

Robert Walpole

The English statesman Robert Walpole, 1st Earl of Orford (1676-1745), was the first minister to maintain continuing support for royal government by exercising both careful use of Crown patronage and untiring leadership in the House of Commons.

Robert Walpole entered political life during the turbulent era of party strife that marked the reigns of William III and Anne. Walpole dominated English politics from 1722 to 1742, and when he departed from political life, Britain enjoyed the benefits of stable government. This change was in large measure a fruit of his efforts.

The son of a leading Norfolk squire, Walpole was born at Houghton, the family seat, on Aug. 26, 1676. After Eton he attended King's College, Cambridge, but had to withdraw to manage the family estate. He first entered the House of Commons in 1701 as member for Castle Rising, his deceased father's seat; the following year he stood successfully for King's Lynn, which he represented for the rest of his career. A blunt, cheerful man, adept at parliamentary business and impressive in debate, he quickly made his mark in the Commons. In 1708 he was appointed war secretary and in 1710 treasurer of the navy.

Walpole and the Whigs

From the outset Walpole was firmly attached to the Whig party, a party pledged to continuing the war against France; when war weariness eroded its strength in 1710, he suffered accordingly. By 1711 he was out of office—not merely dismissed, but subjected to an investigation of his War Office dealings. After voting him guilty of shaking down several forage contractors, the House expelled him in 1712 and sent him to the Tower. His guilt cannot be doubted. Yet, by the standards of the time the crime was not serious, and his conduct was not censured by his friends. Indeed, he became a Whig martyr. Like the voters of King's Lynn, who reelected their imprisoned candidate, he judged himself a victim of party malice and he vowed revenge.

Walpole's fortunes rose when George I's accession restored the power of the Whig party. Walpole became paymaster general of the forces. The job offered manifold opportunities for self-enrichment, and he made the most of them. Indeed, throughout his career he used public office for personal gain, and the results, if not the precise methods, were plainly visible: he lived high, indulged his wife's expensive whims, rebuilt Houghton on a grand scale, poured money into his London town house, and assembled a magnificent art collection. But power, not wealth, was the main object of his driving ambition. In 1715 he entered the Cabinet as chancellor of the Exchequer and first lord of the Treasury, thus acquiring command of a vast resource of

patronage. He did not have it long, because neither he nor his ally and brother-in-law, Lord Townshend, who was a secretary of state, were in close touch with George I. Isolated from the court when the King visited Hanover, they could not answer the accusations of their enemies, and by April 1717 Townshend and Walpole felt obliged to resign.

Attainment of Power

At once, and with no qualms about using Tory support, Walpole launched a vigorous opposition. His object was not to oust the King's ministers but to make political management so difficult for them that they would have to take him back. He would demonstrate that no government could long ignore an aroused House of Commons. Indeed, the success of the strategy he developed in his 4-year struggle to regain the Treasury stood as an object lesson for 18th-century politicians.

Walpole's first step was to stir up the Commons. A talented debater, expert in government business, he spoke often and with telling authority. Attacking abuses in the army and probing the Hanoverian basis of foreign policy, he played on the suspicions of independent minded gentlemen in the Commons. In 1719 a pet Cabinet measure, the Peerage Bill, was sent down to defeat. This was not enough; Walpole also needed acceptance at court. To gain influence over the mind of the Prince of Wales, he developed an intimate friendship with the princess. By bribing George I's most trusted mistress, he established a line of communication with the King. Thus, in 1720 he could offer George I, who hated his son and had openly quarreled with him, the prince's submission. He could also offer safe passage through Parliament of funds to meet the Civil List debt. These were tempting offers, and no one but Walpole could make good on them. The King's ministers, shaken by their defeat on the Peerage Bill, agreed to take him back, and he again became paymaster general.

The leading ministers in 1720 were Lord Sunderland and Lord Stanhope. Although Walpole had joined their government, they remained his rivals, and his indispensability would depend on their need for his skills. The need soon arose. When the "South Sea Bubble" burst, the cries of the wounded echoed in the Commons. The opposition wanted blood, and the leading ministers, having accepted free options on South Sea shares, were deeply implicated. Walpole, newly in office, was clear of the scandal. He could have sided with the opposition and brought the government down. It would have meant political chaos—a mixed ministry containing unruly dissidents. He sided instead with the men in power and then he labored to screen Sunderland and Stanhope from the attacks. It was a supreme test of his talents and his courage. Patiently he answered the government's critics in the Commons. His reward was the Treasury, once again, in 1721. It was, however, luck—the deaths within a year of Stanhope and Sunderland— that accounted for the speed with which he became the King's leading minister, because George I had not yet learned to trust him.

Walpole's Policy

Walpole dominated British government for 20 years, from 1722 to 1742. He may be considered the first "prime minister," but in those days the title implied an unwarranted usurpation of royal authority, so Walpole disclaimed it. His long supremacy stemmed from his unwavering dedication to the task of governing and from the willingness of the first two Georges to avoid wild adventures in politics. He never took royal confidence for granted.

To an unprecedented degree, Walpole mobilized Crown patronage for the purpose of obtaining majorities in Parliament. Allying himself with powerful aristocrats, such as the Duke of Newcastle, he melded their influence and patronage with that of the Crown. He refused a peerage during active political life (while accepting one for his son), being the first leading minister to perceive the necessity of forceful defense of policy in the House of Commons. There the same talents that he had formerly employed to incite, he now used to calm. His object was always to win over the independent-minded gentlemen. Drawing on his vast knowledge of affairs, he regularly exhibited to them the reasonableness of government policy. As the years passed, his foreign policy was increasingly adjusted to the wishes of such men. They hated military involvement on the Continent and the high taxes that war meant. Walpole gave them peace, and he tried to limit diplomatic commitments. In order to reduce the land tax, which the independent squires of the Commons hated, he was prepared to increase the amounts raised by excise taxes, which hit the lower orders of society. Walpole did not care about the lower orders. When his excise scheme gave rise to a popular uproar in 1733, he ignored the London mob as best he could; although he backed down and withdrew his bill, it was because he feared the way in which the uproar was being used by ambitious men to undermine his position at court and in the House of Lords.

But Walpole was never ruled by ideals or hatreds. Like most successful politicians, he dealt with problems immediately before him and sought the least troublesome solutions. Truthfully he said, "I am no saint, no Spartan, no reformer."

At length Walpole's power waned. The death of Queen Caroline rendered his influence at court less secure. When William Pitt the Elder and the Patriots excited the Commons by clamoring for war with Spain, Walpole proved unable to calm either the House or his colleague the Duke of Newcastle, and war was allowed to begin in 1739. By 1742 Walpole no longer commanded the situation, and he resigned. A grateful George II created him Earl of Orford. He died on March 18, 1745, and was buried at Houghton.

Further Reading

The most readable and reliable biography is J. H. Plumb, *Sir Robert Walpole* (1956—); the two volumes now completed bring the story to 1734. The political situation of Walpole's last years is examined in J. B. Owen, *The Rise of the Pelhams* (1957). For background the most important book is J. H. Plumb, *The Origins of Political Stability in England, 1625-1725* (1967), which places Walpole's political achievement in context. Also useful are Basil Williams, *The Whig Suprem-* acy, *1714-1760* (1939; 2d ed. 1962), and E. N. Williams, *The Eighteenth-century Constitution* (1960), both of which contain good bibliographies.

Additional Sources

Hill, Brian W., *Sir Robert Walpole: sole and prime minister,* London: H. Hamilton; New York, NY, USA: Penguin, 1989.
Kemp, Betty, *Sir Robert Walpole,* London: Weidenfeld and Nicholson, 1976. ☐

Marie Esprit Léon Walras

The French economist Marie Esprit Léon Walras (1834-1910) influenced modern economic theory by his discovery of the general equilibrium theory, which was designed to include within a single logically coherent model the theories of exchange, production, capital, and money.

Léon Walras was born in Évreux in Normandy, son of the economist Auguste Walras, who was forced by the low esteem in which economics was held in France in his day to waste his talents in the performance of administrative functions within the French centralized system of education. Auguste vowed to realize his cherished ambition to renovate economics and place it on a firm scientific basis through his son. This is precisely what Léon eventually did.

Career as an Economist

Léon's initiation in economics was late, hesitant, and singularly unpropitious. He was self-taught, having had no one but his father to guide his first steps, for there was no provision in the curriculum of French universities up to the 1870s to train professional economists. To satisfy his parents, who were eager to see him assured of a recognized career, he enrolled in the Paris School of Mines in 1854 after twice failing, for want of adequate mathematics, to gain admission into the prestigious Polytechnic School. Finding engineering distasteful, he neglected his studies and never became a mining engineer. Instead, he wrote novels (*Francis Sauveur* and *La Lettre*), but in 1858 his father persuaded him to abandon his literary pursuits and become an economist.

With this in view Walras tried his hand first at journalism, then as an employee on the clerical staff of a railway company, then as manager of a bank for cooperatives, and finally as secretary in a private bank, until he was called in 1870 to occupy a newly founded chair in political economy at the Academy (later the University) of Lausanne in Switzerland. He owed this call to his early economic publications in book and journal form, and particularly to his participation in an International Congress on Taxation held in 1860 at Lausanne, where he had impressed Louis Ruchonnet, a young lawyer destined to become a leading Swiss statesman.

In the formative pre-Lausanne years Walras's attention had been devoted almost exclusively to working out normative principles inspired in the main by his father's ideas. At Lausanne, however, where he could call upon the aid of his mathematical colleagues, he began systematically to lay theoretical foundations for his father's and his own pet policy proposals. These proposals aimed at a "socialist" regeneration of society through the nationalization of land to be acquired by repurchase and through the state ownership of such enterprises as could not operate under conditions of perfect competition. The underlying purpose of his mathematical model was to define the limits within which free enterprise could contribute to maximum social welfare. He also advocated a scheme for the long-run stabilization of the purchasing power of money by means of a regulatory silver token currency.

In the course of developing his pure theory, Walras utilized his independently, but belatedly, discovered theory of marginal utility to derive more rigorously than any of his precursors the relationship between the utility function and the demand function. His theory of production, or of the determination of prices of production services, foreshadowed the modern conception of linear programming. His theory of capital formation was formulated as a theory of the determination of prices of capital goods. His theory of money represented a heroic attempt to integrate the monetary sector with the real sector of the economy instead of considering them as dichotomized entities. The concept of "desired cash balances," which he utilized in his definitive statement of monetary theory, largely anticipated the Keynesian liquidity-preference approach.

The appearance of the first edition of Walras's *Éléments d'économie politique pure* (1874-1877) marked a major event in the "marginal revolution" of the 1870s. For all its novelty his contribution still remained within the classical tradition. However, he drew his inspiration directly from celestial mechanics. Making use of the models and methods of earlier mathematical economists, especially A. N. Isnard and A. A. Cournot, he created a well-defined theory of a network of interrelated markets which had been only vaguely and intuitively perceived by his classical predecessors.

In 1892 Walras retired from teaching. Besides producing his third and fourth substantially revised editions of the *Éléments* in 1896 and 1900, he published two volumes of collected papers: the *Études d'économie sociale* (1896), dealing primarily with distribution considered from a normative standpoint; and the *Études d'économie politique appliquée* (1898), containing applications of his theory to monetary policy and the organization of production. Since his death in 1910, his renown as an innovator of modern trends in economic theorizing has never ceased growing.

Further Reading

Walras's major work was translated by William Jaffé as *Elements of Pure Economics* (1954). The principal source of biographical material on Walras is William Jaffé ed., *Correspondence of Léon Walras and Related Papers* (3 vols., 1965). Joseph A. Schumpeter, *History of Economic Analysis* (1954), contains the most readily accessible summary of Walras's theory and is

recommended for historical background. More technical discussions of the Walrasian model are in Don Patinkin, *Money, Interest and Prices: An Integration of Monetary and Value Theory* (1956; 2d ed. 1965); Robert E. Kuenne, *The Theory of General Economic Equilibrium* (1963); and Bent Hansen, *General Equilibrium Systems* (1970).

Additional Sources

Jaffé, William, *William Jaffé's Essays on Walras,* Cambridge Cambridgeshire; New York: Cambridge University Press, 1983.
Léon Walras: critical assessments, London; New York: Routledge, 1993. □

Thomas James Walsh

The U.S. senator Thomas James Walsh (1859-1933) is probably best known for his role in exposing the Teapot Dome oil-lease scandal.

Thomas J. Walsh was born on June 12, 1859, in Two Rivers, Wis., the son of Irish immigrants. After receiving his law degree from the University of Wisconsin in 1884, he practiced law at Redfield, Dakota Territory, for seven years. He then moved to Helena, Mont., and quickly became one of the state's leading lawyers.

A Democrat, he was elected in 1912 to the U.S. Senate and retained that seat until his death. In the Senate, he was sympathetic to labor and social welfare legislation. He led the fight for the confirmation of the nomination of Louis Brandeis to the Supreme Court, assailed the anti-Red raids of Attorney General A. Mitchell Palmer, and opposed Herbert Hoover's appointment of an antilabor judge to the Supreme Court.

On the other hand, Walsh avoided battle locally in Montana with the powerful Anaconda Copper Mining Company. He was also an advocate of the opening of the western public lands to development. A loyal Wilsonian, he supported American membership in the League of Nations and later the World Court.

After the passage of the resolution for an investigation of the leasing of Navy oil-reserve lands, Walsh took charge of the investigation in the fall of 1923 and uncovered evidence that Secretary of the Interior Albert B. Fall had corruptly leased the reserves at Elk Hills, Calif., and Teapot Dome, Wyo., to two oilmen. Though he was criticized by many newspapers and Republicans for his alleged sensationalism and partisanship, Walsh's labors led to the resignation under fire of Secretary of the Navy Edwin L. Denby, who had cooperated with Fall in transferring the reserves to the Interior Department, and to the conviction of Fall for bribery. His work also forced President Calvin Coolidge to appoint two special prosecutors, who voided the leases in the courts.

Although a devout Roman Catholic, Walsh was personally and politically a "dry." He was an unsuccessful dark-horse candidate for the Democratic presidential nomination in 1924 and 1928. He was the overwhelming choice

orn in Kahla (Thuringia), Johann Walter spent his formative years in the chapel of Frederick the Wise, Elector of Saxony. From 1520 until Frederick's death five years later, Walter not only directed the electoral chapel but also began his career as musical spokesman of the Lutherans. Martin Luther wrote a preface to a collection of 43 polyphonic works by Walter, the *Geystliche gesangk Buchleyn* (1524). Planned for young people in Lutheran schools, the collection went through many editions, the last one of which (1551) contained 47 Latin and 74 German pieces. In 1525 Luther consulted Walter about a projected sacred service in German, a service that was published as the *Deudsche Messe* (1526).

Walter became cantor (musical director) of the town choir of Torgau in 1525 and held the post until 1548, when he was named court composer at Dresden to Moritz, Duke of Saxony. Walter remained at the Saxon court only a short time. By 1554 he accepted a pension from the duke and returned to Torgau, where he lived the rest of his life.

Probably during his Dresden residence Walter composed his "dramatic" or "responsorial" Passion in German. In earlier musical versions of the Passion story the entire narrative was a succession of polyphonic motets, but Walter used a monophonic reciting tone for the Evangelist and *dramatis personae*, reserving for the people and disciples simple *falsobordone* (chordal) polyphony.

Walter wrote his motets and lieder, often of high quality, in two distinct styles. For the first style he employed a polyphonic manner derived from the Franco-Flemish school. In the tenor voice of these compositions was a *cantus firmus* sounding as an unbroken succession of sustained notes or as a melody fragmented into short sections separated by rests. Above and below the *cantus firmus* were counterpoints that sometimes imitated the tenor but more often moved independently of it. In either case the melodic flow of four or more voices avoided simultaneous rests.

For the second style Walter rejected imitative or independent voice-leading for chordal writing in which each fragment of the *cantus firmus* rested simultaneously with the other parts. In a few such cases he placed the borrowed tune in the top voice, thereby inaugurating the favorite manner of chorale setting of the succeeding 2 centuries.

Further Reading

A stylistic discussion of Walter's music is offered by Gustave Reese, *Music in the Renaissance* (1954; rev. ed. 1959), and in *The New Oxford History of Music,* vol. 4 (1968). □

---

of the delegates for the 1924 vice-presidential nomination, but his refusal was adamant. In 1933 president-elect Franklin Roosevelt selected Walsh to be attorney general, but Walsh died on March 2, 1933, on the way to Washington for the inaugural.

Further Reading

The only available published biography of Walsh is by a relative, Josephine O'Keane, *Thomas J. Walsh: A Senator from Montana* (1955). Information on Walsh's position in the Versailles Treaty debate appears in Thomas A. Bailey, *Woodrow Wilson and the Great Betrayal* (1945); and on his role in the Teapot Dome revelations, in Burl Noggle, *Teapot Dome: Oil and Politics in the 1920's* (1962). For general background on the period see Francis Russell, *The Shadow of Blooming Grove: Warren G. Harding in His Times* (1968), and Robert K. Murray, *The Harding Era: Warren Harding and His Administration* (1969). □

Johann Walter

As musical adviser to Luther, the German composer Johann Walter (1496-1570) helped construct a new liturgy and composed tunes for many Lutheran hymns. He also pioneered the "dramatic" musical setting of the Passion in German.

Barbara Walters

Drawing the highest pay in the history of television broadcasting at the time, Barbara Walters (born 1931) became the first woman co-anchor of a network evening newscast. She developed to a high art the interviewing of public figures.

Barbara Walters was born to Dena (Selett) and Lou Walters. Her father operated a number of nightclubs, resulting in Barbara attending schools in Boston, New York, and Miami Beach. She earned a B.A. degree in English from Sarah Lawrence College (1954). After working briefly as a secretary she landed a job with NBC's (the National Broadcasting Company's) New York affiliate WRCA-TV where she quickly rose to producer and writer. She also held various writing and public relations jobs, including a stint as women's-program producer at WPIX-TV in New York.

Her abilities and experience in research, writing, filming, and editing earned her a job as news and public affairs producer for CBS (Columbia Broadcasting System) television. There she wrote materials for noted personalities who appeared on the CBS morning show that competed with NBC's *Today* program. She left CBS because she believed further advancement was unlikely.

In 1961 she was hired by NBC as a writer with an occasional on-the-air feature for the *Today* show. Within three years Walters became an on-camera interviewer and persuaded such notables as Mamie Eisenhower, Anwar Sadat, and H. R. Haldeman to appear with her.

Meanwhile, a number of different "show-business" women held the post as the "*Today* girl," but none held news credentials. Mainly they engaged in small talk and read commercials. Some at NBC began to think a different kind of woman might help the show. When the spot was unexpectedly vacated, Walters was given the "*Today* girl"

slot on a trial basis. The public readily accepted this bright, on-the-air newswoman, who also continued to write and produce much of her own material. A few months later Hugh Downs said Walters was the best thing that had happened to the *Today* show during his time as host. They would later be teamed on ABC's program *20/20* as competition to CBS's *Sixty Minutes*.

Today feature stories by Walters included socially significant topics, and frequently she got on-the-spot experience which gave her reports even more credibility. As her reputation grew, NBC made her a radio commentator on *Emphasis* and *Monitor*. She also participated in such NBC specials as "The Pill" and "The Sexual Revolution" (1967), and in 1969 she covered the investiture of Prince Charles as the Prince of Wales.

Finally in 1974 Walters was named co-host of the *Today* show. By then, her status as a broadcaster had risen to such heights that she had twice been named to *Harper's Bazaar's* list of "100 Women of Accomplishment" (1967 and 1971), *Ladies Home Journal's* "75 Most Important Women" (1970), and *TIME's* "200 Leaders of the Future" (1974). As the most influential woman on television, others soon vied for her talents.

In 1976 she accepted a million-dollar-a-year contract for five years to move to ABC, where she became television's first network anchor-woman, the most prestigious job in television journalism. She also anchored and produced four prime-time specials and sometimes hosted or appeared on the network's other news and documentary programs. Her contract stirred professional criticism and jealousy. It not only doubled her income from NBC and her syndicated show, *Not For Women Only,* but it also made her the highest-paid newscaster in history at that time. (Walter Cronkite, John Chancellor, and Harry Reasoner then received about $400,000.) Reasoner, with whom she was to co-anchor, seemed especially miffed at first but later was mollified.

Executives of other networks fumed that their established anchors might demand salary increases, questioned what they perceived as a "show-biz" tint to the sober task of news reporting, and questioned whether the public would accept a woman news-anchor. (ABC's private polls before they made their record offer indicated only 13 percent preferred a male anchor, and they knew her presence could easily increase advertising revenues far exceeding her salary.)

Despite Walters' tart, probing interviewing techniques, she seldom seemed to alienate the person she was interviewing. She revealed some of the secrets of her success in her book *How to Talk With Practically Anybody About Practically Anything* (1970). Others attributed her interviewing success to her uncanny ability to ask primarily those questions which the public would want answered.

Still, Walters was not without her critics. Some interview-subjects said her nervousness distracted them. Others claimed she was so eager that disastrous mistakes occurred, citing the instance when she grabbed another network's microphone as she dashed to get a unique interview. Washington press corps members charged that she acted more as a "star" than as a reporter on presidential trips. However, her professional admirers outnumbered her detractors. Walter Cronkite noted her special interviewing talents. Sally Quinn, former rival on *CBS Morning News,* commented how "nice" Walters was to her.

Walters' personal life held considerable interest to the public. Her brief marriage to businessman Bob Katz was annulled; her 13-year marriage to Lee Guber, a theatrical producer, ended in divorce. Still they remained congenial, sharing mutual love for their daughter, Jacqueline Dena. In 1985 she married Merv Adelson, who had also previously been wed twice.

Walters' elevation to top-paid broadcaster was credited with raising the status of other women journalists. Her own prowess as a broadcaster exploring socially-important issues and as top-notch interviewer were undeniable. In addition, she excelled at bringing to the television public reluctant interview-subjects that ranged from show business personalities to heads of state.

Walters has had a reputation for often being the first to interview world leaders. During the 1996 presidential campaign she interviewed the first African American Chair of the Joint Chiefs of Staff, General Colin Powell, after his retirement. She has also had exclusive interviews with both Christopher Dardin and Robert Shapiro of the O.J. Simpson murder trial, noted by the media as one of the most controversial murder trials of the twentieth century. Walters also had exclusive interviews with billionaire David Geffen and with Christopher Reeves following the horseback riding fall that left him paralyzed.

In 1996 Walters celebrated 20 years with ABC. At the time, she was earning $10 million per year.

Further Reading

Biographical data for Barbara Walters is primarily found in her book *How to Talk With Practically Anybody About Practically Anything* (1970). In addition to the periodicals cited in the biography see *Newsweek* (May 19, 1969); *Reader's Digest* (May 1974); *Vogue* (June 1975); *Newsweek* (May 3, 1976); *Time* (May 3, 1976); and *Ladies Home Journal* (July 1983; June 1984). □

Ernest Walton

Physicist Ernest Walton (1903-1995) shared the achievement of the first artificial disintegration of an atomic nucleus without the use of radioactive elements. For this work, Walton and John D. Cockroft shared the 1951 Nobel Prize in physics.

Ernest Walton was an Irish experimental physicist who gained renown for achieving, with physicist John D. Cockcroft, the first artificial disintegration of an atomic nucleus, without the use of radioactive elements. Their breakthrough was accomplished by artificially accelerating a beam of protons (basic particles of the nuclei of atoms that carry a positive charge of electricity) and aiming it at a target of lithium, one of the lightest known metals. The resultant emission of alpha particles, that is, positively charged particles given off by certain radioactive substances, indicated not only that some protons had succeeded in penetrating the nuclei of the lithium atoms but also that they had somehow combined with the lithium atoms and had been transformed into something new. Although the process was not an efficient energy producer, the work of Walton and Cockcroft stimulated many theoretical and practical developments and influenced the whole course of nuclear physics. For their pioneering work, Walton and Cockcroft shared the 1951 Nobel Prize in Physics.

Ernest Thomas Sinton Walton was born October 6, 1903, in Dungarven, County Waterford, in the Irish Republic. His father, John Arthur Walton, was a Methodist minister, while his mother, Anna Elizabeth (Sinton) Walton, was from a very old Ulster family, who had lived in the same house in Armagh for over two hundred years. The young Walton was sent to school at Belfast's Methodist College, where he demonstrated an aptitude for science and math. It was no surprise, then, that he decided to enroll in math and experimental science at Dublin's Trinity College in 1922. He graduated in 1926 with a B.A. degree, in 1928 with a M.Sc., and in 1934 with a M.A.

The following year he headed to Cambridge University, England, on a Clerk Maxwell research scholarship. There, he joined the world-famous Cavendish Laboratory, headed by the great New Zealand-born physicist Ernest

Rutherford. Walton was assigned cramped laboratory space in a basement room. While his quarters were less than luxurious, he was at least blessed by having roommates with whom he struck up an immediate friendship, physicists T. E. Allibone and John D. Cockcroft. Walton would go on to make scientific history, in collaboration with the latter, for a project that would pave the way for the development of the atom bomb. At the suggestion of Rutherford, Walton began attempting to increase the velocity of electrons (the negatively charged particles of the atom) by spinning them in the electric field produced by a changing circular magnetic field as a method of nuclear disintegration. Although the method was not successful, he was able to figure out the stability of the orbits of the revolving electrons, and the design and engineering problems of creating an accelerating machine with minimal tools and materials. This early work of Walton's later led to the development of the betatron, that is, a particle accelerator in which electrons are propelled by the inductive action of a rapidly varying magnetic field.

Next, Walton tried to build a high frequency linear accelerator. His goal was to produce a stream of alpha particles traveling at high speed which could be used to shed light on various aspects of the atomic nucleus. Rutherford had long been keen to get his hands on such a source of alpha particles but despaired of any short-term breakthrough. As Walton's work progressed, Rutherford's wish was granted sooner than he expected.

What was needed was a fundamentally different way of viewing the problem. Walton and his colleagues at the Cavendish were trying to accelerate electrons to a speed sufficient to enable them to penetrate an atomic nucleus. Such high velocities were necessary, they believed, in order to counteract the repulsive charge of the nuclei. The speeding electrons, they figured, would literally bully their way through. However, achieving such high speeds was easier said than done. It required the application of enormous amounts of electricity, about four million volts, which at that time was impossible to generate in a discharge tube (a tube that contains a gas or metal vapor which conducts an electric discharge in the form of light). A crucial breakthrough came in 1929, when the Russian physicist George Gamow visited the Cavendish laboratory. With physicist Niels Bohr in Copenhagen, he had worked out a wave-mechanical theory of the penetration of particles, in which they believed particles tunneled through rather than over potential barriers. This meant that particles propelled by about 500,000 volts, as opposed to millions, could possibly permeate the barrier and enter the nucleus if present in sufficiently large numbers. That is, one would need a beam of many thousands of millions of moving particles to produce atomic disintegrations that would be capable of being observed.

Rutherford gave Walton and Cockcroft the go-ahead to test the supposition. It was a measure of his confidence in them—the high voltage apparatus they constructed to enable them to accelerate atomic particles cost almost £1,000 (British pounds) to build. It was an enormous sum in those

days, and represented almost the entire annual budget for the laboratory.

The machine, the first of its kind ever built, and today on view at the London Science Museum in South Kensington, was built out of an ordinary transformer, enhanced by two stacks of large condensers (or what would today be called capacitors), which could be turned on and off by means of an electronic switch. This arrangement generated up to half a million volts, which were directed at an electrical discharge tube. At the top of the tube protons were produced. The velocity of the protons was increased into a beam which could be used to hit any mark at the bottom of the tubes. Although it would be considered primitive by today's standards, their apparatus was, in fact, an ingenious construction, cobbled together from glass cylinders taken from old fashioned petrol pumps, flat metal sheets, plasticene, and vacuum pumps. The current generated by the discharge tube was almost one hundred-thousandth of an ampere, which meant that about 50 million protons per second were being produced. The availability of such a large and tightly controlled source of particles—compared with that produced by, say, a radioactive source—greatly increased the odds of a nucleus being penetrated by the speeding atomic particles.

Halfway through 1931, while their experiment was still in its early stages, Walton and Cockcroft were forced to vacate their subterranean basement when it was taken over by physical chemists. They were obliged to deconstruct their installation and build it again. As it happened, it turned out to be a lucky break. Their new laboratory was an old lecture theater, whose high ceiling was much more suitable for their purposes. When Walton and Cockcroft went to reassemble their massive apparatus, they used the opportunity to introduce a few modifications. This time around, they incorporated a new voltage multiplying circuit, which Cockcroft had just developed, into their apparatus. It took them until the end of 1931 just to produce a steady stream of five or six hundred volts.

When the accelerator was finally completed, they restarted the laborious process of trying to penetrate an atomic nucleus using a stream of speeded up protons. They positioned a thin lithium target obliquely across from the beam of protons in order to observe the alpha particles on either side of it. In order to detect the alpha particles that they hoped would be produced, they set up a tiny screen made of zinc sulfide, which they observed with a low-power microscope, a technique borrowed from Rutherford.

The first few months of 1932 were spent in rendering the installation more reliable and measuring the range and speed of the accelerated protons. It was not until April 13, 1932, that they achieved a breakthrough. On that fateful date, Walton first realized that their experiment had been successful. On the tiny screen, he detected flashes, called scintillations. These indicated that not only had the steam of protons succeeded in boring through the atomic nuclei but also that, in the process, a transformation had occurred. The speeding protons had combined with the lithium target to produce a new substance, the alpha particles, which appeared on the screen as scintillations.

Walton and Cockcroft confirmed these observations using a paper recorder with two pens, each operated by a key. Walton worked one key, Cockcroft the other. When either noticed a flash, he pressed his key. As both keys were consistently pressed at the same time, it was clear that the alphas were being emitted in pairs. The implication was that the lithium nucleus, with a mass of seven and a charge of three had, on contact with an accelerated proton, split into two alpha particles, each of mass four and charge two. In the transformation, a small amount of energy was lost, equivalent to about a quarter of a percent of the mass of lithium.

Walton and Cockcroft's achievement was groundbreaking and historic in many ways. It represented the first time that anyone had produced a change in an atomic nucleus by means totally under human control. They had also discovered a new energy source. Furthermore, they had confirmed George Gamow's theory that particles could tunnel or burrow their way into a nucleus, despite the repulsion of the electrical charges. And finally, they furnished a valuable confirmation of physicist Albert Einstein's theory that energy and mass are interchangeable. The extra energy of the alpha particles, when allowance was made for the energy of the proton, exactly corresponded to the loss of mass.

Walton and Cockcroft's achievement was announced in a letter in *Nature* and later at a meeting of the Royal Society of London on June 15, 1932. By that time, they had succeeded in splitting the nuclei of 15 elements, including beryllium, the lightest, to uranium, the heaviest. All produced alpha particles, although the most spectacular results were obtained from fluorine, lithium, and boron. The news caused a sensation throughout the world. As a result of their discovery, Walton and Cockcroft were the star attractions at the Solvay Conference, an important gathering of international physicists, held in 1933, and at the International Physics Conference, held in London in 1934.

Walton and Cockcroft's particle accelerator spawned many more sophisticated models, including one built by their colleague physicist Marcus Oliphant at the Cavendish. It was capable of producing a more abundant supply of particles; not only protons, but also deuterons (nuclei of heavy hydrogen). With this, many groundbreaking nuclear transformations were carried out. Their invention also inspired the American nuclear physicist Ernest Orlando Lawrence to build a cyclotron, a cyclical accelerator, capable of reaching tremendous speeds. Although scientists in the close of the twentieth century may regard the equipment Walton and Cockcroft used as primitive, the basic idea behind the particle accelerator has stayed the same.

In 1932, Walton received his Ph.D from Cambridge and two years later returned to Dublin as a fellow of Trinity College, his reputation preceding him. That same year he married Winifreda Wilson, a former pupil of the Methodist College, Belfast. They had two sons and two daughters, Alan, Marian, Philip, and Jean.

The next few years passed rather uneventfully for Walton. While his erstwhile partner, John D. Cockcroft went from one high profile position to another, Walton preferred to remain slightly aloof from the mainstream of physics. He concentrated instead on establishing his department's reputation for excellence. His efforts were rewarded in 1946 when he was appointed Erasmus Smith Professor of Natural and Experimental Philosophy.

In 1951, almost twenty years after achieving the breakthrough that changed the face of nuclear physics, Walton and Cockcroft finally achieved the recognition that many believed was long overdue. The Nobel Prize for Physics was awarded to them jointly for their pioneering work on the transmutation of atomic nuclei by artificially accelerated atomic particles. The following year, Walton became chairman of the School of Cosmic Physics of the Dublin Institute for Advanced Studies. He was elected a senior fellow of Trinity College in 1960.

Outside of his scientific work, Ernest Walton was active in committees concerned with the government, the church, research and standards, scientific academies, and the Royal City of Dublin Hospital. He died on June 25, 1995, at the age of 91.

Further Reading

Andrade, E.N. da C, *Rutherford and the Nature of the Atom,* Doubleday Anchor, 1964.
Biographical Dictionary of Scientists, Volume 2, Facts-on-File, 1981, pp. 823.
Crowther, J. G., *The Cavendish Laboratory, 1874–1974,* Science History Publications, 1974.
Modern Men of Science, McGraw-Hill, 1966, pp. 509.
Oliphant, Mark, *Rutherford: Recollections of the Cambridge Days,* Elsevier Publishing Co., 1972.
Weber, Robert L., *Pioneers of Science: Nobel Prize Winners in Physics,* Bristol and London, The Institute of Physics, 1980, pp. 141.
Wilson, David, *Rutherford: Simple Genius,* MIT Press, 1983.
Dicke, William, "Ernest T. S. Walton, 91, Irish Physicist Dies," in *The New York Times,* June 28, 1995, p.B8. ☐

Izaak Walton

The English writer and biographer Izaak Walton (1593-1683) was the author of *The Compleat Angler.* His works show him to have been a kindly and religious man with a quiet sense of humor and rare common sense.

Izaak Walton was born at Stafford on Aug. 9, 1593. Little is known of his childhood and early youth. By 1624 he was established in London as a cloth merchant after a period of apprenticeship, perhaps to his uncle, a haberdasher. Walton's shop was located in St. Dunstan's parish, and he became acquainted with John Donne, who was then vicar. In 1626 Walton married Rachel Floud, a great-grandniece of Archbishop Thomas Cranmer. She died in 1640.

That same year Walton's first literary work, a life of Donne, was published. Donne had died in 1631, and a mutual friend, Sir Henry Wotton, had asked Walton to collect material for a life he was writing to preface an edition of Donne's sermons. Wotton died before writing the life, and Walton took on the task.

Walton continued in his business until 1644, when the civil war turned to the favor of the Puritans. He seems to have retired from business shortly before the battle of Marston Moor. In 1646 he married Anne Ken, half sister to Bishop Thomas Ken. In 1651 Walton published a life of Sir Henry Wotton as a preface to *Reliquiae Wottonianae*.

In 1653 Walton published his most famous book, *The Compleat Angler; or, The Contemplative Man's Recreation*. Ostensibly a book on fishing, the volume mingles philosophy and politics with directions for hooking a worm or catching a trout. It is filled with apt quotations, songs, poems, and anecdotes and gives one a full sense of Walton's personality—his gentle disposition, his cheerful piety, and his Anglican politics. The book was so popular with his contemporaries that it was expanded considerably and underwent five editions during Walton's lifetime.

Very little is known of the way in which Walton spent the last 30 years of his life. His second wife died in 1662. After this time he seems to have made his home at Farnham Castle with Bishop George Morley. In 1665 Walton published his life of the great Anglican bishop of Elizabethan times, Thomas Hooker. Five years later Walton published his life of the Anglican poet and clergyman George Herbert. In 1670 Walton's four lives were collected and revised. In 1678, at the age of 85, he published his last biography, a life

of Bishop Robert Sanderson. Walton died at Winchester on Dec. 15, 1683.

Further Reading

The standard biography is that of Sir Harris Nicolas, prefixed to an edition of Walton's *The Compleat Angler* (1836). More recent full-length studies are Stapleton Martin, *Isaak Walton and His Friends* (1904), and Edward Marston, *Thomas Ken and Izaak Walton* (1908). An interesting study of Walton as a biographer is David Novarr, *The Making of Walton's Lives* (1958).

Additional Sources

Haim, José, *Twenty ballads stuck about the wall: a dramatic biography of Izaak Walton*, Pittsburgh, Pa.: Dorrance Pub., 1993. □

Sam Moore Walton

Businessman Sam Moore Walton (born 1918) built Wal-Mart into one of the nation's largest retailers and became one of the richest Americans.

Sam Moore Walton was born in Kingfisher, Oklahoma, March 29, 1918. The older of two boys, his father was a banker. A product of the Great Depression of the 1930s, he graduated from the University of Missouri in 1940. He married Helen Robson after graduation and eventually had four children. He served three years as an Army intelligence officer during World War II.

Walton had started in retailing with the J. C. Penney Company in Des Moines, Iowa, as an $85-a-month trainee. He spent the period 1938-1942 with them. After his army service, in 1945 Walton used his savings plus a $25,000 loan to buy a Ben Franklin store in Newport, Arkansas, where his brother joined him. In 1950, when his landlord failed to renew his lease, Walton moved to Bentonville, Arkansas, now a town of about 10,000 and headquarters to the Wal-Mart empire.

From 1945 through 1962 he operated Ben Franklin stores; by 1962 he had nine stores—Walton's 5 & 10—operated under a franchising agreement with the Chicago-based Ben Franklin. Then began what became one of America's most successful retail operations—Wal-Mart, which he co-founded in 1962.

At that time Walton decided that the future of retailing was in discount stores, not dime stores. He studied chains such as K Mart and Zayre and then proposed to the Ben Franklin management the starting of a discount store. When they showed no interest, he, along with his younger brother James, opened his first Wal-Mart outlet in Rogers, Arkansas, five miles from Bentonville.

Walton avoided publicity about himself, preferring that his stores occupy the spotlight, and he took a direct role in the administration of those stores at all levels. He was, indeed, perhaps a corporate evangelist, and in his articula-

chain of warehouse stores—Sam's Wholesale Club—and was moving into the hypermarket area, Wal-Mart Supercenters. In 1990 there were more than 1,000 stores and more than 150,000 employees.

Walton was the epitome of modern retailing, adapting to contemporary demographic trends. He built his empire not in the large urban areas of the North, East, and West—the politically and economically dominant regions of the first two-thirds of the 20th century—but in the South and Midwest (the former once depressed and neglected, the latter the "heartland" of the nation). His strategy was not to take on the large chains and department stores of the urban centers, but rather to compete with the local chains and individual merchants of smaller urban areas and their rural surroundings. When his stores did approach larger population centers, they went first to the periphery of the urban area. That strategy changed in the 1980s with the extension of stores to the other geographic areas of the nation—in order to build a truly national chain—and the movement in toward the center of the urban areas.

Sam Walton died on April 5, 1992 at 74 years of age. He left behind a fortune that amounted to over $23 billion in Wal-Mart stock alone. Before his death, Walton penned a book in 1992 entitled *Sam Walton, Made in America*. By 1997, five years after Walton's death, Wal-Mart had grown to over 2,300 stores with annual revenues of $104.8 billion per year.

Further Reading

The major biography of Sam Walton is Vance H. Trimble, *Sam Walton: The Inside Story of America's Richest Man* (1990), which discusses his rise and wealth and also describes the common man who continued to live in a small Arkansas town and drives an inexpensive car. Other sources are Art Harris, "The Richest Man in America" in *Reader's Digest* (May 1986); Howard Rudnitsky, "Play It Again, Sam" in *Forbes* (August 10, 1987); and Michael Barrier, "Walton's Mountain" in *Nation's Business* (April 1988). Information on both Sam Walton and Wal-Mart can be found on the World Wide Web at http://www.wal-mart.com. □

tion of a vision for his firm is a good example of the conscious creation of a corporate culture—a set of shared values which define a business and those who work in it. Preferring to be called "Sam," or "Mr. Sam" at most, he might appear at a Wal-Mart checkout, or loading dock, or at a rally at a new store opening.

His business has been described as an extremely well managed one. Although the stores tended to operate as relatively inexpensive, no-frills units and appeal to a lower-middle-class market, the company was quite willing to invest at the cutting edge of technology. The stores were clustered around warehouses in order to permit one-day delivery of goods, and advertising costs were minimized. An early innovation was the decision to buy directly from manufacturers rather than through wholesalers. In addition, the company was firmly committed to a "Buy American" program. Walton built his firm into the fastest growing and most influential force in the retail industry, with stores averaging an annual growth rate of more than 35 percent for more than a decade—a rate more than three times that of the retail industry in general. An investor who spent $1,650 for 100 shares of stock in 1970, when the firm went public, would have had $700,000 worth of stock at 1987 prices. In the process, Walton became one of the richest men in the world, with estimates of his worth varying widely and growing constantly.

This early and phenomenal growth—Wal-Mart stood behind only Sears and K Mart in the retail field and was challenging them—was achieved as essentially a regional chain, operating in the Sunbelt. In later years it created a

Sir William Turner Walton

Sir William Turner Walton (1902-1983) was one of the principal composers among the enlightened conservatives of 20th-century England.

William Walton received his first music lessons from his father, who was a singing teacher. At the age of 10 William was enrolled in the Cathedral Choir School at Oxford; at 16 he entered the university, where it appears that he received little systematic training in music. From an early age, however, he was composing, and this self-tutelage must have been effective, for at 20 he wrote a String Quartet that was accepted for performance at a Festival of the International Society for Contemporary Music. In the same year (1922) he collaborated with the poet Edith Sitwell on *Facade,* a clever "entertainment" for speaking voice and six instrumental players, which epitomizes certain aspects of the smart set in the era after World War I.

During the next decade Walton's reputation was solidly established with a lively overture about ships and sailors entitled *Portsmouth Point* (1925); a *Sinfonia concertante* for orchestra and piano (1927); a Concerto for viola (1929), which is one of the few important solo works for that instrument; and *Belshazzar's Feast* (1931), a vivid and very popular addition to the long line of English oratorios. From then on he continued to compose steadily in an unhurried fashion and usually on commission or with distinguished sponsorship which ensured performance. Although his catalog after *Belshazzar* was not long, the items are substantial. In addition to a few songs, marches and incidental and film music, there are the large works, including two Symphonies (1935, 1960), a Concerto for violin (1939), a ballet entitled *The Quest* (1943), a second String Quartet (1947), a Sonata for violin and piano (1949), the opera *Troilus and Cressida* (1954), a Concerto for cello (1956), a *Partita* for orchestra (1958), the orchestral *Variations on a Theme by Hindemith* (1963), a *Missa brevis* (1966), the one-act extravaganza *The Bear* (1967) and *Capriccio burlesco* for orchestra (1969).

Walton composed slowly and meticulously. Paul Hindemith complimented him on the "honest solidity of workmanship" in his scores; yet they do not give a labored effect, for a rhythmic vigor permeates everything Walton wrote. His style is also marked by a harmonic idiom that is tonal though modernized and a preference for melodic lines of considerable amplitude as against the highly condensed mode of the post-Anton Webern school. In *Troilus,* for example, Walton said that he wanted to write a *bel canto,* or "singing" opera, which in his case is more a statement of artistic independence than merely a look backward.

Walton's music shows that he knew what other composers were doing in the 20th century and profited from observation of such diverse men as Hindemith, Igor Stravinsky, Arnold Schoenberg, and Jean Sibelius. Nevertheless, Walton did not subscribe to any cult or try to be especially English in his work.

Knighted in 1951, he died March 8, 1983, at his home on Ischia, an island off the coast of Italy.

Further Reading

Walton's general position in the modern music world is sketched in Joseph Machlis, *Introduction to Contemporary Music* (1961), and his place among English composers is described in Frank Howes, *The English Musical Renaissance* (1966). For a detailed analysis of his music see Frank Howes, *The Music of William Walton* (1965). □

An Wang

An Wang (1920-1990) made important inventions relating to computer memories and to electronic calculators. He was the founder and longtime executive officer of Wang Laboratories Incorporated, a leading American manufacturer of computers and word processing systems.

An Wang was born February 7, 1920, in Shanghai, China. He became interested in radio as a high school student, built his own radio, and went on to study communications engineering at Chiao-Tung University in his native city. After graduation he stayed on at the university another year as a teaching assistant. With the outbreak of World War II Wang moved to inland China, where he spent the war designing radio receivers and transmitters for the Chinese to use in their fight against Japan.

Wang left China in the spring of 1945, receiving a government stipend to continue his education at Harvard University in Massachusetts. He completed his master's degree in communications engineering in one year. After graduation, he worked for an American company for some months and then for a Canadian office of the Chinese government. In 1947, he returned to Harvard and rapidly completed a doctorate in engineering and applied physics. Wang married in 1949, and he and his wife had three children. Six years later Wang became an American citizen.

In the spring of 1948 Howard Aiken hired Wang to work at the Harvard Computation Laboratory. This institution had built the ASSC Mark I, one of the world's first digital computers, a few years earlier. It was developing more advanced machines under a contract from the U.S. Air Force. Aiken asked Wang to devise a way to store and

retrieve data in a computer using magnetic media. Wang studied the magnetic properties of small doughnut-shaped rings of ferromagnetic material. He suggested that if the residual magnetic flux of the ring was in one direction, the ring might represent the binary digit 1. Flux in the opposite direction could represent 0. One could then read the information stored in a ring by passing a current around it. Researchers at the nearby Massachusetts Institute of Technology and elsewhere were intrigued by the idea of magnetic core storage of information and greatly refined it for use in various computers. Wang published an account of his results in a 1950 article coauthored by W.D. Woo, another Shanghai native who worked at Harvard. He also patented his invention and, despite a protracted court fight, earned substantial royalties from International Business Machines and other computer manufacturers who used magnetic core memories. These cores were a fundamental part of computers into the 1970s.

Wang was not content to have others develop and sell his inventions. In 1951 he left the Computation Laboratory and used his life savings to start his own electronics company. He first sold custom-built magnetic shift registers for storing and combining electronic signals. His company also sold machines for magnetic tape control and numerical control. In the mid-1960s Wang invented a digital logarithmic converter that made it possible to perform routine arithmetic electronically at high speeds and relatively low cost. Wang desktop calculators were soon available commercially, replacing traditional machines with mechanical parts. Several calculators operated on one processing unit.

These early electronic calculators sold for over $1,000 per keyboard. They were used in schools, scientific laboratories, and engineering firms. By 1969, Wang Laboratories had begun to produce less expensive calculators for wider business use. However, Wang saw that the introduction of integrated circuits would allow competitors to sell electronic handheld calculators at a much lower price than the machines his company offered.

Confronted with the need to find a new product, Wang directed his firm toward the manufacture of word processors and small business computers. The first Wang word processing systems sold in 1976. They were designed for easy access by those unfamiliar with computers, for broad data base management, and for routine business calculations. In addition to such computer networks, the company developed personal computers for office use.

Wang began his business in a room above an electrical fixtures store in Boston with himself as the only employee. By the mid-1980s the company had expanded to over 15,000 employees working in several buildings in the old manufacturing town of Lowell, Massachusetts, and in factories and offices throughout the world. To acquire money to finance this expansion and to reward competent employees, Wang Laboratories sold stock and acquired a considerable debt. The Wang family retained control of the firm by limiting administrative power to a special class of shareholders. In the early 1980s when company growth slowed while debt remained large, Wang made some effort to reduce his personal control of the business and follow more conventional corporate management practices. While remaining a company officer and leading stockholder, he gave increased responsibilities to his son Frederick and to other managers. Wang intended to devote even more time to educational activities. He served as an adviser to several colleges and as a member of the Board of Regents of the University of Massachusetts. Wang also took a particular interest in the Wang Institute of Graduate Studies which he founded in 1979. This fully accredited school gives advanced degrees in software engineering. Difficult times in the computer industry soon led Wang to turn his concentration from these projects and resume full-time direction of Wang Laboratories.

In the last decades of the twentieth century, Wang's economic structure teetered. In 1982 the organization generated more than a billion dollars a year, and by 1989 sales were $3 billion a year. But Wang Laboratories fell on hard times as well. In the early 1990s the former minicomputer maker fell into Chapter 11 bankruptcy and Wang died of cancer in March of 1990 at the age of 70.

On Jan. 30, 1997, the Eastman Kodak Company bought the Wang Software business unit for $260 million in cash. The deal put Kodak into the document imaging and workflow business and took Wang out of software. Wang also began an affiliation with Microsoft, and Michael Brown, chief financial officer for Microsoft, sat on Wang's board of directors. The reorganization enabled the company to prosper once again.

Wang's engineering acumen and business success resulted in him being made a fellow of the Institute of Electrical and Electronic Engineers and a fellow of the American Academy of Arts and Sciences. He received an honorary doctoral degree from the Lowell Technological Institute.

Further Reading

Wang, with Eugene Linden, published *Lessons: An Autobiography* in 1986. For brief accounts of his career see "The Guru of Gizmos," *TIME* (November 17, 1980) and "Wang Labs' run for a second billion: One-man rule will fade into professional management," *Business Week* (May 17, 1982). On the history of magnetic core memories see E. W. Pugh, *Memories that Shaped an Industry* (1984). On electronic calculators see H. Edward Roberts, *Electronic Calculators,* edited by Forrest M. Mimms III (1974). Wang is also included in *Historical Dictionary of Data Processing: Biographies,* by James Cortada (1987). The *Wall Street Journal* covered the fall and resurgence of Wang Laboratories in two articles, *Steep Slide: Filing in Chapter 11, Wang Sends Warning to High-Tech Circles* (Aug. 1992), and *Wang Labs Reorganization is Cleared, Allowing Emergence from Chapter 11* (Sept. 1993). □

Wang An-shih

Wang An-shih (1021-1086) was the most famous reformer in Chinese history, a poet, and a scholar. He developed a program of far-reaching reforms which was vigorously attacked in his own day and has been controversial ever since.

The 11th century in China was a period of rare intellectual brilliance, the most creative phase of the Confucian revival, which imparted new force and vitality to old values and produced lasting achievements in philosophy, history, and literature. Yet, China was troubled by the military threat of the Khitans and Tanguts in the North and Northwest, economic problems associated with the growth of population and increasing economic complexity, acute fiscal problems, an expensive and ineffective military establishment, and a bureaucracy which was far removed from the ideal of competent, devoted, and disinterested service. Concerned scholars widely supported the reform attempts undertaken by Fan Chung-yen in the 1040s, but the more extensive program of Wang An-shih in the 1070s in the end antagonized most of his illustrious contemporaries.

Wang An-shih was born on Dec. 18, 1021, in Ch'ing-chiang prefecture, Kiangsi, where his father, Wang I, was serving as an official. Originally from Shansi, the family had for several generations made its home in Lin-ch'uan, Fuchou prefecture, Kiangsi, where An-shih's great-grandfather prospered in farming. The family began producing officials when An-shih's granduncle Wang Kuan-chih succeeded in passing the highest civil service examination his *chin-shih* degree. Wang I received his *chin-shih* in 1015, and four members of Anshih's own generation were similarly successful. Wang I's family was a large one: An-shih was the third of seven sons, and there were also three younger sisters. During his youth Wang An-shih accompanied his

family as his father moved from post to post and devoted himself to his books. He continued his studies after his father's death in 1038 and obtained his *chin-shih* 4 years later, placing fourth out of 435 successful candidates.

Early Career

From 1042 to 1060 Wang An-shih served mostly in local posts, although he was in the capital in 1046 and again in 1054-1056, when he held positions in the bureau charged with the maintenance and rearing of horses; he then spent a very brief period in a post in the capital prefecture. When feasible, Wang turned down opportunities for serving in the capital during these years, preferring provincial appointments, partly for financial reasons, since the death of his elder brother left him, in the early 1050s, responsible for the family.

Wang's service as a local administrator began in Yangchou, Kiangsu (1042-1045), and included posts in Chenhsien, Chekiang (1047-1049), Suchou in Anhwei (1051-1054), another term in Kiangsu, this time in Ch'ang-chou (1057-1058), and an appointment as judicial intendant for Chiang-tung (1058-ca. 1060), an area including portions of modern Anhwei, Kiangsu, and Chekiang. His duties gave him insight into local economic and political conditions and allowed him to gain practical administrative experience, particularly in economic matters, including irrigation and finance. His literary ability and reputation for forthrightness won him important friends, including Ou-yang Hsiu, who admired Wang's writings as early as 1044, recommended him for an important appointment even before meeting him in 1056, and did not allow later political disagreements to destroy their friendship.

This period saw Wang's marriage to a lady who, like his mother, belonged to the Wu family, and at least two of his five children were born during these years. Although he developed some close friendships, there are indications that he was not a sociable man but preferred the company of his books to the niceties of social life. The allegations that he did not wash his clothes and was careless in personal appearance and hygiene may have originated in this period, but there is no way of separating truth and fiction in dealing with various anecdotes. In any case, the image that has been passed down of his mature character is one of integrity, persistence carried to the point of stubbornness, lofty ambition, and personal eccentricity.

Ten Thousand Word Memorial

Even while serving in the provinces, Wang An-shih was deeply concerned over problems affecting the whole empire; it was as a provincial official that he submitted to Emperor Jen-tsung in 1058 his famous *Ten Thousand Word Memorial,* in which he urged the Emperor to return to the principles of the sage rulers of antiquity, and in which he concentrated on personnel policy, including especially the training of men for civil office and military command, the support and control of officials, and the selection and appointment of men to office. His advocacy of specialization and his insistence that the Emperor must be firm and vigorous in enforcing regulations demonstrated Wang's tough-mindedness and foreshadowed his later reforms.

From 1060 to 1064 Wang served in a number of positions in the capital: a very short term in the Finance Commission was followed by service in the Chi-hsien Library as well as an appointment as special drafting official, which ran concurrently with the other assignments from 1061 to 1063. During these years Wang was involved in several controversies, but his political activities were interrupted by the death of his mother in 1063 and the two years of prescribed mourning.

After the accession of Emperor Shen-tsung in 1067 and a brief stint as governor of Nanking, Wang was appointed Hanlin academician and called to the capital in 1068. The following year he became a second privy councilor and initiated his reform policies.

Wang in Power: The Reforms

Wang became chief councilor in 1070 and held this position until 1074, when Cheng Hsia's dramatic portrayal of famine conditions in the Northwest and discontent in the capital caused the Emperor to waver in his support for Wang, who resigned and became governor of Nanking. During these years he initiated major irrigation projects near the capital and scored military successes in the Northwest and Southwest, but of greatest importance were his reforms. When he resigned, the reform policy was continued by his associates, and Wang himself returned as chief councilor in 1075. He remained in office until his permanent retirement in 1076, but during this second term in power his position was weaker than before. His last year in office also saw a victory in the South against an Annamese invasion.

Wang was greatly interested in finance and economics; one of his first acts, in 1069, was the creation of a finance planning commission to investigate and recommend changes in fiscal matters and to administrate many of the subsequent innovations. Another measure initiated in the same year was to reform the system under which certain provinces were responsible for contributing and shipping to the capital particular commodities under a schedule of fixed quotas. This inflexible arrangement had become out of date and proved burdensome to the provinces and the central government alike, benefiting only a group of wealthy merchants who took advantage of the shortage of some items and a surplus of others. The new plan called for the collection of these goods in the area close to the capital when possible and a general rationalization of the procurement of these products. An active government role in the economy was also called for in the state trade system of 1072, under which the government purchased goods directly from small merchants and extended loans, thus again depriving wealthy guild merchants of a lucrative source of profit.

Similarly concerned with trade was the guild exemption tax of 1073, substituting cash payments for the hitherto customary deliveries of supplies to the palace. This illustrates Wang's positive acceptance of the increased use of money and contrasts sharply with the attitude of his conservative opponents. His confidence in money also appeared in the hired service system, begun as an experiment in the

capital in 1069 and applied to the whole country in 1071. Hired personnel were employed to perform duties in local government previously assigned on a rotating basis to relatively well-off families, and a service exemption tax was instituted. In the specific area of monetary policy, the reformers rescinded a prohibition against private dealing in copper and on several occasions expanded the volume of the bronze currency, but not sufficiently to prevent a currency shortage created by the increased demand for money brought on by the reform policies.

Wang shared the general Confucian belief in the primacy of agriculture. To relieve the small farmer of the burden of interest rates of 60 to 70 percent for the period from spring sowing to autumn harvest, he devised, in 1069, the farming loans, whereby the government itself, through its district granaries, extended loans in the form of "young shoots money" to farmers at a maximum interest rate of 20 percent for the season. In 1072, in order to assist peasants and government alike by providing for more equitable and efficient taxation, Wang initiated a program of land survey and equitable taxation involving a resurvey of landholdings with the land to be measured in squares, classified under one of five categories of productivity, and taxed accordingly.

These reforms demonstrate the importance Wang attached to financial and economic policies as positive aspects of government, and beyond that they reflect his belief that the government could and should encourage productivity even if this meant increased government spending. This conflicted with the conventional view of his opponents, which, predicated on a static economy, held that the less the government spent, the more would remain for the people.

Many of Wang's reforms which were not primarily economic in intent nevertheless had important economic aspects and implications. For example, Wang's *paochia* system, which organized people into groups of 10, 50, and 500 families, was primarily intended to ensure collective responsibility for local policing and tax collecting and was further used to guarantee repayment of loans under the farming loans program. Forces composed of men conscripted through the system were given military training and helped to supply at least internal military security when they were stationed in the capital region and certain sensitive border areas, a program financed by the transfer of funds released when retiring regular army personnel were not replaced. Later these forces were also used as army reserve units.

Other military measures included the establishment of a directorate of weapons in 1073 and the horse breeding system in 1072 to deal with the problem caused by the Liao and Hsi Hsia horse export embargo. In the North and Northwest the state now provided a horse and fodder, or the equivalent in money, to a family, allowed it the use of the horse in peacetime, and exempted it from certain taxes in return for raising the animal and supplying it to the army when needed. A system of annual inspection controlled the operation of the system, and households were fined if the horse died.

Since farm horses do not make good war horses, the horse breeding system was faulty in its basic conception and would have failed even if it had been faithfully administered by officials devoted to the reform program. However, the fate of many reforms lay ultimately in the hands of the officials charged with their implementation. Wang realized that reform of the bureaucracy was crucial. Furthermore, despite his belief in regulatory systems, he shared the traditional Confucian conviction that the quality of officials was the determining factor in government, which was responsible for the moral edification as well as the security and welfare of the people.

Wang's *Ten Thousand Word Memorial* had already discussed matters of personnel policy, and he gave top priority to the reform of the civil service. He was not the first to object to the emphasis placed on poetry in the examinations or to demand that candidates be judged on their understanding of the principles of the classics rather than on their literary abilities or the sheer power of their memories, but he went beyond his predecessors in insisting that the criteria of the examinations be relevant to a man's future career as an official, and he emphasized examination questions dealing with policy matters, included the new field of law among the topics for the lesser degree, and in 1073 decided to administer a test in law to men who had obtained their *chin-shih* and to others awaiting official appointments.

Most controversial as well as indicative of Wang's intellectual orientation was his treatment of the classics in the examinations. Like other Chinese reformers, he was attracted to the idealized social, political, and economic order depicted in the *Rituals of Chou* (*Chou Li*), which provided classical justification for his emphasis on institutional reform. For the purpose of the examinations, Wang assigned his own commentary to this classic as the official interpretation. Compounding the outrage of his opponents, he removed from the examinations the *Spring and Autumn Annals* (*Ch'un-ch'iu*), widely revered as containing the moral judgments of Confucius himself and used to support the absolute primacy of ethics in government.

Wang also influenced education by establishing additional prefectural schools and founding a medical and a law school. In 1071 he reorganized the university into three consecutive "colleges" and excused graduates of the top "college" from the *chin-shih* examination.

Wang also concerned himself with the reform of the clerical subbureaucracy, which was responsible for much of the routine work of government. Underpaid, low in status, and generally corrupt, the clerks were extremely influential since they constituted the permanent staff of local government and were often more familiar with local conditions than the regular civil service official serving his tour of duty. In addition to the hired service system, which dealt with one aspect of local government service, Wang provided for a reduction in the number of clerks, improvement in their pay, and close supervision and control, and he gave the most capable clerks an opportunity for promotion into the regular bureaucracy. Since the details of the system involved the local government storehouses, it was called the granary system.

Wang's reforms did something to improve the standards of the subbureaucracy but ultimately fell far short of their goal. The dishonesty of clerks did much to damage the execution of such major reforms as the farming loans, the land survey and equitable tax system, and the state trade system. Nor could Wang rely on the honesty, let alone the devotion, of the regular bureaucracy. Furthermore, he was faced with continual criticism encouraged by illustrious elder statesmen, such as Han Ch'i, Fu Pi, and Ou-yang Hsiu, and led by such capable leaders as the historian Ssu-ma Kuang and the more moderate Su brothers, Su Shih the great poet and Su Ch'e. Wang's firm conviction that he was right helped him to continue his program despite opposition, but his intolerance of criticism and tendency to overreact to it lost him valuable support. In 1185, after the death of Emperor Shen-tsung, Ssu-ma Kuang came into power and proceeded to rescind Wang's measures.

Retirement and Death

In retirement near Nanking from 1076 until his death on May 21, 1086, Wang devoted himself to literary pursuits. His book on etymology, the *Tzu Shuo*, and some essays and commentaries on the classics date from this period. Unlike some of his contemporaries, Wang had great respect for Mencius, whose political and economic views he admired, but he disagreed with Mencius on the much-disputed thesis of the goodness of human nature, arguing instead that human nature is neutral and inseparable from the emotions and emphasizing the importance of social custom and government for the development of human goodness.

Famous as an essayist and included among the traditional Eight Prose Masters of the T'ang and Sung dynasties, Wang is also famous as a poet. Some of his poetry shows signs of Buddhist influence, an inclination also revealed in some of his friendships and the donation of property to a Buddhist temple after recovery from an illness in 1083 during which he was treated by a doctor especially sent from the court. His poems are marked by their lyricism and their concern for the common man, qualities Wang admired in the poetry of Tu Fu.

Further Reading

James T. C. Liu, *Reform in Sung China: Wang An-shih and His New Policies 1021-1086* (1959), is a modern interpretative study incorporating valuable Chinese and Japanese scholarship. The most extensive treatment in English remains Henry R. Williamson, *Wang An-shih: A Chinese Statesman and Educationalist of the Sung Dynasty* (2 vols., 1935-1937). A range of modern and traditional assessments is presented in John T. Meskill, ed., *Wang An-shih: Practical Reformer?* (1963). A section on Wang's poetry is in Kojiro Yoshikawa, *An Introduction to Sung Poetry,* translated by Burton Watson (1967). Recommended for general background are Edward A. Kracke, Jr., *Civil Service in Early Sung China* (1953), and James T. C. Liu and Peter J. Golas, eds., *Change in Sung China: Innovation or Renovation?* (1969). □

Wang Ching-wei

The Chinese revolutionary leader Wang Ching-wei (1883-1944) was an early follower of Sun Yat-sen and served as president and prime minister of the Nationalist government. During World War II he headed the Japanese puppet regime at Nanking.

Born at Canton in a minor gentry family, Wang Ching-wei was a brilliant student in traditional Chinese subjects. A good poet, an excellent calligrapher, and a master of Chinese prose, he later became a powerful orator. In 1903 he passed the first civil service examination and won a government scholarship to Japan. He earned a degree at Tokyo Law College and was a founding member of a revolutionary association, the T'ung Meng Hui. A major propagandist for the revolution, he became a national figure through an abortive attempt to assassinate the prince regent in 1910, which left him in jail until after the 1911 Revolution. He played a major role in negotiations between the revolutionaries and Yüan Shih-k'ai over the new government organization in 1912.

Wang married Ch'en Pi-chün in 1912 and left for France to further his education. He returned in 1917 and again became an active supporter of Sun Yat-sen. After Sun's death in 1925, Wang was made head of the Kuomintang party (KMT) and of its revolutionary government. He was forced to flee the revolutionary territory by Chiang Kai-shek's military coup in 1926, returning early in 1927. As head of the Nationalists' Wuhan government, Wang continued to support the Communist alliance for several months after Chiang's Shanghai coup in April but broke with the Communists himself in July. Forced out of his leadership position in the KMT, Wang became the chief opponent of Chiang in the party. He supported attempts to overthrow Chiang from 1929 to 1932.

As a result of the Manchurian incident in late 1931, Wang and Chiang formed a coalition to support a policy of minimal resistance to Japanese encroachment until the Chinese government could be strengthened. Wang was prime minister until the end of 1935, when he was forced to retire for medical reasons after being shot by an assassin.

With the outbreak of the Sino-Japanese War in 1937, Chiang's control of the party increased, and, although Wang held high position in the government, he was powerless. Hoping to ease the suffering of the helpless Chinese people in the war, avoid a Communist victory, and weaken Chiang's power, Wang urged a peace settlement with Japan. In December 1938 he fled China and ultimately accepted Japanese assurances of autonomy as head of a new regime in occupied China. In effect, he became a puppet of the Japanese until his death, resulting from an attempt to remove the bullet left from the 1935 attack.

Further Reading

Some of Wang's writings have been translated into English. *The Poems of Wang Ching-wei* (trans. 1938) has an introduction to his life and work by T. Sturge Moore. Wang's *China's Problems and Their Solution* (trans. 1934) contains a biographical sketch of him by T'ang Leang-li. There is no standard biography of Wang. The best study of him in English is T'ang Leang-li, *Wang Ching-wei: A Political Biography* (1931), which was intended to support his career. The biography by Don Bates, *Wang Ching Wei, Puppet or Patriot* (1941), also presents him in a favorable light. For general background see O. M. Green, *The Story of China's Revolution* (1945); Ch'ien Tuan-sheng, *The Government and Politics of China* (1950); and Li Chien-nung, *The Political History of China, 1840-1928* (trans. 1956). □

Wang Ch'ung

Wang Ch'ung (27-ca. 100) was a Chinese philosopher who questioned the validity of contemporary belief and applied a new standard of critical inquiry to the problems of the natural world.

Wang Ch'ung may be described as a rationalist in the sense that he sought explanations that were intellectually satisfying to his reason; as a naturalist insofar as he believed in the independent working of the world of nature; and as a protestant as he rejected current beliefs as ill-founded, misleading, and pernicious. Of his several writings the *Lun-heng,* or *Balanced Discourses,* survives complete except for one of the 85 chapters. The work set a new standard of ordered systematic thinking in Chinese philosophy, with separate treatment of subjects as diverse and as all-embracing as the creation and working of the universe, the place of man in creation, or the acceptance of dogma.

Wang Ch'ung's clarity of thought is apparent in his application of strict methods of inquiry. He identifies the subject at issue, and while isolating it from extraneous and irrelevant problems he sets it within its main context. He calls on the results of earlier thinkers, citing passages from literature or historical precedents, and indicates fallacies in their conclusions. Both in such refutations and in providing support for his own positive views, he presents his own observations of material evidence together with arguments by analogy; and he invites his reader to conduct experiments which have been shown to produce satisfactory results. For instance, he explains thunder in terms of the interaction of fire and other forces, and he rejects as disproved the view that thunder is caused by divine or supernatural anger.

In seeking a rational explanation of the universe Wang Ch'ung rejected many of the extravagant conclusions that had followed the popularization of a belief in *yin* and *yang* and the powers of the Five Elements. While some of his predecessors, notably Tung Chung-shu, had discerned the operation of regularity or design in the creation of the material world by these forces, Wang Ch'ung held that it was only through their impersonal, undirected, and independent action that matter is created, through processes such as rarefaction and condensation. Man is subject to such forces in the same way as are the other parts of the creation; and just as different crops do not possess moral qualities which will save them from the destruction of field fires, so man's practice of moral precepts does not affect his destiny or save him from natural catastrophe.

Wang Ch'ung thus had no place for the active attention by heaven to human affairs, or for its willingness to interfere on behalf of human happiness, such as Tung Chung-shu had postulated. In a number of chapters Wang Ch'ung reverts to this subject, disproving the concept that heaven expressed its warnings to a ruler of men in the form of rare or outrageous phenomena. Similarly he refutes a belief in the power of omens and disparages the guiding influence that they exerted on human decisions.

There was a prevalent belief in Wang Ch'ung's day that the spirits of the dead possessed powers of cognition and that they were capable of utterance; and that if they were left unpropitiated, they would show their displeasure or anger by wreaking malevolent actions on mankind. Wang Ch'ung rejected such beliefs as superstitious and untenable and sought to relieve the human fears and anxieties that they had engendered. He provided a number of reasons to show why powers of cognition and utterance depend on the possession and command of effective faculties and material substances. He cited the many tales of the appearance of ghosts and their acts of revenge for wrongs that they had suffered and exposed such tales as imagined, unfounded, or lacking in significance. In addition he argued against the validity of paying extravagant services to the spirits of the dead as a means of propitiation, on the grounds that such services both failed to achieve their purpose and involved the participants in ruinous expense.

In writings contemporary with Wang Ch'ung's, the force of ethical precept and of historical precedent had been considerably enhanced by referring to personages of a mythical nature or to historical individuals to whom the possession of superhuman powers had been attributed. In addition there had been a tendency to glorify the achievements of China's past, of which wisdom some periods were represented as a golden age in which wisdom and goodness had ruled unquestioned.

Wang Ch'ung criticized such opinions as being unsubstantiated. He denied flatly that some of the mythical sovereigns of long ago had possessed abnormal physical features which corresponded with inspired powers of government. He refused to accept that Confucius possessed superhuman powers or that all his statements were of unquestionable authority; and he would not accept that the decades of the recent past had necessarily been of poorer value or quality than those of earlier ages such as the reigns of the kings of Chou.

Wang Ch'ung's views were evolved before Buddhism had become established in China. His skepticism has sometimes been compared with that of his near contemporary Lucretius (99-50 B.C.), whose writings were partly devoted to the same objective—that of dispelling the unnecessary fears to which mankind had subjected itself. In the surviving Chinese literature of the period the *Lunheng* is a somewhat exceptional work, owing to its unorthodox contents, its trenchant style, and its ordered argumentation. At the time, its radical point of view was received with small acclaim or popularity, and it is only in the last few decades that interest has steadily increased in the book, both in the East and the West.

Further Reading

For the place of Wang Ch'ung in the development of Chinese thought see Fêng Yu-lan, *A History of Chinese Philosophy* (trans. 1937; 2d ed. in 2 vols., 1952-1953); Joseph Needham, *Science and Civilization in China* (4 vols., 1954-1965); William T. De Bary, *Sources of Chinese Tradition* (1960); and Wing-tsit Chan, ed. and trans., *A Source Book in Chinese Philosophy* (1963). □

Wang Fu-chih

The Chinese philosopher Wang Fu-chih (1619-1692) was well known for his "nationalist" beliefs and his theory of historical evolution. One of the outstanding thinkers of the 17th century, he provides an important intellectual link between imperial and revolutionary China.

Wang Fu-chih was born on Oct. 7, 1619, in the province of Hunan in central China, later the home of such famous revolutionaries as Huang Hsing and Mao Tse-tung. Mao, in fact, facetiously proposed the theory that Hunanese are natural rebels because they eat so many red peppers. Wang's father and brother were noted scholars, and they seem to have influenced his career in the direction of scholarship. As a child, Wang exhibited an enormous capacity for reading, and it was said that he had a phenomenal memory and could read ten times faster than the average educated individual. He passed the rigorous provincial civil service examination in 1642, and it seemed that he had a great future as a scholar-official.

Fall of the Ming Dynasty

Wang was on the way to Peking to take the examination for the highest civil service degree (*chin-shih*) when suddenly his career ambitions were crushed. The rebel Li Tzu-ch'eng took Peking in April 1644, overthrowing the Ming dynasty as the last Ming emperor hanged himself in despair. Two months later the Manchus from the North ousted Li Tzu-ch'eng and placed themselves as foreign conquerors on the Chinese throne.

Wang, irate that barbarian people now ruled China, devoted the next six years to resisting the Manchus. He raised an army in his native province and, after suffering defeat at the hands of the Manchus, fled to southeastern China, where he attached himself to a Ming descendant, the prince of Kuei. For a few years he followed the Ming prince around southern China but finally realized that military action against the powerful Manchu armies was hopeless, and he retired in 1651 as a hermit to his native town.

From then until his death, Wang immersed himself in thought and writing. He often lived an impoverished existence, sometimes able to write only with the ink and paper donated by his few friends and students. Although his writings were extensive (amounting to some 358 Chinese volumes, or *chüan*), few of his works were published in his lifetime, and some he gave away in repayment for gifts of food and money.

Student of Neo-Confucianism

Wang was a devoted student of Neo-Confucian philosophy of the Sung dynasty, and he took the philosopher Chang Tsai as his favorite. Neo-Confucian thought is somewhat difficult for the Westerner to fully grasp, but it basically fell into two different schools: the first, with Chu Hsi as its great spokesman, argued that the universe was composed of "ether" (*ch'i*) and that behind all matter was "principle" (*li*); the second, led by Wang Yang-ming, believed that the human mind consisted of "pure principle," and thus one could achieve understanding by introspection.

During the 16th century a great philosophical debate raged between the two schools, the first advocating a dualistic theory and encouraging the scholar to "investigate things" in search of "principle," the second advocating a monistic outlook and urging one to "look within himself." Wang suggested a compromise which he had discovered in his readings of Chang Tsai. Wang felt that principles were

manifested only in matter and thus believed that the universe could be explained in a monistic fashion, but that one must diligently investigate not only himself but also his environment in order to achieve understanding. Wang's compromise led him into a variety of areas of unusual research, including the study of mathematics, astronomy, and geography, with the assistance of some Jesuit missionaries.

New Theory of History

Believing that human society takes on radically different forms in different historical periods and geographical areas, Wang developed his evolutionary theory of history. He rejected the prevalent Chinese idea that there was a "golden age" in the past, and instead he asserted that "the present is better than the past, and the future will be still better than the present; each period has its own characteristics." To Wang, the ruler had an obligation to alter policies and institutions in order to meet changing times and to better the material livelihood of his subjects.

In one of his most famous works, the *Yellow Book* (*Huang shu*), Wang proposed an interesting corollary in which later commentators have seen the seeds of "nationalism." He wrote that "if the Chinese do not mark themselves off from the barbarians, then the principle of earth is violated . . . if men do not mark themselves off and preserve an absolute distinction between societies, then the principle of man is violated." Wang was not a racist, but he did believe that different cultures and geographical areas should keep to their own customs and should have their own rulers and forms of government. In this argument one can see a veiled attack against the Manchu regime; Wang clearly felt that the Manchus belonged in Manchuria, not in China. He was an ardent patriot, and throughout his historical writings he praised those who remained loyal to their dynasties and condemned those who acted as traitors.

Since most of Wang's writings remained in manuscript form until the 19th century, he died as he had lived, a relatively obscure hermit. With the concern for institutional change and the growing nationalist sentiments in the face of the Western threat, however, Wang's writings rapidly gained popularity. Several editions of his collected works were published in the late 19th and early 20th centuries. Thousands of young Chinese, many of them nationalists and revolutionaries, began to read Wang's writings and to venerate him as a national hero.

In 1915 students and intellectuals in Wang's own province of Hunan honored him by establishing the Society for the Study of Wang Fu-chih (*Ch'uan-shan hsüehshe*). Mao Tse-tung attended several of the society's meetings, elated to discover that one from his own province had held such radical views over 2 centuries earlier. In 1962, in commemoration of the 270th anniversary of his death, more than 90 scholars gathered in the capital of Hunan to discuss Wang Fu-chih's writings and his historical legacy. Few Chinese thinkers who lived prior to the 20th century have received such laudatory treatment by the People's Republic of China.

Further Reading

Some of Wang Fu-chih's translated writings, along with a short critical interpretation, can be found in W. T. De Bary, ed., *Sources of the Chinese Tradition* (1960). A biography of Wang is in the publication by the U.S. Library of Congress, Orientalia Division, *Eminent Chinese of the Ch'ing Period, 1644-1912,* edited by Arthur W. Hummel (2 vols., 1943-1944). □

Wang Kon

Wang Kon (877-943) was the founder of the Korean Koryo dynasty and a descendant of a powerful clan at Songdo which controlled maritime trade on the Yesong River. The legends of his ancestors and his rise to power bespeak the clan's intimate association with the sea.

Wang Kon first served as a general under Kungye of Later Koguryo, one of the Later Three Kingdoms. A Silla prince who took to the hills on account of political squabbling at court, Kungye was something of a megalomaniac and Buddhist fanatic, styled himself a Maitreya, and indulged in butchery in his sumptuous palaces. Finally, Wang's colleagues decided to make Wang king, and he ascended the throne at Ch'orwon, the capital of Later Koguryo (918). A year later, Wang transferred the capital to Songdo (modern Kaesong), his clan's stronghold, for personal, strategic, and geomantic reasons.

The destruction of Later Paekche, established by Kyonhwon in the southwestern part of the peninsula, was Wang's next objective. The battle line was drawn along the west of the Naktong River, where battles were fought from 930 to 936. Wang's fleet also invaded the enemy's coast, especially Naju and Chin islands, in order to sever its communication routes with China and Japan. Later Paekche finally fell in 936, owing chiefly to the internecine feud that sapped the country's energy. Thus the peninsula was reunified after half a century of war and chaos.

Wang's policy toward Silla, the other major Korean kingdom, was that of comity. When the Later Paekche army ravaged the Silla capital and caused the reigning Silla monarch to commit suicide (927), Wang personally took the field and fought the enemy. When King Kyongsun (reigned 927-935), the last Silla ruler, surrendered in the eleventh month of 935, Wang gave Kyongsun his eldest daughter in marriage and did his utmost to absorb peacefully the traditional authority of the vanquished state. Thus Wang was able to display that he inherited the Silla throne not just as a local strong man, but as a legitimate successor to Silla tradition and authority.

The political structure of Koryo was basically the same as that of Silla, and Koryo continued the use of the T'ang administrative system. In order to unite the nation under a single authority, Wang succeeded in consolidating some 20 local magnates, his erstwhile comrades-in-arms, chiefly by marriage alliances.

The foreign policy of Wang was at once dynamic and conciliatory. He attempted to regain the old territory of Koguryo; and the western capital, P'yongyang, the erstwhile Koguryo capital, served as the base for his northern expansion. He protected refugees from Parhae, the successor state of Koguryo, when it fell to the hands of the Khitans (926). He also subjugated the Jürchen, east of the Yalu, thus extending his sway to the Yalu River. A devout Buddhist, Wang believed that the country's peace and prosperity depended upon the Buddha's protection and mercy.

Further Reading

Information in English on Wang Kon must be gleaned from general works on Korea, such as Cornelius Osgood, *Koreans and Their Culture* (1951), and Takashi Hatada, *A History of Korea* (1969). □

Wang Mang

Wang Mang (45 B.C.-A.D. 23) was a Chinese statesman and emperor. An official under the former Han dynasty, he took the Han throne and founded his own Hsin dynasty. He attempted many economic and political reforms, all of which failed.

Wang Mang owed his positions, first as an official of the Han dynasty and then as emperor of his own dynasty, to the fact that he was the nephew of the Empress (née Wang) of Emperor Yüan (reigned 48-33 B.C.). Because of her, the Wang family dominated the Han government for about a quarter century.

Wang Mang, who became known for his diligence, studied Confucianism, particularly its ritual ceremonies. He treated family members and eminent government figures with the utmost respect. About 22 B.C. his uncle recommended him for official position, and as he moved upward through the ranks of officialdom, he became ever more humble in his behavior.

By 8 B.C. Wang was promoted to the highest position in the bureaucracy. About this time he brought charges against another minister, who was executed even though he was a relative of Wang's famous aunt. This case added to Wang's reputation of being straightforward and scrupulously honest.

Power behind the Throne

In 7 B.C. Wang had to leave the government. Because of a dynastic crisis in 1 B.C., his aunt recalled him, and he was instrumental in putting Emperor P'ing (reigned 1 B.C.-A.D. 6) on the throne. Since the Emperor was only 9 years old, Wang dominated the government. In order to protect his own position, Wang prevented the family of the Emperor's mother from moving into positions of authority. There were objections to this, including the use of omens to threaten Wang Mang. Wang's son, who was among the objectors, was arrested and died in prison. The event increased Wang's fame for impartiality. In the following year, A.D. 4, Wang married his daughter to the young emperor, thus securing his own position in the government.

By this time the Han dynasty was in grave difficulties. There was dissatisfaction in officialdom, and since recent emperors had died without sons, there were rumors that heaven was indicating that the dynasty had run its course. Wang attempted to deal with these problems by attracting scholars to the court, by enlarging the educational system, by granting pay raises and pensions to officials, and by restoring prestige to members of the imperial family. These measures, in conjunction with a bountiful harvest in A.D. 3, produced a general feeling of well-being. It was believed that Wang Mang had rescued the faltering dynasty from collapse. In A.D. 5 it was proposed that he become regent. However, before any action was taken on that proposal, Emperor P'ing died at the age of 14.

Wang now moved to seize the throne. At this time there were no male descendants of any of the past four emperors. Wang passed over the adult descendants of Emperor Hsüan (reigned 73-47 B.C.) and selected a two-year-old infant who was not enthroned but was given the title Heir Apparent and Young Prince. Soon (A.D. 6) a portent appeared, supposedly sent by heaven, directing that Wang become emperor. This step was not taken, but Wang was elevated to regent and then to acting emperor. During the next two years there were many portents "proving" that Wang should become actual emperor. Finally, on Jan. 10, A.D. 9, he took the throne, announcing the founding of the Hsin (New) dynasty (9-23).

The fact that relatively little effort was needed to take over the throne was due to a combination of factors. Briefly, there was a general feeling that the Han dynasty had lost its heaven-granted mandate to rule; the deaths of several emperors without sons tended to encourage this belief. Furthermore, the numerous portents and omens were positive proof that heaven had chosen Wang Mang to succeed to the Han throne. And, since Wang had a well-established reputation, it was felt that he was eminently suited for the position. Hence, except for a brief uprising in A.D. 7, there was very little opposition to his "usurpation" of the Han throne, even by members of the Han house.

His Reforms and Policies

Wang Mang's activities as emperor can be treated under four headings: land reform, administrative reforms, foreign policies, and economic and currency reforms. Land tenure and slavery presented acute socioeconomic problems that Wang tried to face directly. For a century and a half officials had tried to limit the amount of land that an individual could own. A similar problem had arisen with regard to slaveholding by the wealthy. Wang Mang ordered the nationalization of all land, which he planned to redistribute periodically. Slavery was abolished. However, because of opposition from the aristocracy Wang had to countermand these order in A.D. 12, less than 3 years after they had been issued.

Wang's attempts to improve the administration amounted to little more than repeated changes of names of offices and administrative units. Wang sincerely believed that he was acting as the perfect Confucian ruler when he substituted Chou-dynasty designations for Han official titles and when, for these and other reasons, he altered place names. However, decrees and orders were sent to the wrong places because of the confusion that permeated the bureaucracy, and his attempt at restoring Confucian purity ended in a chaotic array of titles.

In foreign affairs Wang Mang enjoyed no success whatsoever. He insulted the tribal leaders on all his frontiers when he changed their titles. Furthermore, there were droughts along the northern border which caused the Hsiung-nu to raid Chinese settlements. Beginning in A.D. 10 most of the frontiers were in an uproar. Wang began preparations to send a huge 300,000-man army against his northern enemy. Although these plans were canceled and peace was restored in 13, the situation did not remain stable very long. By 18 the Chinese were again sending armies against the Hsiung-nu. New taxes were levied, and the ruler again prepared to send thousands of troops to the north. Comparable unrest existed in all of China's border areas until after the end of his reign. Wang's foreign problems accounted for many of his economic policies.

In order to raise money, state monopolies were created or existing ones were more rigorously enforced. Wang also reintroduced a system for equalizing prices. However, the monopolies created an additional hardship on the already-strained peasantry, and the system for equalizing prices was badly abused by avaricious officials. He attempted currency reforms by issuing new coins. But the coinage was in confusing denominations, and it was debased. Both officials and commoners rejected the money, even though that meant severe punishments. Wide-scale discontent was the main result of these measures.

By the late teens of the first century, Wang Mang had little left to his credit. His reforms were failing. The various military preparations had been extremely hard on the commoners. His economic policies had been counter-productive, for they had created great hardship and resentment. In addition, eastern China suffered from a flood of the Yellow River in A.D. 11 which sent thousands of people from their homes and into a life of vagabondage or banditry.

Then droughts were so severe in the years 18-22 that cannibalism was reported in the area. Wang Mang offered succor by teaching the people how to eat grass and tree bark. In 18 many bandit groups began disrupting eastern China. Descendants of emperors of the Former Han ruling house saw the rising disorders as an opportunity to restore the Han dynasty. Several of them joined with bandit groups in Honan. The nature of these hordes now changed; instead of consisting largely of illiterate peasants plundering the countryside, they became organized military units with the avowed political aim of restoring the Han dynasty.

Wang Mang by this time was in no condition to rule. He had become psychotically distrustful of everyone and felt compelled to rule single-handedly. More urgent business took precedence over appointments, and offices remained empty for as long as three years. Administration almost ground to a halt. As the advancing troops, now called the Han army, moved toward the palace, Wang Mang surrounded himself with religious paraphernalia and pathetically begged for supernatural intervention. On Oct. 6, A.D. 23, Wang's defenders were defeated, and Wang Mang was killed.

Wang Mang's Legacy

Wang Mang was originally hailed as the hero who had saved the Han dynasty from extinction; he ended up vilified as the usurper who had brought the Former Han to its end. In spite of his many failures, he was a significant, though tragic, historical figure. For over 200 years no one again tried to cope with China's land problem, but Wang's bold attempts dramatize clearly the extent to which remedial measures were needed and the magnitude of aristocratic power. His manipulation of omens and portents led directly to a new body of Confucian literature, known as the Apocryphal Texts, which was to become the dominant trend within Confucianism for almost 2 centuries. But his commitment to the ritualistic and ceremonial aspects of Confucianism contributed to the growth of another trend within Confucianism which by about 200 supplanted the omenistic thought of the earlier period.

Further Reading

Wang Mang's life and activities are extensively treated in Pan Ku, *The History of the Former Han Dynasty: A Critical Translation,* with annotations by Homer H. Dubs (3 vols., 1938-1955).

Additional Sources

Pan, Ku, *Wang Mang: a translation of the official account of his rise to power as given in the history of the former Han dynasty,* Westport, Conn.: Hyperion Press, 1977. □

Wang Ming

Wang Ming (1904-1974) was the leader of the "Internationalist" group within the Chinese Communist Party that opposed Mao Tse-Tung's (Zedong's) nationalist "deviation" and favored, instead, disciplined compliance with each shift in the Comintern line. As such, Wang emerged as a major rival of Mao in the 1930s.

Wang Ming, the pseudonym by which Chen Shaoyu was commonly known, was born in Anwei province in Central China in 1904. Influenced by socialist ideas during his middle school years in Wuhan, in 1925 Wang entered Shanghai University where he became involved in the anti-imperialist agitation then shaking Shanghai. In November 1925 Wang was sent to Moscow by the newly founded Chinese Communist Party (CCP) for a two year course of study at Sun Yat-sen University, a school designed to train future Chinese cadre. In Moscow Wang rapidly mastered the Russian language and

Marxist-Leninist theory, joined the CCP, and emerged as the leader of the foreign students at Sun Yat-sen University.

Wang formed close ties with a number of other Chinese students in Moscow, ties which were an important source of strength in his subsequent contest with Mao. He also became the star protegé of Pavel Mif, one of the Soviet Union's leading sinologists and rector of Sun Yat-sen University. From 1927 to 1929 Wang served as a Comintern functionary, acting as Russian language interpreter at the CCP's fifth and sixth congresses in 1927 and 1928 and assisting the Comintern's representative Borodin in Wuhan in 1927.

In 1930 Wang Ming led a small group of Chinese students from Moscow back to China, where they challenged the leadership of CCP head Li Lisan. Wang's "Returned Students" or "28 Bolsheviks" charged that Li's "political errors" were responsible for the setbacks the CCP had recently suffered in implementing the Comintern's directives. Although Li had in fact faithfully implemented Moscow's orders, he was made a scapegoat for the failures resulting from those orders, and in January 1931 he was ousted as leader of the CCP. Li's removal involved the direct intervention of Pavel Mif, who was then Comintern representative to China. Wang Ming's group took over leadership of the CCP from Li; a number of "Returned Students" were made Politburo members, and Wang became secretary general. In 1932 Wang returned to Moscow to serve as CCP representative to the Comintern, leaving his Returned Student followers Zhang Wentien, Qin Bangxian, and Shen Zemin in control of the CCP's central organs.

From 1931 through 1934 Wang Ming's group struggled to take over control of the peasant armies and rural base areas Mao Tse-Tung and Zhu De had built up in Jiangxi province. Years later, in 1945, the orthodox CCP interpretation of this period characterized it as "the third left deviation" and charged that Wang and his group wanted to use the Red Army to seize major cities so that the urban proletariat could be mobilized for the revolution, in line with Soviet teachings. From Moscow Wang wrote many articles applying the Comintern's line to Chinese circumstances. In 1933 Wang was elected to the Comintern's Central Executive Committee (CEC).

Comintern policy shifted as Stalin began to realize the threat posed to the U.S.S.R. by Nazi rule of Germany. By 1934-1935 Moscow desired collective security with the capitalist democracies to deal with the two-front threat posed by Nazi Germany and Japan. This meant that the attitude of the Comintern's "branch parties" toward the rulers of those capitalist democracies would have to be moderated. Wang Ming played a major role in interpreting and applying to China Moscow's new line of an "antifascist united front." He drafted the "August First Manifesto" of 1935 which set the CCP on a course of an anti-Japanese united front with Chiang Kai-shek and his Nationalist Party (or KMT) against Japan, thus dropping the previous line of revolutionary civil war to overthrow Chiang and the KMT. The Seventh Comintern Congress, which reoriented the Comintern toward the "anti-fascist united front," also elected Wang a member of the Presidium of the

Comintern's CEC—a higher Comintern post than was held by any other member of the CCP.

During the Long March Mao won over key members of Wang's Internationalist faction and used the opportunity of severance of radio contact with Moscow to push aside Wang's people and have himself elected leader of the CCP at an expanded Politburo conference at Sunyi, Kueizhou province, in January 1935. Once the Long March was over and the CCP was ensconsed in Northern Shaanxi, Wang Ming attempted to use the Comintern's new united front line to undermine Mao's newly established leadership. From mid-1935 through the fall of 1938 there were important differences between Wang and Mao over the terms of the CCP-KMT united front.

These differences became acute once the Sino-Japanese war began in July 1937. The specific points in dispute were many and complex, but, in sum, Wang argued that the CCP should subordinate itself to the KMT for the sake of keeping the KMT in the war against Japan, to ensure a pro-Soviet foreign policy on the part of Chiang Kai-shek, and to facilitate collective security between the U.S.S.R. and Britain, France, and the United States. Mao, on the other hand, saw the destruction of KMT power in vast areas of north and central China as an unprecedented opportunity to expand Communist power and was unwilling to forgo this opportunity for the sake of Moscow's interests. At a critical juncture of the Sino-Japanese war in late November 1937, Wang Ming returned to China to try to force Mao to alter his radical line. After a year of complex maneuvering, Mao and Stalin finally reached a compromise. One aspect of this compromise was Comintern endorsement of Mao's leadership of the CCP and the demotion of Wang Ming at the Sixth Plenum of the CCP's Sixth Central Committee in the fall of 1938.

After 1938 Wang Ming never again posed a serious challenge to Mao, although he did continue to dispute Mao's policies. Wang's influence was progressively reduced after the fall of 1938 and became negligible after the 1942-1943 rectification campaign in the CCP against ''foreign dogmatism'' and ''foreign formalism''—euphemisms for Wang's penchant for Soviet Marxism.

Wang held relatively unimportant posts through the 1940s and into the mid-1950s. As late as 1956 he was elected to the CCP's Central Committee, but he was listed last of the 97 Central Committee members. Wang returned to the Soviet Union in 1956, with the permission of the CCP and for reasons of ''health.'' During the Cultural Revolution Wang was an active propagandist for Moscow, making Chinese language broadcasts to China and writing several books and articles condemning Mao's rule. He died after an illness in Moscow on March 27, 1974, at the age of 70.

Further Reading

Wang Ming's life is discussed in the standard biographic dictionaries of China: Donald W. Klein and Anne B. Clark, *Biographic Dictionary of Chinese Communism, 1921-1965* (1971); Howard L. Boorman, *Biographic Dictionary of Republican China* (1967); and *Who's Who in Communist China* (Hong Kong, 1969). An unpublished doctoral dissertation dis-

cusses Wang's early years in the Soviet Union: Zora A. Brown, *The Russification of Wang Ming* (Mississippi State University, 1977). Wang's conflict with Li Lisan is discussed in Robert North, *Moscow and the Chinese Communists* (1953) and Charles B. McLane, *Soviet Policy and the Chinese Communists, 1931-1946* (1958). Tetsuya Kataoka discusses the wartime conflict between Wang and Mao in *Resistance and Revolution in China* (1974). This is also discussed by Gregor Benton in ''The 'Second Wang Ming Line' (1935-38),'' in *China Quarterly* (March 1977). □

Wang Pi

Wang Pi (226-249) was one of the most brilliant Chinese philosophers. He reinterpreted the *Tao-te ching* and the *I ching* and laid the basis for an entirely new metaphysics that inspired Chinese philosophers for centuries to come.

The year 226, when Wang Pi was born, found China divided into three separate kingdoms, each straining to regain control of the entire empire. The fall of the Han, which occurred at the end of the 2nd century A.D. and gave rise to the Three Kingdoms, was a catastrophe that had its repercussions in every aspect of life in China, not least of all in philosophy. Once the imperial state had disappeared, the extraordinarily complex and complete philosophical systems the Han scholastics had compounded were seen to be what they really were: lifeless and arbitrary conglomerations of old theories and superstitions that crudely attempted to provide a metaphysical foundation for the Han hegemony. The disappearance of the great Han state thus created an intellectual vacuum that thinkers hastened to fill; it also left a period of comparative liberty, very rare in China, that was to allow them to present new and bold formulations.

Family and Social Background

If Wang Pi accomplished so much in so short a space of time, it was perhaps in part due to the fact that he was born into a family active in the most progressive philosophical circles at the end of the Han period and had at his disposition close to 1,000 chapters (*chüan*) of books, the important library of Ts'ai Yung, given to his father by the first emperor of the Wei dynasty.

Wang Pi seems to have been a somewhat conceited young intellectual aristocrat, good at a traditional dart game, in which the player threw sticks into a long-necked bottle; fond of feasting and carousing; very discriminating in music; and somewhat apt to laugh at others who did not come up to his extraordinary high intelligence. There is a strong streak of something that at first reading looks like frivolity in his work, an overindulgence in paradox and in farfetched analogies, that probably reflects his youth and his playboy tendencies—but only on first reading, for further study shows that he was deadly serious.

Wang's biography tells us that, when he was being interviewed for an important post by the regent Ts'ao Shuang, Wang Pi spoke with the busy head of state on nothing but metaphysics. He did not get the job and caused Ts'ao Shuang to "snicker at him," but the incident is revealing: Wang Pi's metaphysics, which at first seems gratuitous and disembodied, was for its author a vital, "committed" philosophy, something essential for the good administration of the empire. He truly intended to replace the worn-out philosophies of the Han with something new and all-encompassing.

His Works and Philosophy

Wang Pi's most important works are two commentaries: one on the *Tao-te ching* and the other on the *I ching*. On both these works he has left his indelible mark, but his work on the *I ching* completely reorganized the book and made it much as it is today; of the extremely numerous early commentaries, moreover, his is the only one to survive in its entirety. It is, of course, very difficult to study a man's philosophy solely by studying his commentaries on other works, but that is what we have to do in Wang Pi's case; for aside from these commentaries, all that remains of his work are fragments of a commentary on the Analects of Confucius, a fragmentary short work on the *Tao-te ching* (the *Lao-tzu chih-lüeh*), and the slightly longer, complete *Chou-i lüeh-li* on the *I ching*.

Putting it succinctly but without too much distortion, we may say that Wang Pi's philosophy is a combination of Confucian ethics and Taoist metaphysics. He suggests that the Taoist absolute, or ontological substratum of the universe (the *tao*), is indeed the metaphysical basis of the Confucian social organization, with a single ruler and a hierarchical society harmoniously cooperating according to ritual and the traditional Confucian virtues.

In his commentary to the *Tao-te ching*, Wang Pi brilliantly shows that the *tao* is in fact *wu*. *Wu* is a term difficult to translate; it is a negation but definitely does not mean "nothing" or "nothingness," as it is often translated. It is "non-," "un-," "without," meaning that it is "undefined," "undetermined"—a true absolute in the Western philosophical meaning of the word. All of creation, all of the diversified universe, all *yu* (the opposite of *wu*) —"having" or "with" determination or definition—ultimately depends upon the undefined and undefinable *wu* for its existence. We must thus model ourselves upon this absolute if we wish to "develop our natures to their full" (*ch'üan-hsing*) and live out our lives to their limits under the best conditions.

The ancient Taoists did not give much concrete information on just how this was to be done. Wang Pi says we can find this information in the *I ching*, which for him, as for all his compatriots, contains in its 64 hexagrams all the possible combinations of conditions that a man can encounter in life. His commentary brilliantly exploits the methods and terminology of the *I ching*, showing the subtle and changing relations between the six lines of each hexagram and explaining in abstract terms just what the obscure remarks of the ancient explanations really mean for us in our moral life.

The fine points of Wang's philosophy have not yet been fully studied, but the underlying nucleus, the motive force that gives the philosophy its basic impulsion, is that the ontological substratum underlying the universe and the universe as we see it are actually only different phases of a single entity: *wu* is the essence, *yu* its manifestation (*t'i* and *yung* as they are called in later philosophy). Just as the outward manifestations of the world are really only differentiations of a basic unity, so must we, in our activities, attempt to conform to our basic "principle" or "reason for being" (*li*) in sticking "spontaneously" (*tzu-jan*) to our "lot" (*fen*) in life and society. The *I ching* is a guide to accomplish this, but its traditional Confucianism takes on a new metaphysical dimension in Wang Pi's version as he teaches us that conforming to our "reason for being" and our "lot" enables us to return to the undifferentiated, mystical *wu* that underlies all reality.

Wang Pi was not only closely studied and imitated by the early Buddhist thinkers of the 4th and 5th centuries, but his first coherent and complete Confucian metaphysics seems, consciously or unconsciously, to have inspired the Sung Neo-Confucianists.

Further Reading

There is little on Wang Pi in English. Short introductions to his work are in Feng Yu-lan, *A History of Chinese Philosophy*, vol. 2 (new ed. 1953); Hellmut Wilhelm, *Change: Eight Lectures on the I Ching* (1960); and Wing-tsit Chan, ed. and trans., *A Source Book in Chinese Philosophy* (1963). □

Wang T'ao

The Chinese reformer and scholar Wang T'ao (1828-1897) was a pioneer of modern journalism in China and one of the earliest advocates of economic and political modernization.

On Nov. 10, 1828, Wang T'ao was born in Kiangsu Province, near the city of Soochow. Wang endeavored in his youth to become a scholar, like his father, and he studied the Confucian classics in preparation for the civil service examinations. He successfully completed the first examination in 1845, but he failed in the second, or provincial, examination the following year. This was his last attempt to find a career in the state bureaucracy.

In 1848 Wang went to Shanghai, where he met several foreign missionaries, one of whom invited him in 1849 to become Chinese editor in the publishing operations of the London Missionary Society. He remained in this position until 1862, when he had to flee Shanghai after being accused of passing information to the Taiping rebels. Thereafter his life was in danger, and he took refuge in the British colony of Hong Kong.

Soon after his arrival in Hong Kong, Wang began a close and fruitful association with the British missionary James Legge. For over ten years Wang assisted Legge in the monumental undertaking of translating the Confucian classics. Legge developed a keen admiration for his Chinese assistant, writing that Wang "far excelled in classical lore any of his countrymen whom the Author had previously known." In December 1867 Wang followed Legge to Great Britain, where they continued their scholarly cooperation. Wang stayed in Europe, mostly in Scotland, for two years, during which time he delivered a highly successful lecture at Oxford University. He returned with Legge to Hong Kong in 1870, and their work continued there until Legge left permanently for England in 1873.

Wang T'ao, meanwhile, had embarked on an independent career of writing and publishing. As early as the 1860s, he began his journalistic endeavors as editor of the foreign-owned *Hong Kong News*. And in 1873 he founded his own Chinese-language newspaper. As a result of his bold innovation, provocative editorials, and intelligible style, he became renowned as a founder of modern Chinese journalism.

Advocate of Reform

During the 1870s and 1880s Wang wrote prolifically on an almost infinite variety of subjects, among which were books on the general history of France (1871) and a detailed account of the recent Franco-Prussian War (1873). But it was his writings advocating the adoption in China of Western learning that ensured him of an enduring historical importance. While most of his contemporaries favored the adoption of Western techniques only as a means to preserve Chinese culture, Wang T'ao suggested that even Confucian values and Chinese institutions might have to be altered if the Chinese nation was to become strong and prosperous. By granting primacy to the Chinese "nation" rather than to the "culture," Wang displayed a characteristic of modern nationalism that most Chinese literati did not reveal until the late 1890s.

In his reformist writings, Wang stressed that military modernization alone would not suffice to protect China from the Western intrusion. Instead, he argued that China must develop a modern and dynamic economy—complete with banks, railroads, telegraphs, and machine industry—to compete with the foreigners. Wang was also a warm admirer of Western constitutional democracy. He never explicitly advocated the establishment of parliamentary government in China, yet he clearly believed this was a source of the power of the European states. He expressed the hope that in China there could exist the same spirit of mutual trust and cooperation between the government and the people that he thought existed in the democratic countries of the West. While expressing admiration for the West, he bitterly criticized the corruption, waste, and inefficiency of the ruling government in Peking.

In 1879 Wang toured Japan, where he was welcomed enthusiastically. In 1884 he finally felt it safe to resume residence in Shanghai, where he remained until his death.

Further Reading

An informative chapter on Wang T'ao is in Roswell S. Britton, *The Chinese Periodical Press, 1800-1912* (1933). Also helpful is Lin Yutang, *A History of the Press and Public Opinion in China* (1936). For general background see O. M. Green, *The Story of China's Revolution* (1945).

Additional Sources

Cohen, Paul A., *Between tradition and modernity: Wang T'ao and reform in late Ch'ing China*, Cambridge: Harvard University Press, 1974. ☐

Wang Wei

The Chinese poet and painter Wang Wei (699-759) was one of the greatest poets of the golden age of Chinese poetry, the T'ang dynasty, 618-907. He was also regarded by later critics as the founder of the Southern school of landscape painting.

Wang Wei was also called Mo-chieh (or ch'i, the name Wei-moch'i being a transliteration of the Sanskrit name Vimalakirti, the great lay disciple of Buddha) and Yuch'eng (assistant minister of the right, after his last government position). He was born in P'u-chou (the present Fen-yang county in Shansi Province) into a family which had contributed 13 prime ministers to the T'ang court. Because the traditional family seat was in T'ai-yüan, Shansi, Wang Wei is usually called a native of T'ai-yüan.

By the age of 15, Wang Wei was a skillful poet and musician. In 717 he won first place in the metropolitan examination in preparation for a government career, and in 719 he was awarded the highest degree in the examination system, the *chin-shih*. His long official career began immediately thereafter with his appointment as assistant director of the Imperial Directorate of Music; at the time of his death in 759, he directed the administration of 12 departments in the ministries of war, justice, and works. His career was not uneventful, however, and included demotion, exile, and forced service under the usurper An Lu-shan. Two personal losses also left deep imprint: when he was about 30, his wife died childless, and Wang never remarried; 20 years later, the death of his mother left him grief-stricken. Though he continued to hold office thereafter, he tended more and more to withdraw from public society to the solace of his country home at Lan-t'ien along the Wang River. There, in the company of fellow poets, Buddhist monks, and other friends, he roamed the hills and waters, studied Taoism and the Buddhist sutras, wrote, and painted.

Achievement as a Poet

Wang Wei is sometimes classed as one of the three greatest poets of the T'ang dynasty, along with Tu Fu and Li Po. While he was neither as brilliant a craftsman as Tu Fu nor as exuberant a genius as Li Po, he excelled in imagery, and his poems often hold a subtle metaphysical flavor testifying to his long study of Buddhism. Many of his works are such perfectly crystallized visual images that they became favored subjects of later artists, as in this couplet: "White herons drift across flooded rice fields/ Yellow orioles warble in shadowed summer trees." Or: "I walk to where the waters end/And sit and watch the clouds arise." Something of the personal warmth of Wang Wei's poems may be suggested in this translation of his "Answering Magistrate Chang": "In my late years I am only fond of quiet,/ The ten thousand affairs do not involve my heart./ I look to no long-range plans,/ Only the knowledge that I shall return to the old forests-/ The wind through the pines will loosen my belt,/ The moon in the mountains shine on my lute./ You ask me, sir, the cause of success and failure:/ The fisherman's song carries deep into the mountains."

His Landscape Painting

The great Sung poet, painter, and critic Su Shih (1036-1101) described Wang Wei's art in terms that suggest the complex interaction between poetry and painting in the later history of Chinese art: "Taste Wang Wei's poetry- there are paintings in it; look at his paintings-they are full of poetry." Just as his older contemporary Wu Taotzu carried painting to new levels through his study of calligraphy, so too did Wang Wei achieve a breakthrough because of his understanding of poetry. His poems convey thought by means of carefully chosen visual images; his paintings borrow the same technique. That is, it is no longer solely the image with which the painter is concerned, but mood, rhythm, key, the ineffable qualities of expression that ultimately escape definition.

Much earlier, the figure painter Ku K'ai-chih had sought to achieve a similar goal by "conveying the spirit" of men, the inner man, not his appearance. Wang Wei now brought the same purpose to an art form that had been largely decorative in function theretofore: landscape painting. Typical of the preceding taste was the courtly "blue and green" style of the father and son Li Ssu-hsün and Li Chao-tao. Rich color, hard and even outlines, a somewhat decorative concept of natural form, and the use, still, of landscape elements as a backdrop for human narratives are characteristics of this art.

Some historians credit the crucial innovation to the great figure painter Wu Tao-tzu. His loose, fluctuating brushwork described form in a more organic, lively manner and thus allowed the creation of a new, vital landscape art. But it was Wang Wei who lent his name to the concept of pure landscape, enjoyed for its own sake. To Wang as well is credited the first systematic use of ink wash in conjunction with brush lines, and the initial development of monochrome landscape—all of which would thoroughly dominate the later history of Chinese painting.

As in his poetry, qualities, not forms per se, were pursued. One T'ang critic speaks of the "profound" expressive power of his landscape and elevates him above Li Ssuhsün, whose colorful style was still the standard to most critics. But in general Wang Wei was overshadowed by the more renowned masters of the day, and it was not until the 10th and 11th centuries that his stature began to grow toward its present eminence.

The Painting of the Wang-ch'üan Villa

Wang Wei's most celebrated work was his "portrait" of the estate he owned at Wang-ch'üan. Originally painted on the walls of Ch'ing-yüan monastery, it was a long, rambling portrayal of the favorite scenic sites in and around his country home.

Later it was copied on silk, recopied by the 10th-century painter Kuo Chung-shu and 11th-century painter Li Kung-lin, and finally engraved on stone in 1617. Through its successive reincarnations it has remained the most influential single landscape composition in Chinese history.

His Snowscapes

Among the 126 works by Wang Wei owned by the Sung emperor Hui-tsung, snow scenes predominate. And among extant works still attributed to the master, it is snowscapes which appear to best reflect the nature of his achievement. While none of these works can be considered original, several of them are consistent enough among themselves, and in sufficiently close harmony with genuine but anonymous works of the T'ang period, to warrant consideration.

Best is the composition surviving in one complete but very late copy (Honolulu Academy of Arts), one shorter but earlier and better copy (Ogawa Collection, Kyoto), and a fragmentary recension on Taiwan (Palace Museum), known as *Clearing after Snow over Mountains and River*. The composition is the prototype of the continuous landscape handscroll format, a classical sequential mode equivalent to the sonata form of Western musical composition. The painter introduces: themes in the form of basic motifs; a spatial structure within which the themes are elaborated; elements of anticipation and surprise; a key or mood—here the minor key of frozen winter; and movements, here, as is usual, a beginning, middle, and final development.

The only break in the dominance of landscape elements is an occasional tiny human figure or house. Such paintings are to be understood as journeys: the mental journey through snow-covered landscape, and the spiritual journey into metaphysical realms. The landscape hand scroll, which begins at that time, deserves to be recognized as one of the unique art forms of world art.

Patriarch of the Southern School

When the great Ming critic and painter Tung Ch'ich'ang (1555-1636) drew up his ambitious and extraordinarily influential theory of the Northern and Southern schools of landscape painting, he honored Wang Wei as patriarch of the Southern school, which included all of the great literati, or scholar-painters. As poet, painter, and scholar; as innovator in ink-wash landscape painting; and as one of the first masters to lodge poetic expression in painted forms, Wang Wei stands at the opposite pole from the professional and academic masters of the Northern school. He has been honored since the 11th century by every great landscape painter who sought to perpetuate this ideal.

When Wang Wei died in 759, he was buried in the deer park on his beloved estate, not far from the tomb of his mother.

Further Reading

A collection of Wang Wei's poetry, translated by Ching Yin-nan and Lewis Walmsley, is *Poems by Wang Wei* (1968). There is a monograph in English on Wang Wei by Lewis and Dorothy Brush Walmsley, *Wang Wei, the Painter-Poet* (1968).

Additional Sources

Wagner, Marsha L., *Wang Wei*, Boston: Twayne Publishers, 1981. □

Wang Yang-ming

Wang Yang-ming (1472-1529) was a Chinese philosopher and government official. He led the revolt against the orthodox Neo-Confucianism of Chu Hsi and founded the Yang-ming school, which later dominated Chinese thought.

Born Wang Shou-jen into a scholar-official family in a district southeast of Hangchow, Chekiang, Wang Yang-ming exhibited in his teens a spirit of adventure and a questioning of orthodox beliefs. He became obsessed with Neo-Confucianism at age 17, when a noted Confucian scholar told him that one could become a sage through learning. Besides his classical studies, Wang interested himself in the military arts, the practice of Taoist technique of breathing to prolong life, and Buddhist philosophy.

Official Career

Wang passed the examination for *chin-shih,* the highest academic degree, in 1499, and then served as a secretary in the Ministry of Justice, later of War. But he twice left office, first because of illness, then because of his offending a powerful eunuch in trying to save an official's life, but these temporary reliefs from public duties gave him the leisure to deepen his thinking. In 1508, during a banishment in Kweichow, he came to the realization that to investigate the principle of things is not to seek for them externally on actual objects, as Chu Hsi had taught, but to look for them in one's own mind. A year later he formulated the epoch-making theory that knowledge and action are one.

Emerging from his exile in 1510, Wang was appointed a district magistrate in Kiangsi. There he initiated several reform measures that were prototypes in his later administration and made him famous in government. In the following year he served in various ministries at Nanking and Peking, returning to Kiangsi as governor in 1516. He suppressed the bandits, reorganized the administration, and introduced social reforms, the most significant of which was the setting up of the community compact. Meanwhile, he

further developed his philosophy and took a position against the criticism of the followers of the Chu Hsi school.

In 1519 Wang took charge of the suppression of an imperial prince who staged a rebellion in Kiangsi. Wang succeeded in capturing the rebel, but his victory aroused the jealousy of his opponents at court; only when Wang submitted a report deemphasizing his own efforts did criticism subside. Late in 1521 he was made the Earl of Hsin-chien, but he retired shortly upon his father's death.

During these years Wang made significant strides in his philosophical achievements. In 1521 he enunciated the doctrine of the extension of innate knowledge, which he described as the "original substance of the mind." His last official assignment occurred in 1527, when he was recalled from retirement to crush a tribal uprising in Kwangsi. There he contracted an illness and died 2 years later. Despite his meritorious service, he fell under the malice of his enemies at court and the traditional honors were withheld. Only in 1567 was he honored with the title of Marquis and the posthumous name Wen-ch'eng, meaning "completion of culture."

Wang's Philosophical Concepts

The Neo-Confucian idealist movement of Wang Yangming arose as a reaction against the Neo-Confucian rationalism of Chu Hsi, which had dominated Chinese thought since the 12th century but which had become stereotyped, narrow, and devoid of originality by the time of the Ming dynasty. Championing against this empty and lifeless tradition, Wang advocated sincere convictions and outright actions emanating from one's own intuitive mind and presented four basic concepts: love as exemplified in the great man's forming one body with the universe, the identification of one's mind with principle (*li*), the extension of native knowledge, and the unity of knowledge and conduct.

These concepts can be briefly illustrated as follows. First, in forming one body with heaven and earth, the great man eliminates selfish desires and obscurations, reveals his true character, and fully develops his nature. This is love, which, by extension, is the will to live, the process of unceasing production and reproduction; it is also filial piety, brotherly respect, and the like.

Second, following Lu Hsiang-shan (Lu Chiu-yüan), Wang equates principle with mind, of which principle is the order, and material force (*ch'i*) is the function. As this original mind manifests itself, there is native knowledge; to extend this native knowledge is the supreme duty of man.

Third, while extension of knowledge depends on investigation, unlike Chu Hsi who interpreted investigation (*ko*) as intellectual investigation of things, Wang argued that *ko* meant rectification of the mind. To him all principles are contained in the mind and are discoverable if the mind is clear and calm; such a state can be achieved through the method of tranquility, that is, the elimination of self-desires, self-examination, quiet sitting, and the like.

Fourth, as Wang placed equal emphasis on tranquility and activity, extension of native knowledge is not mere contemplation but knowledge translated into action. In his theory, knowledge is not complete until it becomes conduct, and conduct is not complete unless it is knowledge itself at work. Knowledge is the will, the beginning; conduct is the work, the accomplishment. These tenets are the foundation of the philosophy of the unity of knowledge and conduct.

Justification and Influence

That Wang gave priority to firm purpose, a will to work, and social and political responsibilities distinguished him as a true Confucian; and though he adopted Buddhist and Taoist overtones and practices, he rejected selfish renunciation of human relations and of social responsibility. In time his followers spread all over China, and the school set off a strong movement that was to overshadow the Chu Hsi orthodoxy during the next century. His influence also extended to Japan, where, as the O-yo-mei school, Wang's ideas inspired the great leaders of modern reforms and produced some of Japan's leading thinkers.

Although the movement in China declined in vitality toward the end of the 16th century, its impact was again felt in the 20th, especially in Sun Yat-sen and other leaders of the revolution who zealously admired Wang's idealism and personality. Wang left several volumes of philosophical writings and literary works, many of which are available in English translation.

Further Reading

The most useful interpretation of Wang Yang-ming's life and thought is the introductory chapter in his *Instructions for Practical Living and Other Neo-Confucian Writings,* translated with notes by W. T. Chan (1963). Wang's writings are available in *The Philosophy of Wang Yang-ming,* translated by Frederick G. Henke (1916); W. T. De Bary, ed., *Sources of the Chinese Tradition* (1960); and W. T. Chan, comp. and trans., *A Source Book in Chinese Philosophy* (1963). A study of Wang in English is Carsun Chang, *Wang Yang-ming: Idealist Philosopher of Sixteenth-century China* (1962). Fung Yu-lan, *A History of Chinese Philosophy,* translated by Derk Bodde (2 vols., 1952-1953), is recommended for general historical background.

Additional Sources

Ching, Julia, *To acquire wisdom: the way of Wang Yang-ming,* New York: Columbia University Press, 1976.

Tu, Wei-ming, *Neo-Confucian thought in action: Wang Yang-ming's youth (1472-1509),* Berkeley: University of California Press, 1976. □

Otto Warburg

Biochemist Otto Warburg (1883-1970) discovered cell oxidation and identified the iron-enzyme complex, which catalyzes cell oxidation. For this work, he was awarded the Nobel Prize in physiology or medicine in 1931.

Otto Warburg is considered one of the world's foremost biochemists. His achievements include discovering the mechanism of cell oxidation and identifying the iron-enzyme complex, which catalyzes this process. He also made great strides in developing new experimental techniques, such as a method for studying the respiration of intact cells using a device he invented. His work was recognized with a Nobel Prize for medicine and physiology in 1931.

Otto Heinrich Warburg was born on October 8, 1883, in Freiburg, Germany, to Emil Gabriel Warburg and Elizabeth Gaertner. Warburg was one of four children and the only boy. His father was a physicist of note and held the prestigious Chair in Physics at University of Berlin. The Warburg household often hosted prominent guests from the German scientific community, such as physicists Albert Einstein, Max Planck, Emil Fischer—the leading organic chemist of the late-nineteenth century, and Walther Nernst —the period's leading physical chemist.

Warburg studied chemistry at the University of Freiburg beginning in 1901. After two years, he left for the University of Berlin to study under Emil Fischer, and in 1906 received a doctorate in chemistry. His interest turned to medicine, particularly to cancer, so he continued his studies at the University of Heidelberg where he earned an M.D. degree in 1911. He remained at Heidelberg, conducting research for several more years and also making several research trips to the Naples Zoological Station.

Warburg's career goal was to make great scientific discoveries, particularly in the field of cancer research, according to the biography written by Hans Adolf Krebs , one of Warburg's students and winner of the 1953 Nobel Prize in medicine and physiology. Although he did not take up problems specifically related to cancer until the 1920s, his early projects provided a foundation for future cancer studies. For example, his first major research project, published in 1908, examined oxygen consumption during growth. In a study using sea urchin eggs, Warburg showed that after fertilization, oxygen consumption in the specimens increased 600 percent. This finding helped clarify earlier work that had been inconclusive on associating growth with increased consumption of oxygen and energy. A number of years later, Warburg did some similar tests of oxygen consumption by cancer cells.

Warburg was elected in 1913 to the Kaiser Wilhelm Gesellschaft, a prestigious scientific institute whose members had the freedom to pursue whatever studies they wished. He had just begun his work at the institute when World War I started. He volunteered for the army and joined the Prussian Horse Guards, a cavalry unit that fought on the Russian front. Warburg survived the war and returned to the Kaiser Wilhelm Institute for Biology in Berlin in 1918. Now 35 years old, he would devote the rest of his life to biological research, concentrating on studies of energy transfer in cells (cancerous or otherwise) and photosynthesis.

One of Warburg's significant contributions to biology was the development of a manometer for monitoring cell respiration. He adapted a device originally designed to measure gases dissolved in blood so it would make measurements of the rate of oxygen production in living cells. In related work, Warburg devised a technique for preparing thin slices of intact, living tissue and keeping the samples alive in a nutrient medium. As the tissue slices consumed oxygen for respiration, Warburg's manometer monitored the changes.

During Warburg's youth, he had become familiar with Einstein's work on photochemical reactions as well as the experimental work done by his own father, Emil Warburg, to verify parts of Einstein's theory. With this background, Warburg was especially interested in the method by which plants converted light energy to chemical energy. Warburg used his manometric techniques for the studies of photosynthesis he conducted on algae. His measurements showed that photosynthetic plants used light energy at a highly efficient sixty-five percent. Some of Warburg's other theories about photosynthesis were not upheld by later research, but he was nevertheless considered a pioneer for the many experimental methods he developed in this field. In the late 1920s, Warburg began to develop techniques that used light to measure reaction rates and detect the presence of chemical compounds in cells. His "spectrophotometric" techniques formed the basis for some of the first commercial spectrophotometers built in the 1940s.

His work on cell respiration was another example of his interest in how living things generated and used energy. Prior to World War I, Warburg discovered that small amounts of cyanide can inhibit cell oxidation. Since cyanide forms stable complexes with heavy metals such as iron, he inferred from his experiment that one or more catalysts important to oxidation must contain a heavy metal. He conducted other experiments with carbon monoxide, showing that this compound inhibits respiration in a fashion similar to cyanide. Next he found that light of specific frequencies could counteract the inhibitory effects of carbon monoxide, at the same time demonstrating that the "oxygen transferring enzyme," as Warburg called it, was different from other enzymes containing iron. He went on to discover the mechanism by which iron was involved in the cell's use of oxygen. It was Warburg's work in characterizing the cellular catalysts and their role in respiration that earned him a Nobel Prize in 1931.

Nobel Foundation records indicate that Warburg was considered for Nobel Prizes on two additional occasions: in 1927 for his work on metabolism of cancer cells, then in 1944 for his identification of the role of flavins and nicotinamide in biological oxidation. Warburg did not receive the 1944 award, however, because a decree from Hitler forbade German citizens from accepting Nobel Prizes. Two of Warburg's students also won Nobel Prizes in medicine and physiology: Hans Krebs (1953) and Axel Theorell (1955).

In 1931 Warburg established the Kaiser Wilhelm Institute for Cell Physiology with funding from the Rockefeller Foundation in the United States. During the 1930s, Warburg spent much of his time studying dehydrogenases, enzymes that remove hydrogen from substrates. He also identified some of the cofactors, such as nicotinamide derived from vitamin B3 (niacin), that play a role in a number of cell biochemical reactions.

Warburg conducted research at the Kaiser Wilhelm Institute for Cell Physiology until 1943 when the Second World War interrupted his investigations. Air attacks targeted at Berlin forced him to move his laboratory about 30 miles away to an estate in the countryside. For the next two years, he and his staff continued their work outside the city and out of the reach of the war. Then in 1945, Russian soldiers advancing to Berlin occupied the estate and confiscated Warburg's equipment. Although the Russian commander admitted that the soldiers acted in error, Warburg never recovered his equipment. Without a laboratory, he spent the next several years writing, publishing two books that provided an overview of much of his research. He also traveled to the United States during 1948 and 1949 to visit fellow scientists.

Even though Warburg was of Jewish ancestry, he was able to remain in Germany and pursue his studies unhampered by the Nazis. One explanation is that Warburg's mother was not Jewish and high German officials "reviewed" Warburg's ancestry, declaring him only one-quarter Jewish. As such he was forbidden from holding a university post, but allowed to continue his research. There is speculation that the Nazis believed Warburg might find a cure for cancer and so did not disturb his laboratory. Scientists in other countries were unhappy that Warburg was willing to remain in Nazi Germany. His biographer Hans Krebs noted, however, that Warburg was not afraid to criticize the Nazis. At one point during the war when Warburg was planning to travel to Zurich for a scientific meeting, the Nazis told him to cancel the trip and to not say why. "With some measure of courage," wrote Krebs, "he sent a telegram [to a conference participant from England]: 'Instructed to cancel participation without giving reasons.'" Although the message was not made public officially, the text was leaked and spread through the scientific community. Krebs believed Warburg did not leave Germany because he did not want to have to rebuild the research team he had assembled. The scientist feared that starting over would destroy his research potential, Krebs speculated.

In 1950 Warburg moved into a remodeled building in Berlin which had been occupied by U.S. armed forces following World War II. This new site was given the name of Warburg's previous scientific home—the Kaiser Wilhelm Institute for Cell Physiology—and three years later renamed the Max Planck Institute for Cell Physiology. Warburg continued to conduct research and write there, publishing 178 scientific papers from 1950 until his death in 1970.

For all of his interest in cancer, Warburg's studies did not reveal any deep insights into the disease. When he wrote about the "primary" causes of cancer later in his life, Warburg's proposals failed to address the mechanisms by which cancer cells undergo unchecked growth. Instead, he focused on metabolism, suggesting that in cancer cells "fermentation" replaces normal oxygen respiration. Warburg's cancer studies led him to fear that exposure to food additives increased one's chances of contracting the disease. In 1966 he delivered a lecture in which he stated that cancer prevention and treatment should focus on the administration of respiratory enzymes and cofactors, such as iron and the B vitamins. The recommendation elicited much controversy in Germany and elsewhere in the Western world.

Warburg's devotion to science led him to forego marriage, since he thought it was incompatible with his work. According to Karlfried Gawehn, Warburg's colleague from 1950 to 1964, "For him [Warburg] there were no reasonable grounds, apart from death, for not working." Warburg's productivity and stature as a researcher earned him an exemption from the Institute's mandatory retirement rules, allowing him to continue working until very near to the end of his life. He died at the Berlin home he shared with Jakob Heiss on August 1, 1970.

Further Reading

Krebs, Hans, *Otto Warburg: Cell Physiologist, Biochemist and Eccentric,* Clarendon Press, 1981. □

Paul Moritz Warburg

The German-American banker and banking theorist Paul Moritz Warburg (1868-1932), as spokesman for the large bankers of America, favored a highly centralized banking system. In much modified form, this became the Federal Reserve System.

Born in Hamburg to an aristocratic Jewish family of rabbis and merchants who had engaged in banking and commerce in Europe for nearly 300 years, Paul Warburg was educated in a realgymnasium and served an apprenticeship in a Hamburg mercantile house. Completing his commercial education in London and Paris banking houses, he went around the world in 1893 to learn international finance. While in the United States, he married the daughter of one of the partners in the large New York investment banking firm of Kuhn Loeb and Company. On his return to Germany he was admitted as a partner in the family banking firm in Hamburg.

In 1902 Warburg accepted a partnership in Kuhn Loeb and established residence in New York; he became a naturalized American citizen in 1911. During this time banking reform was a constant concern, particularly after the Panic of 1907 wiped out many American banks and brokerage houses, in part because of the inability of the national banking system to funnel credit to areas where it was needed. In a series of noted speeches and essays Warburg proposed establishing a large united reserve bank which would be owned by the nation's banks, would mobilize reserves, emit a flexible banknote currency, and be directed by the banking community immune from political interference. The plan, heartily endorsed by Nelson Aldrich, chairman of a Senate committee considering proposals for banking reform, became, with modifications, central to the committee's report to the Senate in 1911.

Progressives of both parties denounced this proposal, suggesting that it would create a money trust which would

control the nation's credit. Instead, a regional reserve system was worked out, and it reached its final form in the Federal Reserve Act of 1913. Though critical of this approach, Warburg cheerfully endorsed the final solution as better than no system at all, and because of his stature in the banking community President Wilson appointed him to the Federal Reserve Board.

Warburg then served on the Advisory Council of the Federal Reserve Board until 1926, contributing greatly to the smooth implementation of the Federal Reserve System. He foresaw the coming of the crash of 1929. A man of broad culture, he devoted much of his time during his latter years to cultural and civic activities.

Further Reading

Warburg's account of his participation in banking reform and his voluminous essays on the subject are contained in his *The Federal Reserve System: Its Origin and Growth* (2 vols., 1930). There is no biography of Warburg. Sketches of uneven quality can be found in B. C. Forbes, *Men Who Are Making America* (1917; 6th ed. 1922); Harry Simonhoff, *Saga of American Jewry, 1865-1914* (1959); and Tina Levitan, *Jews in American Life* (1969). J. Laurence Laughlin treats Warburg rather critically in *The Federal Reserve Act* (1933). Warburg's position regarding the Federal Reserve Act is briefly described in Henry Parker Willis, *The Federal Reserve System* (1923). □

Aaron Montgomery Ward

American merchant Aaron Montgomery Ward (1843-1913) helped create mail-order merchandising and built the large mail-order house which bears his name.

Born in Chatham, N.Y., A. Montgomery Ward moved to Niles, Mich., with his parents. He went to work at 14 in a barrel factory and later in a brickyard. He worked in the Chicago store that became Marshall Field; then he was a travelling salesman for a wholesale dry-goods house.

Aware of farmers' criticism of the high prices at country stores and their condemnation of what they considered exorbitant middlemen's profits, Ward conceived the idea of founding a mail-order house that would cut the cost of sales by purchasing direct from manufacturers and selling direct to retail purchasers. All transactions would be for cash, thereby eliminating the costs country storekeepers incurred by selling on credit. Ward also inaugurated the policy of allowing purchasers to return, without cost, goods they considered unacceptable.

Ward and his partner started their business with only a $2,400 stock of goods housed in a loft and displayed in a one-page catalog, but the enterprise was immediately successful. The 1876 catalog had 150 pages, and annual sales reached $1 million by 1888. At the time of Ward's death, annual sales were $40 million. There were several reasons for his great success, including his intimate knowledge of

farmers' desires and the prices they would pay, his ability to get lower prices from manufacturers by volume purchasing, and the confidence customers gained by the return guaranty. He was fortunate in obtaining the support of the Farmers' National Grange, so he could advertise as "The Original Grange Supply House."

But Ward's career had its stormy aspects. Competition with Sears, Roebuck was brisk, and Sears passed the Ward company in annual volume of sales in 1902. Also, conflict with country storekeepers was continuous and bitter. Storekeepers, regarding mail-order houses as a grave threat, tried a variety of expedients to curtail their operations, including holding large ceremonies where mail-order catalogs were burned. Ward fought back by sending displays throughout the Midwest and by trumpeting his conviction that mail order had saved farmers millions by forcing country stores to lower prices.

Retiring from active management in 1901, Ward undertook much expensive litigation to preserve Chicago's lake front as a park and guard it against commercial encroachment. After his death his wife gave about $8.5 million to Northwestern University.

Further Reading

There is no biography of Ward, and materials on his career are hard to obtain. There is a sketch of him in Paul Gilbert and Charles Lee Bryson, *Chicago and Its Makers* (1929). An account of the origin of Ward's company and its chief competitor is in Boris Emmet and John E. Jeuck, *Catalogues and Counters: A History of Sears, Roebuck and Company* (1950). Stewart H. Holbrook, *The Age of the Moguls* (1953), evaluates Ward and his work. □

Artemus Ward

Artemus Ward (1834-1867) was an American journalist, humorist, and comic lecturer who achieved fame on both sides of the Atlantic.

Artemus Ward was the pen name of Charles Farrar Browne, who was born in Waterford, Maine. The son of a surveyor, storekeeper, and farmer, at 13 he was apprenticed to a printer. He set type for several newspapers in New England before a Boston printshop hired him in 1851. His first humorous sketches, signed "Chub," appeared in the *Boston Carpet-bag*. During the next 2 years he was a printer in several Ohio towns. In 1853 he became an editor on the *Toledo Commercial;* between 1857 and 1861 he was an editor of the *Cleveland Plain Dealer*.

In 1858 Browne wrote a humorous letter purportedly from a traveling showman, Artemus Ward, for the *Plain Dealer*. Similar pieces appeared in this paper and then in *Vanity Fair*. He soon became a regular contributor to that comic magazine, moved to New York, and became an editor, serving until 1862. His writings were collected in *Artemus Ward: His Book* (1862), *Artemus Ward: His Travels* (1865), and *Artemus Ward in London* (1867). Ward used many of the procedures employed by a large group of very popular American humorists in the post–Civil War period: he assumed the role of a humorless ignoramus whose writings were studded with malapropisms, misspellings, grammatical errors, and strangely constructed sentences. In time, though, Ward dropped the assumed character and illiterate touches without discontinuing his use of the humor of diction. Helped by tricks of language, he wrote many burlesques and parodies, as well as sketches and travel accounts. Among his many readers was Abraham Lincoln, who read one of Ward's pieces to his Cabinet the day he presented his Emancipation Proclamation.

Ward profited not only from writings but also from his lectures between 1860 and 1867. In a period when lecturers—on science, philosophy, literature, mesmerism, travel, and other topics—were appearing throughout the nation, Ward traveled through the East, the Midwest, and the Far West burlesquing these solemn and instructive lecturers. Wearing a funereal expression, he pleased audiences by solemnly saying the most absurd things. He was giving a very popular series of comic lectures in London in 1867 when illness forced him to discontinue; he died there on March 9.

Ward was important to a number of humorous writers, notably Mark Twain. Besides being responsible for the publication of Twain's first big success, his "Jumping Frog" story, in an eastern magazine in 1865, Ward provided an invaluable model for comic lecturing, as Twain himself acknowledged.

Further Reading

The indispensable biography of Ward is Don C. Seitz, *Artemus Ward (Charles Farrar Browne): A Biography and Bibliography* (1919). James C. Austin, *Artemus Ward* (1964), is a systematic, critical analysis of Ward's talents, ideas, aims, and influence. Walter Blair examines Ward in relation to other humorists in *Native American Humor, 1800-1900* (1937) and *Horse Sense in American Humor, from Benjamin Franklin to Ogden Nash* (1942).

Additional Sources

Pullen, John J., *Comic relief: the life and laughter of Artemus Ward, 1834-1867,* Hamden, Conn.: Archon Books, 1983.
Seitz, Don Carlos, *Artemus Ward (Charles Farrar Browne); a biography and bibliography,* New York, Beekman Publishers, 1974; c1919. □

Lester Frank Ward

Lester Frank Ward (1841-1913) was an American paleobotanist, sociologist, and educator. He was the leading American opponent of social Darwinism and of impotent government.

Lester Ward was born in Joliet, Ill., on June 18, 1841. He received a bachelor of arts degree from George Washington University in 1869 and a master's in 1873. From 1865 to 1872 he was with the U.S. Treasury Department and from 1881 through 1888 was assistant and then chief paleontologist with the U.S. Geological Survey. He did considerable research in geology and paleobotany but became intensely interested in sociology as an emerging discipline. His published works in sociology were so well received that, without an academic position, he was elected president of the American Sociological Society in 1906 and 1907. In 1906 Ward was made professor of sociology at Brown University. He died in Washington on April 18, 1913.

Ward approached human society from two perspectives. First, as a successful botanist, he analyzed developments in social organization in terms of energy, and combinations and specialization in the use of energy. These themes were first presented in his *Dynamic Sociology* (1883) and *Pure Sociology* (1903). But Ward also emphasized the role of feelings, motives, and will in social affairs. This was extensively discussed in *Psychic Factors in Civilization* (1893).

In all the previously mentioned works, Ward sought to simplify the entire history of mankind as a relatively blind but somewhat progressive evolution of social order through conflict and resolution of conflict, by means of compromise and various degrees of cooperation (the socalled theory of genesis). Though prefigured in the last section of *Pure Sociology,* Ward's theory of telesis was considerably expanded in his *Applied Sociology* (1906). This theory asserted that the fruits of previous social achievements made possible man's

ability to direct further evolution by rational effort and acquired intelligence.

Consequently, Ward strongly opposed the laissez-faire approach to government and regarded education as the primary mechanism of continued human progress. In short, Ward anticipated the development of modern governmental responsibilities (the welfare state), planning, and the expansion of formal education as a funnel for maximum participation by citizens in public affairs.

Ward epitomized the "engaged" or involved intellectual who values knowledge for its application to the resolution of social problems. He strongly favored cooperation between social welfare and the social sciences—though a divergence between the two was characteristic of the last decades of his life. The movement toward a closer alliance between social science and social practice is a quiet vindication of the visions of a long-neglected social prophet.

Further Reading

Israel Gerver, *Lester Frank Ward* (1963), contains selected portions of Ward's writings and a brief biographical sketch. A comprehensive collection of Ward's essays and selected excerpts, along with a well-reasoned interpretation of his thinking, is in Henry S. Commager, *Lester Ward and the Welfare State* (1967). A full-length biography and interpretation of Ward is Samuel Chugerman, *Lester Frank Ward: The American Aristotle* (1939).

Additional Sources

Scott, Clifford H., *Lester Frank Ward*, Boston: Twayne Publishers, 1976. □

Andy Warhol

Andy Warhol (ca. 1927-1987) was a pioneer American pop artist and film maker. His paintings of Campbell soup cans and other mundane objects both piqued and delighted the art public and brought him fame.

Andy Warhol liked to shroud himself in mystery. "I never give my background, and anyway, I make it all up differently every time I'm asked," he said. His exact birth date and place only add to this mystery. Warhol (born Andrew Warhola) provided no information on the matter, so any definitive statement is subject to question. Based on his early years and college dates, it is estimated he was born in 1927 in Forest City, Pennsylvania, the son of a construction worker and miner from Czechoslovakia. He attended the Carnegie Institute of Technology in Pittsburgh (1945-1949), receiving a bachelor of fine arts degree in pictorial design.

In 1949 Warhol arrived in New York City, where he made a meager living in advertising display work. He took some of his drawings to *Glamour* magazine and received a commission to make drawings of shoes. These were published and admired; he then worked for a shoe chain. In 1957 a shoe advertisement brought him the Art Directors' Club Medal. His work appeared in *Vogue* and *Harper's Bazaar* magazines, and in 1959 he exhibited his gold shoe drawings in a New York City gallery.

In 1960 Warhol began painting pictures with no commercial market in mind. He did a series on comic strips such as Dick Tracy, Popeye, Superman and the Little King. His paintings of Coca Cola bottles and Campbell soup cans, arranged in seemingly endless rows, were ridiculed when they were first shown. He created paintings of money and silk-screen portraits of Marilyn Monroe. His second New York show in 1962 was a critical success and perfectly timed, as pop art was just becoming an acceptable art form. His fascination with silk screen as an instrument for mass production led him to open a studio, dubbed The Factory, where he later made his films.

The Factory became a center for pop and would-be pop stars. It attracted a wide variety of glamorous people and an assortment of characters in the art and performing worlds. Although many of Warhol's films, such as *Sleep* (1963), *Eat* (1963), and *Empire* (1965), were lengthy depictions of the most mundane activity or object, some of his works anticipated future film themes or ridiculed certain subjects. *Lonesome Cowboys* (1968) treated homosexuality when it was taboo as a subject for commercial films and, at the same time, challenged the cowboy myth of courageous, macho riders of the range. With such works as *Flesh* (1968)

and *Trash* (1970), Warhol focused on sexual themes. These were the forerunners of the pornographic film market of the 1970s and 1980s. By the mid-1970s his *Andy Warhol's Dracula* (1974) and *Andy Warhol's Frankenstein* (1974) enjoyed commercial success as satiric yet serious works. From 1963 to 1974, he had been involved in the production of more than sixty films of varying quality and subject matter.

Warhol and other pop artists drew their inspiration and imagery from popular culture, but they heightened the color and changed the scale to make the images larger than life. In doing so they redefined pictorial realism and extended its concept. Warhol's imagery can be classified in four broad categories: commercial products such as Brillo boxes and Heinz ketchup bottles, personality portraits of celebrities, modes of exchange such as trading stamps and bills, and disaster pictures of automobile accidents, electric chairs, gangster funerals and race riots.

In 1968 Warhol's celebrity status nearly cost him his life. A disturbed visitor to The Factory shot him, inflicting serious internal wounds. Warhol's slow recovery included a two-month hospital stay and a turn to a new direction, his post-Pop period. From 1970 onward, he increasingly turned to producing portraits of cult figures, prominent persons, and personal friends. These portraits, of figures such as Mao Tse-tung, Philip Johnson, Mick Jagger, Jimmy Carter, and Merce Cunningham display a softer, more delicate imagery than Warhol's earlier Pop Art paintings. His art of the 1970s moved closer to an abstract expressionist style and away from the figurative or realistic style of his work in the 1960s.

In 1981 he undertook a series of myth paintings in which the subject matter treated mythical figures from popular culture sources, such as advertisements, comic strips and films. These works included Dagwood, Mickey Mouse, and Superman. Later in 1983 he created a series of endangered species paintings which depicted various threatened wildlife. As in all of his work, Warhol selected subjects with great popular imagery and treated the symbol and image as much as he does the real object itself.

As a social commentator (a role he denied), Warhol had the uncanny ability to mirror the trends and fads of his time. Recognizing the elements of an urban mass society heavily influenced by symbols, images, and the mass media, he made those symbols and images the subjects of his art. For Warhol and other Pop artists, these images have taken on a reality of their own. They were not only shaped by but also reshaped popular culture. Warhol left social and cultural historians visual documents of the significant elements from America's consumerist society of the postwar era—an important legacy.

Warhol died of heart failure hours after undergoing gall bladder surgery on February 22, 1987, in New York City.

Further Reading

Warhol's *The Index Book* (1970) is an entertaining selection of photographs, mostly of Warhol and his retinue. The most rewarding book on Warhol is John Coplans, *Andy Warhol* (1970), which includes a biographical sketch by Calvin Tomkins, a study and catalog of Warhol's films by Jonas Mekas, and a comprehensive selection of illustrations. See also Pat Hackett's *Andy Warhol Diaries* (1991). □

Helen Mary Wilson Warnock

British philosopher Baroness Helen Mary (Wilson) Warnock (born 1924) was one of the leading lights in the philosophical community of the 20th century.

Helen Mary Wilson (later Warnock) was born on April 14, 1924, in Winchester, England. She received her formal university education at Oxford and earned both the B.A. and D.Phil. degrees. She was the headmistress of the Oxford High School, 1966-1972, research fellow and tutor at Lady Margaret Hall, Oxford, 1972-1976, senior research fellow at St. Hugh's College, Oxford, 1976-1984, and mistress of Girton College, Cambridge, England, from 1985 to 1991.

Married to another British philosopher, Sir Geoffrey James Warnock, in 1949, they had three children. She was awarded a Dame Commander of the British Empire (DBE) in 1984 and was created a baroness a year later.

Over a long career in academia Warnock demonstrated a keen understanding of many and disparate fields of philosophy. Her intellectual interests were broad and varied. But it was the discipline of ethics that dominated her interest, as demonstrated by her books on the history of *Ethics Since 1900, Utilitarianism,* and *Existentialist Ethics.* She was well versed in the distinctive analytical philosophical methodology of England, but she also introduced into the British philosophical discussion the continental existentialist tradition and wrote a definitive philosophical study of the thought of Jean-Paul Sartre, as well as surveys of *Existentialism* and *Existentialist Ethics.* Her books on *Imagination* (1976) and *Memory* (1987) are careful analyses of these complex subjects, much discussed by contemporary philosophers in England, the Continent, and the United States. She continued her publishing activity with substantial studies of educational and university issues.

She was especially active in British committees that examined the moral issues of governmental, political, and educational institutions; included are the Committee of Inquiry into Special Education, the Royal Commission on Environmental Pollution, the Advisory Committee on Animal Experiments, the United Kingdom's National Commission for UNESCO, the Committee of Inquiry into Human Fertilization, the Committee of Inquiry into Validation of Public Sector Higher Education, and the Committee on Teaching Quality.

A Study of Ethics

Warnock's book *Ethics Since 1900* presents the broad sweep of moral philosophy from what is called metaphysical ethics (best represented in the late 19th and early 20th centuries by F.H. Bradley) to the philosophy of existentialism in the 20th century. The chief characteristic of ethics since 1900 is the rejection of ethical naturalism (or utilitarianism) by the empiricist philosophers. G.E. Moore invented the phrase "The Naturalistic Fallacy" and set the agenda for later moral philosophers to argue in an antinaturalistic manner. Moore was interested to show that moral values are distinct from facts. "Goodness" had a unique kind of property that the philosopher was able to intuit. The antinaturalists were not concerned with the problem of moral choices. Rather, they were chiefly interested in judging things to be good or bad, right or wrong. The property of goodness is a property of things in the external world, "there to be discovered." The positivists (such as A.J. Ayer) followed Moore and the antinaturalists and further restricted the competency of moral judgments, arguing that the language of morality was basically "emotive" and nonpropositional. At Oxford, then, after World War II, moral philosophy concerned itself with the logic of the words used in framing ethical propositions.

Warnock, on the other hand, argued that the analysis of ethical language leads inevitably to the trivialization of ethics. Warnock saw ethics not so much as the categories we use to describe the world, but rather "as our own impact upon the world, our relation to other people and our attitude to our situation and our life." Moral philosophy ought not to distinguish between those who theorize about the logic of moral discourse and the moralists who act as moral agents in the world. Ethics is all about "deliberating, wishing, hating, loving, choosing; these are things which characterize us

as people and therefore as moral agents." Warnock believed, too, that the future of ethics (to save ethics from boredom, as she said) must be characterized by an appreciation of the philosophical significance of feelings, scruples, desires, intentions, and other psychological phenomena.

Warnock was appreciative of the efforts of several moral philosophers to reopen, as she said, the *grounds* of our moral convictions. She maintained, "For is it not a *fact* that some types of behaviour tend to do good, and others do harm? And how, in the end, if not on the basis of this fact, can we make sense of discriminating some actions as *right* in morals, and others as *wrong?*' She believed that an answer to this question leads us back to the point of the reappraisal of our moral convictions. She then argued that moral philosophers might begin to take seriously the phenomenologists and the existentialists.

Warnock was especially attracted to the philosophical perspectives of Jean-Paul Sartre, though never without maintaining the kind of critical distance that a British analytical philosopher would want always to maintain. She complained about the general vagueness of the language of the existentialists and about their lack of objectivity, so that there are no criteria for making moral judgments (which is, of course, precisely what the existentialists are affirming). Warnock argued that there is a substantial difference between moral formalism—that is, the view that there is just one right thing waiting to be done in each situation—and the existentialist's attempt to "interiorize" morals, to make them both individual and concrete. She believed that the latter attempt is both worthwhile and necessary, given the hypothetical and ultrarationalistic nature of the former. However, to assert that moral theory consists only of the assertion that there is no moral code is to assert something that is meaningless.

Warnock believed that what the existentialists ultimately did in their earnest endeavor to expurgate the worthless, the insincere, and the disingenuous from the moral discussion of the philosophers was to destroy morality altogether. Existentialism, however, had an impact upon the mood of the culture of the 20th century, but it was a mood, a way of thinking more suited to drama and novels than it was a serious way of thinking about moral issues.

Books on Sartre and Imagination

Warnock's book *The Philosophy of Sartre* (1965) provides the reader with a splendid introduction to the complex, at times unintelligible, thought of the French literary genius, the existentialist who later became a Marxist. Warnock confessed that as a reader of Sartre she at times could not understand what he was talking about. Sartre espoused a radical view of human freedom and argued that "They are free not only to do as they choose but to feel as they choose—in short, to be whatever they choose." Warnock called Sartre "a metaphysical moral theorist" who offered little or no prospect for individuals who attempt to answer the question "What ought we to do?" The world is a perverse place for Sartre, and there is little that individuals in their freedom can do about it. But then Sartre underwent what Warnock calls "the radical conversion" and offered to desperate individuals a new way out, that of becoming Marxists. Warnock did not believe that this was an attractive option, and proceeded to demonstrate the contradictory nature of the later Marxist Sartre over against the early existentialist one. She did find in her study of Sartre that he at times made interesting philosophical moves, but moves which finally lead away from a coherent philosophical system.

Warnock's book on *Imagination* (1976) is a philosophical *tour de force*. The philosophical analysis of the activity of the imagination is a complex, indeed a stupefying, task. She acknowledged that Hume's and Kant's analyses of imagination are seminal for all later philosophical discussions. Imagination for Hume is related to the perception of a series of images with which one builds up an intelligible world. For Kant, the imagination is the same image-making faculty that works in our minds to enable us to recognize objects in our world and to relate our concepts of them to our actual experience. But Warnock constructed a theory of imagination that is independent of Hume and Kant:

> Imagination is a power in the human mind which is at work in our everyday perception of the world, and is also at work in our thoughts about what is absent; which enables us to see the world, whether present or absent as significant, and also to present this vision to others, for them to share or reject. And this power, though it gives us 'thought-imbued' perception (it 'keeps the thought alive in the perception'), is not only intellectual. Its impetus comes from the emotions as much as from the reason, from the heart as much as from the head. (Imagination)

Warnock's bold statement would not be accepted by many of her positivist colleagues in Great Britain and the United States. For the faculty of imagination is not only the intellectual perception of those similar images that make up our world, but also the emotional power that enables ideas to exist within us. Such a concept, of course, has broad consequences for education, a subject matter that concerned Warnock for almost all of her adult life.

Also from *Imagination* is this concept:

> The fact is that if imagination is creative in all its uses, then children will be creating their own meanings and interpretations of things as much by looking at them as by making them. . . . In so far as they begin to feel the significance of the forms they perceive, they will make their own attempts to interpret this significance. It is the emotional sense of the infinity or inexhaustibleness of things which will give point to their experience. . . .

Lady Warnock's influence upon the direction of philosophy will be felt long into the 21st century.

Further Reading

Mary Warnock was a prolific author, both of books and of articles in scholarly and popular journals. The most significant of her philosophical texts are: *Ethics Since 1900* (1960); *J.P. Sartre* (1963); *Existentialist Ethics* (1966); *Existentialism* (1970);

Imagination (1976); *Schools of Thought* (1977); with T. Devlin, *What Must We Teach?* (1977); *Education: A Way Forward* (1979); *A Question of Life* (1985); *Teacher Teach Thyself* (1985); *Memory* (1987); *A Common Policy for Education* (1988); *Universities: Knowing Our Minds* (1989); *The Uses of Philosophy* (1992); and *Imagination and TIme* (1994).

Accounts of Warnock's life and work can be found in Ann Evory and Linda Metzger, eds., *Contemporary Authors* (1983) and the British *Who's Who: An Annual Biographical Dictionary* (1993). □

Earl Warren

During the 16-year term of Earl Warren (1891-1974), a chief justice of the U.S. Supreme Court, the Court decided a series of landmark cases regarding individual civil liberties and civil rights, particularly for minority groups.

Earl Warren's legal philosophy was opposed to the laissez-faire doctrine that had previously prevailed. His public life before he came to the Supreme Court had been pragmatic rather than activist. He had a natural flair for administration; his prosecutive experience gave him broad insights into the inequities of criminal justice, and he had a realistic understanding of the debilitating effects of racial segregation.

Warren, the son of a Norwegian immigrant, was born in Los Angeles, California, on March 19, 1891, and grew up in Bakersfield. He attended the School of Jurisprudence of the University of California at Berkeley, where he supported himself by working as a law clerk in a local office. Admitted to the bar in 1914, he had a meager practice in California before he enlisted in the Army in 1917.

In 1919 Warren became the clerk to the Judiciary Committee, a potent force in the California Legislature. He rose quickly to deputy city attorney of Oakland and then to deputy district attorney, chief deputy (1923), and district attorney (1925) of Alameda County. In 1925 he married Nina P. Meyers. During his 14 years as district attorney, he prosecuted thousands of criminal cases in an unrelenting fight against crime. Still, he said, "I never heard a jury bring in a verdict of guilty but what I felt sick in the pit of my stomach."

Attorney General

In 1939 Warren began campaigning for attorney general of California. In the midst of this, the tragedy of his life struck; his father was murdered as he sat by the window in the living room. Made more determined by this, Warren pledged to pursue strict law enforcement and to conduct a nonpartisan office. He was easily elected and soon became one of the best-known state attorneys general in the country. He was the resolute foe of the gambling syndicates as well as organized crime.

World War II was in progress, and these were tumultuous times. In 1941 Pearl Harbor catapulted Warren into

controversy. California had long been the base of the aircraft industry and was now producing military planes and "liberty ships." At the outbreak of the war between the United States and Japan it was imperative that war matériel production be maintained. Public sentiment against Japanese people reached a frenzy, especially in California, which had over 100,000 residents of Japanese extraction, two-thirds of whom were American citizens. Violence against these people began to break out, and accusations of disloyalty to the United States were made. Minisubs of the Japanese fleet were off the coast of California; bombs from balloons fell in the forests of Oregon and Washington. The West Coast became a virtual powder keg. Though history may treat the internment of some 112,000 of these Japanese residents as a brutal violation of the Constitution, Warren made this decision in a desperate hour, and it was approved by the Supreme Court.

Governor of California

Warren was elected governor of California by an overwhelming majority in 1942 and was reelected in 1946 and 1950, serving until he was appointed chief justice of the United States in 1953. A progressive governor, he brought about many statutory reforms, including a unified judiciary, water control, prison modernization, and a new higher education system. In 1944 he was a darkhorse candidate for the presidency of the United States but failed to be nominated. In 1948 he was the vice-presidential running mate of Thomas E. Dewey on the Republican ticket. In a third try for national office, Warren headed the California delegation to the Republican convention in 1952, but Dwight Eisenhower was nominated. Warren became a strong supporter of Eisenhower in the subsequent campaign.

Chief Justice

When President Eisenhower appointed Warren to the Supreme Court, he said that he "wanted a man whose reputation for integrity, honesty, middle of the road philosophy, experience in government, experience in the law . . . will make a great Chief Justice." A great chief justice was long overdue. In its 163d year, the Supreme Court had accomplished little in establishing "equal justice under law" in the actual lives of most Americans. While some of the chief justices who preceded Warren doubtless aspired to give real meaning to the phrase, they could not quite bring it about. Though the due-process clause of the 14th Amendment had been written into the Constitution 85 years before Warren came to the bench, only portions of the Bill of Rights had been applied through that clause against action by individual states. Further, the equal-protection clause of the 14th Amendment had been recognized only in very limited areas. It had not been utilized in the grade schools, in public facilities, or in transportation.

In the field of criminal justice, though lip service had been given to individual rights, the fact is that in state cases poor persons were not furnished a transcript of the trial for appeal or given counsel at any stage of the litigation, save in capital cases. And while the right to vote is the sine qua non of a free society, America had for a century and a half permitted invidious discrimination in legislative reapportionment. Finally, the doctrine of lack of standing in taxpayers' suits had for years acted as an impenetrable barrier to the testing of the constitutionality of many acts of Congress.

Racial Desegregation

The 14th Amendment to the Federal Constitution, adopted in 1868, declared "all persons born . . . in the United States" to be citizens there of and guaranteed them, among other things, "the equal protection of the laws." However, African Americans struggled long and hard before they obtained these equal rights. It was not until 1954 that an 1896 constitutional rule of "separate but equal" treatment of the races was overturned in *Brown v. Board of Education of Topeka*. In his opinion for the Court, Warren declared that "separate educational facilities are inherently unequal" and concluded that "in the field of public education the doctrine of separate but equal has no place."

The *Brown* decision triggered cases attacking segregated public facilities in transportation, libraries, parks, and so forth. Finally, its doctrine was extended in 1964 to places of public accommodation such as restaurants and hotels. The opinion also sparked a tempest of controversy that brought the dawn of a new day in America's economic, social, and political life.

Criminal Justice

Winston Churchill said that history judges the quality of a civilization by its system of criminal justice. If this be true,

American civilization will owe much of its standing to Warren's leadership. Beginning with *Griffin v. Illinois* (1956), which required states to furnish an indigent criminal defendant with a copy of the evidence adduced at his trial, and extending to *Miranda v. Arizona* (1967), which afforded counsel to an indigent before interrogation, there was a continual wave of cases that gave substance to the guarantees afforded every individual in the Bill of Rights. These included *Mapp v. Ohio,* extending the protection against unreasonable search and seizure of the 4th Amendment to actions of the states; *Gideon v. Wainwright,* giving the 6th Amendment's guarantee of counsel that same coverage; *Malloy v. Hogan,* protecting the individual from self-incrimination by state action, and *Berger v. New York,* guarding the privacy of the individual from self-incrimination by state action; and *Berger v. New York,* guarding the privacy of the individual against eavesdropping by the state.

Like the segregation cases, these opinions aroused a storm of protest. The Chief Justice, as well as the Court, was accused of handcuffing the police, causing a crime wave, and coddling criminals. But the Court continued to follow the principle that when the rights of any individual or group are transgressed, the freedom of all is threatened. In short, it translated the ideals of the Bill of Rights into a strong shield for the individual against both the federal and state governments.

Political Process

As Warren said in *Reynolds v. Sims,* "The right to vote freely for the candidate of one's choice is of the essence of a democratic society, and any restrictions on that right strike at the heart of representative government." This right includes not only casting one's vote but also the right to have the vote counted at its full value. Nevertheless, prior to *Baker v. Carr* (1962), the ballots of rural voters had from 10 to 30 times the weight of those of city dwellers. Warren said in *Reynolds v. Sims,* "Legislators represent people, not trees or acres. Legislators are elected by voters, not farms or cities or economic interests . . . The weight of the citizen's vote cannot be made to depend on where he lives."

The impact of the voting cases was tremendous. Thus, there were some 25 cases subsequent to *Baker.* The political process in representative governments was completely transformed. In the long run the effect of these cases may be more important than those condemning segregation. The right to vote is the citizen's most powerful weapon in a democratic society. Because legislators listened to the voices of voters, the equality of those voices foced them to listen more attentively. One of the basic problems America faced in the city ghettoes included the result of the dominance of the rural voter. The new "one man, one vote" slogan changed the politics of every state in the Union. The decisions of the Chief Justice in segregation, criminal law, and apportionment cases culminated in a campaign to impeach him. He completely ignored it. When asked why he did not fight back, he replied, "A senator or governor may explain or defend his position publicly but not members of the Court. We can't be guided by what people think or say

. . . by public appraisal. If we were we would be deciding cases on other than legal bases."

Taxpayer Suits

In his decision in *Flast v. Cohen,* which the Chief Justice wrote in 1968, he made it possible for citizens to bring "test suits" to the Court. This was one of his last opinions and one of the most important. Because the Court can pass only on legal controversies brought to it, the number of people able to litigate a question is important. *Flast* was an opening wedge in enlarging the ways and means by which any taxpayer can bring a suit to the Supreme Court. This contributed to opening the door of litigation, bringing forth the greatest surge of citizen participation that any democracy has attained.

Through self-discipline and public experience Warren learned never to permit the clamor of the public or the private pressures of individuals or groups to influence his decisions. Some critics called him a crying liberal, but he classified himself as a conservative-liberal. He had courage, a simple but strong faith in humanity, a practical and varied public experience, and a determination to improve the lot of the common man. As Chief Justice, he extended those horizons in five categories of the law, including racial desegregations, criminal justice, the political process, taxpayer standing to test legislative action, and the all-important field of judicial administration, which enables the courts to function efficiently.

Improved Court Administration

The job of the judge is twofold: first, to determine the rule of law and second, to apply the rule determined. Warren soon found that the legal profession was placing greater emphasis on substantive problems than on administration. As a consequence, court dockets had become congested, the trial bar had decreased in size, and criminal law had become degraded. For over 16 years Warren preached the dogma of improved court administration. In his final address to the American Law Institute on June 2, 1969, he summed up the problem in these words, "We have never come to grips with . . . court administration. . . . We should make bold plans to see that our courts are properly managed to do the job the public expects . . . We must do everything that modern institutions these days do in order to keep up with growth and changes in the times."

In fact, Warren made "bold plans" for the federal system and implemented them. The Judicial Conference of the United States was transformed from a club for chief judges of the courts of appeals into an effective general administrator for the federal courts. Its membership was increased to include trial court representation; the rule making power for federal courts was transferred to it from the Supreme Court; and a complete reorganization of the conferences was effected through a reduction of the number of committees. The administrative office of the federal courts was thus strengthened and reorganized. The Federal Judicial Center, Warren's brainchild, was authorized by Congress and organized into a potent force in judicial administration.

After Robert Kennedy's assassination, Warren feared that nothing could stop Richard M. Nixon from winning the 1968 presidential race. The two men had been bitter enemies since their days as California politicians nearly twenty years before. At age seventy-seven, the chief justice knew that he could not outlast a four-year conservative administration. To prevent Nixon from appointing his successor, Warren submitted his resignation to President Lyndon Johnson on June 11, 1968. He served until 1969. At the request of President Lyndon Johnson, Warren reluctantly headed the commission of inquiry into the circumstances of the assassination of President John Kennedy. He concluded that the killing was not part of a domestic or foreign conspiracy.

He was honorary chairman of the World Peace through Law Center. As chairman of the World Association of Judges from 1966 to 1969, he brought to the judicial forums of the world the message that he had written indelibly into American jurisprudence: only equal justice under law will bring peace, order, and stability to the world.

Warren died on July 9, 1974, in Washington, D.C.

Further Reading

The most significant papers of Warren's early career are collected in *The Public Papers of Chief Justice Earl Warren,* edited by Henry M. Christman (1959). The most complete biography is John D. Weaver, *Warren: The Man, the Court, the Era* (1967). A shorter work is Bill Severn, *Mr. Chief Justice: Earl Warren* (1968).

A superficial, laudatory account is Luther A. Huston, *Pathway to Judgment: A Study of Earl Warren* (1966). Biographical sketches and excellent photographs of Warren and other members of his Court are in John P. Frank, *The Warren Court* (1964). A critical analysis of the Warren Court and its work was edited by Richard H. Sayler and others, *The Warren Court* (1969). Other books on the Court include Alexander M. Bickel, *Politics and the Warren Court* (1965), and Archibald Cox, *The Warren Court* (1968). Clifford M. Lytle collected various statements from critics of the Warren Court in *The Warren Court and His Critics* (1968). □

Mercy Otis Warren

The American writer Mercy Otis Warren (1728-1814), the first significant woman historian, wrote an eyewitness account of the American Revolution.

Mercy Otis was born at West Barnstable, Mass., on Sept. 14, 1728. She had no formal education, but the tutor of her elder brother, James Otis, permitted her to use his library. She married James Warren of Plymouth in 1754. Her husband became a distinguished political leader and served for a time as paymaster to George Washington's army during the Revolution.

During the Revolutionary period Warren became a poet and pamphleteer. Her particular enemy was Thomas Hutchinson, who had served as chief justice and governor of Massachusetts and had been prominent in the "writs of assistance" controversy. In 1773 she wrote a pamphlet, *The*

Adulateur, and a play, *The Defeat,* based upon letters that Hutchinson and his lieutenant governor, Andrew Oliver, had written to England criticizing the colonists. In 1775 she wrote *The Group,* a satirical play. The Warrens took a consistently anticonstitution, pro-states'-rights position in the debates over ratification of the Constitution in 1787-1788, and Warren even wrote a tract against the Constitution. Her *Poems Dramatic and Miscellaneous* was published in 1790.

Warren began writing the *History of the Rise, Progress, and Termination of the American Revolution* (3 vols., 1805) during the Revolutionary War, and after the peace treaty was signed she continued to work on it. The first volume covers the period from the Stamp Act to Valley Forge, the second goes to the end of the Revolutionary War, and the third to 1800. She based her history on firsthand sources, which included her own observations, the Benjamin Lincoln papers, and John Adams's correspondence concerning his diplomatic attempts to involve the Dutch in the war.

The history is not parochial, as Warren included British domestic affairs and the war in other theaters as well as in the continental United States. Her Revolutionary nationalism showed in her praise of Sam Adams, Patrick Henry, and Thomas Jefferson and in her castigation of Hutchinson. Despite her opposition to the Constitution, she praised Washington. Her treatment of John Adams helped alienate a friendship, and her description of Alexander Hamilton as a "foreign adventurer" won her no support from his friends. Merrill Jensen (1966) characterized Warren's history by saying, "Her view of the revolution is

simple and anticipates in every way the views of the 'Whig historians' of the latter part of the nineteenth century." She died in Plymouth on Oct. 19, 1814.

Further Reading

Alice Brown, *Mercy Warren* (1896), is dated, while Katherine Anthony, *First Lady of the Revolution: The Life of Mercy Otis Warren* (1958), is adulatory. The most complete evaluation of Warren as a historian is in William Raymond Smith, *History as Argument: Three Patriot Historians of the American Revolution* (1966). Merrill Jensen's "Historians and the Nature of the American Revolution" in Ray Allen Billington, ed., *The Reinterpretation of Early American History* (1966), places Warren in the larger context of Revolutionary historiography. □

Robert Penn Warren

Robert Penn Warren (1905-1989), American man of letters, was dedicated to art as a way of exploring the meaning of contemporary existence.

Writer and poet Robert Penn Warren (1905-1989) was born in Guthrie, Kentucky on April 24, 1905. He twice received the Pulitzer Prize: one for fiction in 1947 and another for poetry in 1958. He earned his baccalaureate at Vanderbilt University in 1925 where he knew John Crowe Ransom, Allen Tate, and other Southern Agrarian poets who published the *Fugitive* magazine (1922-1925). His essay, *I'll Take My Stand,* published by Fugitive in 1930, was among the most persuasive and reasonable defenses of the South's cultural and social heritage to that date.

After receiving his master's in 1927 from the University of California, Warren attended Oxford University on a Rhodes scholarship and took his doctorate in 1930. *Pondy Woods and Other Poems* (1930) was his first published volume of verse. During the 1930s, he was managing editor with Cleanth Brooks of the *Southern Review.* Warren taught at Southwestern College, Vanderbilt, Louisiana State University, University of Minnesota, and Yale University after 1950.

Warren's fiction, usually historically based, considers the implications of man's initiation into awareness of the potential evil in himself and the world. It has much in common with the work of Nathaniel Hawthorne.

His pre-eminent work was *All the King's Men* (1946), ostensibly a fictionalized account of the rise and fall of the Louisiana demagogue Huey Long. Warren's central theme throughout the book was man's capacity for evil. This book garnered the first of his two Pulitzer Prize awards. *World Enough and Time* (1950), based on a famous 19th-century murder case, examines the conjunctions between idealism and evil, innocence and guilt. *Wilderness* (1961), a Civil War tale, describes a youth's acceptance of moral responsibility.

Although Warren's early poems were examples of the so-called New Critical school (as presented in his text book,

Understanding Poetry, written with Cleanth Brooks in 1938), his later verse was more romantic and transcendental, reflecting the influence of American writers such as Ralph Waldo Emerson, Hawthorne, and Herman Melville. "The Ballad of Billie Potts" retells a folk legend involving the unwitting murder of a child by his parents. *Brother to Dragons* (1953), a book-length "tale in verse and voices," tells of the wanton murder of an African American slave by Thomas Jefferson's two nephews in 1811. Jefferson represents the idealist enmeshed in evil and the institution of slavery. Warren himself appears as the seeker of some solution to universal moral complicity that slavery needed to survive. *Promises: Poems 1954 to 1956* (1957) won for Warren his second Pulitzer Prize.

Warren's *Segregation: The Inner Conflict in the South* (1956) argued that only by coming to terms with the common humanity of the African Americans could the South ever realize its ideals. The new poems in *New and Selected Poems* (1966) provide conclusive evidence that Warren's concerns changed considerably after his New Critical period. *Homage to Emerson: On a Night Flight to New York* entertains the possibility that Emerson's faith may still be relevant. Other works by Warren include the novels *Night Rider* (1939), *Band of Angels* (1955), *The Cave* (1959), and *Flood* (1964). He also published *Selected Essays* (1958) and *Who Speaks for the Negro?* (1965). Later works by Warren include such volumes of poetry as *Selected Poems, 1923-1975* (1976), *Being Here: Poetry, 1977-1980* (1980), *Chief Joseph of the Nez Perce* (1983), and *New and Selected Poems, 1923-1985* (1985); works of fiction include *Meet*

Me in the Green Glen (1971) and *A Place to Come Home To* (1977). His nonfiction pieces include *Democracy and Poetry* (1975), *Jefferson Davis Gets His Citizenship Back* (1980), *Portrait of a Father* (1988), and *New and Selected Essays* (1989). Warren also wrote the play *Ballad of a Sweet Dream of Peace: An Easter Charade* (produced in 1981).

Warren died of cancer September 15, 1989, in Stratton, Vermont. During his long and respected career, he was the recipient of many awards, including his two Pulitzer Prizes; Caroline Sinkler Prize, Poetry Society of America (1936, 1937, and 1938); Shelley Memorial Prize for *Eleven Poems on the Same Theme* (1942); National Book Award for *Promises: Poems 1954 to 1956* (1958); Bollingen Prize in Poetry, Yale University, 1967 for *Selected Poems: New and Old, 1923-1966* (1967); National Medal for Literature for *Audubon: A Vision* (1970); Copernicus Prize, American Academy of Poets (1976); Presidential Medal of Freedom, 1980; National Book Critics Circle Award nomination for *Being Here: Poetry, 1977-1980* (1980); named first Poet Laureate of the United States (1986); National Medal of Arts (1987); and numerous honorary degrees from such institutions as University of Louisville (1949), Swarthmore College (1958), Yale University (1959), Harvard University (1973), Johns Hopkins University (1977), Oxford University (1983), and Arizona State University.

Further Reading

An excellent critical study is Victor H. Strandberg, *A Colder Fire: The Poetry of Robert Penn Warren* (1965). Other studies include Leonard Casper, *Robert Penn Warren* (1960); Charles H. Bohner, *Robert Penn Warren* (1965); and the section on Warren in Hyatt H. Waggoner, *American Poets, from the Puritans to the Present* (1968). A useful critical anthology is John Lewis Longley, Jr., ed., *Robert Penn Warren: A Collection of Critical Essays* (1965); Connelly, Thomas L., et al.,*A Southern Renascence Man: Views of Robert Penn Warren*, Louisiana State University Press (1984); Koppelman, Robert S., *Robert Penn Warren's Modernist Spirituality*, University of Missouri Press (1995). □

Earl of Warwick and of Salisbury

The English nobleman Richard Neville, Earl of Warwick and of Salisbury (1428-1471), known as the Kingmaker, was the most powerful noble of his time in England and the principal baronial figure in the Wars of the Roses.

The eldest son of the Earl of Salisbury and nephew to Richard, Duke of York, Richard Neville was born on Nov. 22, 1428. He married Anne Beauchamp, through whom he inherited in 1449 the Warwick estate of a hundred manors. This wealth supplied troops for the 1455 street fight at St. Albans in which York, Salisbury, and Warwick captured the pliable Henry VI.

Warwick's reward was the captaincy of Calais, a position he filled with vigor and independence. Surviving a premature Yorkist demonstration in 1459 but forced to flee the country, in June 1460 Warwick and York's son Edward invaded England with 2,000 troops from the Calais garrison and captured Henry VI at Northampton on July 10. Parliament resisted York's claim to the throne on the argument of real-property inheritance laws. Warwick promoted the political compromise of having York named Henry's heir.

Henry VI's spirited queen, Margaret of Anjou, took up the cause of their son, Prince Edward of Lancaster. Her "northern army" defeated and killed Richard of York and the Earl of Salisbury at Wakefield on Dec. 30, 1460, out maneuvered Warwick at St. Albans on Feb. 17, 1461, and then liberated Henry VI. But her army failed to assault London. Warwick then stage-managed the "popular election" of York's eldest son as King Edward IV, the first monarch of the Yorkist line. With the help of Warwick, the 18-year-old king crushed the Lancastrians in a 10-hour slaughter at Towton on March 29, 1461. Margaret and Prince Edward fled to France, and Henry VI was later captured.

With his brother George installed as chancellor and with a trusted lawyer, Sir James Strangways, elected Speaker, Warwick was given the assignment of "pacifying the north," and from 1461 to 1464 he governed this region during unrest, Scottish invasions, and forays by Margaret of Anjou. His superintendence of diplomacy centered on possible marriage alliances for the King in the tangled rivalry of Burgundy, France, Brittany, Aragon, and Castile. By 1464 Warwick had decided on a policy of alliance with Louis XI of France and pressed Edward to marry Bona of Savoy, Louis's sister-in-law. Warwick's clamor on this subject eventually forced Edward to announce that he had already secretly married Elizabeth Woodville in 1464. The Queen's many relatives hencefourth received rapid advancement. Warwick gained a retaliatory advantage by the success with which he brought his daughters Isabel and Anne to the attention of King Edward's brothers, George of Clarence and Richard of Gloucester. Each of these romances, however, was delayed by royal policy. Edward sent Warwick to France for negotiations in 1467. During this absence Edward concluded an alliance by marrying Margaret, his sister, to Charles the Bold of Burgundy. At the same time, George Neville was dismissed as chancellor, and on the instance of Edward IV, Warwick's 79-year-old wealthy aunt was married to a 19-year-old nephew of the King.

The Kingmaker

In 1469, however, Warwick turned the usual unrest in northern England to his own purposes. The July 11 marriage at Calais of his daughter Isabel to George of Clarence was followed by another expedition to England. Edward's inadequate forces deserted him, and he became Warwick's captive. Warwick, however, found himself unable to raise sufficient troops to deal with the increasing disorders. With both Henry VI and Edward IV as his prisoners, and with George of Clarence at hand as a willing aspirant, the Kingmaker found himself overstocked with royal candidates and under equipped in soldiery. Edward resumed the government, and in 1470 he was "reconciled" to his brother and to Warwick as a curious prelude to a belated public discovery that both were rebels and must be driven from the land.

Warwick, with Clarence, fled to the court of Louis XI, embraced the Lancastrian cause, and betrothed his daughter Anne to Prince Edward, the son of Henry VI and Margaret of Anjou. Warwick's 1470 invasion of an unarmed England forced Edward IV to take refuge with Charles the Bold of Burgundy. Warwick recrowned an apathetic Henry VI and committed England to war against Burgundy as Louis's price for the escort of Margaret and Prince Edward to England.

The projected invasion of Burgundy did not materialize. When Edward IV returned in 1471 "to claim the duchy of York," Clarence made peace with his brother, Louis made peace with Burgundy, and Warwick could not muster an army significantly larger than Edward's. Against Edward that was not enough. Warwick was beaten at Barnet on April 14, 1471, and killed in flight. His Lancastrian candidate was slain at Tewkesbury on May 4, 1471, and the Neville estates were divided between Clarence and Gloucester (later Richard III), following the latter's marriage to the widowed Anne Neville.

Warwick's 1460 rebellion showed how armed wealth and public dissatisfaction could be combined to seize the seat of government in a nation without a standing army and, thus, to establish a legally accepted new regime. This action marked a change from the baronial factionalism of the past, and it looked toward the "popular politics" of the future.

Further Reading

Sir C. W. Oman, *Warwick the Kingmaker* (1893), and Paul Murray Kendall, *Warwick the Kingmaker* (1957), are sympathetic and readable biographies. J. R. Landers, *The Wars of the Roses* (1966), presents extensive quotations of primary sources translated into modern English. More general surveys of the period are Sir James H. Ramsay, *Lancaster and York* (2 vols., 1892), and S. B. Chrimes, *Lancastrians, Yorkists, and Henry VII* (1964).

Additional Sources

Young, Charles R. (Charles Robert), *The making of the Neville family in England, 1166-1400,* Rochester, NY: Boydell Press, 1996. □

Washakie

Washakie (1804–1900) was a Shoshoni tibal leader who helped passengers westward and remained friends with mountain men and trappers.

An ally of the white fur trappers, traders, immigrants, and the U.S. government, Chief Washakie and the Eastern Shoshonis were instrumental in assisting the Anglo-Americans in settling the western United States. His father, Paseego, was an Umatilla or Flathead Indian; his mother was a Shoshoni, possibly of the Wind River or Lemhi band.

Shortly after his birth in Montana's Bitterroot Mountains, he was named Pinquana ["Sweet Smelling"]. Later in life, he took the name Washakie—derived from Shoshonean *Wus'sik-he,* variously interpreted as "Gourd Rattle," "Rawhide Rattle," or "Gambler's Gourd." Washakie did not acquire this name until he had killed his first buffalo: after skinning the buffalo and curing the hide, he made a stone-filled rattle out of a dried, pouch-like piece of the animal's skin. During battle, Washakie would ride toward his enemies and shake his rattle to frighten their horses. Early on, he earned a reputation as a fierce warrior against the Sioux, Blackfeet, and Crow Indian nations. He also gained several other names from his fighting exploits: "Scar Face" or "Two Scar Chief" because of the deep scars on his left cheek, which had been pierced by a Blackfoot arrow, as well as "Shoots Straight" and "Sure Shot," for his keen eye and steady hand.

Became the Eastern Shoshonis' Leader

The Shoshonis were known as the Snake Indians, among not only whites but also the Great Plains tribes, apparently because they painted snakes on sticks to frighten their enemies. The origin of the word "Shoshoni" is unknown, but the name is believed to have been given them by whites. Bands of Shoshoni Indians—Southern, Western, Eastern, and Northern—occupied vast portions of the Rocky Mountain and plains areas of the American West.

Washakie's Eastern or Wind River Shoshonis roamed over most of Wyoming and a small part of southeastern Idaho.

When Washakie was a small child, his father was killed during a Blackfoot raid on their village. His mother escaped with her five young children and returned to her people, who lived along the Rocky Mountains in Wyoming. Washakie stayed with them until he was a young man, then is believed to have lived for about five years with the Bannocks.

As chief of the Eastern Shoshonis during the second half of the nineteenth century, Washakie became the most powerful leader of the migratory horse-owning tribe. He was chief at a time when his people's way of life was being threatened by the westward expansion of white American society. Washakie exerted great influence over the Northern Shoshonis and was temporarily allied with other Shoshoni and Bannock chiefs. Chief Pocatello, for whom a city in Idaho was named, had an alliance with Washakie. The Bannock chief Taghee of the Northern Paiutes, also offered Washakie his allegiance for a time.

Forbade His People from Fighting the Whites

During the 1820s through the 1830s, Washakie and the Shoshonis were on good terms with Anglo frontiersmen, trappers, and traders. They attended the fur trappers' Rocky Mountain rendezvous, establishing an alliance with their brigades and joining them in battles against the Sioux, Blackfeet, and Crows—all traditional enemies of the Shoshonis. By the mid-1840s, Washakie was principal chief of the Eastern Shoshoni band and waves of settlers were crossing his country on their way west along the Oregon Trail.

Washakie continued to maintain cordial relations with this new group of immigrants, assisting them in many ways. The Shoshonis helped the settlers recover lost stock and cross the region's swift rivers. Washakie also provided regular patrols of Shoshoni warriors to protect the immigrants from Sioux, Cheyenne, and Arapaho raiding parties. Perhaps even more important was his refusal to allow Shoshoni reprisals against settlers who were wiping out game and whose stock was destroying valuable Indian root grounds. According to Russell Freedman's *Indian Chiefs,* Washakie told his people: "You must not fight the whites. I not only advise against it, I forbid it!" The settlers were so appreciative of Washakie's assistance that 9,000 of them signed a document commending the Shoshonis and their chief. He was even on friendly terms with the Mormon leader "Big-Um" or Brigham Young.

Between the fall of 1858 and the spring of 1859, Washakie fought at the Battle of Crowheart Butte, the climax of the intertribal warfare between the Shoshonis and the Crows. He also met and became friends with famous mountain man Jim Bridger and Missouri hunter, trapper, and guide Christopher "Kit" Carson. In 1863 Washakie led his people to the safety of Fort Bridger, keeping them out of the Americans' Bear River Campaign against Bear Hunter's band of Northwestern Shoshonis.

In exchange for a 20-year-long payment agreement, Washakie signed the 1863 Treaty of Fort Bridger, guaranteeing U.S. travelers safe passage through his band's territory. His good relations with the U.S. government made it possible for him to secure the Wind River reservation, in present-day Wyoming, for the Eastern Shoshonis. In 1868 Washakie signed a second treaty establishing the 3 million-acre reservation; his people had given up their claims to other lands in Wyoming and Utah for the reservation, a remnant of their traditional territory. He also agreed to a clear path through the Green River Valley for the Union Pacific Railroad Company.

Even after the Shoshoni treaties were signed, the Sioux continued to hunt and raid the Eastern Shoshonis' reservation. Washakie complained to the U.S. Army, but they did little to stop the Sioux, adding to the animosity the chief already felt towards his traditional enemies. Washakie had old scores to settle with the Sioux: they had raided his people's villages many times and killed and scalped his oldest son. Later, when the army requested assistance in their war against the Sioux, Washakie jumped at the proposition.

The Eastern Shoshonis served as scouts and warriors for the U.S. Army against the Arapahos, Cheyennes, Sioux, and Utes. In 1876 Washakie and 200 warriors rode to the aid of General George Crook. Arriving too late to help Crook fight the Sioux at the Battle of the Rosebud in southern Montana, he joined forces with the general's troops and together they followed Crazy Horse's warriors all the way to the Powder River in eastern Montana.

A big and imposing man, Washakie took great pride in his appearance. He is said to have enjoyed looking at a framed photograph of himself hanging on the wall of a reservation store. Washakie was also proud of his possessions. With the help of his son Charlie, he painted pictures of his war exploits and then decorated his cabin with them. He was especially fond of a handsome saddle, decorated in silver, given to him by President Ulysses S. Grant. And he proudly posed for photographs wearing a silver peace medal sent to him by President Andrew Johnson. Always popular with politicians, Washakie was visited by President Chester A. Arthur in 1883.

But the United States did not always satisfy Washakie. In 1878 the government decided to put Chief Black Coal's Northern Arapahos on the Wind River reservation. The Arapahos were traditional enemies of the Shoshonis, but since they were destitute and starving Washakie agreed to let them stay on his reservation for a limited time. In spite of Washakie's protests, the Arapahos' temporary stay turned into a permanent one. Washakie had other complaints against the government; he objected to white hunters killing off large numbers of deer and antelope on the reservation. He also protested against trespassing gold miners and cowboys who were rustling the Shoshonis' cattle. Washakie reminded officials that the government had promised to keep both whites and other Indian tribes off Shoshoni land, but his arguments seemed to fall on deaf ears.

Washakie's Importance in Native American History

Washakie's peaceful relations with Anglo-Americans kept the Eastern Shoshoni from experiencing the devastating effects of removal to the Indian Territory, located in what is today the state of Oklahoma. Their alliance with the Americans also kept the Native American band from suffering casualties at the hands of the U.S. Army. Washakie's cooperation with the Americans benefited his people more than a war with the white settlers could have.

In 1897 Washakie was baptized an Episcopalian. He died three years later at Flathead Village in Montana's Bitterroot Valley and was buried with full military honors at Fort Washakie, Wyoming. In a life that spanned nearly an entire century, he had married twice and fathered at least 12 children, including a son, Cocoosh (Dick Washakie), who succeeded him as chief of the Eastern Shoshonis.

Further Reading

Dockstader, Frederick J., *Great North American Indians,* New York, Van Nostrand Reinhold, 1977; 323-25.

Freedman, Russell, *Indian Chiefs,* New York, Holiday House, 1987; 73-89.

Native North American Almanac, edited by Duane Champagne, Detroit, Gale, 1994; 1184.

Trenholm, Virginia Cole, and Maurine Carley, *The Shoshonis: Sentinels of the Rockies,* Norman, University of Oklahoma Press, 1964; 97-99.

Waldman, Carl, *Who Was Who in Native American History,* New York, Facts On File, 1990; 372. □

Booker Taliaferro Washington

Booker Taliaferro Washington (1856-1915), African American educator and racial leader, founded Tuskegee Institute for black students. His "Atlanta Compromise" speech made him America's major black leader for 20 years.

Booker Taliaferro (the Washington was added later) was born a slave in Franklin County, Va., on April 5, 1856. His mother was the plantation's cook. His father, a local white man, took no responsibility for him. His mother married another slave, who escaped to West Virginia during the Civil War. She and her three children were liberated by a Union army in 1865 and, after the war, joined her husband.

Growing Up Black

The stepfather put the boys to work in the salt mines in Malden, W.Va. Booker eagerly asked for education, but his stepfather conceded only when Booker agreed to toil in the mines mornings and evenings to make up for earnings lost while in school. He had known only his first name, but

when pupils responded to roll call with two names, Booker desperately added a famous name, becoming Booker Washington. Learning from his mother that he already had a last name, he became Booker T. Washington.

Overhearing talk about a black college in Hampton, Va., Washington longed to go. Meanwhile, as houseboy for the owner of the coal mines and saltworks, he developed scrupulous work habits. In 1872 he set out for Hampton Institute. When his money gave out, he worked at odd jobs. Sleeping under wooden sidewalks, begging rides, and walking, he traveled the remaining 80 miles and, bedraggled and penniless, asked for admission and assistance. After Hampton officials tested him by having him clean a room, he was admitted and given work as a janitor.

Hampton Institute, founded in 1868 by a former Union general, emphasized manual training. The students learned useful trades and earned their way. Washington studied brickmasonry along with collegiate courses. Graduating in 1876, he taught in a rural school for two years. Studying at Wayland Seminary in Washington, D.C., he became disenchanted with classical education, considering his fellow students to be dandies more interested in making an impression and living off the black masses than in serving mankind. He became convinced that practical, manual training in rural skills and crafts would save his race, not higher learning divorced from the reality of the black man's downtrodden existence. In 1879 he was invited to teach at Hampton Institute, particularly to supervise 100 Native Americans admitted experimentally. He proved a great success in his two years on the faculty.

Tuskegee Institute

In 1881 citizens in Tuskegee, Ala., asked Hampton's president to recommend a white man to head their new black college; he suggested Washington instead. The school had an annual legislative appropriation of $2,000 for salaries, but no campus, buildings, pupils, or staff. Washington had to recruit pupils and teachers and raise money for land, buildings, and equipment. Hostile rural whites who feared education would ruin black laborers accepted his demonstration that his students' practical training would help improve their usefulness. He and his students built a kiln and made the bricks with which they erected campus buildings.

Under Washington's leadership (1881-1915), Tuskegee Institute became an important force in black education. Tuskegee pioneered in agricultural extension, sending out demonstration wagons that brought better methods to farmers and sharecroppers. Graduates founded numerous "little Tuskegees." African Americans mired in the poverty and degradation of cotton sharecropping improved their farming techniques, income, and living conditions. Washington urged them to become capitalists, founding the National Negro Business League in 1900. Black agricultural scientist George Washington Carver worked at Tuskegee from 1896 to 1943, devising new products from peanuts and sweet potatoes. By 1915 Tuskegee had 1,500 students and a larger endowment than any other black institution.

"Atlanta Compromise"

In 1895 Washington gave his famous "Atlanta Compromise" speech. Although he shared the late Frederick Douglass's long-range goals of equality and integration, Washington renounced agitation and protest tactics. He urged blacks to subordinate demands for political and social rights, concentrating instead on improving job skills and usefulness. "The opportunity to earn a dollar in a factory just now is worth infinitely more than the opportunity to spend a dollar in an opera-house," he said. He appealed to white people to rely on loyal, proven black workers, pointing out that the South would advance to the degree that blacks were allowed to secure education and become productive.

Washington's position so pleased whites, North and South, that they made him the new black spokesman. He became powerful, having the deciding voice in Federal appointments of African Americans and in philanthropic grants to black institutions. Through subsidies or secret partnerships, he controlled black newspapers, stifling critics. Overawed by his power and hoping his tactics would work, many blacks went along. However, increasingly during his last years, such black intellectuals as W.E.B. Du Bois, John Hope, and William Monroe Trotter denounced his surrender of civil rights and his stressing of training in crafts, some obsolete, to the neglect of liberal education. Opposition centered in the Niagara Movement, founded in 1905, and the National Association for the Advancement of Colored People, which succeeded it in 1910.

Although outwardly conciliatory, Washington secretly financed and encouraged attempts and lawsuits to block southern moves to disfranchise and segregate blacks. He had lost two wives by death and married a third time in 1893. His death on Nov. 14, 1915, cleared the way for blacks to return to Douglass's tactics of agitating for equal political, social, and economic rights. Washington won a Harvard honorary degree in 1891. His birthplace is a national monument.

Further Reading

Washington's autobiographical works are *The Story of My Life and Work* (1900), *Up from Slavery* (1901), and *My Larger Education* (1911), the last two especially revealing. Collections of his writings along with contemporary opinions are Hugh Hawkins, ed., *Booker T. Washington and His Critics* (1962), and Emma Lou Thornbrough, ed., *Booker T. Washington* (1969). There are three major biographies: Emmett J. Scott and Lyman Beecher Stowe, *Booker T. Washington* (1916), an unscholarly glorification, is useful because Scott was Washington's assistant; Basil Mathews, *Booker T. Washington: Educator and Interracial Interpreter* (1948), is also highly laudatory; Samuel R. Spencer, Jr., *Booker T. Washington and the Negro's Place in American Life* (1955), the most balanced account is still not sufficiently critical of Washington. The best account of Washington's times is August Meier, *Negro Thought in America, 1880-1915: Racial Ideologies in the Age of Booker T. Washington* (1963). □

George Washington

George Washington (1732-1799) was commander in chief of the American and French forces in the American Revolution and became the first president of the United States.

George Washington was born at Bridges Creek, later known as Wakefield, in Westmoreland County, Va., on Feb. 22, 1732. His father died when George was eleven years old, and the boy spent the next few years with his mother at Ferry Farm near Fredericksburg, with relatives in Westmoreland, and with his half brother at Mount Vernon. By the time he was 16 he had a rudimentary education, studying mathematics, surveying, reading, and the usual subjects of his day. In 1749 Washington was appointed county surveyor, and his experience on the frontier led to his appointment as a major in the Virginia militia in 1752.

French and Indian War

Virginia governor Robert Dinwiddie appointed the 21-year-old Washington to warn the French moving into the Ohio Valley against encroaching on English territory. Washington published the results of this expedition, including the French rejection of the ultimatum, in the *Journal of Major George Washington . . .* (1754). Dinwiddie then commissioned Washington a lieutenant colonel with orders to dislodge the French at Ft. Duquesne, but a superior French force bested the Virginia troops. This conflict triggered the French and Indian War, and Great Britain dispatched regular troops under Gen. Edward Braddock in 1755 to oust the French. Braddock appointed Washington as aide-de-camp.

Later in the year, after Braddock's death, Dinwiddie promoted Washington to colonel and made him commander in chief of all Virginia troops. Throughout 1756 and 1757 Washington pursued a defensive policy, fortifying the frontier with stockades, recruiting men, and establishing discipline. In 1758, with the title of brigadier, he accompanied British regulars on the campaign that forced the French to abandon Ft. Duquesne. With the threat of frontier violence removed, Washington resigned his commission, soon married the widow Martha Custis, and devoted himself to life at Mount Vernon.

Washington took seriously his role of stepfather and guardian of Martha's two children; it was his duty, he wrote, to be "generous and attentive," and he was. His stepdaughter's death at 17 was an emotional shock to him. When his stepson died in 1781, after serving in the Virginia militia at Yorktown, Washington virtually adopted two of his four children.

Early Political Career

Washington inherited local prominence from his family, just as he inherited property and social position. His grandfather and great-grandfather had been justices of the peace, a powerful county position in 18th-century Virginia, and his father had served as sheriff and church warden, as well as justice of the peace. His half brother Lawrence had been a representative from Fairfax County, and George Washington's entry into politics was based on an alliance with the family of Lawrence's father-in-law, Lord Fairfax.

Washington was elected as a representative to the Virginia House of Burgesses in 1758 from Frederick County. From 1760 to 1774 he served as a justice of Fairfax County, and he was a longtime vestryman of Truro parish. His experience on the county court and in the colonial legislature molded his views on Parliamentary taxation of the Colonies after 1763. He opposed the Stamp Act in 1765, arguing that Parliament "hath no more right to put their hands into my pocket, without my consent, than I have to put my hands into yours for money." As a member of the colonial legislature, he backed nonimportation as a means of reversing British policy in the 1760s, and in 1774 he attended the rump session of the dissolved Assembly, which called for a Continental Congress to take united colonial action against the Boston Port Bill and other "Intolerable Acts" directed against Massachusetts.

In July 1774 Washington presided at the county meeting which adopted the Fairfax Resolves, which he had helped write. These resolves influenced the adoption of the Continental Association, the plan devised by the First Continental Congress for enforcing nonimportation of British goods. They also proposed the creation in each county of a militia company independent of the royal governor's control, the idea from which the Continental Army developed. By May 1775 Washington, who headed the Fairfax militia company, had been chosen to command the companies of six other counties. The only man in uniform when the Second Continental Congress met after the battles of Lexington and Concord, he was elected unanimously as commander in chief of all Continental Army forces. From June 15, 1775,

until Dec. 23, 1783, he commanded the Continental Army and, after the French alliance of 1778, the combined forces of the United States and France in the War of Independence against Great Britain.

Revolutionary Years

Throughout the Revolutionary years Washington developed military leadership, administrative skills, and political acumen, functioning from 1775 to 1783 as the de facto chief executive of the United States. His wartime experiences gave him a continental outlook, and his Circular Letter to the States in June 1783 made it clear that he favored a strong central government.

Washington returned to Mount Vernon at the end of the Revolution. "I have not only retired from all public employments," he wrote his friend the Marquis de Lafayette, "but I am retiring within myself." But there was little time for sitting "under the shadow of my own vine and my own fig tree." He kept constantly busy with farming, western land interests, and navigation of the Potomac. Finally, Washington presided at the Federal Convention in 1787 and supported ratification of the Constitution in order to "establish good order and government and to render the nation happy at home and respected abroad."

First American President

The position of president of the United States seemed shaped by the Federal Convention on the assumption that Washington would be the first to occupy the office. In a day when executive power was suspect—when the creation of the presidency, as Alexander Hamilton observed in *The Federalist,* was "attended with greater difficulty" than perhaps any other—the Constitution established an energetic and independent chief executive. Pierce Butler, one of the Founding Fathers, noted that the convention would not have made the executive powers so great "had not many of the members cast their eyes toward General Washington as President, and shaped their ideas of the Powers to be given a President, by their opinions of his Virtue."

After his unanimous choice as president in 1789, Washington helped translate the new constitution into a workable instrument of government: the Bill of Rights was added, as he suggested, out of "reverence for the characteristic rights of freemen"; an energetic executive branch was established, with the executive departments—State, Treasury, and War—evolving into an American Cabinet; the Federal judiciary was inaugurated; and the congressional taxing power was utilized to pay the Revolutionary War debt and to establish American credit at home and abroad.

As chief executive, Washington consulted his Cabinet on public policy, presided over their differences—especially those between Thomas Jefferson and Hamilton—with a forbearance that indicated his high regard for his colleagues, and he made up his mind after careful consideration of alternatives. He approved the Federalist financial program and the later Hamiltonian proposals—funding of the national debt, assumption of the state debts, the establishment of a Bank of the United States, the creation of a national coinage system, and an excise tax. He supported a national policy for disposition of the public lands and presided over the expansion of the Federal union from eleven states (North Carolina and Rhode Island ratified the Constitution after Washington's inaugural) to 16 (Vermont, Kentucky, and Tennessee were admitted between 1791 and 1796). Washington's role as presidential leader was of fundamental importance in winning support for the new government's domestic and foreign policies. "Such a Chief Magistrate," Fisher Ames noted, "appears like the pole star in a clear sky. . . . His Presidency will form an epoch and be distinguished as the Age of Washington."

Despite his unanimous election, Washington expected that the measures of his administration would meet opposition, and they did. By the end of his first term the American party system was developing. When he mentioned the possibility of retirement in 1792, therefore, both Hamilton and Jefferson agreed that he was "the only man in the United States who possessed the confidence of the whole" and "no other person . . . would be thought anything more than the head of a party." "North and South," Jefferson urged, "will hang together if they have you to hang on."

Creation of a Foreign Policy

Washington's second term was dominated by foreign-policy considerations. Early in 1793 the French Revolution became the central issue in American politics when France, among other actions, declared war on Great Britain and appointed "Citizen" Edmond Genet minister to the United States. Determined to keep "our people in peace," Washington issued a neutrality proclamation, although the word "neutrality" was not used. His purpose, Washington told Patrick Henry, was "to keep the United States free from political connections with every other country, to see them independent of all and under the influence of none. In a word, I want an American character, that the powers of Europe may be convinced we act for ourselves and not for others."

Citizen Genet, undeterred by the proclamation of neutrality, outfitted French privateers in American ports and organized expeditions against Florida and Louisiana. For his undiplomatic conduct, the Washington administration requested and obtained his recall. In the midst of the Genet affair, Great Britain initiated a blockade of France and began seizing neutral ships trading with the French West Indies. Besides violating American neutral rights, the British still held posts in the American Northwest, and the Americans claimed that they intrigued with the Indians against the United States.

Frontier provocations, ship seizures, and impressment made war seem almost inevitable in 1794, but Washington sent Chief Justice John Jay to negotiate a settlement of the differences between the two nations. Although Jay's Treaty was vastly unpopular—the British agreed to evacuate the Northwest posts but made no concessions on neutral rights or impressment—Washington finally accepted it as the best treaty possible at that time. The treaty also paved the way for Thomas Pinckney's negotiations with Spanish ministers, now fearful of an Anglo-American entente against Spain in the Western Hemisphere. Washington happily signed

Pinckney's Treaty, which resolved disputes over navigation of the Mississippi, the Florida boundary, and neutral rights.

While attempting to maintain peace with Great Britain in 1794, the Washington administration had to meet the threat of domestic violence in western Pennsylvania. The Whiskey Rebellion, a reaction against the first Federal excise tax, presented a direct challenge to the power of the Federal government to enforce its laws. After a Federal judge certified that ordinary judicial processes could not deal with the opposition to the laws, Washington called out 12,000 state militiamen "to support our government and laws" by crushing the rebellion. The resistance quickly melted, and Washington showed that force could be tempered with clemency by pardoning the insurgents.

Washington's Contributions

Nearly all observers agree that Washington's 8 years as president demonstrated that executive power was completely consistent with the genius of republican government. Putting his prestige on the line in an untried office under an untried constitution, Washington was fully aware, as he pointed out in his First Inaugural Address, that "the preservation of the sacred fire of liberty and the destiny of the republican model of government are justly considered, perhaps, as deeply, as finally, staked on the experiment entrusted to the hands of the American people."

Perhaps Washington's chief strength—the key to his success as a military and a political leader—was his realization that in a republic the executive, like all other elected representatives, would have to measure his public acts against the temper of public opinion. As military commander dealing with the Continental Congress and the state governments during the Revolution, Washington had realized the importance of administrative skills as a means of building public support of the army. As president, he applied the same skills to win support for the new Federal government.

Despite Washington's abhorrence of factionalism, his administrations and policies spurred the beginnings of the first party system. This ultimately identified Washington, the least partisan of presidents, with the Federalist party, especially after Jefferson's retirement from the Cabinet in 1793. Washington's Farewell Address, though it was essentially a last will and political testament to the American people, inevitably took on political coloration in an election year. Warning against the divisiveness of excessive party spirit, which tended to separate Americans politically as "geographical distinctions" did sectionally, he stressed the necessity for an American character free of foreign attachments. Two-thirds of his address dealt with domestic politics and the baleful influence of party; the rest of the document laid down a statement of firs principles of American foreign policy. But even here, Washington's warning against foreign entanglements was especially applicable to foreign interference in the domestic affairs of the United States.

His Retirement

Washington's public service did not end with his retirement from the presidency. During the "half war" with

France, President John Adams appointed him commander in chief, and Washington accepted with the understanding that he would not take field command until the troops had been recruited and equipped. Since Adams settled the differences with France by diplomatic negotiations, Washington never assumed actual command. He continued to reside at Mount Vernon, where he died on Dec. 14, 1799, after contracting a throat infection.

At the time of Washington's death, Congress unanimously adopted a resolution to erect a marble monument in the nation's capital "to commemorate the great events of his military and political life"; Congress also directed that "the family of General Washington be requested to permit his body to be deposited under it." The Washington Monument was finally completed in 1884, but Washington's remains were never moved there.

Further Reading

The most thorough biography of Washington is Douglas Southall Freeman's monumental six-volume *George Washington,* completed in a seventh volume by John A. Carroll and Mary Wells Ashworth (1948-1957). The one-volume condensation of Freeman's work by Richard Harwell (1968) offers a well-rounded portrait of Washington as a person and as a public figure. Another major work is the splendidly written study by James Thomas Flexner, *George Washington* (1965-1972).

The best brief surveys are Esmond Wright, *Washington and the American Revolution* (1957); Marcus Cunliffe, *George Washington: Man and Monument* (1958); and James Morton Smith, ed., *George Washington: A Profile* (1969), a group of essays by 11 historians. Assessments of Washington by contemporaries and by historians appear in Morton Borden, comp., *George Washington* (1969). For details on the first presidential elections see Arthur M. Schlesinger, Jr., ed., *History of American Presidential Elections* (4 vols., 1971).

Recommended for general historical background are Merrill Jensen, *The New Nation: A History of the United States during the Confederation, 1781-1789* (1950), John C. Miller, *Federalist Era, 1789-1801* (1960); and John Richard Alden, *A History of the American Revolution* (1969). □

Juan Carlos Wasmosy

Juan Carlos Wasmosy (born 1939) became president of Paraguay in 1993 after winning the country's first truly democratic elections.

At the age of 54, Juan Carlos Wasmosy, conservative in his politics and a long-time member of the Colorado party (which had ruled Paraguay continuously since 1947), took the presidential oath on August 15, 1993, Paraguay's first democratically-chosen president since the nation's founding in 1811.

After the fall of longtime dictator Alfredo Stroessner in 1988, Paraguay's politics had been stormy. Stroessner's successor, General Andrés Rodríguez, had pledged a fair election, but opposition candidates (notably Domingo Laíno of the Authentic Radical Liberal party and Guillermo Caballero Vargas of National Encounter) expressed concerns about irregularities. A nonpartisan agency that monitored the election, Saka, tried to carry out a separate vote count, but the state telephone company cut its phone lines and police in the capital of Asunción prevented Saka employees from hand-delivering the count. The telephone service of the two major opposition parties was also discontinued.

Former U.S. President Jimmy Carter (who with Canadian Senator Ed Graham headed an international inspection team that visited more than 1,800 polling tables in the country) personally appealed to President Rodríguez, and three opposition phone lines were restored. In related harassing actions, the military, citing a 1992 election law, prevented Paraguayans exiled in Argentina and Brazil from crossing the border in order to cast their ballots. When the vote was finally in, Wasmosy won with 40 percent of 1.7 million votes cast. The Colorado party also won a majority of the country's 17 governor's races, but the Authentic Liberals garnered enough support to prevent a Colorado domination of either legislative house. In the closing days of the campaign, a prominent military officer, General Lino Oviedo, declared that the army and the Colorado party would continue to govern Paraguay for a hundred years. These events reinforced beliefs that the military, which has had a close relationship with the Colorado party, would dominate Wasmosy's government.

Educated as an engineer, Wasmosy made a fortune in business in the 1970s as head of a consortium that won contracts to build Itaipu Dam, the world's biggest, on the Paraguayan-Brazilian border. A free-market disciple, he supported Paraguay's role in Mercosur, the regional common market. Though a longtime Colorado party member, his only political office before assuming the presidency was that of minister of integration in the Rodríguez administration.

In economic policy Wasmosy was little different from his two major opponents, both of whom called for a transition to market-oriented doctrine and ridding the country of the widespread fraud tolerated during the Stroessner dictatorship. Caballero Vargas (also a millionaire), candidate of National Encounter, appealed to business classes in the capital who were openly critical of military-run monopolies. He also did well among young urbanites. Laíno, candidate of the Authentic Liberals, made his mark as a critic of the Stroessner regime.

In his inaugural address Wasmosy promised to carry out the free-trade policies of his predecessor and to confront the growing problems in transportation, health, and education. Recognizing the strength of the legislative opposition, he called for a "governability pact" with those who had opposed him. Paraguay appeared headed for political as well as economic modernization. Still, political differences can create divisions among those who generally agree on economic policies, and the political animosities of the past reared to disrupt the plans of even the best-intentioned.

Following the 1993 elections, animosities between the new president and then supporter General Lino Oviedo grew. In 1996 Wasmosy requested Oviedo retire his command but the general refused, setting off the biggest challenge faced to date by the young democracy. Rumors swept through the government that Oviedo was planning a coup. With Oviedo in control of greater military resources, Wasmosy was faced with either surrendering to the general's demand that he resign or sending his less powerful forces into battle. To avoid certain bloodshed, Wasmosy and Oviedo stuck a deal. In exchange for ending the coup attempt and his military resignation, Oviedo would be given the post of Defense Minister.

Although Wasmosy saw the action as "a gesture of reconciliation," the people of Paraguay were outraged, accusing the president of giving into blackmail. Supporters of the democracy, such as the United States, responded in kind, saying they would not recognize a government that came to power by military threat. This placed Oviedo on the brink of political alienation and provided Wasmosy with the strength to calm the public turmoil by forcing Oviedo to resign without the Defense Minister offer and sending him to jail. As investigations into these events continued, the success of the young government remained uncertain. Oviedo claimed there was no coup attempt, accusing Wasomosy of creating the crisis as a means to restructure his government. Wasmosy denied those charges and claimed his resolution of the crisis as a strong victory for democracy. Consequently, both Wasmosy and Oviedo resolved to run in the 1998 elections.

Further Reading

As a contemporary political figure, Wasmosy was not widely known outside Paraguay. There is little about him in English, though the story of modern Paraguayan politics can be followed in the *Christian Science Monitor, The New York Times,* and *Facts–On–File.* Recent developments are documented in various news sources including: Stephen Brown, "Paraguay says citizens will defend democracy,"*Reuters* (April 26, 1996); IPS Correspondents, "Paraguay: confusion regarding end of crisis persists," *Inter Press Service English News Wire* (April 26,1996); Jos De Mar Dia Amarilla, "Paraguay army rebel says president wanted coup," *Reuters* (June 5,1996). □

Jakob Wassermann

The German author Jakob Wassermann (1873-1934) combined a romanticized psychoanalysis with an almost journalistic sensationalism. He used a narrative technique that verged at times on the surrealistic and was heavily laden with symbol and constructed myth.

Jakob Wassermann was born on March 10, 1873, in Fürth, the son of a Jewish merchant. After a childhood with many restrictions, he began his career as an office clerk, in Munich and then in Freiburg. In 1898 he moved to Vienna and eventually established himself as a writer. Derivative and imitative, Wassermann's novels showed from the outset a strong dependence upon Fyodor Dostoevsky—particularly in his fondness for the psychological probing of criminals and social outcasts—as well as the influence of

the master of the romantic horror and detective story, E. T. A. Hoffmann.

Wassermann's first significant work is *Die Juden von Zirndorf* (1897; *The Jews of Zirndorf*), in which his deep knowledge of his own community in Fürth and Nuremberg stands him in good stead. As in many of his other works, Wassermann's preoccupation with innocence and redemption is here interleaved with a somewhat crass depiction of depravity and superstition. *Der Moloch* (1902) pays tribute to the contemporary literary cult of the great city (here Vienna), seen as an all-devouring monster of sin and perversion. *Caspar Hauser* (1908) is probably the author's best novel; the book, based on fact, deals with the case of the mute youth who appeared one day in 1828 on the streets of Nuremberg. Resemblances to Dostoevsky's *The Idiot* may also be noted in this tale of the rejection and contamination of innate purity by corrupt society.

After *Caspar Hauser* Wassermann's novels and short stories become increasingly preoccupied with bizarre and perverse anecdotes and intrigue, often initially drawn from biography or the newspapers. *Das Gänsemännchen* (1915; *The Goose Man*) illuminates the problem involved in simultaneous cohabitation with two wives. *Christian Wahnschaffe* (1919) exploits the theme of the rich man's son who rejects the world to turn toward Buddhism. *Der Fall Maurizius* (1928; *The Mauritius Case*) is a type of detective novel made colorful by excursions into hypnosis but also weighed down by a tedious mass of psychological dissection. Like Honoré de Balzac, whom he imitated, Wassermann introduces the same characters into different novels;

thus *Etzel Andergast* (1931) is a sequel to *The Mauritius Case,* and its hero, Joseph Kerkhoven, reappears in *Joseph Kerkhovens dritte Existenz* (1934; *Joseph Kerkhoven's Third Existence*).

Wassermann is a somewhat uneven and labored writer, and he cannot in any sense be considered a stylist. His novels are often marred by diffuseness and miasmic obscurity. At the same time his extensive output is of considerable historical interest and illuminates rather well the consequences of marriage between the new depth psychology and the popular novel of sensation and crime. He died on Jan. 1, 1934, in Alt-Aussee.

Further Reading

The standard study in English is John C. Blankenagel, *The Writings of Jakob Wassermann* (1942). A penetrating account of Wassermann, placing him in his tradition and period, is also in Jethro Bithell, *Modern German Literature* (1939; 3d ed. 1959). □

Benjamin Waterhouse

The American physician Benjamin Waterhouse (1754-1846) introduced cowpox vaccination against smallpox in the Boston area in 1800.

B enjamin Waterhouse was born at Newport, R.I., on March 4, 1754, the son of Timothy Waterhouse, a chairmaker. His mother was a cousin of Dr. John Fothergill, an eminent London physician. This family connection, plus the influence of the Scottish physicians practicing in Newport, led Waterhouse into medicine as an apprentice to Dr. John Haliburton. He spent most of 1777-1778 studying medicine in London and Edinburgh, then went to Leiden in late 1778.

Waterhouse returned to Newport in 1782 and joined the medical department of Harvard College the next year as professor of the theory and practice of physic. He married Elizabeth Oliver in 1788; she died in 1815, after giving birth to six children, and he remarried in 1819.

In 1799 Waterhouse learned of Edward Jenner's work in England, using cowpox as a vaccination against smallpox. Waterhouse immediately published a paper on this procedure, pointing out the advantage of cowpox as a very mild disease. Securing some cowpox matter in 1800, he inoculated his five-year-old son and a servant boy. He then exposed the servant boy to smallpox, resulting in a very mild infection, limited to the arm. While continuing to vaccinate with cowpox matter, Waterhouse began publicizing the method, notably in *A Prospect of Exterminating the Small Pox* (1800). Unfortunately, the need for pure cowpox material for inoculation and the need for medical supervision of inoculation procedures were not realized, and soon inoculation was being administered by the general populace, resulting in an epidemic. Criticism directed against Waterhouse was allayed when he demanded a complete investigation by the Boston board of health in 1802, which verified all his claims for cowpox vaccination. From 1802 he continued to publicize and encourage vaccination in Massachusetts and neighboring states, constantly stressing the need for purity of vaccine.

In 1804 Waterhouse began an attack on the Harvard students for their use of tobacco and liquor, which he was convinced was responsible for the rise in incidence of consumption and nervous disorders. By 1810 Waterhouse was involved in a dispute with college officials and a number of younger medical men over the future direction of the medical school. He was committed to the lecture system exclusively and opposed the development of clinical facilities at a new site near the proposed Massachusetts General Hospital. After trying to establish a rival medical school, called the College of Physicians, Waterhouse was forced to resign from Harvard in 1812.

Waterhouse was medical superintendent of military posts in New England (1813-1820), which gave him time for a literary career. His best-known work is *A Journal of a Young Man of Massachusetts,* the story of a ship's doctor imprisoned by the British in the War of 1812. He died at his home in Cambridge on Oct. 2, 1846.

Further Reading

Some mention of Waterhouse's life and work is in Thomas F. Harrington, *The Harvard Medical School: A History, Narrative and Documentary, 1782-1905* (1905), and Henry R. Viets, *A Brief History of Medicine in Massachusetts* (1930). Brooke Hindle, *The Pursuit of Science in Revolutionary*

America, 1735-1789 (1956), is the best source for general background.

Additional Sources

The Life and scientific and medical career of Benjamin Waterhouse: with some account of the introduction of vaccination in America, New York: Arno Press, 1980. □

Maxine Waters

After serving in the California State Assembly, Maxine Waters (born 1938) was elected by Californians to the U.S. House of Representatives in 1990. As a member of Congress she fought for legislation promoting aid to poor and minority neighborhoods in American cities and combating apartheid in South Africa.

"If you believe in something, you must be prepared to fight. To argue. To persuade. To introduce legislation again and again and again," stated Maxine Waters in *Essence.* During the fourteen years that she served in the California State Assembly, Waters earned a reputation as a both a fighter and the most powerful black woman in politics. In 1984 M. Carl Holman, head of the National Urban League, was quoted in *Ebony* as saying that Waters was "one of the brightest, ablest and most effective legislators without regard to race or sex that I've ever seen." After her 1990 election to the U.S. House of Representatives, Waters moved to Washington ready to continue what she had done in California—champion black issues. In an *Essence* article entitled "Woman of the House," Waters reiterated her belief that "too many Black politicians want to be in the mainstream. . . . My power comes from the fact that I am ready to talk about Black people."

Born in 1938, Waters was one of thirteen children in a poor family living in a St. Louis housing project. She credits her childhood for what she is today—competitive, outspoken, and determined. "Just getting *heard* in a family that size is difficult," she explained in *Ebony.* Waters's mother, Velma Moore Carr, struggled to support her family by working intermittently at a series of low-paying jobs augmented by welfare. Waters described her mother in *Ebony* as "a strong woman, a survivor," whose determination served as an inspiration to her.

Although Waters's high school yearbook had predicted that one day she would be the Speaker of the House of Representatives, Waters found that possibility to be extremely remote. After graduating from high school, she married and had two children. In 1960 the family moved to Los Angeles, where Waters worked at a few menial jobs before taking an opportunity to organize a Head Start program in the suburb of Watts. " Head Start made a significant difference in my life," Waters stated in *Essence.* "It helped me see how I could help people, and it helped steer me into politics."

In the late 1960s she entered California State University at Los Angeles to study sociology. By the time she earned her degree, she was divorced and raising her children alone. Waters's background is frequently cited to explain why she fights so passionately for such issues as education and affirmative action. She explained in *Essence:* "I just want to make life better for some people. Everybody deserves a good quality of life. There is too great a divide between the haves and the have-nots, and I believe I can do something to change that."

Entered Politics

Waters got her start in politics as the chief deputy to Los Angeles city councilman David Cunningham. She managed Councilman Cunningham's campaigns and was actively involved in the campaigns of Senator Alan Cranston and Los Angeles mayor Tom Bradley. She gained a reputation for superb legislative ability and determination. Although her move into state politics was natural, it was also a rough transition. Because some of her colleagues regarded her as a maverick, Waters found all sorts of roadblocks when she arrived at the California State Assembly. Waters told *Ebony* that the early difficulties she had were a result of "this perception they had of the Black woman coming from Los Angeles who needed to be taught a lesson."

The first thing Waters did was to take on women's issues and travel throughout California, organizing and talking to women who had never before heard from a legislator. Waters believes that this experience helped to shape her leadership ability. The Speaker of the Assembly, Willie

Brown, Jr., provided support and guidance as Waters learned the system.

Waters was instrumental in the formation of the National Political Congress of Black Women in August of 1984. Born of the frustration of black women leaders, the organization emphasized mainstream electoral politics as a way to focus on what they felt were unique and neglected problems facing women. The organization's goal was to encourage every black woman in America to become involved in political activity. "It is important that Black women understand that we can seek leadership roles and not lose our identity," proclaimed Waters in *Essence.* "We don't have to do a song and dance because we're afraid we might alienate others. I'm not interested in making everyone comfortable—some people need to be made uncomfortable. Black women need to feel a sense of our own power."

Sponsored Minority Legislation

While a member of the California State Assembly, Waters introduced and passed legislation on minority and women's tenants' rights and on limits on police strip searches. Her greatest challenge, however, was maintaining patience throughout the eight years it took her to pass legislation divesting California state pension funds from companies doing business with South Africa. She reintroduced the bill six times before it passed in September 1986, demonstrating the perseverance that she feels is necessary for success in politics.

Waters also succeeded in passing an affirmative action bill that required California to set aside 15% of all state contracts for companies owned by members of minority groups and 5% for companies owned by women. The bill was acclaimed as landmark legislation because it was the first major statewide bill to mandate such programs. Another of Waters's pieces of legislation resulted in the creation of the nation's first statewide Child Abuse Prevention Program. In 1984 Waters's accomplishments were acknowledged when she was selected to chair the California State Assembly's Democratic Caucus, the first woman to ever hold this post.

Worked on Jesse Jackson's Campaigns

Waters was Jesse Jackson's most vocal backer in both the 1984 and 1988 presidential races and was his campaign manager in the latter. When presidential candidate Michael Dukakis chose Texas Senator Lloyd Bentsen instead of Jackson as his vice presidential running mate, Waters appeared on ABC's *Nightline* declaring that Jackson would break off talks with the Dukakis campaign.

In an article for the *Nation,* Waters wrote: "That Jackson speaks for large numbers of others as well is one indication that blacks serve as a barometer for the nation. . . . The Democrats cannot win the presidency without us and without Jackson and others who will work for the party." In the same article, Waters further addressed what she considered the Democratic party's lack of commitment to black issues. She wrote of the hopelessness of young black people crowded into inner-city ghettos, not only in Los Angeles but across the nation, and of the "lethal infestation of drugs" in

such communities. Waters noted: "An elementary lesson in life is that if people cannot survive in one way they will try another. In an affluent society in which only dollars appear to matter, some young people will find drug-pushing a seductive (or desperate) alternative to low-paying jobs."

Waters advocated breaking away from the Democratic party and possibly creating a third party that would be responsive to the concerns of blacks and other people of color. In the *Nation* she commented: "When I look at what is currently happening to the masses of black people, to America's poor in general and the entire nation, I am angry and frustrated. But we cannot yield to feelings of helplessness; we must transform anger and frustration into bold and direct action. . . . As for the Democratic Party, it must prove itself in these critical times or stand, like the Republicans, as just another instrument for betrayal and suppression of the people."

"That's the thing about Waters," remarked Julianne Malveaux in *Essence.* "She pushes her causes openly. She raises her voice while everyone else whispers. She wears red when everyone else wears gray. She makes a difference." That Waters has made a difference is evidenced by such programs as Project Build, which she established in her district to provide educational and job training services for residents in six Watts housing projects. Late in 1990 the Maxine Waters Vocational Educational Center was under construction in South Central Los Angeles, a symbol of hope in an area of boarded-up buildings and vacant lots.

When Waters was elected to Congress in 1990 she was one of five new African American representatives. She was appointed to the House Banking, Finance and Urban Development and the veteran Affairs Committees but vowed to remain an activist in civil rights, women's issues, and peace. She explained: "Activists don't shut down when they get to Congress, they try to be more activist." On gender issues she remained adamant in inspiring the "average" woman to succeed. "People who come from backgrounds like mine are not supposed to serve in the U.S. Congress. When a little girl who came out of poverty in St. Louis has an opportunity to serve in Congress, it is like thumbing your nose at the status quo."

Waters exploded onto the national scene during the Los Angeles fires, beatings, and rioting which followed the verdict of the policemen in the Rodney King beating. Much of the destruction and mayhem was in Waters's district and she quickly returned home to lend a helping hand and take advantage of the media spotlight by excoriating the urban policies of President Bush and former President Reagan. She was also in turn excoriated for defending the rioters, looters, and arsonists when she remarked on national television: "Riot is the voice of the unheard." In a scathing editorial the conservative National Review claimed she was trying to shift the blame for the riots from the rioters to everybody and everything else and in the process was giving tacit permission to riot again.

As promised, Waters continued her form of activism from Washington D.C. In 1992 she introduced a bill which would have provided $10 billion to fight urban decay. In defending her proposed legislation she claimed that America's cities deserve the same consideration as Russia and Israel, both recipients of massive U.S. foreign aid. Waters also called for job training for black males aged 17 to 30, increased African American ownership of small businesses, and tougher anti-discrimination banking laws. In 1994 she joined a coalition against violent and sexually explicit song lyrics and came out against so-called "gangsta rap." She told *Jet* that little was being done to curb music's obscenities and vulgarities. But ever the street populist, Waters pointed the finger of blame at industry executives for not exercising more control over their recording artists and said it was ". . .foolhardy to single out rap artists as instigators of violence among young people."

In 1996, Waters was elected to chair the Congressional Black Caucus. Following that, she was involved in pushing for further investigation of reports that the CIA was involved in a plan to distribute drugs to African Americans in Los Angeles in the early 1980s.

Further Reading

Black Enterprise, November 1981; January 1985; August 1985; December 1988; January 1989; April 1991; December 1991.
Ebony, August 1984; January 1991.
Essence, March 1984; May 1985; November 1990.
Glamour, January 1991.
Jet, April 6, 1987; October 22, 1990; December 9, 1991.
Los Angeles Times, September 8, 1989; February 1, 1990; March 17, 1990; March 20, 1990; October 1, 1990; May 12, 1991; March 4, 1997.
Maclean's, November 1, 1982.
Mother Jones, February 1984.
Ms., January-February 1991.
Nation, July 24, 1989.
Time, August 22, 1983.
Washington Post, February 19, 1991; March 15, 1991; March 20, 1991. □

Muddy Waters

From the 1950s until his death, Muddy Waters (1915-1983) literally ruled Chicago with a commanding stage presence that combined both dignity and raw sexual appeal with a fierce and emotional style of slide guitar playing.

How many blues artists could boast of an alumni of band members that includes Otis Spann, Little Walter, Junior Wells, Fred Below, Walter Horton, Jimmy Rogers, James Cotton, Leroy Foster, Buddy Guy, Luther Johnson, Willie Dixon, Hubert Sumlin and Earl Hooker, just to name a few? Muddy Waters gave these and many more their first big break in music while creating a style known now as Chicago blues (guitar, piano, bass, drums, and harmonica). "Contemporary Chicago blues starts, and in some ways may very well end, with Muddy Waters," wrote Peter Guralnick in *Listener's Guide To The Blues.*

Waters was born McKinley Morganfield in Rolling Fork, Mississippi, in 1915 but grew up in Clarksdale, where his grandmother raised him after his mother died in 1918. His fondness for playing in mud earned him his nickname at an early age. Waters started out on harmonica but by age seventeen he was playing the guitar at parties and fish fries, emulating two blues artists who were extremely popular in the south, Son House and Robert Johnson. "His thick heavy tone, the dark coloration of his voice and his firm almost stolid manner were all clearly derived from House," wrote Guralnick in *Feel Like Going Home,* "but the embellishments which he added, the imaginative slide technique and more agile rhythms, were closer to Johnson."

In 1940 Waters moved to St. Louis before playing with Silas Green a year later and returning back to Mississippi. In the early part of the decade he ran a juke house, complete with gambling, moonshine, a jukebox and live music courtesy of Muddy himself. In the summer of 1941 Alan Lomax came to Stovall, Mississippi, on behalf of the Library of Congress to record various country blues musicians. "He brought his stuff down and recorded me right in my house," Waters recalled in *Rolling Stone,* "and when he played back the first song I sounded just like anybody's records. Man, you don't know how I felt that Saturday afternoon when I heard that voice and it was my own voice. Later on he sent me two copies of the pressing and a check for twenty bucks, and I carried that record up to the corner and put it on the jukebox. Just played it and played it and said, 'I can do it, I can do it.'" Lomax came back again in July of 1942 to record Waters again. Both sessions were eventually released as *Down On Stovall's Plantation* on the Testament label.

In 1943 Waters headed north to Chicago in hopes of becoming a full-time professional. He lived with a relative for a short period while driving a truck and working in a factory by day and playing at night. Big Bill Broonzy was the top cat in Chicago until his death in 1958 and the city was a very competitive market for a newcomer to become established. Broonzy helped Waters out by letting him open for the star in the rowdy clubs. In 1945 Waters's uncle gave him his first electric guitar, which enabled him to be heard above the noisy crowds.

In 1946 Waters recorded some tunes for Mayo Williams at Columbia but they were never released. Later that year he began recording for Aristocrat, a newly-formed label run by two brothers, Leonard and Phil Chess. In 1947 Waters played guitar with Sunnyland Slim on piano on the cuts "Gypsy Woman" and "Little Anna Mae." These were also shelved, but in 1948 Waters's "I Can't Be Satisfied" and "I Feel Like Going Home" became big and his popularity in clubs began to take off. Soon after, Aristocrat changed their name to Chess and Waters's signature tune, "Rollin' Stone," became a smash hit.

The Chess brothers would not allow Waters to use his own musicians (Jimmy Rogers and Blue Smitty) in the studio; instead he was only provided with a backing bass by Big Crawford. However, by 1950 Waters was recording with perhaps the hottest blues group ever: Little Walter Jacobs on harp; Jimmy Rogers on guitar; Elgin Evans on drums; Otis Spann on piano; Big Crawford on bass; and Waters handling vocals and slide guitar. The band recorded a string of great blues classics during the early 1950's with the help of bassist/songwriter Willie Dixon's pen. "Hoochie Coochie Man" (Number 8 on the R & B charts), "I Just Want To Make Love To You" (Number 4), and "I'm Ready." These three were "the most macho songs in his repertoire," wrote Robert Palmer in *Rolling Stone*. "Muddy would never have composed anything so unsubtle. But they gave him a succession of showstoppers and an image, which were important for a bluesman trying to break out of the grind of local gigs into national prominence."

Waters was at the height of his career and his band steamed like a high-powered locomotive, cruising form club to club as the Headhunters, crushing any other blues band that challenged their musical authority. "By the time he achieved his popular peak, Muddy Waters had become a shouting, declamatory kind of singer who had forsaken his guitar as a kind of anachronism and whose band played with a single pulsating rhythm," wrote Guralnick in his *Listener's Guide.*

Unfortunately, Waters's success as the frontman led others in his group to seek the same recognition. In 1953 Little Walter left when his "Juke" became a hit and in 1955 Rogers quit to form his own band. Waters could never recapture the glory of his pre-1956 years as the pressures of being a leader led him to use various studio musicians for quite a few years following.

He headed to England in 1958 and shocked his overseas audiences with loud, amplified electric guitar and a thunderous beat. When R & B began to die down shortly after, Waters switched back to his older style of country

blues. His gig at the Newport Folk Festival in 1960 turned on a whole new generation to Waters's Delta sound. As English rockers like Eric Clapton and the Rolling Stones got hip to the blues, Waters switched back to electric circa 1964. He expressed anger when he realized that members of his own race were turning their backs to the genre while the white kids were showing respect and love for it.

However, for the better part of twenty years (since his last big hit in 1956, "I'm Ready") Waters was put on the back shelf by the Chess label and subjected to all sorts of ridiculous album themes: *Brass And The Blues, Electric Mud,* etc. In 1972 he went back to England to record *The London Muddy Waters Sessions* with four hotshot rockers—Rory Gallagher, Steve Winwood, Rick Grech, and Mitch Mitchell—but their playing wasn't up to his standards. "These boys are top musicians, they can play with me, put the book before 'em and play it, you know," he told Guralnick. "But that ain't what I need to sell my people, it ain't the Muddy Waters sound. An if you change my sound, then you gonna change the whole man."

The Waters sound was basically Delta country blues electrified, but his use of microtones, in both his vocals and slide playing, made it extremely difficult to duplicate and follow correctly. "When I plays onstage with my band, I have to get in there with my guitar and try to bring the sound down to me," he said in *Rolling Stone.* "But no sooner than I quit playing, it goes back to another, different sound. My blues look so simple, so easy to do, but it's not. They say my blues is the hardest blues in the world to play."

Fortunately for Waters and his fans there was one man who understood the feeling he was trying to convey: Johnny Winter, an albino Texan who could play some of the nastiest guitar east or west of the Mississippi. In 1976 Winter convinced his label, Blue Sky, to sign Waters and the beginning of a fruitful partnership was begun. Waters's "comeback" LP, *Hard Again,* was recorded in just two days and was as close to the original Chicago sound he had created as anyone could ever hope for. Winter produced/played and pushed the master to the limit. Former Waters sideman James Cotton kicked in on harp on the Grammy Award-winning album and a brief but incredible tour followed. "He sounds happy, energetic and out for business," stated Dan Oppenheimer in *Rolling Stone.* "In short, Muddy Waters is kicking in another mule's stall."

In 1978 Winter recruited Walter Horton and Jimmy Rogers to help out on Waters's *I'm Ready* LP and another impressive outing was in the can. The roll continued in 1979 with the blistering *Muddy "Mississippi" Waters Live.* "Muddy was loose for this one," wrote Jas Obrecht in *Guitar Player,* "and the result is the next best thing to being ringside at one of his foot-thumping, head-nodding, downhome blues shows." *King Bee* the following year concluded Water's reign at Blue Sky and all four LP's turned out to be his biggest-selling albums ever.

In 1983 Muddy Waters passed away in his sleep. At his funeral, throngs of blues musicians showed up to pay tribute to one of the true originals of the art form. "Muddy was a master of just the right notes," John Hammond, Jr., told *Guitar World.* "It was profound guitar playing, deep and simple. . . . more country blues transposed to the electric guitar, the kind of playing that enhanced the lyrics, gave profundity to the words themselves." Two years after his death, the city that made Muddy Waters (and vice versa) honored their father by changing the name of 43rd Street to Muddy Waters Drive. Following Waters's death, B.B. King told *Guitar World,* "It's going to be years and years before most people realize how great he was to American music."

Further Reading

Christgau, Robert, *Christgau's Record Guide* Ticknor & Fields, 1981.
Guralnick, Peter, *Feel Like Going Home,* Vintage Books, 1981.
Guralnick, Peter, *The Listener's Guide to the Blues,* Facts on File, 1982.
Harris, Sheldon, *Blues Who's Who,* Da Capo, 1979.
Kozinn, Allan, Pete Welding, Dan Forte, and Gene Santoro, *The Guitar: The History The Music The Players,* Quill, 1984.
The Rolling Stone Record Guide, edited by Dave Marsh with John Swenson, Random House/Rolling Stone Press, 1979.
Guitar Player, July 1979; July 1983; August 1983.
Guitar World, September 1983; January 1986; March 1989; March 1990.
Living Blues, September-October 1989.
Rolling Stone, March 24, 1977; October 5, 1978. □

Elkanah Watson

Elkanah Watson (1758-1842), American merchant, banker, and promoter, was noted for his efforts in organizing agricultural societies and fairs.

Elkanah Watson was born in Plymouth, Mass., on Jan. 22, 1758. His family was descended from early Pilgrim stock. Other than that his family lived comfortably, little is known about Watson's youth.

Watson went to grammar school until he was 14. Then he began his apprenticeship in Providence, R.I., with John Brown, a prosperous merchant and one of the founders of Brown University. During the American Revolution, Watson joined a local militia unit, but Brown would not release him to serve in the Army. Brown was one of the Army's chief suppliers of gun powder.

Watson completed his apprenticeship in 1779 but, lacking capital, continued to work for Brown. Sent to France for Brown, he remained in Europe for five years, becoming involved in several private commercial ventures and traveling extensively.

Returning to the United States in 1784, Watson established himself in Edenton, N.C. He engaged in the West Indies trade and purchased a plantation. Business failures, however, forced him to sell his estate, and he moved to Albany, N.Y. He organized and helped secure a charter for the State Bank at Albany. He continued to urge the construction of canals and turnpikes and worked actively for a free system of public schools.

At the age of 50 Watson purchased a farm near Pittsfield, Mass. He was particularly interested in wool manufacturing and introduced Merino sheep to improve the quality of raw wool. He also organized a cattle show, which by 1810 had become an annual affair. He next organized the Berkshire Agricultural Society, which became a prototype for organizations throughout the country devoted to improving agriculture. Working through the society, he changed the character of the cattle show. Prizes were awarded for cattle, articles of domestic manufacture, and agricultural products. Gradually, a "county fair" emerged that encompassed social, political, educational, and recreational activities, as well as the desire to improve agriculture.

In his later years Watson returned to New York, continuing, however, to work for agricultural improvement. He traveled extensively and wrote numerous pamphlets on agricultural subjects. He attempted to secure state funds for agricultural societies and urged the formation of a state department of agriculture. As one biographer suggests, Elkanah Watson was a crusader, a reformer, and a dreamer. He made a significant contribution to the improvement of agriculture in the United States.

Further Reading

Watson's autobiography was completed by his son, Winslow C. Watson, *Men and Times of the Revolution; or, Memoirs of Elkanah Watson* (1857). Additional biographical information is in Wayne C. Neely, *The Agricultural Fair* (1935). □

James Dewey Watson

The American biologist James Dewey Watson (born 1928) was a discoverer of the double-helical structure of the deoxyribonucleic acid molecule.

James D. Watson was born April 6, 1928, in Chicago, Illinois. At age 15 he entered the University of Chicago. He graduated in 1947 and went on to pursue graduate study in the biological sciences at Indiana University. There he came under the influence of some distinguished scientists, including Nobel laureate Hermann J. Muller, who were instrumental in shifting his interests from natural history toward genetics and biochemistry. In 1950 Watson successfully completed his doctoral research project on the effect of x-rays upon the multiplication of bacteriophages (viruses that attack bacterial cells).

Watson spent 1950-1951 as a National Research Council fellow in Copenhagen doing postdoctoral work with biochemist Herman Kalckar. He had hoped to learn more about the biochemistry of the genetic material deoxyribonucleic acid (DNA). These studies proved unproductive. It was not until the spring of 1951, when he heard the English biophysicist Maurice Wilkins speak in Naples on the structure of the DNA molecule, that Watson enthusiastically turned his full attention to the DNA problem.

Watson's next research post at Cavendish Laboratory, Cambridge, England, brought him into contact with the physicist turned biologist Francis Crick. Together they shared an interest in DNA while he was preparing for his doctorate. Thus began the partnership between Watson and Crick which resulted in their joint proposal of the double-helical model of the DNA in 1953. Watson, Crick, and Wilkins shared the 1962 Nobel Prize in physiology or medicine for their DNA studies.

The structure of the giant and complex DNA molecule reveals the physical and chemical basis of heredity. Watson and Crick were convinced that the molecular subunits which made up DNA were arranged in a relatively simple pattern that could be discovered by them. Their mode of operation stressed the conception and construction of large-scale models that would account for the known chemical and physical properties of DNA. To this model-building endeavor Watson contributed the double-helical structure, along with other fruitful, intuitive suggestions, while Crick provided the necessary mathematical and theoretical knowledge. After their work on DNA was completed, Watson and Crick collaborated again in 1957, this time in clarifying the structure of viruses.

After a two-year stay at the California Institute of Technology, Watson accepted a position as professor of biology at Harvard University in 1956 and remained on the faculty until 1976. In 1968 he became the director of the Cold Spring Biological Laboratories but retained his research and teaching position at Harvard. That same year he published *The Double Helix,* revealing the human story behind the discovery of the DNA structure, including the rivalries and deceits which were practiced by all.

While at Harvard Watson wrote *The Molecular Biology of the Gene* (1965), the first widely used university textbook on molecular biology. This text has gone through seven editions and exists in two large volumes as a comprehensive treatise of the field. He gave up his faculty appointment at the university in 1976, however, and assumed full-time leadership of Cold Spring Harbor. With John Tooze and David Kurtz, Watson wrote *The Molecular Biology of the Cell,* originally published in 1983.

In 1989 Watson was appointed the director of the Human Genome Project of the National Institutes of Health. Less than two years later, in 1992, he resigned in protest over policy differences in the operation of this massive project. He continued to speak out on various issues concerning scientific research and upheld his strong presence concerning federal policies in supporting research. In addition to sharing the Nobel Prize, Watson received numerous honorary degrees from institutions, including one from the University of Chicago (1961) when Watson was still in his early thirties. He was also awarded the Presidential Medal of Freedom in 1977 by President Jimmy Carter.

Watson, as his book *The Double Helix* confirms, has never avoided controversy. His candor about his colleagues and his combativeness in public forums have been noted by critics. Nevertheless, his scientific brilliance is attested to by Crick, Delbruck, Luria, and others. The importance of his role in the DNA discovery has been well supported by Gunther Stent, a member of the Delbruck phage group, in an essay which discounts many of Watson's critics through well-reasoned arguments.

Most of Watson's professional life has been spent as a professor, research administrator, and public policy spokesman for research. More than any other location in Watson's professional life, Cold Spring Harbor (where he is still director) has been the most congenial in developing his abilities as a scientific catalyst for others. His work there has primarily been to facilitate and encourage the research of other scientists.

In 1968 Watson married Elizabeth Lewis. They had two children, Rufus Robert and Duncan James.

Further Reading

Ruth Moore, *The Coil of Life: The Story of the Great Discoveries in the Life Sciences* (1961), has a chapter describing Watson's personality and work in detail. George and Muriel Beadle, *The Language of Life: An Introduction to the Science of Genetics* (1966), and Leonard Engel, *The New Genetics* (1967), provide lucid discussions of Watson's life and his scientific work. General appraisals of the significance of DNA in modern biology are in Ernest Borek, *The Code of Life* (1965; rev. ed. 1969), and John C. Kendrew, *The Thread of Life: An Introduction to Molecular Biology* (1966). □

John Broadus Watson

John Broadus Watson (1878-1958) founded the behaviorist movement in American psychology. His view that only observable events, and not mental states, are the substance of psychology provided the behavioristic flavor that still characterizes much of psychology today.

John B. Watson was born on Jan. 9, 1878, on a farm near Greenville, S.C. At 16 he enrolled at Furman University and graduated 5 years later with a master's degree. He then entered the University of Chicago and in 1901 received his doctorate. His major in psychology was under J. R. Angell, his philosophy minor under John Dewey, and his neurology major under H. H. Donaldson.

Watson remained at Chicago as an assistant and instructor until 1908. During this period he married Mary Ickes. His empirical work focused on animal behavior and relied on white rats, monkeys, and birds as objects of study. In 1908 he moved to Johns Hopkins, where he remained until 1920. A widely publicized divorce action precipitated his resignation, withdrawal from academics, and a second marriage.

Watson was a highly productive scientist. During his time at Johns Hopkins, he published more than 35 papers, reports, and books. He was elected president of the American Psychological Association in 1915 and served as editor on a number of professional journals into the 1920s.

In 1913 Watson published the theoretical paper "Psychology as the Behaviorist Views It." This paper presented for the first time an articulated statement of behaviorism as a reaction to Wundtian psychology, characterized by the study of consciousness and the reliance on introspection to obtain data. For Watson, psychology was to become an "objective experimental branch of natural science." Consciousness could no longer be the substance of psychology, and introspection was an unreliable method because they both required mentalities language construction.

Watson strongly rejected any belief in instincts and indicated that it was a misnomer for early experiences. Differences in ability and talent originate in early experience in contrast to being innately determined.

In 1920 Watson went to work in advertising, where his perseverance and ability again caused him to be successful. Despite his withdrawal from professional psychology, he continued to write articles relevant to psychology for popular consumption. His second wife, Rosalie Rayner, died in 1934; Watson went into retirement in 1946 and lived in Woodbury, Conn. He died on Sept. 25, 1958, in New York City.

Further Reading

Watson's own account of his life and work appears in Carl A. Murchison, ed., *A History of Psychology in Autobiography* (4 vols., 1930-1952). He figures in such general works on psychology as Edwin G. Boring, *A History of Experimental Psychology* (1929; rev. ed. 1957), and Robert I. Watson, *The Great Psychologists from Aristotle to Freud* (1963).

Additional Sources

Buckley, Kerry W. (Kerry Wayne), *Mechanical man: John Broadus Watson and the beginnings of behaviorism,* New York: Guilford Press, 1989.

Cohen, David, *J. B. Watson, the founder of behaviourism: a biography,* London; Boston: Routledge & Kegan Paul, 1979.

□

Thomas Edward Watson

Thomas Edward Watson (1856-1922) was an American political leader in the South. His degeneration from idealism and equalitarianism to racial and religious bigotry is indicative of problems affecting the nation at this time.

Thomas E. Watson was born in Columbia County, Ga., on Sept. 5, 1856, into a wealthy family. His father was ruined by the Civil War, so Tom, emotional and hungry for knowledge, had to leave Baptist Mercer University to work. He taught school unhappily for two years. Then he passed the bar requirements in 1875 and began a spectacular rise as a criminal lawyer.

Watson turned against not only those who had dispossessed his family but those who dominated Georgia politics. Violent and threatening, he accused them of using the state's black citizens as a force with which to divide the poor. He defied the Democratic party and won election to the U.S. Congress in 1890 as a partisan of the Farmers' Alliance.

Although Watson gained fame by reform speeches and congressional proposals, he could not control his state and lost his congressional seat in 1892. In 1896 an agreement between the Populists and William Jennings Bryan, the Democrats' presidential candidate, gave Watson the vice-presidential nomination on the Populist fusion ticket. Neither he nor the Populists gained votes or prestige by this plan.

Watson turned to writing as a career, but his major themes were never far from his politics. *The Story of France* (1898), filled with rhetoric, saw that nation's progress as a struggle between oppressors and oppressed. His biographies of Napoleon (1902), Thomas Jefferson (1900, 1903), and Andrew Jackson (1912) utilized history and biography to make contemporary points.

In 1904 Watson became the presidential candidate of the nearly defunct Populists. His more than 117,000 votes attested to his personal popularity, and backers helped him issue *Tom Watson's Magazine,* which mixed muckraking with a new, unleashed racism. In 1908, his last national campaign year, he took pride in being the only candidate to stand "squarely for White Supremacy." Yet his hatred of finance capital continued to give him the respect of many liberals and socialists. Watson continued to see himself as a "farmer," but he was actually a man of wealth and many interests.

One of Watson's most notorious causes became "popery," which he discerned in numerous national and international events. He interceded, too, in the Georgia case of Leo Frank, falsely accused of the murder of a factory girl in Atlanta. Frank's sentence was commuted by the governor. Watson roused his followers with such slogans as "When 'mobs' are no longer possible, liberty will be dead." Frank was taken by force from the state penitentiary and lynched.

Watson was against American entry into World War I, denounced the Espionage and Sedition Acts, and fought conscription. Elected U.S. senator in 1920, he continued to pursue a mixed set of objectives. He died on Sept. 26, 1922, in Washington. Although all did not agree with Eugene V. Debs that Watson was a great man who fought his whole life for the common people, none denied the *New York Times*'s view that he was a "strange and vivid public character."

Further Reading

C. Vann Woodward, *Tom Watson* (1938), is the definitive biography. William W. Brewton, *The Life of Thomas E. Watson* (1926), is the laudatory authorized biography, justifying Watson's attitude and actions. Gerald W. Johnson, *American Heroes and Hero-Worship* (1943; new ed. 1966), offers extended interpretation of Watson's career. □

Thomas J. Watson

Thomas J. Watson (1874-1956), American business executive, assumed the management of International Business Machines in 1914 and built it into one of the world's largest corporations.

Thomas J. Watson was born Feb. 17, 1874, in Campbell, N. Y. He attended the Adison Academy but turned down his father's offer to pay his college expenses. Instead, he took a short course in the Elmira School of Commerce and became a salesman in Painted Post, N.Y.

In 1898 Watson joined the fast-growing National Cash Register Company as salesman. His first efforts were less than spectacular, but he received encouragement from his superiors, who realized the difficulty of the product market. During the next 15 years he moved steadily up the ladder, eventually becoming general sales manager. While working on advertising material, Watson produced a sign which read "THINK." This attracted John Patterson, the company's founder, who ordered copies for all offices.

Watson left National Cash Register in 1913 after a dispute over an antitrust legal issue and became president of Computing-Tabulating-Recording Company. The firm was a small holding company which controlled four other small firms that produced a punch-card tabulator, time clocks, and other machines. About this time Watson married Jeannette M. Kittredge, who bore him four children.

One of Watson's first tasks with his new firm involved the negotiation of a loan for expansion. Watson, like many other businessmen of his era, embraced the concept of research and development, and much of the borrowed funds went into an engineering laboratory. From this and other laboratories came new machines such as the key punch, card sorters, tabulators, and eventually the computer. In 1924 the firm merged with International Business Machines Corporation (IBM) and took its name. The success of Watson's leadership is dramatically revealed by investment data. One hundred shares, which would have cost $2,750 in 1914, by 1956 were equivalent to 3,990 shares valued at $2,164,000. By 1941 IBM held nearly 1,400 patents on various types of business machines.

Having been a salesman, Watson placed great emphasis on that area of company activity. He insisted that IBM salesmen know how to install and service products as well as sell them. Labor conditions and benefits were always regarded as excellent.

IBM became a virtual monopoly, largely because of its patents and because the firm chose to rent its equipment rather than sell it. In 1952 the Federal government instigated an antitrust suit against IBM, charging that the firm controlled over 90 percent of all the tabulating machines in the country. The company agreed to a consent decree in 1956, by which competition was ensured.

Watson had many other interests outside the business world. For many years he served as a trustee for Columbia University. He participated in many ways to encourage and support the fine arts and gave financial assistance to all religious groups. He served as president of the International Chamber of Commerce. Watson acted as an adviser to several U.S. presidents. He died on July 19, 1956, in New York City.

Further Reading

Two biographies of Watson are Thomas Graham Belden and Marva Robins Belden, *The Lengthening Shadow: The Life of Thomas J. Watson* (1962), and William Rodgers, *Think: A Biography of the Watsons and IBM* (1969).

Additional Sources

Simmons, W. W. (William W.), *Inside IBM: the Watson years: a personal memoir*, Bryn Mawr, Pa.: Dorrance, 1988. □

Sir Robert Alexander Watson-Watt

Sir Robert Alexander Watson-Watt (1892-1973) was a British scientific civil servant who pioneered the development of radar.

Robert Watson-Watt, the youngest son of a carpenter, was born on April 18, 1892, at Brechin, Angus, Scotland. He studied electrical engineering and physics at University College, Dundee, and became assistant to the professor of natural philosophy there in 1912. In 1915 he was assigned to the Meteorological Office to assist in the location of thunderstorms by their radio emissions for the information of aviators. This led to fundamental research into atmospherics (the transient radio emissions from lightning discharges) at the Radio Research Station, Slough, England, under the aegis of government departments. By the 1930s much had been achieved there through *inter alia,* the development of the cathode-ray oscillograph and aerial systems. Atmospherics were located by direction finding at two or more receivers and associated with the movements of cold-air fronts.

In 1935 Watson-Watt was asked to consider the possibility of radio destruction of aircraft (the "death ray"), but with A. F. Wilkins he soon confirmed its impracticability. However, further calculations indicated the possibility of radio detection, and in February 1935 Watson-Watt's memorandum on the "location of aircraft by radio methods" was taken up by the Tizzard Committee for the scientific survey of air defense. Watson-Watt showed that a metal aircraft approximated to a linear oscillator and indicated that the secondary radiation induced when aircraft were illuminated from the ground with 50-meter radiation could be detected at ranges of tens of miles. He proposed transmitting short pulses both to increase peak output and to use the time delay in the return of the echo from the aircraft to determine range. Cross bearings from other stations could fix positions. Pulse techniques had been developed for echo-sounding the generally reflective ionosphere, but extensive refinement was required for its application to the detection of small targets. At an establishment on the North Sea coast Watson-Watt, with Wilkins, L. H. Bainbridge-Bell and E. G. Bowen, brought the system to reality and added direction finding from crossed horizontal halfwave aerials. By 1936 a home defense chain of radar stations had been approved; largely completed by 1938, it played a vital role in the Battle of Britain.

The development of radar was very much a team effort with Watson-Watt as captain. Throughout the war he was increasingly concerned in coordinating the expanding effort in the radar field. He visited the United States in 1941-1942 as an adviser. In 1946 he left government service to practice as a consultant. He was elected a fellow of the Royal Society in 1941 and was knighted in 1942.

Watson-Watt claimed the invention of radar, but, as with other classic science-based inventions, it evolved. There were precursors and simultaneity of discovery in several countries. Suffice it to say that no other saw the possibilities so clearly, and no government took up the implications more quickly. Perhaps more than any other in the history of invention, Watson-Watt was the right man in the right place at the right time.

For his work, Watson-Watt received the United States Medal for Merit in 1946. He lived in Tuxedo, New York, and briefly in Canada. But he died December 5, 1973, in his homeland of Scotland after a long illness.

Further Reading

Watson-Watt describes the development of radar from a personal point of view in his *Three Steps to Victory* (1957) and *The Pulse of Radar: The Autobiography of Sir Robert Watson-Watt* (1959). A biography is John Rowland, *The Radar Man: The Story of Sir Robert Watson-Watt* (1963). Briefer accounts appear in Egon Larsen, *Men Who Changed the World: Stories of Invention and Discovery* (1952), and Patrick Pringle, *Great Discoveries in Modern Science* (1955). □

James Watt

The British instrument maker and engineer James Watt (1736-1819) developed an efficient steam engine which was a universal source of power and thereby provided one of the most essential technological components of the early industrial revolution.

James Watt was born on Jan. 19, 1736, in Greenock, Scotland, the son of a shipwright and merchant of ship's stores. He received an elementary education in school, but of much more interest to him was his father's store, where the boy had his own tools and forge and where he skillfully made models of the ship's gear surrounding him. In

1755 he was apprenticed to a London mathematical instrument maker; at that time the trade primarily produced navigational and surveying instruments. A year later he returned to Scotland. By late 1757 Watt was established in Glasgow as "mathematical instrument maker to the university."

About this time Watt met Joseph Black, who had already laid the foundations of modern chemistry and of the study of heat. Their friendship was of some importance in the early development of the steam engine.

Invention of the Steam Engine

In the meantime, Watt had become engaged in his first studies on the steam engine. During the winter of 1763/1764 he was asked to repair the university's model of the Newcomen steam engine. After a few experiments, Watt recognized that the fault with the model rested not so much in the details of its construction or in its malfunctioning as in its design. He found that a volume of steam three or four times the volume of the piston cylinder was required to make the piston move to the end of the cylinder. The solution Watt provided was to keep the piston at the temperature of the steam (by means of a jacket heated by steam) and to condense the steam in a separate vessel rather than in the piston. Such a separate condenser avoided the large heat losses that resulted from repeatedly heating and cooling the body of the piston, and so engine efficiency was improved.

There is a considerable gap between having a good idea for a commercial invention and in reducing it to practice. It took a decade for Watt to solve all the mechanical

problems. Black lent him money and introduced him to John Roebuck of the Carron ironworks in Stirlingshire, Scotland. In 1765 Roebuck and Watt entered into a partnership. However, Watt still had to earn his own living, and his employment as surveyor of canal construction left little time for developing his invention. However, Watt did manage to prepare a patent application on his invention, and the patent was granted on Jan. 5, 1769.

By 1773 Roebuck's financial difficulties brought not only Watt's work on the engine to a standstill but also Roebuck's own business. Matthew Boulton, an industrialist of Birmingham, England, then became Watt's partner, and Watt moved to Birmingham. He was now able to work full time on his invention. In 1775 Boulton accepted two orders to erect Watt's steam engine; the two engines were set up in 1776 and their success led to many other orders.

Improvements in the Steam Engine

Between 1781 and 1788 Watt modified and further improved his engine. These changes combined to make as great an advance over his original engine as the latter was over the Newcomen engine. The most important modifications were a more efficient utilization of the steam, the use of a double-acting piston, the replacement of the flexible chain connection to the beam by the rigid threebar linkage, the provision of another mechanical device to change the reciprocating motion of the beam end to a rotary motion, and the provision of a centrifugal governor to regulate the speed.

Having devised a new rotary machine, the partners had next to determine the cost of constructing it. These rotary steam engines replaced animal power, and it was only natural that the new engine should be measured in terms of the number of horses it replaced. By using measurements that millwrights, who set up horse gins (animal-driven wheels), had determined, Watt found the value of one "horse power" to be equal to 33,000 pounds lifted one foot high per minute, a value which is still that of the standard American and English horsepower. The charge of erecting the new type of steam engine was accordingly based upon its horsepower.

Other Inventions

On Watt's many business trips, there was always a good deal of correspondence that had to be copied. To avoid this irksome task, he devised letter-press copying, in which, by writing the original with a special ink, copies could be made by simply placing another sheet of paper on the freshly written sheet and then pressing the two together.

Watt's interests in applied chemistry led him to introduce chlorine bleaching into Great Britain and to devise a famous iron cement. In theoretical chemistry, he was one of the first to argue that water was not an element but a compound.

In 1794 Watt and Boulton turned over their flourishing business to their sons. Watt maintained a workshop where he continued his inventing activities until he died on Aug. 25, 1819.

Further Reading

Excellent biographies of Watt are H. W. Dickinson and Rhys Jenkins, *James Watt and the Steam Engine* (1927), and Dickinson's *James Watt* (1936). Eric Robinson and A. E. Musson, *James Watt and the Steam Revolution* (1969), is a documentary history that commemorates the bicentenary of Watt's patent for the separate condenser in his steam engine and includes extracts from Watt's personal letters and other documents not before published. For background material see H. W. Dickinson, *A Short History of the Steam Engine* (1939), and T. S. Ashton, *The Industrial Revolution* (1948). □

Antoine Watteau

The French painter Antoine Watteau (1684-1721) was the catalyst of the Regency period of the rococo style. His painterly language is an elegant camouflage of strong emotion by kindly sentiments and gentle manners.

Antoine Watteau was born on Oct. 10, 1684, in Valenciennes, the son of a prosperous roof tiler. Because Antoine was the second son, his parents did not oppose his training with the local religious painter J. A. Gérin. When Watteau was about 18, nevertheless, his father declined to continue paying for his apprenticeship, and the youth moved to Paris, where he made his way copying paintings for dealers.

It was probably through Pierre and Jean Mariette, dealers in engravings, that he met in 1703 Jean's cousin, the painter Claude Gillot, designer of costumes and stage sets inspired by themes from the Italian commedia dell'arte, a troupe of traveling actors noted for satirical improvisation. They had been banished from France since 1697, when they had imprudently staged *La Fausse Prude,* a parody, it seemed, upon Madame de Maintenon, King Louis XIV's second wife. This pious woman exercised considerable influence over the King and delayed the natural evolution of the arts until his death in 1715, when all of France, including Watteau, who had previously functioned largely as a decorator and painter of small genre scenes, went on a holiday of unconstrained creativity.

Watteau worked with Gillot until 1707/1708, when a professional rivalry developed, and Watteau went to work with Claude Audran III for about two years. Audran was a great decorator, and Watteau is known to have assisted in some of his commissions for the King. Through Audran he mastered his quick, supple line and his feathery brushstroke for foliage, figures, and facial accents. Audran was also the curator of the Medici Gallery of the Luxembourg Palace, which contained the celebrated series of paintings of the life of Marie de Médicis by Peter Paul Rubens, whose art had a profound influence upon Watteau.

After Watteau won second place in the Royal Academy's competition for the Prix de Rome in 1709, he returned to Valenciennes for a brief visit and then brought with him to Paris a young colleague, the artist Jean Baptiste Pater, who followed, almost slavishly, Watteau's style and themes, especially the military subjects Watteau was painting during this period. The landscape and figure sketches Watteau made at this time constituted a repertory of motifs which served him thereafter for his paintings, the arbitrary compositions of which precluded the necessity of his observing nature directly.

In 1712, on the recommendation of Charles de La Fosse and Antoine Coypel, Watteau became an associate member of the academy. His presentation piece was the painting *Les Jaloux,* known only from an engraving. La Fosse introduced Watteau to the financier and art collector Pierre Crozat, who invited Watteau to stay with him in 1715 at his country place at Montmorency, which housed a superb collection of Flemish and Venetian paintings and drawings, including works by Titian, Domenico Campagnola, and Paolo Veronese. Close study of these masterworks instantly inspired Watteau's most notable theme, the *fêtes galantes,* which represent the pleasures of country life enjoyed by Paris society during the Regency.

Works like Watteau's *Musical Party,* probably representing Crozat's friends amusing themselves in the park at Montmorency, are less turbulent than works of his previous period like the *Accordée de village* and though more polite, reminiscent of the blooming conviviality of Rubens's *Garden of Love*. Gallantry and splendid refinement of manners and dress perfume these pastoral scenes of Watteau; demure gesture and physiognomical charm alone reveal the emotional intensity experienced by prospective young lovers, who register in infinite variety the first shock of infatuation. Watteau's sensitivity to nuance, in the gamut of amorous emotions, apparent in these group compositions and isolated in works representing single figures, such as *L'Indifférent,* bespeaks the shy lover in love with love, ever at dalliance but seemingly incapable of gratification.

In 1717 Watteau became a member of the academy. His diploma piece was the *Embarkation for Cythera* (later he made another version of it). This work was officially qualified as a *fête galante* and the artist as a painter of *fêtes galantes.*

Though Watteau is reputed to have been of a nervous and impatient nature, little is really known of him except that he was indifferent to money, devoted to his art, delicate in health, retiring, discreet with women, and always surrounded by a few loyal friends. The frequent changes of residence or studio in which he worked is perhaps attributable not only to restlessness of temperament but also to carelessness of bachelor habits, apparent in his untidy painting techniques, occasioning the deterioration of a number of his most prized works. In 1711 he had lived in Paris with his close friend, the art dealer Pierre Sirois, where, seeking a less social milieu than that found with Crozat, he returned in 1715/1716. Between 1716 and 1719 Watteau resided with Nicolas Vleughels in Paris, when he painted many of his masterpieces.

Watteau's painting *Gilles* (ca. 1719) seemingly deals with two levels of thought, the worldly and the philosophical. Glamorous actors with sensuous faces and fanciful hats amuse themselves by teasing a donkey ridden by a grinning jackanapes dressed in black who leers provocatively at the observer as if eager for recognition. The pagan god Pan is represented as a herm figure in profile with closed eyes. In front of the actors, raised on an eminence, looms their fellow player Gilles, like an immemorial Pagliacci, alone and ludicrous. Dressed in white satin, with his head set off against the blue sky by a hat rounded like a nimbus, Gilles mutely awaits a cue that is not given here. The world of his cohorts is unaware of his overwhelming awareness. Only the donkey seems to know what Gilles, in fact, Watteau, knows, and their eyes solemnly meet the observer's.

In 1719 Watteau went to London, possibly to consult the noted physician Richard Mead, who became his patron and friend. The rigors of the London winter are said to have undermined Watteau's health. During his brief sojourn there he met artists of the French colony, who passed on his style; thus Watteau profoundly influenced the course of 18th-century painting in England.

On Watteau's return to Paris in 1720 he lodged with E. F. Gersaint, Sirois's son-in-law, for whom he painted the famous signboard known as the *Enseigne de Gersaint* which hung outside the picture dealer's shop. This work is remarkable for the painterly spontaneity with which it was executed, presumably within a very few days, its diminutive figure scale, and the graceful informality of genre realism typifying the modern style which Watteau helped to create. Because of increasing ill health, he moved to Nogent-sur-Marne, where he died on July 18, 1721. His last work, *The Halt during the Chase,* is uncoordinated and in particularly poor condition, indicative, no doubt, of the artist's final illness.

Of the approximately 300 paintings executed by Watteau between 1704 and 1721, none is signed or dated, making the establishment of a chronological development purely conjectural. Most of these works were engraved under the direction of Jean de Jullienne between 1721 and 1735.

Further Reading

Previous to Karl T. Parker's pioneering book, *The Drawings of Antoine Watteau* (1932), many Watteau drawings were scattered and known only from the Jean de Jullienne engravings. Though their art-historical scholarship is far from negligible, the essay on Watteau by Edmond and Jules Goncourt in their *French XVIII Century Painters: Watteau, Boucher, Chardin, Latour Greuze, Fragonard,* edited by Robin Ironside (trans. 1948), is important humanistic literature; as a verbal reincarnation of the 18th-century spirit, it should it should not be missed. More recent studies of Watteau include Anita Brookner, *Watteau* (1967); Pierre Schneider, *The World of Watteau, 1684-1721* (1967); and René Huyghe, *Watteau* (1968; trans. 1970). See also François Fosca, *The Eighteenth Century: Watteau to Tiepolo* (1952).

Additional Sources

Posner, Donald, *Antoine Watteau,* Ithaca, N.Y.: Cornell University Press, 1984.

Wine, Humphrey, *Watteau,* London: Scala Books; New York, NY: Distributed in the USA and Canada by Rizzoli International Publications, 1992. □

Alan Wilson Watts

Alan Wilson Watts (1915-1973) was a naturalized American author and lecturer who interpreted Zen to the West. His writings were particularly popular among the so-called "beat generation" of the late 1950s and early 1960s.

A lan Wilson Watts was born in Chislehurst, England, on January 6, 1915. Raised in the county of Kent, his introduction to Eastern culture came at about the age of 11 when he read the novels of Sax Rohmer and Edgar Wallace about Fu Manchu, the inscrutable Chinese detective, "and other sophisticated Chinese villains." Watts received his secondary education at King's School, Canterbury, where he did some creative writing and participated in fencing, rowing, and debate.

He worked in his father's office from 1932 to 1939 while serving as a council member and member of the executive committee of the World Congress of Faiths in London. He read Bergson, Nietzche, Havelock Ellis, Jung, Bernard Shaw, and Eastern texts through the understandings of modern interpreters such as Swami Vivekananda, D. T. Suzuki, and Madame Blavatsky. In 1934 a Theosophical Society member introduced him to a Yugoslavian mystic,

Dmitrije Mitrinovic, with whom he identified. From 1934 to 1938 he edited the Buddhist Lodge of London's journal, *The Middle Way,* and his first book, *The Spirit of Zen,* appeared in 1936.

Watts came to the United States in 1939 and was naturalized in 1943. Upon arrival in New York he studied under a local Zen master, Sokei-an Sasaki. But, believing that Christianity could be understood as a form of a mystical and perennial philosophy, he affiliated with the Episcopal Church. He received his Master of Sacred Theology degree from Seabury-Western Theological Seminary in Evanston, Illinois, in June 1948 and was given an honorary Doctor of Divinity from the University of Vermont in 1958. Ordained an Episcopal priest, he served from 1944 until 1950 as Episcopal chaplain at Northwestern University. He then left the church. In an interview in *LIFE* magazine in 1961 Watts said that he left the church "not because it doesn't practice what it preaches, but because it preaches."

Watts returned to his early interest in Eastern thought. He sought to apply its principles to modern psychology in *The Meaning of Happiness* (1940). Among other writings in which he argued for a common mystical core underlying all religions, reflecting the influence of Aldous Huxley, a major attempt to reconcile Christianity and Eastern thought was *Myth and Ritual in Christianity* (1953). In 1964 in *Beyond Theology* he argued that they were in fact incompatible: "My previous discussions did not take proper account of that whole aspect of Christianity which is uncompromising, ornery, militant, rigorous, imperious, and invincibly self-righteous."

From 1951 to 1957 Watts taught comparative philosophy and psychology at the new American Academy of Asian Studies in San Francisco, which became a graduate school of the College of the Pacific, and served as its dean from 1953 to 1956. Feeling as out of place in academy as he did in the church, he retired to a career of writing and lecturing. In 1959-1961 he was director and writer of the National Educational Television series *Eastern Wisdom and Modern Life.*

He was married three times—to Eleanor Everett (1938; divorced 1950); to Dorothy DeWitt (1950; divorced 1963); and to Mary Jane Yates King (1963)—and had seven children. He described himself as "an unrepented sensualist, an immoderate lover of women and the delights of sexuality," as well as of fine food, drink, tobacco, clothes, books, and jewelry and of nature. From 1957 until his death on November 16, 1973, he continued to write and lecture at colleges, universities, medical schools, and mental health institutions in the United States, Canada, Europe, and Asia, including Harvard; Yale; Cambridge; the Universities of Chicago, Michigan, Indiana, and Hawaii; and the C. J. Jung Institute (Zurich).

Although his thought is associated with Rinzai Zen Buddhism, Watts did not wish to identify himself with any religious group, "on the ground that partisanship in religion closes the mind." He once called himself a spiritual "entertainer." His own mystical idealism, however, was more an amalgamation of ideas than traditional Zen, for he also borrowed from the Taoist philosophy of Lao-tzu and Chuang-tzu and the Advaita Vedanta of Shankara, treating all Eastern thought monolithically and interpreting it in modern terms.

Watts believed that the key to the universe is fundamentally a higher consciousness or mind. The world is an emanation of the one Being or Consciousness. Unity is the nature of the universe while the distinctions between knowing subject and the objects of knowledge are actually expressions of unity. This fact, he said, is gaining support from the discoveries of science, such as those of the British biologist Joseph Needham, in whose work he was especially interested. The human predicament is the mistaken belief in the individual ego and the forms of activity which result. This places the individual in conflict with all of reality and results in the ego feeling ultimately responsible. Christianity in all its forms, Watts said, has reinforced this delusion, while Chinese and Indian thinkers have discovered the unity of the depths of the human being and the One which makes one "at home in the world." Watts even criticized the applications of Zen by the "beat generation" of the 1950s and traditional Japanese Zen schools as egoconscious.

True Zen, he said, was not that of the "solemn and sexless ascetic," but the liberation of the mind from traditional thought forms to raise human consciousness to identify with the Consciousness which is Reality. It is essentially a mystical experience of Reality "felt directly in a silence of words and meanings." Mystical thinkers of all traditions have discovered this, he said, and modern psychotherapy is coming to agree. In *Psychotherapy East and West* (1961) Watts referred to Carl Jung, Erich Fromm, Rollo May, Norman O. Brown, Abraham Maslow, and others as those who were bringing science closer to Eastern insight.

Further Reading

In My Own Way (1972), Watt's autobiography, is the best place to begin. Among his scores of works, his most systematic attempt to present his thought and relate it to Christianity is *Beyond Theology* (1964). *Psychology East and West* (1961) exhibits his attempt to harmonize his thought with psychotherapy. A full-length critical study of Watts is David Clark, *The Pantheism of Alan Watts* (1978).

Additional Sources

Brannigan, Michael C., *Everywhere and nowhere: the path of Alan Watts,* New York: P. Lang, 1988.

Furlong, Monica, *Zen effects: the life of Alan Watts,* Boston: Houghton Mifflin, 1986.

Stuart, David, *Alan Watts,* New York: Stein and Day, 1983, 1976.
□

Evelyn Arthur St. John Waugh

The English author Evelyn Arthur St. John Waugh (1903-1966) ranks as one of the outstanding satiric novelists of the 20th century. Hilariously savage wit

and complete command of the English language were hallmarks of his style.

Evelyn Waugh was born in London on Oct. 28, 1903. He was the son of Arthur Waugh, critic, author, and editor of many books, who was the influential chairman of the London publishing firm Chapman and Hall. Evelyn's elder brother, Alec, became a novelist and writer of travel books. Evelyn was educated at Lancing and at Oxford University, where his deeply religious temperament and literary abilities, which had manifested themselves early, received encouragement. He became a convert to the Roman Catholic Church in 1930.

Waugh enlisted in the Royal Marines in 1939 at the outbreak of World War II. He later shifted to the commandos, with the rank of major, and served until 1945. He saw service in West Africa and Crete, and as a British liaison officer he parachuted into Yugoslavia, where he narrowly escaped death in the crash of a transport plane. After the war he settled in Gloucestershire, with his wife and their three sons and three daughters. In 1946 he wrote: "I live in a shabby stone house in the country, where nothing is under a hundred years old except the plumbing and that does not work. I collect old books in an inexpensive, desultory way. I have a fast-emptying cellar of wine and gardens fast reverting to the jungle. I am very contentedly married. I have numerous children whom I see once a day for ten, I hope, awe-inspiring minutes."

In 1946 Waugh made a widely acclaimed lecture tour in the United States. One interviewer described him as looking "a little like a boyish Winston Churchill." Another wrote of him: "Conservatively dressed, bland and cherubic in appearance, his manner sardonic, he brought to life the spirit of his work." At this time Waugh announced that in his future work he had two primary concerns: "a preoccupation with style and the attempt to represent man more fully, which, to me, means only one thing, man in his relation to God."

The English critic Philip Toynbee, in reviewing a biographical portrait of Waugh written by a country neighbor, Frances Donaldson, wrote in the *Observer* in 1968: "What does emerge with great freshness is that Waugh was a man who could charm the birds off a tree; that he could be the best possible company—witty, extravagant, ebullient; that his aggressiveness, exclusiveness, fear of boredom and fierce love of privacy were all far stronger emotions than his 'soft-centred' (Mrs. Donaldson's good phrase) regard for the upper classes. What emerges, too, is that he was exceptionally kind and considerate to unknown writers—a great and rare quality in a successful author—and that he was capable of the most notable self-sacrifice." Waugh died in Taunton, Somerset, on April 10, 1966.

Early Literary Works

Waugh's literary production divides into three categories: novels, travel books, and biographies (the latter category including his incomplete autobiography). He also wrote a small number of short stories.

Waugh burst upon the literary scene, taking the British public by storm and making his youthful reputation, with his first novel, *Decline and Fall,* in 1928. In the same vein of farce and burlesque, always mordant, Waugh published *Vile Bodies* (1930), *Black Mischief* (1932), *Scoop* (1938), *Put Out More Flags* (1942), *Scott-King's Modern Europe* (1947), *The Loved One* (1948), and *Love among the Ruins* (1953). In a more serious vein he published *A Handful of Dust* (1934), *Work Suspended: Two Chapters of an Unfinished Novel* (1942), and *Helena* (1950).

In his novels of the 1920s and 1930s Waugh looked coldly through very conservative eyes on modern technology and encroaching democracy as the ancient British class system began to atrophy. Seeing his disenchanted world clearly, he expressed his cynicism with savage fantasy and satire. His early novels were brilliantly funny, attacking real follies. His satire was sharp, unencumbered, and to the point; his stories were furiously witty and inventive. His later novels became petulant at the disintegration of the staid, stable, snobbish, values of the England he knew.

Later Literary Works

Waugh's greatest popular success was *Brideshead Revisited: The Sacred and Profane Memories of Charles Ryder* (1945). It was a frankly serious novel about the decline of an aristocratic English Catholic family. Many critics consider it his finest book. John K. Hutchens wrote of it: "*Brideshead Revisited* has the depth and weight that are found in a writer working in his prime, in the full powers of an eager, good mind and a skilled hand, retaining the best of what he has already learned. It tells an absorbing story in imaginative terms.'' Other critics, particularly English ones, complained that the book was a Catholic tract.

The Loved One, displaying Waugh's satiric brilliance, was a farce set in a deluxe funeral park in Hollywood. It was based upon burial customs at Forest Lawn Cemetery there. Orville Prescott described it as ''brilliantly amusing satire,'' and Wolcott Gibbs wrote that it was ''as rich and subtle and unnerving as anything its author has ever done.''

The *Men at Arms* trilogy—*Men at Arms* (1952), *Officers and Gentlemen* (1955), and *The End of the Battle* (1961)—was based on Waugh's experiences in World War II. The final text of the trilogy, revised to be read as a single story, was published as *Sword of Honor* (1966). Other fiction of the 1950s included *Tactical Exercise* (1954), a collection of shorter satiric works that contained *Love among the Ruins. The Ordeal of Gilbert Pinfold* (1957) reveals much about Waugh's attitudes toward his own work and personality.

Biographies and Travel Books

Aside from an early biography of Dante Gabriel Rossetti (1928), Waugh wrote two other biographies: *Edmund Campion, Jesuit and Martyr* (1935) and *The Life of Ronald Knox* (1959). The first volume of his projected three-volume autobiography appeared in 1964. Entitled *A Little Learning: The Early Years,* it is an amusing and thoughtful chronicle of the author's early life.

Waugh traveled extensively throughout the 1930s and 1940s and he recorded his impressions of the impact of Western civilization on indigenous social patterns in a series of travel books. They include *Labels* (1930), *Remote People* (1932), *Ninety-two Days* (1934), *When the Going Was Good* (1947), and *A Tourist in Africa* (1960).

Further Reading

Biographical works on Waugh include Christopher Hollis's pamphlet, *Evelyn Waugh* (1954); Frances Donaldson, *Evelyn Waugh: Portrait of a Country Neighbour* (1967); and Alec Waugh, *My Brother Evelyn, and Other Portraits* (1968). The best overall general survey of Waugh's career is James Francis Carens, *The Satiric Art of Evelyn Waugh* (1966), although it lacks the acute insights into Waugh's comedy found in Malcolm Bradbury, *Evelyn Waugh* (1964), and the perceptions of Waugh's artistry in Frederick J. Stopp, *Evelyn Waugh: Portrait of an Artist* (1958). □

Archibald Percival Wavell

The English general, statesman, and writer Archibald Percival Wavell, 1st Earl Wavell (1883-1950), is best known for his devastating victories over the Italians in 1940 and 1941.

Archibald Percival Wavell, the son of Maj. Gen. Archibald Graham Wavell, was born on May 5, 1883, at Colchester. After spending 3 years in Summer Fields, the famous preparatory school at Oxford, he won a scholarship to Winchester and entered in 1896. As a student, he developed a well-disciplined and comprehensive intellectual ability. When he was 17 he passed on to Sandhurst; a year later he was commissioned into the Black Watch. In 1901 he was sent to South Africa, where he served as a subaltern in the later stages of the Boer War.

After the war Wavell continued his vigorous pursuit of a military career. In 1903 he went to India, where he remained for five years and served with distinction. Leaving there in 1908, he entered the staff college at Camberly, which, at that time, represented the stepping-stone to extraregimental promotion. He then spent several years in Russia studying the language and customs of the people and attending army maneuvers. In 1912, at the age of 29, he was appointed to the War Office.

When World War I broke out, Wavell was eager to serve in France, and in September 1914 his opportunity came. He spent most of the next two years in France, but in 1915 he managed a short leave to marry Eugenie Marie Quirk in England. In 1916 he was back in France and engaged in an attack at Ypres Salient, where he was wounded and lost his left eye. After a short convalescence he returned to France for another brief tour, and then later in the year he was sent to Russia to serve as the British military representative on the staff of the Grand Duke Nicholas. With the outbreak of the Russian Revolution, however, he

was again reassigned and rounded out the war years serving in the Near East under Gen. Allenby, a man from whom he learned lasting lessons about conduct of war.

In the interwar years Wavell gained a wide reputation in public as well as professional quarters. In spite of some unorthodox ideas, such as his statement that "my ideal infantryman has the qualities of a successful poacher, a cat burglar and a gunman," he advanced steadily. In 1930 he received command of the 6th Brigade at Blackdown, and in 1935 he was appointed commander of the 2d Division at Aldershot. Two years later he was appointed to assume the command in Palestine, and in 1938 he was called home to receive the important Southern Command. One year later, on the eve of World War II, he accepted the appointment of general officer commander in chief, Middle East, in which capacity all of his talents would be tested severely.

In the Middle East, Wavell not only commanded a vast area but also faced an enemy much larger and better supplied than his own forces. Once the war began, he was, moreover, under constant pressure from Prime Minister Winston Churchill to achieve victory immediately and at all cost. But Wavell possessed a quiet resolve, a sense of daring, and a grasp of strategy that made him equal to his task. When, on Sept. 12, 1940, the Italians invaded Egypt, he successfully defended his position and in December launched his own devastating counteroffensive. Under his direction the Italians were completely defeated; Tobruk and Benghazi were captured, and Mussolini's empire in Ethiopia was liquidated.

In the spring of 1941, however, the Germans were successful in Greece and Crete, and Wavell's counteroffensive in North Africa failed. Churchill, consequently, decided to replace Wavell with Sir Claude Auchinleck. Wavell, in turn, assumed Auchinleck's position as commander in chief in India. After Japan entered the war, he became allied commander of the Southwest Pacific, and, fighting again against great odds, he lost Malaya and Burma. From 1943 to 1947 he served as one of the last viceroys of India. In 1943 he also was promoted to field marshal and was created Viscount Wavell of Cyrenaica and Winchester. In 1947 he was created earl.

Wavell was a likable and many-sided man who always had the respect and confidence of his men. As a soldier, he was uncomplaining and professional. His reputation survived all of his misfortunes; he was a general of exceptional quality. He also was a scholar and a talented writer. He published *The Palestine Campaigns* (1928), *Allenby: A Study in Greatness* (1940), *Generals and Generalship* (1941), *Allenby in Egypt* (1943), *Other Men's Flowers: An Anthology of Poetry* (1944), *Speaking Generally* (1946), *The Good Soldier* (1947), and *Soldiers and Soldiering* (1954). In 1947 he retired to London, where he died on May 24, 1950.

Further Reading

The best book on Wavell is John H. Robertson (John Connell, pseudonym), *Wavell: Scholar and Soldier* (1964), a brilliant, exciting biography that thoroughly relates Wavell's career up to June 1941. Winston Churchill's *The Grand Alliance* (1950) and *The Hinge of Fate* (1950), along with Anthony Eden, *The*

Reckoning (1965), provide interesting reflections on Wavell. Useful specialized studies include Corelli Barnett, *The Desert Generals* (1960); Anthony Heckstall-Smith and H. T. Baillie-Grohman, *Greek Tragedy: 1941* (1961); and B. N. Pandey, *The Break-up of British India* (1969). For a full appreciation of Wavell his own works should be consulted.

Additional Sources

Lewin, Ronald, *The chief: Field Marshall Lord Wavell, Commander-in-Chief and Viceroy, 1939-1947*, New York: Farrar, Straus, Giroux, 1980. □

Francis Wayland

Francis Wayland (1796-1865), American educator and clergyman, was in the forefront among educators who urged reforms in American collegiate education.

Francis Wayland was born in New York City on March 11, 1796, to a Baptist family recently emigrated from England. He entered Union College, Schenectady, at the age of 15. After his graduation in 1813, he began studying medicine with doctors in Troy. He received his license to practice medicine but decided to study theology and went to Andover Theological Seminary in Massachusetts in 1816.

Financial difficulties interrupted Wayland's theological studies. He accepted a tutorship at Union, where he associated with the president of the college, Eliphalet Nott. After 4 years in teaching, he became pastor of the First Baptist Church of Boston in 1821. In 1825 he married Lucy L. Lincoln, and the next year he resigned his pastorate to become a professor of moral philosophy at Union. In 1827 he became president of Brown University.

At this time Brown was suffering from a decline in applicants, faculty dissension, and a breakdown in student discipline. To correct the abuses, Wayland called for more faculty responsibility in teaching and in the supervision of student life and for greater student discipline.

Wayland also tackled the problems of declining enrollments and financial crises. In 1842 his "Thoughts on the present Collegiate System in the United States" cast him nationwide as a critic of higher education who urged drastic reforms. He charged that college education did not meet the needs of an American public with increasing diversity of backgrounds and educational needs. His reforms stressed an expanded curriculum, including science; a student's election of his own course of study; flexibility in the required residence for a degree; thoroughness in teaching; increased fees; and better library facilities. In 1850 his report to the Brown board of trustees called for an overhaul of the college's educational program in order to attract more students and improve the college's usefulness to society.

Wayland's proposals ultimately won disfavor, and he resigned in 1855. After his first wife's death in 1834, he had

tary career was varied and honorable. First assigned to the Army unit covering the retreat of American forces from Canada, he fought in the Battle of Three Rivers, where he was wounded. Next he joined George Washington and the main body of the Army at Morristown, N.J., in February 1777, receiving promotion to brigadier general. He distinguished himself in several battles, but his greatest exploit was the capture of Stony Point, a British stronghold on the Hudson River, in July 1779. In command of a picked corps of 1,300 men, Wayne attacked at midnight. In a brilliant tactical maneuver, he took the garrison by surprise, killing or wounding 123 and capturing 575 men. A grateful Congress voted him a gold medal. The whole country acclaimed him, and Washington praised his "judgment and bravery."

For the remainder of the war, Wayne served with the Marquis de Lafayette in Virginia until the British surrendered at Yorktown. When peace came in 1783, he retired as brevet major general. In 1792 President Washington recalled him to serve as commander in chief of the Army. His assignment was to destroy the Indian power north of the Ohio River. For a year Wayne gathered and trained an army; in the spring of 1793 they set out for the west. At Fallen Timbers (near present-day Toledo) he defeated the Indians in August 1794. He negotiated the Treaty of Greenville with the chiefs (1795), by which the several tribes acknowledged American supremacy in the region. This ended a generation of warfare on the frontier.

While on a tour of inspection of frontier posts, Wayne died on Dec. 15, 1796, at Presque Isle (Erie) in Pennsylva-

married again in 1838. His later years were spent in writing and as pastor of a Baptist church in Providence, R.I. He died on Sept. 30, 1865.

Further Reading

The standard biography is James O. Murray, *Francis Wayland* (1891). For background see Walter C. Bronson, *The History of Brown University, 1764-1914* (1914); R. Freeman Butts, *The College Charts Its Course* (1939); H.G. Good, *A History of American Education* (1956); and Frederick Rudolph, *The American College and University* (1962). □

Anthony Wayne

The American soldier Anthony Wayne (1745-1796) became a hero during the American Revolution and in his later campaigns against the Indians.

Anthony Wayne was born in Easttown, Pa., on Jan. 1, 1745. He attended local schools and the Philadelphia academy. In 1763 he began a career in surveying, principally in Nova Scotia. In 1766 he and his wife settled down at Waynesborough, Pa., the family property, where Wayne helped his father in the profitable business of farming and of operating a tannery.

When the Revolution began in 1775, Wayne organized a regiment of infantry and was appointed colonel. His mili-

nia. Often impetuous and occasionally rash, he was called "mad," but none disputed his courage and competence.

Further Reading

Wayne's activities in the Old Northwest are recorded in *The Wayne-Knox-Pickering-McHenry Correspondence,* edited by R. C. Knopf (1960). The best study of Wayne is Charles J. Stillé, *Major-General Anthony Wayne and the Pennsylvania Line in the Continental Army* (1893); complete and judicious, it contains many of Wayne's letters. Harry Emerson Wildes, *Anthony Wayne: Trouble Shooter of the American Revolution* (1941), does not add much new. An interesting and colorful biography, but not as scholarly as Stillé's, is Thomas Boyd, *Mad Anthony Wayne* (1929).

Additional Sources

Fox, Joseph L., *Anthony Wayne, Washington's reliable general,* Chicago, Ill.: Adams Press, 1988.

Isaac, Norm, *Wayne—Ohio's wilderness warrior,* Richmond, Ind.: N. Isaac, 1982.

Nelson, Paul David, *Anthony Wayne, soldier of the early republic,* Bloomington: Indiana University Press, 1985. □

John Wayne

American actor John Wayne (1907-1979) played characters who typically exuded decisiveness, virility, and an American "can-do" spirit in over 75 films.

John Wayne was born Marion Mitchell Morrison on May 26, 1907, in Winterset, Iowa. He received his nickname "Duke" while still a child, because of his love for a dog of that name. The family's circumstances were moderate. His father was a pharmacist whose business ventures did not succeed. The family moved to California in 1914. His parents were divorced in 1926.

From the age of 12 he was forced to help support himself. He did so with a variety of odd jobs, including stints as a delivery boy and as a trucker's helper. A star football player on the Glendale High School team, he was accepted at the University of Southern California on a football scholarship. An accident ended his playing career and scholarship; without funds to support himself he left the university in 1927 after two years there.

He had spent some time while at college working at the Fox studio lots in Los Angeles as a laborer, prop boy, and extra. While doing so he had met John Ford, the director, who took a shine to him (and would over the years have a major impact on his career). In 1928, after working at various odd jobs for some months, he was again employed at the Fox studios, mostly as a laborer but also as an extra and bit player. His efforts in the main went unbilled, but he did attain his first screen credits as Duke Morrison.

His first real break came in 1929, when through the intervention of Ford he was cast as the lead in a major Fox production, the Western movie *The Big Trail.* According to some biographers Fox executives found his name inappro-

priate and changed it to John Wayne, the surname being derived from the American Revolutionary general "Mad Anthony" Wayne.

The Big Trail was not a success, and Fox soon dropped him. During the 1930s he worked at various studios, mostly those on what was known as "Poverty Row." Wayne appeared in over 50 feature films and serials, mostly Westerns. He even appeared in some films as "Singing Sandy." Tall, personable, able to do his own stunts, it appeared that he was doomed to be a leading player in low-budget films.

However, thanks to Ford, with whom he had remained friends, Wayne was cast as the lead in that director's film *Stagecoach,* a 1939 Western that became a hit and a classic. This film was a turning point in Wayne's career. And although it took time for him to develop the mythic hero image which propelled him to the top of the box office charts, within a decade he was voted by movie exhibitors one of the top ten box office attractions of the year, a position he maintained for 23 of the next 24 years.

Wayne appeared in over 75 films between 1939 and 1976 when *The Shootist,* his last film (and appropriately enough a Western), was released. In the vast majority of these films he was a man of action, be it in the post Civil War American West or in contemporary U.S. wars. As an actor he had a marvelous sense of timing and of his own persona, but comedy was not his forte. Action was the essence of his films. His characters exuded decisiveness, confidence, virility, strength, and an American "can-do" spirit. Indeed, critics have emphasized over and over again the manner in which he represented a particular kind of "American Spirit."

As a box-office superstar he had his choice of roles and vehicles, but he chose to remain with the genre he knew best. As the years passed his only concession to age was the gradual elimination of romance from the roles he played. He went from wooing leading ladies such as Marlene Dietrich (*Pittsburgh,* 1942), Gail Russell (*Angel and the Badman,* 1947), and Patricia Neal (*Operation Pacific,* 1951) to more mature roles as a rowdy pater familias (*McClintock,* 1963), an older brother (*The Sons of Katie Elder,* 1965), and an avuncular marshal (*Rio Lobo,* 1970).

Wayne's politics were not always right-of-center, but in the latter part of his life he became known for his active anti-Communism. His ultra conservatism began in the mid-1940s. He served as head of the extremist anti-Communist Motion Picture Alliance for the Preservation of American Ideals; supported various conservative Republican politicians, including Barry Goldwater and Richard Nixon; and spoke out forcefully on behalf of various causes such as American participation in the Vietnam War.

His politics also influenced his activities as a producer and director. Wayne's production companies made all kinds of films, but among them were *Big Jim McClain* (1951), in which he starred as a process server for the House Un-American Activities Committee fighting Communists in Hawaii, and *Blood Alley* (1955), in which he played an American who helps a village to escape from the Communist Chinese mainland to Formosa. The two films that Wayne directed also are representative of his politics: *The Alamo* (1960) is an epic film about a heroic last stand by a group of Texans in their fight for independence against Mexico and included some sermonizing by the Wayne character about democracy as he saw it; *The Green Berets* (1968), in which Wayne played a colonel leading troops against the North Vietnamese, was an outspoken vehicle in support of America's role in the war.

Wayne was married three times. He had four daughters and three sons by two of his wives (Josephine Saenez, 1933-1945, and Pilar Palette Weldy, after 1954). His second wife was Esperanza Diaz Ceballos Morrison (1946-1954). Wayne was the recipient of many awards during his career, including an Oscar for his role as the hard-drinking, one-eyed, tough law man in *True Grit* (1969) and an Academy Award nomination for his playing of the career marine noncom in *Sands of Iwo Jima* (1949). Plagued by various illnesses during the last few years of his life, he publicly announced his triumph over lung cancer in 1964. But a form of that disease claimed him on June 11, 1979.

Further Reading

For additional information, see the biographies by Maurice Zolotow (1974), Mike Tomkies (1971), and Donald Shepherd and Robert Saltzer with David Grayson (1985).

Additional Sources

Riggin, Judith M., *John Wayne: a bio-bibliography,* New York: Greenwood Press, 1992.

Levy, Emanuel, *John Wayne: prophet of the American way of life,* Metuchen, N.J.: Scarecrow Press, 1988.

Roberts, Randy, *John Wayne: American,* New York: Free Press, 1995. □

James Baird Weaver

James Baird Weaver (1833-1912) was an American political leader of reform movements who twice ran for the presidency.

James Baird Weaver was born on June 12, 1833, at Dayton, Ohio. His family soon moved to the virgin prairies of Iowa to farm. Weaver attended country schools. When gold was discovered in California, he longed to go west. In 1853 he accompanied a relative to the gold fields but soon returned disillusioned. He entered and graduated from Cincinnati Law School in a single year; then he opened law practice in Bloomfield, Iowa, in 1856.

Weaver immediately became absorbed in local politics as a Republican opposed to the expansion of slavery into the territories. When the Civil War came, he volunteered as an officer and participated in the bloody battles at Ft. Donelson and Shiloh. At Corinth he assumed field command when his superior officers were mortally wounded, and he received a promotion to major. He returned to Iowa in 1864 and at war's end was breveted brigadier general. He was known subsequently as "General" Weaver.

As a staunch Republican and a Civil War veteran, Weaver was destined for a political career. He was successful in obtaining a place as district attorney in 1866. Between 1867 and 1873, while holding the appointive position of assessor of revenue for the Federal government, he found himself at odds with the Republican leadership over currency policies and the subsidization of corporate endeavor, chiefly railroads, that he thought were exploitive. His militant moralism, ardent prohibitionism, and evangelical Protestantism compounded his difficulties. His political enemies blocked his nomination for Congress in 1874 and for governor in 1875.

Weaver wanted the currency expanded to meet the needs of the economy; his party wanted to appreciate the value of the dollar to aid the creditor. Conservatives unfairly branded him as an advocate of unlimited inflation and debt repudiation. Finally, Weaver joined the Greenback party, which favored his views on monetary reform. He was elected to Congress in 1878, ran for president in 1880, lost the congressional election in 1882, but won two additional terms after 1884 as a candidate for this minor party.

Weaver joined the Farmers' Alliance, which also championed his views on money matters, and played a major role in bringing that organization into the Populist party, which succeeded the Greenback party as a vehicle for reform. As the party's candidate for president in 1892, he received over a million popular votes and 22 votes in the Electoral College. Four years later he led the fusionist group within the Populist party that brought about a merger with the Democrats behind William Jennings Bryan's unsuccessful presidential campaign. This terminated the Populist crusade, and Weaver's career as a national politician was over. He returned to Iowa, on occasion serving as mayor of his hometown, Colfax. He died in Des Moines on Feb. 6, 1912.

Further Reading

A biography, published during the 1892 presidential campaign, is Emory Adams Allen, *The Life and Public Services of James Baird Weaver*. Frederick Emory Haynes, *James Baird Weaver* (1919), is largely an account of Weaver's political career based upon his unpublished autobiography and his scrapbooks of newspaper articles. John D. Hicks, *The Populist Revolt* (1931), contains a brief critical and interpretive sketch of Weaver's life.

Additional Sources

Haynes, Frederick Emory, *James Baird Weaver,* New York: Arno Press, 1975. □

Robert C. Weaver

Robert C. Weaver (born 1907) was a housing expert who served as administrator of the Housing and Home Finance Agency and then became the first African American cabinet officer when President Lyndon B. Johnson appointed him secretary of the Department of Housing and Urban Development in 1966.

Born into a middle-class family in 1907, Robert C. Weaver grew up in a nearly all-white Washington, D.C. neighborhood. The grandson of Robert Tanner Freeman, the first African American, Harvard-educated dentist, Weaver followed his grandfather's footsteps and enrolled at Harvard after graduation from Dunbar High School. At Harvard he majored in economics and graduated *cum laude* in 1929. Two years later he received a master's from Harvard. After teaching economics one year at the Agricultural and Technical College of North Carolina, Weaver returned to Harvard in 1932 on a scholarship and pursued a Ph.D. in economics conferred in 1934.

Deeply concerned that African Americans receive their fair share from the New Deal, Weaver joined Clark Foreman as an adviser on African American affairs for Harold Ickes' Department of the Interior. Under Weaver's prodding, the DOI's Public Works Administration (PWA) achieved a fine record for its treatment of African Americans. The Harvard economist particularly made sure that they received adequate consideration in PWA-sponsored public housing. Weaver remained in the federal government until 1944, serving in a number of advisory roles with the United States Housing Authority, the National Defense Advisory Commission, the Office of Production Management, the War Production Board, and the War Manpower Commission.

Just as important as these official positions was Weaver's leadership role in the informal Federal Council on Negro Affairs. Created in 1936, the council served as President Roosevelt's adviser on African American affairs, helped sensitize FDR to their needs and aspirations, and assured unprecedented commitments to African Americans.

Upon leaving the federal government in 1944, Weaver joined the Mayor's Committee on Race Relations in Chicago as its first executive secretary. While in Chicago he also served on the Metropolitan Housing Council. In 1946 he traveled to the former Soviet Union as a member of the United Nations Relief and Rehabilitation Administration's mission to the Ukraine.

After his return, Weaver taught at Northwestern University, Columbia University Teachers College, New York University, and the New School for Social Research between 1947 and 1951. He also completed his two most important books after leaving government work: *Negro Labor; A National Problem* (1946) and *The Negro Ghetto* (1948). The latter was one of the first works to explore segregation in the North.

Besides his writing and teaching, Weaver assumed the directorship of the John Hay Whitney Foundation in 1949 and oversaw the distribution of fellowships to deserving African Americans for further study. He remained with the foundation until 1955, when Governor W. Averell Harriman of New York named him deputy state rent commissioner. Within a year Harriman promoted Weaver to state rent administrator, the first cabinet level position ever held by an African American in New York state.

Weaver soon broke additional ground and became the highest federal administrator ever when John F. Kennedy nominated him administrator of the Housing and Home Finance Agency (HHFA) and overseer of the Federal Housing Administration (FHA), Community Facilities Administration, Federal National Mortgage Association, Urban Renewal Administration, and Public Housing Administration. Kennedy's choice for the HHFA job proved controversial, primarily because he chaired the board of directors of the National Association for the Advancement of Colored People. In addition, he strongly opposed segregated public housing, advocated the use of FHA mortgage insurance to integrate the suburbs, and insisted that the Urban Renewal Program stop uprooting so many poor African Americans. As a result, the nomination faced congressional delay and defiance, particularly from southerners. Nevertheless, Congress finally confirmed him and he took office February 11, 1961.

Unlike his predecessors, the new HHFA head wished to create a more rational urban complex rather than merely more housing production. He also believed that the independent agencies under HHFA needed more coordination and attempted to control better their personnel and budgets. Meanwhile, Weaver helped write the Housing Act of 1961, which he described as "a blend of the old and the new." Overall, it relied more on existing machinery rather than new programs. Among its features were provision for 100,000 public housing units and a four-year authorization of $2.5 billion for reviving center cities.

Although Congress willingly agreed to pass the omnibus bill, its refusal to approve another bill directly affected Weaver's career. From the beginning of his administration, John F. Kennedy firmly believed that the nation needed a cabinet post on urban affairs. Only then, Kennedy believed, could order and direction be given to the many federal programs operating in metropolitan areas. Weaver, it appeared, would be the obvious choice to head the new cabinet post. But the prospect of having an African American cabinet officer seemed too much for Southern congressmen who felt little need for such a position anyway. As a result, they defeated all efforts by the president to create such a department.

Not until after Kennedy's assassination did urban America attain its own department, and then many expected that a white mayor would be selected to head it. After reviewing more than 200 applications, however, Johnson named Weaver as secretary of the Department of Housing and Urban Development (HUD) in 1966. Weaver helped organize and manage the growing department for the next two years, leaving after Richard Nixon's victory over Hubert Humphrey in 1968. On retiring from federal service, the former HUD chief became the first president of Bernard M. Baruch College, a new component of the City University of New York system. He left Baruch in 1970 to become Distinguished Professor of Urban Affairs at Hunter College in New York City. For the next eight years he taught and directed the Urban Affairs Research Center. Weaver also maintained

involvement in the civil rights movement and served on the boards of 13 prestigious companies. Later, Mayor Edward Koch of New York appointed the then 75-year-old Weaver as a member of a nine member board to supervise the city's rent-stabilized apartments in 1982.

Further Reading

A treatment of Weaver's early career can be found in Harvard Sitkoff, *A New Deal for Blacks: The Emergence of Civil Rights as a National Issue* (1978) and Richard Bardolph, *The Negro Vanguard* (1959). Mark I. Gelfand provides a good analysis of Weaver's career heading the HHFA in *A Nation of Cities: The Federal Government and Urban America, 1933-1965* (1975). □

Beatrice Potter Webb

The English social reformer Beatrice Potter Webb (1858-1943) was a leading Fabian socialist and a partner with her husband, Sidney Webb, in their projects for social and educational reform and in their research into the history of political and economic institutions.

Beatrice Potter was born on Jan. 2, 1858, at Standish House near Gloucester. Her father, Richard Potter, was a man with large railroad interests and many contacts among politicians and intellectuals. She was educated at home by governesses and also by extensive travel, wide reading, and direct contact with many of the leading figures of politics, science, and industry. Herbert Spencer in particular gave her the attention and encouragement that she thought denied to her by her family.

Potter's involvement with social problems began in 1883, when she became a rent collector in London. This work, in turn, led to her participation in Charles Booth's survey published as *Life and Labour of the People in London*. In 1887 the results of her inquiries into dock life in the East End of London were published in *Nineteenth Century,* soon followed by other articles and studies of sweated labor.

Increased confidence and deeper study culminated in Potter's *The Co-operative Movement in Great Britain* (1891). It was in connection with this that she met Sidney Webb. They were married in 1892, and their life together became one of single-minded dedication to research and social reform. Together they produced a veritable torrent of books, pamphlets, essays, and memoranda amounting to over a hundred items.

Until 1906 Potter's role in the partnership was primarily that of researcher, writer, and hostess for gatherings of Cabinet ministers and members of Parliament who came to hear the Webb opinion on social legislation. At the end of 1905 Beatrice was appointed a member of the Royal Commission on the Poor Laws, which sat from 1906 to 1909. The minority report, drafted by the Webbs, played an im-

portant role in the dismantling of the old Poor Law and in its replacement by the new systems of social insurance.

In the period after 1910 the Webbs abandoned their nonpartisan stance and became an important force in building the Labour party. Another cornerstone of their earlier philosophy was abandoned with the publication of their *Soviet Communism: A New Society?* (1935). They, who had always held that social change cannot come about by the violent destruction of existing institutions, endorsed the Russian Revolution in spite of its totalitarianism. Beatrice Webb died at Liphook, Hampshire, on April 30, 1943. In 1947, shortly after Sidney's death, their ashes were buried in Westminster Abbey.

Further Reading

The two volumes of *Beatrice Webb's Diaries, 1912-1924,* edited by Margaret Cole (1952), with an introduction by Lord Beveridge, offer many insights missing from the standard biographies. Beatrice Webb's memoirs are *My Apprenticeship* (1926) and *Our Partnership* (1948). One of the best books on Beatrice Webb was written by her niece, Kitty Muggeridge, and Ruth Adam, *Beatrice Webb: A Life, 1858-1943* (1967). Margaret Cole, ed., *The Webbs and Their Work* (1949), is a collection of appraisals of the Webbs written by acquaintances and colleagues. Margaret Cole, *Beatrice Webb* (1945), is also well written, informative, and accurate. Mary Agnes Hamilton, *Sidney and Beatrice Webb* (1933), is an interesting account of the Webbs' activities up to the early 1930s.

Additional Sources

MacKenzie, Jeanne, *A Victorian courtship: the story of Beatrice Potter and Sidney Webb,* New York: Oxford University Press, 1979.

Muggeridge, Kitty, *Beatrice Webb: a life, 1858-1943,* Chicago: Academy Publishers, 1983, 1967.

Nord, Deborah Epstein, *The apprenticeship of Beatrice Webb,* Amherst: University of Massachusetts Press, 1985.

Radice, Lisanne, *Beatrice and Sidney Webb: Fabian Socialists,* New York: St. Martin's Press, 1984.

Seymour-Jones, Carole, *Beatrice Webb: a life,* Chicago: I.R. Dee, 1992.

Webb, Beatrice Potter, *My apprenticeship,* Cambridge; New York: Cambridge University Press, 1979. □

Sidney James Webb

Sidney James Webb, Baron Passfield (1859-1947), was an English social reformer and a leading Fabian Socialist, a historian of social and economic institutions, founder of the London School of Economics and Political Science, and Cabinet minister.

Sidney Webb was born in London on July 13, 1859. He was educated in Switzerland, Germany, the Birkbeck Institute, the City of London College, and through his own intensive reading. After a brief period of employment in the office of a firm of colonial brokers, he entered the civil service in 1878. In 1885 he was called to the bar and in the following year received his bachelor of laws degree from London University.

In 1885 Webb joined the Fabian Society and soon became a dominating influence on that organization. In 1891 he resigned from the civil service to run successfully for the London County Council. During most of the next 2 decades he was chairman of the Technical Education Committee of the council and brought about a thoroughgoing reform and centralization of the educational system in London. In 1895 he became the founder of the London School of Economics and Political Science.

In 1892 Webb married Beatrice Potter. From that time on, their work merged so thoroughly that it is impossible to distinguish their individual contributions. Among the earliest and most notable of their works are *The History of Trade Unionism* (1894) and *Industrial Democracy* (1897). Later there were nine massive volumes of the history of *English Local Government,* the first of which appeared in 1906 and the last in 1929.

By 1910 the Webbs decided that the Fabian policy of working through the existing political parties without partisan involvement had outlived its usefulness, and the Fabian Society threw its weight behind the Labour party. From 1915 to 1925 Sidney was a member of the party executive. In 1920 he was elected to Parliament, and in 1924 he was appointed president of the Board of Trade. Although he retired from office in 1928, he was called out of retirement in 1929 to serve (as Baron Passfield) as secretary of state for the colonies.

After the fall of the Labour government in 1932, the Webbs toured the Soviet Union and extolled it in their *Soviet Communism: A New Society?* (1935). Beatrice died in 1943, and Sidney on Oct. 13, 1947.

Further Reading

Sidney Webb has received much less attention from biographers than has Beatrice. Margaret Cole, ed., *The Webbs and Their Work* (1949), is a collection of appraisals of the Webbs written by acquaintances and colleagues. Mary Agnes Hamilton, *Sidney and Beatrice Webb* (1933), examines the Webbs' activities up to the early 1930s. For Sidney Webb's role in the Fabian movement consult Anne Fremantle, *This Little Band of Prophets: The Story of the Gentle Fabians* (1960); Margaret Cole, *The Story of Fabian Socialism* (1961); and A. M. McBriar, *Fabian Socialism and English Politics, 1884-1918* (1962).

Additional Sources

MacKenzie, Jeanne, *A Victorian courtship: the story of Beatrice Potter and Sidney Webb,* New York: Oxford University Press, 1979.

Radice, Lisanne, *Beatrice and Sidney Webb: Fabian Socialists,* New York: St. Martin's Press, 1984.

The Webbs and their work, Westport, Conn.: Greenwood Press, 1985. □

Andrew Lloyd Webber

The British musician Andrew Lloyd Webber (born 1948) was the composer of such musical theater hits as *Joseph and the Amazing Technicolor Dreamcoat,* *Jesus Christ Superstar, Evita, Cats, Starlight Express,* *The Phantom of the Opera,* and *Aspects of Love.* His early successes brought him four Tony awards, four Drama Desk awards, and three Grammys.

Andrew Lloyd Webber was born on March 22, 1948, in London, England. His father was the director of the London College of Music and his mother, a piano teacher. Thus, Lloyd Webber came by his musical ability naturally. As a boy he played piano, violin, and French horn. Excerpts from his first musical composition, *The Toy Theatre,* were published in a British music magazine.

As a child, Webber aspired to become Britain's chief inspector of ancient monuments. He won a Challenge Scholarship to Westminster and in 1965 entered Oxford as a history major. In the 1980s he exercised his love for history via Sydmonton Court, his country estate, whose oldest section dates from the 16th century and where his compositions were tried out at yearly festivals.

Other childhood pastimes of Webber's surface in his works and his approach to their staging. His keen ability to envision fully-mounted productions of even his most spec-

tacular pieces may have emanated, at least in part, from his experience as an 11-year-old working with his elaborate toy theater, built to scale. Webber's lifelong fascination with trains was exhibited in *Starlight Express* (1984). Some consider this his childhood fantasy gone awry, an adulteration of the famous story of the little engine that could.

Webber's formal education ended after only one term at Oxford. He left to begin work on the never-to-be-produced musical *The Likes of Us,* which is based on the life of British philanthropist Dr. Bernardo. Webber's career was inextricably linked with that of lyricist Tim Rice, and their partnership began with this musical.

The duo's next effort was *Joseph and the Amazing Technicolor Dreamcoat* (1968, extended 1972), at first a concert piece, then expanded into a two-act production. The score demonstrates what were to become the Webber trademarks of shifting time signatures and styles, ranging from French cafe music to calypso, country, jazz, and the popular rock idiom.

In *Jesus Christ Superstar* (1971), popular music was presented in classical operatic form. Conceived first as a demonstration disc for Decca, it began the Webber/Rice tradition of recording first, then producing. The score boasts the hit single "I Don't Know How To Love Him." The 1971 Broadway version was directed by Tom O'Horgan, of *Hair* notoriety.

When Rice became disenchanted with a proposed musical based on the works of P. G. Wodehouse, Webber teamed up with British playwright Alan Ayckbourn on the

unsuccessful *Jeeves* (1974). During this period Webber also composed the film scores for *Gumshoe* (1971) and *The Odessa File* (1973).

Webber and Rice were paired once again for *Evita* (1976), the story of the dangerously manipulative actress-courtesan who married Argentinean dictator Juan Peron. Veteran Broadway producer Harold Prince was commandeered to direct the 1978 and 1979 productions on both sides of the Atlantic. *Evita* faced the criticisms that have consistently plagued Webber's compositions. He was accused of "borrowing" songs and his work was called "derivative," "synthetic," and a "pastiche."

Webber's next (and less impressive) production, *Song and Dance* (1982), was the result of the fusion of two of his earlier pieces: *Variations* (1978) and *Tell Me on a Sunday* (1979). *Variations* (1978) is a set of cello variations written for his brother, Julian, and *Tell Me on a Sunday* (1979), is the story of an English working girl who moves to New York and through a series of relationships.

Cats (1981) constituted the composer's personal and professional watershed. Based on T. S. Eliot's volume of children's verses, *Old Possum's Book of Practical Cats,* the production was staged by Royal Shakespeare director Trevor Nunn and its extravagant scenery was created by John Napier. Rice was called in to provide assistance on the lyrics for the now-famous "Memory," but his words were abandoned in favor of Nunn's.

Webber found himself attracted at first vocally, then romantically, to performer Sarah Brightman. She was a castmember in *Cats,* and in 1983 he abandoned his first wife, Sarah Hugill, for her. He later married Brightman and she was cast as the female lead, Christine Daae, in *The Phantom of the Opera.*

With *Cats,* spectacle became the key to success both in London and on Broadway. It was only natural that a production like *Starlight Express* would follow on its heels. Webber and Prince were paired again for the romantic 1986 production of *Phantom of the Opera.*

Webber's production *Aspects of Love* (1989) was in many ways a "retread." The score is filled with tunes retrieved from Webber's past, reworked for the occasion.

Webber turned his attention toward his production company, Really Useful Theatre Group, Inc., in the 1980s. In April 1990 he announced his intention to take a hiatus from writing musicals and to turn to moviemaking, perhaps even a film version of *Cats* with Stephen Spielberg.

Ironically, in July 1990 Webber announced his impending divorce from Sarah Brightman while she was completing her summer concert tour of *The Music of Andrew Lloyd Webber.* However, after the November divorce the couple planned to continue working together, despite Webber's early marriage in London to Madeleine Gurdon.

Webber went on to produce *Sunset Boulevard,* in London, 1993, and in Los Angeles and on Broadway, both in 1994. Besides *The Likes of Us* (lyrics by Rice), his other unproduced plays include *Come Back Richard, Your Country Needs You* (with Rice) and *Cricket.*

Further Reading

A behind-the-professional-scenes perspective permeates Gerald McKnight's 1984 biography *Andrew Lloyd Webber. TIME* magazine music critic Michael Walsh's 1989 *Andrew Lloyd Webber: His Life and Works* (dealt with chronologically) deftly combines intelligent criticism of the composer's works with biographical detail. Richard Melcher, "The Roar of the Greasepaint Is Too Quiet for Lloyd Webber" (*TIME,* April 23, 1990) discusses the business career and financial position of Webber as he seeks to broaden his talents into other media. □

Carl Maria Friedrich Ernst von Weber

The operas of Carl Maria Friedrich Ernst von Weber (1786-1826) are the cornerstone of the German romantic opera, and he is often heralded as the father of musical romanticism.

The son of an itinerant musical family, Carl Maria von Weber was born on Dec. 18, 1786, near Lübeck, where his father was a town musician and his mother a singer. The family was distantly connected with Constanze Weber Mozart's family. There was no justification for the claim of nobility or the use of the "von." Weber spent his early years in nearly constant travel. His father, an unscrupulous eccentric, attempted to turn him into a prodigy, but young Weber was unable to live up to these expectations.

In 1796 the family settled temporarily in Salzburg, where Weber entered the school for choristers directed by Michael Haydn. Two years later Weber's mother died, and his father resumed his itinerant existence, carrying his son first to Vienna and then to Munich, where the boy again formally studied music. In 1800 he composed his first opera, *Die Macht von Liebe* (The Power of Love), a piano sonata, some variations for piano, and several songs, all highly amateurish.

In 1801 Weber and his father returned to Salzburg, where Weber resumed his study with Michael Haydn. Beginning in 1804 Weber studied off and on over the next few years with Georg Vogler.

During this time the handsome young Weber managed to survive on his wits, charm, and ability to manipulate people and circumstances. He was involved in various court imbroglios and intrigues through his own culpability, to say nothing of his father's notoriously disreputable behavior. The turning point in Weber's career seems to have taken place when he was arrested and eventually banished from Stuttgart as a result of an unsavory scandal concerning a possible charge of bribery in connection with the court. Although proved innocent of this charge, he was shaken enough, it seems, to settle down and become seriously concerned with establishing himself as a performer and composer.

Weber traveled extensively throughout Germany and Austria, playing his own compositions and composing. In 1813 he became an opera conductor in Prague. The following year he fell in love with Caroline Brandt, a singer in his company, whom he married in 1817, a year after he had been appointed conductor of German opera in Dresden. He served in this post and remained active in the city's musical life until his untimely death.

Creation of the German Romantic Opera

Weber's vast and varied theatrical experience in the provincial opera houses of central Europe bore fruit in *Der Freischütz* (The Freeshooter), produced in Berlin in 1821. Composed to a libretto by Friedrich Kind and heavily indebted to folk superstition and sentimentalized medieval German history, the opera was an enormous success. In this one composition Weber succeeded in creating a prototype for the German romantic opera which he himself was unable to equal.

In 1824 Weber's second major opera, *Euryanthe,* with a libretto by Helmine von Chézy, was produced in Dresden. Overly complicated and without the instant popular appeal of *Freischütz, Euryanthe* did not live up to expectations. That year Weber received an offer to go to London to prepare an English opera based on C. M. Wieland's *Oberon.* Although seriously ill, Weber agreed to undertake this work since he was financially straitened. He left for England in 1825 to supervise the performances of *Oberon,* which was a great success. He died in London on June 5, 1826, of tuberculosis.

Other Works

Weber was a prolific composer in many forms. In addition to his piano music—several sonatas, variations, two concertos, and the fanciful *Konzertstück*—his production includes symphonies, chamber music, vocal works, and two clarinet concertos. His major accomplishment, however, was to create the first great popular success for German romantic opera. The folklike quality of much of his vocal writing has ensured his popularity in Germany, but elsewhere he is a composer more honored by name than in performance. The overtures of his three major operas have long been repertoire items in the concert hall, but the operas themselves deserve to be better known. Weber was also a respectable prose writer, especially of music criticism, thus proving himself to be entirely in keeping with 19th-century romantic aspirations.

Further Reading

Good biographies of Weber are William Saunders, *Weber* (1940), and Lucy and Richard Poate Stebbins, *The Enchanted Wanderer: The Life of Carl Maria von Weber* (1940). His operas are examined in Donald J. Grout, *A Short History of the Opera* (1947; rev. ed. 1965).

Additional Sources

Benedict, Julius, Sir, *Carl Maria von Weber,* New York: AMS Press, 1980.
Friese-Greene, Anthony, *Weber,* London; New York: Omnibus, 1991.
Warrack, John Hamilton, *Carl Maria von Weber,* Cambridge, Eng.; New York: Cambridge University Press, 1976.
Warrack, John Hamilton, *The New Grove early romantic masters 2: Weber, Berlioz, Mendelssohn,* New York: Norton, 1985. □

Max Weber

The German social scientist Max Weber (1864-1920) was a founder of modern sociological thought. His historical and comparative studies of the great civilizations are a landmark in the history of sociology.

The work of Max Weber reflects a continued interest in charting the varying paths taken by universal cultural history as reflected in the development of the great world civilizations. In this sense, he wished to attempt a historical and analytical study of the themes sounded so strongly in G. W. F. Hegel's philosophy of history, especially the theme, which Weber took as his own, of the "specific and peculiar rationalism of Western culture." Along with this emphasis on universal cultural history, Weber's detailed training as a legal and economic historian led him to reject the overly simplistic formulas of economic base and corresponding cultural superstructure that were so often used to account for cultural development and were a strong part of the intellectual environment of Weber's early years as student and professor. His historical and comparative erudition and analytical awareness required that he go beyond both the Hegelian and Marxian versions of historical development toward a deep historical and comparative study of sociocultural processes in West and East.

Weber was born on April 21, 1864, in Erfaut, Thuringia, the son of a lawyer active in political life. An attack of meningitis at the age of 4 and his mother's consequent overprotectiveness helped contribute to Weber's sedentary yet intellectually precocious youth. He read widely in the classics and was bored with the unchallenging secondary education of his time, which he completed in 1882. He then attended Heidelberg University, where he studied law, along with history, economics, and philosophy.

After three terms at Heidelberg, Weber served a year in the military, which he found to be largely an "incredible waste of time" with its continued attempts to regiment the human intellect. Resuming his studies at the universities of Berlin and Göttingen in 1884, he passed his bar examination in 1886 and would later practice law for a time. He completed his doctoral thesis in 1889 with an essay on the history of the medieval trading companies, which embodied his interests in both legal and economic history. His second major work, a customary "habilitation" thesis that would qualify him to teach at the university level, appeared in 1891 and involved a study of the economic, cultural, and legal foundations of ancient agrarian history.

In 1893 Weber married Marianne Schnitger. The following year he received an appointment as professor of economics at Freiburg University; in 1896 he accepted a

professorship at Heidelberg. Shortly after his father's death in 1897, Weber began to suffer from a psychic disturbance that incapacitated him almost completely until 1902. By the next year he was well enough to join Werner Sombart in editing the *Archiv für Sozialwissenschaft and Sozialpolitik* (Archives for Social Science and Social Policy), the most prominent German social science journal of the period.

Protestantism and Capitalism

Having assumed his full work load again, Weber began to write perhaps his most renowned essays, published in the *Archiv* in 1904-1905 under the title *The Protestant Ethic and the Spirit of Capitalism.* In them he attempted to link the rise of a new sort of distinctly modern capitalism to the religious ethics of Protestantism, especially the Calvinist variety, with its emphasis on work in a calling directed toward the rational ascetic mastery of this world.

Weber argued that, when the asceticism of the medieval Catholic monastery, oriented toward salvation in a world beyond this one through self-denial exercised by a religious few, was brought into the conduct of everyday affairs, it contributed greatly to the systematic rationalization and functional organization of every sphere of existence, especially economic life. He viewed the Reformation as a crucial period in western European history, one that was to see a fundamental reorientation of basic cultural frameworks of spiritual direction and human outlook and destined to have a great impact on economic life as well as other aspects of modern culture. Within the context of his larger questions, Weber tended to view Protestant rationalism as one further step in the series of stages of increasing rationalization of every area of modern society.

In 1904 Weber was invited to attend the St. Louis Exhibition in Missouri and to deliver a popular sociological lecture. While in America, he had substantial opportunity to encounter what he saw as added evidence for his special thesis in *The Protestant Ethic and the Spirit of Capitalism,* as well as for his more general philosophic and historical concerns. In the United States the religious foundations of modern economic life had seen perhaps their greatest fruition in the enormous "towers of capital," as Weber called them, of the eastern industrial centers of the country. However, he also recognized that the contemporary American economic life had been stripped of its original ethical and religious impulse. Intense economic competition assumed the character almost of sport, and no obvious possibilities appeared for the resuscitation of new spiritual values from what appeared to be the extensive mechanization of social and economic existence.

Employing a method that isolated the similarities and differences between features of sociocultural development in different societies, Weber attempted to weigh the relative importance of economic, religious, juridical, and other factors in contributing to the different historical outcomes seen in any comparative study of world societies. This larger theme formed one of his central intellectual interests throughout the remainder of his life, and it resulted in the publication of *The Religion of China* (1915), *The Religion of India* (1916-1917), and *Ancient Judaism* (1917-1919). Although he also planned comparable works on early Christianity, medieval Catholicism, and Islamic civilization, he died before they could be completed.

Later Work

After the essays of 1904-1905, Weber took on an even heavier burden of activities than before his illness. His break with the Verein für Sozialpolitik (Union for Social Policy), a long-standing German political and social scientific organization, over the question of the relation of social scientific research to social policy led to the establishment in 1910, with the collaboration of other great social scientists of his day, of the new Deutsche Soziologische Gesellschaft (German Sociological Society).

Weber and his collaborators argued that social science could not be simply subordinated to political values and policies. Rather, there was a logical distinction between the realms of fact and value, one which required a firmly grounded distinction between the analyses of the social scientist and the policies of any political order. Social science must develop "objective" frames of reference, ones "neutral" to any particular political policies and ethical values. This ever-renewed tension between particular ethical stances and "objectivity" in the sciences remained a central part of Weber's concerns in his political activities during and after World War I as well as in his academic writings and lectures.

Economy and Society

In 1909 Weber took over the editorship of a projected multivolume encyclopedic work on the social sciences entitled *Outline of Social Economics*. It was to contain volumes authored by prominent social scientists of the time. Although he was originally to contribute the volume *Economy and Society* to this effort, difficulties in obtaining completed manuscripts from some participants led Weber to expand his contribution into what became a prodigious attempt at the construction of a systematic sociology in world historical and comparative depth, one which was to occupy a large portion of his time and energies during the remainder of his life. He published his first contributions in 1911-1913, other still unfinished sections being published after his death.

Economy and Society differed in tone and emphasis from Weber's comparative studies of the cultural foundations of Chinese, Indian, and Western civilizations. This massive work was an attempt at a more systematic sociology, not directed toward any single comparative, historical problem but rather toward an organization of the major areas of sociological inquiry into a single whole. Weber never believed it possible to write a truly systematic sociology that would have separate analytical sections on each area of interest and that would form a general system of theory. Containing large sections on sociological analysis, the economy and social norms, economy and law, domination, and legitimacy, and still unsurpassed sections on religion, the city, and political rulership, *Economy and Society* remains today perhaps the only systematic sociology in world historical and comparative depth.

Last Years

Despite time spent in the medical service during World War I, Weber's efforts were largely devoted from 1910 to 1919 to the completion of his studies on China, India, and ancient Judaism and to his work on *Economy and Society*. Many younger as well as more established scholars formed part of Weber's wide intellectual circle during these years. Always desirous of championing the cause of scholars whose work was judged unfairly because of religious, political, or other external criteria, Weber on numerous occasions attempted to aid these young scholars—despite sometimes substantial intellectual differences with them—by securing for them the academic appointments they deserved. Often these attempts were unsuccessful and led Weber into bitter conflicts with many established scholars and political figures over the relation of science to values and the application of extrascientific criteria to the evaluation of a writer's work.

In 1918 Weber resumed his teaching duties. One result was a series of lectures in 1919-1920, "Universal Economic History," which was published posthumously from students' notes as *General Economic History*. Along with this lecture series, Weber delivered two addresses in 1918, "Science as a Vocation" and "Politics as a Vocation," in which he voiced ethical themes that had occupied him in his scholarly work and in his numerous discussions of social policy. In these two addresses he contrasted the ethic of unalterable ultimate ends so characteristic of uncompromising religious and political prophets with the ethic of consequences so necessary in political life, in which possible outcomes of actions and policies are agonizingly weighed and the least undesirable course determined in light of a plurality of given goals. Variants of this distinction pervaded much of Weber's own view of political and religious life and formed a central aspect of his ethical philosophy.

Thus, Weber sounded ethical themes that have become a central part of the "existentialist" philosophical orientation of our time. Understanding the dilemma of modern men caught between the older religious systems of the past and the cynical power politics of the present, he gave no simple solutions and was willing neither to wait for new prophets nor to abdicate all ethical responsibility for the conduct of life because of its seeming ultimate "meaninglessness."

Weber died in Munich on June 14, 1920. His work forms a major part of the historical foundation of sociology.

Further Reading

Biographical background on Weber as well as an analysis of his major intellectual orientation can be found in the "Introduction" to *From Max Weber: Essays in Sociology,* edited by Hans H. Gerth and C. Wright Mills (1946). An interpretation of Weber's life and work, emphasizing analytical motifs derived from Freudianism and the sociology of knowledge, is provided by Arthur Mitzman, *The Iron Cage: An Historical Interpretation of Max Weber* (1970).

There are a number of readily accessible general treatments of Weber's sociology. Volume 2 of Raymond Aron, *Main Currents of Sociological Thought* (2 vols., 1965-1967), contains an excellent treatment of Weber, recommended for beginning students. Julien Freund, *The Sociology of Max Weber* (1966; trans. 1968), is overly systematic, yet chapters 1 and 2 are helpful as an introduction to Weber's vision of society and his method. Reinhard Bendix, *Max Weber: An Intellectual Portrait* (1960), gives a depth analysis of Weber's historical works but is recommended for more advanced study. Talcott Parsons, *The Structure of Social Action* (1937; 2d ed. 1949), gives a penetrating and difficult treatment of some elements of Weber's theoretical perspective.

In addition to Mitzman's study, helpful insights into the social, political, and intellectual background of the period are in Koppel S. Pinson, *Modern Germany: Its History and Civilization* (1954; 2d ed. 1966), and Walter M. Simon, *Germany: A Brief History* (1966). □

Max Weber

The American painter Max Weber (1881-1961) sampled various styles, including cubism, before turning to representation in 1918. Thereafter, he developed a style which was personal and expressionistic but incorporated elements from his earlier, experimental phase.

Max Weber was born on April 18, 1881, in Belostok, Russia, the son of a tailor. In 1891 the family emigrated to America, settling in Brooklyn, N.Y. Max entered Pratt Institute in 1898; he took courses in manual training and art with a teaching career as his goal. After he graduated in 1900, he studied with Arthur Wesley Dow for a year. Weber then taught manual training and drawing in Virginia and Minnesota.

In 1905 Weber went to Paris, where he studied with Jean Paul Laurens at the Académie Julian and went to life classes at the Académie de la Grande Chaumière and Académie Colarossi. In 1907 he saw the Paul Cézanne retrospective at the Salon d'Automne. Weber soon acquired an interest in Fauve art and began to paint in a style inspired by it. In 1907 he helped form a class with Henri Matisse as its teacher and joined the class for a year. Weber exhibited in 1906 and 1907 at the Indépendants and in 1907 and 1908 at the Salon d'Automne.

In 1909 Weber returned to New York City. By 1912 his style had changed, as he embraced cubism more and more. His best-known work of this period is *Chinese Restaurant* (1915). Though it is an abstraction, he epitomizes in it the atmosphere of a restaurant, with tile floors, festive decorations, and frenetic waiters. His use of bright color and varieties of robust patterns allied him more with such cubists as Albert Gleizes and Jean Metzinger than Pablo Picasso or Georges Braque. By 1918 Weber had moved away from abstraction. His paintings of the 1920s and 1930s feature figures in compositions, which are Cézannesque, contemplative, and poetic. In the late 1930s he turned to the contemporary scene in such paintings as *At the Mill* (1939), *The Haulers* (1939), and *The Toilers* (1942).

Mindful of his Jewish heritage, Weber began to exploit Hasidic themes in a highly mannered, expressionist fashion. His giddy Talmudic scholars respond to the mildest occasion with an excess of agitation and bounce. One work in this style is *Adoration of the Moon* (1944). He had his first one-man show in New York City in 1909, was represented in the famous Armory Show of 1913, and exhibited regularly thereafter. In 1929 he moved to Great Neck, Long Island, where he died on Oct. 4, 1961.

Further Reading

The only generally available work on Weber is Lloyd Goodrich, *Max Weber* (1949). Discussions of Weber are in Jerome Mellquist, *The Emergence of an American Art* (1942); James T. Flexner, *A Short History of American Painting* (1950); Daniel M. Mendelowitz, *A History of American Art* (1960); and Samuel M. Green, *American Art: A Historical Survey* (1966). □

Anton Webern

The Austrian composer Anton Webern (1883-1945), one of the first important disciples of Schoenberg, carried many of that master's ideas to their logical extremes. Webern's music was very influential on postwar European composers.

Anton von Webern was born in Vienna on Dec. 3, 1883, to the mining engineer Karl von Webern and his wife, Amalia. When he was ten years old, the family moved to Klagenfurt. There Webern began his first music lessons; he studied piano, cello, and the rudiments of theory and began to compose songs. At the gymnasium he studied the traditional courses in the humanities.

After graduation in 1902, Webern traveled to Bayreuth to hear performances of Richard Wagner's works. This experience impressed Webern deeply, and on entering the University of Vienna in the fall of 1902, he devoted himself more intensely to studies in harmony and counterpoint, as well as to courses in musicology under Guido Adler. A typical piece of this period is a ballade with orchestral accompaniment, *Jung Siegfried,* which shows the influence of Wagnerian ideas.

In 1904, after an abortive attempt to study with Hans Pfitzner in Berlin, Webern began lessons with Arnold Schoenberg, who was the dominating figure of his life, even though Webern carried some of Schoenberg's ideas further than the older composer could entirely approve. At this time, too, Webern became friendly with another Schoenberg pupil, Alban Berg. The friendship lasted till Berg's death in 1935; it was a personally and artistically stimulating relationship for both composers.

While Webern was developing his distinctive style under Schoenberg's guidance, he was also completing a major project in musicology. In 1906 he received his doctorate from the University of Vienna for his dissertation on Hein-

rich Isaac's *Choralis Constantinus,* an important Renaissance collection of liturgical compositions. His edition of part two of this work is still standard.

Webern's studies with Schoenberg lasted till 1908. Some works written during this 4-year period are the *Passacaglia for Orchestra,* the chorus *Entflieht auf leichten kähnen* (text by Stefan George), and the Five Songs (also with texts by George), as well as a Piano Quintet in C Major. In the Five Songs, Webern already followed Schoenberg in transcending the limitations of classical tonality. His following works are atonal, that is, written without reference to a key center.

Webern's compositions of the next 10 years became more and more concise; some are less than a minute long. His dynamic effects were often delicate; he made use of the idea of *Klangfarbenmelodie* (tone-color melody), frequently dividing a melody among a succession of different instruments with resultant subtle changes in tone color. Works representative of this new style are the Five Pieces for String Quartet (1909), the Four Pieces for Violin and Piano (1910), the Six Bagatelles for String Quartet (1913), and the Three Little Pieces for Cello and Piano (1914), as well as groups of orchestral pieces and songs. Schoenberg's preface to the Six Bagatelles, which he wrote in 1924 for their publication by Universal-Edition, gives a vivid impression of the style:

"Just as the brevity of these pieces speaks in their favor, even so it is necessary to speak in favor of this brevity. Think of the concision which expression in such brief form demands! Every glance is a poem, every sigh a novel. But to achieve such concentration—to express a novel in a single gesture, a great joy in a single breath—every trace of sentimentality must be correspondingly banished."

During these years Webern was going from job to job as theater conductor. He worked in Bad Ischl, Vienna, Teplitz, Danzig, and Stettin. But these positions did not suit him. The introverted, sensitive composer was unhappy with the low standards of the opera houses in provincial towns, and he did not like theatrical life. His marriage to his cousin Wilhelmine Mörtl in 1911 brought a welcome stability to this rather frustrating existence. In 1915 he joined the Austrian army as a volunteer but was dismissed after a year because of poor eyesight.

After World War I Webern took an active part in Schoenberg's Society for Private Performances in Vienna. This organization did valuable work in presenting major contemporary compositions to a highly selective audience. When it had to dissolve in 1922 because of rising costs, Webern took over the direction of the Vienna Workers' Symphony Orchestra and, in the following year, added the responsibility of the Vienna Workers' Singing Society. The performance of Mahler's Eighth Symphony by these groups under his direction in 1926 was long remembered.

Webern's adoption of the twelve-tone method came in 1924, with the *Drei Volkstexte* for soprano, violin, clarinet, and bass clarinet. These songs, based on religious folk poetry, were the first works in which Webern used strict twelve-tone rows in the Schoenbergian sense. His acceptance of the new technique was wholehearted, and he used it till the end of his life. Important twelve-tone compositions

of the 1920s were the String Trio (1927) and the Symphony (1928), as well as two groups of songs.

After 1933 Webern led a very retired existence. Political conditions in Germany and Austria did not favor his radical kind of music. He earned his living mainly by giving private lessons; after 1941 he was employed as a reader by Universal-Edition, evaluating new scores that were sent to them for consideration. Major works composed between 1933 and 1945 included the Concerto for Nine Instruments (1934), Variations for Piano (1936), String Quartet (1938), First Cantata for soprano solo, mixed chorus, and orchestra (1939), Variations for Orchestra, and Second Cantata for soprano and bass solo, mixed chorus, and orchestra (1941-1943). The texts for the two cantatas are by Hildegard Jone; she and her husband, the sculptor Josef Humplik, were among Webern's closest friends.

Webern remained in retirement during World War II, staying in his home in Mödling near Vienna. In Easter, 1945, he moved his family to Mittersill, near Salzburg, where he thought they would be safer. There, through a tragic error, he was shot to death by an American occupation soldier on Sept. 15, 1945.

After World War II it was Webern's work rather than Schoenberg's that inspired the young European composers. Webern's radical position led these composers to consider him as the true founder of the new music.

Further Reading

Webern's ascetic personality is glimpsed in his writings, *The Path to the New Music* (trans. 1963) and *Letters to Hildegard Jone and Josef Humplik* (1963; trans. 1967). Friedrich Wildgans, *Anton Webern* (1966), is a straightforward narrative with brief comments on the works. A moving account of the mysterious circumstances surrounding his death is Hans Moldenhauer, *The Death of Anton Webern: A Drama in Documents* (1961). Detailed musical analysis are in Walter Kolneder, *Anton Webern: An Introduction to His Works* (1961; trans. 1968), and in *Anton von Webern: Perspectives,* compiled by Hans Moldenhauer and edited by Demar Irvine (1966).
René Leibowitz, *Schoenberg and His School* (1947; trans. 1949), offers an enthusiastic introduction to Webern, as does George Perle, *Serial Composition and Atonality: An Introduction to the Music of Schoenberg, Berg, and Webern* (1962; 2d rev. ed. 1968). Also useful are the sections on Webern in Pierre Boulez, *Notes of an Apprenticeship* (1966; trans. 1968); Wilfrid Mellers, *Caliban Reborn: Renewal in Twentieth-century Music* (1967); and Joan Peyser, *The New Music: The Sense behind the Sound* (1971).

Additional Sources

Moldenhauer, Hans, *Anton von Webern, a chronicle of his life and work,* New York: Knopf: distributed by Random House, 1979, 1978.
Neighbour, O. W. (Oliver Wray), *The New Grove Second Viennese School: Schoenberg, Webern, Berg,* New York: Norton, 1983. □

Daniel Webster

Daniel Webster (1782-1852), a notable orator and leading constitutional lawyer, was a major congressional spokesman for the Northern Whigs during his 20 years in the U.S. Senate.

Daniel Webster was born in Salisbury, N. H., on Jan. 18, 1782. After graduating from Dartmouth College, he studied law and was admitted to the bar in 1805. He opened a law office in Portsmouth, N. H., in 1807, where his success was immediate. He became a noted spokesman for the Federalist point of view through his addresses on patriotic occasions. In 1808 he married Grace Fletcher.

Early Years in Politics

Elected to the U.S. House of Representatives in 1813, Webster revitalized the Federalist minority with his vigorous attacks on the war policy of the Republicans. Under his leadership the Federalists (with the help of dissident Republicans) often successfully obstructed war measures. After the War of 1812 he advocated the rechartering of the Bank of the United States, but he voted against the final bill, whose provisions he considered inadequate. As the representative of a region where shipping was basic to the economy, he voted against the protective tariff.

Webster's congressional career ended temporarily in 1816, when he moved to Boston. As a result of his success in pleading before the U.S. Supreme Court, his fame as a lawyer grew, and soon his annual income rose to $15,000 a year. In 1819 he experienced a notable victory for the trustees of Dartmouth College, who were seeking to prevent the state from converting the college into a state-supported institution. Chief Justice John Marshall's opinion in the Dartmouth College case was not so much colored by Webster's emotion-charged argument as by Marshall's determination to take the opportunity to further bolster the contract clause. A few weeks later Webster secured an even greater triumph in defending the Bank of the United States in *McCulloch v. Maryland*. On this occasion Marshall drew from Webster's brief the doctrine that the power to tax is the power to destroy. In 1824 Webster was also successful on behalf of his clients in *Gibbons v. Ogden*.

When Webster returned to the U.S. House of Representatives in 1823, his speeches in behalf of the popular cause of the Greek revolution attracted national attention. President James Monroe, however, was able to prevent the passage of Webster's resolutions announcing American sympathy for the rebels. From 1825 to 1829 Webster was one of the staunchest backers of President John Quincy Adams, endorsing Federal internal improvements and supporting Adams in his conflict with Georgia over the removal of the Cherokee Indians.

The Senator

Upon his election to the Senate in 1827, Webster made the first about-face in his career when he became a proponent of the protective tariff. This shift reflected the growing importance of manufacturing in Massachusetts and his own close involvement with factory owners both as clients and as friends. It was largely due to his support that the "Tariff of Abominations" was passed in 1828. His first wife died shortly after he entered the Senate, and in 1829 he married Catherine Le Roy of New York.

In January 1830 Webster electrified the nation by his speeches in reply to the elaborate exposition of the Southern states'-rights doctrines made by John C. Calhoun's close friend Senator Robert Y. Hayne of South Carolina. In memorable phrases Webster exposed the weaknesses in Hayne's views and countered them with the argument that the Constitution and the Union rested upon the people and not upon the states. These speeches, delivered before crowded Senate galleries, defined the constitutional issues which agitated the nation until the Civil War.

Webster was at the height of his powers in 1830. Regarded by contemporaries as one of the greatest orators of the day, he delivered his speeches with tremendous dramatic impact. He modulated his voice, speaking at one moment in stentorian tones, the next in a whisper. Yet, in spite of his emotional style and the florid character of his oratory, he rarely sacrificed logic for effect. His striking appearance contributed to the forcefulness of his delivery: tall, rather gaunt, and always clad in black; his face was dominated by deep, luminous black eyes under craggy brows and a shock of black hair combed straight back. As he

grew older, his figure remained erect, but his eyes seemed to be more cavernous and to burn with greater intensity.

In private Webster was less formidable. He was fond of convivial gatherings and was a lively talker, although at times given to silent moods. His taste for luxury often led him to live beyond his means. While his admirers worshiped the "Godlike Daniel," his critics felt that his constant need for money deprived him of his independence. During the Panic of 1837, he was in such desperate circumstances as a result of excessive speculation in western lands that only loans from business friends saved him from ruin. Again, in 1844, when it seemed that financial pressure might force him to leave the Senate, he permitted his friends to raise a fund to provide him with a supplementary income.

Secretary of State

Although Webster was one of the leaders of the anti-Jackson forces which coalesced in the Whig party, he unhesitatingly endorsed President Andrew Jackson's stand during the nullification crisis in 1832. In 1836 the Massachusetts Whigs named Webster as their presidential candidate, but in a field against other Whig candidates he polled only the electoral votes of Massachusetts. In recognition of his standing in the party and in gratitude for his support during the campaign, President William Henry Harrison appointed him secretary of state in 1841. He continued in this post under John Tyler, who succeeded to the presidency when Harrison died a month after the inauguration. Webster was the only Whig to remain in the Cabinet after Tyler refused to approve the party program formulated by Henry Clay. Webster stayed on in the hope of using Tyler's influence to build up a following which would ensure his nomination as Tyler's successor. He won general approval for his skill in settling the Maine-Canada dispute in the Webster-Ashburton Treaty in 1843. This dispute had been a major source of Anglo-American tension for nearly a decade. He also sent Caleb Cushing to the Orient to establish commercial relations with China, although he was no longer in office when Cushing concluded the agreement. Late in 1843 Webster, feeling that he no longer enjoyed Tyler's confidence, yielded to Whig pressure and retired from office.

In spite of his disappointment at not receiving the presidential nomination in 1844, Webster actively campaigned for Henry Clay, his archival within the party. On his return to the Senate in 1844, Webster opposed the annexation of Texas and denounced the expansionist policies that culminated in the war with Mexico. After the war he worked to exclude slavery from the newly acquired territories and voted for the Wilmot Proviso. Yet, when confronted by the crisis precipitated by California's application for admission to the Union as a free state in 1849, he dismayed his constituents by supporting Clay's compromise.

Although Northern businessmen, desiring domestic tranquility, approved Webster's speech of March 1850 in defense of the new Fugitive Slave Law, the average citizen was outraged. Webster again became secretary of state in July 1850, in Millard Fillmore's Cabinet. In 1852 he lost his last hope for the presidency when the Whigs passed over him in favor of Gen. Winfield Scott, a former Democrat. Deeply outraged, he refused to support the party candidate. He died just before the election on Oct. 24, 1852.

Further Reading

Until the modern edition of Webster's correspondence under the editorship of Charles M. Wiltse appears, the old, inadequate editions must be used: *The Private Correspondence of Daniel Webster,* edited by Fletcher Webster (2 vols., 1857), and *The Writings and Speeches of Daniel Webster,* edited by J. W. McIntyre (18 vols., 1903). The standard biography is Claude M. Fuess, *Daniel Webster* (2 vols., 1930). Richard N. Current, *Daniel Webster and the Rise of National Conservatism* (1955), is an excellent brief survey. Webster's important influence on American constitutional development is examined in Maurice G. Baxter, *Daniel Webster and the Supreme Court* (1966). □

John Webster

The reputation of the English dramatist John Webster (ca. 1580-ca. 1634) rests on two blank-verse trage-dies, *The White Devil* and *The Duchess of Malfi*. He was a painstaking literary craftsman, much con-cerned with the philosophy and the psychology of evil.

Nothing definite is known of John Webster's birth or parentage. He has been tentatively identified as the son of a merchant-tailor of London, and it is thought he was born about 1580; but no solid evidence on either of these points exists. From his plays it is clear that Webster was a learned man, but nothing is known of his education.

The earliest definite reference to Webster occurs in the diary of the theatrical manager Philip Henslowe. Henslowe's records reveal that in 1602 Webster collabo-rated with Anthony Munday, Thomas Middleton, Michael Drayton, and others on a play called *Caesar's Fall,* which has not survived. Two years later John Marston's play *The Malcontent* was performed by the King's Men with an In-duction written by Webster. The Induction provides a re-vealing picture of an early Jacobean audience. In 1605 and 1606 Webster worked on two plays with Thomas Dekker. These were *Westward Ho!* and *Northward Ho!,* both realis-tic comedies performed by the Children of Pauls.

None of this early work gives more than the vaguest hint of the dramatic genius that is displayed in Webster's twin tragic masterpieces, *The White Devil* and *The Duchess of Malfi.* The first was probably written in 1611 or 1612, the second in 1613 or 1614. Both are powerful tragedies domi-nated by strong-willed female protagonists, each of whom suffers a violent death for defying the conventions of a corrupt society. The strain of morbidity evident in each play is frequently considered the most distinctive feature of Web-ster's work.

Webster's later dramatic work was sporadic and undis-tinguished. The most interesting of his nondramatic writings are found in the second edition of Sir Thomas Overbury's *Characters* (1615). Although Webster's name does not ap-pear in this collection of Theophrastian sketches, it is gener-ally agreed that he was responsible for a number of those sketches added to the original edition of 1614.

The circumstances of Webster's death are as obscure and uncertain as those of his birth. There is some reason to believe that he was dead before the end of 1634, but no more precise information has been uncovered.

Further Reading

Frank L. Lucas, *The Complete Works of John Webster,* vol. 1 (1927), contains the fullest treatment of Webster's life. Critical analyses of his two major works are Clifford Leech, *John Webster: A Critical Study* (1951), and Travis Bogard, *The Tragic Satire of John Webster* (1955). The introductions to John Russell Brown's editions of *The White Devil* (1960) and *The Duchess of Malfi* (1964) also contain valuable critical commentary.

Additional Sources

Bradbrook, M. C. (Muriel Clara), *John Webster, citizen and dra-matist,* New York: Columbia University Press, 1980. □

Noah Webster

Noah Webster (1758-1843), American lexicog-rapher, remembered now almost solely as the com-piler of a continuously successful dictionary, was for half a century among the more influential and most active literary men in the United States.

Noah Webster was born on Oct. 16, 1758, in West Hartford, Conn. In 1774 he entered Yale, sharing literary ambitions with his classmate Joel Barlow and tutor Timothy Dwight. His college years were inter-rupted by terms of military service. After his graduation in 1779, he taught school in Hartford, Litchfield, and Sharon, read widely, and studied law. He was admitted to the bar and received his master of arts degree in 1781. Dissatisfied with the British-made textbooks available for teaching, he determined to produce his own. He had, he said, "too much pride to stand indebted to Great Britain for books to learn our children."

Schoolmaster to America

Webster devised the first of his long series of American schoolbooks, a speller ponderously titled *A Grammatical Institute of the English Language, Part I* (1783). Known for generations simply as *The Blue-back Speller,* it was in use for more than a century and sold over 70 million copies. His book's effect on students is said to have been unparalleled in the history of American elementary education. Part II of the *Grammatical Institute,* a grammar, reprinted often under

In New York, Webster established the *American Magazine* (1787-1788), which he hoped might become a national periodical. In it he pled for American intellectual independence, education for women, and adherence to Federalist ideas. Though it survived for only 12 monthly issues, it is remembered as one of the most lively, bravely adventuresome of early American periodicals. He continued as a political journalist with such pamphlets as *The Effects of Slavery on Morals and Industry* (1793), *The Revolution in France* (1794), and *The Rights of Neutral Nations* (1802).

Language Reform

But Webster's principal interest became language reform. As he set forth his ideas in *Dissertations on the English Language* (1789), theatre should be spelled theater; crumb, crumb; machine, masheen; plough, plow; draught, draft. For a time he put forward claims for such reform in his readers and spellers and in his *Collection of Essays and Fugitiv Writings* (1790), which encouraged "reezoning," "yung" persons, "reeding," and a "zeel" for "lerning"; but he was too canny a Yankee always to allow eccentricity to stand in the way of profit. In *The Prompter* (1790) he quietly lectured his countrymen in corrective essays written plainly, in simple aphoristic style.

After his marriage in 1789, Webster practiced law in Hartford for 4 years before returning to New York to edit the city's first daily newspaper, the *American Minerva* (1793-1798). Tiring of the partisan controversy brought on by his forthright expression of Federalist opinion, he retired to New Haven to write *A Brief History of Epidemic and Pestilential Diseases* (1899) and to put together a volume of *Miscellaneous Papers* (1802).

The Dictionaries

From this time on, Webster gave most of his attention to preparing more schoolbooks, including *A Philosophical and Practical Grammar of the English Language* (1807). But he was principally concerned with compilation of *A Compendious Dictionary of the English Language* (1806); its abridgment, *A Dictionary . . . Compiled for the Use of Common Schools* (1807, revised 1817); and finally, in two volumes, *An American Dictionary of the English Language* (1828). In range this last surpassed any dictionary of its time. A second edition, "corrected and enlarged" (1841), became known popularly as *Webster's Unabridged*. Conservative contemporaries, alarmed at its unorthodoxies in spelling, usage, and pronunciation and its proud inclusion of Americanisms, derided it as "Noah's Ark." However, after Webster's death the rights were sold in 1847 to George and Charles Merriam, printers in Worcester, Mass.; and the dictionary has become, through many revisions, the cornerstone and bulwark of effective American lexicography.

Webster's other late writings included *A History of the United States* (1832), a version of the Bible (1832) cleansed of all words and phrases dangerous to children or "offensive especially to females," and a final *Collection of Papers on Political, Literary and Moral Subjects* (1843). Tall, redheaded, lanky, humorless, he was the butt of many cruel

various titles, appeared in 1784. Part III, a reader, in the original 1785 edition included excerpts from yet-unpublished poetry by Dwight and Barlow. Though the reader had shorter life and more vigorous competition than other parts of the *Institute,* it set a patriotic and moralistic pattern followed by rival books, some of which were thought to attract attention because more religiously orientated. Webster stressed what he called the "art of reading" in later volumes, including two secularized versions of *The New England Primer* (1789, 1801), *The Little Reader's Assistant* (1790), *The Elementary Primer* (1831), and *The Little Franklin* (1836).

Copyright Reform

Webster toured the United States from Maine to Georgia selling his textbooks, convinced that "America must be as independent in *literature* as she is in *politics,* as famous for *arts* as for *arms,*" but that to accomplish this she must protect by copyright the literary products of her countrymen. He pleaded so effectively that uniform copyright laws were early passed in most of the states, and it was largely through his continuing effort that Congress in 1831 passed a bill which ensured protection to writers. On his travels he also peddled his *Sketches of American Policy* (1785), a vigorous Federalist plea. In Philadelphia, where he paused briefly to teach school and see new editions of his *Institute* through the press, he published his politically effective *An Examination into the Leading Principles of the Federal Constitution* (1787).

criticisms in his time. He died in New Haven on May 23, 1843.

Further Reading

Webster's *Letters* were edited by Harry R. Warfel (1953). Biographies include Emily E. (Ford) Skeel, *Notes on the Life of Noah Webster* (1912); Ervin C. Shoemaker, *Noah Webster: Pioneer of Learning* (1936); and Harry R. Warfel, *Noah Webster: Schoolmaster to America* (1936). See also Robert K. Leavitt, *Noah's Ark, New England Yankees, and the Endless Quest* (1947), a history of the first century of Merriam-Webster dictionaries. □

Frank Wedekind

The German dramatist, cosmopolite, and libertarian Frank Wedekind (1864-1918) was a foe of middle-class hypocrisy and a moralist eager to reform the world through sexual emancipation.

Frank Wedekind was born Benjamin Franklin Wedekind on July 24, 1864, in Hanover, Germany. He was the son of a German who had emigrated to America, practiced medicine in San Francisco, then returned to his home in Germany. Dissatisfied with Otto von Bismarck's Prussian policy, the elder Wedekind left again and settled in Switzerland, where his son grew up. After working as a freelance journalist, an advertising copywriter, and a secretary for a circus, and spending long sojourns as a painter in England and France, young Wedekind moved to Munich, joining the staff of the satirical magazine *Simplizissimus,* in which his first political poems appeared. He remained in Munich until his death, occasionally making guest appearances in his own plays, giving public readings, and reciting and singing his ballads in a famous cabaret called Die Elf Scharfrichter (Eleven Executioners).

Wedekind's psychological insight into daydreams, emotions, and conversations among adolescents is reflected in his first successful play, *Frühlings Erwachen* (1891; *The Awakening of Spring*). Here he developed his own dramatic style and technique, characterized by many short and loosely connected scenes, calling to mind George Büchner's *Wozzek* and, in his frank exposure of sexual problems, anticipated many of the later insights of modern depth psychology. Wedekind's next major work was a "monster tragedy" consisting of two parts: *Erdgeist* (1893; *Earth Spirit*) and *Büchse der Pandora* (1906; *Pandora's Box*). Significantly, its central character, Lulu, the femme fatale, has no second name; indeed, even her first name changes with each suitor. Representing pure instinct, lust, desire, and flesh, she destroys each man who pursues her. It was the final act of part II, set in London and written in English for reasons of censorship, with Lulu as a prostitute supporting her father and her lover Alwa, which won for Wedekind his reputation as an immoralist and pornographic enemy of society.

Of Wedekind's plays, one relatively widely known in the United States is his character study, *Der Kammersänger* (1897; *The Tenor*). In a hotel room the hero, the famous tenor Gerardo, receives in turn a number of unwelcome guests: a 16-year-old girl admirer, an old composer anxious to get his opera produced, and finally a married woman who, refused by Gerardo, commits suicide. *Der Kammersänger* was followed, in 1900, by a full-length play in five acts, *Der Marquis von Keith,* which deals not with an adventurer in love but with an adventurer of life, a reckless swindler and social climber involved in shady financial dealings.

These five works mark Wedekind's first and most important creative period. After the turn of the century, he became more and more autobiographical, feeling an urge to "explain" himself and his work and to defend his ideas against the attacks leveled against him from all sides. Among the plays of this period are *Karl Hetman der Zwergriese* (1900; *Hidalla*) and *König Nicolo oder So ist das Leben* (1905; *Such Is Life*). These years were marked by critical abuse, censorship (he once spent 6 months in jail for lèse majesté), and difficulties with his publishers.

After the publication of *Nicolo,* Wedekind's dramatic art deteriorated. *Totentanz* (1905; *The Dance of Death*) and *Schloss Wetterstein* (1910; *Hunted by Every Hound*) both deal with prostitution, while *Zensur* (1907; *Censorship*) is purely autobiographical. His last play, *Bismarck* (1916), is hopelessly dull and undramatic.

Wedekind is also remembered for his short, pointed tales, reminiscent of Heinrich von Kleist and Guy de Maupassant. Here again, as in his dramas, his theme is love and eros. One of the best prose tales in modern German literature is his story *Der Brand von Egliswyl* (1905; *The Fire of Egliswyl*), which reveals his psychological insight into the relationship between arson and sexual anxiety. And he was a master, as well, of slightly frivolous, mocking, flirtatious love songs and ballads, some of which call to mind Heinrich Heine. Wedekind died in Munich on March 9, 1918.

Further Reading

The first full-length study in English of Wedekind is Sol Gittleman, *Frank Wedekind* (1969). It has a useful chronology and a selective bibliography. Wedekind's dramas are analyzed at length in Alex Natan, ed., *German Men of Letters,* vol.2 (1963). A brief introduction is in Hugh Garten, *Modern German Drama* (1962).

Additional Sources

Best, Alan D., *Frank Wedekind,* London: Wolff, 1975. □

Cicely Veronica Wedgwood

The British writer Cicely Veronica Wedgwood (1910-1997) was a narrative historian of the 17th century. She depended on primary documents to make sense of history.

One of Britain's most celebrated historians, Cicely Veronica Wedgwood was born on July 20, 1910, in Stocksfield, Northumberland, England. She was the descendant of the great 18th-century Staffordshire potter Josiah Wedgwood, about whom she wrote a biography. Her father, Sir Ralph Wedgwood, was chairman of British Railways during World War II. Her mother, Iris Pawson, was the author of several books of history and topography.

Her mother's father, a formidable patriarch, doted on his favorite granddaughter. He was well-travelled and well-read and had a great influence on her. At age 12 she was encouraged by her father to write history because he thought she was writing too much poetry and fiction. She wrote history from then on.

Early Works

In 1927-1928 Wedgwood studied at Bonn University and learned German. She then studied at Oxford University, where her history tutor was the famed A. L. Rowse. She graduated with honors in history in 1931 and published her first book with the support of Rowse and historian G. M. Trevelyan, a family friend. This was *Strafford, 1593-1641* (1935), the story of the brilliant, tragic adviser to King Charles I.

Her second book is a study of "that squalid struggle," as Wedgwood called it, *The Thirty Years War* (1938). She relied on primary sources in the relevant languages and on seeing for herself the locales she was to describe in her history. Written with clarity, detachment, and freshness, it was the first good book on the subject, written when she was 28.

William the Silent (1944), a book about William I, prince of Orange, the Dutch statesman and the father of Dutch independence, has been criticized for being unfair to Philip II of Spain, but the book points out that William was a happy man until his country's sufferings made him "Silent." It has been translated into six languages and won the James Tait Black Memorial Prize from the University of Edinburgh, Scotland.

The Civil War Study

In *The Great Rebellion* in two volumes (*The King's Peace, 1637-1641* [1955] and *The King's War, 1641-1647* [1958]), Wedgwood concentrated not on the "underlying causes" of the English civil war, but on the "admitted motives and illusions of men of the seventeenth century." Wedgwood sought "to restore their immediacy of experience."

A great narrative stylist, Wedgwood was criticized by some historians whose writing was more analytical or interpretive. Wedgwood shunned interpretation and let the narrative speak for itself. She was interested in how things happened, rather than why they happened. "I have tried to describe the variety, vitality and imperfections as well as the religion and government of the British Isles in the seventeenth century, *deliberately avoiding analysis,* and seeking rather to give an impression of its vigorous and vivid confusion," she wrote in *The King's Peace.* Later she explained in *Contemporary Authors* (Vol. 21), "I am by nature an optimist. I continue stubbornly to believe that if an intelligent reader is given all the facts (or should I say all the available facts), he should be able to work out his own conclusions about the underlying causes . . . I have a very deep suspicion of the modern habit of analyzing causes without a close attention to facts."

Wedgwood was at ease with the primary documents of her trade for the 17th century. "I enjoy the unexacting company of the dead," she once said of her addiction for churchyards.

Wedgwood went on from *The Great Rebellion,* the British civil war, to give the conclusion of the story in *A Coffin for King Charles: The Trial and Execution of Charles I* (1964). The book is the "finest account of the trial that has ever been written," according to the historian J.H. Plumb. She also wrote about Oliver Cromwell, the other leading political figure of the 17th century, in *Oliver Cromwell* (1939, rev. ed. 1973) and *Oliver Cromwell and the Elizabethan Inheritance* (1970).

Wide Interests

Her studies of poetry and literature are also impressive. She published *Seventeenth Century English Literature* (1950, rev. ed. 1977), *Poetry and Politics Under The Stuarts* (1960), *The World of Rubens* (1967), *Milton and His World* (1969), and *The Political Career of Peter Paul Rubens*

(1975). She also edited poetry: *New Poems, 1965: A P.E.N. Anthology of Contemporary Poetry* (1966). Wedgwood also was successful as a German translator. Several universities in America and the British Isles gave her honorary degrees.

Wedgwood lived off her books, lectures, talks for the British Broadcasting Corporation, reviews, and fellowships. She was literary editor of *Time and Tide,* a London journal (1944-1950), and a member of the Institute of Advanced Studies at Princeton University (1953-1968). She was a trustee of the National Gallery in London (1960-1976) and a member of the Royal Commission on Historical Manuscripts (1952-1978), the Arts Council Literature Panel (1956-1967), and the Advisory Council of the Victoria and Albert Museum (1959-1969). Wedgwood was president of the English Association (1955-1956) and of the Society of Authors (1972-1977). She was a fellow of the British Academy, the Royal Historical Society, and the Royal Society of Literature of the United Kingdom. In 1968 she was named a ''dame'' of the British Empire, and in 1969 she became one of the 24 members of the Order of Merit.

Her writings include her essays, which are interesting for autobiographical reasons: *Velvet Studies: Essays on Historical and Other Subjects* (1946) and *Truth and Opinion: Historical Essays* (1960). She spent her later years working mainly on a volume of world history, *The Spoils of Time: A World History from the Dawn of Civilization through the Early Renaissance* (1985).

Unlike many academic histories, Wedgwood's books were highly readable and sold in great numbers. ''She had a novelist's talent for entering into the character of the giants of history,'' noted an obituary in *The Economist.* Wedgwood, who died in 1997, respected the power of historians' view of truth and believed that ''historians should always draw morals,'' so that villains could not use their work to deceive the public. She was also willing to change her assessment of historical figures when new information was unearthed. ''The stuff of history is by no means coherent,'' she wrote. ''No agreed consensus has yet emerged, nor ever will.''

Further Reading

C. V. Wedgwood's *Velvet Studies: Essays on Historical and Other Subjects* (London, 1946) contains autobiographical material. A thorough source is Richard Ollard and Pamela Tudor-Craig, eds., *For Veronica Wedgwood These: Studies in Seventeenth-Century History* (1986). Other sources of information on her include John Kenyon, *History Men* (1983); *Time and Tide* (January 8, 1955); *New York Review of Books* (September 10, 1964); *New York Times Book Review* (September 29, 1964); *History and Theory* I (1961); and *New Yorker* (December 15, 1962). □

Josiah Wedgwood

The English potter Josiah Wedgwood (1730-1795) established the Wedgwood pottery factory. His work is most associated with the neoclassic style.

Josiah Wedgwood was born in August 1730 at Burslem, Staffordshire, into a family which had been engaged in the manufacture of pottery since the 17th century. His father owned a factory called the Churchyard Pottery, and Josiah began working in this family enterprise as an apprentice in 1744. He left the factory in the early 1750s and until 1759 was engaged with various partners in the manufacture of standard types of earthenware, including salt-glaze and stoneware products and objects in the popular agate and tortoiseshell glazes. During these years he experimented with improving glazes in color, and he achieved a particularly refined green glaze.

In 1759 Wedgwood set up his own factory at Ivy House in Burslem. The Ivy House pottery was so successful that in 1764 he moved his factory to larger quarters nearby; the new factory was first known as the Brick House Works and later as the Bell House. During this period Wedgwood created his first creamware, a palecolored earthenware frequently decorated with painted or enameled designs. Wedgwood's creamware won the approval of Queen Charlotte and after about 1765 became known as ''Queen's ware.''

During the first half of the 18th century the prevailing taste was for the rococo, a decorative style which used sensuous and delicate colors, lavish ornament, and a complex interplay of curved lines and masses. From about the middle of the century, however, the exuberant gaiety of the rococo began gradually to be replaced by neoclassicism and a return to the comparative severity of the art of antiquity. In the early 1760s Wedgwood met Thomas Bentley, a

cultivated man devoted to neoclassicism, and in 1769 they opened a factory near Burslem which was called Etruria and dedicated to the creation of ornamental pottery designed in the neoclassic manner. The factory at Bell House was retained for the production of functional tableware until the 1770s, when it was absorbed into Etruria.

The two products of the Etruria factory which became most fashionable were the basaltes and the jasperware objects. The basaltes were decorative and functional pieces made of a hard black stoneware, often with lowrelief decoration, in designs based upon antiquity. The jasperware became the most famous of the Wedgwood products and is still the pottery most associated with the Wedgwood name. Jasperware, which Wedgwood perfected about 1775, is a fine stoneware with a solid body color in blue, soft green, lavender, pink, black, or other colors and generally decorated with delicate low-relief designs in white adapted from Greek vase paintings, Roman relief sculpture, and other antique sources. Jasperware was produced in a great variety of functional and decorative objects ranging from teapots to cameos and including vases, bowls, candlesticks, and portrait reliefs.

Bentley died in 1780, and Wedgwood continued the work at Etruria, producing some of the factory's finest jasper in the late 18th century. He employed many artists to provide designs for his products and to adapt designs from classical antiquity. The most notable of these modelers was John Flaxman, a famous sculptor who supplied designs for the Etruria factory from 1775 to 1800. From 1787 Flaxman was in Rome for several years studying antique sculpture and sending Wedgwood elegant interpretations of ancient art.

Wedgwood died at Etruria on Jan. 3, 1795. His tombstone states that he "converted a rude and inconsiderable Manufactory into an elegant Art and an important part of National Commerce." The factory remains in the family and since 1810 has been known as Josiah Wedgwood and Sons. The modern factory is primarily concerned with the production of dinnerware and functional objects but continues to manufacture the jasper and basaltes that Josiah made so popular.

Further Reading

An excellent account of Wedgwood's career and of the Wedgwood product in general is William B. Honey, *Wedgwood Ware* (1948), a brief but thorough and critical work with illustrations of high quality. Wolf Mankowitz and Reginald G. Hagger, *The Concise Encyclopedia of English Pottery and Porcelain* (1957), is handsomely illustrated, has an excellent bibliography, and contains basic information concerning Josiah Wedgwood and the Wedgwood family and factory. Older but still important standard biographies are Sir Arthur H. Church, *Josiah Wedgwood, Master Potter* (1903), and William Burton, *Josiah Wedgwood and His Pottery* (1922). Also useful is Wolf Mankowitz, *Wedgwood* (1953).

Additional Sources

Burton, Anthony, *Josiah Wedgwood: a biography,* London: A. Deutsch, 1976.

Reilly, Robin, *Josiah Wedgwood 1730-1795,* London: Macmillan, 1992. □

Thurlow Weed

Although he held only a few minor offices, American politician Thurlow Weed (1797-1882) was a leading figure in the Whig party and later in the Republican party. He was a master behind-the-scenes manipulator and a skilled lobbyist.

Thurlow Weed was born in Greene County, N.Y., on Nov. 15, 1797. His farm family was so impoverished that he had to begin working at the age of 8. Except for a few years of primary schooling, he was self-educated. After serving as apprentice and journeyman on several newspapers, he became foreman of the *Albany Register* and in 1821 moved to Rochester as editor of the *Telegraph.* In 1822 he married Catherine Ostrander.

Weed soon made the *Telegraph* one of the most important newspapers in western New York; he became part owner in 1825. His strong anti-Jackson feelings led him to participate in the Anti-Masonic party, whose leaders helped him establish the *Albany Evening Journal* in 1830. After the Anti-Masonic movement collapsed in 1836, Weed threw the weight of the *Journal* to the new Whig party. His enormous political influence was based upon his vigorous editorials, his friendship with William H. Seward, and his great personal charm. Warm, affable, and good-natured, he entertained generously and had a host of friends. His contacts made him such a potent lobbyist that his enemies dubbed him the "Lucifer of the Lobby."

In politics Weed was a moderate. Thus he equally condemned abolitionists and nativists. However, in spite of his antipathy for the abolitionists, he shared Seward's antislavery views and opposed the extension of slavery into the territories acquired during the Mexican War. When he joined the ranks of the Republicans in 1854, he continued advocating moderate policies.

As a loyal supporter of Abraham Lincoln and Seward, Weed was sent to Europe in 1861 as a special agent to counteract Confederate propaganda. Returning in 1862, he became increasingly concerned about what he termed abolitionist influence over Lincoln. So strongly did he object to the Emancipation Proclamation that he contemplated supporting the Democratic candidate during the presidential election of 1864, but he considered Gen. George B. McClellan unacceptable. At the end of the war he threw his support to President Andrew Johnson and the National Union party. Although the failure of the Union party marked the end of his influence, he continued active in state politics. He died in New York on Nov. 22, 1882, leaving an estate of over a million dollars in stocks and bonds.

tainer. Intellectuals ignored his writings, but the mass of people seemed not to get enough of them. Weems had a remarkable ability to give the populace the untarnished heroes it craved. He ardently believed that books should be uplifting. He wrote moral tales—*The Drunkard's Looking Glass* (ca. 1812), *God's Revenge against Adultery* (1815), *God's Revenge against Murder* (1827)—and others.

The histories and biographies then being written of men noted during the American Revolution were sober tomes. Weems's fictionalized biographies, which mixed pleasant myth with fact, were better known than the writings of any other American in the first half of the 19th century. More than a million copies of his books were sold, and they are still being reprinted. His books inculcated the prized virtues of industry, temperance, and frugality.

Weems wrote biographies of Benjamin Franklin, William Penn, and Gen. Francis Marion, but his fame rested mainly on *The Life and Memorable Actions of George Washington* (1800). A strong supporter of Jefferson, Weems wanted to prevent Federalists from monopolizing Washington's fame. The Father of His Country, said Weems, was no aristocrat "but a pure Republican." In its fifth edition, Weems added the story of the cherry tree, which soon entered the national folklore. "George," said his father, 'do you know who killed the beautiful little cherry-tree yonder in the garden?' This was a tough question and George staggered under it for a moment. . . . 'I can't tell a lie, Pa, you know I can't tell a lie. I did cut it with my hatchet.'"

Weems's biographies contained many inaccuracies. Yet his clear, simple, warm, enthusiastic writing revived the human presence of men grown austere and remote. The endearing mythmaker died in Beaufort, S.C., on May 23, 1825.

Further Reading

Weed's autobiography, with a memoir by his grandson, is *The Life of Thurlow Weed* (2 vols., 1883-1884). An excellent biography is Glyndon G. Van Deusen, *Thurlow Weed: Wizard of the Lobby* (1947). Also useful are De Alva S. Alexander, *A Political History of the State of New York* (4 vols., 1906-1923), and New York State Historical Association, *History of the State of New York,* edited by Alexander C. Flick (10 vols., 1933-1937; new ed., 5 vols., 1962). □

Further Reading

Weem's *Life of Washington* was edited by Marcus Cunliffe (1962). The most important work on Weems is Paul L. Ford, *Mason Locke Weems,* edited by Emily E.F. Skeel (3 vols., 1928-1929). Lawrence C. Wroth, *Parson Weems* (1911), is an excellent short biography. William A. Bryan, *George Washington in American Literature 1775-1865* (1952), is useful.

Additional Sources

Leary, Lewis Gaston, *The book-peddling parson: an account of the life and works of Mason Locke Weems, patriot, pitchman, author, and purveyor of morality to the citizenry of the early United States of America,* Chapel Hill, N.C.: Algonquin Books, 1984. □

Mason Locke Weems

Mason Locke Weems (1759-1825) was an American Episcopal minister, book salesman, and popular writer.

Mason Locke Weems was born in Anne Arundel County, Md., on Oct. 1, 1759. He was admitted to the priesthood in 1784, serving in Maryland parishes until 1792. In 1795 he married Frances Ewell; they had 10 children. For 31 years Weems roamed, gypsylike, from New York City to Savannah selling books. He was a star salesman for Mathew Carey of Philadelphia, the nation's leading publisher.

As compiler, editor, and original author, Weems revealed a good knowledge of the Bible and general literature. He was an interesting combination of preacher and enter-

Alfred Lothar Wegener

The German meteorologist, Arctic explorer, and geophysicist Alfred Lothar Wegener (1880-1930) is remembered for his theory of continental drift.

Alfred Wegener son of an Evangelical preacher, was born in Berlin on Nov. 1, 1880. He attended university at Heidelberg, Innsbruck, and Berlin. He became interested in arctic climatology and joined the 1906-1908 Danish expedition to Greenland as meteorologist. He returned there in 1912-1913 and, wintering on a high glacier, completed studies begun on his first visit.

In 1908 Wegener settled at Marburg, lecturing there with enviable clarity on meteorology and astronomy. The next years were perhaps his most fruitful: he wrote up his Greenland material; produced his *Thermodynamik der Atmosphäre* (1911), a standard textbook which ran through several editions; and conceived his idea of continental drift. He saw active service in World War I.

Wegener was a scientific civil servant at the Meteorological Department of the Deutsche Seewarte in Hamburg (1919-1924) and professor of meteorology and geophysics at the University of Graz (1924-1930). There he drew together aspects of subjects hitherto considered disparate while planning for a two-winter expedition to Greenland, scheduled to begin in 1930. He made a preliminary visit in 1929. Early in November 1930, in attempting to cross Greenland from an ice-cap camp to the Kamarujuk base on the west coast, he lost his life.

Most of Wegener's life was spent in conventional meteorology, and his contributions both there and in polar exploration have been recognized. But Wegener is most widely remembered for his theory of continental drift. In 1910 he was struck by the congruity of the east and west Atlantic shorelines. This, coupled with his fortuitous reading of evidence indicative of a land bridge from Brazil to Africa, led him to examine the geologic and paleoclimatologic evidence for his rapidly burgeoning continental drift theory. He suggested that until Mesozoic times the light material of the earth's crust formed one continental block floating on the dense core, that relative movement has since occurred, and that the geographic poles have wandered. These views he published in 1912 and expanded into book form as *Die Entstehung der Kontinente und Ozeane* (1915; *The Origins of Continents and Oceans,* 1924). The theory first received adverse criticism and then interested discussion. Many objections were overcome in later editions of the work, but in seeking a mechanism for the movements, Wegener failed. Thus the theory was long discounted. Recent work based on new information has led to a general acceptance of the concept.

Further Reading

Wegener's biography by his daughter, Else Wegener, *Alfred Wegener* (1960), is in German. S.K. Runcorn, ed., *Continental Drift* (1962), includes a memoir on Wegener. Background on Wegener is in Johannes Georgi, *Mid Ice: The Story of the Wegener Expedition to Greenland* (trans. 1934).

Additional Sources

Schwarzbach, Martin, *Alfred Wegener, the father of continental drift,* Madison, Wis.: Science Tech, 1986. □

Franz Weidenreich

The German anatomist and physical anthropologist Franz Weidenreich (1873-1948) made outstanding contributions in the areas of hematology and human evolution.

Franz Weidenreich the son of a merchant, was born on June 7, 1873, in Edenkoben in the Bavarian Palatinate. He studied medicine and biology for 6 years at the universities of Munich, Kiel, Berlin, and Strassburg, from the last of which he received a medical degree in 1899. After graduation he worked with Gustav Schwalbe at Strassburg and Paul Ehrlich at Frankfurt am Main. In 1904 he was appointed professor of anatomy at the University of Frankfurt. During his earlier academic life Weidenreich carried on researches chiefly in the field of hematology, and by 1914 he had published nearly 50 papers relating to that subject.

World War I brought an interruption to Weidenreich's academic career. Following the French occupation of Alsace-Lorraine in 1918, he lost his post at the University of Strassburg, and it was not until 1921, when he became professor of anatomy at the University of Heidelberg, that he returned to academic life. From that time on, his studies dealt chiefly with the skeleton, especially with its relation to human evolution, resulting in nearly 100 publications.

In 1935 Weidenreich was appointed visiting professor of anatomy at Peking Union Medical College and honorary director of the Cenozoic Research Laboratory, Geological Survey of China. For the next 7 years he was engaged, together with Chinese colleagues and Father Teilhard de Chardin, in excavating and studying the fossil remains of Peking man, *Sinanthropus pekinensis* (*Homo erectus pekinensis*). This produced a series of famous papers and monographs by Weidenreich that are of truly unsurpassed excellence in the field of paleoanthropology. The original remains of Peking man mysteriously disappeared with the Japanese invasion of China during World War II. Notwithstanding, Weidenreich's superb casts and detailed descriptions of these important fossils have made the loss relatively unimportant.

In 1937 Weidenreich made a trip to Java to visit the sites where *Pithecanthropus erectus* (*Homo erectus erectus*) and other human fossils had been discovered by G.H.R. von Koenigswald. They collaborated in producing several papers on fossil man.

In 1941 Weidenreich left China for the United States. For the remainder of his life this man of friendly and engaging personality was an honored guest of the American Museum of Natural History in New York City, where he continued his studies of fossil man and other aspects of human evolution. Despite the soundness of his researches, some of his interpretations of the fossil evidence provoked wide discussion. He concluded, for example, that the immediate ancestors of man were giants, a theory that has been generally rejected.

Weidenreich was president of the American Association of Physical Anthropologists in 1944-1945 and was the first recipient of the Viking Fund Medal and Award in Physical Anthropology in 1946. He died on July 11, 1948.

Further Reading

A biographical account of Weidenreich appears in *The Shorter Anthropological Papers of Franz Weidenreich, 1939-1948: A Memorial Volume* (1949). Thomas K. Penniman, *A Hundred years of Anthropology* (1935; 3d ed. 1965), is recommended for general historical background. □

Simone Weil

The French thinker, political activist, and religious mystic Simone Weil (1909-1943) was known for the intensity of her commitments and the breadth and depth of her analysis of numerous aspects of modern civilization.

Simone Weil was born in Paris on February 3, 1909, the second child of an assimilated Jewish family. She received a superb education in the French lycées and the Ecole Normale Supérieure. A brilliant and unusual student, she was admired by some of her teachers and held in awe by some of her peers, while others mocked her for her radical political opinions and the intensity of her convictions. Her political activism and life-long interest in work and in the working class began in her student years.

Following the completion of her Ecole Normale studies in 1931 she taught philosophy for several years in various provincial girls' lycées. These were years of severe economic depression and great political upheaval in Europe, and Weil's interest in the worker and her passionate concern for social justice led her to devote all of her time outside of teaching to political activism in the French trade-union (syndicalist) movement. She taught classes for workingmen, took part in meetings and demonstrations, and wrote for a variety of leftist periodicals.

At first she shared her comrades' belief in the imminence of a proletarian revolution; soon, however, both her experience within the revolutionary Left and her observation of the international political situation led her to conclude that what had developed in the 1930s was different from anything Marx had expected, that there were no premonitory signs of the proletarian revolution, and that a new oppressive class was emerging—the managerial bureaucracy. Though she was an admirer of Marx, she became a trenchant critic of Marxism, which she accused of being a dogma rather than a scientific method of social analysis. In the last half of 1934 she wrote a lengthy essay called "Oppression and Liberty" in which she summed up the inadequacies of Marxism, attempted her own analysis of the mechanism of social oppression, and sketched a theoretical picture of a free society.

Experiences in Factories and the Spanish Civil War

In 1934-1935 Weil's intense sympathy for the workers and her desire to know first-hand what the working-class condition was like led her to take a leave of absence from teaching to spend eight months as an anonymous worker in three Paris factories. A modern worker's experience, she concluded, far from being a hard but joyous contact with "real life," was entirely comparable to that of the slaves of antiquity. This experience also reinforced her conviction that political revolution without a total transformation of the methods of production—methods that depended on the subordination of the worker both to the machine and to the managerial bureaucracy—would do nothing to alleviate working-class oppression.

Although her experience with the organized Left disillusioned her with political activism, when the Spanish Civil War broke out in July 1936 Weil, hoping that a genuine working-class revolution was under way in Spain, went immediately to Barcelona. She made her way to the front and was accepted into a militia unit, but after only a week her foot and ankle were badly burned in a camp accident, and she returned to Barcelona, where she was hospitalized. Her experience in Spain further disillusioned her; her observations in the several weeks she remained there convinced her that the atmosphere created by civil war was fatal to the ideals for which the war was being fought.

After Weil returned to France, ill health kept her from returning to teaching; her burn was slow to heal, she was anemic, and the debilitating migraine headaches from which she had suffered for years became worse. She spent the last years of the 1930s reflecting and writing on war and peace and beginning to formulate her thoughts on the nature of force, on the human spirit's tragic subjection to it, and on mankind's temptation to worship it. These reflections found expression in two remarkable essays, "The Iliad, or the Poem of Force," and "The Great Beast," a long essay on the origins of Hitlerism, both of which were written early in 1940.

The late 1930s also brought a significant new dimension to Weil's thinking. Though an agnostic from childhood, she found herself in situations—contemplating the beauty of St. Francis' little chapel in Assisi, listening to a Gregorian chant at a Benedictine monastery during Holy Week, reciting George Herbert's poem "Love" as an object of concentration to help her endure the climax of an excruciating headache—in which she suddenly felt overwhelmed by the presence of God. After these experiences she began to regard Plato, whom she had always loved, as a mystic and began to search for what she called the "mystical core" in other religions. She came to believe that a non-oppressive society must be based on a common conviction that every human being is deserving of respect because he has an eternal destiny. Her longstanding belief in the radical equality of human beings (based on the Cartesian teaching that every human being is capable of knowing as much as the greatest genius if only he exercises his mind properly) was now given a supernatural sanction.

World War II Flight to England

Following the German occupation of Paris in June 1940, Weil and her parents fled to the unoccupied south of France, residing in Marseilles from September 1940 until May 1942. During this period Weil read extensively in Greek, Hindu, and other texts and thought and wrote a great deal. She believed she had found a truly Christian civilization, a model of the type of the hierarchical but non-oppressive society she was beginning to formulate as an ideal, in the 11th- and 12th-century cities of the Languedoc, where for more than 100 years Catholicism existed side by side with a form of Gnosticism known as Catharism.

Though she was strongly drawn toward Catholicism, Weil also found many elements of the Catharist faith attractive; as a result of this, some commentators have judged her to be a Manichean and a Gnostic—essentially, a heretic—who rejected the material realm as evil and sought escape from it and from the body into a realm of pure spirit. In fairness to Weil it should be pointed out that there is a great deal in her writing about the beauty of the world and the necessity of loving it as God's creation, even when it brings pain and death. Moreover, there is nothing Manichean in her belief in the humanity and divinity of Christ and in his presence in the Eucharist. Though she desired the sacraments she was never baptized, feeling that it was her vocation to remain a Christian outside the Church.

During the time she spent in Marseilles she was phenomenally productive. In addition to the essays on the Languedoc (see "A Medieval Epic Poem" and "The Romanesque Renaissance" in *Selected Essays*), she wrote essays on problems in modern science (see *On Science, Necessity, and the Love of God*), a large number of essays on religious subjects (see *Waiting for God* and *Intimations of Christianity Among the Ancient Greeks*), and her Marseilles *Notebooks*. She also spent several weeks as a hired laborer working the vineyards of the Rhone valley during the grape harvest.

Though reluctant to leave France, Weil was persuaded to accompany her parents to New York in May 1942. She hoped once in New York to be able to interest the United States government in a plan she had conceived to organize a corps of nurses who would go into battle with the soldiers in order to give immediate first aid and thus save lives that would otherwise be lost because of shock and loss of blood. Needless to say, Weil wanted to be one of these nurses. Her proposal was turned down, and after five months in New York City she made her way to London to work for the French Resistance. Desperately wanting to be exposed to the risks and suffering of war—she felt she was called by God to do so—she begged to be parachuted into France as a saboteur; however, she was given a desk job reviewing reports of Resistance committees in France. Told to draw up her own ideas on how France should be reconstructed after the war, she wrote *The Need for Roots*, an extremely condensed summary of her thinking on the causes of the modern loss of rootedness in the sacred and suggestions for its possible cure.

Stress and malnourishment (she refused, out of solidarity with the French living on short rations under the German occupation, to eat more than the amount of food that would have been available to her in France) took their toll on her health, and in April 1943 she was hospitalized with tuberculosis. Even in the hospital, however, she was unwilling or unable to eat more than meager amounts. In July digestive problems caused her to eat even less than before, and she went downhill rapidly. She died in a sanitarium in Ashford, Kent, on August 24, 1943, at the age of 34. The Ashford newspaper, which carried a story on her death, described it as a suicide. When her books began to be published and translated after her death, this story of her supposed suicide out of sympathy with the starving French captured the popular imagination, and she was widely seen as a kind of crazy secular saint, admirable but ludicrous in her intense seriousness and impossible and impractical idealism. As more of her large body of writings was published and translated in the 1950s and 1960s, this image began to give way to a serious study of her work and to a recognition of her as one of the most lucid, challenging minds of the 20th century.

Further Reading

The major biography of Weil is Simone Petrement's *Simone Weil: A Life* (1976). Shorter but also valuable are Jacques Cabaud's *Simone Weil: A Fellowship in Love* (1964) and Richard Rees's *Simone Weil: A Sketch for a Portrait* (1966). Dorothy Tuck McFarland's *Simone Weil* (1983) is a study of her writings. Robert Cole wrote a reflective account of Weil's faith in *Simone Weil: A Modern Pilgrimage* (1987).

Additional Sources

Coles, Robert, *Simone Weil: a modern pilgrimage,* Reading, Mass.: Addison-Wesley, 1987.

Fiori, Gabriella, *Simone Weil, an intellectual biography,* Athens: University of Georgia Press, 1989.

McFarland, Dorothy Tuck, *Simone Weil,* New York: F. Ungar Pub. Co., 1983.

McLellan, David, *Utopian pessimist: the life and thought of Simone Weil,* New York: Poseidon Press, 1990.

Nevin, Thomas R., *Simone Weil: portrait of a self-exiled Jew,* Chapel Hill: University of North Carolina Press, 1991.

Petrement, Simone, *Simone Weil: a life,* New York: Schocken Books, 1988.

Rees, Richard, *Simone Weil: a sketch for a portrait,* Carbondale: Southern Illinois University Press, 1978, 1966.

Simone Weil, interpretations of a life, Amherst: University of Massachusetts Press, 1981. □

Kurt Weill

The operas and other stage works of Kurt Weill (1900-1950), German-American composer, had considerable influence on contemporary Western musical theater.

Kurt Weill was born in Dessau, Germany, on March 2, 1900. He studied piano as a child and composed several works before enrolling at the Berlin Hochschule für Musik at age 18. He left to work in provincial opera houses, returning to Berlin to study with Ferruccio Busoni from 1921 to 1924.

Weill's early compositions were largely instrumental concert works written in the current "advanced" style, but in 1926 he composed a one-act opera, *Der Protagonist* (The Protagonist; libretto by Georg Kaiser), and concentrated henceforth on stage works. Two short operas containing elements of popular music followed: *Royal Palace* (1926; by Kaiser) and *Der Zar lässt sich photographieren* (1927, The Czar Has His Photograph Taken; by Ivan Goll).

As a composer, Weill achieved maturity in his collaboration with the poet-playwright Bertolt Brecht. On the eve of the Nazi victory in Germany, the team produced thinly veiled attacks on status-quo social attitudes and corrupt politics. Weill's music—trenchant, ironic, bittersweet—was the perfect setting for Brecht's pessimistic texts. *Die Dreigroschenoper* (1928, *The Threepenny Opera*) is their most famous work. This play with music, starring Lotte Lenya (Weill's young bride), was an immediate sensation and was performed throughout Europe. An English-language revival in 1955 ran for over 2,000 performances.

Other Weill-Brecht stage works included the opera *Aufstieg und Fall der Stadt Mahagonny* (1927-1929, *The Rise and Fall of the City of Mahagonny*), the musical play *Happy End* (1929), and the school opera *Der Jasager* (1930, The Yes-sayer). With other librettists Weill composed the operas *Die Bürgschaft* (1930, The Pledge) and *Der Silbersee* (1932, The Silver Lake) before his works were banned by the Hitler regime and he fled Berlin in February 1933.

Weill lived briefly in Paris and London. His last collaboration with Brecht was an unusual ballet with songs, *Die Sieben Todtsünden* (1933, *The Seven Deadly Sins*), with choreography by George Balanchine, and he composed the scores for two musical plays, *Marie Galante* (1934) and *A Kingdom for a Cow* (1934). He became a naturalized American citizen in 1936.

The larger American compositions of Weill comprise 10 stage works, including the operas *Street Scene* (1946; by Elmer Rice and Langston Hughes) and *Down in the Valley* (1948; by Arnold Sundgaard); the musicals *Johnson Johnson* (1936; by Paul Green), *Knickerbocker Holiday* (1938; by Maxwell Anderson), *Lady in the Dark* (1940; by Moss Hart); and the "musical tragedy" *Lost in the Stars* (1949; by Anderson).

Weill was a creative genius, an innovator worthy of considerable study, whose music always bears unique stylistic traits of melody, harmony, rhythm, and orchestral color. His best stage works contain a sophistication of technique and a grasp of character delineation often belied by the use of simple means and "ordinary" elements from German folk tradition and the contemporary dance hall. As a whole, the works are innovative in their mixing of singing actors with opera singers, use of films and unconventional staging and design, and their explosive political and social content. Two Weill songs are worldwide popular standards:

"Moritat" (or "Mack the Knife") from *Threepenny Opera* and "September Song" from *Knickerbocker Holiday,* both characteristic of his best work. He died on April 3, 1950.

Further Reading

Weill's career is recounted in David Ewen, *European Light Opera* (1962) and *The World of Twentieth Century Music* (1968). His work with Brecht is discussed in Frederick Ewen, *Bertolt Brecht* (1967).

Additional Sources

Jarman, Douglas, *Kurt Weill, an illustrated biography,* Bloomington: Indiana University Press, 1982.

Sanders, Ronald, *The days grow short: the life and music of Kurt Weill,* Los Angeles: Silman-James Press; Hollywood, CA: Distributed by Samuel French Trade, 1991.

Schebera, Jurgen, *Kurt Weill: an illustrated life,* New Haven: Yale University Press, 1995.

Taylor, Ronald, *Kurt Weill: composer in a divided world,* Boston: Northeastern University Press, 1992. ☐

Steven Weinberg

Steven Weinberg (born 1933) shared the 1979 Nobel Prize in Physics with two other scientists for their work in the field of elementary-particle forces.

Steven Weinberg was born on May 3, 1933, in New York City. He graduated from the Bronx High School of Science in 1950; one of his classmates was Sheldon Lee Glashow, with whom Weinberg would share the Nobel Prize in 1979. Weinberg received his B.A. from Cornell (1954) and then for a year went to the Institute for Theoretical Physics (now the Niels Bohr Institute) in Copenhagen before returning to the United States to complete his Ph.D. at Princeton (1957). Weinberg taught at Columbia University (1957-1959), the University of California at Berkeley (1959-1966), the Massachusetts Institute of Technology (1969-1973), and Harvard University (1973-1982). In 1982 he became Josey Professor of Science at the University of Texas in Austin, where he remained into the 1990s. He met his wife, Louise, while an undergraduate at Cornell, and they were married in 1954; their only child, Elizabeth, was born in Berkeley in 1963.

Weinberg was awarded the Nobel Prize in recognition of his contributions to the unification of elementary-particle forces. "Unification" refers to the process by which scientists succeed in describing apparently disparate phenomena in terms of a few simple principles. Success in unification often goes hand-in-hand with progress in science. Isaac Newton's demonstration in the 17th century that the forces that pull objects to the ground were the same as those that keep the planets in their orbits was an example of unification. Likewise, James Clerk Maxwell's discovery two centuries later that electricity and magnetism are but different manifestations of the same phenomenon, electromagnetism.

When Weinberg entered Princeton as a graduate student in 1955, four fundamental forces (also called interactions) were known: gravitation, electromagnetism, weak forces, and strong forces. The latter three are called elementary-particle forces because they govern the behavior of the subatomic realm. Although periodic attempts had been made to unify them, the efforts had been unsuccessful. Of the three forces, the theory describing electromagnetism was the most elaborately developed and was couched in a mathematical language known as quantum field theory. According to quantum field theory, a force is carried by a type of particle called a vector or "spin-one" boson; the vector boson carrying the electromagnetic force, for instance, is the photon.

In the early 1960s Weinberg began exploring a version of quantum field theory called gauge theory and wondered whether it could also be used to describe the strong force in a manner analogous to the already successful description of the electromagnetic force. But, if written as a gauge theory, the strong force would have to be carried by massive vector bosons while the photon was massless, making the attempt appear hopeless, because in a unified theory the bosons would have to be described symmetrically. Weinberg tried to overcome the apparent discrepancy by utilizing a new type of symmetry principle called broken symmetry. Weinberg was thoroughly familiar with broken symmetry, having exploited it in inventing the successful modern theory of the low-energy interactions of the particles known as hadrons (particles that feel the strong interaction). In the context of gauge theories, however, the application of symmetry breaking generated a new problem, for it seemed to entail the postulation of a kind of particle already known not to exist. Weinberg tried for years to find a loophole in the apparent requirement without success.

"A Model of Leptons"

One day while driving to his Massachusetts Institute of Technology office, he suddenly realized that he had been applying the right idea to the wrong problem. The mathematical apparatus involving broken symmetry that he had been trying to fit to the strong interaction would work when applied to the weak. This involved a major shifting of conceptual gears, for whereas Weinberg's models previously had involved hadrons, they would now have to involve another set of particles called leptons, which only experience the weak and electromagnetic interactions. The result was "A Model of Leptons," which was published in *Physical Review Letters* in November 1967. This short paper, only two and a half pages long, crystallized years of effort and represents the work for which Weinberg would receive his Nobel Prize.

"Leptons interact only with photons, and with the intermediate bosons that presumably mediate weak interactions," the paper began. "What could be more natural than to unite these spin-one bosons into a multiplet of gauge fields?" Weinberg then acknowledged that the attempt would immediately run into the same problem that he had faced in his models of the strong interaction of the mass differences between photons and the vector bosons of the weak interaction. Furthermore, attempts to use broken symmetry to finesse the problem would create unwanted bosons. Weinberg's paper then proposed a solution to the problem involving a spontaneously broken model that avoids the troublesome particles by introducing the photons and intermediate bosons as gauge fields.

In retrospect, the model described in the paper was a major step forward in the unification of elementary-particle interactions. It is the most frequently cited paper on elementary-particles physics in the last half-century. But this was hardly apparent at the time. The model had two serious problems. One was that the gauge theory that Weinberg used contained certain inconsistencies (it was apparently not "renormalizable"), and though the paper asserted the difficulty could be eliminated, the claim was unsubstantiated. A second problem was that the model implied that so-called "neutral" weak interactions, in which no charge was exchanged, ought to exist. Thus far none had been detected.

These two problems were soon overcome. In 1971 a Dutch theorist, Gerard 't Hooft, showed that Weinberg's hunch was correct, and that the scheme was indeed renormalizable. Around the same time several theorists, including Weinberg, demonstrated that if a fourth quark existed, the rate of neutral weak interactions would be less than the existing observational limit.

A similar model was also proposed by Weinberg's school colleague Sheldon Glashow and by the Pakistani physicist Abdus Salam. The electroweak theory, as it is now called, made several important predictions that were confirmed one by one throughout the 1970s: neutral weak interactions at the reduced rate (1973), the existence of the fourth quark (1974), and an effect known as atomic parity violation (1978). Weinberg's Nobel Prize came the following year in 1979, shared with Glashow and Salam. The electroweak theory forms a major part of what has come to be known as the standard model of elementary-particle physics. This provides a comprehensive picture of the basic units of matter and their behavior and explains virtually all the experimental data physicists have been able to obtain.

Tying High-Energy Physics to Cosmology

Meanwhile, Weinberg had already been at work on other important steps in the drive toward unification. In 1974 he co-authored a paper describing how the coupling constants, or measures of strength, of the electromagnetic, weak, and strong interactions would converge at extremely high energies, such as existed in nature only fractions of a second after the Big Bang. This result gave further impetus to a growing convergence of interests between high-energy physicists and cosmologists. Three years later Weinberg wrote a book, *The First Three Minutes* (1977), which awakened many scientists and nonscientists to the importance of cosmology in understanding the present-day universe.

Though his Nobel Prize was for work in unification, Weinberg made significant contributions in a wide range of areas in particle physics and even in plasma physics. Among colleagues he was known more for versatility than for mathematical strength. One consequence of the stunning success of the standard model was that it outran the ability of experimental physicists to produce data that will enable theoretical physicists to make further advances. Concerned by this fact, Weinberg was one of the staunchest proponents of the superconducting supercollider (SSC), an ill-fated particle accelerator that would have been able to produce data whose implications reached beyond the standard model. However, that project was killed by the U.S. Congress in the fall of 1993.

At the University of Texas Weinberg became a senior statesman in the field of physics and a champion for the further development of elementary-particle physics. By 1994 *The First Three Minutes* had been translated into 22 foreign languages. He continued writing and made notable contributions to both the scientific and general literature. Writing for a general audience in *Dreams of a Final Theory* (1994) he argued the case for the SSC, reminding readers that "science has always had its enemies throughout history." Included among numerous theoretical publications, papers and presentations were *Unbreaking Symmetries* (1995), *Pion Scattering Lengths* (1996), *Theories of the Cosmological Constant* (1996), and *Precise Relations Between the Spectra of Vector and Axial Vector Mesons* (1997). He also wrote the highly regarded two-volume textbook *The Quantum Theory of Fields, Vol. 1: Foundations* (1995) and *The Quantum Theory of Fields Vol. 2, Applications* (1997). His colleagues considered him the foremost champion of the value and dignity of the scientific enterprise, an attitude of which the concluding line of *The First Three Minutes* offers a typical expression: "The effort to understand the universe is one of the very few things that lifts human life a little above the level of farce, and gives it some of the grace of tragedy."

Further Reading

Aside from scientific articles, Weinberg wrote several books, including *The Theory of Subatomic Particles, Gravitation and Cosmology: Principles and Applications of the General Theory of Relativity* (1990) and *Dreams of a Final Theory: The Search for the Fundamental Laws of Nature* (1993), whose cover displays a wheat field in Texas near the site of the former SSC project, over which is superimposed a simulated particle collision from the device. The story of the drive towards unification, with a long description of Weinberg's role, is contained in *The Second Creation: Makers of the Revolution in Twentieth Century Physics* by Robert P. Crease and Charles C. Mann (1986). Reviews of general and scientific works can be found in publications such as *Science* and *Physics Review* . □

Casper Willard Weinberger

Casper Willard Weinberger (born 1917) served in the administrations of three U.S. presidents, as director of the Office of Management and Budget, as secretary of health, education and welfare, and as secretary of defense. He was noted for His budget-cutting ability until, as secretary of defense, he pressed for huge annual increases in military spending.

Casper W. Weinberger was born in San Francisco on August 18, 1917. He was the son of Herman Weinberger, an attorney, and Cerise Carpenter Hampson. After attending public schools in San Francisco, Caspar won a scholarship to Harvard University, where he earned a bachelor of arts degree with honors in 1938 and a law degree in 1941. In his senior year as an undergraduate, he was editor of the *Crimson,* the Harvard newspaper, and wrote conservative editorials that angered his liberal colleagues.

Weinberger enlisted in the army in 1941. He met his future wife Jane, a nurse, aboard a troop ship carrying them to the Pacific theater, and they married in 1942. He saw action in New Guinea and was promoted to captain under General Douglas MacArthur. He was honorably discharged in 1945. After the war he returned to California to practice law, serving a two-year clerkship with a U.S. Court of Appeals judge and entering private law practice in 1947.

Early Political Career

In 1952 he was elected to the first of three two-year terms in the California State Assembly. During his second term Weinberger was voted the most able member of the state legislature in a poll of newspaper correspondents. During his stint in the legislature he also worked as a freelance

journalist, writing book reviews. He lost a race for state attorney general in 1958, but remained active in politics while practicing law. He was vice-chairman of the California Republican State Central Committee from 1960 to 1962 and chairman from 1962 to 1964.

While in private law practice from 1959 to 1968, he moderated a televised public affairs program and wrote a newspaper column. In 1968 California Governor Ronald Reagan appointed him the state's director of finance. As director, Weinberger carried out Reagan's mandate to reduce state expenditures and budget deficits.

"Cap the Knife"

In 1970 President Richard Nixon named Weinberger chairman of the Federal Trade Commission. His mandate was to clean house, and within a year 50 lawyers had left the agency. Besides streamlining the organization, Weinberger adopted an aggressive program of consumer protection.

In 1971 Nixon named Weinberger deputy director of the Office of Management and Budget. In 1972 he succeeded George Shultz as director. At OMB he made unprecedented use of impoundment, forbidding federal agencies to spend authorized funds. He was so effective in cutting public spending, impounding $11.2 billion in 1972, that he was labeled "Cap the Knife," a nickname that stuck throughout his career.

In 1973 Weinberger became secretary of health, education and welfare. He again cut costs and attempted to transfer control of many social programs to state and local governments. He frequently clashed with Congress and lost most of the fights, but his policies of social cuts would become dominant in the 1980s and 1990s under Presidents Reagan, Bush, and Clinton.

Weinberger returned to the private sector in 1975. He followed his former boss, Shultz, to join the Bechtel Corporation, a San Francisco-based international construction and engineering firm with close ties to the U.S. government. For the next six years he served as its general counsel, vice president, and director, making over $500,000 a year.

Secretary of Defense

When Reagan became president in 1981 he named Weinberger secretary of defense. Immediately, Weinberger started warning of an increased threat from the Soviet Union and a need to upgrade the U.S. military. He presided over an unprecedented peacetime military spending program. He resurrected the B-1 bomber program, which had been scuttled by President Jimmy Carter. He pushed for more ships, fighter planes, and tanks. Fighting for an increased arsenal of nuclear weapons, he became the leading advocate of the Strategic Defense Initiative, an enormously expensive space-based anti-missile system known popularly as *Star Wars*. Weinberger's reputation for cutting costs was replaced by a reputation for giving the military everything it wanted, contributing greatly to massive budget deficits which worried the nation and Congress. Critics charged that "Weinberger has often let hardware dictate strategy, with a resulting surfeit of gold-plated weapons systems," noted William R. Doerner in *Time* (February 11, 1985). "He became known around the Pentagon as Mr. Yes," according to *Fortune* (July 21, 1986). Supporters credited Weinberger with upgrading the quality of America's military personnel, as well as their pay and other personal benefits, and with modernizing the nation's defense system.

Despite his enthuasism for the arms buildup, Weinberger was somewhat cautious about the use of U.S. military force overseas. He supported the U.S. invasion of the Caribbean nation of Grenada and air strikes against Libya, but opposed sending Marines as peacekeeping forces to Lebanon.

Iran-Contra Controversy

Citing his wife's battle with cancer, Weinberger resigned from the cabinet late in 1987. In 1988 Queen Elizabeth made Weinberger a knight of the British Empire for his support of the British 1982 war against Argentine in the Falkland Islands. Also that year *Forbes* named Weinberger its publisher.

In 1990 Weinberger published his memoirs, *Fighting for Peace: Seven Critical Years in the Pentagon,* which received mixed reviews. Lawrence J. Korb in *Washington Monthly* noted, "Most memoirs are somewhat self-serving, but Weinberger carries his to the extreme . . . Throughout the book, he simply dismisses the problems that plagued his tenure in office and undermined support for national defense." In the book Weinberger glossed over his role in the Iran-contra affair, the secret and illegal shipment of arms from the U.S.-backed Nicaraguan rebels, the contras, to the regime of Iran in November 1985 in exchange for the release of hostages. Weinberger initially had opposed the deal, but became involved in an attempt to keep it quiet.

In 1992 Lawrence Walsh, the independent prosecutor investigating the Iran-contra affair, brought a five-count felony indictment against Weinberger, charging him with obstructing justice by concealing more than 1,700 pages of personal notes about the arms-for-hostages swap and with perjury for lying to Congress and hiding his knowledge of the deal. Later that year a federal judge dismissed the obstruction of justice charge, and on Christmas Eve in 1992 President George Bush, who was about to leave office, pardoned Weinberger, who was awaiting trial in January, and other officials involved in the scandal.

Out of government, Weinberger continued to sound warnings about what he believed was a lack of military preparedness. His strong criticism of military cuts under President Bill Clinton fueled his 1996 book, *The Next War,* co-written with Peter Schweitzer, which detailed five fictional scenarios of nuclear blackmail and other disasters for the United States in the future. "As the nation weakens [its] military . . . the numbers of people who feel safe in attacking or seeking revenge or in using terrorism increases exponentially," Weinberger told journalist Stephen Goode in *Insight on the News* (October 28, 1996).

Weinberger's hero was British Prime Minister Winston Churchill, and he quoted Churchill frequently. One of his favorite Churchill quotes, framed on the wall of Weinberger's office, was, "Never give in; never give in; never, never, never, never in nothing great or small, large or petty—never give in."

Further Reading

Weinberger's account of his stint as defense secretary is *Fighting for Peace: Seven Critical Years in the Pentagon* (1990). Some biographical material is in Ronald Brownstein and Nina Easton, *Reagan's Ruling Class* (1982). Weinberger's views on the national defense budget can be found in his *The Defense Budget* (1972), and his warnings about military cuts of the 1990s are in *The Next War,* co-written with Peter Schweitzer (1996). Background reading about Weinberger's participation in public office is in Gary C. Hamilton and Nicole W. Biggart, *Governor Reagan, Governor Brown* (1984); A. James Reichley, *Conservatives in an Age of Change: The Nixon and Ford Administrations* (1981); and Laurence I. Barrett, *Gambling With History: Ronald Reagan in the White House* (1984). A good short overview of Weinberger's career is William R. Doerner, "Man with a Mission: Seeking Fire and Vision," *Time* (February 11, 1985). □

August Freidrich Leopold Weismann

The German biologist August Freidrich Leopold Weismann (1834-1914) was one of the founders of the science of genetics.

ugust Weismann was born on Jan. 17, 1834, at Frankfurt am Main. He early showed intense interest in natural history, and while still a schoolboy he made extensive collections of butterflies, moths, beetles, and plants from the country around Frankfurt. He entered the University at Göttingen in 1852 and took a four-year course in medicine.

Weismann became an assistant in a hospital at Rostock (1856-1857) and then an unpaid assistant to a chemist in Rostock Chemical Institute. He soon decided he was not suited to chemistry and in 1858 went to Baden and to Italy as an army doctor. In 1861 he worked in Giessen for 2 months under Rudolf Leuckart, whom Weismann much admired and to whom he dedicated *The Germ Plasm* (1892). Weismann then obtained an appointment as private physician to the Archduke Stephen of Austria.

In 1863 Weismann joined the University of Freiburg im Breisgau as a privatdozent in the medical faculty, teaching zoology and comparative anatomy. In 1865 he was appointed professor extraordinarius, and thanks to his enthusiasm, a zoological institute and museum, of which he was appointed head, was built. About 1874 he was appointed professor ordinarius at Freiburg, being the first occupant of the chair in zoology in the university, where he remained until his retirement in 1912. He died in Freiburg on Nov. 5, 1914.

Early Embryological Work

Weismann's early research was mainly in the field of embryology. He published six classical studies on the embryonic and postembryonic development and metamorphosis of insects between 1862 and 1866. In a monograph on the postembryonic development of the Muscidae (1864), he described in detail the building up of the perfect form of the pupa, and he showed that in insects with a complete metamorphosis the tissues break down into an apparently simple, primitive mass, from which the imago is built up afresh by a kind of second embryonic development.

This work on insect development was followed by a series of memoirs on minute Crustacea and by a very thorough study of the sex cells of the *Hydrozoa,* which was published in four papers between 1880 and 1882. His eyesight became too weak for him to continue microscope work, and he turned to more general theoretical problems, such as heredity and reproduction.

Evolution Studies

From the first Weismann was a strong supporter of the theory of evolution by natural selection, as put forward by Charles Darwin and Alfred Wallace. In his book *The Evolution Theory* (2 vols., 1904) Weismann stated that Darwin's *Origin of Species,* when it was published in German in 1859, fell "like a bolt from the blue."

In spite of his enthusiastic support of Darwin, Weismann felt it necessary to disagree with that part of the theory in which Darwin had accepted the Lamarckian view of the inheritance of acquired characters. Weismann disagreed strongly with this concept, both on technical grounds and from experimental evidence (or the lack of it). He first publicly expressed his views on the matter in 1883 in the essay "Heredity," presented as his inaugural address as prorector of the University of Freiburg. He pointed out the impossibility of proposing a mechanism whereby changes in the external organs and tissues of an animal, induced by environmental stimuli, would be conveyed to the reproductive organs and the germ cells within them and thence to ensuing generations.

Weismann realized it was necessary to suggest some other mechanism for producing the variations necessary for evolution. In this he was not very successful. He spoke as though natural selection could itself act in this way, but he was vague about the details. In *The Germ Plasm* he mentioned "chance nutritive fluctuations" in the germ plasm as giving rise to variations.

Germ Plasm Theory

The idea for *The Germ Plasm* appears to have stemmed from Weismann's early embryological studies, especially with *Hydra,* where he observed that only certain predetermined cells were capable of giving rise to the germ line and to daughter individuals. He extended the idea to the contents of these cells and proposed that there was a certain substance, or "germ plasm," which could never be formed anew but only from preexisting germ plasm. It was transmitted unchanged from generation to generation and controlled all the characters of the individual animals. The idea of the germ plasm seemed (and seems) to some people to be somewhat mystical, as it postulates a completely self-determining substance, which apparently does not obey the laws of the physical world, since it proceeds along a path determined only by itself, unaffected by the surrounding environment.

Weismann made his germ plasm theory all-embracing, in that he attempted to explain not only heredity but also development. In fact, at times he seems to place greater significance on the latter aspect than on the former and allows his imagination to get rather out of hand. He proposed that the total hereditary substance of a cell should be called idioplasm. Every cell contained idioplasm, while the idioplasm of the germ cells was the germ plasm. The idioplasm was composed of smaller entities called ids. Each id in its turn consisted of determinants, each controlling the development of a particular part of the organism. The determinants contained certain groups of biophors, the simplest living units, which were thought to consist of "albumen molecules, water and salts."

Surprisingly, Weismann did not appear to appreciate the full significance of Gregor Mendel's work even after 1900. In *The Evolution Theory,* apropos Mendel's work, Weismann states, "We must postpone the working of this new material into our theory until a very much wider basis of facts has been supplied." (To most of us today, Mendel's experiments seem completely convincing.)

Yet in some respects Weismann was remarkably farseeing. In his discussion on the "inheritance" of musical ability and other cultural activities, he clearly sets out the distinction between biological heredity, based on a transmission of material through the germ cells, and cultural inheritance, resulting from a process of learning of skills and traditions by individuals of each generation from their parents and other individuals in the surrounding society. Again, in regard to the origin of life on earth, which Weismann discusses in the last chapter of *The Evolution Theory,* he dismisses the possibility that life was brought to the earth in a meteorite and comes out firmly in favor of spontaneous generation—not however of any form of life like that now familiar to us, but of some extremely primitive bodies (biophors). These "albuminoid substances," he assumed, could have arisen spontaneously through purely chemicophysical causes, from inorganic materials, under conditions which may no longer exist on the earth. Such views are not far removed from the speculations on the origin of life currently in vogue.

Further Reading

Major works on Weismann are in German. A study in English is George J. Romanes, *An Examination of Weismannism* (1893). See also Gavin De Beer, *Streams of Culture* (1969). □

Wei Yüan

The Chinese historian and geographer Wei Yüan (1794-1856) was one of the first Chinese to advocate learning about the West; he collected and edited available facts in the "Illustrated Gazetteer of the Countries Overseas."

Wei Yüan was born on April 23, 1794, in Shaoyang, Hunan. He passed the first of the official examinations at the age of 14 and is said to have exhibited an interest in history and philosophy. In 1822, after having received the *chujen* (the second-highest academic degree), he accepted the post of editor of the *Collected Essays on Statecraft under the Reigning Dynasty,* in which were reprinted over 2,000 essays on economics and other administrative matters. This book, which was completed in 1826, became the model for an entire genre of such collections.

Through his work as editor, Wei developed an interest in current affairs and in 1829 purchased a position as a secretary in the Grand Secretariat. His new job, which gave him access to the imperial library and the archives, made it possible for him to become thoroughly familiar with national affairs and government procedures. His work also motivated him to write a history of the military campaigns of the Ch'ing dynasty (1644-1912), *Record of Imperial Military Exploits,* which he finished in 1842. In his book he described the Ch'ing conquests of China, Mongolia, Tibet, Sinkiang, and Taiwan and the victories over the Russians, Burmese, Vietnamese, and the White Lotus rebels.

Wei was not satisfied being just a scholar, as he believed that learning should be applied to the practical problems of government. In 1825, when the Grand Canal was blocked by ice, he wrote a treatise advocating that the tribute rice be sent to Peking by sea. His admirer, the reforming governor of Kiangsu, T'ao Chu, put his plan into effect in 1826 with exemplary results. During the 1830s T'ao Chu relied on Wei's advice to reform the Northern Huai salt monopoly.

Wei Yüan is known primarily for his authorship of the *Illustrated Gazetteer of the Countries Overseas,* which he produced in 1844. Wei had witnessed the decline of the Ch'ing, the growing internal unrest, and the encroachment of the Western nations which climaxed in the Opium War (1839-1842). His concern prompted him to write his book as a guide on how to control the Western barbarians. The imperial commissioner for the suppression of the opium trade at Canton, Lin Tse-hsü, who was Wei's old friend, had devoted a great deal of time and energy while in Canton to gathering information about the West, much of it from Western sources which he had translated into Chinese. These materials were compiled into a *Gazetteer of the Four Continents,* which was turned over to Wei in 1841 and became the basis of his book.

Wei's work is unique in China's relations with the West since it represents the first systematic attempt to provide educated Chinese with a realistic picture of the outside world. His general thesis was that the Western barbarians in their desire for power and profit had devised techniques and machines to conquer the civilized world. China, committed to spiritual and moral virtue, learning, and peace, should arouse itself to the danger and apply itself to the practical problems involved so that it could triumph over the enemy.

The book is divided into four parts: history, geography, and recent political conditions in the West; the manufacture and use of foreign guns; shipbuilding, mining, and the practical arts of the West; and methods of dealing with the West. In the preface Wei stated that his reasons for compiling this book were so that China could use barbarians to fight barbarians, use barbarians to negotiate with barbarians, and learn the superior techniques of the barbarians to control barbarians. This last statement presaged the ideas of the later-generation "self-strengtheners."

In the same year that Wei completed his *Illustrated Gazetteer* he also received a *chin-shih* (the highest academic degree) and in the next year (1845) was appointed an acting district magistrate in Kiangsu. The remainder of his official career was spent in relatively minor posts, in which he dealt with matters of more traditional concern, such as local administration, flood control and irrigation, water transport, and salt administration.

Even so, Wei Yüan was recognized by his contemporaries as one of the outstanding scholars of his age, and his *Illustrated Gazetteer* was reprinted many times, expanded and supplemented, and translated into Japanese. Wei was working on a revised history of the Yüan dynasty (1260-1368) at the time of his death in Hangchow.

Further Reading

The preface to Wei Yüan's *Illustrated Gazetteer of the Countries Overseas* is presented in translation in William T. De Bary, ed., *Sources of Chinese Tradition* (2 vols., 1964). There is no book in English on Wei Yüan. The only complete biography is in the publication by the U.S. Library of Congress, Orientalia Division, *Eminent Chinese of the Ch'ing Period, 1644-1912*, edited by Arthur W. Hummell (2 vols., 1943-1944). □

Ezer Weizman

Ezer Weizman (born 1924) was an Israeli air force commander and statesman who became president of Israel in 1993. Weizman changed from a hard-liner to a leading advocate of peacemaking with the Arab nations.

Ezer Weizman's career was a stormy one, with a number of sharp personal transitions: from the professional military to civilian life, from politics to the private business sector and back to politics, and from membership in the right-wing Gahal party to affiliation with the

left-wing Labour party. Throughout his life, Weizman remained one of the more colorful and controversial figures in Israel.

Love of Flying

Weizman was born in Tel-Aviv, Palestine (now Israel), in 1924. His uncle was Chaim Weizman, leader of the Zionist movement during the period before the two World Wars and later first president of the state of Israel. Soon after his birth Weizman's parents moved to Haifa where his father, Yehiel, taught agronomy. When he was 16 Weizman trained with the infantry of the Palestinian Jews' underground military organization, but he soon became fascinated with flying. "The air force is full of fine fancies," he later wrote in his autobiography, *On Eagle's Wings* (1976). "Planes, flying, spreading your wings; the clouds and the roar of the engines; and that wonderful feeling of power, of being different."

In 1942 Weizman earned his pilot's license and saw service during World War II in Egypt and India as a Royal Air Force fighter pilot. Demobilized in 1946, he became a strong advocate of the need for Jewish civil and military aviation as part of preparations for independence. In 1947 Weizman was given charge of a squad of Piper Cub aircraft. The squad supplied isolated Jewish settlements and became the nucleus for the modern Israeli air force.

Modernized Air Force

During the 1948 Israeli war of independence Weizman took part in Israeli's first air strike against Egypt, which then had a vastly superior air force. Following the war he remained as a career air force officer and helped build the fledgling air force into a strong, separate wing of the Israeli military. In 1950 he was promoted to lieutenant colonel and chief of operations for the air force. In 1951 he studied in England at the Royal Air Force Air Command College. Back in Israel Weizman served as commander of an air base from 1953 to 1956, then became chief of the air force general staff. Weizman's efforts to make the air force more modern and independent culminated in May 1966 when he was promoted to chief of operations of the Israeli Defense Forces.

Weizman's advocacy of air superiority and the use of pre-emptive air strikes was vindicated in the dramatic success of the 1967 Six-Day War. During the first hours of the war Egypt's air force was virtually destroyed on the ground, assuring Israel victory. Nevertheless, Weizman did not hide his disappointment in January 1968 at being denied promotion to chief-of-staff.

Entry Into Politics

In 1969 Weizman, then a major general, resigned from the military. Known publicly for his hard-line stance, he entered politics, becoming minister of transportation in the government of national unity led by Golda Meir. Weizman was a member of the right-wing Gahal political faction of the Likud party. When Gahal protested Meir's call for a cease-fire to end the conflict with Egypt in January 1970, Weizman resigned his post. He engaged in a variety of business enterprises as well as in Gahal politics and maintained an uneasy relationship with Likud leader Menachem Begin because of his outspoken views. Weizman's hard-line policies were evolving into support of peace through power. In *On Eagle's Wings* he explained, "We must be sensitive to any hint of peace and open our hearts to any Arab attempt to put an end to the wars. But there is no prospect of this happening if we don't build up our military, economic and social might."

As director of Begin's 1976-1977 campaign for prime minister, Weizman was instrumental in engineering the political upset of May 1977, which saw Begin and his Likud party victorious at the polls after 29 years in opposition. When the new Likud-dominated coalition government assumed office, Weizman was named minister of defense. With typical energy and zeal, he continued the efforts of his predecessor, Shimon Peres, at rebuilding the armed forces. Weizman personally pursued a closer military supply relationship with the United States.

Promoter of Peace

Following Egyptian President Anwar Sadat's dramatic peace initiative in November 1977, Weizman became an architect of Begin's strategy. He argued strongly that Egypt's willingness to recognize Israel and to negotiate a settlement of the Middle East conflict posed an historic opportunity. "My job had changed," Weizman noted in his second book

of memoirs, *The Battle for Peace* (1981). "Instead of a war room, I found myself in the negotiating chamber—and again I urged full speed ahead." During months of tedious negotiations Weizman used his warm personal relationship with Sadat to encourage the peace process, which eventually resulted in the 1979 Israel-Egypt Treaty. However, the process involved him in frequent sharp policy differences and heated exchanges with Premier Begin and other cabinet members. Finally, in 1980 Weizman resigned from the cabinet. He withdrew completely from politics, retiring to his home in Caesaria and various business projects.

In 1984 Weizman re-entered politics. He organized and headed a new political party, Yahad (Together), hoping to fill the center of the Israeli political spectrum. Expected to do well at the polls following an active campaign, the party did poorly, gaining only four seats. The two largest parties, Labour and Likud, were locked in a stalemate, and Weizman's seats were crucial. He helped form the National Unity government of both parties, becoming a minister in the Prime Minister's Office. Eventually, he completed his political metamorphosis by integrating his party into the Labour Alignment.

Weizman by the 1990s advocated Israel's withdraw from occupation of the Golan Heights, direct negotiations with Arafat's Palestinian Liberation Organization, and the establishment of a Palestinian state. Weizman's advocacy of peace continually led to clashes with other officials. Named minister of science in the Likud-Labour coalition government headed by Yitzhak Shamir, Weizman secretly met with members of Arafat's PLO, which was then off-limits. Shamir threatened to fire him, then relented partially, but Weizman was drummed out of the inner cabinet, which decided on foreign policy.

In 1993 the Knesset, the Israeli parliament, named Weizman to a five-year term as president, a largely ceremonial office that carries prestige but little power. During peace talks in 1995 he questioned whether interim Prime Minister Shimon Peres could make decisions after many sleepless nights. He defied the prime minister by refusing for months to free some Palestinian prisoners because, Weizman said, they had "blood on their hands." With the peace process of the mid-1990s unraveling, Weizman pressured Israeli prime minister Benjamin Netanyahu to meet with Palestinian leader Yasser Arafat. Weizman "sees himself as the voice of the people," *The Economist* noted (August 31, 1996). Throughout his career in the delicate realm of Israeli politics, Weizman steadfastly remained his own man.

Further Reading

Weizman's book *On Eagles' Wings* (1976) provides insights into his political career. His book *The Battle for Peace* (1981) details the long peace negotiations of 1977-1979 and his key role in them. A helpful source is William Stevenson, *Zanek!: A Chronicle of the Israeli Air Force* (1971). □

Chaim Weizmann

**The Zionist leader Chaim Weizmann (1874-1952)
was president of the World Zionist Organization and
first president of the state of Israel.**

Chaim Weizmann, son of Oizer and Rachel
Weizmann, was born on Nov. 2, 1874, in Motele,
Russia. After receiving a religious education, Chaim
was admitted to the gymnasium of Pinsk, where he continued his Hebraic studies. At the age of 18, he received his
baccalaureate. He majored in chemistry at the universities
of Darmstadt and Berlin, and he received his doctor of
science degree from the University of Freiburg in 1900.
From 1900 to 1904 Weizmann was a lecturer in chemistry
at the University of Geneva and from 1904 to 1916 a
lecturer in biochemistry at the University of Manchester.

While in Switzerland, Weizmann joined the active
Zionist leadership. He participated in all Zionist congresses
after 1898 and was a delegate after 1901. He urged a
synthesis of settlement, cultural work, and political propaganda to secure international recognition of Zionist goals in
Palestine. He opposed the British proposal for Jewish settlement in Uganda. As an exponent of cultural Zionism,
Weizmann suggested the creation of a Hebrew University in
Palestine. The university opened in Jerusalem in 1925. In
appreciation of his efforts in building the university, he was
elected its honorary president.

During World War I, Weizmann, because of his connections with British authorities, emerged as the leader of
the Zionist movement. As a result of his efforts, the British
government issued on Nov. 2, 1917, the Balfour Declaration, in which it declared its support of the establishment of
a Jewish national home in Palestine. As the head of a Jewish
delegation, Weizmann appeared before the Paris Peace
Conference in 1919 and submitted the Zionist claims to
Palestine. These claims were recognized by the League of
Nations, and the British government was appointed to further Jewish settlement and to assist the development of a
Jewish national home there.

In 1921 Weizmann was elected president of the World
Zionist Organization, a post he held until 1931 and later
from 1935 to 1946. When the Jewish Agency for Palestine
was established in 1929, he served simultaneously as its
president. In this dual capacity, he cooperated with Great
Britain except for a time in 1930, when he resigned from his
Zionist post in protest against the new British policy curtailing Jewish immigration to Palestine. After 1946, in spite
of his unofficial position, Weizmann served with the Jewish
Agency's delegation before the United Nations Special
Committee for Palestine in October 1947. When Israel was
proclaimed an independent state, he was elected the president of its Provisional Council of State. After the elections to
the Parliament, he was elected, on Feb. 17, 1949, as Israel's
first president, and he was reelected on Nov. 19, 1951.

In addition to his political activity, Weizmann also
engaged in scholarly scientific work. He founded the Sief
Research Institute in Rehovoth and served as its director
from 1932 to 1952. This institute was later enlarged and
named the Weizmann Institute of Science.

During his terms of office as president, he was in poor
health and could not perform many of his official duties. He
died in office on Nov. 9, 1952.

Further Reading

Considerable information on Weizmann can be gleaned from his
Trial and Error: The Autobiography of Chaim Weizmann
(1949), and the first volume of a projected multivolume collection, *The Letters and Papers of Chaim Weizmann*, edited
by Leonard Stein and Gedalia Yogev (1968), which covers the
years from his youth to 1902. Works on Weizmann include
Paul Goodman, ed., *Chaim Weizmann: A Tribute* (1945);
Isaiah Berlin, *Chaim Weizmann* (1949); and M. W. Weisgal
and Joel Carmichael, eds., *Chaim Weizmann: A Biography by
Several Hands* (1962).

Additional Sources

Blumberg, H. M. (Harold M.), *Weizmann, his life and times,* New
York: St. Martin's Press, 1975.
*Chaim Weizmann: statesman of the Jewish renaissance: the
Chaim Weizmann centenary, 1874-197,* Jerusalem: Zionist
Library, 1974.
Litvinoff, Barnet, *Weizmann: last of the patriarchs,* New York:
Putnam, 1976.
Reinharz, Jehuda, *Chaim Weizmann: the making of a statesman,*
New York: Oxford University Press, 1993.
Rose, Norman, *Chaim Weizmann: a biography,* New York, N.Y.,
U.S.A.: Viking, 1986.

Weizmann, Chaim, *The essential Chaim Weizmann: the man, the statesman, the scientist,* New York: Holmes & Meier Publishers, 1982. □

Robert Welch

Political ideologue Robert Welch (1899-1985) founded the John Birch Society to promote his conspiracy theory that Communists controlled American society.

Robert H. W. Welch, Jr., was born in Chowan County, North Carolina, on December 1, 1899. A bright boy, he graduated from the University of North Carolina in 1916 and studied at the U.S. Naval Academy, 1917-1919, and at Harvard Law School, 1919-1921. In 1922 he joined his brothers in a candy manufacturing business in Boston from which he retired as vice president in 1956. A prosperous and well-regarded businessman, Welch was little known outside Massachusetts.

Like many Americans, Welch became increasingly alarmed as Communist regimes seized power in Eastern Europe and Asia in the years following the end of World War II. Convinced of the need to educate Americans about the danger of Communist subversion, he founded the John Birch Society in 1958. Welch named the society after a 26-year-old American soldier and missionary killed by Chinese Communist forces on August 25, 1945, just ten days after the Japanese surrender that ended the war. For Welch, Birch's death marked the beginning of the final struggle between the defenders of freedom and Christianity and the forces of Communist oppression and atheism.

In the 1950s and 1960s many American conservatives opposed the U.S. policy of "containment" and wanted to "roll-back" Communist expansion. They believed government policymakers were unwilling to use U.S. power effectively to combat the Soviet Union. Welch became convinced that this failing was deliberate: top American officials were engaged in a calculated plan to protect the Communist enemy. Welch formed the John Birch Society to alert loyal Americans to the alleged existence of a conspiracy of Communists and Communist sympathizers whose positions in government put them in control of the United States.

Welch's monthly magazine, *American Opinion,* claimed in 1960 that 40 percent to 60 percent of the United States was under Communist control. Communists either controlled the presidential nominations of candidates John F. Kennedy and Richard Nixon or "the conspiracy is so powerful that the candidates dare not offend it by recognizing its existence." In his 1958 book *The Politician,* Welch declared that President Dwight Eisenhower was "a dedicated, conscious agent of the Communist conspiracy." Such extreme views were repudiated by such conservative leaders as Senator Barry Goldwater and columnist William

F. Buckley, Jr., but many Americans nevertheless joined the Birch Society.

Between 1962 and 1966 membership in the John Birch Society rose from an estimated 25,000 to 85,000 organized into 4,000 local chapters across the country. Birch members, mainly older upper-income whites, were encouraged to work on projects at the local community level, in school parent-teacher associations and in business and church groups, to awaken their neighbors to the Communist influence inside America. Birch members called for U.S. withdrawal from the United Nations, the impeachment of Supreme Court Chief Justice Earl Warren, the abolition of the income tax, and the disclosure of Communist control of the civil rights movement. At its peak in 1966 the society maintained 350 bookstores and had a staff of 220 and an estimated annual budget of five to eight million dollars. Robert Welch kept personal control over the society and the causes it favored. Secretive and distrustful of politicians, he declared that the society would avoid political organizing and emphasize public education and community action.

Nonetheless, the John Birch Society became a major issue in national politics in the early 1960s. Critics said Welch was the authoritarian head of a secret society whose immediate goal was the infiltration and takeover of the Republican Party. Many Republican leaders were alarmed by the selection of "Birchers" to positions in the party and their involvement in the 1964 presidential campaign of party nominee Barry Goldwater. By 1965 Republican conservatives had joined liberal Democrats in denouncing Welch and the society.

The society tried unsuccessfully to improve its public image by claiming that members did not have to agree with everything Welch said. Indeed, many members were simply patriotic conservatives worried about Communism. But loyalty to Welch's leadership was the foundation of the society, and Welch's thinking was the core of its philosophy. If America's leaders refused to follow his policies for fighting Communism, Welch reasoned that they must be Communists or Communist sympathizers, "comsymps." And if American citizens foolishly denied that their country was under Communist control, this proved the success of Communist propaganda! The John Birch Society began to lose members and financial support once Welch's view of President Eisenhower became widely known. Conservative anti-Communists found the attack bizarre and politically harmful. The society continued to exist, but it no longer played a part in the rise of conservative ideas that culminated in the election of Ronald Reagan. Robert Welch's ideas grew more strange over the years. In old age he decided that Communists were merely a front group formed by a more powerful and secret group of "Insiders" which he linked to the Bavarian Illuminati of the 18th century. Robert Welch died on January 6, 1985.

Further Reading

The best sources are Welch's own writings, especially *The Politician* and *The Blue Book* published by the John Birch Society. A sympathetic biography is G. Edward Griffin, *The Life and Words of Robert Welch* (1975). Benjamin R. Epstein and Arnold Forster's *The Radical Right* (1966) is a critical examination of the John Birch Society and other rightist groups.

Additional Sources

Griffin, G. Edward, *The life and words of Robert Welch, founder of the John Birch Society,* Thousand Oaks, Calif.: American Media, 1975. □

William Henry Welch

The American pathologist, bacteriologist, and medical educator William Henry Welch (1850-1934) established a firm foundation for the development of the medical sciences in the United States.

William H. Welch was born on April 8, 1850, in Norfolk, Conn. He entered Yale at the age of 16, where the study of the classics was his major interest. After graduating in 1870, he taught Greek and Latin in Norwich.

Although his father and grandfather were physicians, Welch had little interest in medicine while at Yale. Gradually his attitude changed, and in 1871 he became an apprentice to his father and then a student at Yale's scientific school, where he learned basic science. In 1872 he entered the College of Physicians and Surgeons in New York, graduating in 1875. After an internship at New York's Bellevue Hospital, Welch went to Germany to study pathology and physiology and had a first contact with the rising science of bacteriology. When he returned to the United States, he established the first laboratory for pathology in the United States, at the Bellevue Hospital Medical School. On a second trip to Europe, in 1884, Welch concentrated specifically on bacteriology and became one of the earliest proponents of this science in the United States.

In 1884 Welch was appointed professor of pathology at Johns Hopkins Hospital and Medical School in Baltimore, which was then under construction. When the medical school opened in 1893, Welch was appointed dean of the medical faculty, a position he held until 1898. His selection of department heads exerted a powerful influence on the modern direction in which medicine in the United States was to go. Equally important in this regard were his many positions in organizations, including service as president of the Board of Scientific Directors of the Rockefeller Institute (1901-1933), president of the American Medical Association (1910-1911), and president of the National Academy of Sciences (1913-1916).

Medicine was also public health to Welch, and a great dedication to this area characterized his life. He was, for example, president of the Maryland State Board of Health (1898-1922), and he was the leading figure in the establishment of the important School of Hygiene and Public Health at Johns Hopkins, of which he was director (1918-1926).

At the age of 76 Welch accepted a new chair in medical history at Johns Hopkins and guided the development of the Institute of the History of Medicine. Through his efforts a

fine medical library was also established, which was dedicated in 1929 and bears his name.

Welch's greatest factual contribution to medicine was the discovery of the bacillus causing gas gangrene, first reported in 1892. Far more important than such specific discoveries was his far-reaching impact on medicine, expressed through a general emphasis on the new sciences like bacteriology and through brilliant leadership. He died in Baltimore on April 30, 1934.

Further Reading

Walter C. Burket edited Welch's *Papers and Addresses* (3 vols., 1920). The most complete biography of Welch is Simon and James Thomas Flexner, *William Henry Welch and the Heroic Age of American Medicine* (1941). Donald Fleming, *William H. Welch and the Rise of Modern Medicine* (1954), is a popular account.

Additional Sources

Fleming, Donald, *William H. Welch and the rise of modern medicine,* Baltimore: Johns Hopkins University Press, 1987, 1954. □

Theodore Dwight Weld

Theodore Dwight Weld (1803-1895) was an American reformer, preacher, and editor. He was one of the most-influential leaders in the early phases of the antislavery movement.

Theodore Weld was born in Hampton, Conn., on Nov. 23, 1803, the son of a Congregational minister. Sent to Phillips-Andover to prepare for the ministry, he was forced to leave because of failing eyesight; he tried lecturing and later entered Hamilton College in New York. Here he was especially influenced by evangelist Charles Grandison Finney, who conducted revivalist meetings in the area. Weld toured with Finney's "holy band," leaving for Oneida Institute in 1827 to complete his ministerial studies.

Weld soon converted to the antislavery cause. "I am deliberately, earnestly, solemnly, with my whole heart and soul and mind and strength," he wrote in 1830, "for the immediate, universal, and total abolition of slavery." The New York philanthropists Lewis and Arthur Tappan hired Weld as an agent for the Society for the Promotion of Manual Labor to lecture and also to choose a site for a theological seminary for Finney. Weld chose Lane Seminary, and when the Tappans installed the Reverend Lyman Beecher as president, Weld remained as a student. However, Weld and other "Lane rebels" left in 1834 to train agents for the new national American Antislavery Society. Weld himself was a powerful speaker, and his famous agents, the "Seventy," preached abolition across the West.

In 1837, his voice failing, Weld went to New York to edit the society's books and pamphlets. His *The Bible* *against Slavery* (1837) summarized religious arguments against slavery, while *American Slavery as It Is* (1839, published anonymously), a compilation of stories and statistics, served as an arsenal for abolitionist speakers and writers. In 1838 Weld married Angelina Grimké, one of two sisters he had helped train as antislavery speakers.

By the late 1830s antislavery forces formed a significant bloc in Congress, led by John Quincy Adams. Weld helped to develop the "petition strategy," which forced the slavery issue into open debate. In 1843, feeling that abolition was established as a political issue, Weld, in poor health, retired to New York. In 1854 he founded an interracial school in New Jersey. He died Feb. 3, 1895, in Massachusetts.

Weld's passion for anonymity and fear of pride tended to osbcure his role in the antislavery movement, on which he exerted an enormous influence. He trained more than a hundred agents for the cause, directed its strategy for a decade, and influenced many of its leaders.

Further Reading

The best biography of Weld is Benjamin P. Thomas, *Theodore Weld* (1950). Additional information is in Gilbert H. Barnes and Dwight L. Dumond, *Letters of Theodore Dwight Weld, Angelina Grimké Weld and Sarah Grimké* (2 vols., 1934). For Weld's place in the antislavery movement see Gilbert H. Barnes, *The Antislavery Impulse, 1830-1844* (1933); Louis Filler, *The Crusade against Slavery, 1830-1860* (1960); and Martin Duberman, ed., *The Antislavery Vanguard: New Essays on the Abolitionists* (1965).

Additional Sources

Abzug, Robert H., *Passionate liberator: Theodore Dwight Weld and the dilemma of reform,* New York: Oxford University Press, 1980. □

Fay Birkinshaw Weldon

British novelist, dramatist, essayist, and feminist Fay Birkinshaw Weldon (born ca. 1931) was famous for her witty and satirical evocations of contemporary mores and morals as they affect the lives of women.

Whether Fay Birkinshaw Weldon was born on September 22 of 1931 or of 1933 is uncertain; what is certain, however, is that this British author of internationally acclaimed novels, short stories, screen plays, and television and radio dramas, as well as works of biography and historical criticism, descended from a line of writers. Her mother, Margaret Birkinshaw, reportedly published two novels under her maiden name and wrote serial novels under the pseudonym Pearl Bellairs. Weldon's maternal grandfather, Edgar Jepson, edited *Vanity Fair* and wrote popular romance-adventure stories, and his brother Selwyn authored mystery-thrillers and plays for screen, television, and radio. Understandably, Weldon saw her literary ability as, at least in part, genetic.

Weldon and her family moved to New Zealand soon after her birth in Alvechurch, Worcestershire, England. Her father, Frank Thornton Birkinshaw, was a doctor. He and his wife divorced when Weldon was five or six, and for the next eight years she lived with her mother and sister in New Zealand and went to Girls' High School in Christchurch. Her mother did domestic work to support the family. When the war ended and Weldon was about 14, the three returned to England to live with her grandmother. Here Weldon attended London's Hampstead High School, a convent school. After graduating, she entered St. Andrew's University in Scotland on scholarship. When she completed her master's degree in economics and psychology, Weldon was only 20 years old.

Weldon was married in the early 1950s to a schoolmaster who was 25 years her senior. But this union lasted only six months. When her son Nicholas was born in 1955, Weldon found herself ill-equipped to support them both. She tried unsuccessfully to write novels and worked for 18 months at the Foreign Office writing Cold War propaganda. In 1960 she married Ronald Weldon, an antiques dealer.

During the 1960s Weldon found work doing market research for the London *Daily News* and writing advertising copy for Ogilvy, Benson, & Mather and other firms. This work paid better and brought her some renown when she coined the popular British slogan, "Go to work on an egg." While decrying advertising as a "shameful business," Weldon acknowledged that her years as a copywriter forced her to make every word count, an ability that is reflected in her sharply succinct prose style.

According to an interview, Weldon went through psychoanalysis in her early thirties and it was this "dreadfully painful and very interesting" experience that enabled her to try writing fiction again. In the mid-1960s she began writing television plays, which were produced by BBC and one of which, *The Fat Woman's Joke,* was published in the United States as the novel *And the Wife Ran Away.* So began her career as a prolific writer of dramas and novels. By 1990 Weldon had written more than 50 scripts for British television, including two episodes of *Upstairs, Downstairs,* one of which won an award from the Society of Film and Television Arts in 1971. She wrote adaptations for the screen of her own fiction, as well as that of Penelope Mortimer and Elisabeth Bowen. Her five-part dramatization of Jane Austen's *Pride and Prejudice* was produced on BBC in 1980 after Weldon spent four years completing the adaptation. In 1984 she wrote *Letters to Alice on First Reading Jane Austen,* a nonfiction work comprised of 16 witty and informative letters to a fictional niece with literary aspirations, explaining the life and times of both Austen and Weldon. Throughout the 1970s and 1980s Weldon wrote plays for television and radio and even the libretto for an operatic version of Ibsen's *A Doll's House.*

However impressive her other work, it is for her 18 novels that she is best known. One, *The Life and Loves of a She-Devil,* published in 1984, was serialized on BBC and made into a popular movie in the United States. Her short and fast-paced novels are pastiches of science fiction, economic theory, surreal imagery, psychological insight, and political satire. The reader turns the pages of a Weldon novel not so much to discover what its characters will do next, but rather to learn what brilliant comic moves Weldon herself will engineer to drive the story. Most of her work is translated into many languages and distributed around the world.

Weldon's childhood experience in a largely female world as a child of divorce raised by a working mother, as well as her own later struggle as a single mother, are reflected in the characters who people her fictional worlds. However, her later life was very different. Married to Ronald Weldon for over thirty years, they raised a family of sons. Weldon's oldest son, Nicholas, was a jazz musician as well as a chef and Weldon's business manager. Daniel (1963) was a filmmaker, Thomas (1970) was described by his mother as a "practicing punk," and Samuel (1977) lived with his parents in the Somerset town of Shepton Mallet. Weldon herself commuted two days a week to a house in Kentish Town, London. In 1997 Weldon provided yet another unique profile on women in *Wicked Women,* a collection of short stories taking place in the 1990s.

Further Reading

Weldon's writing is reviewed in American newspapers and periodicals such as *The New York Times, Los Angeles Times, New Yorker, The Washington Post,* and *Village Voice.* For interviews see Marjorie Williams in *The Washington Post* (April 24, 1988) and Eden Ross Lipson in *Lear's* (January 1990). Brigitte Salzmann-Brunner in *Amanuenses to the Present: Protagonists in the Fiction of Penelope Mortimer, Margaret Drabble, and Fay Weldon* (1988) looks at Weldon's work in the context of that of her peers. See also Carolyn Nizzi Warmbold, ''Books: Reviews and Opinion: In Brief: 'Wicked Women' by Fay Weldon,'' *The Atlantic Journal and Constitution* (June 22, 1997). □

Sir Roy Welensky

Sir Roy Welensky (1907-1991) was prime minister of the Federation of Rhodesia and Nyasaland from 1956 to 1963. He was a chief architect and defender of the ill-fated, white-dominated federation in British south-central Africa.

Roy Welensky was born on Jan. 20, 1907, in Salisbury, Southern Rhodesia (now Zimbabwe), the 13th child of a Polish father and an African mother. Born Christened Roland, he was always called Roy. He left school at age 14, held several jobs, and in 1924 began work for Rhodesia Railways, first as a fireman and then as an engine driver. He was heavy-weight boxing champion of the Rhodesias (1926-1928). In 1933 he was transferred to Broken Hill, Northern Rhodesia, and rose rapidly as a railway trade union leader. Elected from Broken Hill to the Northern Rhodesia Legislative Council (1938-1953), he served on its executive council (1940-1953). For his work as director of manpower during the war (1941-1946) he received the C.M.G., or Companion (of the Order) of St. Michael and St. George.

In 1941 Welensky formed the Labour party, pledging to protect white workers from African competition. In 1946 he became chairman of the unofficial (that is, the elected) members of the Legislative Council. He long urged a single, independent, white-dominated government for both Rhodesias. In 1950 when ruling British Conservatives showed favor for a multiracial federation including Nyasaland, Welensky urged this course on Southern Rhodesia's prime minister, Sir Godfrey Huggins (later Lord Malvern). Under Huggins as federal prime minister, Welensky served as deputy prime minister and minister of transport (1953-1956).

Welensky succeeded Lord Malvern as federal prime minister, was president of the United Federal party (both 1956-1963), and served as minister of defense (1956-1959). His honors included knighthood in June 1953 and the K.C.M.G. (Knight Commander) in 1959. The federation's demise in 1963, deplored by Welensky, resulted from bitter agitation by black Africans. In October 1964 as leader of the new Rhodesia party, he lost a by-election in Southern Rhodesia and wrote *Welensky's 4,000 Days: The Life and Death of the Federation of Rhodesia and Nyasaland*. In December he retired from politics to his farm near Salisbury.

A powerfully built and hard-fighting politician, Welensky was, during the federation period, a dominant white supremacist in central Africa. He stood for Cecil Rhodes's concept of civilized standards and opposed the one-man, one-vote principle. Yet he saw Nyasaland (now Malawi) and Northern Rhodesia (now Zambia) become independent African-ruled states in 1964. In Southern Rhodesia, strangely, he saw a more intransigent white government than he had represented illegally break with Great Britain (1965) and become a republic (1970)—a course which he deplored. Welensky died on December 5, 1991.

Further Reading

The most intimate account of Welensky is his own *Welensky, 4000 Days: The Life and Death of the Federation of Rhodesia and Nyasaland* (1964). Biographies are Don Taylor, *The Rhodesian: The Life of Sir Roy Welensky* (1955), and the authorized biography, which includes the federation period, Garry Allighan, *The Welensky Story* (1962). Useful for historical background are A. J. Hanna, *The Story of the Rhodesias and Nyasaland* (1960), and Kenneth Young, *Rhodesia and Independence* (1967). □

Gideon Welles

Gideon Welles (1802-1878), a member of Lincoln's Cabinet, is known especially for the diary he kept throughout the Civil War period.

Gideon Welles was born at Glastonbury, Conn. He was educated at the Episcopal Academy at Cheshire, Conn., and at the American Literary, Scientific, and Military Academy at Norwich, Vt. (later Norwich University). Though he studied law, his interest in writing led him, at the age of 24, to become part owner and editor of the *Hartford Times*. His writing up until then had consisted of "romantic trifles," but his style now developed rapidly, and his vigorous editorials in support of Andrew Jackson attracted wide attention. Soon the *Times* was one of the leading Democratic papers in New England.

Welles's effort for the Democratic party revealed important mental and moral qualities which were to characterize his life. Few New Englanders had much use for Thomas Jefferson or those who came after him. The courage it took to support Jackson revealed a sincere and honest mind. With Welles's support the Democratic party gained in respectability.

In 1826 Welles was elected to the Connecticut Legislature. He labored for reform: his most important act was that of pushing through a bill removing the requirement that a person profess belief in God and in a future life in order to qualify as a witness in court. Although Welles himself was a deeply religious man, he insisted that this requirement denied religious liberty and freedom of thought. His efforts brought bitter criticism and insinuations that he had been corrupted by the lack of belief of men such as Jefferson and Jackson. He left the legislature in 1835 with the blunt statement, "I am ashamed to say regarding the civil and judicial complexion of my state, that a degraded, bigoted, hidebound, autocratic, proud, arrogant and contemptible policy governs her, through . . . unprincipled knaves."

Jackson appointed Welles postmaster at Hartford in 1836, a post he held to 1841. This office made him virtually

the Democratic leader in the state. In 1845 President James K. Polk appointed him chief of the Bureau of Provisions and Clothing in the Navy Department. It was not a particularly important post, but it did give him some naval experience and connected him in the minds of others with the Navy.

Meanwhile Welles continued to write political articles for important newspapers and established friendly relations with such prominent men as jurist David Dudley Field and poet and editor William Cullen Bryant. He broke with his party over the slavery issue and in 1854 helped to organize the Republican party. He served as a national committeeman from 1856 to 1864 and headed the Connecticut delegation to the 1860 convention and favored Salmon P. Chase as the Republican presidential nominee. He did not support Abraham Lincoln even on the important third ballot, but he was completely satisfied with the final choice of Lincoln.

In his effort to construct a Cabinet which represented all sections and all parties, Lincoln knew he must appoint someone from New England and that this person must be a former Democrat. Welles was by all odds the best choice and was offered the Navy Department.

With only the limited experience gained earlier in the Bureau of Provisions and Clothing, Welles took over a Navy Department short on both men and ships. The secession of the Southern states had created an even more serious problem. As he himself said: "When I took charge of the Navy Department, I found great demoralization and deflection among the naval officers. It was difficult to ascertain who among those that lingered about Washington could [be trusted] and who were not to be trusted." Furthermore Congress had adjourned without providing funds or authorizing the enlistment of additional seamen. Almost all of the naval force was scattered about the world, some in European waters and most of "the small Home Squadron" in the Gulf or the West Indies, "nearly as remote and inaccessible."

Welles reorganized his department, bought ships where possible, and did his best to keep the Norfolk Navy yard from falling into Confederate hands. He might have saved the navy yard if Gen. Winfield Scott had been able to supply troops and if Lincoln, anxious to avoid provoking Virginia into seceding, had not insisted on a fatal delay. Welles made mistakes at first, but he was well ahead of public opinion in the building of ironclad ships. While congressmen ridiculed the idea, he went ahead and was ready with these ships when the battle between the *Monitor* and the *Merrimac* made them a national necessity.

Welles checked favoritism in building new navy yards. He opposed the blockade of the South at first, but when the tactic was adopted, he made it increasingly efficient. In all he created an adequate navy where there had been almost none.

As a member of the Cabinet, Welles was loyal both to Lincoln and his successor, Andrew Johnson. He was rather conservative even regarding slavery and opposed Radical Reconstruction and military rule of the South after the war. He disapproved of the suppression of newspapers, the suspension of the writ of habeas corpus, and the too rapid granting of Negro suffrage.

Most important of all, Welles kept a diary. Always tolerant and fair-minded, with a keen ability to understand men and their basic worth, he made a record which is an invaluable historical document. He was on the inside of events, and from his early newspaper days he had acquired an uncanny ability to pass judgment on men and events. He recognized Lincoln as "in every way large—brain included."

Further Reading

Welles's *Diary,* edited by Howard K. Beale (3 vols., 1960), offers considerable insights into his life. A full-length work is Richard S. West, Jr., *Gideon Welles: Lincoln's Navy Department* (1943).

Additional Sources

Niven, John, *Gideon Welles: Lincoln's Secretary of the Navy,* Baton Rouge: Louisiana State University Press, 1994. □

Orson Welles

Orson Welles (1915-1985) was a Broadway and Hollywood actor, radio actor, and film director. His earliest film production, *Citizen Kane,* was his most famous, although most of his other productions were notable.

Orson Welles was born George Orson Welles in Kenosha, Wisconsin, on May 6, 1915, the second son of Richard Welles, an inventor, and Beatrice Ives, a concert pianist. The name George was soon dropped. The family moved to Chicago when Welles was four; two years later his parents separated formally. The comfortable circumstances in which Welles was born gradually diminished. An important early influence on his life was Maurice Bernstein, an orthopedist and passionate admirer of his mother until her death in 1926. That year he was enrolled in the progressive Todd School (Woodstock, Illinois). His formal education ended with graduation in 1931.

After a sojourn to Ireland, where he was involved in the theater as an actor, Welles returned to Chicago where he briefly served as a drama coach at the Todd School and coedited four volumes of Shakespeare's plays. He made his Broadway debut with Katharine Cornell's company in December 1934. He and John Houseman joined forces the next year to manage a unit of the Federal Theatre Project, one of the work-relief arts projects established by the New Deal. Welles' direction was inspired, injecting new life into various classics, including an all-African American *Macbeth,* the French farce *The Italian Straw Hat,* and the Elizabethan morality play *Dr. Faustus.*

Welles and Houseman broke with the Federal Theatre Project over its attempt to censor their June 1937 production of Marc Blitzstein's pro-labor *The Cradle Will Rock.* They organized the Mercury Theatre, which over the next two seasons had a number of extraordinary successes, including a modern dress anti-Fascist *Julius Caesar* (with Welles playing Brutus), an Elizabethan working-class comedy *Shoemaker's Holiday* (re-written by Welles), and Shaw's *Heartbreak House* (with the 24-year-old Welles convincingly playing an octogenerian). Welles also found time to play "The Shadow" on radio and to supervise a "Mercury Theatre on the Air," whose most notorious success was an adaptation of H. G. Wells' *War of the Worlds,* which resulted in panic as many listeners believed that Martians were invading New Jersey.

In 1939 the Mercury Theatre collapsed as a result of economic problems; Welles went to Hollywood to find the cash to resurrect it. Except for a stirring dramatization of Richard Wright's *Native Son* in 1940, an unhappy attempt to stage Jules Verne's *Around the World in 80 Days* (music and lyrics by Cole Porter) in 1946, and an unsatisfactory *King Lear* in 1956, his Broadway career was over. He did continue theater activity overseas: during the 1950s he successfully staged *Moby Dick* in England, directed Laurence Olivier in the London production of Ionesco's *Rhinoceros,* and wrote a script for a Roland Petit ballet.

Following an early flirtation with movies and after casting around some months for a subject, Welles filmed *Citizen Kane* in 1939-1940. Since its release in 1941 this film has generally been awarded accolades and in recent years has been acclaimed as one of the best movies of all time. It is a fascinating study of a newspaper publisher (obviously modeled on William Randolph Hearst, despite Welles' disclaimers). Controversy surrounds the production of this film, which Welles is credited with producing, directing, and co-scripting. He also played the leading role. However one views the making of this film, there is no doubt about his role as catalyst.

Years later Welles declared "I began at the top and have been making my way down ever since." All the films he directed are of interest, but none matched his initial achievement. Among his other films are *The Magnificent Ambersons* (1942), *The Lady From Shanghai* (1946), *Othello* (1952), *Touch of Evil* (1958), *The Trial* (1962), and *F Is for Fake* (1973). Most of these films have been marked by disputes; Welles often disowned the final version. His critics argue that a self-destructive tendency caused these problems and cite his experiences with the unfinished *It's All True,* which he embarked on in Brazil in 1942 before finishing the final editing of *The Magnificent Ambersons.* But his partisans called it a destroyed masterpiece (in his absence 131 minutes were edited down to a final release print of 88 minutes).

A somewhat hammy actor with a magnificent voice, Welles appeared in over 45 films besides his own. In some of these films, such as *The Third Man* (1949) and *Compulsion* (1959), he was superb. But all too many were junk movies such as *Black Magic* (1949) and *The Tarters* (1960); he accepted these so that he might earn the funds necessary to finance films of his own such as *Chimes at Midnight* (released in 1966, an exciting film based on various Shakespeare plays and dealing with Falstaff).

For various reasons Welles left the United States after World War II and for three decades lived a kind of gypsy existence abroad, with occasional visits back to America for movie assignments or other work. An intelligent, multifaceted individual, Welles during World War II had put in a stint as a columnist at the liberal *New York Post* and later gave some thought to a political career. During the latter part of his life, despite being dogged by ill health, he earned a comfortable living doing television commercials for companies such as Paul Masson wines, putting much of what he earned into the production of various films, including *The Other Side of the Wind* (which dealt with an old film-maker and which was unfinished at the time of his death as well as being involved in litigation). A superb raconteur, Welles—after moving back to the United States in the mid-1970s—was much in demand as a guest on television talk shows.

Welles was found dead in early October 1985 in his Los Angeles home. Married three times, he had children with each wife: Virginia Nicolson (Christopher), Rita Hayworth (Rebecca), and his widow Paola Mori (Beatrice). He had many friends in his lifetime, including Oja Kodar, a Yugoslav artist who was his companion and assistant from the mid-1960s onward. Welles shared an Academy Award for the script of *Citizen Kane* and in 1975 was honored by the American Film Institute with a Life-Achievement Award. Welles' other awards include a 1958 Peabody Award for a TV pilot.

Further Reading

See biographies by Charles Higham (1985), Barbara Leaming (1985), and John Russell Taylor (1986). See also Roger Carringer, *The Making of Citizen Kane* (1985) and Pauline Kael, *The Citizen Kane Book* (1973). □

Sumner Welles

Sumner Welles (1892-1961) was an American diplomat who helped create the good-neighbor policy with Latin America during the 1930s.

Sumner Welles was born in New York City on Oct. 14, 1892. He was educated at Groton School and graduated from Harvard in 1914. Entering the diplomatic service in 1915, he served as chargé d'affaires in Japan. In 1921 he was placed in charge of Latin American affairs in the U.S. State Department. During his short term he undertook a special mission for the department in the Dominican Republic, assisting in the reorganization of Dominican finances. From this assignment came his most important literary work, *Naboth's Vineyard,* still the best history of the area.

In 1933 Welles was appointed undersecretary of state in Franklin Roosevelt's administration, an appointment made easier by his earlier association with Roosevelt. His service in this post for more than a decade was the most distinguished part of his career.

Welles was one of the architects of the good-neighbor policy aimed at a better understanding between the United States and Latin America. During one of his earlier assignments as ambassador to Cuba (troubled by revolution in 1932-1933), he seemed to toy with the idea of intervention, and he did play a part in removing the radical Grau San Martín regime from office. But as his career developed, he came more and more to advocate nonintervention. He attended the series of Latin American conferences that distinguished the Roosevelt administration—the conferences at Buenos Aires in 1933 and in 1936, at Lima in 1938, at Havana in 1940, and at Rio de Janeiro in 1942. In 1940 he also made a special trip to Europe by order of the President to assess the war situation and to talk with European leaders. Nothing came of this mission.

Welles was a highly competent diplomat, but he did not always get along well with Roosevelt's secretary of state, Cordell Hull, and his personal intimacy with the President was irksome to Hull. A serious dispute arose in the Rio conference of 1942 as to the form by which the nations of Latin America would declare their solidarity with the United States. Hull and Welles both appealed to Roosevelt, and Roosevelt sustained Welles's idea. The rift between Welles and Hull widened, and in the fall of 1943 Welles resigned.

During the last 18 years of his life, Welles wrote several books: *A Time for Decision* (1946), *Where Are We Heading* (1948), *Seven Decisions* (1951). He also edited, with Donald McKay of Harvard, an important series of volumes on the relations of the United States with Latin America. He died on Sept. 24, 1961, in Bernardsville, N.J.

Even before he arrived in India as governor general in April 1798, Wellesley had developed a plan to fight renewed French interest in India. He pursued the expansion of British power by annexation and subsidiary alliances with native princes, often against the orders of the East India Company.

Mysore, a dynamic South Indian state ably ruled by Tipu Sultan, posed an immediate challenge, as Tipu was known to be corresponding with Napoleon I. As a preliminary to a direct attack upon Mysore, Wellesley contracted his first "subsidiary alliance" with the nizam of the powerful state of Hyderabad. By this treaty the French mercenaries training the troops of Hyderabad were replaced by British. The nizam's armies joined in the three-month campaign against Mysore, ending when Tipu Sultan was killed and his forces defeated at Seringapatam. The settlement saw additions to the East India Company's territories in southern India and to the nizam's. The latter turned over his acquisitions to the company to pay the British soldiers in the nizam's armies.

Wellesley (newly created marquess) employed the subsidiary alliance, like that arranged with the nizam of Hyderabad, as the main means of extending British power. Treaties with Tanjore (1799), Surat (1800), the Carnatic (1801), and Oudh (1801) would all be criticized in England, but none as much as the Treaty of Bassein (1802) with the fugitive peshwa of Poona, titular head of the powerful Maratha Confederacy. This treaty directly provoked a Maratha war which brought several British defeats before

Further Reading

A good account of Welles' career is Julius W. Pratt, *Cordell Hull,* in Samuel Flagg Bemis, ed., *American Secretaries of State and Their Diplomacy,* vols. 12 and 13 (1964).

Additional Sources

Graff, Frank Warren, *Strategy of involvement: a diplomatic biography of Sumner Welles,* New York: Garland, 1988. □

Richard Colley Wellesley

The British colonial administrator Richard Colley Wellesley, 1st Marquess Wellesley (1760-1842), served as governor general of India. He was one of the most vigorous expansionists to hold that office.

Richard Wellesley was born June 20, 1760, at Dangan Castle, Ireland, the eldest son of the 1st Earl of Mornington. He was educated at Eton and at Christ Church, Oxford. On his father's death in 1781, he inherited the title and seat in the Irish House of Lords. Three years later he entered the English House of Commons, and in 1786 he was made a lord of the Treasury. In 1793 William Pitt the Younger appointed him to the Board of Control, where he was initiated into the problems of British India.

final victory. Intense criticism of Wellesley's policy forced his resignation in 1805.

Between 1806 and 1808 repeated attempts were made to impeach Wellesley, but he was finally exonerated by Parliament. During 1809 he served as ambassador to Spain before becoming foreign secretary. He left office in February 1812 and thereafter was noted as a Catholic emancipationist and opponent of both the East India Company and the peace terms of 1814. In 1821 Wellesley became lord lieutenant of Ireland and achieved the suppression of Catholic and Protestant secret societies. Wellesley resigned in 1828, when his younger brother, the Duke of Wellington, formed a ministry committed to Protestant ascendancy. Wellesley resumed the same post in 1833 but resigned when the Grey ministry fell the following year. Wellesley died at Kingston House, Brompton, on Sept. 26, 1842, and was buried in the Eton College Chapel.

Further Reading

Montgomery Martin edited *Despatches, Minutes, and Correspondence of the Marquess Wellesley* (5 vols., 1836-1837). Books on Wellesley's life include W. McCullagh Torrens, *The Marquis Wellesley* (1880); G. B. Malleson, *Life of the Marquess Wellesley* (1889); and W. H. Hutton, *Marquess Wellesley* (1893). The best study of Wellesley's administration is P. E. Roberts, *India under Wellesley* (1929). Ainslie T. Embree, *Charles Grant and British Rule in India* (1962), clarifies Wellesley's relations with the East India Company.

Additional Sources

Malleson, G. B. (George Bruce), *Life of the Marquess Wellesley, K.G.,* Delhi: Daya Pub. House, 1985. □

1st Duke of Wellington

The British soldier and statesman Arthur Wellesley, 1st Duke of Wellington (1769-1852), was one of the pacifiers of British India, an important architect of the downfall of Napoleon I, and a major political figure.

The third son of the Earl of Mornington, Arthur Wellesley was born in Dublin, Ireland, on or about May 1, 1769. He was educated at Eton, in Brussels, and at Angers Military Academy. In 1787 he became a lieutenant of foot and aide-de-camp to the lord lieutenant of Ireland. From 1790 he was for five years a member of the Irish Parliament. In 1793, at the age of 24, he purchased a lieutenant colonelcy in the 33d Foot, whose colonel he became in 1806. In 1794 Wellesley participated in the Netherlands campaign, during which he was so struck by the inefficiency of British officers that the next year he began the serious study of warfare.

From 1797 to 1804 Wellesley was the commanding officer of the 33d Foot in India, where from 1797 to 1805 his brother Richard, Marquess Wellesley, was governor general. In India, Wellesley came into his own as a soldier,

aiding in the capture of Mysore in 1799 and leading the two campaigns in 1799-1802 that crushed Dhundia Wagh, the robber chieftain. In 1802 Wellesley was promoted to major general, and from 1803 to 1805 he was chief administrator as well as military commander of the Deccan, where on Sept. 23, 1803, at Assaye he defeated the vaunted Marathas. Wellesley resigned when his brother was recalled in 1805.

The next year Wellesley became commander of a brigade at Hastings and was elected a member of Parliament. He married Kitty Pakenham on April 10, 1806, but she was never his equal and eventually became almost a recluse. In 1807 he moved to Ireland as chief secretary for 2 years; but in the same year he was sent on an expedition against the Danes. In 1808 he was posted to Portugal, beginning what was to be his major campaign.

Portugal and Spain

Wellesley had conceived the idea of thwarting Napoleon on the Iberian Peninsula, and in 1808 he led an expedition to assist the Portuguese in their revolt against the French. He defeated the French at Rolica and Vimeiro, but Sir Harry Burrard prevented his pursuit of the routed French. Both Wellesley and Burrard returned to England to stand courts-martial, but both were acquitted. In 1809 Wellesley resumed command in Portugal. He captured Oporto, advanced into Spain on the strength of Spanish promises of support, won at Talavera, and then retreated when the Spanish promises fell flat to carefully prepared lines at Torres Vedras. He did not reach Torres Vedras, however, until after he had been created Viscount Wellington and had bloodied André Massena's nose at Bussaco. The French commander made no progress at Torres Vedras in spite of the fact that Wellington was ill-supported from England both in the quality of his officers and in the number of reinforcements.

In 1811 Massena pulled back and Wellington pursued, but he soon found himself facing larger forces. In 1812 he incurred heavy casualties storming Ciudad Rodrigo and in the capture of Badajoz; he entered Madrid on August 12. His efforts to take Burgos were bloodily repulsed, and he then beat a hasty retreat to Ciudad Rodrigo. He was created Marquess of Wellington.

Late in May 1813, after mending political fences in Spain and Portugal, Wellington began his final advance into France, beating Joseph Bonaparte at Vitoria and crossing into France over the Pyrenees. After much hard fighting, he penned the French into Bayonne and defeated them at Orthez. Following this victory he went to Paris to negotiate a peace. On entering France he had been created field marshal, to which title was now added Duke of Wellington.

Waterloo and After

Wellington remained as ambassador in Paris only through late 1814, for he then joined other European leaders at the Congress of Vienna. He was participating in these negotiations when Napoleon returned from Elba. Wellington was at once sent to command the Allied armies in the Netherlands, where he cooperated with the Prussian general Gebhard von Blücher. Wellington was surprised by

Marshal Ney at Quatre Bras and fell back on Waterloo, where on June 18 he held on until Blücher could fulfill his promise to come to his aid after the Prussian defeat at Ligny. Together they routed the French. At the age of 46 Wellington had fought one of the most decisive battles in history and won. After advancing on Paris, effecting Napoleon's abdication, and restraining Blücher from taking reprisals or territory, Wellington was variously engaged in France until the Allied army of occupation was withdrawn in 1818.

As a general, Wellington was respected by his troops, who admired his sangfroid and his imperturbability under fire. "Nosey" was a known battlefield figure who had the loyalty of his varied forces, and he carried this over into his later career as a political leader. His successes were due to his study of war, to careful planning including that of supply, and to his realism, which led him to rely heavily on his British infantry and to choose so often defensive positions in which he had to be attacked, usually uphill, because he flanked the enemy's line of advance.

Man on Horseback

In the years after his great victory, Wellington reverted more and more to the aristocratic mold from which he had been cast. Not only was he an 18th-century nobleman, but also he was a man whose career had been spent leading officers and men not noted for their intellectual brilliance. Thus he was used to speaking bluntly and to the point. At the same time he was accustomed to giving orders and to being obeyed. That was his public image. Yet privately he displayed a great sense of humor and was much beloved by the ladies.

In the second half of his life, Wellington had to spend a good deal of time dealing with politics and civilians, for neither of which he had much tolerance. Yet these were the difficult times of the Peterloo Massacre, the Great Reform Bill, the Chartists, and the repeal of the Corn Laws. Moreover, in these years he was exposed to examination by journalists and liberals who became unsympathetic to his outlook and actions since he was no longer leading victorious armies in popular wars. Yet he had emerged from the Napoleonic Wars as the one great man in England, the man on horseback.

Political Leader and Prime Minister

On his return from France, Wellington divided his time between occasional attendance at international peace conferences and military and political appointments at home. From 1818 to 1827 he was master general of the ordnance with a seat in the Cabinet. In 1827 he became commander in chief. George Canning asked him to join the government when he succeeded Lord Liverpool, but Wellington professed himself happy as commander in chief. Moreover, he was staunchly Tory and Irish anti Catholic, while Canning leaned the other way. The upshot, when coupled to personal dislike, was that Wellington resigned both as master general of the ordnance and as commander in chief, and for the first time since he had joined the army in 1787 he was unemployed. Canning died within three months, and by September 1827 the duke was back as commander in chief.

But when Goderich's caretaker government faded early in 1828, the King sent for Wellington and asked him, as leader of the Tories, to form a new government. So at the age of 58, with doubts about the rising tide for Catholic emancipation, Wellington became prime minister. Suddenly he was back in public favor as he had not been since Waterloo.

Once in office, the duke, resigning again as commander in chief, discovered that he had to move to unite the Tories, especially after the Canningites left him. He therefore favored Catholic emancipation in an attempt both to unite his Party and to provide a sound government for Ireland. In this he was successful. The government survived until late 1830, when a combination of factors caused by the accession of William IV and the Revolution of 1830 in France made Wellington's position weak, even without his announced opposition to reform. The government resigned. The Tories were out of office for the first time in decades. Wellington refused to lead the opposition for he had been a royal servant too long.

Later Years

Unpopular for a while, Wellington beat a gradual retreat on reform in the House of Lords and was willing in 1832 to be prime minister again if the King desired, but he could not form a Cabinet. He then withdrew his opposition to the Reform Bill to prevent the Whigs from packing the House of Lords. When the Whigs went out of office in 1834, the duke acted as prime minister and all three secretaries of state until Sir Robert Peel could return from Italy; then Wellington briefly retained the Foreign Office until the elections went against the Tories.

Nevertheless, Wellington's personal popularity was high once again, and he decided that the country would survive reform. In 1841 Peel formed a new government with Wellington as leader of the House of Lords. The next year the incumbent commander in chief died, and the "Iron Duke" resumed the post that he held until his death a decade later. He constantly worried about national defense. During the Chartist troubles in 1848 he organized the defense of London. He died on Sept. 14, 1852.

Deaf in his last years, Wellington was the elder states man of Great Britain, honored and consulted by many. A gradualist and a realist, he was one of the best-informed persons in the kingdom, especially on foreign affairs. He carried on a voluminous correspondence, and he was always careful of his dignity and honor. Plain of speech, sometimes tart, he generally cut to the heart of the matter. At the same time, his distinctive features made him one of the few personalities well known to the people in the days before photography. His reputation was enhanced by the publication of his dispatches (1834-1880) and his parliamentary speeches (1854).

Further Reading

The most useful biography of Wellington is Elizabeth Longford, *Wellington: The Years of the Sword* (1969), which carries his career through 1815 and whose bibliography provides the best starting point for research on him; a second volume is under way. The older standard work is Philip Guedalla, *Wel-*

lington (1931). An excellent illustrated work on the duke is Victor Percival, *The Duke of Wellington: A Pictorial Survey of His Life* (1969), composed for the Victoria and Albert Museum. E. L. Woodward, *The Age of Reform, 1815-1870* (1938; 2d ed. 1962), provides an adequate introduction to the later period of Wellington's life. Dealing with Wellington and the army are Godfrey Davies, *Wellington and His Army* (1954); Jac Weller, *Wellington in the Peninsula, 1808-1814* (1963), narrating the 6-year war against Napoleon's forces in Spain, and *Wellington at Waterloo* (1967); and Albert Tucker's chapter in Robin Higham, ed., *A Guide to the Sources of British Military History* (1971).

Additional Sources

Barthorp, Michael, *Wellington's generals,* London: Osprey, 1978.

James, Lawrence, *The Iron Duke: a military biography of Wellington,* London: Weidenfeld and Nicolson, 1992.

Thompson, Neville., *Wellington after Waterloo,* London; New York: Routledge & Kegan Paul, 1986.

Wellington Commander: the iron duke's generalship, Boston: Faber and Faber, 1986. □

Herbert George Wells

The English author Herbert George Wells (1866-1946) began his career as a novelist with a popular sequence of science fiction that remains the most familiar part of his work. He later wrote realistic novels and novels of ideas.

On Sept. 21, 1866, H. G. Wells was born in Bromley, Kent. His origins were lower middle class, his father being a semiprofessional cricket player and his mother an intermittent housekeeper. At the age of 7 Wells entered Morley's School in Bromley, leaving at the age of 14, when he became apprenticed to a draper. He rebelled against this fate in 1883. After a year of teaching at a private school, he won a scholarship to the Normal School of Science at South Kensington in 1884, where he studied under the biologist T. H. Huxley. Wells left Kensington without a degree in 1887, returning to teaching in private schools for three years. He received a degree in science from the University of London in 1890.

Wells began teaching at a correspondence college in London in 1891 after his marriage to his cousin Isabel. The marriage was both difficult and brief. In the same year he published his article "The Rediscovery of the Unique" in the *Fortnightly Review*. After three years of writing on educational topics, he published his first novel, *The Time Machine*. Divorcing his first wife, Wells remarried in 1895 and abandoned teaching. A series of scientific fantasies followed *The Time Machine: The Island of Dr. Moreau* (1896), *The Invisible Man* (1897), *The War of the Worlds* (1898), *When the Sleeper Awakes* (1898), *The First Men in the Moon* (1901), and *The War in the Air* (1908). Wells's involvement with socialism and radicalism had begun in 1884 and continued for the remainder of his life.

Love and Mr. Lewisham (1900), Wells's first nonscience fiction novel, concerned the relationship of men and women and introduced sex as an integral part of that relationship. His semiautobiographical novels continued with *Kipps* (1905), *Tono-Bungay* (1909), and *The History of Mr. Polly* (1910). These novels are considered his greatest achievement.

As his novels indicate, Wells was hostile to the Victorian social and moral orders. His criticism became explicit as his involvement with radical causes grew. Wells as prophet wrote *Anticipations* (1901), *Mankind in the Making* (1903), and *A Modern Utopia* (1905). He joined the Fabian Society, a socialist group that included George Bernard Shaw and Sydney Webb, in 1903; after an unsuccessful attempt four years later to turn Fabianism to mass propaganda and political action, Wells resigned. *The New Machiavelli* (1911), a novel, was a response to his experience in the society. After *The New Machiavelli* he began producing dialogue novels that expressed his current preoccupations. His *Boon* (1915) parodied the late style of Henry James.

Wells became during World War I an expert publicist, particularly in *Mr. Britling Sees It Through*. Initially believing that the war would end all war, he wrote that "my awakening to the realities of the pseudo-settlement of 1919 was fairly rapid." His solution was what he identified as world education. The intention of *The Outline of History* (1920) was to "show plainly to the general intelligence, how inevitable, if civilization was to continue, was the growth of political, social, and economic organizations into world federation." After the *Outline*'s appearance, Wells led an increasingly public life, expressing his opinions through syndicated articles. *The Open Conspiracy: Blue Prints for a World Revolution* (1928) urged the case for an integrated global civilization.

Experiment in Autobiography (1934) was "an enormous reel of self-justification." Wells continued to average two titles a year. *Apropos of Delores* (1938) was a hilarious tribute to a former mistress. *Mind at the End of Its Tether* (1945), his last book, was a vision of the future as nightmare. He died on Aug. 13, 1946, in London.

Further Reading

One of the first critical biographies of Wells was Van Wyck Brooks, *The World of H. G. Wells* (1915). Other full-scale reviews are R. Thurston Hopkins, *H. G. Wells* (1922); Ivor Brown, *H. G. Wells* (1923); Norman Nicholson, *H. G. Wells* (1950); and Richard Hauer Costa's scholarly study of Wells as a literary figure, *H. G. Wells* (1967). Wells's political and philosophical beliefs provoked a large commentary. He is discussed in Edwin E. Slosson, *Six Major Prophets* (1917); his educational theories are reviewed in F. H. Doughty, *H. G. Wells: Educationist* (1926); and his politics in G. D. H. Cole, *British Working Class Politics: 1832-1914* (1941). George Bernard Shaw considers him in *Pen Portraits and Reviews* (1932). Other useful studies are in G. K. Chesterton, *Autobiography* (1936), and George Orwell, *Critical Essays* (1946). □

Horace Wells

The American dentist Horace Wells (1815-1848) was the first practitioner to publicly advocate the use of nitrous oxide as an anesthetic and one of the first to use an anesthetic.

Horace Wells was born in Hartford, Vt., on Jan. 21, 1815. He attended schools in Hopkinton and Walpole, N. H., and Amherst, Mass. There were no dental schools, and his education in dentistry was gained through study with several practicing dentists.

Wells was probably a traveling dentist before settling in Hartford, Conn., in 1836, where he developed a large practice. In 1838 he published *An Essay on Teeth, Comprising a Brief Description of Their Formation, Disease, and Proper Treatment.*

Wells was actively interested in finding some method of reducing the pain of dental procedures. Nitrous oxide had been discovered in the 18th century, but its potential value as an anesthetic was, for the most part, overlooked. Instead, nitrous oxide was valued because it produced a state of euphoria, and "laughing gas" parties were common in the 19th century. On Dec. 10, 1844, Wells attended one of these parties and witnessed a man under the influence of the gas injure himself and yet feel no pain. The following day Wells had a tooth pulled after inhaling the gas and felt no pain. After several experiments he arranged to demonstrate his discovery before a group of medical students and physicians in Boston, but the demonstration was not completely successful because an insufficient amount of nitrous oxide was administered. Although rebuffed by those in attendance because of this failure, Wells returned to Hartford and continued his use of the gas.

In 1846 William Morton used ether as an anesthetic and claimed credit as the discoverer of anesthesia. In 1846 Wells went to Europe to make his work known there and in 1847 presented his claim as the discoverer of anesthesia to several French scientific societies. His claim was generally acknowledged in France, and in later years it was also recognized in the United States. In 1847 Wells returned to the United States and published his claim in *A History of the Discovery of the Application of Nitrous Oxide Gas, Ether, and Other Vapors to Surgical Operations.*

Wells continued his study of anesthesia and was led to experiment with chloroform. These experiments brought on a state of mental derangement that resulted in a hostile act for which Wells was arrested. He committed suicide on Jan. 23, 1848.

Further Reading

Considerable information on Wells is in W. Harry Archer, *Life and Letters of Horace Wells* (1944), but there is no full biography of him. A centenary celebration of Wells's discovery was held in 1944, and the proceedings were edited by William J. Gies and published as American Dental Association, Horace Wells Centenary Committee, *Horace Wells, Dentist: Father of Surgical Anesthesia* (1948). □

Mary Georgene Berg Wells

Advertising Woman of the Year in 1971, Mary Georgene Berg Wells (born 1928) was an advertising executive who rose from a department store copywriter to the chief executive officer of one of the largest advertising firms in the world.

Born Mary Georgene Berg on May 25, 1928, she was the only child of Waldemar, a furniture-maker, and Violet in Youngstown, Ohio. When Mary was five years old, her mother enrolled her in elocution classes to help the child overcome shyness. Subsequently, she took music, drama, and dance lessons and participated in amateur and semiprofessional theater productions. Upon finishing high school, Mary moved to New York City to enroll in the Neighborhood School of the Theater. After one year she left to pursue a career in merchandising at the Carnegie Institute of Technology in Pittsburgh, where she met and married Burt Wells, an industrial design student. The couple moved back to Youngstown where she worked as an advertising writer for Mckelvey's department store bargain basement.

When she and her husband settled in New York City in 1952, Wells was promptly hired by Macy's as a copywriter. There she learned to write convincing copy that was well received by customers. At 23 years of age, she was promoted to the position of fashion advertising manager for Macy's. Then she was approached by several Madison Avenue advertising agencies that were impressed with her effective advertisements.

Her introduction to Madison Avenue, the heart of the advertising industry, came with a job offer from McCann-Erickson. There she learned to create ads using a variety of media, including television, radio, magazines, newspapers, and billboards, for many different businesses. But it was not until she accepted a job with Doyle, Dane, Bernbach that Wells was truly challenged. DDB was one of the most innovative agencies at that time; it took a low-key approach to advertising and had created humorous and successful campaigns for Avis Rent-A-Car and Volkswagen, among others. The climate at DDB was most stimulating, and she garnered respect as a creative, insightful writer, advancing her career by designing original campaigns. By 1963 Wells was vice-president and copy chief with an annual salary of $40,000. Over the years her elocution lessons paid off, and she became a dynamic speaker and communicator. These skills were further honed and perfected during her employment with DDB.

Feeling the need for more independence, Wells elected to move to Jack Tinker and Partners. This agency encouraged employees to participate in a cooperative, freethinking, and loosely-organized setting. At a salary of $60,000, Wells was given virtually free rein. For her first account, she was teamed up with Richard Rich and Stuart Greene to handle Alka-Seltzer. The campaign produced wryly humorous commercials that won several industry awards. She then landed the Braniff International Airline account. Harding Lawrence, the president of Braniff, wanted the agency to create a new image for the airline, one which would result in increased revenues. Wells, Rich, and Greene created an avant-garde campaign that was an overwhelming success. The slogan, "The End of the Plain Plane," was substantiated by painting each of the planes one of several bright colors. In addition, Emilio Pucci was hired to design new uniforms for the flight attendants, and Alexander Girard was commissioned to restyle the airplane interiors. Despite being dubbed "the Easter-egg airline" by industry critics, sales increased 41 percent and profits rose 114 percent.

Wells' career also took off. By 1966 she was making almost $80,000 a year, but when Jack Tinker and Partners requested that she sign a long-term contract she opted to leave the company. Rich and Greene resigned at the same time. Ultimately, the three colleagues decided to start their own agency. With an investment of $30,000 each and a $100,000 bank loan, they created Wells, Rich and Greene, Incorporated. They were immediately flooded with calls both from potential employees and from clients eager to sign a contract. Their first client was Braniff, a $6.5 million account. WRG proved their ability and gained momentum without ever soliciting business. Within six months they had billings of $30 million, landing such accounts as Benson and Hedges cigarettes and Personna razor blades.

After the first year they signed Hunt-Wesson Foods, General Mills, and American Motors and had reached annual billings of $70 million. Wells soon advanced up the corporate ladder, assuming the roles of chairman of the board, chief executive officer, chief administrator, and chief "presenter." In 1965 she divorced her first husband and married Harding Lawrence of Braniff in 1967. WRG resigned the Braniff account, whose parent company feared a conflict of interest. To replace it, WRG signed on the TWA account, which had an advertising budget of $22 million.

WRG's dynamic growth can be directly credited to Wells. She was considered the best conceptualizer in the advertising industry, and in 1971 she was honored as Advertising Woman of the Year by the American Advertising Federation. She was also awarded the Clio Award for TV spots with recurring taglines, "I can't believe I ate the whole thing" and "Try it— you'll like it." The philosophy of WRG was "to create tasteful, respectful, attention-getting advertising capable of increasing sales and market share promptly." By staying with this credo, WRG grew to be one of the top advertising agencies in the United States.

Wells' skills as a creator and planner of advertising were matched by her executive abilities. She was a hard-driving, ambitious, and particularly demanding boss. Wells' astute financial sense benefited both the company and Wells personally. The company's billing increased from $36.7 million in 1967 to $767 million in 1988. During that same time, Wells' salary increased to over $300,000, and she was one of the best-paid women executives in the world. In 1968 WRG went public, at which time Wells took out $1,208,000 in cash and retained shares valued at more than $4 million. When she returned the company to private ownership in 1974, through a bonds-for-stock exchange, she again profited handsomely.

Wells' impact on the advertising industry was enormous. Her awards included Marketing Stateswoman of the Year, the Clio Award, and Advertising Woman of the Year. She was inducted into the Copywriter's Hall Fame as its youngest member in 1969. In the 1980s Wells continued to hold the position of WRG chief executive officer, although she was less involved in the day-to-day operations of the company. In 1990 she announced her retirement as president of WRG at the age of 62. The advertising giant she created reported annual billings of $850,348,000 with a staff of more than 300 employees in 1995.

Further Reading

The most comprehensive account of Mary Wells' career appears in *Possible Dream* by Marthe Gross (1970). A shorter account appears in *Enterprising Women* (1976) by Caroline Bird. There is also a full biography in Ingham, editor, *Biographical Dictionary of American Business Leaders* (1978). She is also included in standard reference works such as *Biography Almanac,* 3rd edition, *Who's Who in Business and Finance* (1974), and *Who's Who in the East* (1974). There are a number of good magazine articles on Mary Wells and her agency. Among the best are: *Journal of Marketing* (January 1972), *Vogue* (February 1978), *Fortune* (August 1966), and *Newsweek* (October 3, 1966). Later information on Mary Wells and her agency appears in *Advertising Age* (August 1, 1988) and *Business Week* (October 3, 1988). Stewart Fox, *The Mirror Makers* (1985), provides information on Wells and other advertising industry figures. After retirement in 1990 Wells was reported to not accept interviews. □

Ida. B. Wells-Barnett

Ida B. Wells-Barnett (1862-1931), an African American journalist, was an active crusader against lynching and a champion of social and political justice for African Americans.

Ida B. Wells was born a slave in Holly Springs, Mississippi, on July 16, 1862, six months before the Emancipation Proclamation freed all of the slaves in the Confederate states. Her father, James, was a carpenter and her mother, Elizabeth, a cook. James Wells was a hardworking, opinionated man who was actively interested in politics and in helping to provide educational opportunities for the liberated slaves and for his own eight children. He was on the board of trustees of Rust College, a freedmen's school, where his daughter Ida received a basic education. Elizabeth Wells supervised her children's religious training by escorting them to church services and by insisting that the only book that they could read on Sunday was the Bible. Young Wells was an avid reader and stated that as a result of this rule she had read through the Bible many times.

Tragedy struck the Wells family when she was about 16 years old. Her parents and some of her brothers and sisters died in a yellow fever epidemic while Wells was in another town visiting relatives. With a small legacy left by her parents, she was determined to assume the role of mothering her younger brothers and sisters. By arranging her hair in an adult style and donning a long dress, Wells was able to obtain a teaching position by convincing local school officials that she was 18 years old. A few years later, after placing the older children as apprentices, she moved to Memphis with some of the younger children to live with a relative. She was eventually able to earn a teaching position there by obtaining further education at Fisk University.

In 1884, while she was travelling by train from school, Wells was forcibly thrown out of a first-class car by the conductor because she refused to ride in the car set aside for African Americans which was nicknamed the "Jim Crow" car. She had purchased a first-class ticket and was determined not to move from her seat, but she was not able to defend herself against the conductor, who literally dragged her from her seat while some of the white passengers applauded. However, Wells, who was determined to fight for justice, sued the railroad and won her case. When the decision was later overturned by the Tennessee Supreme Court, Wells just became more determined to fight against racial injustice wherever she found it.

When Wells joined a literary society in Memphis, she discovered that one of their primary activities was to write essays on various subjects and read them before the members. Wells' essays on social conditions for African Americans were so well received that the society members began to encourage her to write for church publications. When she was offered a regular reporting position and part ownership of the *Memphis Free Speech and Headlight* in 1887 she eagerly accepted. The name of the newspaper was later

shortened to the *Free Press,* and Wells eventually became its sole owner. She was not afraid to speak out against what she perceived to be injustices against African Americans, especially in the school system where she worked. She believed that the facilities and supplies available to African American children were always inferior to those offered to whites. As a consequence of her editorials about the schools, Wells lost her teaching position in 1891.

One year later, in 1892, three of Wells' friends, who were successful businessmen in Memphis, were killed and their businesses destroyed by whites who Wells accused of being jealous of their success. The *Free Speech* ran a scathing editorial about the murders in which Wells harshly rebuked the white community. It was probably not coincidental that she was out of town by the time local whites read her paper. An angry mob of whites broke into her newspaper office, broke up her presses, and vowed to kill her if she returned to Tennessee.

Wells became a journalist "in exile," writing under the pen name "Iola" for the *New York Age* and other weekly newspapers serving the African American population. She systematically attacked lynching and other violent crimes perpetrated against African Americans. She went on speaking tours in the northeastern states and England to encourage people to speak out against lynching. She wrote well-documented pamphlets with titles such as *On Lynchings, Southern Horrors, A Red Record,* and *Mob Rule in New Orleans.*

In 1895 Wells moved to Chicago, where she married a widower named Frederick Barnett. She remained active after she was married and carried nursing children with her during her crusades. She and her husband owned a newspaper for a while, and she continued to write articles for other journals. She actively participated in efforts to gain the vote for women and simultaneously campaigned against racial bigotry within the women's movement. In 1909 she attended the organizational meeting of the National Association for the Advancement of Colored People (NAACP) and continued to work with the organization's founders during its formative years, although her association with the organization was not always peaceful. Wells-Barnett did agree with one of the major thrusts of the organization, however, and that was their desire to see the enactment of federal anti-lynching legislation. She found a settlement house in Chicago for young African American men and women, regularly taught a Bible class at the house, and also worked as a probation officer there. After her death in 1931 her contributions to the city of Chicago were acknowledged when a public housing project was named after her.

Further Reading

Wells-Barnett's autobiography, which was edited by her daughter, Alfreda M. Duster, is entitled *Crusader for Justice: The Autobiography of Ida B. Wells* (1970). Several of Wells-Barnett's pamphlets have been reprinted by Arno Press in *On Lynchings: Southern Horrors* (1969). There is a short biography of Wells-Barnett in *Mississippi Black History Makers* (1984) by George A. Sewell and Margaret L. Dwight. An article entitled "The Lonely Warrior: Ida B. Wells-Barnett," by Thomas Holt is a part of a volume edited by John Hope Franklin and August Meier, *Black Leaders of the Twentieth Century* (1982). □

Eudora Welty

Eudora Welty (born 1909) is considered one of the most important authors of the twentieth century. Although the majority of her stories are set in the American South and reflect the region's language and culture, critics agree that Welty's treatment of universal themes and her wide-ranging artistic influences clearly transcend regional boundaries.

Born in Jackson, Mississippi at a time when that city had not yet lost its rural atmosphere, Welty grew up in the bucolic South she so often evokes in her stories. She attended the Mississippi State College for Women and the University of Wisconsin, where she majored in English Literature, then studied advertising at Columbia University; however, graduating at the height of the Great Depression, she was unable to find work in her chosen field. Returning to Jackson in 1931, Welty worked as a part-time journalist and copywriter and as a WPA photographer. The latter job took her on assignments throughout Mississippi, and she began using these experiences as material for short stories. In June, 1936, her story "Death of a Traveling Salesman" was accepted for publication in the journal *Manuscript,* and within two years her work had appeared in such prestigious publications as the *Atlantic* and the *Southern Review.* Critical response to Welty's first collection of stories, *A Curtain of Green* (1941), was highly favorable, with many commentators predicting that a first performance so impressive would no doubt lead to even greater achievements. Yet when *The Wide Net, and Other Stories* was published two years later, several critics, most notably Diana Trilling, deplored Welty's marked shift away from the colorful realism of her earlier stories toward a more impressionistic style, objecting in particular to her increased use of symbol and metaphor to convey themes. Other critics responded favorably, including Robert Penn Warren, who wrote that in Welty's work, "the items of fiction (scene, action, character, etc.) are presented not as document but as comment, not as a report but as a thing made, not as history but as idea."

As Welty continued to refine her vision her fictional techniques gained wider acceptance. Indeed, her most complex and highly symbolic collection of stories, *The Golden Apples,* won critical acclaim, and she received a number of prizes and awards throughout the following decade, including the William Dean Howells Medal of the Academy of Arts and Letters for her novella *The Ponder Heart* (1954). Occupied primarily with teaching, traveling, and lecturing between 1955 and 1970, Welty produced little fiction. Then, in the early 1970s, she published two novels, *Losing Battles* (1970), which received mixed re-

views, and the more critically successful *The Optimist's Daughter* (1972), which won a Pulitzer Prize. Although Welty has published no new volumes of short stories since *The Bride of Innisfallen* in 1955, the release of her *Collected Stories* in 1980 renewed interest in her short fiction and brought unanimous praise. In addition, the 1984 publication of Welty's *One Writer's Beginnings,* an autobiographical work chronicling her own artistic development, further illuminated her work and inspired critics to reinterpret many of her stories.

In his seminal 1944 essay on *The Wide Net, and Other Stories,* Robert Penn Warren located the essence of Welty's fictional technique in a phrase from her story "First Love": "Whatever happened, it happened in extraordinary times, in a season of dreams." It is, states Warren, "as though the author cannot be quite sure what did happen, cannot quite undertake to resolve the meaning of the recorded event, cannot, in fact, be too sure of recording all of the event." This tentative approach to narrative exposition points to Welty's primary goal in creating fiction, which is not simply to relate a series of events, but to convey a strong sense of her character's experience of that specific moment in time, always acknowledging the ambiguous nature of reality. In order to do so, she selects those details which can best vivify the narrative, frequently using metaphors and similes to communicate sensory impressions. The resulting stories are highly impressionistic. Welty typically uses traditional symbols and mythical allusions in her work and, in the opinion of many, it is through linking the particular with the general and the mundane with the metaphysical that she attains her transcendent vision of human existence.

Welty's stories display a marked diversity in content, form, and mood. Many of her stories are light and humorous, while others deal with the tragic and the grotesque. Her humorous stories frequently rely upon the comic possibilities of language, as in both "Why I Live at the P.O." and *The Ponder Heart,* which exploit the humor in the speech patterns and colorful idiom of their southern narrators. In addition, Welty employs irony to comic effect, and many critics consider this aspect of her work one of its chief strengths. Opinions are divided, however, on the effectiveness of Welty's use of the grotesque. While Trilling and others find Welty's inclusion of such elements as the carnival exhibits in "Petrified Man" exploitative and superfluous, Eunice Glenn maintains that Welty created "scenes of horror" in order to "make everyday life appear as it often does, without the use of a magnifying glass, to the person with extraordinary acuteness of feeling."

Critics of Welty's work agree that these same literary techniques which produced her finest stories have also been the cause of her most outstanding failures, noting that she is at her best when objective observation and subjective revelation are kept in balance and that where the former is neglected, she is ineffective. They remark further, however, that such instances are comparatively rare in Welty's work. Many contemporary critics consider Welty's skillful use of language her single greatest achievement, citing in particular the poetic richness of her narratives and her acute sensitivity to the subtleties and peculiarities of human speech.

Yet the majority of commentators concur with Glenn's assertion that "it is her profound search of human consciousness and her illumination of the underlying causes of the compulsions and fears of modern man that would seem to comprise the principal value of Miss Welty's work."

While critics do not concur on all aspects of Welty's fiction, the preeminence of her work remains unquestioned. Despite some early resistance to her style, Welty has garnered much critical and popular respect for both her humorous colloquial stories and her more experimental works. Although she is known chiefly as a southern writer, the transcendent humanity conveyed in her stories places her beyond regional classification, and she is widely regarded as one of the foremost fiction writers in America.

Further Reading

Abadie, Ann J. and Louis D. Dollarhide, editors, *Eudora Welty: A Form of Thanks,* University Press of Mississippi, 1979.

Aevlin, Albert J., *Welty: A Life in Literature,* 1987.

Appel, Alfred, Jr., *A Season of Dreams: The Fiction of Eudora Welty,* Louisiana State University Press, 1965.

Balakian, Nona and Charles Simmons, editors, *The Creative Present,* Doubleday, 1963.

Bloom, Harold, editor, *Welty,* 1986.

Bryant, Joseph A., Jr., *Eudora Welty,* University of Minnesota Press, 1968.

Carson, Barbara Harrell, *Eudora Welty: Two Pictures at Once in Her Frame,* Whitston, 1992. □

Wenceslaus

Wenceslaus (1361-1419) was Holy Roman emperor from 1376 to 1400 and as Wenceslaus IV was king of Bohemia from 1378 to 1419.

Wenceslaus, son of the emperor Charles IV, succeeded his father as emperor-elect in 1376 but was deposed on the grounds of his alleged "worthlessness" by German opponents in 1400. As emperor, Wenceslaus was faced with the problems raised in the Church by the Great Schism and with those raised in the empire by the rivalry of political factions, which, unlike his father, he proved unable to control. In Bohemia, Wenceslaus's reign was marked by increasing aristocratic and ecclesiastical opposition to the growing power of the royal house of Luxemburg, to Wenceslaus's attempts to strengthen the power of the Crown, and to the early force of Czech nationalism.

Wenceslaus grew up and was educated during the years of his father's greatest prestige and effectiveness. Charles IV had devoted great energy to Bohemia, and his political and artistic influence was particularly strong in Prague and in the great castle of Karlstein, from which he governed both Bohemia and the empire. The flowering of Bohemian art and education that took place during Charles's reign coincided with the first stirrings of Czech national feeling, which the Emperor supported. Wenceslaus

was a product of his father's cosmopolitan interests. He possessed considerable native intelligence and absorbed effectively the education his father provided for him. He appears to have been a talented diplomat in his early years, and he gave every sign of following in his father's footsteps. Wenceslaus, however, early evinced passions for hunting and drinking that later contributed to serious failures in his reign.

As king of the Romans (the title possessed by a ruler who has been elected as successor to the Holy Roman emperor but not yet crowned by the pope), Wenceslaus was faced with the problems caused by the Great Schism (1378-1415). A supporter of Pope Urban VI in Rome, Wenceslaus was opposed by those who supported Pope Clement VI in Avignon. Another cause of dissension lay in the dynastic rivalry between the house of Luxemburg on the one hand and the houses of Hapsburg and Wittelsbach on the other, dynasties that had once provided Holy Roman emperors and were eager to do so again. A third source of trouble for Wenceslaus was the political dissension in Germany. Charles IV had granted considerable privileges to the electors and to other aristocratic dynasties and to town leagues. The lesser nobility then attempted to claim the same privileges, and the result was political chaos. For the first 20 years of his reign, Wenceslaus managed to impose some degree of order upon his German subjects, but his resources were drained in military campaigns to support his brother (later Emperor Sigismund) in Hungary, and in disputes after 1394 with the Bohemian aristocracy. As long as he could use his Bohemian resources to maintain order in Germany,

Wenceslaus was successful. During the last decade of the 14th century, however, those resources were fully engaged in Bohemian affairs, and Wenceslaus encountered ferocious opposition from the electors and the nobility of Germany. That opposition culminated on Aug. 20, 1400, when a meeting of the electors declared Wenceslaus deposed on the grounds of incompetence, inability to restore peace, and failure to heal the schism.

As king of Bohemia, Wenceslaus encountered problems of a different kind. His insistence upon royal rights quickly precipitated a series of quarrels with the higher clergy of Bohemia, and his employment of the lower nobility and bourgeoisie alienated the higher nobility. In 1394 the first of a series of aristocratic revolts broke out, possibly related to the breakdown in the relations between Wenceslaus and John of Jenstein, Archbishop of Prague. The revolt was led by Wenceslaus's cousin Jobst of Moravia and purported simply to force the King to reform the government and dismiss his advisers. In fact, the revolt, like those that quickly followed in 1397, 1401, and 1403, was an attempt on the part of the aristocracy to defend its individual rights and privileges against the more broadly based government of the King. Between 1394 and 1403 Wenceslaus was at the mercy of the aristocracy; and after 1403 the broken royal government was faced with yet a third domestic crisis, the revolutionary movement of piety and Czech national feeling that centered on John Hus and opened Bohemia to several decades of religious and social revolution.

The 14th century had witnessed a great upsurge of devotional feeling in Bohemia, and such great vernacular preachers as Milic of Kremsier had stirred criticism of the Church and of an Old Testament fundamentalist attitude toward dogma. When John Hus became the leader of this movement in 1402, Wenceslaus was powerless to check its excesses. Torn between Czech Hussitism and the demands of the Church for orthodoxy, Wenceslaus extended protection to the ''heretics'' while conciliating the Church. The burning of Hus, ordered by the Council of Constance in 1415, however, touched off great resistance. In 1419 a mob of Hussites attacked several of Wenceslaus's officials in Prague and killed them. The King, encountering the same tensions in Bohemia that he had found in the empire, could do nothing. His political and temperamental weakness—and his career of increasing political frustration—came to an end when he died of an apoplectic seizure on Aug. 16, 1419.

Further Reading

There is no biography of Wenceslaus in English. The best accounts in English are in *The Cambridge Medieval History* (8 vols., 1911-1936); R. W. Seton-Watson, *A History of the Czechs and Slovaks* (1943); and Frederick G. Heymann, *John Zizka and the Hussite Revolution* (1955). □

Wen-hsiang

The Manchu official and statesman Wen-hsiang (1818-1876) was influential in China's change of policy toward the West in the 1860s and a leading figure in the Self-strengthening movement.

Wen-hsiang was born on Oct. 16, 1818, in Mukden into a Manchu family. Through the aid of his wealthy father-in-law, he purchased the rank of a student in the Imperial Academy in 1837. He passed the provincial examinations in Peking in 1840, and five years later he attained a *chin-shih* (the highest academic degree).

When the Taiping rebels advanced toward Peking in 1853, despite the ensuing panic, Wen-hsiang courageously remained at his post as a secretary in the Board of Works. His exemplary conduct brought him to the attention of his superiors, and he was rapidly promoted. By the end of 1855 he was chief supervisor of imperial instruction, a junior vice president of the Board of Ceremonies, and concurrently a grand councilor (one of the five officials who daily advised the Emperor as a sort of privy council).

Early Official Career

When Tientsin fell to the allied British and French forces in 1860, Wen-hsiang repeatedly urged the Hsienfeng emperor (reigned 1851-1862) to remain in Peking. However, as the enemy advanced on the capital, other counsels prevailed, and the Emperor fled to Jehol. Wen-hsiang insisted on remaining, however, and, along with Prince Kung (the Emperor's half brother) and Kuei-liang, was ordered to handle the peace negotiations and to maintain order in the city. The allies occupied Peking on Oct. 13, 1860, and on October 24 the Treaty of Tientsin of 1858 was ratified and the supplementary Convention of Peking was signed. The foreign troops withdrew on November 5 and not long after left China.

The events of 1860 brought home to Wen-hsiang and Prince Kung the superiority of Western military power. Prince Kung, who previously had been rabidly antiforeign, now did a complete about-face and came to respect and even admire the British. He also discovered that the foreigners did not have any designs on Chinese territory and, surprisingly, were willing to share their military secrets by offering to help China train its army and manufacture Western-style weapons.

Learning about and from the West, which had been advocated as early as 1839 by Lin Tse-hsü, now found favor in the capital among the chief ministers of the state. Prince Kung and Wen-hsiang, on Jan. 11, 1861, memorialized the throne that a new office be established to direct foreign affairs and that there be a general change in China's policy toward the West, based on peace through diplomacy and Self-strengthening.

Diplomatic Service

The new Foreign Office was formally established on March 11, 1861, as the Tsungli Yamen, with Wen-hsiang as the principal minister and at times the acting head. Although Prince Kung was the nominal head of the Tsungli Yamen, he and Wen-hsiang worked together so closely that it is difficult to determine who was really responsible for its policies. Nevertheless, to the foreigners, Wen-hsiang came to be known as "Mr. Tsungli Yamen." Because of his honesty (he was proud of being poor), straightforwardness, efficiency, and intelligence, he gained the highest praise of the entire foreign diplomatic community.

Between 1861 and the early 1870s the Tsungli Yamen effectively advanced the cause of Westernization and peaceful relations with the foreigners. As its working director, Wen-hsiang, who once referred to himself as a small donkey pulling a far too heavy load, was responsible for its everyday operation, its relations with foreign diplomats, and, with Prince Kung, for its general overall policies. Under their leadership the Tsungli Yamen promoted modern schools—the T'ung-wen Kuan, which was China's first foreign-language school, was established in 1862 on Wen-hsiang's recommendation—Western science, industry, and commerce. Wen-hsiang also initially suggested sending Anson Burlingame, the former U.S. minister to China, to the Western nations as China's special representative in 1868.

As grand councilors, Prince Kung and Wen-hsiang were able to protect the Tsungli Yamen from the attacks of the conservatives until about 1869-1870, when Prince Kung was severely chastised by the empress dowager Tz'u-hsi, and when Li Hung-chang, as the superintendent of trade for northern ports, began to overshadow it. Nevertheless, Wen-hsiang, despite his multifarious other duties and a serious illness in 1870, remained loyal to the Tsungli Yamen until his death.

Further Reading

There is no book in English on Wen-hsiang. Facets of his career are dealt with in Ssu-yu Teng and John K. Fairbank, *China's Response to the West* (1954), and throughout Mary C. Wright, *The Last Stand of Chinese Conservatism* (1957; rev. ed. 1966). A short biography of him appears in the publication by the U.S. Library of Congress, Orientalia Division, *Eminent Chinese of the Ch'ing Period, 1644-1912,* edited by Arthur W. Hummel (2 vols., 1943-1944). □

Wen T'ien-hsiang

The Chinese statesman Wen T'ien-hsiang (1236-1283) served the Sung dynasty in its closing years. For later Chinese he was the ideal model of the loyal minister.

Wen T'ien-hsiang was born on June 6, 1236, in Chi-an, Kiangsi. He grew into a tall man of imposing physique with a clear complexion and bushy brows setting off flashing eyes. He performed brilliantly on his *chin-shih* examination in 1256, placing first, but since his father died 4 days later, Wen T'ien-hsiang did not begin his official career until after the completion of the prescribed period of mourning. In 1259 he was appointed an assistant to the Ning-hai regional commander

and soon attracted considerable attention by calling for the decapitation of an official who had suggested moving the capital because a strong Mongol attack seemed imminent. Wen's request was not granted, and the Sung dynasty was given a respite when, still in 1259, Kublai Khan, on the death of Möngke (Mangu) Khan, turned north to claim the Mongol throne.

When the Mongols in 1274 again embarked on a major offensive under General Bayan, Wen T'ien-hsiang was in charge of a prefecture in Kiangsi. In 1275 in response to an imperial edict, he recruited loyalist soldiers and, paying them out of his own pocket, led them to the capital, where he was ordered to proceed to Wu-hsien in Kiangsu. His advice to organize South China into four armies, each to advance north, and to use local inhabitants to combat the Mongols was rejected. When the Sung lost an important prefecture in northwestern Kiangsu, Wen fell back to a position near the capital and then was placed in charge of the capital itself. Promoted to right grand councilor, he was sent to negotiate with General Bayan in 1276, but his recalcitrant attitude and evident determination to save the dynasty led the Mongol general to keep him a prisoner and send him north. Wen, however, managed to escape on the way and was able to rejoin the Sung court, which had fled to Fukien.

In 1277 Wen T'ien-hsiang was able to retake a number of prefectures in Kiangsi before being defeated and forced to retreat. Confronted by the superior Mongol armies, Wen was unable to reverse the military situation and early in 1279 suffered a final defeat in Kwantung. Unsuccessful in attempting suicide by poison, he was captured and taken to the Yüan capital, Peking, where in prison he composed his most famous poem, "Song of the Upright Spirit." Even after the death of the last Sung prince and the end of armed resistance, and despite Kublai Khan's offers of high office, Wen T'ien-hsiang refused to submit to the Yüan dynasty and asked only for death. On Jan. 9, 1283, his wish was granted.

Further Reading

There are no works in English on Wen T'ien-hsiang. Recommended for background on the Southern Sung and the Mongol conquest of China are: L. Carrington Goodrich, *A Short History of the Chinese People* (1943; 3d ed. 1959); Wolfram Eberhard, *A History of China* (trans. 1960); Edwin O. Reischauer and John K. Fairbank, *East Asia, The Great Tradition* (1960); Kenneth Scott Latourette, *The Chinese, Their History and Culture* (1964); and René Grousset, *The Rise and Splendour of the Chinese Empire* (1968). □

William Charles Wentworth

William Charles Wentworth (1790-1872) was an Australian statesman and writer who achieved repute as an explorer.

In the 1820s William Wentworth came to typify the spirit of the radical native-born Australians, conscious of their difference from the "English ascendancy," exulting in their love of country, and determined to obtain civil rights and representative institutions and control the development of what they claimed was their country.

By 1830 the overwhelming majority of the inhabitants of New South Wales were convicts, former convicts, or the children of convicts, collectively, if loosely, known as emancipists. They were opposed by the exclusives, the civil and military officers and the free settlers, not numerous, but generally rich. The exclusives adopted a conservative political stance, being relatively happy to cooperate with the governor and coming to seek a measure of constitutional reform that would place them in positions of power commensurate with their wealth and their view of their social worth and that, at the same time, would leave the emancipists politically and socially inferior.

Most of the native-born Australians were among the emancipists, but there were also some among the exclusives. Both groups also shared in the wealth that was accumulating as New South Wales developed a pastoral-commercial economy. By the mid-1830s the emancipist-exclusive conflict was blurred.

Wentworth's mother was Catherine Crowley, a convicted thief who arrived with her infant son at Norfolk Island on Aug. 7, 1790. She died at Parramatta in 1800. D'Arcy Wentworth, who acknowledged him as son, had aristocratic connections but had been accused, and found not guilty, of highway robbery in 1787 in England; he had come to New South Wales as an assistant surgeon on the ship with Catherine Crowley.

William was educated in England and returned to New South Wales in 1810. In 1813, with a growing reputation as a headstrong and fearless young man, he accompanied William Lawson and Gregory Blaxland in the first crossing of the Blue Mountains west of Sydney. Wentworth received 1,000 acres for the exploit but, although a relatively large landholder, was unacceptable to the exclusives because of his father's dubious background. His resentment was softened by the exercise of a great talent for satire and invective and later by the writing of poetry.

Originally intended for an army career, Wentworth returned to London in 1816 and read for the bar. In 1819 he published *A Statistical Description of the Colony of New South Wales . . .* , an influential emancipist analysis of the settlement that revealed a sound grasp of economic principles. Wentworth was made aware for the first time of his father's misadventures, and his developing radicalism was consolidated by 1822, when he was called to the bar. After studying for some time at Cambridge, he returned to Sydney in 1824.

Emancipist Leader

With William Wardell, Wentworth soon founded the *Australian,* which became an insistent and effective champion of the emancipists' aims. Attacks on Governor Sir Ralph Darling led to Wentworth's prosecution for seditious libel; his vindication strengthened the freedom of the colonial press. In 1829-1830 Wentworth's support of the campaign for reform of the jury system was successful. By this time his fierce patriotism had made him a colonial hero.

Wentworth had led the movement that had gained important civil concessions connected with the press and juries, and he was now one of the chief leaders of the growing impetus for self-government. But by 1840 his wealth was tending to place him with a new group of conservatives, some of whom were also native-born. In the 1840s his conservatism took a liberal form, and he helped to prepare the way for more constitutional change. The emphasis of his campaign changed: he sought self-government but not a democracy. In 1842 he contributed to the establishment of a partly elective legislative council. In the council in the 1840s he fought for further constitutional and social advances, especially in education, and supported the interests of the great pastoralists, to whom he now belonged.

Wentworth's plan of responsible government was not so radical as that of several younger reformers in the early 1850s, but his great reputation and skill played an essential part in the advent of the new system in 1855. He spent the rest of his life in England, where he died at Dorset on March 20, 1872.

Further Reading

There is no biography of Wentworth. His life is sketched in all histories of Australia. The most complete and satisfying portrait is in Charles M. H. Clark, *A History of Australia* (2 vols., 1962-1968). A.C.V. Melbourne, *William Charles Wentworth* (1934), gives an account of Wentworth's constitutional work, and Arthur Jose, *Builders and Pioneers of Australia* (1928), an outline of his career. Wentworth's keen insight into the early colonial economy is analyzed in G. J. Abbott and N. B. Nairn, eds., *Economic Growth of Australia, 1788-1821* (1969).

Additional Sources

Liston, Carol, *Sarah Wentworth: mistress of Vaucluse,* Glebe, N.S.W.: Historic Houses Trust, New South Wales, 1988. □

Franz Werfel

The Austrian poet, novelist, and playwright Franz Werfel (1890-1945) was a leading representative of the expressionist movement in German literature.

Franz Werfel was born on Sept. 10, 1890, in Prague, the son of a Jewish businessman. He studied at the universities of Prague, Leipzig, and Hamburg and then worked (1912-1914) as a reader for a publishing house. After service in World War I (1915-1917) he lived and worked as a professional writer.

Werfel's first achievement was a play, *Besuch aus dem Elysium* (1909), which was followed by *Die Troerinnen* (1915), an expressionistic reworking of Euripides's *The Trojan Women.* However, his reputation was made by his lyric poetry, which he published in such collections as *Der*

Weltfreund (1911) and *Wir Sind* (1913). His lyric poetry is distinctive and of considerable quality; like his plays, it is passionate, often ecstatic and rhapsodic, but equally often inclined toward the abstruse and the ratiocinative; tightly knit and full of rhetorical figures, it suffers from a certain lack of color and tactile quality.

A strong vein of religious feeling runs through Werfel's poems. In his earlier work this ardor is less overtly religious than philanthropic and humanitarian. The struggle to overcome selfishness is the theme of his trilogy of dramas in verse, *Spiegelmensch* (1920), a work that fluctuates between the profound and the trivial, the pithy and the diffuse. The element of social criticism in Werfel's work, often pungent, is well exemplified by his novel *Der Abituriententag* (1928), which deals with the problem of sadism in a school. His novellas, such as *Nicht der Mörder, der Ermordete ist schuldig* (1920) and *Der Tod des Kleinbürgers* (1926), reveal their author as a gifted narrator, a scholar of psychoanalytic lore, a shrewd psychologist, and the possessor of an acerbic and cynical wit.

In his later career the novel became Werfel's primary field of endeavor, and he developed for the most part a conventional but sophisticated realism. *Verdi* (1924), one of his most interesting and evocative novels, attacked the cult of the musical genius established in the German mind by the example of Richard Wagner. In *Barbara, oder die Frömmigkeit* (1929) Werfel combined an impressive portrayal of postwar Viennese life with the development of a moral theme. *Die Geschwister von Neapel* (1931; *The*

Pascarella Family) studied the effects of fascism upon a small-time Italian banker, a pillar of austerity and morality.

Werfel fled from Nazi-occupied Austria to France and after the fall of France to the United States. *Das Lied von Bernadette* (1941; *The Song of Bernadette*) was written to fulfill a vow he had made when he found temporary refuge in Lourdes. The novel is a fictionalized history of the life and experiences of Bernadette Soubirous, and his choice of theme enabled him to illuminate that essential supremacy of the spiritual over the material that his writings constantly sought to assert. Werfel's posthumously published novel, *Stern der Ungeborenen* (1946), is a fantastic, futuristic vision of a world in which the intellect succumbs to the profusion and vitality of instinctive life. He died on Aug. 26, 1945, in Beverly Hills, Calif.

Further Reading

Biographical material may be gleaned from Alma M. Werfel, *And the Bridge Is Love* (1958). The only booklength literary study of Werfel in English is Gore B. Foltin, ed., *Franz Werfel, 1890-1945* (1961). Werfel's dramatic work is discussed in Hugh F. Garten, *Modern German Drama* (1959). For material on the expressionist background see Richard Samuel and R. Hinton Thomas, *Expressionism in German Life, Literature and the Theatre, 1910-1924* (1939), and Walter H. Sokel, *The Writer In Extremis: Expressionism in Twentieth-century German Literature* (1939).

Additional Sources

Giroud, Francoise, *Alma Mahler, or, The art of being loved,* Oxford; New York: Oxford University Press, 1991.

Jungk, Peter Stephan, *Franz Werfel: a life in Prague, Vienna, and Hollywood,* New York: Grove Weidenfeld, 1990.

Steiman, Lionel B. (Lionel Bradley), *Franz Werfel, the faith of an exile: from Prague to Beverly Hills,* Waterloo, Ont., Canada: W. Laurier University Press; Atlantic Highlands, N.J.: Distributed in the U.S.A. by Humanities Press, 1985. □

Abraham Gottlob Werner

The German naturalist Abraham Gottlob Werner (1749-1817) wrote the first modern textbook of descriptive mineralogy and was the major proponent of the Neptunian theory of the earth.

Abraham Werner was born on Sept. 25, 1749, at Wehrau in Upper Lusatia (Prussian Silesia). His ancestors had been employed in the mining industry for several hundred years, and his father was the overseer of a foundry in Wehrau. When he was 10 years old, Werner went to school at Bunzlau, Silesia, but five years later he returned home to become his father's assistant. However, his interest in mineralogy became so strong that he abandoned this practical career and in 1769 entered the Mining Academy of Freiberg. After two years there he matriculated in 1771 at the University of Leipzig.

Investigations in Mineralogy

During his stay at Leipzig as a student, Werner became acutely aware of the unsatisfactory character of the numerous systems used at the time to describe and classify minerals. Two conflicting approaches, based respectively on the chemical composition and on the physical characters of minerals, had created a confused association of unrelated observations, imprecise definitions, and impractical tabular arrangements. In the amazingly short time of a year, Werner wrote and then published *Vonden äusserlichen Kennzeichen der Fossilien* (1774; On the External Characters of Fossils, or of Minerals), the first modern textbook of descriptive mineralogy. Although Werner recognized that a true and final classification of minerals should be based on their chemical composition, he emphasized that it should be preceded by a method which would allow a precise identification of the various minerals by means of their external characters and physical properties.

Werner's description of the external characters of minerals, which occupies the major part of his book, remains an outstanding illustration of his unusual gift of observation and his knowledge of minerals. However, the quality of his work on mineralogy decreases abruptly with the discussion of the crystalline forms, for he was a practical or applied mineralogist to whom the mathematical aspect of mineralogy was superfluous. He never realized the basic importance of crystallography, which he thought was applied mathematics rather than a branch of mineralogy.

Geognosy and Neptunism

Upon publication of his book on minerals, Werner left Leipzig and returned to his home in Wehrau, where he became involved in the preparation of field trips to collect minerals and visit mines. However, the Mining Academy of Freiberg, strongly impressed by his performance, appointed him in 1775 inspector and teacher of mining and mineralogy. His dogmatic but stimulating teaching filled his students with enthusiasm, and they returned to their respective countries zealously spreading Werner's geological concepts. Therefore, a full account of his ideas is obtainable only through their writings and particularly those of his foremost follower, Robert Jameson.

Werner's concept of the earth's crust may be visualized as an extension of his great desire for rigid classification. He had only contempt for the speculative naturalists who were concerned with theories about the origin of the earth, and therefore he called his subject "geognosy," or "earth knowledge," which he defined as the science concerned with the arrangement of minerals in the various layers, and with the relationship of such layers, in order to reach an understanding of the constitution of the earth. He emphatically stressed the precision of his observations but did not hesitate to make sweeping generalizations about the whole earth from his very limited experience in Saxony. He gradually changed his hypotheses into so-called "facts" by the simple process of repeating them many times with unshakable confidence. Therefore, Werner's system, which pretended to avoid speculation, actually became the most speculative and erroneous attempt at explaining the origin of the earth.

Werner subdivided the earth's crust into a series of superposed and distinct "formations." He believed that these formations could be recognized all over the world and would therefore provide the key to the understanding of the geology of any country. He adopted the old idea that the earth originally consisted of a solid core completely surrounded by a universal ocean, which was at least as deep as the highest mountains and contained great quantities of mineral matter. Since the sea played a fundamental role in this system, the name of Neptunism was given to Werner's school. In this universal body of water, chemical precipitation took place, generating and depositing all forms of rocks in a constant succession.

Because Werner did not believe that the earth had any kind of internal fire or other deep-seated source of energy, he was forced to consider volcanic rocks as recent and accidental products, which he explained by means of the old concept of the combustion of underground coal beds. A further strange characteristic of Werner's was his denial of the disturbances of the earth's crust, such as folding or tilting, as proofs of the internal energy of the earth. Beds were supposed to have been deposited essentially in a horizontal position, and those dipping more than 30° were considered as having been "locally disturbed" by processes which were not elaborated upon. This refutation of mountain-building processes as an expression of internal energy was naturally coupled with Werner's equally dogmatic refutation of the occurrence of past volcanic activity.

Origin of Ore Deposits

Werner's ideas on the origin of ore deposits were corollaries of his general theory on geognosy. He stated that mineral veins were due to the filling by precipitates of fissures developed on the bottom of the universal ocean. The fissures were formed either by contraction or by the effects of earthquake movements. Consistent with his negation of the earth's internal fire, he refuted the idea that veins could have been filled by the products deposited by solutions or vapors originating from within the earth. Despite his ever present dogmatism, Werner did, however, demonstrate the value of a geometrical classification of veins, and he also gave excellent descriptions of their internal structures.

In bad health, Werner retired to Dresden, where he died, a bachelor, on June 30, 1817. His death was felt by most of the profession as a relief from a unique example of scientific despotism during which a man of genius tried unsuccessfully, for his entire life, to mold nature into an inflexible framework.

Further Reading

Biographical accounts of Werner are in Sir Archibald Geikie, *The Founders of Geology* (1897; new ed. 1962); Karl A. von Zittel, *History of Geology and Palaeontology* (1901); and Frank D. Adams, *The Birth and Development of the Geological Sciences* (1938; new ed. 1954). □

Max Wertheimer

The German psychologist Max Wertheimer (1880-1943) was the originator of Gestalt psychology, which had a profound influence on the whole science of psychology.

Max Wertheimer was born in Prague on April 15, 1880. At the University in Prague he first studied law and then philosophy; he continued his studies in Berlin and then in Würzburg, where he received the doctorate in 1904. During the following years his work included research on the psychology of testimony, deriving no doubt from his early interest in law and his abiding interest in the nature of truth; he also carried on research in music, another lifelong interest.

In 1910 Wertheimer performed his now famous experiments on apparent movement, that movement which we see when, under certain conditions, two *stationary* objects are presented in succession at different places (a phenomenon familiar in moving pictures). This was the beginning of Gestalt psychology—a major revolution in psychological thinking.

The phenomena which Wertheimer was investigating could not be explained by the then-prevailing psychology. Psychology was, in 1910, characteristically analytical: in naive imitation of the natural sciences, it attempted to reduce every complex phenomenon to simpler ones, the elements which were supposed to make up the whole.

But it was already clear that this analytical procedure could not account for many well-known psychological facts. Some advocates of the older psychology tried to patch it up by adding assumptions to take care of troublesome findings, while leaving the old framework intact. Other scholars, seeing the inadequacy of the customary approach, denied that the problems of psychology could be treated scientifically.

For Wertheimer, neither line of criticism went to the core of the problem. The difficulties of the older psychology went far beyond its failure to explain special laboratory findings. Everything that was vital, meaningful, and essential seemed to be lost in the traditional approach. The trouble, he held, was not in the scientific method itself but rather in an assumption generally made about that method—that it must be atomistic.

But science need not only be analytical in this sense. The viewing of complex wholes as "and-sums," to be reduced to accidentally and arbitrarily associated elements, Wertheimer described as an approach "from below," whereas many situations need to be approached "from above." In these cases what happens in the whole cannot be understood from a knowledge of its components considered piecemeal; rather the behavior of the parts themselves depends on their place in the structured whole, in the context in which they exist.

These are precisely the situations which are most important for psychology, those in which we find meaning, value, order. Thus, apparent movement cannot be under-

stood if one knows only the "stills" by which it is produced; nor can the form of a circle, the peacefulness of a landscape, the sternness of a command, the inevitability of a conclusion be understood from a knowledge of independent elements. Here whole properties are primary, and the characteristics of parts are derived from the dynamics of their wholes.

Wertheimer became a lecturer in Frankfurt in 1912. Later he went to Berlin and in 1929 returned to Frankfurt as professor. All this time he was developing his ideas and influencing students who themselves became distinguished psychologists. Although he preferred the spoken to the written word as a vehicle for communication, he wrote some notable articles applying the new approach "from above" to the organization of the perceptual field and to the nature of thinking.

Just before the German elections in 1933, Wertheimer heard a speech by Hitler over a neighbor's radio. He decided that he did not want his family to live in a country where such a man could run, with likelihood of success, for the highest office in the land; and the next day the family moved to Marienbad, Czechoslovakia. Soon Wertheimer realized that Hitler was not a passing phenomenon, and he accepted an invitation from the New School for Social Research in New York City to join its University in Exile (later the Graduate Faculty of Political and Social Science). He resumed his studies of thinking, completing his major work, *Productive Thinking,* a highly original and penetrating examination of the processes that occur in thinking at its best. In a series of articles he showed the application of Gestalt thinking to problems of truth, ethics, freedom, and democracy. Unfortunately he did not live to write his projected Gestalt logic.

Further Reading

Wolfgang Köhler, *The Task of Gestalt Psychology* (1969), is an overview of Gestalt psychology by one of its founders and shows Wertheimer's role in its development. □

Charles Wesley

The English hymn writer and preacher Charles Wesley (1707-1788) joined his brother John in starting Methodism and composed thousands of hymns to express its religious ideals.

Charles Wesley was born on Dec. 18, 1707, the eighteenth child of the rector of the Anglican church in Epworth, Lincolnshire. All 19 Wesley children received individual weekly instructions in religious matters from their mother, who gave them some of her own independent spirit. Although Charles was bright, he wasted much of his energy looking for good times when he began his studies at Christ Church, Oxford, in 1726. In 1729, after he had settled down, Charles, his older brother John, and several other Oxford students formed the Holy Club, for the

purpose of studying the Bible and receiving the Sacrament of the Eucharist. The group soon became known as the "Methodists" because of the regularity of their religious activities.

By the time Wesley received his master's degree in 1733, he had proved himself an excellent scholar and a master of Latin. In 1735 he was ordained a priest in the Church of England. With his brother John he left England for the New World. He became secretary to Col. James Oglethorpe, governor of the colony of Georgia. But he had a hard time adapting to Georgia's climate and had to return to England the next year.

In the spring of 1738 Wesley experienced a profound religious awakening. He became vividly convinced of the power of the New Testament message of salvation and saw more clearly than ever before how faith in Jesus Christ could change one's life. For the next 50 years Wesley brought this message to as many people as he could, particularly to the poor and uneducated workers in London's slums. Along with his brother and their "Methodist" friends from Oxford, Wesley preached that the value of one's life is to be measured by his faith and decent sober conduct, rather than by his church attendance. Many Anglican officials were displeased by the Methodists' approach. Less devout people often ridiculed their fervent preaching. After Wesley married in 1749, he lived for a while in Bristol, where opposition to his ideals was less severe, but 12 years later he resumed his preaching in London.

Wesley was a master of the English language. Over the years of his ministry he wrote some 6,500 hymns to spread the New Testament message as he understood it. When he died in London on March 29, 1788, he was known as a preacher of great power and wisdom. Many of his hymns (among them *Hark! The Herald Angels Sing* and *Jesus, Lover of My Soul*) are sung in churches today, and it is for them that he is famous.

Further Reading

The most recent and readable biography is by Frederick C. Gill, *Charles Wesley: The First Methodist* (1964). A deeper insight into Wesley's character can be gained from Frank Baker, *Charles Wesley as Revealed by His Letters* (1948). John E. Rattenbury, *The Eucharistic Hymns of John and Charles Wesley* (1948), analyzes the religious ideas behind Wesley's principal contribution to the Church.

Additional Sources

Dallimore, Arnold A., *A heart set free: the life of Charles Wesley*, Westchester, Ill.: Crossway Books, 1988.

Mitchell, T. Crichton, *Charles Wesley: man with the dancing heart*, Kansas City, Mo.: Beacon Hill Press of Kansas City, 1994.

Wesley, Charles, *Charles Wesley: a reader*, New York: Oxford University Press, 1989.

Wilder, Franklin, *The Methodist riots: the testing of Charles Wesley*, Great Neck, N.Y.: Todd & Honeywell, 1981. □

John Wesley

The English evangelical clergyman, preacher, and writer John Wesley (1703-1791) was the founder of Methodism. One of England's greatest spiritual leaders, he played a major role in the revival of religion in 18th-century English life.

The 18th century found the Church of England out of touch with both the religious and social problems of the day. Its leadership was constituted largely by political appointees, its clergy were riddled with ignorance, and churchmen of genuine concern were rare. The influence of rationalism and deism even among dedicated clergymen caused the Anglican Church to be unaware of the spiritual needs of the masses. John Wesley's great achievement was to recognize the necessity of bringing religion to this wide and neglected audience.

Wesley was born in Epworth, Lincolnshire, on June 17, 1703. He was the fifteenth of the 19 children of Samuel Wesley, an Anglican minister who took his pastoral duties seriously and instilled this idea in his son. John's mother, a woman of great spiritual intensity, molded her children through a code of strict and uncompromising Christian morality, instilling in John a firm conception of religious piety, concern, and duty.

In 1714 Wesley entered Charterhouse School, and in 1720 he became a student at Christ Church, Oxford. Re-

ceiving his bachelor of arts degree in 1724, he was ordained a deacon in the Church of England in 1725 and was elected a fellow of Lincoln College, Oxford, in 1726. He became curate to his father in the following year and was ordained a priest in 1728. Returning to Oxford in 1729, Wesley, in addition to the duties of his fellowship at Lincoln, became active in a religious club to which his younger brother Charles belonged. The Holy Club, nicknamed "Methodists" by its critics, met frequently for discussion and study. Its members engaged in prayer, attended church services, visited prisoners, and gave donations to the needy. The Holy Club was one of Wesley's formative influences, and he soon became its acknowledged leader.

Ministry in Georgia

Buoyed by his years at Oxford and desirous of putting the principles of the Holy Club to work elsewhere, Wesley in 1735 accepted the invitation of James Oglethorpe to become a minister in the recently founded colony of Georgia. Accompanied by his brother Charles, Wesley spent two disappointing years in the New World. Despite his zeal to bring them the Gospel, he was rebuffed by the colonists and received unenthusiastically by the Indians. Moreover, he became involved in an unsuccessful love affair, the aftermath of which brought him the unwanted publicity of a court case. In 1737 Wesley returned to England.

Wesley's stay in Georgia was, however, not without benefit. Both on his trip over and during his two-year stay, he was deeply influenced by Moravian missionaries, whose

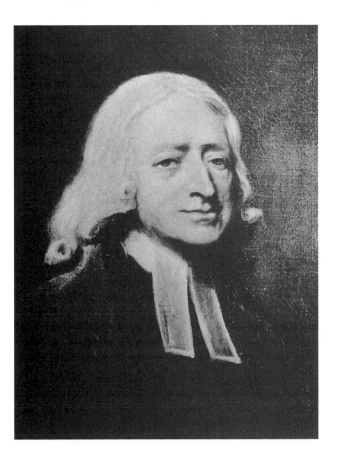

sense of spiritual confidence and commitment to practical piety impressed him.

Conversion and Preaching

In England, Wesley continued to keep in close touch with the Moravians. At one of their meetings—in Aldersgate Street, London, on May 24, 1738—he experienced conversion while listening to a reading of Martin Luther's preface to the Epistle to the Romans. "I felt I did trust in Christ, Christ alone, for salvation," Wesley wrote, "and an assurance was given me that He had taken away *my* sins, even *mine,* and saved *me* from the law of sin and death."

Through this personal commitment Wesley, though he later broke with the Moravians, became imbued with the desire to take this message to the rest of England. Finding the bishops unsympathetic or indifferent and most clergymen hostile to the point of closing their churches to him, Wesley, following the example of such preachers as George Whitefield, began an itinerant ministry that lasted more than 50 years. Forced to preach outside the churches, he became adept at open-air preaching and, as a result, began to reach many, especially in the cities, about whom the Church of England had shown little concern.

A small man (he was 5 feet 6 inches in height and weighed about 120 pounds), Wesley always had to perch on a chair or platform when he preached. He averaged 15 sermons a week, and as his *Journal* indicates, he preached more than 40,000 sermons in his career, traveling the length and breadth of England—altogether more than 250,000 miles—many times during an age when roads were often only muddy ruts. A contemporary described him as "the last word . . . in neatness and dress" and "his eye was 'the brightest and most piercing that can be conceived.'"

Preaching was not easy; crowds were often hostile, and once a bull was let loose in an audience he was addressing. Wesley, however, quickly learned the art of speaking and, despite opposition, his sermons began to have a marked effect. Many were converted immediately, frequently exhibiting physical signs, such as fits or trances.

Organization of Methodism

From the beginning Wesley viewed his movement as one within the Church of England and not in opposition to it. As he gained converts around England, however, these men and women grouped themselves together in societies that Wesley envisioned as playing the same role in Anglicanism as the monastic orders do in the Roman Catholic Church. He took a continual and rather authoritarian part in the life of these societies, visiting them periodically, settling disputes, and expelling the recalcitrant. Yearly conferences of the whole movement presented him with the opportunity to establish policy. Under his leadership each society was broken down into a "class," which dealt with matters of finance, and a "band," which set standards of personal morality. In addition, Wesley wrote numerous theological works and edited 35 volumes of Christian literature for the edification of the societies. A tireless and consummate organizer, he kept his movement prospering despite a variety of defections.

Yet the continual opposition of the Anglican bishops, coupled with their refusal to ordain Methodist clergy, forced Wesley to move closer to actual separation toward the end of his life. In 1784 he took out a deed of declaration, which secured the legal standing of the Methodist Society after his death. In the same year he reluctantly ordained two men to serve as "superintendents" for Methodists in North America. He continued the practice to provide clergymen for England but very sparingly and with great hesitation. Wesley always maintained that he personally adhered to the Church of England.

Methodism had a significant impact on English society. It brought religion to masses of people who, through the shifts of population brought about by the industrial revolution, were not being reached by the Anglican Church. In addition, it had a beneficial effect on many within both the Church of England and dissenting congregations. By emphasizing morality, self-discipline, and thrift to the deprived classes, Wesley has been credited by some historians as being a major force in keeping England free of revolution and widespread social unrest during his day. He himself was politically conservative, a critic of democracy, and a foe of both the American and French revolutions.

Throughout his life Wesley's closest confidant was his brother and coworker Charles, the composer of a number of well-known hymns. Wesley, always extraordinarily healthy, remained active to the end, preaching his final sermon at an open-air meeting just 4 months before his death on March 2, 1791, in London.

Further Reading

The best source for an understanding of Wesley is *The Journal of the Rev. John Wesley,* edited by Nehemiah Curnock (8 vols., 1909-1916). J. H. Overton, *John Wesley* (1891), is a short, sympathetic, well-written biography. Francis J. McConnell, *John Wesley* (1939), is a full reinterpretation and reevaluation of Wesley in the light of modern experience and research. Valuable background material is in Basil Williams, *The Whig Supremacy, 1714-1760* (1939; 2d ed. rev. 1962), and Elie Halevy, *A History of the English People in the Nineteenth Century* (4 vols., 1961). The economic changes of the Wesley era are well treated in T. S. Ashton, *The Industrial Revolution, 1760-1830* (1948; rev. ed. 1964). ☐

Benjamin West

Benjamin West (1738-1820), the first of America's emigré artists, became one of Europe's most important neoclassic painters.

Benjamin West was born on Oct. 10, 1738, in Springfield Township, Pa., to a struggling innkeeper who had emigrated from England. Though the Wests lived among Quakers, who habitually frowned upon art, Benjamin seems to have been encouraged by all about him from the time he began to draw at the age of six years. He gained a reputation in eastern Pennsylvania as a child prodigy. At first he was self-taught, but later, before his departure for Italy in 1759, he knew the paintings of William Williams and Gustavus Hessalius, whose work he soon surpassed.

Among West's American works produced during the 1750s were the *Death of Socrates,* forecasting his later neoclassic work; a somewhat fantastic *Landscape with Cow* (1748), revealing his early dreams of storybook castles; and a lustrous portrait of the young Thomas Mifflin. While in Pennsylvania, West aspired to be the companion of emperors and kings. He sought, then, the social opportunities which Europe offered.

Absorbing Neoclassicism

Because of his quaint charm and the remoteness of his origins (in the eyes of the Italians), West interested important patrons, critics, and literati in Rome. Cardinal Albani introduced him to the treasures of the Vatican; and the English painter Gavin Hamilton, the German painter Anton Raphael Mengs, and the esthetician Johann Joachim Winckelmann schooled West in the niceties of neoclassic art, which was then supplanting the more frivolous rococo style. Excavations at Pompeii and Herculaneum had fostered the growth of neoclassicism, and partisans of the new nationalisms saw in the glories of the ancient world pretexts for their own ambitions.

When West arrived in London in 1763, he was prepared by temperament and training for the success he would enjoy. He was immediately encouraged by Joshua Reynolds and was deluged by portrait commissions. But he

aspired to history painting, which he saw as a higher art form than portraiture. He wished to choose lofty themes, idealize figures, and dramatize scenes according to the principles he had learned in Rome. Robert Hay Drummond, Archbishop of York, commissioned West to paint *Agrippina with the Ashes of Germanicus* (1767), a story, of faithfulness and self-sacrifice based on a theme from Tacitus. West endowed his figures with a grave dignity, clearly stratified his space in the manner of Nicolas Poussin, and took his composition, in part, from the ancient reliefs of the Ara Pacis in Rome.

Relations with the King

King George III heard of West through Archbishop Drummond and commissioned from West a painting on a theme of nobility, *Regulus Leaving Rome* (1769). The painter and the King became intimate friends, and not even West's sympathy with the American colonists marred the friendship. The *Death of Wolfe* (1771), a major painting and one of George's favorites, marked a temporary break with neoclassic formulas. In this scene from the battle of the English and French for Quebec in 1759, West used contemporary costumes rather than Roman togas because the event had not taken place in Europe. To ennoble Wolfe, West showed the general in the attitude of a dying Christ with his lieutenants neatly placed beside him like attendant saints.

In 1788 it was obvious that the King was suffering from madness, and West lost his support. In 1792, upon the death of Joshua Reynolds, West was elected president of the Royal Academy, a position that was made increasingly difficult because of George's capricious behavior. Moreover, West's financial position became precarious, as he had lent large sums of money to the Crown and was unable to recover these. Royal commissions dwindled, then disappeared.

Yet West's reputation had not really suffered, and the public continued to support him. His *Christ Healing the Sick* (1811), commissioned by the Pennsylvania Hospital in Philadelphia, was bought by the British Institute for 3,000 guineas before its completion (the largest sum paid in England up to that time for a contemporary work), and a replica was sent to Philadelphia.

West's Style

West's work has been classified as being in three modes: stately, pathetic, and dread. The stately mode includes classicizing, elevating ancient themes, featuring idealized forms and gravity of demeanor, as in the *Agrippina.* *Christ Healing the Sick,* showing milder sentiments and more relaxed figures, falls within the pathetic mode. Subjects stirring the astonishment and awe of the beholder, like *Death on the Pale Horse* (1802), are in the dread mode.

Death on the Pale Horse, which was exhibited at the Paris Salon of 1802, marked a departure from the staidness of neoclassicism and forecast the emotionality of romanticism. The painting was an apocalyptic subject of terror and sublimity. Space, rather than being clearly stratified (as in the stately mode), was here vast and unmeasurable; and color, rather than being applied to neat outlines, was handled in a free, Rubenesque manner.

West died in London on March 11, 1820. He played a fundamental role in the history of American art by encouraging and training the most gifted younger American painters of his time. In spite of his position, he was friendly and helpful to any artist, American or English, who stopped at his studio.

Further Reading

John Galt, *The Life and Studies of Benjamin West* (2 vols., 1816-1820), is an amusingly anecdotal biography by a contemporary Scottish novelist and the source for later studies. Also useful is Henry E. Jackson, *Benjamin West: His Life and Work* (1900). Grose Evans, *Benjamin West and the Taste of His Times* (1959), groups West's work into the stately, pathetic, and dread modes.

Additional Sources

Alberts, Robert C., *Benjamin West: a biography,* Boston: Houghton Mifflin, 1978.
Flexner, James Thomas, *America's old masters,* New York: McGraw-Hill, 1982, 1980. □

Cornel West

An American philosopher, Cornel West (born 1953) quickly won recognition as a critic of culture, an interpreter of African American experience, an advocate of social justice, and an analyst of Post-Modern art and philosophy.

Cornel West, born in Tulsa, Oklahoma, in 1953, lived most of his childhood and youth in segregated working-class neighborhoods in Oklahoma, Kansas, and California. In high school he excelled in scholarship and athletics. He earned his A.B. at Harvard University, then completed his doctorate in philosophy at Princeton in 1980. While a graduate student, he was a teaching assistant in humanities and ethics at Harvard and in philosophy at Princeton.

In 1977 he joined the faculty of Union Theological Seminary in New York, teaching classical and contemporary philosophy. From 1984 to 1987 he taught at the Yale University Divinity School, then returned to Union in 1987-1988. In 1988 Princeton University tapped him to be the director of its African American Studies Program and as professor of religion. In the former program he drew together a multi-disciplinary group of literary artists and scholars who interpreted the African American experience in history and literature.

West earned an early reputation as a scholar of infectious enthusiasm, sharp insight, and wide-ranging interests. Within a decade of earning his doctorate, he accepted visiting appointments at Barnard College, Williams College, Princeton Theological Seminary, Haverford College, City University of New York (Center for Worker Education), Harvard Divinity School, and the University of Paris. In addition, he lectured at more than a hundred colleges and

universities in the United States. He taught philosophy to inmates of a federal prison, an unusual distinction for an academic philosopher. Within the same decade he produced dozens of essays and reviews, published in books and in journals, both scholarly and popular.

In an age of scholarly specialization, West cultivated widely diverse interests. His nimble mind danced from one subject to another with dazzling virtuosity. On one side of his thought he was a social philosopher, drawing much from the Marxist tradition but uninhibited by allegiance to any Marxist orthodoxies. His scholarship was closely related to active involvement in movements for social and racial justice. He was simultaneously an interpreter of African American experience to white Americans, of American philosophy to Europeans, of democratic beliefs to South Africans, of religious insights to secularists, and of secular themes to the religious. As a philosopher, he showed special interest in pragmatism, Post-Modern thought, and philosophy of religion. His artistic interests included literature (he had published one short story and friends predicted that he would write a novel), opera (he was seen occasionally at Salzburg), cinema (he was a fellow at the British Film Institute), and architecture (he lectured at the School of Architecture at Milan, Italy).

The unifying center for these diverse interests was a concern for cultural criticism: intellectual, esthetic, ethical, and religious. Whatever area of human interest he entered, from the arts to the most technical philosophy, he soon related to its expressions in contemporary society and its meaning for human self-understanding and justice. West appreciated culture as an expression of human creativity; he also saw that culture often oppresses human beings, especially marginalized people. He united intellectual analysis and social involvement, scholarship and action, the academic world and political life.

Even as he boldly acknowledged his roots in the African American church, West made trenchant criticisms of religious belief and practice, and he asked no favoritism for religion in the intellectual discussions of universities and society. He drew inspiration from the prophetic tradition of the Bible, and the words "prophetic" and "prophecy" appear often in his writings.

West was an eloquent lecturer, whose lithe and energetic body was totally involved in the torrent of words and ideas that tumbled from his mouth. He asked his listeners not only to hear what he said, but to enter into his thought processes and share his enthusiasms or generate their own thoughts and enthusiasms. His speaking style was symbolic of his convictions, which rejected the divorce of body from mind, of emotion from intellect, characteristic of much philosophy since Descartes. In a time when many philosophers would be horrified to be called preachers, West (although not an ordained minister) was not embarrassed to preach an occasional sermon. For him a passion for social justice was as intellectually respectable and demanding as the most rigorous intellectual analysis of propositions, and the two were never far apart in his philosophy.

West wrote and co-authored numerous books on philosophy, race and sociology. His *Race Matters* won a Critics Choice Award and was listed as a *New York Times* Notable Book of the Year in 1992. Other works included *Keeping the Faith: Philosophy and Race in American* (1993) and *Jews and Blacks: Let the Healing Begin* (1995), co-authored with Michael Lerner. In 1996 he co-authored *The Future of Race* with his Harvard colleague, Henry Louis Gates, Jr.

West was a frequent guest lecturer on university campuses nationwide. He joined the Harvard Faculty in 1994 as professor of Religion and African American Studies. During the 1996 Fall Semester he was a visiting professor at the University of Arizona. West was a featured speaker during the 1997 Martin Luther King, Jr./ Human Rights Week Celebration at Boise State University. At Harvard, West was known for his electrifying presentations that inspired students to critically analyze their own beliefs on race, culture, and class. Gates once described West as "the pre-eminent African American intellectual of our generation."

Further Reading

West's first book was *Prophesy Deliverance! An Afro-American Revolutionary Christianity* (1982). He co-edited *Post-Analytic Philosophy* (1985), a collection of essays by numerous scholars. *Prophetic Fragments* (1988) is a gathering of some 50 of West's essays and reviews. *The American Evasion of Philosophy: A Genealogy of Pragmatism* by West (1989), is a study of an America n intellectual tradition. *Out There: Marginalities and Contemporary Culture,* co-edited by West (1990), explores artistic interests. Jervis Anderson interviews West in *The New Yorker* (Jan 17,1994). Critical reviews of West's work can be found in major newspapers and magazines such as *Time.* Campus newspapers where West was a guest speaker provide information on current interests and social causes. □

Nathanael West

The work of the American novelist Nathanael West (1903-1940) is strikingly original. It is characterized by its use of Mythic themes in contemporary settings, terrifying symbolism, profound pessimism, and grisly humor.

Nathanael West was born Nathan Weinstein in New York City of affluent Russian-Jewish immigrants. After graduating from Brown University in 1924 with a bachelor of philosophy degree, he held a number of nonwriting jobs. In 1927 he became manager of the Kenmore Hotel in New York City and in 1928 of the Sutton Hotel; he frequently gave rooms rent-free to indigent friends. West's acquaintance with poverty grew more directly personal in 1929, when his family suffered complete financial ruin.

The Dream Life of Balso Snell (1931), West's first novel, was written at college and is generally regarded as the weakest of his four novels. It is based on a Quest motif, but settles into a misanthropic, scatological attack on Christianity and Judaism.

West's next novel should have marked an upturn in his writing fortunes, but he was the victim of freakishly bad luck. His masterpiece, *Miss Lonelyhearts* (1933), was enthusiastically reviewed, but the publisher went bankrupt, the printer refused to deliver most of the edition, and the book sold fewer than 800 copies. (It has sold over 300,000 copies since West's death.) A variation on the Scapegoat theme, *Miss Lonelyhearts* explores attitudes toward the problem of suffering. Its hero, who is never named but is identified by his role as a newspaper columnist, is an idealist; he refuses to accept the other newsmen's cynical view of his lonelyhearts newspaper column as a joke. Moved by his correspondents' grotesque but genuine pleas for help, he becomes caught up in their lives and is ultimately killed by one of them. A contemporary projection of a Christ figure, the novel is a masterpiece of economy. Critic Stanley Edgar Hyman called it "one of the three finest American novels of our century."

Ironically, although *Miss Lonelyhearts* sold badly, it led West to a job in Hollywood as adviser on the film adaptation. The movie, an artistic disaster, reduced his morally centered theme to a simple murder melodrama. (A remake 25 years later was somewhat better.)

West's third novel, *A Cool Million* (1934), utilizing the myth of the Holy Fool, is a bitterly satiric treatment of American politics. Lemuel Pitkin, who is in the Candide—Horatio Alger mold, sets forth with naive good will, only to be consistently victimized, often violently.

West spent his last five years in Hollywood as a scenarist. His final novel, *The Day of the Locust* (1939), is based on the Mythic Dance of Death. A group of characters on the fringe of Hollywood are used as a quintessential symbol of American violence and emptiness. Especially jarring is its final scene, a grotesque, surrealistic treatment of a film premiere which deteriorates into mob frenzy. The book received favorable reviews but sold fewer than 1500 copies. (It, too, has sold over 300,000 copies since West's death.) On Dec. 22, 1940, West and his wife, Eileen McKenney, were killed in an automobile accident near El Centro, Calif., just a few days before the opening of *My Sister Eileen,* the hit play immortalizing Mrs. West, written by her older sister, Ruth McKenney.

Further Reading

Since publication of *The Complete Works of Nathanael West* (1957), critical treatments have proliferated. Probably the best study of his life and work is Stanley Edgar Hyman, *Nathanael West* (1962). Other good accounts are the critical biography by Victor Comerchero, *Nathanael West: The Ironic Prophet* (1964), and the more comprehensive biography by Jay Martin, *Nathanael West: The Art of His Life* (1970). A recent useful critical study is Randall Reid, *The Fiction of Nathanael West: No Redeemer, No Promised Land* (1968). □

Ruth Karola Westheimer

Ruth K. Westheimer (born 1928) has gained fame for giving practical and straightforward advice for sexual problems.

Known to her public simply as "Dr. Ruth," the New York psychologist, broadcaster, and writer Dr. Ruth Westheimer became known for giving out sexual advice "like good hot chicken soup" to Americans in the 1980s. Orphaned by the Third Reich when her German-Jewish family perished after sending her to safety in Switzerland, she immigrated to Palestine where she became a fervent Zionist and member of the Haganah, the Jewish underground movement. The tiny woman, only four feet seven inches tall, briefly married a young Israeli soldier, and the couple moved to Paris where she earned a degree in psychology from the Sorbonne. In 1956 Dr. Ruth moved to New York with her second husband. After this marriage ended, she supported herself and her young daughter by working as a maid while she learned English and earned a master's degree at the New School for Social Research. After meeting her third husband on a ski trip to the Catskills, she earned her doctorate in education at Columbia University.

Media Celebrity

Dr. Ruth learned about sex early when she sneaked into her father's library to read his hidden marriage manual. At Columbia she studied family counseling and sex counseling, and her big break came in 1977 when she gave a lecture to a group of New York broadcasters about the need for more broadcast programs to promote "sexual literacy." Contacts at this lecture evolved into a phenomenally popular two-hour syndicated radio talk show called *Sexually Speaking,* a cable television show, *The Dr. Ruth Show,* several best-selling books, and celebrity status throughout the country.

"Grandma Freud"

Dr. Ruth's accent, witty humor, eccentric style, and commonsense advice made her enormously popular with the American public. On a typical night four thousand callers jammed the radio station's switchboards, and her talk show became the top-rated radio show in the New York City area in 1983. She stirred controversy with both political and religious leaders because of her frank answers about homosexuality, sex education, and contraception. Her ability to say anything and get away with it gave her both detractors and admirers. Critics warned she verged on entertainment rather than psychology and accused her of being frivolous and irresponsible. Her admirers praised her conviction and "knack of translating new technological information about sex into sound practical advice." A firm believer in traditional marriage and family, her enthusiasm for her work also kept her in her active private practice as a psychologist and family counselor.

Spicy Advice and the Ratings

To her loyal followers who counted on her, no question was too outrageous and no problem was insoluble. When a caller asked what to do about his girlfriend who had given him an inflatable love doll and "wants to watch," Dr. Ruth fired back, "Give the doll a name and have a good time." Concern about instant advice to unseen callers prompted the American Psychiatric Association to caution the growing ranks of media therapists against providing actual therapy or trying to solve a problem conclusively over the air. But Dr. Ruth's spicy advice, conventional morality, and upbeat approach continued to help media ratings whether or not they actually helped the nation's sexual psyche.

Further Reading

Ruth K. Westheimer and Jonathan Mark, *Heavenly Sex: Sexuality in the Jewish Tradition,* New York University Press, 1995, 188 p.

Ruth K. Westheimer, *Dr. Ruth's Guide to Good Sex,* Warner Books, 1983.

Ruth K. Westheimer, *Dr. Ruth's Guide for Married Lovers,* Warner Books, 1986.

Ruth K. Westheimer and Ben Yagoda, *All in a Lifetime: An Autobiography,* Warner Books, 1987.

Ruth K. Westheimer and Louis Lieberman, *Sex and Morality: Who is Teaching Our Sex Standards,* Harcourt Brace Jovanovich, 1988.

Ruth K. Westheimer and Louis Lieberman, *Dr. Ruth's Guide to Erotic and Sensuous Pleasures,* Shapolsky, 1991.

Ruth K. Westheimer, *Dr. Ruth Talks to Kids: Where You Came From, How Your Body Changes, and What Sex is All About,* Macmillan, 1993.

Ruth K. Westheimer and Steven Kaplan, *Surviving Salvation: The Ethiopian Jewish Family in Transition,* New York University Press, 1992.

Ruth K. Westheimer, *Dr. Ruth's Guide to Safer Sex,* Warner Books, 1992.

Ruth K. Westheimer, *Sex for Dummies,* IDG Books Worldwide, 1995.

Ruth K. Westheimer and Ben Yagoda, *The Value of Family: A Blueprint for the 21st Century,* Warner Books, 1996.

Ruth K. Westheimer and Pierre Lohu, *Dr. Ruth Talks About Grandparents: Advice for Kids on Making the Most of a Special Relationship,* Farrar Strauss Giroux, 1997.

Ruth K. Westheimer, ed., *Dr. Ruth's Encyclopedia of Sex,* Continuum, 1994, 319 p.

Ruth Westheimer, *The Art of Arousal,* Abbeville Press, 1993, 180 p.

Patricia Bosworth, "Talking with Doctor Goodsex," *Ladies' Home Journal* (February 1986): 82 + ;

Georgia Dullea, "Therapist to Therapist: Analyzing Dr. Ruth," *New York Times,* 26 October 1987, p. 8B;

George Hackett, "Talking Sex with Dr. Ruth," *Newsweek* (3 May 1982): 78. □

George Westinghouse

George Westinghouse (1846-1914), American inventor and manufacturer, made substantial contributions to railroad transportation safety and efficiency and to the transmission of electrical power.

George Westinghouse was born in Central Bridge, N.Y., on Oct. 6, 1846. After working in his father's machine factory in Schenectady, George served in the Union Army during the Civil War and then attended Union College for a short time. He received his first patents in 1865. His rotary steam engine proved impractical, but the car-replacer he designed to restore derailed cars to their tracks was successfully marketed.

Westinghouse laid the basis for his fortune when he patented his first air-brake invention in 1869 and organized the Westinghouse Air Brake Company. A number of patented improvements followed, including the truly revolutionary automatic air brake for trains (1872). He also worked to make all air-brake apparatus standardized and interchangeable and later developed a complete signal system for railroads. He formed the Union Switch and Signal Company in 1882.

Early in the 1880s Westinghouse applied his knowledge of compressed-air problems to the new natural-gas industry and patented several devices for the transmission and measurement of natural gas. This work in turn enabled him to comprehend the problems involved in distributing electrical power. An early convert to alternating current, he acquired European patents covering single-phase alternating-current transmission and organized the Westinghouse Electric Company in 1886. The company soon acquired the rights to a new polyphase alternating-current motor designed by Nikola Tesla and thus was equipped to produce power for both lights and motors. Westinghouse successfully advocated the alternating-current system, and in the early 1890s he received contracts to light the World's Co-

lumbian Exposition in Chicago and to develop a power system at Niagara Falls.

An incredibly prolific inventor, Westinghouse obtained an average of more than a patent a month during the 1880s. Among his most significant inventions were the friction gear, geared turbine, and air springs. He lost control of the Westinghouse Electric and the Westinghouse Machine companies in the business crisis of 1907, but his reputation for integrity and wisdom was such that he was one of three trustees appointed to reorganize the mammoth Equitable Life Assurance Company after its collapse at the same time. He died in New York City on March 12, 1914.

Further Reading

Good biographies of Westinghouse are Francis E. Leupp, *George Westinghouse: His Life and Achievements* (1918), primarily a personal account of the man, and Henry G. Prout, *A Life of George Westinghouse* (1921), chiefly useful for its technical explanations of Westinghouse's inventions. Also useful is H. Gordon Garbedian, *George Westinghouse: A Fabulous Inventor* (1943). For a good but dated appreciation of Westinghouse's financial achievements see Theodore J. Grayson, *Leaders and Periods of American Finance* (1932), as well as various Westinghouse Company publications. □

William Childs Westmoreland

William Childs Westmoreland (born 1914) was commander of all American forces in the Vietnam War from 1964 until 1968, when he became chief of staff of the U.S. Army.

B y the time the political and military situation in South Vietnam had become almost chaotic Westmoreland had risen to the rank of general. He had acquired a reputation for efficiency and was a protegé of General Maxwell D. Taylor, a leading proponent of the "Flexible Response" and the popular counterinsurgency strategies of the Kennedy administration.

In early 1964 President Lyndon Johnson sent Westmoreland to Saigon as deputy commander, U.S. Military Assistance Command, Vietnam. Within a few months, at the rank of full general, he succeeded to command American forces assisting the Republic of Vietnam in its war against the Communist Viet Cong insurgents. Westmoreland's assumption of command coincided with a decisive change in the nature of the conflict. The Viet Cong began shifting from small-scale guerrilla warfare to larger, more conventional attacks. Beginning early in 1965, regular North Vietnamese army units came south down the Ho Chi Minh Trail to reinforce the insurgents. In the same period the administra-

tion of President Lyndon B. Johnson further escalated the conflict, first with a limited bombing campaign against North Vietnam and then by introducing U.S. combat forces into South Vietnam.

Westmoreland did not determine overall American strategy and had no control over most of the air war against North Vietnam. He did direct American operations within South Vietnam. He attempted to carry out a balanced campaign of attacks on enemy regular units and their bases on the one hand, and assistance to the South Vietnamese in pacification and population security on the other. Many observers, however, criticized him for emphasizing the first part of the strategy at the expense of the second. His name became associated with tactics of "search and destroy." In February 1968 the Viet Cong launched their Tet offensive. Although Westmoreland, with considerable reason, regarded the outcome as an allied victory, this display of enemy strength convinced much of the American public that the war was a failure. President Johnson then turned toward de-escalation and negotiation. In the aftermath of Tet in July 1968, Westmoreland returned to Washington to become chief of staff of the army.

As chief of staff, Westmoreland faced a difficult task. He had to extricate the army from Vietnam, reorient it toward the future, and make the transition from the draft to an all-volunteer service, all in a period of virulent antimilitary sentiment. Although hampered by his own identification with an unpopular war, Westmoreland contributed much toward the post-Vietnam rebuilding of the army. He also championed his service's cause by extensive public speaking, despite antiwar and anti-military heckling and abuse.

Westmoreland retired as chief of staff on June 30, 1972. After that he made his home in South Carolina and continued an active public career. In 1974 he sought the Republican nomination for governor but was decisively defeated in the primary election. The controversies of the Vietnam War continued to follow him. In a January 1982 television documentary, "The Uncounted Enemy," the Columbia Broadcasting System accused Westmoreland of manipulating figures on enemy strength to deceive President Johnson concerning progress in the war. In response, Westmoreland sued CBS for libel. The case ended in February 1985 in an out-of-court settlement which left the factual issues unresolved and both sides claiming victory.

Further Reading

The earliest full-length biography of Westmoreland is the highly favorable one by Ernest B. Furgerson, *Westmoreland: The Inevitable General* (1968). Westmoreland tells the story of his command in Vietnam in *A Soldier Reports* (1976). His strategy is sharply criticized by David Halberstam in *The Best and the Brightest* (1972). Gen. Bruce Palmer, Jr., in *The Twenty-Five Year War: America's Military Role in Vietnam* (1984) also analyzes and is critical of Westmoreland's conduct of operations. Don Kowet in *A Matter of Honor* (1984) tells the story of the CBS controversy, as does Renata Adler in *Reckless Disregard: Westmoreland v. CBS et al.; Sharon v. TIME* (1986). The crucial Tet offensive is recounted in Don Oberdorfer's *Tet!* (1971).

In 1994, Vietnam veteran Samuel Zaffiri published a biography, *Westmoreland: A Biography of General William C. Westmoreland.* A book reviewer stated that the book offered "a fair hearing for a man who has been alternately overlooked and maligned by history." Articles of interest can be found in the *New York Times* (January 25, 1991; September 30, 1990; and November 28, 1988) and the *Los Angeles Times* (April 22, 1991 and March 25, 1991). □

Vivienne Westwood

British designer Vivienne Westwood (born 1941) is often credited with being the creator of "punk fashions," among other trend-setting styles.

Vivienne Westwood was born in Tinwhistle, England, in 1941. Following just one term at the Harrow Art School, Westwood left and trained to become a primary school teacher. She earned her living teaching until she crossed paths with Malcolm McLaren, the man behind the punk rock group The Sex Pistols.

Under McLaren's guidance and influence, Westwood slid into the world of youthful fashion, which reflected the turmoil of those rebellious times. She was responsible for mirroring and outfitting the social movements characterized by the growing segments of British population known as the Teddy Boys, Rockers, and, finally, the Punks.

In 1971 the duo began making drastic changes in British style with a series of shops located at 430 Kings Road. The first was Let It Rock, a 1950s revival boutique, coinciding with the Teddy Boys movement and zoot suits. The store also sold 1950s memorabilia and rock music. Then in 1972 the shop was changed to Too Fast To Live, Too Young To Die, a name stolen from a biker's jacket. In 1974 Westwood and McLaren opened their infamous Sex Shop, selling bondage and fetish fashions of rubber and leather. Rock star Adam Ant has commented that, "Sex was one of the all-time greatest shops in history."

The concept of satirical style and subversive chic was foremost in Westwood and McLaren's minds. Both were once prosecuted for wearing T-shirts that depicted a homosexual cowboy.

In 1975 they opened Seditionaries, the first authentic punk clothing shop in London. Jon Savage, a *Face* magazine writer, then called their look "the only modern look of the '70s." The shop translated the hard edges of street style in an interior filled with photos of a bombed-out, war-torn London. When her Pirate collection coincided with the New Romantic fashion movement in London, the shop changed focus again, becoming Worlds End, with a bizarre fantasy interior of slate tiles, cuckoo clocks, and sloping floors. Her next collection was dubbed Clothes for Heros, and her patrons included the soon-to-be-famous Boy George.

Westwood's next three collections, Savage (1981) and Hobo and Buffalo (both in 1982), were highly innovative, and her wildly staged shows (models square dancing to Appalachian music covered with mud makeup) affected the show styles of other designers.

Soon after, another shop opened in London's fashionable West End with a 3-D map of Africa. It was called Nostalgia of Mud, the name a slam of middle-class longings for low-life seedy chic. Westwood's clothing at this time consisted of rags tangled in hair, bras worn outside disheveled clothing, and ripped and torn T-shirts.

In 1983 Westwood's alliance with McLaren came to an explosive and painful end. Without his tutelage and often overbearing guidance, Westwood began to extend her design range. The Witches Collection (summer of 1983), the first completely on her own, was a highly successful showing of oddly shaped, cut, and proportioned garments (the neckline often found under the arm) based on a book about voodoo she had read. Her clothing was cut, not on a board, but on the body, pulling, draping, and then, finally, cutting.

After several seasons' absence, Westwood came back strong with her fall 1985 collection centered on the bubble-shaped hooped skirt with thigh-high stockings. Westwood's Mini-Crinis caused a shift in silhouette that was swiftly picked up, first by Jean Paul Gaultier, then by almost every other designer in Europe and New York. In fact, 1986 was dubbed by fashion seers as The Year That Went Pouf, and all because of Vivienne Westwood. Through the 1990s Westwood continued to reign as Queen of Punk Fashion. She scandalized and outraged the world of fashion with bare-breasted models and bizarre creations at yearly shows in

Paris and other centers of design. A childhood friend, Fred Vermorel, wrote a biography of Westwood in 1996.

Westwood and McLaren can be justified in claiming that they invented "punk fashions," and, despite her rebellious nature, the fashion establishment recognized her work as important. Her Pirate outfit was the centerpiece of the modern dress collection in London's Victoria & Albert Museum. Decadent, depraved, and demented are all words that describe the fashions of Vivienne Westwood. She once said of her designs, "My aim is to make the poor look rich and the rich look poor."

Further Reading

Additional information on designers and fashions can be found in the *Fairchild Dictionary of Fashion* (1988), *McDowell's Directory of 20th Century Fashion* (1987), and Catherine McDermott's *Street Style* (1987). See also Andrew Edelstein's *The Pop Sixties* (1985), Alison Lurie's *The Language of Clothes* (1983), and Melissa Sones' *Getting into Fashion* (1984). A biography was written in 1996, Fred Vermorel, *Vivienne Westwood: Fashion, Perversity and the Sixties Laid Bare*. Articles and reviews of fashion shows include "Marion Hume, Portrait of a Former Punk," *Vogue* (September, 1994) and Amy M. Spindler, "Treating History with a Sense of Pride," *New York Times* (March 17, 1997). □

Nancy Wexler

Psychologist Nancy Wexler (born 1945) researched Huntington's disease and developed a presymptomatic test for the condition as well as the identification of the genes responsible for the disease.

Nancy Wexler's research on Huntington's disease has led to the development of a presymptomatic test for the condition as well as the identification of the genes responsible for the disease. The symptoms of this fatal, genetically based disorder (for which Wexler herself is at risk) usually appear around middle age, and the disease leads to the degeneration of mental, psychological, and physical functioning. For her pivotal role in these achievements, Wexler was granted the Albert Lasker Public Service Award in 1993.

Nancy Sabin Wexler was born on July 19, 1945, to Milton Wexler, a Los Angeles psychoanalyst, and Leonore Sabin Wexler. She studied social relations and English at Radcliffe and graduated in 1967. Wexler subsequently traveled to Jamaica on a Fulbright scholarship and studied at the Hampstead Clinic Child Psychoanalytic Training Center in London.

In 1968 Wexler learned that her mother had developed the symptoms of Huntington's disease, a condition to which Wexler's maternal grandfather and three uncles had already succumbed. Efforts to fight the disease became a primary mission for Wexler and her family: Her father founded the Hereditary Disease Foundation in 1968, and Wexler herself, who was then entering the doctoral program in

clinical psychology at the University of Michigan, eventually wrote her doctoral thesis on the "Perceptual-motor, Cognitive, and Emotional Characteristics of Persons-at-Risk for Huntington's Disease," and received her Ph.D. in 1974.

After graduating from University of Michigan, Wexler taught psychology at the New School for Social Research in New York City and worked as a researcher on Huntington's disease for the National Institutes of Health (NIH). In 1976 she was appointed by congress to head the NIH's Commission for the Control of Huntington's Disease and its Consequences. In 1985 she joined the College of Physicians and Surgeons at Columbia University.

In 1979 Wexler's research led her to Lake Maracaibo in Venezuela, where she studied a community which had a high incidence of Huntington's disease. Wexler kept medical records, took blood and skin samples, and charted the transmission of the disease within families. Wexler sent the samples she collected to geneticist James Gusella at Massachusetts General Hospital, who used the blood samples to conduct a study to locate the gene—the first such genetic mapping of a disease. Gusella eventually discovered a deoxyribonucleic acid (DNA) marker close to the Huntington's gene. Based on this study, Gusella introduced a test that was ninety-six percent accurate in detecting whether an individual bears the Huntington's gene. Because there was still no cure for the Huntington's disease, the test proved to be controversial, raising many issues involving patient rights, childbearing decisions, and discrimination by employers and insurance companies. In her interviews and writings Wexler has stressed the importance of keeping such genetic information confidential.

In 1993 the Huntington's gene was identified through research based on the Venezuelan blood samples and the work of the Huntington's Disease Collaborative Research Group. In October, 1993, Wexler received an Albert Lasker Public Service Award for her role in this effort. In addition, she has served as an advisor on social and medical ethics issues to the Human Genome Project—a massive international effort to map and identify the approximately 100,000 genes in the human body. Wexler also has assumed directorship of the Hereditary Disease Foundation founded by her father, to which she donated the honorarium that accompanied the Lasker Award.

As a pioneer in the field of geriatric care management, Wexler was a founding member of the National Association of Professional Geriatric Care Managers. Sher served on the organization's first National Board of Directors, as well as the association's first standards committee. She serves as director of Gerontology Associates, Alzheimer's Case Management Professional Placement Services in Los Angeles and is on the staffs of UCLA Neuropsychiatric Institute, Encino-Tarzana Regional Medical Center, and Northridge Hospital.

Further Reading

About Nancy Wexler, MA, MFCC, "http://www.nancy-wexler.com/bio.htm," July 23, 1997.
Newsmakers, Gale, 1992, pp. 530–33.
U.S. News & World Report, April 22, 1985, pp. 75–76.
Bluestone, Mimi, "Science and Ethics: The Double Life of Nancy Wexler," in *Ms.,* November/December 1991, pp. 90–91.
Grady, Denise, "The Ticking of a Time Bomb in the Genes," in *Discover,* June 1987.
Jaroff, Leon, "Making the Best of a Bad Gene," in *Time,* February 10, 1992, pp. 78–79.
Konner, Melvin, "New Keys to the Mind," in *New York Times Magazine,* July 17, 1988, pp. 49–50.
New York Times, October 1, 1993, p. A24. □

Rogier van der Weyden

The Flemish painter Rogier van der Weyden (1399-1464) was the most influential northern artist of the 15th century. His style is characterized by fluency of line, rhythmic composition, and expressive intensity.

Rogier van der Weyden, Jan van Eyck, and Robert Campin were the founding fathers of the main traditions of early Netherlandish painting. The formal beauty and spiritual intensity of Weyden's art, however, made Netherlandish painting more readily accessible to succeeding generations of artists than the work of his two major contemporaries.

Rogier van der Weyden, probably born at Tournai, was the son of a master cutler. Weyden was apprenticed to Campin on March 5, 1427. In 1432 he was received into the

Tournai guild as a master and presumably remained in that city for the next 3 years. In 1436 he is recorded in Brussels, where he was appointed city painter. With the exception of a pilgrimage to Rome in 1450, Weyden resided in Brussels the rest of his life.

Weyden: Master of Flémalle Controversy

Weyden neither signed nor dated his paintings and thus created major stylistic and chronological problems for recent historians of his art. The central issue is the relationship of Weyden to his master, Campin. This is especially critical in light of the fact that Campin is now most generally identified as the painter of a group of works formerly attributed to the anonymous Master of Flémalle.

Weyden's close connection to the style of these paintings can be seen most clearly in the *Annunciation* in Paris, which is one of the earliest works attributable to him. Numerous details of the setting as well as the spatial construction plainly rely on works by Campin (compare Campin's *Mérode Altarpiece*), yet major stylistic differences are also apparent. In place of Campin's earthy, robust figures, Weyden has substituted longer, more elegant types who enact the religious scene before, rather than within, the deep space of the room. A tendency to emphasize line over plastic shape and a greater sensibility to color are also marked features of Weyden's style that clearly demarcate his work from that of the Master of Flémalle. In short, few scholars today would subscribe to the once fashionable thesis that Weyden and the Master of Flémalle are one and the same painter.

Early Style

The work of the period from about 1435 to 1445 is characterized by a developing awareness of the style of Jan van Eyck and a lessening of the Campin influence. Weyden's *St. Luke Painting the Virgin* in Boston (ca. 1435-1437) is largely based upon an Eyckian scheme but contains several typical Weydenian transformations. In place of Van Eyck's detailed treatment of the complexity and multiplicity of the external world, Weyden has substituted a reduced and simplified setting in order to heighten the spiritual content. This evidence of the painter's instinctive austerity confirms Erwin Panofsky's view (1953) that "Weyden's world was at once physically barer and spiritually richer than Jan van Eyck's."

The *Crucifixion Triptych* in Vienna (1440-1445) marks the boundary between the early style and the mature phase of Weyden's work. The painting still retains several Eyckian features, such as the continuous landscape background across all three panels, but it also introduces a new emotive quality in the sense of dramatic immediacy. In this connection another important innovation is the inclusion of two donors directly within the drama.

Close in spirit to the Vienna *Crucifixion* is the great *Deposition* panel in Madrid. The date of this work and the source of many of the influences that inspired it are still widely disputed, but the painting is universally recognized for its unique expression force. Based upon a sculptural device of compressing a maximum of form into a minimum of space, the work evokes sentiments of profound religiosity and emotional intensity. As one of the most influential paintings of its time, Weyden's *Deposition* firmly established the iconography for this subject for over half a century.

Mature Style

This period is initiated by the magnificent *Last Judgment Altarpiece* in Beaune (late 1440s), executed for Nicolas Rolin, Chancellor of Burgundy. This gigantic altarpiece measures about 18 feet across when the wings are opened. Of all Weyden's paintings, none more fully reveals the artist's fundamental "Gothicism" in combination with a creative approach to the art of the past. In its austere and hieratic frontality, the painting displays the influence of Gothic sculpture, yet the absence of demons and other traditional symbols of the tortures of hell suggests a highly subjective, almost modern conception of Christian eschatology. Stylistically the work is distinguished by a greater attenuation of form and a more sophisticated treatment of line and color.

Weyden's journey to Rome in 1450 is evidenced by two paintings, the *Entombment* in Florence and the *Virgin and Child with Peter, John the Baptist, Cosmas, and Damian* in Frankfurt, which are based on unique Italian iconographies, yet remain thoroughly northern in style. The *Braque Triptych* in Paris, however, reveals a new, monumentalized conception of form that could only derive from a close study and appreciation of Italian painting.

The synthesis of the newly acquired "monumental style" with Weyden's inherently abstemious outlook is achieved in the *Bladelin Triptych* in Berlin-Dahlem (ca. 1452), an altarpiece painted for Pierre Bladelin, Receiver General of Burgundy. The theme of the Nativity is here treated in a manner that effectively fuses the painter's concern for both planar and spatial values. This is partially achieved by the use of a classic, triangular composition to stabilize the fluid, interlocking movement of forms upon the surface of the painting.

Late Period

Weyden's so-called *ultima maniera,* which dates from about 1456 until his death in 1464, is based upon a sense of heightened spiritual refinement in combination with an increasing pictorial asceticism. This late style is first revealed in the austerely beautiful *Crucifixion Diptych* in Philadelphia, in which the artist has reduced the setting to a bare stone wall to heighten and dramatize the emotional content. Forms are elongated and dematerialized, thus conveying the spiritual message of the work in essentially abstract and stylized terms.

The *St. Columba Altarpiece* in Munich (ca. 1462) is the latest of Weyden's surviving works and forms a noble conclusion to his career. In this painting, his only treatment of the theme of the Adoration of the Magi, Weyden attains a total harmony of fluid surface design with formal balance and clarified spatial organization. Graphic beauty is achieved without sacrifice of mass or volume, while grace and elegance are revealed within a context of significant spirituality. One of the most passionate of all religious painters, Weyden has created a magisterial synthesis as his final legacy to northern painting.

Weyden's portraits reflect a stylistic development similar to that found in the religious works. The *Portrait of a Young Lady* in Berlin is an early work composed in the cold and detached manner of Jan van Eyck. The elegant *Portrait of a Lady* in Washington (ca. 1455) conforms to the more refined style of Weyden's middle period. Stylization and linear abstraction are here employed in order to impose the painter's own sense of aristocratic reserve upon the sitter. As a consequence, the work becomes a study of Weyden's own character rather than an objective statement of fact concerning another individual.

The impact of Weyden's art on European painting was so great as to virtually defy calculation. His influence can be seen in the next generation of Flemish painters and was also present to some degree in the work of almost every important French, German, and Spanish artist of the second half of the 15th century.

Further Reading

A brilliant appreciation of Rogier van der Weyden's work is in Erwin Panofsky *Early Netherlandish Painting* (2 vols., 1953), which contains a sensitive analysis of the painter's stylistic development and definitive survey of all the major paintings. For an older and now partially discredited view of Weyden's work, see volume 2 of Max J. Friedländer, *Early Netherlandish Painting,* translated by H. Norden (2 vols., 1967). Rogier is discussed in R. H. Wilenski, *Flemish Painters, 1430-1830* (2 vols., 1960); Margaret Dickens Whinney, *Early Flemish Painting* (1968); and Charles D. Cuttler, *Northern Painting from Pucelle to Bruegel* (1968).

Additional Sources

Campbell, Lorne, *Van der Weyden,* New York: Harper & Row, 1980. □

Edith Wharton

Edith Wharton (1861-1937), American author, chronicled the life of affluent Americans between the Civil War and World War I.

Edith Wharton was born Edith Newbold Jones in New York City, probably on Jan. 24, 1861. Like many other biographical facts, she kept her birth date secret. Gossip held that the family's English tutor—not George Frederic Jones—was really Edith's father. The truth may never be known, but Edith evidently believed the story. After the Civil War, George Jones took his family to Europe, where they could live more cheaply.

Back in New York, by the age of 18 Edith had published poems in magazines and in a privately printed volume and had experimented with fiction. However, events deferred her writing career. The family's second long European trip ended in her father's death. In New York again, she evidently fell in love with Walter Berry; yet she became engaged to Edward Wharton, eleven years her senior, a wealthy Bostonian. They were married in 1885.

Marriage brought Edith Wharton two things she valued most, travel and leisure for writing. In the early 1890s her stories began appearing in magazines, but her first commercial success was a book written with an architect, *The Decoration of Houses* (1897). She sought help on it from Walter Berry, who remained in some uncertain way part of her life until his death (1927). Soon after this book, Mrs. Wharton suffered a nervous breakdown. For therapy her physician suggested she write fiction. In 1899 a collection of stories, *The Greater Inclination,* appeared—the first of her 32 volumes of fiction.

In 1905, after she began her friendship with Henry James, Wharton's first masterpiece, *The House of Mirth,* laid bare the cruelties of New York society. Her range was apparent in *Tales of Men and Ghosts* (1910), a collection of chillers, and in the celebrated novella *Ethan Frome* (1911). In 1910 the Whartons moved to France, where Edward Wharton suffered a nervous breakdown and was placed in a sanitorium. After their divorce in 1913, Edith Wharton stayed in France, writing lovingly about it in *French Ways and Their Meanings* (1919) and other books.

The Age of Innocence, a splendid novel of New York, won the Pulitzer Prize (1921), and a dramatization of Mrs. Wharton's novella *The Old Maid* won the Pulitzer Prize for drama (1935). She died of a cardiac attack on Aug. 11, 1937, and was buried in Versailles next to Walter Berry.

Further Reading

The first edition of all of Wharton's short stories, edited with an introduction by R. W. B. Lewis, is *The Collected Short Stories of Edith Wharton* (1968). Wharton's autobiographical work, *A Backward Glance* (1934), and the book by her friend Percy Lubbock, *Portrait of Edith Wharton* (1947), convey a sense of the woman. A detailed, enthusiastic biography is Grace (Kellogg) Griffith, *The Two Lives of Edith Wharton: The Woman and Her Work* (1965), but it was written without access to the Wharton Papers in the Yale University Library. The more scholarly work by Millicent Bell, *Edith Wharton and Henry James: The Story of Their Friendship* (1965), although restricted to part of Mrs. Wharton's life, makes use of materials not available to Griffith. Useful critical studies include Blake Nevius, *Edith Wharton: A Study of Her Fiction* (1953); Irving Howe, *Edith Wharton: A Collection of Critical Essays* (1962); and Louis Auchincloss's short *Edith Wharton: A Woman in Her Time* (1971). □

Phillis Wheatley

Phillis Wheatley (ca. 1753-1784), the first African American woman poet, was a celebrated literary figure in Boston during the Revolutionary era.

n 1761, a frail child of seven or eight years, Phillis Wheatley came to America by slaveship from Senegal and was auctioned to Mrs. John Wheatley, wife of a prosperous Boston tailor. The Wheatleys and their children, Mary and Nathaniel, found Phillis, as they named her, highly intelligent and responsive. Mary taught Phillis to read and write. She read the Bible, Alexander Pope's translations of Homer, the Latin classics, books on mythology, and the English poets. At 13 she wrote her first poem.

Menial tasks were not expected of Phillis. She accompanied the family on social occasions, although she asked to eat at a table separate from the other guests. She kept writing supplies by her bed so that she could write at all times. She was raised a strict Congregationalist and at 18 belonged to the Old South Meeting House, though ordinarily slaves were excluded from church membership. In 1773 she was formally freed.

Never very strong, Wheatley was sent with Nathaniel to England for her health in 1773. There her *Poems on Various Subjects, Religious and Moral* was published, dedicated to her hostess, the Countess of Huntington. Another volume was planned, but the Revolutionary War prevented its appearance. Her trip was cut short by the sudden illness of Mrs. Wheatley, who died in 1774.

Wheatley married John Peters, a free black man who had several trades but was unable to support her. After her husband deserted her and their two children, she worked for room and board in a boarding house. She died penniless in Boston on Dec. 5, 1784.

The poetry in *Poems on Various Subjects* is imitative and conventional. Wheatley's attitudes are deeply religious. The poetry is often elegaic. Her first poem, ''On the Death of the Reverend Mr. George Whitefield'' (1770), commemorates the English evangelist so instrumental in the Great Awakening. Her poems often honor a person or an occasion: ''His Excellency, General Washington'' (1775) prompted a personal note from Washington. Some subjects are general—''On Recollection,'' ''On Imagination,'' ''On Virtue''; others retell stories from Ovid or the Bible.

Wheatley evidently did not preserve her African heritage. Saunders Redding said her work had a ''negative, bloodless, unracial quality'' and seemed ''superficial, especially to members of her own race.'' Apparently, her only memory of Africa was of her mother at dawn pouring water in a ritual to the rising sun. Strikingly, there is scarcely a Wheatley poem that does not celebrate the rising sun. She repeatedly rejoices that ''darkness ends in everlasting day.'' She interprets her slavery and her ''darkness'' (note the italicized words in the following) as typical of all mankind: ''On *Death's* domain intent I fix my eyes,/ where human nature in vast ruin lies.'' She, an ''*Ethiop*,'' has experienced ''those dark abodes'' and that ''*Egyptian* gloom'' that make her so fully appreciate freedom's ''genial ray.''

Further Reading

The Poems of Phillis Wheatley was edited by Julian D. Mason, Jr. (1966), and *Poems and Letters* was edited by Charles Frederick Heartman (1915; repr. 1969). Vernon Loggins, *The Negro Author* (1931), discusses Phillis Wheatley's life and work; Langston Hughes, *Famous American Negroes* (1954), devotes a chapter to her; Martha S. Baconhas, *Puritan Promenade* (1964), contains a long section on her; and Benjamin G. Brawley, *The Negro Genius: A New Appraisal of the Achievement of the American Negro in Literature and the Fine Arts* (1966), offers a short, informative account of her life. An assessment of Wheatley's work in the context of black poetry is in J. Saunders Redding, *To Make a Poet Black* (1939). □

Eleazar Wheelock

Eleazar Wheelock (1711-1779), American clergyman and educator, was the founder of Dartmouth College and led efforts to educate the Indians of New England.

E leazar Wheelock was born on April 22, 1711, in Windham, Conn. In 1733 he graduated from Yale. The following year he continued his theological studies in New Haven. In May 1734 he was licensed to preach and the following February was called to the pulpit of the Second (or North) parish in Lebanon, Conn. In April he married Sarah Davenport Maltby, a widow, by whom he had six children.

When the movement of religious fervor known as the Great Awakening swept over New England in 1740, Wheelock was its warmest supporter in Connecticut. He traveled extensively, preached persuasively, and served as the chief intelligencer of revival news. Assailed by orthodox persons for his itinerancy, the neglect of his own parish, and the promulgation of "a meer *passionate* Religion," he was deprived of his salary in 1743 by the General Assembly.

Though Wheelock owned considerable farmland, the loss of his salary prompted him to take a few boys into his house for college preparation. In 1743 Samson Occam, a Mohegan Indian youth who had learned English and been converted to Christianity in his childhood, entered Wheelock's tutelage to prepare for the ministry. Wheelock was so encouraged by Occam's progress that he decided to found an Indian school that would send educated natives back to their people as missionaries and teachers.

To finance his school, Wheelock appealed, with good result, to charitable groups and the benevolent rich at home and in Great Britain. His school was initially successful. In 1765 it had 46 charity students. But internecine Indian strife, the attrition rate of his students, and the half successes of his graduates caused Wheelock to look toward an expanded institution. He was offered a tract of land in New Hampshire and on Dec. 13, 1769, obtained a charter for Dartmouth College.

In 1770 Wheelock moved his family to the virgin forests of New Hampshire. Living in a few log huts, he and 30 students sought to preserve Anglo-American civilization and to bring the word of God to the Indian. Wheelock was president, professor of divinity, pastor of the Dartmouth

church and oversaw the building of a town, its supply, and farming operations.

Because it was removed from the paths of war, Dartmouth survived the Revolution unscathed. But Wheelock's health failed, and he died on April 24, 1779. A son by a second marriage succeeded to the college presidency.

Further Reading

Wheelock's only important writing was his continuing *Plain and Faithful Narrative of the Original Design, Rise, Progress and Present State of the Indian Charity-School at Lebanon in Conn.* (1763, 1765-1775). James D. McCallum is Wheelock's best biographer in *Eleazar Wheelock: Founder of Dartmouth College* (1939), although Leon B. Richardson, *History of Dartmouth College* (2 vols., 1932), places many details in a rich educational setting. □

William Wheelwright

William Wheelwright (1798-1873) was an American promoter who pioneered South American steamship, railroad, and telegraph construction.

Willliam Wheelwright was born in Newburyport, Mass., on March 18, 1798. After attending Phillips Academy in Andover (1812-1814) he sailed as a cabin boy aboard one of his father's ships trading in the West Indies. In 1817 he captained a family ship to Brazil. When a vessel under his command ran aground off Buenos Aires in 1823, he shipped out as a supercargo on a vessel bound for Chile. He subsequently founded a prosperous mercantile firm and served as U.S. consul in Guayaquil, Ecuador.

In 1828 Wheelwright returned to Newburyport, married Martha Bartlet, and took her on a mule-back honeymoon trip across Panama en route to Ecuador. Finding his enterprise had collapsed, he moved to Valparaiso in Chile and established a coastal shipping business. Several sidelines—development of port facilities and gasworks, mineral explorations, and experimentation with desalting ocean water—also absorbed his attentions.

Wheelwright's navigational experience stimulated his interest in introducing the recently perfected steamship on the Pacific coast of South America, where contrary winds and currents severely hamper wind-driven vessels. Although this scheme was considered to be highly impractical, in 1835 Chile's government granted a 10-year concession to operate steamers on that country's long coastline. After unsuccessfully seeking financial support in the United States in 1836, Wheelwright went to London and in 1838 influenced a British investment group to form the Pacific Steamship Navigation Company, which he served as managing director until 1852. A British government mail contract helped defray expenses.

In 1840 Wheelwright sailed two 700-ton steamers, the *Chile* and the *Peru,* through the Strait of Magellan to initiate steamship service from Callao to Valparaiso. After a 5-year struggle against seemingly insuperable obstacles, especially that of obtaining enough coal for fuel, the company began to show a profit.

While residing in Chile, Wheelwright inaugurated South America's first railroad and telegraph lines. He built a spectacular 51-mile railroad from Caldera to Copiapó (1849-1852) and wanted to extend the railway across the Andes to Argentina. Finding little support for this scheme in Chile, he moved to Argentina and, using English capital, constructed the Argentine Central Railroad between Rosario and Córdoba (1863-1870). He developed the La Plata portworks with a connecting railroad serving Buenos Aires in 1872. Regrettably, Argentina's war with Paraguay (1864-1870) and internal political strife obstructed Wheelwright's plans and deferred completion of the trans-Andean line until 1910. He died in London on a business trip on Sept. 26, 1873.

Further Reading

A notable Argentine philosopher, Juan Bautista Alberdi, wrote a commemorative biography, *Life and Industrial Labors of William Wheelwright in South America* (trans. 1877). Arthur C. Wardle, Steam *Conquers the Pacific* (1940), outlines Wheelwright's career. ☐

George Hoyt Whipple

The American pathologist George Hoyt Whipple (1878-1976) found that certain foods, especially liver, stimulate the regeneration of hemoglobin in animals suffering anemia.

George Hoyt Whipple was born in Ashland, New Hampshire, on August 28, 1878. He attended local schools until, at age 13, he transferred to a school in Tilton 15 miles away. Then in 1892 his widowed mother moved to Andover, Massachusetts, so that George could attend Phillips Academy. After graduation he entered Yale, received a degree in 1900, and in 1901 entered Johns Hopkins Medical School. He received his medical degree in 1905 and joined the department of pathology at John Hopkins almost immediately.

Whipple's early work led to the discovery in 1907 of a rare disease now commonly called "Whipple's disease," which is related to a breakdown in fat storage in the body. In 1907 he accepted a one-year position in pathology at Ancon Hospital in the Panama Canal Zone but returned to Hopkins in 1908 as assistant resident pathologist. He advanced to resident pathologist and assistant professor of pathology in 1909, and in 1911 he was made associate professor.

On June 24, 1914, Whipple married Katharine Ball Waring. That same year he accepted a position as professor of research medicine and director of the Hooper Foundation for Medical Research in San Francisco. The foundation was

a new, independent unit of the University of California, and Whipple was responsible for its organization. There he continued experiments started at Hopkins on the metabolism of bile pigments, which are made from hemoglobin that has been released from broken-down red blood corpuscles.

In 1920 Whipple was appointed dean of the University of California Medical School. In 1921 he became professor of pathology and dean of the new School of Medicine and Dentistry at the University of Rochester. The researches of Whipple and his colleagues on bile pigments and hemoglobin regeneration continued and were reported in a long series of scientific articles. The specific use of liver as an agent that stimulates the regeneration of hemoglobin was reported in the *American Journal of Physiology* in 1925. This discovery paved the way for the use of a raw liver diet in the treatment of pernicious anemia by George Richards Minot and William Parry Murphy. Minot and Murphy shared the 1934 Nobel Prize with Whipple.

Whipple's studies continued unabated, and among many other things he, with his collaborators, determined a long list of specific dietary factors, such as iron and copper, that influence hemoglobin regeneration.

Whipple was an active member of many scientific societies and was associated with the Rockefeller Foundation from 1927 until 1960. He retired as dean in 1953 and as professor of pathology in 1955. Whipple died on February 1, 1976.

Further Reading

George W. Corner, *George Hoyt Whipple and His Friends: The Life-story of a Nobel Prize Pathologist* (1963), is an informative and detailed biography that includes a complete bibliography of Whipple's publications. Brief accounts of Whipple's life and work are in Lloyd G. Stevenson, *Nobel Prize Winners in Medicine and Physiology* (1954), and Nobel Foundation, *Nobel Lectures: Physiology or Medicine, 1922-1941*, vol. 2 (1965). □

James Abbott McNeill Whistler

The American painter, etcher, and lithographer James Abbott McNeill Whistler (1834-1903) created a new set of esthetic principles, championed art for art's sake, and introduced a subtle style of painting in which atmosphere and mood predominated.

James McNeill Whistler was born in Lowell, Mass., on July 10, 1834, the son of Major George Whistler, a railroad engineer. In 1842 Czar Nicholas I of Russia invited Major Whistler to build a railroad from St. Petersburg to Moscow and offered the princely salary of $12,000 a year. In St. Petersburg the family lived luxuriously, with several servants, and James and his brother had a governess and a Swedish tutor. Because French was the court language, the boys soon became fluent in it. On one occasion the Whistlers took a trip 15 miles out of St. Petersburg to Tsarkoe Selo. Here, in the palace built by Catherine the Great, there was a suite of apartments in the Chinese style containing many fine examples of Oriental porcelain. James was fascinated by this collection and later became a collector of blue-and-white porcelain.

James's interest in drawing, which had begun when he was 4, greatly increased during the years in Russia, and in 1845 he was enrolled in a drawing course at the Academy of Fine Arts in St. Petersburg. In 1849 Major Whistler died, and Mrs. Whistler returned to America with her sons, settling in Pomfret, Conn. James decided he wanted to go to the U.S. Military Academy at West Point, which his father had attended, and obtained an appointment in 1851. At West Point he stood first in the drawing course but was deficient in chemistry. Because he constantly broke the rules, he accumulated 218 demerits and as a result was dismissed in 1854.

After an unsuccessful apprenticeship with the Winaas Locomotive Works in Baltimore, Whistler obtained a job in Washington, D.C., with the Coast and Geodetic Survey. He was always late, often absent, and was the despair of his employer. However, he had the finest training in etching and learned the basic principles of printmaking.

Departure for Europe

With a $350-a-year inheritance from his father, Whistler went abroad to study art. He arrived in Paris in 1855 and at once threw himself into the bohemian life of the French students. He spent two years in the atelier of Charles Gabriel Gleyre but learned little from his master, who came only once a week to give perfunctory criticism. While copying in the Louvre in 1858, Whistler met Henri Fantin-Latour, who in turn introduced him to Alphonse Legros and other artists, including the great realist painter Gustave Courbet. In 1858 Whistler brought out *Twelve Etchings from Nature,* known as the French Set. The next year his first important painting, *At the Piano,* influenced by Fantin-Latour and Dutch 17th-century interiors, was rejected by the Paris Salon, although it was accepted by the Royal Academy in London in 1860.

Whistler settled in London, where he had relatives, but spent much time at an inn in Wapping, and his early Thames etchings and paintings were done in this area. He depicted people at ease in their own environment and his work never told a story or pointed a moral, which was very much against the trend of mid-Victorian England. He was already anticipating the concept of "art for art's sake."

Whistler's painting *Wapping* (1861) shows the influence of Courbet's realism. One of the figures in the foreground is the redheaded Irish beauty Joanna Hiffernan, known as Jo, who became both Whistler's model and mistress. He painted her as *The White Girl* (1862), standing in a white dress, against a white background, with her red hair over her shoulder. The figure is medieval in feeling with a remoteness and introspective gaze that place it close to the Pre-Raphaelite painters. Whistler knew their work; he had met Dante Gabriel Rossetti in 1862 and was decidely influenced by the Pre-Rapahelites at this time. Although *The White Girl* was rejected by the Royal Academy in 1862 and the Paris Salon of 1863, it was a sensation at the Salon des Refusés, admired by artists though laughed at by the public.

In 1863 Whistler leased a house in the Chelsea section of London, where he set up housekeeping with Jo. His mother arrived late that year and spent the rest of her life in England. Whistler became a collector of blue-and-white porcelain as well as Oriental costumes, in which he posed his models for such pictures as *La Princess du Pays de la Porcelaine* (1864). Despite the Oriental trappings, these paintings are essentially Victorian. Influenced by his friendship with Albert Joseph Moore, whose subjects were drawn from classical antiquity, Whistler did numerous classical subjects.

The Nocturnes

In 1871 Whistler published the 16 etchings *Views of the Thames,* known as the Thames Set. He also did a series of atmospheric paintings which he called nocturnes. He liked to go out on the river at twilight and was fascinated by the foggy or misty effects in the fading light. In putting these impressions on canvas from memory, he made use of the Japanese concept of space as a well-balanced design in which perspective plays no part. In the famous *Arrangement in Grey and Black, the Artist's Mother* (1872) he composed the picture with disarming simplicity, keeping compartmental Japanese spatial relationship in mind.

During 1877 Whistler exhibited several paintings, including *Falling Rocket,* a nocturne showing the mysterious and elusive effects of fireworks at night at Cremorne Gardens. It outraged John Ruskin, considered the arbiter of taste in England, and he wrote an insulting review of the exhibition. Whistler sued him for libel in what was the most sensational art trial of the century and was awarded a farthing damages without costs. The trial ruined Whistler financially, and he had to sell the house which architect E. W. Godwin had just built for him and dispose of his porcelain collection.

Fortunately, the Fine Arts Society commissioned Whistler to do 12 etchings of Venice. He spent 14 months in Venice doing many etchings as well as small oils, watercolors, and pastels. His etching style was now completely changed. He treated his themes with the utmost delicacy, using a spidery line and lively curves, and he often wiped the plates to give tone. His Venetian work sold well and he was financially re-established. He took a house in London with Maud Franklin, who had replaced Jo as model and mistress.

On the evening of Jan. 31, 1885, Whistler delivered at Prince's Hall the "Ten O'Clock," his famous lecture summing up his theories of esthetics in beautifully polished prose. He mentioned the poetry that evening mists produce when "the tall chimneys become campanili and the warehouses are palaces at night."

Master Lithographer

One of Whistler's finest achievements was in the field of lithography, which he concentrated on for a 10-year period beginning in 1887. Drawing in the most spirited way, he used a stump as well as a pencil and obtained effects never achieved by a lithographer before him. He had great facility with watercolors and small oils which sometimes depicted the seaside or shop fronts in Chelsea. In portraiture he favored full-length standing poses, influenced by Diego Velázquez, and was more concerned with subtle tones and atmosphere than he was with exact likenesses.

In 1888 Whistler married E. W. Godwin's widow, Beatrix. The Whistlers moved to Paris in 1893 but 2 years later were back in England. Trixie, as his wife was called, died of cancer in 1896. After her death, Whistler maintained studios in both Paris and London. He died in London on July 17, 1903.

Further Reading

Whistler set forth his ideas on art in *The Gentle Art of Making Enemies* (1890). Studies of Whistler and his work include Joseph and Elizabeth Robbins Pennell, *The Life of James McNeill Whistler* (2 vols., 1908); Frederick A. Sweet, *Sargent, Whistler, and Mary Cassatt* (1954); Denys Sutton, *Nocturne: The Art of James McNeill Whistler* (1964); and Frederick A. Sweet, *James McNeill Whistler* (1968). □

Andrew Dickson White

Andrew Dickson White (1832-1918), American educator and diplomat, helped found Cornell University and became its first president.

Andrew Dickson White was born in Homer, N.Y., on Nov. 7, 1832. At the age of 17 he entered the Episcopal-oriented Geneva (Hobart) College in western New York, but he disliked it and after a year dropped out and entered Yale. Upon graduating in 1853, he and his friend Daniel Gilman went to Europe. White studied languages and history in Paris and Berlin, and during 1854-1855 he served for 6 months as an attaché to the American minister in St. Petersburg, Russia.

In 1856 White received his master of arts degree from Yale and then accepted an offer to be professor of history at the nonsectarian University of Michigan. The young, innovative teacher was an immediate success. During his 6 years there he conceived of a new university for central New York that would be shorn of outworn traditions and would offer the broadest opportunities for study in higher education.

When his father died in 1862, White returned to New York to handle the business affairs of his father's bank. In 1864 he became a state senator, and in the New York Legislature he joined with another senator, Ezra Cornell, on the problem of utilizing the land grant of the Morrill Act (1862), which provided the state with the means of offering education in agriculture and mechanical arts. White fought to concentrate the Federal aid in one institution, and Cornell agreed to give $500,000 and land for a site to bolster that aim. The result was Cornell University, officially inaugurated in October 1868, with White as its president. He retired from this post in 1885.

During his years at Cornell, where White taught history as well as being chief administrator, he brought to reality his earlier concept of a nonsectarian, coeducational university where not only the classics but also modern subjects including science, agriculture, mechanical arts, and even military science would be taught—a place where every student could study just what interested him or her. White's reforms in teaching and in the curriculum gained him national attention.

White took a leave of absence from Cornell to serve as U.S. minister to Germany (1879-1881). After he retired from the university he served as U.S. minister to Russia (1892-1894) and U.S. ambassador to Germany (1897-1902). He was also minister to the Hague Peace Conference in 1899. He spent his later years in writing and influencing educational projects. He died on Nov. 4, 1918, in Ithaca, N.Y.

Further Reading

The main sources for White's life are *Autobiography of Andrew Dickson White* (2 vols., 1905), and Walter P. Rogers, *Andrew D. White and the Modern University* (1942). A good summary of his educational career is in Carl L. Becker, *Cornell University: Founders and the Founding* (1943).

Additional Sources

Altschuler, Glenn C., *Andrew D. White, educator, historian, diplomat*, Ithaca, N.Y.: Cornell University Press, 1979. □

Byron R. White

Byron R. White (born 1917) was a football star, a successful lawyer, a deputy U.S. attorney general, and a U.S. Supreme Court justice. On the high court, he was considered an independent and often served as a swing vote in close decisions, though he most often sided with the conservatives.

Byron R. White was born on June 8, 1917, in Fort Collins, Colorado, and grew up in Wellington, a small farming and trading town in northern Colorado. His father was a branch manager for a local lumber supply company. From their early youth White and his brother worked long hours at hard-labor jobs in sugar beet fields or on section crews for the railroad, their income vital to the family during the bleak years of the Great Depression of the 1930s. Though neither of White's parents had gone through high school, they valued academics and sports, and Byron was accomplished at both. He graduated from high school first in his class and won an academic scholarship to the University of Colorado.

Glory Days

In college White excelled in sports and academics, winning numerous varsity letters in football, basketball, and baseball and being elected Phi Beta Kappa. Nicknamed "Whizzer" for his speed, White as a junior received national attention as Colorado's star running back. Graduating with one of the highest averages in the university's history, White accepted a prestigious Rhodes scholarship to study at Oxford University. Before going to Oxford, he played the 1938-1939 season with the Pittsburgh Steelers, receiving what was at the time the highest salary ever paid to a professional football player. White led the National Football League in rushing, the first rookie ever to lead the league in any department.

After a short time studying at Oxford, White returned to the United States in the fall of 1939 to enter Yale University Law School. He won the Edgar Cullen Award for receiving the highest grades of the freshman class and was appointed to a coveted job on the *Law Review*. But he declined in order to "play football and make some money instead," he later recalled. White played the 1940-1941 season with the Detroit Lions, then continued law study during the summer at the University of Colorado. White signed another pro football contract for 1941-1942, but after the Japanese attack on Pearl Harbor he enlisted in the Navy. During World War II White was a naval intelligence officer in the South Pacific, winning two bronze stars for courage in action. He also renewed his acquaintance with another decorated offi-

cer, PT-boat commander John F. Kennedy, whom he first had met at Oxford.

To the Supreme Court

After the war White married his college sweetheart, Marion Stearns. He then returned to Yale and finished the final year of law school, graduating in November 1946 *magna cum laude*. During the 1946-1947 term White held a prestigious law clerkship at the U.S. Supreme Court under Chief Justice Fred Vinson. Again he met Kennedy, who was then a freshman congressman. Although he received offers from leading Washington law firms, White returned to Colorado to begin practice in Denver.

In the 1950s White established a successful legal career, achieving recognition throughout the state. When Kennedy began his campaign for the presidency in 1959, White organized local Colorado-for-Kennedy clubs and successfully gained the bulk of the state's delegate votes for his old friend at the 1960 Democratic convention. White helped Kennedy in his national campaign as well, and the new president named him deputy attorney general. White served capably, especially during the civil rights struggles in the South. In March 1962, to fill the vacancy created by the resignation of Justice Charles E. Whittaker, Kennedy nominated White to the Supreme Court. Six months later Justice Felix Frankfurter also resigned, and the president called on Arthur J. Goldberg to fill that seat.

The two new justices came on the Court at a tumultuous time. Under the leadership of Chief Justice Earl Warren during the 1950s and 1960s, the Supreme Court was leading the nation in an effort to improve the lot of dispossessed minorities and other disadvantaged groups. A majority of the justices embraced an activist role as civil rights confrontations, student anti-war protests, and other struggles shook America. A minority of the Court urged greater restraint. Goldberg aligned himself with the activists, and White tended to side with the proponents of judicial self-restraint.

By the 1970s and 1980s, a new conservative Court majority emerged, with White often a part of it. He did not adhere rigidly to any ideological position and often represented a vital swing vote in close decisions. But on key issues, he tended to side with the conservatives. He was one of two dissenters in the Court's landmark decision approving a woman's right to abortion, *Roe v. Wade* (1977) and remained a consistent foe of abortion rights in subsequent cases. White opposed broad use of affirmative action, favored closer ties between church and state, and strongly sided with law enforcement officials on law-and-order issues. He rarely ventured to overturn laws passed by Congress. In his most personal opinion, in *Bowers v. Hardwick* (1986), he argued that states are free to ban sodomy and oral sex because there is a long tradition of intolerance against homosexuality.

White's pragmatic approach to law did not sit well with critics. "White was uninterested in articulating a constitutional vision," author Jeffrey Rosen wrote in *The New Republic* of April 12, 1993. "Despite his ability as a first-rate legal technician, White never transcended his initial incarnation as the jock justice. . . . White's jurisprudence . . . was essentially reactive and obsessed with scoring points. . . . Despite his reputation for independent voting, White's lack of an independent vision reduced him to defining himself in relation to those with more coherent views."

In 1993 White retired after 31 years on the Supreme Court. His career as athlete, attorney, and justice was unique in American history.

Further Reading

White's entry in *The Justices of the United States Supreme Court, 1789-1969, Their Lives and Major Opinions,* Leon Friedman and Fred L. Israel, Volume IV (1969), provides an excellent overview from his birth to the end of the Warren Court era. Volume V of the same series, edited by Leon Friedman, examines White's contribution to the Court from 1969 to 1978. For treatment of his place on the Warren Court see Bernard Schwartz, *Super Chief: Earl Warren and His Supreme Court— A Judicial Biography* (1983). White's role on the Burger Court is discussed in Vincent Blasi, *The Burger Court, The Counter Revolution That Wasn't* (1983). A critical assessment of his tenure as justice is Jeffrey Rosen, *The New Republic* (April 12, 1993). □

E. B. White

E. B. White (1899-1985) was one of the most influential modern American essayists, largely through his work for *The New Yorker* magazine. He also wrote

two children's classics and revised Strunk's *The Elements of Style,* **widely used in college English courses.**

Elwyn Brooks White was born on July 11, 1899, at Mount Vernon, New York, the son of a piano manufacturer who was comfortably well off, but not wealthy. He attended Cornell, graduating in 1921.

He was offered a teaching position at the University of Minnesota, but turned it down because his goal was to become a writer. He worked for the United Press International and the American Legion News Service in 1921 and 1922 and then became a reporter for the *Seattle Times* in 1922 and 1923. As he put it, he found that he was ill-suited for daily journalism, and his city editor had already reached the same conclusion, so they came to an amicable parting of the ways.

White then worked for two years with the Frank Seaman advertising agency as a production assistant and copywriter. During this time he had poems published in "The Conning Tower" of Franklin P. Adams, the newspaper columnist who helped so many talented young people achieve prominence during the 1920s and 1930s.

In 1925 he published the article "Defense of the Bronx River" in *The New Yorker* magazine, his first piece in that publication. It led to his being named a contributing editor in 1927, an association which continued until his death in 1985.

From the time of its origin, *The New Yorker* was one of the most prestigious periodicals in the nation. It featured such celebrities as Alexander Woolcott, Dorothy Parker, Robert Benchley, and George S. Kaufman as contributors, so White was in the company of the best when he was added to the staff.

At some time he became the principal contributor to the magazine's column "Notes and Comment" and set the tone of informed, intelligent, tolerant, faintly amused urbanity in observations on the passing scene, a feature which continued after his death. A typical example is this brief note, "Barred from Barnard," written in 1929:

> *April 20.* Our failure to attend the Greek games in the Barnard College gymnasium last Saturday was a bitter disappointment. The fact is, we wrote the dean of the college and she replied that she couldn't send us tickets because "through long experience we have found that it is much better not to have the games written up by visitors who do not understand them." We regard the dean's attitude as hardly Greek. Our public reply is that we *do* understand Greek games, that simplicity is our watchword, and that Demeter and Persephone are our favorite goddesses. Further, we think that Miss Gildersleeve ought to know that, as a result of being kept out of the games, we moped around all Saturday afternoon and in the evening went to a night club owned by a couple of Greeks.

That same year White published a poetry collection, *The Lady Is Cold,* and then joined fellow *New Yorker* writer James Thurber in *Is Sex Necessary?* Freudian psychology had been enormously influential in America in the 1920s, giving rise to a spate of volumes analyzing or presenting advice on the subject. The time was ripe for a parody of such books, and these two came up with a witty, low-key work featuring passages like this:

> The sexual revolution began with Man's discovery that he was not attractive to Woman, as such. . . . His masculine appearance not only failed to excite Woman, but in many cases it only served to bore her. The result was that Man found it necessary to develop attractive personal traits to offset his dull appearance. He learned to say funny things. He learned to smoke, and blow smoke rings. He learned to earn money. This would have been a solution to his difficulty, but in the course of making himself attractive to Woman by developing himself mentally, he had inadvertently become so intelligent an animal that he saw how comical the whole situation was.

Also in 1929, White married *New Yorker* editor Katharine Sergeant Angell; the marriage produced one son.

He published *Ho Hum* in 1931, *Another Ho Hum* in 1932, *Every Day Is Saturday* in 1934, and in 1936, in the *New Yorker,* under the pseudonym Lee Strout White, the essay "Farewell My Lovely!" One of his best-known pieces, it was suggested to him by a manuscript submitted by Richard L. Strout of the *Christian Science Monitor.* It served as the basis for the book *Farewell to the Model T,* published later that same year.

White's next work was a poetry collection, *The Fox of Peapack* (1938), the same year that he began the monthly column "One Man's Meat" for *Harper's* magazine, a column which lasted five years. There followed the essay collection *Quo Vadimus?* in 1939; an editing job with his wife, *The Subtreasury of American Humor,* in 1941; and *One Man's Meat,* an anthology of his *Harper's* columns, in 1942.

In 1945 he entered a new field with great success, writing *Stuart Little* for children. The story of a mouse born to normal human parents was clearly intended to console young people who thought themselves different or odd, and it carried the message that Stuart's parents never batted an eye when their son turned out to be a mouse and that the hero, debonair, even jaunty, could build himself a good life.

After *The Wild Flag* in 1946 and *Here Is New York* in 1949, White returned to children's literature with his most popular book in the genre, *Charlotte's Web,* in 1952. The story of the bond between the young pig Wilbur and the clever spider who saves his life is a paean to the power of friendship and a reminder to young readers that death is a part of life.

The Second Tree from the Corner came in 1954. Three years later White and his wife gave up their New York apartment and moved permanently to North Brooklin, Maine.

While an undergraduate at Cornell, White had taken a course with Professor William S. Strunk, Jr. Strunk used a text he had written and published at his own expense, a thin volume titled *The Elements of Style.* White edited it, revised it, and added the chapter "An Approach to style," offering such advice as "Place yourself in the background; do not explain too much; prefer the standard to the offbeat." The book sold widely and became a college campus fixture for the next 20 years in several editions (1959, 1972, 1979).

Honors began to pour in on the author. He won the Gold Medal for Essays and Criticism from the National Institute of Arts and Letters in 1960, the Presidential Medal of Freedom in 1963, the Laura Ingalls Wilder Medal for his children's books in 1970, and the National Medal for Literature in 1971. In 1973 he was elected to the American Academy of Arts and Letters.

He published *The Points of My Compass* in 1962; *The Trumpet of the Swan,* another children's book, in 1970; and collections of his letters (1976), essays (1977), and poems and sketches (1981).

E. B. White's influence was profound, particularly in the popular essay. His poetry is not exceptional and his sketches tend to the precious, but his essays served as models for two generations of readers. In the 1930s, 1940s, and 1950s, *The New Yorker* was judged by critics to be a model of elegant yet simple style in non-fiction, and White was in no small measure responsible for that reputation. He died October 1, 1985.

Further Reading

An early biography is *E. B. White* by Edward C. Sampson (1974). There are accounts of him in several books, such as Dale Kramer's *Ross and the* New Yorker (1951). A good discussion of his life and influence is Scott Elledge's *E. B. White: A Biography* (1985). □

Edward Douglass White

Edward Douglass White (1845-1921), ninth chief justice of the U.S. Supreme Court, is known for his enunciation of the "rule of reason" for interpreting and applying antitrust legislation.

B orn on Nov. 3, 1845, at the family plantation at Thibodaux, La., Edward Douglass White was the son of a lawyer and sugar planter. A Roman Catholic, White was educated mainly by Jesuits. He was attending Georgetown College when the Civil War began; he returned to Louisiana and fought in the Confederate Army. After the war he studied law at what became Tulane University and was admitted to the bar in 1868.

A conservative Democrat identified with the overthrow of the Radical Reconstruction government, White was named to the Louisiana Supreme Court in 1878. When his faction of the party lost power, he returned to a lucrative private practice; when it regained influence, he was elected to the U.S. Senate in 1891. Save on the lowering of sugar tariffs, which was detrimental to Louisiana, White was loyal to President Grover Cleveland, who appointed him to the U.S. Supreme Court in 1894. White refused the appointment until after modifications favorable to Louisiana were made in the tariff reform bill.

A hardworking but not innovative justice, White fitted comfortably into a Court committed to encouraging business as the best insurance of national prosperity and stability. He broke from this pattern to dissent in *Pollock v. Farmers' Loan and Trust Co.* (1895), which held an income tax to be unconstitutional, and, he voted with the minority in *Lochner v. New York* (1905), which disallowed a state's regulation of the length of working hours of bakers. White also wrote a significant concurrence in one of the Insular cases, *Downes v. Bidwell* (1901), which required explicit congressional action if constitutional privileges of American citizens were to extend to persons in the nation's newly acquired overseas territories.

During White's 27 years on the Court, justices Stephen Field, John Marshall Harlan, Oliver Wendell Holmes, Charles Evans Hughes, and Louis Brandeis all overshadowed him. White was appointed chief justice in 1910 largely because of the ambition of President William Howard Taft, who hoped that, by appointing a man of 65, he himself could succeed him.

White did not lead the Court into bold new areas of judicial thought; he prescribed, instead, the "rule of reason." Undercutting antimonopoly efforts, White's Court ap-

pealed to the common law to allow "reasonable" restraint of trade in *Standard Oil Co. v. U.S.* (1911) and *U.S. v. American Tobacco* (1911). Thus White was reflecting the pragmatic spirit of the day and, from a viewpoint favorable to business, testing whether a business combination was workable rather than whether it complied with the letter of the law.

On May 19, 1921, White died in Washington. With a Republican back in the White House, former president Taft made good his ambition: he was named chief justice.

Further Reading

A full-length work on White is by Sister Marie Carolyn Klinkhamer, *Edward Douglass White: Chief Justice of the United States* (1943). A section on White by Alfred F. Watts, Jr., appears in Leon Friedman and Fred L. Israel, eds., *The Justices of the United States Supreme Court, 1789-1969: Their Lives and Major Opinions* (4 vols., 1969).

Additional Sources

Highsaw, Robert Baker, *Edward Douglass White, defender of the conservative faith,* Baton Rouge: Louisiana State University Press, 1981. □

Kevin H. White

The reform mayor of Boston, Kevin H. White (born 1929), was concerned with the revitalization of the downtown area to make Boston a "world-class city."

K evin Hagan White was born on September 25, 1929, in Boston of a family which was noted in city politics. His parents were Irish Catholics, and both his father and his mother's father had been Boston City Council presidents. He married Kathryn Galvin in 1956, daughter of another Boston City Council president. He was educated at Tabor Academy, Williams College (AB, 1952), Boston College Law School (LLB, 1955), and the Harvard Graduate School of Public Administration.

He first sought public office as a Democrat, as secretary of state for Massachusetts, supplanting Edward W. Brooke in 1960. He held that office for the next three elections and was subsequently elected as mayor of Boston in November 1967.

In 1967 White was a sample of the new breed of urban mayors: extremely liberal, impartial, concerned with equity, and, in the end, aggressive. White modeled himself after Mayor John Lindsay of New York, who lusted after a wider stage on which to display his talents. White could play to the crowd; once when the Rolling Stones were arrested on the way to Boston, the mayor released them into his own

custody. "The Stones have been busted, but I have sprung them!" he told an audience at Boston Garden.

His opponent in 1967 was Louise Day Hicks, a popular anti-bussing spokeswoman. He defeated her with African American and liberal support. In 1970 he made an attempt to be governor of Massachusetts, but a Republican won. In his second mayor's election against Hicks (1971), he defeated her again. White was seriously considered as vice-presidential running mate to Senator George McGovern in 1972, but was passed over for Senator Thomas Eagleton (and later for R. Sargent Shriver, Jr.). In 1975 in his third election to the mayor's office, he won a narrow victory, and his attitude changed considerably, becoming more dictatorial, embattled, and cynical. In 1979 he won his last electoral victory. White served for 16 years in office as mayor of Boston, 1967 to 1983.

In the beginning White maintained a racial balance in his administration: liberals, Jews, African Americans, Italians, Irish, and some Hispanics. He pioneered by forming "Little City Halls" (as John Lindsay did) in the neighborhoods to decentralize power. For the summer months, he organized outdoor activities known as the "Summerthing." But the most important ingredient of his policy towards Boston was the revitalization of the downtown parts of the city, especially the shops and restaurants of Quincy Market near city hall. He believed that the downtown renaissance would make Boston a "world-class city."

In the mid-1970s Boston began to change. Federal efforts to integrate neighborhood schools, particularly in South Boston, turned the school system into an armed camp. In 1974 Federal District Court Judge W. Arthur Garrity ordered bussing. White protected the schoolchildren from violence (with federal and state assistance) during the period of crisis. One school was taken into federal receivership for a time to guard against social outbreaks.

The bussing issue nearly cost White the election in 1975. Gradually, he became an iron-fisted ruler. White closed his "Little City Halls"; he used instead a network of ward henchmen ("corner boys"), who gave city jobs and contracts to all who helped the mayor, notably in the election of 1979. At one time Boston's schools, jails, housing authority, and even part of its tax structure were under court jurisdiction, and the city was desperate for money; the desegregation and the bussing costs were onerous.

In 1983 the job proved too stressful for White, especially because seven aides to the mayor were under indictment on charges of fraud and extortion. White himself was not implicated in these charges, though the State Ethics Commission had an extensive 10-month enquiry which found "reasonable cause" that White had violated conflict-of-interest laws. In June 1983 White ("King Kevin," as his enemies would say) dropped out of the race for mayor. Consequently, Raymond L. Flynn won the November election.

In a 1993 interview with Margo Howard, *Boston Magazine,* White characterized Boston as an "international, cosmopolitan lady." Later that same year he published "Making Trouble: Essays on Gay History, Politics, and the University" in the *Journal of American History.* White will be remembered as the man who changed Boston's downtown.

Further Reading

Alan Lupo, *Liberty's Chosen Home: The Politics of Violence in Boston* (1977) and Eric A. Nordlinger, *Decentralizing the City: A Study of Boston's Little City Halls* (1972) deal with some of the events of Mayor White's 16 years of administration of Boston. The *Biographical Dictionary of American Mayors, 1820-1980,* edited by M.G. Holli and Peter d'A. Jones, contains an entry on White by R.H. Gentile. *Macleans* magazine (January 31, 1983) and *Newsweek* (June 6, 1983) include items on White. In *Common Ground* (1985) J. Anthony Lukas describes Boston's turbulent decade of school integration through the eyes of three families. An interview with Margo Howard appears in *Boston Magazine* (February 1993). Biographical information is provided by George Higgins in *Style Versus Substance: Boston, Kevin White, and the Politics of Illusion,* (1984). □

Leslie A. White

The American anthropologist Leslie A. White (1900-1975) was known for his fieldwork among the Keresan-speaking Indians, his "culturological" theory of human behavior, and his energy theory of cultural evolution.

L eslie White was born at Salida, Colorado, on January 19, 1900. He took his B.A. and M.A. degrees in psychology at Columbia University in 1923 and 1924. At the same time he took some courses at the New School for Social Research which he later said were the most important intellectual influences on him; his teachers there were Alexander Goldenweiser, William I. Thomas, Thorstein Veblen, and John B. Watson. In 1924 White decided that sociology would be his field, and he moved to the University of Chicago to take his Ph.D. degree in what was then a combined anthropology-sociology department. At that time he began the summer field expeditions to the Keresan pueblos in New Mexico which he continued for many years.

White taught briefly at the University of Buffalo and for 40 years at the University of Michigan, and after retirement he taught at Rice University, San Francisco State College, and the University of California at Santa Barbara. The wide interest in his work is demonstrated by the fact that his writings have been translated and published in several European languages and in India, China, and Japan. Several of his essays have been reprinted many times in prestigious publications representing a wide variety of disciplines. His 1940 article "The Symbol: The Origin and Basis of Human Behavior" was reprinted at least 14 times in collections representing anthropology, sociology, linguistics, philosophy, and social psychology. Several others, now published in his volume called *The Science of Culture* (1949), were also reprinted several times.

These essays were all on the subject of what he called *culturology,* the science of human behavior as based on culture—socially learned activities made possible by the uniquely human capacity to create symbols. Culturology, with White's definition of it, eventually made *Webster's International Dictionary,* and he contributed the articles on it for *The International Encyclopedia of the Social Sciences* and for the 15th edition of the *Encyclopedia Britannica.*

But White is remembered not so much for his positive contribution of culturology as for his affirmation of 19th century evolutionism, opposing the negative stand of American anthropology toward that important legacy. As Bohannan and Glazer put it (1973): "Leslie White for years stood alone in his conviction that evolutionary theory as expounded by Herbert Spencer, Lewis H. Morgan, and Edward Tylor was the beginning of the right track for a science of culture. He can now look about him in full awareness that the whole field [of anthropology] knows he was right."

The greatest amount of time and effort in White's early career was spent on field work and library research connected with his five monographs and many articles on the culture of the Keresan-speaking Indians of the American Southwest. The militant secrecy of the Indians toward their ancient culture—their religion particularly—made White's achievements in describing and analyzing it truly remarkable. This field work was mostly of the confidential-informant kind, based on hard-won trusted friendships that he was able to achieve with a few Indians whom he convinced that the information would be valuable to preserve for future generations of whites and Indians alike.

In his later years White fully devoted himself to the study of modern civilizational problems, particularly those related to the rise and spread of industrial capitalism. This interest had actually begun early: he said that as a student he studied psychology, switched to sociology, and finally to anthropology because of his intense desire to discover why modern nations behaved as they did. This progression of disciplines was due to his gradual realization that *culture,* in the anthropological sense, was the appropriate subject for him, not the psychology of people either in its individual or collective aspects.

White's early and middle years were attended by intense controversy over his pro-evolutionism. This reaction in the anthropological discipline was largely caused by an unusual feature of American anthropology; the nearly total adherence of the academic anthropologists to the teachings of Fran Boas. Boas wielded enormous influence in America because he became the founder and chairman of the Anthropology Department at Columbia University between 1899 and 1936, the first important school to train Ph.D. candidates in anthropology. Most of the university teachers of anthropology in the United States were powerfully and directly influenced by Boas, accepting his intellectual weaknesses as well as his very considerable strengths. The most important weakness was his anti-evolutionism. Beginning in the 1930s and until the 1960s White waged an unremitting crusade against anti-evolutionism which meant, as well, that he made mordant criticisms of Boas himself, who was idolized by most of White's contempo-

raries. This, of course, aroused wide hostility against White in most anthropology departments.

But White's writings and teaching eventually had a snowballing intellectual impact. His strong stand against the anthropological establishment of his day created a strong following for Whitean "neoevolutionism." But White distrusted schools-of-thought and tried to combat this tendency among his own students. In order to discourage the rise of an ingrown "Michigan School" he made these rules: that Michigan Ph.D. candidates also should have studied anthropology at some other major department; that no Michigan ethnology Ph.D. could be hired there; that a balanced representation of faculty from other major graduate schools be maintained in the Michigan department; and that the department be run democratically by an elected executive committee, with all faculty members having one vote. Former students from Michigan all agree that White should be honored for this achievement as well as many others.

Despite his unpopularity in many important quarters, White received numerous academic honors. He was given an honorary doctorate of sciences in 1952 by the University of Buffalo and an honorary doctor of laws in 1970 by the University of Colorado. He received the annual award for distinguished service voted by the faculty of the University of Michigan in 1957—the first year the award was made. He was Viking Medalist of the Wenner-Gren Foundation in 1959, vice-president of the American Association for the Advancement of Science in 1958, and president of the American Anthropological Association in 1964.

These awards, however impressive and numerous, came late in his career, and we may be sure the recognition was entirely by merit, for he never courted the politicians of the association nor his university's administrators, never deviated one step from his course in order to gain any kind of academic approval—his life was unblemished by any hint of careerism or any other kind of self-seeking, including high salary, large grants, or special academic chairs.

White died suddenly of a heart attack on a visit to Death Valley in 1975.

Further Reading

White's most famous books are *The Science of Culture* (1949), a collection of his most important essays, and *The Evolution of Culture* (1959). See also his general article "culturology" in *The International Encyclopedia of the Social Sciences* (1968). Some of his most important arguments appear in Elman R. Service, *A Century of Controversy* (1965), and in Richard K. Beardsley's article "An Appraisal of Leslie A. White's Scholarly Influence" in the *American Anthropologist.* □

Patrick Victor Martindale White

Patrick Victor Martindale White (1912-1990) was the first Australian to win the Nobel Prize for literature. He used religious experience and symbolism to

show man's struggle to transcend the "dreary, every-day life."

Patrick White was born in London on May 28, 1912, of Australian parents. His early education was at Tudor House, Moss Vale, New South Wales (an Anglican school). He went to England to attend Cheltenham College, then returned to Australia, where he gained experience as a jackeroo, or "gentleman stockman," on sheep- and cattle-grazing properties in New South Wales. At 22 he returned to England to study at King's College, Cambridge. Subsequently, he traveled extensively in Europe and the United States.

White's first novel, *Happy Valley* (1939), a somewhat ironic story of a doctor in a mountain township of New South Wales, uses the stream-of-consciousness method and shows White's attention to suffering and solitude as essential elements of the human condition. Concern for unfulfilled lives is central to *The Living and the Dead* (1941). Set in Bloomsbury in the 1930s, the novel explores especially the problems of a Londoner who has tried to "build a cocoon of experience away from the noises of the street," while other characters represent acceptance of life at any level. The theme is repeated in *The Ham Funeral,* a play written in the late 1940s but not performed until 1960.

During the war years White served in the Middle East and Greece in the Royal Air Force's intelligence section. He

returned to Australia in 1948, settling in Sydney. Thereafter he showed a surer touch in his writing.

The Aunt's Story (1948) reflects an underlying concern with resistance to the conformity that other lives impose. The main character is seen first as a thin, sallow child leading a solitary life in an Australian country town, then in Sydney, where she becomes subordinated to her mother. Next she is seen as a spinster struggling to reconcile opposing aspects of her experience abroad. Later, during a journey across America, she decides to leave the train and cast aside her identity. Finally she is confronted by a hallucinatory figure who foretells her end in a mental hospital.

The Tree of Man (1955) was the next in a succession of novels in which White attempted, in his words, "to discover the extraordinary behind the ordinary, [to uncover] the mystery and poetry." It traces the lives of a settler and his wife who establish a holding in the Australian wilderness and see their homestead absorbed within a settlement, then a wider community. Eventually, their old fulfilling world is threatened with submergence in soulless suburbia. The central character's final vision suggests that fulfillment lies in liberation from the ordinariness of living: in transcendence.

A way to transcend is examined in *Voss* (1957), a story enshrining the theme of eclipse of self in the natural world. Recreating the challenge of 19th-century exploration in Australia, it is primarily a book about spiritual need. A German explorer who places a high value on his soul, Voss welcomes the privations of the desert and insists on blotting out all emotion of camaraderie. The expedition's total disappearance is a natural outcome.

In *Riders in the Chariot* (1961), White organized his story around four withdrawn or misfit characters in Sydney's suburbia through whom he tells of the alienated, tortured consciousness. Similar distorted personalities are seen in the play *The Season at Sarsaparilla* (1962) and in the short-story collection *The Burnt Ones* (1964). In showing the rejection of the "illuminates" by the society in which they are placed, White presents a condemnation of life as it is commonly lived. The play *Night on Bald Mountain* (1964) also scarifies those who might claim most need of compassion.

In *The Solid Mandala* (1966) White draws upon a body of mystical and visionary material derived from the observations and writing of the psychiatrist Carl Jung to set forth the mandala as a symbol of divine perfection and transcendence. The choice of characters, especially twin brothers who are strongly contrasted as a warmhearted halfwit and an arid intellectual, heightens the intensity of the symbolism. The dolt, as a cause of humiliation, breeds such hatred in his twin that the latter dies of it, while through the perfection he finds in four glass marbles treasured from his childhood the simpleton comes painfully to articulate his vision.

With the publication of *The Vivisector* (1970), critics began taking note of an increasing bleakness in White's vision and an implied darkening of the novelist's view of his own efforts. (Vivisection is the practice of cutting into, or dissecting, the body of a living organism.) This work, however, clinched White's status as a major figure in contemporary literature, and in 1973 he was awarded the Nobel Prize.

Evaluation of His Work

The central purpose of White's works was to explore the underlying problems of humanity, the impossibility of building a bridge from one life to another, and the individual's relationship with God. He developed a striking and distinctive style, sometimes with surrealist overtones, to match his increasingly powerful and emotional themes.

White consistently used religious experience and a high degree of symbolism in exploring man's relationship with the unknown and in adumbrating means whereby the individual might achieve a totality of serenity and insight. Throughout, his work shows a preoccupation with emotional incapacity and a predilection for investing emotions very heavily on the analysis of social pretensions. He creates figures whom middle-class society finds worthless or repellent and explains through them the mysticism he wishes to convey. Overall, his writing suggests an aversion to the comfortable urban life and dwells upon ways in which transcendence might be achieved. His most moving characters, often questing, eccentric, and sometimes bizarre personalities, manifest a high degree of "psychic isolation" and include some cases of extreme alienation.

White acknowledged his books to be outgrowths of his interest in religion. His preoccupation was "the relationship between the blundering human being and God." Although disclaiming affiliation with any Church, he said in 1969 that he had a religious faith and that his work was "an attempt to express that, among other things." He saw mankind as having got out of hand ("a kind of Frankenstein monster"); as the world became pagan, it was still desirable to lead people in the direction of religion, even though in a different way.

Before dying September 20, 1990, in Sydney after a long illness. White wrote 12 novels, three books of poetry, three collections of short stories, nine plays, and a number of pieces of non-fiction, including his autobiography, *Flaws in the Glass: A Self-Portrait* (1981).

Further Reading

A chapter on White by Vincent Buckley in Geoffrey Dutton, ed., *The Literature of Australia* (1964), contains a penetrating analysis of White's method and content, particularly emphasizing White's mythmaking propensity. A close consideration and generally sympathetic appreciation of White is in G. A. Wilkes, *Australian Literature: A Conspectus* (1969), focusing on the characters to explain the method by which White's central theme and ethic are evolved. John McLaren's essay "The Image of Reality in Our Writings, with Special Reference to the Work of Patrick White," collected in Clement Semmler, ed., *Twentieth Century Australian Literary Criticism* (1967), provides a thorough but less favorable assessment of White's novels. □

Stanford White

The American architect Stanford White (1853-1906), a partner in the architectural firm of McKim, Mead & White, was noted for his decorative inventiveness.

Stanford White was born on Nov. 9, 1853, in New York City. His father, Richard Grant White, was a distinguished Shakespearean scholar and a music and drama critic. At the age of 19 Stanford became an apprentice in the architectural office of Gambrill and Richardson, where he met Charles Follen McKim. By 1878 White felt that he must study architecture in Europe. For almost two years he lived in Paris and traveled extensively, sometimes with McKim and the sculptor Augustus Saint-Gaudens, making sketches of buildings and architectural details, medieval ornaments, and armour.

In September 1879 White entered into partnership with McKim and William Rutherford Mead, creating the firm that would be responsible for setting a high standard of taste in America for the next three decades. The firm's greatness grew out of the fine blending of individual talents: Mead, the level-headed business man; McKim, the man of impeccable taste and determined persuasiveness; and White, the brilliant, imaginative artist-architect. Many of the firm's apprentices became the next generation's best architects.

White's first commissions were for houses and monuments. During the 1880s he built homes on Long Island with Renaissance decoration, Robert Goelet's mansion at Newport, R.I. (1883), and many residences for rich clients in New York City. He designed the pedestal for Saint-Gaudens's Farragut Monument (1881) in Madison Square, New York City.

To commemorate George Washington's first inauguration, White was commissioned to design a wooden arch (1889) in New York City's Washington Square. After the celebration, the public insisted on a permanent arch in stone, which he completed in 1892. The precedent for this arch is Roman; the clear, concise combination of classical ornamental ideas is White's.

White designed Madison Square Garden (1890) as a center for spectacular events. Backed by rich New Yorkers, including White himself, this daring project proved financially unstable, yet it continued for many years to serve a public need. His design offered color, gaiety, a Spanish exoticism, and consistency in style.

During the 1890s White was at his prime. He was involved with more than 70 projects, from tombs to fashionable men's clubs. The best tomb is in the Adams Memorial in Rock Creek Cemetery, Washington, D.C.; its sculpture—a deeply moving, shrouded figure—is by Saint-Gaudens. The Metropolitan Club, New York, is outstanding for White's authoritative borrowing of Italian Renaissance and English 19th-century ideas; however, it is less imaginative than many of his residential designs. In planning residences he had the best opportunity to display his talent for small-scale ornament, often of an exquisite quality and always original in spite of its eclecticism.

Among White's other well-known projects in New York City are the Italianate Herald Building (1894); St. Bartholomew's Church facade (1903), imitating St-Gilles near Arles, France; the Gorham Building (1906), which shows his familiarity with Louis Sullivan's work; and the Tiffany Building (1906), resembling a Venetian palace. At the Military Academy at West Point, White, with the sculptor Frederick MacMonnies, executed the Battle Monument (1896).

In 1884 White had married Bessie Springs Smith; they had one child. White died tragically on June 25, 1906, when Harry Thaw, believing that White had seduced his wife, shot him in Madison Square Garden while White was watching an evening show.

Further Reading

A full-length account of White's life is Charles C. Baldwin's interesting *Stanford White* (1931). This may be supplemented by Gerald Langford, *The Murder of Stanford White* (1962). There is no thorough study of White's architecture. Lawrence Grant White outlines his father's career in a book of drawings called *Sketches and Designs by Stanford White* (1920), which contains mostly momentary records of what fascinated White in Europe.

Additional Sources

Baker, Paul R., *Stanny: the gilded life of Stanford White*, New York: Free Press; London: Collier Macmillan, 1989. □

T. H. White

A pioneering political journalist, T. H. White (1915-1986) gained prominence for his indepth coverage of American political campaigns. His book *The Making of the President—1960* helped to alter the style and character of presidential campaigns as well as the way reporters cover them.

Born May 6, 1915, in Boston, Massachusetts, Theodore H. White (known as Teddy) was the son of David and Mary Winkeller White. His father, a Jewish immigrant from Russia, was a poor neighborhood lawyer until his death in 1931. After graduating from the Boston Latin School in 1932, White could not afford to attend college. He found a job selling newspapers on a streetcar—his start in journalism.

After working two years as a newsboy and Hebrew teacher, White enrolled at Harvard in 1934 with the help of a scholarship from Harvard and a grant from the Newsboy Foundation. He studied Chinese and graduated *summa cum laude* with a degree in history. Awarded a travelling fellowship, he arranged to write articles for the Boston *Globe* and headed for the Far East. He sold articles to the *Globe* and to the Manchester *Guardian* and obtained a job with the Chinese Information Committee. After witnessing the Japanese bombing of Peking (now Beijing) in 1939 he decided to remain a journalist rather than return to Harvard and become a professor.

While in China White accepted a job as a stringer for *Time* magazine. He became a staff reporter in 1940. Among his early contacts was the future Communist leader Chou En-lai. In 1941 White moved to New York to become *Time*'s Far East editor, but after the United States entered World War II he returned to Asia as a war correspondent and chief of *Time*'s bureau there. During the war he covered the Honan famine in 1943, followed the internal political struggles in China, interviewed Mao Tse-tung [Zedong], observed the conflict in American war strategies, and reported the formal Japanese surrender above the U.S.S. *Missouri* on September 2, 1945.

After the war White's unfavorable opinion of the nationalist Chinese leader Chiang Kai-chek, whom *Time* publisher Henry Luce admired, led to a break with *Time* magazine. White elaborated his own views of China in a book, *Thunder Out of China* (written with Annalee Jacoby), which was selected by the Book-of-the-Month Club and became an immediate best-seller in 1946. He served briefly as an editor of *The New Republic* magazine, but found the demands of Henry Wallace too restricting. White edited the papers of Gen. Joseph Stilwell whom he had met in China and respected.

Given the political atmosphere in America in the early Cold War years, White's stand on China was considered radical, and he found the pages of major publications closed to his writings. With the sizable amount of money he received for *Thunder Out of China* he left for Paris to work

for the Overseas News Agency. When the agency went broke, he became a free-lance writer and then in 1951 the chief European correspondent for *The Reporter* magazine. He spent over five years in Europe covering the major postwar stories, the economic recovery program (the Marshall Plan), and the formation of a Western military defense alliance (NATO). He wrote a book summarizing his European experience, *Fire in the Ashes,* which was also accepted by the Book-of-the-Month Club.

White returned to the United States in 1953 to concentrate on American politics. Almost immediately he became a victim of the politics of the McCarthy era for defending his old China friend John Patton Davies, who was under investigation by the State Department. White found himself targeted and had his passport temporarily revoked. The experience not only frightened him but also inhibited him (which he later regretted) from writing again about foreign policy or defense issues. In 1954 he became national political correspondent for *The Reporter* and then for the mass magazine *Colliers.* He wrote stories on a wide range of topics, including aviation and the emerging national highway system.

When *Colliers* folded in late 1956, as the growing popularity of television undermined the market for general-interest periodicals, White was unable to find a job in journalism he liked. He turned to fiction and wrote two best-selling novels. *The Mountain Road,* set in China, was accepted by the Book-of-the-Month Club and was made into a movie. His second book, *The View From the Fortieth Floor,* depicted his experience at *Colliers.* It was a Literary Guild

selection, and the film rights were sold to the actor Gary Cooper for $80,000.

With his financial independence temporarily secure, White embarked on the major project of his career, a study of presidential campaigns, which earned him respect as a political reporter and as a contemporary historian. He chose to view presidential elections as a dramatic story—with an eye for anecdotal details and an awareness of historical themes—in books that would be published after the votes were counted. Auspiciously he began his quest with the 1960 presidential election which featured a ready-made hero—John Kennedy—and villain—Richard Nixon. Journalistically, he had the field to himself as the media tended to ignore primaries.

His book, *The Making of the President—1960,* was enormously successful. Combining a novelist's skill for storytelling with an historian's sense of the wider significance, White initiated a new genre of political reporting. Another Book-of-the-Month Club selection, the book sold over four million copies and earned him about half a million dollars. With his accomplishment, presidential campaigns would never be the same again for either the news media or the candidates.

White regarded Kennedy not only as a personal hero but as a watershed figure in American politics. In the aftermath of Kennedy's death, White met with Jacqueline Kennedy at her request and in an article for *LIFE* magazine attached the label "Camelot" to the Kennedy myth. Looking back, White pointed to Kennedy's assassination as the moment of division in American politics between a period of stability and what he called the stormy era. Yet, despite the turbulence of the later stage, White remained a fascinated and optimistic observer of American politicians.

White continued his coverage of elections with books on the 1964, 1968, and 1972 campaigns. After President Nixon's resignation he wrote *Breach of Faith: The Fall of Richard Nixon.* He skipped the 1976 campaign while he wrote his autobiography, *In Search of History: A Personal Adventure.* White's later effort, *America in Search of Itself* (1982), focused on the 1980 campaign but also served as a review of 25 years of history, culminating his project.

White received numerous journalism awards, including a Pulitzer Prize (1962) and two Emmys for his television writing. White had two children by his first wife and lived with his second wife, Beatrice Hofstadter, in Bridgewater, Connecticut. He died in New York City on May 15, 1986, following a stroke.

Further Reading

For biographical information, the best book is White's autobiography, *In Search of History: A Personal Adventure* (1978). To appreciate White's contribution to political literature and presidential elections, read *The Making of A President—1960.* For a sense of history and how American politics has changed in the last quarter century in White's view, see *America in Search of Itself.* □

Walter Francis White

Walter Francis White (1893-1955), general secretary of the National Association for the Advancement of Colored People for 24 years, was an outspoken critic of lynching and racial injustice in America.

Walter White was born in 1893 in Atlanta, Georgia. His father, George, was a postman, and his mother, Madeline, a former school-teacher. The younger of two sons in a family of seven children, all light enough to pass for white, he was raised in an eight room, two story house on the edge of the ghetto. Their light complexion caused them a variety of problems. Aboard Atlanta's Jim Crow cars, the family found that if they sat in the "white" section, African Americans accused them of passing; if they sat in the African American section, they faced embarrassing stares and rude remarks. To avoid humiliation, the children walked everywhere or rode in the surrey their father had purchased.

When he was 13, Walter learned "that there is no isolation from life." In 1906 Atlanta was engulfed in a race riot and Walter and his father found themselves in the midst of an angry white mob. But their color shielded them from violence as white rioters bypassed them in search of victims to kill or maim. Back in the African American section father and son stood guard as whites invaded their neighborhood. With guns cocked they waited as whites planned to torch their home. Shots from a neighboring building scared away the would-be arsonists.

The Atlanta public school system was "separate" but decidedly "unequal." White attended school from eight to two in the afternoon in a poorly staffed, "double shifted" elementary school. His father sent him to the private high school department of an Atlanta African American college because there were no high schools for African Americans in Atlanta.

After graduation from Atlanta University in 1916, he worked for a time for Standard Life, a major African American insurance company, and helped organize the Atlanta National Association for the Advancement of Colored People (NAACP). As secretary of the new branch, he led the drive to force the city to improve its public facilities for African Americans and attracted the attention of James Weldon Johnson, the first African American general secretary of the organization. A year later Johnson secured White's appointment as assistant to the organization's chief administrative officer. While visiting Chicago, he narrowly escaped an ambush during the 1919 race riot. This time the assailant was an African American man who fired at what he thought was a white man walking through the ghetto.

Twelve days after his appointment, White volunteered to go to Tennessee to investigate a lynching on Lincoln's birthday. An African American sharecropper had been slowly burned by a white mob for defending himself against a beating by his employer. White learned that the employer was widely disliked by the townspeople, but that they figured African Americans might get out of hand if any African American, no matter what his justification, resisted any white authority.

In the next few years White personally investigated a dozen race riots and two dozen lynchings. Posing as a white reporter who wanted to give the South's side of the story, he was invited to join the Ku Klux Klan, and one southern sheriff pinned a badge on him, gave him a gun, and took him along on a hunt for African Americans.

In Helena, Arkansas, on the way to interview Negroes jailed for joining a sharecroppers' union, an African American man whispered that a mob had planned to ambush him. On a northbound train, he talked to a conductor who told him that he was leaving too soon. The townspeople, he was told, were preparing a surprise lynching for an African American who was passing through town. White's observations formed the basis for *Rope and Faggot: The Biography of Judge Lynch,* published in 1929.

White was assistant secretary of the NAACP from 1918 to 1929, when he replaced Johnson as acting secretary. In 1931 Johnson decided not to return to active leadership and White replaced him, presiding over the organization during the Depression, New Deal, World War II, and the Supreme Court's historic *Brown* v. *Board of Education* decision outlawing school segregation.

During his tenure White faced several crises. He opposed W. E. B. DuBois' call for "black economic self-determination" as contrary to the integrationist aims of the organization. Younger African American intellectuals such as Abram Harris, Ralph Bunche, and E. Franklin Frazier, while critical of the organization, joined White in criticizing DuBois' plan for an economic "Negro Nation Within a Nation" scheme. DuBois, the longtime editor of the organization's *Crisis* magazine, resigned in protest in 1934.

The young intellectuals supported, however, a 1934 internal report by Abram Harris on "Future Plans and Programs of the NAACP" which called for greater decentralization, more direct action, and class and labor alliances between African Americans and white workers. White weathered these criticisms of the traditional legal, political, and educational strategies of the organization, and after 1935 he focused much of the organization's energies toward a long, hard-fought, but ultimately fruitless campaign to pass a national anti-lynching bill.

Yet, as Ralph Bunche observed, White showed increased responsiveness to the economic problems facing African Americans. He supported the establishment of the Joint Committee on National Recovery, an umbrella organization of several civil rights organizations monitoring the impact of New Deal programs on African American life. Although a confidant of first lady Eleanor Roosevelt and sympathetic to the social vision of the New Deal, he criticized National Recovery Administration (NRA) and Agricultural Adjustment Administration (AAA) policies and called for a congressional investigation of racial discrimination in government programs. In 1938 he urged President Franklin D. Roosevelt to extend social security benefits to agricultural and domestic workers and to amend the National Labor Relations Act to prohibit union discrimination. He opposed the creation of a segregated African American division in the United States Army and endorsed A. Phillip Randolph's March on Washington Movement in 1940 and 1941.

Critics charged that White was too close to the New Deal, that he failed to build a mass base for his organization, and that his autocratic style led him to view other African American organizations and leaders as rivals rather than as potential allies. But it is clear that White was devoted to bringing African Americans into the mainstream of American life and that he shared the liberal, reformist aspirations of his age. When he died, ten months after the historic *Brown* v. *Board of Education of Topeka, Kansas* decision (1954), he had lived long enough to see the legal basis of that exclusion overturned. He was a consistent and articulate spokesman in the cause of human rights.

Further Reading

A Man Called White: The Autobiography of Walter White (1948) is the best introduction to the NAACP leader's career. Brief biographical sketches also appear in the *Dictionary of American Negro Biography* (1983) edited by Rayford Logan and Michael Winston and in *A Biographical History of Blacks in America Since 1528* by Edgar A. Toppin (1969). White himself was the author of *Fire in the Flint* (1924); *Flight* (1926); *Rope and Faggot: The Biography of Judge Lynch* (1929); *A Rising Wind: A Report of Negro Soldiers in the European Theatre of War* (1945); and *How Far Is the Promised Land* (1955).

Additional Sources

Waldron, Edward E., *Walter White and the Harlem Renaissance*, Port Washington, N.Y.: Kennikat Press, 1978.
White, Walter Francis, *A man called White: the autobiography of Walter White*, Athens, GA: University of Georgia Press, 1995.
□

William Alanson White

William Alanson White (1870-1937) was an American psychiatrist and hospital administrator. Physician, writer, teacher, and humanitarian, he represented an integral part of the development of modern psychiatry.

Williriam Alanson White was born on Jan. 24, 1870, in Brooklyn, N.Y. His home was only half a block from a hospital and medical school, and his friendship with the sons of a surgeon instilled an early desire to become a physician. He won a scholarship to Cornell at the age of 15 and eventually obtained his degree in medicine in 1891 from Long Island Medical School. A year later he was appointed to the staff at Binghamton State Hospital.

White considered crucial to the development of his interest in psychiatry his association with Boris Sidis, then working with hypnosis on problems of dissociation. This laid the groundwork for his acceptance of Freud's doctrine of the unconscious, which later gained acceptance in the United States largely through White's efforts. He also formed a close friendship with Dr. Smith Ely Jelliffe, with whom he subsequently founded and edited the *Psychoanalytic Review*.

White's distinguished contributions at Binghamton led to an appointment in 1903 by President Theodore Roosevelt to the superintendency of the Government Hospital for the Insane, in Washington, now Saint Elizabeths Hospital. There followed several difficult years of reorganization and building construction, complicated by congressional investigations. White's calm, logical presentation of his ideas and plans, with emphasis upon patient welfare, prevailed.

Among White's innovations were the establishment of a psychological laboratory (1907) and later the Medical and Surgical Building (1920). He encouraged scientific investigations and publications, developed the School of Nursing, and started social work and occupational therapy at the hospital.

Among White's approximately 200 papers and 19 books were *Outlines of Psychiatry* (1907), a major medical textbook for 30 years; *Modern Treatment of Nervous and Mental Diseases* (with Jelliffe, 1913); and the personally revealing *Autobiography of a Purpose*, published posthumously (1938). Some of the earliest American writings on psychiatry and the law came from his pen. He attempted to secure changes in commitment laws and permit voluntary admissions. His testimony in the famous Loeb-Leopold murder trial is well known.

With his singular lucidity of thought and expression, White influenced, perhaps more than anyone else, the acceptance of psychiatry by other physicians and by the public. He was professor of neurology and psychiatry at both the George Washington and Georgetown universities and held the presidency of the American Psychiatric Association in 1924-1925. He was president also of the American Psychopathological Association, the American Psychoanalytic Association, and the First International Congress on Mental Hygiene (1930).

Under his aegis Saint Elizabeths Hospital prospered. By the time of White's death in Washington on March 7, 1937, it was perhaps the best-known hospital of its kind in the world. To this day it has endeavored to fulfill a unique function within the Federal service. The William Alanson White Foundation, established in 1933, sponsors the Washington School of Psychiatry and publishes *Psychiatry*, a journal dedicated to White's memory.

Further Reading

Autobiographical material which provides rich insight into White's personality is in his *Forty Years of Psychiatry* (1933) and *William Alanson White: The Autobiography of a Purpose* (1938). Otherwise, material on white is largely found in journals rather than in books. Gregory Zilbourg in the American Psychiatric Association's *One Hundred Years of American Psychiatry* (1944) covers the general background very well and pays tribute to White. Dr. Winfred Overholser, who succeeded White as superintendent of St. Elizabeths, describes White's work in some detail in the Centennial Commission's *Centennial Papers, Saint Elizabeths Hospital, 1855-1955* (1956).

Additional Sources

White, William A. (William Alanson), *William Alanson White,* New York: Arno Press, 1980, 1938. □

William Allen White

William Allen White (1868-1944), American journalist, was a spokesman for small-town America. His folksy wisdom and political commentaries were read and loved by millions.

On Feb. 10, 1868, William Allen White was born in Emporia, Kan. While attending Emporia College and the University of Kansas, he became involved in newspaper work and left, before receiving a degree, to work on various newspapers. After valuable years of experience writing for Kansas City newspapers, in 1895 he purchased the *Emporia Gazette,* the small-town weekly which he edited for the next 49 years.

The heat of a political campaign soon thrust White, a Republican, into national prominence. He was a virulent foe of the Populists and William Jennings Bryan, and during the presidential campaign of 1896 he published a vitriolic editorial attacking populism entitled "What's the Matter with Kansas?" The Populists, said White, were "gibbering idiots" intent on despoiling the rich and driving business and capital from the state. The editorial was reprinted by various Republican newspapers and magazines, and soon thousands of copies were being circulated in pamphlet form by the Republican campaign committee.

White did not long remain the darling of the conservatives. He soon moved toward progressivism and became a friend and supporter of President Theodore Roosevelt. When Roosevelt bolted the Republican party in 1912 to run on the Bull Moose ticket, White backed him. During World War I White became an ardent supporter of Woodrow Wilson's form of internationalism and fought for American entry into the League of Nations. In the 1920s White battled both the nativist Ku Klux Klan and the urban sophisticates who disparaged rural America. He came to stand for all that was decent and tolerant in small-town America, all the virtues that were rapidly being lost in an industrializing and urbanizing country. During the 1930s he supported most of Franklin Roosevelt's New Deal legislation but voted against Roosevelt in elections.

In 1940 White lent the great weight of his name to an organization lobbying for American support for the opponents of Nazism in Europe. "The Committee to Defend America by Aiding the Allies" became popularly known as the "White Committee." He died on Jan. 31, 1944, in Emporia.

Further Reading

White was a prolific writer and published many books, of which the best is his Pulitzer Prize-winning *The Autobiography of William Allen White* (1946). The finest biography is Walter Johnson, *William Allen White's America* (1947), written with loving care and considerable insight, whose bibliography lists 22 books written by White. As a supplement, Johnson edited the *Selected Letters of William Allen White: 1899-1943* (1947). Also of interest are Everett Rich, *William Allen White: The Man from Emporia* (1941), and David Hinshaw, *A Man from Kansas: The Story of William Allen White* (1945), the recollections of a friend supplemented by selected editorials from the *Emporia Gazette*.

Additional Sources

Griffith, Sally Foreman, *Home town news: William Allen White and the Emporia gazette,* New York: Oxford University Press, 1989.

Johnson, Walter, *William Allen White's America,* New York: Garland Pub., 1979, 1947.

White, William Allen, *The autobiography of William Allen White*, Lawrence, Kan.: University Press of Kansas, 1990. □

George Whitefield

George Whitefield (1714-1770) was an English evangelist whose preaching in America climaxed the religious revival known as the Great Awakening.

George Whitefield was born in the Bell Tavern, Gloucester. This tavern, of which his father was proprietor, located in a rough neighborhood, was his childhood home. His later confessions of early wickedness were probably exaggerated, but they can be understood as belonging to this setting. His first religious raptures also belong to these early years. When he was 12 years old, he left grammar school and became a tapster in the tavern. However, hope of a university education sent him back to his former teacher, who continued his preparation for college, and in his thirteenth year George matriculated at Pembroke College, Oxford, as a servitor.

At Oxford, Whitefield met John and Charles Wesley, joined the Holy Club, and practiced religious asceticism for a time. Through the Wesleys he learned of the Methodist mission recently established in the colony of Georgia in America. At 21 he professed personal religious conversion, and thereafter to the last day of his life his all-consuming desire was to tell of the "new birth" he had experienced. At 22 he was ordained at Gloucester Cathedral and received his bachelor of arts degree from Oxford.

Young Preacher

Whitefield began to preach with amazing success. His youth, his histrionic ability, his beautiful voice, and a compulsive personal conviction enabled him to hold an audience with remarkable power. As he preached in Bristol, Bath, and London, his popularity increased. Multitudes clamored to hear him, for it was the common people who were most deeply affected by his preaching. Those whom he could not reach with convictions of their sins were nevertheless moved by the power of his eloquence.

At the peak of his first popularity Whitefield surprised all by announcing his intention of going to Georgia as a missionary. In February 1738 he embarked on the first of his seven voyages across the Atlantic. His first stay in Georgia was brief. He returned to England to take priest's orders in the Church of England and to collect money to build an Orphan House for the Georgia mission. The money came, for he had influential friends among the upper classes, and philanthropy of this sort was current in London.

During his two-year sojourn in England, Whitefield's success as a preacher increased beyond all expectation. He was almost a phenomenon. Very soon, however, criticism began to be voiced, at first by churchmen, because of the Calvinistic tone of his sermons. When churches of the settled ministry began to be closed against him, he took to churchyards and fields; with this innovation his popularity with the masses greatly increased. So did the criticism. The press gave him more space. On the eve of his second departure for America he was a front-page controversial figure, the idol of thousands and the target of sometimes unseemly abuse. Word of all this reached America before his arrival, giving him the best preparation he could have asked.

American Success

After another brief time in Georgia, planning the Orphan House, Whitefield had the greatest triumph of his life during his month-long tour through New England. Welcomed by ministers and officials of colonies and towns, he found shops closed and business suspended during his stays, thousands of people at his heels, and many following him to the next town. No wonder his head was turned by such adulation. He was only 26 years old at this time, a fact often forgotten in making up his account. Success had come too early.

Whitefield's Boston visit lasted 10 days. Met on the road by a committee of ministers and conducted into the town, he found all meetinghouses except King's Chapel open to him. He preached in all of them and also on the Common, where thousands could assemble. The contemporary record was set down in superlatives. Benjamin Colman's words are typical: "admired and followed beyond any man that ever was in America."

The suddenness of Whitefield's acclaim for a time disarmed skeptics and silenced criticism, but before the 10 days were over, more realistic second thoughts began to be expressed by the more discerning. His criticism of the settled ministry as "unconverted" sparked the first criticism, though it did not bother the multitudes who were as clay in his hands. After his departure, the declarations of several leading ministers, and later still the testimonies of Harvard College and Yale against him, provided considerable check to the earlier unqualified admiration.

Later Revivals

Whitefield's five later visits were less spectacular, but none lacked extravagance and sensationalism. He was a magnet, and to his last sermon, preached the day before his death, he could cast a spell over his hearers, even though by now they knew his power was of the moment only.

After two centuries George Whitefield remains something of a controversial figure, although the controversy no longer deals with praise or blame or the accuracy of his own accounting of 18,000 sermons preached. Rather, modern critics meditate upon his impact on the mid-18th century. He broke the familiar meetinghouse pattern and released the membership to new ways of thought and action; he encouraged men to righteousness through their own individual decision; he put new hope in men's hearts and made the good life more attainable in response to their own desire for it; he made God kinder. He was not a thinker; he was not the originator of a new doctrine. He was a man with a conviction, and in some way not easily analyzed, as he stood before an audience of thousands, he seemed the living evidence of the gospel he preached. More than any other preacher of his day, he made the Great Awakening a vital, far-reaching force, religiously, socially, and politically, in America.

Further Reading

Sources of information of Whitefield are his own *A Continuation of the Reverend Mr. Whitefield's Journal* (1740); Luke Tyerman, *Life of the Rev. George Whitefield, B.A. of* *Pembroke College* (2 vols., 1876-1877); and Stuart C. Henry, *George Whitefield: Wayfaring Witness* (1957). □

Alfred North Whitehead

English-born American mathematician and philosopher Alfred North Whitehead (1861-1947) pioneered in mathematical logic, demonstrating that all mathematics may be derived from a few logical concepts. He also produced a comprehensive philosophical system in accord with contemporary science.

Alfred North Whitehead was born on Feb. 15, 1861, in Kent, England. His father, an Anglican clergyman, had a keen interest in education. Whitehead's character and intellectual orientation were largely shaped by his father's personality. After studying Latin, Greek, and mathematics in Dorsetshire, he entered Trinity College, Cambridge, in 1880 as a scholarship student in mathematics. Elected to a fellowship in 1884, Whitehead remained at Cambridge until 1910, rising to the position of senior lecturer.

In 1890 Whitehead married Evelyn Willoughby Wade, to whom he attributed his interests in moral, esthetic, and other humane values. The Whitehead's had three children; the youngest son's death in World War I profoundly affected Whitehead's later reflections on human life.

Early Work

At Cambridge, Whitehead concentrated on mathematical logic. He sought to develop an abstract (that is, nonnumerical) algebra. For the first volume of *A Treatise on Universal Algebra* (1898) he was elected to the Royal Society. His second volume was never published. Meanwhile, Bertrand Russell had worked independently on the logical foundations of mathematics and published *Principles of Mathematics* (1903). Whitehead and Russell collaborated for nearly a decade; the result was *Principia Mathematica* (3 vols., 1910-1913).

Widely recognized as one of the great intellectual achievements of all time, *Principia Mathematica* sought to demonstrate that mathematics could be deduced from postulates of formal logic. No work in logic since Aristotle's *Organon* has had a greater impact on the field than *Principia Mathematica*. Its influence on mathematics has also been considerable, manifest in the teaching of "new mathematics" in American schools today.

In 1910, in London, Whitehead wrote *Introduction to Mathematics*. In 1911 he began teaching at the University College, London, and in 1914 he became professor at the Imperial College of Science and Technology, subsequently becoming dean of the faculty of science in the University of London. During this period his interests centered on the philosophy of science.

Philosophy of Science

His 1906 paper, "On Mathematical Concepts of the Material World," had shown Whitehead's concern with connecting the formal concepts of a logicomathematical system, such as he conceived geometry to be, with features of the experienced world of space, time, and matter. In *Enquiry concerning the Principles of Natural Knowledge* (1919) he introduced the method of extensive abstraction. This method defines, for example, a formal element, like a point, in terms of a whole convergent set of volumes of a certain shape extending over others of the same shape, like a nest of Chinese boxes.

These investigations were pressed further in *The Concept of Nature* (1920). Whitehead rejected the prevailing dualism. He defined nature as that which is "disclosed in sense experience"; and he stressed, not our simple awareness of particular sensations, but rather our deep-seated feeling of a spatiotemporally extended passage going on in nature. Moreover, Whitehead analyzed the passage of nature into events and objects. Events are happenings which, while they may overlap, come into being and pass away. Objects, on the contrary, are constant; they are patterns which recur. Whitehead claimed that such a pervasive pattern, an element of permanence in the flux, accounts for nature's uniformity. It is bound up with the categories of space, time, causation, and matter.

Whitehead, keenly interested in Albert Einstein's relativity theory, could not, however, accept it without a revision so radical as to constitute an alternative. *The Principle*

of Relativity (1922) proposed a homaloidal conception of space and an absolutistic conception of measurement. (Physicists, however, have preferred Einstein's version of relativity for experimental reasons.)

Move to America

In 1924 Whitehead transported his family to America, where he became a philosophy professor at Harvard University. He devoted his Harvard years to elaborating a comprehensive philosophy.

Whitehead's 1925 Lowell Lectures at Harvard, published as *Science and the Modern World* (1925), immediately appealed to avant-garde thinkers not only in the sciences but also in religion and in the humanities. On the one hand, Whitehead wrote clearly about difficult points in the history of literature and science, such as romantic poetry and the new discoveries in quantum mechanics. On the other hand, he wrote numerous technical paragraphs which invited painstaking exegesis. The work, widely read and discussed, introduced Whitehead's own "philosophy of organism."

In 1926 Whitehead published his influential *Religion in the Making*. In *Symbolism, Its Meaning and Effect* (1927) he presented his theory of perception, marking his epistemology off from that of the empiricists. He noted two modes of perception: perception by presentational immediacy and perception by causal efficacy. Perception by presentational immediacy is the apprehension of distinct sense data—colors, sounds, shapes, and so on. Empiricists take this mode of perception to be fundamental, whereas Whitehead saw it as derivative from the mode of perception by causal efficacy. This second mode presents the deep-seated pervasive feelings that the perceiving organism has by virtue of its causal relations to other beings. By stressing perception by causal efficacy, Whitehead believed he would escape the subjectivism and skepticism into which traditional empiricism fell.

Process and Reality

Process and Reality (1929), probably Whitehead's most famous book in philosophy, presents his system of speculative philosophy, which he called "cosmology." According to Whitehead, speculative philosophy is the endeavor to frame a coherent set of basic concepts capable of interpreting every item of experience; he unveiled a technical system of 36 categories. It suffices here to cite four: actual entities, eternal objects, nexus, and creativity. Actual entities are the ultimately real things, coming into being and passing away. As momentary entities, they may be equated with the event constituting the leap of an electron from one orbit in its atom to another, or with an occasion of experience. Eternal objects, by contrast, are forms or qualities which recur in the passage of actual entities. A nexus is a society whose components are actual entities. Nexūs, or societies of actual entities, constitute the enduring objects—for example, trees and persons—encountered in ordinary experience. Creativity is the ultimate category, accounting for the novelty, the creative advance in the world. God is a derivative notion; it is an accident of creativity.

Process and Reality is widely considered the final formulation of the evolutionary, process philosophies which, stimulated in the first instance by the scientific achievement of Charles Darwin, were espoused by Herbert Spencer, Henri Bergson, and others.

As a result of his contributions, Whitehead was elected a fellow of the British Academy in 1931. In his last major work, *Adventures of Ideas* (1933), he further clarified his key ideas, relating them to earlier ideas in the history of thought, particularly the basic concepts of Plato. He also offered an interpretation of history and civilization, revealing the extent to which a few leading ideas shape human destiny. Because of its lucidity, profundity, and relevance, *Adventures of Ideas* is the best introduction to Whitehead's philosophy.

In 1937 Whitehead became emeritus professor of philosophy at Harvard. He stayed on in Cambridge, Mass., continuing discussions with students, former students, colleagues, and friends. A sample of these was published by Lucien Price as *The Dialogues of Alfred North Whitehead* (1954). In 1945 the British crown awarded Whitehead the Order of Merit, the highest honor it bestows on a man of learning. Whitehead died in Cambridge, Mass., on Dec. 30, 1947.

Further Reading

The basic study of Whitehead is Paul A. Schlipp, ed., *The Philosophy of Alfred North Whitehead* (1941; 2d ed. 1951). The best guide to Whitehead's thought is Victor Lowe, *Understanding Whitehead* (1962). Also noteworthy are Nathaniel Lawrence, *Whitehead's Philosophical Development* (1956), and Wolfe May, *The Philosophy of Whitehead* (1959). Special aspects of Whitehead's philosophy are dealt with in Dorothy M. Emmet, *Whitehead's Philosophy of Organism* (1932; 3d ed. 1966); A. H. Johnson, *Whitehead's Theory of Reality* (1952) and *Whitehead's Philosophy of Civilization* (1958); Ivor Leclerc, *Whitehead's Metaphysics: An Introductory Exposition* (1958); Robert M. Palter, *Whitehead's Philosophy of Science* (1960); Donald Sherburne, *A Whiteheadian Aesthetic: Some Implications of Whitehead's Metaphysical Speculation* (1961); John B. Cobb, Jr., *A Christian Natural Theology: Based on the Thought of Alfred North Whitehead* (1965); and Edward Pols, *Whitehead's Metaphysics* (1967). □

Edward Gough Whitlam

Gough Whitlam (born 1916), prime minister of Australia from 1972 to 1975, was one of the most skillful and controversial leaders of the Australian Labor party.

Edward Gough Whitlam was born on July 11, 1916, in Kew, an upper-class suburb of Melbourne, Australia. He dropped the "Edward" and was known usually as "Gough." His father, H.F.E. Whitlam, was Australian Crown Solicitor and Australia's representative on the United Nations' Human Rights Commission.

Whitlam attended schools in Canberra and Sydney and enrolled in Sydney University, where he got a law degree in 1946. In World War II he served in the Royal Australian Air Force (1941-1945), rising to the rank of flight lieutenant. He was admitted to the bar in 1947, served as a member of the New South Wales Bar Council from 1949 to 1953, and served as a junior counsel assisting the Royal Commission into the Liquor Trade in 1951-1952.

Broadened Labor Party's Appeal

In 1952, Whitlam was chosen as the Australian Labor party candidate for an election in the district of Werriwa. He won and kept that seat in the House of Representatives until his retirement in 1978. In contrast to his upbringing, Whitlam lived in the working-class suburban section of Sydney which he represented. Most of his Labor colleagues had working-class backgrounds and were suspicious of upper-class people. But Whitlam worked hard in his electorate to earn the trust of his constituents.

His first major position in government was on the Joint Parliamentary Committee on Constitutional Review between 1956 and 1959. By 1959 Whitlam had gained enough support in the party to become a member of the party's federal parliamentary executive, and in 1960 he became deputy leader of the party. On February 8, 1967, Whitlam was elected leader in a fiercely contested election, succeeding Arthur Calwell.

Under Whitlam the Labor party reorganized its internal decision-making structures and broadened its electoral ap-

peal to include the middle-class. Whitlam helped the party put aside its longstanding ideological disputes long enough to appear as a united party with a sense of direction.

Though Labor lost the 1969 election, it increased its seats in the 125-seat House of Representatives from 42 to 59. Whitlam had a mandate within his party to develop a broad range of policies seeking more attention to education, health, urban life, the environment, and equality for women, migrants, and aboriginal peoples. Whitlam's moderate, respectable tone helped the party shed its longstanding onus of being pro-communist. Whitlam's prestige in foreign policy was established in 1971 when he led a delegation to China, shortly before U.S. President Richard Nixon made his historic China trip.

Headed Labor Government

With a vigorous campaign whose slogan was "It's Time," Whitlam led the Labor party to victory on December 2, 1972. The party gained a majority in the House of Representatives, winning 67 seats, and Whitlam became the first Labor prime minister in 23 years. But Labor did not gain a majority in the Senate.

Whitlam overturned the slow-moving bureaucracy of the Liberal-Country party coalition which had ruled since 1949 and instituted rapid changes in policy. He pushed for better treatment for aborigines and a limit to U.S. and British influence in Australia. He ordered Australian troops to return from Vietnam, where they were fighting in support of American policies, and ended the military draft. But soon the international oil shortage and Whitlam's dramatic increases in government spending led to serious economic problems: first inflation and then stagnation.

The Liberal-Country majority in the Senate blocked several major pieces of Labor's legislative package. Seeking a stronger mandate, Whitlam called an election in May 1974. He remained prime minister, but Labor lost seats in the House of Representatives and failed to gain a majority in the Senate. Despite the deteriorating economic situation and bitter disputes within his own party, Whitlam continued his attempts to create a "new" Australia, changing the relationships between the central, state, and local levels of government. He introduced ideas about participatory democracy at the local level and using the public service to set the pace for wages and workers' rights. But many of his policies were bitterly opposed at home and by the United States. His efforts to develop a more independent role for Australia and his criticism of American policies in southeast Asia antagonized Washington.

The rising Liberal party under the new leadership of Malcolm Fraser and a critical mass media put Whitlam's government on the defensive. Scandals undermined public trust. The most damaging was the Loans Affair, in which the government tried improper means of raising several hundred million dollars from Arab oil sources. The deputy prime minister was forced to resign, and the minister for minerals and energy was fired. The Senate, under Fraser, challenged the Labor government by refusing to pass the budget. Whitlam called for an immediate election in the Senate. Instead, on November 11, 1975, the governor-gen-

eral, Sir John Kerr, a Labor appointee, dismissed Whitlam as prime minister, appointed Fraser as "caretaker" prime minister, dissolved both houses of Parliament, and called an election. Shocked, Whitlam declared it a day of shame and called for Australians to "maintain their rage" and carry it into the election. His appeal failed. The Labor party soundly lost the 1975 election, with only 40 percent of the vote.

Respected Statesman

Whitlam continued as leader of the Labor party until 1977 and retired from politics in 1978. After that he taught at the Australian National University (1978-1980), at Harvard (1979) and at the University of Sydney (1981-1983, 1986-1989).

Whitlam led the revival of the Labor party and made it more appealing to voters. Despite the failure of many of his policies, Whitlam changed the political map of Australia. After his defeat in 1975 he remained a respected figure in Australia. He was Australia's representative to the United Nations' Educational, Scientific, and Cultural Organization (UNESCO) in Paris (1983-1989). He was on UNESCO's executive board from 1985 to 1989. He served on Australia's Constitutional Commission from 1986 to 1988 and was chairman of the Australia-China Council from 1986 to 1991.

Further Reading

Whitlam wrote extensively on policy and constitutional issues. His books include *The Constitution vs. Labor* (1957), *Australian Foreign Policy* (1963), *Beyond Vietnam: Australia's Regional Responsibility* (1968), *The New Federalism* (1971), *Living with the United States: British Dominions and New Pacific States* (1990), and his spirited defense of his 1975 position in *The Truth of the Matter* (1979), a book which should be read in conjunction with *Matters for Judgement* by Sir John Kerr. He also wrote *Labor Essays* (1980), *The Cost of Federalism* (1983), and a retrospective on his leadership years, *The Whitlam Government 1972-75* (1985). Books about Whitlam include G. Freudenberg, *A Certain Grandeur* (1978); L. Oakes, *Crash Through or Crash* (1976); P. Kelly, *The Unmaking of Gough* (1976); and A. Reid, *The Whitlam Venture* (1976). □

Christine Todd Whitman

Christine Todd Whitman (born c.1947) managed to defeat her opponent, James Florio, the incumbent Governor of New Jersey, with very little political experience.

From the beginning, Whitman was perceived as a long shot for the office—a woman *and* a Republican was considered an awkward mix. She advocated sweeping tax cuts, as well as abortion rights. And, in the beginning of her campaign, her platform was very disorganized. However, Florio had so offended his constituents by raising taxes and reacting slowly to the plummeting economy in his state, that in the end Whitman won.

Whitman has definitely been characterized as a woman of privilege—a millionaire who made much of her money on Wall Street. She descended from a well-to-do family with strong ties to the Republican party. Whitman's husband also has ties to the Republican party—his grandfather was once governor of New York. Whitman's siblings have also been involved in politics.

Whitman was not a career politician by any means when she ran for the New Jersey governor's office. Her only previous political experience had been winning election to the Somerset County Board of Chosen Freeholders, which is the governing body of that county. She served there for five years. Republican governor Thomas H. Kean subsequently appointed her to the New Jersey Board of Public Utilities, where she served until 1990.

That year she took a major plunge into the political spotlight by running against New Jersey Democratic senator Bill Bradley, a very popular incumbent. It seemed at first that she would be token opposition against Bradley. However, Florio had just been elected as governor, and as such raised taxes by $2.8 billion and instigated an unpopular increase in the state sales tax. This infuriated many New Jersey residents. Whitman kept her campaign focused on Florio's unpopular tax hikes, instead of on Bradley's work. Her technique succeeded, and she won an unprecedented 47 percent of the vote—hardly the margin of an "easy walkover" opponent.

Her finish in this campaign put her in an excellent position to run for the governor's office. She had such an

impressive showing against Bradley that she was considered a prime contender. And Florio's tax policies would make her job easier. After his tax program went into effect, New Jersey dove into a recession deeper than that being experienced by the rest of the country. "Rarely has a state fallen so quickly from economic grace. . . . Its . . . disaster is entirely Florio-made," wrote Malcolm S. Forbes, Jr. in a *Forbes* editorial.

Florio's approval rating plunged to 20 percent. In 1991, the Democrats lost their majority in the state legislature, for the first time in 20 years. This made Florio's job even more difficult, since his ideas went against the politics of the Congress. They tried to repeal a sales tax increase, he vetoed it; they tried to repeal a ban on semiautomatic weapons, he vetoed it. When election time rolled around in 1993, Florio had an unimpressive approval rating of roughly 50 percent. However, he had the backing of the newly-elected president, Bill Clinton.

But Whitman's campaign was not without foibles either. She hired Larry McCarthy as her media consultant in August of 1993, to the outrage of many—he was responsible for the allegedly racist "Willie Horton" advertisements which aired during George Bush's campaign against Michael Dukakis. In response, Whitman countered that someone else had been in charge of the infamous ads, but McCarthy soon quit. While the controversy simmered, Whitman removed herself to go on a remote biking trip in Idaho.

Another scandal broke after she released her tax returns, which indicated that she and her husband had grossed an impressive $3.7 million in 1992. This fact made it harder for Whitman to seem like a "regular person" to the voters. Journalists also called into question her use of two rural homes as working farms. To respond to this, Whitman conducted a press party at one of the properties. Reporters found themselves at a real down-home event, with baked beans being served, and Whitman conducting tours in blue jeans. Her candor about the matter and willingness to answer questions scored points with many people.

Another problem with Whitman's campaign was her perceived lack of direction. It took her a long time to put together a clear tax package that would appeal to voters. In September of 1993 she finally unveiled her economic plan, which included many tax cuts, including one to slash income taxes 30 percent over several years. While the news sounded good, the voters seemed skeptical rather than enthused.

Whitman also attacked Florio's record on social programs. In a move to gain favor with conservatives, Florio had advocated making tighter restrictions on welfare allocations to mothers. One of the proposed changes involved forcing the women into naming the fathers of their babies. Outraged, Whitman attacked his ideas. "What is the governor's next idea in his headlong rush to embrace right-wing radicalism?" she was quoted as asking in *Congressional Quarterly*. "A program of tattoos for welfare mothers? A badge sewn on to their clothing identifying them as welfare recipients?" Her tactics backfired, however, when the Florio camp countered with angry letters from Jewish leaders who were outraged at Whitman's use of a Holocaust analogy for comparison.

Malcolm Forbes, one of Whitman's campaign advisers, wrote that "What makes Mrs. Whitman's tax ideas and approach so different, indeed so truly breathtaking, is that she plans to make her tax cuts the *core* of the budgeting process. Spending decisions will be made around the cuts, not vice-versa." Despite news like this, the public for the most part remained unconvinced, and the race was very close in the month leading up to the election.

Something changed that helped Whitman turn around the election. As her campaign gained momentum, she put increasing confidence into her campaign manager, Ed Rollins. A political analyst who had helped achieve Ronald Reagan's 1984 win, Rollins became a controversial figure when he switched camps to assist H. Ross Perot in his 1992 presidential bid. Shortly after taking the job with Perot, he left in disgust. In the last weeks of Whitman's campaign, Rollins simply took the reins, and immediately began to reorganize her campaign approach. "For much of the campaign," according to *Congressional Quarterly*, "Whitman seemed unable or even unwilling to capitalize on the anyone-but-Florio sentiment." Rollins changed all that by focusing on Florio's unpopular record in her stump speeches. Rollins also advised her to keep her own promises on the back burner, because she had encountered so much skepticism about them.

The tactic worked. The Eagleton Institute poll showed the incumbent governor as being ahead just one week before election day. But the undecided vote was just too close to call. Whitman won the November 2, 1993 election by just 26,000 votes. Constituents were just too concerned with Florio's previous records to place any confidence in him.

With her long campaign over, Whitman should have been able to breathe a sigh of relief. But, just a short time after the votes were in, Rollins told the press that the reason they had won was because they had paid African-American ministers to suppress the vote among their parishioners. "We went into black churches and we basically said to ministers who had endorsed Florio, 'Do you have a special project? And they said, 'We've already endorsed Florio.' We said, 'That's fine—don't get up on the Sunday pulpit and preach. We know you've endorsed him, but don't get up there and say it's your moral obligation that you go on Tuesday to vote for Jim Florio,'" Rollins was reported as saying in *Time*. Money was also supposedly paid to election workers in Democratic neighborhoods (who were supposed to be getting people to the polls) to stay home. Rollins bragged that these measures were key in Whitman's election to governor.

His comments unleashed a furor of responses from many people, most notably black ministers. Edward Verner, head of a Newark black minister's organization, commented in *Time:* "To suggest that the black vote or the black church is up for sale is a racist lie." Whitman herself was appalled, and claimed that her manager's statement was an unequivocated lie. Rollins soon retracted his statements, telling *People* that his remarks were "an exaggeration that

turned out to be inaccurate." However, a federal judge ruled that an investigation would be necessary. Whitman assured the voters that she would agree to a new vote if any illegalities were uncovered.

Rollins's wife, Sherrie, claimed in *People* that her husband "feels awful about this furor he has created. He did not intend to hurt anyone. He feels so badly for Christie. He did not want to taint her victory." It turned out that no proof could be found to substantiate Rollins's initial claims, and by November 29, 1993, the Democrats abandoned their campaign to have the election results decertified. On January 12, 1994, state and federal investigators ended their investigation into the campaign and deemed Whitman innocent of the charges.

"Don't let the hullabaloo over the alleged antivoting activities of campaign manager Ed Rollins blind the nation to the significance of Christie Whitman's victory last month in the New Jersey gubernatorial election. She won on character and substance," Malcolm Forbes asserted in one of his magazine's editorials. After the election, Whitman went right ahead with her daring tax-cut proposals, even declaring that if they didn't work, she wouldn't run for reelection.

Whitman was very busy making personnel and policy decisions shortly after the Rollins controversy cleared. She made headlines when she added female state troopers to the group who were assigned to protect her and her family. She complained to Governor Florio that he had violated an understanding between the two of them and extended contracts, endorsed salary increases, and appointed people to positions before she took office.

On January 18, 1994, Christine Todd Whitman was officially inaugurated into the office of governor. And she faced serious challenges—the size of New Jersey's deficit had swelled to $1 billion. She nixed a proposal to use taxpayer's money to lure the Philadelphia 76ers from their home in Pennsylvania to Camden, New Jersey, and fully outlined her plans to cut state income taxes. In her inaugural address, she was so bold as to ask the Legislature to put into effect a five-percent tax cut retroactive to January 1. Her campaign promise had been to start cutting taxes by July 1, but she felt it necessary to start her proposals immediately.

Whitman's ultimate goal was to see state income taxes reduced by 30 percent within her first three years in office. She went on record as saying that she hoped these cuts would not force municipalities to raise taxes to cover missing state aid, but also said that she would not be responsible if this did happen.

Whitman outdid herself by reaching her goal in just two years, as opposed to the three she promised. She has also been involved in educational, environmental, and auto insurance reforms, and has taken steps to balance the state budget.

Whitman's popularity has swelled not only in her home state. *People* named Whitman one of their twenty-five most intriguing people of 1994, calling her "a one-woman political slogan."

Whitman was the first-ever governor chosen by the GOP to give the rebuttal to President Clinton's State of the Union address in 1995. Her audience was impressed with her response and the buzz began about the possibilities of her candidacy for vice president in 1996. Robert Dole, the Republican candidate, ultimately chose Jack Kemp as his running mate.

With ambitious and far-reaching tax plans, Whitman has impressed many political leaders. As Malcolm Forbes commented: "Opponents and pundits underestimated her backbone."

Further Reading

Aron, Michael, *Governor's Race: A TV Reporter's Chronicle of the 1993 Florio/Whitman Campaign,* 1993.
Congressional Quarterly, October 13, 1990; September 25, 1993; November 6, 1993.
The Economist, October 23, 1993.
Editor & Publisher, October 30, 1993.
Forbes, October 11, 1993; February 13, 1995.
Nation, January 3/10, 1994.
National Review, August 23, 1993; November 1, 1993.
New York, September 6, 1993.
People, December 26, 1994.
Time, November 15, 1993; November 22, 1993; February 6, 1995.
U.S. News & World Report, November 22, 1993.
Village Voice, October 12, 1993; November 23, 1993. □

Marcus Whitman

Marcus Whitman (1802-1847) was an American physician, missionary, and pioneer whose death, at his medical and agricultural mission, was instrumental in passage of the act to make Oregon a Federal territory.

Born at Rushville, N.Y., on Sept. 4, 1802, Marcus Whitman was educated in Plainfield, Mass., and then studied medicine with a doctor at Rushville. After receiving his medical degree from the College of Physicians and Surgeons of New York, he practiced as a doctor for eight years: four years in Canada and four years at Wheeler, N.Y.

In 1835 Whitman applied for a missionary position as "physician, teacher, or agriculturist" with the American Board of Commissioners for Foreign Missions and was sent to Oregon with the Reverend Samuel Parker. At the Green River rendezvous they met several Indian tribes who so fervently requested missionary help that the two men returned east to ready men to go west.

In 1836 Whitman married Narcissa Prentiss in New York. Then, in company with the Reverend and Mrs. Henry H. Spaulding, they departed for Oregon. On this overland trip, Whitman drove a light cart from Ft. Hall to Ft. Boise, thereby opening a portion of the Oregon Trail to wagon traffic. Mrs. Whitman and Mrs. Spaulding were the first American women to cross the Rockies overland.

Whitman established his mission at Waiilatpu in the Walla Walla Valley, teaching irrigated farming, ranching, home construction, and other aspects of civilization to the Indians. A dynamic, vigorous, resourceful, even stubborn man, he was often overly optimistic. When the board threatened to close his mission because of scant results, he made a dramatic 3,000-mile ride east in the winter of 1842/1843 to plead to keep it open (not to save Oregon from British domination, as was later stated).

Successful, Whitman returned to Oregon in 1843 with a large wagon train. His work at Waiilatpu was hampered in the next years by the excesses of renegade whites, unruly half-breeds, and denominational quarrels. Then in 1847 a wagon train brought measles to Oregon. Whitman's medicine kept white children alive, but the Indian young had no resistance and could not be saved. The Cayuse Indians believed that he was poisoning their children. On Nov. 29, 1847, they killed Whitman, his wife, and 12 others at Waiilatpu, triggering a long, savage war between Indians and whites in Oregon.

Joe Meek carried news of this war to Washington, pleading for protection so eloquently that Congress created the territory of Oregon and sent troops to it—just at the time the American Board for Foreign Missions was abandoning the region.

Marcus Whitman (left)

Further Reading

For Whitman's surviving correspondence see A. B. and D. P. Hulbert, eds., *Marcus Whitman, Crusader* (3 vols., 1936-1941). Myron Eells, *Marcus Whitman* (1909), is eulogistic but contains the letters and journals of Narcissa Whitman. The best biography is Clifford M. Drury, *Marcus Whitman, M.D.* (1937).

Additional Sources

Sager, Catherine, *Across the plains in 1844,* Fairfield, Wash.: Ye Galleon Press, 1989.

Whitman, Marcus, *More about the Whitmans: four hitherto unpublished letters of Marcus and Narcissa Whitman,* Tacoma, Wash.: Washington State Historical Society, 1979. ☐

Walt Whitman

Walt Whitman (1819-1892) is generally considered to be the most important American poet of the 19th century. He wrote in free verse, relying heavily on the rhythms of native American speech.

In all, over a 37-year period, Walt Whitman published nine separate editions of his masterpiece, *Leaves of Grass.* The final, 1892 edition, is the one familiar to readers today. He has strongly influenced the direction of 20th-century American poets, especially Ezra Pound, William Carlos Williams, Carl Sandburg, and, most recently, Allen Ginsberg and other "beat" poets.

Whitman was born on May 31, 1819, in West Hills, Huntington town, Long Island, the second of nine children. His family soon moved to Brooklyn, where he attended school for a few years. By 1830 his formal education was over, and for the next five years he learned the printing trade. For about five years, beginning in 1836, he taught school, on Long Island; during this time he also founded the weekly newspaper *Long-Islander.*

Journalist and Editor

By 1841 Whitman was in New York City, where his interests turned to journalism. His short stories and poetry of this period were highly derivative and indistinguishable from the popular sentimental claptrap of the day, as was his temperance novel, *Franklin Evans, or the Inebriate* (1842).

For the next few years Whitman edited several newspapers and contributed to others. He was dismissed from the *Brooklyn Eagle* because of political differences with the owner. In 1848 he traveled south and for three months worked for the *New Orleans Crescent.* The sheer physical beauty of the new nation made a vivid impression on him, and he was to draw on this experience in his later poetry. His brief stay in New Orleans also led his early biographers to suggest an early romance with a Creole woman, for which there is no evidence. In his later years, Whitman spoke of fathering six illegitimate children (one being a "living Southern grandchild"), but there is no evidence for

this claim either. In 1848 he returned to Brooklyn, where he edited a "free-soil" newspaper. Between this time and 1854, he worked as a carpenter, operated a printing office, did free-lance journalism, built houses, and speculated in real estate.

First Edition of *Leaves of Grass*

Not much is known of Whitman's literary activities that can account for his sudden transformation from journalist and hack writer into the iconoclastic and revolutionary poet.

The first edition (1855) opened with a rather casual portrait of Whitman, the self-professed "poet of the people," dressed in workman's clothes. In a lengthy preface Whitman announced that his poetry would celebrate the greatness of the new nation—"The Americans of all nations at any time upon the earth have probably the fullest poetical nature. The United States themselves are essentially the greatest poem"—and of the peoples—"The largeness of nature or the nation were monstrous without a corresponding largeness and generosity of the spirit of the citizen." Of the 12 poems (the titles were added later), "Song of Myself," "The Sleepers," "There Was a Child Went Forth," and "I Sing the Body Electric" are the best-known today. In these Whitman turned his back on the literary models of the past. He stressed the rhythms of native American speech, delighting in colloquial and slang expressions. He wrote in free verse, that is, poetry of irregular meter, usually (or in Whitman's case, almost always) without rime.

Whitman stressed contemporary events and everyday happenings. He drew his vocabulary from commerce and industry. He exalted the commonplace: "I believe a leaf of grass is no less than the journeywork of the stars,/ And the pismire is equally perfect, and a grain of sand, and the egg of a wren." The worker, the farmer, and the trapper were his muses. He identified strongly with the outcasts of society. Rebelling against the restrictive puritanical code of the day, he delighted in conveying in graphic terms the beauty of the "undraped" human body; he stressed in his poetry the purity of the sexual act—"Urge and urge and urge,/ Always the procreant urge of the world."

The first edition of *Leaves* sold poorly. Fortunately, Whitman had sent Ralph Waldo Emerson a complimentary copy, and in his now famous reply, Emerson wrote: "I find it the most extraordinary piece of wit and wisdom that America has yet contributed. . . . I greet you at the beginning of a great career." Emerson's enthusiasm for *Leaves of Grass* was understandable, for he had strongly influenced the younger poet. Whitman echoed much of Emerson's philosophy in his preface and poems. Emerson's letter had a profound impact on Whitman, completely overshadowing the otherwise poor reception the volume received.

Second Edition of *Leaves of Grass*

For the second edition (1856), Whitman added 20 new poems to his original 12. With this edition, he began his lifelong practice of adding new poems to *Leaves of Grass* and revising those previously published in order to bring them into line with his present moods and feelings. Also, over the years he was to drop a number of poems from *Leaves.*

Among the new poems in the 1856 edition were "Crossing Brooklyn Ferry" (one of Whitman's masterpieces), "Salut au Monde!," "A Woman Waits for Me," and "Spontaneous Me." Most of the 1855 preface he reworked to form the nationalistic poem "By Blue Ontario's Shore." Like the first edition, the second sold poorly.

Third Edition of *Leaves of Grass*

The third edition (1860) was brought out by a Boston publisher, one of the few times in his career that Whitman did not have to publish *Leaves of Grass* at his own expense. This edition, referred to by Whitman as his "new Bible," contained the earlier poems plus 146 new ones. For the first time, Whitman arranged many of the poems in special groupings, a practice he continued in all subsequent editions. The most notable of these "groups" were "Children of Adam," a gathering of heterosexual love poems, and "Calamus," a group of poems celebrating the brotherhood and comradeship of men, or, more properly, in Whitman's phrase, "manly love."

In addition to the pervading optimism and nationalistic fervor he generated in many of the poems in the third edition, Whitman was also very much concerned with the theme of death, the result of some emotional crisis (whose source is unknown) he had experienced in the late 1850s. Several of his great poems of this period testify to this—"As I Ebb'd with the Ocean of Life," "Out of the Cradle Endlessly Rocking," and "Scented Herbage of My Breast." Other well-known poems of this edition were "Starting from Paumanok," "I Saw in Louisiana a Live-Oak Growing," "As the Time Draws Nigh," and "I Sit and Look Out."

The critical reception of the third edition was mixed, although as usual the unfavorable reviews outnumbered the favorable. Many were repelled by the frank and open sexuality of a number of his poems. (One reviewer's reaction was so violent that he thought Whitman ought to kill himself.) The third edition was selling well—a new experience for Whitman—when his usual bad luck in such matters caught up with him: his publisher went into bankruptcy soon after the beginning of the Civil War. To add to Whitman's troubles, the plates of the third edition later came into the possession of an unscrupulous printer, who is believed to have issued over the years some 10,000 pirated copies of the book.

Whitman and the Civil War

Soon after the outbreak of the Civil War, Whitman went to Virginia to search for his brother George, reported wounded in action. Here Whitman experienced the war at first hand. He remained in Washington, working part-time in the Paymaster's Office. He devoted many long hours serving as a volunteer aide in the hospitals in Washington, ministering to the needs of the sick and wounded soldiers. Whitman's humanity was such that he brought comfort to Federal as well as Confederate soldiers. His daily contact with sickness and death took its toll. Whitman himself became ill with "hospital malaria." Within a few months his health was "quite reestablished." In January 1865 he took a clerk's position in the Indian Bureau of the Department of the Interior.

The impact of the war on Whitman was reflected in his separately published *Drum-Taps* (1865). In such poems as "Cavalry Crossing a Ford," "The Wound-Dresser," "Come Up from the Fields Father," "Vigil Strange I Kept on the Field One Night," "Sight in Camp in the Daybreak Gray and Dim," and "Year That Trembled and Reel'd Beneath Me," Whitman caught with beautiful simplicity of statement the horror, loneliness, and anguish caused by this national calamity.

Fourth Edition of *Leaves of Grass*

Whitman's revisions for the fourth edition (1867) were made in a blue-covered copy of the third, the so-called Blue Book, which he kept in his desk in the Indian Bureau. The secretary of the interior managed to get hold of it and was scandalized by its sexual references. In June 1865 he discharged Whitman from the clerkship, but an influential friend interceded in the poet's behalf. The next day Whitman was placed in the Attorney General's Office, where, safe from outraged moralists, he remained until 1873.

The upshot of the episode was the publication in 1866 of *The Good Gray Poet: A Vindication*, written by Whitman's good friend William Douglas O'Connor. The book was so adulatory that Whitman emerged looking less like a poet than a candidate for sainthood. This book marked the beginning of a fiercely partisan, uncritical approach to

Whitman and his poetry by his followers that persisted until recent times. Late in 1865, Whitman published *Sequel to Drum-Taps,* whose best-known poem was the great elegy on Abraham Lincoln, "When Lilacs Last in the Dooryard Bloom'd."

If Whitman was neglected at home, his fame was beginning to spread abroad. In England, William Rossetti's selection of poems from *Leaves of Grass* (1868) was well received.

A Different Emphasis in Themes

Following the Civil War and the publication of the fourth edition, Whitman's poetry became increasingly preoccupied with themes relating to the soul, death, and immortality. He was entering the final phase of his career. Within the span of some dozen years, the poet of the body had given way to the poet of internationalism and the cosmic. Such poems as "Whispers of Heavenly Death," "Darest Thou Now O Soul," "The Last Invocation," and "A Noiseless Patient Spider," with their emphasis on the spiritual, paved the way for "Passage to India" (1871), Whitman's most important (and ambitious) poem of the post-Civil War period.

In "Passage to India," Whitman explored the implications to mankind of three great scientific achievements of the age—the completion in 1869 of the Union Pacific Railroad, spanning the continental United States and of the Suez Canal, connecting Europe with Asia, and the completion, a decade earlier, of the Atlantic cable, connecting America and Europe. To Whitman, these three great events had symbolically brought mankind together in a one-world federation. After centuries of struggle against bitter odds, man had at last achieved a harmony and unity with nature. What remained was for him to achieve his complete spiritual union with God, a transcendent universal spirit, or life force. This was the soul's "Passage to India," a passage to the very cradle of civilization.

Democratic Vistas

In 1871 Whitman published *Democratic Vistas,* perhaps his most important prose work. He was thoroughly disenchanted with the pervading corruption in the United States during the period of Reconstruction. However, he believed in the ultimate triumph of the democratic ideal in the United States: "Many will say it is a dream . . . but I confidently expect a time when there will be seen . . . running . . . through . . . America, threads of manly friendship, fond and loving, pure and sweet, strong and life-long, carried to degrees hitherto unknown."

In 1871-1872 and 1876, Whitman published the fifth and sixth editions of *Leaves.* The most notable poems were "The Base of All Metaphysics," "Prayer of Columbus," and "Song of the Redwood-Tree." In 1873 Whitman suffered a paralytic stroke and moved from Washington to Camden, N.J. Thereafter, he devoted much of his time to putting *Leaves of Grass* into final order. He had recovered sufficiently from his stroke to take a trip West in 1879 and to Ontario a year later.

In 1881 Whitman settled on the final arrangement of the poems in *Leaves of Grass,* and thereafter no revisions were made. (All new poems written after 1881 were added as annexes to *Leaves* .) The seventh edition was published by James Osgood. The Boston district attorney threatened prosecution against Osgood unless certain objectionable poems were expurgated. When Whitman refused, Osgood dropped publication of the book. However, a Philadelphia publisher reissued the book in 1882.

Specimen Days and Collect

Whitman's reminiscences of the Civil War and other prose pieces were published as *Specimen Days and Collect* (1882). The so-called "Death-bed Edition" of *Leaves of Grass,* published in 1892, is the one familiar to readers today.

In his last years Whitman received the homage due a great literary figure and personality. He died on March 26, 1892, in Camden. *Leaves of Grass* has been widely translated, and his reputation is now worldwide. His emphasis on his native idiom, his frank approach to subject matter hitherto thought unsuitable to poetry, and his variety of poetic expression have all contributed to making him a strong influence on the direction of modern poetry.

Further Reading

The standard edition of Whitman's major work is *Leaves of Grass: Comprehensive Reader's Edition,* edited by Harold William Blodgett and Sculley Bradley (1965), one volume of the projected 16-volume *Collected Writings* now in progress under the editorship of Gay Wilson Allen and Sculley Bradley. The definitive, scholarly biography is by Gay Wilson Allen, *The Solitary Singer: A Critical Biography of Walt Whitman* (1955; rev. ed. 1967). Allen's *Walt Whitman* (1961; rev. ed. 1969) is a short, illustrated biography. Worth reading is Newton Arvin's study, *Whitman* (1938; repr. 1969).

The most comprehensive treatment of Whitman's thought and literary techniques is Gay Wilson Allen, *Walt Whitman Handbook* (1946). Allen's *A Reader's Guide to Walt Whitman* (1970) is a balanced analytical introduction to Whitman's thought. A stimulating psychological study is Edwin Haviland Miller, *Walt Whitman's Poetry: A Psychological Journey* (1968). Other sound studies include Frederik Schyberg, *Walt Whitman* (1933; trans. 1951); James E. Miller, Jr., *A Critical Guide to Leaves of Grass* (1957); Roger Asselineau, *The Evolution of Walt Whitman* (trans., 2 vols., 1960-1962); and V. K. Charl, *Whitman in the Light of Vedantic Mysticism* (1964). See also Joseph Beaver, *Walt Whitman: Poet of Science* (1951), and Richard Chase, *Walt Whitman Reconsidered* (1955). F. O. Matthiessen's study of the mid-19th-century literary milieu, *American Renaissance* (1941), includes a sensitive account of Whitman's "Language Experiment." Recommended for general background are Roy Harvey Pearce, *The Continuity of American Poetry* (1961), and Hyatt H. Waggoner, *American Poets from the Puritans to the Present* (1968). □

Kathryn Jean Niederhofer Whitmire

Certified public accountant and public official Kathryn Jean Niederhofer Whitmire (born 1946) was mayor of Houston, Texas and later taught at Harvard's School of Government.

First elected mayor of Houston, Texas, in 1981, Kathryn. J. Whitmire took office in January 1982 just as the Houston oil boom had crested and was beginning to decline. Mayor Whitmire proved a durable chief executive who rode out the oil recession and was elected to five consecutive two-year terms as mayor.

Kathryn Jean Niederhofer was born on August 15, 1946, to Karl Niederhofer, a Houston electrician, and his wife Ida. She was raised in a blue-collar, lower-middle-income neighborhood on the northeast side of the city. A hardworking and brilliant student, she graduated from the University of Houston with honors in business administration and two years later earned a master's degree in accounting and joined the firm of Coopers and Lybrand.

Fascinated by politics since her father's spare-time dabbling at the precinct level, Kathy fantasized about marrying a politician and did that in 1966 when she married Jim Whitmire. Twice an unsuccessful candidate for the Houston city council, her husband died in 1976 after a

debilitating bout with diabetes. Whitmire, who had risen to audit manager at Coopers and Lybrand, had resigned her job to attend to the daily needs of her ailing husband. She never exploited politically the compassion shown for her dying husband, an oversight that would later help earn for the cool and dispassionate mayor such epithets as "ice princess."

Inspired by her deceased husband and the women's movement, Whitmire in 1977 ran for Houston's second most powerful political office, controller, and won, becoming the first woman elected to citywide office. Aggressive and serious of purpose, as controller Whitmire became a leading critic of the sitting mayor for his inefficiency and lax administration. At the same time she reformed the pension system, avoided tax hikes by innovative adjustments in the water department, and put the brakes on large salary increases for city employees. She denounced the mayor's street survey as a frivolous expenditure of $1.3 million for what she called a "pothole study." Also critical of the mayor's poor management of explosive growth and its attendant problems, Whitmire entered the 1981 mayoralty race promising to bring efficiency and to run the city like a business corporation. Supported by an unlikely (in Texas) coalition of women's groups, African American leaders, Hispanics, some unions, and the gay political caucus, she drew ahead in a crowded field of candidates in a nonpartisan election and went on to win the runoff election, defeating the local sheriff.

When Whitmire assumed office in January 1982 as Houston's first female mayor, the oil boom was cooling. As oil prices fell, so did city tax revenues. Vacancies in office space went up. By 1983 Houston was in a recession, with a former labor shortage transformed into a 10 percent unemployment rate. Nevertheless, Whitmire fulfilled her campaign promises by repairing city streets, improving garbage collection, and stepping up the efficiency of city workers. Delivering on her promise to fight crime, she hired more than one thousand new police and put 50 percent more officers on the street by hiring lower-salaried civilian clerical workers to replace deskbound cops. She helped defuse racial tensions by bringing in the city's first African American police chief, a highly regarded former Atlanta safety commissioner. Her prudent fiscal management retained for the city its prized triple-A bond rating.

Whitmire's first term had a down side. She failed to win public support for a new transit system, worked poorly with the city council, and outraged the police when she increased their insurance payments while offering them only a modest pay increase. The disgruntled police officers besieged city hall, shouting obscenities at the mayor. In addition, the city was a mess, littered with broken tree limbs and rubble from Hurricane Alicia. However, she was elected for another term.

Re-elected in 1985, 1987, and 1989 Whitmire faced a number of tough challenges in her administrations. Cool, detached, and with the demeanor of a technocrat, she generally sought efficiency by paring away waste, pushing for higher productivity from city workers instead of relying on tax increases during serious drops in city revenue. During a precipitous fall in 1986 oil prices which saw tax revenues sag even further, Whitmire adamantly refused to raise taxes and downsized the city workforce, including the sanitation department where she cut salaries by 3 percent and got higher production from the remaining force. She also fought for and wrung more efficiency (in an earlier term, her second) by moving highly paid firemen out of desk jobs and chauffeur duty to the fire-ready force. She stumbled, however, when it came to ridding the department of an inside chief and bringing in an outsider as she had done with the police. She yielded to union demands and permitted a deputy officer to become fire chief.

It was also in her second term that she pushed through an ordinance barring discrimination against homosexuals in city hiring, which provoked a fire storm of criticism and a popular referendum in January 1985 which repealed the ordinance by an overwhelming 82 percent. The gay rights question became a heated issue in the 1985 mayoral election campaign when a former five-term mayor, Louis Welch, turned it to his favor and led the incumbent in the public opinion polls by 17 percent. She managed re-election in 1985 with 56 percent of the vote. During her last term as Houston's mayor, Whitmire served as president of the U.S. Conference of Mayors (1989-1990). She received the Good Heart Humanitarian Award in 1990, presented by the Jewish Women International.

After her defeat in a hotly contested race in 1991 to Bob Lanier, she directed a policy institute at Rice University and briefly served as president of Junior Achievement. This was followed by an appointment to Harvard's JFK School of Government. In 1996 Whitmire was selected by a national search committee to be president for the American Public Transit Association, but old political foes in Houston blocked her appointment. Later that same year, while addressing the North Houston Greenspoint Chamber of Commerce, she announced she was leaving her teaching position at Harvard to accept a new job with the University of Maryland.

Further Reading

For general information on Kathryn Whitmire see Mayor's Biography File, City of Houston. For her political career, see Molly Ivins, "Kathy Whitmire," *Working Woman* (March 1987); "Whitmired," *The Economist* (May 14, 1988); Lisa Belkin, "The Women Mayors of Texas," *New York Times Magazine* (March 20,1988); and Eileen Ogintz, "Texas Mayor," *Chicago Tribune* (November 29, 1983). Interviews with Whitmire, during the 1990s, can be found in the *Houston Chronicle* and other Texas publications. □

Eli Whitney

The American inventor and manufacturer Eli Whitney (1765-1825) perfected the cotton gin. He was a pioneer in the development of the American system of manufactures.

Eli Whitney was born in Westboro, Mass., on Dec. 8, 1765. He took an early interest in mechanical work. Although he worked on his father's farm, he preferred his father's shop, where, by the age of 15, he was engaged part-time in making nails for sale. He taught school to earn money to continue his education and graduated from Yale College in 1792.

It was Whitney's intention to study law, and he undertook to tutor children on a plantation near Savannah, Ga., to support himself. In Georgia he attracted a great deal of attention by inventing a number of domestic contrivances for his hostess. He was informed of the need for a machine to clean green-seed cotton. Cotton gins of various designs were then in use in different parts of the world, and models had been imported and tried in Louisiana as early as 1725. None had ever worked well, however, and when Whitney arrived in Georgia, cleaning was still a hand job. It took a slave a full day to clean one pound of cotton. Whitney set his hand to the problem and within ten days had produced a design for a gin. By April 1793 he had made one which cleaned 50 pounds a day.

Whitney went into partnership in May 1793 with Phineas Miller and returned to New England to build his gins. He received a patent for his machine in March 1794, by which time word of his design had spread and imitations were already on the market. It was the initial hope of Whitney and Miller to operate the gins themselves, thus cornering the cotton market, but a lack of capital and the large number of pirated machines made this impossible. Whitney took infringers to court, but he lost his first case, in 1797,

and it was to be ten years before he won decisively and was able to establish his right to the machine.

During this decade of frustration and financial uncertainty, Whitney turned to the manufacture of small arms as a way of repairing his fortune and saving his reputation. He signed his first contract with the Federal government on June 14, 1798, and promised to deliver 4,000 arms by the end of September 1799 and another 6,000 a year later. Whitney had no factory and no workmen, knew nothing about making guns, and had thus far been unable even to manufacture in quantity the relatively simple cotton gins. The inducement for him was that the government agreed to advance him $5,000.

Judged by the terms of the contract, however, Whitney was a failure. He had no idea of how to go about fulfilling his obligation, and indeed he delivered his first 500 guns in 1801, three years late. The last guns were not delivered to the government until January 1809, almost nine years late. By this time the government had advanced him over $131,000. He died in New Haven, Conn., on Jan 8, 1825.

Whitney's claims of novel methods of production have led many scholars to assume that he had worked out and applied what came to be called the American system of manufactures. By this method, machines were substituted for hand labor, parts were made uniform, and production was speeded up. Thus it became possible to dispense with the skilled but expensive master craftsmen required previously.

This idea was not a new one. The Swedish inventor Christopher Polhem had used such a system in the 1720s, but no one had carried on his work. By 1799 the government armory at Springfield, Mass., had cut the number of man-days needed to make a musket from 21 to 9 through the use of machines.

The question thus becomes: where did Whitney fit into this growing concept of the American system? We know practically nothing of what went on within his armory. The records show that he tried to hire workmen away from the Springfield Armory to build machines for him. We know also that in a recent test of Whitney muskets not all their parts were in fact interchangeable and that some parts were not even approximately the same size. The answer then must be that Whitney was only one of a number of men who, about 1800, began to experiment with a relatively new and potentially revolutionary method of production—mass manufacture, by special-purpose machines, of products made up of uniform and interchangeable parts.

Further Reading

The basic biography is still Denison Olmsted, *Memoir of Eli Whitney* (1846). Two modern studies which tend perhaps to overemphasize Whitney's contributions to the development of American technology are Jeannette Mirsky and Allan Nevins, *The World of Eli Whitney* (1952), and Constance (McLaughlin) Green, *Eli Whitney and the Birth of American Technology* (1956). □

Josiah Dwight Whitney

The American chemist and geologist Josiah Dwight Whitney (1819-1896) was instrumental in placing mining geology on a firm scientific basis.

Josiah Dwight Whitney was born in Northampton, Mass., on Nov. 23, 1819, the son of a local banker. After graduating from Yale in 1839, he studied chemistry with Robert Hare in Philadelphia. In 1840 Whitney joined Charles T. Jackson as an unpaid assistant in the geological survey of New Hampshire. Whitney studied chemistry and geology with some of the leading scientists of France and Germany from 1842 to 1847.

In 1847 Jackson engaged Whitney to assist in a survey of the mineral lands of the upper peninsula of Michigan. Then followed a period as a consulting expert in mining, and during this time he compiled the information that appeared in his book *Metallic Wealth of the United States* (1854), which remained the standard reference for nearly two decades. Also in 1854, he married Louisa Goddard Howe of Brookline, Mass. In 1860 he was appointed state geologist of California, where he began an elaborate survey that was to include paleontology, zoology, and botany as well as the conventional mineral survey. The work progressed smoothly at first, but by 1868 legislators, becoming impatient with his scholarly ideals and his failure to produce quick results, suspended his activities. Although he remained in office until 1874, the work was not resumed, and the final reports were published at Whitney's own expense.

In 1865 Whitney had been appointed to the Harvard faculty to found a school of mines and had been granted an indefinite leave of absence to carry on the work of the California survey. In 1868 he returned to Cambridge to open the school, and the following year he took a party of his students to do fieldwork in Colorado. With the definite suspension of the survey in 1874, Whitney took up permanent residence in Cambridge and resumed his professorship, which he held for the rest of his life.

Whitney's second great work, *Climatic Changes of Later Geological Times* (1882), was based on his western experiences. Although it was an important contribution to the subject at the time of publication, many of his conclusions have since been modified or overturned. Whitney also wrote the articles on America for the ninth edition of the Encyclopaedia Britannica and prepared a revised version for separate publication in two volumes: *The United States: Facts and Figures Illustrating the Physical Geography of the Country and Its Material Resources* (1889). Equally important for the development of the profession was his preparation for *The Century Dictionary and Cyclopedia* of the terms in the fields of mining, metal and metallurgy, geology, lithology, physical geography, and fossil botany.

Whitney was a member of the American Philosophical Society and a founding member of the National Academy of Sciences; he was the fourth American to be elected a foreign

member of the Geological Society of London. He died on Sept. 25, 1896.

Further Reading

The source for Whitney's life is Edwin T. Brewster, *Life and Letters of Josiah Dwight Whitney* (1909). For background see George P. Merrill, *The First One Hundred Years of American Geology* (1924). □

Charles Evans Whittaker

Charles Evans Whittaker (1901-1973) was named to the U.S. Supreme Court by President Dwight Eisenhower. Supreme Court justices receive a lifetime appointment, but Whittaker resigned after serving only five years.

Charles Whittaker was born in Troy, Kansas, on February 22, 1901, and was raised on his father's farm. Grief-stricken at the death of his mother on his 16th birthday, he quit high school and buried himself in full-time farm work. In describing this difficult period in his life, Whittaker movingly commented to the Senate Judiciary Committee many years later: "I rode a pony to school through six miles of mud night and morning for about a year

and a half. When my mother died, it broke my heart; she died on my birthday, 1917. I felt I couldn't go on and I quit high school."

After agreeing to be tutored in high school subjects, Whittaker was accepted into the night program at the University of Kansas City Law School in 1921. The future justice financed his education, in part, through money he earned from selling the furs of animals he trapped. While a law student, Whittaker also worked in the Kansas City law firm of Watson, Gage, and Ess as an office boy, putting in a nine-hour day before attending classes from 4:30 to 9:30 in the evening. He would then study until midnight. Whittaker passed the Missouri Bar Exam in 1923—one year *before* he received his law degree. After passing the bar, he joined the Watson firm and became a partner after two years. In 1928 Whittaker married Winifred R. Pugh, with whom he had three sons.

In his private practice Whittaker was a litigator who represented both national and local corporations, including Union Pacific and Montgomery Ward. From 1953 to 1954 he served as president of the Missouri Bar Association, but was otherwise uninvolved in social or political activities. Nevertheless, his position as the leader of the local bar made him well-known to state political leaders.

When a vacancy occurred on the United States District Court for the Western District of Missouri in 1954, Whittaker received strong backing from state and local political and bar leaders. In addition, Roy Roberts, Republican publisher of the *Kansas City Star,* and Arthur Eisenhower, brother of the president and a close friend of Whittaker, pushed his nomination. Thus, President Dwight Eisenhower named him a U.S. District Court judge. Two years later Whittaker was nominated to the United States Court of Appeals for the Eighth Circuit and was confirmed by the Senate on July 22, 1956.

In 1957 Justice Stanley Reed retired from the U.S. Supreme Court, and President Eisenhower nominated Judge Whittaker to take Reed's seat on March 2, 1957, apparently at the recommendation of U.S. Attorney General Herbert Brownell. Eisenhower's selection criteria and Whittaker's background were a perfect match. Like Kentuckian Reed, Whittaker was from a border state; he was a reasonable age (56); he had compiled an outstanding record as a regional corporate lawyer; he was a conservative Republican but had succeeded in being a nonpartisan attorney and jurist; and he had the all-important (to Eisenhower) experience of serving on the lower federal courts. The Senate confirmed him on March 19, 1957, without a formal roll call, making him the first justice born in Kansas and appointed from Missouri.

Justice Whittaker served only five years on the Supreme Court. Despite his previous legal and judicial experience, he found himself temperamentally unsuited for the pressured life of a U.S. Supreme Court justice. Decision-making and opinion-writing were excruciating exercises for him. Thus, during his short tenure he wrote only eight majority opinions, and none is of particular note. He voted with the majority in a number of close 5-to-4 decisions, however.

One major case in which Whittaker participated and wrote a separate opinion was *Gomillion v. Lightfoot* in 1960, which involved the gerrymandering of Tuskegee, Alabama. The state had redrawn the city boundaries to exclude all African American voters, making Tuskegee's city limits into a 28-sided figure. This left only four or five African American voters within the city. The affected African American voters argued that they were denied due process and equal protection under the Fourteenth Amendment and the right to vote under the Fifteenth Amendment. Whittaker wrote a concurring opinion to the unanimous decision. The majority opinion written by Justice Felix Frankfurter argued that segregating a racial minority was discriminatory and violative of the Fifteenth Amendment. Whittaker stated that this application extended the amendment to include the right to vote, as well as the right to vote in a particular district. Whittaker, however, believed that the equal protection clause of the Fourteenth Amendment was better suited to the ruling because redistricting is not a true violation of voting rights. The redrawing of the Tuskegee city limits was a clear violation of the equal protection clause of the Fourteenth Amendment.

After five years on the Court, Justice Whittaker retired, succumbing to physical exhaustion on April 1, 1962. Eventually, he went to work on the legal staff of General Motors. The ex-justice died on November 26, 1973, at the age of 72, in Kansas City, Missouri.

Further Reading

Because of Justice Whittaker's short and undistinguished career on the U.S. Supreme Court, no major biographies of him exist. A longer biographical entry, however, appears in Leon Friedman and Fred Israel's *Justices of the United States Supreme Court, 1789-1978*, vol. 4, 1980. □

John Greenleaf Whittier

John Greenleaf Whittier (1807-1892) was an American poet whose humanitarianism and great popular appeal established him as an important 19th-century figure.

John Greenleaf Whittier was born on a farm near Haverhill, Mass., on Dec. 17, 1807, of poor Quaker parents. His formal education was meager. At the age of 14 he discovered Robert Burns's poetry, with its Scottish dialect and humble, rural subjects. He began writing poems; one caught the eye of abolitionist William Lloyd Garrison, who published it in 1826 in his paper, the *Newburyport Free Press*. Garrison encouraged him to continue his schooling, and Whittier attended Haverhill Academy on and off for two years. For a time he also taught school. Meanwhile, his poems were being published in local newspapers.

Between 1829 and 1846 Whittier edited various journals, including the abolitionist *Pennsylvania Freeman* (1838-1840). In 1835 he served in the Massachusetts Legislature.

With his vigorous antislavery essay *Justice and Expediency* (1833), Whittier firmly committed himself to the abolitionist cause. His antislavery poems such as "The Yankee Girl," "The Slavery-Ships," "The Hunters of Men," "Massachusetts to Virginia," and "Ichabod" were equally vigorous. He was well aware of his limitations as a poet; his was poetry in service of a cause, a poetry, often, of declamation. As he had put it in "Proem," he was concerned with "Duty's rugged march through storm and strife" and viewed the "softer shades of Nature's face,/ . . . with unanointed eyes." His volumes *Lays of My Home* (1843), *Voices of Freedom* (1846), and *Songs of Labor and Other Poems* (1850) reflected his belief in art as a weapon.

Poor health caused Whittier to curtail his editorial duties, but he was able to serve as contributing editor from 1847 to 1859 of the abolitionist journal *National Era*.

There was another, gentler side to Whittier. After about 1850 he also wrote folksy New England ballads and narrative poems, sentimental country idylls, and simple religious poems that appealed strongly to his readers. Among the most popular are "Skipper Ireson's Ride," "John Underhill," "Maud Muller," "Telling the Bees," "The Barefoot Boy," "Snow-Bound" (his masterpiece), "The Eternal Goodness," and "My Psalm."

In his later years many honors came to Whittier. He died on Sept. 7, 1892, at Hampton Falls, N.H.

Further Reading

The standard edition of Whittier's work is *The Complete Poetical Works,* with a biographical sketch by Horace E. Scudder (1894). The standard biography is Samuel T. Pickard, *Life and Letters of John Greenleaf Whittier* (2 vols., 1894; rev. 1907). Edward Wagenknecht, *John Greenleaf Whittier: Portrait in Paradox* (1967), is compact and balanced. Other sound studies include John A. Pollard, *John Greenleaf Whittier: Friend of Man* (1949; repr. 1969), a thorough work; Lewis G. Leary, *John Greenleaf Whittier* (1961); and John B. Pickard, *John Greenleaf Whittier: An Introduction and Interpretation* (1961).

Additional Sources

Burton, Richard, *John Greenleaf Whittier,* Philadelphia: R. West, 1977 c1901.

Fields, Annie, *Whittier: notes of his life and of his friendships,* Norwood, Pa.: Norwood Editions, 1977 c1893.

Woodwell, Roland H., *John Greenleaf Whittier: a biography,* Haverhill, Mass.: Trustees of the John Greenleaf Whittier Homestead, 1985. □

Sir Frank Whittle

The British Royal Air Force officer and engineer Sir Frank Whittle (1907-1996) invented the turbojet method of aircraft propulsion.

Frank Whittle was born on June 1, 1907, in Coventry, England, the son of a mechanical engineer. He joined the Royal Air Force as an aircraft apprentice at Cranwell in 1923, where he underwent three years of training as an aircraft mechanic. Then he entered the R.A.F. College at Cranwell as an officer-cadet. Although he was just 21 years old by the time he graduated in 1928, Whittle was already focusing on ways to produce higher speeds and greater altitude for the propellor-driven aircraft of the time. The title of his final thesis, according to the magazine *Aviation Week & Space Technology,* was *Future Developments in Aircraft Design.* Its theme was a discussion of rocket propulsion and gas turbine-driven propellors, and ways in which they could be used as alternatives to the conventional piston engines then available.

After graduating from Cranwell Whittle became a fighter pilot and was then posted to an instructor's course at the Central Flying School. Here, despite day-to-day responsibilities, he painstakingly designed his first turbojet.

Although sound in theory, Whittle's invention was in advance of its time in its material demands, and the Air Ministry rejected it. Nevertheless, he sought patent protection for his invention in 1930 and tried to interest manufacturers in production. He was granted a patent in 1932, but because of the Great Depression he had little success in finding manufacturers.

This was frustrating, but he did not allow this disappointment to interfere with his service career. He attended the Officers' Engineering Course at Henlow (1932-1933) and Cambridge University (1934-1937), where he completed his engineering training while continuing to seek interested investors for his engines.

In 1935, having found no factories interested in his engine, he formed his own company together with two partners named Williams and Tinling. Power Jets, Ltd. opened its doors in 1936 and immediately took out further patents with financial backing from O.T. Falk and Company.

By now the Royal Air Force was beginning to take Whittle's work seriously enough to transfer him to the special-duty list, enabling him to continue working on his engine. An experimental version ran in the British Thomson-Houston works at Rugby in April 1937, and by mid-1938 the feasibility of jet propulsion had been established. After the outbreak of World War II, development of the engine became dependent on Air Ministry finance. However, progress remained slow because of an ambiguous attitude by civil servants toward the unconventional organization of Power Jets, Ltd.

By April 1941 the Gloster Aircraft Company had completed an experimental airframe, and this was fitted with an early Whittle engine for taxiing trials. After an airworthy engine had been fitted, the Gloster-Whittle E28/39 made its first test flight on May 15, 1941.

Meanwhile, Whittle did not realize that he had a competitor for his invention in Nazi Germany. Hans von Ohain had not only produced a turbojet, but had also flown it in a

Heinkel plane as early as 1939. But though his engine was the first to fly, von Ohain did not have the last word.

Whittle had been generous with his research, sharing his technology with both the British Rolls Royce and the American General Electric Company. His foresight led to renewed interest in both the design of production engines and the airplane which was to become the Gloster *Meteor* twin-engine jet fighter. In the U.S. collaboration on the development of jet engines with the General Electric Company and the Bell Aircraft Corporation began in September 1941, while Britain was not far behind, putting its *Meteor* aircraft powered by Rolls-Royce "Welland" into service by May 1944.

In 1946 Prime Minister Clement Attlee's Labour government nationalized Whittle's Power Jets company and forced it to limit its activities to components research. Angrily, Whittle and several coworkers resigned from the company, following up, two years later, with his retirement from the R.A.F. with the rank of Air Commodore, an award of 100,000 pounds, and a knighthood.

In 1976 after several mental breakdowns, Sir Frank emigrated to the U.S. permanently to marry a retired U.S. Navy nurse named Hazel Hall and to take an appointment as a visiting research professor of Aerospace Engineering in the Division of Engineering and Weapons at the U.S. Naval Academy, in Annapolis, Maryland. He was deep into new research in 1978 when the Federal Aviation Administration decided to honor him by giving him the Extraordinary Service Award, the highest accolade the office can bestow. It was a shining moment in an otherwise quiet appointment, which ended in September 1979.

Whittle was now an elderly man, but he had no intention of fading quietly from view. In 1987 Smithsonian Institution Press published his autobiography, *Whittle, The True Story* which, in a collaboration with John Golley, gave his personal account of the jet engine's development and how it transformed aeronautical design.

Whittle then lived out of the limelight until October 1993, when an article on his achievements appeared in *Aviation Week & Space Technology*. The article's many inaccuracies infuriated him. Within a month of the magazine's appearance, he presented the editor with a list of 11 corrections, worded with enough military curtness to stress that the 86-year-old author had lost neither his formidable intellect nor his prodigious memory. Although Whittle lived until January, 1996, his letter was his last appearance in print.

Further Reading

Whittle's account of his development of the jet engine is in his *Jet: The Story of a Pioneer* (1953). Briefer accounts appear in Egon Larsen, *Men Who Changed the World: Stories of Invention and Discovery* (1952); James Gerald Crowther, *Six Great Inventors* (1954); and Patrick Pringle, *Great Discoveries in Modern Science* (1955). General background works include Charles H. Gibbs-Smith, *The Aeroplane: An Historical Survey of Its Origins and Development* (1960); Oliver Stewart, *Aviation: The Creative Ideas* (1966), which devotes a chapter to Whittle; and Ronald Miller and David Sawers, *The Technical Development of Modern Aviation* (1968).

Additional Sources

Air & Space, October/November, 1993; December, 1992; January, 1993.
Annapolis Evening Capitol, October 19, 1978.
Aviation Week & Space Technology, August 19, 1996.
Whittle, Frank, and John Golley, *Whittle, the True Story,* Smithsonian Institution Press, 1987. □

Sheila E. Widnall

Sheila E. Widnall (born 1938) was the first woman to head one of the country's military branches, the United States Air Force. While at the Massachusetts Institute of Technology (MIT), she developed the anechoic wind tunnel to study the phenomenon of noice and V/STOL aircraft.

Sheila E. Widnall is an accomplished researcher, educator, and writer in the field of aerospace engineering. A specialist in fluid dynamics at the Massachusettes Institute of Technology (MIT) for nearly three decades, she has also served in numerous administrative and advisory posts in industry, government, and academia. In August, 1993, Widnall was appointed Secretary of the United States Air Force, the first woman to head one of the country's military branches.

Sheila Evans Widnall was born to Rolland John and Genievieve Alice Evans in Tacoma, Washington, on July 13, 1938. Her father worked as a rodeo cowboy before becoming a production planner for Boeing Aircraft Company and, later, a teacher. Her mother was a juvenile probation officer. Interested in airplanes and aircraft design from her childhood, Widnall decided to pursue a career in science after she won the first prize at her high school science fair. She entered MIT in September, 1956, one of twenty-one women in a class of nine hundred, and received her Bachelor of Science degree in aeronautics and astronautics in 1960. She continued on at MIT to earn a Master of Science degree in 1961 and the Doctor of Science degree in 1964, both in aeronautics and astronautics. Upon graduation, MIT awarded Widnall a faculty post as assistant professor in mathematics and aeronautics. She was the first alumna to serve on the faculty in the school of engineering. In 1970 MIT promoted her to associate professor, and in 1974 to full professor. During her tenure at MIT, Widnall served as head of the Division of Fluid Mechanics from 1975 to 1979, and as director of the Fluid Dynamics Laboratory from 1979 to 1990.

Widnall specialized in the theories and applications of fluid dynamics, particularly in problems associated with air turbulence created by rotating helicopter blades. Her research focused on the vortices or eddies of air created at the ends and at the trailing edge of helicopter blades as they swirl through the air. These vortices are the source of noise, instability, and vibrations that affect the integrity of the blades and the stability of the aircraft. Widnall pursued

similar interests in relation to aircraft that make vertical, short take-offs and landings (that is, V/STOL aircraft) and the noise associated with them. To this end, her studies led her to establish the anechoic wind tunnel at MIT, where researchers study the phenomenon of noise and V/STOL aircraft. During her tenure at MIT, Widnall established a reputation as an expert in her field and lectured widely on her research in vortices and their relation to aerodynamics. Widnall is the author of seventy papers on fluid dynamics as well as other areas of science and engineering; she has also served as associate editor for the scientific publications *Journal of Aircraft, Physics of Fluids,* and the *Journal of Applied Mechanics.*

In addition to writing about aerodynamics, Widnall has also published articles and delivered talks about the changing attitudes and trends in education for prospective engineers and scientists. In 1988, as newly elected president of the American Association for the Advancement of Science (AAAS), Widnall addressed the association on her long-standing interest in seeing more women become scientists and engineers and the problems they face in attaining higher degrees and achieving professional goals. In recognition of Widnall's efforts on behalf of women in science and engineering, in 1986 MIT awarded her the Abby Rockefeller Mauze chair, an endowed professorship awarded to those who promote the advancement of women in industry and in the arts and professions.

Along with her technical and scientific interests, Widnall has been active in administration, public policy, and industry consulting. In 1974 she became the first direc-

tor of university research of the U.S. Department of Transportation. In 1979 MIT nominated Widnall to be the first woman to chair its 936-member faculty; she chaired MIT's Committee on Academic Responsibility for a year beginning in 1991; and she was named associate provost at the university in 1992. In addition to her term as president of the AAAS, Widnall has served on the board of directors for the American Institute of Aeronautics and Astronautics, as a member of the Carnegie Commission on Science, Technology, and Government, and as a consultant to businesses and colleges, including American Can Corporation, Kimberly-Clark, McDonnell Douglas Aircraft, and Princeton University. Her career has been recognized with numerous awards, including the Lawrence Sperry Award from the American Institute of Aeronautics and Astronautics in 1972, the Outstanding Achievement Award from the Society of Women Engineers in 1975, and the Washburn Award from the Boston Museum of Science in 1987. She was elected to the National Academy of Engineering in 1985. In 1996 she was named New Englander of the Year by the New England Council and was admitted into the Women in Aviation Pioneer Hall of Fame.

Widnall's association with the Air Force developed through her appointment by President Carter to two three-year terms on the Air Force Academy's board of visitors, which she chaired from 1980–1982. She also served on advisory committees to the Military Airlift Command and to Wright-Patterson Air Force Base in Dayton, Ohio. As Secretary of the Air Force, Widnall is responsible for all administrative, training, recruiting, logistical support, and prsonnel matters, as well as research and development operations.

She married William Soule Widnall, also an aeronautical engineer, in June, 1960. The couple has two grown children, William and Ann Marie. In her spare time, Widnall enjoys bicycling, wind surfing, and hiking in the Cascade Mountains with her husband in her native Washington. In September 1997, Widnall announced that she would resign as secretary of the Air Force, effective October 31, to return to academia.

Further Reading

Dr. Sheila E. Widnall, ''http://www.af.mil:80/news/biographies/ widnall_se.html,'' July 23, 1997.

Air Force Times, August 2, 1993, p. 4.

Jehl, Douglas, ''M.I.T. Professor Is First Woman Chosen as Secretary of Air Force,'' in *New York Times,* July 4, 1993, sec. 1, p. 20.

Sears, William R., ''Sheila E. Widnall: President-Elect of AAAS,'' in *Association Affairs,* June 6, 1986, pp. 1119–1200.

Stone, Steve, ''Air Force Secretary Salutes Female Aviators,'' in *Norfolk Virginian-Pilot,* October 10, 1993, p. B3.

''USAF Head Approved,'' in *Aviation Week & Space Technology,* August 9, 1993, p. 26.

Physics Today, February 1986, p. 69.

Biography, *Dr. Sheila E. Widnall,* Office of the Secretary of the Air Force/Public Affairs, November 1993. □

Christoph Martin Wieland

The German poet and author Christoph Martin Wieland (1733-1813), sometimes called the German Voltaire, was a typical stylist of the German rococo period.

Christoph Martin Wieland was born on Sept. 5, 1733, in Oberholzheim zu Biberach in Württemberg. His father a pastor, had been influenced by the Pietistic movement of A. H. Francke. As a student, Wieland attended the University of Erfurt and then the University of Tübingen, where he studied law. His real interest, however, was literature.

While still at the University of Tübingen, Wieland wrote the epic *Hermann; Zwölf moralische Briefe in Versen;* and *Anti-Ovid* (1752). J. J. Bodmar's attention was attracted by this Pietistic literature, and he invited Wieland to Zurich in the summer of 1752. However, he was soon disillusioned by Wieland's "frivolity." Wieland remained in Switzerland as a tutor until 1760. An inner change had come over him by the time he returned to Biberach as town clerk. Instead of austere Pietism he now held a lighthearted philosophy of life. Thus in his prose translation of William Shakespeare's works (1762-1766), Wieland—who now responded to the elegant and playful tastes of the rococo—failed to grasp the depth of Shakespeare's genius. However, he excelled as a translator of Horace's epistles and satires, of Cicero's letters,

and of the complete works of Lucian. *Don Sylvio von Rosalva,* an imitation of *Don Quixote,* appeared in 1764, and his *Comische Erzählungen* was issued in 1765.

Wieland's novel *Agathon* (1766-1767) remains a psychological masterpiece. Gotthold Ephraim Lessing praised and recommended it as "a novel of classic taste." Its background is ancient Greece, but symbolically Wieland described his own artistic and spiritual development. Platonic philosophy is set against hedonistic irony, sex against Eros. In the end the hero gains only a Pyrrhic victory over sophism. His *Musarion oder die Philosophie der Grazien* (1768) can be considered a continuation of Agathon, but the conflict between sensuous delight and purity of character is here softened by a spirit of renuciation and a determination to seek pleasure.

In 1769 Wieland was appointed to a chair of philosophy at the University of Erfurt. In 1772 he published a political novel, *Der goldne Spiegel oder die Könige von Scheschian.* This volume, an enthusiastic defense of an absolute but enlightened monarch whose one aim is the happiness of his people, so impressed the Duchess Anna Amalia of Saxe-Weimar that she invited Wieland to become, with the title of *Herzoglicher Hofrat,* tutor to the princes Karl August and Konstantin in Weimar. Wieland remained in Weimar until his death.

In 1773 Wieland founded the journal *Der Teutsche Merkur,* later continued as *Der neue Teutsche Merkur* until 1810. In 1774 *Die Geschichte der Abderiten,* his best-known political satire, appeared. In it he blended mythology and philosophy and personal and social allusions to the contemporary scene in a vivid satire aimed at intellectual snobs and spineless sycophants.

Wieland's greatest literary achievement was *Oberon: Ein romantisches Heldengedicht in zwölf Gesängen* (1780). This verse narrative, in a romantic-heroic vein, was greatly admired by Johann Wolfgang von Goethe. This epic of great rococo virtuosity was based on a 16th-century prose version of the Old French *Huon de Bordeaux,* into which Wieland wove Shakespeare's story of Oberon and Titania.

In 1797 Wieland purchased a small estate at Ossmannstädt near Weimar, but financial troubles forced him to give it up after six years. In 1800 he composed an epistolary novel entitled *Aristipp und einige seiner Zeitgenossen* about life and thought in 4th-century Greece. On Oct. 6, 1808, he was presented to Napoleon Bonaparte in Weimar. Wieland died on Jan. 20, 1813.

The formal elegance of Wieland's works has misled many critics and literary historians. They have misinterpreted his sensitive personality, his inner change from a pious protégé of Bodmer's to an Epicurean, and his change from a Platonist to a skeptic and satirist. Wieland's artistic and human vision strove toward ultimate reconciliation of pleasure-seeking materialism and spiritual integrity. His enlightened vision was rooted in a passionate belief in human progress and perfectibility.

Further Reading

An extensive treatment of Wieland in English is Derek M. van Abbe, *Christopher Martin Wieland: A Literary Biography* (1961). An older study of Wieland is Charles Elson, *Wieland and Shaftesbury* (1913). Extensive material on Wieland and his times is in W. H. Bruford, *Culture and Society in Classical Weimar, 1775-1806* (1962). Useful background studies are J. G. Robertson, *A History of German Literature,* revised by Edna Purdie (1902; 5th ed. 1966); Ernst Rose, *A History of German Literature* (1960); and Ernest L. Stahl and W. E. Yuill, *Introductions to German Literature,* vol. 3: *German Literature of the 18th and 19th Centuries* (1970).

Additional Sources

McCarthy, John A. (John Aloysius), *Christoph Martin Wieland,* Boston: Twayne Publishers, 1979. □

Henry Nelson Wieman

The American philosopher and theologian Henry Nelson Wieman (1884-1975) developed an "empirical theology" which opposed both orthodoxy and humanism and claimed that through the scientific method one could discover "God"—that is, "that creative good which transforms us in ways in which we cannot transform ourselves."

Born on August 19, 1884, the son of a Presbyterian minister in Richhill, Missouri, Henry Nelson Wieman became the most famous proponent of theocentric naturalism and empirical method in American theology. As a student at Park College, he had dreamed of following his uncle into a career in journalism—until a fateful experience one April evening in 1907. As he sat alone looking over the Missouri River in the faint light of dusk, a sudden conviction came over Wieman—a conviction that he should devote his life to religious inquiry and its central problem.

The central problem of religious inquiry, as it presented itself so forcefully to him that evening, was to seek a better understanding of the nature of whatever it is in human life and experience that transforms us in ways that we cannot transform ourselves, that rightfully deserves the kind of ultimate commitment and total self-giving that we associate with "religious faith." What is the nature of that process or structure of events or reality actually at work in the universe which, in religious language, has been designated "God"? And how can human lives be so adjusted to this reality that the power of creative good can be unleashed and thereby human life enriched? It was this problem, and the attendant questions which emerged from it, that came to consume Wieman during all the rest of his life.

Graduating from Park College and San Francisco Theological Seminary, he later earned a Ph.D. in philosophy at Harvard. His attempts to construct a philosophy of religion which paid virtually no heed to supernatural revelation or to biblical authority or to historic Christianity soon brought Wieman to public attention, and he was invited to join the faculty of the University of Chicago Divinity School, an institution known in the 1920s as a hotbed of Modernism in religious thought. There the question of the reality of God was at the center of controversy. Some professors were opting for humanism, while others were attempting to develop a form of "conceptual theism." For example, some believed that "God" was the concept people have for the forces or activities in the cosmos that give rise to personality. It was suggested by many at Chicago that in the study of religion we could examine the history and development of people's concepts and ideas about God; we could study cultural ideals and human values, but we could not know anything about the existence or nature of divine reality itself.

Into this setting Wieman came in the 1920s proclaiming that "God is an object of sensuous experience," that God is "as real as a toothache," and therefore that religious inquiry should not be focussed on socio-historical issues or on human ideals. Thus, he sought to clarify the nature and workings of "God," which Wieman defined as "that Something upon which human life is most dependent for its security, welfare, and increasing abundance." This approach caused Wieman to develop and support definite ideas about how religious inquiry should be reformed. It should not concentrate upon biblical studies, church history, or ecclesiastical doctrine. Neither should it utilize some trans-experiential method which gives authority to "revelation" or ecclesiastical dogma. Rather, religious inquiry must give centrality to sense experience, guided by reason, as the inquiry seeks to discover how we can put ourselves in the keeping of that good not our own, that power which is the integrative activity at the heart of the cosmos. While a number of scholars felt that Wieman's empirical method truncated religious inquiry, and while many criticized his disregard for history, Wieman gained a tremendous following.

His major books included *Religious Experience and Scientific Method* (1926), *The Wrestle of Religion with Truth* (1927), *The Source of Human Good* (1946), *Man's Ultimate Commitment* (1958), and *Creative Freedom: Vocation of Liberal Religion* (1982). In these works Wieman developed his defense of naturalism and empiricism in religion, his opposition to humanism, his assurances concerning the reality of God, and his focus on creativity and creative interchange. His was a naturalistic world-view. In religion, just as in science, said Wieman, there are not two realms of reality, namely, natural and supernatural. There is but one dimension of reality, and it must be studied through the observations of the senses. This does not mean there is no god. But God, for Wieman, is a natural creative process or structure—superhuman, but not supernatural. Our supreme devotion, then, must be to the creative good that is the activity of God, not to the created relative goods of human construction or the social ideals of the human mind. For Wieman, this was an ultimate commitment to what in his later years he increasingly came to label "creative interchange."

Through charting a course which at once affirmed the scientific method instead of reliance on revelation and which advocated theism instead of the new humanism, Wieman offered a unique alternative in theology between orthodoxy and liberalism. Many scholars have argued that he is the most distinctively "American" of our theologians and that his system is the most profound and well-developed attempt to provide an empirical and naturalistic theology. Wieman died on June 19, 1975, at the age of 90, having influenced generations of American theologians who sought to carry on his legacy, his commitment to scientific method in religious inquiry and to creative interchange in the human community.

Further Reading

The most substantive set of commentaries on Wieman's theology is Robert W. Bretall, editor, *The Empirical Theology of Henry Nelson Wieman* (1963). Also very helpful, though uneven, is a more recent collection, John A. Broyer and William S. Minor, editors, *Creative Interchange* (1982). Important studies of the movements of which Wieman was a part, or to which he was reacting, are Kenneth Cauthen, *The Impact of American Religious Liberalism* (1962); Bernard E. Meland, editor, *The Future of Empirical Theology* (1969); Randolph Crump Miller, *The American Spirit in Theology* (1974); and William R. Hutchinson, *The Modernist Impulse in American Protestantism* (1976). □

Norbert Wiener

The American mathematician Norbert Wiener (1894-1964) studied computing and control devices. Out of these studies he created the science of cybernetics.

Norbert Wiener was born on Nov. 26, 1894, at Cambridge, Mass. His father, Leo Wiener, professor of Slavonic languages and literature at Harvard University, determined to train the boy actively and singlemindedly as a scholar. Norbert was driven hard on the way to becoming a prodigy; fortunately he had the intellect and energy to emerge without undue suffering. He graduated with a bachelor's degree from Tufts College at the age of 14 and obtained his doctorate at Harvard four years later.

Wiener was awarded a traveling fellowship which he spent at the two centers where learning, especially in the mathematical and physical sciences, was perhaps the most significant and the most exciting in Europe: the University of Cambridge, England, and the University of Göttingen, Germany. After a varied career during World War I, he joined the Massachusetts Institute of Technology in 1919 as an instructor in the department of mathematics, and he remained on its staff for the whole of his career. There he was introduced to the work of the chemist Josiah Willard Gibbs, whose research on statistical mechanics, published in 1902, was a decisive influence in the development of Wiener's intellectual career.

Wiener had been instructed in the Lebesgue integral by G. H. Hardy at Cambridge, and with this grounding and his recognition of the importance of Gibbs's writings, he attacked the problem of the Brownian motion and produced one of his first major contributions to research. About the same time he began work on harmonic analysis. He brought to bear on this problem the method of Tauberian theorems and by this means refined his theory of harmonic analysis and also produced simple proofs of the prime-number theorem. He also worked on Fourier transforms and wrote *Fourier Transforms in a Complex Domain*.

At the same time that he pursued these studies into the field of quasi-analytic functions, Wiener was developing his interest in electrical circuits. The knowledge he gained on the problems of feedback control was of use when he became engaged in World War II on fire-control apparatus for antiaircraft guns. His interest in the parallels between feedback control in circuits and mental processes led to the creation of a new discipline which he called cybernetics, the study of control, communication, and organization. In *Cybernetics* (1948), his most influential work outside the field of pure mathematics, he propounded a new approach to the study of man in his technological environment, a science of man as component of an age of automation. On March 18, 1964, Wiener died in Stockholm.

Further Reading

The best sources of biographical material are Wiener's two volumes of memoirs, *Ex Prodigy: My Childhood and Youth* (1953) and *I Am a Mathematician: The Later Life of a Prodigy*

(1956). See also Mitchell Wilson, *American Science and Invention* (1954). ☐

Elie Wiesel

Elie Wiesel (born 1928), a survivor of the Holocaust, is a writer, orator, teacher and chairman of the United States Holocaust Memorial Council.

Elie Wiesel was born in Sighet, Transylvania, on September 30, 1928. The third of four children and the only son, Wiesel was educated in sacred Jewish texts. When he was 15, Wiesel was taken off with his family to the concentration camps at Birkenau and Auschwitz, where he remained until January 1945 when, along with thousands of other Jewish prisoners, he was moved to Buchenwald in a forced death march. Buchenwald was liberated on April 11, 1945, by the United States army, but neither Wiesel's parents nor his younger sister survived. After the war Wiesel went to France where he completed secondary school, studied at the Sorbonne, and began working as a journalist for an Israeli newspaper. In 1956 he moved to New York to cover the United Nations and became a U.S. citizen in 1963. He was the Andrew Mellon Professor of Humanities at Boston University in the mid-1980s.

Wiesel's writings bear witness to his year-long ordeal and to the Jewish tragedy. In 1956 Wiesel's first book, a Yiddish memoir entitled *And the World Was Silent,* was published in Argentina. Two years later a much abbreviated version of the work was published in France as *La Nuit.* After the 1960 English language publication of *Night,* Wiesel wrote more than 35 books: novels, collections of short stories and essays, plays, and a cantata. His works established him as the most widely known and admired Holocaust writer.

Only in *Night* does Wiesel speak about the Holocaust directly. Throughout his other works, the Holocaust looms as the shadow, the central but unspoken mystery in the life of his protagonists. Even pre-Holocaust events are seen as warnings of impending doom. In *Night* he narrates his own experience as a young boy transported to Auschwitz where suffering and death shattered his faith in both God and humanity. *Night* is widely considered a classic of Holocaust literature.

Night was followed in 1961 by *Dawn,* the story of a young Holocaust survivor brought to work for the underground in pre-independence Israel. Young Elisha is ordered to execute a British Army officer in retaliation for the hanging of a young Jewish fighter. Through Elisha's ordeal, Wiesel describes the transformation of the Jewish people from defenseless victims into potential victimizers. The execution occurs at dawn, but the killing is an act of self-destruction with Elisha its ultimate victim.

The struggle between life and death continues to dominate Wiesel's third work of the trilogy, but in *The Accident* (*Le Jour* in French), published in 1962, God is not implicated in either life or death. The battle is waged within the protagonist, now a newspaper correspondent covering the United Nations, who is fighting for life after an accident. In these three early works Wiesel moved from a God-infused universe to a godless one. The titles of his books grow brighter as the presence of God becomes dimmer, yet the transition is never easy.

Wiesel's next two novels come to terms with suffering and hope, reaffirming his commitment to man and his duel with God. In *The Town Beyond the Wall* (1964), a young Holocaust survivor returns to his home town to confront indifference and discovers instead the meaning of suffering and the transcendent power of friendship. A Spaniard whose encounter with his nation's civil war (1936-1939) shaped his consciousness instructs the survivor, "To say 'I suffer, therefore I am' is to become the enemy of man. What you must say is 'I suffer, therefore you are.' Camus [once] wrote . . . that to protest against a universe of unhappiness you had to create happiness. That's an arrow pointing the way: it leads to another human being. And not via absurdity." In *The Gates of the Forest* (1966), a novel describing a survivor's unsuccessful attempts to bury the past and live in the present, this same need for relationship is reaffirmed as the protagonist discovers his own weakness and need for love.

In addition to his literary activities, Wiesel played an important role as a public orator. Each year he gave a series of lectures on Jewish tradition at New York's 92nd Street Young Men's Christian Association. These lectures formed the basis for his retelling of Jewish tales: stories of Hasidism

(18th-and 19th-century Jewish pietists) which Wiesel published in *Souls on Fire* (1972), *Somewhere a Master* (1982), and *Four Hasidic Masters* (1978). Biblical and rabbinic legends are recounted in *Messengers of God* (1975), *Images from the Bible* (1980), and *Five Biblical Portraits* (1981). Wiesel spun his own tales in such works as *Legends of Our Time* (1968), *One Generation After* (1970), and *A Jew Today* (1978). The themes of these stories remained tragedy and joy, madness and hope, the fragility of meaning, and the quest for faith.

As a social activist, Wiesel used his writing to plead for Jews in danger and on behalf of all humanity. *The Jews of Silence* (1966) describes Wiesel's visit with Soviet Jews during trips to Russia in 1965 and 1966. Wiesel captured the spiritual reawakening that was to mark the struggle of Soviet Jewry during the 1970s and 1980s. Soviet Jews were not Wiesel's Jews of silence. Western Jews, who dared not speak out on their brothers' behalf, were the silent ones. Wiesel also wrote a play set in the Soviet Union, entitled *Zalman or the Madness of God* (1974), which dramatizes the fate of a rabbi who defied the Soviet system and spoke out on Yom Kippur eve.

Wiesel's novels usually involve spiritual dilemmas that confront his narrators. In *A Beggar in Jerusalem* (1970) Wiesel dealt with the implications of Israel's victory in the Six Days' War. In *The Oath* (1973) he explored the difficulty of recounting an event without betraying it. In *The Testament* (1981) Wiesel grappled with the legacy of suffering transmitted in Jewish history. *The Trial of God* (1978) returns to the theme of *Night* and questions God's justice, and *The Fifth Son* (1985) examines the meaning of revenge for the Holocaust. Among Wiesel's other works of both fiction and nonfiction are *The Golem: The Story of a Legend as Told by Elie Wiesel* (1983), *The Six Days of Destruction* (1989, with Albert H. Friedlander), *The Forgotten* (1995), *All Rivers Run to the Sea: Memoirs* (1995), *Memoir in Two Voices* (1996, with Francois Mitterrand), and *From the Kingdom of Memory* (a collection of essays, 1996).

Wiesel was the recipient of numerous awards throughout his career, including the Nobel Peace Prize in 1986. He was awarded France's Prix Medicis in 1969, and three years later the Prix Bordin from the French Academy. Other book awards include the Remembrance Award (1965), Jewish Heritage Award for excellence in literature (1966), Frank and Ethel S. Cohen Award from the Jewish Book Council (1973) and Prix Livre-International (1980), and Prix des Bibliothecaires (1981). Wiesel's humanitarian activities were rewarded with many honors, such as Eleanor Roosevelt Memorial Award (1972), Jabotinsky Medal from the state of Israel (1980), the International League for Human Rights humanitarian award (1985), Profiles in Courage Award from B'nai B'rith (1987), Human Rights Law Award from the International Human Rights Law Group (1988), Human Rights Campaign Fund Humanitarian award (1989), Award of Highest Honor from Soka University (1991), Ellis Island Medal of Honor (1992), Golden Slipper Humanitarian award (1994), and Interfaith Council on the Holocaust Humanitarian award (1994). Wiesel was named Humanitarian of the Century by the Council of Jewish Organizations. He

was also named a commander of the Legion of Honor in France, and in the United States he was awarded a Congressional Gold Medal. Numerous honors have been established in his name, including the Elie Wiesel Chair in Holocaust Studies at Bar-Ilan University, the Elie Wiesel Chair in Judaic Studies at Connecticut College, and the Elie Wiesel Endowment Fund for Jewish Culture at the University of Denver.

In 1979 President Jimmy Carter named Wiesel chair of the President's Commission on the Holocaust, which recommended creation of a memorial museum and educational center in Washington, D.C. In 1980 Wiesel was appointed chair of its successor body, the U.S. Holocaust Memorial Council. In 1985 Wiesel led the opposition to President Ronald Reagan's trip to a German military cemetery which contained the graves of Adolf Hitler's elite S.S. Waffen soldiers.

Speaking in 1984 at the White House, where President Reagan presented him with the Congressional Gold Medal, Wiesel summarized his career, "I have learned that suffering confers no privileges: it depends on what one does with it. This is why survivors have tried to teach their contemporaries how to build on ruins; how to invent hope in a world that offers none; how to proclaim faith to a generation that has seen it shamed and mutilated."

Further Reading

Carole Greene, *Elie Wiesel, Messenger from the Holocaust,* 1987; Carol Rittner (ed.), *Elie Wiesel: Between Memory and Hope,* 1990; Michael Berenbaum, *The Vision of the Void: Theological Reflections on the Works of Elie Wiesel* (1979); Robert McAfee Brown, *Elie Wiesel: Messenger to All Humanity* (1989); Harry J. Cargas, *Conversations with Elie Wiesel* (1976); Ellen Fine, *Legacy of Night: The Literary Universe of Elie Wiesel* (1982); and John Roth, *A Consuming Fire: Encounters with Elie Wiesel and the Holocaust* (1979). Chapter three of Lawrence Langer's Versions of *Survival* (1982) is a good description of Wiesel as a literary figure. □

Simon Wiesenthal

Simon Wiesenthal (born 1908) was a Ukrainian Jew caught in the horrors of World War II. Having lost most of his family to the death camps of the Holocaust, he spent the years following the war tracking down and seeking the conviction of Nazi war criminals.

Simon Wiesenthal was born on December 31, 1908, in what is now the Lvov section of the Ukraine. Turned away from higher educational opportunities at home because of a strict anti-Jewish quota system, he attended the Technical University of Prague. There he received his degree in architectural engineering in 1932. He married Cyla Muller in 1936 and the young couple set out to establish their life together in Lvov. However, like millions of his fellow Jews in Central and Eastern Europe, Simon Wiesenthal's life was to be traumatized by the policies of the two most notorious dictators of the 20th century: Joseph Stalin and Adolph Hitler.

Wartime Horrors

At the outset of World War II in 1939, the Soviet Union occupied the Lvov region. The Russians immediately set out to purge society of its "bourgeois" elements. The results were devastating for the Wiesenthal family. Simon's stepfather was arrested by the Soviet secret police and eventually died in prison. His stepmother was shot. Wiesenthal was forced to close his architecture business and barely avoided deportation to Siberia.

Life Under Nazi Rule

When the Germans displaced the Soviets in 1941, Wiesenthal escaped execution through the intervention of a former employer who was collaborating with the Nazis. But he was sent to the Janowska concentration camp. Later both he and his wife were assigned to a forced labor camp, where inmates worked servicing and repairing Lvov's Eastern Railroad. Compared to other Jews, those in the Ostbahn work camp were treated humanely by its German director, who did not adhere to the murderous anti-Semitic policies of the Nazis.

After invading the Soviet Union, Germany executed over 1.5 million civilians, mostly Jews, in captured Soviet territory. In the late summer and fall of 1942, Wiesenthal's

mother, along with most of his and Cyla's relatives, were deported and murdered. In all, 89 members of their families perished in the Holocaust. In late 1942 Wiesenthal secured his wife's safety by persuading the Polish underground to provide her with "Aryan" papers identifying her as "Irene Kowalska." She lived in Warsaw and later was a forced laborer in Germany, but her true identity was never revealed.

The "island of sanity," as Wiesenthal described the Ostbahn camp, crumbled in late 1943. Wiesenthal escaped before the camp was liquidated, but was detained again in June 1944 at Janowska. As the Eastern Front moved closer to Lvov, 200 retreating Nazi SS guards took Wiesenthal and 33 other prisoners westward, the only survivors of an original camp population of 149,000. Eventually, the few survivors were brought to the infamous Mauthausen concentration camp in Austria. There, on May 5, 1945, Wiesenthal, little more than a 90-pound skeleton, was liberated by a U.S. Army armored unit.

Becoming a Nazi Hunter

As his health and strength were restored, Wiesenthal began to help the war crimes section of the American army pursue Nazi war criminals. At the end of 1945 Simon was reunited with his wife, whom he thought had long since died.

In 1947, after working for the U.S. Office of Strategic Services and Army Counter Intelligence Corps, Wiesenthal headed the Jewish Central Committee of the U.S. Zone of Austria, a relief and welfare organization for Holocaust survivors.

When reflecting back on his initial period of "Nazi hunting," Wiesenthal said he never thought that gathering and preparing evidence on Nazi atrocities would occupy him all his life. "I assumed that the Allied governments and free nations of Europe would mount a serious effort to ferret out the estimated 150,000 criminals who committed crimes against humanity' as part of Germany's Final Solution of the Jewish Problem,'" he said. But the Cold War rapidly became the focus of the former Allies, and many war criminals, including Adolf Eichmann, Josef Mengele, and Klaus Barbie, escaped to South America.

Wiesenthal and 30 volunteers established the Jewish Historical Documentation Center in Linz, Austria, to gather data for future trials. By 1954 the frustrations of the staff over the inaction and apathy of world governments led Wiesenthal to close the center. Its documents were sent to the Yad Vashem Holocaust Memorial in Israel, except the dossier on Adolf Eichmann, the architect of the blueprint used to destroy six million Jews. It was the one case which continued to interest Wiesenthal throughout the 1950s, even as he worked for refugee relief and welfare agencies. Eichmann was eventually located, kidnapped by Israeli agents, tried, and hanged in Israel. Wiesenthal characterized the hunt for Eichmann as a "mosaic to which many contributed," including himself.

Buoyed by the renewed interest in Nazi war criminals which the Eichmann trial generated, Wiesenthal reopened the Jewish Documentation Center, this time in Vienna. By the end of the 1960s "Holocaust deniers" and neo-Nazis had launched an intensive propaganda campaign to whitewash the crimes of the Nazi era. Dutch fascists attacked the *Diary of Anne Frank* as a hoax, claiming that Anne Frank never had lived. That lie was exposed by Wiesenthal in 1963, when he located and confronted Karl Silberbauer, who was then serving as a police inspector of Austria. Silberbauer confessed, saying, "Yes, I arrested Anne Frank."

Wiesenthal's efforts also helped bring to trial in 1966 in Stuttgart, West Germany, nine major SS participants in the mass murder of Jews in his native region of Lvov. In 1967 Wiesenthal tracked down Franz Stengl, the commandant of two of the most notorious death camps, Treblinka and Sobibor, who was hiding in Brazil. He was extradited to West Germany for trial. Other major criminals apprehended through his efforts included Franz Murer, the "Butcher of Wilno," and Erich Rajakowitsch, who was in charge of transporting Jews from Holland to Nazi death camps.

Conscience for the World

During one of his earliest visits to the United States, Wiesenthal revealed that Hermine Braunsteiner Ryan, a murderer of several hundred children at Majdanek, was living in Queens, New York. It took several years, but in 1973 she was returned to Germany, tried, and jailed. Through the efforts of Weisenthal and others, Americans were confronted with the fact that the United States had become a haven for thousands of Nazi criminals. As a result, in the late 1970s the U.S. Department of Justice established a special office to identify and deal with Nazi war criminals.

The most notorious criminal pursued by Simon Wiesenthal since Eichmann was Josef Mengele, the infamous Auschwitz doctor wanted for the murder of 200,000 to 400,000 people. For many years Wiesenthal was the only public figure to raise the issue of Mengele's continued freedom in South America. In 1979 he led the successful effort to pressure Paraguay into revoking Mengele's citizenship. In June 1985 came the startling revelation that Mengele had lived since 1961 as a recluse in Sao Paulo, Brazil, and had apparently died in 1979. After receiving reports from forensic experts, Wiesenthal concluded that Mengele had died. "Although I know there is no proper man-made punishment for Mengele, it is unfortunate that his crippled victims could not face him in a court of law," Wiesenthal said. "But God has chosen to close the case."

Although Wiesenthal fought a lonely battle for many years in helping to bring more than 1,100 Nazi war criminals to justice, he touched the lives of millions of people throughout the world through his writings, lecture tours, and meetings with world leaders. Nominated twice for the Nobel Peace Prize, Wiesenthal was decorated by the Austrian and French resistance movements and received the Dutch and Luxembourg Medals of Freedom, the Diploma of Honor from the United Nations, and many other awards. In 1980 President Jimmy Carter presented him with the U.S. Congressional Medal of Honor on behalf of the American people.

In 1977, in recognition of his humanitarian work, the Simon Wiesenthal Center was established in Los Angeles. It became the largest institution in North America dedicated to the study of the Holocaust and its contemporary implications. In 1988 a made-for-TV movie of Wiesenthal's 1967 autobiography *The Murderers Among Us* was produced, with Ben Kingsley playing Wiesenthal.

Asked why he maintained his efforts to track down Nazis all his life, Wiesenthal said, "I believe in a world to come . . . When confronted by the martyred millions . . . I will be able to say . . . 'I did not forget you.'"

Further Reading

Wiesenthal's account of the unpunished war criminals is told in his *The Murderers Among Us* (1967), edited by Joseph Wechsberg. In *The Sunflower* (1970; revised edition, 1997) Wiesenthal deals with individual responsibility, justice, revenge, and repentance. His *Max and Helen* (1982) is about the lives of survivors of the Holocaust and the impact on their offspring. He told the plight of the Jews under Hitler in *Every Day Remembrance Day* (1987) and retold his own story in *Justice, Not Vengeance* (1990). In a lighter vein he wrote a historical detective novel about Christopher Columbus titled *Sails of Hope* (1973). For additional information on Wiesenthal, see Iris Noble, *Nazi Hunter, Simon Wiesenthal* (1979) and Lydia C. Triantopolus, *Simon Wiesenthal: The Man and His Legacy* (1983). □

Michael Wigglesworth

Michael Wigglesworth (1631-1705) was an American Puritan poet, physician, and minister. His poem "The Day of Doom" enjoyed a popular success unequaled in America before Longfellow.

Michael Wigglesworth was born probably in Yorkshire, England, on Oct. 18, 1631. The family went to Charlestown, Mass., in 1638 and soon settled in New Haven, Conn. There was no shelter on the land allotted to the Wigglesworths, and they spent the first winter in a cellar hole. Wilderness hardships took their toll. The father, broken in health, was unable to manage the farm alone and had to ask Michael to interrupt his New Haven schooling and come home. Michael, so frail that he was of limited help, was finally encouraged to prepare for Harvard College; he graduated first in his class in 1651; he continued on as fellow and as tutor. After receiving his master's degree in 1656, he became minister of the Congregational Church at Malden.

Wigglesworth had had some medical training in college and, in 1663, on a trip for his health, took up medicine again. Afterward he was both physician and minister, but poor health plagued him. In 1697 he was elected a fellow of Harvard; some say that he was offered the presidency but refused it because of his health.

Introspective and often despondent, Wigglesworth worried unceasingly about his spiritual and physical wellbeing. Yet his contemporaries loved and respected this "feeble little shadow of a man," as Cotton Mather called him. He married three times (outliving two wives) and had eight children. He died in Malden on May 27, 1705.

In the long ballad, *The Day of Doom*, written in 1662, Wigglesworth attempted to make Christ's judgment vivid to a popular audience. The damnation of sinners on that day is terrifyingly described; the elect reign eternally with Christ. Almost 1,800 copies were sold in a year; four editions of the poem appeared in Massachusettts and in England before 1701. Doubtless most New Englanders read, heard about, or owned this electrifying piece. Also in 1662, a year of severe drought, he wrote a poetic interpretation of New England's decline, "God's Controversy with New England," first published in 1873. His last verses appeared in *Meat out of the Eater or Meditations Concerning the Necessity, End and Usefulness of Affliction unto God's Children* (1669).

Wigglesworth's verse is poetry in the service of doctrine; his personality is suppressed. He tried a variety of styles and modes, always with the intention of finding the most effective means of presenting his theological vision of particularly his vision of Christ's imminent return to judge the world.

Further Reading

The Diary of Michael Wigglesworth, 1653-1657: The Conscience of a Puritan was edited, with an interpretative introduction, by Edmund S. Morgan (1951; new ed. 1965). A generous selection of Wigglesworth's poetry is in Perry Miller and Thomas H. Johnson, eds., *The Puritans* (2 vols., 1938; rev. ed. 1963). An authoritative biography is Richard Crowder, *No Featherbed to Heaven: A Biography of Michael Wigglesworth* (1962). □

Mary Wigman

The German dancer, choreographer, and teacher Mary Wigman (1886-1973) is considered one of the founders of the modern dance movement.

Mary Wigman was born Marie Wiegmann on November 13, 1886, in Hanover, Germany. The daughter of a manufacturer, Wigman obtained her secondary education at schools in Germany, England, and Switzerland. During a visit to Amsterdam she attended a dance performance by students of Emile Jaques-Dalcroze, originator of the system of musical instruction known as eurythmics. The experience instilled in Wigman an awareness of dance as an expression of life.

Despite the objections of her parents, Wigman enrolled in Jaques-Dalcroze's school in Dresden-Hellerau in 1911. The system of rhythmical gymnastics taught there became too rigidly academic and too confining for her because it forced dance to play a secondary role to music. On the advice of the German expressionist painter Emil Nolde she went to Ascona, Switzerland, in 1913 to enroll in the summer course given by Rudolf von Laban, whose theories helped pave the way for the modern dance movement. She remained with the Laban school—through the summer sessions in Switzerland and the winter sessions in Munich—until 1919 and served for a time as Laban's assistant. In 1914 she gave her first student solo performance.

After leaving the Laban school, Wigman went into solitude in the mountains of Switzerland. She worked intensively, creating dances and developing her unique expressionist or "absolute" style of dance, which was independent of any literary or interpretive content. She called this dance style "New German Dance," partly to express its break with the sterility of the prevailing classical ballet and partly to reaffirm ancient principles of the dance as an expression of human passions and aspirations.

In 1919 she gave her first professional solo concert in Berlin, followed by performances in Breman and Hanover. These concerts were poorly received, but later that year she won acclaim from audiences and critics in Hamburg, Zurich, and Dresden, and her reputation began to be established. By the mid-1920s Wigman became known as the leading exponent of the new "Ausdruckstanz," or Expressionist Dance, in Germany.

In 1920 Mary Wigman opened a school in Dresden, which soon became the focal point of German modern dance. At the school she trained dancers and experimented with choreography. Among her pupils were Holm, Georgi, Palucca, Wall, and Kreutzberg. These dancers also appeared in her dance troupe, which made its first public appearance in 1923. During the following years she toured extensively, alone and with her troupe. She made her London debut in 1928 and her triumphant U.S. debut in 1930,

followed by two more U.S. tours between 1931 and 1933. Although Wigman's style was often characterized as tense, introspective, and sombre, critics of the time described the quality of ecstasy and radiance to be found beneath even her "darkest" compositions.

In her early performances Wigman danced at times to no music at all or to the accompaniment of flutes or percussion instruments, such as African drums, Oriental gongs, or cymbals. Later she had music composed to accompany the movements of her individual dances—a new approach to dance accompaniment that proved to be widely influential.

Offshoots of her Dresden Central School were set up all over Germany, and in the United States by Hanya Holm. In addition, educational authorities prescribed her dance training for the public schools. She had become the center of a national movement and was honored officially in the early 1930s by the German government.

The Nazi authorities, however, considered her to be a leftist and her dances to be decadent. They took her school away from her, but allowed her to teach in Leipzig during World War II. The last work in which she appeared as a soloist was "The Dance of Niobe" (1942), in which she danced the title role.

After the war ended Wigman continued to work in Leipzig under Soviet occupation until 1949, when she fled to West Berlin. She opened a school there which became a meeting place for modern dance enthusiasts from all over the world well into the 1960s. Her last public appearance as a dancer was in 1953. During the 1950s she also worked as a guest choreographer. Her most important productions for German opera houses include Handel's "Saul" (Mannheim, 1954), Orff's "Carmina Burana" (Mannheim, 1955), and Stravinsky's "Sacre du Printemps" (Municipal Opera, Berlin Festival, 1957).

Mary Wigman was a major influence on American modern dance, largely through the work of Hanya Holm and other disciples who kept alive, developed, and extended her concepts.

Further Reading

Biographical material on Wigman can be found in Hanya Holm, "The Mary Wigman I Know," in Walter Sorell, editor, *The Dance Has Many Faces*, 2d ed. rev. (1966), and in Ernst Scheyer, "The Shape of Space: The Art of Mary Wigman and Oskar Schlemmer," *Dance Perspectives* (1970). Wigman's own writing includes *The Language of Dance,* translated by Walter Sorell (1966); *The Mary Wigman Book,* edited and translated by Walter Sorell (1975); "The New German Dance," in Virginia Stewart and Merle Armitage, editors, *The Modern Dance* (1935 and 1970); and "The Philosophy of Modern Dance," in Selma Jeanne Cohen, editor, *Dance as a Theatre Art* (1974).

Additional Sources

Manning, Susan, *Ecstasy and the demon: feminism and nationalism in the dances of Mary Wigman,* Berkeley: University of California Press, 1993. □

Eugene Paul Wigner

The Hungarian-born American physicist Eugene Paul Wigner (1902-1995) formulated symmetry principles and, together with group theory, applied them in atomic, nuclear, and elementary particle physics.

On November 17, 1902, Eugene P. Wigner was born in Budapest, the son of Anthony Wigner, a leather manufacturer, and Elisabeth Einhorn Wigner. In 1920 he entered the Technical Institute in Budapest, where, at his father's urging, he concentrated on chemical engineering although his principal interest lay in mathematics. A year later he transferred to the Technische Hochschule in Berlin, still majoring in engineering. However, before long he was a regular visitor at the physics colloquia attended by some of the chief leaders in physics in Germany at that time, including Albert Einstein, Walther Nernst, and Max Planck.

Wigner's doctoral thesis was on the formation and disintegration of molecules. After a year and a half of work as leather chemist, Wigner eagerly accepted the offer of an assistant professorship at the Technische Hochschule in Berlin, where, in the late 1920s and early 1930s, his attention turned toward the exploration of symmetry principles in atomic physics. Related to this was Wigner's recognition that group theory, a branch of mathematics inaugurated almost 100 years earlier, could be used to great advantage in accounting for the quantummechanical interpretation of atomic spectra. His book on this topic, *Gruppentheorie and ihre Anwendung auf die Quantenmechanik der Atomspektren* (1931; trans. in 1959 as *Group Theory*), is a classic in the field.

Wigner's stay in Berlin ended in 1933 when the Nazis came to power. His first post in the United States was at Princeton University, the second at the University of Wisconsin (1937-1938). In 1938 he returned to Princeton as Thomas D. Jones professor of mathematical physics. During the 1930s Wigner followed with keen interest research on neutron capture, and he was one of the first to realize its awesome and immediate potentialities.

In 1936 Wigner married Amelia Z. Frank. She died the following year. In 1941 he married Mary Annette Wheeler, and they had two children, David and Martha. After her death Wigner married Eileen Hamilton and had another daughter, Erika.

Among his early efforts to alert the government of the United States was his visit, in the summer of 1939 with Leo Szilard, to Albert Einstein on Long Island. What happened made history. At Wigner's and Szilard's pleading, Einstein consented to address a letter to President Roosevelt about the urgency of producing atomic weapons. In the actual production of the first atomic bomb, Wigner's role was crucial.

Wigner not only took a most active part in achieving the first controlled nuclear reaction in Chicago in December 1942, but it became his task to design the first large-scale

nuclear reactor. His secret report of January 9, 1943, outlined the details of the huge reactor, a million times more powerful than the first, to be built near the banks of the Columbia River. The gigantic measure of problems to be solved can be gauged from the fact that Wigner's design called for 200 tons of uranium and 1,200 tons of graphite. He also successfully argued that the cooling should be done by water running throughout the whole graphite structure in pipes whose central part contained the uranium. It is safe to assume that Wigner's feat saved about a year in the production of the bomb and also in the duration of the war. After the war he remained a leader in the investigation of the very essence of reactor theory, the neutron chain reaction, as evidenced by his authoritative work written jointly with A.M. Weinberg, *The Physical Theory of Neutron Chain Reactors* (1958).

In the 1950s but especially in the 1960s, Wigner's attention increasingly turned to some fundamental questions of physical science and to their major philosophical implications. His articles "Invariance in Physical Theory" (1949), "Conservation Laws in Classical and Quantum Physics" (1954), "The Problem of Measurement" (1963), and "Symmetry and Conservation Laws" (1964) have already proved their lasting value. As to the philosophical ramifications of physics, the same holds for his papers "The Limits of Science" (1950), "The Unreasonable Effectiveness of Mathematics in Natural Sciences" (1960), "Two Kinds of Reality" (1964), and "The Probability of the Existence of a Self-reproducing Unit" (1961).

Wigner's main scientific distinctions are the Nobel Prize in physics for 1963 and the Max Planck Medal of the German Physical Society (1962). His adopted country gave him the Medal for Merit, the Enrico Fermi Prize, the Atoms for Peace Award, and the Albert Einstein Award. In 1990 Wigner received the Order of the Banner of the Republic of Hungary with Rubies from his newly democratized birthplace, Hungary. In 1994, he was presented with Hungary's highest recognition, the Order of Merit.

Most significantly, in 1963, is Wigner's award of the Nobel physics prize for "systematically improving and extending the methods of quantum mechanics and applying them widely." Specifically, he was commended for his contribution to the theory of atomic nuclei elementary particles, especially for his discovery and application of fundamental principles of symmetry. This marked an unusual departure for the Nobel Committee, which normally awards the prize for a single discovery or invention.

Wigner, who retired from Princeton in 1971, was also active on behalf of other scientists. He was one of thirty-three Nobel Prize winners who sent a telegram to President Podgorny of the former Soviet Union asking that Andrei Saktlarov be permitted to receive the Nobel Peace Prize in Stockholm.

His dedication to the defense of America's freedom, and of freedom everywhere, constitutes indeed a major aspect of his life and activities. It was the same unconditional appreciation of freedom, whether threatened by dictatorship from the right or the left, that determined Wigner's position amidst the debates on nuclear armament and civil defense. His philosophy is best evidenced by his insistence on the crucial importance of the role of nonscientists in the modern scientific world: "The struggle for men's minds continues and it is quite possible that the conflict between democracy and dictatorships will be won not by armies, not even by scientists, but by philosophers, psychologists, and missionaries who articulate and communicate our ideals."

Wigner died from pneumonia at the age of 92 on Sunday, January 1, 1995.

Further Reading

Wigner's *Symmetries and Reflections: Scientific Essays* (1967) contains a selection of his less technical papers on a wide range of subjects. There is no comprehensive account of Wigner's life and work. A profile of him appears in Robert H. Phelps, *Men in the News—1958: Personality Sketches from the New York Times* (1959). The history of modern physics, of which he was a part, is entertainingly given in George Gamow, *Biography of Physics* (1961). The extensive use of group theory in physics is fully discussed in Morton Hamermesh, *Group Theory and Its Application to Physical Problems* (1962). □

William Wilberforce

The English statesman and humanitarian William Wilberforce (1759-1833) was a prominent an-

tislavery leader. His agitation helped smooth the way for the Act of Abolition of 1833.

William Wilberforce was born to affluence at Hull on Aug. 24, 1759. He attended Hull Grammar School and St. John's College, Cambridge. He was elected to Parliament from Hull in 1780 and from Yorkshire in 1784. In 1812 he moved his constituency to Bramber, Sussex. He retired from the House of Commons in 1825.

Wilberforce was a friend and lifelong supporter of William Pitt the Younger, the great British prime minister and war leader. Like his leader, Wilberforce moved toward a more conservative position following the French Revolution and Britain's involvement in the French Revolutionary Wars and Napoleonic Wars. His antislavery ideas arose not out of a background of secular liberalism but out of his religious beliefs. England in the late 18th century experienced a powerful religious revival, and in 1785 Wilberforce was converted to Evangelical Christianity.

In 1787 Wilberforce was approached by the antislavery advocate Thomas Clarkson, who was already in touch with the abolitionist lawyer Granville Sharp. The three formed the nucleus of a group ridiculed as the "Clapham sect" (after the location of the house where they held their meetings). They were joined by such slavery opponents as John Newton, Hannah More, Henry Thornton, Zachary Macaulay, E. J. Eliot, and James Stephen. Clarkson

organized a propaganda campaign throughout the country, while Wilberforce represented the group's interests in the House of Commons. Wilberforce created two formal organizations in 1787: the Committee for the Abolition of the Slave Trade and the Society for the Reformation of Manners.

The Claphams won a growing number of converts to their cause, but they were unable to make any legal headway against the West Indies slave traders and planters. Pitt personally supported the petitions presented to the House by Wilberforce; yet the slave trade was regarded as essential to economic health, and the West Indies interests were an important component of Pitt's Whig coalition. The 1790s witnessed some reform of the worst practices of the slavers and a resolution supporting the gradual abolition of the slave trade.

However, Wilberforce held firm in his views. His persistence was finally rewarded in 1807, when, following Pitt's death, a temporary Radical government coalition led by Charles James Fox united liberals and Evangelicals behind passage of an act prohibiting the slave trade. This act represented the culmination of Wilberforce's active participation in the movement.

In 1823 younger followers of Wilberforce founded the Antislavery Society, of which Wilberforce became a vice president. Once again a prolonged period of agitation produced results. Wilberforce, however, had been dead for a month when the Emancipation Act became law in August 1833.

Further Reading

The most authoritative volumes on Wilberforce are Reginald Coupland, *Wilberforce* (rev. ed. 1945), and Oliver Warner, *William Wilberforce and His Times* (1963). The struggle over slavery and the slave trade is examined within the framework of British imperial history in Charles E. Carrington, *The British Overseas: Exploits of a Nation of Shopkeepers,* vol. 1 (2d ed. 1968). J. H. Parry and P. M. Sherlock deal with the colonial aspect of the question in *A Short History of the West Indies* (2d ed. 1963).

Additional Sources

Catherwood, H. F. R. (Henry Frederick Ross), Sir, *The difference between a reformer and a progressive,* London: Shaftesbury Society, 1977.

Everett, Betty Steele, *Freedom fighter: the story of William Wilberforce, the British parliamentarian who fought to free slaves,* Fort Washington, Pa.: Christian Literature Crusade, 1994.

Furneaux, Robin, *William Wilberforce,* London, Hamilton, 1974.

Lean, Garth, *God's politician: William Wilberforce's struggle,* Colorado Springs: Helmers & Howard, 1987.

Ludwig, Charles, *He freed Britain's slaves,* Scottdale, Pa.: Herald Press, 1977.

Pollock, John Charles, *Wilberforce,* New York: St. Martin's Press, 1978, 1977. □

Richard Purdy Wilbur

Richard Wilbur (born 1921) was a distinguished translator and the most accomplished formalist poet of his generation. In 1987 he became poet laureate of the United States.

The son of portrait artist Lawrence Lazear, Richard Wilbur took the surname of his mother, Helen Ruth Wilbur. He was born in 1921 in Manhattan, New York, but two years later his family moved to North Caldwell, New Jersey, at the time a rural village, where he spent his boyhood. Following graduation from Amherst College in 1942, he served with the U.S. Army in Europe, where he witnessed the World War II horrors of Anzio, Cassino, and the Siegfried Line. He later said that these experiences led him to be a poet.

Prolific Poet

For awhile he toyed with the idea of becoming a political cartoonist, but he soon turned to writing poetry full-time. Wilbur's first book, *The Beautiful Changes and Other Poems,* was published in 1947, the same year he completed his masters degree at Harvard. From 1950 to 1954 he was an assistant professor of English at Harvard. He later taught at Wellesley University (1955-1957), Wesleyan University (1957-1977), and Smith College (1977-1986). In 1987-1988 he was the second poet laureate of the United States, succeeding Robert Penn Warren.

Wilbur was a prolific poet who continued to write in traditional forms no matter what the current trend in poetry. His books include *Ceremony and Other Poems* (1950), *Things of This World* (1956), *Poems, 1943-1956* (1957), *Advice to a Prophet, and Other Poems* (1961), *Walking to Sleep: New Poems and Translations* (1969), *The Mind-Reader: New Poems* (1976), *Seven Poems* (1981), *New and Collected Poems* (1988), and *Runaway Opposites* (1995).

Wilbur was also the premier English translator of Moliére, with acclaimed translations of *The Misanthrope* (1955), *Tartuffe* (1963), *The School for Wives* (1971), and *The Learned Ladies* (1978). *The Whale and Other Collected Translations* and his translation of Racine's *Andromache* appeared in 1982. He also wrote books for children, edited works by Shakespeare, Poe, and Witter Bynner, and collaborated with Lillian Hellman and Leonard Bernstein on the operetta *Candide.* A collection of prose works, *Responses,* was published in 1976, and another collection, *The Catbird's Song: Prose Pieces 1969-1995* in 1997. Wilbur won Pulitzer Prizes in 1957, for *Things of This World,* and in 1989 for his *New and Collected Poems.* He also won the National Book Award, Bollingen Prizes for poetry and translation, the Drama Desk Award, and innumerable other honors.

Formal Grace

None of Wilbur's contemporaries equalled his mastery of traditional poetic form, but he insisted that none of his works was a formal construction for its own sake. Each arose from an ideal union of form and substance, though followed by years of exacting work as the poem assumed its final shape. Those who considered Wilbur to be merely a self-conscious craftsman and poet of ideas missed the point; he was essentially a visionary poet for whom traditional structure provided ideal forms of poetic expression. In his work the form is a kind of pressure chamber, which by constraining emotion intensifies it, giving it a contained force that would dissipate in less rigorous poetic forms.

Wilbur belongs to the tradition of New England transcendentalists and their immediate successor, Robert Frost. Nature is a frequent subject in Wilbur's poetry, and from Frost and Henry David Thoreau he seems to have acquired an ability to see the natural world with precision. Frost's poetic voice can at times be heard clearly and intentionally in Wilbur's verse, notably in "Seed Time: Homage to R.F." But his poetry also has an elegance and grace largely foreign to Frost and Thoreau.

Wilbur's verse can assume a baroque elegance and complexity that one might expect to find in the work of a European poet. His poetry is often a delicate movement of image, wit, irony, and sound. He can make highly complex syntactical statements seem airy and inevitable.

One of the finest translators of the late 20th century, Wilbur created highly regarded versions of works from Old English, Russian, Latin, Italian, and Spanish, but he was best known for his translations from French. His translations of Villon are perhaps the best in English. As a translator of

Moliére he was unequalled, and he successfully adapted English verse to the high passion of Racine's *Andromache*.

From the beginning of his work (as the title of his first book, *The Beautiful Changes* suggests), Wilbur was concerned with a theme of change that obsessed the Romantic poets. During the course of his career he shifted from the personal lyric to the dramatic poem, but his obsessive concern with the inevitability of change remained.

Some critics accused Wilbur of ignoring political matters in his poetry, and he usually did, except for works such as "Speech for the Repeal of the McCarren Act" and "To the Student Strikers." His apolitical stance and his refusal to try experimental verse forms harmed Wilbur's reputation in the 1960s and early 1970s. But by the time he was named poet laureate of the United States, those criticisms were largely forgotten and the more traditional poetic forms were making a comeback. In a world forever changing, Wilbur did not try to use poetry to make political statements, but tried to find aesthetic perspectives in which chaos and confusion were momentarily outwitted and a higher, formal order took their place.

Reviewer William F. Bell, in *America* (October 15, 1994) called him "a poet of virtuosic skill, with remarkable sensitivity to melody and a true genius for metaphor." In the poem, "For Dudley," on the death of poet translator Dudley Fitts, Wilbur wrote, "All that we do/ Is touched with ocean, yet we remain/ On the shore of what we know."

Further Reading

Most of the studies of Wilbur's poetry and translations have been published in critical and scholarly journals. An impressive and well-balanced selection of these articles is available in *Richard Wilbur's Creation* (1983), edited by Wendy Salinger. Donald L. Hill's *Richard Wilbur* (1967) should also be consulted. A good, brief overview of Wilbur's work is William F. Bell, *America* (October 15, 1994). □

Oscar Fingall O'Flahertie Wills Wilde

The British author Oscar Fingall O'Flahertie Wills Wilde (1854-1900) was part of the "art for art's sake" movement in English literature at the end of the 19th century. He is best known for his brilliant, witty comedies.

Oscar Wilde was born in Dublin, Ireland, on Oct. 16, 1854. His father, Sir William Wilde, was a well-known surgeon; his mother, Jane Francisca Elgee Wilde, wrote popular poetry and prose under the pseudonym Speranza. For three years Wilde was educated in the classics at Trinity College, Dublin, where he began to attract public attention through the eccentricity of his writing and his style of life.

At the age of 23 Wilde entered Magdalen College, Oxford. In 1878 he was awarded the Newdigate Prize for his poem "Ravenna." He attracted a group of followers, and they initiated a personal cult, self-consciously effete and artificial. "The first duty in life," Wilde wrote in *Phrases and Philosophies for the Use of the Young* (1894), "is to be as artificial as possible." After leaving Oxford he expanded his cult. His iconoclasm contradicted the Victorian era's easy pieties, but the contradiction was one of his purposes. Another of his aims was the glorification of youth.

Wilde published his well-received *Poems* in 1881. The next six years were active ones. He spent an entire year lecturing in the United States and then returned to lecture in England. He applied unsuccessfully for a position as a school inspector. In 1884 he married, and his wife bore him children in 1885 and in 1886. He began to publish extensively in the following year. His writing activity became as intense and as erratic as his life had been for the previous six years. From 1887 to 1889 Wilde edited the magazine *Woman's World*. His first popular success as a prose writer was *The Happy Prince and Other Tales* (1888). *The House of Pomegranates* (1892) was another collection of his fairy tales.

Wilde became a practicing homosexual in 1886. He believed that his subversion of the Victorian moral code was the impulse for his writing. He considered himself a criminal who challenged society by creating scandal. Before his conviction for homosexuality in 1895, the scandal was essentially private. Wilde believed in the criminal mentality. "Lord Arthur Savile's Crime," from *Lord Arthur Savile's*

Crime and Other Stories (1891), treated murder and its successful concealment comically. The original version of *The Picture of Dorian Gray* in *Lippincott's Magazine* emphasized the murder of the painter Basil Hallward by Dorian as the turning point in Dorian's disintegration; the criminal tendency became the criminal act.

Dorian Gray was published in book form in 1891. The novel celebrated youth: Dorian, in a gesture typical of Wilde, is parentless. He does not age, and he is a criminal. Like all of Wilde's work, the novel was a popular success. His only book of formal criticism, *Intentions* (1891), restated many of the esthetic views that *Dorian Gray* had emphasized, and it points toward his later plays and stories. *Intentions* emphasized the importance of criticism in an age that Wilde believed was uncritical. For him, criticism was an independent branch of literature, and its function was vital.

His Dramas

Between 1892 and 1895 Wilde was an active dramatist, writing what he identified as "trivial comedies for serious people." His plays were popular because their dialogue was baffling, clever, and often epigrammatic, relying on puns and elaborate word games for its effect. *Lady Windermere's Fan* was produced in 1892, *A Woman of No Importance* in 1893, and *An Ideal Husband* and *The Importance of Being Earnest* in 1895.

On March 2, 1895, Wilde initiated a suit for criminal libel against the Marquess of Queensberry, who had objected to Wilde's friendship with his son, Lord Alfred Douglas. When his suit failed in April, countercharges followed. After a spectacular court action, Wilde was convicted of homosexual misconduct and sentenced to 2 years in prison at hard labor.

Prison transformed Wilde's experience as radically as had his 1886 introduction to homosexuality. In a sense he had prepared himself for prison and its transformation of his art. *De Profundis* is a moving letter to a friend and apologia that Wilde wrote in prison; it was first published as a whole in 1905. His theme was that he was not unlike other men and was a scapegoat. *The Ballad of Reading Gaol* (1898) was written after his release. In this poem a man has murdered his mistress and is about to be executed, but Wilde considered him only as criminal as the rest of humanity. He wrote: "For each man kills the thing he loves,/ Yet each man does not die."

After his release from prison Wilde lived in France. He attempted to write a play in his pretrial style, but this effort failed. He died in Paris on Nov. 30, 1900.

Further Reading

R. Hart-Davis's edition of Wilde's *Letters* (1962) contains an excellent portrait of Wilde. Frank Harris, *Oscar Wilde: His Life and Confessions* (2 vols., 1916), is one of the first and most comprehensive biographies. Frances Winwar, *Oscar Wilde and the Yellow 'Nineties* (1940), emphasizes Wilde's position in that decade. Other standard biographies are Boris L. Brasol, *Oscar Wilde: The Man, the Artist, the Martyr* (1938), and André Gide, *Oscar Wilde* (1951). The major critical studies of Wilde's work are George Woodcock, *The Paradox of Oscar Wilde* (1950), and St. John Ervine, *Oscar Wilde* (1951). Arthur Ransome, *Oscar Wilde: A Critical Study* (1912), has influenced Wilde criticism. William Butler Yeats discusses Wilde in his *Autobiography* (1938; many later eds.).
□

Amos Niven Wilder

The American New Testament scholar, poet, minister, and literary critic Amos Wilder (1895-1993) was a seminal interpreter of biblical language. His work showed the need to understand how much imaginative vision underlies the language of early Christianity, as well as the theology and literature of the 20th century.

Amos Niven Wilder was born on September 18, 1895, in Madison, Wisconsin. His father, a journalist with a doctorate from Yale, worked at the U.S. consulate in China. His mother was the daughter of a Presbyterian minister. Pulitzer-Prize-winning writer Thornton Wilder was his brother. After two years at Oberlin College (1913-1915), Wilder interrupted his education to volunteer in the American Ambulance Field Service in 1916. In World War I he served in the U.S. Field Artillery and was awarded the *Croix de Guerre*.

Resuming his education, he graduated from Yale in 1920. He also studied at the *Faculte de Theologie,* Montauban, France (1919), the University of Brussels (1920-1921), and Mansfield College, Oxford University, England (1921-1923). In college he was a champion tennis player, and he competed at the Wimbledon tournament in England in 1922. Wilder's first book, *Battle Retrospect* (1923), was a volume of verse about his war experiences. In later years he published several other collections of poetry.

His keen interest in the New Testament dated to 1922, when he served briefly as a secretary to Albert Schweitzer at Oxford. He completed his study for the ministry at Yale in 1924, was ordained a minister, and was pastor of the Congregational Church in North Conway, New Hampshire, from 1925 to 1928. He then entered graduate study in the field of the New Testament at Yale. During his graduate years he studied at Harvard Divinity School (1929-1930) and taught at Hamilton College (1930-1933).

After earning his doctorate in 1933, he began teaching at Andover Newton (1933-1943). In 1935 he married Catharine Kerlin and their union lasted 58 years until his death. He taught at Chicago Theological Seminary and the Federated Theological Faculty of the University of Chicago (1943-1954) and at Harvard Divinity School (1954-1963) as Hollis Professor of Divinity, teaching New Testament interpretation.

Although he officially retired in 1963 and became Professor Emeritus at Harvard, Wilder continued to write on the literary art of the New Testament. His analysis of the oral forms and novelty of speech of early Christianity stimulated

an entirely new vein of literary and interpretive studies by New Testament scholars.

Wilder occupies a unique position in American literary history, combining the vocations of poet and scholar, critic and pastor. He brought together the heritage of the Bible with the visions of the 20th century. His wartime experience recorded in his early poetry opened him up to the catastrophic depths of humanity, while his vision of hope, derived from his biblical story, allowed him to press beyond the negative limits of his time. His poetic eye enabled him to see connections between the Bible and literature, the Kingdom of God and modern ethics, religious experience and contemporary symbols.

The appreciation of the depths and multi-dimensionality of language led Wilder to reject any reductionist interpretation of biblical material. In order to understand the historical evidence of the First century imagination and heart, Wilder employed a wide-ranging mode of interpretation, using literary criticism, social psychology, the studies of archetypes and folklore, and anthropology.

Wilder's inclusive mode of interpretation differed from other New Testament scholars, particularly in the relation of scripture to social ethics. In contrast to the existentialist position of Rudolf Bultmann, Wilder maintained that an individualistic approach did not do justice to the full dimensions of the New Testament message. For Wilder the revelation of God comes through the New Testament's varied symbols and myths, which need to be interpreted in their socio-historical context. Once interpreted, these mythological expressions can speak to the social dimension of humanity and open up the possibility of seeing the corrupt structures of present society.

The challenge to link the issues of the contemporary world with the biblical story came not only from Wilder's experience with postwar poetry but also from his pastoral sensitivity. His critical works on modern literature as well as his ecumenical endeavors attempted to lead beyond parochial and dogmatic limits to an enjoyment of the deeper and wiser vision of faith.

Wilbur also wrote extensively on the relationship of religion to modern poetry and literature. He also wrote about the life and work of his brother, Thornton Wilder. Before his death at age 97, the tireless Amos Wilder had just completed a book that brought him full circle to his seminal wartime experiences, *Armageddon Revisited* (1993).

Further Reading

Kerygma, Eschatology, and Social Ethics (1966) and *Early Christian Rhetoric, The Language of the Gospel* (1971) provide readable access to the thought of Amos Wilder. His work *New Testament Faith for Today* (1956) is a well-written attempt to make sense of biblical interpretation for the general reader. *Eschatology and Ethics* (revised 1950) remains the essential work for a critical understanding of Wilder's biblical scholarship. Awarded the Decennial Bross Prize, *Modern Poetry and the Christian Tradition* (1952) explores the relationship of Christianity to culture. *The New Voice* (1969) continues Wilder's literary and theological criticism. His book *Theopoetic: Theology and the Religious Imagination* (1976) is a brief but seminal work of Wilder's interdisciplinary concerns. A fine collection of his essays can be found in James Breech, editor, *Jesus' Parables and the War of Myths* (1982). A collection of his selected poetry is *Grace Confounding* (1972). A critical appraisal and scholarly discussion of the work of Amos Wilder is John Dominic Crossan's *A Fragile Craft* (1981). A career summary and bibliography (up to 1978) of Amos Wilder was compiled by Arthur J. Dewey in *Semeia*, vol. 13 (1978). □

Lawrence Douglas Wilder

Lawrence Douglas Wilder (born 1931) was the first African American elected governor in the United States. He rose from waiting tables in the segregated country clubs of the Jim Crow South to become a powerful Virginia state legislator who broke the color line by winning statewide elections as lieutenant governor in 1985 and then as governor four years later.

Lawrence Douglas Wilder was born January 17, 1931, in Richmond, Virginia, the youngest of Robert and Beulah Wilder's ten children. Robert Wilder sold insurance for an African American-owned insurance company, making the Wilders middle-class for their day. Wilder remembered his childhood as "gentle poverty."

Starting at age 13, Wilder held a variety of jobs to earn money for college. For example, he worked as a shoeshine boy, elevator operator, and paper boy. In 1947 at age 16, Wilder entered Virginia Union University, where he studied chemistry. He also began waiting tables at the city's segregated hotels and country clubs where Virginia politicians often gathered. Unlike the other waiters, Wilder always stayed in the room to listen to the speeches.

After graduation in 1951 Wilder was drafted by the U.S. Army and sent to Korea, where he saw duty on the front lines. In Korea Wilder demonstrated his aptitude for politics, organizing a meeting of African American soldiers with their commanding officer to complain about a lack of promotions. The promotions were soon forthcoming; Wilder became a sergeant. He also won a Bronze Star for heroism when he and another man helped capture 19 Chinese prisoners on Pork Chop Hill.

After the war Wilder returned home to Richmond, working as a toxicologist in the state medical examiner's office. But Wilder soon concluded that his laboratory work was a dead-end job and he sought a new profession. In 1956, enthused by the opportunities opened by the Supreme Court's decision striking down segregation, he decided to go to law school. Because Virginia law schools still barred African Americans, he attended Howard University in Washington, D.C.

After graduation in 1959 Wilder began practicing law in Richmond. In 1969 one of Richmond's state senators ran for higher office. While that campaign was still in progress,

the upstart Wilder, with the foresight and chutzpah that later became his trademarks, announced that he would run in the special election to fill a vacancy. Wilder's abrupt announcement preempted senior African American leaders who might have otherwise made the run. With two white candidates splitting the white vote, Wilder had an easy victory, becoming the first African American to serve in the Virginia Senate since Reconstruction.

Wilder immediately shocked conservative whites with what they considered his militance on racial matters. Wilder made headlines by stalking out of a reception where the state song, "Carry Me Back to Old Virginia," was played. He claimed its lyrics were racist and tried unsuccessfully to have the song repealed.

Wilder was considered a liberal in a decidedly conservative legislature, but because the 1970 redistricting gave Wilder a predominantly African American district, he faced no opposition for re-election. Wilder gradually gained seniority, and with it, committee chairmanships. In time, a newspaper poll ranked Wilder as the Senate's fifth most influential member. Wilder was easily the most prominent African American leader in Virginia.

In 1981 some African Americans were skeptical of Charles Robb, the Democratic candidate for governor. But Wilder was instrumental in organizing a large turn-out of African American voters that helped make Robb the state's first Democratic governor in 16 years. In return, Robb consulted Wilder on almost a daily basis about appointments.

However, Wilder objected to Robb's choice of conservative Owen Pickett as the Democratic candidate for the U.S. Senate in 1982 and threatened to run as an independent. Thus, Pickett was forced to withdraw. Wilder's threat angered many Democrats, but it dramatized his growing political clout. In 1985 when Wilder sought the Democratic nomination for lieutenant governor, no one dared oppose him lest they alienate African American voters the party needed.

Nevertheless, most party officials were convinced Virginia wasn't ready for an African American candidate and feared that Wilder would drag the 1985 ticket down to defeat. Republicans were so confident of victory that they denied the nomination to their strongest candidate, who had angered conservatives, and instead nominated John Chichester, a littleknown state legislator more acceptable to the right wing.

Knowing he had to do something dramatic to win in a state that was only 19 percent African American, Wilder set out on a two-month tour of the state by stationwagon, vowing to stop in every town he passed through. This "backroads tour" captured the citizens' imaginations and Wilder became an unlikely folk hero among white, rural Virginians. The tour also enabled Wilder to save money for a television blitz featuring a rural policeman with a distinct Southern drawl declaring his support for the African American candidate. The ads were a sensation that the lackluster Chichester was unable to match. A vote for Wilder became synonymous with a vote to distance Virginia from its racist past. Wilder won with 52 percent of the vote, becoming the first African American to win a statewide election in Virginia.

As lieutenant governor, Wilder feuded openly with Governor Gerald Baliles and former Governor Charles Robb, both fellow Democrats. But Wilder's constituency base made him invulnerable to attack. In 1989 Wilder faced only token opposition for the Democratic nomination for governor. Despite their differences, Wilder sought to portray himself as the logical heir to Robb and Baliles. He also tried to paint Republican Marshall Coleman as a rightwing extremist and used Coleman's opposition to abortion even in cases of rape and incest to dominate the campaign. Coleman was on the defensive for much of the campaign and blamed the news media for cheering on Wilder to make history. Nevertheless, the election was the closest in Virginia history, a development most political analysts attributed to some whites' reluctance to support an African American in the privacy of the voting booth. But a recount, the state's first in a statewide contest, upheld Wilder's 7,000-vote margin.

On January 11, 1990, Wilder was sworn in as the first African American elected governor in the United States. As governor, he astonished friends and foes alike. He distressed allies by purging state boards of many Robb and Baliles appointees. Yet the Wilder administration saw no major increase in the number of Black appointees; most of his key advisers were whites who were personally loyal to him.

But Wilder surprised opponents by stressing fiscal conservatism. He insisted on a surplus in the state budget. He won a modest tax cut. He ordered state colleges to reduce proposed tuition increases. Then, as soon as the legislature adjourned, Wilder set out on a nationwide speaking tour to tell Democrats that the way to win the White House in 1992 was to follow his example. He suggested they practice "fiscal discipline" and free themselves from "special interests."

He also took swipes at the party's leading liberals, specifically Jesse Jackson and Mario Cuomo, by suggesting that he was part of a "New Mainstream" of fiscal conservatism and social liberalism while they were not. Many commentators predicted Wilder would be a likely candidate for vice-president in 1992; others saw Wilder positioning himself as a moderate alternative to Jackson. In the fall of 1991 Wilder began campaigning for the Democratic nomination for president.

Some African Americans were upset with Wilder for his attacks on Jackson. They also complained that Wilder refused to pay enough attention to African American concerns. For instance, Wilder came out against proposals to create an African American-majority congressional district in Virginia after the 1990 census. Wilder declared that his election proved African Americans did not need special treatment to win office. Stung by the criticism, however, Wilder looked for a dramatic way to respond. In May 1990 Wilder ordered state agencies and universities to divest themselves of investments with ties to South Africa, the first Southern state to take such an action. And despite Virginia's economic problems in the national recession, Wilder held to his pledge of not increasing taxes.

In January of 1992 Wilder wirthdrew his presidential candidacy. He pointed to the deteriorating fiscal state of Virginia, claiming that governing the commonwealth and conducting a presidential campaign at the same time allowed him to do neither job full justice.

After finishing his term as governor in 1994, Wilder began a two-hour weekday radio show, *The Douglas Wilder Show,* which lasted only months before it was canceled.

At a news conference Wilder announced he would hang up his hat. "I will not run for another elected office and I almost rule out serving in any governmental capacity," he said.

Further Reading

Three books have been written about Wilder: *When Hell Froze Over* (1988, updated 1990), by *Roanoke Times & World-News* reporter Dwayne Yancey, details Wilder's political career, with special emphasis on his breakthrough campaign for lieutenant governor. *Wilder: Hold Fast to Dreams* (1989), by *Washington Post* reporter Don Baker, is a biography that follows Wilder through his nomination for governor. *Claiming the Dream* (1990), by *Norfolk Virginian-Pilot* reporter Margaret Edds, is an account of Wilder's campaign for governor. □

Thornton Niven Wilder

Novelist and playwright Thornton Niven Wilder (1897-1975) won two Pulitzer Prizes for his plays *Our Town* and *The Skin of Our Teeth,* written in 1938 and 1942 respectively. His most renowned novel, *The Bridge of San Luis Rey,* also accorded him a Pulitzer Prize in 1927.

Born April 17, 1897, in Madison, Wisconsin, Thornton Niven Wilder lived in China as a teenager where his father was a United States Consul-General in Hong Kong. He attended the English China Inland Mission School at Cheefoo but returned to California in 1912. Graduating in 1915, he attended Oberlin College before transferring to Yale University in 1917. He served with the First Coast Artillery in Rhode Island in 1918 during World War I, returning to Yale after the war. In 1920 he received his bachelor's and saw the first publication of his play *The Trumpet Shall Sound* in *Yale Literary Magazine.*

Wilder began his novel *The Cabala* at the American Academy in Rome in 1921. In New Jersey he taught at the Lawrenceville School while earning a master's at Princeton University. He received his degree in 1926, the publication year of *The Cabala.* Its publication coincided with the first professional production of *The Trumpet Shall Sound* by the American Laboratory Theater. But his breakthrough work was *The Bridge of San Luis Rey* (1927) that thrust him to the forefront of American literature.

A cosmopolitan lifelong traveler, he later taught at the University of Chicago (1930-1936) and the University of Hawaii (1935). He volunteered in World War II and served in Africa, Italy, and the United States. A lecturer at Harvard in the early 1950s, he received the Gold Medal for Fiction from the Academy of Arts and Letters in 1952. In 1962 he retired to Arizona for almost two years, then renewed his travels. Wilder was awarded the Presidential Medal of Freedom in 1963 and the National Book Committee's National Medal for Literature (first time presented) in 1965.

Career as a Playwright

Wilder's first successful dramatic work, which he started at Oberlin, was *The Angel That Troubled the Waters* (1928). A four-act play, *The Trumpet Shall Sound* (1919-1920), was produced unsuccessfully off-Broadway in 1926. *The Long Christmas Dinner and Other Plays in One-Act,* published in 1931, contained three plays that gained popularity with amateur groups: *The Long Christmas Dinner, Pullman Car Hiawatha,* and *The Happy Journey to Trenton and Camden.* This last series marked Wilder's trademark use of a bare stage for the actors.

Wilder's first Broadway shows were translations: André Obey's *Lucrece* (1932) and Henrik Ibsen's *A Doll's House* (1937). His dramatic reputation soared with *Our Town* (1938). Written for a bare stage, guided throughout by a narrator, his script examines a small town for the "something way down deep that's eternal about every human being."

His subsequent dramatic work, *The Merchant of Yonkers,* failed initially in 1938. When produced with slight revisions as *The Matchmaker* in 1954, it proved a fascinating farce. (It later re-emerged as the musical play *Hello, Dolly!* in 1963, then an overwhelming success.) Wilder intermingled style and forms even more daringly in *The Skin of Our Teeth.* Here, Wilder described the human race as flawed but worth preserving. A complex and difficult play with an indebtedness to James Joyce's *Finnegans Wake,* it became the work cited for his final Pulitzer Prize in 1943.

The essentially conservative thematic material staged in radical styles made Wilder's plays unique. His later work included an unsuccessful tragedy, *A Life in the Sun* (or *The Alcestiad,* 1955) and three short plays of an intended 14-play cycle: *Someone from Assisi, Infancy,* and *Childhood* (produced as *Plays for Bleecker Street* in 1962).

Career as a Novelist

Wilder established his reputation as a novelist with *The Cabala,* a minor work that showed Wilder's moral concerns. *The Bridge of San Luis Rey,* set in 18th-century Peru, proved immensely popular and led to the Pulitzer Prize in 1928. *The Woman of Andros* (1930), based on Terence's play *Andria* and set in a pagan and Christian epoch, was not well received. Although Wilder's view of life elicited a strong communist attack, *Heaven's My Destination* (1934), set in the American Midwest, grew in favor over the years. In *The Ides of March* (1948) Wilder tried a novel approach to Julius Caesar. *The Eighth Day* in 1967 returned Wilder to a 20th-century American setting that examined the lives of two families. Wilder's last novel, *Theophilus North,* was published in 1973.

In line with his diverse interests and scholarly bent, Wilder lectured and published extensively. His Harvard lectures "Toward an American Language," "The American Loneliness," and "Emily Dickinson" appeared in the *Atlantic Monthly* (1952). His topics addressed play writing, fiction, and the role of the artist in society. His range spanned from the works of the ancient Greeks to modern dramatists, particularly Joyce and Gertrude Stein. His observations and letters were published in a variety of works, from André Maurois's *A Private Universe* (1932) to Donald Gallup's *The Flowers of Friendship* (1953).

Wilder died of a heart attack December 7, 1975, in Hamden, Connecticut.

Further Reading

Biographical details appear most cohesively in Malcolm Goldstein's perceptive study, *The Art of Thornton Wilder* (1965). Other critical works include Rex Burbank, *Thornton Wilder* (1961); Bernard Grebanier, *Thornton Wilder* (1964); Donald Haberman, *The Plays of Thornton Wilder: A Critical Study* (1967), useful as an interesting source book; and Helmut Papajewski, *Thornton Wilder,* translated by John Conway (1968). For more information, please see David Castronovo, *Thornton Wilder* (1986); Richard Henry Goldstone, *Thornton Wilder, an annotated bibliography* (1982); Idy Martouskie, *Thornton Wilder, 1897-1975* (videotape, 1993); Theophius North, *Thornton Wilder, 1897-1975* (1975). Other works include *The Journals of Thornton Wilder: With Two Scenes of an Uncompleted Play, "The Emporium"* (1985), and *Mirrors of Friendship: The Letters of Gertrude Stein and Thornton Wilder* (1996). □

Harvey Washington Wiley

The American chemist Harvey Washington Wiley (1844-1930) established the methods and philosophy of food analysis. His writings and influence made him the "father of the Food and Drug Administration."

Harvey Wiley was born in Kent, Ind., on Oct. 18, 1844, the son of a farmer. His oldest sister Elizabeth Jane Wiley Corbett, became an early woman physician. A sturdy boy with a fine and receptive mind, Wiley advanced from a log-cabin schoolhouse to Hanover College in Indiana, where he majored in the humanities. He interrupted his studies to serve in the Union Army and then returned, graduating from Hanover in 1867.

Wiley became an instructor in Latin and Greek (1868-1871) at Butler University while continuing his studies at Indiana Medical College, from which he received his medical degree in 1871; subsequent studies took him to Harvard and the University of Berlin. Meanwhile he became a professor of chemistry at Butler, then at Purdue University. Having served as Indiana's state chemist, he became chief chemist of the U.S. Department of Agriculture in 1883.

Wiley did a series of studies of food products and published several papers which established him among agricultural chemists. His achievements while at the Department of

Agriculture were of both a technical and, uniquely, social character: he devised instruments and methods for processing glucose, grape sugar, and sorghum sugar and practically established the beet-sugar industry in the United States. Wiley also supervised the preparation of his landmark *Bulletin No. 13: Foods and Food Adulterants* (1887-1889), which covered all classes of food products and described methods of analysis. However, Wiley's dynamic personal qualities, expressed on the public platform and, informally, in such a private publication as *Songs of Agricultural Chemists* (1892) carried the subject beyond the arguments of technicians.

In 1902 Wiley established his famous "poison squad," a group of volunteers who became "human guinea pigs" to help determine the effect on digestion and health of preservatives, coloring matter, and other substances. His work was the base from which a variety of exposés and sensations, including patent medicines and processed beef, roused the nation, resulting in the passage of the Pure Food and Drug Act of 1906.

Subsequently Wiley found himself under fire by interests dissatisfied with his rigid application of standards. Controversy over administration of the act and its specific effect on industries continued through the presidencies of Theodore Roosevelt and William Howard Taft. Wiley, persuaded that the act had been betrayed, resigned his government post in 1912.

Wiley then became director of the bureau of foods for *Good Housekeeping,* published books on health and adul-

teration, and lectured widely and effectively. A man of excellent presence, magnetic and witty, he stirred general and professional audiences and was accorded national and international honors. In 1929 his retrospective *History of a Crime against the Food Law* provided inspiration for later crusaders. Active to the end, he died in Washington, D.C., on June 30, 1930.

Further Reading

Wiley's *An Autobiography* (1930) is also valuable as history. Oscar E. Anderson, Jr., *The Health of a Nation* (1958), provides details on Wiley's major battle. Wiley is examined in the context of the Progressive era in Louis Filler, *The Muckrakers: Crusaders for American Liberalism* (1968 ed.). □

Wilhelmina

Wilhelmina (1880-1962) was queen of the Netherlands from 1890 to 1948. During her reign the royal house maintained a strong commitment to parliamentary institutions and the principle of parliamentary government.

Born on Aug. 31, 1880, Whilhelmina was the daughter of the king of the Netherlands, William II, and his second wife, Princess Emma of Waldeck-Pyrmont. On Nov. 23, 1890, William II died, and Wilhelmina succeeded to the throne. A regency reigned in her name until Aug. 31, 1898, when she was declared of age; she was crowned queen of the Netherlands on Sept. 6, 1898. On Feb. 7, 1901, Wilhelmina married Prince Henry of Mecklenburg-Schwerin (1876-1934). Although Wilhelmina's personal political inclinations were conservative, the Crown remained above politics and did not attempt to alter the rules of the political game in the Netherlands.

During the years before World War I, the Netherlands was confronted with a certain measure of labor unrest and demands for social reform plus a revision of the suffrage law which would extend the right to vote to all adult males. The Netherlands remained neutral throughout World War I; however, severe food shortages and concomitant social dislocation triggered demonstrations in Amsterdam, Rotterdam, and other cities. The parliamentary leader of the Social Democratic Workers party (SDAP), Pieter Troelstra, seemed to be calling for social revolution in November 1918. Troelstra was quickly disavowed by other SDAP leaders, and the prospect of revolution proved to be momentary. Within this context, however, the socially conservative governing parties responded by legislating universal manhood suffrage and a modest measure of social reform.

With the coming of the depression crisis and the resultant rise of National Socialism in Germany, the Dutch nation faced yet a new set of problems. Facing mass unemployment internally and a Dutch Nazi movement, the NSB, Wilhelmina maintained a stance of pro-British neutrality and at no time attempted to weaken the parliamen-

Charles Wilkes was born on April 3, 1798, in New York City. He was educated mainly at home by tutors. He began a naval career at the age of 17 aboard the merchant ship *Hibernia.* In 1818 he received his midshipman's warrant and entered the British navy. He spent three years in the Mediterranean on board the *Guerriere* and later cruised the Pacific.

Wilkes's nautical investigations won scientific recognition and led to his appointment as head of the Depot of Charts and Instruments (later the Naval Observatory and Hydrographic Office). In 1836 he headed a commission to Europe to purchase scientific instruments for naval explorations. In 1838 his dream of a great seagoing exploration was fulfilled when President Martin Van Buren authorized the U.S. Exploring Expedition. In spite of Wilkes's junior rank, he was chosen to lead the five vessels and numerous explorers and scientists. They charted 1,600 miles of the Antarctic coast and hundreds of Pacific islands and collected fossils, observed habits of seals, whales, and strange birds, investigated geological formations, and studied esoteric languages. On his return in 1842, however, Wilkes was courtmartialed for "illegal punishment" of men under his command; he received only a public reprimand, and his promotion to commander followed in less than a year.

tary institution. With the coming of World War II, the Netherlands continued the policy of neutrality until the German attack of May 10, 1940. Wilhelmina, her daughter Juliana (born April 30, 1909), and her son-in-law Prince Bernhard of Lippe-Biesterfeld (married Juliana on Jan. 7, 1937) were able to flee to London and there served as a symbol of Dutch freedom and a rallying point for the Dutch government-in-exile. The Crown returned to the liberated Netherlands with enhanced prestige, and Wilhelmina's conduct during the war all but eliminated antimonarchical forces in Dutch society. On Sept. 4, 1948, Wilhelmina abdicated and was succeeded by her daughter Juliana. Wilhelmina died on Nov. 28, 1962.

Further Reading

Wilhelmina's autobiography is *Lonely but Not Alone* (trans. 1960). A biographical account is Philip Paneth, *Queen Wilhelmina, Mother of the Netherlands* (1943), which also includes considerable Dutch history. For historical background see A. J. Barnouw, *Holland under Queen Wilhelmina* (1923). Alden Hatch, *Bernhard: Prince of the Netherlands* (1962), contains extensive material on Wilhelmina. □

Charles Wilkes

Charles Wilkes (1798-1877), American naval officer, is remembered for his exploration of the Antarctic

Wilkes's wife died in 1848, and in 1854 he married again. Soon after, he was promoted to captain, and for some years the family lived in Washington, D.C.

In 1861 Wilkes received orders to command the Union ironclad warship *Merrimac,* but when he arrived he found that it had been destroyed by the Confederates. His next assignment was the command of the *San Jacinto* off the coast of Africa. On the voyage homeward Wilkes intercepted the British mail steamer *Trent,* bound for England with Confederate commissioners James M. Mason and John Slidell on board. With characteristic audacity, he seized the commissioners. This victory, however, gave way to political embarrassment when Britain demanded an apology and the immediate release of the two men. Still, Wilkes's popularity remained undimmed, and in 1862 he was promoted to commodore and then to acting rear admiral. His orders were to capture the Confederate destroyers plaguing Union supply ships. Secretary of the Navy Gideon Welles recalled him in 1863, complaining that instead of capturing destroyers he had used his office to collect prize monies. His commission was withdrawn, and he retired as captain (although his rank of commodore had been restored several months before his recall).

Wilkes's angry letter to Welles, which appeared in the newspapers, led to another court-martial. His sentence of a 3-year suspension from the Navy was reduced by Abraham Lincoln to a year. In 1866 he was given the rank of rear admiral, retired. Wilkes remained active, editing the unfinished volumes of the U.S. Exploring Expedition, confident that his career and reputation would be vindicated by history. On Feb. 8, 1877, he died in Washington.

Further Reading

Wilke's account of the Antarctic voyage, *Narrative of the United States Exploring Expedition* (5 vols., 1845; repr. 1970), is a valuable scientific work. A recent biography is Robert Silverberg, *Stormy Voyager: The Story of Charles Wilkes* (1968). Daniel Henderson, *The Hidden Coasts* (1953), is a good popular biography. The best account of the *Trent* affair is Charles Francis Adams, *The Trent Affair: An Historical Retrospect* (1912).

Additional Sources

Wilkes, Charles, *Autobiography of Rear Admiral Charles Wilkes, U.S. Navy, 1798-1877,* Washington: Naval History Division, Dept. of the Navy: for sale by the Supt. of Docs., U.S. Govt. Print. Off., 1978. □

John Wilkes

As a focus and spokesman of radical discontent, the English politician John Wilkes (1727-1797) made an important contribution to the movement for parliamentary reform.

John Wilkes was born on Oct. 17, 1727, at Clerkenwell. He entered Lincoln's Inn in 1742 and studied for two years (1744-1746) at the University of Leiden. In 1747 he married the daughter of a Buckinghamshire squire, a connection which enabled him to become sheriff of the country in 1754-1755 and to enter Parliament as member for Aylesbury in 1757.

On meeting Wilkes in 1762, Edward Gibbon wrote: "I scarcely ever met with a better companion; he has inexhaustible spirits, infinite wit and humour, and a great deal of knowledge; but a thorough profligate in principle as in practice.... He told us himself that in this time of public dissension he was resolved to make his fortune. Upon this noble principle he has connected himself closely with Lord Temple and Mr. Pitt [and] commenced public adversity to Lord Bute, whom he abuses weekly in the *North Briton.*"

Wilkes gained little from pursuit of his "principle." The resignation of his friends William Pitt the Elder and Lord Temple spoiled his chance of obtaining office; and a libel published in the *North Briton* resulted in his arrest on an illegal general warrant and imprisonment in the Tower. Released on a warrant of habeas corpus, he withdrew to France and in January 1764 was expelled from the Commons. His expulsion and the matter of general warrants were taken up by the opposition as political issues; but Wilkes himself they disowned.

In 1768, impoverished and frustrated, Wilkes decided to return to England. Defeated as parliamentary candidate for London, he was head of the poll for Middlesex. His

imprisonment, expulsion from the Commons, and finally the seating of his defeated rival constituted a small price to pay for the popularity which Wilkes now assumed. His debts were settled by public subscription, and a party under his leadership was formed in the City of London. He became the martyr of the London radicals and the idol of the London mob. Yet he showed no sympathy with their economic grievances and took resolute action against them during the Gordon riots. But he did adopt the radical demands of the urban middle class: shorter Parliaments, exclusion of placemen and pensioners from the Commons, parliamentary reform, and proAmericanism. However, Edmund Burke, James Boswell, and Gibbon all noted the lack of seriousness in Wilkes's political conduct.

In 1774 Wilkes finally secured admittance to the House as member for Middlesex and 5 years later was elected to the lucrative office of chamberlain of the City of London. He never formally discarded his radicalism, but his behavior during the last seven years of his parliamentary career reflected his new respectability. By the time of the 1790 election his popularity in Middlesex had sunk so low that he was forced to decline the poll. He thereupon retired from national politics. Wilkes died at Rouen, France, on Dec. 26, 1797.

Further Reading

Modern biographies of Wilkes include R. W. Postgate, *That Devil Wilkes* (1929; rev. ed. 1956); O. A. Sherrard, *A Life of John Wilkes* (1930); and Charles Chenevix-Trench, *Portrait of a Patriot: A Biography of John Wilkes* (1962). Two important works set Wilkes in historical context: Ian R. Christie, *Wilkes, Wyvill and Reform: The Parliamentary Reform Movement in British Politics, 1760-1785* (1962), and George Rudé, *Wilkes and Liberty: A Social Study of 1763 to 1774* (1962).

Additional Sources

Kronenberger, Louis, *The extraordinary Mr. Wilkes: his life and time,* Garden City, N.Y., Doubleday, 1974.

Thomas, Peter David Garner, *John Wilkes, a friend of liberty,* New York: Clarendon Press, 1996.

Williamson, Audrey, *Wilkes, a friend to liberty,* New York: Reader's Digest Press: distributed by Dutton, 1974. □

Sir George Hubert Wilkins

Sir George Hubert Wilkins (1888-1958) was an Australian explorer, scientist, and adventurer who imaginatively used scientific techniques in widely diverse conditions in the Australian bush, the Arctic, and the Antarctic.

Hubert Wilkins was born at Mount Bryan near Adelaide, South Australia, on Oct. 31, 1888, the son of a pioneer farming family. Three years' drought brought disease and starvation to his father's sheep and cattle and an abrupt end to George's education at the local school. He gave ample and early evidence of his most remarkable personal energy, however, and displayed an extraordinary talent for improvisation. His interests, which were to expand still further as his curiosity about nature and humanity grew, spread to include music, botany, zoology, meteorology, geology, and particularly photography. He quickly became an inveterate and bold traveler.

In 1909 Wilkins arrived in England after an adventurous journey through the Mediterranean and Middle East as a stowaway. He lost no time in learning to navigate and fly both airplanes and dirigibles; and he established himself as a professional photographer, correspondent, and film editor. In 1912 he reported on the brutal Balkan War and the next year accompanied Vilhjalmur Stefansson's expedition to the Arctic. During the next 3 years he laid the firm foundations of a distinguished record in the field of polar science and exploration.

Wilkins served during World War I as an outstanding and intrepid pilot and aerial photographer. In 1919 he attempted to win the *Daily Mail* £10,000 prize for a record-making flight across the globe from Britain to Australia, but he crashed his plane in Crete.

Fascinated by polar exploration, and already an old hand, Wilkins seized the offer of a place in E. H. Shackleton's last expedition to the Antarctic, in 1921. The next year he spent in Europe and the Soviet Union as a photographer and relief worker for the Society of Friends. In 1923 he was appointed by the British Museum to lead a valuable and eventful two-year scientific expedition to

northern Australia, the results of which he summarized in his book *Undiscovered Australia.*

By 1925 Wilkins had returned to his earlier project of flying in the Arctic, and his plans received the support and approval of the American Geographical Society. His pioneering Arctic flights from 1926 to 1928 earned him many honors, among them a knighthood from king George V. Many Antarctic flights followed throughout the next decade, and Wilkins consolidated his reputation as a major figure in polar exploration and the application of technology to harsh polar conditions. He spent 5 "summers" and portions of 26 "winters" in the Arctic regions and 8 "summers" in the Antarctic.

Wilkins supported submarine investigation under the ice caps in his work *Under the North Pole,* and in 1931 he carried out important experiments in the *Nautilus,* preceding the atomic-powered *Nautilus* by 27 years.

During World War II and afterward, Wilkins was respectfully consulted by the American, British, Australian, and Canadian governments as a scientific specialist, and he lived chiefly in the United States. His travels in the Antarctic continued until 1958, and he died in Framingham, Mass., on November 3 of that year.

Further Reading

Works on Wilkins include John Grierson, *Sir Hubert Wilkins* (1960), and Lowell Thomas, *Sir Hubert Wilkins* (1961). □

Roy Wilkins

Roy Wilkins (1901-1981) was one of the most important leaders in the civil rights struggle of African Americans.

B orn Aug. 30, 1901, in St. Louis, Missouri, of struggling African American parents, Roy Wilkins received his bachelor of arts degree from the University of Minnesota in 1923. During his college career he served as secretary to the local National Association for the Advancement of Colored People (NAACP), beginning a relationship which became his career. As managing editor of the *Call,* a militant African American weekly newspaper in Kansas City, he attracted the attention of the NAACP national leadership through vigorously opposing the reelection of a segregationist senator.

In 1931 Wilkins became assistant executive secretary at NAACP National Headquarters. His first assignment, to investigate charges of discrimination on a federally financed flood control project in Mississippi in 1932, led to congressional action for improvement. The first of his few arrests on behalf of equal rights occurred in 1934 when he picketed the U.S. attorney general's office for omitting the subject of lynching from a national conference on crime.

From 1934 to 1949 Wilkins served as editor of the *Crisis,* the official organ of the NAACP. He was chairman of the National Emergency Civil Rights Mobilization in 1949.

This organization, composed of more than 100 national and local groups, was responsible for sending over 4,000 delegates to Washington in January 1950 to lobby for fair employment and other civil rights.

Wilkins became the NAACP's administrator of internal affairs in 1950, and in 1955 the Board of Directors unanimously elected him executive secretary. This was a postion he held until 1977. When Wilkins began, he played a key role in helping plan and implement ways to eliminate segregation on all fronts and advance African Americans to first-class citizenship. He conferred with presidents, congressmen, and Cabinet officials. Furthermore, Wilkins testified before congressional committees, appeared on television and radio, addressed innumerable groups, and wrote extensively for both the African American press and general publications.

An articulate speaker and accomplished writer and organizer, Wilkins condemned the idea that African Americans must earn their rights through good behavior. He emphatically stated that no American is required to earn rights because human rights come from God, and his citizenship rights come from the Constitution. In support of President John Kennedy's civil rights bill, he testified in 1963 that African Americans "are in a mood to wait no longer, at least not to wait patiently, and silently and inactively." He was chairman of the Leadership Conference on Civil Rights, which led the civil rights march on Washington in 1963.

Wilkins won the NAACP's Spingarn Medal for distinguished service in civil rights in 1964 and received the

Medal of Freedom from President Richard Nixon in 1969. He received honorary degrees and awards from 21 universities and colleges. President Lyndon Johnson named him a member of the National Advisory Commission on Civil Disorders in 1967.

In 1968 Wilkins announced a new plan to harness the energies and talents of young African American activists while maintaining a firm line against those who counseled violence and separation. Wilkins stood firmly against these militant movements, and he encouraged the NAACP not to back them either. By 1969 he was being vilified as an "Uncle Tom" by some African Americans and even found himself on the assassination list of one revolutionary group. "No matter how endlessly they try to explain it," Wilkins told Reader 's Digest, "the term 'black power' means anti-white power. [It is] a reverse Mississippi, a reverse Hitler, a reverse Ku Klux Klan."

At the sixty-first annual NAACP meeting in 1970, he warned that "there can be no compromise with the evil of segregation", meanwhile calling upon African Americans to reject separatism and join to build a single society with common opportunity.

He chose to keep his position as executive director year after year, even when high-ranking members of the organization asked him to step down. Wilkins never groomed a successor for his job and refused until 1976 even to court the idea of retirement. When he finally did leave his post in 1977, he was more or less forced to do so by the board of directors, who accused him off-the-record of mismanaging funds. Others supported Wilkins until the end, convinced that without his charismatic leadership, the NAACP would splinter into competing groups with separate directors.

Wilkins' health had been good for many years following surgery for cancer in 1946, but he began to decline in 1980. He died September 9, 1981, of kidney failure aggravated by heart trouble. Wilkins was eulogized by his successor as executive director of the NAACP, Dr. Benjamin Hooks. Hooks told the *New York Times*, "Mr. Wilkins was a towering figure in American history and during the time he headed the NAACP. It was during this crucial period that the association was faced with some of its most serious challenges and the whole landscape of the black condition in America was changed, radically, for the better." Jesse Jackson also praised Wilkins in the *New York Times* as "a man of integrity, intelligence and courage who, with his broad shoulders, bore more than his share of responsibility for our and the nation's advancement."

Wilkins' lifelong devotion to civil rights was fueled by a passion for justice. As he stated in his autobiography, he sought to fight against "a deep, unreasoning, savagely cruel refusal by too many white people to accept a simple, inescapable truth—the only master race is the human race, and we are all, by the grace of God, members of it." Years after his death, Wilkins remained one of the most respected voices in the battle for racial equality in the United States. He received numerous awards, including the NAACP's Spingarn Medal, the Presidential Medal of Freedom, bestowed upon him by Lyndon Johnson in 1969, and the Congressional Gold Medal, bestowed posthumously in 1984.

Further Reading

Elton C. Fox, *Contemporary Black Leaders* (1970), and George R. Metcalf, *Black Profiles* (1970), contain chapters on Wilkins. Biographical sketches of Wilkins appear in Richard Bardolph, *The Negro Vanguard* (1959), and in *Historical Negro Biographies* of the *International Library of Negro Life and History*, edited by Whilhelmena S. Robinson (1968). Considerable biographical background is in Marcus H. Boulware, *The Oratory of Negro Leaders, 1900-1968* (1969). Langston Hughes, *Fight for Freedom: The Story of the NAACP* (1962), includes references to Wilkins. □

Ellen Wilkinson

Ellen Wilkinson (1891-1947), British Labour politician and crusader for the unemployed during the Depression, was part of the World War II coalition government and Labour minister of education from 1945 to 1947. She was a lifelong socialist, feminist, and politician.

Born in 1891 in working-class Manchester, England, Ellen Wilkinson's devout Methodist father was a cotton operative, but became an insurance clerk while Ellen was growing up. As a teenager she supported women's suffrage, participated in socialist activities, and joined the Independent Labour Party (ILP). A successful scholarship student, Wilkinson first planned to be an elementary school teacher, but in 1909 she won a national scholarship to attend university.

A history student at Manchester University, Wilkinson joined the University Debating Society and the Fabian Society. After graduating in 1913 Wilkinson was an organizer for the nonmilitant National Union of Women's Suffrage Societies. In 1915 she became the national woman organizer to the Amalgamated Union of Cooperative Employees, a union with a large female membership, particularly in wartime. A 1921 merger made the union part of the National Union of Distributive and Allied Workers (NUDAW).

During the 1910s and early 1920s Wilkinson was exposed to various radical groups such as the Guild Socialists, the Women's International League for Peace and Freedom, and the emergent Communist Party, which she belonged to between 1920 and 1924. She also kept up her membership in the Fabian Society, the ILP, and the Labour Party.

Elected to the Manchester City Council in 1923, she moved on quickly: in 1924 she entered Parliament, representing Middlesbrough East, Yorkshire. Only 33 years old, Wilkinson was one of four female members of Parliament (MP). In Parliament Wilkinson fought to extend the 1918 act giving women over 30 the vote to include women above the age of 21 (finally passed in 1928) and for other measures to grant women equality and protection; she supported MPs who were critical of the short-lived Labour government of 1924; and in 1926 she supported the general strike and subsequent miners' strike.

She was a critic of Ramsay Macdonald's second Labour administration, elected in 1929. With other radical Labourites and even many moderates, Wilkinson urged the government to take more resolute action against unemployment, which was reaching peak levels with the Depression. Her parliamentary experience was enhanced by working as secretary to Susan Lawrence, the parliamentary secretary to the minister of health.

Macdonald dissolved the Labour government in 1931, and with that year's Labour defeat, Wilkinson lost her seat. Between 1931 and 1935 she worked for NUDAW, lectured, and wrote. Already a published author—she had written a thinly veiled autobiographical novel, *Clash* (1929), and a thriller, *The Division Bell Mystery* (1932)—Wilkinson also contributed to newspapers and magazines. In 1934 she coauthored, with Edward Conze, a work entitled *Why Fascism* tracing the rise of fascism in Europe.

Returning to Parliament in 1935 as representative for Jarrow, a Tyneside shipbuilding town devastated by the Depression, Wilkinson achieved national fame for leading the 1936 Jarrow Crusade, one of the most publicized Depression hunger marches. Becoming more influential in the left wing of the Labour Party, she also began a slow drift to the right. For instance, she agreed to separate the Jarrow march from other marches organized with the help of Communists. Yet the Jarrow march made a strong statement, which was reinforced by Wilkinson's *The Town That Was Murdered,* a history of Jarrow's economic exploitation published by the Left Book Club in 1939.

In the mid-and late 1930s Wilkinson joined other left wing Labourites in groups such as the Socialist League and the journal *Tribune* to support the Republicans in the Spanish Civil War and to fight against fascism. In Parliament she initiated important consumer legislation for a more equitable system of installment purchasing.

By the late 1930s Wilkinson was on the National Executive Committee (NEC) of the Labour Party. Her personal relationship with Herbert Morrison, a more conservative and influential Labourite, involved Wilkinson in internal party struggles. She played a balancing act between trying to push the party leftward and staying in its good graces. For instance, in 1939, when Stafford Cripps was expelled from the Labour Party by the NEC for urging unity between Labour, socialists, and Communists in order to fight fascism, Wilkinson voted against the expulsion, but did not oppose it once it was passed; thereafter she did not appear on platforms urging such a unity.

In Winston Churchill's wartime coalition government Wilkinson was briefly parliamentary secretary to the ministry of pensions and then a parliamentary secretary for Herbert Morrison, the wartime home secretary and minister of home security; Wilkinson was in charge of air raid shelters. Energetic at this job, she constantly visited sites, urged the conscription of women for home defense, and generally strengthened Britain's civil defense.

By 1945 Wilkinson was a key Labour leader. As chair of that year's annual party conference she called for the development of socialist policies. After Labour's landslide victory Wilkinson became minister of education, only the second woman to achieve Cabinet rank in Britain. (The first was Margaret Bondfield, 1929.)

The Labour government had to implement the 1944 Education Act, which called for raising the school leaving age to 15 and providing access to secondary education for all. Labour's left urged the development of "comprehensive" schools which would enroll all classes of students, as an alternative to middle-class academic "grammar" schools and technical and "secondary modern" schools meant for working-class youth.

Wilkinson's record as minister of education is disputed. Plagued by ill-health for years, she served less than two years before she died. Committed to raising the school leaving age (accomplished in 1947) and to recruiting more teachers, she did not get far in developing comprehensive schools. Whether this was due to her lack of experience in education, her inability to motivate career civil servants, or a belief that reforming the existing system—which, after all, had served her well enough—would be sufficient is hard to say. What is clear is that just as the Labour government was building the welfare state, a crucial issue in education was not attended to.

During this post-war period Wilkinson was also active in the founding of the United Nations Educational, Scientific and Cultural Organization (UNESCO).

Wilkinson's legacy lies in the pattern of her political development. She was a feminist; a pioneer politician who never forgot her working-class origins; a fighter against poverty, unemployment, and fascism; a person who never abandoned her socialism yet found that, once in power, she had to compromise some of her more radical beliefs.

Further Reading

A useful biography of Wilkinson is Betty D. Vernon's *Ellen Wilkinson 1891-1947* (1982). For women in Parliament see Elizabeth Vallance, *Women in the House: A Study of Women Members of Parliament* (1979). An important general work on the period is Ralph Miliband, *Parliamentary Socialism* (1972).

Additional Sources

Vernon, Betty, *Ellen Wilkinson, 1891-1947,* London: Croom Helm, 1982. □

James Wilkinson

James Wilkinson (1757-1825), an American army general and frontier adventurer, was deeply involved in western land intrigues with Spain and in Aaron Burr's scheme to disrupt the Union.

James Wilkinson was born in Calvert County, Md. His father, a successful planter, died when James was seven. After schooling with a private tutor, he studied medicine in Maryland and then in Philadelphia. In 1775 he returned to his home state and opened practice. Medicine, however, was too tame for the restless and ambitious Wilkinson. The American Revolution provided the opportunity to enter into the military and begin his permanent career.

Career in the Revolution

After some involvement with the Maryland militia, Wilkinson was commissioned captain in the Continental Army. He demonstrated a remarkable capacity for ingratiating himself with men of influence, and his rise through the ranks was meteoric. By December 1776 he was a lieutenant colonel and aide-de-camp to Gen. Horatio Gates, the commander of Continental forces in the Northern Department and a man who was to prove Wilkinson's frequent benefactor. Largely through the good offices of Gates, Wilkinson was named deputy adjutant general for the Northern Department. In November 1777, just 20 years old, he was appointed brigadier general. When Gates became head of the Continental Congress's Board of War, Wilkinson followed him as secretary. During the next several months, however, a rift developed as a result of rumors Wilkinson apparently spread concerning Gates. The immediate consequence was that Wilkinson resigned from the Board of War.

In July 1779 Wilkinson obtained the potentially lucrative post of clothier general for the Continental forces, but within a year he resigned under fire for suspected irregularities in accounts. In November 1778 he married and settled on a farm in Bucks County, Pa. During the next several years, he was returned for two terms to the Pennsylvania Assembly, the only political office he seems ever to have held.

Spanish Intrigue

By early 1784 Wilkinson had sold his Pennsylvania properties and moved to Kentucky, where he became involved in continuous and deepening controversy as he engaged in a series of intrigues with the Spanish authorities in New Orleans. His maneuvers were probably motivated mostly by his never-ending quest for financial gain and his compulsion to fashion roles of importance for himself.

Persuading Spanish authorities that certain American groups were conspiring to occupy Spanish territory in Louisiana and the Floridas, Wilkinson explained that opening the Mississippi River to western trade would encourage separatist tendencies among western settlers. If he was granted a monopoly of this trade, he suggested, he could promote Spanish interests. As a result, he briefly secured the monopoly, took an oath of allegiance to the Spanish monarchy, received the promise of an annual pension, and secured a permanent loan of $7,000. By 1791, however, the Spanish apparently suspected that his promises exceeded his capacity to deliver and revoked his trade monopoly.

His debts mounting rapidly, Wilkinson liquidated his personal affairs and returned to military life in March 1792 as brigadier general in the American army. In the fall of 1796 he became commandeer of all western forces. Though rumors of his Spanish dealings circulated back east, tangible proof of wrongdoing was lacking. Moreover, President George Washington wanted peace with Spain and believed Wilkinson might serve as an effective intermediary with the Spanish in the southwest.

By the end of 1796, Spain had dispensed some $32,000 to Wilkinson for his services (which included reporting on American troop movements and plans), but his personal finances remained shaky. Under fire for irregularities both in Army contracts and his personal land speculations, Wilkinson's luck nonetheless continued to hold. In 1801 he was commissioned by President Thomas Jefferson to deal with some of the southern Indian tribes and two years later helped take formal possession of Louisiana from France.

Burr Conspiracy

During the winter of 1804/1805, Wilkinson began his fateful relationship with Aaron Burr. His actual involvement in the Burr conspiracy to separate western lands from the Union remains somewhat unclear. It is known that he corresponded frequently with Burr and was privy to the vice president's plans. In 1805 he furnished Burr with a barge, escort, and letter of introduction to the Spanish officials at New Orleans. Later, in his position in St. Louis as governor of the upper Louisiana Territory, Wilkinson was visited by Burr and then kept in regular communication with him.

As Burr's intrigue deepened, however, and as Wilkinson found his own name listed in western newspapers as

one of the conspirators, he pulled back. To disentangle himself, Wilkinson sent a rather frantic and effusive letter to President Jefferson, proclaiming his loyalty and warning of Burr's plans. In return, Wilkinson received an order to proceed to New Orleans, where, in a characteristically aggressive and high-handed manner, he readied the city's defenses, placed suspected Burrites under military arrest, and sent a small force upriver to intercept Burr himself.

At the trial following the collapse of the conspiracy, Wilkinson's involvement with Burr and the Spanish government came to the surface, and he narrowly escaped indictment. In several congressional investigations and courts-martial, he was formally acquitted, but the suspicions surrounding his career were too great, and he was removed from command.

Many of Wilkinson's last years were spent composing a turgid three-volume defense of his career. He died in Mexico City on Dec. 28, 1825.

Further Reading

Thomas R. Hay and M. R. Werner, *The Admirable Trumpeter: A Biography of General James Wilkinson* (1941), is the most balanced and judicious of the biographical studies. Useful for Wilkinson's military exploits is James R. Jacobs, *Tarnished Warrior: Major-General James Wilkinson* (1938). See also John E. Weems, *Men without Countries: Three Adventurers of the Early Southwest* (1969). □

George Frederick Will

Syndicated columnist, television commentator, and conservative intellectual, George Frederick Will (born 1941) was influential in shaping the arguments that drove American conservatism.

Arguably the most distinguished of conservative newspaper columnists, George F. Will, with weekly television appearances and syndication by the *Washington Post,* had particular impact on American public discourse after the election of President Ronald Reagan in 1980. Born into an academic family in 1941, Will attributed his attitude, if not his politics, to the influences of his parents, Frederick L. Will, then a philosophy professor at the University of Illinois, and Louise Will, a high school teacher and editor of a children's encyclopedia. He attended Trinity College in Connecticut, Oxford University in England, and received a Ph. D. from Princeton University in political science in 1967.

Will taught at Michigan State and the University of Toronto, but in 1970 left the academic world to serve on the staff of Republican Senator Gordon Allott of Colorado. After Allott failed to win reelection in 1972, Will became the Washington editor of *National Review*. He resigned as editor in 1975, but by this time he was already syndicated by the Washington Post Writers Group, and by 1976 he became a contributing editor for *Newsweek*. Beginning in

1977 Will was a television commentator for *Agronsky and Company* and in 1981 for *This Week with David Brinkley*. At a time when conservative ideas were being seized by both the religious right and a new form of America First, Will provided a counterpoise, suggesting that conservatism could support defense, encourage law and order, and also provide for the unfortunate. He even had little difficulty suggesting the virtues of a graduated income tax.

In 1960 Will served as co-chair of Trinity Students for Kennedy. By the time he completed his dissertation in 1967, he was firmly in the conservative camp. The route by which he arrived at conservatism, however, may help explain why he has a vision that transcends the average writers of the right. At Oxford Will became dismayed with a pervasive anticapitalism. He reacted against intellectual pretension and trendiness. In rejecting the debilitating spirit of British academic conventions, Will moved toward the influence of Friedrich von Hayek and his vision of the power of the free market. By the time Will accepted his first teaching position, his view of the free market had softened and he was working his way toward a conservatism that acknowledged the possibility of government as a positive force.

In their work *Column Right: Conservative Journalists in the Service of Nationalism* (1988), David Burner and Thomas R. West identify the development of civic virtue as Will's central concern. As part of such development he sought justice. In his book *Restoration: Congress, Term Limits, and the Recovery of Deliberative Democracy* (1992), Will wrote, "There is a kind of scorched-earth, pillage-and-burn conservatism that is always at a rolling

boil, and which boils down to a brute animus against government . . . that is not my kind of conservatism . . . Patriotism properly understood simply is not compatible with contempt for the institutions that put American democracy on display."

Will rejected a conservatism based on self-interest rather than on conservation. One of his works, *Pursuit of Virtue and Other Tory Notions* (1982), argued against self-indulgence and for a measured stability to public and private life. In short, Will argued for conserving traditional American values rather than having a free-market trample all values, traditional or not. For example, he argued, following along with Leo Strauss, that government should be a force to ensure justice, because market forces alone cannot be concerned with such a concept. Certainly, Will was not an advocate of withdrawal from the world but was more interested in promoting some vision of America on an international basis. And even though he shared much of the sense of defense and preparedness with other conservatives, his sense of such matters always moved back to America, civic virtue, and moral responsibility.

To the end of establishing American values and securing America in what he perceived as a hostile world, Will wholeheartedly endorsed Reagan's presidency. At the beginning of the 1980 election year Will supported Howard Baker. As Reagan received the Republican nomination, however, Will turned to Reagan as a possibility for the promotion of civic virtue. In the process, Will, through his friendship with the Reagans, became journalist as advocate rather than journalist as adversary. This vision of civic virtue, presumably, caused him to turn away from the George Bush-Dan Quayle campaign of 1992, essentially arguing that virtue was gone from the Republican campaign and that Republicans and conservatives would be better to begin anew.

In 1977 Will received a Pulitzer Prize for distinguished commentary. After that date his productive output was, if anything, even more impressive. In addition to the *Pursuit of Virtue* book, four other collections of Will's columns have been published: in 1978, *The Pursuit of Happiness and Other Sobering Thoughts;* in 1986, *The Morning After: American Successes and Excesses;* in 1990, *Suddenly: The American Idea Abroad and At Home;* and in 1994, *The Leveling Wind.* A sixth collection of Will's essays, *The Woven Figure,* was scheduled for publication in 1997.

Besides the *Restoration* book Will published two books of political theory: *Statecraft as Soulcraft: What Government Does* (1983), originally the Godkin Lecture at Harvard University; and *The New Season: A Spectator's Guide to the 1988 Election,* published in 1987. *Men At Work: The Craft of Baseball,* based on in-depth interviews with players and managers, was published in April 1990 and became a bestseller.

Will received more than a dozen academic degrees and awards. He married Madeleine Marion in 1967. They had three children, two sons and a daughter. He remarried in 1991 and had a son by that marriage. In 1995 Will was appointed a visiting professor of government at Harvard University. Will's driving passion, almost beyond politics and political philosophy, was National League baseball and the Chicago Cubs. He even sought, in writing, to make the Cubs the metaphor for his view of mankind and vision of civic virtue.

Further Reading

There is no single biographical source on George F. Will. Other than those listed in this article, many works on current political philosophy, on contemporary newsmakers, or on modern commentators will deal with Will, and his individual body of work is massive. David Astor, "Should George Will be a Harvard prof?"*Editor & Publisher* (May 2, 1995). □

Adrian Willaert

Adrian Willaert (ca. 1480-1562), a Franco-Flemish composer active in Italy, founded the Venetian school of composers.

It is supposed that Adrian Willaert was born in Bruges, and almost nothing is known of his earliest years. He was intended for the law and went to Paris for legal training but soon switched to music, becoming a student of Jean Mouton, a disciple of Josquin des Prez. After completing his musical studies, Willaert sojourned briefly in Rome and then entered the service of Duke Alfonso d'Este I at Ferrara (1522-1525). For the following three years (1525-1527) he was employed by the duke's brother, Ippolito d'Este II, Archbishop of Milan. Finally, in 1527, Willaert was named choir director of St. Mark's in Venice, and he retained this important post for his last 35 years, training many illustrious composers who constitute the Venetian school.

Willaert's works include all the major forms of his time, such as Masses, motets, madrigals, villanescas, and chansons. Among the secular genres, first place must go to the madrigals. Willaert grafted northern polyphony onto the simple Italian form, raising it to the artistic level of the imitative motet; at the same time he continued to write uncomplicated native forms such as the villanesca. His French chansons may be divided into two groups: melismatic, canonic, *cantus-firmus* pieces from his early years; and syllabic, text-oriented, and occasionally chromatic pieces reflecting the influence of the Italian madrigal.

Much more significant are the sacred works, as befitted the choirmaster of the second most important church in Italy. Most of his ten surviving Masses are "parodies", that is, elaborations of preexistent motets, madrigals, or chansons. Despite their beauty, they rank below the approximately 350 motets in which he carried forward, and even went beyond, the brilliant models of Josquin des Prez. The Latin texts of Willaert's motets included such diverse sources as the *Aeneid* of Virgil, devotional lyrics of contemporary poets, and the liturgical books of the Roman Catholic Church. The music of these masterful creations is filled with canons, thoroughgoing imitation, mild chromaticism, and polychoral writing.

Willaert's polychoral psalms of 1550 popularized this already known style of composition and influenced later composers such as Andrea and Giovanni Gabrieli to the degree that Willaert was credited until recently with the invention of *chori spezzati,* or scoring for two antiphonal choirs. His experiments with chromaticism influenced such students as Nicolò Vicentino; and another pupil, Gioseffo Zarlino, derived from his polyphonic achievements the most complete analysis of 16th-century counterpoint.

Further Reading

For an analysis of Willaert's style see Alfred Einstein, *The Italian Madrigal* (3 vols., trans. 1949), and Gustave Reese, *Music in the Renaissance* (1954; rev. ed. 1959). The role of Willaert's music in Renaissance society is treated in Paul Henry Lang, *Music in Western Civilization* (1941). □

Emma Hart Willard

The American educator and author Emma Hart Willard (1787-1870) was a leader in the early movement for women's education and the founder of the Troy Female Seminary.

mma Hart was born in Berlin, Conn., on Feb. 23, 1787. Her early education was in the district school and local academy. When she was 17 she began teaching in the village school while continuing her preparation at women's academies in Hartford.

Miss Hart accepted a position in the Westfield Academy at Middlebury, Vt., in 1807 but interrupted her career to marry John Willard, a physician. With the help of a student at Middlebury College she mastered the college's curriculum but was not allowed to attend classes or win a degree. The experience heightened her awareness of the educational advantages which were denied to women. (Popular opinion and religious tradition held that intensive study would endanger women's health and morals and divert them from their domestic duties.) When, in 1814, she was obliged by financial necessity to open the Middlebury Female Seminary, she taught the higher studies, as an experiment, along with the customary secondary school subjects. The success of the seminary confirmed her conviction that women could survive advanced study without peril.

In 1818 Mrs. Willard sent to Governor DeWitt Clinton of New York *An Address to the public: Particularly to the Members of the Legislature of New York, Proposing a plan for Improving Female Education,* a lucid argument supporting women's education and outlining a scheme for a female seminary financed by the state. The proposal failed to persuade the legislature, although it was published and widely praised. Sympathetic citizens in Waterford, N.Y., induced Mrs. Willard to establish a school there, but she moved the enterprise to Troy in 1821, when that community offered

greater support. The Troy Female Seminary, following the pattern of the Middlebury experiment, grew in influence and enrollment, its graduates spreading the new gospel of female education. Emma Willard supervised every detail of the school's development, frequently teaching herself a subject in order to introduce it to her students.

For 18 years Mrs. Willard managed the seminary, pausing in 1830 to visit Europe and in 1833 to agitate for women's education in Greece. The sale of her *Journal and Letters from France and Great Britain,* describing the European voyage, helped to support a female seminary in Athens. Her husband died in 1825, and her second marriage ended in divorce in 1843. But by then she had left the management of the seminary to her son, John Hart Willard, to work with Henry Barnard in advancing the common-school movement in Connecticut. She served briefly as superintendent of the Kensington, Conn., common schools and lectured before teachers' groups, attempting always to recruit women into teaching.

Sometimes drawn into public controversy, Mrs. Willard was never genuinely a part of the feminist movement, but by the example of her life and through the institution she founded at Troy, she was identified with the cause. She died in Troy on April 15, 1870.

Further Reading

Alma Lutz, *Emma Willard: Pioneer Educator of American Women* (1964), which describes Mrs. Willard's career within the larger context of American social history, is an updating of an earlier volume, comprehensive and well written but inadequately documented. Willystine Goodsell, *Pioneers of Women's Education in the United States* (1931), contains a short chapter on Mrs. Willard and reprints selections from her writings.

Additional Sources

Lutz, Alma., *Emma Willard: daughter of democracy,* Washington: Zenger Pub. Co., 1975, 1929.

Lutz, Alma., *Emma Willard: pioneer educator of American women,* Westport, Conn.: Greenwood Press, 1983, 1964. ☐

Frances Elizabeth Caroline Willard

Frances Elizabeth Caroline Willard (1839-1898) was a prominent American temperance crusader and women's suffrage leader.

Frances Willard was born on Sept. 28, 1839, in Churchville, N.Y. Her idealistic parents moved to Oberlin, Ohio, in 1841, where both attended college. In 1846 they moved to Janesville, Wis. Frances (or "Frank," as she was called), her elder brother, and younger sister lived vigorous youths, despite the intense moral tone at home. At the age of 18 Frances informed her father that she would thenceforward determine right and wrong for herself.

Her views, however, were a modernization of, rather than a deviation from, her parents'.

In 1857 Miss Willard attended Milwaukee Female College, moving the next year to Northwestern Female College. She was class valedictorian. In 1860 she began teaching and three years later taught science at Northwestern. She taught successively at Pittsburgh Female College and Genesee Wesleyan Seminary in New York. She also wrote essays. Her first book, *Nineteen Beautiful Years* (1864), memorialized her deceased sister. During 1869-1870 she toured Europe, spending some time at the Collège de France and the Sorbonne.

Appointed president of Northwestern Female College in 1871, Miss Willard was ambitious to see women's opportunities expanded. When the college merged with Northwestern University, she became her college's dean and professor of esthetics. By 1874 she was convinced that her program would not be aided, and she resigned.

That year was a revivalist one for temperance advocates; Miss Willard participated in prayer and singing sessions. Rejecting outstanding teaching opportunities, she accepted the presidency of the Chicago Women's Christian Temperance Union (WCTU), and rose rapidly as secretary of the state organization and then of the national organization. By 1881, when she became president of the WCTU, she was an outstanding lecturer, organizer, writer, and policy maker. Her distinguished presence—warm, clear–minded, and eloquent, with an attractive sense of humor—was one of the WCTU's principal assets.

Miss Willard's unique contribution was her feeling that women's work and views were needed in all fields. One of her most famous slogans was "Do Everything." This point of view was opposed by temperance advocates who narrowed their goals to suppressing the liquor trade. Though Miss Willard helped form the Prohibition party, which influenced the election of 1884, she was also concerned about women's suffrage, peace, labor problems, "social purity" (a topic which many of her associates found indelicate), and Populism, among other causes. Her innumerable correspondents, audiences, conferences, projects, and devoted admirers took her to all parts of the country and abroad. In 1891 she became president of the World's WCTU. Her influence was especially strong in Great Britain. During a visit to New York City she developed influenza and died on Feb. 17, 1898.

Further Reading

Francis Willard's *Glimpses of Fifty Years: The Autobiography of an American Woman* (1889) reflects her era and its goals. Mary Earhart, *Frances Willard* (1944), is judicious and scholarly. Ray Strachey, *Frances Willard* (1912), helps explain what Miss Willard meant to her generation. Anna Adams Gordon, *The Life of Frances E. Willard* (1898; rev. ed. 1912), though adulatory, contains valuable abstracts of Frances Willard's writings.

Additional Sources

Bordin, Ruth Birgitta Anderson, *Frances Willard: a biography,* Chapel Hill: University of North Carolina Press, 1986.
Leeman, Richard W., *"Do everything" reform: the oratory of Frances E. Willard,* New York: Greenwood Press, 1992. □

William I

The English king William I (1027/1028-1087), called the Conqueror, subjugated England in 1066 and turned this Saxon-Scandinavian country into one with a French-speaking aristocracy and with social and political arrangements strongly influenced by those of northern France.

William I was the illegitimate son of Robert I the Devil, Duke of Normandy, and Arletta, a tanner's daughter. Before going on pilgrimage in 1034, Robert obtained recognition of William as his successor, but a period of anarchy followed Robert's death in 1035. As he grew up, Duke William gradually established his authority; his victory over a rival at Val-ès-Dunes in 1047 made him master of Normandy. One chronicle relates that in 1051 or 1052 he visited his childless cousin king Edward the Confessor of England, who may have promised him the succession to the English throne.

About 1053 William married a distant relative, Matilda, daughter of Baldwin V, Count of Flanders. She bore him four sons and four daughters, including Robert, Duke of Normandy; King William II; King Henry I; and Adela, Countess of Blois, mother of King Stephen.

William's military ability, ruthlessness, and political skill enabled him to raise the authority of the Duke of Normandy to an entirely new level and at the same time to maintain practical independence of his overlord, the king of France. William completed the conquest of Maine in 1063, and the next year he was recognized as overlord of Brittany.

Norman Conquest of England

In the same year, according to Norman sources, Harold, Earl of Wessex, son of Godwin, chief of the Anglo–Saxon nobility, fell into William's hands and was forced to swear to support William's claim to the English throne. Harold was nonetheless crowned king following the death of Edward on Jan. 6, 1066. William secured for his claim the sanction of the Pope, who was interested in correcting abuses in the English Church; at the same time, he ordered transports to be built and collected an army of adventurers from Normandy and neighboring provinces. William was also in touch with Harold's exiled brother, who with the king of Norway attacked the north of England. Harold defeated these enemies at Stamford Bridge on Sept. 25, 1066, but his absence allowed William to land unopposed in the south three days later. Harold attempted to bar William's advance, but he was defeated and killed in the Battle of Hastings on Oct. 14, 1066. After a brief campaign William was admitted to London and crowned king on Christmas Day.

In the next four years William and his Norman followers secured their position; after the last serious rising, in Yorkshire in 1069, he "fell upon the English of the North like a raging lion," destroying houses, crops, and livestock so that the area was depopulated and impoverished for many decades. William took over the old royal estates and a large part of the land confiscated from Saxon rebels. He kept for himself nearly a quarter of the income from land in the kingdom. About two-fifths he granted to his more important followers, to be held in return for the service of a fixed number of knights. This feudal method of landholding was common in northern France, but it was rare if not unknown in England before the Conquest.

Government of England

Claiming to be King Edward's rightful heir, William maintained the general validity of Anglo-Saxon law and issued little legislation; the so-called Laws of William (Leis Willelme) were not compiled until the 12th century. William also took over the existing machinery of government, which was in many ways more advanced than that of France. Local government was placed firmly under his control; earl and sheriff were his officers, removable at his will. He made use of an established land tax and a general obligation to military service.

William also controlled the Church. In 1070 he appointed Lanfranc, abbot of St. Stephen's Abbey at Caen, as archbishop of Canterbury. Lanfranc became William's trusted adviser and agent. The higher English clergy, bishops, and abbots were almost entirely replaced by foreigners. In a series of councils Lanfranc promulgated decrees intended to bring the English Church into line with developments abroad and to reform abuses. Though encouraging reforms, William insisted on his right to control the Church and its relations with the papacy. He controlled the elections of prelates; he would allow no pope to be recognized and no papal letter to be received without his permission; and he would not let bishops issue decrees or excommunicate his officials or tenants-in-chief without his order. About 1076 William rejected the demand of Pope Gregory VII that he should do fealty to the Roman Church for England, and the matter was dropped.

Domesday Book and Death

At Christmas, 1085, William ordered a great survey of England to be carried out, primarily in order to record liability to the land tax, or "geld." The results were summarized in the two great volumes known as the Domesday Book. Six months later, at a great gathering in Salisbury, William demanded oaths of fealty from all the great landowners, whether or not they were tenants-in-chief of the Crown. In this as in the Domesday survey, he was asserting rights as king over subjects, not simply as feudal lord over vassals.

Throughout his life William was involved in almost ceaseless campaigning: against rebels in Normandy and England, enemies in France, and the Welsh and the Scots. The Scottish king was forced to do homage to William in 1072. William died in Rouen, France, on Sept. 9, 1087. He was respected for his political judgment, his interest in

Church reform, the regularity of his private life, and his efforts to maintain order. But above all he was feared; the *Anglo-Saxon Chronicle* says that "he was a very stern and harsh man, so that no one dared do anything contrary to his will."

Further Reading

The standard biography of William I is David C. Douglas, *William the Conqueror* (1964). R. Allen Brown, *The Normans and the Norman Conquest* (1970), treats the invasion in detail, while F. M. Stenton, ed., *The Bayeux Tapestry* (1947; 2d ed. 1965), offers a vivid contemporary record from the Norman viewpoint. The best general history of the period is Stenton's *Anglo-Saxon England* (1943; 3d ed. 1971), which concludes with the death of William. □

William I

William I (1772-1843) was king of the Netherlands from 1815 to 1840. He was one of the restored rulers of post-Napoleonic Europe whose power derived from no clearly settled precedent.

W illiam I was born at The Hague on Aug. 24, 1772. His father was the Dutch stadholder (executive ruler) William V, Prince of Orange. In 1791 the younger William married his cousin, Princess Wilhelmina of Prussia; and in 1792 the couple had a son, who, as William II, succeeded his father as king of the Netherlands.

In the administrative system of the Dutch Republic (United Provinces of the Netherlands), inherited from the long revolutionary war against Spain in the 16th and 17th centuries, the office of stadholder played a prominent role in affairs. In the 18th century the formal power of the stadholder was greatly augmented. But the strengthening of the executive power in the hands of traditional Orangeist leadership was by no means sufficient to halt the gradual decline of the Netherlands into weak-power status. William V, a rigid conservative, ruled with an iron hand, using Prussian troops to put down the native revolutionary Patriot movement (1787). But when the French Revolution began to spill across the borders of its homeland, William V, his son, and his grandson were forced to flee the Netherlands into English exile.

The younger William at first showed liberal tendencies in marked contrast to the autocratic temperament of his father. In 1802 both men returned to Europe, the elder to take up residence in the family's hereditary estates in Nassau, the younger to German territories granted him as a favor by Napoleon. The father's death in 1806 left William the title of Prince of Orange (as William VI) and the Nassau lands. But his switch to the Prussian side against Napoleon in the same year deprived him of all his holdings and turned him into a pensioner of the Prussian court.

In 1813, however, the French pulled out of the Netherlands, to which William returned first as "sovereign

prince," then as king (March 16, 1815). His original grant of territory made him sovereign not only of the former United Provinces but of Belgium and Luxembourg as well. The restoration that reunited, if briefly, those territories which had once coexisted in tenuous unity under their Burgundian and Hapsburg overlords until the Dutch Revolution and partial Spanish reconquest, set them on different historical paths.

This history of separation—rather than any semimythical Netherlandish unity—was to prove William's undoing. The joining of the Netherlands to Belgium upset the linguistic balance in the latter country, antagonizing the French-speaking Walloons of the south. Religious tensions in the Low Countries, long divided by the Reformation, were also aggravated. Although not as conservative as his father, William ruled as a restored enlightened despot rather than as the liberal monarch his subjects desired. In 1830, the year which ended the restoration regime in France, Belgium successfully broke away from its northern ruler; but William I learned little from this experience. He continued his opposition to liberal demands, and on Oct. 7, 1840, he was forced to abdicate in favor of his son. William once again retreated to Prussia, where he died in Berlin on Dec. 12, 1843.

Further Reading

Two general surveys of Dutch history are G. J. Renier, *The Dutch Nation* (1944), and B. H. M. Vlekke, *Evolution of the Dutch Nation* (1945). Practically all significant historical and bio-graphical literature on the Netherlands is in the Dutch lan-guage; but for a brilliant synthesis of modern Dutch history down to William's reign see Charles H. Boxer, *The Dutch Seaborne Empire, 1600-1800* (1965). □

William I

William I (1797-1888) was king of Prussia from 1861 to 1888 and emperor of Germany from 1871 to 1888. He was the first of the three Hohenzollern rulers of the German Empire of 1871-1918.

Born in Berlin on March 22, 1797, William I was the second son of Prussian king Frederick William III and Queen Luise. William spent much of the Napoleonic Wars as a somewhat sickly refugee in Konigsberg, Memel, and St. Petersburg. He participated in the 1813-1814 War of Liberation, gaining an Iron Cross for action at Bar-sur-Aube and being promoted to general major on his twenty-first birthday.

After a brief "forbidden romance" with Princess Elizabeth Radziwill, in 1829 William wed the lively Princess Augusta of Saxe-Weimar, with whom he enjoyed a happy marriage despite habitual arguments. William became heir presumptive in 1840 on the accession of his childless brother, Frederick William IV. This fact, and his military conservatism, made William the "Cartridge Prince," whom the revolutionaries of 1848 hounded from Berlin to a diplomatic refuge in England. He returned in a few months, advocating order and enforcing it in an 1849 "campaign" against rebels in the Palatinate, where military administration brought William promotion to field marshal in 1854.

William became deputy sovereign in 1857 and regent in 1858 for his expiring brother, whom he succeeded on Jan. 2, 1861. The authoritarian policy and advisers of the new reign soon created a constitutional crisis. William sought to conscript a larger regular army to support his foreign policy, while pursuing a progressive "new era" in domestic politics. This united only the Landtag opponents of the military budget. War Minister Albrecht von Roon persuaded William to appoint Otto von Bismarck as minister president in 1862, and thenceforth Bismarck's skill as a diplomatist soon made him so indispensable that his right to advise William became in effect a power to rule in the King's name.

William presided over, without directing or controlling, the political and military conflicts by which Bismarck and chief of staff Count Moltke drove Austria from the German Confederation (1866) and then led the remaining German states to victory over Napoleon III (1870). The united *Deutsches Reich* under Kaiser William was acclaimed at Versailles on Jan. 18, 1871, during the siege of Paris. William regarded his new title as a burden of doubtful value and complained that "it is very difficult being Kaiser under a Chancellor like Bismarck." However, Bismarck was kept as chancellor to the end of William's long reign.

The new German Empire needed more modern institutions of government than the old kaiser could develop or tolerate. This proved a misfortune for his successors, Frederick III and William II, as well as for Germany, but William's generation was content to understand "German freedom" simply as national independence. The diplomatic effort to preserve this by averting another war consumed the old king's declining years. The last hours before his death on March 9, 1888, were expended in royal monologues on foreign policy, and the dying monarch rejected suggestions that he rest with the ironic retort, "I have no time to be tired now."

Further Reading

A full-length study of William I in English is Paul Wiegler, *William the First* (1927; trans. 1929). See also Walter H. Nelson, *The Soldier Kings* (1970), and Theo Aronson, *The Kaisers* (1971). For historical background see Golo Mann, *The History of Germany since 1789* (trans. 1968), and Hajo Holborn, *A History of Modern Germany, 1840-1945* (1969). □

William II

William II (ca. 1058-1100) called William Rufus, "the Red," was king of England from 1087 to 1100. He attempted to wrest Normandy from his brother, and he quarreled about his rights over the Church with Anselm, Archbishop of Canterbury.

illiam II was the second surviving son of William I and Matilda of Flanders. On the death of William I his lands were divided; his elder son Robert became Duke of Normandy, while William Rufus received England. He was crowned on Sept. 26, 1087. He had almost at once to face a rebellion in favor of Robert, led by their uncle Odo, Earl of Kent and Bishop of Bayeux. The rebels were defeated largely with the help of English levies, to whom William promised, among other things, less taxation and milder forest laws, but he did not keep his promise. In 1091 he attacked Normandy with some success; by the treaty of Rouen, Robert let him hold what he had won in return for help in restoring order and regaining the county of Maine. These promises too were only partially fulfilled.

Archbishop Lanfranc died in 1089. William, who seems to have been openly irreligious, kept the see vacant and exploited the leaderless Church through his able and unpopular minister Ranulf Flambard. But in 1093, thinking he was dying, he appointed as archbishop Anselm, Abbot of Bec, a leading theologian, who made every effort to decline the office. The King recovered, shook off his superstitious fears, and soon quarreled with the archbishop. The first dispute arose over the recognition of one of two rival popes; more trouble arose over the poor quality of the archbishop's knights; in addition William would not allow Anselm to visit the Pope to obtain his pallium. A council at Rockingham (February 1095) failed to make a decision about the archbishop's rights. The King wished for his deposition but was outmaneuvered by a papal legate to England.

In 1096 Duke Robert decided to go on crusade. To finance his expedition he offered to pledge the duchy to William for 100,000 marks. William raised the money in England and so got control of Normandy, where he restored order and attacked Maine and the French Vexin. He was considering a similar bargain with the Duke of Aquitaine, but on Aug. 2,1100, while hunting in the New Forest with his brother Henry, he was killed by an arrow shot by Walter Tirel. His body was brought by a forester to Winchester and buried without ceremony in the Cathedral, while his brother seized his treasure and his throne.

William was an able ruler and in his disputes with Anselm was only claiming rights which his father had exercised. His reputation suffered because he was a homosexual and an irreligious man in an age when prejudices were strong and nearly all history was written by churchmen.

Further Reading

Useful information about William Rufus is provided in the biography of his brother by Charles Wendell David, *Robert Curthose, Duke of Normandy* (1920). A good account of the England of William's time is in A. Lane Poole, *From Domesday Book to Magna Carta, 1087-1216* (1951; 2d ed. 1955), and of Normandy in Charles Homer Haskins, *Norman Institutions* (1918).

Additional Sources

Barlow, Frank, *William Rufus,* Berkeley: University of California Press, 1983. □

Bismarck considered him a more acceptable successor to his grandfather (and to Frederick the Great) than his liberal father. Conservative circles in Germany breathed a sigh of relief when the death of William I in 1888 was quickly followed by that of Frederick III. William II ascended the throne that year.

Differences between the young kaiser and the aging Bismarck soon were public knowledge. Serious questions of policy separated them, such as whether to renew the anti-Socialist legislation on the books since 1878, and in foreign affairs, whether to keep the alliance with Russia as well as with Austria, as Bismarck insisted. But basically the split was a personal one, the question being which man was to rule Germany. William forced Bismarck to resign in 1890, and thereafter he steered his own course.

It seemed to mark the beginning of a new era. William was the representative of a new generation that had grown up since German unification, and he was at home in the world of technology and of neoromantic German nationalism. Indeed, William gave the impression of dynamism. He was always in the public eye and caught, for a time, the imagination of his country. But he cared little for the day-to-day problems of government, and his "policies" were often shallow, short-lived, and contradictory. Thus the "Labor Emperor" of the early years of the reign soon became the implacable enemy of the Social Democratic working-class movement. In foreign policy his inconsistencies were even more glaring. England and Russia, in particular, were alternately wooed and rebuffed; both ultimately ended up as foes. Sometimes the Kaiser's sounder instincts

William II

The last of the Hohenzollern rulers, William II (1859-1941) was emperor of Germany and king of Prussia from 1888 until his forced abdication in 1918.

In the crucial years before World War I, William II was the most powerful and most controversial figure in Europe. His domineering personality and the comparatively vague political structure of the post-Bismarck state combined to make his reign over the most advanced country in Europe both authoritarian and archaic.

William was born on Jan. 27, 1859. He was the son of Frederick III and Princess Victoria of England. William's views of his prerogatives were strongly influenced by his Prussian military education, amidst the subservience and flattery of his fellow cadets. After completing his studies at the University of Bonn, William entered the army and in 1881 married Princess Augusta Victoria of SchleswigHolstein.

William was an intelligent, dashing, impulsive young man who loved military display and believed in the divine nature of kingship; his strong personality overcame the serious handicap (for a horseman) of a withered left arm. His father found William immature, but Chancellor Otto von

were overridden by his advisers, as in the Morocco crisis of 1905, which William, who was essentially peaceful in intent, had not wished to provoke. But mainly his mistakes were his own.

Foreign opinion concerning the Kaiser was much more hostile than German opinion, and his often bellicose and pompous utterances did much to tarnish Germany's image abroad. Nevertheless, World War I and postwar depictions of him as the incarnation of all that was evil in Germany were grossly unfair. So little was he the martial leader of a militaristic nation that his authority in fact faded during World War I, and the military assumed increasing control. Belatedly, William tried to rally a warweary nation with promises of democratic reforms, but at the end of the war the German Republic was proclaimed without serious opposition. William abdicated in November 1918.

After his abdication William lived in quiet retirement in Doorn, Holland, not actively involved with the movement for a restoration of the monarchy. He died in Doorn on June 4, 1941.

Further Reading

Most studies of William II have been in a popular vein. Two good recent biographies are Virginia Cowles, *The Kaiser* (1963), and Michael Balfour, *The Kaiser and His Time* (1964). William's autobiographical *My Early Life* (trans. 1926) ends at 1888. □

William III

William III (1650-1702), Prince of Orange, reigned as king of England, Scotland, and Ireland from 1689 to 1702. He was also stadholder of the United Netherlands from 1672 to 1702.

As perhaps the pivotal European figure of the late 17th century, William of Orange remains most noted for having fought France, the dominant power in Europe, to a standstill in three wars. In this process he reunited his native Netherlands and became king of England. In his English role William fostered the legal bulwarks of the Glorious Revolution of 1688: religious toleration for Protestant dissenters, a prescribed monarchy, and parliamentary partnership with the Crown concerning legislation. As William drew England into his wars against France, he concluded more than a century's isolation for England and initiated a series of victories that later yielded Great Britain a worldwide empire.

Early Years and Education

Eight days before William was born at The Hague on Nov. 4, 1650, his father, William II, Prince of Orange and Stadholder of the United Netherlands, died, bequeathing a divided Netherlands to his son. William's mother was Mary, the oldest daughter of Charles I of England. The De Witt brothers, Jan and Cornelius, heads of an urban and commer-

cial coalition, assumed power and pursued a policy of autonomy for the seven provinces of the Netherlands. The house of Orange, aristocratic leader of the landed interests, had stood for unity as the only means of protection against foreign interests. Despite the De Witts' control over his education, William nurtured plans to restore the stadholdership. In the meantime, the young prince prepared himself, mastering four languages, studying politics and war, and exercising the Spartan self-control and taciturnity for which he became famous.

In 1667 the prince's popularity rose dramatically when Louis XIV of France made the first of his many attempts to conquer the Dutch. Public exasperation greeted the De Witts' inactivity while Louis's armies occupied neighboring Flanders. When the southern Dutch provinces were invaded in 1672, William was advanced quickly from captain general in February to stadholder in July. In August a panicked mob murdered the De Witts, and a year later William's office was made hereditary.

Stadholder of the United Provinces

The war with France raged from 1672 to 1678, and while William battled against armies that were sometimes five times the size of his own, he built an alliance with Spain, Denmark, and Brandenburg. He fought the Great Condé—Louis II de Bourbon, Prince de Condé—to a draw at the Battle of Seneff in August 1674. Despite a near-fatal bout with smallpox in 1675 and a severe arm wound in 1676, William wrung from the French a recognition of Dutch independence in the Treaty of Nijmegen in 1678.

Toward the end of the French war, William married—in 1677—Mary, the Protestant elder daughter of James, Duke of York, later King James II of England. With England as the Netherlands' partner there could be no doubt about maintaining Dutch independence. The match was advanced by the pro-Dutch English minister, the Earl of Danby, and after the marriage William slowly intruded himself into English politics. He ostensibly visited Charles II in 1681 to seek aid against renewed French hostilities, but he actually came to observe the increasing antagonism of the Whigs to the proposed succession of York, whose autocracy and Roman Catholicism displeased many Englishmen. William quietly let it be known that if Charles should die without issue, he would be willing to be named regent over his father-in-law in case James should be excluded from the throne.

Glorious Revolution of 1688

During the War of the League of Augsburg, William brought to the alliance the overwhelming support of England in 1689. James II's precipitate illegalities in favor of his Roman Catholic subjects after he became king in 1685 alienated most English leaders, who in turn sought the alternative earlier suggested by William. William invaded England in November 1688 with a force of 15,000. Met by many of England's important men, he proceeded under such careful circumstances that not one shot was fired. James's flight to France in December cleared the path for William and Mary to assume the vacated throne. Their reign became the only jointly held monarchy in English history. In May 1689 England declared war on France.

Between 1689 and 1693 William, equipped with an army often numbering 90,000, remained mostly in the field, leaving duties at home in Mary's hands. In Ireland, William defeated an attempt by French and Irish troops to dethrone him, nearly being killed in the Battle of the Boyne in July 1690. At sea the English repelled an invasion at La Hogue in May 1692; but on the Continent, William barely held his own. William's defeat at Neerwinden in July 1693 cost the French so many lives that Louis XIV began peace overtures. Sporadic campaigning continued until lengthy negotiations finally resulted in the Treaty of Ryswick (September 1697), in which Louis XIV recognized William as the legitimate ruler of England (Mary had died in 1694).

Last Years

William's domestic relations in England were intermittently strained because he understood little of the compromise required under the parliamentary system of broad-based consultation and administration. He was the last English king to use the veto extensively, although he usually yielded to Parliament's wishes rather than risk losing support for his wars. William fostered the Toleration Act of 1689 and the establishment of the Bank of England to fund the war debt in 1694. He assented to the Declaration of Right and to the Triennial Act.

William's frequent absences from England and his reliance upon Dutch counselors accounted for his general unpopularity. However, the discovery of the Turnham Green Plot against his life in 1696 prompted a personal loyalty lasting until the end of his reign. In 1702 William fell from his horse, seriously undermining his fragile health. He died on March 8, 1702, as he was constructing a new alliance against France for the War of the Spanish Succession.

Further Reading

The most thorough of the modern biographies, focusing particularly on William III's role and importance during England's crisis with France, is Stephan B. Baxter, *William III and the Defense of European Liberty, 1650-1702* (1966). An anecdotal glimpse into William's private life is provided by Nesca A. Robb's highly readable *William of Orange: A Personal Portrait* (2 vols., 1962-1966). David Ogg, *William III* (1956), is an attractive brief sketch. Three indispensable works on William's age are John B. Wolf, *The Emergence of the Great Powers, 1685-1715* (1951); David Ogg, *England in the Reigns of James II and William III* (1955; corrected 1963); and Maurice Ashley, *The Glorious Revolution of 1688* (1966). Peter Geyl, *Orange and Stuart, 1641-1672* (trans. 1970), is superb.

Additional Sources

Miller, John, *The life and times of William and Mary,* London, Weidenfeld and Nicolson 1974. □

William IV

William IV (1765-1837), called the "Sailor King" and "Silly Billy," was king of Great Britain and Ireland from 1830 to 1837. He reigned during the struggle over the great Reform Bill, and his actions helped to establish important constitutional precedents.

Willliam Henry, third son of George III, was born at Buckingham Palace on Aug. 21, 1765. The shortest of the royal brothers and closely resembling his mother, Queen Charlotte, William was perhaps the least physically attractive of the Hanoverians. He was, however, the best-natured, bluff, hearty, and unassuming. Like that of all the children of George III, his early childhood was sheltered, and he was educated by tutors. At the age of 13, however, he was launched on a not unsuccessful naval career, which probably accentuated his basic personality traits. He rose to the rank of rear admiral, seeing active service in America and the West Indies, and became a fast friend of the future Lord Nelson.

William's active naval career ended in 1790, and until he ascended the throne 40 years later, his life was spent in retirement. Like his brothers, he sought solace in love. Until 1817 he lived happily with the actress Mrs. Dorothea Jordan, producing ten illegitimate children. The death of Princess Charlotte, the daughter of his eldest brother, changed William's life. He was now third in line for the throne, after the older brothers George, who served as regent from 1811 to his accession in 1820, and the Duke of York. In 1818 William married the German princess Adelaide; it was a

most happy marriage. The Duke of York died in 1827, and on George IV's death in 1830 William IV ascended the throne.

The new king was more than a little eccentric, but his reputation as a "character" probably did him no harm, and his informality gained him considerable popularity. William did his best to be a strictly constitutional monarch, and, despite his personal fears of parliamentary reform, he firmly supported his ministers, save on one occasion. That was in May 1832, when William faltered over packing the House of Lords to carry the Reform Bill and tried to bring in a Tory ministry. Neither the House of Commons nor the country would have it, and William had to give way and bring back Lord Grey. It was a clear indication that a king could no longer actually appoint his own ministers. And the lesson was underlined by William's unsuccessful attempt in 1834-1835 to replace the Whig Lord Melbourne by the Tory Sir Robert Peel, again against the wishes of a majority in the House of Commons.

By and large, however, William demonstrated a strong sense of reality, and he was always ready to yield to necessity. These qualities, which were not marked in his Hanoverian predecessors, were undoubtedly of the first importance in carrying the British monarchy over a most difficult period. By the time he died on June 20, 1837, William had done much to restore the tarnished reputation of the crown which George IV had left him.

Further Reading

W. Gore Allen, *King William IV* (1960), is a recent biography, but uneven in quality. A charming short treatment of William is in Roger Fulford, *Hanover to Windsor* (1960). Asa Briggs, *The Making of Modern England, 1783-1867* (1959), gives an excellent, balanced account of the political background.

Additional Sources

Marples, Morris, *Wicked uncles in love,* London, Joseph, 1972.
Pocock, Tom, *Sailor King: the life of King William IV,* London: Sinclair-Stevenson, 1991.
Somerset, Anne, *The life and times of William IV,* London: Weidenfeld and Nicolson, 1980. □

William of Malmesbury

William of Malmesbury (ca. 1090-ca. 1142) was the foremost English historian of his day and a leading representative of 12th-century clerical humanism.

Of mixed Norman and English descent, William of Malmesbury was born in England between 1090 and 1095. At an early age he was admitted to Malmesbury (Benedictine) Abbey, where he became a monk and, later, librarian of the monastery. His earliest major work was *Gesta regum Anglorum* (*Deeds of the Kings of England*) a compendium of English history in five books, first published in 1125 and later revised. *Gesta regum* is the finest historical work of 12th-century England, although it is less the product of original research than a skillful combination of sources featuring colorful anecdotes and placing special emphasis on the reigns and characters of the Anglo-Norman kings.

William wrote history for moral and didactic purposes, both pious and patriotic (the latter imitative of classical Roman historiography). He reveals his hybrid attitude in this passage from the *Historia novella:* "What gives more aid to virtue, what is more conducive to justice, than to learn of God's indulgence toward good men and vengeance on traitors? What, moreover, is more pleasant than to record in literary writings the deeds of brave men, by whose example others may abandon cowardice and be armed to defend the fatherland?" In William's description of the Norman conquest, both these assumptions are at work. The victory belongs to the godly Normans, the defeat results from English sinfulness; yet there are also laments, couched in classical rhetoric, for England's loss of liberty under the Norman yoke.

The year after he finished the *Gesta regum,* William completed the *Gesta pontificum* (1126; *Deeds of the Bishops*), a compilation of the lives and deeds of English bishops. During the next few years he wrote the *Vita sancti Wulfstani* (*Life of Saint Wulfstan*) and *De antiquitate Glastoniensis ecclesiae* (1129-1135; *Concerning the Antiquity of Glastonbury*), a history of that ancient and celebrated abbey. William's last work, and the most valuable to modern historians, is the *Historia novella* (*New History*) a continuation to 1142 of the *Gesta regum* in three books, which includes eyewitness, though not impartial, testimony to the progress of the civil war in England between King Stephen and the house of Anjou. The comparative roughness of the style and the absence of a promised fourth book indicate that the *Historia novella* was unfinished, William apparently having died soon after he finished book 3 in 1142. He owes his considerable reputation today to his feeling for the sweep of history, the complexities of human character, and the rhetorical possibilities of Latin narration.

Further Reading

Biographical and critical material on William of Malmesbury appears in Reginald R. Darlington, *Anglo-Norman Historians* (1947), and in the introduction to K. R. Potter, ed. and trans., *The Historia Novella* (1955). See also the chapter on historical writing in Charles H. Haskins, *The Renaissance of the Twelfth Century* (1927; repr. 1952).

Additional Sources

Thomson, Rodney M., *William of Malmesbury,* Woodbridge, Suffolk; Wolfeboro, N.H., USA: Boydell Press, 1987. □

William of Ockham

The English philosopher and theologian William of Ockham (ca. 1284-1347) was the most important intellectual figure in the 14th century and one of the major figures in the history of philosophy.

The first half of the 14th century was one of the most active, creative periods in medieval thought. Building on the solid foundation of the 13th-century achievements in science, logic, metaphysics, and epistemology, William of Ockham and his immediate followers developed an approach to philosophy and theology that became known as nominalism. This school of thought, alongside the humanist movement, aided in the transition from the medieval to the modern world.

Early Life

William was born in the village of Ockham in Surrey. Having received his early education in Latin grammar and the liberal arts, possibly at the nearby monastic house of Augustinian canons at Newark, he joined the Franciscan order and studied arts and philosophy at their convent in London. In February 1306 he was ordained a subdeacon at the church of St. Saviour at Southwark in London, where Southwark Cathedral now stands. The following fall Ockham began his 13 years of theological study at Oxford.

During the years 1317 to 1320 Ockham lectured on the *Sentences* of Peter Lombard, the standard theological textbook from the 12th to the 16th centuries. After the completion of his theological studies, he became lecturer at the Franciscan convent in Reading, where he taught off and on until 1324. There he revised the first book of his commentary on the *Sentences,* lectured on logic and Aristotle's *Physics,* and engaged in quodlibetic disputes with other theologians.

In these various works Ockham set forth ideas which, within 20 years, earned him an international reputation and placed him alongside Thomas Aquinas and John Duns Scotus as one of the most significant minds of the age. Like Thomas and Scotus, the different areas of Ockham's thought are closely interrelated and marked by distinctive features that give his thought a special character. Ockham's ideas should not, however, be seen as a rejection or destruction of 13th century thought. He borrowed from the past and perfected constructive tendencies already present in the previous period.

Epistemology and Empiricism

The 13th-century tendency to base scientific knowledge, knowledge of the physical world, on sense experience was accepted and extended by Ockham. In place of the Aristotelian description of how man comes to know (a description that sees the human mind primarily as a passive receptacle that abstracts the universal form or concept from particular things that are experienced and transmitted through a multistage process), Ockham described the mind as an active agent that knows the particular immediately and directly through intuitive cognition. Intuitive cognition is the direct apprehension by the mind of a particular, existing thing according to which the mind forms a judgment that such a thing exists and apprehends those facts contingent upon its existence, such as size, shape, color, and so on. In addition to intuitive cognition, which is the initial and primary means of knowledge, there is abstractive cognition, closely related to memory, which can reflect on an object but does not convey any knowledge of whether the object presently exists.

This direct apprehension of the existing particular thing by means of intuitive cognition increased the empirical quality of medieval thought at the expense of the Platonic reliance on forms or ideas. It also meant that man initially and primarily knows the particular, and only on the basis of that and similar experiences does he begin to form a more general concept known as the universal.

It is because of Ockham's rejection of the "realistic" interpretation of the universal or general concept that the term "nominalist" is applied to him. Ockham rejected the idea that there is similarity among things of the same species because there exists a "common nature," prior to existing individual things, which inheres in the latter and makes them similar. While recognizing similarities among things in nature, Ockham saw that similarity as the result of a generic relationship that does not endanger the peculiar individuality of each object. The concept is formed when several individuals of the same species are considered at the same time, and when one forms a composite in the mind of those features they have in common. One of the results of this approach, with its stress on the priority and importance of knowledge of the particular, was to give added impulse to the scientific tradition of the 13th and 14th centuries by stressing both empiricism and an inductive method.

Theology and Ethics

By restricting the objects of scientific knowledge to those individuals known directly through sense experience and by rejecting the idea of a common nature prior to and inherent in the things experienced, Ockham limited the kind of things man could know by reason apart from revelation, and he thus changed the character of metaphysical discussion. In much the same way, Ockham limited the number of truths in theology that can be established by reason alone, thus making theological propositions depend much more on revelation and the teaching of the Church than would be true for earlier scholastic theologians from Anselm to Aquinas. Most "truths" of natural theology are, for Ockham, learned by way of revelation.

Because most theological propositions are known only through revelation, this does not make them any the less certain for Ockham, who saw certainty as the result of different types of evidence. Scientific knowledge produces a certainty based on belief in the way man's mind operates and in the validity of human sense experience. For Ockham this form of knowledge is so compelling that it is impossible not to acknowledge its certainty. The certainty of theological knowledge is based on belief that what God has revealed through Scripture and the Church cannot be in error. Such "knowledge" is compelling only for the Christian and is not of the same order as scientific knowledge.

The overriding conception of Ockham's theology is the freedom and omnipotence of God, an idea that shapes much of his philosophy as well. The realm of God's choice is limited only by the principle of contradiction, namely, that God cannot do that which is logically impossible. Since God wills from eternity and not within time, the choices made by God have become the reliable principles upon which the human world depends. The uniformity in nature which Ockham continually asserted is basically a uniformity in God's will, which can never be arbitrary because it is one with His intellect and wisdom. By His initial choices God has freely bound Himself to act in reliable, definable ways, both within the physical world and within the Church.

The contingency of the universe and the theological order upon the will of God includes the ethical system according to which God rewards and punishes. Good deeds are defined by their conformity to God's revealed law, and although God retains his freedom to reject as meritorious those good deeds done in a state of grace, he has in fact committed himself to accept them as meritorious of eternal life.

Final Years

In 1324 Ockham was called to Avignon to answer charges of heretical doctrine in his writings. Two lists of suspect opinions were drawn up, but neither resulted in a formal condemnation.

While living in Avignon near the papal court awaiting the results of the investigation, Ockham wrote a defense of his theories on the Eucharist, which was one of the major areas of his thought under attack. In addition, at the urging of the head of the Franciscan order, Michael of Cesena, Ockham undertook a study of the concept of apostolic poverty, a concept basic to the Franciscan ideal and one under attack by Pope John XXII. When in 1328, Ockham came to the conclusion that John XXII was incorrect on the issue of apostolic poverty and perhaps even heretical—and when it appeared that the Pope was about to deliver a pronouncement on the issue that would make the Franciscan position appear heretical—Ockham, Cesena, and several others fled Avignon on the night of May 26 toward Italy, and they sought and received the protection of John's major enemy, Emperor Louis of Bavaria.

The remainder of Ockham's life was spent at the Franciscan convent in Munich, where he wrote political treatises against the positions of John XXII and his successors. In these treatises Ockham argued that Scripture and the established theological tradition of the Church are the two sources for authority in doctrine. Neither the papacy nor secular political powers have the authority to proclaim doctrines that go against Scripture or tradition. Ockham agreed with Marsilius of Padua that Christ did not establish the papacy, and one can find in Ockham a strong defense of the authority of a general Church council. However, unlike Marsilius, Ockham believed that the pope did possess administrative authority within the Church, and as long as he did not fall into heresy he should not have his administrative or judicial power questioned.

Further Reading

The best introduction in English to Ockham's thought is *The Collected Articles on Ockham* (1958) by Philotheus Böehner, who, more than anyone else, was responsible for the revised understanding of Ockham. Particular aspects of Ockham's thought are examined in Ernest A. Moody, *The Logic of William of Ockham* (1935); Damascene Webering, *The Theory of Demonstration according to William Ockham* (1953); and Herman Shapiro, Motion, *Time and Place according to William Ockham* (1957). For background see Philotheus Böehner, *Medieval Logic: An Outline of Its Development from 1250 to c. 1400* (1952); Gordon Leff, *Medieval Thought: St. Augustine to Ockham* (1958) and *Paris and Oxford Universities in the 13th and 14th Centuries* (1968); David Knowles, *The Evolution of Medieval Thought* (1962); and Arthur Hyman and James J. Walsh, eds., *Philosophy in the Middle Ages: The Christian, Islamic and Jewish Traditions* (1967).

Additional Sources

Adams, Marilyn McCord, *William Ockham*, Notre Dame, Ind.: University of Notre Dame Press, 1987. □

William of Tyre

William of Tyre (ca. 1130-1184) was archbishop of Tyre, chancellor of the Latin Kingdom of Jerusalem, and historian of the last years of the kingdom before its fall to Saladin in 1187.

Born in the crusading Kingdom of Jerusalem, William of Tyre also grew up there. Besides the French language, he acquired a knowledge of Eastern languages: Arabic, Greek, Hebrew, and Persian. These stood him in good stead in his later career. William's parents were probably of humble origin, but William's scholastic aptitude made him a likely candidate for the priesthood. He became a protégé of the archbishop of Tyre, and was sent sometime before 1163 to Europe, probably to study law.

Between 1163 and 1167 William was a canon in the cathedral church of Tyre. In 1167 he was chosen by King Amalric to become the historian of the kingdom and was promoted to archdeacon of Tyre. William traveled to Rome and Constantinople in the next few years before being appointed tutor to Amalric's son Baldwin (later King Baldwin IV) in 1170. Upon Amalric's death William planned to stop writing, but the rise to power of Count Raymond III of Tripoli brought William the appointment of chancellor of the kingdom, and in 1175 he was made archbishop of Tyre.

From 1176 on, William was engaged in diplomacy as well as in his official duties as chancellor and historian. William attended the Third Lateran Council in Italy in 1178, but from then on he became less powerful as the court intrigues which surrounded the dying young king Baldwin IV moved him farther from centers of real power. William now concentrated upon the writing of his history as the chaos of the court of Jerusalem began to reveal that inner weakness which would make it vulnerable to Saladin's attacks a few years later. William's history in this period became more than a royally commissioned work. From 1180 on, William wrote with a skill and tragic insight which few historians have surpassed.

William's use of documents in different languages, his lack of bias toward the men of different religions and races whose actions he described, his intimate knowledge of political and diplomatic events, and his skill as a Latin prose writer contributed to the greatness of his *History of Deeds Done beyond the Sea*. Toward the end of his life, when he felt the external and internal threats to the survival of the kingdom, William's commentary and narrative rise to eloquent heights of political tragedy. His somber account of the decline of the crusading kingdom is addressed not only to posterity but to all of the Christian world. William's work was continued and translated in his own time, and it has been widely used since and is still of immense interest, not only to professional historians but to students of history as well. It is the primary historical narrative contemporary with the last years of the Latin Kingdom and is an excellent example of the best 12th-century chronicle-writing technique.

Further Reading

The best account of William's life, along with a complete listing of source materials concerning his works, is in the introduction to his *History of Deeds Done beyond the Sea,* translated by Emily Atwater Babcock and A. C. Krey (2 vols., 1943). □

William the Silent

The Dutch statesman William the Silent (1533-1584), or William I, Prince of Orange and Count of Nassau, led the revolt of the Low Countries against Spain and created the independent republic of the United Provinces.

A German nobleman by birth, William the Silent became the leader of a rebellion in the Netherlands against the king of Spain. Passionately devoted to the cause of the unity of the Netherlands, he saw the country dividing into distinct northern and southern states under the impact of military events and religious antagonisms. At various times a Lutheran, a Roman Catholic, and a Calvinist, William was most of all dedicated to Erasmian tolerance in religion; yet in the end he had to rely upon fanatical Calvinists in order to stand up to the assaults of conquering Spanish armies. A wealthy, luxury-loving noble in his younger years, he learned to live the meager life of an exile and rebel and came to love the Dutch people, high and low, for whom he gave his life and who loved him as Father of the Fatherland. Trying ceaselessly to persuade foreign princes to take over the sovereignty of the Low Countries in order to save it, he ended by becoming the founder of a free and independent Dutch republic, and only his assassination prevented Holland from making him its count.

Early Years

William was born on April 24, 1533, at Dillenburg, the ancestral castle of the Nassaus near Wiesbaden, Germany, to Count William of Nassau-Dillenburg and Juliana von Stolberg. His early life was one of simple comforts and close family affection—a rough and easy life in a castle in the countryside. His mother raised him as a Lutheran, but after he inherited the vast possessions of his cousin, René of Châlon-Nassau, in 1544 (including the principality of Orange and numerous baronies and manors in France and in the Low Countries), Emperor Charles V, as a condition of his receiving his heritage in the Netherlands, required that William come there in 1545 to be raised as a Roman Catholic.

Under the guidance of the regent, Mary of Hungary, William grew into a handsome young nobleman, elegant and well-spoken in French and Dutch as well as in his native German, and intelligent and at ease with people. He married a wealthy heiress, Anne of Egmont and Büren, in 1551, thus becoming the richest nobleman in the Netherlands. Charles V was particularly fond of him, and during his abdication at Brussels on Oct. 25, 1555, he rested his weary arms upon young Orange's shoulders.

Appointment as Stadholder

Given military commands in the war against France in 1555, William proved to have little talent as a warrior, but he clearly displayed political ability on diplomatic missions to Germany and in the peace negotiations at Cateau-Cambrésis in 1559. Philip II, who had inherited the Nether-

Opposition to the Duke of Alba

William was shocked by the "image-breaking" movement of fanatical Calvinists in 1566, which made Philip decide to replace Margaret of Parma with the Duke of Alba, who brought an army of Spanish regulars to the Low Countries in 1567 in order to crush all resistance to the King's will. William, forewarned of Alba's task of terror, resigned his offices and withdrew beyond the duke's reach into Germany, where from his refuge at Dillenburg he renewed efforts to thwart the suppression of the Netherlands. Military expeditions led by himself and by Louis of Nassau in 1568 failed in the face of Alba's superior generalship and the people's passivity. During the next 4 years, while Alba ruled the Netherlands without visible hindrance, William and his brother Louis spent their time, after a year in service with the French Huguenots under Admiral Gaspard de Coligny, in preparing to return to the struggle in the Low Countries.

In 1570 the secret resistance movement in Holland encouraged William to attempt another expedition against Alba, which also failed. However, in 1572, after the "Sea Beggars" had seized Brill, they attempted a second campaign in the southern Netherlands, which failed. William, whose hopes of help from the French Huguenots were dashed by their destruction in the massacre of St. Bartholomew's Day, thereupon decided to join the rebels in Holland and Zeeland "to find my grave there." These provinces, which continued to recognize William as their stadholder, thus maintaining the fiction that they were fighting not Philip II but only his general, Alba, became the base of William's new strategy of resistance. William became a Calvinist, although a moderate one, in order to hold the support of the most vigorous opponents of Spain, and he reorganized the governments of Holland and Zeeland upon the basis of the authority of their States, with himself as governor and commander. William was able to relieve Leiden in 1574 after a long siege, and he established a university there as the city's reward.

Pacification of Ghent

Also in 1574, William's marriage to Anne of Saxony, who had run off with another man and was obviously mentally unbalanced, was annulled, and in 1575 he married Princess Charlotte de Bourbon-Montpensier, who became an affectionate stepmother to his children. Negotiations in Breda for peace the same year with Luis de Lúñiga y Requesens, the Spanish commander, shortly before Requesens' death, failed over the question of religion. After a mutiny of Spanish troops in 1576, William was able to arrange an agreement among all the provinces, north and south, called the Pacification of Ghent, which enabled him to maintain their common resistance to Don John of Austria, the new governor general from Spain. He persuaded the Austrian archduke Matthias to accept appointment as governor general from the States General, but William's attempt to preserve the unity of the provinces failed due to the intransigence of religious extremists on both sides. The northern provinces, under the urging of his oldest brother, John of Nassau, joined together in the Union of Utrecht in January 1579, a union that William accepted reluctantly at

lands as well as Spain from Charles V, made William a member of the Council of State in 1555 and a knight of the Golden Fleece, the Burgundian chivalric order, in 1556. In 1558 Anne of Egmont and Büren, who had given him a son, Philip William, and a daughter, died. Philip II recognized William's preeminence among the nobility by making him stadholder of Holland, Zeeland, and Utrecht in 1559.

William's second marriage was to Anne, the daughter of Elector Maurice of Saxony; she was a Lutheran princess who was even wealthier than Anne of Egmont and Büren had been. This 1561 marriage was a sign that William was not a passive instrument of his sovereign. When he returned to Brussels from the wedding in Leipzig, William joined the counts of Egmont and Hoorn, his colleagues in the Council of State, in resistance to the centralizing absolutist policies of Cardinal Antoine Perrenot de Granvelle, who was Philip's principal agent in the Netherlands while Margaret of Parma, the King's half sister, acted as regent. They were able to compel the King, who depended upon them as the most influential persons in the country for effective government, to recall Granvelle in 1564. But Philip would make no concession in the matter of repression of Protestant heresy, although William, a nominal Roman Catholic at the time, strongly urged a policy of tolerance on the principle that men's consciences should not be forced. However, William was aware that his young brother, Louis of Nassau, was one of the leaders of the movement of the lower nobility to prevent enforcement of the ordinances introducing the Inquisition.

first. Meanwhile Alessandro Farnese forged the almost simultaneous Union of Arras among Roman Catholics and Walloons in the opposite camp. The civil war resumed with new fury.

Last Years and Assassination

Philip II put William under the ban of outlawry in 1580, to which he replied in a bitter *Apology*. The States General abjured the sovereignty of Philip in 1581, and the French Duke of Alençon and Anjou was called in to take his place as a constitutional sovereign. An attempt upon William's life by Jean Jaureguy on March 18, 1582, almost succeeded; Princess Charlotte, who nursed him through a difficult recovery, died of overstrain. In January 1583 Anjou, revealing his true purpose of becoming an absolute lord in the Netherlands, unleashed his troops on Antwerp in the so-called French Fury, but he was saved from the revenge of the populace by William. That April, William married Louise de Coligny, a French Huguenot noblewoman, at Antwerp, and then moved his residence to Holland, despairing at last of keeping the Low Countries, though divided in religion, united against Spain.

During 1584 the States of Holland and Zeeland proposed to give William the title of count with limited powers, but he was slain on July 10 by Balthasar Gérard, a Roman Catholic from Franche-Comté, at the Prinsenhof in Delft before any action was taken. The last words attributed to him, "God, have pity on me and this poor people," expressed his devotion to the cause for which he had fought so long. This cause was to triumph, although not before 6 more decades had passed, under the leadership of his sons Maurice of Nassau and Frederick Henry, and then only in the northern provinces, which became the Dutch Republic. The United Provinces, which accepted the Union of Utrecht, constituted only a fragment of the Low Countries that he had sought to hold together. But it endured, became rich and powerful, and was the direct historical origin of the modern kingdom of the Netherlands (Holland).

Further Reading

As readable biographies, Frederic Harrison, *William the Silent* (1910; repr. 1970), and Ruth Putnam, *William the Silent, Prince of Orange, and the Revolt of the Netherlands* (1911), have been superseded by C. V. Wedgwood's brilliant *William the Silent* (1944). For historical background see Pieter Geyl, *The Revolt of the Netherlands, 1555-1609* (1931; trans. 1932), and B. H. M. Vlekke, *Evolution of the Dutch Nation* (1945).

Additional Sources

Swart, K. W. (Koenraad Wolter), *William the Silent and the revolt of the Netherlands,* London: Historical Association, 1978. □

Daniel Hale Williams

Daniel Hale Williams (1856-1931), African American surgical pioneer and innovator, founded the first black voluntary hospital in the United States.

Daniel Hale Williams was born on Jan. 18, 1856, in Hollidaysburg, Pa. He attended school there and in Annapolis and Baltimore, Md. He eventually settled in Janesville, Wis., where he worked his way through the Janesville Classical Academy as a barber and bass violin player. After a medical preceptorship in Janesville, he received his medical degree from Chicago Medical College (affiliated with Northwestern University) in 1883. Following internship at Mercy Hospital in Chicago, he was appointed surgeon to the South Side Dispensary and demonstrator of anatomy at Northwestern. He continued to improve his surgery through anatomical dissection.

In 1891 Dr. Williams founded Provident Hospital in Chicago, where black patients were freely admitted and African American nurses trained. This was the first black voluntary hospital in America. It had an interracial staff and board of trustees. Newspaper reports of an operation he performed in 1893 gave him instant fame, as he was acclaimed the first physician to operate on the human heart. He did not publish his case until 1897, and there may, in fact, have been an earlier pericardial suture; the point remains unclear.

In 1894 Dr. Williams was appointed surgeon in chief of Freedmen's Hospital in Washington, D.C., then the most prestigious medical post open to an African American, but hardly an inviting one. He remained here until 1898, when he resigned after controversies. He wrought many improvements in Freedmen's. He reduced its mortality rate, established its School of Nursing, appointed the first interns,

acquired the first ambulance, and imposed discipline geared to the highest standards of excellence.

Returning to the Provident Hospital, Dr. Williams found a hostile climate engendered by a rival there. He continued to do excellent surgery but resigned in 1912. Thereafter, he did his surgery at St. Luke's Hospital, one of Chicago's largest and wealthiest hospitals, where, as an associate attending surgeon, he was held in high esteem by his white colleagues.

In 1913 Dr. Williams was inducted into the American College of Surgeons as a charter fellow, the first of his race. He had helped organize the National Medical Association in Atlanta, Ga., in 1895 to afford opportunities for improvement to black professionals. In 1900 he began annual visits to Meharry Medical College in Nashville, Tenn., serving without salary for over 25 years as visiting clinical professor of surgery. One writer commented: "He not only taught scientific medicine and surgery by precept and example but encouraged the founding of hospitals and training schools. His greatest pride was that directly or indirectly, he had a hand in the making of most of the outstanding Negro surgeons of the current generation."

Dr. Williams published nine creditable scientific papers. Wilberforce University and Howard University awarded him honorary degrees. He died on Aug. 4, 1931, at Idlewild, Mich. The Daniel Hale Williams Medical Reading Club in Washington, D.C., memorializes him.

Further Reading

Full-length biographical studies of Williams are Helen Buckler, *Daniel Hale Williams: Negro Surgeon* (1968), and Lewis Fenderson, *Daniel Hale Williams: Open Heart Doctor* (1970). A long account of his career is in Herbert M. Morais, *The History of the Negro in Medicine* (1968). Good accounts of his life are in Langston Hughes, *Famous American Negroes* (1954); Jay Saunders Redding, *The Lonesome Road* (1958); and Louis Haber, *Black Pioneers of Science and Invention* (1970). A brief biography is in Wilhelmena S. Robinson, *Historical Negro Biographies* (1968). The general medical background is given in Robert G. Richardson, *Surgery: Old and New Frontiers* (1970). □

Henry Sylvester Williams

The Trinidadian lawyer Henry Sylvester Williams (1869-1911) organized the First Pan-African Conference in London in 1900. He traveled widely to promote pan-African solidarity.

Henry Sylvester Williams was born of ambitious, lower-middle-class parents in the British colony of Trinidad on Feb. 15, 1869. He attended the Normal School in Port-of-Spain and qualified as a primary school teacher at the age of 17. For the next five years he served as a headmaster. In 1891 he went to the United States, where he worked at odd jobs for two years. This was a time when the gains made by black Americans in the

Reconstruction years (1867-1877) were being rapidly lost: blacks were being disfranchised, subjected to a Jim Crow mentality, and virtually reenslaved economically. William's experience in the United States doubtless stimulated his racial consciousness. In 1893 he became a law student at Dalhousie University but did not complete his degree.

In 1896 Williams emigrated to England, settling in London. Here he supported himself as a temperance and thrift lecturer. In 1897 he resumed his study of law at Gray's Inn, passed the bar examination in 1900, and began practice in 1902. In 1898 he married a middle-class English woman, by whom he had several children.

First Pan-African Conference

In London Williams's feelings of racial solidarity were further strengthened by meeting blacks from various parts of the world. He learned from Africans of their exploitation and degradation by Europeans. In 1897 he formed the African Association to publicize injustices against African peoples everywhere and to promote their interests.

To do this more dramatically as well as to foster a sense of unity among all African peoples, Williams convened the First Pan-African Conference in London, July 23-25, 1900, with himself as general secretary. It was attended by some 30 delegates from the United States, Liberia, and Ethiopia, among whom were the African Americans Alexander Walters of the African Methodist Episcopal Zion Church (Williams's chief collaborator) and W. E. B. Du Bois, who was to play a leading role in the five Pan-African Conferences held between 1919 and 1945.

The tone and demands of the conference were moderate. It called for friendly relations between the Caucasian and African races; it appealed to the British government "not [to] overlook the interest and welfare of the native races" in its colonies; and in an address to the "nations of the world," it protested against "denying to over half the world the right of sharing to their utmost ability the opportunities and privileges of modern civilization." The conference formed the Pan-African Association with Williams as honorary secretary, and it was decided to hold a conference every two years. It was this conference which gave currency to the term pan-Africanism.

Proselytizing Pan-Africanism

After the conference Williams remained virtually the sole organizer of the Pan-African Association. In 1901 he visited Trinidad and Jamaica, where he established branches of the Pan-African Association, and the United States, where he propagandized for the pan-African cause primarily at the annual meeting in Philadelphia of the National Afro-American Council, then the leading African American civil rights organization. Williams returned to London that year and published the *Pan-African,* a monthly journal which collapsed after a few issues. Williams did not succeed in organizing a second Pan-African Conference, partly because of shortage of funds—perhaps partly, too, because of doubts of black leaders as to the efficacy of such conferences.

In 1903 Williams visited South Africa. He practiced law in Cape Town and played the role of agitator in his quest to promote African interests against minority white domination. He was regarded as dangerous by the ruling South African whites and was probably forced to leave. Back in London in 1905, he became involved in leftist British politics. In 1906 he won a seat on the St. Marylebone Borough Council, becoming probably the first black elected official in Britain.

Between 1905 and 1907 Williams played host and lawyer to individual Africans as well as to African delegations seeking redresses from the British government. In 1908 he visited Liberia; it is very likely that while there he conferred with Edward Blyden, the outstanding pan-African intellectual. Later that year Williams returned via London to his native Trinidad. He practiced law, lectured on Africa, and was actively connected with the Working Men's Association, one of Trinidad's earliest political organizations. Williams died on March 26, 1911.

Further Reading

There are no studies of Williams. Background studies include Colin Legum, *Pan-Africanism: A Short Political Guide* (1962; rev. ed. 1965), and Joseph L. Anene and Godfrey N. Brown, *Africa in the Nineteenth and Twentieth Centuries* (1966). □

Roger Williams

Roger Williams (ca. 1603-1683), Puritan clergyman in America, founded Providence, R.I. He was the first American spokesman for religious toleration and the separation of church and state.

Roger Williams's views on the relationship of church and state sprang from his religious beliefs. Like his contemporaries, Williams believed that Christ's second coming was imminent and that, in the time remaining, it was a Christian's duty to help gather the most perfect church possible. Williams's search for the spiritually pure congregation eventually led him to a conviction that the world was so deeply sinful that it would not be redeemed until Christ's return. In view of the world's unredeemable state, all a Christian could do was to keep his spiritual life uncontaminated by the world's evil. This view put Williams at odds with the Massachusetts Puritans, who, because they thought their whole society was being redeemed, maintained that civil authority must protect churches.

Born in London, educated at the Charterhouse School and Cambridge, Williams in 1629 became chaplain to Sir William Masham of Essex. That same year he married Mary Barnard. In 1630 Williams and his wife sailed for Massachusetts. Williams's discontent with the Massachusetts Church was quickly evident: he refused to serve as the first minister to the Boston Church because it had not "separated" itself from the spiritual corruption of the Anglican Church. Williams thought of joining the Salem Church, but when the authorities intervened he went to Plymouth. Finding the Plymouth Church too impure, Williams returned to Salem in 1633 as assistant minister.

In 1634 the Salem Church defied the Massachusetts authorities and chose Williams minister. Williams taught that civil authorities could not punish transgressions against the first four commandments of the decalogue, that an oath of loyalty is a religious act, and that the English had no proper title to American land because the English king was in league with antichrist.

Banished to Rhode Island

In 1635, banished from Massachusetts for his teachings, Williams went to Rhode Island, where he founded Providence. He worked as a farmer, Indian trader, and civil magistrate. When visiting the Indians, Williams worked on a dictionary, entitled *A Key into the Language of America* (1643), which he hoped would serve future apostles who, after Christ's return, would travel in the wilderness to convert the Indians. Williams himself did not attempt to convert the Indians. Williams's own search for spiritual perfection made him first a Baptist and, next, a Seeker rejecting adherence to any specific creed. Williams even refused to pray with his wife because he did not consider her fully regenerate. During the Pequod War, Williams did great service to the Massachusetts colony in his negotiations with the Narragansett Indians.

Believing all present societies, Indian and Puritan, to be unredeemable, Williams thought that men's propensity for evil needed tight control. Consequently he helped pass strict laws for Providence. At the same time, he also believed that, since all men are naturally evil, they have the same natural rights and should share land equally. To that end, Williams assisted in setting up a democratic land association.

Williams in England

In 1643 Williams went to England to secure a charter for Providence. The colony was torn by internal strife and threatened by the other New England colonies. With the help of Sir Henry Vane, Williams got the charter in 1644. While in England, Williams published several books and pamphlets. In *Queries of Highest Consideration* (1644), he urged Parliament not to establish a national church, Congregational or Presbyterian. In *Mr. Cottons Letter Lately Printed, Examined and Answered* (1644), he argued for religious toleration. A church, he proclaimed, which in Christ's name persecutes people of different faiths and denies them the right to live in the community, is anti-Christian.

In these, as in all his writings, Williams's arguments for separation of church and state are drawn from his interpretation of the relationship between the Old and New Testaments. The Massachusetts Puritans believed that their churches were the successors to the Jewish temples; the Massachusetts governor was as responsible for the churches as David was for the Temple. Williams, on the other hand, maintained that after Christ's coming the church is spiritual only and must remain apart from the world.

Reuniting the Colony

On his return from England, Williams found that William Coddington had received a land grant from England which split the colony. In 1652 Williams again went to England and got Coddington's land title annulled. In London, Williams continued publishing his books. John Cotton had answered William's 1644 work *The Bloudy Tenent of Persecution* . . . , so, in turn, Williams in *The Bloudy Tenent Yet More Bloudy* (1652) refuted Cotton's views.

Returning to Providence, Williams united the colony and served as its president. In these years Jews and Quakers came to Providence and were granted religious toleration. However, some extreme sects, like the Ranters, were excluded. In 1659 Williams began a bitter but successful struggle against William Harris, who was trying to defraud the Narragansett Indians of their land. In King Philip's War, which he had striven to prevent, Williams served as captain for Providence. Though he granted them toleration, Williams disagreed with the Quakers, and in 1672 he debated with them in Newport. In 1675 Williams published his side of the argument in *George Fox Digg'd out of His Burrowes.* . . . Williams died in providence.

Further Reading

Williams's works are collected in *The Complete Writings* (7 vols., 1963). Biographies are Cyclone Covey, *The Gentle Radical* (1966), and John Garrett, *Roger Williams* (1970). Edmund S. Morgan, *Roger Williams: The Church and the State* (1967), is a good introduction to Williams's thought. An important study

of Williams's idea of history is Perry Miller, *Roger Williams: His Contributions to the American Tradition* (1953). Irwin H. Polishook, *Roger Williams, John Cotton and Religious Freedom: A Controversy in New and Old England* (1967), is a short, valuable introduction to one of the most important debates in American history. □

Shirley Vivien Teresa Brittain Williams

The British politician Shirley Vivien Teresa Brittain Williams (born 1930) was a Labour party minister who later helped to form the Social Democratic party in the 1980s.

Shirley Williams was born on July 27, 1930, in London, the daughter of two eminent socialists, Sir George Catlin and Vera Brittain. She was raised comfortably in the Roman Catholic faith in Cheyne Walk, Chelsea, where her parents entertained T.S. Eliot, Arthur Greenwood, and other celebrities; Jawaharal Nehru bounced her on his knee when she was an infant.

Her father taught political science at Cornell University in New York and at McGill University in Montreal. Catlin was a special adviser to Wendell Willkie in 1940 when Willkie was Republican contender for the presidency of the United States. In British politics he was adviser to the Labour party from 1930 to 1979. He wrote extensively on U.S.-British cooperation. Her mother, Vera Brittain, was a feminist and a pacifist, a nurse in World War I, and a gifted writer between the two world wars.

During World War II, Williams was evacuated to the United States. She lived in St. Paul, Minnesota, and attended the Summit School there from 1939 to 1943. She also was educated at St. Paul's, a private school in London, and at Somerville College in Oxford, England. She joined the Labour party at the age of 16. A member of Britain's Labour League of Youth, she became the first woman to chair the Labour Club in 1948. She worked in factories and at waitressing jobs in England, then pursued graduate studies, focusing on trade unions, at Columbia University in New York. There she met her future husband.

To Parliament

For two years Williams worked as a gossip columnist for the *Daily Mirror,* a London newspaper which then was associated with Labour causes. She then joined the staff of the *Financial Times.* In 1955 she married Professor Bernard Williams, a philosopher and, beginning in 1979, provost of King's College, Cambridge. Their marriage was annulled in 1974. They had a daughter, Rebecca Clair.

Nicknamed the "schoolgirl candidate," Williams ran for Parliament in 1954 and 1955 at Harwich, Essex, but lost. For three years she lived in Africa with her husband, teaching at the University of Ghana in Accra. She returned to England to run for a seat in Parliament from Southampton in

1959; she again failed. Williams became general secretary of the Fabian Society, the nucleus of socialism in England, from 1960 to 1964. Finally she was elected to Parliament at Hitchin, Hertfordshire, in October 1964. That year, after 13 years in opposition, the Labour party returned to power, with Harold Wilson as prime minister.

Wilson gave Williams minor posts in the government. She served in the Ministry of Health (1964-1966), the Ministry of Labor (1966-1967), the Ministry of Education and Science (1967-1969), and the Home Office (1969-1970), where she concentrated on the Northern Ireland issue. The Protestants of Ulster never trusted her because she was a Catholic. During the 1960s she voted against liberalizing divorce laws and against abortion rights.

Williams was a self-confident, ebullient, popular, and decidely unglamorous politician. With a rumpled appearance and unruly hair, she noted, "People like me because I look as crummy as they do."

When Wilson was defeated and the Labour party became the opposition government in 1970, Williams became a member of the party's national executive board. She also became party spokesperson on Social Services, Home Affairs, and Prices and Consumer Protection. In May 1971 she was among 100 Labour members of Parliament who signed a declaration endorsing the Common Market despite criticism of the Common Market by many leftists in the party. Williams vehemently opposed isolationist policies and advocated joining the European Economic Community. Wilson proclaimed that the Labour party was opposed to the Common Market, and Williams threatened to resign from the opposition cabinet unless Labour adopted a "more constructive" stance toward Europe. The Conservative government of Prime Minister Edward Heath brought Britain into the Common Market in July 1972, aided by Williams and other Labour party members. "I am not as much a passionate European, as I am a passionate internationalist . . . with a deep sense of the special and unique nature of Britain," she said in an interview with the *Guardian* on April 15, 1975. "I see staying in Europe as being part of the price of living with reality."

In the election of February 1974 Williams won a new seat in Parliament, representing Hertford and Stevenage, and Wilson regained power. Williams was appointed minister of prices and consumer protection, her first cabinet office. As minister, Williams endorsed voluntary guidelines for combating inflation.

When Wilson, in a surprise move, resigned in March 1976, Williams removed herself from consideration for party leadership. The new leader was James Callaghan, who appointed Williams minister of education and science, where she led a campaign for comprehensive education but cut teacher training positions. She also served as paymaster-general from 1976 to 1979.

Social Democratic Party Founder

In May 1979 the Conservatives under Margaret Thatcher swept the elections, routing Labour. Williams lost her seat in Parliament and turned to a job as a senior research fellow at the Policy Studies Institute in London

until 1985. Within the Labour party, the leftists and the centrists battled. At a Labour party conference in January 1981, the left, led by Anthony Wedgwood Benn, staged a showdown with the leaders of the center: Williams, Roy Jenkins, David Owen, and William Rogers, known as the "Gang of Four." Instead of letting the party's members of Parliament choose the party leader by themselves, Benn moved to give 40 percent of the vote to unions and 30 percent to local party organizations. Benn's faction won platform fights endorsing unilateral disarmament and withdrawal from the Common Market. Williams and others who opposed the platform resigned from the party. With Owen, Rogers, and Jenkins, she formed a new party, the Social Democratic party, in March 1981.

Eight months later she was elected to Parliament at Crosby, a suburb of Liverpool, as a candidate for the Social Democratic party. By the end of 1981 the fledgling Social Democrats had 23 seats in the House of Commons and were gaining popularity. Williams became the party's president in 1982 and remained its leader until 1988.

The Social Democrats quickly went into decline. By 1983 they had only six seats in the House of Commons, and Williams lost her seat at Crosby in 1984. Popular support for the Falklands War against Argentina carried Margaret Thatcher's government and the Conservative party to new heights of popularity, and the SDP never regained its initial momentum.

In 1985 Williams became director of the Turing Institute in Glasgow, Scotland. In 1987 Williams married Richard Neustadt, a Harvard political economist. That same year she ran again for Parliament at Cambridge and lost. In the 1990s she became a member of the House of Lords, a Harvard University professor of electoral politics, and a director of Project Liberty, which assisted developing democracies in eastern and central Europe. She continued to play an active role in trying to bring peace to Northern Ireland.

Further Reading

Williams wrote *Politics is for People* in 1981 and *A Job to Live* in 1985. Information on Williams can be found in *New York Times Magazine* (December 13, 1981); John Newhouse, "Profiles: Breaking the Mold," *New Yorker* (May 21, 1984); Hugh Stephenson, *Claret and Chips: The Rise of the SDP* (London, 1982); *Newsweek* (February 9, 1981; December 7, 1981; and June 6, 1983); and *The Nation* (December 19, 1981). A good analysis of the Social Democratic party is Polly Toynbee, "The Rise and Fall of Britain's Neoliberals" *Washington Monthly* (November 1987). □

Tennessee Williams

Tennessee Williams (1914-1983), dramatist and fiction writer, was one of America's major mid-20th-century playwrights.

Tennessee Williams was born Thomas Lanier Williams in Columbus, Mississippi, on March 26, 1914. His father was a traveling salesman, and for many years the family lived with his mother's parents. When Williams was about 13, they moved to a crowded tenement in St. Louis, Missouri. At the age of 16 he published his first story. The next year he entered the University of Missouri but left before taking a degree. He worked for two years for a shoe company, spent a year at Washington University (where he had his first plays produced), and earned a bachelor of arts degree from the State University of Iowa in 1938, the year he published his first short story under his literary name.

In 1940 the Theatre Guild produced Williams' *Battle of Angels* in Boston. The play was a total failure and was withdrawn after Boston's Watch and Ward Society banned it. Between 1940 and 1945 he lived on grants from the Rockefeller Foundation and the American Academy of Arts and Letters, on income derived from an attempt to write film scripts in Hollywood, and on wages as a waiter-entertainer in Greenwich Village.

With the production of *The Glass Menagerie* Williams' fortunes changed. The play opened in Chicago in December 1944 and in New York in March; it received the New York Drama Critics Circle Award and the Sidney Howard Memorial Award. *You Touched Me!*, written in collaboration with Donald Windham, opened on Broadway in 1945. It was followed by publication of 11 one-act plays, *27 Wagons Full of Cotton* (1946), and two California productions. When *A Streetcar Named Desire* opened in 1947,

New York audiences knew a major playwright had arrived. It won a Pulitzer Prize. The play combines sensuality, melodrama, and lyrical symbolism. A film version was directed by Elia Kazan; their partnership lasted for more than a decade.

Although the plays that followed *Streetcar* never repeated its phenomenal success, they kept Williams's name on theater marquees and films. His novel *The Roman Spring of Mrs. Stone* (1950) and three volumes of short stories brought him an even wider audience. Some writers consider *Summer and Smoke* (1948) Williams's most sensitive play. *The Rose Tattoo* (1951) played to appreciative audiences, *Camino Real* (1953) to confused ones. *Cat on a Hot Tin Roof* (1955) won the New York Drama Critics Circle Award and a Pulitzer Prize.

Baby Doll (an original Williams-Kazan film script, 1956) was followed by the dramas *Orpheus Descending* (1957), *Garden District* (1958; two one-act plays, *Something Unspoken* and *Suddenly Last Summer*), *Sweet Bird of Youth* (1959), *Period of Adjustment* (1960), and *The Night of the Iguana* (1961). With these plays, critics charged Williams with public exorcism of private neuroses, confused symbolism, sexual obsessions, thin characterizations, and violence and corruption for their own sake. *The Milk Train Doesn't Stop Here Anymore* (1963), *The Seven Descents of Myrtle* (1963; also called *Kingdom of Earth*), and *In the Bar of a Tokyo Hotel* (1969) neither exonerated him of these charges nor proved that Williams's remarkable talent had vanished.

Through the 1970s and 1980s, Williams continued to write for the theater, though he was unable to repeat the success of most of his early years. One of his last plays was *Clothes for a Summer Hotel* (1980), based on the American writer F. Scott Fitzgerald and his wife, Zelda.

Two collections of Williams's many one-act plays were published: *27 Wagons Full of Cotton* (1946) and *American Blues* (1948). Williams also wrote fiction, including two novels, *The Roman Spring of Mrs. Stone* (1950) and *Moise and the World of Reason* (1975). Four volumes of short stories were also published. *One Arm and Other Stories* (1948), *Hard Candy* (1954), *The Knightly Quest* (1969), and *Eight Mortal Ladies Possessed* (1974). Nine of his plays were made into films, and he wrote one original screenplay, *Baby Doll* (1956). In his 1975 tell-all novel, *Memoirs,* Williams described his own problems with alcohol and drugs and his homosexuality.

Williams died in New York City, February 25, 1983. In 1995, the United States Post Office commemorated Williams by issuing a special edition stamp in his name as part of their Literary Arts Series.

For several years, literary aficionados have gathered to celebrate the man and his work at The Tennessee Williams Scholars Conference. The annual event, held in conjunction with the Tennessee Williams/New Orleans Literary Festival, features educational, theatrical and literary programs.

Further Reading

There is no uniform edition or omnibus collection of Williams's plays. His mother's reminiscences, Edwina Dakin Williams, *Remember Me to Tom* (1963), and the account of a friend, Gilbert Maxwell, *Tennessee Williams and Friends* (1965), provide biographical data. Taped interviews with various artists who worked with Williams give a multifaceted view in Mike Steen, *A Look at Tennessee Williams* (1969). Accounts of Williams' words were gathered to put together *Memoirs* (1975); *Tennessee Williams' Letters to Donald Windham 1940-65* (1977); Albert J. Devlin, *Conversations with Tennessee Williams* (1986); and *Five O'Clock Angel: Letters of Tennessee Williams to Maris St. Just 1948-1982* (1990).

The best critical studies are Signi Lenea Falk, *Tennessee Williams* (1961); Benjamin Nelson, *Tennessee Williams: The Man and His Work* (1961); Louis Broussard, *American Drama: Contemporary Allegory from Eugene O'Neill to Tennessee Williams* (1962); Francis Donahue, *The Dramatic World of Tennessee Williams* (1964); Gerald Weales, *Tennessee Williams* (1965); and Louis Broussard, *American Drama: Contemporary Allegory from Eugene O'Neill to Tennessee Williams*. □

William Carlos Williams

William Carlos Williams (1883-1963), American writer and pediatrician, developed in his poetry a lucid, vital style that reproduced the characteristic rhythms of American speech.

William Carlos Williams's major work, *Paterson* (1946-1958, published entire 1963), a five-volume impressionistic poem, is an attempt to define the duties of the poet in the context of the American environment. Its appearance firmly established him as a major poet, and his work became greatly influential on the new generation of American poets.

Williams was born on Sept. 17, 1883, in Rutherford, N.J. He was educated in Geneva, Switzerland, and at the University of Pennsylvania. He received his medical degree in 1906 from Pennsylvania, where he met poets Ezra Pound and Hilda Doolittle. After interning for two years in New York hospitals and studying pediatrics at the University of Leipzig, Williams began practicing pediatrics in Rutherford in 1910. He continued his medical career for more than 40 years, writing in his spare time. That his profession allowed little time for study and writing probably accounts for both the unevenness of much of his verse and the naiveté of his poetic theory. He died in Rutherford on March 4, 1963.

Development of the Poet

The lifelong tension in Williams between a romantic poetic sensibility and a confused modernist poetic theory was largely the result of the conflict between the two major influences in his development: his loyalty to Ezra Pound and his devotion to his mother. Pound had actually launched him as a poet in 1912, when he arranged for publication of six poems in the English *Poetry Review* and wrote an encouraging and affectionate introduction to his friend's verse. Williams acknowledged the influence of Pound's teachings (which he never fully understood) in *I Wanted to Write a Poem* (1958). Here Williams wrote, "Before meeting Ezra Pound is like B.C. and A.D." *The Tempers* (1913), Williams's first commercially published volume, was accepted by the publisher primarily through Pound's influence. *Kora in Hell* (1920) was partly inspired by a book Pound had left in Williams's house.

But if it was Pound who shaped Williams's ideas about poetry, it was his mother who shaped the man himself and the verse he actually created. As a result, he consistently uttered contradictory statements and often appeared to deny the poetry written out of his deepest self. If Pound represented "realism" and "science," authority and discipline, and the conscious will, Williams's mother stood for romance, freedom and impulse, and the unconscious springs of the creative miracle itself. A Spanish Jew, Williams's mother seemed out of place in industrial New Jersey. The feelings Williams held for her are evident in his statements in *I Wanted to Write a Poem* about her "ordeal" as a woman and a foreigner, about her interest in art, which became, as he says, his own, and about his feeling that she was a "mythical" figure, a heroic "poetic ideal."

The conflict between the influences of Pound and his mother affected Williams all his life and finally resolved itself into the artistic problem of how to write essentially "romantic" poetry while professing an antiromantic, behavioristic theory of poetics. The conflict came violently to the surface twice in Williams's career. T. S. Eliot's *The Waste Land,* published in 1922, should have been an occasion for rejoicing for Williams, as it was for Pound, because Eliot's masterpiece exemplified the characteristics Pound and Williams had been demanding of contemporary poetry.

Yet for Williams the poem was clearly a shattering experience. Eliot's poem seemed to him, reflecting on it years later in *I Want to Write a Poem,* a "great catastrophe to our letters," a work of genius which by its very brilliance seemed to make unnecessary his own groping experiments in developing a distinctively American poetry written in a native idiom. Overawed by the stylistic brilliance and the learning of Eliot's poem, yet profoundly unsympathetic to its description of modern culture as a "waste land," Williams felt defeated in his effort to create a new sort of poetry rooted in common experience in a specific locality, his "Paterson."

The second trauma involved the awarding of the Bollingen Prize to Pound's *Pisan Cantos* in 1948 while Pound was under indictment for treason for making broadcasts during World War II for the Italian Fascist dictator, Mussolini. Williams's inability to accept an appointment to the chair of poetry at the Library of Congress, because of a stroke, just at the time when Eliot and the other fellows of the Library were voting to grant the prize to Pound, and the resulting congressional controversy over the award, exacerbated Williams's difficulty in reconciling his sincere patriotism with his affection for Pound. His deferred appointment was attacked in Congress as a strengthening of the un-American Ezra Pound "clique" among the fellows; the attacks delayed Williams's recovery. As his wife later wrote, "Coming after the stroke, it was too much; it set him back tragically, kept him from poetry and communication with the world for years."

In many respects Williams's *Autobiography* (1951) was a form of therapy, for within it he was able to exorcise many of his frustrations and resentments. In the end, the shock and painful self-examination resulting from the affair had a salutary effect on his work; his chief poems after this period, *Journey to Love* (1955), "Asphodel, That Greeny Flower," and *Paterson, Book V* (1958), are the most self-assured and fully achieved of his career. He was freed from an excessive dependence on Pound's example, and his mother's influence became increasingly dominant. He did not live to complete the book he planned about her, but his projected *Paterson, Book VI* clearly revealed the essentially romantic sensibility she had nurtured.

Although Williams thought of himself as a "realist," in reaction against what Pound had called the "messy, blurry, sentimentalistic" 19th century, he was actually a sort of modern Walt Whitman. Under Pound's tutelage he had denigrated Whitman, only to reverse himself later when postwar critics demonstrated that it was neither naive to approve Whitman nor unflattering to be said to resemble him. Williams never seemed to realize that Pound himself was much more indebted to Whitman than he ever cared to admit. Over a lifetime of contradictory writing and lecturing, Williams revealed little understanding of *Leaves of Grass,* and it is likely that he read it only superficially.

It was typical of Williams's critical innocence that in the 1940s and 1950s he vehemently continued to expound the modernist poetics first elaborated by Eliot and Pound a generation earlier, seemingly unaware that these theories had long since ceased to be revolutionary and were, in fact, the essence of the academic New Criticism he scorned. Unwittingly, Williams theoretically agreed with the very critics who slighted his work for its romanticism.

Williams's Works

As always, there was a tremendous gap between what Williams intended—"autotelic," "pure," aristocratic poetry exhibiting primarily metrical expertness—and what he actually wrote—Whitmanesque poetry celebrating the native and the local that affirmed the beauty and meaning of the commonplace in American democracy. Williams's best work, from *Al Que Quiere* (1917) on, was characterized by a tension between romantic feeling and the concern to confront the brute facts of reality.

"Gulls," one of the best early poems, suggests that the harshness of the gulls' cries makes a better hymn than those sung in the churches, which outrage "true music." "By the Road to the Contagious Hospital," which Williams intended as a pure imagist poem, actually concludes with the supposedly "neutral" poet affirming the possibility of life even in the urban wasteland. The workmen in "Fine Work with Pitch and Copper" are not machines that react to stimuli but artists who shape and create their own ends.

When Williams tried to "think out" poetry in terms of the imagist theory of the separation between the artist and his material, he usually failed. His greatest poems, such as the late "A Unison," resemble the opposite sort of response, wherein the poem itself becomes a religious celebration of the union of man, nature, life, and reality in the Emersonian tradition.

Wallace Stevens's insightful Preface to Williams's *Collected Poems* (1934), calling him a "romantic," deeply offended the poet, who thought he had been writing "scientific" poetry like his idol, Pound. Yet Stevens's assessment of the real sensibility behind the poetry was penetrating: "He is a romantic poet. This will horrify him. Yet the proof is everywhere." Williams indeed was so horrified that he never allowed the Preface to be reprinted. Randall Jarrell's Introduction to Williams's *Selected Poems* (1949) is still the best short criticism of the poet's work. Ignoring Williams's often contradictory and confused opinions, Jarrell pinpointed the central qualities of the best poems, "their generosity and sympathy, their moral and human attractiveness."

Williams's major work, *Paterson,* begins at the headwaters of the Passaic River in the past and proceeds downstream, both geographically and temporally. *Book IV,* which takes place at the currently polluted mouth of the river, seems an exception to the affirmations of most of his work. But he was committed to using the actual facts of his locale and refused to ignore the decline and degeneration, the blight and perversion that characterized contemporary Paterson. The measure of his commitment to affirmation, however, can be marked in *Book V* and the unfinished *Book VI* of the poem, in which he strove to correct *Book IV's* impression of despair and denial. "Asphodel, That Greeny Flower," one of his last and finest poems, seems completely free of irrelevant imagist baggage; in it Williams stands firm as a prophet of creative personality.

Other volumes of verse by Williams are *Collected Later Poems* (1950), *Collected Earlier Poems* (1951), and *Desert Music* (1954). His essays include the reinterpretations of American history in *In the American Grain* (1925), *Selected Essays* (1954), and *I Wanted to Write a Poem* (1958). His plays include *A Dream of Love* (1948) and *Many Loves* (1950). He also wrote novels: *A Voyage to Pagany* (1928); a triology concerning an American immigrant family, *White Mule* (1937); *In the Money* (1940); and *The Build-up* (1952). The *William Carlos Williams Reader* (1966) brings together whole poems and excerpts from his most important prose.

Further Reading

Williams's *Autobiography* appeared in 1951, and his *Selected Letters* was published in 1957. See also John Malcolm Brinnin, *William Carlos Williams* (1963). Specialized studies include Linda Welsheimer Wagner, *The Poems of William Carlos Williams* (1964) and *The Prose of William Carlos Williams* (1970); J. Hillis Miller, ed., *William Carlos Williams: A Collection of Critical Essays* (1966); and Joel Conarroe, *William Carlos Williams' "Paterson": Language and Landscape* (1970). There are sections on Williams in Randall Jarrell, *Poetry and the Age* (1953), and Hyatt H. Waggoner, *American Poets: From the Puritans to the Present* (1968). ☐

Richard Willstätter

A Nobel Prize winning chemist, Richard Willstätter (1872-1942) studied the chemical composition of chlorophyll and other plant pigments.

A gifted experimentalist, Richard Willstätter's pioneering work on natural products, especially chlorophyll and anthocyanins (plant pigments), was honored with the 1915 Nobel Prize in chemistry. In 1924 Willstätter, who was Jewish, resigned from his position at the University of Munich in protest against the anti-Semitism of some of the faculty. This act of conscience seriously hampered his research activity. In 1939 the anti-Semitic policies of the Third Reich forced him to emigrate to Switzerland, where he spent the remaining few years of his life.

Richard Martin Willstätter was born in Karlsruhe, Germany on August 13, 1872, the second of two sons of Max and Sophie Ulmann Willstätter. Willstätter's father was a textile merchant and his mother's family was in the textile business. Willstätter's education began in the classical Gymnasium in Karlsruhe. When he was eleven years old, his father moved to New York in search of better economic opportunities and to escape the circumscribed life in Karlsruhe; although this separation was meant to be short, it lasted seventeen years. Willstätter's mother took him and his brother to live near her family home in Nürnberg, a change to which Willstätter had difficulty adjusting, in part because of the more overt anti-Semitism he experienced there.

One effect of the move to a new school was that, although receiving good grades in his other subjects, he did poorly in Latin, the most important subject in the gymnasia of the time. A family council decided he should switch to the Realgymnasium and be educated for business instead of a profession. Ironically, it was at this time, stimulated by some home experiments and good teachers, that he decided to become a chemist. In his autobiography, Willstätter observed that excellence in academic subjects caused one to be disliked, while athletic excellence resulted in popularity. He was also attracted to medicine and might have become a physician instead of a chemist, but because of the longer schooling required his mother would not permit him to change. An interest in biological processes remained with him, though, and is evident in the kinds of chemical problems he attacked. Much later, while teaching at Zurich, he still thought of studying physiology and internal medicine, but the death of his wife ended the idea.

In 1890 the eighteen-year-old Willstätter entered the University of Munich and also attended lectures at the Technische Hochschule. In 1893 he began his doctoral studies and was assigned to do his research under Alfred Einhorn on some aspects of the chemistry of cocaine. It was at this time that Adolf von Baeyer, the leading organic chemist in Germany, began to take Willstätter under his wing. Although Willstätter never worked directly for Baeyer, he thought of himself as Baeyer's disciple. Willstätter completed his doctoral work in a year and stayed on doing independent research, becoming a privatdocent, or unsalaried lecturer, in 1896.

In his work with Einhorn, Willstätter had come to suspect that the structure assigned to cocaine by Einhorn and others was incorrect. When he started his independent research, Einhorn forbade him to work on the cocaine problem. Willstätter, with Baeyer's approval, decided to work instead on the closely related chemical tropine, whose structure was suspected to be similar to that of cocaine; once the structure of tropine was known, the structure of cocaine could be easily derived. Willstätter showed that, indeed, the cocaine structure was not what it had been thought to be; for the remainder of his stay at Munich, Einhorn refused to speak to him. In 1902 Willstätter was appointed professor extraordinarius (roughly equivalent to associate professor), although Baeyer thought he should have accepted an industrial position. Baeyer, himself partly Jewish, also recommended that Willstätter be baptized, an act that would have removed the legal barriers he faced as a Jew. This Willstätter refused to consider. During Easter vacation in 1903 Willstätter met the Leser family from Heidelberg, and that summer he and Sophie Leser were married. Their son Ludwig was born in 1904 and their daughter, Margarete, in 1906.

In 1905 Willstätter accepted a call to the Eidgenössische Technische Hochschule in Zurich as professor of chemistry, beginning the most productive phase of his career. While at Munich he had begun an investigation into the chemical nature of chlorophyll, the green pigment in plants that converts light into energy through photosynthesis; at Zurich, he and his students made great strides in understanding this important material. They developed methods for isolating chlorophyll from plant materials without changing it or introducing impurities. Willstätter was then able to prove that the chlorophyll from different plants (he examined over two hundred different kinds) was substantially the same—a mixture of two slightly different compounds, blue-green chlorophyll a and yellow-green chlorophyll b, in a 3 to 1 ratio.

He also showed that magnesium, which had been found in chlorophyll by earlier workers, was not an accidental impurity but an essential component of these chlorophyll molecules, bonded in a way very similar to that in which iron is bonded in hemoglobin, the oxygen-carrying constituent of blood. The later work of others, especially Hans Fischer, in elucidating the detailed structures of the chlorophylls and hemoglobin would not have been possible without the pioneering work of Willstätter and his students. In 1913, Willstätter, in collaboration with his former student and good friend, Arthur Stoll, reviewed the work on chlorophyll in a book, *Untersuchungen über Chlorophyll*. In all, between 1913 and 1919, Willstätter published twenty-five papers in a series on chlorophyll. A preliminary step in the isolation of chlorophyll from plant materials yielded a yellow solution that on further study proved to contain carotenoid pigments. These had been described before, but Willstätter's work marked the beginning of our understanding of these materials that produce the color of tomatoes, carrots, and egg yolk.

In 1908, Willstätter suffered a devastating blow in the death of his wife after an operation for appendicitis had been delayed for thirty-six hours after the appendix had ruptured. He consoled himself with the care of his two children and with his work; in his autobiography he wrote that he took no vacations for the next ten years. During his stay at Zurich, Willstätter also did work on quinones and the mechanism of the oxidation of aniline to aniline black—a process of importance to the dye industry. He also completed a project begun eight years earlier, by synthesizing the chemical cyclooctatetraene and showing that it did not behave as an aromatic compound despite its structural similarities to benzene.

The Kaiser Wilhelm Institutes were founded in 1910 to afford outstanding scientists the chance to do research on problems of their own choosing, free of any teaching obligations. In 1911 Willstätter accepted the position of director of the Kaiser Wilhelm Institute of Chemistry and in 1912 moved into the new building at Berlin-Dahlem. The institute was situated next to the Institute for Physical Chemistry and Electrochemistry, headed by Fritz Haber, and a deep and lasting friendship developed between the two directors.

At Zurich, Willstätter had initiated a study of the pigments of various red and blue flowers, a class of compounds now known as anthocyanins. He began with dried cornflowers, or bachelor's button, because it was winter and they were commercially available. This choice, as it turned out, was not a good one; cornflowers only contained a percent or less of the pigment. In Berlin, Willstätter planted fields of double cornflowers, asters, chrysanthe-

mums, pansies, and dahlias around the Institute and his residence. In these fresh flowers he found a much higher pigment content, up to 33 percent in blue-black pansies. Before World War I brought an end to this line of research, Willstätter published eighteen papers in an anthocyanin series between 1913 and 1916. He showed that the various shades of red and blue in these flowers as well as in cherries, cranberries, roses, plums, elderberries, and poppies all arose mainly from three closely related compounds, cyanidin, pelargonidin, and delphinidin chlorides, and were very dependent on the acidity or alkalinity of the flower. During the first year of the war, most of Willstätter's co-workers went into military service, and the flowers were taken to military hospitals instead of to the laboratory. Willstätter was bitterly disappointed by this interruption and could not bring himself to return to the problem after the war.

In 1915 Haber, who was in charge of Germany's chemical warfare work, asked Willstätter's assistance in developing the chemical absorption unit for a gas mask that would protect against chlorine and phosgene (a severe respiratory irritant). In five weeks, Willstätter came up with a canister containing activated charcoal and hexamethylenetetramine (also called urotropin). The use of charcoal was not new, but the use of hexamethylenetetramine was. When asked after the war how he had come to try so unusual a compound, he said that the idea had just popped into his head. For this work he received an Iron Cross, Second Class. He was also involved in an industrial research project with Friedrich Bergius on the hydrolysis of cellulose with hydrochloric acid to give dextrose, which could then be fermented to produce alcohol. The process, which was only perfected later, is now known as the Bergius-Willstätter process.

In the spring of 1915 Willstätter's ten-year-old son, Ludwig, died suddenly, apparently from diabetes. Willstätter wrote that his memory of the months following was blurred. Ironically, in November, while engaged in the work on gas masks, Willstätter learned that he had been awarded the 1915 Nobel Prize in chemistry in recognition of his work on chlorophylls and anthocyanins. Because of wartime conditions he did not travel to Stockholm to receive the prize until 1920, when a ceremony was held for a group of those who had been honored during the war. Willstätter made the trip in the company of fellow German awardees Max Planck, Fritz Haber, Max von Laue, and Johannes Stark.

An offer of a full professorship to succeed Baeyer at Munich also came in 1915. This offer, recommended by Baeyer, was precipitated by an offer to succeed Otto Wallach, a pioneer in natural product chemistry, at Göttingen. Willstätter maintained that left to his own inclinations, he would have preferred Göttingen, because a medium-sized university would provide more contact with colleagues and greater interaction with different disciplines than was possible at large institutions. However, he accepted the appointment as professor and director of the state chemical laboratory in Munich and moved there in the spring of 1916.

He made two major demands before accepting the offer: that the old institute building be remodeled and a large addition to the chemical institute be built housing laboratories and a large lecture hall, and that a full professorship in physical chemistry be established. The first of these was contrary to the advice that the physical chemist Walther Nernst gave him before he left Berlin, "Don't ever build!" In fact, the construction, delayed by the war and post-armistice turmoil in Munich, was not completed until the spring of 1920.

At Munich, as before, Willstätter experienced the anti-Semitism that had troubled him during his earlier residence, and that finally brought about his resignation in 1924. The final straw was the refusal of the faculty to appoint the noted geochemist Victor Goldschmidt of Oslo, Norway, to succeed the mineralogist Paul von Groth, who had himself named Goldschmidt as the only one who could take his place. The sole reason for the refusal was that Goldschmidt was Jewish. When Willstätter's resignation became known, students and faculty joined in expressions of respect and confidence, urging him to reconsider. Nonetheless, he remained only for the time needed to see his students finish their research and to install Heinrich Wieland in his place. He received offers of positions at universities and in industry in Germany and abroad, but he declined all of them, finally leaving the university in September 1925 never to return.

Some of Willstätter's assistants continued work at the University, and in 1928 Wieland made room in what had been Willstätter's private laboratory for Willstätter's private assistant, Margarete Rohdewald, one of his former students. From 1929 until 1938 she collaborated with him in a series of eighteen papers on various aspects of enzyme research. It was an odd collaboration, conducted almost entirely over the telephone; Willstätter never saw her at work in the laboratory.

During the few years at Munich before his resignation, Willstätter began to concentrate his research on the study of enzymes. He had first encountered these biological catalysts in his early work on chlorophyll. Now he worked to develop methods for their separation and purification. His method for separation was to adsorb the materials on alumina or silica gel and then to wash them off using solutions of varying acidity, among other solvents. In this connection, Willstätter carried out a systematic study (comprised of nine papers) of hydrates and hydrogels during which he, with his assistants Heinrich Kraut and K. Lobinger, was able to show that aluminum hydroxide, silicic acid, ferric hydroxide, and stannic hydroxide do actually exist in solution and are not colloidal sols (dispersions of small solid particles in solution) of the corresponding oxides. Willstätter reported that this foray of an organic chemist into inorganic chemistry was not well received by inorganic chemists.

The enzyme studies were not as successful, in part because Willstätter thought that enzymes were relatively small molecules absorbed on a protein or some other giant (polymer) molecule. The modern view, of course, is that enzymes are themselves proteins. Though Willstätter's chemical intuition failed him, there were positive results—for example, the enzymatic reduction of chloral and bromal

resulted in the formation of trichloroethanol, a sedative (Voluntal), and tribromoethanol, an anesthetic (Avertin).

In 1938 the situation for Jews in Germany was becoming impossible. On a visit to Switzerland, Stoll tried to persuade Willstätter to stay, but he insisted on returning to Munich. There, after some trouble with the Gestapo, he was ordered to leave the country. After much red tape, which entailed the confiscation of much of his property, papers, and art collection, and an abortive attempt to leave unofficially, he entered Switzerland in March 1939 to stay for a while with Stoll and then to settle in the Villa Eremitaggio in Muralto. There he wrote his autobiography to pass the time. On August 3, 1942, Willstätter died of cardiac failure in his sleep. Among the honors received by Willstätter in addition to the Nobel prize were honorary membership in the American Chemical Society (1927), honorary fellowship in the Chemical Society (1927), the Willard Gibbs Medal for distinguished achievement in science from the Chicago Section of the American Chemical Society (1933), and election as foreign member of the Royal Society (1933). Willstätter's obituary by Sir Robert Robinson in *Obituary Notices of Fellows of the Royal Society,* has an eleven page bibliography, probably incomplete, listing over three hundred papers between 1893 and 1940.

Further Reading

Dictionary of Scientific Biography, Volume 14, Scribner, 1976, pp. 411–412.
Obituary Notices of Fellows of the Royal Society, Volume 8, Morrison & Gibb, 1954, pp. 609–634.
Partington, J. R., *A History of Chemistry,* Macmillan, 1964, pp. 860–866.
Huisgen, Rolf, "Richard Willstätter," in *Journal of Chemical Education,* Volume 38, number 1, 1961, pp. 10–15.
Robinson, Robert, "Willstätter Memorial Lecture," in *Journal of the Chemical Society,* 1953, pp. 1012–1026. □

David Wilmot

As the author of the Wilmot Proviso, David Wilmot (1814-1868), U.S. congressman, initiated the legislative effort to prohibit the expansion of slavery.

David Wilmot, the son of a prosperous merchant, was born in Bethany, Pa., on Jan. 20, 1814. He studied law, was admitted to the Pennsylvania bar in 1834, and opened a practice in Towanda, Pa., in 1836, shortly after his marriage. He became more interested in politics than in law. An active and ardent Jacksonian Democrat, noted for his extemporaneous oratorical skills, he played a major role in Pennsylvania's Democratic state convention in 1844 and won a congressional seat, which he held from 1845 to 1851.

Initially Wilmot loyally supported the measures of James K. Polk's administration, although he had strongly supported Polk's opponent, Martin Van Buren, in the 1844 Democratic National Convention. During the Mexican

War, however, Wilmot and other Northern and Western Democrats became convinced that Polk's policies would give the Southern wing of the party permanent dominance. Proslavery political power had already been enhanced by the acquisition of Texas. Northern and Western Democrats feared its further growth through the potential acquisition of more slave territory from Mexico.

Thus, when Polk requested funds to conduct peace negotiations with Mexico in 1846, Wilmot attached to the appropriations bill his famous proviso that slavery be absolutely prohibited in any territory acquired through those negotiations. Wilmot's measure passed in the House of Representatives but was blocked in the Senate. The Southern congressional bloc, led by John C. Calhoun, immediately countered with resolutions stating that property rights ("property" including slaves) were guaranteed by the Constitution and had to be fully protected in all Federal territories.

The principles stated in this debate permanently polarized proslavery and antislavery factions. Attempts at reconciliation—in the Compromise of 1850 and the 1854 Kansas-Nebraska Act—only temporarily averted the confrontation. Ultimately the controversy over slavery in the territories split the nation's political parties asunder. When Abraham Lincoln, pledging unalterable opposition to any future extension of slavery in the United States, was elected in 1860, the slave states refused to accept their political defeat, and the stage was set for the Civil War.

Wilmot made no further notable political contributions. He held a judgeship from 1851 until 1861 and served in the U.S. Senate from 1861 to 1863. Lincoln appointed him to a Federal judgeship which he retained until his death on March 16, 1868, in Towanda.

Further Reading

Charles B. Going, *David Wilmot: Free-Soiler* (1924; new ed. 1966), is a thorough and competent biography. A lengthy discussion of the Wilmot Proviso is in Allen Nevins, *Ordeal of the Union* (2 vols., 1947). ☐

Alexander Wilson

The 13-volume *American Ornithology* of Alexander Wilson (1766-1813), Scottish-American ornithologist and poet, was the first great comprehensive descriptive and illustrated work on the birds of the eastern United States.

Alexander Wilson was born on July 6, 1766, in Paisley, Scotland, into a large, poor family. Apprenticed at the age of 13 in the weaving trade, he spent ten years as a weaver. He then began tramping about Scotland as a peddler and writing dialect poems, which he published in *Poems* (1790). Discouraged by poverty and by political persecution because of some satires he wrote, he emigrated to America in 1794.

Though entirely self-educated, Wilson supported himself as a teacher around Philadelphia. The turning point in his life came in 1802, when he took charge of a school at Gray's Ferry, near the home and gardens of William Bartram, the Philadelphia naturalist. Bartram helped channel Wilson's natural love of birds and the outdoors into systematic scientific endeavors. Wilson became convinced that no single work on American birds was free from defect, and he decided to produce a comprehensive illustrated work on the birds of the eastern United States.

Wilson spent 10 years gathering specimens and materials for his classic work, *American Ornithology;* the first seven volumes were published in 1808-1813, the others posthumously. In 1807 he secured a position as assistant editor with a Philadelphia publisher, which relieved him of the drudgery of teaching and undoubtedly made possible the completion of his massive work. In 1808, to assure publication of his masterpiece, Wilson traveled all over the eastern United States in search of 250 subscribers.

American Ornithology is noted for the elegance of the essays on individual birds and for the excellent illustrations, which Wilson did himself. Although skilled as an artist, he needed the help of Alexander Lawson to translate his drawings into the plates from which the illustrations were printed. *American Ornithology* was acclaimed by both American and European scientists as the best work on American birds, and it went through two subsequent editions.

Wilson's health broke down while he was preparing the eighth volume of *American Ornithology* for publication, and he died in Philadelphia on Aug. 23, 1813. His friend George Ord completed the eighth and ninth volumes from Wilson's manuscript notes and saw them through publication in 1814. Charles Lucien Bonaparte published the four final volumes in 1825-1833.

Further Reading

The best biography of Wilson is Robert Cantwell, *Alexander Wilson, Naturalist and Pioneer* (1961), which replaces the older work by James S. Wilson, *Alexander Wilson, Poet-Naturalist* (1906). Some general background can be found in William Dunlap, *A History of the Rise and Progress of the Arts of Design in the United States* (1834; rev. ed. 1965).

Additional Sources

Wilson, Alexander, *The life and letters of Alexander Wilson,* Philadelphia: American Philosophical Society, 1983. □

August Wilson

Two-time Pulitzer Prize-winning American playwright August Wilson (Frederick August Kittell; born 1945) embarked upon a mission to write a cycle of ten plays addressing central issues that have impacted African Americans in each decade of the 20th

century. **The first five evolve from the playwright's own commentary upon illconceived, ill-advised, yet sometimes unavoidable choices made by past generations of African Americans and their too frequent negative consequences.**

Christened Frederick August Kittell was born in 1945 and later changed his name to August Wilson. He was the namesake of an irresponsible German baker. His father spent little time with his family in their two-room apartment in Pittsburgh's Hill District where Wilson, his mother, and five brothers and sisters survived on public assistance and earnings from her janitorial job. Wilson's move to adopt the maiden name of his African American mother, Daisy Wilson, in the 1970s was not just a means of disavowing his estranged white father. His decision to call himself August Wilson also represented a significant rite of passage marking both his discovery and celebration of ties with Africa. His identification with his mother's roots later became the driving force behind young Wilson's fascination with the language and culture of African Americans.

Against the pleas of his mother, Wilson gave up on formal education in the ninth grade. Memories of former years spent in the Pittsburgh public school system included a devastating accusation by one of his teachers that he was not the original author of a term paper that he had, in fact, written on Napoleon Bonaparte. Offended by the affront to his integrity and bored with the stifling regimentation of

Pittsburgh's schools, Wilson turned to the city's tobacco shops, barber shops, and street corners for schooling of a different sort. While mingling among fellow African American residents of the working-class neighborhood where he grew up listening to their uncensored language, Wilson developed an intimate knowledge of their lifestyles. His time spent in this environment would later serve him well in creating credible characters for his cycle of plays depicting the African American experience.

But Pittsburgh's streets and shops did not satisfy Wilson's appetite for knowledge about African Americans. He was drawn to the city's public libraries where he poured over the works of Ralph Ellison, Richard Wright, Langston Hughes, and other African American writers. A reader since the age of four, Wilson had no trouble comprehending these works that gave direction to the quest for his own racial consciousness.

From Poet to Playwright

After finally moving out of his mother's house in 1965, Wilson found lodging at a nearby rooming house, took a job as a short-order cook, and tried his hand at verse. Armed with a $20 typewriter he purchased with money from his sister Freda, Wilson tried desperately to become a successful poet and writer. This newfound freedom allowed Wilson to mingle with the Bohemian set. He learned their language and their ideals, emerging as a self-proclaimed Dylan Thomas. During this time he also identified with the cultural nationalists such as Amiri Baraka, (then known as LeRoi Jones), who argued for heightened racial consciousness. His initiation into African American aestheticism culminated in a heightened awareness of the importance of the blues, Bessie Smith, Ma Rainey, and writers of the Harlem Renaissance.

In the late 1960s an interest in Malcolm X led him to a total acknowledgement of African American culture as his own. Renouncing his white father, moving out from his mother's house, and living among day to day reminders of this culture cleared the way for Wilson to find out more about his African American ancestors' trek from the fields of North Carolina to the cramped urban shelters of Pittsburgh. What followed this phase of cultural enlightenment in Wilson's life were organized efforts to raise consciousness among Pittsburgh natives. With such an agenda, Wilson co-founded, with director Rob Penny, Pittsburgh's Black Horizons Theater in 1968.

Although Wilson chose to imitate the style of flamboyant British poet Dylan Thomas during an early stage in his evolution into an artist, he soon realized that his African American heritage, grounded in the blues tradition, was at odds with the alien persona he had chosen to idolize. Serendipity was largely responsible for his discovery of the tremendous role music, in particular the blues, played in his writing. After buying a three-dollar record player that only played 78s, he discovered a record store that proved to be a veritable gold mine of the records that were no longer in circulation. Here he found a copy of Bessie Smith's "Nobody in Town Can Bake a Sweet Jelly Roll Like Mine" and was so moved by its lyrics that he played it repeatedly.

He later recalled, "I'd never heard of Bessie Smith. I listened to it twenty-two times, and I became aware that this stuff was my own. Patti Page, Frank Sinatra—they weren't me. This was me. The music became the wellspring of my work. I took the stuff and ran with it."

It took numerous rejection slips from magazines and several uninspired poetry readings to finally dissuade the would-be poet and nudge him in the direction of the theater. His conversion from poet to playwright was coerced by a supportive friend, Claude Purdy. In 1977 Wilson's poetry reading in Pittsburgh about a character named Black Bart so impressed Purdy that he encouraged Wilson to turn the material into a play. After much complaining that he could not write a play, Wilson sat down to complete the work in one week (*Black Bart and the Sacred Hills* [1981]).

In 1982 Lloyd Richards—artistic director of the Eugene O'Neill Theater in Waterford, Connecticut, dean of Yale's School of Drama, and director of the Yale Repertory Theater—discovered that among the hundreds of scripts sent to him was Wilson's *Ma Rainey's Black Bottom*. Although Richards admitted that the play had structural problems, he realized that, aside from these weaknesses, it evidenced an incredibly gifted talent. Over the next eight years Wilson and Richards formed a close alliance. Some have described their unique relationship with words like "avuncular," "paternal," or simply "compatible." At any rate, the two men blended their playwriting and directing talents to produce a string of successful plays. Wilson wrote the plays while Richards directed and polished them in workshop environments such as the Yale Repertory Theater and various regional theaters throughout the United States. Beginning with the initial Broadway success of *Ma Rainey's Black Bottom* in 1984, the two men collaborated successfully on four more of Wilson's plays: *Fences, Joe Turner's Come and Gone, The Piano Lesson,* and *Two Trains Running.* During his collaboration with Richards, all of Wilson's works took similar routes, preliminary staging at the O'Neill Theater Center followed by presentations at the Yale Repertory Theater and other resident non-profit theaters and an eventual Broadway production.

Chronicles of African American History

Gaining confidence as a playwright from close associations with important contacts such as directors Purdy and Richards, Wilson committed himself to writing a series of plays addressing central issues that have impacted African Americans in each decade of the 20th century. Although he initially did not set out to write a history of his people, he rather accidentally realized a pattern of sorts developing in his early works; he had written plays that addressed issues peculiar to 1911, 1927, 1941, 1957, and 1971. The idea of writing one play per decade pleased Wilson, for once he discerned a pattern, he then was able to focus his playwriting skills on what he felt were the most important issues confronting African Americans each decade and then committed himself to writing ten plays emphasizing these issues.

Wilson's first Broadway success, *Ma Rainey's Black Bottom* (1984), was based upon an imagined day in the life of Gertrude Pridgett "Ma" Rainey, often called the "Mother of the Blues.'' The play focuses upon rampant greed, insensitivity, and racism in the 1920s recording business. The victims of the time period are typified by Ma Rainey and her band of talented yet frustrated musicians. His second play to reach Broadway, *Fences* (1985), earned him his first Pulitzer Prize. It portrays the frustration of a former African American League baseball player in the industrial North of the 1950s. In *Joe Turner's Come and Gone* (1986), Wilson concentrated upon the cultural fragmentation as well as the emotional and physical effects of the accompanying displacement of newly freed African Americans following the Civil War.

The Piano Lesson (1987) earned Wilson a second Pulitzer Prize in the spring of 1990. Central to this play's conflict is an old piano, which simultaneously functions as an emblem of both African folk tradition and American capitalism. The pictorial history carved into its surface by the great-grandfather of the currently embattled siblings, Berneice and Boy Willie, appreciates both its monetary and sentimental values. Berneice wants to preserve it as a family heirloom, while Boy Willie wants to sell it to afford a piece of land. Wilson's chronicle of the 1960s, *Two Trains Running,* debuted at the Yale Repertory Theater in March 1990 and was making its way through various regional theaters on its way to an almost certain Broadway finale. Set in 1968 in a small restaurant in an African American section of Pittsburgh (apparently its Hill District), Wilson's play tells the story of neighbors sorting out problems, complaining about injustices, loving, fighting, and communing.

Wilson's *Seven Guitars* hit Broadway in 1995, reuniting him with longtime collaborator Richards. The story, set in Pittsburgh in the 1940s, tells the story of Floyd ''Schoolboy'' Barton, who died before his career as a blues guitarist could take off. The *San Diego Sun* reviewed the show as containing ''rich, casually revealing language.'' The Broadway version featured Keith David, famous for his role in *Jelly's Last Jam.*

''All the ideas and attitudes of my characters come straight out of the blues,'' Wilson said, during an interview with *People* magazine. ''I look behind the lyrics.'' *Seven Guitars* is no exception.

Along with his two Pulitzers, Wilson received the Black Filmakers Hall of Fame Award in 1991. In 1992 he earned the Antoinette Perry Award nomination for best play, as well as the American Theatre Critics' Association Award, for *Two Trains Running.* He also received the Clarence Muse Award in 1992.

Wilson moved to Seattle in 1990 with his third wife, Constanza Romero, a costume designer who worked on *The Piano Lesson* with him. Wilson's only daughter, Sakina Ansari, found her career as a social worker in Baltimore.

Further Reading

Because August Wilson is relatively new to the literary world, a critical study of his work remains to be done. However, several excellent sources are available in the form of interviews, feature articles, and theater reviews. For detailed biographical information consult Chip Brown's ''The Light in August'' in *Esquire* (April 1989). For information of his plays and his aesthetics, see Bill Moyers' *A World of Ideas: Conversations with Thoughtful Men and Women about American Life Today and the Ideas Shaping Our Future* (1989) and David Savran's *In Their Own Words: Contemporary American Playwrights* (1988). Magazine feature articles include Nick Charles' ''August Wilson: Stages of Black America,'' in *Emerge* (April 1990); Hillary DeVries' ''A Song in Search of Itself: August Wilson Is a Chronicler of Black America's Recent Past,'' in *American Theater* (January 1987); and Ishmael Reed's ''A Shy Genius Transforms American Theater,'' in *Connoisseur* 217 (March 1987). □

Charles Erwin Wilson

Charles Erwin Wilson (1890-1961), engineer, businessman, and secretary of defense during the Eisenhower administration, is popularly remembered for his remark comparing the welfare of the United States with that of General Motors Corporation.

Charles E. Wilson was born in Minerva, Ohio, on July 18, 1890. At the age of four Wilson moved with his family to Mineral City, Ohio. There he struck up a boyhood friendship with two railroad engineers who frequently took Wilson on the local railroad and showed him how the new Westinghouse air-braking system worked. Fascinated with mechanics, he enrolled at the Carnegie Institute of Technology and completed the four-year program in three years, graduating near the top of his class.

After graduation, Wilson employed his engineering skills first at Westinghouse Electric and then at Remy Electric, a subsidiary of General Motors. At Remy he rose from chief engineer to president and oversaw the company's merger in 1926 with Delco. As head of Delco-Remy of Anderson, Indiana, Wilson and his 12,000 employees produced the ignition systems for General Motors automobiles.

Promoted by General Motors to corporate headquarters in Detroit, Wilson again rose rapidly and became president of the mammoth company in 1941. During World War II Wilson helped transform General Motors into the nation's chief producer of war materiel. Between 1941 and 1945 the company built one-fourth of U.S. tanks, armored cars, and airplane engines and one-half of the machine guns and carbines.

Wilson's industrial management skills were also evident in employee relations. During the 1930s auto workers conducted a series of strikes against General Motors because the company refused to recognize their right to organize unions and bargain collectively. Wilson, however, negotiated labor peace with the United Auto Workers union and its leader, Walter Reuther. During contract negotiations in 1948 and 1950 General Motors agreed to tie workers' salaries to the rate of inflation, the so-called ''escalator clause,'' to award raises for increased worker productivity; and to establish a company-wide pension plan. Thereafter, other industrial corporations would negotiate labor con-

tracts with features similar to those that Wilson and Reuther designed.

Impressed by Wilson's managerial abilities, President-elect Dwight Eisenhower asked Wilson in late 1952 to take charge of the government's largest agency, the Department of Defense. But compared to his business career, Wilson's tenure as secretary of defense (1953-1957) was controversial. A blunt, outspoken man, Wilson seemed uncomfortable in a political world. His public comments left the impression that he was an insensitive tycoon. Wilson's most difficult moment came in 1953 when, during congressional testimony, he declared: "What was good for our country was good for General Motors and vice versa."

As secretary of defense, Wilson played a limited role in shaping the nation's military policies. In view of his vast military experience, President Eisenhower decided that he would set defense policies. Eisenhower expected Secretary Wilson to carry out his detailed instructions and to run his department in an efficient and business-like manner.

As commander-in-chief, Eisenhower chose to streamline the Department of Defense's budget by reducing manpower and basing the nation's defense on atomic weaponry, a policy tagged "more bang for the buck." Critics within the Pentagon and Congress charged that these policies left the nation incapable of waging conventional and guerrilla wars. Because he had to defend these policies in public, Wilson was often blamed for them. Eisenhower, on the other hand, complained to aides that Wilson should have quelled dissent within the Pentagon.

Secretary Wilson resigned from Eisenhower's Cabinet in late 1957. He returned to the board of directors of General Motors and also served as chair of a civil rights commission in Michigan. Charles E. Wilson died in his sleep of a coronary thrombosis on September 26, 1961, at his plantation near Norwood, Louisiana.

Further Reading

There is no complete biography of Wilson. For Wilson's background and a favorable assessment of his career as secretary of defense, see E. Bruce Geelhoed, *Charles E. Wilson and Controversy at the Pentagon* (1979). Fred I. Greenstein, in his *The Hidden-Hand Presidency* (1982), analyzes President Eisenhower's relationship with his Cabinet. Stephen E. Ambrose's *Eisenhower: The President* (1984) is a solid account of the Eisenhower administration. Ambrose argues that the president was disappointed with Wilson's work. Wilson's private papers are located at Anderson College in Anderson, Indiana. □

Charles Thomson Rees Wilson

The Scottish physicist Charles Thomson Rees Wilson (1869-1959) was the inventor and developer of the Wilson cloud chamber.

Charles Wilson was born on Feb. 14, 1869, in Glencorse near Edinburgh. He received his first undergraduate training at Owens College, now part of the University of Manchester, and from there, at the age of 19, he went to Cambridge University with the realization that physics and not medicine was to be his life's vocation.

As Wilson himself disclosed it, two experiences determined the direction and ultimate fortunes of his interest in physics. One was his few weeks' stay in 1894 at the observatory on the top of Ben Nevis, the highest Scottish mountain. The magnificent optical phenomena observable in the interplay of sunshine, mist, and clouds "greatly excited my interest and made me wish to imitate them in the laboratory." The other experience consisted in his being exposed to an electric storm on the summit of Carn Mor Dearg in 1895. From this came Wilson's strong interest in atmospheric electricity, while the first experience inspired his efforts culminating in the construction of the first cloud chamber.

In the beginning of 1895 Wilson concluded that even after the removal of all dust particles, droplets still appeared whenever a volume of moist air was suddenly expanded. He attributed this to a residual conductivity in the air. His reasoning was fully verified a year later when his primitive cloud chamber was exposed to the newly discovered x-ray radiation. In 1904 he also proved that these droplets could be removed from the chamber by an electric field. Not until 1910, however, did he conceive the idea of making visible and of photographing the path of an ionizing particle. The

Further Reading

The most authoritative account of Wilson's life and work is the lengthy essay by P. M. S. Blackett in *Biographical Memoirs of Fellows of the Royal Society* (1960). For background see William Dampier, *A History of Science* (1949), and Mitchell Wilson, *American Science and Invention* (1954). □

Edmund Wilson

The American critic Edmund Wilson (1895-1972) pursued an independent course that secured him respect and eminence.

Edmund Wilson was born in Red Bank, N.J., on May 8, 1895, the son of a railroad lawyer. He attended Princeton University (1912-1916), where he was editor of the *Nassau Literary Magazine* and a friend of writers John Peale Bishop and F. Scott Fitzgerald. With Bishop, he was later to publish a miscellany, *The Undertaker's Garland* (1922); after Fitzgerald's death, Wilson compiled in *The Crack-up* (1945) the tragic story of the disaster which overtook that novelist.

After taking a bachelor of arts degree, Wilson was briefly a reporter for the *New York Sun*. Drawn into World War I, he served in a French hospital and in United States intelligence. He then became managing editor of *Vanity Fair*. The first of his four marriages took place in 1923. He was, in turn, book review editor and associate editor of the *New Republic* (1926-1931); later he was a book reviewer for the *New Yorker* (1944-1948).

Despite his very great endowment as a critic, Wilson never settled comfortably into that role and tried his hand repeatedly at other things. *Discordant Encounters* (1926) is a volume of "dialogues and plays." *Five Plays* (1954) and other works are theatrical efforts. *I Thought of Daisy* (1929) and *Memoirs of Hecate County* (1946), the latter banned as pornographic, are fiction. *Poets, Farewell!* (1929) is a second volume of verse. It is hard to classify *The American Jitters* (1932), *Europe without Baedeker* (1947), *The Scrolls from the Dead Sea* (1955), and *Apologies to the Iroquois* (1959) as anything but journalism, albeit journalism of a high order. Marked by the influence of Karl Marx, whether it be criticism or journalism, Wilson's writing shows a strong social consciousness.

Wilson's reputation, however, rests solidly on his critical works: *Axel's Castle* (1931), *The Triple Thinkers* (1938), *To the Finland Station* (1940), *The Wound and the Bow* (1941), *The Boys in the Back Room* (1941), *Classics and Commercials* (1950), *The Shores of Light* (1952), and individual essays collected in miscellánies. The encompassing and organizing power of his mind, his ability to state with exceptional clarity, his range of learning, and his sensibility are brilliantly displayed in these volumes. He opened new perspectives on novelists Henry James, Rudyard Kipling, Edith Wharton, and Charles Dickens.

chamber he designed for that purpose was simplicity itself but rested on many years of painstaking effort. It was a flat cylindrical vessel, 16.5 centimeters in diameter and 3.4 centimeters deep, with a fixed glass roof, and a glass floor that could be rapidly moved downward by a piston into an evacuated vessel.

For almost 20 years Wilson's design remained the standard form of cloud chamber by which he took his famous series of photographs of ionization tracks in 1911 and 1921-1922 respectively. The analysis of those tracks proved to be an invaluable tool for all early investigators of nuclear phenomena. Wilson himself provided the experimental evidence for Arthur Compton's theory that in x-ray scattering, the recoil electron takes up the momentum of the quantum of radiation. Fittingly enough, the two shared the Nobel Prize in physics in 1927. It was again the cloud chamber that revealed the existence of positrons and made possible the visual demonstration of "pair creation" and "annihilation" of electrons and positrons.

Upon his retirement from the Jacksonian chair at Cambridge (1925-1934) Wilson took up residence in the village of Carlops near Edinburgh. There he completed his final great study of thundercloud electricity, submitting the manuscript to the Royal Society in 1956, at the age of 87. An indomitable energy and a zest for life were the chief characteristics of Wilson, who took to airplanes for the first time at the age of 86 to observe atmospheric phenomena. He was also possibly the most serene and unassuming among the great scientists of his time. He died at Carlops on Nov. 15, 1959.

On June 13, 1972, Wilson died at his home in Talcottville, N.Y. The house was the setting of his last work: *Upstate: Records and Recollections of Northern New York* (1971).

Further Reading

Wilson's autobiographical writings are *A Piece of My Mind: Reflections at Sixty* (1956), *A Prelude: Landscapes, Characters and Conversations from the Earlier Years of My Life* (1967), and *Upstate* (1971). Paul Sherman, *Edmund Wilson: A Study of Literary Vocation in Our Time* (1965), and Warner Berthoff, *Edmund Wilson* (1968), are surveys of Wilson's life and work. An important new book is Leonard Kriegel, *Edmund Wilson* (1971). Appreciative assessments are in Lionel Trilling, *A Gathering of Fugitives* (1955), and Delmore Schwartz, *Selected Essays of Delmore Schwartz,* edited by Donald A. Dike (1971).

Additional Sources

Costa, Richard Hauer, *Edmund Wilson, our neighbor from Talcottville,* Syracuse, N.Y.: Syracuse University Press, 1980.

French, Philip, *Three honest men: Edmund Wilson, F. R. Leavis, Lionel Trilling: a critical mosaic,* Manchester: Carcanet New Press, 1980.

Meyers, Jeffrey, *Edmund Wilson: a biography,* Boston: Houghton Mifflin, 1995. □

Edward Osborne Wilson

The American biologist Edward O. Wilson (born 1929) was a leading authority on ants and social insects and an influential theorist of the biological basis of social behavior. He promoted the controversial discipline of sociobiology.

Born June 10, 1929, in Birmingham, Alabama, to Inez (Freeman) and Edward Osborne Wilson, Edward O. Wilson became a naturalist at an early age, after a fishing accident damaged his right eye and he learned to examine insects closely with his left eye. Growing up in Alabama, Florida, Georgia, and Washington, D.C., he collected insects and decided to specialize in ants even before entering the University of Alabama. While still in college, in 1949 he published his first paper on fire ants. He continued research on these insects at the Alabama Department of Conservation and earned his master's degree in science in 1950 at the University of Alabama. After a year at the University of Tennessee, he entered graduate study at Harvard University.

Wilson's research on ants at Harvard involved him in theories of evolution and classification. He collaborated with William L. Brown on two influential papers on the field of new systematics, the attempt to classify species based on evolutionary theory. The first paper in 1953 critiqued the category of subspecies. In 1956 they proposed the concept of character displacement, by which closely related species diverge genetically when they come into competition. Wilson's Ph.D. from Harvard, granted in 1955, was based on work dealing with the taxonomy and ecology of ants.

In 1955 he married Irene Kelley. They had one daughter. After serving as a junior fellow, Wilson was appointed in 1956 to the Harvard faculty, where he remained through his career. Beginning in 1973 he was curator of entomology at the university's Museum of Comparative Zoology.

"Dr. Ant"

Wilson's graduate work included research in the American tropics, Australia, and the South Pacific. His studies of native ants soon made him the world's foremost authority on these insects and he gained the nickname "Dr. Ant." In the late 1950s he proposed a "taxon cycle," later found also among birds and other insects, to explain how Melanesian ants adapted to poor habitats by colonizing new places and splitting into new species. In 1959, influenced by the rise of molecular biology, Wilson discovered how ants communicate by chemical releasers known as pheromones, and he later collaborated with William Bossert on a wide-ranging theory of chemical communication in other species.

In the 1960s Wilson and ecologist Robert MacArthur developed a quantitative theory of species equilibrium, relating the size of islands to the number of species they contain and proving that the number of species on a small island would remain constant while the variety of species changed. Their *Theory of Island Biogeography* (1967) was highly influential in theoretical population ecology and its practical application to designing wildlife preserves. They argued that large areas and pathways between preserves are crucial for the survival of diversity. In 1971 Wilson summarized his own and other work on social insects in a comprehensive survey, *The Insect Societies.*

Father of Sociobiology

As an insect researcher, Wilson demonstrated the genetic underpinnings of the complex social behavior of ants and other species. In 1975 he extended his theories to all species, including humans, with the publication of the sweeping and controversial book *Sociobiology: The New Synthesis.*

The term "sociobiology" had already been in use, but Wilson's work was the first in the field to challenge scientific and popular thinking about human behavior. Wilson's goal was to unify all the behavioral sciences on the basis of ecology and evolutionary biology into a "systematic study of the biological basis of all social behavior." Knowing the environmental pressures facing a species and its genetic constraints should allow scientists to predict the social organization and behavior of the species, he believed. Wilson argued that social behavior is a survival trait, and natural selection preserves patterns of useful behavior.

Since Charles Darwin proposed his theory of evolution, scientists had tried to explain animal behavior as an outcome of evolution. But Wilson was the first to argue that the pathway to the survival of the species was the survival of individuals possessing favorable traits. Wilson explained the genetic basis of kinship, communication, specialization of labor, and even altruism. In ants, he observed, the welfare of the colony, not the individual, is paramount, and he believed the same was true for all species. "Genes hold culture on a leash," Wilson said.

The Sociobiology Debate

Wilson's boldness in reducing complex behavior to patterns with a genetic basis and further extending that analysis to humans set off a storm of controversy. Initially favorable reviews of *Sociobiology: The New Synthesis* noted the well-reasoned and extensively documented text on animals, but the focus of criticism was on the chapter about humans. Wilson wrote that humans always have been characterized by "aggressive dominance systems, with males generally dominant over females." He argued further, "Even with identical education and equal access to all professions, men are likely to continue to play a disproportionate role in political life, business and science." Such statements prompted a firestorm of protests from feminists and humanists, and some critics saw an ethnocentric or racist basis to his judgments about the determination of behavior.

At a 1978 meeting of the American Association for the Advancement of Science, protesters yelled at Wilson and poured a pitcher of water over his head. A letter of protest was signed by two of Wilson's colleagues at Harvard and other scholars. Public protests followed Wilson on lecture tours. Insisting he had no political motivation for his theories, Wilson denied the charges of racism and sexism, calling the attacks "slander" and saying his theories were misunderstood. He was partly vindicated in 1982 when the *Humanist* magazine named him its Distinguished Humanist of the year.

Wilson's next book, *On Human Nature* (1978), was an elegantly written essay on the biological basis for human actions and culture. Reviewer Nicholas Wade in the *New Republic* called it "a work of high intellectual daring." It became a best-seller and helped make Wilson's theories even more widely known. It was awarded the 1979 Pulitzer Prize in general non-fiction, to which Wilson responded, "It's not necessarily a certification that I'm right, but an affirmation that this is an important thing we should be talking about."

Next, Wilson and physicist Charles Lumsden tried to create appropriate mathematical models for the genetic evolution of culture. Their two books were *Genes, Mind, Culture: The Coevolutionary Process* (1981), a scholarly work, and *Promethean Fire: Reflections on the Origin of the Mind* (1983), a popular book on the same subject, which they labeled "the gene-culture coevolution." Again, Wilson's theories drew criticism. Writing about *Promethean Fire* in *Commentary*, sociologist Howard Kaye said, "questionable assumptions about mind and culture and an extreme reductionism mar their thought and inflate their claims." While controversy over Wilson's work continued, the field of sociobiology expanded into a thriving biological discipline, mostly devoted to animal behavior.

Besides his books and scientific papers, Wilson co-authored biology textbooks and edited the Scientific American Readings series. His ecological interests led to his partly autobiographical *Biophilia: The Human Bond to Other Species* (1984), an eloquent discussion of human love for nature and a plea for conservation. Wilson served on the board of directors of the World Wildlife Fund from 1984 to 1990. In 1990 his lifelong fascination with ants culminated in the publication of *The Ants,* a comprehensive work co-authored with German entomologist Bert Holldobler. In 1992 he wrote *The Diversity of Life,* affirming his devotion to all the species on Earth, from ants to human beings.

Further Reading

Wilson was the subject of many reports and stories in both the scientific press (*Nature, Science, New Scientist*) and the popular press during the years of debate over sociobiology, from 1975 to 1980. Many of the dimensions of that debate are laid out in A. Caplan's *The Sociobiology Debate* (1980). See also Arthur Fisher, "Sociobiology: Science or Ideology?, *Science* (July/August 1992), and *Scientific American* (March 1993). □

Harriet E. Wilson

Considered the first African American woman to publish a novel in English, Harriet E. Adams Wilson (c. 1827-c. 1863) is also distinguished as the first black, male or female, to publish a novel in the United States.

arriet E. Adams Wilson's book, *Our Nig; or, Sketches From the Life of a Free Black, in a Two-Story White House, North. Showing that Slavery's Shadows Fall Even There,* is a thinly veiled fictional autobiography depicting the brutality of white racism in the antebellum North. The protagonist is a free, mulatto girl named Alfrado. Abandoned by her parents at the age of six, she is sentenced to years of cruel indentured servitude. The book was originally printed in Boston in 1859, and apparently soon sank into literary obscurity, as virtually no early critical comment on the novel exists. Discovered in 1981 in a Manhattan bookstore by Henry Louis Gates, Jr., a Cornell University professor, the book was republished in 1983, with an introduction by Gates. Its discovery forced literary historians to restructure the chronology of black literature, displacing William Wells Brown from his previously accepted position as the first African American novelist. His *Clotel: or, The President's Daughter: A Narrative of Slave Life in the United States* was originally published in London in 1853, but did not appear in the United States until 1864, when it was published in Boston as *Clotelle: A Tale of the Southern States.*

Details of Life are Scarce

Almost all that is known of Wilson's life is confined to the ten-year period between 1850 and 1860, the time frame covered by her novel. In the tradition of the slave narrative, letters of support appear as an appendix to the novel, establishing the truth of its autobiographical aspects. Gates conducted exhaustive research in an attempt to confirm the author as the subject of its biographical detail. Although it yielded pitifully few facts about Wilson's tragic life, this research did verify enough to rescue Wilson and her novel from literary oblivion.

The dates of Wilson's birth and death remain unknown. Census reports provide conflicting records of her possible birth date and birthplace. The 1850 federal census of New Hampshire lists Harriet Adams, age 22, as living in Milford, New Hampshire, suggesting a birth date or 1827 or 1828. Her birthplace is listed merely as "New Hampshire." The 1860 Boston federal census records a Mrs. Harriet E. Wilson, age 52—a 20-year discrepancy from the previous record—born in Fredericksburg, Virginia. If this age is correct, her birth date would be 1807 or 1808. In both census reports she is listed as "black."

Other records indicate that in 1850 Harriet Adams lived with the white Samuel Boyles family in Milford, New Hampshire. On October 6, 1851, she married Thomas Wilson in Milford. Their son, George Mason Wilson, was likely born in May or June of 1852. He was probably their first and only child. He was born at Goffstown, New Hampshire, which was near Milford and was the location of the Hillsborough County Farm. As Gates explained in his introduction to the second edition of *Our Nig,* "One of the letters appended to *Our Nig* states that, abandoned by her husband, the author . . . was forced . . . to go to the 'County House,' where she gave birth to a child."

A "Harriet Wilson, Widow" is listed in the *Boston City Directory* in 1855. Two Harriet Wilsons are listed in the 1856 *Directory,* one a "widow" and one a "dressmaker." Gates has suggested these two Harriet Wilsons may well be the same person. Between 1857 and 1863, only "Harriet Wilson, Widow" appears. After 1863, Harriet Wilson disappears from public record completely. As Margo Jefferson wrote in the *Nation* in 1983, "That we do not know the date of Harriet Wilson's death says a great deal about the remainder of her life."

The facts gleaned from the public records search, Gates wrote, "correspond dramatically to assertions about the life of the author . . . that were made by three acquaintances who endorsed her novel. . . . When brought together, these facts leave no doubt that the author of *Our Nig,* who signed her copyright as 'Mrs. H. E. Wilson' and Harriet E. Adams Wilson, are the same person." Gates continued, "Another source of confirmation is the of *Our Nig*—described as autobiographical by her supporters—which parallels major events of Mrs. Wilson's life that we have been able to verify."

Wrote Novel for Economic Reasons

An examination of both the plot of *Our Nig* as well as the letters of testimonial appended to the book reveal that Harriet Adams lost her parents at an early age, and was then indentured to a white family, which overworked her mercilessly and ruined her health. It was this precarious health which caused her, finally, to place her son in a foster home. She subsequently wrote her novel in an attempt to raise enough money to be reunited with her child. In her preface, Wilson wrote, "In offering to the public the following pages, the writer confesses her inability to minister to the refined and cultivated, the pleasure supplied by abler pens. It is not for such these crude narrations appear. Deserted by kindred, disabled by failing health, I am forced to some experiment which shall aid me in maintaining myself and child without extinguishing this feeble life." Toward that end, Wilson asked, "I sincerely appeal to my colored brethren universally for patronage, hoping that they will not condemn this attempt of their sister to be erudite, but rally around me a faithful band of supporters and defenders."

Unfortunately, the hoped-for patronage did not materialize, and tragically, Wilson's son George died of fever less than six months after her novel was published. Gates noted in 1987, "The irony is profound. George's death certificate made possible the confirmation of a number of details about Wilson, which parallel rather closely statements made about her by three of her friends and printed as an 'appendix' to *Our Nig.* George's death serves as a convenient emblem of the tragic irony of his mother's life and subsequent literary reputation."

Several factors may have contributed to the many years of obscurity to which *Our Nig* was subjected after publication. The most compelling factor may have been what Gates called "the boldness of her themes." In his introduction to *Our Nig* he wrote, "Interracial marriage, it is fair to say, was not a popular subject for representation in either antislavery or proslavery novels." A further likely cause for rejection of the novel can be found in the subject of the book, which is clearly depicted in its lengthy subtitle: the hypocrisy of the brutal racism practiced by Northern whites. Although in her preface Wilson anticipated "severe criticisms" from Northern abolitionists, she further wrote, "I have purposely omitted what would most provoke shame in our anti-slavery friends at home." Nevertheless, "the book did not gain attention or a ready market—perhaps because she had brought that shame she had feared to the antislavery people of the North," wrote Ann Allen Shockley in *Afro-American Women Writers, 1746-1933.* Another reason the book was overlooked may have been due to the fact that Wilson was erroneously identified as white. Monroe Work's *A Bibliography of the Negro in Africa and America* lists Mrs. H. E. Wilson as a white author who wrote novels "relating to the Negro."

Novel Considered a Literary Landmark

While many critics hesitate to imbue *Our Nig* with classic literary status, it is considered a black literary landmark. Francis Browne wrote in 1987 that the novel "is an indictment, not alone of oppression, but of the hypocritical liberalism that held sway in the North during the middle years of the nineteenth century when all eyes were focused on the heinous legalized servitude in the South. The irony resonates when one recognizes that the locales of the novel, New Hampshire and Massachusetts, were hotbeds of abolition. . . ." Similarly, Shockley stated, "Aside from its firsts, the novel can be deemed important for other reasons. It attests to prejudice and a different kind of black bondage in the North as a time when Abolitionists were violently attacking slavery in the South. . . . Harriet E. Adams Wilson unknowingly set a precedent with her personal fictionalized memoir of a free—yet unfree—black northern woman of her time."

As the forerunner of the African-American literary tradition, Gates argued in 1983 that "*Our Nig* stands as a 'missing link,' as it were, between the sustained and well-developed tradition of black autobiography and the slow emergence of a distinctive black voice in fiction." He has suggested that Wilson's combination of "the received conventions of the sentimental novel with certain key conventions of the slave narratives" became a unique new literary form. Had it been available much earlier, "perhaps the black literary tradition would have developed more quickly and more resolutely than it did." Francis Browne concluded in 1987, "Wilson's art might indeed be defective, but her imaginative effort . . . has proven itself worthy and signally prophetic." Gates stated in 1987, "We can cogently argue . . . that Wilson is the most accomplished and subtle black novelist of the nineteenth century."

Further Reading

Bell, Bernard W., *The Afro-American Novel and Its Tradition,* 1987.
Smith, Jessie Carney, editor, *Black Firsts: 2000 Years of Extraordinary Achievement,* Gale Research, 1995, pp. 414-415.
Draper, James P., *Black Literature Criticism,* Gale Research, Vol. 3, 1975-1983.
Browne, Francis, *Fiction International,* Vol. 17:2, 1987, pp. 149-154.
Harris, Trudier, editor, "Afro-American Writers Before the Harlem Renaissance," in *Dictionary of Literary Biography,* Gale Research, Vol. 50, 1986, pp. 268-271.
Pryse, Marjorie J., and Hortense Spillers, editor, "Adding Color and Contour to Early American Self-Portraitures: Autobiographical Writings of Afro-American Women," in *Conjuring: Black Women, Fiction, and Literary Tradition,* Indiana University Press, 1985.
Gates, Henry Louis, Jr. "Introduction," in *Our Nig: or, Sketches From the Life of a Free Black, In a Two-Story White House, North. Showing That Slavery's Shadows Fall Even There,* 2nd ed., Vintage Books, 1983, pp. xi-lv.
Gates, Henry Louis, Jr., *Figures in Black: Words, Signs, and the "Racial" Self,* 1987, pp. 125-163.
Jefferson, Margo, "Down & Out & Black in Boston," in *Nation,* May 28, 1983, pp. 675-677.
Smith, Jessie Carney, editor, *Notable Black American Women,* Gale Research, 1992, pp. 1266-1268.
Shockley, Ann Allen, *Afro-American Women Writers, 1746-1933,* G. K. Hall & Co., 1988, pp. 84-88.
Reprint, 1970
Work, Monroe, *A Bibliography of the Negro in Africa and America,* Octagon Books, 1928. □

Henry Wilson

U.S. Vice President Henry Wilson (1812-1875) was effective in helping to shape the Republican party's antislavery measures and politics.

Henry Wilson, born on Feb. 16, 1812, in Farmington, N.H., was originally named Jeremiah Jones Colbath (he changed his name by act of legislature in 1833). Of a poor family, at 10 he was indentured to a farmer. Such was his hunger for self-improvement that he studied grammar and read widely in books on history and literature.

Free at 21, and with $85 in hand, Wilson became a shoemaker in Natick, Mass. He was debilitated by overwork and in 1838 went south for a change in climate. His view of slavery in Washington, D.C., and Virginia filled him with enduring libertarian sentiments. He became a successful shoe manufacturer. In 1840 he was elected to the Massachusetts House of Representatives as a Whig, and the "Natick cobbler" became a force in state politics.

Wilson's keen faith in free enterprise and scorn of slavery made him a likely representative of those Northerners who feared what they saw as abolitionist excesses but who were unwilling to countenance slavery expansion. Wilson's most striking achievement was to provide a "halfway house" for Northerners in the disintegrating Whig party while the Republican party was being built. In 1854 he joined the nativist American party and attempted to influence it on the slavery issue. But when his pleas were rejected, he led his contingent out of the convention. Elected by the Massachusetts Legislature to the U.S. Senate in 1855, he advocated all legal measures to curb slavery.

During the Civil War, Wilson served as the influential and responsible chairman of the Committee on Military

James Wilson

James Wilson (1742-1798) was a patriot leader during the American Revolution and an influential delegate at the Federal Convention of 1787. He served on the first U.S. Supreme Court.

James Wilson was born on Sept. 14, 1742, on a farm in Fifeshire, Scotland. His family expected him to become a minister, and at 15 he entered St. Andrews University, but a family crisis interrupted his education. He took passage for America in 1765. In Philadelphia, Wilson turned to law studies; admitted to the bar in 1767, within six months he began practicing in Reading, Pa.

Wilson started his patriotic career in 1774 as head of the Carlisle Committee of Correspondence. In his pamphlet *Considerations on the Nature and Extent of the Legislative Authority of the British Parliament* (1774) he argued that the colonists, promoting genuine British constitutionalism, were being victimized by a corrupt ministry. He was sent to the Second Continental Congress in 1775. Wilson stood as a moderate but surrendered his early caution on July 2, 1776.

For the next decade, Wilson was mainly committed to the law and to his dream of vast wealth. He speculated in bank shares, land warrants, and similar ventures on borrowed capital. These involvements gave a misleading impression of great wealth, which in turn enabled Wilson to borrow more for speculations. In the Continental Congress

Affairs and worked earnestly for emancipation measures. He joined other Radical Republicans to oppose President Andrew Johnson's program for bringing the seceded Southern states peaceably back into the Union at the expense of the newly freed Negroes. Wilson's services gained him the vice-presidential office when Ulysses S. Grant won the 1872 election.

Wilson prepared pedestrian but useful accounts of congressional debates and acts during the Civil War and Reconstruction crises. His most ambitious work was his three-volume *History of the Rise and Fall of the Slave Power in America* (1872-1877), which reflected the simplistic but forthright viewpoint of the Northern workers and farmers. A sick man during his last several years, he was stricken with apoplexy in the Capitol and died in the Vice President's Room on Nov. 22, 1875.

Further Reading

Wilson's life is covered in Ernest McKay, *Henry Wilson: Practical Radical* (1971). Another biography is the sympathetic work by the Reverend Elias Nason and Thomas Russell, *The Life and Public Services of Henry Wilson* (1872; repr. 1969). See also George F. Hoar, *Autobiography of Seventy Years* (2 vols., 1903). □

he sought a national fiscal policy far sounder than that he personally practiced.

Wilson welcomed the Federal Convention call. He served on the Pennsylvania delegation, was on the powerful Committee of Detail, and was a persistent advocate for the direct election of both Congress and the president. His plan for an electoral college was ultimately accepted. His influence helped carry ratification of the Constitution in Pennsylvania in 1787.

With the establishment of the national government, Wilson vainly hoped to become chief justice of the Supreme Court but accepted an associate justiceship. On the Court he consistently favored the nationalistic position, and in *Chisholm v. Georgia* (1793) he insisted that states were as liable to a "controlling judiciary" as an individual citizen.

Wilson enjoyed the thrill of speculation but was ultimately unsuccessful at it. His health and his credit began to fail perceptibly. In the winter of 1796/1797, he took flight to escape imprisonment for debt. A defaulted $197,000 debt sent him to jail. He died at Edenton, N.C., on Aug. 21, 1798.

Further Reading

The Works of James Wilson, edited by Robert Green McCloskey (1967), contains a lengthy, thoughtful introduction and analysis of Wilson's main ideas. *Selected Political Essays of James Wilson,* edited by Randolph G. Adam (1930), also contains an assessment of Wilson's contribution to American political ideas. The best biography of Wilson is Charles Page Smith, *James Wilson, Founding Father: 1742-1798* (1956).

Additional Sources

Seed, Geoffrey, *James Wilson,* Millwood, N.Y.: KTO Press, 1978.
☐

James Harold Wilson

The English statesman Harold Wilson (1916-1995), who served as prime minister and leader of the Labour party, was one of the most skillful political tacticians in 20th-century British history.

James Harold Wilson was born on March 11, 1916, in Huddersfield, Yorkshire. He distinguished himself early, capturing a scholarship to Oxford University, where he earned a first-class honors degree in politics, philosophy, and economics. In 1937, at a mere 21 years of age, Wilson became a lecturer in economics at New College, Oxford, and a fellow of University College the following year. When World War II broke out he was drafted into the civil service, where he first became director of the manpower, statistics, and intelligence branch of the Ministry of Labour, then switched to the directorship of statistics at the Ministry of Fuel and Power. Here he compiled his extensive research on the coal industry into a statistical digest, which was published in 1945 under the title *New Deal for Coal.*

Parliamentary Career

The same year the Labour party ousted the aristocratic Sir Winston Churchill from office in a landslide victory. Wilson made his debut in parliament at the age of 29 as the representative of Ormskirk. He spent his first two years as parliamentary secretary to the Ministry of Works (1945-1947), following this appointment with two as president of the Board of Trade (1947-1951).

A Man for the Middle Class

By the beginning of the 1950s Wilson was becoming a familiar figure on the parliamentary scene. Proud of his middle-class roots, he had long since simplified his identity by dropping his first name, "James," in favor of a simpler "Harold Wilson." Now other signs of his determinedly middle-class image became instantly recognizable. Among them included the Yorkshire accent he did not bother to smooth, the raincoat he invariably wore over a rumpled suit, and his preference for beer rather than champagne.

In 1951 Wilson's unpretentious image received a further boost when the government announced that the National Health Service would bill its patients for the first time since its introduction in 1946. This change of policy caused two resignations from the government. The first came from Minister of Health Aneurin Bevan, who had designed the plan with the express intention that it offer free service. The second was from Wilson, whose gesture was seen then as support for the middle class. Voters later remembered this

gesture when the time came to elect a new leader for the Labour party.

The occasion arose in 1963 with the death of Party leader Hugh Gaitskell. Wilson faced off against competitor George Brown for the top slot. Despite Brown's popularity with the labour unions, Wilson defeated him to take Gaitskell's place as leader of the opposition until his election victory in October 1964.

A Prime Minister Without Pretension

From his first months in office Prime Minister Wilson handled his responsibilities with flair. He worked well with the cloistered Queen Elizabeth II, introducing her to the middle-class viewpoint for the first time. Furthermore, he managed his party with dexterity, replacing conflict in the ranks with the first unity Labour had known since the early 1950s. Pragmatic and willing to listen to all viewpoints, Wilson ended a vicious round of miners' strikes, froze rents, announced government subsidies on certain food staples, and imposed price controls, all to convey to the electorate that each governmental decision was motivated by an idea of the national interest rather than by an idea of socialism. Later, he was not only credited with the establishment of the Open University which allowed working people to study for degrees by correspondence, but was also praised by supporters for refusing to join America in sending troops to Vietnam.

Nevertheless, by the end of the decade Wilson's popularity was fading because of growing tensions in Northern Ireland, a breakaway white minority government in colonial Rhodesia, and abrasiveness between the domestic government and the powerful British trade unions. Rising unemployment spurred Wilson to gamble by calling for general elections in 1970, but the Labour party was resoundingly defeated by Edward Heath.

His defeat proved temporary, for in February 1974 a miners' strike in response to a wage freeze brought Wilson and the Labour party back into power. He seemed to be on solid political ground, but in 1976 he suddenly chose to resign and largely disappeared from public view despite his elevation to a baron's status in 1983.

His decision led to a rash of speculation in the media. One rumor had him fighting cancer, while a second stated that the British counter-intelligence agency was trying to destabilize his government. The truth was concealed until after Wilson's death in 1995. According to the influential British medical journal *The Lancet,* Harold Wilson was one of 500,000 British patients suffering from Alzheimer's Disease.

Further Reading

Books by Harold Wilson include *Purpose in Politics: Selected Speeches,* Houghton Mifflin, 1964; *A Personal Record: The Labour Government 1964-1970,* Little, Brown, 1971; *The Governance of Britain,* Harper & Row, 1976; *The Chariot of Israel: Britain, America and the State of Israel,* Norton, 1981. The popular biography by Leslie Smith, *Harold Wilson: The Authentic Portrait* (1964), is a sympathetic "inside" view by an admirer. There are two predominantly hostile books about him, one from the political right by Dudley Smith, *Harold Wilson: A Critical Biography* (1964), the other from the left by Paul Foot, *The Politics of Harold Wilson* (1968), the latter a brilliant example of political journalism at its polemical but accurate best.

Additional Sources

New York Times Biographical Service (May, 1995); *The Lancet* (June 10, 1995). □

Joseph Chamberlain Wilson

Joseph Chamberlain Wilson (1909-1971) was the manager of the Haloid Company which, through Wilson's vision, bought the rights to developing the process later called xerography and became, in 1961, the Xerox Corporation. Xerography revolutionized the world of office management in the 1960s.

Joseph Chamberlain Wilson was born on December 19, 1909, in Rochester, New York. His grandfather, also named Joseph C. Wilson, settled in the city in the late 19th century and in 1903 helped found M. H. Kuhn Co., which in 1906 became the Haloid Company, and still later would become the Xerox Corporation. The elder Wilson was absorbed with politics, serving as alderman, city treasurer, and mayor, so management of the firm devolved upon his son, Joseph R. Wilson.

The name haloid referred to chemicals known as halogens, salts of which are used in the making of conventional photographic emulsions. During the 1920s the firm undertook extensive research to find a better sensitized paper for photocopying, which resulted in 1930 in Haloid Record, a greatly improved type of photographic paper. This product met with instant success, allowing the firm to maintain a full production staff throughout the Depression years.

It was at this time in the mid-1930s that young Joseph C. Wilson joined the family business. Having graduated from the University of Rochester in 1931, Wilson got an M.B.A. at Harvard in 1933. He was named secretary of Haloid in 1936 and in 1944 became vice-president. During these years Joseph C. Wilson assisted his father, who was president of Haloid, in directing most of the firm's business toward the war effort in World War II. This helped to greatly expand the company's business, so that annual sales, which stood at just $1.8 million in 1938, were at $6.8 million in 1946. Profits on these sales, however, were only $150,000. The younger Wilson was keenly aware that the firm needed a new product and a new technology if it were to have any kind of a future. He thus began a search which would end with the purchase of the rights to a new technique called xerography.

John H. Dessauer, research director at Haloid, found an old article in *Radio News* by Chester F. Carlson, then an employee of Bell Labs. In the article Carlson described a process which he called electrophotography. The process, as described by Carlson, did not require sensitized paper or liquid chemicals. Instead, it used an application of a fine powder upon the electrostatic deposition of an image and the fixing on ordinary stationary of the resultant image through the application of heat to the powdered surface of the paper. Later the process would be renamed xerography, which means dry writing.

Carlson had developed the process in 1938 and then spent six fruitless years trying to interest someone in it. During this time he was turned down by more than 20 companies, including IBM, Remington Rand, RCA, and General Electric. Even the National Inventors Council dismissed his idea as impractical. He did get the Battelle Memorial Institute in Columbus, Ohio, to help him develop the process, and it was to them and Carlson that Wilson turned with his negotiations which resulted in the granting to Haloid of limited commercial rights to the process in 1946. The rights were subsequently broadened, and in 1948 the process was demonstrated publically by Haloid and Battelle under a new name—xerography. Over the next six years Wilson paid out over $3.5 million to develop the process, but the payoff to him and his company was enormous, as Xerox Corporation became one of the industrial phenomenons of the mid-20th century. In 1956 Haloid Xerox had net sales of under $7 million, employed 735 workers, and had ten research scientists and engineers. By the time of Wilson's death in 1971, sales had mushroomed to over $3 billion and there were over 25,000 employees. Joseph C. Wilson served as chief executive officer until his death. In 1961 the firm's name was changed to Xerox Corporation.

Wilson and Xerox's main breakthrough came in 1960, when the Xerox 914, the first production-line copier, was introduced. This was a desk-size, pushbutton machine capable of copying anything (printed, written, drawn, or three dimensional); it was able to do it fast and dry and on ordinary paper. This was a revolution in office copying and the great fulfillment of Wilson's vision of a dozen years earlier. The machines were rented out by Xerox and the unit charge for their use decreased as larger numbers of copies were made. Whole new office systems were developed, adapted to fit the particular needs of larger clients, and Xerox turned heavily to television as the best method for advertising their revolutionary new machine. And revolutionary it was. The new copier not only transformed its own industry, but also set in motion a vast metamorphosis of basic office practice in industry, government, and schools. Fast, convenient, relatively inexpensive copying was now possible for even small firms and organizations; the days of carbon copies or of routing individual letters up and down a bureaucratic chain were over; filing systems were streamlined; and a whole new world of office management came into being.

Perhaps Wilson's biggest mistake as head of Xerox came in 1969 when he attempted to challenge IBM for a share of the computer manufacturing business. Xerox purchased Scientific Data Systems, a California maker of scientific computers. IBM immediately countered with an announcement of their intention to enter the dry-copy in-

dustry. Xerox battled it out with IBM for five years, losing over $100 million, and finally pulled out of the computer business in 1975. But Wilson's concern about the wisdom of remaining so closely tied to the copier business was well founded. By the mid-1970s the market was pretty well saturated. In response, Xerox began moving toward the world of the electronic office—"intelligent" copiers, word processors, high-speed printers, and the like.

Joseph C. Wilson early became convinced that a corporation had a duty to support the institutions which made possible a free, healthy, and educated society. To this end, Xerox pioneered a new era of television in 1964 when it sponsored a six-part prime-time series on the United Nations which was largely devoid of commercials. Xerox was also the first company in the nation to adopt a social service leave program through which employees could take as much as a year off, with full pay and benefits, to devote themselves to some worthy cause. When an irate stockholder complained of the corporation's largess, he was told: "You can sell your stock or try to throw us out, but we are not going to change."

Wilson served as a trustee of the University of Rochester for many years, and in 1965 named the university as the ultimate beneficiary of an irrevocable trust upon the death of his wife, set up with 90,000 shares of Xerox stock. In 1967 he gave the university an additional 50,000 shares. He died on November 22, 1971.

Further Reading

There is no biography of Joseph Wilson. The best coverage of the birth and development of Xerox is in John H. Dessauer, *My Years With Xerox* (1971). Daniel J. Boorstin, *The Americans: The Democratic Experience* (1973) nicely summarizes the social impact of the Xerox copier. □

Pete Wilson

Republican Peter Barton Wilson (born 1935) was elected the governor of California in 1991.

As governor of the most populous and economically powerful state in the United States, Pete Wilson is faced with both problems and opportunities of monumental size. His 1990 triumph over Dianne Feinstein for the governor's position made the 60-year-old Wilson an instant candidate for national office—as former California governor and U.S. president Ronald Reagan demonstrated earlier, California politics often become American policies—but for the time being Wilson has his hands full coping with California's massive budgetary, environmental, and population problems. In his first year as governor, Wilson outraged the right wing of the Republican party by raising state taxes $7 billion to help cover California's growing budget deficit, caused by a slow economy and the state's extensive system of social welfare programs. In the land of Reaganism, tax hikes by a Republican governor are viewed as nothing less than treason by many party members; as

California Assemblyman Tom McClintock lamented to the *New Republic,* "All the advantages we [Republicans] had in the 1980s have been thrown away."

Wilson's situation is far more complex than those faced by earlier Republican governors of California, however. The population of the state grew from 23 million in 1980 to 30 million in 1990, with much of the increase in the child population or people too poor to contribute to the state's tax base. At the same time, Californians have grown used to a broad range of social services and tight environmental controls, while simultaneously expressing growing frustration with the size of government and especially with taxes, signaled most clearly by the passage of Proposition 13 in 1978, which imposed a cap on real estate taxes. The net result of these disparate forces was a 1991 budget deficit of $14 billion, a rude welcome to the governor's mansion for Pete Wilson.

Peter Barton Wilson was born August 23, 1935, in Lake Forest, Illinois, an affluent suburb north of Chicago. His father, James Wilson, was originally a jewelry salesman who later became a successful advertising executive. The Wilson family moved to St. Louis when Pete was in junior high school. There he attended St. Louis Country Day School, an exclusive private institution, winning an award in his senior year for combined scholarship, athletics, and citizenship. In the fall of 1952 Wilson enrolled at Yale University, where he majored in English and won a Marines ROTC scholarship. A former Yale classmate later described Wilson to the *Los Angeles Times* as "not the kind of guy

who put himself forward a lot," a capable student but not exceptionally gifted nor much interested in student politics.

After graduation from Yale, Wilson served three years in the Marines as an infantry officer, eventually becoming a platoon commander. His Marines service gave Wilson his first taste of leadership, a kind of political initiation which would prove decisive for his later career. After writing a novel in 1958 (which has not been published), Wilson attended law school at Berkeley, having decided that he wanted to live in California while visiting the state as a Marine. He was an average student at Berkeley but became active in political circles, starting a local chapter of Young Republicans and working on various election campaigns. In 1962, while working for Republican gubernatorial candidate Richard M. Nixon, Wilson got to know one of Nixon's top aides, Herb Klein. Klein suggested that Wilson might do well in San Diego politics, and in 1963 the ambitious young Republican moved to San Diego and began his long climb to the governor's mansion. He was attractive, well-spoken, and conservative, all of which made him a good match for San Diego's rather sedate political climate.

Wilson had to take the California bar exam four times before passing, which speaks for his persistence if nothing else. He began his practice as a criminal defense attorney in San Diego, but found such work to be low-paying and personally repugnant—as he later commented to the *Los Angeles Times,* "I realized I couldn't be a criminal defense lawyer because most of the people who do come to you are guilty." Wilson switched to a more conventional law practice and continued his activity in local politics, working for Barry Goldwater's unsuccessful presidential campaign in 1964. Wilson soon discovered that he genuinely liked politics and that he was good at managing the day-to-day details of the political process. He put in long hours for the Goldwater campaign, earning the friendship of local Republican boosters so necessary for a political career, and in 1966, at the age of thirty-three, he ran for and won a seat in the California state legislature.

As a young state assemblyman Wilson spent much of his time working with Frank Lanterman, a long-time power in Republican state politics. Under the tutelage of Lanterman, Wilson learned the intricacies of the political maneuvering by which the political process is conducted among a host of competing factions. As has always been his fashion, Wilson tended to be quiet and diligent as an assemblyman, neither a brilliant speaker nor visionary policy maker but willing to do the hard work needed for success. In the Republican party, Wilson defined himself as a moderate, while then-governor Ronald Reagan was forging the new coalition of extreme right-wing Republicans that would later carry him to the White House. The two men did not see eye to eye ideologically and were never close personally. At times, Wilson's moderate brand of Republicanism ran head-on with Reagan's conservatism, as when the young assemblyman sponsored a bill that would have created a master plan for controlling use of the California seashore. For the most part, however, Wilson benefitted from the strength of Reagan's popularity, and it was not until the 1991 tax crisis that the philosophical gulf between the two men became apparent.

In 1968, Wilson married Betty Robertson. The couple bought a house in Sacramento, the capital of California, but soon returned to San Diego when Wilson decided to run for mayor of that city in 1971. His experience as chairman of the state Urban Affairs and Housing Committee between 1968 and 1970 had whetted Wilson's appetite for urban government, and San Diego was the natural arena for his ambitions. Not only was the city Wilson's home and political base, but San Diego had also recently seen the indictment of several city officials for bribery and was in the mood for a change. Wilson's youthful good looks and conservative record made a perfect combination, and he beat thirteen other candidates to become mayor of California's second largest city in 1971. Voters were impressed by Wilson's refusal to accept campaign contributions from certain controversial land developers and his commitment to a program of controlled growth for the San Diego area. As he repeatedly said in campaign speeches, "We don't want to become another sprawled-out Los Angeles monster"—a platform that did not jibe well with Reagan-style laissez-faire economics but was in keeping with the growing environmental awareness of many San Diegans.

Wilson remained a very popular figure in San Diego during his terms as mayor. His habitually long work days and concern for the smallest details of city government earned him the respect of voters, while he also extended his political base by leadership in organizations such as the League of California Cities and the president's Citizens' Advisory Committee on Environmental Quality. Wilson's style of living was modest—at $20,000, his salary was less than that of some municipal bus drivers—adding to his image among San Diego residents as a young Mr. Clean. As mayor, his government was fiscally conservative but relatively liberal on social issues, particularly care of the environment. Wilson appealed to his fellow citizens as a sober but not insensitive politician, often described as being rather dull ("Button-Down Pete" was one of his nicknames, referring to his Ivy League dress) but never as insincere or dishonest. San Diego is itself often thought of as rather dull, and in 1976 its voters returned Pete Wilson to the mayor's office with a resounding 61.7% majority.

In 1978, Wilson attempted the next step in what appeared a surefire political career by running for the Republican gubernatorial nomination. He failed miserably, coming in fourth out of five candidates, a defeat that taught him a good deal about politics on a large scale. His poor showing was mainly due to two factors, Proposition 13 and Wilson's own lack of charisma. Proposition 13 was a state referendum intended to put a stop to California's rising property taxes; its approval in 1978 marked the triumph of Ronald Reagan's "supply-side economics" and deeply conservative social policy. Wilson's opposition to Proposition 13 contributed heavily to his poor performance in the gubernatorial election and, ironically, to the fiscal crisis confronting Wilson twelve years later when he succeeded in the governor's race. Of more permanent significance was Wilson's inability to inspire excitement in the voting public. As Wilson's media consultant Paul Keye told the *Los Angeles Times,* "What you have to do is convey Pete's seriousness without letting it become so earnest it fogs your glasses." Or, as Ronald Brownstein wrote in the *New Republic,* Wilson has an "unerring instinct for the gray."

Four years later, however, Wilson ran against and defeated then-governor Jerry Brown in the 1982 race for the United States Senate. Many Californians were weary of Brown's eccentricities (his nickname was "Moonbeam"), and the Senate race itself was an excellent opportunity for Wilson's "dullness" to shine—the Senate is traditionally the more conservative house of Congress, and Brown's much-publicized liberalism was out of place in the atmosphere inspired by Reagan's conservative presidency. Wilson won the Senate race with the same mix of conservatism and progressivism that had carried him to victory twice in San Diego—he was hawkish on defense, opposed to taxes, and a supporter of the death penalty, but in favor of abortion rights, the Equal Rights Amendment, and environmental planning. In many ways, his political make-up resembled that of George Bush, a moderate, Yale-educated Republican, and it succeeded for Wilson in both the 1982 and 1988 Senate elections. In the latter campaign, Wilson was reelected easily over challenger Leo T. McCarthy, as Senate incumbents generally are when the economy is strong.

As Senator of California, Wilson was best known for being unremarkable—"obscure" was the *New Republic's* characterization of his eight-year tenure in the Senate. His one brush with national recognition came in 1986, when the Senator had to be wheeled into the Capitol after an appendectomy to cast a decisive vote for the 1986 Republican budget. Wilson's record as Senator earned him neither great love nor enmity from most Californians; in fact, it was not until his defeat of Dianne Feinstein for governor in 1990 that Wilson generated much attention. The race with Feinstein (a former mayor of San Francisco) degenerated into a campaign of negative advertising and mudslinging, as the candidates held common opinions on nearly every substantial issue. Perhaps simply because he was the candidate from the more populous southern half of the state, Wilson won the election by three percentage points over Feinstein and entered the governor's office in January of 1991.

His decisive action of raising taxes in the face of California's fiscal problems brought Wilson's level of popularity to the lowest mark ever recorded for a California governor. An advocate of what he calls "preventive government," aimed at solving problems before they arise, Wilson raised taxes and cut social programs with equal vigor, denouncing along the way his more conservative fellow Republicans as "gutless" for their tax phobia.

Wilson, who ran unsuccessfully for the 1996 Republican presidential nomination, received much public attention for his controversial and conservative agenda for California. In August of 1993, stated *Christian Science Monitor* contributor Daniel B. Wood, Wilson "called on President Clinton to 'repeal the perverse incentives that now exist for people to emigrate to this country illegally.'" In open letters reprinted in several national newspapers, he detailed a broad plan to deny citizenship to the children of undocumented aliens, cut off health and education benefits, and create a legal-resident eligibility card that would be required for anyone seeking such benefits. Wilson told the *Monitor* that "enough people to fill a city the size of Oakland [Calif., population 372,242] got past the border patrol over the past four years. The almost $3 billion in state tax dollars we are required to spend by federal law on services for illegal immigrants is causing us to be unable to spend [on], and in some cases to [have to] cut, needed services for legal residents." "To me, it is terribly unfair and wrong," Wilson concluded, "to be spending state tax dollars for illegal immigrants and declining it to working poor who are legal residents."

In the summer of 1995, Wilson made another controversial decision when he convinced the University of California's Board of Regents to end the university's affirmative action policy. "At a moment when affirmative action is under attack across the country—and just one day after President Bill Clinton told Americans that it had been 'good for America'—the vote made California the first state to eliminate race preferences in college admissions and put the state at the forefront of eliminating them nationwide," declared *Time* contributor Margot Hornblower. Although Wilson's actions were opposed by many national figures, including Rev. Jesse Jackson, the governor's stance was popular with many California voters. "Next year," wrote Hornblower, "Californians will vote in a referendum on a measure that would forbid the state to use affirmative action not only in public education but also in state employment and contracting. Polls show three-fourths of the state's voters supporting it."

But although voters in California accepted the measure, the Clinton administration has decided to press its challenge of Proposition 209 that was deemed constitutional by a federal appeals court panel. The decision by the White House means that the Justice Department will continue to participate in the legal challenge to the proposition as a friend of the court. Thus, the Justice Department may file a legal brief outlining why it views the affirmative action ban as unconstitutional in future legal proceedings. However, the key decisions in the case will continue to be made by others.

In 1997 Wilson has also found time to volunteer as a mentor. A teenage boy from an underprivileged neighborhood and Wilson met in April through a mentoring program. Policymakers nationwide have high hopes for such programs. Leaders of the volunteerism are searching for new ways to avert the tragedies of crime, drugs, and violence that afflict too many youth in the U.S.

Further Reading

Business Week, October 14, 1987.
Christian Science Monitor, October 4, 1993.
Los Angeles Times, March 7, 1976; October 11, 1982; April 11, 1997, p. A3; April 28, 1997, p. A3.
New Republic, August 22, 1988; April 15, 1991; December 9, 1991.
Newsweek, October 11, 1982.
New York Times Magazine, September 30, 1990.
Time, November 18, 1991; July 31, 1995. □

Richard Wilson

The British painter Richard Wilson (1713/1714-1782) raised English landscape painting to new heights by uniting its topographical traditions with those of the great 17th-century landscape masters on the Continent.

The third son of the rector of Penygoes in Montgomeryshire, Wales, Richard Wilson received an excellent grounding in classical literature from his father. In 1729 Richard went to London "to indulge his prevailing love for the arts of design," and there he trained under an obscure portrait painter, Thomas Wright. Family connections with the aristocracy helped Wilson to get portrait commissions, including one from the royal family, but his reputation among artists was chiefly for topographical landscapes imbued with a strong feeling for open-air naturalism. In 1746 he painted the *Founding Hospital* and *St. George's Hospital* for the Founding Hospital.

In 1750 Wilson went to Venice and about a year later to Rome, where Salvator Rosa was his chief model for dramatic landscapes with storms, shipwrecks, and bandits. For six years Wilson made an intensive study of the Italian landscape, especially scenes with classical associations, working up his open-air sketches into studio pictures, strongly influenced in his handling of light and air by the Dutch masters and in his composition by Gaspard Dughet, Nicolas Poussin, and Claude Lorrain.

After his return to England in 1756 or 1757, Wilson took an apartment in the Great Piazza in Covent Garden, where he also had a studio for his pupils. He made his chief bid for fame with a number of versions of the *Destruction of the Daughters of Niobe,* one of which was exhibited at the Society of Artists in 1760. The verdict of Sir Joshua Reynolds was unfavorable, but in any case the taste of the aristocracy was not for heroic essays in the sublime, corresponding to the theories of Edmund Burke, but for pictures of their country houses elevated by the style of Claude Lorrain and for Italian scenes that reminded them of their grand tours.

Between 1765 and 1769 Wilson gave up his apartment in Covent Garden. Elected a foundation member of the Royal Academy in 1768, he established a practice both substantial and lucrative, but sporadic ill health, generosity, touchiness, and the unremunerative proportion of his time devoted to uncommissioned heroic landscapes all contributed to the decline of his fortune. His appointment as librarian to the Royal Academy in 1776 was largely a charitable gesture.

Wilson frequently visited his beloved Wales, and he retired there in 1781. He died in Colomendy, Denbighshire, the following year. His Welsh landscapes, such as *Snowdon* (ca. 1766) and *Cader Idris* (ca. 1774), and views of the English countryside are highly original paintings which announce the romantic exaltation of nature and solitude.

Further Reading

The standard authority for Wilson's life and work is W. G. Constable, *Richard Wilson* (1953), which contains nearly 400 illustrations. An excellent appreciation of Wilson is in Ellis Waterhouse, *Painting in Britain, 1530-1790* (1953; 2d ed. 1962). □

Thomas Woodrow Wilson

Thomas Woodrow Wilson (1856-1924), twenty-eighth president of the United States, led the country into World War I and was a primary architect of the League of Nations.

Woodrow Wilson was born in Staunton, Va., on Dec. 28, 1856. His father, a Presbyterian minister, communicated his moral austerity to his son, resulting in an inflexibility that sometimes revealed itself. Wilson attended Davison University in North Carolina for a brief time but graduated from Princeton in 1879. In his senior year he published an important essay in the *International Review,* revealing his early interest in American government. He studied law briefly and, though he did not complete the course, practiced for a time in Atlanta, Ga., without much success. He pursued graduate studies at Johns Hopkins University, receiving his doctorate in 1886.

In his doctoral thesis Wilson analyzed the American political system, pointing to the fracturing of power that flowed from the committee system in Congress. This thesis foreshadowed his intense belief in the role of the presidency as the only national office and in the duty of the president to lead the nation. He was to put these views into practice when he occupied the White House.

From 1886 to 1910 Wilson was in academic life—as a professor of political science at Bryn Mawr, Wesleyan, and Princeton and, after 1902, president of Princeton. A magnificent teacher, Wilson was a strong and imaginative college executive. His establishment of the preceptorial system at Princeton was an important contribution to university education that emphasized intimacy between teacher and student. He also fought for democracy in education.

Governor of New Jersey

By 1910 Wilson had established a wide reputation but had also aroused many enmities at Princeton. Thus he was ready to accept when, in 1910, the Democratic party in New Jersey offered him the nomination for governor. He was elected by a large plurality.

As governor, Wilson demonstrated masterly leadership, pushing through the legislature a direct primary law, a corrupt-practices act, an employers' liability act, and a law regulating the public utilities. His success made him a prominent candidate for the presidency in 1912. He was nominated, after a long convention battle, and easily elected in November. At the same time the Democratic

party secured a substantial majority in both houses of Congress.

First Term as President

Once elected, Wilson proceeded to put into practice his theory of presidential leadership. In the first 2 years of his presidency he dominated Congress and secured legislation of long-term historical significance. The tariff was revised downward, initiating a policy which was to be of substantial importance later. The Federal Reserve Act created a banking system under governmental control. The Federal Trade Commission Act, directed against monopoly, created a body which has had an important role in preventing overwhelming concentration of power in industry.

Wilson from the beginning confronted difficult questions of foreign policy. In Mexico a revolution was taking place, but just before Wilson's inauguration a military dictator, Victoriano Huerta, seized the presidency. Wilson refused to recognize Huerta, setting a course sympathetic with the struggle of the Mexican masses for social reform. He prevented Huerta from consolidating power, and in 1914 he ordered the occupation of Veracruz to prevent the dictator from receiving arms from abroad. He was saved from the possibility of war by the proffered mediation of Argentina, Brazil, and Chile; and Huerta was overthrown. But the Mexican question continued causing trouble.

Beginning of World War I

In August 1914 World War I broke out in Europe. The basis of Wilson's policy was the preservation of neutrality. But there can be little doubt that in his heart he sympathized with France and Great Britain and feared the victory of imperial Germany. The warring powers soon began interfering with American trade. The British more and more restricted American commerce, but the Germans proclaimed a new kind of warfare, submarine warfare, with the prospect of American ships being sunk and their passengers and crew being lost. Wilson took German policies more seriously, not only because of his innate partiality for the British, but because German policies involved the destruction of human life, whereas the British interfered only with trade. As early as February 1915, in response to a German declaration instituting the U-boat war, the President declared that Germany would be held to "strict accountability" for the loss of American lives.

For a time thereafter Wilson took no action. But on May 7, 1915, the liner *Lusitania* was sunk, with over a hundred American lives lost. The President addressed a stiff note to Germany but clung to the hope that the war might be ended by the good offices of the United States. He engaged in a debate with Berlin and, after other painful submarine episodes, got Germany to abandon the U-boat war in 1916.

Wilson then addressed himself to Great Britain but made little headway. In the meantime the presidential campaign of 1916 was approaching. He was renominated virtually by acclamation; the Democratic platform praised him for keeping the country out of war. He won in a very close campaign. It is important to note that though the President profited from his stand in preserving peace, and though the Democratic politicians made the most of the slogan "He kept us out of war," Wilson promised nothing for the future.

Second Term as President

Wilson's efforts to bring the belligerents together were ineffectual. When the German government cast the die for unlimited warfare on the sea, Wilson severed diplomatic relations with Berlin but continued to hope that a direct challenge could be avoided. No president has ever taken more seriously the immense responsibility of leading the American people into war. But on April 2, 1917, Wilson demanded a declaration of war against Germany from Congress, and Congress responded by overwhelming majorities.

There is every reason to regard Wilson as a great war president. He put politics aside, appointing a professional soldier to head American forces in Europe. Fully as important, he appealed to American idealism in a striking way. Though he believed that the defeat of Germany was necessary, he held out hope that at the end of the war a League of Nations might be established which would make impossible the recurrence of another bloody struggle. As early as April 1916 he had begun to formulate his views on this. He advocated an association of nations which would act together against any nation which broke the peace. There was much support for his point of view.

Fourteen Points

Throughout the war Wilson insisted on two things: the defeat of German militarism and the establishment of peace resting on just principles. In January 1918 he gave his speech of the Fourteen Points. In the negotiations that autumn he made the acceptance of these points the primary condition on the part of his European associates and of the Germans as well. Wilson was at the apogee of his career in November 1918, when the armistice was signed. No American president had ever attained so high a position in world esteem, and millions looked to him as the prophet of a new order.

But difficulties loomed. The 1918 elections returned a Republican majority to Congress. The President himself stimulated partisanship by his appeal to elect a Democratic legislature. Though he selected able men for his delegation to the forthcoming peace conference at Paris, he did not think of conciliating the Republican opposition. By insisting on going to Paris in person and remaining there until the treaty was finished, he cut himself off from American opinion.

Versailles and the League Covenant

At the peace conference Wilson strove to realize his ideals. He was able to win the negotiating powers' consent for drafting the Covenant of the League of Nations. This provided for a League Council of the five Great Powers and four elective members and for an Assembly in which every member state would have a vote. The signatories bound themselves to submit disputes to either arbitration or conciliation through the Council. If they failed to do this, they would be subjected to economic and possibly to military sanctions. They were also to agree to respect and preserve the territorial integrity and political independence of the members of the League.

Wilson fought also for what he conceived to be a just peace. On territorial questions he strove to apply the principle of nationality; he fought successfully against French ambitions to detach the Rhineland from Germany and against the Italian desire for Dalmatia, a province peopled by Yugoslavs. Many of the new boundaries of Europe were to be determined by plebiscite. At times, however, the principle of nationality was violated. On the question of reparations Wilson was unsuccessful in limiting German payments in amount and time, and he accepted a formula which was subject to grave criticism. In the Orient, much against his will, he was compelled to recognize the claims of Japan (which had in 1914 entered the war on the side of the Allies) to economic control of the Chinese province of Shantung (formerly in the hands of Germany).

The Treaty of Versailles was not to stand the test of time. In detaching substantial territories from Germany and in fixing Germany with responsibility for the war, it furnished the basis for that German nationalism which was to come to full flower with Adolf Hitler.

Wilson returned to the United States with a political battle ahead. There was much partisanship in the opposition to him but also a genuine dislike of the Treaty of Versailles and honest opposition to "entanglement" in world politics. He erred in demanding ratification of the treaty without modification. He made his appeal in a countrywide tour. He was hailed by tremendous crowds and greeted with immense enthusiasm, but his health gave way, and he was compelled to go back to the White House. A stroke temporarily incapacitated him.

The Senate in November rejected unconditional ratification but adopted the treaty with reservations which the President refused to accept. In January a compromise was attempted. But Wilson spoiled these efforts by taking the issue into the 1920 presidential campaign. That campaign resulted in an overwhelming Republican victory and the election of Warren G. Harding as president. The new chief executive never sought to bring the Treaty of Versailles to the Senate or to bring the United States into the League, which was by now actually in existence. Wilson's presidency ended in a stunning defeat.

Evaluation of Wilson's Policies

Despite his failure to secure American adherence to the League, the long-run judgment on the President must be that he was one of the few great presidents of the United States. In his first term he exerted a presidential leadership that has rarely been equaled and won legislation of far-reaching importance. In his policy toward Germany he faithfully interpreted the majority opinion of the nation, neither rushing passionately into war at the possible cost of national unity nor hesitating to face the issue once it seemed clear. He was a war leader of the first magnitude. In his campaign for a world order, moreover, he has lasting significance. He bequeathed to his generation, and that which followed, a passionate faith in the possibility of such an order.

The Charter of the United Nations reflects in no small degree Woodrow Wilson's aspirations. Whether such an order as he dreamed will ever eventuate in fact is a question that must be left to the prophets. But if a day comes when men seek the means of settling their disputes in international organization, the failure of Woodrow Wilson will appear a transitory thing, and his idealism and his vision will receive their due praise from posterity.

Wilson was twice married. His first wife bore him three daughters. She died in the White House shortly after the outbreak of World War I. In 1916 he married Edith Bolling Galt, who survived him by many years. He died on Feb. 3, 1924.

Further Reading

The foremost biographer of Wilson is Arthur S. Link, whose still uncompleted definitive work, *Wilson* (5 vols., 1947-1965), takes Wilson's life up to 1917; Link's work is a monumental, detailed record of Wilson's times. The biography by Arthur Walworth, *Woodrow Wilson* (2 vols., 1958; 2d rev. ed., 2 vols. in 1, 1964), presents a fine understanding of Wilson the man. Henry Wilkinson Bragdon, *Woodrow Wilson: The Academic Years* (1967), describes Wilson's years as writer, teacher, and scholar, and George C. Osborn, *Woodrow Wilson: The Early Years* (1968), relates his prepolitical years generally.

A critical study of Wilson is John M. Blum, *Woodrow Wilson and the Politics of Morality* (1956). Other biographies include William Allen White, *Woodrow Wilson* (1924); H. Hale Bellot, *Woodrow Wilson* (1955); John A. Garraty, *Woodrow Wilson: A Great Life in Brief* (1956); and Silas Bent McKinley, *Woodrow Wilson* (1957). See also Eleanor Wilson McAdoo, *The Woodrow Wilsons* (1937). A synoptic view of Wilson's personality emerges from Arthur S. Link, ed., *Woodrow Wilson: A Profile* (1968), an anthology by persons who knew Wilson or who assessed his impact during their lifetimes. The papers of Wilson's confidant, Edward Mandell House, *The Intimate Papers of Colonel House,* arranged by Charles Seymour (4 vols., 1926-1928), provide intimate glimpses of Wilson.

Specialized studies include excellent works by Thomas A. Bailey dealing with the peace treaty and the struggle that followed, *Woodrow Wilson and the Lost Peace* (1944) and *Woodrow Wilson and the Great Betrayal* (1945); Arthur S. Link, *Woodrow Wilson and the Progressive Era, 1910-1917* (1954) and *Wilson the Diplomatist* (1957); the well-documented study of Wilson's relations with Congress during World War I by Seward W. Livermore, *Politics Is Adjourned: Woodrow Wilson and the War Congress, 1916-1918* (1966); and Norman Gordon Levin, Jr., *Woodrow Wilson and World Politics: America's Response to War and Revolution* (1968). The elections of 1912 and 1916 are covered in Arthur M. Schlesinger, Jr., ed., *History of American Presidential Elections* (4 vols., 1971). □

Johann Joachim Winckelmann

The German archeologist Johann Joachim Winckelmann (1717-1768) redefined archeology as

a history of ancient art. His high regard for Greek art greatly influenced German classical literature and stimulated classicism.

The only son of a cobbler, Johann Joachim Winckelmann was born on Dec. 9, 1717, in Stendal, Prussia, and grew up in modest circumstances. From 1738 he studied theology and medicine, then taught in Salzwedel from 1743 to 1748, and from 1748 until 1754 he was librarian for the Count of Bühnau in Nöthnitz near Dresden. Here, in addition to his historical studies, he turned to the fine arts and prepared a description of the paintings in the Dresden Gallery.

In 1754-1755 Winckelmann studied art in Dresden with the painter Adam Friedrich Oeser and came in contact with Italian artists. A result of his studies was his essay "Thoughts on the Imitation of Greek Works in Painting and Sculpture," in which he portrayed an idealized picture of Greek art and saw its spirit as "noble simplicity and silent greatness." Since Greek art was to him the highest artistic achievement, he advocated its imitation by all later cultures. The contemporary, baroque art was to be dismissed since it had grown too remote from the Greek simplicity.

Winckelmann's essay received great acclaim and prepared his way to Rome, where he went in 1755 after becoming a Catholic. In Italy, which he called the land of humanity, he fulfilled his human and intellectual purpose. The southern freedom of mores and ideas recalled his ideal

Greece and enabled him to pursue the cult of male beauty which he found embodied in Greek art. Thus Winckelmann devoted his "Dissertation on the Ability to Appreciate the Beautiful in Art and Its Instruction" to his young friend Reinhold von Berg.

As equal, Winckelmann met with Roman scholars and clerics, even lived for a time in the papal residence at Castel Gandolfo. His special friends were the German painter Anton Raphael Mengs and Cardinal Alessandro Albani, in whose palace he lived before moving with him into a newly built villa in the Via Salaria. On the outfitting of this villa with antique sculptures, Winckelmann had a decided influence.

In 1763 Winckelmann was named prefect of Roman antiquities, and he worked also in the Vatican library. In his studies he combined historical awareness with vivid feeling for the present; in his writings he was at once scholar and poet. His descriptions of the statues in the Vatican's Belvedere (only the descriptions of the Apollo and of the Torso were finished) are in their enthusiastic language genial prose poems.

Winckelmann included these descriptions in his major work, *History of the Art of Antiquity* (1764), the first historical overview of the entire ancient art, born of profound knowledge of the sources and his personal views. His thorough erudition is also apparent in his catalog of the gem collection of Baron Stosch (1758) and in publications on unknown antiques. Winckelmann published lively reports on the excavations in Pompeii and Herculaneum, which he got to know on three journeys, and he wrote also about ancient architecture and allegories in art.

Most of Winckelmann's writings appeared in German, and he never relinquished his bonds with Germany. In 1765 he almost became the librarian of Frederick the Great in Berlin. But as Winckelmann traveled to Germany in April 1768, his love of Rome proved the stronger; beset with deep melancholy he interrupted his journey in Regensburg, traveled to Vienna where he was honored by Empress Maria Theresa, and arrived in Trieste in June. There he met a former-convict cook who robbed and killed him on June 8, 1768.

Further Reading

Wolfgang Leppmann, *Winckelmann* (1970), is the first biography in English; it provides interesting material on life and education in 18th-century Germany, the first excavations of Pompeii and Herculaneum, and the attitude and policy of the papacy. More specialized are two studies by Henry C. Hatfield: *Winckelmann and His German Critics, 1755-1781* (1943) and *Aesthetic Paganism in German Literature* (1964). □

Oprah Gail Winfrey

America's first lady of talk shows, Oprah Gail Winfrey (born 1954), is well known for surpassing her competition to become the most watched daytime

show host on television. Her natural style with guests and audiences on the *Oprah Winfrey Show* earned her widespread adoration, as well as her own production company.

Oprah Gail Winfrey was born to Vernita Lee and Vernon Winfrey on an isolated farm in Kosciusko, Mississippi, on January 29, 1954. Her name was supposed to be Orpah, from the Bible, but because of the difficulty of spelling and pronunciation, she was known as Oprah almost from birth. Winfrey's unmarried parents separated soon after she was born and left her in the care of her maternal grandmother on the farm.

Winfrey made friends with the farm animals and, under the strict guidance of her grandmother, she learned to read at two and a half years old. She addressed her church congregation about "when Jesus rose on Easter Day" when she was two years old. Then Winfrey skipped kindergarten after writing a note to her teacher on the first day of school saying she belonged in the first grade. She was promoted to third grade after that year.

It was her last year on the farm; at six years old she was sent north to join her mother and two half-brothers in the Milwaukee ghetto. Because she missed the farm animals and could not afford a dog, she made pets out of cockroaches and kept them in a jar. Her career as a young

Oprah Winfrey (standing)

speaker continued with poetry readings at African American social clubs and church teas. At 12 years old she was staying with her father in Nashville and earned $500 for a speech at a church. She knew then that she wanted to be "paid to talk."

The poor, urban lifestyle had its negative effect on Winfrey as a young teenager, and her problems were compounded by repeated sexual abuse, starting at age nine, by men that others in her family trusted. Her mother worked strenuously at odd jobs and did not have much time for supervision.

Winfrey became a delinquent teenager, frequently acting out and crying for attention. Once she faked a robbery in her house, smashed her glasses, feigned amnesia, and stole from her mother's purse, all because she wanted newer, more stylish glasses. Another time she spotted Aretha Franklin getting out of a car and convinced her she was a poor orphan from Ohio looking for a way back home. Franklin gave her $100, with which Winfrey rented herself a hotel room for three days until a minister brought her home. Her mother tried to send her to a detention center only to discover there was no room; so she sent her troubled daughter to live with her father in Nashville.

Winfrey said her father saved her life. He was very strict and provided her with guidance, structure, rules, and books. He required his daughter to complete weekly book reports, and she went without dinner until she learned five new vocabulary words each day.

She became an excellent student, participating as well in the drama club, debate club, and student council. In an Elks Club oratorical contest, she won a full scholarship to Tennessee State University. The following year she was invited to a White House Conference on Youth. Winfrey was crowned Miss Fire Prevention by WVOL, a local Nashville radio station, and was hired by that station to read afternoon newscasts.

During her freshman year at Tennessee State, Winfrey became Miss Black Nashville and Miss Tennessee. The Nashville CBS affiliate offered her a job; Winfrey turned it down twice, but finally took the advice of a speech teacher, who reminded her that job offers from CBS were "the reason people go to college." Now seen each evening on WTVFTV, Winfrey was Nashville's first African American female co-anchor of the evening news. She was 19 years old and still a sophomore in college.

When she graduated in 1976, she went to Baltimore to become a reporter and co-anchor at ABC affiliate WJZ-TV. The station sent her to New York for a beauty overhaul, which Winfrey attributes to her assistant news director's attempt to "make her Puerto Rican" and from an incident when she was told her "hair's too thick, nose is too wide, and chin's too big." The New York salon only made things worse by giving her a bad permanent, leaving her temporarily bald and depressed. Winfrey comforted herself with food; so began the weight problem that became so much a part of her persona.

In 1977 WJZ-TV scheduled her to do the local news updates, called cut-ins, during *Good Morning, America,* and soon she was moved to the morning talk show *Baltimore Is Talking* with co-host Richard Sher. After seven years on the show, the general manager of WLS-TV, ABC's Chicago affiliate, saw Winfrey in an audition tape sent in by her producer, Debra DiMaio. At the time her ratings in Baltimore were better than Phil Donahue's, and she and DiMaio were hired.

Winfrey moved to Chicago in January 1984 and took over as anchor on *A.M. Chicago,* a morning talk show which was consistently last in the ratings. She changed the emphasis of the show from traditional women's issues to current and controversial topics, and after one month the show was even with Donahue's program. Three months later it had inched ahead. In September 1985 the program, renamed the *Oprah Winfrey Show,* was expanded to one hour. Consequently, Donahue moved to New York.

One of the reasons her show became so successful was she decided against using stifling prepared scripts. She refused to research her topics, and, in her own words, she "wings it" in order to carry on normal conversations with her guests. It succeeds because of her sharp personality and quick wit.

In 1985 Quincy Jones saw Winfrey on television and thought she would make a fine actress in a movie he was co-producing with director Stephen Spielberg. The film was based on the Alice Walker novel *The Color Purple.* Her only acting experience until then had been in a one-woman show, *The History of Black Women Through Drama and Song,* which she performed during an African American theater festival in 1978.

Winfrey was cast as Sofia, a proud, assertive woman whose spirit is broken by neither an abusive husband nor white authorities. Critics praised her performance, and she was nominated for an Academy Award as Best Supporting Actress.

In 1986 she appeared in Jerrold Freedman's film of Richard Wright's *Native Son,* playing the crucial role of Bigger Thomas' mother. The film was not as well received as *The Color Purple,* and critics considered Winfrey's performance overly sentimental.

The popularity of Winfrey's show skyrocketed after the success of *The Color Purple,* and in September 1985 the distributor King World bought the syndication rights to air the program in 138 cities, a record for first-time syndication. That year, although *Donahue* was being aired on 200 stations, Winfrey won her time slot by 31 percent, drew twice the Chicago audience as Donahue, and carried the top ten markets in the United States.

The *Oprah Winfrey Show* featured such topics and guests as a group of nudists without clothing in the studio (with only their faces shown), a live birth, white supremacists, transsexuals, pet death, gorgeous men, well-dressed women, and Winfrey's own struggle with her weight and coming to terms with the abuse she endured as a child. She holds interviewees' hands during difficult discussions and often breaks into tears right along with them. One show's topic was incest, during which she revealed to her audience she had been raped by a cousin when she was nine years old.

She once taped a show with an all-white audience in Forsyth County, Georgia, where no African American had lived since 1912. This program was prompted after an incident on the anniversary of Martin Luther King Jr.'s birthday, when 20,000 people marched in Forsyth County to protest racism after the Ku Klux Klan had broken up a previous civil rights march in that town. Another program featured a man who had contracted AIDS and as a result had been harassed, beaten, jailed, and run out of his hometown. The studio audience was made up of the residents of that town.

In 1986 she received a special award from the Chicago Academy for the Arts for unique contributions to the city's artistic community and was named Woman of Achievement by the National Organization of Women. The *Oprah Winfrey Show* won several Emmys for Best Talk Show, and Winfrey was honored as Best Talk Show Host.

Winfrey formed her own production company, Harpo, Inc., in August 1986 in order to produce the topics that she wanted to see produced, including the television drama miniseries based on Gloria Naylor's *The Women of Brewster Place,* in which Winfrey was featured, along with Cicely Tyson, Robin Givens, Olivia Cole, Jackee, Paula Kelly, and Lynn Whitfield. The miniseries aired in March 1989, and a regular series called *Brewster Place,* also starring Winfrey, debuted on ABC in May 1990. Winfrey also owned the screen rights to *Kaffir Boy,* Mark Mathabane's autobiographical book about growing up under apartheid in South Africa, as well as Toni Morrison's novel *Beloved.*

Winfrey is also politically active. In 1991 the tragic story of a four-year-old Chicago girl's molestation and murder prompted Winfrey, as a former abuse victim, "to take a stand for the children of this country," she explained in *People.* With the help of former Illinois governor James Thompson, she proposed federal child protection legislation designed to keep nationwide records on convicted child abusers. In addition, Winfrey pursued a ruling that would guarantee strict sentencing of individuals convicted of child abuse.

In September 1996 Winfrey started an on-air reading club. For 10 years publishers had watched as self-help, inspirational, and celebrity titles rose to best-seller status on the tides of telegenic emotion flooding each day across the screens of Winfrey's 14 million American viewers. Think of *Simple Abundance, The Soul's Code, Don't Block the Blessings, Down in the Garden,* and Winfrey's own *Make the Connection,* written with Bob Greene. They all received their sales starts because of Winfrey's reading club. The book club has taken her power to sell books to a different level. On September 17 Winfrey stood up in an evangelist mode and announced she wanted "to get the country reading." She told her adoring fans to hasten to the stores to buy the book she had chosen. They would then discuss it together on the air the following month.

The initial reaction was astonishing. *The Deep End of the Ocean* had generated significant sales for a first novel; 68,000 copies had gone into the stores since June. But between the last week in August, when Winfrey told her plans to the publisher, and the September on-air announcement, Viking printed 90,000 more. By the time the discussion was broadcast on October 18, there were 750,000 copies in print. The book became a number one best-seller, and another 100,000 were printed before February 1997.

The club ensured Winfrey as the most powerful book marketer in the United States. She sends more people to bookstores than morning news programs, other daytime shows, evening magazines, radio shows, print reviews and feature articles combined. As of May 1997, *Make the Connection* was rated number nine on the *New York Times* Best Seller List.

On April 30, 1997, Winfrey appeared in the role of a therapist on a controversial episode of the sitcom *Ellen,* in which the show's character reveals her homosexuality. The controversey deepened when the show's star, comedian Ellen DeGeneres, announced that she herself was a lesbian. As a result, rumors quickly spread questioning Winfrey's sexuality. Distressed by the rumors, Winfrey issued a statement declaring that she is heterosexual.

Although one of the wealthiest women in America and the highest paid entertainer in the world, Winfrey has made generous contributions to charitable organizations and institutions such as Morehouse College, the Harold Washington Library, The United Negro College Fund, and Tennesse State University.

In addition to her numerous Daytime Emmys, Winfrey has received other awards. She was inducted into the Television Hall of Fame in 1994 and received the George Foster Peabody Individual Achievement Award following the 1995-1996 season, one of broadcasting's most coveted awards. Further, she received the IRTS Gold Medal Award, was named one of "Americas's 25 Most Influential People of 1996" by *Time* magazine, and was included on Marjabelle Young Stewart's 1996 list of most polite celebrities. In 1997 Winfrey received TV Guide's Television Performer of the Year Award and was named favorite Female Television Performer at the 1997 People's Choice Awards.

Winfrey lives in a condominium on Chicago's Gold Coast and owns a 162-acre farm in Indiana. She spends four nights a week lecturing for free at churches, shelters, and youth organizations. Winfrey also spends two Saturdays a month with the Little Sisters program she set up at Chicago's Cabrini-Green housing project.

Further Reading

Three informative and anecdotal books have been written about Oprah Winfrey: *Everybody Loves Oprah!* (1987) by Norman King, *Oprah* (1987) by Robert Waldron, and *Oprah Winfrey* by Lillie Patterson (1988). "The Importance of Being Oprah," a June 11, 1989, feature story in the *New York Times Magazine* by Barbara Grizzuti Harrison, is an excellent in-depth profile of Winfrey. She is the subject of countless magazine articles in the popular media. □

Sarah Winnemucca

Sarah Winnemucca (1844?-1891) was active as a peacemaker, teacher, and defender of the rights of Native Americans. She published *Life among the Paiutes, Their Wrongs and Claims* and founded a school for Indians.

Sarah Winnemucca was a skilled interpreter, an Army scout, a well-known lecturer, a teacher, and the first Indian woman to publish a book. She was born near Humboldt Lake about 1844 in the part of Utah Territory that later became Nevada, the fourth child of her father, Chief Winnemucca, called Old Winnemucca and mother, Tuboitonie. They named her Thocmetony, meaning Shell Flower. Later she took the name Sarah, a name she kept the rest of her life. The homelands of the Northern Paiutes extended over parts of present day Idaho, Nevada and Oregon. Over those lands, the Paiutes hunted, gathered seeds (especially pine nuts), and fished in the rivers and lakes. During Winnemucca's lifetime, however, they were crowded onto reservations and deprived of much of their land. Winnemucca became nationally known for her fight for her people's rights and for her struggle to keep the peace between her people and the white newcomers.

Winnemucca's own friendship may have been influenced by her maternal grandfather, the leader of the tribe. He was known as Truckee, from a Paiute word meaning "good" or "all right." The name was given to him by Captain Fremont when they met soon after Winnemucca was born. Truckee and eleven Paiutes went with Fremont to California to help fight Mexican influence there. They returned full of stories of the ways of white people. Truckee, impressed by Fremont and the culture he had been exposed to in California, told his people to welcome the "white brothers."

As more emigrants moved west, however, the Paiutes heard horror stories about the killing of Indians. They apparently also heard a garbled account of the Donner Party, who survived a winter trapped in the Sierra Nevadas by eating their dead. These stories terrified Winnemucca. Her fears were intensified by an experience she described in her book *Life Among the Piutes*. Truckee was in California, and Old Winnemucca had become chief. One morning, hearing that white men were coming, the entire tribe fled in terror. Tuboitonie, who was carrying a baby on her back and pulling Winnemucca by the hand, found that she couldn't keep up. She and another mother decided to hide their older children by partially burying them in the ground and arranging branches to shade their faces. "Oh, can any one imagine my feelings," Winnemucca says, *"buried alive,* thinking every minute that I was to be unburied and eaten up by the people that my grandfather loved so much?"

At nightfall, the mothers returned and dug up the girls. It was an experience Winnemucca never forgot. It was long before she would look at white people or forgive her grandfather for his love of them. Finding that the white men had set fire to the tribe's stores of food and that all their winter supply was gone, Chief Winnemucca could no longer agree with his father-in-law that the white men were his "brothers."

Winnemucca's distrust of white folk lasted for some time. In the spring of 1850, Truckee traveled again to California, taking fifty people, including Tuboitonie and her children. Carrying a letter of commendation given him by Fremont, Truckee was able to get friendly receptions and occasional gifts of food or clothing from the settlers they met. Winnemucca, herself, hid from the strangers, refusing to speak or to look at them. Her attitude changed, however, after she fell sick with poison oak and was nursed back to health by a white woman. Although she never came to believe as strongly as her grandfather in the goodness of the "white brothers," she did try to understand them and to learn about their customs, without losing touch with her own traditions.

Serves as Interpreter and Scout as the Wars Begin

Winnemucca showed an early facility for languages, learning English, Spanish, and several Indian languages during the time she spent in California. She also came in close contact with white people when she, her mother and her sisters started to work in the houses of white families. When Winnemucca was thirteen, she lived with her younger sister Elma in the home of Major William M. Ormsby, a trader. Ormsby's wife, Margaret, and their daughter taught the girls to sew and cook. They learned and became quite proficient at English, even began to learn to read and write.

As contacts between the whites and Indians increased, Winnemucca often served as interpreter for her father when he met with Indian agents, army officers and in inter-tribal councils. In 1875, she was hired as interpreter for the Indian agent S. B. (Sam) Parrish at Malheur Reservation, which had been established three years earlier. In 1868 Winnemucca served as interpreter at Camp McDermit, while her father and almost 500 of his followers lived at the camp, under the protection of Captain Jerome and the U.S. Army. Parrish and Jerome were two men that Winnemucca trusted, men she believed treated her people fairly.

Winnemucca served as scout, along with her brother, Natchez, while she was at Camp McDermit, but it was during the Bannock War in 1878 that she met her greatest challenge. On her way to Washington, D.C., where she hoped to get help for her people, she learned that the Bannock tribe was warring with the whites and that some Paiutes, her father among them, were being held by the Bannocks. On the morning of June 13, she left the Camp McDermit for the Bannock camp with two Paiutes, arriving at nightfall of the second day. Wrapped in a blanket, her hair unbraided so she wouldn't be recognized, she crept into the camp. There she found her father, her brother, Lee, and his wife, Mattie, among those held captive. They escaped during the night, but were soon pursued by the Bannocks. Winnemucca and her sister-in-law raced their horses to get help, arriving back at Sheep Ranch at 5:30 on June 15. She had ridden a distance of 223 miles. "It was," Winnemucca said, "the hardest work I ever did for the army."

Winnemucca was poorly rewarded for her hard work for the U.S. Army. Both she and Mattie served as scouts during the Bannock War. After the war, the Paiutes were to be returned to Malheur Reservation, but to Sarah's distress, they were ordered to be taken to Yakima Reservation on the other side of the Columbia River, a distance of about 350 miles. It was winter, and the Paiutes did not have adequate clothing. Many people died during the terrible trip, and others, including Mattie, died soon after.

Writes and Speaks Out for Her People

Over the years the situation worsened. Winnemucca sent messages, complaints and entreaties to anyone she thought might help. She traveled to San Francisco and spoke in great halls, telling of the mistreatment of her people by the Indian agents and by the government. She was labelled 'The Princess Sarah' in the *San Francisco Chronicle* and her lecture was described as "unlike anything ever before heard in the civilized world—eloquent, pathetic, tragical at times; at others her quaint anecdotes, sarcasms and wonderful mimicry surprised the audience again and again into bursts of laughter and rounds of applause." News of her lectures reached Washington, and in 1880 she was invited to meet with the President. Together with Chief Winnemucca, and her brother Natchez, she met with Secretary of the Interior Carl Schurz and, very briefly, with President Rutherford B. Hayes. However, Winnemucca was not allowed to lecture or talk to reporters in Washington, and the small group were given promises that were not kept.

Elizabeth Palmer Peabody and her sister, Mary Peabody Mann, the widow of Horace Mann, helped arrange speaking engagements for Winnemucca in Boston and many other cities in the East. They encouraged her to write, as well as speak. She wrote many letters, at least one magazine article and a book. Her friends also encouraged Winnemucca in her dream to start an all-Indian school. Winnemucca had been an assistant teacher on the Malheur Reservation, even though her formal education was limited to three weeks at a Californian Catholic school. In 1884, she founded the Peabody School for Indian children near Lovelock, Nevada, on land that had been given to Natchez. It was to be a model school where Indian children would be taught their own language and culture as well as learning English. Unable to get government funding or approval, however, she had to close the school after four years.

Winnemucca's own life was cut short a few years later by disease. After brief marriages to 1st Lieutenant Edward Bartlett and to Joseph Satwaller, she married Lewis H. Hopkins in 1881. He traveled east with her when she went to lecture there. Hopkins died at their ranch at Lovelock on October 18, 1887 of tuberculosis. On October 16, 1891, Winnemucca died at the home of her sister Elma at Henry's Lake, Idaho, probably of tuberculosis as well. In his book *Famous Indian Chiefs I Have Known,* General Oliver Otis Howard said of Winnemucca's Army career, "She did our government great service, and if I could tell you but a tenth part of all she willingly did to help the white settlers and her own people to live peaceably together, I am sure you would think, as I do, that the name of Thocmetony should have a place beside the name of Pocahontas in the history of our country."

Although Winnemucca ended her life believing that she had failed to make the changes she worked for, she has not been forgotten. Her name is in most reference books about North American Indians. Many books have been written about her life and accomplishments, several especially for young people. The book she wrote in 1883, with the encouragement and editorial assistance of Mary Peabody Mann, *Life Among the Piutes: Their Wrongs and Claims,* was republished in 1969 and remains an important source book on the history and culture of the Paiutes. In Nevada, on the McDermit Indian Reservation, there is a historical marker, erected in 1971, honoring Sarah Winnemucca with the words "she was a believer in the brotherhood of mankind." The name of Sarah Winnemucca, as General Howard hoped, stands high among those Native Americans who have fought for the rights of their people.

Further Reading

American Indian Intellectuals, edited by Margot Liberty, West Publishing, 1976.

Bataille, Gretchen M., and Kathleen M. Sands, *American Indian Women: A Guide to Research,* Garland, 1991.

Brumble, H. David III, *American Indian Biography,* University of California Press, 1988.

Canfield, Gae Whitney, *Sarah Winnemucca of the Northern Paiutes,* University of Oklahoma Press, 1983.

Egan, Ferol, *Sand in a Whirlwind: The Paiute Indian War of 1860,* University of Nevada Press, 1985.

Gehm, Katherine, *Sarah Winnemucca: Most Extraordinary Woman of the Paiute Nation,* O'Sullivan Woodside and Co., 1975.

Gridley, Marion E., *American Indian Women,* Hawthorn, 1974.

Handbook of American Indians North of Mexico, edited by Frederick Webb Hodge, Pageant Books, 1959.

Hirschfelder, Arlene B., Mary Gloyne Byler, and Michael A. Dorris, *Guide to Research on North American Indians,* American Library Association, 1983.

Howard, O. O., *Famous Indian Chiefs I Have Known,* Century Co., 1908.

Kloss, Doris, *Sarah Winnemucca,* [Minneapolis, MN], 1981.

Luchetti, Cathy and Carol Olwell, *Women of the West,* Antelope Island Press, 1982.

Miluck, Nancy Christian, *Nevada, This is Our Land: A Survey from Prehistory to Present,* Dragon Enterprises, 1978.

Morrow, Mary Frances, *Sarah Winnemucca,* Steck-Vaughn, 1992.

Notable American Women 1607-1950: A Biographical Dictionary, edited by Edward T. James, Janet Wilson James and Paul S. Boyer, Belknap Press/Harvard University Press, 1974.

Peabody, Elizabeth P., *The Piutes: Second Report of the Model School of Sarah Winnemucca,* John Wilcox and Son, 1887.

Peabody, Elizabeth P., *Sarah Winnemucca's Practical Solution of the Indian Problem,* John Wilcox and Son, 1886.

Scordato, Ellen, *Sarah Winnemucca: Northern Paiute Writer and Diplomat,* Chelsea House, 1992.

Heizer, Robert F., "Ethnographic Notes on the Northern Paiute of the Humboldt Sink, West Central Nevada, in *Languages and Cultures of Western North America,* edited by Earl H. Swanson, Jr., Idaho State University Press, 1970.

Waltrip, Lela, and Rufus Waltrip, *Indian Women,* David McKay, 1964.

Brimlow, George F., "The Life of Sarah Winnemucca: The Formative Years," *Oregon Historical Quarterly,* June, 1952, pp. 103-34.

Egan, Ferol, "Here in Nevada a Terrible Crime," *American Heritage,* June, 1970, pp. 93-100.

Egan, Ferol, "Victims of Justice: Tragedy at Carson City," *American West,* September, 1972, pp. 42-47, 60-61.

Stewart, Patricia, "Sarah Winnemucca," *Nevada Historical Society Quarterly,* Winter, 1971, pp. 23-28. □

Edward Winslow

Edward Winslow (1595-1655) was a Pilgrim leader in colonial America. He conducted Plymouth's diplomatic business on both sides of the Atlantic and wrote histories of the colony.

The son of a salt dealer, Edward Winslow received a classical education and later became a printer's apprentice in London. Probably employed by William Brewster, he moved to Leiden, Holland, in 1617. Once associated with the Pilgrims there, he became an important supporter and invaluable servant.

Winslow sailed to America with the Pilgrims on the *Mayflower* and from the first bore the Pilgrims' diplomatic responsibilities. He attended to Indian relations and was the colony's major trade representative. He went to the Maine coast to buy provisions from fishing ships and was active in the creation and defense of furtrading posts. He also served three terms as Plymouth's governor.

However, it was as Plymouth's agent in England that Winslow performed his greatest service. He went to England in 1623 to sell a supply of boards and furs and to report to the colony's investors. He returned to Plymouth the next year with a patent for a fishing center at Cape Ann and with three heifers and a bull, the beginnings of Plymouth's herd. In 1630 he replaced the questionable Isaac Allerton as Plymouth's agent to the London investors and in 1634 defended Plymouth's jurisdiction over its Maine trading fort. During the latter visit Winslow proposed that New England create a united military front against the encroachments of the Dutch and French. The proposal aroused political opposition, and he was imprisoned for 4 months for being a Separatist in religion. He undertook his last journey to England in 1646 as the agent of both Massachusetts and Plymouth to defend them from the attacks of their English enemies, notably Robert Childe and Samuell Gorton.

Winslow did not return to Plymouth but instead joined Oliver Cromwell's government in England. He was appointed one of the three joint commanders of the expedition that captured Jamaica in 1655, and he died on the return voyage. His departure from Plymouth and his death were sad losses for the colony.

Winslow wrote a number of pamphlets and tracts recording Plymouth's early history. *Mourt's Relation,* of

which he was coauthor, and his *Good Newes from New England* were Plymouth's first authoritative histories.

Further Reading

There is no recent biography of Winslow. One of the best sources of information, especially on Winslow's contribution to Plymouth, is William Bradford, *Of Plimoth Plantation,* edited by Samuel Eliot Morison (1952). Specific information as well as general background can be found in George F. Willison, *Saints and Strangers* (1945); Bradford Smith, *Bradford of Plymouth* (1951); and George D. Langdon, Jr., *Pilgrim Colony: A History of New Plymouth, 1620-1691* (1966). □

John Winthrop

John Winthrop (1588-1649) was an American colonial political leader and historian. He was a very effective governor of the Massachusetts Bay Colony, and his journal constitutes an important historical record.

John Winthrop was the dominant figure in the early years of the Massachusetts Bay Colony. His actions and ideas gave the Puritan colony much of its essential character. He had close dealings with other important Puritan leaders, such as John Cotton, minister of the church to which he belonged, and Roger Williams, with whom he disagreed.

Winthrop was born on Jan. 22, 1588, near the family seat at Groton in Suffolk County, England. He was the only son of a prosperous landowner, Adam Winthrop. After an education near home, John was admitted to Trinity College, Cambridge, in 1602; he studied there less than two years. At the age of 17, by family arrangement, he was married to Mary Forth. Sometime during his early years Winthrop had a religious experience. He adopted a zealous Puritanism as a result, although he decided not to enter the ministry.

Winthrop's wife produced six children before she died in 1615. He remarried but his wife died a year later. In 1618 he married Margaret Tyndale, and their relationship is one of the most attractive in history. During these years Winthrop devoted himself to the tasks of a country landholder and also to the study of law; he was admitted to Gray's Inn in 1613 for legal studies. In 1617 he was made a justice of the peace in Suffolk, where he lived at Great Stambridge on dowry lands. In 1627 he was appointed attorney in the Court of Wards and Liveries. But Winthrop found several sources of dissatisfaction. The government's religious and political policies and his unprosperous personal circumstances led to a concern to provide for his sons.

Massachusetts Bay Colony

In 1629 Winthrop agreed to go to America with the Massachusetts Bay Company, and in October, after a decision had been reached to put the government of the colony in the hands of resident leaders, he was elected governor. He was involved in all of the elaborate financial arrange-

it has been called *The History of New England*. In it he reports nearly all important events of the day; he also offers profound insights into the essential nature of the Massachusetts Bay Colony.

Religious Controversies

Among the problems that Winthrop and the colony had to deal with was the highly individualistic Roger Williams. The separatist religious tendencies that Williams had demonstrated in Salem (he urged the church there to renounce the other churches of the colony) led to his being banished. But Winthrop, who recognized that Williams's views were potentially destructive to the colony he had helped create, also recognized the virtues of the man and maintained a friendship with him.

Winthrop was much less sympathetic to another member of the church in Boston, Anne Hutchinson. She had arrived in Massachusetts in 1634 to enjoy the preaching of the Reverend John Cotton, whom she had admired in England. As early as 1636 Winthrop began to record a list of the theological errors that she was teaching in weekly meetings. Her fundamental teaching was that "the person of the Holy Ghost dwells in a justified person," in a person called to eternal salvation, and that the presence of the indwelling spirit, not good works, was the evidence that one was of the elect. This antinomianism undercut the Puritan emphasis on the Bible as interpreted by learned ministers, and Mrs. Hutchinson went so far as to declare that only two ministers in the colony, Cotton and John Wheelwright, were among the elect.

At this time, 1636, Winthrop was not governor; the man who held the post was Henry Vane, also a member of Cotton's church and an admirer of Mrs. Hutchinson. Many of the other members of the church also admired her, but she and her views were much less popular outside Boston. Eventually Winthrop was reelected governor, replacing Vane, and Wheelwright and Mrs. Hutchinson were banished. Though Winthrop had been in the minority in his church, his position once more triumphed. In both the Williams episode and the antinomian controversy Winthrop's role was to create unity within the colony, unity necessary for survival.

Winthrop's governorship was intermittent (he served 1630-1633, 1637-1639, 1642, 1646-1648). The General Court recognized his services in 1637 by granting him substantial acreage in Concord. Unfortunately his incapable overseer brought Winthrop deeply into debt. When he put up his Boston house and much of his land for sale, the colony gave him gifts of land and money.

Political Spokesman

The Puritan Revolution in England in the early 1640s led many American colonists to feel a sense of responsibility to their mother country. Some of Winthrop's friends urged his return. But Winthrop felt that it was his duty to remain in Massachusetts. When Dr. Robert Child announced that he was asking Parliament to reduce the colony's independence and abolish the right to limit the vote to church members, Child was promptly fined for contempt, and Winthrop an-

ments and preparation of supplies, and in April 1630 he sailed on the *Arbella,* one of the four ships that brought 400 Puritan men, women, and children to America. Under his direction the colonists settled in the area around the Charles River. Despite courageous and able leadership, 200 colonists died during the first winter, and 80 returned home in the spring. Among the earliest deaths was that of Winthrop's son Henry. Because of the discouragement that resulted among the colony's backers, Winthrop was obliged to invest increasing amounts of his money to provide supplies. The rest of his family did not arrive until the fall of 1631, by which time the colony was solidly established.

Winthrop provided a rationale for the colony in a sermon, "A Model of Christian Charity," which he delivered on the *Arbella*. Here he argued for the creation of a community covenanted with God, and "a due form of government civil and ecclesiastical." The colony was to be "as a city upon a hill" for all to observe. The key provision was that full citizenship in the colony was to be available only to church members. The churches first established adopted a congregational polity, and thenceforth only congregational churches were permitted. The government took great authority unto itself, though it was based on a principle of representative government. Though in 1634 the citizens elected Thomas Dudley as the colony's governor, Winthrop continued to be the most influential man in the colony.

In 1630 Winthrop had begun keeping a diary, which he continued to the year of his death. It is a dry, cold, and impersonal document in style, but it is of immense interest because of its contents. He referred to it as a journal, though nounced that the colony recognized no appeal to higher authority.

One of Winthrop's most important roles in the life of the colony was his spokesmanship for its political position; he sometimes created public policy as well. In July 1645 he delivered a speech to the General Court in which he defined two kinds of liberty: natural (liberty to do as one wishes, "evil as well as good," a liberty that should be restrained) and civil (liberty to do good). It is only the latter, according to Winthrop, that is "the proper end and object of authority." In other words, it is the duty of government to stop corruption and to promote justice, not to promote the general welfare.

Winthrop died on March 26, 1649. Although circumstances in time changed the nature of the colony, many of the features of the New England way he had established remained. He more than anyone else gave the colony its distinctive character, and he was largely responsible for the flourishing state of its 15,000 inhabitants at the time of his death. Of his several children, the most notable was John, who became governor of the colony of Connecticut.

Further Reading

The best edition of Winthrop's journal, *The History of New England, 1630-1649,* is that of James Savage (2 vols., 1825-1826; rev. ed. 1853). The Massachusetts Historical Society's *Winthrop Papers* (5 vols., 1929-1947) is also of great value. Other important sources are Robert C. Winthrop, *Life and Letters of John Winthrop* (1864-1867), and the splendid biography by Edmund S. Morgan, *The Puritan Dilemma: The Story of John Winthrop* (1958). A valuable discussion of Winthrop in relation to Boston's growth is Darrett B. Rutman, *Winthrop's Boston: A Portrait of a Puritan Town, 1630-1649* (1965). □

John Winthrop

John Winthrop (1606-1676), American colonial statesman and scientist, founded several New England settlements. He obtained Connecticut's favorable charter and served as its chief executive.

Oldest child of Massachusetts Bay Colony's first governor, John Winthrop was born at Groton, England, on Feb. 12, 1606. His mother died when he was nine, and his well-to-do father sent him to Bury St. Edmunds Grammar School and Trinity College, Dublin. John studied law desultorily, then served as captain's secretary in the fleet sent to relieve La Rochelle in 1627. After that expedition's failure, he embarked on a European tour.

Returning to London, Winthrop found his father determined to join the Puritan migration to America. John remained behind to sell the family estate and marry his cousin Martha Fones in 1631. Late that year the couple arrived in Boston.

For the next 14 years Winthrop roamed restlessly. In 1633 he led a party to found Ipswich, where his wife and infant daughter died. Returning to England, John visited leading Puritans and obtained the governorship for a projected colony in Connecticut. He reappeared in Boston in 1635 with men, supplies, and a second wife. An advance party erected a fort at Saybrook, Conn., but Winthrop resettled at Ipswich and soon moved the family to Salem.

When the elder Winthrop encountered financial difficulties, John aided his father. This necessitated selling some Ipswich lands; he began salt manufacturing and then journeyed again to England for capital. In 1644 Massachusetts granted him 3,000 acres to establish iron-works, and with imported workers and machinery he built furnaces at Lynn and Braintree. That year he also founded New London, Conn., for the same purpose.

After his father's death in 1649 Winthrop surrendered his Massachusetts public offices, concentrating on Connecticut. Elected governor in 1657, he made Hartford his permanent residence. After 1658 he was annually chosen chief executive the remainder of his life. King Charles II gave Winthrop a most liberal charter for Connecticut in 1662; it included New Haven within Connecticut's jurisdiction. During 1673-1675 he successfully defended the colony's claims against the Dutch and New York's governor Edmund Andros.

Winthrop was more concerned with science than theology. Noted for his library and knowledge of medicine, he pioneered in industrial chemistry and was first resident American member of the Royal Society.

As a New England Confederation commissioner, Winthrop attended a meeting in Boston, where he died on April 5, 1676. Able and charming, he was noted for his tolerance in a generally bigoted age.

Further Reading

The best book on Winthrop is Robert C. Black III, *The Younger John Winthrop* (1966), a thorough and objective treatment, although there are some admitted assumptions. Also worthwhile are Lawrence S. Mayo, *The Winthrop Family in America* (1948), and the penetrating analysis in Richard S. Dunn, *Puritans and Yankees: The Winthrop Dynasty of New England* (1962). □

John Winthrop

John Winthrop (1714-1779), American educator and scientist, helped liberalize the curriculum of Harvard College and received English recognition as America's leading astronomer.

John Winthrop was born in Boston, Mass., on Dec. 19, 1714, the great-great-grandson of Massachusetts Bay's first governor. He early demonstrated scholarly ability, completing Boston Latin School at 14 and graduating from

Harvard in 1732. He studied science at home for six years and at 24 was named professor of mathematics and natural philosophy at Harvard.

Winthrop's public lectures and demonstrations in physical science attracted wide attention, and the results of his continuous and extensive research were published by London's Royal Society. His series of sunspot observations in 1739 were the first in Massachusetts and necessitated close cooperation with both the Royal Society and Greenwich Observatory. He noted transits of Mercury in 1740, 1743, and 1769 and also accurately recorded the longitude of Cambridge, Mass. Other studies included work on meteors (1755), the transit of Venus (1761), and solar parallax and distance (1769).

In 1751 Winthrop inaugurated a new era in American mathematical study by introducing the elements of calculus at Harvard. His study of the New England earthquake of 1755 was a pioneering approach to seismology. He established America's first laboratory of experimental physics in 1746, and his demonstrations on mechanics, heat, and light are thought to have influenced both Benjamin Franklin and Count Rumford.

Winthrop carried on meteorological observations for some 20 years; in 1759 he first predicted the return of Halley's comet. His study of the 1761 Venus transit in Newfoundland was Harvard's first astronomical expedition. His other interests included extensive research on magnetism, eclipses, and light aberrations. In fact, his chief defect as a teacher was said to be his range of subjects which was

so vast that he sometimes failed to go into them deeply enough.

Twice Winthrop declined the presidency of Harvard. However, he served for a time as Massachusetts probate judge and member of the governor's council. During the period of the American Revolution he enthusiastically promoted the colonial cause, encouraged munitions production, and advised George Washington and other American leaders. He was a fellow of the Royal Society (1766) and a member of the American Philosophical Society (1769), and he received honorary doctorates from the University of Edinburgh (1771) and Harvard (1773-the institution's first).

Winthrop married twice; his first wife, Rebecca Townsend, died after seven years (1753), and in 1756 he married Hannah Fayerweather Tolman. She survived him, together with three sons by his first wife, when he died in Cambridge on May 3, 1779.

Further Reading

Information on Winthrop must be gleaned from a number of sources. The best accounts are in Lawrence S. Mayo, *The Winthrop Family in America* (1948), and in Brooke Hindle, *The Pursuit of Science in Revolutionary America* (1956). Robert C. Winthrop, Jr., *A Pedigree of the Family of Winthrop* (1874), is somewhat outdated. □

Isaac Mayer Wise

Isaac Mayer Wise (1819-1900), American Jewish religious leader, was the builder of Reform Judaism in the United States.

I saac M. Wise was born on March 29, 1819, in Steingrub, Bohemia. He attended various traditional Jewish schools in Bohemia, studied at the Universities of Prague and Vienna, and was ordained a rabbi in 1842. After several years as rabbi in the Bohemian town of Radnitz, he emigrated to the United States in 1846. His first pulpit in America was Temple Beth El in Albany, N.Y., where he served from 1846 until 1854, when he became rabbi of Congregation Bene Yeshurun in Cincinnati. He held this post until his death on March 26, 1900.

Reform Judaism

Wise's greatest achievement was the establishment of the three key institutions of Reform Judaism in America. In 1873 he founded, and was elected president of, the Union of American Hebrew Congregations, the organization of Reform Jewish congregations in the United States. Feeling that a rabbinate trained in America could best serve American Judaism, Wise founded in Cincinnati in 1875 the Hebrew Union College, the Reform rabbinical seminary. He served as its president and as a professor of theology for the rest of his life. In 1889 he founded the main organization of American Reform rabbis, the Central Conference of American Rabbis, and served as its president for 11 years. These three

organizations provided the structure for Reform Judaism in America.

Wise's philosophy of moderate Reform Judaism affirmed the historicity of the revelation at Sinai and the divine origin of the Ten Commandments. The latter was for him the basis of Judaism as a universal, rational religion whose destiny was to be mankind's universal religion. Wise accordingly proceeded to "reform" American Jewish ritual and ceremony, removing many of the features of rabbinic Judaism and formulating a new synagogue liturgy (Minhag America) in 1857. Influenced by the universal ideals of American nationalism as well, Wise became an outspoken opponent of the Zionist movement.

His Writings

In addition to his ministerial and organizational labors, Wise was a prolific writer. He edited (1854-1900) the weekly publication *Israelite* (later *American Israelite*), and he published in it numerous articles on Jewish theology and history as well as novels in serial form. The *Israelite* served Wise not only as a platform for expounding his views on Judaism but also as a vehicle for defending Jewish rights. He wrote a number of books on Jewish theology, including *The Essence of Judaism* (1861), *Judaism, Its Doctrines and Duties* (1872), and *The Cosmic God* (1876). In addition he published works on the relationship between Judaism and Christianity: *The Origin of Christianity, and A Commentary to the Acts of the Apostles* (1868), *The Martyrdom of Jesus of Nazareth* (1874), *Judaism and Christianity: Their Agreements and Disagreements* (1883), and *A Defense of Judaism*

versus Proselytizing Christianity (1889). Among his works on Jewish history and literature were *The History of the Israelitish Nation from Abraham to the Present Time* (1854), *The History of the Hebrews' Second Commonwealth* (1880), and *Pronaos to Holy Writ* (1891).

Further Reading

The most comprehensive work on Wise is James G. Heller, *Isaac M. Wise: His Life, Work, and Thought* (1965), a lengthy study published by the Union of American Hebrew Congregations. A shorter, more popular work is Israel Knox, *Rabbi in America: The Story of Isaac M. Wise* (1957).

Additional Sources

Temkin, Sefton D., *Isaac Mayer Wise, shaping American Judaism,* Oxford England; New York: Published for the Littman Library by Oxford University Press; Washington, DC, USA: Distributed in the U.S. by B'nai B'rith Book Service, 1992. ☐

John Wise

John Wise (1652-1725), American Congregational minister, effectively defended the autonomy of individual congregations. His opinions regarding religious and civil democracy foreshadowed the logic of the Declaration of Independence.

John Wise was born in Roxbury, Mass., in August 1652. He studied in the Roxbury free school and graduated from Harvard in 1673. He then studied theology and preached at Branford, Conn. (serving as chaplain during King Philip's War), and Hatfield, Mass. In 1680 he was called to the Second (Chebacco) Church in Ipswich. A dispute with the First Church, from which the body was separating, delayed official organization but Wise was installed in 1683 and remained throughout his life.

Known for his democratic principles, Wise encouraged Ipswich citizens to resist Governor Edmund Andros's attempt to raise money by a province tax without legislative authorization. He was tried, convicted, and fined for the remonstrance, and Andros briefly deprived him of his ministerial functions. When Andros was deposed, Wise sued Chief Justice Joseph Dudley in 1689 for refusing his earlier plea for habeas corpus; tradition has it that, though the town had paid his fine and costs, he recovered damages. That year he was a delegate from Ipswich to reorganize the Massachusetts colonial legislature.

The General Court appointed Wise chaplain of the unsuccessful 1690 expedition against Quebec, and Wise upon his return wrote a report of the undertaking. He petitioned in 1703 for reversal of the sentence for one of the victims in a witchcraft trial, and he opposed the moves of Increase and Cotton Mather to subordinate Massachusetts churches to associations of clergymen. Wise viewed their proposal as hierarchical and infringing upon the rights of individual congregations. Some years after Increase

Mather's advocacy of it in a pamphlet (1705), Wise published a devastating and satirical reply, *The Churches' Quarrel Espoused* (1710), which reputedly crushed the effort.

Wise's *A Vindication of the Government of New-England Churches* (1717) reemphasized his position and dealt with the bases of both religious and civil government. His pamphlet *A Word of Comfort to a Melancholy Country* (1721) advocated paper money for the colony.

Tall and graceful in appearance, and possessing almost legendary physical strength, Wise was an impressive speaker and an earnest, witty, and forceful writer. He married Abigail Gardner, who bore him seven children. He died in Ipswich on April 8, 1725.

Wise's 1710 and 1717 pamphlets, reprinted in 1772 for use in the Revolutionary ideological controversy with England, have been adjudged among the finest colonial expositions of democratic principles. An edition of 1860 noted that the Declaration of Independence utilized several passages strikingly similar to those in *A Vindication. . . .*

Further Reading

Wise's own *Narrative* of the Quebec expedition is in *Proceedings of the Massachusetts Historical Society,* 2d series, vol. 15 (1902). A good account of him is George A. Cook, *John Wise: Early American Democrat* (1942). Helpful comments are in Vernon L. Parrington, *Main Currents in American Thought* (3 vols., 1927-1930; 3 vols. in 1, 1930). □

Political Activist

Wise's career was marked by a long and distinguished record of service to the American public. In Oregon he had been active in civic affairs and served as commissioner of child labor. In New York City he became active in efforts to improve municipal government and served as a member of the City Affairs Committee. He fought to better the lot of the workingman and was a founder of the National Association for the Advancement of Colored People. Active in interfaith activities, he inaugurated, with his close friend Protestant minister John Haynes Holmes, a series of nonsectarian services. Wise participated actively in various presidential campaigns, supporting Woodrow Wilson and Franklin Roosevelt. He was appointed to the President's Advisory Committee on Political Refugees (1940) and to the President's Commission on Higher Education (1946). He numbered among his friends the Supreme Court justices Benjamin Cardozo and Louis Brandeis, both of whom worked with Wise in the Zionist movement.

It was in the area of Jewish communal affairs that Wise made his greatest contributions. He was a lifelong Zionist and devoted much time to the development of a Jewish state in Palestine. In 1897 he was among the founders of the Federation of American Zionists. In 1898 he attended the Second Zionist Congress in Basel and met—and was greatly influenced by—Theodor Herzl, founder of the Zionist movement. Herzl appointed him American secretary of the Zionist Organization. Wise first visited Palestine in 1913, returning again in 1922 and 1935. In 1914, with Brandeis,

Stephen Samuel Wise

Stephen Samuel Wise (1874-1949), American Jewish religious leader and Zionist, played an important role in Jewish communal affairs.

Stephen S. Wise was born on March 17, 1874, in Budapest, Hungary, into a family with a long tradition of rabbinic leadership. He was brought to the United States in 1875. After graduating from Columbia University in 1892, he pursued postgraduate studies at Oxford and rabbinical studies in Vienna, where he was ordained by the chief rabbi of Vienna. He received his doctorate from Columbia in 1902. In 1900 he married Louise Waterman. Wise's scholarly work included an English translation (1901) of the Book of Judges for the Bible published by the Jewish Publication Society of America in 1917.

Wise's first ministerial post was Congregation Bnai Jeshurun in New York City (1893-1899). He then became rabbi of Temple Beth Israel in Portland, Ore. In 1906 he returned to New York City and founded the Free Synagogue, of which he was spiritual leader until his death. Feeling a need for a seminary in New York to train students for the liberal rabbinate, Wise founded the Jewish Institute of Religion in 1922 and served as its president until it merged with Hebrew Union College in 1948.

he established the Provisional Committee for General Zionist Affairs. In 1918 he was elected to a 2-year term as president of the Zionist Organization of America and served a second term in 1936.

Zionist Leader

As a leader of the Zionist movement, Wise represented the movement on many historic occasions. He advised Woodrow Wilson with regard to the British government's Balfour Declaration, which supported the establishment of a Jewish state in Palestine (1917). He attended the Paris Peace Conference (1918) and the London Conference of Arabs and Jews (1939). Also, he testified before the Anglo-American Commission of Inquiry on Palestine (1946). When British policy in Palestine during the 1930s and 1940s became increasingly anti-Jewish, Wise fought against it, and as early as 1930 he had written *The Great Betrayal,* with Jacob de Haas. In 1947 Wise fought for the adoption of the Palestine Partition Plan, which brought about the establishment of the State of Israel in 1948.

In 1916, together with Brandeis and others, Wise founded the American Jewish Congress, and in 1936 he founded the World Jewish Congress. He served both congresses as president until his death. In the 1930s he played a leading role in mobilizing American opposition to the Nazis and in focusing attention on the Jewish refugee problem created by Nazi persecution. During the 1940s he brought reports on the Nazi efforts to exterminate European Jewry to public attention. Wise died on April 19, 1949.

Further Reading

The main source of information on Wise is his autobiography, *Challenging Years* (1949). This is supplemented by two collections of his correspondence: *Personal Letters,* edited by Wise's children, Justine Wise Polier and James Waterman Wise (1956); and *Stephen S. Wise: Servant of the People,* selected letters edited by the Protestant clergyman Carl Hermann Voss (1969). Voss also wrote an account of Wise's friendship with John Haynes Holmes, *Rabbi and Minister* (1964).

Additional Sources

Shapiro, Robert Donald, *A reform rabbi in the progressive era: the early career of Stephen S. Wise,* New York: Garland Pub., 1988.

Urofsky, Melvin I., *A voice that spoke for justice: the life and times of Stephen S. Wise,* Albany: State University of New York Press, 1982.

Voss, Carl Hermann, *Rabbi and minister: the friendship of Stephen S. Wise and John Haynes Holmes,* Buffalo, N.Y.: Prometheus Books, 1980. □

Frederick Wiseman

Frederick Wiseman (born 1930) was an American documentary filmmaker whose "fly-on-the-wall" films revealed what happens in a hospital, school, meat-packing plant, police department, modeling agency, department store, zoo, and other public institutions. Many of his films focused public attention on problems in the places he portrayed.

Frederick Wiseman was born in Massachusetts on January 1, 1930. He graduated from Williams College and Yale Law School. Wiseman was a graduate fellow at Harvard for a year and was then drafted into the army. He worked for a short time as an assistant to the attorney general of Massachusetts, then lived in Paris for two years (1956-1958). On his return to the United States he taught at Boston University's Institute of Law and Medicine, often taking his students to visit law courts and prisons.

Titicut Follies

Increasingly bored with the abstractions of the law, Wiseman bought the film rights to *The Cool World* (1963), a novel about Harlem delinquents, and produced the film, which was directed by Shirley Clarke. After taking his law students to the Massachusetts Correctional Institution at Bridgewater, a prison for the criminally insane, to show them the conditions there, Wiseman decided to make his own film. *Titicut Follies* (1967) is a brutally realistic, extended gaze at the oppressive conditions at Bridgewater, offered without any commentary.

Titicut Follies was widely celebrated by critics and academics, but was attacked in courts by the Commonwealth of Massachusetts. In 1968 Judge Harry Kalus ruled in *Commonwealth* v. *Wiseman* that Wiseman had breached an oral contract with the state and had invaded the privacy of one of the Bridgewater inmates. Kalus ordered the film banned in Massachusetts. On appeal, the Massachusetts Supreme Court softened the decision and permitted showings of the film to special audiences; in 1991 the injunction was lifted completely.

In *Titicut Follies* and the documentaries that followed, Wiseman used a small, unobtrusive crew, including a cameraman using lightweight equipment and no additional lights. Wiseman recorded sound, while an assistant supplied fresh film and tape. His straightforward films contain no on-camera interviews or commentary by the filmmaker. All scenes are unstaged to achieve what Wiseman called "a natural history of the way we live." His films are shot in black and white with no music. Wiseman's method gave the films the feel and texture of reality, but they were deftly and slowly edited in a way that encouraged the viewer to make connections, to speculate about social themes, and to reflect about the subject. "The whole point of this technique is to put you right into the middle of things so you have to think through your relationship to them," Wiseman said in 1993 to *Vogue* magazine.

"Reality Fictions"

Wiseman called his films "reality fictions," acknowledging that he was employing his own perspective. "All the material is manipulated so that the final film is totally fictional in form although it is based on real events," he explained. Wiseman's films have both the gravity of reality and the pleasures of art. They examine the oppressive, silly, and mundane procedures of human institutions, but they are not cynical, depressing, or vicious. Wiseman's wry, detached tone, accompanied by the patient's probing curiosity of his films, resulted in a humanistic focus on the quality of our everyday lives.

After *Titicut Follies,* Wiseman produced *High School* (1968), filmed at the middle-class Northeast High School in Philadelphia, a widely admired exposure of the oppressiveness and boredom imposed on adolescents and their apathetic response. After the angry tone of *Titicut Follies* and *High School,* Wiseman turned increasingly to a more complex interest in cultural issues, in which problems and victims are seldom clear-cut. Wiseman's subsequent documentaries were produced under contracts with New York City Public Television station WNET and were often shown on TV's Public Broadcasting System, but rarely in movie theaters.

Wiseman's *Law and Order* (1969) follows police procedures in Kansas City. *Hospital* (1970) explores the routines of an urban hospital. *Basic Training* (1971) shows a group of young draftees being prepared for infantry service in Vietnam. *Essene* (1972) focuses on a group of Benedictine monks. *Juvenile Court* (1973) explores a juvenile justice system in Memphis, presenting the paradoxes of attempting to combine justice and therapy. *Primate* (1974), one of Wiseman's most controversial films, shows the destructive results of human curiosity on a colony of captive apes at the Yerkes Primate Research Center in Atlanta. The PBS broadcast of the film brought viewer complaints and a bomb threat.

Many consider Wiseman's *Welfare* (1975) to be his most effective work; it shows the frustrating interaction of a New York City welfare center and its clients. *Meat* (1975) is a dark comedy about a meat-packing plant in Colorado, where bleating animals are reduced to stacks of neat plastic packages for supermarkets.

Institutions Laid Bare

Wiseman said his goal in his films was to "discover what kind of power relationships exist and differences between ideology and the practice in terms of the way people are treated. The theme that unites the films is the relationship of people to authority."

Wiseman ventured outside the United States in *Canal Zone* (1977), which shows how American residents of the Panama Canal Zone try to keep their American cultural routines intact. In *Sinai Field Mission* (1978) Wiseman explored American soldiers on a peacekeeping mission in the Sinai Desert. In *Manoeuvre* (1979) Wiseman watched a National Guard unit participating in war games in Germany, rehearsing for a war with the Soviet Union.

Model (1980) extended Wiseman's analysis of American culture by looking at how images are constructed in the advertising business. In *The Store* (1983) Wiseman moved from modeling to merchandising, choosing the Neiman-Marcus store in Dallas as his setting.

Wiseman released one fiction film, *Seraphita's Diary* (1982), which explores the theme of self-awareness. He went to Belmont Race Track in New York to film *Racetrack* (1985), then in 1987 released a pair of films on people with disabilities: *Blind* and *Deaf.* Also in 1987 he released *Missile.* In 1989 his *Near Death* chronicled the intensive care unit of Boston's Beth Israel Hospital. In 1990 he returned to New York City to shoot *Central Park.* In 1993 his look at Miami's Metrozoo, *Zoo,* was widely praised. In 1994 he returned to an earlier subject with *High School II,* about Central ParkEast Secondary School in East Harlem, New York. In 1995 he chronicled the American Ballet Theatre in *Ballet.* In 1996 Wiseman released *La Comedie-Francaise Ou L'Amour Joue,* a tribute to a three-century-old Paris theater. "Wiseman at last has made a totally positive case for a human institution," wrote Robert Brustein in the *New Republic.*

For his work, Wiseman won three Emmys. Melissa Pierson noted in the June 1993 *Vogue,* "Under Wiseman's steady, perseverant gaze, these almost banal institutions yield fascinating information on their customary play of power, or what happens to individuals venturing into their works, or the gap between what society professes and what it ends up doing. His films require patience, but the viewer is rewarded with crucial truths about the way we live—and lie."

Wiseman told Pierson that he considered his earlier films, *Titicut Follies* and *High School,* too "didactic." Thus, in his later years Wiseman tried to avoid being too partisan. "There's a lot of heavy freight connected with the documentary," he said. "It's supposed to instruct us, uplift us, right a social wrong. But it can be other things; it doesn't have to be an exposé. That's too simpleminded. Why bother?"

Further Reading

Wiseman's films are the central texts that he has produced, and they are available for rental or lease from his distribution company, Zipporah Films, in Cambridge, MA. A standard reference work is Liz Ellsworth, *Frederick Wiseman: A Guide to References and Resources* (1979), which provides descriptive material, and in some cases transcripts, of the films up to 1977, as well as an extensive bibliography. Tom Atkins, *Frederick Wiseman* (1976), contains several useful interviews and reviews. Several books provide material on Wiseman in the context of documentary film in general; see Richard Meran Barsam, *Nonfiction Film: A Critical History* (1973); Lewis Jacobs, *The Documentary Tradition,* 2nd edition (1979); G. Roy Levin, *Documentary Explorations: 15 Interviews with Filmmakers* (1971); Stephen Mamber, *Cinema Verite in America: Studies in Uncontrolled Documentary* (1974); and Bill Nichols, *Ideology and the Image* (1981). □

John Witherspoon

John Witherspoon (1723-1794) was a Scottish-born American Presbyterian divine and educator. He transformed the College of New Jersey (later Prince-

ton) from a poor theological seminary into a vigorous academic community.

John Witherspoon was born into a ministerial family near Edinburgh on Feb. 5, 1723. He matriculated at the University of Edinburgh at 13 and took his master of arts degree in 1739 and his divinity degree 4 years later. In 1745 he accepted the call to the pulpit of Beith in Ayrshire. There he married Elizabeth Montgomery, who bore him ten children, only five of whom survived.

In 1757 the town of Paisley offered him its church and he served there for the next eleven years. An eloquent spokesman for the Popular (conservative) church party, he deplored the spiritual vacuity of the "paganized Christian divines" of his day and attracted the attention of intellectuals at home and abroad for his courage and leadership. As moderator of the synod of Glasgow and Ayr, he delivered a powerful sermon, "The Trail of Religious Truth by Its Moral Influence" (1759), in which he decried the flabby "theory of virtue" that was replacing "the great and operative views of the Gospel."

President of the College of New Jersey

Witherspoon was just the man for the presidency of the College of New Jersey, which was torn between new-and old-side factionalism, and the job was offered him in 1766. But his wife thought that to leave home "would be as a sentence of death to her." The persuasiveness of Benjamin

Rush, an alumnus of the college, and now a medical student at Edinburgh, finally allayed her fears. Witherspoon and his family arrived in America in August 1768, loaded with valuable books for the college library.

The call to the college in Princeton, N.J., was more than an educational mission. The Presbyterian Church was divided in counsel and looked to the new president to heal its wounds. As Rush explained to Witherspoon, the college president "was from his office as it were the bishop of all our American churches and ruled in all our church judicatories," and his voice "has hitherto been a law in our synods." Under Witherspoon the schism was healed, the organization strengthened, and the church grew rapidly toward its union with Congregationalism in 1801.

As a college administrator, Witherspoon had equal success. His personal energy and magnetism filled the mismanaged and inadequate coffers. He pressured his trustees into purchasing substantial additions to the library and the finest scientific additions to the library and the finest scientific equipment, of which David Rittenhouse's orrery was the most coveted item. For the traditional recitations he substituted lectures on the largely neglected fields of history and rhetoric, and he encouraged his professors to promote more science and mathematics, while he himself taught French to those who wanted it. As the Colonies drew closer to revolution, he promoted public speaking and literary exercises on current events in an effort to fashion the civil leaders of the next generation. But his most abiding intellectual achievement was to introduce to America the Scottish commonsense philosophy, which quickly made short shrift of his tutors' infatuation with the idealism of George Berkeley.

Political Activities

The American Revolution put a damper on this progress. The students dispersed, Nassau Hall was mutilated in turn by British and colonial troops, and Witherspoon was drafted into a frantic round of political duties. From an early involvement in New Jersey committees of correspondence, he went on to sign the Declaration of Independence and to serve on a hundred congressional committees, including two important standing committees—the Board of War and the Committee on Secret Correspondence, or Foreign Affairs. He took an active part in the debates over the Articles of Confederation and helped organize the executive branch and draw up the instructions of the American peace commissioners.

Though Witherspoon was often absent from the college, leaving his son-in-law Samuel Stanhope Smith in charge, the institution was never far from his thoughts. While in Congress, he criticized the galloping depreciation of currency that was pinching endowed institutions, extracted a grant of £7,250 from Congress for damages to Nassau Hall, and fought for military deferments for students and teachers. When he returned to full-time teaching in 1782, the college was in relatively sound condition, though it never fully recovered from the war during his lifetime.

The remainder of Witherspoon's busy years were spent in rebuilding the college. He lost an eye on a fruitless fundraising trip to Great Britain in 1784, and his total sight in 1792. When his wife died, the 68-year-old president delighted the college community by marrying a young widow of 24, by whom he had two daughters. On Nov. 15, 1794, ''our old Scotch Sachem'' (as Benjamin Rush affectionately called him) died at his farm near Princeton.

Further Reading

The definitive, scholarly biography of Witherspoon is Varnum L. Collins, *President Witherspoon* (2 vols., 1925). Thomas Jefferson Wertenbaker places the man in his academic setting in *Princeton, 1746-1896* (1946).

Additional Sources

Stohlman, Martha Lou Lemmon, *John Witherspoon: parson, politician, patriot,* Louisville, Ky.: Westminster/John Knox Press, 1989, 1976. □

Johan de Witt

The Dutch statesman Johan de Witt (1625-1672), as councilor pensionary of Holland from 1653 to 1672, led the Dutch Republic after the end of its war of independence.

A man of keen intelligence, displayed notably in his contributions to mathematics and actuarial science, Johan or Jan de Witt used his post as chief minister of the States of Holland to prevent or limit the restoration of the powers of the Prince of Orange. The era of his government is known in Dutch history as the first stadholderless period because no stadholder (governor) was named in Holland and four other Dutch provinces from the death of William II in 1650 until the election of William III in 1672.

De Witt was born at Dordrecht on Sept. 24, 1625, into a family of prosperous merchants and lawyers. With his older brother Cornelius, he studied law at Leiden (1641-1644), and he also studied mathematics with great enthusiasm. The brothers visited Sweden in 1644 as part of a diplomatic mission led by their father, and then they went on a tour of France and England (1645-1647), taking their law degrees at Angers in 1645. Upon their return, Johan practiced law at The Hague until 1650.

When his father, a deputy to the States of Holland, was arrested during the coup d'etat of William II on July 30, 1650, Johan obtained his release, with the loss of his father's offices but not his honor. This coup totally estranged the De Witt family from the house of Orange, to which it had been closely bound since the struggle between Maurice of Nassau and Johan van Oldenbarnevelt 3 decades before. When William II died in November, leaving only a posthumous son, William III, to claim his offices of stadholder and captain general, Johan and his father were among the leaders in creating a fully republican regime, in which no one was appointed to these quasi-monarchical positions. The name ''True Freedom'' was given to this regime by its advocates.

Leader of Holland

De Witt was named pensionary (chief legal and political officer) of Dordrecht in December 1650, and as such he was its principal deputy to the States of Holland. He became councilor pensionary in 1653. As such, he was in practice, although not in law, the political leader of Holland, director of foreign and fiscal policies for the United Provinces, and leader of a party committed to ''True Freedom.'' His republican principles were put to the test when Oliver Cromwell demanded the perpetual exclusion of the Prince of Orange from the stadholdership and captaincy general as the price of peace in the first of the Anglo-Dutch Wars (1652-1654). De Witt persuaded the States of Holland to accept this admittedly distasteful interference, from which Cromwell could not be swerved, because the war was irredeemably lost. The Act of Seclusion (May 4, 1654) caused a tremendous furor among the still strongly Orangeist preachers and populace and in the other provinces; but De Witt defended Holland's sovereign right to act in his *Deduction,* published in the name of the States of Holland.

De Witt used the years of peace to strengthen Dutch finances and encourage trade and shipping. After the outbreak of the First Northern War in 1658, the pressure of Amsterdam overwhelmed his preference for neutrality, and the Dutch Republic took the side of Denmark, rescuing it from conquest by Sweden. Meanwhile, De Witt watched as the English called Charles II to the throne. Only too aware that the restored king was William III's uncle, he tried to win the King to a policy of friendship, proposing during Charles's stay in The Hague, enroute home, that the young prince become a "Child of State," educated by the States of Holland with the promise of office upon coming of age. This compromise failed when William's mother, Mary Stuart, died in 1660, leaving Charles by testament as his sole guardian.

Sharp commercial rivalries between the English and the Dutch increased until the second of the Anglo-Dutch Wars began in 1664 in West Africa and in 1665 in Europe. By now De Witt had the Dutch navy ready for war. He pursued a policy of vigorous naval offensive, culminating in the triumphant campaign of June 1667 that compelled the English to make peace in the Treaty of Breda in July.

Soon afterward, Holland adopted an Eternal Edict, which abolished the stadholdership but assured eventual military office to the prince. On Jan. 23, 1668, De Witt completed negotiation of an alliance with England (called the Triple Alliance following Sweden's entry in March) to halt French advances in the Spanish Netherlands in the War of Devolution.

De Witt attempted without success to retain an alliance with France made in 1662. Louis XIV persuaded England and Sweden to betray their alliance with Holland, and England joined him in an invasion of the Republic (the Third Anglo-Dutch War, 1672-1674, or the "Dutch War" of France, 1672-1678) which began in April. De Witt had not given the Dutch land forces the same attention as the navy, and he had delayed as long as possible the election of William III as captain general. When the French invaders plunged into the heart of the United Provinces in June, De Witt was held responsible, denounced as a traitor, and badly wounded in an assassination attempt on June 21. Upon recovery he resigned as councilor pensionary on August 4. He and his brother were massacred by an Orangeist mob in The Hague on August 20.

De Witt's mathematical work, praised by Christiaan Huygens and Sir Isaac Newton, was a study of conic sections appended to a Latin translation of René Descartes's *Geometry* (1661). De Witt's study of the relative values of life annuities and redeemable bonds, given to the States of Holland in 1671, was one of the earliest actuarial works, although not concerned with insurance as such.

Further Reading

The best study of De Witt is in Dutch. In English, James Geddes, *History of the Administration of John De Witt, Grand Pensionary of Holland* (1879), is very detailed but goes only to 1654. Germain Antonin Lefèvre-Pontalis, *John De Witt, Grand Pensionary of Holland; or, Twenty Years of a Parliamentary Republic* (2 vols., 1885), is comprehensive, based on long research, but suffers from an anachronistic interpretation. De Witt figures prominently in the excellent history by Pieter Geyl, *Orange and Stuart, 1641-1672* (trans. 1970).

Additional Sources

Rowen, Herbert Harvey, *John de Witt, grand pensionary of Holland, 1625-1672*, Princeton, N.J.: Princeton University Press, 1978.

Rowen, Herbert Harvey, *John de Witt, statesman of the "true freedom"*, Cambridge; New York: Cambridge University Press, 1986. □

Count Sergei Yulyevich Witte

The Russian statesman Count Sergei Yulyevich Witte (1849-1915) is noted for his policy of Russian industrialization, for his role in negotiating the Peace of Portsmouth between Russia and Japan, and for his formulation of the Manifesto of October 1905.

Sergei Witte was born in Tiflis. His parents gave him little attention, and he was exposed to the harmful influences of his foster-mother and to her drunkard husband and to tutors of questionable character. He was a poor student in the local classical gymnasium. At the age of 17 Witte received the certificate of maturity which entitled him to enter a university, and he matriculated in the faculty of physico-mathematical sciences at the University of Odessa.

Upon finishing his studies Witte entered the service of the Odessa government railroad. In 1877, when war broke out between Russia and Turkey, he was named head of the Odessa railroad. It was of strategic importance, for the railroad transported soldiers to the front. After the war Witte was appointed director of the exploitation department of the newly formed railroad system. His office was in St. Petersburg, and there he married Madame Spiridonov, a beautiful woman and the daughter of the marshal of the nobility of the Chernigov Province. Since the northwestern railroads were running at a deficit, Witte was named director of southwestern railroads in order to reorganize the entire management of the roads through centralization. In 1892 he was appointed minister of ways of communication. His administration in this capacity lasted some 6 months. He was then appointed minister of finance by Alexander III and served in that powerful post until Nicholas II dismissed him in 1903.

Industrialization of Russia

Like Peter the Great, Witte believed that Russia must industrialize. He held that Russia must avoid war and that domestic policy must be coordinated with foreign policy. He was realistic in opposing Asian wars and the Japanese-Russian war. He erred, however, in the notion that he could control the general bureaucracy of the army.

Witte advocated autocracy and a strong state. His program included not only economic but also political reforms. He was a friend of the middle class engaged in industry and thus made many enemies among the nobility. He believed that, if sacrifices had to be made so that Russia would be industrially strong, the peasants could be exploited because in the future their standard of living would rise.

strike of October took place, he advised Nicholas II to decide between a constitutional regime and a military dictatorship, but informed the Czar that he would take part only in the former. On Oct. 30, 1905, Nicholas II issued the October Manifesto, which was drafted by Witte, and simultaneously named Witte Russia's first prime minister. The October Manifesto recognized the civil liberties of the Russian people; it called for the election of a state Duma; it established as a rule that no law should be passed without its confirmation by the Duma.

Witte served as prime minister during a very difficult period and was forced to resign in May 1906; he was replaced by a more conservative premier. Witte died in St. Petersburg on March 12, 1915.

Further Reading

The Memoirs of Count Witte (trans. 1921) provides a good picture of the man and his times. Theodore H. Von Laue, *Sergei Witte and the Industrialization of Russia* (1963), gives an account of the impact of the reforms enacted by Witte. For a good discussion of the general historical period and Witte's career see Lionel Kochan, *Russia in Revolution, 1890-1918* (1966). □

Witte, through the construction of railroads, provided necessary links and stimulants to industry and lowered the prices. The state took over the railroads in order to achieve greater efficiency. Witte believed in foreign investments and was not afraid of increasing government debt. He wanted a favorable balance of trade and a stable currency, convertible and based on gold. In 1897 he put Russia on the gold standard to attract investments. He also put a high tariff on imports in order to protect Russian production and to overcome industrial backwardness. He believed that grain would serve as the currency to pay for Russian imports. Russia, however, had to compete with America, Australia, and Argentina, which produced grain more cheaply. Witte tried to solve this problem by exploiting the peasants ruthlessly.

Diplomatic Activities

On July 29, 1905, Witte was appointed chief plenipotentiary for the purpose of conducting a peace treaty with Japan at Portsmouth, N.H. He negotiated a peace with Japan on Sept. 5, 1905. Russia recognized Japanese hegemony in Korea, the annexation of southern Sakhalin, and the lease of the Liotung Peninsula and the southern Manchurian railway. Although these concessions were large, the cost of peace did not seem excessive in light of the domestic problems which the government was facing at home. For his services he was given the title of count.

When Witte had returned from making peace at Portsmouth, he found the country torn by strikes, demonstrations, and mutiny in the armed forces. When the general

Ludwig Wittgenstein

After making important contributions to logic and the foundations of mathematics, the Austrian philosopher Ludwig Wittgenstein (1889-1951) moved away from formalism to an investigation of the logic of informal language.

Ludwig Wittgenstein was born in Vienna on April 26, 1889, the last of eight children in a wealthy and highly cultured family. He was educated at home, particularly in music, which both parents pursued, and raised as a Catholic. At the age of 14, having shown a talent for mechanics, Ludwig was sent to a school in Linz that emphasized mathematics and physical sciences. Three years later he entered the Hochschule in Berlin to pursue a course in mechanical engineering. Becoming dissatisfied, Wittgenstein moved to England, where he did experimental work in aeronautics and eventually registered as a research student in engineering at the University of Manchester.

In 1912 Wittgenstein read Bertrand Russell's *Principles of Mathematics* and became fascinated with the question of the foundation of mathematics. Immediately he applied to enter Trinity College, Cambridge, where Russell lectured. Wittgenstein made rapid progress in his studies of logic and mathematics at Cambridge, but within two years his restless temperament moved him on again, this time to a solitary life in a primitive hut in Norway. Several times in his life Wittgenstein responded to an underlying passion for a simple and authentic life, what he called "purity," by abandoning academic society for a hermit's existence.

On the outbreak of World War I, Wittgenstein returned to Austria and saw service on the Eastern front and later in the Tirol, where he was taken prisoner by the Italians. From his prison camp he was able to send Russell the draft of the only book published in his lifetime. After years of discussion and disagreement, the work was finally published in 1922 under the title *Tractatus Logico-Philosophicus*. At the time Wittgenstein regarded it as his definitive contribution to philosophy.

After the war, having been profoundly influenced by reading Leo Tolstoy on the Gospels, Wittgenstein gave away his considerable fortune and became a school-teacher in an Austrian village. For years he resisted the overtures of the group of philosophers known as the Vienna Circle, who were excited by his book, and turned down the invitations of Cambridge friends. Finally, in 1929, he returned to Cambridge as a lecturer and resumed his work in philosophy. His classes there were always small seminars of about 20 students who had passed Wittgenstein's stringent requirements of seriousness and dedication. He refused to take part in the social amenities of a don's life.

In the *Tractatus* Wittgenstein had stated that all positive inquiry falls into the domain of one of the sciences and had relegated philosophy to the clarification of what can meaningfully be said. He believed he had set final limits to the expressible and exposed the remainder as either nonsense or inexpressible. Now he began to doubt the finality of these results. He became more sensitive to the importance of shifting contexts in meaningful expression. He now thought it mistaken to search for invariant forms or rules of expression. Sentences are meaningful within the rules of a particular "language game," but each game is nothing more than a part of language, and the various parts do not share a common essence but only a "family resemblance." In analyses of great subtlety, rich with vivid metaphors and striking examples, Wittgenstein led his students on a search for the implicit rules in various language games, without claiming that everything involved in the communication of meaning can be made explicit—and without claiming that any a priori limits can be set on linguistic inventiveness. Some of this work was published posthumously as *Philosophical Investigations* (1952), and since then his students have issued a steady stream of selections from his notebooks.

Wittgenstein's teaching was interrupted by World War II, during which he insisted on doing menial work in a hospital laboratory. Thereafter he became increasingly dissatisfied with academic philosophy and in 1947 resigned the chair which he had assumed, after G. E. Moore, in 1940. Again he sought seclusion on the Irish coast and in Norway. He visited his family in Vienna and spent three months in the United States. Meanwhile his health had deteriorated, and it was discovered that he had cancer. He died in the home of his Cambridge physician on April 29, 1951.

Wittgenstein had unusual gifts in architecture, sculpture, and music, besides his talents for engineering and philosophy. He was a charismatic teacher and yet was fearful of making disciples. Although melancholy and depressive all his life, he radiated strength and authority. Always longing for solitude, he had many friends and, like Socrates, influenced most by personal contact. He repudiated academic philosophy, but he remains a decisive force in English and American universities.

Further Reading

A convenient place to begin a study of Wittgenstein is the anthology edited by K. T. Fann, *Ludwig Wittgenstein: The Man and His Philosophy* (1967). This contains a number of memoirs by his friends, critical essays on his work, and a good bibliography. Two full-length studies of Wittgenstein are Justus Hartnack, *Wittgenstein and Modern Philosophy* (1960; trans. 1965), and George Pitcher, *The Philosophy of Wittgenstein* (1964). The short biographical essay by a former student, Norman Malcolm, *Ludwig Wittgenstein: A Memoir* (1958), is a moving tribute. A definitive biography is being prepared by B. F. McGuinness. For background information see John Passmore, *A Hundred Years of Philosophy* (1957; rev. ed. 1966). □

Additional Sources

Ludwig Wittgenstein, personal recollections, Totowa, N.J.: Rowman and Littlefield, 1981.

Malcolm, Norman, *Ludwig Wittgenstein: a memoir / Malcol,* Oxford Oxfordshire; New York: Oxford University Press, 1984.

McGuinness, Brian, *Wittgenstein, a life: young Ludwig, 1889-1921,* Berkeley: University of California Press, 1988.

Monk, Ray, *Ludwig Wittgenstein: the duty of genius,* New York: Free Press: Maxwell Macmillan International, 1990.

Pinsent, David Hume, *A portrait of Wittgenstein as a young man: from the diary of David Hume Pinsent 1912-1914,* Oxford, UK; Cambridge, Mass., USA: Basil Blackwell, 1990. □

Konrad Witz

Konrad Witz (ca. 1410-1446) was the first German painter to depict a fully developed three-dimensional space and landscape that is topographically recognizable. His figures have a hieratic monumentality and power.

Konrad Witz was born in the village of Rottweil in the Black Forest. He went to Basel, presumably attracted by the great Church council in progress since 1431. He entered the painters' guild in Basel in 1434. The following year he became a citizen. In 1441-1442 Witz was paid for paintings he executed for the city, and he bought a house in 1443. He died in 1446.

Fate has been unkind to the three major enterprises of Witz, all originally altarpieces composed of many panels, for none is intact today. The earliest certain work is the *Mirror of Salvation Altarpiece* (ca. 1435), an agglomerate of panels depicting scenes from the Old Testament and Roman history which prefigure man's salvation, for example, the scenes of Antipater before Caesar, the Queen of Sheba before Solomon, and Emperor Augustus and the Tiburtine Sibyl. The lost centerpiece was probably the Birth of Christ, signaling the redemption of man. Witz's last known major work, signed and dated 1444, was the *Altarpiece of St. Peter* for a chapel in the Cathedral of Geneva. Only the wings, comprising eight scenes, exist today. Probably dating between these two altarpieces, in the artist's creative life-span of a mere 12 years, are three large paintings which may have formed part of an altarpiece of the Virgin. It was originally in the Dominican nunnery in Basel, and the panels are now dispersed.

From beginning to end, Witz's major artistic aim was to present the illusion of plastic form. He achieved this by bright color contrasts, a strong modeling light that causes the simplified figures and objects to cast strong shadows, and the use of stark architectural settings. His figures thus appear like actors on a stage. Stumpy in proportion, with large heads and hands, these figures move awkwardly but convincingly; and to further the illusion Witz imagined such ancient dignitaries as Caesar and Solomon as homely human beings, a sibyl as a robust housewife. The master's conviction of the force of his technique enabled him to transcend his limitations.

Witz's style is memorable because it is born of forthrightness and sincerity. This combination of naiveté and sophistication is seen in his most memorable picture, the *Miraculous Draught of Fishes,* from the *St. Peter Altarpiece,* wherein the Sea of Galilee becomes a realistically observed portion of Lake Geneva, with the Môle mountain in the distance, as it appeared in the artist's own day. As such, the painting is a landmark in the history of Western landscape painting.

Further Reading

An excellent discussion of Witz's life and work is in Hanspeter Landolt, *German Painting: The Late Middle Ages, 1300-1500* (1968). Briefer comments are in Pierre Descargues, *German Painting from the 14th to the 16th Centuries* (1958), and Horst Vey and Xavier de Salas, eds., *German and Spanish Art to 1900* (1965). □

Wo-jen

Wo-jen (1804-1871) was a Chinese official who, during the 1860s, became the preeminent opponent of the introduction of Western learning. He represents the conservatism encountered by progressive Chinese who attempted the partial modernization of China.

W o-jen was a Mongol, born in Honan Province. His father was a soldier in the banner armies of the Manchu rulers of China. Wo-jen undertook classical studies rather than following his father's military career. At the age of 25 Wo-jen completed successfully the third and highest of the civil service examinations and began his long career in the bureaucracy. Meanwhile, he had become widely acclaimed as a Confucian scholar and for his stern observance of the Confucian ethical code. This philosophical and moral reputation may have impeded Wo-jen's bureaucratic advancement, however, for Emperor Hsienfeng (ruled 1851-1861) thought such persons lacked administrative ability.

The death of Hsien-feng and the accession of a new emperor, T'ung-chih (ruled 1862-1874), marked Wo-jen's leap to the top of the bureaucratic ladder. He now assumed a series of prestigious posts, serving (often concurrently) as president of one of the Six Boards, chancellor of the Hanlin Academy, tutor to the Emperor, and grand secretary. He had become one of the most powerful ministers in the realm.

In 1860 China had been defeated in the Arrow War by the combined British and French forces and was forced to sign a humiliating peace treaty. To resist further foreign aggression, the Ch'ing government adopted a policy of Self-strengthening reforms that had been advocated by such leading officials as Prince Kung, Tseng Kuo-fan, and Li Hung-chang. So long as these reforms were limited to the sphere of the army and diplomacy, Wo-jen made no protest. But in 1867 Prince Kung proposed the inclusion of Western learning (mathematics, astronomy, chemistry, political economy) in the curriculum of the T'ung-wen Kuan (Interpreter's College) and the hiring of foreigners as instructors.

Wo-jen, true to his Confucian learning, believed that national strength could not be obtained by borrowing the techniques and learning of the hated and despised foreigner, but only by the reassertion of the strictest moral principles. In a memorial to the throne, he declared: ''Your humble servant has learned that the way to establish a nation is to lay emphasis on propriety and righteousness, not on power and plotting. . . . From ancient down to modern times, I have never heard of anyone who could use mathematics to raise the nation from a state of decline. . . . The only thing we can rely on is that our scholars should clearly explain the Confucian tenets to the people.''

Wo-jen's arguments had no immediate effect on government policy. His views, however, were supported by conservative and antiforeign literati throughout the country, and they served to impede efforts to modernize China during the 19th century. He died on June 8, 1871, and his name was celebrated in the Temple of Eminent Statesmen.

Further Reading

A biographical sketch of Wo-jen is in Arthur W. Hummel, ed., *Eminent Chinese of the Ch'ing Period, 1644-1912,* vol. 2 (1944). For background see Mary C. Wright, *The Last Stand of Chinese Conservatism: The T'ung Chih Restoration, 1862-1874* (1957), and Joseph R. Levenson, *Confucian China and Its Modern Fate* (1958; repr. as *Modern China and Its Confucian Past: The Problem of Intellectual Continuity,* 1964). □

Friedrich August Wolf

The German classical scholar and philologist Friedrich August Wolf (1759-1824) laid the foundations for modern philology through his scientific treatment of the classical period.

Friedrich Wolf was born at Hagenrode near Hanover on Feb. 15, 1759. When the 18-year-old Wolf entered the University of Göttingen, already proficient in several ancient and modern languages, he demanded that he be enrolled in the faculty of philology. The fiery young scholar was unaware that such a faculty did not exist in the university. The rebellious Wolf persisted, however, and he indeed was enrolled as he desired, only to leave the university 2 years later completely disillusioned by the curriculum and his professors.

In 1783 Wolf became professor of philosophy and pedagogy at the University of Halle, where he taught for the next 23 years. In his early career he published studies on Plato, Hesiod, Lucian, Demosthenes, Herodian, and Cicero. Both these studies and his lectures did much to revive interest in classical studies in Germany. He saw classical philology as a science in itself. His lectures were famous, and he developed a great following among the students, many of whom saw him as a debunker. It is reported that even the great Goethe came to hear the lectures. Wolf lectured on literature, survivals, geography, art, coins, and on almost every aspect of the classical world, with the notable exceptions of philosophy, politics, and economics. Many of these courses were posthumously published on the basis of auditors' notes.

The Napoleonic invasion in 1806 caused the closing of the university, and Wolf went to Berlin, where he helped to reorganize the university and became a professor. His essay outlining the best approaches to classical study might be described as a literate syllabus, and in that sense, a most

unusual work indeed. The central theme was that we should avoid the endless and mere collection of particular facts. Rather, we must begin with a conception of the animating spirit of an age, that which binds all the particulars together and makes them meaningful. He died in Marseilles on Aug. 8, 1824.

The work for which Wolf will always be known is the *Prolegomena to Homer* (1795). Written in Latin, it has been termed "one of the cardinal books of the modern world." The main argument of the book is that the Homeric epics in the form that we know them were of composite authorship. That contention was not a new or radical one. It had been advanced by the scholars of Alexandria in the late classical period, by Perizonius, by Giambattista Vico, and by Robert Wood in 1769 in a work which was translated into German. Indeed, some critics have seen Wolf's preoccupation with establishing his originality as a grave moral fault in that the time would have been better spent, from the standpoint of the development of scholarship, in the application and refinement of his critical methods.

Wolf's argument that the *Iliad* and the *Odyssey* were of composite authorship rested upon the then firmly held belief that writing for literary purposes was unknown prior to Solon (late 7th century B.C.). Thus it would be impossible to compose and transmit long epics. The "Homer" we know is really a blending of various poems written by different authors, probably about the mid-6th century B.C. Wolf admitted that several of the poems were probably composed by a poet named Homer. The Wolfian thesis, however, was perceptively criticized by subsequent scholars who felt that even if everything that Wolf said was true, the next—and most obvious—question would be: who did the "blending"? Thus, in reply to Wolf, we have the famous scholarly joke that the Homeric poems were not composed by Homer but by an entirely different individual whom we now know as Homer. Furthermore, the hypothesis upon which his whole argument rested, concerning the beginning of literary writing, has now been definitively refuted. Thus, this "cardinal book of the modern world" is now read only by litterateurs with antiquarian interests.

Despite the erroneous central contentions of the book, it was of great significance for modern scholarship because of the critical methods that Wolf used. It did more than any other single work to inspire the modern critical approach to the analysis of ancient texts, and it is credited with leading directly to the 19th-century "higher criticism" of the Bible. For these reasons, he is often regarded as the founder of modern philology.

Further Reading

The best brief sketch in English of Wolf's life and work is the noted essay in *Essays by the Late Mark Pattison,* edited by Henry Nettleship (2 vols., 1889; repr. 1967). For Wolf's analysis of the Homeric texts see John E. Sandys, *A History of Classical Scholarship* (1908). More recent discussions of Wolf's life and work are in James Westfall Thompson, *A History of Historical Writing* (2 vols., 1942), and John L. Myres, *Homer and His Critics,* edited by Dorothea Gray (1958). □

James Wolfe

James Wolfe (1727-1759), English general, led the British troops to their famous victory over the French at the Plains of Abraham near Quebec.

James Wolfe was born into a military household on Jan. 2, 1727, at Westerhan, Kent. He attached himself as a volunteer to his father's regiment at the age of 13 and 2 years later received a commission in that regiment. Shortly afterward, he joined the 12th Foot as an ensign. In 1743 he fought at Dettingen as battalion adjutant. In the Jacobite rebellion of 1745, he was brigade major and aide to Gen. "Hangman" Hawley. Wolfe was cited by the Duke of Cumberland for his part in the battle at Lanfoldt, a factor in his being given command of the 20th Regiment at the age of 23. After his promotion to lieutenant colonel in 1750, he served as quartermaster general in the ill-fated attempt on Rochefort.

In the continuing conflict between the French and British in Canada, Wolfe distinguished himself as a brigadier under Gen. Jeffery Amherst in early 1758 during the successful siege of Ft. Louisbourg. After ravaging the settlements of the "Canadian vermin" along the Gulf of St. Lawrence, he returned to England although he had received no specific orders to do so. Then, becoming bored with garrison life, he offered his services to Prime Minister William Pitt, expressing a preference for duty in the St. Lawrence area.

In Pitt's plan to take Canada, Amherst was to drive north to take Ticonderoga and Montreal. Wolfe, now a major-general, was given an independent command to take Quebec. On June 4, 1759, the expedition sailed from Louisbourg with a total of 8,500 troops, and by June 27 the army had disembarked and camped on Île d'Orléans opposite Quebec. A bombardment of Quebec from batteries on Pointe de Lèvis and raiding parties through the countryside failed to lure the French commander, the Marquis de Montcalm, out of the city. On July 31 a British attack at Beauport failed because of strong French resistance and a sudden storm.

Wolfe sent out punitive expeditions, burning homes and killing inhabitants, hoping that the Canadians would desert Montcalm. Illness swept through the British army. Wolfe's personal relations with the officers of the army worsened. The famous statement, "I can only say, Gentlemen, that if the choice were mine, I would rather be the author of these verses [Gray's "Elegy"] than win the battle which we are to fight tomorrow morning," is said to have been uttered by Wolfe in a fit of pique when his officers did not properly appreciate his recitation.

On Sept. 3, 1759, the Pointe de Lèvis camp was evacuated, and preparations were made for an all-out attack on the city before cold weather. On the night of September 13, the British scrambled up a zig-zag path at Anse au Foulon and overpowered the French guard at the top of the cliff. On the following morning the British were drawn up on the

Plains of Abraham. Montcalm sallied out of the city, and the battle began about 2 P.M.

Early in the battle Wolfe received a wound in the wrist from a sniper and later a belly wound from an artillery splinter. He had his ranks hold their fire until the enemy were within 50 yards. The badly mauled French were routed; their general was among the fatalities. Wolfe received another wound, through the lungs, supposedly from the gun of an English deserter. He died shortly afterward with the words: "Now, God be praised. Since I have conquered, I will die in peace." Quebec surrendered on September 18. Wolfe's body was returned to England and was buried in the family vault at Greenwich.

Further Reading

Wolfe has been a popular subject for biographers. Christopher Hibbert, *Wolfe at Quebec* (1959), provides insight into Wolfe's personality. Duncan Grinnell-Milne, *Mad, Is He?: The Character and Achievement of James Wolfe* (1963), is chiefly a defense of Wolfe's military career. Older works include Francis Parkman, *Montcalm and Wolfe* (2 vols., 1884; new intro., 1962); Beckles Willson, *The Life and Letters of James Wolfe* (1909); J. T. Findlay, *Wolfe in Scotland* (1928); W. T. Waugh, *James Wolfe: Man and Soldier* (1928); and Frederick E. Whitton, *Wolfe and North America* (1929). For the struggle between England and France for control of North America see Lawrence H. Gipson's multivolume work, *The British Empire before the American Revolution,* particularly vol. *7: The Great War for Empire: The Victorious Years, 1758-1760* (1949), and vol. 8: *The Great War for Empire: The Culmination, 1760-1763* (1954).

Additional Sources

Garrett, Richard, *General Wolfe,* London: Barker, 1975.

Liddell Hart, Basil Henry, Sir, *Great captains unveiled,* London: Greenhill Books; Novato, Ca., U.S.A.: Presidio Press, 1990.

Pringle, John, Sir, *Life of General James Wolfe, the conqueror of Canada, or, the elogium of that renowned hero, attempted according to the rules of eloquence with a monumental inscription, Latin and English, to perpetuate his memory,* Montreal: Grant Woolmer Books, 1974. □

Thomas Clayton Wolfe

Thomas Clayton Wolfe (1900-1938) was an American novelist of prodigious talent and equally formidable failings. His highly autobiographical novels are notable for fervent energy, uninhibited emotion, and grandly rhetorical language.

Thomas Wolfe achieved critical acclaim for his unabashed romanticism and visionary faith in the inherent greatness of America and the heroism of its people. He possessed an extraordinary ability for portraiture and a gift for visual detail and sensory impressions, but his brilliance is often diminished in a diffuse sea of inflated irrelevancies and ranting incantations and exhortations. Modern critics have grown less infatuated with his prose and become more aware of the lack of thematic focus, structural cohesion, and controlling artistic intelligence in even his most disciplined work.

The most striking irony in Wolfe's work is that despite his spontaneous emotionalism there is an absence of compassion for any character other than his self-identifying protagonist, and despite his mystic exaltation of sex there is little credible sexuality and even less love.

Lonely Childhood

Wolfe was born on Oct. 3, 1900, in Asheville, N.C. His mother had been a schoolteacher before marrying William O. Wolfe, a stonecutter and a man of towering assertiveness and drive. After the parents split up, Wolfe's lonely childhood was spent shuttling between the two. The death of his older brother Ben, whom he idolized, left an emotional scar from which he never recovered.

After an outstanding scholastic record, at the age of 15 Wolfe was admitted to the University of North Carolina, where he became active in various publications and theater groups. Two plays were produced: *The Return of Buck Gavin* (published 1924) and *The Third Night* (1938). Upon graduation the embryonic author continued at Harvard University, eventually earning a master of arts degree. His involvement with the famous Playwright Workshop led to *Welcome to Our City* (produced at Harvard, 1923) and to work on *Mannerhouse* (published 1948), concerning the disintegration of a southern family. His professors' enthusiasm encouraged Wolfe to move to New York in 1923 to seek success in the theater. Failure forced him to accept a position as English instructor at New York University. In 1924 in Europe he met Aline Bernstein, a married mother of two, 16 years his senior, with whom he had a brief but intense love affair.

Look Homeward, Angel

In 1926 Wolfe began work on an enormous novel which would explore and explain "the strange and bitter magic of life." After some 20 months of furious writing, Wolfe left the huge, sprawling manuscript with Maxwell Perkins, editor of Scribner's. Though impressed with the author's genius, Perkins would not publish the novel until it was considerably revised and drastically cut. After a great deal of reworking and editing, *Look Homeward, Angel* appeared in 1929. Opening with a 90-page account of the early lives of his father and mother, the novel is a thinly disguised autobiographical record of the author's early years in the person of Eugene Gant.

In contrast to the critics' instant praise, Wolfe earned the hostility of many relatives and friends who easily recognized themselves in the novel. Though recent critical judgment of the work has been tempered by the recognition of its romantic and at times adolescent pretentiousness, *Look Homeward, Angel* contains vigorous prose and sequences of unquestionable power, such as the chilling conversation between Eugene and the ghost of his brother Ben, and the graphic description of his father's struggle against cancer. It is Wolfe's major contribution to American literature.

Wolfe resigned from New York University in 1930 and returned to Europe for a year on a fellowship. He had in mind a vast novel of several volumes which would range in time from the Civil War to the present and would replace Eugene Gant with a less autobiographical protagonist. After nearly five years of grappling with this conception—while living in extreme loneliness and near poverty in Brooklyn Heights, New York City—Wolfe recognized his inability to achieve a structural unity for the work.

Of Time and the River

Perkins insisted that Wolfe return to his previous auto-biographical mode. Despite Wolfe's bitter protestations, a mammoth, haphazardly organized novel, *Of Time and the River,* appeared in 1935. Here the story of Eugene Gant continues, from his journey to Harvard University, through his period of personal turmoil in Europe, including an unhappy love affair, concluding with his return to the United States. The work's two outstanding sections are a vivid description of Eugene's ride to Boston and the horrifyingly effective account of the death of Gant's father.

Alternating between hysterical affirmation and maudlin self-pity, the novel's young protagonist is a rather unpleasant individual whose heroic conception of himself is never sustained by objective facts. Most of the other characters are sketchily drawn, with the exception of the friend Starwick, who, like Eugene, is endowed with a tragic dimension, whose basis is never made clear. Eugene's relationship with Starwick and his horror at discovering his friend's homosexuality are psychologically ambiguous and absurdly melodramatic. The study maintains a strange effectiveness, however, because of its frequent insights into the abyss of human loneliness and the sterility of self-love.

Several months after publication of *Of Time and the River,* Perkins collected several short stories and sketches extracted from Wolfe's earlier uncompleted novel. Under the title *From Death to Morning,* the uneven work was severely attacked by critics, although it included two of Wolfe's finest pieces of controlled narration—"Only the Dead Know Brooklyn" and "Death the Proud Brother." In 1936 Wolfe terminated his association with Perkins, largely to quell the rumor that the editor had acted as a near collaborator in the creation of his fiction, and signed with Edward C. Aswell, editor of Harper and Brothers.

Posthumous Publications

Forgiven by his family and friends in North Carolina, for the first time in many years Wolfe returned home, where he spent several months writing and discovering that "you can't go home again." He presented a voluminous manuscript to Aswell, the working outlines for a new series of novels. On vacation in the West, Wolfe suddenly contracted pneumonia, which activated a tubercular condition. He died on Sept. 15, 1938, in Baltimore.

From the eight-foot pile of manuscript left him, Aswell compiled two novels, *The Web and the Rock* (1939) and *You Can't Go Home Again* (1940), and a volume of short stories, *The Hills Beyond* (1941). The novels are no less autobiographical than Wolfe's earlier ones, and despite

some impressive prose in *The Web and the Rock,* there is no indication that Wolfe had begun to achieve mastery of his medium or to discover fresh thematic material. Wolfe's other posthumous writings include *Letters to His Mother* (1943), *Western Journal* (1951), and *Letters* (1956).

Further Reading

The only biography of Wolfe is Andrew Turnbull, *Thomas Wolfe* (1968). An intimate but adulatory view emerges from the reminiscences of Robert Raynolds, *Thomas Wolfe: Memoir of a Friendship* (1965). Critical studies are Pamela Hansford Johnson, *Thomas Wolfe* (1947); Herbert J. Muller, *Thomas Wolfe* (1947); Louis D. Rubin, *Thomas Wolfe: The Weather of His Youth* (1953); Richard G. Walser, *Thomas Wolfe* (1961); and Bruce R. McElderry, *Thomas Wolfe* (1964).

Collections of critical opinion on Wolfe are Richard G. Walser, ed., *The Enigma of Thomas Wolfe: Biographical and Critical Selections* (1953), and Thomas Clark Pollock and Oscar Cargill, eds., *Thomas Wolfe at Washington Square* (1954). For briefer discussions see the relevant sections in Joseph Warren Beach, *American Fiction, 1920-1940* (1941); Maxwell Geismar, *Writers in Crisis: The American Novel between Two Wars* (1942); Alfred Kazin, *On Native Grounds: An Interpretation of Modern American Prose Literature* (1942); Edwin B. Burgum, *The Novel and the World's Dilemma* (1947); and Frederick J. Hoffman, *The Modern Novel in America, 1900-1950* (1951). □

Thomas Kennerly Wolfe Jr.

American journalist and novelist Thomas Kennerly Wolfe, Jr. (born 1931), was a major figure in the "New Journalism" which began in the 1960s.

Thomas Kennerly Wolfe, Jr., was born in Richmond, Virginia, on March 2, 1931, the son of Thomas Kennerly and Helen (Hughes) Wolfe. He graduated from Washington and Lee University (1951) and earned a doctorate in American studies at Yale University in 1957, with a dissertation on "The League of American Writers: Communist Organizational Activity among American Writers, 1929-1942." Wolfe married Sheila Berger (art director of *Harper's* magazine) in 1978. They had two children: Alexandra and Thomas.

He began his career as a journalist, including positions at the Springfield, Massachusetts, *Union, The Washington Post,* and the *New York Herald Tribune,* where he was a feature writer. In 1963 Wolfe won recognition for a series of articles in *Esquire* and *New York,* the Sunday magazine of the *Herald Tribune.* Some of Wolfe's articles were collected in his first book, *The Kandy-Kolored Tangerine-Flake Streamline Baby,* whereupon he was generally acknowledged as a master of the New Journalism.

Wolfe described his version of the New Journalism as an appropriation of the techniques of realistic fiction writers, building a nonfiction account of a person or group after an intense period of observation and interviews, mixing exposition with reconstructed dramatic "scenes" that rely

upon dialogue and access to the interior experience of the subjects. Wolfe experimented with a flamboyant style, switching freely between the point of view of the narrator and his subjects, employing an energetic vocabulary that mixed the subject's colloquialisms with his own vivid and esoteric diction, and constructing a detailed awareness of the subject's social status. At its best, the New Journalism opened a new world to nonfiction writing, both enriching the reader's sense of the lived experience of the subject and expanding the range of interpretation open to the writer, whose voice had an entirely new range. By abandoning the rules of objectivity, stylistic simplicity, authorial distance, and decorum of contemporary journalism, Wolfe also made of New Journalism a vehicle for parody and social criticism, freed from the responsibility for connected argument or earnest sobriety—which he implicitly blamed for turning conventional journalism into a tame creature.

In Wolfe's hands, the New Journalism was a celebration for life as lived, and at the same time an instrument for the disparagement of pretension and self-destructiveness. In his story on Junior Johnson, a race driver schooled in backcountry whiskey running, Wolfe described an escape from revenue agents: "They had the barricades up and they could hear this souped-up car roaring around the bend, and here it comes—but suddenly they can hear a siren and see a red light flashing in the grille, so they think it's another agent, and boy, they run out like ants and pull those barrels and boards and sawhorses out of the way, and the— Ggghhzzzzzzzzhhhhhhggggggzzzzzzzeeeeeong!—

gawdam! there he goes again, it was him, Junior Johnson! with a gawdam agent's si-reen and a red light in his grille!"

In 1968 Wolfe published *The Electric Kool-Aid Acid Test,* an account of novelist Ken Kesey and his followers, the Merry Pranksters, on a drug-saturated cross-country bus tour. In 1973 he published his manifesto on "The New Journalism," along with an anthology of other new journalists he admired, with special praise and acknowledgement of such figures as Truman Capote, Gay Talese, Michael Herr, Hunter Thompson, and Garry Wills.

In 1979 Wolfe published *The Right Stuff,* which is about the Apollo 7 astronauts, a work with greater intellectual sweep and less satirical attitudes than his earlier work. In the book he tells the story of the Apollo mission within the frame of the "right stuff," an ethos epitomized by fighter ace and test pilot Chuck Yeager, who never became an astronaut. The astronauts, in Wolfe's account, were at first regarded as human guinea pigs—"spam in a can." *The Right Stuff* describes their attempts to achieve the status of true test pilots. This book earned Wolfe both the American Book Award and the National Book Critics Circle Award in 1980.

Wolfe's *Bonfire of the Vanities* (1987) is a sweeping satirical novel about New York City in which a rich, young Wall Street bond salesman becomes the object of a criminal investigation and trial motivated by a venal media and self-serving descendants of the civil rights movement. The novel was a best seller. But although it was praised by critics as a good read, it was criticized for the flatness of its characterizations, driven by Wolfe's polemical intentions. In 1989 Wolfe published a manifesto in *Harper's* magazine, echoing his 1973 essay on the New Journalism in his claims that America's major novelists had abandoned realistic fiction and, in effect, claiming the mantle of America's chief realistic novelist—just as he had, in the earlier essay, declared the realistic novel dead and claimed for New Journalism the inheritance of the 19th-century realistic novel.

Further Reading

The works of Tom Wolfe include *The Kandy-Kolored Tangerine-Flake Streamline Baby* (1965), *The Pump House Gang* (1968), *The Electric Kool-Aid Acid Test* (1968), *Radical Chic and Mau-Mauing the Flak Catchers* (1970), *The Painted Word* (1975), *Mauve Gloves and Madmen, Clutter and Vine and Other Stories, Sketches, and Essays* (1976), *The Right Stuff* (1979), *Bonfire of the Vanities* (1987), "Stalking the Billion-Footed Beast: A Literary Manifesto for the New Social Novel," *Harper's Magazine* (November 1989), and Tom Wolfe and E. W. Johnson, editors, *The New Journalism* (1973).

For commentaries and critiques of Tom Wolfe and the New Journalism, see Marshall Fishwick, editor, *New Journalism* (1975); John Hellmann, *Fables of Fact: The New Journalism as New Fiction* (1981); John Hollowell, Fact and *Fiction: The New Journalism and the Nonfiction Novel* (1977); Nicholas Mills, editor, *The New Journalism* (1974); Ronald Weber, *The Literature of Fact: Literary Nonfiction in American Writing* (1980); and W. Ross Winterowd, *The Rhetoric of the "Other" Literature* (1990). □

Baron Christian von Wolff

The German philosopher Baron Christian von Wolff (1679-1754) systematized the doctrines of Leibniz. He is best known for his broad concept of philosophy.

Christian von Wolff was born in Breslau, Silesia, on Jan. 24, 1679. His father, a tanner, vowed that his son would enter the Lutheran ministry. At the University of Jena, Wolff studied theology but found that he was more interested in mathematics, physics, and philosophy. He took a master of arts degree at the University of Leipzig, where he taught from 1703 to 1706. He wrote a paper on universal practical philosophy, which he submitted to Gottfried Wilhelm von Leibniz, and on the strength of Leibniz's recommendation Wolff was appointed professor of mathematics at Halle in 1706. He remained there until 1723, when Frederick William I expelled him from Prussia for anti-Pietist teachings.

Wolff then taught at the University of Marburg, where he continued to publish various sections of his unified and deductive system of all branches of human knowledge. His productivity can be gauged by the fact that the collected edition of his major works fills 26 volumes. With the accession of Fredrick II (the Great) in 1740, Wolff was recalled in triumph to Halle. He was honored as professor, vice-chancellor, and finally chancellor of the university (1743). He died at Halle on April 9, 1754.

Wolff was well acquainted with the major developments of modern science and philosophy. He met and corresponded with Leibniz, and, like his mentor, Wolff knew ancient philosophy as well as the Roman Catholic and Protestant traditions of scholasticism. His aim was to systematically organize all knowledge in terms of logical deductions from first principles.

The metaphysics of this endeavor was Leibnizian in origin: the principles of identity and sufficient reason. Wolff believed that every idea or concept expresses a possibility. That some possibilities are actualized is a matter of historical fact. Thus the role of sensation and experience in general is historical. The transition from historical knowledge to philosophical knowledge is the difference between "the bare knowledge, the fact" and the reason for this fact. Philosophy is "the science of all possible things." Insofar as things are definite they have quantitive relations, and mathematics is the clearest expression of the demonstrable scientific connections between objects. Therefore the purview of all knowledge is encompassed in the disciplines of history, philosophy, and mathematics. With this plan, which Wolff presented in *Preliminary Discourse on Philosophy in General* (1728), he was able to offer a complete division of the sciences.

Further Reading

Richard J. Blackwell's translation of *Preliminary Discourse on Philosophy in General* (1963) is Wolff's only work available in English. For secondary literature in English consult John V. Burns, *Dynamism in the Cosmology of Christian wolff: A Study in Pre-critical Rationalism* (1966). Further information on Wolff can be found in Etienne Gilson and Thomas Langan, *Modern Philosophy: Descartes to Kant* (1963). □

Hugh Wolff

Hugh Wolff (born 1953) achieved a national reputation as a talented conductor and in the 1990s was considered one of a handful of Americans who would lead the major orchestras of the future. He was musical director of the New Jersey Symphony and principal conductor of the St. Paul Chamber Orchestra. He had also been a guest conductor with many of the best-known orchestras in the United States.

His family was living in Paris when Hugh Wolff was born in 1953. His father was a U.S. foreign service officer, and the family subsequently moved to postings in London and the Washington, D.C. area. When Wolff was 10 years old he became fascinated by the piano while watching his sister practice. Later, in his own words, he became "one of those obnoxious twelve-year-olds who practiced every day, entered local piano competitions, and endured the jeers of the neighborhood kids because I spent so much time at the piano." While still in high school, Wolff was fortunate to be able to study piano with Leon Fleisher and composition with George Crumb. In choosing a college, Wolff avoided conservatories, viewing them as intellectually confining, and attended Harvard College instead. He majored in composition there and studied piano with Leonard Shure and composition with Leon Kirchner while also studying physics, mathematics, and chemistry.

It was at Harvard that Wolff had his first experiences as a conductor, leading the student-run Bach Society Orchestra. Some of the instrumentalists were "pre-med students who wanted to get away from organic chemistry for a while," according to Wolff. He found the experience invaluable. "I learned from the bottom up," he says, "planning programs, selling tickets, setting up chairs. That's how you get the bug."

Wolff graduated from Harvard *magna cum laude* and Phi Beta Kappa in 1975. During the next year he attended the Paris Conservatoire on a fellowship. There he studied conducting with Charles Bruck and composition with Oliver Messiaen. In the fall of 1976 he returned to the United States to continue his piano studies with Leon Fleisher at the Peabody Conservatory. It was at this time that Wolff decided to give up composing and to concentrate on conducting. He became the conductor for a community orchestra in Annapolis, Maryland, and sat in during rehearsals of the Baltimore Symphony. It was during these rehearsals that Wolff observed the subtle interplay between conductor and orchestra members, the combination of persuasion and pressure that is needed to forge and then project a single interpretation of a piece.

Conducting with the National Symphony Orchestra

After three years of study, Wolff decided to apply for a position as assistant conductor with a major American orchestra. As a result of sending out dozens of letters to orchestras around the country, he was invited to audition for the position of Exxon/Arts Endowment conductor with the National Symphony Orchestra (NSO). He was awarded the position and began his association with the orchestra in the 1979-1980 season. Antol Dorati, who was scheduled to give a two-week series of concerts, became indisposed and Wolff conducted the National Symphony Orchestra in his absence to critical acclaim, proving that he was able to work well under pressure.

Under the tutelage and with the support of Mstislav Rostropovich, the musical director of the National Symphony, Wolff appeared with an increasing number of orchestras around the country. In the 1980-1981 season he was a guest conductor of the Hartford Symphony and the Chicago Civic Orchestra. He also made his debut at Carnegie Hall with the National Symphony.

In the 1981-1982 season the fast pace he had set for himself continued with a debut with the London Philharmonic and a new appointment as music director of the Northeastern Pennsylvania Philharmonic. Of this appointment he said, "[It was] a remarkable orchestra based in

Scranton . . . They capitalize on the presence of New York and Philadelphia near by, getting outside musicians to supplement a core of locals . . . I learned a lot there, including fund-raising and project-planning." Over the summer he returned with the NSO to the music festival at Wolf Trap.

At the end of the three-year Exxon/Arts Endowment funding, Wolff was retained for three more years as an associate conductor of the NSO. It was during these three seasons that his guest conducting increased to include the Seattle Symphony, Stockholm Philharmonic, Chicago Symphony, and the New Jersey Symphony Orchestra. It was this last orchestra that provided Wolff with his first musical directorship of an important orchestra.

Director of the New Jersey Symphony Orchestra

In the 1985-1986 season he began his tenure with the New Jersey Symphony. One of Wolff's goals was to develop interesting programs by using unifying themes, by juxtaposing works in some way related to each other, and by re-enacting concert programs from the past. His first concert as music director was a re-creation of a concert of Beethoven's music held in Vienna on December 22, 1808. The program, the length of which required a dinner break in the middle of the performance, included Symphonies No. 5 and No. 6 plus the G major piano concerto and three movements from the Mass in C and the Choral Fantasia. Michael Redmond remarked in *Musical America* that, "[Wolff] appears to have a particular gift for music of extended lyrical character. He never permitted the songful lines of the Sixth Symphony to sag; instead, they seemed to pick up tensile strength the longer they got."

During the years that he was musical director of the New Jersey Symphony he was in great demand and his schedule was astonishingly full. He conducted concert versions of operas, including *Fidelio* by Beethoven and a program called "Star-Crossed Lovers" which included Prokofiev and Tchaikovsky's music based on the story of Romeo and Juliet. In addition to the many responsibilities that came from directing the New Jersey Symphony, he also accepted the position of principal conductor of the St. Paul Chamber Orchestra.

As music director of The Saint Paul Chamber Orchestra (SPCO), Wolff continued delighting audiences and critics alike. Under his direction the SPCO made tours on both the national and international scene. Wolff's recordings regularly made *Billboard's* top-selling classical music charts. While associated with the SPCO, he also found time for guest conducting engagements with the National Symphony Orchestra, the San Francisco Symphony and the Atlanta Symphony. The 1990's included two nationally-televised concerts: a "Live from Lincoln Center" Christmas program (1990) and "A Capitol Fourth" Independence Day concert from Washington, D.C. (1992). In 1993 Wolff served as artistic director of the American Russian Youth Orchestra with performances in both Russia and the U.S.

Wolff was already one of the leading American conductors by the 1990s. His extensive training, excellent teachers, and broad experience gave him a particularly rich background from which to develop his own interpretations of orchestral music, enabling him to transmit to an audience all of the subtlety and intricacy of the symphonic repertoire.

Further Reading

Many of Wolff's performances have been reviewed in newspapers and magazines. Good articles about him appeared in the *New York Times* on February 1, 1989, and in *Musical America* in September 1987 in which he discussed his career. Regular reviews of his recordings can be found in magazines such as; *Stereo Review* and *American Record Guide*. □

Wolfram von Eschenbach

Wolfram von Eschenbach (ca. 1170-ca. 1230), a German writer of chivalric romances, was one of the greatest poets of the Middle Ages. His masterpiece, *Parzival*, deals with the problem of man's attitude and relationship to God.

Wolfram von Eschenbach was born into a family of ministerial or lackland knights, probably in Wolframs Eschenbach (so named since 1917) in central Franconia near Ansbach. Roving, he practiced knighthood in Bavaria, Swabia, and Styria, as well as at home. In 1203 he visited the Wartburg court of Landgrave Hermann I of Thuringia. Wolfram probably wrote a part of his 25,000-line *Parzival* in Wildenberg Castle in the Odenwald. He held an unproductive fief near his hometown and thus was a vassal of the Count of Wertheim.

Early in his career Wolfram composed nine short poems, mostly "dawn songs"—a genre based upon the alba of Provençal troubadours, in which two lovers must end their nocturnal tryst. With their taunting mood and mastery of language they exhibit Wolfram's superiority to the courtly minnesingers.

From 1197 to 1210 Wolfram worked on *Parzival*, revising, filing, deepening, and completing it in conventional four-foot couplets, with only three beats when the rhyme is feminine. It is written in a lapidary language pregnant with meaning and in a versatile style, the whole revealing stern independence, creative power, and sly humor.

Parzival is based only in part upon the fragmentary *Perceval* (ca. 1179) of the French *trouvère* Chrestien de Troyes. Wolfram's basic themes of morality and respect for others, richness of humor, and individuality of style derive little from Chrestien. Nor does Chrestien dwell upon the slow, painful educative development of Perceval from an eager, well-meaning lad, gauche but pure of heart, to noble, mature manhood, embodying the medieval ideals of human perfection, as does Wolfram in *Parzival*. Parzival progresses from despair of heaven to compassion and to humble, confident reliance upon God. His story is one of the gradual awakening of man's best instincts. Wolfram employs much symbolism but little allegory. Parzival's quest for purity and nobility and his struggle for true religious devotion are sym-

Wolfram von Eschenbach (with horse)

bolized by his search for the Grail, which succeeds only upon his second attempt. The Grail, a familiar object in the romances of chivalry, acquires a deeper meaning in Wolfram's treatment. He describes it as a "stone" from heaven with miraculous powers. It becomes a cornucopia, a preserver of life, and a bearer of divine messages. Significant too is the poet's idea of the fellowship of knights sworn to perform noble deeds—a fellowship on two levels: the worldly Arthurian Round Table and the sacred company of the Knights of the Grail.

Wolfram not only deepened the meaning of Chrestien's tale; he also expanded the plot. He added the story of Gahmuret, Parzival's father, and his first marriage to a Moorish princess, Balakane, who bore him the pagan piebald son Feirefiz, the exemplar of heathen nobility, which Wolfram rated as high as its Christian counterpart. This receives stress when Feirefiz and Parzival meet in combat unrecognized.

Perhaps to conceal his originality, which was no asset to a medieval poet, Wolfram emphasized another source, the work of Kyot, a mysterious writer of Provençal provenance. Scholars have vainly expended much ingenuity to ferret out Kyot. To account for Wolfram's not always orthodox religious views, some critics have discovered traces of Albigensian heresies in *Parzival,* but most writers credit Wolfram with a devout layman's piety.

Titurel, one of Wolfram's two unfinished epic poems, is written in four-line stanzas with feminine rhyme, each line divided by a caesura. Only two fragments of this poem exist. It deals with the earlier history and love of two of the minor characters of *Parzival.* More important is the compactly written but also incomplete knightly legend of *Willehalm,* composed between 1212 and Wolfram's death. It is based upon several *chansons de geste.* The titular hero, a vassal of Louis the Pious, is a devout fighter for God who does not share the scruples that trouble young Parzival. His heathen wife, Gyburg, converted to Christianity, is drawn as a noble character.

Wolfram's reputation remained high even after knighthood had faded. In the *Wartburgkrieg* of the late 13th century, he is pictured as the defender of Christianity against the heathen sorcerer Klingsor. The Meistersingers of the 15th century regarded him as one of their founders. In the 19th century Richard Wagner paid Wolfram homage in his operas *Tannhäuser* and *Parsifal.* In the latter opera he dealt freely with the source but showed respect for the poem's deeper meaning.

Further Reading

Two recent English translations of *Parzival,* both of which contain a critical introduction, are Edwin H. Zeydel and Bayard Q. Morgan, *Parzival* (1951), which, with the exception of less important passages, is in the original meter; and Helen M. Mustard and Charles E. Passage, *Parzival* (1961), presented in prose, which divorces the highly important form from the content. See the chapter on *Parzival* by Otto Springer in Roger S. Loomis, ed., *Arthurian Literature in the Middle Ages: A Collaborative History* (1959). Recommended for historical background are Frederick B. Artz, *The Mind of the Middle Ages, A.D. 200-1500: An Historical Survey* (1953; 3d rev. ed. 1965), and Maurice O. Walshe, *Medieval German Literature: A Survey* (1962). ☐

Harry Austryn Wolfson

The American scholar and educator Harry Austryn Wolfson (1887-1974) spent half a century as Harvard University's Littauer Professor of Hebrew Literature and Philosophy. He was a leading historian of medieval philosophy in Islam, Judaism and Christianity.

Harry Austryn Wolfson was born in Austryn, Lithuania, on November 2, 1887. He received a thorough traditional education in the legendary yeshivot of Slobodka, Kovno and Vilna before abject poverty and oppression by the czarist regime caused his family to join the great emigration to America. Following his father in 1903, Wolfson settled in Scranton, Pennsylvania, where he supported himself by part-time Hebrew teaching while he completed the requirements for his new homeland's high school curriculum.

A $250 scholarship, won by a competitive examination, brought Wolfson to Harvard University, where he was to remain with few interruptions for the rest of his life. In 1911 he earned a bachelor's degree, then followed up with a travelling fellowship in Europe. He spent two years visiting the great libraries at the Vatican, Paris, London, and Vienna in order to exhume, annotate, and classify scores of neglected Hebrew texts. With these two years behind him, he went home to Harvard to earn a Ph.D., awarded in 1915, and to become an instructor in the fledgling Department of Hebrew Language and Literature.

The Essential Academic

In 1925, thanks to a wealthy Harvard alumnus named Lucius Littauer who was looking for a suitable way to memorialize his father, Wolfson became the Nathan Littauer Professor of Hebrew Literature and Philosophy. The appointment was a double coup. Not only was Wolfson the first professor to occupy this post, but he was also the first in any American university to occupy a chair devoted solely to Jewish studies.

It was not long before he proved himself worthy of this great honor. A stream of scholarly papers and books entrenched Jewish studies firmly within the realm of humanistic research in the United States, while close attention to the university library's acquisitions on all his topics of interest soon built the Judaica Collection into one of the country's finest research resources.

Principal Areas of Interest

Wolfson wrote more than 150 books and articles, primarily on Jewish, Christian, and Islamic philosophy. His research was devoted to an examination of the structure and growth of philosophy stretching between the writings of Philo Judeas, a first-century Jewish thinker who had lived in Alexandria, Egypt, and those of Baruch Spinoza, a 17th-century Jewish counterpart in Amsterdam.

Wolfson viewed Philo as the originator of a philosophical trend because, living during a time of increasing Hellenization, he had found ways to interpret the incoming Greek philosophy "in terms of certain fundamental teachings of Hebrew Scripture." Adopted first by Christian thinkers and then by scholars of Islam, Philo's ideas influenced all of medieval philosophy until Spinoza arrived on the intellectual scene to pose maddeningly rational questions that challenged an all-accepting Jewish faith. Despite his presence in a metaphysically-conscious academic era, Spinoza was excommunicated by the Jewish community. Nevertheless, he left his massively detailed *Ethics* as a permanent record of his scholarship.

Although few other scholars dared to undertake the daunting task of studying Spinoza's works, Wolfson tackled the project with enthusiasm, publishing *The Philosophy of Spinoza* in 1934, following up with *Philo: Foundations of Religious Philosophy in Judaism, Christianity and Islam* in 1947. Finally, over a period of years, he produced *The Structure and Growth of Philosophic Systems from Plato to Spinoza,* which tied together these two works plus several others published on Christianity and Islam. The over-arching theme of all these works summed up his belief that the philosophies of all three religions, stemming from the same root, could be viewed essentially as one philosophy written in Arabic, Hebrew, and Latin, with Hebrew's senior spot giving it the central and most important position.

To support this theory on the history of ideas, Wolfson had a particular method of analyzing even the most intricate philosophic texts. He called it the "hypothetico-deductive" method, or the method of conjecture and verification, which was the traditional way in which Talmud had been taught in the Lithuanian yeshivot. Although each of these long-dead philosophers were worthy of lifetime study, Wolfson did not confine his attention to them.

Selected Works

Other major works from Wolfson include *Crescas' Critique of Aristotle: Problems of Aristotle's Physics in Jewish and Arabic Philosophy* (1929), *The Philosophy of the Church Fathers* (1956), and *The Philosophy of the Kalam* (1972). In addition, a number of his essays were collected and published as *Religious Philosophy: A Group of Essays* (1961).

Afterword

Constantly immersed in his academic work, Wolfson never found time to marry. After he retired in 1958, he continued to write and to study, leaving a memory of distinguished scholarship behind him when he died of cancer in 1974.

His legacy is greater than the just the contribution he made to the study of religious philosophy and its history. Because he used the rigorous analytical methods he had learned in yeshivot which were later obliterated by Hitler's minions, later scholars were granted a glimpse of the intellectual heights which had made these schools an accepted part of academic history. A member of many learned societies, he was president of the American Academy for Jewish Research (1935-1937) and of the American Oriental Society (1957-1958).

Further Reading

The best reference source on Wolfson is Leo W. Schwarz's "A Bibliographical Essay" in *Harry Austryn Wolfson Jubilee Volume on the Occasion of His Seventy-fifth Birthday* (1965).

Additional Sources

Commentary, April, 1976. □

Stefan Wolpe

In his career the German-born composer Stefan Wolpe (1902-1972) crossed paths with most of the Modernist movements. His greatness lay in the ability to absorb divergent styles and ideas and to produce out of them music of striking and compelling originality.

Stefan Wolpe was born in Berlin on August 25, 1902, the third of four children to David and Hermine Wolpe. His father had established a successful manufacturing business after emigrating from Moscow, and his mother, who was Viennese, played the piano a little. Wolpe began to develop his musical gifts early, composing by the age of 14. At the same age he began formal studies at the Klindworth-Schwarwenka Conservatory but was expelled for a composition he had written.

In 1918, the year of the November Revolution, Wolpe left home to join the *Wandervögeln,* the name given to roving bands of young people in search of lost ideals. He supported himself at the start with menial jobs but was soon offered patronage by the wife of a wealthy attorney, who allowed him the use of a studio with a piano in her home. Her friendly assistance ended only when Wolpe had to flee Berlin in 1933. In the years 1919 to 1921 Wolpe made two more attempts at formal education, both unsuccessful.

Wolpe's needs and temperament benefitted much more from lectures at the Bauhaus, which he attended shortly after its founding in 1919. There Paul Klee, Laszio Maholy-Nagy, and others recognized the advantages of allowing students to pursue an individual artistic identity through experimentation rather than making them submit to a rigid, pre-established methodology. It was also at the

Bauhaus that he met his first wife, Ola Okuniewska; their daughter Katerina Wolpe became a pianist.

Learns from the Dadaists

At about the same time that he was attending lectures at the Bauhaus, Wolpe began associating with the Berlin Dadaists—George Grosz, Kurt Schwitters, Hans Richter, and others—who were no doubt largely responsible for his inclination toward the combination of irreconcilable opposites, a major thesis of his later music. It is noteworthy that among the many artists Wolpe had come in contact with, few were musicians. The principal exception was Ferruccio Bussoni, whom he met in 1920 and who, in advocating what he called "*junge Klassizimus*" (the young classicism), succeeded to some extent in steering Wolpe away from the expressionistic abandon of some of his music.

In 1922 Wolpe joined the *Novembergruppe,* a leftist group originally made up of visual artists and architects, but by that time also including writers and musicians. Wolpe served as a pianist and composer for *Novembergruppe,* possibly until its demise in 1932. He was said to have been an exceptional pianist.

Wolpe found additional outlets for his combined musical/political interests. He was musical director for Die Truppe '31, the first fully professional agitprop theater group. The troupe staged three productions in the two following years, of which the first, *Die Mausefalle,* was the most successful, with over 300 performances in Germany and Switzerland. As a communist, a Jew, and a radical artist,

Wolpe found it increasingly difficult to co-exist with Germany's rising National Socialism. The third play of Die Truppe '31 was closed by Nazi edict on March 4, 1933, shortly after Hitler became chancellor. When Nazi storm troopers invaded the district in which Wolpe was living, he escaped to Zurich aided by the pianist Irma Schoenberg.

Although he destroyed most of the music he had written before 1925, a few extant piano pieces from 1920 display a thorough grasp of freely atonal expressionism. His encounter with the Dadaists engendered several pieces employing mixed media and prefabricated sound. But greater recognition probably came from the *Kampfmusik* (music for the struggle) composed for agitprop groups. One song, *Es wird die neue Welt geboren,* remained in East German political songbooks until the fall of communism. Jazz elements appear in his works after 1925.

But neither the rapidity with which he moved from style to style nor his readiness to draw from more individual traits of composers so diverse as Arnold Schoenberg, Eric Satie, Bela Bartok, and Igor Stravinsky could be taken as the mere immature groping of a young composer. His later works would continue to acknowledge these sources and to add to them.

In the fall of 1933 he made his way to Vienna, where he studied for three or four months before the threat of deportation back to Germany again compelled him to flee, now to Jerusalem in May 1934. There he was married to Irma Schoenberg. Delighted by the Palestinian folk music and the sound of Semitic languages, he responded with simple songs for the kibbutzim and by incorporating oriental scales into his stylistic vocabulary. Two important pieces from the period, *Four Studies on Basic Rows* and *Duo im Hexachord,* show the influence of others in the partitioning and relatively free ordering of pitch-classes and of Anton Webern in their economy of material. However, the cosmopolitan situation and the uncertain politics in Jerusalem did not offer Wolpe the stability he sought. He emigrated to the United States in 1938 and became a citizen in 1945.

In the United States he quickly won the respect of composers but remained unknown to the larger public. He taught at the Settlement Music School in Philadelphia (1939-1942), the Brooklyn Free Music Society (1945-1948), and the Philadelphia Academy of Music (1949-1952). Gaining a reputation for his enthusiatic and capable teaching at these institutions and among private students, he founded the Contemporary Music School in New York in 1948. In that year he also met the poet Hilda Morley, whom he married in 1952.

In 1952 he became music director at Black Mountain College in North Carolina, an experimental school that attracted many of the leading exponents of Modernism. Among its faculty were several of the newly-ascendant Abstract Expressionists, including Willem DeKooning and Franz Kline, with whom Wolpe developed lasting friendships.

Studies Still Another Art Group

The Abstract Expressionist ethos no doubt encouraged Wolpe's tendency to view the problem of contemporary music as resolvable strictly within its traditional parameters. But music, too, had long partaken of the literary model in its dialectical resolution of thematic and tonal differences. Wolpe's originality lay in his abandoning of this model and replacing it with the constant, never resolving interaction of opposites posited as non-hierarchical, non-thematic shapes, and filling out what he called a "constellatory" rather than a layered space. Opposition occurs not only within fundamental syntactical components, but also as the rapid succession of stylistic clashes. But the systematic unfolding of pitch and interval relationships that nevertheless controls the succession of disparate events results in a language that is at once unpredictable and yet highly ordered, fragmented and yet musically logical.

Wolpe's duties at Black Mountain left him ample time to compose, and he responded with several notable compositions of extreme complexity, among them *Enactments* for three pianos and the *Symphony*. But the college was soon to fold, and Wolpe, sensing its end, left for Europe on a Fulbright scholarship in 1956. He spent that summer, the first of several, lecturing at the Darmstadt Summer Course for New Music. In 1957 he became chairman of the music department at C.W. Post College, Long Island University, a post he held until 1968.

In the compositions of these years, beginning with *Form* for piano (1959), all excesses were stripped away in a style now taut and lean, conveying an urgency born of stark images thrust forward by propulsive rhythms. Other pieces from this period include *Chamber Piece No. 1* (1964) and *II* (1967), the *Trio* (1964), *From Here on Farther* (1969), the *String Quartet* (1969), and his last composition, *Piece for Trumpet and Seven Instruments* (1971). Beginning in 1963 his health declined slowly but steadily due to Parkinson's disease, the illness to which he succumbed on April 4, 1972.

Given the reluctance of the public to accept advanced music, and in spite of the fact that he had strong populist leanings, Wolpe may never claim a large following. But a growing interest in his music has led to an increase in recordings and publications, frequent performances at new music festivals, and the founding of the Stefan Wolpe Society for the purpose of promoting his music. Among his students were Ralph Shapey, Morton Feldman, David Tudor, Robert Man, and many jazz musicians, including Tony Scott, George Russell, and Eddie Sauter. The composers Charles Wuorinen and Harvey Sollberger also acknowledged his influence.

Further Reading

Two extended reviews of Wolpe's music appeared in *The New York Times* (April 5 and August 30, 1992). The latter, written by his former student Austin Clarkson, is especially illuminating, as are all Clarkson's writings on Wolpe. Clarkson is also responsible for *Stefan Wolpe: A Brief Catalogue of Published Works* (1981), which contains biographical information as well as the catalogue. His essay "Stefan Wolpe's Berlin Years" is included in *Music and Civilization: Essays in Honor of Paul Henry Lang* (1964). The composer's widow, Hilda Morley, wrote a book of poems, *What Are Winds and What Are Waters,* about their relationship, and her book *A Thou-*

sand Birds: A Memoir of Stefan Wolpe is forthcoming. Several of Wolpe's lectures have been published. The best known of these is "Thinking Twice," contained in *Contemporary Composers on Contemporary Music* (1967). A complete bibliography can be obtained from the Stefan Wolpe Society, York University, Ontario. Of the ensembles that have championed and recorded his music, the Contemporary Chamber Ensemble (now defunct) and Parnassus deserve special mention. □

Thomas Wolsey

The English statesman and prelate Thomas Wolsey (ca. 1475-1530) was virtual ruler of England as chief minister to Henry VIII. He fell from favor because of his inability to secure the King's divorce.

Thomas Wolsey was born in Ipswich, where his father, Robert, was a butcher and dealer in meat. A precocious child, Thomas was probably educated by churchmen at Ipswich before he proceeded to Oxford. He received his bachelor of arts degree when he was only 15 years old and was called the "boy bachelor." He was appointed bursar of Magdalen College in 1498 but was forced to resign two years later because he had applied funds without authority to the construction of the college's great tower, which still stands.

Wolsey, who took Holy Orders in 1498, then became rector of Limington in Dorset. He was also appointed chaplain to the archbishop of Canterbury, Henry Deane. After Deane's death in 1503, Wolsey became chaplain to Sir Richard Nanfan, the deputy of Calais. Through Nanfan, Wolsey gained an introduction at court, and by 1507 he had become chaplain to King Henry VII. Henry successfully employed Wolsey on several diplomatic missions to Scotland and the Netherlands.

In the Service of Henry VIII

Henry VIII appointed Wolsey royal almoner upon his accession to the throne in 1509. Wolsey rapidly accumulated additional positions in the Church: he became dean of Lincoln in 1509, a canon of Windsor in 1511, bishop of Lincoln in 1514, and archbishop of York later that year. He received additional revenues from various bishoprics and from the wealthy monastery of St. Albans.

As archbishop of York, Wolsey was the second-ranking churchman in England. He was not satisfied with this position, but he could not become archbishop of Canterbury because the incumbent, William Warham, steadfastly refused to accommodate him by retiring or dying. In 1515 Wolsey gained prestige by being created a cardinal—he had the red hat carried through the streets of London in a solemn procession—and in 1518 he was named a papal legate a *latere,* thus gaining preeminence over Warham.

By this time Wolsey's influence dominated the state also. He had successfully organized an army for the invasion of France in 1513 and had accompanied the King on the campaign. By Wolsey's treaty with France (1514), En-

gland held the balance of power between France and the Hapsburgs. In 1515 Wolsey was named lord chancellor, Warham having been persuaded to resign that office. Wolsey owed his power, however, more to the King's favor than to his tenure of any specific office. The young Henry VIII was more inclined to martial and sporting pursuits than to the transaction of routine governmental business, and he was delighted to find a minister as competent as the cardinal. In 1518 Wolsey engineered a treaty of universal peace embracing the principal European states.

Wolsey undertook minor reforms in both Church and state. He secured papal permission to close several small monasteries and applied the revenues to the foundation of a grammar school at Ipswich and a college at Oxford. The school did not survive his fall, but Henry VIII allowed the college to continue, changing its name from Cardinal's College to Christ Church. Wolsey also attempted to provide better regulation for the King's household by drawing up the Eltham Ordinances of 1526.

Wolsey's greatest interest lay, however, in foreign affairs. While it has been argued that he wished mainly to preserve a balance of power in Europe, to become pope, or to maintain peace, his real motives may have been less precise, and he may have responded to European situations and to Henry VIII's desires without developing any overriding policy. In 1518 Wolsey negotiated an alliance between England and France, to be cemented by the marriage of Henry VIII's daughter Mary to the French Dauphin. In 1520 he arranged a meeting between Henry and Francis I of France on the "Field of the Cloth of Gold," a tent city

erected in Flanders, and a more significant conference between Henry and Emperor Charles V at Gravelines. When Francis I drifted into war with the Holy Roman Empire, Wolsey sided with the Emperor. In 1523 English forces invaded France, without notable success, and Wolsey obtained unusual taxation from Parliament only after very stormy debates. In 1527 England abandoned the Emperor, signing a new treaty with France.

Fall from Favor

By this time Henry's mind was preoccupied with his desire for a divorce from Catherine of Aragon. As the Queen had not borne him a male heir, he wished to be free to remarry. Wolsey conducted elaborate negotiations with Rome, and in 1529 he and Cardinal Lorenzo Campeggio began a trial of Henry's suit in London. But Pope Clement VII, who was dominated by the Emperor, Catherine's nephew, revoked the case to Rome and concluded the trial without a decision. The King's wrath focused on Wolsey, who was dismissed as chancellor in October 1529 and forced to leave London.

Although Wolsey's revenues were greatly reduced, he still managed to live in considerable magnificence. In 1530 he planned his enthronement as archbishop of York, never having been officially installed, but he was found in correspondence with foreign powers, contrary to the King's order. Wolsey was arrested at Cawood near York and ordered to London. He would doubtless have been executed on false charges of treason had he not died a natural death on the way to London. Lamenting that he had not served God as well as he had the King, Wolsey succumbed at Leicester on Nov. 29, 1530.

Despite Wolsey's supreme influence in Church and state, his achievements in both spheres were ephemeral. His greatest lasting monument is perhaps Hampton Court Palace, which he constructed on the Thames River west of London and where he lived in great pomp surrounded by an enormous retinue of servants and retainers.

Further Reading

George Cavendish, the cardinal's gentleman-usher, wrote *The Life and Death of Cardinal Wolsey* (1641), one of the masterpieces of early biography. The best edition is that by Richard S. Sylvester (1959). Modern biographies include Albert F. Pollard, *Wolsey* (1929), and Charles W. Ferguson, *Naked to Mine Enemies: The Life of Cardinal Wolsey* (1958). There is related material in Albert F. Pollard, *Henry VIII* (1902; new ed. 1913), and J. J. Scarisbrick, *Henry VIII* (1968).

Additional Sources

Cardinal Wolsey: church, state, and art, Cambridge; New York: Cambridge University Press, 1991.

Gwyn, Peter, *The king's cardinal: the rise and fall of Thomas Wolsey,* London: Barrie & Jenkins, 1990.

Harvey, Nancy Lenz, *Thomas Cardinal Wolsey,* New York, N.Y.: Macmillan; London: Collier Macmillan, 1980.

Pollard, A. F. (Albert Frederick), *Wolsey,* Westport, Conn.: Greenwood Press, 1978.

Ridley, Jasper Godwin, *Statesman and saint: Cardinal Wolsey, Sir Thomas More, and the politics of Henry VIII,* New York: Viking Press, 1983, 1982.

Williams, Neville, *The Cardinal and the Secretary: Thomas Wolsey and Thomas Cromwell,* New York: Macmillan, 1976, 1975. □

Anna May Wong

Anna May Wong (1907-1961) is chiefly remembered as the first actress of Asian extraction to achieve stardom as the epitome of the "Oriental temptress," so much a fixture of melodramas in the late 1920s and 1930s.

Anna May Wong became America's first Asian American movie star before films could even talk. In fact, with more than 80 film credits to her name, Wong is the all-time leading Asian American presence on film. She maintained her popularity for more than a quarter of a century, and she remained one of the highest-salaried stars of her time. She built a career around being the mysterious evil villainess, repeatedly playing stereotypical Oriental roles. She was the exotic slave girl, the powerful dragon lady, the mysterious woman of the Orient with deadly charms.

However, despite her success, Wong was torn between her two cultures. Twice, at the height of her fame, she moved to Europe to protest the limited, stereotypical roles she and other Asians were offered in Hollywood. Yet during a later trip to China to learn more about her native culture, Wong was heavily criticized for her degrading portrayals of Chinese women and was told that many of her films were banned in China.

Born on Flower Street in Los Angeles, California, in 1907, Anna May Wong was named Wong Liu Tsong, which in Cantonese means "frosted yellow willow." Wong was third-generation Chinese American; her father was born in Sacramento and his father had immigrated to California during the Gold Rush.

Growing up, Wong and her six brothers and sisters lived in an apartment over the family's run-down laundry. Her first memories were of constant steam and the strong odor of hot-ironed linen. As a young child, Wong became fascinated with the brand-new world of movies. She began skipping Chinese school in the evenings to watch such movies as *The Perils of Pauline* (1914) at the local theater. By the time she was 11, Wong decided she was going to be a movie actress. Against all odds, she got her first part at age 12 when an agent hired three hundred Chinese girls as extras in the 1919 film *The Red Lantern.* Hardly visible in the film, she went on to get a few more minor roles.

For two years, Wong worked after school as an extra without telling her parents, who, she knew, would not approve. At age 14, her father found her a job as a secretary, but Wong was fired as unqualified one week later. When she returned home, fearing her father's anger, she found a letter from a director's office offering her a role in the film *Bits of Life* (1921). It would bring Wong her first screen credit. Although Wong's father strongly objected to his daughter's chosen career, he eventually gave in on the condition that an adult escort, often he himself, would chaperon the young Wong on the film sets at all times. When she was not in front of the cameras, her father locked her into her room on the set.

At age 17, Wong had one of the few romantic lead roles she would ever play in *Toll of the Sea* (1923), the first Technicolor feature ever made. As a young village girl who marries an American sailor, Wong captured the media's attention for the first time. Reporters began to appear at the laundry in the hopes of catching Wong for an interview or a photo.

International fame came in 1924 with *The Thief of Bagdad,* in which Wong played an exotic Mongol slave girl opposite star Douglas Fairbanks, Sr. Wong's role embarrassed her family. Although Wong would continue to support her family for many years, she remained close only to her brother, Richard.

The success of *Bagdad* led to countless new offers. She appeared as an Eskimo in *The Alaskan* and a Native American girl in *Peter Pan.* In addition to film roles, Wong also worked as a model. She made a few more films, but soon became disillusioned with the roles and with Hollywood's practice of casting non-Asians in the few leading Asian roles. Wong finally fled to Europe where, in London, she costarred with Charles Laughton in *Piccadilly.* After the film, director Basil Dean produced a Chinese play, *A Circle of Chalk,* specifically for Wong. She successfully played opposite the rising new talent, Laurence Olivier, in London's New Theater.

Wong remained in Europe for three years, where she was hailed for her film and stage appearances. In Germany and France, she made foreign versions of her British films, including Germany's first sound picture. She spoke both German and French so fluently that critics could hardly believe they were hearing her voice instead of a native actress. During her career, Wong taught herself to speak English, Chinese, French, German, and Italian.

In 1931 a leading role on Broadway lured Wong back to the United States. The play, *On the Spot,* ran for 30 weeks, until Wong was called back to Los Angeles when her mother died in an automobile accident.

Wong's next screen role, *Daughter of the Dragon,* cast her in yet another stereotypical role as the daughter of the infamous Dr. Fu Manchu. Wong then appeared in the thriller *Shanghai Express,* starring Marlene Dietrich. Wong's portrayal of the bad-girl-turned-good inspired better reviews than Dietrich received. Years later, the star would complain that Wong had upstaged her.

Wong then made one independent Sherlock Holmes picture and returned to England, where she felt her true audiences were. Like many minority artists at the time, Wong felt Europe was a less racist place to work. There she enjoyed the company of royalty and the wealthy. Wong remained in England for almost three years, appearing in more films and traveling in a variety show.

After failing to win the lead role in *The Good Earth,* which was given to a non-Asian German actress, a furious and frustrated Wong traveled to China, the home of her ancestors. In spite of those who criticized her for playing degrading Asian roles, Wong remained in China for ten months, studied Mandarin Chinese, purchased costumes for films and plays, and wrote articles on her travels. Unfortunately, she learned that she was too westernized for the Chinese stage. At the same time, she knew she never would be considered American enough for Hollywood's racist views.

After returning to the United States, Wong starred in one sympathetic role before World War II. In *Daughter of Shanghai,* she played a detective. She then appeared in two war epics, *Bombs over Burma* and *The Lady from Chungking.* The war brought another difficult situation for Wong. As more war movies were being cast, she was not hired as an actress, but as a coach to teach Caucasian actors how to be more believable as Asians.

In 1942, finally fed up with the Hollywood system, Wong retired from films at the age of 35. "I had to go into retirement for the sake of my soul. I suddenly found no more pleasure in acting. My screen work became a weary and meaningless chore—and Hollywood life a bore!" Wong told *New York Enquirer* in 1957. Throughout the war, she contributed to the war efforts by working for the United China Relief Fund and touring with the USO. During the 1940s and 1950s, Wong took occasional small parts on television, even starring in her own series, *Mme. Liu Tsong,*

in which she played the owner of an international chain of art galleries who was also a sleuth.

Seventeen years after retirement, Wong attempted a film comeback. She returned as Lana Turner's mysterious housekeeper in the 1950 film, *Portrait in Black.* In 1961, while she was preparing for the role of the mother in *Flower Drum Song,* Wong died of a heart attack in her sleep.

Further Reading

Parish, James Robert, and William T. Leonard, *Hollywood Players: The Thirties,* New Rochelle, New York, 1976.
Pictures, August 1926 and September 1926. □

Fernando Wood

Fernando Wood (1812-1881), American politician, was mayor of New York City, and a leading Peace Democrat during the Civil War.

Fernando Wood was born in Philadelphia on June 14, 1812. After a meager education, he worked at a number of jobs, twice failing in businesses of his own. By 1836 he had entered shipping, and in 1849 he made great profits shipping goods to San Francisco as the gold rush began. Wood invested his profits in New York and San Francisco real estate and acquired a great fortune, which enabled him to devote full attention to politics, long his major interest.

In 1836 Wood joined Tammany Hall, the powerful Democratic organization in New York City, and rapidly became one of its leaders. In 1841 he entered the U.S. Congress for a single term. Wood ran unsuccessfully for mayor of New York in 1850, when the Tammany organization split, but in 1854 he won the post in a heated campaign. As mayor, Wood labored to reform city government and through patronage to increase his political power. In 1856 he was reelected.

Opposition to Wood from disappointed office seekers and the Republican state legislature led to confusion in city administration and the establishment of two police groups (one of which tried to arrest Wood). Wood was defeated for reelection in 1857 and expelled from Tammany Hall. Although he had sponsored a number of liberal programs, including the preservation of Central Park from business exploitation, his administration was marred by excessive graft and generally poor management.

As a rival to Tammany, Wood established Mozart Hall, an amalgam of businessmen, mechanics, immigrants, and stevedores, which helped Wood reestablish his power on the local level. In 1859 he was again elected mayor. He also became a large contributor to the national Democratic party.

Wood espoused compromise with the South before the Civil War and opposed the war once it began. In 1860 he headed a pro-Southern delegation to the National Democratic Nominating Convention. In January 1861, during the

secession crisis, he proposed the secession of New York City from the state and the establishment of the city as a free port, independent of the "tyranny" of Albany.

After the battle of Ft. Sumter, Wood supported the war effort momentarily. When defeated for reelection as mayor in 1861, he reverted to the opposition. In 1863 he joined Clement Vallandingham in organizing the Peace Democrats and, capitalizing on New York's war weariness and dissatisfaction with the Emancipation Proclamation, won election to Congress for a second time. Except for the years 1865 to 1867, Wood served until 1881 in the House, where he was an ardent opponent of Radical Reconstruction. His greatest success came in achieving tariff reform. Wood died at Hot Springs, Ark., on Feb. 14, 1881.

Further Reading

The best biography of Wood is Samuel A. Pleasants, *Fernando Wood of New York* (1948), which is essentially a political study, balanced in interpretation but generally sympathetic. Wood's milieu is excellently treated in Philip S. Foner, *Business and Slavery: The New York Merchants and the Irrepressible Conflict* (1941).

Additional Sources

Mushkat, Jerome, *Fernando Wood: a political biography*, Kent, Ohio: Kent State University Press, 1990. □

Grant Wood

The American painter Grant Wood (1891-1942) was one of the principal Regionalists of the 1930s. He depicted his Iowan subjects in a deliberately primitivizing style, sometimes satirizing them.

G rant Wood was born on Feb. 13, 1891, at Anamosa, Iowa. His father, a farmer, died in 1901, and the family moved to Cedar Rapids. There Grant took drawing lessons from local artists and attended high school. He studied design briefly in Minneapolis at the Handicraft Guild, taught school near Cedar Rapids, and then took a job in 1913 in a silversmith shop in Chicago and attended night classes at the Art Institute. In 1916 he registered at the Art Institute for full-time study as a "fresco painter."

During World War I Wood served in Washington, D.C., where he made clay models of field gun positions and helped camouflage artillery pieces. After teaching art in a Cedar Rapids high school, he left for Europe in 1923. He spent most of the next 14 months in Paris, where he studied at the Académie Julian. The paintings he did in Paris were in an impressionistic manner. On his return to America he spent the summer of 1925 painting pictures of workers at a dairy equipment and manufacturing plant in Cedar Rapids. His paintings began to sell, and he was able to give up teaching. To supplement his income he decorated house interiors.

In 1927 Wood received a commission for a stained-glass window memorializing the veterans of World War I to be installed in the Cedar Rapids City Hall. To learn the technique of stained glass he went to Munich. There he admired the work of the 15th-century French and German primitive painters and began to work in a linear, primitivizing style. In the late 1920s he painted portraits of his mother and local Iowans.

Wood's work is usually seen as espousing the homespun virtues of the people of Iowa. The acid overtones in such works as his well-known *American Gothic* (1930) are generally missed. Wood's maiden sister and the local dentist posed for the picture. Behind the prim, straightlaced couple, who stand self-consciously erect and stiff, is a flimsy Gothic-like structure. Wood had a special distaste for the conservatively patriotic organization, Daughters of the American Revolution, which he satirized in his *Daughters of Revolution* (1932). Here he posed a group of proud, self-righteous, elderly ladies, obviously insular in their experiences and philosophies, gingerly holding their teacups, before the familiar Emanuel Leutze painting, *Washington Crossing the Delaware*. In Wood's *Victorian Survival* (1931) he shows a stiffly grim, elderly Iowan woman. Here the insularity is combined with a certain diabolical quality.

After the Works Progress Administration was established, Wood directed the 34 artists working at the University of Iowa and planned and executed a series of frescoes at Iowa State University in Ames and elsewhere. He died in Iowa City on Feb. 12, 1942. He was one of the major Regionalists, a group of painters who in the 1930s employed a variety of naturalistic styles (in marked contrast to the modernistic idioms of the previous two decades) for a subject matter that was obviously American in content.

Further Reading

Darrell Garwood, *Artist in Iowa: A Life of Grant Wood* (1944), is chronological and anecdotal; the few illustrations of paintings are of poor quality. University of Kansas Museum of Art, *Grant Wood, 1891-1942: A Retrospective Exhibition of the Works of the Noted Painter from Cedar Rapids* (1959), is useful.

Additional Sources

Graham, Nan Wood, *My brother, Grant Wood,* Iowa City: State Historical Society of Iowa, 1993. □

Leonard Wood

Leonard Wood (1860-1927), American Army officer and colonial administrator, was an ardent advocate of military preparedness.

A doctor's son, Leonard Wood was born in Winchester, N.H., on Oct. 9, 1860. After graduating from Harvard Medical School in 1884, he joined the Army Medical Corps as a contract surgeon. While advancing to the grade of captain, which he reached in 1891, he proved himself an effective troop leader in the West and won the friendship of influential generals and politicians. Stationed in Washington after 1895, he was part of the White House inner circle of presidents Grover Cleveland and William McKinley and made friends in 1897 with Assistant Secretary of the Navy Theodore Roosevelt.

When the Spanish-American War began in 1898, Wood and Roosevelt raised the famous "Rough Riders." As colonel of the regiment, Wood permanently left the Medical Corps for troop command. After participating in the Santiago de Cuba campaign, he was commissioned a brigadier general of volunteers in July 1898. In October he was appointed governor of Santiago Province, the first Cuban province to fall under United States control. Physically tireless, an inspiration to his staff, at once overawing the Cubans and winning their loyalty, Wood relieved suffering and restored order. As military governor of Cuba from 1899 to 1902, he repeated these achievements on a larger scale while preparing the island for independence. Wood advanced to the permanent grade of brigadier general in 1901 and to major general in 1903.

Wood served in administrative capacities in the Philippines and in the United States until 1910, when he was made Army chief of staff. He used his four-year term to assert power over the War Department bureaus, reorganize

the Regular Army for greater wartime effectiveness, and launch a program of citizens' military-training summer camps. The camps constituted a step toward Wood's ultimate goal—universal military training, which to him meant schooling in patriotism and community service as well as in the use of arms. From 1914 to 1917 he was commander of the Department of the East. He spoke and wrote constantly about universal service and preparedness during America's years of neutrality early in World War I. Associating openly with Republican critics of Woodrow Wilson's administration, he went beyond the bounds of proper military conduct in advocating defense policies. In retaliation, the administration kept him from the front when the United States entered the war in 1917.

As political heir of Theodore Roosevelt, Wood made a strong bid for the Republican presidential nomination in 1920 but lost to Warren G. Harding. Wood was appointed governor of the Philippines by Harding in 1921 and served there until his death on Aug. 7, 1927.

Further Reading

The standard if excessively laudatory biography of Wood is Hermann Hagedorn, *Leonard Wood* (1931). For Wood's work in Cuba see David F. Healy, *The United States in Cuba, 1898-1902* (1963). Samuel P. Huntington, *The Soldier and the State* (1957), discusses Wood's military theories and political activities.

Additional Sources

Chapman, Ronald Fettes, *Leonard Wood and leprosy in the Philippines: the Culion Leper Colony, 1921-1927,* Washington, D.C.: University Press of America, 1982.

Lane, Jack C., *Armed progressive: a study of the military and public career of Leonard Wood,* San Rafael, Calif.: Presidio Press, 1978. □

Robert Elkington Wood

Robert Elkington Wood (1879-1969), American Army officer and business executive, pioneered in modern retailing and was responsible for building Sears, Roebuck and Company into the world's largest merchandising operation.

Robert E. Wood was born on June 13, 1879, in Kansas City, Mo. He won an appointment to the U.S. Military Academy and graduated in 1900. After tours of duty in the Philippines and Montana and teaching at the academy, he wrangled a transfer to Panama, where canal construction was beginning in 1905. He became a captain in 1907 and later was made chief quartermaster. When the canal was completed in 1915, he retired as a major under a special congressional act. He joined E. I. du Pont de Nemours and Company but left for General Asphalt Company when he saw no room for advancement.

When the United States entered World War I in 1917, Wood returned to the Army as a colonel and was placed in

charge of ports in France. In 1918 he was promoted to brigadier general and made acting quartermaster general in Washington. His rapid reorganization of chaotic Army procurement greatly impressed his civilian assistant Julius Thorne, the president of Montgomery Ward, who made Wood a vice president of his mail-order firm in 1919. He clashed with the older executives and left in 1924. He was quickly hired by Julius Rosenwald, chairman of Sears, Roebuck and Company. Wood's plan to expand into retail stores that were outside urban business districts and easily accessible to the automobile was a great success, and he was made president in 1928.

Wood encouraged, advised, lent money to, and sometimes bought control of hundreds of small manufacturers around the country in order to obtain merchandise for his retail stores at competitive prices. This policy was in line with his hope of strengthening the American economic system through industrial democracy, which also inspired the Sears profit-sharing plan, which Wood called his proudest achievement.

Although a conservative Republican, Wood supported the New Deal until 1940, when his isolationist views prompted him to form the American First Committee to oppose American entry into World War II. However, he gave full support to Franklin Roosevelt's administration after Pearl Harbor and served as a civilian adviser to the Army. After the war he was a strong supporter of anti-internationalists, especially Wisconsin senator Joseph McCarthy.

Wood became chairman of the board at Sears in 1939. He launched the largest expansion in merchandising history in 1946, just when most businessmen were predicting a postwar recession. This successful gamble made Sears the undisputed leader in retailing before Wood retired in 1954. He died on Nov. 6, 1969.

Further Reading

There is no biography of Wood, but Herman Kogan, *The Great E. B.: The Story of the Encyclopedia Britannica* (1958), contains a full discussion of Wood's publishing career. Wood figures prominently in Boris Emmet and John E. Jeuck, *Catalogues and Counters: A History of Sears Roebuck and Company* (1950).

Additional Sources

Worthy, James C., *Shaping an American institution: Robert E. Wood and Sears, Roebuck,* New York: New American Library, 1986. □

Victoria C. Woodhull

Victoria Claflin Woodhull (1838–1927) was a promoter of women's rights. An 1872 candidate for president, she founded the first women's owned stock brokerage.

Victoria Claflin Woodhull was one of the most controversial figures of her time. Though she did much to promote the cause of women's rights—even announcing herself as a candidate for president in 1872—her espousal of free love (which rejected sexual monogamy) and her involvement in a number of highly publicized scandals gained her as many enemies as she had supporters. Along with her sister, Tennessee Claflin, Woodhull founded the first female-owned stock brokerage in the United States and published an influential newspaper, *Woodhull and Claflin's Weekly*. In the biography *Mrs. Satan*, Woodhull was quoted on the philosophy that led to her many accomplishments: "All this talk about women's rights is moonshine. Women have every right. They have only to exercise them. That's what we're doing."

Woodhull's unusual upbringing contributed to the deep convictions and free spirit she evidenced later in life. She was born in Homer, Ohio, on September 23, 1838, the seventh of ten children born to Reuben Buckman Claflin and Roxanna Hummel Claflin. Her mother was a fervently religious woman who enjoyed taking the family to evangelical revival meetings, while her father was a jack-of-all-trades who would try anything if it seemed to hold the potential for financial reward. Victoria and Tennessee, the youngest Claflin child, followed their mother's lead and proclaimed themselves clairvoyant at an early age. Their father soon created a traveling spiritualist show, featuring folk medicine and fortune-telling, in an attempt to profit from his daughters' talents.

Victoria Woodhull (standing, forefront)

Victoria left the family's show before she turned sixteen to marry Dr. Canning Woodhull, partly at her father's urging. During their marriage she worked at a number of odd jobs to help support her husband, who was an alcoholic, and their two children. Though the couple divorced in 1864, they continued to live together for some time afterward. Woodhull would remarry twice, but she practiced free love for most of her life. In 1868 Woodhull and her sister traveled to New York City, where they met wealthy industrialist Cornelius Vanderbilt. Although Tennessee refused the elderly man's marriage proposal, he maintained an interest in the sisters and gave them financial advice. Eventually Woodhull and her sister became proficient enough in the financial markets to establish the first female-owned stock brokerage, Woodhull, Claflin and Company. Their company opened amidst a huge wave of publicity and became quite successful.

Woodhull and her sister used some of the profits from this venture to found a newspaper, *Woodhull and Claflin's Weekly*, in 1870. By this time their home had become a sort of literary salon that attracted many well-known radical intellectuals. Many friends from this circle contributed to the paper, which articulately supported such controversial goals as equal rights for women, free love, and socialism. *Woodhull and Claflin's Weekly* even published the first English translation of Karl Marx's *The Communist Manifesto* in 1872. Woodhull used her newfound stature to speak out on the issue of women's suffrage. Many of the women who had taken up this cause before her, however, resented her views on free love and deemed her an unworthy spokesperson.

In April 1870 Woodhull shocked the nation with a sensational letter to the editor of the New York *Herald* entitled "First Pronunciamento." In it, as quoted in *Mrs. Satan,* she proclaimed: "While others argued the equality of women with men, I proved it by successfully engaging in business; while others sought to show that there was no valid reason why women should be treated, socially and politically, as being inferior to men, I boldly entered the arena. . . . I now announce myself candidate for the Presidency." Thus Woodhull became the first woman candidate for president, headlining the ticket of the National Radical Reform Party (also known as the Equal Rights Party). Her running mate was abolitionist and former slave Frederick Douglass—though he declined to take part in the unlikely campaign—and her rallying call was "Victory for Victoria in 1872!" Woodhull presented her views on women's rights in a passionate speech to the House Judiciary Committee in 1871, which marked the first personal appearance before such a high congressional committee by a woman. Besides impressing legislators, the speech also helped Woodhull win over many of her detractors in the women's suffrage movement, who began to recognize that Woodhull's visibility might be valuable enough to outweigh their reservations about her morality.

Following her failed bid for the presidency, however, Woodhull continued to be the subject of rumors and gossip. Two of her most prominent detractors were novelist Harriet Beecher Stowe and her sister, Catherine Beecher. Partly to get back at her critics and partly to expose what she saw as blatant hypocrisy, Woodhull used her paper to accuse Henry Ward Beecher—one of the most prominent clergymen of the day and brother of her detractors—of having adulterous affairs with several of his parishioners. After the scandalous story was printed, Beecher was put on trial for adultery, and he responded by charging Woodhull and her sister with libel. Though Woodhull was acquitted in 1873, many of her former supporters found that they could no longer stand by her.

In 1877 Woodhull moved to England, where she continued to lecture and publish books and pamphlets. Her writings include *Stirpiculture, or the Scientific Propagation of the Human Race,* 1888; *The Human Body the Temple of God* (written with her sister), 1890; and *Humanitarian Money,* 1892. From 1892 to 1910, Woodhull published *Humanitarian* magazine with her daughter, Zulu Maud Woodhull. Woodhull married a wealthy English banker, John B. Martin, in 1882. In her efforts to obtain the blessing of his respectable family, she made several trips to the United States, where she faced her critics and disavowed her previous stance on free love. She died at their English country estate on June 10, 1927. □

Robert W. Woodruff

Businessman Robert W. Woodruff (1889-1985) was the head of the Coca-Cola Company from 1923 until 1984, during which time sales increased from $31 million a year to $7.36 billion. He was also a political and economic power in Atlanta and nationally and a major philanthropist of the period.

Born in Columbus, Georgia, on December 6, 1889, Robert Winship Woodruff was the son of Ernest Woodruff, who later became a prominent businessman in Atlanta. Robert Woodruff was educated at Georgia Military Academy and attended Emory University from 1908 to 1910. In the latter year he became a machinist's apprentice and then salesman at General Fire Extinguisher Company. Having proven himself in this position, his father hired him as a salesman and buyer for his Atlantic Ice Company in 1911. A couple of years later young Woodruff began negotiating with Walter White, head of White Motor Company, to purchase a fleet of trucks to replace the horse-drawn delivery wagons used by his father's firm. Upon hearing of this, an irate Ernest Woodruff fired his son, but White hired him as a salesman for White Motor. Woodruff moved rapidly up the ranks as he proved himself to be the firm's top truck salesman. In 1919 he was named vice-president and general manager, serving in that position until 1923.

In 1923 Ernest Woodruff, finding himself in desperate straits, convinced his son to return to Atlanta to help with a recent business acquisition. In 1919 the elder Woodruff, along with others, had purchased the Coca-Cola Company. The cola firm, after reaching peak sales of $31 million in 1920, had suffered a series of business reverses, and it was clear that new, aggressive, and innovative management was needed.

Coca-Cola was invented in 1886 by John S. Pemberton, an Atlanta pharmacist who manufactured several patent medicines. It was a modification of something called French Wine Cola and was marketed as a cure-all for headaches, sluggishness, indigestion, and hangovers. The business changed hands a few times over the next couple of years, and in 1891 was purchased by Asa Griggs Candler, another Atlanta druggist, who coincidently had been Robert Woodruff's Sunday school teacher. Candler soon realized that the product had greater potential as a soda fountain drink and began erecting Coca-Cola signs on barns all over the country. By 1895 the drink was sold in every state and territory of the nation, and in 1899 Candler set up the franchise system for dealers. In 1916 Candler stepped down as president of the company, giving all but one percent of his stock to family members. Three years later, without consulting him, they sold out to Woodruff's syndicate for $25 million.

Under Robert Woodruff's regime, the Coca-Cola Company was rapidly invigorated. Sales rose in seven years from $24 million to $30 million, while net profits climbed from $5 million to $13 million. This transformation was accomplished in a number of ways. First, Woodruff employed a massive advertising campaign, with the goal of making Coca-Cola as "American" as baseball and hot dogs. The famous advertising slogan "The Pause that Refreshes" was penned at this time, and over the years "Coke" became a symbol of the United States more widely recognized than the flag itself. Woodruff also abolished the sales department, substituting instead a service department, the principal function of which would be assisting Coca-Cola bottlers, distributors, and fountain operators to increase their profits. A large number of people were also put to work in market research, determining why people drink the beverages they do and developing advertising which exploited these findings.

Robert Woodruff remained president of Coca-Cola until 1939, when he became chairman of the board. He retained the latter position until 1942, when he became chairman of the executive committee. From 1955 until 1981 he served as a director and chairman of the finance committee. He finally left the board in 1984, having served the company for 61 years. During all this time, whatever his title, there was never much question who ran the company. "Mr. Bob," as he was deferentially known, seldom issued a direct order, signed a contract, or dispatched a memorandum. Nevertheless, he dominated the company by the force of his personality, by unremitting energy and attention to detail, and by delegating functions to men of special talent.

By the time of his death in 1985 Coca-Cola had become a massive company with sales of $7.36 billion. Although Woodruff diversified the company somewhat in the 1950s, soft drinks in 1983 still accounted for 80 percent of its profits. Woodruff's major accomplishment was the transformation of Coca-Cola from a national to a universal drink. In 1985 it was the world's single largest selling product, accounting for some $2.3 billion of the company's $5 billion in sales. Coke was sold in 135 countries. Around the globe, Coca-Cola is consumed about 60 million times a day, and only a few areas have not been visited by the cola invasion. Much of this expansion has been due to Woodruff's style of advertising. As he explained: "We've tried to show Coca-Cola as a pleasant, unassuming social amenity. I guess that's what they now call the soft sell. We've never made claims. We've tried to do with our advertising what we always try to do with everybody inside and outside the company—to be liked."

Outside of Coca-Cola, Robert Woodruff was an enormous economic and political power in Atlanta, in Georgia, and in the nation. The extent of his national political power was shown during World War II when, despite sugar rationing, Coke got its requirements on the plea that G.I.s shouldn't be deprived of the morale effects of a handy bottle of Coke. In Atlanta itself it was often commented that the power structure was split 50/50—with Woodruff one 50 and everyone else the other 50. As one intimate commented: "It's not that he decides all kinds of things, it's just that the others won't do anything they know he is really against." As an economic power Woodruff sat on the boards of a large number of major American corporations and was also a longtime member of the Business Advisory Council of the U.S. Department of Commerce.

A major philanthropist, during his lifetime Woodruff gave away an estimated $350 million, much of it anonymously, to medicine, the arts, and education. His principal benefaction, however, was Emory University. Towards the end of 1979 he gave Emory three million shares of Coca-Cola stock, then worth about $100 million. It was called the largest single benefaction in American history and brought to over $200 million the total he had given the university. Emory, with five million shares of stock, became one of the largest owners of Coca-Cola. Woodruff also established the R. W. Woodruff Memorial Clinic and the Emily and Ernest Woodruff Foundation. He and his wife were childless, and it was often speculated that he lavished his paternal affections on Coke. Shortly before he died in Atlanta on March 7, 1985, Coke executives brought Woodruff the new formula they had developed, the first change in nearly 100 years. He evidently approved, but would undoubtedly be aghast at the massive consumer resistance which developed against the new product, forcing the return to the marketplace of the original formula under the name Classic Coca-Cola.

Further Reading

There is no biography of Woodruff. The best source on Coca-Cola is E. J. Kahn, Jr., *The Big Drink* (1959).

Additional Sources

Elliott, Charles., *A biography of the "boss": Robert Winship Woodruff,* S.l.: R.W. Woodruff, 1979.

Elliott, Charles Newton, "Mr. Anonymous," Robert W. Woodruff of Coca-Cola, Atlanta: Cherokee Pub. Co., 1982. □

Robert Archey Woods

Robert Archey Woods (1865-1925), American social worker, founded South End House, the first settlement house in Boston. His pioneer surveys of ethnic communities taught method to settlement workers and helped create social-work institutions.

Robert A. Woods was born in Pittsburgh, Pa., on Dec. 9, 1865. After attending Amherst College, he entered Andover Theological Seminary in 1886. Affected by the "Christian Socialist" ideas of the time, he considered how to dedicate himself to useful works. In 1890 he graduated from Andover, served briefly as a chaplain at the Concord, Mass., Reformatory, then became a resident student at Toynbee Hall, a settlement house in London, England.

When Woods returned to America, he was determined to emulate the work of the settlement. He offered a series of lectures at Andover, published as *English Social Movements* (1891), and opened Andover House in Boston in 1891 to minister to the immigrant poor. He directed the settlement house until his death. In 1896 its name was changed to South End House. He also began a career as a civic figure, seeking improved public facilities such as baths, gymnasiums, and industrial schools.

Inspired by Charles Booth's study of the London poor, *Life and Labour of the People* (1904), Woods determined to apply a similar method of survey to Boston. Essentially, his goal was to utilize the neighborhood as a means for enriching the city. The result, the first such American survey, conducted under his direction, was *The City Wilderness: A Study of the South End* (1898) and *Americans in Process: A Study of the North and West Ends* (1902). These and later surveys have been criticized for seeking to teach middle-class Anglo-Saxon values, rather than attempting to understand the nature of the separate groups; nevertheless, they broke the ground for later investigators.

Woods helped organize the National Federation of settlements in 1911. He and Albert J. Kennedy, a younger associate, edited *Handbook of Settlements* (1911) and *Young Working Girls* (1913). They also prepared *The Settlement Horizon: A National Estimate* (1922). Woods was particularly troubled by the debilitating influence of hard liquor and was a leading prohibitionist. His continuing faith in rural values and neighborhood virtues was shown in his study *The Preparation of Calvin Coolidge: An Interpretation* (1924). He died on Feb. 18, 1925, in Boston.

Further Reading

The book by Woods and Albert J. Kennedy, *The Zone of Emergence,* abridged and edited with an introduction by Sam B. Warner, Jr. (1962), was a pioneering examination of ethnic groups that had transcended their original environments. A biography of Woods by his wife, Eleanor H. Woods, is *Robert A. Woods: Champion of Democracy* (1929). Extensive material on Woods and his career is in Allen F. Davis, *Spearheads for Reform: The Social Settlements and the Progressive Movement, 1890-1914* (1967). Woods figures prominently in Albert Boer, *The Development of USES: A Chronology of the United South End Settlements, 1891-1966* (1966). □

Carter Godwin Woodson

Called the "Father of Negro History," Carter Godwin Woodson (1875-1950) was instrumental in the founding of the Association for the Study of Negro Life and History in 1915. During his lifetime he was probably the most significant scholar promoting the history and achievements of African Americans.

Carter Woodson was born in New Canton, Virginia, in 1875—ten years after the 13th Amendment, abolishing slavery, was written into law. His grandparents and his father, James, a tenant farmer, and mother, Anne, had been slaves. Consequently, when freedom was a reality, they were poor like thousands of newly freed families of African descent in the United States. Because of the close ties to his family and a strong sense of responsibility to them, Woodson worked throughout his early school years to help support his parents and siblings. By the time he was able to attend school, he was well past his teens.

Creative and imaginative as well as independent at an early age, Woodson taught himself by reading avidly in his spare time. As a result of his innate intelligence, personal accomplishments, and dedication to learning, he was able to complete high school. In 1903 he graduated with honors from Berea College, a unique college in the slave state of Kentucky. Founded in 1855, Berea introduced integrated education in the 19th century and thus permitted the enrollment of African Americans. Yet Kentucky had profited from the slave market and the psychology of its people could not accept racially-integrated classrooms. One year after Woodson's graduation the "Day Law" was passed, which prevented white and African American students from being in the same classroom or school community together. Integrated schooling became illegal. The pernicious "Day Law" was actually enforced for nearly half a century, a fact that was not lost on Woodson in his writings about the social customs and laws that served as obstacles to the progress of "the Negro race." He recorded these events as he pursued his interests in the study of African American history.

In 1907 and 1908, respectively, Woodson earned an undergraduate degree and his M.A. from the University of Chicago. Just four years after completing graduate training at the University of Chicago, he was awarded the doctorate from Harvard. This educational background in the country's leading universities challenged Woodson's creative imagination. He became increasingly interested in documenting for the permanent historical record the talents and accom-

plishments of the sons, daughters, grandsons, and grand-daughters of slaves.

Promoting African-American History

In 1916, during the height of World War I, the Association for the Study of Negro Life and History, which Woodson had founded, issued the *Journal of Negro History.* This would become one of his most significant scholarly contributions for recording the backgrounds, experiences, and writings of Americans of African ancestry. He served as the sponsor and editor of the *Journal of Negro History* for many years. This important medium became a significant milestone in promoting the history and contributions of African Americans to the culture. African Americans themselves became aware of their own influence in the intellectual sphere and in the whole society.

In addition to establishing and publishing the *Journal of Negro History,* while Woodson was dean of West Virginia Collegiate Institute he served as president of Associated Publishers. The primary purpose of this innovative outlet was to publish and distribute writings by and about African Americans. When Woodson left West Virginia to continue his research, he involved himself more deeply in the work of the Association for the Study of Negro Life and History. It remains today as a monument to his dedication and foresight.

The broad spectrum of the life of Africans in America was of central interest to Woodson. He studied all facets of their experiences and rich cultural contributions. These in-cluded myths, patterns of migration, roles as wage earners, entrance into medicine, work in rural America, inventions and writings, and their unique history. In 1926, during the zenith of the Harlem Renaissance, he launched a movement to observe ''Negro History Week.'' Woodson felt that an annual celebration of the achievements of the African American should occur during the month of February, since both the gifted abolitionist and orator Frederick Douglass and President Abraham Lincoln were born in that month. In the 1960s what was once only a week of recognizing the outstanding achievements of Americans of African heritage to science, literature, and the arts became transformed into ''Black History Month.''

The Writings of Woodson

Carter G. Woodson was one of the country's prominent historians and a prolific writer. From the moment he received the doctorate from Harvard, he initiated a career in publishing. In 1915 he wrote *The Education of the Negro Prior to 1861,* in which he concentrated on both the obstacles and the progress characterizing the schooling of the descendants of slaves. Three years later he published *A Century of Negro Migration.* This was introduced in 1918, as World War I was coming to a close. The examination of patterns of migration was followed by *The Negro in Our History,* published in 1922. This work has been defined as ''the first textbook of its kind.''

Among Woodson's basic writings are those that describe patterns of migration and family composition. For example, under the auspices of the Association for the Study of Negro Life and History he prepared two important documents—one on slave holding and the other on heads of families: *Free Negro Owners of Slaves in the United States in 1830,* together with *Absentee Ownership of Slaves in the United States in 1830* (1924) and *Free Negro Heads of Families in the United States in 1830* together with *A Brief Treatment of The Free Negro* (1925).

African Americans who had entered the professions of medicine and law during the eras of Reconstruction and post-Reconstruction were of particular interest to Woodson. In 1934 Negro Universities Press published his documentation of *The Negro professional man and the community, with special emphasis on the physician and the lawyer.* Perhaps his most important work, and the one for which he is widely known in the late 20th century, is *The Mis-Education of the Negro* (1933, reprinted 1990). Woodson is remembered as a leading historian who promoted the rich intellectual and creative legacy of the African American.

Further Reading

Probably the two best books about Carter Woodson are Jacqueline Goggin, *Carter G. Woodson: A Life in Black History* (1993) and Pat McKissack, *Carter G. Woodson: The Father of Black History* (1991). Woodson's writings, in addition to those listed in the text, include *The African background outlined or Handbook for the study of the Negro* (1936), *Freedom and slavery in Appalachian America* (1973), *Negro makers of history* (1958), *Negro orators and their orations* (1925), *The rural Negro* (1969), *The history of the Negro church* (2nd ed., 1922), and *Historical genealogy of the*

Woodsons and their connections (1915). See also Doris Y. Wilkinson, "Forgotten Pioneers," *Think,* the newsletter of the Kentucky Humanities Council (October 1988), and *Encyclopedia of Black America* (3rd ed., 1988). □

James Shaver Woodsworth

The Canadian humanitarian, reformer, and political leader James Shaver Woodsworth (1874-1942) contributed significant observations on the life of immigrants to Canada and fought vigorously for social reforms in Parliament.

Born near Toronto, Ontario, on July 29, 1874, J. S. Woodsworth as a boy moved to Manitoba, where his father was for many years superintendent of Methodist missions for the North West Territory. He was educated at Wesley College, Winnipeg, and subsequently studied theology at Victoria University, Toronto. He spent a year in England, attending lectures at Oxford and observing social work in the slums of London. On returning to Canada he was ordained to the Methodist ministry in 1900 and served a brief time in rural pastorates until his appointment as assistant pastor of the prosperous downtown Grace Methodist Church in Winnipeg. In 1904 he married a college classmate from Ontario, Lucy Staples.

As the center of the great wheat boom, Winnipeg was the gateway to the west for thousands of British and European immigrants. A growing interest in the "Social Gospel" fed Woodsworth's feeling that his current work in the church was socially irrelevant, and in 1907 he accepted appointment as superintendent of All Peoples' Mission in the north end of Winnipeg. His observations on the problems of immigrants there became the subject of two books, *Strangers within Our Gates* (1908) and *My Neighbour* (1910).

Woodsworth's increasing involvement in secular approaches to social reforms and the confirmation of his pacifist views during World War I deepened his longstanding doubts about the doctrines of Methodism, and he resigned from the ministry in 1918. After a brief period as a longshoreman in British Columbia, he became involved, while on a visit, in the Winnipeg general strike of 1919 and was arrested for sedition, although the charge was not pressed. In 1921 he was elected to Parliament on a Labour ticket in Winnipeg North Centre, a seat he held continuously until his death.

In Parliament, Woodsworth initially cooperated with the agrarian Progressive party, and in that party's decline after 1924 he became the leader of the "Ginger group," composed of members speaking for labor and the more radical agrarian interests. He fought vigorously for various social reforms, and in 1926, when Mackenzie King's minority government was in a precarious position, Woodsworth pushed through a measure establishing old-age pensions. In 1932, when the impact of the Depression brought together representatives of labor, farm, socialist, and intellectual groups across the country to form a broad Socialist party, the Cooperative Commonwealth Federation (CCF), Woodsworth automatically became its leader.

Woodsworth was the key figure in securing the cooperation of urban and agrarian reformers within the new party. More radical than many of the farmers but less so than many labor leaders, he represented moderation in the advance toward a democratic socialist society. Woodsworth was neither a great orator nor an outstanding party politician, but his integrity and passionate sincerity made him a powerful figure, and even his opponents sometimes paid him tribute as "a saint in politics." The CCF won seven seats in the federal election of 1935 and eight in 1940. Woodsworth ceased to lead his party when his pacifist convictions made him the sole opponent in Parliament of Canadian participation in World War II, but he remained in the House of Commons until his death in Vancouver on March 21, 1942.

Further Reading

The most important study of Woodsworth is the biography by Kenneth McNaught, *A Prophet in Politics* (1959). Also valuable is the memoir by Woodsworth's daughter, Grace MacInnis, *J. S. Woodsworth: A Man to Remember* (1953). The best study of the CCF and Woodsworth's role in it is Walter D. Young, *The Anatomy of a Party: The National CCF, 1932-1961* (1969).

Additional Sources

Mills, Allen George, *Fool for Christ: the political thought of J.S. Woodsworth,* Toronto; Buffalo: University of Toronto Press, 1991. □

Woodward and Bernstein

Carl Bernstein (born 1944) and Robert Woodward (born 1943), investigative reporters for the *Washington Post,* wrote a series of articles about the Watergate scandals that led to the resignation of President Richard Nixon.

Carl Bernstein, born on February 14, 1944, in Washington, D.C., began part-time work at the *Washington Star* at the age of 16 and later dropped out of the University of Maryland to work full-time as a reporter. He joined the *Washington Post's* metropolitan staff in 1966, specializing in police, court, and city hall assignments, with occasional self-assigned feature stories.

Robert Upshur Woodward, born on March 26, 1943, in Geneva, Illinois, attended Yale University on a Naval Reserve Officers Training Corps (ROTC) scholarship, after which he served for five years as a naval officer. He joined the *Washington Post's* metropolitan staff in 1971.

On June 17, 1972, Woodward was assigned to cover a story about an attempted burglary the night before in which five men had been arrested at the headquarters of the

Democratic National Committee in the Watergate complex. Woodward was soon joined on the story by Bernstein, and together the two young reporters undertook a series of investigative reports that gradually revealed the connections between the burglary and a converging pattern of crimes that finally implicated President Richard M. Nixon himself, forcing his resignation in the face of otherwise certain impeachment. The burglary was revealed as part of an extensive program of political espionage and sabotage run by Nixon subordinates at the White House and its political campaign organization, the Committee to Re-Elect the President (CRP, or, as referred to in most later press coverage, CREEP). In addition to the espionage and sabotage, another series of felonies stemmed from the attempt to cover up the earlier crimes by perjury and other obstructions of justice.

Bernstein and Woodward did not, all by themselves, bring about the destruction of the Nixon presidency, but some historians of the period do credit their early investigations with both informing and stimulating the official investigations by a special prosecutor, the courts, the Senate Watergate Committee, and the Judiciary Committee of the House of Representatives that eventually forced Nixon to resign when it was revealed that he had participated in the cover-up almost from the beginning.

Starting with the Watergate burglars, the two young reporters traced the money used to finance the break-in, following it by October 1972 to John Mitchell, formerly Nixon's attorney general and at the time of the break-in the head of the CRP. Bernstein and Woodward pursued documentary evidence by cross-checking telephone books, airline records, building directories, hotel records, and—in what some claimed were violations of journalistic ethics—confidential credit card and telephone company records. In addition, they tracked down and interviewed a large number of people who gradually revealed various pieces of the puzzle. Their editors at the *Post* allowed them to keep most of their sources confidential, but demanded that alleged facts be confirmed by more than one witness. This practice was usually followed scrupulously, but broke down when Bernstein and Woodward wrongly claimed that Hugh Sloan, a CRP official, had implicated H. R. "Bob" Haldeman, Nixon's chief of staff, in testimony before a grand jury. (They later discovered that Sloan meant to communicate to them that Haldeman was guilty, but that Sloan had not said so to the grand jury because he had not been asked.) Woodward relied on one source whom he refused to identify even to his editors except by the code-name "Deep Throat."

From the time of the break-in, and through the fall and winter of 1972-1973, Bernstein and Woodward, under increasing public attack from White House spokesmen, worked virtually alone on the story. In February the U.S. Senate voted seventy to zero to establish a committee of four Democrats and three Republicans to investigate the Watergate affair. Then in March 1973 one of the Watergate burglars, James McCord, a former CIA official, wrote a letter to Judge John Sirica, who was trying his case, that essentially confirmed the Bernstein and Woodward stories. Soon other newspapers began to investigate the Watergate story more energetically, and legislative and judicial agencies began to uncover a larger and larger pattern of lawbreaking. Bernstein and Woodward stayed on the story, though the government agencies they had helped to prod into activity now began to resent their continuing revelations. Samuel Dash, the Democratic counsel to the Senate Select Committee chaired by Senator Sam Ervin of North Carolina, argued in his later book on the Senate investigation, *Chief Counsel*, that the admirable, early investigative reporting of Bernstein and Woodward had now degenerated into what he called "hit and run" journalism based on leaks from the committee and jeopardized the ability of the legal system to track down and punish the guilty.

But Bernstein and Woodward were already branching out into another form of journalism, having secured a contract to write a book on their Watergate investigations. Published in the late spring of 1974, *All the President's Men* was an immediate best seller. Whereas the Bernstein and Woodward stories in the *Washington Post* had consisted of straight investigative reports, *All the President's Men* told not only the story of Watergate but the story of Woodward and Bernstein. Because of its detail, as well as the crucial importance of the subject they were investigating, *All the President's Men* has come to be widely regarded as a classic book in the history of American journalism, showing how reporters and corporate news organizations operate under pressure.

Woodward (right) and Bernstein

Nixon resigned from the presidency on August 9, 1974, after tape recordings that he had ordered made, and then tried to conceal from and deny to investigators, were made public. The tapes incontrovertibly showed that he had participated in an attempt to obstruct justice from as early as six days after the Watergate burglary. Vice President Gerald Ford was sworn in as president on August 9. (Spiro Agnew, who had been elected as Nixon's vice president in 1968 and 1972, had resigned in October 1973 after pleading no contest to a charge of tax evasion.)

Soon after the Nixon resignation, Bernstein and Woodward began work with a team of researchers on *The Final Days,* an account of the last months of Nixon's presidency, based on interviews with 394 people. *All the President's Men* was made into a hit motion picture starring Robert Redford as Woodward and Dustin Hoffman as Bernstein (1976). Both men continued to work for the *Post.* Woodward, with Scott Armstrong, wrote a study of the Supreme Court, *The Brethren* (1979); and Woodward wrote a study of the death by drug overdose of comedian John Belushi, *Wired: The Short Life and Fast Times of John Belushi* (1984). Nora Ephron's novel *Heartburn* (1983) caused a minor journalistic sensation with its fictionalized description of her divorce from Bernstein. The five Watergate burglars and several other Nixon subordinates, including former U.S. Attorney General Mitchell, were sentenced to prison terms. On September 8, 1974, President Gerald Ford pardoned Richard Nixon for any crimes he might have committed while in office, thereby cutting off further criminal investigation of the former president.

As of 1997 Woodward is an assistant managing editor of the *CIA in Veil (1987),* the Pentagon and the Gulf War in *The Commanders* (1991), and the Clinton White House in *The Agenda* (1994). In *The Choice,* he uses his proven research methods for an illuminating examination of the quest for the presidency.

Woodward lives in Washington, D.C., with his wife, Elsa Walsh, a writer for *The New Yorker* and the author of *Divided Lives.* His daughter, Tali, attends the University of California at Berkeley.

Further Reading

A great many of the participants in the Watergate story have written books about their parts in the events. Bernstein and Woodward's *All the President's Men* (1974) and *The Final Days* (1976) capture the excitement of the chase, the enormity of the constitutional crisis, and the agony of the downfall. J. Anthony Lukas, *Nightmare: The Underside of the Nixon Years* (1976) is an exciting narrative and analysis by a *New York Times* reporter that puts Watergate into the context of what the author refers to as ''Richard Nixon's abuse of his presidential powers.'' *The End of a Presidency* (1974) by the staff of the *New York Times* provides a useful combination of analysis and chronology with a sampling of the major documents. David Halberstam, *The Powers That Be* (1979) places the Bernstein and Woodward story into a history of recent American journalism. Richard Nixon's *RN: The Memoirs of Richard Nixon* (1978) gives the former president's version of the events surrounding Watergate. See also Myron J. Smith, *Watergate: An Annotated Bibliography* (1983).Updated information gathered from simonsays.com, an online service. □

Comer Vann Woodward

Comer Vann Woodward (born 1908), American historian, is one of the leading interpreters of southern history and race relations.

Comer Vann Woodward was born in Vanndale, Arkansas in 1908. He graduated from Emory University in 1930, earned his master's degree at Columbia University in 1932, and received his doctorate at the University of North Carolina in 1937. As part of the requirements for the degree, Woodward chose to try the difficult art of historical biography and wrote his dissertation on Thomas Watson, a member of Georgia's liberal Populist movement who later became an editor known for his virulently anti-African American and anti-Semitic views, and who was almost certainly an instigator of mob violence.

Against Desegregation

Woodward's thesis was published in 1938 as *Tom Watson: Agrarian Rebel* to praise from the critics, who were just as complimentary when the book received further notice in the late 1960s.

In 1940 Woodward was called to testify before a congressional committee in support of an anti-lynching bill. Deeply immersed in his life's work, which is the unravelling of post-reconstructionist southern history, Woodward took this responsibility seriously.

In 1943 Woodward was commissioned into the U.S. Navy, where he was sent to the Office of Naval Intelligence in Washington. There, his duties included the creation of monographs on battles in the Pacific, which were later collected together under the title *The Battle for Leyte Gulf,* published in 1947.

Released from active Navy duty in 1946, Woodward accepted a professorship at Johns Hopkins University. Woodward now found his own insistence on desegregation pressed into practical service. He did not hesitate to move academic conventions and meetings from hotels or restaurants unwilling to serve colleagues of all faiths and various heritages, and he also supplied Thurgood Marshall, then chief counsel for the NAACP and later a Supreme Court justice, with detailed background research used extensively for the 1954 *Brown vs. Board of Education of Topeka* court case which ultimately outlawed academic segregation.

What Really Happened after Reconstruction?

In 1951 he published *Reunion and Reaction: The Compromise of 1877 and the End of Reconstruction* and *Origins of the New South 1877-1913*. Both books were pioneering efforts in clarifying the complex political situation at the end of the Reconstruction period, when the laws of segregation had first been boldly set forth in the South, and their publication made him one of the most significant historians of the period.

The "Bible of the Civil Rights Movement"

By the early 1950s Woodward's works on Southern history were extensively used and quoted in university history departments all over the country. He was highly respected, but his reputation had not yert acquired the distinction it would shortly receive. In 1954 he was asked to deliver the Richard lectures at the University of Virginia. The contract for the lectures on the subject of desegregation happened to include the stipulation that any profits from publication were to go to the university. Woodward had not been expecting to publish his remarks. Nevertheless, collected for publication in 1955, they were lavishly praised by Dr. Martin Luther King, Jr. As a result, a paperback edition appeared under the title *The Strange Career of Jim Crow.* Forty years later, this book was still regarded as the Bible of the civil rights movement.

Yale and Afterwards

In 1961 Woodward took an appointment as Sterling Professor of History at Yale University. Here he published some of his most highly-esteemed work, including a collection of essays called *The Burden of Southern History.* He remained at Yale for 16 years, becoming Professor Emeritus in 1977. But official retirement, while relieving him of responsibility the day-to-day running of the department, did not mean the end of writing and his continual search for the truths of history.

In 1981 his name came to the fore once again when he edited a new edition of *The Diary of Mary Boykin Chesnut.* Chesnut, whose husband had been first the United States senator from South Carolina and later an aide to the brilliant, doomed Jefferson Davis, had been a perceptive and witty woman, and Woodward felt her diaries, covering the years 1861 and 1865, had much to say about one of America's most important historical periods.

With more time on his hands, Woodward also turned an increasing amount of time to criticism a crucial necessity if students of history are to distinguish between over-interpreted or justified versions of historical events. Many thoughtful essays have appeared in such widely respected publications as *The New York Review of Books.* In 1994 he also joined 34 other distinguished historians in their fight against the Walt Disney Company's intention to build a huge new theme park close to the Manassas battlefield and many other Civil War sites in Virginia. His advanced age did not prevent him from pointing an acid-tipped pen in the direction of the Disney headquarters. Comparing the advance of the 1990s corporation to the clash of Civil War troops that had once taken place in the area, he wrote, in an article in *The New Republic,* "the battalions of the Walt Disney Company advance their cause with subtler strategy, more sophisticated weaponry and a long barrage of propaganda."

Further Reading

The best assessment and biographical account of Woodward and his work is David Potter's essay "C. Vann Woodward" in Marcus Cunliff and Robin Winks, eds., *Pastmasters: Some Essays on American Historians* (1969). John Higham and others, *History* (1965), contains references to Woodward's ideas.

Additional Sources

American Heritage, April/May, 1981.
The Historian, autumn, 1991.
The New Republic, June 20, 1994. □

Ellen S. Woodward

Ellen S. Woodward (1887-1971) was the director of work relief programs for women during the New Deal in the 1930s. As a leader among women's clubs and political groups in the United States, she was an effective advocate for economic security for women and children.

Ellen Sullivan Woodward was born on July 11, 1887, in Oxford, Mississippi. Her father, William Van Amberg Sullivan, was a lawyer who served briefly in the U.S. Congress both as a representative and as a senator from 1897 to 1901. Thus, young Ellen lived in Washington and developed an early interest in politics and public affairs. She went to private schools in Washington and to Sans Souci, a female seminary in Greenville, South Carolina.

In 1906, at the age of 19, Ellen Sullivan married an attorney, Albert Young Woodward, who lived in Louisville, Mississippi. Soon after she moved there, Ellen Woodward became involved in club work and civic activities that made her aware of the many possibilities and opportunities available to organized women to improve the lives of citizens in their communities and states. After her husband died suddenly in 1925, leaving her with a son, Albert Jr., to support, she was elected to complete her husband's term in the Mississippi legislature. She was the third woman to serve in that body.

When her term ended in 1926, Woodward took a promotional job with the Mississippi State Board of Development, an agency created to encourage civic and industrial growth in the state. At first she was assigned to work with club women to help them improve their towns and counties, but she was soon made the executive secretary of the board. She became the most informed woman in Mississippi about matters of economic and social welfare. As the Democratic national committeewoman from Mississippi, she was a strong supporter of the candidacy of Franklin D. Roosevelt in 1932. Her work came to the attention of public welfare leaders outside her state, and in August 1933 Harry L. Hopkins, the head of the Federal Emergency Relief Administration, asked her to come to Washington to be his assistant administrator. She was put in charge of creating and supervising relief projects that would provide work for

unemployed women. When a larger program—the Works Progress Administration (WPA)—was set up in 1935, Woodward's duties and influence greatly expanded; at its peak in 1936 her division had 480,000 women at work. In 1936, when she was given the direction of the professional workers (artists, musicians, writers, and actors) who had jobs with the WPA, the numbers of workers and projects under her supervision increased and also included men whose work fell within the jurisdiction of her division of the WPA for the first time. Next to First Lady Eleanor Roosevelt and Secretary of Labor Frances Perkins, Woodward was said to be the most important woman in the New Deal. She once said, "Unemployment and unhappiness are synonymous. Our programs aim to end both."

In 1938 Woodward resigned from the WPA to accept an appointment from President Roosevelt as one of the three members of the Social Security Board (SSB). She remained in that position until the executive branch of the government was reorganized in 1946. At that time her work was transferred to the Bureau of Inter-Office and International Relations in the new Federal Security Agency (FSA). She remained the head of that office until she retired in 1953, but by then the work of the FSA had been subsumed by the new Department of Health, Education, and Welfare (now the Department of Health and Human Services).

During her tenure as an SSB member (1938-1946) Woodward concentrated on making the benefits of the social security system understood by American housewives and women workers. She also devoted much time to advocating that the Social Security Act be amended to provide protection to additional workers such as farmers, nurses, and domestics. Her ally in these endeavors was Eleanor Roosevelt, who had also given Woodward full support earlier during her administration of women's work relief. Through World War II Woodward spoke out often on subjects of importance to women war workers and professional and political women who did not want to see the number of policy-making positions in government for women diminished.

New assignments came to Woodward in the area of international social welfare. From 1943 to 1946 she attended six international meetings of the United Nations Relief and Rehabilitation Administration (UNRRA) as an adviser to the United States delegation. In 1945 the State Department sent her to Germany as an UNRRA observer of camps for displaced persons. In 1947 she was one of two women delegates at the organizational meeting at Lake Success, New York, of the United Nations Economic and Social Council (which became the organizational link between the UN and such specialized agencies as UNESCO, WHO, and FAO).

After she retired in 1953, Woodward remained in Washington and died there of arteriosclerosis on September 23, 1971. She was buried in her old hometown, Louisville, Mississippi.

Further Reading

Sketches on Ellen Woodward appear in *Notable American Women: The Modern Era* (1980) and in the *Historical Dictio-*

nary of the New Deal (1985). She is one of the women whose work is described in a book by Susan Ware, *Beyond Suffrage: Women in the New Deal* (1981). An essay on her friendship with Eleanor Roosevelt is in Joan Hoff-Wilson and Marjorie Lightman, editors, *Without Precedent: The Life and Career of Eleanor Roosevelt* (1984).

Additional Sources

Swain, Martha H., *Ellen S. Woodward: New Deal advocate for women,* Jackson: University Press of Mississippi, 1995. □

Virginia Woolf (left)

Virginia Stephen Woolf

The English novelist, critic, and essayist Virginia Stephen Woolf (1882-1941) ranks as one of England's most distinguished writers of the period between World War I and World War II. Her novels can perhaps best be described as impressionistic.

Dissatisfied with the novel based on familiar, factual, and external details, Virginia Woolf followed experimental clues to a more internal, subjective, and in a sense more personal rendering of experience than had been provided by Henry James, Marcel Proust, and James Joyce. In the works of these masters the reality of time and experience had formed the stream of consciousness, a concept that probably originated with William James. Virginia Woolf lived in and responded to a world in which certitudes were collapsing under the stresses of changing knowledge, the civilized savagery of war, and new manners and morals. She drew on her personal, sensitive, poetic awareness without rejecting altogether the heritage of literary culture she derived from her family.

Early Years and Marriage

Virginia Stephen was born in London on Jan. 25, 1882. She was the daughter of Sir Leslie Stephen, a famous scholar and agnostic philosopher who, among many literary occupations, was at one time editor of *Cornhill Magazine* and the *Dictionary of National Biography.* James Russell Lowell, the American poet, was her godfather. Virginia's mother died when the child was 12 or 13 years old, and she was educated at home in her father's library, where she also met his famous friends.

In 1912, eight years after her father's death, Virginia married Leonard Woolf, a brilliant young writer and critic from Cambridge whose interests in literature as well as in economics and the labor movement were well suited to hers. In 1917, for amusement, they originated the Hogarth Press by setting and handprinting on an old press *Two Stories* by "L. and V. Woolf." The volume was a success, and over the years they published many important books, including *Prelude* by Katherine Mansfield, then an unknown writer; *Poems* by T. S. Eliot; and *Kew Gardens* by Virginia Woolf. The policy of the Hogarth Press was to publish the best and most original work that came to its attention, and the Woolfs as publishers favored young and obscure writers. Virginia's older sister Vanessa, who married the critic Clive Bell, participated in this venture by designing dust jackets for the books issued by the Hogarth Press.

Quite early in her career Virginia Woolf's home in Tavistock Square, Bloomsbury, became a literary and art center, attracting such diverse intellectuals as E. M. Forster, Lytton Strachey, Arthur Waley, Victoria Sackville-West, John Maynard Keynes, and Roger Fry. These artists, critics, and writers became known as the Bloomsbury group. Roger Fry's theory of art may have influenced Virginia's technique as a novelist. Broadly speaking, the Bloomsbury group drew from the philosophic interests of its members (who had been educated at Cambridge) the values of love and beauty as preeminent in life.

As Critic and Essayist

Virginia Woolf began writing essays for the *Times Literary Supplement* when she was young, and over the years these and other essays were collected in a two-volume series called *The Common Reader* (1925, 1933). These studies range with affection and understanding through all of English literature. Students of fiction have drawn upon these criticisms as a means of understanding Virginia Woolf's own direction as a novelist. One passage frequently studied occurs in "Modern Fiction" in the *First Series:* "Life is not a series of . . . big lamps symmetrically arranged; but a luminous halo, a semitransparent envelope surrounding us from the beginning of consciousness to the end. Is it not the task of the novelist to convey this varying, this unknown and uncircumscribed spirit, whatever aberration or complexity it may display, with as little mixture of the alien and external as possible?''

Another essay frequently studied is ''Mr. Bennett and Mrs. Brown,'' written in 1924, in which Virginia Woolf describes the manner in which the older-generation novelist Arnold Bennett would have portrayed Mrs. Brown, a lady casually met in a railway carriage, by giving her a house and furniture and a position in the world. She then contrasts this method with another: one that exhibits a new interest in the subjective Mrs. Brown, the mysteries of her person, her consciousness, and the consciousness of the observer responding to her.

Achievement as Novelist

Two of Virginia Woolf's novels in particular, *Mrs. Dalloway* (1925) and *To the Lighthouse* (1927), follow successfully the latter approach. The first novels covers a day in the life of Mrs. Dalloway in postwar London; it achieves its vision of reality through the reception by Mrs. Dalloway's mind of what Virginia Woolf called those 'myriad impressions—trivial, fantastic, evanescent, or engraved with the sharpness of steel.'' *To the Lighthouse* is, in a sense, a family portrait and history rendered in subjective depth through selected points in time. Part I deals with the time between six o'clock in the evening and dinner. Primarily through the consciousness of Mrs. Ramsay, it presents the clash of the male and female sensibilities in the family; Mrs. Ramsay functions as a means of equipoise and reconciliation. Part II: Time Passes, is a moving evocation of loss during the interval between Mrs. Ramsay's death and the family's revisit to the house. Part III moves toward completion of this intricate and subjective portrait through the adding of a last detail to a painting by an artist guest, Lily Briscoe, and through the final completion of a plan, rejected by the father in Part I, for him and the children to sail out to the lighthouse. The novel is impressionistic, subjectively perceptive, and poignant.

Last Years and Other Books

Virginia Woolf was the author of about 15 books, the last, *A Writer's Diary,* posthumously published in 1953. Her death by drowning in Lewes, Sussex, on March 28, 1941, has often been regarded as a suicide brought on by the unbearable strains of life during World War II. The true explanation seems to be that she had felt symptoms of a recurrence of a mental breakdown and feared that it would be permanent.

Mrs. Dalloway, To the Lighthouse, and *Jacob's Room* (1922) constitute Virginia Woolf's major achievement. *The Voyage Out* (1915) first brought her critical attention. *Night and Day* (1919) is traditional in method. The short stories of *Monday or Tuesday* (1921) brought critical praise. In *The Waves* (1931) she masterfully employed the stream-of-consciousness technique. Other experimental novels include *Orlando* (1928), *The Years* (1937), and *Between the Acts* (1941). Virginia Woolf's championship of woman's rights is reflected in the essays in *A Room of One's Own* (1929) and in *Three Guineas* (1938).

Further Reading

Virginia Woolf's diary was edited by her husband, Leonard Sidney Woolf, *The Dairy of Virginia Woolf* (1953). Leonard Woolf's five-volume autobiography not only deals in great detail with his life with Virginia Woolf but reveals much about English social and literary history since 1939: *Sowing: An Autobiography of the Years, 1880-1904* (1960), *Growing: An Autobiography of the Years, 1904-1911* (1962), *Beginning Again: An Autobiography of the Years, 1911 to 1918* (1964), *Downhill All the Way: An Autobiography of the Years, 1919-1939* (1967), and *The Journey, Not the Arrival Matters: An Autobiography of the Years, 1939-1969* (1970).
Much has been written about Virginia Woolf. Her experimental technique as well as her psychological depth made her, in a sense, a critic's writer. Interesting and helpful studies include David Daiches, *Virginia Woolf* (1942; rev. ed. 1963); Joan Bennett, *Virginia Woolf: Her Art as a Novelist* (1945; 2d ed. 1964); Bernard Blackstone, *Virginia Woolf: A Commentary* (1949); James Hafley, *The Glass Roof: Virginia Woolf as Novelist* (1954); Aileen Pippett, *The Moth and the Star: A Biography of Virginia Woolf* (1955); Dorothy Brewster, *Virginia Woolf* (1962); Jean Guiguet, *Virginia Woolf and Her Works* (trans. 1966); Carl Woodring, *Virginia Woolf* (1966); and Jean O. Love, *World of Consciousness: Mythopoetic Thought in the Novels of Virginia Woolf* (1970). □

John Woolman

John Woolman (1720-1772), American Quaker merchant and minister, was known for his opposition to slavery, poverty, and war. His journal is one of the finest statements of Quaker inner life.

John Woolman was born in Ancocas, N.J., and raised in Quaker schools and meetings. He read widely and prepared himself for a variety of occupations. Primarily a tailor and shopkeeper, he also kept an apple orchard, taught school, wrote, maintained a lending library, and was a surveyor and conveyancer. As conveyancer, he wrote bills of sale for slaves; this was his introduction to slavery. His meeting recorded him as a minister in 1743.

Woolman's was an itinerant ministry; his territory included the Atlantic seaboard, England, and Ireland. He traveled twice to the South, where he witnessed plantation life. His advocacy of the abolition of slavery, *Some Considerations on the Keeping of Negroes,* was published in two parts in 1754 and 1762. In 1763 Woolman visited the Indians on the Pennsylvania frontier, converting many to the Quaker ideals of peace and Christian brotherhood. In 1772, in Yorkshire, England, he made a walking tour in protest against the treatment of postboys. He died of smallpox at York on Oct. 7, 1772.

The mystical experience underlies Woolman's positions on social and economic questions. Convinced of the universal brotherhood of man with Christ, he regarded no distinction of nationality, race, or education as more basic to human nature. Woolman identified with the evildoer and with the slaveholder as well as the slave. He was a keen student of his own motives. He located first in himself the tendencies he sought to eradicate from the world. He devised a theory of action, which he called "passive obedience," similar to contemporary nonviolence. Woolman found the causes of war in the economic self-aggrandizement of nations.

Woolman strove to strengthen his community at Mount Holly, N.J., and resisted oppression by every lawful means. He gave up dyed clothes when he discovered the dyes were harmful to the workers. He ate no sugar because of his convictions about slavery. When his own merchandising business succeeded, he withdrew to concentrate on the "inward business" of living.

Woolman's publications included *An Epistle* (1772), defining his religious beliefs; his *Journal* (1774); and *Plea for the Poor* (1793). Modern peace and civil rights advocates feel akin to this quiet radical.

Further Reading

Biographies of Woolman are Janet (Payne) Whitney, *John Woolman, American Quaker* (1942), and C. O. Peare, *John Woolman* (1954). Reginald Reynolds, *The Wisdom of John Woolman* (1948), is the most perceptive appreciation of Woolman. For general background on Quakerism see Frederick B. Tolles, *Quakers and the Atlantic Culture* (1960).

Additional Sources

Kohler, Charles., *A quartet of Quakers: Isaac and Mary Penington, John Bellers, John Woolman,* London: Friends Home Service Committee, 1978. ☐

Frank Winfield Woolworth

Frank Winfield Woolworth (1852-1919), American merchant, was a pioneer in retailing methods. He established the great chain of "five-and-ten-cent" stores which bear his name.

Born to a poor farm family in upstate New York, F. W. Woolworth began his career by clerking in a general store in the local market center. Impressed with the success of a five-cent clearance sale, he conceived the novel idea of establishing a store to sell a variety of items in volume at that price. With $300 in inventory advanced to him by his employer, Woolworth started a small store in Utica in 1879, but it soon failed. By 1881, however, Woolworth had two successful stores operating in Pennsylvania. By adding ten-cent items, he was able to increase his inventory greatly and thereby acquired a unique institutional status most important for the success of his stores.

The growth of Woolworth's chain was rapid. Capital for new stores came partly from the profits of those already in operation and partly from investment by partners whom Woolworth installed as managers of the new units. Initially, many of the partners were Woolworth's relatives and colleagues.

Convinced that the most important factor in ensuring the success of the chain was increasing the variety of goods offered, Woolworth in 1886 moved to Brooklyn, New York, to be near wholesale suppliers. He also undertook the purchasing for the entire chain. A major breakthrough came when he decided to stock candy and was able to bypass wholesalers and deal directly with manufacturers. Aware of the importance of the presentation of goods, Woolworth took the responsibility for planning window and counter displays for the whole chain and devised the familiar red store front which became its institutional hallmark.

The success of the chain between 1890 and 1910 was phenomenal. The company had 631 outlets doing a business of $60,558,000 annually by 1912. In that year Woolworth merged with five of his leading competitors, forming a corporation capitalized at $65 million. The next year, at a cost of $13.5 million, he built the Woolworth Building in downtown New York, the tallest skyscraper in the world at the time.

By 1915 Woolworth spent much of his time in Europe. When he died in 1919, the F. W. Woolworth Company, with over 1,000 stores, was perhaps the most successful retail enterprise in the world.

Further Reading

The fullest source of information on Woolworth is the partially fictionalized biography by John K. Winkler, *Five and Ten: The*

Fabulous Life of F. W. Woolworth (1940). Other accounts of Woolworth and of the company are in Godfrey M. Lebhar, *Chain Stores in America* (1952; 3d ed. 1963); the Woolworth Company, *Woolworth's First 75 Years* (1954); Tom Mahoney, *The Great Merchants* (1955; new ed. 1966); and Robert C. Kirkwood, *The Woolworth Story at Home and Abroad* (1960).

☐

Barbara Adam Wootton

The British social scientist Barbara Adam Wootton (1897-1988) began as an economist, progressing to a student of social policy and in particular the problems of welfare and social deviance. She was among the first "Life Peers" in Parliament and the first woman to chair that assembly by sitting on the Woolsack.

Barbara Wootton died in the summer of 1988 in her 92nd year. She was born in 1897 into an academic family in Cambridge, the daughter of James Adam, a classical scholar and senior tutor of Emmanuel College. Her mother taught at Girton, the college founded for women who were, until the 1920s, excluded from full membership of the university. Mrs. Adam taught her daughter at home until she was nearly 14, after which she went first to the Perse School in Cambridge and then to Girton. Her father died in 1907 when she was only 10 and the younger of her two brothers was killed in World War I in 1916. At the age of 20, having begun to read classics, she married Jack Wootton, a young army officer whom she had met when he was a research student at Trinity College. Their honeymoon lasted less than two days as he was recalled to his regiment in France at short notice; five weeks later he was killed in action. She remarked in *In a World I Never Made,* her autobiography published in 1967, that "in ten years I had learned little about life, much about death. . . ."

Wootton moved from the study of classics to that of economics, and such was her enthusiasm that she is known to have annotated every line of her copy of Alfred Marshall's *Principles of Economics.* In her examinations she achieved a first class with a special mark of distinction; owing to the rules of the university she was not, as a woman, entitled to be formally awarded the degree of B.A. Her early training in classics gave her an unusually fine command of language, to be demonstrated in her later writings, and her sound foundation in economics gave an equally firm foundation to her work in applied social science. She embarked at a relatively early age upon a teaching career, which continued until 1952 when she resigned her professorial post.

Wootton's talents as a teacher were formidable, although her lectures at Cambridge had to be listed under the name of a man for whom she would, by arrangement, act as a substitute. She left Cambridge in 1922 to become a research officer for the Trades Union Congress and the Labour Party though continuing to teach part time at Westfield and Bedford Colleges. In 1926 she decided to move into the field of adult education and became principal of Morley College for Working Men and Women. She was not to stay there for very long before she was offered and accepted the post of director of tutorial studies for the University of London, a branch of the university which was also concerned with adult education. In 1944 she moved to Bedford College where she became head of the Department of Economics, Sociology and Social Studies, having the title of professor conferred upon her four years later.

But Bedford, then a women's college, was not an easy place in which a social scientist might flourish and in the course of an internecine squabble over the allocation of a government grant—in which she was the principal victim— Wootton resigned and applied for a research fellowship with the Nuffield Foundation. The fruits of this fellowship were to be found in a major work, *Social Science and Social Pathology* (1959). Nine years earlier she had published *Testament for Social Science: An Essay in the Application of Scientific Method to Human Problems,* in which she set out her essentially positivistic belief that only through the application of scientific method could human problems in the area of economic and social planning have any serious hope of solution. It was an idealistic work that inspired many of the rising generation. *The Social Foundations of Wage Policy* appeared in 1955; it was a polemical analysis of the structure of wages and salaries in British society, and in a seminar she summarized it in the aphorism, "The more you earn the less hard you have to work to get it." It contained some strange echoes of her earlier work, *Lament for Economics,* which had appeared in 1938.

Always a supporter of the Labour Party, she became one of the first of the new Life Peers in 1958 with the title of the Baroness Wootton of Abinger and was to become a deputy speaker in the House of Lords. Curiously, when the Wilson government was formed after the Labour election victory of 1964 she was never given any office but continued to serve as a member of the Advisory Council on the Penal System, chairing notable subcommittees on the subjects of noncustodial penalties (subsequently incorporated into legislation) and on cannabis (whose recommendations were rejected by government).

Wootton performed many other public services. She was a magistrate and specialized in the juvenile courts, a member of the University Grants Committee, a governor of the BBC, and the first chairman of the Countryside Commission. She was made a companion of honour in 1977. Her record of public work alone was a formidable achievement, but in addition she was able to produce a continuous stream of books and pamphlets in which her scholarship as a social scientist was blended with a strong political commitment to liberty and a social justice predicated upon the notion of equality. Among sociologists she left little if any mark, but among the analysts of social policy, not least in the criminal justice field, her influence was considerable if not always immediately apparent.

Further Reading

Probably the most useful introduction to Wootton and her work is to be found in Philip Bean and David Whynes, editors, *Bar-*

bara Wootton: Social Science and Public Policy (1968). Wootton's work, which addresses issues in social economics, planning, and criminal justice policy, is representative of the British tradition of social democratic thought in the period 1935 to 1970. Her autobiographical writing is a useful source of information for the period 1920-1970 in which she was active in academic and public life. □

William Wordsworth

William Wordsworth (1770-1850), an early leader of romanticism in English poetry, ranks as one of the greatest lyric poets in the history of English literature.

William Wordsworth was born in Cookermouth, Cumberland, on April 7, 1770, the second child of an attorney. Unlike the other major English romantic poets, he enjoyed a happy childhood under the loving care of his mother and in close intimacy with his younger sister Dorothy (1771-1855). As a child, he wandered exuberantly through the lovely natural scenery of Cumberland. At Hawkshead Grammar School, Wordsworth showed keen and precociously discriminating interest in poetry. He was fascinated by "the divine John Milton," impressed by George Crabbe's descriptions of poverty, and repelled by the "falsehood" and "spurious imagery" in Ossian's nature poetry.

From 1787 to 1790 Wordsworth attended St. John's College, Cambridge, always returning with breathless delight to the north and to nature during his summer vacations. Before graduating from Cambridge, he took a walking tour through France, Switzerland, and Italy in 1790. The Alps gave him an ecstatic impression that he was not to recognize until 14 years later as a mystical "sense of usurpation, when the light of sense/ Goes out, but with a flash that has revealed/ The invisible world"—the world of "infinitude" that is "our beings's heart and home."

Sojourn in France

Revolutionary fervor in France made a powerful impact on the young idealist, who returned there in November 1791 allegedly to improve his knowledge of the French language. Wordsworth's stay in Paris, Orléans, and Blois proved decisive in three important respects. First, his understanding of politics at the time was slight, but his French experience was a powerful factor in turning his inbred sympathy for plain common people, among whom he had spent the happiest years of his life, into articulate radicalism. Second, in 1792 Wordsworth composed his most ambitious poem to date, the *Descriptive Sketches*. An admittedly juvenile, derivative work, it was in fact less descriptive of nature than the earlier *An Evening Walk,* composed at Cambridge. But it better illustrated his vein of protest and his belief in political freedom.

Finally, while Wordsworth's political ideas and poetic talent were thus beginning to take shape, he fell passion-ately in love with a French girl, Annette Vallon. She gave birth to their daughter in December 1792. Having exhausted his meager funds, he was obliged to return home. The separation left him with a sense of guilt that deepened his poetic inspiration and that accounted for the prominence of the theme of derelict womanhood in much of his work.

Publication of First Poems

Descriptive Sketches and *An Evening Walk* were printed in 1793. By then, Wordsworth's wretchedness over Annette and their child had been aggravated by a tragic sense of torn loyalties as war broke out between England and the French Republic. This conflict precipitated his republicanism, which he expounded with almost religious zeal and eloquence in *A Letter to the Bishop of Llandaff,* while his new imaginative insight into human sorrow and fortitude found poetic expression in "Salisbury Plain." The influence of William Godwin's ideas in *Political Justice* prompted Wordsworth to write "Guilt and Sorrow," and this influence is also perceptible in his unactable drama, *The Borderers* (1796). This *Sturm und Drang* composition, however, also testified to the poet's humanitarian disappointment with the French Revolution, which had lately engaged in the terrorist regime of Maximilien de Robespierre.

The year 1797 marked the beginning of Wordsworth's long and mutually enriching friendship with Samuel Taylor Coleridge, the first fruit of which was their joint publication of *Lyrical Ballads* (1798). Wordsworth's main share in the volume was conceived as a daring experiment to challenge "the gaudiness and inane phraseology of many modern writers" in the name of precision in psychology and realism in diction. Most of his poems in this collection centered on the simple yet deeply human feelings of ordinary people, phrased in their own language. His views on this new kind of poetry were more fully described in the important "Preface" that he wrote for the second edition (1800).

"Tintern Abbey"

Wordsworth's most memorable contribution to this volume was "Tintern Abbey," which he wrote just in time for inclusion in it. This poem is the first major piece to illustrate his original talent at its best. A lyrical summing up of the poet's experiences and expectations, it skillfully combines matter-of-factness in natural description with a genuinely mystical sense of infinity, joining self-exploration to philosophical speculation. While tracing the poet's ascent from unthinking enjoyment of nature to the most exalted perception of cosmic oneness, it also voices his gnawing perplexity as the writer—prophetically, as it turned out—wonders whether his exhilarating vision of universal harmony may not be a transient delusion. The poem closes on a subdued but confident reassertion of nature's healing power, even though mystical insight may be withdrawn from the poet.

In its successful blending of inner and outer experience, of sense perception, feeling, and thought, "Tintern Abbey" is a poem in which the writer's self becomes an adequate symbol of mankind; undisguisedly subjective reminiscences lead to imaginative speculations about man and the universe. This cosmic outlook rooted in egocentricity is a central feature of romanticism, and Wordsworth's poetry is undoubtedly the most impressive exponent of this view in English literature.

The writing of "Tintern Abbey" anticipated the later spiritual evolution of Wordsworth; it clarified the direction that his best work took in the next few years; and it heralded the period in which he made his imperishable contribution to the development of English romanticism. Significantly, this period was also the time of his closest intimacy with Dorothy—who kept the records of their experiences and thus supplied him with an unceasing flow of motifs, characters, and incidents on which to base his poetry—and with Coleridge, whose constant encouragement and criticism provided the incentive to ever deeper searching and to more articulate thinking. The three lived at Nether Stowey, Somerset, in 1797-1798; took a trip to Germany in 1798-1799, which left little impression on Wordsworth's mind; and then settled in Grasmere in the Lake District.

Poems of the Middle Period

Even while writing his contributions to the *Lyrical Ballads,* Wordsworth had been feeling his way toward more ambitious schemes. He had embarked on a long poem in blank verse, "The Ruined Cottage," later referred to as "The Peddlar"; it was intended to form part of a vast philosophical poem that was to bear the painfully explicit title "The Recluse, or Views of Man, Nature and Society." In it the poet hoped to "assume the station of a man in mental repose, one whose principles were made up, and so prepared to deliver upon authority a system of philosophy." This grand project, in which Coleridge had a considerable share of responsibility, never materialized as originally contemplated; its materials were later incorporated into *The Excursion* (1815), which centers on the poet's own problems and conflicts under a thin disguise of objectivity. This distortion is significant. Abstract impersonal speculation was not congenial to Wordsworth; he could handle experiences in the philosophical-lyrical manner that was truly his own only insofar as they were closely related to himself and therefore genuinely aroused his creative feelings and imagination. During the winter months that he spent in Germany, he started work on his *magnum opus,* the "poem on his own mind," which was to be published posthumously as *The Prelude, or Growth of a Poet's Mind.*

As yet, however, such an achievement was still beyond Wordsworth's scope, and it was back to the shorter poetic forms that he turned during the most productive season of his long literary life, the spring of 1802, when the great loss anticipated in "Tintern Abbey" came over him. The output of these fertile months, however, mostly derived from his earlier, twofold inspiration: nature and the common people. In "To a Butterfly," "I wandered lonely as a cloud," "To the Cuckoo," "The Rainbow," and other poems, Wordsworth went on to express his inexhaustible delight and participation in nature's "beauteous forms." Such poems as "The Sailor's Mother" and "Alice Fell, or the Beggar-Woman" were in the *Lyrical Ballads* vein, voicing "the still, sad music of humanity" and exhibiting once more his unfailing understanding of and compassion for the sufferings and moral resilience of the poor.

Changes in Philosophy

The crucial event of this period was Wordsworth's loss of the sense of mystical oneness, which had sustained his highest imaginative flights. Indeed, a mood of despondency as acute as Coleridge's in "Dejection" at times descended over Wordsworth, now 32 years old, as life compelled him to outgrow the joyful, irresponsible gladness of youth. He became engaged to Mary Hutchinson, a girl he had known since childhood. Marriage in 1802 entailed new cares and responsibilities. One was to secure some sort of financial stability, and another was somehow to wind up the Annette Vallon episode.

In the summer of 1802 Wordsworth spent a few weeks in Calais with Dorothy, where he arranged a friendly separation with Annette and their child. Napoleon Bonaparte had just been elected first consul for life, and Wordsworth's renewed contact with France only confirmed his disillusionment with the French Revolution and its aftermath. During this period he had become increasingly concerned with Coleridge, who by now was almost totally dependent upon opium for relief from his physical sufferings. Both friends were thus brought face to face with the unpalatable fact that the realities of life were in stark contradiction to the visionary expectations of their youth. But whereas Coleridge recognized this and gave up poetry for abstruse pursuits that were more congenial to him, Wordsworth characteristically sought to redefine his own identity in ways that would allow him a measure of continuity in purposefulness. The new turn that his life took in 1802 resulted in an inner change that set the new course that his poetry henceforth followed.

In earlier days, Wordsworth's interest in the common people, whom he knew and loved and admired, had prompted him to assume a revolutionary stance. He now relinquished this stance, his attachment to his "dear native regions" extending to his native country and its institutions, which he now envisioned as a more suitable emblem of genuine freedom and harmony than France's revolutionary turmoils and republican imperialism. Poems about England and Scotland began pouring forth from his pen, while France and Napoleon soon became Wordsworth's favorite symbols of cruelty and oppression. His nationalistic inspiration led him to produce the two "Memorials of a Tour in Scotland" (1803, 1814) and the group entitled "Poems Dedicated to National Independence and Liberty."

Poems of 1802

The best poems of 1802, however, deal with a deeper level of inner change: with Wordsworth's awareness of his loss and with his manly determination to find moral and poetic compensation for it. In his ode "Intimations of Immortality" (March-April), he plainly recognized that "The things which I have seen I now can see no more"; yet he emphasized that although the "visionary gleam" had fled, the memory remained, and although the "celestial light" had vanished, the "common sight" of "meadow, grove and stream" was still a potent source of delight and solace. And in "Resolution and Independence" (May), he in fact admonished himself to welcome his loss in a spirit of stoic acceptance and of humble gratefulness to God.

Thus Wordsworth shed his earlier tendency to a pantheistic idealization of nature and turned to a more sedate doctrine of orthodox Christianity. Younger poets and critics soon blamed him for this "recantation," which they equated with his change of mind about the French Revolution. While it is true that lyrical outbursts about duty and religion are apt to sound conventional and sanctimonious to modern ears, one cannot doubt the sincerity of Wordsworth's belief, expressed in 1815, that "poetry is most just to its own divine origin when it administers the comforts and breathes the spirit of religion." His *Ecclesiastical Sonnets* (1822), which purport to describe "the introduction, progress, and operation of the Church of England, both previous and subsequent to the Reformation," are clear evidence of the way in which love of freedom, of nature, and of the Church came to coincide in his mind.

The Prelude

Nevertheless, it was the direction suggested in "Intimations of Immortality" that, in the view of later criticism, enabled Wordsworth to produce perhaps the most outstanding achievement of English romanticism: *The Prelude*. He worked on it, on and off, for several years and completed the first version in May 1805. *The Prelude* can claim to be the only true romantic epic because it deals in narrative terms with the spiritual growth of the only true romantic hero, the poet. Thus Wordsworth evolved a new genre peculiarly suited to his temperament. In this poem as in most of his best poetry—but here on a larger scale—the egocentricity for which he has often been rebuked was validated through symbolism. The inward odyssey of the poet was not described for its own sake but as a sample and as an adequate image of man at his most sensitive.

Wordsworth shared the general romantic notion that personal experience is the only way to gain living knowledge. The purpose of *The Prelude* was to recapture and interpret, with detailed thoroughness, the whole range of experiences that had contributed to the shaping of his own mind. Such a procedure enabled him to rekindle the dying embers of his earlier vision; it also enabled him to reassess the transient truth and the lasting value of his earlier glorious insights in the light of mature wisdom. It lies in the nature of such an extended process of reminiscence and revaluation that only death can end it, and Wordsworth wisely refrained from publishing the poem in his lifetime, revising it continuously. The posthumously printed version differs in several ways from the text he read to Coleridge in 1807. It is surprising, however, that the changes from the early version should not be more radical than they are. Most of them are improvements in style and structure. Wordsworth's youthful enthusiasm for the French Revolution has been slightly toned down. Most important and, perhaps, most to be regretted, the poet also tried to give a more orthodox tinge to his early mystical faith in nature.

Later Years

This type of modification toward orthodoxy had already been introduced in 1804, by which time the basic features of Wordsworth's mature personality had begun to stabilize. Of his later life, indeed, little needs to be said. He was much affected by the death of his brother John in 1805, an event that strengthened his adherence to the consolations of the Church. But he was by no means reduced to utter conformity, as his tract *On the Convention of Cintra* (1808), a strongly worded protest against the English betrayal of Portuguese and Spanish allies to Napoleon, shows. Important passages in *The Excursion,* in which he criticizes the new industrial forms of man's inhumanity to man, witness this also.

Wordsworth's estrangement from Coleridge in 1810 deprived him of a powerful incentive to imaginative and intellectual alertness. Wordsworth's appointment to the office of distributor of stamps for Westmoreland in 1813 relieved him of financial care, but it also dissipated his suspicion of the aristocracy and helped him to become a confirmed Tory and a devout member of the Anglican Church. Wordsworth's unabating love for nature made him view the emergent industrial society with undisguised diffidence, but although he opposed the Reform Bill of 1832, which, in his view, merely transferred political power from the landed to the manufacturing class, he never stopped pleading in favor of the victims of the factory system. In 1843 he was appointed poet laureate. He died on April 23, 1850.

Further Reading

Mary Moorman, *William Wordsworth: A Biography* (2 vols., 1957, 1965), is the standard work. On the poet's personality, Herbert Read, *Wordsworth* (1930), and Wallace W. Douglas, *Wordsworth: The Construction of a Personality* (1968), are of interest.

General introductions to the poetry include Peter Burra, *Wordsworth* (1936); James C. Smith, *A Study of Wordsworth* (1944); Helen Darbishire, *The Poet Wordsworth* (1950); John F. Danby, *The Simple Wordsworth* (1960); Frederick W. Bateson, *Wordsworth: A Re-interpretation* (2d ed. 1963); and Carl Woodring, *Wordsworth* (1965). More specialized studies include David Ferry, *The Limits of Mortality* (1959); Colin C. Clarke, *Romantic Paradox: An Essay on the Poetry of Wordsworth* (1963); Geoffrey H. Hartman, *Wordsworth's Poetry, 1787-1814* (1964); David Perkins, *Wordsworth and the Poetry of Sincerity* (1965); Bernard Groom, *The Unity of Wordsworth's Poetry* (1966); and James Scoggins, *Imagination and Fancy: Complementary Modes in the Poetry of Wordsworth* (1966).

Important discussions of Wordsworth's philosophy are Arthur Beatty, *William Wordsworth: His Doctrine and Art in Their Historical Relation* (1922); Raymond D. Havens, *The Mind of a Poet* (1941); Newton P. Stallknecht, *Strange Seas of Thought: Studies in William Wordsworth's Philosophy of Man and Nature* (1945; 2d ed. 1958); Enid Welsford, *Salisbury Plain: A Study in the Development of Wordsworth's Mind and Art* (1966); and Melvin Rader, *Wordsworth: A Philosophical Approach* (1967).

The poet's literary theories are discussed in Marjorie Greenbie, *Wordsworth's Theory of Poetic Diction* (1966), and his political outlook in Francis M. Todd, *Politics and the Poet: A Study of Wordsworth* (1957), and in Amanda M. Ellis, *Rebels and Conservatives: Dorothy and William Wordsworth and Their Circle* (1968). Analyses of individual works include Judson S. Lyon, *The Excursion: A Study* (1950); Abbie F. Potts, *Wordsworth's Prelude: A Study of Its Literary Form* (1953); Herbert Lindenberger, *On Wordsworth's Prelude* (1963); John F. Danby, *Wordsworth: The Prelude* (1963); and Roger N. Murray, *Wordsworth's Style: Figures and Themes in the 'Lyrical Ballads' of 1800* (1967). □

Monroe Work

Monroe Work (1866-1945), a sociologist, published the *Negro Year Book* and an extensive bibliography on African Americans. He was also active in the anti-lynching campaign and the Negro Health Week movement.

Monroe Nathan Work was born to ex-slaves on August 15, 1866, in Iredell County, North Carolina. Shortly after his birth Work's family moved to Cairo, Illinois, where his father worked as a tenant farmer. Like many freedmen, the Works wanted to own land, and in the 1870s they preempted a 160-acre farm in Summer County, Kansas. Work remained there—completing his elementary education at a nearby school located in a church—until 1889 when his mother died and his father went to live with one of the married children.

At the age of 23 Work was finally free to pursue the education he had long desired. He entered a bi-racial high school in Arkansas City, working to support himself while a student. After graduating third in his class, Work tried teaching, preaching, and homesteading before resuming his education at the Chicago Theological Seminary. Instead of becoming a minister, however, Work became a sociologist, transferring to the Sociology Department of the University of Chicago in 1898.

From an early age Work apparently wanted to contribute to the welfare of his fellow African Americans, and in Chicago he found his proper role. African Americans at that time faced crippling and bewildering discrimination, ranging from segregation to disfranchisement to lynching and based on irrational white fear and hatred of African Americans. Work once noted, "In the end facts will help eradicate prejudice and misunderstanding, for facts are the truth and the truth shall set us free." While still a student he began seeking the facts. His paper on Negro crime in Chicago later became the first article by an African American to be published in the *American Journal of Sociology*. Under the influence of Professor William I. Thomas, Work also developed an interest in Africa, and his articles on African culture marked him as one of the pioneer scholars on that subject.

After receiving his Masters degree on June 16, 1903, Work accepted a faculty position at Georgia State Industrial College in Savannah. He went to the Deep South where the largest number of African Americans experienced the most discrimination and where he could continue a research relationship with W. E. B. DuBois through the Atlanta University Studies. DuBois was the foremost African American intellectual of the age and a militant leader who opposed Booker T. Washington's moderate, accommodationist program of African American advancement.

While in Savannah Work joined DuBois' anti-Washington Niagara Movement and founded the Savannah Men's Sunday Club, an African American organization dedicated to protest and to the improvement of living conditions among poor African Americans. Following an unsuccessful, disillusioning campaign to prevent passage of Savannah's first segregation law in 1906, Work accepted a job at Booker T. Washington's Tuskegee Normal and Industrial Institute in Alabama in 1908. He thus became the only person closely affiliated with both of the main rivals for African American leadership in that period.

Overcoming numerous obstacles, Work founded and developed the Department of Records and Research at Tuskegee, where he compiled and catalogued a wide assortment of materials on the African American experience. In 1912 these data provided the basis for the first edition of the *Negro Year Book,* an annual and then periodic publication that was a permanent record of current events, an encyclopedia of historical and sociological facts, a directory of persons and organizations, and a bibliographic guide to the subjects discussed. Published by the respected Tuskegee Institute, the book became an accepted source of facts for newspapers, schools, and other organizations in both the North and South—as did Work's biannual lynching reports, established that same year.

In 1928 Work fulfilled another long-term dream with the publication of *A Bibliography of the Negro in Africa and America.* Containing 17,000 references in 74 classified chapters, the book was the first comprehensive bibliography of its kind and has been widely used by scholars and laymen.

Although the bulk of his efforts provided factual tools for others in the battle against discrimination, Work also became actively involved in interracial organizations and the movements to prevent lynching and to improve African American health. When he died on May 2, 1945, he was survived by his wife, Florence Hendrickson Work, and had published his bibliography, 66 lynching reports, nine editions of the *Negro Year Book,* and more than 70 articles. Leading an undramatic, scholarly life, Work was a quiet crusader who helped lay the foundation for the later civil rights movement.

Further Reading

Although Work is included in many biographical directories and is the subject of two journal articles, the only biography is Linda O. McMurry's *Recorder of the Black Experience, A Biography of Monroe Nathan Work* (1985).

Additional Sources

McMurry, Linda O., *Recorder of the Black experience: a biography of Monroe Nathan Work,* Baton Rouge: Louisiana State University Press, 1985. □

Manfred Wörner

Manfred Wörner (1934-1994), the former West German minister of defense, was appointed secretary-general of NATO and chairman of the North Atlantic Council in July 1988. He had to steer the Atlantic Alliance through times of formidable changes in East-West relations after the fall of the Berlin Wall in November 1989.

Manfred Wörner was born in Stuttgart, (West) Germany, on September 24, 1934. In 1953 he finished high school and went on to study law at the Universities of Heidelberg, Paris, and Munich. In 1957 he passed his first final examination in law in Munich, and in 1961 his second final examination in Stuttgart. The same year he received a Ph.D. in international law from the University of Munich. His dissertation was entitled "The Stationing of Foreign Forces in Friendly Countries."

In 1956 Wörner joined the Christian Democratic Union (CDU), a right-of-center German political party, after having been a member of the Junge Union, a youth organization linked to the CDU, since 1953. His official public career began in 1961 when he became executive councillor for the Department of the Interior of the state of Baden-Württemberg. From 1962 to 1964 he was a CDU state parliamentary adviser in Baden-Württemberg. He moved into national politics with his election to the West German Bundestag in 1965, where he remained until July 1988. His special interests as an elected representative were parliamentary reform and security policy.

Wörner led an extremely active political career, as can be inferred from his many positions within the Bundestag and the Christian Democratic Union/Christian School Union (CDU/CSU) party apparatus. His political career also benefited from the support of Chancellor Helmut Kohl, member of the same political party. Wörner was deputy chairman of the CDU parliamentary group between 1969 and 1971 and chairman of the Baden-Württemberg Bundestag deputies of the CDU from 1970 to 1982. He combined the latter position with that of chairman of the Defense Working Group of the CDU/CSU Bundestag parliamentary party (1972-1976) and with his membership on the Federal CDU Executive Committee from 1973 to 1988. He was chosen as chairman of the Bundestag Defense Committee (1976-1980) and elected deputy chairman of the CDU/CSU parliamentary group (1980-1982), with special responsibility for foreign policy, defense policy, development policy, and internal German relations.

From October 1982 until May 1988 Wörner was West Germany's federal minister of defense. One of the difficult issues with which he had to deal during his term as defense minister was the reduction of intermediate-range nuclear weapons in Europe, eventually consecrated in a treaty. West German public opinion was extremely reluctant at first to host the majority of these weapons on its soil. The North Atlantic Treaty Organization (NATO) two-track approach, whereby the missiles were deployed while negotiations to eliminate them were still ongoing, proved successful at last, but not without serious objections against the missiles' deployment in Germany, Italy, Belgium, and The Netherlands.

Wörner was appointed secretary-general of NATO and chairman of the North Atlantic Council on July 1, 1988, and became the first German to serve in those positions. His term had no official expiration date, although there was a general understanding that he would keep this position until 1992 or 1993. He succeeded Lord Carrington, the former British foreign secretary, who had served since 1984. The secretary-general of NATO is the chief executive of the 16-member alliance, whose headquarters is in Brussels, but important decisions are made by consensus of the leaders of the member countries. The secretary-general of NATO chairs all meetings of the North Atlantic Council, the highest authority in NATO, except at the opening and closing of ministerial sessions when he gives way to the council president, held on a rotational basis by the member countries' foreign ministers.

Soon after his election as secretary-general of NATO, Wörner was confronted with a series of disarmament initiatives pushed forward by the Soviet leader, Mikhail Gorbachev, culminating in the reunification of the two Germanies. The inclusion of the former state of East Germany in NATO and the perception of a fading role for a Western military alliance due to a reduced Soviet threat, compounded by the disintegration of the Warsaw Pact, challenged the traditional role and cohesion of the NATO alliance. However, Wörner was a strong advocate of maintaining U.S. troops in Europe and believed that NATO should not de-nuclearize Europe or Germany. Still, long delayed negotiations on the reduction of conventional forces in Europe (CFE) received a sudden impetus. Wörner was a firm believer in the necessity of a CFE treaty as he hoped that it would create a set of binding obligations for the Soviets, opening the way for a new European military and political order. Given the new emerging world order, Wörner believed NATO and the Soviet Union should look toward each other as "partners in security" rather than as antagonists.

It was the task of NATO's secretary-general in the 1990s to help redefine a comprehensive role for NATO and to find new missions which might reinforce NATO solidarity in the future. Wörner was firmly convinced that NATO could become more of a political alliance rather than purely military, confronting also matters such as economic rivalry among member states. During trips on behalf of NATO, Wörner used his extensive diplomatic skills to extend a hand of cooperation and to establish new partnerships for upholding security in Europe. When he visited Albania in 1993, Wörner addressed the Parliament, the first ever by a NATO Secretary General, saying that the purpose of his visit was "to discuss what we can do together to deepen our cooperation and make it as relevant as possible to your concerns." In August 1994 Wörner was succeeded by Willy Claes of Belgian, as Secretary General. Colonel Anatoly Andrievsky of Ukraine was the first recipient of the Manfred Wörner memorial scholarship in 1995.

Wörner had many outside interests. Beginning in 1970 he held the position of deputy chairman of the Konard Adenauer Foundation. On June 8, 1985, he received an honorary Doctor in Law degree from Troy State University, Alabama. Manfred Wörner was an enthusiastic aviator and a lieutenant colonel of the Air Reserve, having flown over 1,200 hours. He enjoyed soccer and hiking and was a medieval history enthusiast. He was married to Elfriedo Reinsch; he had a son by a previous marriage.

Further Reading

Manfred Wörner wrote several articles in English. Two of these are "Managing European Security," in *Survival* (1989), and "Current Prospects for European Security," in *The Atlantic Quarterly* (1983). He was co-author of "Germany: Keystone to European Security," in *American Enterprise Institute: Foreign Policy and Defense Review* (1983). On NATO's organization and role see "NATO Handbook," available free from the NATO Information Service, Brussels (1989; periodically updated), and "NATO Facts and Figures" (1989). □

Wovoka

In response to a vision, Wovoka (1856-1932) founded the Ghost Dance religion. A complex figure, he was revered by Indians while being denounced as an impostor and a lunatic by the local settlers throughout his entire life.

Based on a personal vision, Wovoka created the Ghost Dance religion of the late 1880's. A distorted interpretation of his beliefs and teachings was a contributing factor in the events leading to the Wounded Knee Massacre in late December of 1890. Wovoka's impact on the local Paiute people, and Native Americans throughout the West, continued beyond his death in 1932.

Until 1990 the documentation about Wovoka's life was scattered, and he was the subject of both speculation and misrepresentation. He was considered to have little importance after 1890. The only general account of his life was Paul Bailey's 1957 biography, which leaves the reader with the impression that Wovoka was a benign huckster. However, the meaning and effects of his life are much more complex. Key primary sources and a biographical summary are provided in *Wovoka and the Ghost Dance* by Michael Hittman, a Long Island University anthropologist. Hittman began studying the Yerington Paiute Tribe of Nevada in 1965, and the source book, completed twenty-five years later, is an extraordinary compilation (over 300 pages) of commentary and sources, including original manuscripts by personal acquaintances of Wovoka, photographs, newspaper accounts, government letters and reports, ghost dance songs, the views of other anthropologists, comments of surviving tribal members, and an extensive bibliography. Any serious study of the life of this famous prophet should start with this publication. According to Hittman, Wovoka was "a great man and a fake."

Wovoka was born about 1856 in Smith Valley or Mason Valley, Nevada, as one of four sons of Tavid, also known as Numo-tibo's, a well-known medicine man. (A link of Wovoka's father to an earlier Ghost Dance of 1870 in the region is unclear.) Both of Wovoka's parents survived into the twentieth Century. At about the age of fourteen Wovoka was sent to live with and work for the Scotch-English family of David Wilson. During this period he acquired the names Jack Wilson and Wovoka, meaning "Wood Cutter."

The religious influences upon Wovoka were diverse. Wovoka was clearly affected by the religious values of the pious United Presbyterian family; Mr. Wilson read the Bible each day before work. He lived in a region where traveling preachers were common and Mormonism prevalent. There is a possibility that Wovoka traveled to California and the Pacific Northwest, where he may have had contact with reservation prophets Smohalla and John Slocum.

At about the age of twenty he married Tumm, also known as Mary Wilson. They raised three daughters. At least two other children died.

The Ghost Dance Religion

Wovoka had promoted the Round Dance of the Numu people and was recognized as having some of his father's qualities as a mystic. A long-time acquaintance described the young Wovoka as "a tall, well proportioned man with piercing eyes, regular features, a deep voice and a calm and dignified mien.'' A local census agent referred to him as ''intelligent,'' and a county newspaper added that he resembled ''the late Henry Ward Beecher.'' Wovoka was known to be a temperate man during his entire life.

The turning point in Wovoka's life came in the late 1880's. In December of 1888 Wovoka may have been suffering from scarlet fever. He went into a coma for a period of two days. Observer Ed Dyer said, ''His body was as stiff as a board.'' Because Wovoka's recovery had corresponded with the total eclipse of the sun on January 1, 1889, he was credited by the Numus for bringing back the sun, and thereby saving the universe.

After this apparent near death experience, Wovoka proclaimed that he had a spiritual vision with personal contact with God who gave him specific instructions to those still on earth. According to Wovoka, God told him of a transformation by the spring of 1891 when the deceased would again be alive, the game would again flourish, and the whites would vanish from the earth. He had also been instructed to share power with the President of the East, Benjamin Harrison. Until the time of the apocalypse, Wovoka counselled the living to work for the dominant population and attempt to live a morally pure life. The plan for the future could only be assured if believers followed the special patterns and messages of the Ghost Dance, which Wovoka taught his followers.

Local believers had already adopted a dependence on him to bring much needed rain. The national setting for Native Americans was such that the message of Wovoka would soon spread throughout the western territory of North America. Scott Peterson, author of Native American Prophesies, explains, ''Wovoka's message of hope spread like wildfire among the demoralized tribes.'' Before long, representatives of over thirty tribes made a pilgrimage to visit Wovoka and learn the secrets of the Ghost Dance.

A Pyramid Lake agent dismissed Wovoka in November of 1890 as ''a peaceable, industrious, but lunatic Pah-Ute,'' who ''proclaimed himself an aboriginal Jesus who was to redeem the Red Man.'' Two weeks later, a writer for the Walker Lake Bulletin expressed concern about the 800 ''sulky and impudent'' male Indians who were participating in a dance at the Walker Lake Reservation. A day later the first known formal interview with Wovoka was conducted by United States Army Indian Scout Arthur I. Chapman. He had been sent to find the ''Indian who impersonated Christ!'' Chapman was not disturbed by what he found.

The most dynamic evidence of Wovoka's impact took place near the Badlands of South Dakota. Regional Sioux delegates, including Short Bull and Kicking Bear, returned with the message that wearing a Ghost Dance shirt would make warriors invulnerable to injury. Among those who accepted the assurance was the famous chief, Sitting Bull. The conditions were ideal for a message of deliverance in the Badlands: the buffalo were vanishing; the native residents were being pushed onto diminishing reservation lands as the designated area was opened to white settlement in 1989. The atmosphere is skillfully presented in a 1992 novel about the Lakota people, Song of Wovoka, which describes,

''The end of their [Lakota] way of life seemed trivial compared to the very real possibility of extermination.'' The Lakota misinterpreted the teachings of Wovoka, namely of passivity and patience to wait for divine intervention, as a call to proactively rid the land of white settlers.

There emerged fear among white settlers and the military in the region. The uncertain future of the newly established states of North and South Dakota was being threatened by ''the Ghost Dance craze.'' Memories of both the 1862 uprising in Minnesota and the debacle at Little Big Horn were still strong. Unable to enforce the ban of the Ghost Dance among the Lakota, Agent James McLaughlin of the Standing Rock Reservation in North Dakota ordered the arrest of Sitting Bull, a respected Lakota leader, intentionally disrupting a plan for Sitting Bull's arrest by old colleague Buffalo Bill Cody, who would have secured the arrest without harming Sitting Bull. As reported by Indian scout Charles A. Eastman, on December 15, 1890, a protest broke out as soldiers seized Sitting Bull, which resulted in gunfire killing Sitting Bull, six Indian defenders, and six Indian police.

A few days later a seriously ill Big Foot and his band were marching to a place of surrender on the Pine Ridge Reservation in South Dakota. An overwhelming force of 470 soldiers confronted them at Wounded Knee. In the process of a final disarmament, gunfire broke out. Over 200 Native Americans, many of them women and children, were killed. The next day, without ceremony, frozen bodies stripped of their Ghost Dance garments were tossed into a mass grave. For many this symbolized the end of resistance.

There is certainly no evidence that Wovoka intentionally promoted the type of confrontation that occurred at Wounded Knee. He later referred to his idea of an impenetrable shirt as a ''joke.'' His associate Ed Dyer evaluated the situation: ''I was thoroughly convinced that Jack Wilson had at no time attempted deliberately to stir up trouble. He never advocated violence. Violence was contrary to his very nature. Others seized upon his prophecies and stunts, and made more of them than he intended . . . in a way, once started, he was riding a tiger. It was difficult to dismount.''

Within a few days of the atrocities at Wounded Knee, the local newspapers in Wovoka's region expressed concern about the fact that there were ''within the radius of 40 miles . . . 1,000 able-bodied bucks, well armed.'' The Paiutes were getting ''very saucy,'' claiming that ''pretty soon they will own stores and ranches and houses . . . that county all belonged to them once, and that pretty soon they will take the farms and horses away from the white man.'' Government sources also expressed concern. Acknowledging that ''the Messiah Craze'' was ''headquartered'' in Nevada, Frank Campbell wrote to the Commissioner of Indian Affairs on September 5, 1891: ''The cause of its spreading so generally among Indians is the hope that these people have that some power greater than themselves may arrest and crush the oncoming flood of civilization that is destined soon to overwhelm them.''

A month later, C. C. Warner, the openly antagonistic United States Indian Agent at Pyramid Lake, said he would not give Wovoka added ''notoriety'' by having him arrested.

''I am pursuing the course with him of nonattention or silent ignoring.'' In December of 1892 he reported that although he found no local agitation, he ''became suspicious that the 'Messiah' Jack Wilson was using an evil influence among foreign Indians which might result in a spring uprising among the Indians.'' His Farmer-In-Charge of the Walker River Reservation did a personal investigation. The following August, Warner announced that the Ghost Dance ''fanaticism'' was ''a thing of the past'' and that ''the strongest weapon to be used against the movement is ridicule.''

The Middle Years, 1890-1920

The role of Wovoka in the years after Wounded Knee has been generally overlooked. But it is clear that he did not fade into oblivion or hesitate to use his unusual fame and powers. An Indian Agent reported in June 1912 ''that Jack Wilson is still held in reverence by Indians in various parts of the country, and he is still regarded by them as a great medicine man.'' Two years later he reinforced that statement, adding, ''the influence of Jack Wilson the 'Messiah' of twenty five years ago is not dead.'' Indian Agent S. W. Pugh took a position quite different than that of C. C. Warner. When Jack Wilson sought an allotment on the reservation, he encouraged the Commissioner of Indian Affairs to help make it possible. ''I would like to have him as he is still a power among his people and could be used to excellent advantage if here. He is a very intelligent Indian, and peaceably inclined apparently. . . . These people will follow him anywhere, and he has advanced ideas.

Although Wovoka had established a reputation as a strong, reliable worker as a young man, the reknown of the Ghost Dance phenomenon resulted in other uses of his time during the balance of his life. Attempts to bring him to both the World's Columbian Exposition in Chicago in 1893 and the Midwinter Fair in San Francisco in 1904 apparently failed, but he made trips to reservations in Wyoming, Montana, and Kansas, as well as the former Indian territory of Oklahoma. Some trips lasted as long as six months. He was showered with gifts and as much as $1,200 in cash on a single trip. In 1924, historian-actor Tim McCoy delivered Wovoka by limousine to the set of a movie he was making in northern California. There he was treated with absolute reverence by Arapahos who had been hired for the film.

While at home Wovoka practiced another brisk form of enterprise. With the aid of his friend Ed Dyer and others he replied to numerous letters and requests for particular items, including thaumaturges and articles of clothing that he had worn. He had a fee for red paint, magpie feathers, etc. Conveniently, Dyer, his frequent secretary, was also a supplier. One of the most popular items was a hat that had been worn by ''the Prophet.'' The usual price to a correspondent was $20. Dyer noted, ''Naturally he was under the necessity of purchasing another from me at a considerable reduced figure. Although I did a steady and somewhat profitable business on hats, I envied him his mark-up which exceeded mine to a larcenous degree.'' Surprisingly, none of the response letters that Wovoka dictated have been found.

Despite his relative notoriety and financial security, Wovoka continued to live a simple life. As late as 1917, he was living in a two-room house built of rough boards. A visitor reported, ''He lives purely Indian customs with very little household effects. They sleep on the floor and from all appearances also use the floor as their table for eating.'''

Wovoka also had an interesting peripheral role in the ''political'' world. As early as November 1890 an ex-Bureau of Indian Affairs employee suggested that an official invitation to Washington, D.C., for Wovoka and some of his followers ''might have a tendency to quiet this craze.'' His early vision of course included the view that he would share national leadership with then President Benjamin Harrison. In 1916, the *Mason Valley News* reported that Wovoka was considering a visit to President Woodrow Wilson to help ''terminate the murderous war in Europe'' (Wovoka's grandson, following the prediction of his grandfather, became a pilot and died a hero in World War II.) In the 1920s, Wovoka was photographed at a Warren G. Harding rally. Perhaps the selection of Charles Curtis, a Sac-Fox from Kansas, as Vice President of the United States was a sign of the predicted millennium. Wovoka sent him a radiogram on March 3, 1929 stating, ''We are glad that you are Vice President and we hope some day you will be President.''

It is not possible to make an absolute judgement about the real talents of this Nevada mystic to determine which of his activities were the product of true inspiration and which merely legerdemain. There are many accounts of his accomplishments varying from making prophesies that came true and returning people from the dead to predicting weather, making rain, surviving shots from guns, and producing ice in the middle of summer. His associate Ed Dyer reflected, it is ''very human to believe what we want to believe.''

Final Years

Anthropologist Michael Hittman explains most of Wovoka's shamatic practice and beliefs in the context of his native culture and concludes, ''Wovoka appears to have maintained faith in his original revelation and supernatural powers to the very end.'' Ed Dyer commented later, ''His prestige lasted to the end.'' His services as a medicine man were in demand until shortly before his own death on September 29, 1932, from enlarged prostate cystitis. His wife of over fifty years had died just one month before. Yerington Paiute tribal member Irene Thompson expressed a local Numu reaction, ''When he died, many people thought Wovoka will come back again.''

A Reno newspaper, although giving a lengthy account of his life, basically dismissed him as a fraud: '''Magic' worked with the aid of a bullet-proof vest; white men's pills and some good 'breaks' in the weather made him the most influential figure of his time among the Indians.'' Scott Peterson, in his 1990 study of Native American prophets, argues that if Wovoka had not ''set a date for the apocalypse . . . the Ghost Dance, with its vision of a brighter tomorrow, might still very well be a vital force in the world today.''

In fact, elements of the Ghost Dance religion pervaded the practices of many tribes even after the tragedy of Wounded Knee. A form of the original dance is still performed by some Lakota today. Historian L. G. Moses describes Wovoka as "one of the most significant holy men ever to emerge among the Indians of North America." John Grim, in *The Encyclopedia of Religion,* gives the mystic credit for promoting "a pan-Indian identity." Hittman asserts that the key elements of "the Great Revelation" remain "honesty, the importance of hard work, the necessity of nonviolence, and the imperative of inter-racial harmony."

Wovoka's role as an "agitator" also remains significantly symbolic. In 1968, a former publisher of the *Mason Valley News* (which ignored the death of the famous resident in 1932) recalled Wovoka's stoical appearance in his elegant apparel on the streets of the small town: "Best human impression of a wooden Indian I ever seen. Oh, he was the only kind of individual that shook up the Army and Washington, D.C. Somebody today should." Five years later, after Dee Brown reminded Americans of the forgotten atrocity of American frontier history, members of the American Indian Movement (AIM) occupied the original site of Wounded Knee and engaged U.S. forces in battle. ☐

Sir Christopher Wren

The English architect Sir Christopher Wren (1632-1723) interpreted the baroque style in England and dominated English architecture for 50 years. His most important work is St. Paul's Cathedral, London.

Christopher Wren was born in East Knoyle, Wiltshire, on Oct. 20, 1632, and educated at Oxford. Apparently destined for a career as a scientific scholar, he became professor of astronomy at Gresham College in London when he was 24. In 1661 he was appointed Savilian professor of astronomy at Oxford.

Wren did not give his attention to architecture until he was 30. No information is available to explain the development of his interest in architecture, but his training in science and mathematics and his ability in solving practical scientific problems provided him with the technical training necessary for a man who was to undertake complex architectural projects. His temperament and education, and the society in which he moved, would naturally have inclined him to wide interests.

Early Career

Wren's first venture into architecture came in 1662, when he designed the Sheldonian Theatre at Oxford, a building intended for university ceremonies. Based upon the concept of a Roman theater, his ingenious interior design left the space free of supports or columns, but for the exterior he had recourse to unimaginative copying from old architectural pattern books.

Wren made only one journey out of England, a visit of several months to France in 1665 to study French Renaissance and baroque architecture. The French journey had significant influence on his work and provided him with a rich source of inspiration.

After the Great Fire of 1666, which destroyed much of London, King Charles appointed Wren a member of the commission created to supervise the reconstruction of the city. He had already drawn up a visionary plan for a new London. His design was typical of 17th-century city planning and called for a combination of radiating and grid-plan streets accented by squares and vistas, but his plan was not accepted.

Wren was given the responsibility for replacing the 87 parish churches demolished by the Great Fire. Between 1670 and 1686 he designed 51 new churches; they constitute a major part of the vast amount of work done by him and are known as the City Churches. They are uneven in quality both in design and execution, and their varied plans and famous steeples reveal Wren's empirical eclecticism and his ingenuity. The churches are essentially classical in design or baroque variations on classical themes as adapted to English taste and the requirements of Anglican worship. His work on the City Churches firmly established his position as England's leading architect; he was appointed surveyor general in 1669, a post which he held until 1718, and was knighted in 1673.

While Wren was working on the City Churches, he undertook many other projects. One of the most important was Trinity College Library at Cambridge (1676-1684), an elegantly severe building derived from the late Italian Renaissance classicism of Andrea Palladio as transmitted to England by Inigo Jones in the early 17th century. By 1670 Wren was also at work on designs for a new St. Paul's Cathedral.

St. Paul's Cathedral

St. Paul's, which took nearly 35 years to build, is Wren's masterpiece. The Great Fire had so damaged the old St. Paul's as to render it dangerous, and the authorities decided that a new cathedral was needed. In 1673 Wren presented an impressive design in the form of a large wooden model known as the Great Model. The Great Model, which still exists, shows a cathedral based on a Greek-cross plan and dominated by a massive central dome. The exterior of the building was to have curved walls and an entrance block faced with a portico of giant Corinthian columns. The design of the Great Model is Wren's expression of baroque vitality tempered by classicism and reveals the influence of French and Italian architecture as well as that of Inigo Jones.

The English were accustomed to cathedrals built on the medieval Latin-cross plan with a long nave; the Great Model design, which was much criticized, departed from this tradition and seemed to the Protestant English to be too Continental and too Catholic. In the face of such opposition, Wren prepared a new design based on the Latin cross with a dome over the crossing and a classical portico entrance. This compromise, known as the Warrant Design, was accepted in 1675, but as the building progressed Wren made many changes which reflected his increasing knowledge of French and Italian baroque architecture gained from books and engravings. The Cathedral as finished in the early 18th century is very different from the Warrant Design; the building, a synthesis of many stylistic influences, is also Wren's uniquely organic creation. With its splendid dome, impressive scale, and dramatic grandeur, St. Paul's is fundamentally a baroque building, but it is English Protestant baroque in its restraint and disciplined gravity.

Later Work

After 1675 English architecture began to turn away from the sober Palladianism of Wren's Trinity College Library and to manifest influences from Continental baroque architecture. These trends are evident in St. Paul's and in his later works. English taste rejected the emotional drama and fluid design of Italian and German baroque and was closer to the classical baroque of France. Nevertheless, during the last quarter of the century English architects began to conceive of buildings in baroque terms, that is, as sculptural masses on a large scale, and to introduce elements of richness, grandeur, and royal splendor which reflected the temper of the age. Important example of Wren's design in the idiom of the English baroque are the Royal Hospital at Chelsea (1682-1689), the work done at Hampton Court Palace (1689-1696) for King William III and Queen Mary, and the Royal Naval Hospital at Greenwich (1696-1705).

Wren died in London on Feb. 25, 1723, and was buried in St. Paul's. His tomb bears a simple inscription: "Reader, if you seek his monument, look about you."

Further Reading

A comprehensive modern biography of Wren is Sir John Summerson, *Sir Christopher Wren* (1953). Older but also excellent is Geoffrey Webb, *Wren* (1937). Margaret Whinney and

Oliver Millar, *English Art, 1625-1714* (1957), is valuable for placing Wren within the context of 17th-century English art. For a brilliant analysis of Wren's place in the history of English architecture see Sir John Summerson, *Architecture in Britain, 1530-1830* (1954; 5th ed. 1969). Edward F. Sekler, *Wren and His Place in European Architecture* (1956), relates Wren's work to that of his contemporaries on the Continent. Ralph Dutton, *The Age of Wren* (1951), places the architect within the framework of his period. □

Wright brothers

The American aviation pioneers Wilbur (1867-1912) and Orville (1871-1948) Wright were the first to accomplish manned, powered flight in a heavier-than-air machine.

Wilbur and Orville Wright were the sons of Milton Wright, a bishop of the United Brethren in Christ. Wilbur was born on April 16, 1867, in Millville, Ind.; Orville was born on Aug. 19, 1871, at Dayton, Ohio. Until the death of Wilbur in 1912, the two were inseparable. Their personalities were perfectly complementary: Orville was full of ideas and enthusiasms, an impetuous dreamer, while Wilbur was more steady in his habits, more mature in his judgments, and more likely to see a project through.

In their early years the two boys helped their father, who edited an evangelical journal called the *Religious Telescope*. Later, they began a paper of their own, *West Side News*. In 1892 they opened the Wright Cycle Shop in Dayton, which was the perfect occupation for the Wright brothers, involving one of the exciting mechanical devices of the time: the bicycle. When the brothers took up the problems of flight, they had a solid grounding in practical mechanics.

The exploits of one of the great glider pilots of the late 19th century, Otto Lilienthal, had attracted the attention of the Wright brothers as early as 1891, but it was not until the death of this famous aeronautical engineer in 1896 that the two became interested in gliding experiments. They then resolved to educate themselves systematically in the theory and state of the art of flying.

The Wrights took up the problem of flight at an auspicious time, for some of the fundamental theories of aerodynamics were already known; a body of experimental data existed; and most importantly, the recent development of the internal combustion engine made available a sufficient source of power for manned flight. Although they sometimes acted as scientists, the basic approach of the Wrights was that of the engineer. They had no formal training as either scientist or engineer, but they combined the instincts of both. They began by accumulating and mastering all the pertinent information on the subject, designed and tested their own models and gliders, built their own engine, and, when the experimental data they had inherited appeared to be inadequate or erroneous, they conducted new and more thorough experiments.

Orville (left) and Wilbur Wright

Armed with this information, the Wright brothers proceeded to fly double-winged kites and gliders in order to gain experience and to test data. After consulting the U.S. Weather Bureau, they chose an area of sand dunes near the small town of Kitty Hawk, N.C., as the site of their experiments. In September 1900 they set up camp there and began the work that culminated three years later in success.

Their first device failed to fly as a kite because it was unable to develop sufficient lift. Instead, they flew it as a free glider and learned a great deal from their experience, partly because of the careful records they kept of their failures as well as of their successes. Their own data showed conclusively that previous tables of information were greatly inaccurate.

Returning to Dayton in 1901, the Wright brothers built a wind tunnel, the first in the United States, and here they tested over 200 models of wing surfaces in order to measure lift and drag factors and to discover the most suitable design. They also discovered that although screw propellers had been used on ships for more than half a century, there was no reliable body of data on the subject and no theory that would allow them to design the proper propellers for their airship. They had to work the problem out for themselves, mathematically.

The Wrights, by this time, not only had mastered the existing body of aeronautical science but also had added to it. They now built their third glider, incorporating their

findings, and in the fall of 1902 they returned to Kitty Hawk. They made over 1,000 gliding flights and were able to confirm their previous data and to demonstrate their ability to control the three axes of motion of the glider. Having learned to build and to control an adequate air frame, they now determined to apply power to their machine.

The Wright brothers soon discovered, however, that no manufacturer would undertake to build an engine that would meet their specifications, so they had to build their own. They produced one that had four cylinders and developed 12 horsepower. When it was installed in the air frame, the entire machine weighed just 750 pounds and proved to be capable of traveling 31 miles per hour. They took this new airplane to Kitty Hawk in the fall of 1903 and on December 17 made the world's first manned, powered flight in a heavier-than-air craft.

The first flight was made by Orville and lasted only 12 seconds, during which the airplane flew 120 feet. That same day, however, on its fourth flight, with Wilbur at the controls, the plane stayed in the air for 59 seconds and traveled 852 feet. Then a gust of wind severely damaged the craft, and the brothers returned to Dayton convinced of their success and determined to build another machine. In 1905 they abandoned their other activities and concentrated on the development of aviation. On May 22, 1906, they received a patent for their flying machine.

The brothers looked to the Federal government for encouragement in their venture, and gradually interest was aroused in Washington. In 1907 bids were asked for an airplane that would meet government requirements—22 bids were received, three were accepted, but only the Wright brothers finished their contract. They continued their experiments at Kitty Hawk, and in September 1908, while Wilbur was in France attempting to interest foreign backers in their machine, Orville successfully demonstrated their contract airplane. It was accepted by the government, although the event was marred by a crash a week later in which Orville was injured and a passenger was killed.

Wilbur's trip to France proved to be a success also, and in 1909 the Wright brothers formed the American Wright Company, with Wilbur taking the lead in setting up and directing the business. His death in Dayton on May 30, 1912, left Orville in a state of desolate isolation. In 1915 he sold his rights to the firm and gave up his interest in manufacturing in order to turn to experimental work. He had little taste for the bustle of commercial life.

After his retirement, Orville lived quietly in Dayton, conducting experiments on mechanical problems of interest to him, none of which proved to be of major importance. His chief public activity was service on the National Advisory Committee for Aeronautics (the predecessor agency of NASA), of which he was a member from its organization by President Woodrow Wilson in 1915 until his death in Dayton on Jan. 30, 1948.

Further Reading

The letters and papers of the Wright brothers are available in Fred C. Kelly, ed., *Miracle at Kitty Hawk: The Letters of Wilbur and Orville Wright* (1951), and Marvin W. McFarland, ed., *The*

Papers of Wilbur and Orville Wright (2 vols., 1953). Fred C. Kelly, *The Wright Brothers* (1943), is a biography authorized by Orville Wright. Other recommended studies are Elsbeth E. Freudenthal, *Flight into History: The Wright Brothers and the Air Age* (1949), and, for young people, Quentin J. Reynolds, *The Wright Brothers: Pioneers of American Aviation* (1950). □

Carroll Davidson Wright

The American statistician and social economist Carroll Davidson Wright (1840-1909) organized the Bureau of Labor Statistics and did much to inspire and produce objective research on labor problems.

Carroll Wright was born on July 25, 1840, in Dunbarton, N. H. His father was a Universalist minister, and the family frequently moved from one town to another. Carroll studied at various academies in New England.

In those days there were no formal law programs in universities, and the path to a law degree was to study and work under a seasoned, respected lawyer and then present oneself under that lawyer's sponsorship for examination. Wright began reading law in Keene, N. H., at the same time teaching in the country schools of that district. He continued his study of law in Dedham and Boston until 1862 and then served in the army during the Civil War.

Wright was admitted to the New Hampshire bar in 1865 and to the Massachusetts bar two years later. He developed a rewarding practice in Boston, dealing mainly in patent law. He was elected to the Massachusetts Senate in 1871 and 1872. His major contribution as a state senator was to sponsor legislation which improved to a great extent the militia system of the state.

In 1873 Wright was appointed chief of the Massachusetts Bureau of Labor Statistics, which had been established four years earlier and was the first in the United States. As its head for 15 years during a period of radical economic change in Massachusetts and the United States itself, Wright attempted to objectively amass statistics in this area, which resulted in criticism from both employers and labor. As a result of these early experiences with partisan factions, he was determined that statistics should be gathered with as much objectivity as possible and that they should be published without regard to whether they were in the interest of one group or another. Wright tried to follow this principle throughout his subsequent life, especially through the National Convention of Chiefs and Commissioners of Bureaus of Statistics of Labor, which he organized in 1883 and served as president for almost 20 years.

Wright's own investigations and collections of data encompassed a very broad scope, dealing with wage rates, cost of living, strikes, lockouts, poverty, crime, divorce, illiteracy, housing, and labor legislation. In many of these areas his work was a pioneering effort. He was a moving force behind the establishment of the U.S. Bureau of Labor

in the Interior Department. President Chester Alan Arthur appointed him the first commissioner of the new bureau, and he held the post for 20 years.

Wright was professor of statistics and social economics at Columbian University (George Washington University after 1900) and supervised the first volumes of the studies on the economic history of the United States. He was president of the American Statistical Association from 1897 to his death; and he received a number of awards from foreign governments. He became the first president of Clark College in Worcester, Mass., in 1902, although he retained his post with the Bureau of Labor until 1905. He died in Worcester on Feb. 20, 1909.

In his own social philosophy, evident in his many works, Wright specifically denied and abhorred the view that there was an inevitable class conflict between capital and labor. Instead, he urged voluntary cooperation, tolerance, and social responsibility for employers.

Further Reading

For information on Wright see James Leiby, *Carroll Wright and Labor Reform: The Origin of Labor Statistics* (1960). □

Elizur Wright

Elizur Wright (1804-1885) was an American reformer whose interests ranged from abolition to

woman's suffrage and to conservation. He was also an intensely practical man as much at home in a government bureau as on the speaker's stump.

Elizur Wright, born in Connecticut on Feb. 12, 1804, was descended from moderately prosperous and typical New England Yankees. His parents moved to Talmadge, Ohio, when Elizur was six, clearing a farm from the forest and gradually prospering as farmers. After attending a local school, Wright entered Yale University. In 1829 he returned to Ohio to teach at Western Reserve College.

Under the influence of William Lloyd Garrison and Theodore Weld, Wright became a leading abolitionist at Western Reserve. With several others, he lost his job, for abolitionism was still regarded as a dangerous heterodoxy, even in the North.

Weld secured a position for Wright as secretary to the New York Antislavery Society. In 1833 Wright took the same position with the American Antislavery Society and, in 1835, became editor of the *Quarterly Antislavery Magazine.* For all his external placidity, Wright was a stormy, tenacious fighter. He split from his employers on the question of third-party action and lost his position.

Remarkably resourceful, Wright published and attempted to sell his own translation of the French writer La Fontaine. The venture was not very successful financially, but it brought Wright into contact with many of the celebrated literati of the day and took him to England in 1846. Back in the United States, he founded a successful antislavery, antitariff newspaper, the *Weekly Chronotype,* but his interests had changed significantly. He became interested in the reform of life insurance then beginning in England; meanwhile, old interests in mathematics and statistics drew him to what was to be his chief field of endeavor.

Though Wright never completely neglected his antislavery interests (acting as the defendant in an important fugitive slave case in 1852), he increasingly turned to life insurance. When he discovered and prepared to publish an exposé of the fraudulent practices of the then largely corrupt business, several companies attempted to buy him off, only to discover that he applied the same fervor and integrity to this project as he had to abolition. He prepared actuarial tables which became the basis for setting premiums and payments of even those companies that were initially hostile, and lobbied successfully for laws to regulate life insurance company policies. He became Massachusetts commissioner of insurance in 1858. In that position he designed other laws and policies governing the business, but in 1866 he lost his job. He continued to work in the business in a private consultation capacity until his death on Nov. 21, 1885. As one eulogist wrote, Wright's reforms "have formed a sort of constitution by which the policy of all life insurance companies is still guided." There is no doubt that his interest improved the ethics and the efficiency of the business.

Further Reading

A biography is Philip G. and Elizabeth Q. Wright, *Elizur Wright: The Father of Life Insurance* (1937). Frank Preston Stearns, *Cambridge Sketches* (1905), contains a convenient if dated and adulatory sketch of Wright.

Additional Sources

Goodheart, Lawrence B., *Abolitionist, actuary, atheist: Elizur Wright and the reform impulse,* Kent, Ohio: Kent State University Press, 1990. □

Frances Wright

Frances Wright (1795-1852), Scottish-American socialist, feminist, and reformer, was the first woman to speak publicly in America.

Frances Wright was born in Dundee, Scotland, on Sept. 6, 1795. Orphaned at the age of two, she inherited substantial means, which enabled her to escape from England and her strict relatives upon coming of age. She went to the United States in 1818, and her play about the struggle for republicanism in Switzerland was performed in 1819 in New York City.

Wright was distinguished for her personal courage, amounting at times to foolhardiness, and for the liberality of her views on public questions. She was especially influenced by the social reformer Robert Dale Owen, and in 1825 she visited New Harmony, Ind., an ambitious experiment in communitarian socialism that his father, Robert Owen, had just founded. There she absorbed the multitude of radical ideas on every conceivable question that flourished in the community. The following year she established her own community at Nashoba on the Tennessee frontier.

Unlike New Harmony, which was founded to demonstrate the superior merits of socialism, Nashoba was aimed directly at the problem of slavery. Wright believed that the most practical way to free the slaves was by establishing facilities where they could work off the costs of their emancipation while acquiring useful skills and the habits appropriate to free men. In some ways this was a farsighted plan. However, like most communal experiments, Nashoba was under financed and badly run. Wright further complicated the enterprise by working into it her own ideas on sex and religion. She came to believe that miscegenation was the ultimate solution of the racial question and that marriage was a limiting and discriminatory institution. Her advocacy of free love and her assistant's public admission that he was living with one of the slave women had a fatal effect on Nashoba's fortunes. In 1830 Wright and Robert Dale Owen arranged for her wards to be sent to the black republic of Haiti.

In 1828-1829 Wright lectured widely in the United States with sensational effect. She spoke on behalf of public education in general and women's education in particular, and she actively supported the Workingman's (Loco-Foco)

party of New York, earning the sobriquet of "the great she-Loco-Foco." She also wrote several books, none of which proved very durable. She returned to Europe in 1830, remaining there until 1835. In later years her lectures attracted little attention. She died on Dec. 13, 1852, in Cincinnati.

Further Reading

Biographies of Frances Wright are William R. Waterman, *Frances Wright* (1924), and A. J. G. Perkins and Theresa Wolfson, *Frances Wright, Free Enquirer* (1939). Among the many works touching on various phases of her career, Arthur E. Bestor, *Backwoods Utopias: The Sectarian and Owenite Phases of Communitarian Socialism in America, 1663-1829* (1950), is especially useful.

Additional Sources

Morris, Celia, *Fanny Wright: rebel in America,* Urbana: University of Illinois Press, 1992. □

Frank Lloyd Wright

The American architect Frank Lloyd Wright (1869-1959) designed dramatically innovative buildings during a career of almost 70 years. His work established the imagery for much of the contemporary architectural environment.

The most famous, although never the most popular or successful, among American architects, Frank Lloyd Wright set himself the task, as no previous architect had, of designing distinctive and varied architecture for the diverse terrains of a nation that stretched over the valleys, deserts, woods, and mountains, spanning an entire continent. Herald of thesis that architecture should express its time, its site, its builders, and its materials, Wright argued from that romantic, specifically Hegelian thesis that the United States, as a new nation with a new society on a new frontier with a new technology, should express those unique conditions and should build its special aspirations into buildings that would be distinctively and wholly its own—a new style that would speak of the American environment, "Usonian," he once called it, an architecture of democracy.

Wright's art was so original, his imagination was so endlessly fertile, and his sense of form was so appropriate to the site and so bold and uninhibited that even the most recent students, although they are more than a generation removed from Wright and nurtured in urban premises and technical resources alien to his, still see in his drawings and his buildings that virtuosity in planning, that command over form, that grace in shaping space which have been the talent of only a few, the greatest masters of architecture.

Wright was born on June 8, 1869, in Richland Center, Wis. When he was 12 years old his family settled in Madison, and Wright worked on his uncle's farm at Spring Green during the summers. He developed a passion for the land that never left him. He attended Madison High School and left in 1885, apparently without graduating. He went to

work as a draftsman and the following year, while still working, took a few courses in civil engineering at the University of Wisconsin.

In 1887 Wright went to Chicago, worked briefly for an architect, and then joined the firm of Dankmar Adler and Louis Sullivan. Wright was very much influenced by Sullivan, and, although their relationship ended in a rupture when Sullivan found out that Wright was designing houses on his own, he always acknowledged his indebtedness to Sullivan and referred to him as "lieber Meister." In 1893 Wright opened his own office.

Master of Domestic Architecture

The houses Wright built in Buffalo and in Chicago and its suburbs before World War I gained international fame wherever there were avant-garde movements in the arts, especially in those countries where industrialization had brought new institutional and urban problems and had developed clients or patrons with the courage to eschew traditional design and the means to essay modernism, as in Germany (the Wasmuth publications of Wright's work in 1910 and 1911), the Netherlands (H. T. Wijdeveld, ed., *The Life Work of the American Architect, Frank Lloyd Wright,* 1925), and, later, Japan, where Wright designed the Imperial Hotel, Tokyo (1916-1922). Similarly, in the United States, Wright's clients were exceptional individuals and small, adventurous institutions, not governments or national corporations. A small progressive private school (Hillside Home School, Spring Green, 1902) and an occasional private, commercial firm (Larkin Company in Buffalo) came to him, but, chiefly, his clients were midwestern businessmen, practical, unscholarly, independent, and moderately successful, such as the Chicago building contractor Frederick C. Robie, for whom Wright designed houses.

Commissions to design a bank, an office building, or a factory were rare; Wright never received any large corporate or governmental commission. These were awarded to the classicists and the Gothicists of the early 20th century; at midcentury, after the case for modernism was won, the corporate commissions continued to go to large, dependable firms who worked in a rectilinear, contemporary idiom. Wright was left for nearly 70 years to exercise his art, always brilliantly and often resentfully, chiefly in domestic architecture, where, indeed, Americans, unlike many other peoples, have long lavished enormous, probably inordinate attention, assigning to their spacious, freestanding, single-family dwellings the inventiveness that some other nations have reserved for public architecture.

Early, Wright insisted upon declaring the presence of pure cubic mass, the color and texture of raw stone and brick and copper, and the sharp-etched punctures made by unornamented windows and doors in sheer walls (Charnley House, Chicago, 1891). He made of the house a compact block, which might be enclosed handsomely by a hipped roof (Winslow House, River Forest, Ill., 1893). Soon, the restrained delight in the simplicity of a single mass gave way to his passion for passages of continuous, flowing spaces; he burst the enclosed, separated spaces of classical architecture, removed the containment, the sense of walls and ceil-

ings, and created single, continuously modified spaces, which he shaped by screens, piers, and intermittent planes and masses that were disposed in asymmetric compositions. By suggesting spaces, but not enclosing them, then by connecting them, Wright achieved extended, interweaving, horizontal compositions of space, and his roofs, windows, walls, and chimneys struck dynamic balances and rhythms. Vertical elements rise through horizontal planes (Husser House, Chicago, 1899); interior spaces flare from a central chimney mass (Willitts House, Highland Park, Ill., 1900-1902); low spaces rise into a high space that is carved into a second story (Roberts House, River Forest, 1908). Unexpectedly, light is captured from a clerestory or a room beyond, and a space flows in vistas seen beyond a structural pier, beneath low roofs and cantilevered eaves, over terraces and courts, and through trellises and foliage into gardens and landscape (Martin House, Buffalo, 1904). All his genius with weaving space, with creating a tension between compact alcove and generous vista, with variegated light, with occult balances of intermittent masses, with cantilevers that soared while piers and chimneys anchored, came to unrivaled harmony in the Robie House, Chicago (1909; now the Adlai Stevenson Institute, University of Chicago).

The Robie House has few antecedents. Perhaps its composition recalls the 19th-century rambling, picturesque houses of Bruce Price and Stanford White; its spaces owe something to Japanese architecture, and something is owed, too, to the master of dramatic balance of bold masses, Henry Hobson Richardson; but the Robie House is Wright's own, a uniquely personal organization of space. While wholly original, the Robie House stands within the principles of Chicago's special theory of architecture, as developed by Sullivan. That the Robie House also reflects an international movement, cubism, which had begun to fascinate pioneering artists in France, the Netherlands, and Germany, shows that Wright, while sensitive to his contemporaries' innovation, subsumed many traditions without any subservience.

Philosophy of Architecture

Wright's philosophy of architecture was compounded of several radical and traditional ideas. There was, first, the romantic idea of honest expression: that a building should be faithful in revealing its materials and structure, as Eugène Emmanuel Viollet-le-Duc had argued, without any classical ornament or counterfeit surface or structure, which John Ruskin abhorred. There was, second, the idea that a building's form should reflect its plan, its functional arrangement of interior spaces, as Henry Latrobe and Horatio Greenough had proposed. There was, third, the conviction that each building should express something new and distinctive in the times (G. W. F. Hegel, Gottfried Semper) and specifically the new technical resources, such as steel skeletons and electric light and elevators, which suggested skyscrapers and new forms of building (John Wellborn Root). There was, fourth, the ambition, even pride, to achieve an art appropriate to a new nation, an American art (Emerson, Hawthorne, Whitman), without Continental or English or colonial dependencies. Finally, there was the theory derived by Sullivan from Charles Darwin and Herbert Spencer that a building should be analogous to a biological organism, a unified work of art, rooted to its soil, organized to serve specified functions, and, as a form, evolved as an organism evolves, fitted to its landscape, adapted to its environment, expressive of its purpose.

Those diverse currents of thought were not readily united. The Unitarianism of Wright's family prepared him to design the humanist Unity Church in Oak Park, Ill. (1906), a cubistic, light-filled meetinghouse, constructed, quite extraordinarily, in concrete. His introduction in kindergarten to F. W. A. Froebel's system of education through construction with blocks prepared Wright to design the playhouse and school of the beautiful Avery Coonley House, Riverside, Ill. (1908); there, significantly, in the progressive architecture of a house and school, John Dewey and his students were educational advisers. Form breaking and function making, the ferment of ideas in late-19th-century Chicago encouraged new thinking about institutions for religion, education, and urban settlement; Wright led a revolt from precedent in form and a celebration of necessity in new functions. His essay "The Art and Craft of the Machine" announced his leadership at Hull House in 1901; and he continued to state his dissatisfaction with America's failure to build institutions and environment adequate to the social problems and opportunities. His theory of an "organic architecture: the architecture of democracy" was broadcast in his Princeton lectures of 1930 and London lectures of 1939, as well as in his *Autobiography* (1932), which also offers some insight into his life and his family, including the apprentices who lived with him and for whom he established the Taliesin Fellowship in 1932 at Taliesin East, the house Wright built over many years (beginning in 1938) at Spring Green.

His Idea and Imagery for Modern Design

If the handsome Taliesin East, whose roofs are rhythmical accents on the brow of a bluff overlooking the confluence of two valleys, were all that Wright left, he would be remembered as the finest architect who worked in the 19th-century tradition of romantic domestic design. But, early, he prepared an idea and an imagery for modern design. He achieved in the Larkin Building, Buffalo (1904; destroyed) an unprecedented integration of circulation, structure, ventilation, plumbing, furniture, office equipment, and lighting; that building, an early example of modern commercial architecture, was emulated by Peter Behrens and Walter Gropius in Germany and Hendrik Petrus Berlage in Holland. Wright's plans for Midway Gardens, Chicago (1914; demolished) and the Imperial Hotel, Tokyo (1916-1922), organized complex modern institutions into new architectural compositions, and they showed inventiveness in structural technique, such as the structure of the Imperial Hotel, which was intended to resist earthquakes, which it did, even though it could not resist the wrecker in 1967. Wright tended to enjoy and to glorify nature and the rural condition, but he attacked various urban problems. Beginning with inexpensive row apartments in 1895, he designed buildings for cities, culminating in his drawing for a high-rise tower whose floors were to be cantilevered from a central shaft, the St. Mark's Tower

project for New York City (1929); that project is reflected in the Price Tower at Bartlesville, Okla. (1953). Like many of his projects, the tower was a fundamental element in the Broadacre City project, the coherent, self-sufficient agricultural and industrial community Wright designed in 1931-1935.

Constant Search for Form

Significantly, Wright's concern for 20th-century problems, including urban form, did not lead him to the mechanistic rectilinear forms and finishes admired by Gropius or the sculptural purism of Le Corbusier. Always distinctive and independent, Wright's style changed often. For about 10 years after 1915 he drew upon Mayan massing and ornament (Barndall House, Hollywood, 1920). He cast ornament in concrete blocks (Millard House, Pasadena, 1923), and he did not achieve his several versions of a decisively modern style until various European architects, including Le Corbusier and others, notably Richard Neutra (who came to the United States in the late 1920s), had dramatized a sheer, stripped geometry. Even then Wright avoided the barrenness and abstraction of the isolated, single parallelepiped; he insisted upon having the multiple form of buildings reflect the movement of unique sites: the Kaufmann House, "Falling Water," at Bear Run, Pa. (1936-1937), where cantilevered, interlocked, reinforced-concrete terraces are poised over the waterfall; the low-cost houses (Herbert Jacobs House, Madison, Wis., 1937); and the "prairie houses" (Lloyd Lewis House, Libertyville, Ill., 1940). No architect was more skillful in fitting form to its terrain: the Pauson House in Phoenix, Ariz. (1940; destroyed) rose from the desert, like a Mayan pyramid, its battered ashlar and shiplapped, wooden walls reflecting the mountains and desert. There is a compatibility, an organic adaptation in stone walls, wooden frames, and canvas that marries Wright's western home, Taliesin West (1938-1959), to Maricopa Mesa, near Phoenix.

Those brilliant rural houses did not reveal how Wright would respond to an urban setting or to the program of a corporate client. But in the Administration Building for the Johnson Wax Company, Racine, Wis. (1936-1939, with a research tower added in 1950), he astonished architects with his second great commercial building (after the Larkin Building). A continuous, windowless red-brick wall encloses a high, clerestory-lighted interior space; that space, which contains tall dendriform columns, is one of the most serene and graceful interior spaces in the world. Thereafter, a college, Florida Southern at Lakeland, Fla., was encouraged to retain Wright to design its campus (1938-1959); unfortunately, it suffers from an obsession with multifaceted form and oblique and acute angles (as does the Unitarian Church in Madison, Wis., 1947). But after those probings toward a new geometry Wright succeeded with complex pyramids (as suggested earlier by his Lake Tahoe project of the 1920s) when he built the Beth Sholom Synagogue at Elkins Park, Pa. (1959), a Mycenaean sacred mountain. Such a temple, a sanctuary of light approached by a continuous spiral, fascinated the elderly Wright. At Florida Southern College he juxtaposed circle and fragmented rhombus, recalling Hadrian's Villa at Tivoli, Italy; he set a helix inside the Morris Gift Shop in San Francisco (1948-1949). Ultimately, he conceived of having the helix surround a tall central space: the six-story Guggenheim Museum in New York City (1946-1959), which paid in significant functional defects to gain a memorable experience in viewing art, especially where the helix affords views into a side gallery below.

Of Wright's colossal helix that he proposed for the Golden Triangle in Pittsburgh (1947), nothing was built. He envisioned ramps for automobiles that would lead to stores and galleries and auditoriums. His drawings, which are in ink and crayon on huge sheets of rice paper, stand among the greatest and most inspiring displays of architectural imagination; what was built in Pittsburgh by other hands is expedient and vulgar. His drawings are magical and lyrical. No one might ever build accordingly, but Wright was never content with the commonplace or servile to the conventional or the practical. He imagined the wonderful where others were content with the probable. Avoidance of the vulgar or probable excited him to ecstatic design: the hyperbole of the Grand Opera and Civic Auditorium for Baghdad, Iraq (1957). The drawings of helix, domes, and finals suggest how far Wright's talent transcended any client's capacity fully to realize his dream: a world of sanctuaries and gardens, of earth and machines, of rivers, seas, mountains, and prairies, where grand architecture enables men to dwell nobly.

Wright died at Taliesin West on April 9, 1959. His widow, Olgivanna, directs the Taliesin Fellowship.

Further Reading

Wright's *An Autobiography* (1932; enlarged 1943) remains the best statement of his architectural theory. Other books by Wright to consult are *An Organic Architecture: The Architecture of Democracy* (1939), essays based on his London lectures of 1939; and *When Democracy Builds* (1945). *An American Architecture,* edited by Edgar Kaufmann (1955), is an anthology of Wright's writings and includes photographs of his work. *Frank Lloyd Wright: Writings and Buildings,* selected by Edgar Kaufmann and Ben Raeburn (1960), is a well-edited compendium. A complication of Wright's work is *Buildings, Plans and Designs,* with a foreword by William Wesley Peters and an introduction by Wright (1963). Arthur Drexler, *The Drawings of Frank Lloyd Wright* (1962), contains some of the finest examples of Wright's art.

The standard monograph on Wright is Henry-Russell Hitchcock, *In the Nature of Materials* (1942; 2d ed. 1969). Grant C. Manson, *Frank Lloyd Wright to 1910* (1958), is a detailed study of his early work. Vincent Scully, *Frank Lloyd Wright* (1960), a sensitive and informative essay about Wright's imagery, covers his entire career. John E. Burchard and Albert Bush-Brown, *The Architecture of America* (1961), interprets Wright in terms of American architectural experience. Wright figures prominently in John Jacobus, *Twentieth-century Architecture: The Middle Years, 1940-65* (1966). □

Richard Wright

The works of Richard Wright (1908-1960), politically sophisticated and socially involved African American author, are notable for their passionate sincerity. He was perceptive about the universal problems that plague mankind.

Richard Wright was born in Natchez, Miss., on Sept. 4, 1908. His mother was a country school teacher and his father an illiterate sharecropper. The family moved to Memphis, Tenn., in 1914, and soon the father abandoned them. Richard's schooling was spotty, but he had experiences beyond his years. He knew what it was to be a victim of racial hatred before he learned to read, for he was living with an aunt when her husband was lynched by a white mob. Richard's formal education ended after the ninth grade in Jackson, Miss. The fact that his "The Voodoo of Hell's Half-acre" had been published in the local black paper set him apart from his classmates. He was a youth upon whom a "somberness of spirit" had already settled.

At 19 Wright decided he wanted to be a writer. He moved to Chicago, where he had access to public libraries. He read all he could of Dostoevsky, Theodore Dreiser, and Henry and William James. His interest in social problems led to an acquaintance with the sociologist Louis Wirth. When Richard's mother, brother, and an aunt came to Chicago, he supported them as a postal clerk until the job ended in 1929. After months of living on public welfare, he got a job in the Federal Negro Theater Project in the Works Progress Administration, a government relief agency. Later he became a writer for the Illinois Writers' Project.

Meantime, Wright had joined the John Reed Club, beginning an association with the Communist party. His essays, reviews, short stories, and poems appeared regularly in Communist papers, and by 1937, when he became Harlem editor of the *Daily Worker,* he enjoyed a considerable reputation in left-wing circles. Four novellas, published as *Uncle Tom's Children* (1938), introduced him to a large general audience.

Native Son

Wright's first novel, *Native Son* (1940), a brutally honest depiction of black, urban ghetto life, was an immediate success. The story's protagonist embodies all the fear, rage, and rebellion, all the spiritual hunger and the undisciplined drive to satisfy it, that social psychologists were just beginning to recognize as common elements in the personality of the underprivileged and dispossessed of all races.

Wright's intention was to make the particular truth universal and to project his native son as a symbol of the deprived in all lands. Contemporary critics, however, unimpressed by the universal symbol, were interested instead in Wright's passionate indictment of white racism and the life-style it imposed upon blacks. Wright's implication that there was another and a better way of social organization than democracy, and that communism was perhaps that better way, also impressed them. This implication was toned down in the stage version (1941). In 1941 Wright also published *Twelve Million Black Voices: A Folk History of the Negro of the United States.*

Black Boy

By 1940 Wright had married and divorced; and a few months after his second marriage, he broke with the communist party. (His "I Tried To Be a Communist," published in the *Atlantic* in 1944, was reprinted in 1949 in *The God That Failed,* edited by Richard Crossman.) The break freed him from social and ideological commitments that were beginning to seem onerous. In *Black Boy,* a fictionalized autobiography, his only commitment is to truth. The book was published in January 1945, and sales reached 400,000 copies by March. Wright accepted an invitation from the French government to visit France, and the three-month experience, in sharp contrast to his experience in his own country, "exhilarated" him with a "sense of freedom." People of the highest intellectual and artistic circles met him "as an equal."

Expatriate Years

Wright and his wife and daughter moved permanently to Paris. Within a year and a half Wright was off to Argentina, where he "starred" in the film version of *Native Son.*

The Outsider, the first of three novels written in France, was deeply influenced by the existentialists, whose most famous spokesmen, Jean Paul Sartre and Simone de Beauvoir, were Wright's warm friends. Following *Savage Holiday* (1954), a potboiler, *The Long Dream* (1958) proved that Wright had been too long out of touch with the American reality to deal with it effectively. None of the novels

written in France succeeded. His experiments with poetry did not produce enough for a book.

Nonfiction Works

In 1953 Wright visited Africa, where he hoped to "discover his roots" as a black man. *Black Power* (1954) combines the elements of a travel book with a passionate political treatise on the "completely different order of life" in Africa. In 1955 he attended the Afro-Asian Conference in Bandung and published his impressions in *The Color Curtain* (1956). *Pagan Spain* (1956), based on two months in Spain, is the best of his nonfiction works. *White Man, Listen* (1957) is a collection of four long essays on "White-colored, East-West relations."

In 1960, following an unhappy attempt to settle in England, and in the midst of a rugged lecture schedule, Wright fell ill. He entered a hospital in Paris on November 25 and died three days later. *Eight Men* (1961), a collection of short stories, and *Lawd Today* (1963), a novel, were published posthumously.

Further Reading

Constance Webb, *Richard Wright* (1968), is a "definitive" but dull biography. Full-length critical works are Edward Margolies, *The Art of Richard Wright* (1969), which emphasizes Wright's role in paving the way for a new generation of Negro authors; Dan McCall, *The Example of Richard Wright* (1969), a fascinating critique; and Russell C. Brignano, *Richard Wright: An Introduction to the Man and His Works* (1970). See also Robert Bone, *Richard Wright* (1969), a brief perspective. James Baldwin's "Alas, Poor Richard" in his *Nobody Knows My Name* (1961) is not to be trusted as a delineation of an episode in Wright's life, and its condescending tone spoils it as literary criticism. David Littlejohn's discussion of Wright in his *Black on White: A Critical Survey of Writing by American Negroes* (1966) is worth reading if only to see how misprized a major black novelist can be. □

Wilhelm Max Wundt

The German psychologist and philosopher Wilhelm Max Wundt (1832-1920) was the founder of experimental psychology. He edited the first journal of experimental psychology and established the first laboratory of experimental psychology.

Wilhelm Wundt was born on Aug. 16, 1832, in Baden, in a suburb of Mannheim called Neckarau. As a child, he was tutored by Friedrich Müller. Wundt attended the gymnasium at Bruschel and at Heidelberg, the University of Tübingen for a year, then Heidelberg for more than 3 years, receiving a medical degree in 1856. He remained at Heidelberg as a lecturer in physiology from 1857 to 1864, then was appointed assistant professor in physiology. The great physiologist, physicist, and physiological psychologist Hermann von Helmholtz came there in 1858, and Wundt for a while was his assistant.

During the period from 1857 to 1874 Wundt evolved from a physiologist to a psychologist. In these years he also wrote *Grundzüge der physiologischen psychologie* (*Principles of Physiological Psychology*). The two-volume work, published in 1873-1874, stressed the relations between psychology and physiology, and it showed how the methods of natural science could be used in psychology. Six revised editions of this work were published, the last completed in 1911.

As a psychologist, Wundt used the method of investigating conscious processes in their own context by "experiment" and introspection. This technique has been referred to as content psychology, reflecting Wundt's belief that psychology should concern itself with the immediate content of experience unmodified by abstraction or reflection.

In 1874 Wundt left Heidelberg for the chair of inductive philosophy at Zurich, staying there only a year. He accepted the chair of philosophy at the University of Leipzig, and in 1879 he founded the first psychological laboratory in the world. To Leipzig, men came from all over the world to study in Wundt's laboratory. In 1879 G. Stanley Hall, Wundt's first American student, arrived, followed by many other Americans. From this first laboratory for experimental psychology a steady stream of psychologists returned to their own countries to teach and to continue their

researches. Some founded psychological laboratories of their own.

In 1881 Wundt founded *Philosophische Studien* as a vehicle for the new experimental psychology, especially as a publication organ for the products of his psychological laboratory. The contents of *Philosophische Studien* (changed to *Psychologische Studien* in 1903) reveal that the experiments fell mainly into four categories: sensation and perception; reaction time; time perception and association; and attention, memory, feeling, and association. Optical phenomena led with 46 articles; audition was second in importance. Sight and hearing, which Helmholtz had already carefully studied, were the main themes of Wundt's laboratory. Some of the contributions to the *Studien* were by Wundt himself. Helmholtz is reported to have said of some of Wundt's experiments that they were *schlampig* (sloppy). Comparing Wundt to Helmholtz, who was a careful experimentalist and productive researcher, one must conclude that Wundt's most important contributions were as a systematizer, organizer, and encyclopedist. William James considered Wundt "only a rather ordinary man who has worked up certain things uncommonly well."

Wundt's *Grundriss der Psychologie* (1896; *Outline of Psychology*) was a less detailed treatment than his *Principles,* but it contained the new theory of feeling. A popular presentation of his system of psychology was *Einführung in die Psychologie* (1911; *Introduction to Psychology*). His monumental *Völkerpsychologie* (1912; *Folk Psychology*), a natural history of man, attempted to understand man's higher thought processes by studying language, art, mythology, religion, custom, and law. Besides his psychological works he wrote three philosophical texts: *Logic* (1880-1883), *Ethics* (1886), and *System of Philosophy* (1889). Wundt died near Leipzig on Aug. 31, 1920.

Further Reading

Virtually all histories of psychology report on Wundt. George Sidney Brett, *Brett's History of Psychology,* edited and abridged by R. S. Peters (1953; 2d rev. ed. 1965), is a standard account. A longer one, written by Wundt's first American student, is G. Stanley Hall, *Founders of Modern Psychology* (1912). J. C. Flugel, *A Hundred Years of Psychology* (1933; rev. 1965), which includes a good account of the development of experimental psychology from its systematic and philosophic antecedents, contains a chapter on Wundt's work. A more scholarly treatment of the same development is Edwin G. Boring, *A History of Experimental Psychology* (1929; 2d ed. 1950). Recommended among the more recent works are Henryk Misiak, *History of Psychology: An Overview* (1966), and Benjamin B. Wolman, *Historical Roots of Contemporary Psychology* (1968).

Additional Sources

Wundt studies: a centennial collection, Toronto: C.J. Hogrefe, 1980. □

Charles Wuorinen

Pulitzer-Prize-winning composer Charles Wuorinen (born 1938) remained at the forefront of the contemporary music scene throughout his prolific career. Following in the tradition of the post-World War II serialists, his works employed techniques to achieve new heights of lyricism, richness, and subtlety.

Charles Wuorinen was born in New York City on June 9, 1938. His father taught history at Columbia University for 40 years, and his early training in composition came from Jack Beeson and Vladimr Ussachevsky, both Columbia University professors. He started playing the piano and composing at age five. At 16, he won the New York Philharmonic's Young Composers Award. Wuorinen enrolled at Columbia in 1956 and studied composition with Otto Luening. He wrote his earliest orchestral work, *Into the Organ Pipes and Steeples,* at 18. While working as a piano accompanist, recording engineer, and singer, Wuorinen attended the Bennington Composers Conference in Vermont for four years. At 21, he composed his first three symphonies.

At Columbia in 1962, Wuorinen founded the Group for Contemporary Music, which became the prototype for many university new music ensembles. Organized in collaboration with Harvey Sollberger, it became one of the most important agencies for the performance and recording of contemporary music. Wuorinen received a bachelor's degree in 1961 and his master's degree in music in 1963. He taught music at Columbia from 1964 to 1971 but resigned when he was not granted tenure. He held Guggenheim fellowships in 1968 and 1972, and taught at the Manhattan School of Music from 1972 to 1979.

Wuorinen's early works use conventional tones but are still modern and exhibit a penetrating control of detail. His *Third Symphony* (1959), for example, shows a mastery of large form orchestration and 12-tone techniques. However, Wuorinen's best-known works feature rigorous serial applications similar to the works of Olivier Messiaen, Pierre Boulez, and Milton Babbitt. His compositions were based in a "time point system" in which pitch, time, and rhythmic divisions are related.

Throughout his career, Wuorinen was receptive to new musical resources. As early as 1961 he incorporated magnetic tape in his *Consort from Instruments and Voices* and combined tape with orchestra in *Orchestra and Electronic Exchanges* (1965). In 1969 Wuorinen created *Times Encomium,* which used synthesized sounds in every element of the composition. In 1970 he was awarded a Pulitzer Prize for *Times Encomium,* the first ever awarded for a composition created solely for a recording.

Wuorinen's works have been widely performed and he is one of the most significant American composers of his generation. Most of his compositions are abstract instrumental music. He created pieces to showcase nearly every musical instrument.

Some of Wuorinen's music may appear dry and uninspired on first listening. Conventional elements such as melody and harmony are superseded by the shaping of melodic contour and the creative interaction of ensemble forces. Wuorinen believed that "art is itself because it demands an active relation with him who perceives it. He cannot appreciate' it; he must himself create the work's meaning." Listeners must absorb a Wuorinen piece several times before they appreciate its depth and dimension.

Wuorinen recorded for Gold Crest, CRI, Cambridge, Advance, Nonesuch, AR-DGG, Mainstream, and Desto Records, and his main publisher was C.F. Peters. He wrote essays and articles for *High Fidelity, Musical America,* the *New York Times, Perspectives of New Music,* the *Saturday Review, Prose, Musik Geschichte und Gegenwart,* and the *New Grove Dictionary,* as well as liner notes for CRI and Nonesuch Records.

Composer, conductor, lecturer, and performer, Wuorinen was so prolific that by the age of 37 he had over 150 compositions to his credit. His reputation allowed him to work exclusively by commission. Wuorinen was a founding member of the American Society of University Composers. He was also notable as the author of *Simple Composition* (1978), a valuable textbook for composition. From 1985 to 1987 he was composer-in-residence for the San Francisco Symphony.

His range of work is extraordinary. Wuorinen's opera *The W. of Babylon* (1975) is a "baroque burlesque" with an assortment of lewd 17th-century French men and women. His *Bambula Squared* (1984) is a piece for orchestra and computer-generated tape. Starting in the 1980s, Wuorinen increasingly composed chamber works with sharp textures, strong rhythms, and sustained, clear melodies.

Further Reading

In addition to his instructive publication *Simple Composition* (1978), recommended reading includes *Introduction to Contemporary Music* by Joseph Machlis (1979), *American Music Since 1910* by Virgil Thompson (1970), David Ewen's *American Composers* (1982), and the *New York Times* (June 7, 1970, and April 10, 1983). Wuorinen is interviewed in T. Caras and C. Gagne, *Soundpieces: Interviews with American Composers* (1982). □

Wu P'ei-fu

Wu P'ei-fu (1874-1939) was a Chinese warlord. As head of the Chihli clique, he controlled significant portions of central and northern China between 1918 and 1926.

Wu P'ei-fu was born into a merchant's household in the northeast province of Shantung. He received a classical education, but family and personal misfortunes drove him into the military, a calling traditionally held in low esteem but increasingly popular during the chaotic years of the late Ch'ing dynasty. In 1902

Wu entered Yüan Shih-k'ai's Paoting Military Academy and became associated with the Peiyang clique. He served as an intelligence officer for the Japanese during the Russo-Japanese War. When Yüan Shih-k'ai emerged as the strongman of China after the Revolution of 1911, Wu became a brigade commander with the rank of colonel.

Under the wing of his division commander, Ts'ao K'un, Wu advanced rapidly during the early years of the republic. Yüan Shih-k'ai's death on June 6, 1916, initiated the warlord era (1916-1928), during which scores of military chieftains struggled for supremacy. After the Peiyang clique split into the Chihli and Anfu factions in 1918, Wu became a leading figure in the Chihli group. In 1920 he helped drive the Anfu leader Tuan Ch'i-jui from Peking. With a base of power in the central provinces of Hupei and Hunan, Wu next defeated Chang Tso-lin, the Manchurian warlord of the Fengtien clique, thereby becoming the most powerful figure in northern China.

During his climb to power, Wu had developed a reputation as a relatively progressive warlord. He persistently advocated the "peaceful unification" of China and generally expressed himself through telegrams before resorting to bullets. He supported student protest against Japanese encroachments and demonstrated sympathy with a civilian movement for good government. However, he was capable of ruthlessness when his vital interests were threatened. In February 1923 his troops killed some 80 striking workers who had halted traffic on the Peking-Hankow Railway, the principal source of Wu's economic and military sustenance.

Furthermore, though scrupulously honest and disdainful of high office, Wu was handicapped by an imperious personality that alienated subordinates. In 1924 one of these, Feng Yü-hsiang, betrayed him at a critical moment in a military campaign and drove him into a brief retirement. Wu quickly reemerged to defeat his treacherous lieutenant, only to fall victim to the forces of the Kuomintang's Northern Expedition. With a mere hundred followers remaining from his once formidable army, Wu found refuge in the province of Szechwan. There he studied Confucianism and Buddhism and wrote a short treatise in praise of loyalty, obedience, social stability, and other traditional virtues. In 1932 he moved to Peiping.

As the Japanese maneuvered for control of northern China, Wu spurned offers to head a puppet government. However Chiang Kai-shek's increasing receptivity to Communist proposals for a united front enhanced his enthusiasm for an anti-Red crusade in cooperation with the Japanese. After the outbreak of the Second Sino-Japanese War on July 7, 1937, Wu offered to cooperate if the Japanese would equip him with a half-million-man army and gradually withdraw their own troops. The Japanese refused to pay so high a price. On Dec. 4, 1939, he succumbed to blood poisoning from an infected tooth. Eulogies from the Nationalist government in Chungking accompanied his elaborate burial in Japanese-occupied Peiping.

Further Reading

There is no biography of Wu P'ei-fu in English. James E. Sheridan's biography of Feng Yü-hsiang, *Chinese Warlord* (1966), provides a perspective on Wu from the viewpoint of his disloyal follower. Detailed accounts of the warlord era are in Li Chien-nung, *The Political History of China, 1840-1928* (trans. 1956), and in O. Edmund Clubb, *20th Century China* (1964).

Additional Sources

Wou, Odoric Y. K., *Militarism in modern China: the career of Wu P'ei-Fu, 1916-39,* Folkestone, Eng.: Dawson, 1978. □

Wu Tao-tzu

Wu Tao-tzu (ca. 689-c. 758) was a Chinese painter and the most admired figure painter in Chinese history.

W u Tao-tzu, also called Wu Tao-hsüan, was born in Yang-ti near Loyang, Honan Province, apparently into a family of humble means. He was orphaned and penniless as a boy and may have begun his study of painting under the professional craftsmen employed to decorate Buddhist temples. According to tradition, he also studied calligraphy with the Buddhist monk Chang Hsü, who was famous for his "crazy cursive" script, emphasizing the madly kinesthetic qualities of the brush.

Wu is also said to have gained insight into the qualities of movement by observing the famous sword dance of Gen. P'ei Min.

Wu Tao-tzu was summoned to the court by Emperor Hsüan-tsung, the extraordinarily cultured ruler to whose palaces were attracted such a glittering array of poets, painters, calligraphers, and musicians that his reign is remembered as the golden age of Chinese culture. There Wu soon acquired a reputation as the most brilliant and untrammeled painter of the dynasty. His genius was legendary, as was his unruly behavior: "He was fond of wine, which brought forth his spirit; before wielding the brush, he would invariably get drunk." He is known to have painted 300 temple walls in the capital alone and is reported to have executed in a single day a mural depicting a hundred miles of scenery along the Chia-ling River.

Wu Tao-tzu's Style

The speed and kinesthetic fury of his brush is the significant aspect of Wu Tao-tzu's art. He was among the first painters to develop a fluid, thickening-and-thinning brushline and to describe forms loosely and suggestively. The early history of Chinese figure painting is written in the successive achievements of three masters: Ku K'aichih, whose brushwork was "like silken thread;" Yen Lipen, who painted with "iron-wire line;" and Wu Taotzu, whose fluctuating, graphic brushwork was the first to acquire qualities of its own, separate from the forms it described. The influence of calligraphy, with its actual kinesthetic properties, was crucial to this development. Wu's emphasis on the brush itself was to have profound impact on the later history of painting.

This brilliant age of Chinese history was ended by the disastrous An Lu-shan rebellion of 755. Wu Tao-tzu survived the tragedy, but the last period of his life is unrecorded. The An Lu-shan rebellion was only the first of countless disasters—rebellions, religious persecutions, dynastic collapse—that have destroyed every trace of Wu's art. He is honored by history as the "Sage of Painting," and he commanded an army of followers, but his material legacy consists only of a few engravings of recent centuries, including the *Spirit of the Heng Mountains,* and a handful of late copies, like the *Rulers of Hell* in Chicago. They may preserve some idea of the master's work but scarcely its reality.

Further Reading

There is little in English on Wu Tao-tzu. He is discussed in Oswald Siren, *Chinese Painting: Leading Masters and Principles* (7 vols., 1956-1958), and Anil De Silva, *The Art of Chinese Landscape Painting* (1964). □

Wu-ti

During the late Han dynasty in ancient China, ruler Wu-ti (156 B.C.-87 A.D.) commanded an empire that stretched eastward to Korea and westward through Central Asia reaching present-day Uzbekistan. He instituted the study of Confucius as a state mandate and created a wealthy and culturally advanced empire.

Through periodic alliances with harsher enemies in the west and subjugation of docile southern farming regions in Vietnam, the empire under Wu-ti consisted of most of the world that was known to him. In the lost city at Chang'an, the Han capitol, Wu-ti presided over his land with a firm hand, relentlessly persecuting his enemies while providing allies with gifts intended to enhance their loyalty. In addition to his military achievements, he was able to maintain authority over Chinese institutions provided for a long period of rule, and he is largely responsible for making Confucianism the state-sanctioned dogma employed by many successive dynasties. The empire's expanse under Wu-ti provided ample opportunities for trade, bringing wealth along with advances in the arts and sciences.

Directed Vast Expansion of Chinese Empire

Born Liu Ch'e in 156 B.C., Wu-ti was reportedly the eleventh son of Han emperor Ching-ti and not in line to ascend the throne. When relatives placed heavy political pressure on the emperor lobbying for Liu Ch'e's nomination as crown prince, Wu-ti managed to overtake his ten brothers and won the throne in 140 B.C. The 14 year-old monarch found his autonomy curtailed by a cabinet composed of relatives and various ministers. Though his power was less than absolute, Wu-ti managed to observe the policies pressed upon him by his political tutors and was not moved by their effectiveness. Chinese territory and influence had recently decreased due in part to raids by nomadic tribes in the northwest, and the government capitulated with defensive, conciliatory policies toward its aggressors. The Hsiung-nu and the Yueh-chih, the two offending tribes, were content to make pacts with the Chinese only to break them at will and raid encampments for provisions and weapons.

Under these circumstances, the explorer Chang Ch'ien set out on the journey that would make him the first Chinese to venture into the Middle East, ranking his discoveries on par with explorers such as Magellan and Marco Polo. Wu-ti wanted to convince Yueh-chih tribesmen to side with him and put an end to the Hsiung-nu raids. He ordered Chang Ch'ien to set out in search of the Yueh-chih and deliver his proposition. The epic mission included a 12-year term as a prisoner of the Hsiung-nu, and when he finally found the Yueh-chih in northwest India, they had found a rich land to tend and presided over their imperial vision upon parts of Central Asia.

The travels of Chang Ch'ien served a purpose more important than historical to Wu-ti. He ordered large armies to follow in Chang Ch'ien's wake, conquering and looting their way across Asia. These armies also opened a valuable trade route connecting east and west, which allowed raw goods and exotic luxury items to pass between the many cultures along the way. While Chang Ch'ien was away, Wu-ti outgrew his handlers and became a strong leader in his own right. He withdrew offers of concessions and instead charged thousands of mounted troops with implementing his will. In 133 B.C., Wu-ti launched an attack against the Hsiung-nu that provided the first of many victories to come. Thirty years later, his forces overran Fergana, an ancient empire in Uzbekistan, marking his domination over all but the most distant civilizations. At his greatest, Emperor Wu-ti commanded troops from southern Vietnam to northern Korea and westward into the far reaches of Asia, recapturing the glory of the empire's grandest days and setting territorial and cultural precedents that would not be met again for several centuries when the Tang dynasty rebuilt a stagnant nation.

Empire Witnessed Cultural Advance

Wu-ti's military exploits set the stage for tremendous growth in Chinese culture. By appropriating much of Confucianism into an encompassing state religion, Wu-ti's government became the first to officially acknowledge Confucius' philosophy, even if it was politically filtered, to further establish the moral authority of the emperor. "What the state religion actually had in common with Confucian ideas was respect for the good old days and for the ancient values said to have been endorsed by the founding fathers of Chinese civilization. But the antiquity of many of these beliefs was counterfeit," wrote Chinese historian Edward Schafer.

Under Wu-ti's Han dynasty significant intellectual and scholarly work was done. The Han emperors employed countless scribes whose work was to codify the ancient myths, legends, and rituals. Among the works completed in the era was the *I Ching,* or *Book of Changes,* a collection of ancient proverbs and the first extensive treatment of the dual concepts of *yin* and *yang.* These ideas, central to much of Chinese philosophy, governed the two fundamental forces of the universe. The *yin* (translated as "shaded") regulated all that was dark, cold, female, and submissive. The winter season was thought to be the annual zenith of *yin* while the summer was the dominant season for *yang.* All that was warm, bright, and male was under the control of *yang* (translated as "sunlit"). Under the Han dynasty, an elaborate system of categorization was worked out classifying nearly every creature, territory, and substance as either a force of *yin* or *yang.* The practice of alchemy also emerged when Li Shao-Chun first claimed to have turned cinnabar into gold around 100 B.C., nearly a thousand years before medieval Europeans were lured by its promise of wealth and eternal life.

In classic Chinese mythology, the earth was divided into "Nine Mansions," each represented in a diagram handed down from Heaven. The diagram showed a square divided into nine equal regions, each containing a single number, one through nine. When the numbers from any three squares in a row were added, the sum was 15. This unity of form was thought to encapsulate one of nature's most divine secrets and the mystical plan was used by later emperors, including the Han, in constructing the capitol city at Chang'an. The Nine Mansions, as the ultimate map of the world, pointed in the eight cardinal directions on the compass, with the ninth reserved for the location of the "Son of Heaven," or emperor. In Wu-ti's case, this Mansion was Chang'an. He built a magnificent palace in the city decorated with jewels and paintings of the Chinese pantheon. The city itself featured wide avenues lined by fruit trees and was guarded by earthen walls 17-feet thick. Chang'an also boasted opulent gardens that served as royal hunting preserves as well as numerous temples and monasteries inhabited by Taoists, Buddhists, and Persian worshippers of Zoroaster. Its residents also enjoyed bath houses, libraries, and two thriving market places.

Managed Economic Reform With Customary Harsh Measures

Wu-ti's expansive conquest, together with his civil building projects, weakened the royal treasuries. Consequently, he was forced to raise taxes, a historically unpopular practice. Wu-ti took firm measures in domestic affairs to stabilize the empire's economy by issuing a standard currency, setting up state monopolies for the production of many commodities, and forcing nobles to purchase their rank for vast sums of money. While many of his economic reforms were successful, foreign policy was less receptive to his dictums. On the northwestern front, the Hsiung-nu were becoming more difficult to keep at bay, and their mounted archers grew increasingly more aggressive as they sensed imperial weakness. Wu-ti had long been known as a harsh ruler, and when one provincial general was forced to surrender to Hsiung-nu, he ordered the man castrated, effectively terminating his family's future nobility by making it impossible to bear a son. The threat from barbaric tribes at the empire's edges was a significant one for Wu-ti because the Chinese enjoyed a substantial trade surplus with their Western neighbors. Cultures as far away as Rome coveted Chinese silk, making its export a prominent contributor to the imperial treasury.

With a state struggling for stability, Wu-ti entered the last years of his life facing an additional problem—who to name as his successor. Court intrigue left his first-born son convicted of witchcraft against the state, and was therefore ineligible for the throne. Wu-ti decided upon his eight-year-old son as the heir apparent. To reduce the threat of undue influence on the next emperor from relatives of his empress (a former slave elevated to the status of courtesan and finally claimed by Wu-ti as his wife for her docility and subservience), Wu-ti ruthlessly ordered the slaying of her relatives, assuring his son a government unfettered by personal rivalry. Nearing the end of his life, Wu-ti developed a strong interest in the mystics that paraded before the court. He offered lavish rewards to any of them that could put him in touch with spirits capable of granting him eternal life. He became very interested in alchemist's claims of offering a measure of immortality through the manipulation of divine substances. When he died in 87 A.D., he left behind a vast empire and an authoritarian tradition duplicated by many later dynasties, but Wu-ti's place in history is secured largely by his military victories.

Further Reading

Schafer, Edward H., *Ancient China,* Time Life Books, 1967.
Fairbank, John K., *China: A New History,* Harvard University Press, 1992.
Reischauer, Edwin O., and John K. Fairbank, *East Asia: The Great Tradition,* Houghton Mifflin, 1958. ☐

Wu Tse-t'ien

Wu Tse-t'ien (623-705) was empress of China. A strong-willed and capable ruler, she was the only female sovereign in China's long history.

Wu Tse-t'ien or Wu Chao is often known as Empress Wu. She was the daughter of a general of the first T'ang emperor, Kao-tsu, and was presented to his son, Emperor T'ai-tsung, as a concubine in 638. When T'ai-tsung died in 649, she, along with the imperial concubines, was required to leave the palace and enter a nunnery in the T'ang capital, Ch'angan.

The following year, unusual circumstances made it possible for Wu to return to the palace. Empress Wang, the wife of the new emperor Kao-tsung, felt insecure because she was not her husband's favorite. Hearing rumors that Wu had earlier attracted Kao-tsung, the Empress thought she could strengthen her position by patronizing and controlling Wu. Once back in the palace Wu turned against her benefactor but could not displace her. She then took the cruel and desperate step of murdering her own newborn infant, the Emperor's child, and accusing Empress Wang of the deed. Kao-tsung believed the accusation, dismissed Empress Wang, and decided to make Wu his empress.

This decision was vigorously opposed by the older ministers. Nevertheless, the Emperor issued a proclamation which listed the virtues of Wu and insisted that there was no reason that she should not become his wife. In 655 Wu became empress. Her position was strengthened when her son was named crown prince in 656.

In 664 Kao-tsung had the first of a series of paralytic strokes that were to affect him for the remainder of his life. Wu quickly took advantage of his infirmity to dominate the court. After a feeble attempt to displace her, Kao-tsung came entirely under her control. Emperor Kao-tsung died in 683, and Wu's son ascended the throne. She had expected to manipulate him, but he soon showed signs of independence. Without hesitation Wu had him deposed and replaced with his younger brother.

As empress dowager, Wu dominated the young emperor. Still unsatisfied, she decided on an unprecedented act. She determined to overthrow her son, change the name of the dynasty, and assume full authority as ruler. In 690 Wu proclaimed the founding of the Chou dynasty. For the first and last time, a woman had become sovereign of China.

Wu's reign, which was traditionally regarded as a regrettable and illegitimate hiatus in T'ang rule, was actually a time of important institutional change. It was a stable period, but the ascendancy of incompetent court favorites finally resulted in her overthrow in 705; she died shortly thereafter. Her older son, whom she had deposed 20 years earlier, was restored to the throne. His first act was to reestablish the T'ang dynasty, which ruled China until the line's extinction in 907.

Further Reading

Readable accounts of Wu Tse-t'ien that emphasize her personal life and career are C. P. Fitzgerald, *The Empress Wu* (1956; 2d ed. 1968), and Lin Yutang, *Lady Wu: A True Story* (1957).

Additional Sources

Guisso, R. W. L., *Wu Tse-T'ien and the politics of legitimation in T'ang China,* Bellingham, Wash.: Western Washington, 1989, 1978. ☐

Wu wang

Wu wang (died ca. 1116 B.C.) was the first ruler of the third Chinese dynasty, the Chou. He was the leader of the forces that overthrew the Shang dynasty.

The original name of Wu wang was Chi Fa. His family had settled in the Wei River valley of Shensi Province during the final years of the Shang dynasty. Archeologists have examined the cultural remains of the area but are yet uncertain to what extent the preconquest Chou people differed from the ruling Shang.

Wu wang's father, known as Wen wang, or the Cultured King, held a ministerial post under Chou Hsin, the Shang ruler. Chou Hsin is depicted in the Chinese tradition as an evil despot and debauchee who delighted in torturing and abusing his subjects. Wen wang, who then held the title of Earl of the West (Hsi po), became alienated from the Shang ruler and established a strong power base for his family in the Wei valley. He engaged in several skirmishes with the Shang, but it was his son, Wu wang, or the Martial King, who undertook large-scale warfare against Chou Hsin.

Assisted by his younger brother, Chi Tan, later known as the Duke of Chou (Chou kung), Wu wang organized an army composed of nobles who had been mistreated by Chou Hsin. Most of the accounts of Wu wang's rise to power are late idealizations and are not particularly reliable, but they are about the only sources presently available.

According to the prevailing tradition, Wu wang first met with his troops at a place called Meng Ford, where they urged him to attack Chou Hsin immediately. Wu wang refused to follow their advice, claiming that the proper time had not yet arrived. Two years later, when resentment against Chou Hsin had reached its peak, Wu wang gathered his troops again at Meng Ford and sent them out against the Shang on the plain of Mu just outside the Shang capital. The

Shang troops were completely routed, and Chou Hsin was forced to commit suicide.

Wu wang immediately proclaimed the end of the Shang reign and the beginning of the Chou dynasty. The traditional date for the founding of the Chou dynasty is 1122 B.C., but as many as nine other dates have been suggested by modern historians, one as late as 1027 B.C. Having conquered the Shang by military might, Wu wang now had the problem of maintaining control. One of his first acts was to bestow parcels of territory on those groups who had helped him defeat the Shang. In order to win over the defeated Shang people, he gave Chou Hsin's son a fief where he could continue the Shang sacrifices.

Several years after the Shang conquest, Wu wang died. The traditional date for his death is 1116 B.C., but this date may not be correct. He was succeeded by his young son Sung, who assumed the title of King Ch'eng (Ch'eng wang). King Ch'eng's uncle, the Duke of Chou, ruled as regent until he became of age.

Further Reading

For background on Wu wang consult Friedrich Hirth, *The Ancient History of China to the End of the Chou Dynasty* (1911), and Herrlee Glessner Creel, *The Birth of China: A Study of the Formative Period of Chinese Civilization* (1937). See also Kenneth Scott Latourette, *The Chinese: Their History and Culture* (1934; 4th rev. ed. 1964), and Creel's *The Origin of Statecraft in China,* vol. 1: *The Western Chou Empire* (1970). □

from the paintings of John Constable and the English landscape school, but an intense and individual naturalism is the dominant quality of Wyant's early work. An outstanding example of this phase of his development is *Mohawk Valley* (1866). He became a full member of the National Academy in 1869.

Interested in America's newly opened western lands, Wyant took a sabbatical from his prospering career and joined a government expedition to Arizona and New Mexico in 1873. En route there, he was subject to exposure and unusual hardships, which evidently brought on the illnesses plaguing him for the rest of his life. His right side was paralyzed, which necessitated that he learn to paint with his left hand. Most remarkably, after 1873 Wyant's style became more intimate and less concerned with aerial perspective and panoramic views. The naturalistic, even photographic effects of the early work gave way to simplified brushwork, a use of broken color, and bolder designs. The later "impressionistic" studies of autumn effects, views in the Adirondacks or along the Ohio River, and the pictures such as *Driving Mists* and *Moonlight and Frost* brought him honors at home and abroad.

Wyant married Arabella Locke in 1880, and they had one son. His later years were uneventful and solitary. Physical infirmities restricted his activities, although he continued to paint each summer in the Catskill Mountains and in his New York studio in winter. He died on Nov. 29, 1892.

Alexander Helwig Wyant

Alexander Helwig Wyant (1836-1892) was one of the outstanding American landscape painters of the late 19th century. His fascination with luminous atmospheric effects led to the creation of a subtle and poetic style.

Alexander Wyant was born on Jan. 11, 1836, in Port Washington, Ohio. The family soon moved to Defiance, where Wyant briefly attended the local grammar school and was later apprenticed to a harness maker. His childhood aptitude for drawing was not encouraged, but after a chance encounter in 1857 with some paintings by the landscapist George Inness, Wyant decided to seek the older artist's guidance. Essentially self-taught, Wyant was able to obtain some encouragement from Inness and small financial assistance from Nicholas Longworth, the Cincinnati patron of innumerable American artists of the period. By 1864 Wyant was listed among the contributors to the National Academy of Design exhibitions.

In 1865 Wyant visited Europe and studied briefly with Hans Gude at Karlsruhe, but the prevailing German taste for highly finished storytelling pictures with a rather dark tonality evidently did not attract him. Visiting England and Ireland on the way home, Wyant no doubt saw and learned

Further Reading

The two books of Eliot Clark, *Alexander Wyant* (1916) and *Sixty Paintings by Alexander H. Wyant* (1920), are the pioneering studies of the artist. No recent objective appraisal of Wyant's art has been made, except for the brief attention given him in Edgar P. Richardson, *Painting in America* (1956). □

Sir Thomas Wyatt

The English poet and diplomat Sir Thomas Wyatt (1503-1542) is chiefly remembered for his 200 songs, many of them intended for lute accompaniment. He also introduced the sonnet and terza rima into English poetry.

Thomas Wyatt was born at Allington Castle near Maidstone, Kent. He was the elder son of Henry Wyatt, afterward knighted, and his wife Anne. In 1515 Thomas entered St. John's College, Cambridge, receiving his bachelor of arts degree in 1518 and his master of arts degree in 1522. His early marriage to Elizabeth Brooke, daughter of Thomas, Lord Cobham, in 1520, proved unhappy. After she had borne him two children, Thomas (ca. 1521-1554) and Bess, Wyatt separated from his wife, apparently because she was unfaithful to him, and they were not reconciled until 1541.

After his early introduction at court, Wyatt quickly secured advancement. Popular and handsome, he was much admired for his skill in music, languages, and arms. As early as 1516 Wyatt became server extraordinary to the king, and in 1524 he became keeper of the king's jewels. Wyatt's father had been associated with Sir Thomas Boleyn, and Wyatt seems to have been early acquainted with Anne Boleyn. He was generally regarded as her lover. He was the fulfillment of the Renaissance ideal—soldier, statesman, courtier, lover, scholar, and poet.

In 1525 Wyatt participated in the Christmas tournament at Greenwich before King Henry VIII, and his diplomatic career began in 1526-1527. In these years he was sent on diplomatic missions to France and to the papacy. These missions were important from the literary standpoint because on them he became acquainted with the work of French and Italian poets. From 1528 to 1530 Wyatt served as high marshal at Calais, and from 1530 to 1536 Henry VIII regularly employed him on diplomatic missions. In 1533 Wyatt deputized for his father as chief fewer at the coronation of Anne Boleyn. At the time of Anne's trial and execution for adultery in 1536, Wyatt was arrested and imprisoned in the Tower. Released from prison after a month, Wyatt returned to full royal favor. Knighted in 1537, Wyatt was sent on embassy to Emperor Charles V in Spain that same year. In May 1539 Wyatt returned to London, and afterward he was sent on missions to France and Flanders. Henry VIII later employed him as overseer of the defense of Calais and as vice admiral of a projected fleet.

In 1542 Wyatt was elected a member of Parliament from Kent, and in October he was sent to meet Charles V's ambassadors upon their arrival at Falmouth. Contracting a fever, Wyatt died at Sherborne, Dorset, on Oct. 11, 1542. Of the numerous commemorative elegies, the one by Henry Howard, Earl of Surrey, remains the most famous: "Wyatt resteth here, that quick could never rest."

His Works

Wyatt's work divides into two groups: the sonnets, rondeaus, songs, and lyric poems treating love; and the satires and the penitential psalms. Ninety-six songs were first published in 1557 in *Songes and Sonettes* (*Tottel's Miscellany*). They have been supplemented by other songs in manuscripts. Wyatt pioneered the sonnet in English verse, writing 31 sonnets, of which 10 were translations from Petrarch. The sonnets do not exhibit Wyatt's poetic gifts at their best because the Petrarchan conventions strained his frank and robust nature. Wyatt's best work is probably contained in his 200 songs, although their main theme—his ill-treatment at the hands of his mistress—becomes monotonous. Wyatt's best songs and poems include "What No, Perdie," "Tagus, Farewell," "Lux, My Fair Falcon," "Forget Not Yet," "Blame Not My Lute," "My Lute, Awake," "In Eternum," "They Flee from Me," and "Once in Your Grace."

Wyatt also wrote three satires, adopting terza rima from Italian poetry. They are "On the Mean and Sure Estate," "Of the Courtier's Life," and "How to Use the Court and Himself." His seven penitential psalms, also written in terza rima, are freely paraphrased and contain much original material. Each one is preceded by a prologue. They were established in 1549 as *Certayne Psalmes . . . drawen into English meter by Sir Thomas Wyat Knyght* by Thomas Raynald and John Harrington.

Further Reading

The standard edition of Wyatt's poetry is *Collected poems of Sir Thomas Wyatt,* edited by Kenneth Muir (1949; rev. ed. 1969). It replaced the two-volume set edited by A. K. Foxwell in 1913 and reprinted in 1964. The standard biography is Muir's *The Life and Letters of Sir Thomas Wyatt* (1963). Critical studies include A. K. Foxwell, *A Study of Sir Thomas Wyatt's Poems* (1911; repr. 1964); Edmund K. Chambers, *Sir Thomas Wyatt and Some Collected Studies* (1933); Catherine M. Ing, *Elizabethan Lyrics: A Study in the Development of English Metres and Their Relation to Poetic Effect* (1951); Raymond Southall, *The Courtly Maker: An Essay in the Poetry of Wyatt and His Contemporaries* (1964); and Patricia Thomson, *Sir Thomas Wyatt and His Background* (1965). □

William Wycherley

The Restoration comedies of the English dramatist William Wycherley (ca. 1640-1716) ridiculed the manners and morals of sophisticated ladies and gentlemen who delighted in illicit intrigue.

William Wycherley was born at Clive, near Shrewsbury, Shropshire, where his father, a royalist, owned a small estate. Because the Puritans were in power, Wycherley was sent to France for his education. He spent several years there studying with the Duchesse de Montausier and her circle of intellectuals. As was the case with many who followed the Stuarts to France, Wycherley was converted to Roman Catholicism. However, he reverted to Protestantism upon his return to England just before the Restoration.

Wycherley entered the Inner Temple, of which his father was a member, ostensibly to study law. But he was more inclined toward literature and later settled in Oxford at the provost's quarters of Queen's College to study at the Bodleian library. He left Oxford without taking a degree.

Early in 1671 Wycherley's first play, *Love in a Wood,* was produced at the Theatre Royal, London. It attracted the attention of Charles II's mistress, the Duchess of Cleveland, who introduced Wycherley to court circles. His second play, *The Gentleman Dancing Master,* a comedy of intrigue based on a play by Pedro Calderón, was performed at Covent Garden late in 1671. It was not well received. Shortly after this Wycherley probably served as a naval officer in the Dutch War.

The Country Wife, Wycherley's best-known play, was first performed in 1672 or 1673. It centers on the attempts of a jealous husband named Pinchwife to keep his young and naive wife out of society because of his fear that she will prove unfaithful. This play was a great success and is still performed today. The next year *The Plain Dealer* was performed with equal success. In both plays he was much influenced by Molière, although his satire is fiercer than Molière's. After *The Plain Dealer* Wycherley stopped writing for the stage.

Wycherley fell ill in 1678, and Charles II sent him to France to recuperate. When he returned, the King entrusted the education of his illegitimate son, the Duke of Richmond, to Wycherley, but he lost the appointment a year later because of Charles's displeasure at his absence from court. This absence was occasioned by his secret marriage to the Countess of Drogheda, who died about a year later. Litigation over her estate proved so expensive that Wycherley was imprisoned for debt. About 7 years later King James II secured his freedom, paid his debts, and gave him a pension.

In 1697 Wycherley succeeded to his father's estate. In 1704 he published *Miscellany Poems,* which caught the attention of young Alexander Pope, who later helped Wycherley to revise them. He died on Jan. 1, 1716.

Further Reading

An excellent, annotated edition of Wycherley's work is *The Complete Plays of William Wycherley,* edited by Gerald Weales (1966). The only full-length biography is Willard Connely, *Brawny Wycherley* (1930). The best study of his plays is Rose A. Zimbardo, *Wycherley's Drama* (1965). More general discussions of Restoration comedy include John Palmer, *The Comedy of Manners* (1913; repr. 1962); Kathleen M. Lynch, *The Social Mode of Restoration Comedy* (1926);

Norman N. Holland, *The First Modern Comedies* (1959); and Virginia Ogden Birdsall, *Wild Civility: The English Comic Spirit on the Restoration Stage* (1970).

Additional Sources

McCarthy, B. Eugene, *William Wycherley: a biography,* Athens: Ohio University Press, 1979. ☐

John Wyclif

The English theologian and reformer John Wyclif (c. 1330-1384) was the most influential ecclesiastical writer in England in the second half of the 14th century.

John Wyclif's denial of the doctrine of transubstantiation, his strong belief in the sole authority of Scripture, and his views on the right of the laity to confiscate Church property brought him under attack by the ecclesiastical leaders of his day. His ideas, however, had an important shaping effect on the Lollard movement in England and on the Hussite movement in Bohemia, and his career and ideas anticipated the work of later English reformers in the 16th century.

During the second half of the 14th century a series of changes took place in England and elsewhere that altered the nature of English society in a manner that was to last for several centuries. In spite of occasional lulls, England was involved throughout this period in a war with France that ultimately resulted in the loss of English territory on the Continent. The war also hastened a growing separation between the English Church and the papacy, which from 1305 until 1378 was resident at Avignon and French-controlled and which after 1378 was split into two rival factions that further eroded respect for the authority and sanctity of the Holy Office. Both in literature and in theological writings many doctrines and practices of the Roman Church were coming under attack, with the result that England increasingly moved in the direction of nonconformity. The political and social discontent of the period, one evidence of which was the Peasants' Revolt in 1381, increased the authority of Parliament as the forum for settling disputes and for altering governmental policy. England also experienced in this period a revival in vernacular literature, in which the leading figure was Geoffrey Chaucer.

Little is known of the life of Wyclif before he arrived at Oxford, where he remained throughout most of his life. It seems most probable that he derived from a family of the lesser gentry in the area around Richmond. In 1356 he completed his arts degree at Oxford as a junior fellow of Merton College. Soon he shifted his affiliation to Balliol College, where, before 1360, he was elected master. During the summer of 1361 Wyclif resigned that position to accept the richest benefice within the gift of that college, namely, the rectorship of Fillingham In Lincolnshire. On the basis of that income he rented rooms in Queen's College and

pursued his theological degree, which he completed in 1372. Although eventually critical of pluralism and absenteeism, as a student he held more than one benefice at a time and was not always conscientious enough to pay a vicar to perform the services for which he was receiving the revenues.

Political Career

In 1372 Wyclif entered the service of the King as a theological adviser and diplomat. The year before, he had attended Parliament in the company of two Austin friars, who argued there the thesis that dominion, or the right to exercise authority and to own property, was granted by God only to those in a state of grace. Sinful clergy might, therefore, be justifiably deprived of their property by a pious layman on behalf of the common good. This concept, known as the lordship of grace, suited the government and the lay members of Parliament who were attempting to raise funds in support of the war against France and who were having difficulty convincing the clergy to undertake half of those expenses.

Wyclif made this issue his own, and in a series of treatises during the next few years he argued for the validity of expropriation by the government of a certain portion of the Church's wealth. His attack was directed primarily against the monastic establishments in England rather than against the mendicant friars who, at least in theory, supported the idea of apostolic poverty and directly served the needs of the people. Although he may have been sincere in his campaign, his antagonism toward the monks resulted in part from his dismissal from the wardenship of Canterbury College at Oxford in 1371 in favor of the monk Henry Woodhall. Moreover, Wyclif's arguments in favor of disendowment brought him opportunities and rewards that he had been slow to acquire before, such as the rectorship of Lutterworth, given to him by the King in 1374 and upon which he eventually retired, and an appointment in the same year to a commission that met with papal delegates in Bruges over the question of papal taxes and the right of filling vacancies in major English sees and abbacies.

In 1376 Wyclif became closely associated with John of Gaunt, Duke of Lancaster, a younger son of the ailing king, Edward III. During the last years of Edward's reign and the minority of Edward's grandson, Richard II, Gaunt exercised control of the royal government. Until 1378 Wyclif was protected by Gaunt from being disciplined by Church leaders as a result of his treatises attacking ecclesiastical possessioners. When, in 1377, Wyclif was called to St. Paul's Cathedral by William Courtenay, Bishop of London, to answer for his writings, Gaunt and his closest associates were there on Wyclif's behalf, hoping to use the occasion to propagandize the cause of taxing the Church. The bishop was frustrated in his attempt to convict Wyclif, but the incident increased the animosity that the people of London held for Gaunt and for his party. The next year Wyclif was summoned to Lambeth Palace, the London residence of the archbishop of Canterbury, to answer charges of false teaching. Again the royal family intervened, and Wyclif was freed with the warning to cease teaching questionable doctrines.

From Harassment to Heresy

The year 1378 was a crucial date in the life of Wyclif. The return of the papacy to Rome and the papal election that year resulted in the election of two popes, an Italian, resident at Rome, and a Frenchman, resident at Avignon. While the papal schism weakened the position of the papacy in taking action against Wyclif in England, it also permitted a reconciliation between the English government and the Italian pope, thus decreasing the usefulness of Wyclif. He was encouraged by his royal protectors to put down his pen and to return to the academic debates of Oxford.

The cause of reform, however, had captured Wyclif's imagination, and he did not cease to write and publicize his views. Beginning in 1378 he wrote a series of polemical and doctrine treatises that slowly carried him in the direction of heresy. The first work was *On the Truth of Holy Scripture;* it was a harmless and somewhat incoherent defense of the inspiration of Scripture and of the importance of its literal meaning. In another work, *On the Church,* Wyclif restricted true membership in the Church to the elect, or predestined, a group known only to God and which might not include the pope. Since one could not alter this judgment of God, prayers for the dead were useless. In his works *On the Office of King* and *On the Power of the Pope* he raised temporal power above that of the Church and tried to demonstrate that the authority claimed by the papacy had no foundation in Scripture or the life of the early Church.

The work of Wyclif that most disturbed his contemporaries was *On the Eucharist,* composed in 1379. In this book he attacked the doctrine of transubstantiation and the idea of Christ's real, or corporeal, presence in the Eucharist after consecration. According to Wyclif, the validity of the sacrament depended upon the sanctity of the one receiving it, not on the consecration of the priest.

Wyclif's attack on such a firmly established doctrine of the Church of his day and his simultaneous attack on the mendicant friars left him almost totally without supporters. Early in 1381 he was condemned by the chancellor of Oxford for teaching heretical doctrine on the Eucharist and prohibited from further expressing his views. Ignoring the advice of friends to remain silent, Wyclif published a defense of his condemned opinions under the title *Confession* and, with that parting shot, left Oxford for his rectorship at Lutterworth, where he remained until his death. In 1382 Wyclif composed his last work, the *Trialogue,* in which he summarized many of his earlier opinions and called for a vernacular translation of the Bible for the use of uneducated priests and the literate laity.

Further Reading

The best introduction to the life and thought of Wyclif is Kenneth B. McFarlane, *John Wycliffe and the Beginnings of English Nonconformity* (1952). Recent works include Edward A. Block, *John Wyclif: Radical Dissenter* (1962), and John Stacey, *John Wyclif and Reform* (1964). For background information consult Herbert B. Workman, *John Wyclif: A Study of the English Medieval Church* (1926), and George M. Trevelyan, *England in the Age of Wycliffe* (repr. 1963). □

Andrew Newell Wyeth

Andrew Wyeth (born 1917) remains one of the most popular American painters of his time. His paintings, meticulously rendered, convey a deep sympathy for people and a sense of the hardness and brevity of life.

Andrew Newell Wyeth came to painting by birth and inheritance. He was born July 12, 1917, in Chadds Ford, Pennsylvania, the son of Newell Convers and Carolyn Wyeth. His father was the great illustrator of such childhood classics as *Kidnapped* and *Treasure Island.* Andrew was a weak and sickly child. His formal schooling consisted of three months in the first grade of a country grammar school. Thereafter, he studied some at home, although he never really mastered spelling. Mostly, he roamed the countryside in solitude or stayed in the house playing with tin soldiers. Imbued with the love of narrative that shines from his father's work, Andrew spent almost a year creating a miniature theater. They were the players, sets, and costumes for a one-man production of Arthur Conan Doyle's romance *The White Company,* which he presented to the family at age 15. Deeply impressed by Andrew's virtuosity, his father immediately took him on as apprentice and student.

When Wyeth was ten his family began spending summers in Maine, a tradition the artist has continued his entire life. During his teenage years, Wyeth's early forays into watercolor painting were of the Maine landscape and ocean vistas, and with these he enjoyed his first one-man show at New York's William Macbeth Gallery in 1937. All of the works were sold, but Wyeth felt almost disheartened by his early success. He began to experiment with rendering the human form, perhaps the most difficult of all subjects. As an exercise, his father recommended that he sketch a skeleton from every possible angle.

His work as a young American artist of this period set him apart from his contemporaries, who were busy experimenting with more radical, abstract styles. Noted art critic John Russell remarked to *Newsweek* that Wyeth's "work has always had a secret and subterranean motivation, conscious or unconscious, which surfaces in strange and unexpected ways."

In 1945 Wyeth's father was killed at a railroad crossing in Chadds Ford, and the sudden death made Wyeth resolve to take his artistic career more seriously. He began to use models, often painting them over several years, a practice which he began in 1939 when he met Christina Olson. The Maine woman was a friend of Betsy Merle James, who would later become Wyeth's wife. Olson was paralyzed from polio, and Wyeth's image of her in a field, *Christina's World* (1948), is perhaps his most famous work. He continued to render Olson, or her Maine house, in a series of works that stretched on until the late 1960s, including *Miss Olson* (1952) and *Weather Side* (1965).

Wyeth and his wife Betsy bought a set of farm buildings in Chadds Ford dating back to the 18th century and restored it as a studio for him and a home for the couple and their two sons, Jamie and Nicholas. (Jamie would eventually become a painter himself). In the late 1940s Wyeth became fascinated with Karl Kuerner, a farmer of German origin who lived nearby, and Wyeth painted images of Kuerner and his property, as well as his wife Anna, over the next few decades. In Maine, where the Wyeth family spent the summer months, the artist also befriended another neighbor who became a frequent subject. Teenaged Siri Erickson was the subject of several portraits that Wyeth painted during the 1960s.

Most major American museums have examples of Wyeth's work. He was given a large retrospective at the Pennsylvania Academy of the Fine Arts in 1967. Earlier, and for many years, he was more or less systematically ignored by American art officials, although not by critics, because his work seemed so completely removed from mainstream American art. President John F. Kennedy awarded him the Medal of Freedom in 1963, and The National Institute of Arts and Letters bestowed its 1965 gold medal for Wyeth's artistic achievements. In 1970 Wyeth then had a one-man exhibition in the White House, the first ever held there.

Wyeth's name, however, remains best associated in the public's mind with the "Helga" media event of 1986. Apparently, the artist had been sketching and painting a German immigrant by the name of Helga Testorf since the early 1970s. A friend of the Kuerners, she also worked as a cleaning woman for Wyeth's sister. With her reddish-blond hair, Teutonic face, and twin braids, Helga made a quietly enigmatic subject, and Wyeth's obsession with her as a subject eventually numbered 240 works of art—supposedly without the knowledge of his wife. In early 1986 he invited Leonard E.B. Andrews, an American art collector who had previously acquired a few Wyeths, into his studio; Andrews later recalled that he was overwhelmed by the drama of the cache, and asserted that the works as a whole were a "national treasure." He purchased the Helga series in its entirety. The stern visage of Helga, as depicted by Wyeth in the 1979 tempera *Braids,* appeared on magazine covers throughout the summer of 1986 in the sensationalist stories that accompanied the unleashing of such a large, secret stash of paintings by an acclaimed American artist.

Later Andrews reportedly tried to sell the series to a buyer in Japan for $45 million, having paid only $6 million for them in 1986. It mirrored a trend in the collection of Wyeth's work, as Japanese high bidders were eagerly carting his paintings off at auctions when they appeared. "They like em; they deserve em," Wyeth noted in a 1990 interview with Thomas Hoving, former Metropolitan Museum Art director, featured in *Connoisseur.* Then 73, Wyeth was still painting, but the artist "has changed in one significant way," asserted Hoving. "He is now bathing his paintings with real light, what the French would call *plein air.*" For example, in *Snow Hill* (1987) anonymous figures dance in the snow around a maypole, and Wyeth called it a summation of his career as an artist. "I've never said anything about it other than to say that it's all the people I've painted who mean a great deal to me—Karl and Anna Kuerner . . . , Helga . . . and X.' It's Kuerner's farm and the railroad tracks where my father was killed." Wyeth admitted that he had tried to infuse the landscape with the spirit of his father. "I got enamored with it and I painted on it like mad. It is my [19th-century French artist Gustave] Courbet's *Studio,* in which all his models are there, watching. My models are watching me and dancing because they all hope I'm dead. Ha! I'm there, but I'm gone."

Further Reading

The best book on Wyeth is Richard Meryman, *Andrew Wyeth* (1968). All the major paintings, as well as a number of the drybrush watercolors, are reproduced in excellent color. In the text Wyeth discusses the people and places of his paintings. A specialized study is Agnes Mongan, *Andrew Wyeth: Dry Brush and Pencil Drawings* (1966).

See also Thomas Hoving, *Andrew Wyeth: autobiography by Andrew Wyeth,* 1995; John Wilmerding, *Andrew Wyeth: the Helga Picgtures,* 1987; Gene Logsdon *Wyeth People: a Portrait of Andrew Wyeth as Seen by His Friends and Neighbors,* 1971. □

George Wythe

George Wythe (1726-1806), American jurist and law teacher, was one of the foremost legal authorities of the Revolutionary period.

George Wythe was born into a prominent Virginia planting family. At his father's death in 1729 the family estate went to an elder brother, and George did not enjoy the advantages of considerable wealth until his brother died in 1755. George's education was therefore largely informal; he learned Latin and Greek from his mother and studied law while working with an attorney.

Wythe served briefly in 1754 as attorney general of the colony of Virginia and held political office almost continuously from then until 1778. He repeatedly served in the House of Burgesses and was its clerk from 1769 to 1775. As the crisis between the Colonies and Great Britain developed, Wythe protested against the new imperial policies. He was a delegate to the Second Continental Congress in 1775 and signed the Declaration of Independence. On the state level he was a member of the committee that designed

Virginia's official seal. The Virginia Legislature appointed him to work with Thomas Jefferson, Edmund Pendleton, and others on the revision and codification of the state's laws. This work resulted in the elimination of feudal land practices from the law.

Wythe's contributions to the history of American jurisprudence were especially significant. He taught law to Jefferson and to many lawyers of future importance in the new republic. In 1779 Wythe was appointed professor of law in the College of William and Mary, the first such position in any American educational institution; he held the post for 11 years. From 1778 until his death he was also a judge in the Virginia chancery (or equity) court. On at least one occasion, he gave early voice to the distinctive American doctrine of judicial review-the power of courts to require that actions of government, particularly legislative enactments, conform to basic or constitutional law.

On June 8, 1806, Wythe died in Richmond-not of natural causes. He had no direct descendants and wrote a will leaving the bulk of his estate to a grand-nephew. The grand-nephew, in financial difficulties, used arsenic in an attempt to eliminate a coheir. The attempt was successful, but Wythe also consumed a fatal dose of the poison. He lived long enough to disinherit his murderer, who was never convicted as the only substantial evidence against him was the word of a black cook. Because of the cook's race his evidence was not admissible in the Virginia courts of the time.

Further Reading

There is no biography of Wythe. He is discussed in David Mays, *Edmund Pendleton* (1952); Charles S. Sydnor *Gentlemen Freeholders* (1952); Alf J. Mapp, Jr., *The Virginia Experiment: The Old Dominion's Role in the Making of America, 1607-1781* (1957); and Clifford Dowdey, *The Golden Age: A Climate for Greatness, Virginia 1732-1775* (1970).

Additional Sources

Blackburn, Joyce., *George Wythe of Williamsburg,* New York: Harper & Row, 1975.

Brown, Imogene E., *American Aristides: a biography of George Wythe,* Rutherford N.J: Fairleigh Dickinson University Press, 1981.

Dill, Alonzo Thomas., *George Wythe, teacher of liberty,* Williamsburg, Va. (Box JF, Williamsburg 23185): Virginia Independence Bicentennial Commission, 1979.

Kirtland, Robert Bevier., *George Wythe: lawyer, revolutionary, judge,* New York: Garland, 1986. □

Iannis Xenakis

Iannis Xenakis (born 1922), Greek-French composer and architect, was one of the first to react against the post-Weberian serialists and pointillists who dominated music in the 1950s. Initially, his most notable achievement was the invention of "stochastic" music based on the mathematical laws of probability. This is a method of composition which uses mathematical formulae to calculate the length and intensity of each sound. As his career has progressed, he became one of the world's best-known composers of electronic music, or music generated by computers.

Iannis Xenakis was was born into a cataclysmic time in pre-World War II history, and like many others who were forced to put their ambitions aside until the world was at peace again, he had to wait until his middle twenties before he was able to follow the desire of his heart and become a composer.

He came from a prosperous Greek family based in Rumania, and was a happy little boy until he was five years old. Then, the death of his mother changed everything. Yearning for her tenderness while in the care of impersonal governesses and nurses, he kept her memory alive by taking a keen interest in the music she had enjoyed.

At the age of ten he was sent to a select Greek boarding school where he did not fit in with the other boys. With few school friends he was intensely unhappy socially, but a natural talent for mathematics and classical Greek literature nevertheless made him blossom in the classroom and gave

him the courage to sign up for piano lessons and the school choir. He graduated from high school in 1938, and eager to shake off his loneliness, he refused his father's offer to send him to England to study naval engineering. Instead, he chose to stay in Athens to attend the Polytechnic School and earn an engineering degree.

World War II: Underground Activities

For his first two years as an undergraduate everything went as expected, and Xenakis was able to immerse himself in the physics, law, mathematics, and ancient literature which were basic curriculum requirements.

But World War II was blasting its way across Europe, and in April 1941, Hitler's soldiers marched into Greece. The Polytechnic was closed. However, its students had no intention of submitting quietly to the famine and the collapse of the economy that accompanied the war. Instead, they quickly organized an underground resistance movement.

Ignoring his father's protests, Xenakis initially joined the Greek Resistance but soon switched to the Communist party. Fervent and idealistic, he even volunteered for a student battalion when savage protests erupted against the British occupiers in 1944. His enthusiasm did not serve him well. During one skirmish he was caught by a shell from a British tank and was left to cope with the loss of an eye and a disfiguring facial scar.

Meanwhile, his worried father had been searching all over Athens for him. As soon as the two were reunited, the wounded warrior was whisked into the hospital, where he remained until March, 1945.

By the time he was well enough to leave the hospital, the war was practically over. Without enthusiasm, because he had privately decided that his heart lay with music,

Xenakis returned to the Polytechnic in April to finish his engineering degree. He graduated in 1946, but was afraid to stay in his shattered homeland and wait for whatever punishment the new anti-Communist government might devise for him.

Starting Afresh in Paris

With his father's help he stowed away on a cargo ship bound for Italy, where the French Communists met him and smuggled him into Paris. By chance, he had his engineering diploma in his pocket, and was therefore qualified to take a job with an architect named Le Corbusier, who happened to be recruiting both engineers and architects to design a large government housing project. The spare, modern architecture favored by Le Corbusier suited Xenakis. Despite the fact that he had entered Paris illegally, he managed to enjoy his work, revelling especially in the rational mathematical calculations which ruled the principles of building design.

At night he wasted no time in frivolous pursuits, but absorbed himself in the music that had been on hold for so long. He studied and wrote, but he was far too intelligent and rational to assume that he could learn everything without the benefit of a teacher. He realized that his knowledge of musical history was sketchy and his understanding of counterpoint and harmony still sadly lacking.

A Difficult Student

He was determined to educate himself, but his own stubborn nature was to prove a real stumbling block. His first attempt to find a teacher took him to the Ecole Normale de Musique, where the distinguished Arthur Honegger was on the faculty. Unfortunately, this association was doomed. At one class Honegger listened to part of a composition Xenakis had written and dared to point out some structural rule-breaking. Xenakis refused to accept the well-meant criticism with grace. Furiously gathering up his music, he accused Honegger of being far too traditional to appreciate such original work, then left the building.

He next tried to find a teacher in 1949 when he started classes with Darius Milhaud, a composer so inventive that he often wrote music set simultaneously in several keys. But Milhaud, too, fell short of Xenakis' expectations. Meticulous in his own creativity, he advised changes to Xenakis' works which Xenakis thought unimportant. These lessons, too, soon came to an end.

Torn between his need to learn and his yearning to be taken seriously as a composer, Xenakis seethed to his boss in frustration. Le Corbusier listened sympathetically, thought about this problem, and eventually suggested a teacher who was to change Xenakis' life.

Creativity Comes to the Fore

Olivier Messiaen was a renowned organist and a composer far ahead of his time. When confronted by Xenakis' questions about whether he should heed all his critics, disregard his previous work, and start learning harmony and counterpoint from the beginning, Messiaen gave him a thoughtful answer. According to Nouritza Matossian, who interviewed Messiaen for the biography *Xenakis,* Messiaen said, "No, you are almost thirty. You have the good fortune of being Greek, an architect, and having studied special mathematics. Take advantage of these things. Do them in your music."

Xenakis took his advice and began to compose music based on the mathematical laws of probability. Rather than start with a melody, he began with one sound and then developed it according to the probability that certain sounds, rhythms, and pitches would recur in the piece a set number of times. To describe this completely new type of music he invented the word "stochastic."

His first publicly presented piece, *Metastis,* was first heard in 1953. As musicologist David Ewen suggests in his book *Composers of Tomorrow's Music,* "Here, and in *Pithoprakata,* a composition that followed a year or so later, Xenakis explored the possibilities of simulating electronically produced sounds and sonorities with conventional instruments." When completed, *Ppithoprakata* featured tapping of string instruments by the players' hands, staccato claps from the woodblock, and Xenakis' characteristic arpeggios played by strings.

From here, it was a natural progression for him to electronic music. At first working with doctored tapes and then, in time, on a computer, he meticulously calculated the interrelationship of elements such as each sound itself, its length and intensity, the instrument on which it was to be played, and its frequency. All these separate components were then combined into suitable musical groups by the computer and retranslated into musical notes by Xenakis himself.

He did not stop there. When synthesizers became available, he made use of them too. Here, because the synthesizer has a battery of switches which can each produce and fine-tune a sound immediately, he was able to work faster on his compositions and produce a huge variety of works.

Recognition

Between the 1960s and the end of the 1980s Xenakis wrote more than 100 musical compositions. He also authored several books, including his *Formalized Music* which appeared in English in 1970. In addition, he held faculty appointments at the University of Indiana, the University of London, and the University of Paris. He also found time to present selected compositions in extremely unusual ways.

In 1971 for instance, in order to show the harmony between his music, history, and a natural topography, he chose to present a light and sound show featuring his composition *Persepolis* at the real Persepolis, a ruin which had been destroyed in the third century by Alexander to avenge the burning of the Acropolis by Xerxes in 480 B.C. Persepolis is in present-day Iran, and transporting all the necessary technological equipment from Europe was extremely difficult. Nevertheless, Xenakis achieved the desired effect.

Fame

By the 1990s Xenakis was a musical legend whose music was no longer appreciated only by other *avant garde* composers. Audiences, always leery of ultra-modern music, were now starting to understand that he had invented an entirely new method of composition.

In 1994 he was the featured composer at the Oslo festival of contemporary music's Ultima 94. A large selection of his music was played, including *Okho,* a 1989 composition for three middle-eastern drums, as well as a 70-minute long concert version of his *Oresteia.* Its performers included a chamber chorus, a children's chorus, an ensemble of winds and percussion, and a cello.

Each of these is now a cherished part of the contemporary music repertoire, as well as a milestone in music's entry into the electronic age.

Further Reading

Bois, Mario, *Iannis Xenakis, the Man and His Music: A Conversation with the Composer and a Description of His Works* (1967). Xenakis is discussed in Peter S. Hansen, *An Introduction to Twentieth Century Music* (3d ed. 1971).

Additional Sources

Ewen, David, *Composers of Tomorrows's Music,* Dodd, Mead & Company, 1971.
Matossian, Nouritza, *Xenakis,* Kahn & Averill, 1986.
American Record Guide, March/April 1995; January/February 1997. □

Xenophon

The Greek historian, essayist, and military expert Xenophon (ca. 430-ca. 355 B.C.) was the most popular of the Greek historians. He facilitated the change from the Thucydidean tradition of history to rhetoric.

The son of Gryllus of the Athenian deme of Erchia Xenophon was of aristocratic background and means. He studied under Socrates. Married to Philesia, he had two sons, both of whom were educated in Sparta. In 401, despite a warning from Socrates and consultation with the oracle at Delphi, he became involved in the expedition of Cyrus against Artaxerxes at the invitation of Proxenus of Thebes. Xenophon was initially unaware of Cyrus's true purpose, which was to gain the crown of Persia. After Cyrus was killed at the battle of Cunaxa in Babylonia, his troops dispersed; Clearchus and other Greek commanders were treacherously murdered by the Persian satrap Tissaphernes, and Xenophon was elected general.

The Spartan general Chirisophus and Xenophon took command of the retreat of the Ten Thousand, the Greek force trapped in the center of the Persian Empire. The generals led the Ten Thousand along the Tigris, across Armenia to Trapezus (modern Trabzon) on the Black Sea, to Chrysopolis (modern Üsküdar) on the Bosporus in 399-an incredible journey of some 1,500 miles. This "March Up Country" is the subject of Xenophon's *Anabasis.*

Some of Xenophon's troops joined Seuthes, King of Thrace. In the spring of 399 others joined the Lacedaemonian Thibron, who warred against Tissaphernes and Pharnabazus. We have no knowledge of Xenophon's activities in the years immediately thereafter. Three years later Xenophon joined the Spartan king Agesilaus in the continuing battle against Persia. A warm and intimate friendship grew up between the two men, and the eulogistic sketch *Agesilaus* is a permanent record of this friendship. When Agesilaus was recalled in 394, Xenophon accompanied him and was present at the battle against the Athenians at Coronea. He was then banished from Athens. There is some dispute as to whether his participation in the expedition of Cyrus against the Persian king, his close association with the Spartans, or his presence at the battle of Coronea with Athens's enemy was the reason.

Agesilaus gave Xenophon an estate at Scillus near Olympia in Elis, and he lived there happily, writing prolifically, until the Spartans were defeated at the battle of Leuctra in 371, when the Eleans expelled him. Xenophon is reported to have removed himself to Corinth, where he may have ended his days. Though the decree of banishment against him was revoked, probably in 369 (presumably because his "Laconism" was acceptable when Athens and Sparta were allies), Xenophon never returned to Athens. The exact date of his death is uncertain; tradition and a reference in the *Hellenica* (IV, 4, 35ff) to the assassination of Alexander of Pherae would seem to point to a time after 357 B.C.,

probably in 355. Apparently all his works have survived, and they may be arbitrarily grouped into three general categories.

Historical Works

The *Anabasis* ("March Up Country"), perhaps Xenophon's most famous and most exciting work, in seven books, was originally published under the pen name Themistogenes of Syracuse. It is a history of the expedition of the Greek mercenaries of the younger Cyrus through the Persian Empire. The *Hellenica,* in seven books, is a continuation of the history of Thucydides, from the Peloponnesian War to the Theban supremacy, and employs the annalistic method and exhibits a pro-Spartan bias. The period covered stretches from the end of Thucydides (411 B.C.) to the Battle of Mantinea (362 B.C.). There is some question about the division and completeness of the work. The encomium to Agesilaus may have been composed shortly after the Spartan king's death in 360. Written in the style of the rhetorician Gorgias, it is not carefully constructed.

Technical and Didactic Works

The *Hipparchus,* which is in two parts—one on memoranda and another on proposals for implementations—is a tract on the duties of a cavalry commander, addressed to one who is about to assume that position. The *Cynegeticus* is a curious medley on hunting, an enumeration of the pupils of Chiron, praise of the hunt, and an attack on the Sophists. *On Equitation,* the oldest treatise on the subject, is authoritatively done and well written.

Philosophical Works

Xenophon's philosophical writings fall into two subdivisions. The first, subject-or theme-oriented (political science, education, economics), includes *The Lacedaemonian Constitution,* an unequal and careless account of Spartan political institutions, adulatory in tone, assigning their origin to Lycurgus, with whom Xenophon identifies his own ideas; and the *Cyropaedia,* in eight books, described as a political romance. Using the history of the elder Cyrus, the founder of the Persian monarchy, Xenophon presents the reader with a dull, monotonous, repetitious handbook of ideal kingly behavior with Cyrus as the model. Considered Xenophon's most polished work, the *Cyropaedia* clearly demonstrates his dislike of democratic constitutions and his preference for a Spartanlike constitution, with practical advice for military commanders, lively descriptions of battle, and suggestions for the education of good citizens. The treatise *On Revenues* (*On Finance*) contains advice for the amelioration of the Athenian public treasury and also an argument for peace.

The second philosophical subdivision is much more concerned with individuals and their ethical behavior, particularly with Socrates. The most famous of this group is undoubtedly *The Memorabilia of Socrates,* in four books. Reflecting his own practical mind, Xenophon here strives to defend his teacher against the charges of impiety and corruption of youth; he proceeds through a series of conversations to illustrate Socrates's moral teachings. It is a limited picture of one side of the great philosopher, and a work whose historicity, construction, depth, credibility, and value have been subject to debate. *The Apology of Socrates* is a brief speech written to justify Socrates's weak defense of himself, and it claims to have recorded material from Hermogenes. Parts of it are found also in Plato. The *Symposium* is also useful for reconstructing the picture of Socrates. Its setting is the house of the rich Athenian Callias during a celebration of the victory of Autolycus at the Great Panathenaia in 422 B.C. The nature of love and friendship is the philosophical subject, and it is discussed with lightness and pleasantness, though Socrates's speech to Callias is pointedly serious. Plato may have written his *Symposium* as a corrective to Xenophon's. The *Hieron,* a dialogue between king Hiero of Syracuse and Simonides of Ceos, who paid a visit to Syracuse in 476, contrasts the lot of the ruler with that of a private person. Which of them is happier is argued out in a way that must have been of particular interest to the Socratics. The *Oeconomicus* is considered a charming work that reflects Xenophon's life at Scillus, though it is a dialogue between Socrates and Critobulus on estate management and records a discussion on the subject between Socrates and Ischomachus.

Although Xenophon's works were admired in antiquity, he is not an author of high critical ability or of outstanding intellectual or moral caliber. His style was simple and straightforward. A man of action as well as a man of letters, he was a nonprofessional in many subjects but a master of military science. More a popularizer and adapter of other people's works, he was not creative, profound, or even original. Nevertheless, he was a meticulous observer and a fair assessor of character, and his sympathies were broad and real.

Further Reading

There have been numerous translations of Xenophon's works, but no recent books of a general nature on Xenophon. G. B. Nussbaum, *The Ten Thousand: A Study in Social Organization and Action in Xenophon's Anabasis* (1967), is a useful study. Xenophon and his works are also discussed in Michael Grant, *The Ancient Historians* (1970), and Stephen Usher, *The Historians of Greece and Rome* (1970). □

Xerxes

Xerxes (reigned 486-465 B.C.), a king of Persia, made an unsuccessful effort to conquer Greece in 480-479, suffering a major naval defeat at the Battle of Salamis.

Xerxes was the son of Darius I and Atossa, daughter of Cyrus I. When Xerxes succeeded his father, Egypt was already in revolt and troubles soon broke out in Babylon; further, there was still pending the matter of the Greeks, where the Persian defeat at Marathon called for vengeance. He crushed the revolts in both Egypt and Babylon with great severity, not sparing even the gods, and then turned to the conquest of Greece.

The superiority of the Greek infantry, man for man, was by then well known, but Xerxes' force outnumbered the Greeks, and he decided to make a land invasion around the northern end of the Aegean. Enormous preparations were made all the way to the borders of Greece. There could be no secrecy, but with overwhelming strength surprise was unnecessary. The Greek historian Herodotus numbered Xerxes' army in the millions, but 300,000 is a frequent modern estimate. The Greeks responded with a "pan-Hellenic" league for defense. Though by no means all the states actually joined, even those that did found it easier to propose plans than to get them agreed on.

In the spring of 480 B.C. Xerxes advanced, and the Greeks finally sent 10,000 men under the Spartan king Leonidas to block the Pass of Thermopylae. A fleet was sent to Artemisium at the northeastern tip of Euboea to keep the Persians from turning the pass by sea. After several days of heroic resistance, the Greeks were defeated when a traitor led a picked Persian force by a mountain track around the pass, laying central Greece open to the Persians. The Greek fleet withdrew to Salamis off Athens.

Xerxes occupied and then burned Athens. What should the Greek fleet do? The army was fortifying a wall across the Isthmus of Corinth to protect the Peloponnesus (southern Greece), and most of the commanders wanted to withdraw to the Isthmus to prevent a Persian landing south of the wall. The Athenian naval leader, Themistocles, however, wanted to fight in the narrow Bay of Salamis, where Persian numbers would not count. He sent a secret letter to Xerxes promising that if the Persians attacked the Athenians would desert to them in return for the restoration of Athens. Xerxes sent in his fleet but the Athenians did not desert, and Xerxes watched the Greeks win a great victory at Salamis.

Xerxes returned to Asia-not in the flight the Greeks later loved to picture but to protect his communications—leaving his general Mardonius with a still large force to complete the conquest. In 479 B.C. Mardonius was defeated and killed at Plataea, and the Persian army disintegrated. Greece was free.

The war dragged on, chiefly a naval affair with Athens leading, until the Persians were cleared from Europe and the coasts of the Aegean, but Xerxes took no further part in it. He retired to his capitals and spent the remainder of his reign building, particularly at Persepolis. He became a drunken, embittered man, a pawn of his scheming courtiers, and was murdered in Susa by the captain of the guards.

Further Reading

The principal source on Xerxes is Herodotus, *Histories,* but it ends with the failure of Xerxes' invasion; information on his later years appears only in isolated references. Among modern works G. B.Grundy, *The Great Persian War* (1901; repr. 1969), and Peter Green, *Xerxes at Salamis* (1970), contain detailed information on Xerxes. Albert T. Olmstead, *A History of the Persian Empire* (1948), and Roman Ghirshman, *Iran, from the Earliest Times to the Islamic Conquest* (1954), discuss Xerxes as a builder. □

Xiang Jingyu

Xiang Jingyu (1895-1928) was a pioneer of the women's liberation movement, who founded China's national women's organization.

In the 1920s, Xiang Jingyu was engaged in the women's liberation movement, primarily in Shanghai, but also in Beijing (Peking) and Guangzhou (Canton). In charge of the publication "Women's Review," she was also instrumental in initiating public schools for girls and organizing working women. She united women of all social strata into the country's struggle for civil rights and founded the China Women's Federation, marking the start of a nationwide movement.

Xupu, where Xiang Jingyu was born, was a distant county 800 miles away from Changsha, the capital of the province. It was September 4, 1895, the last years of the Qing (Ch'ing) dynasty, and China was deep in crisis. Weakened by over population and economic decline, the country was faced with an inability to halt the aggressive and expanding Western nations in the mid-19th century. While the ostensible causes of conflict were China's refusal to trade with the West, the struggle was really a collision of the traditional Chinese system and the modernizing West. The tendency to absorb all things Western prevailed throughout China. Born into a businessman's family, with four brothers sent to study in Japan, Xiang Jingyu was naturally influenced by these trends.

In her youth, she was especially close to her eldest brother Xiang Xianyue, a graduate of Japan's Waseda University and a member of *Tung Men Hui* (Chinese League), founded by Dr. Sun Yat-sen. With Xianyue's support, Xiang Jingyu became the first girl in her county who applied to enter a new type of school based on modern educational ideas. To continue her education, in 1908 she went to Changde, where she often read newspapers edited by revolutionaries and listened to her brother's opinions about the revolutionary activities of foreign countries. When only six or seven, Xiang Jingyu had been very attracted to a story about the legendary Chinese heroine Hua Mulan who had enlisted in the army, disguised as a man to replace her father, and had won awards for her brilliant military merits. As Xiang Jingyu grew older, she also became fascinated with the French revolutionary Madame Roland.

In 1911, in a garden doused with spring sunlight, Xiang Jingyu declared ties of sisterhood with her six fellow schoolgirls in a traditional Chinese ceremonial. The following vow was made: "We seven sisters are of the same will: to boost women's morale, to study hard, to fight for equality between men and women, and to save China by popularizing education." The vow gave testament to the status of Chinese women, who constituted half of the population: they had no opportunity for education and thus could not earn independent livings, making them reliant on men. It was apparent to some that, as the prosperity of the nation was based on well-rounded people from good families, and the center of a

good family was the mother, it was necessary to enlighten women. Such women would serve as moral examples to others, would be concerned with state affairs, and would stand for revolution. By this logic, educated women were vital in the preservation of China. This theory, cherished by Xiang Jingyu until the age of 25, imbued her with persistence and courage.

In Changde, Xiang Jingyu was nicknamed Mo-tse, after the ancient Chinese philosopher, whom she highly regarded, believing that his theory of "multi-love" was equivalent to the Western concept of universal fraternity. Studying hard at Hunan Provincial Number One Girl's Normal School, she became one of the school's finest students. When vacations began, on the boat sailing home, she read and made notes in her cabin, only venturing out on deck for fresh air in the early morning. Strict standards of morale and behavior were self-imposed; she even criticized herself for "giggling following others" in her diary. As health was vital to study, she practiced physical training. In order to temper her will and focus her mind, she learned *qigong*, a traditional deep-breathing exercise. The character and ideals she acquired through study and self-cultivation, which were traditionally advocated by Chinese culture, encouraged her belief that it was her duty to rekindle China. Recognized by teachers as one of the three "excellent girls" in the school, she was known among schoolmates as a saint.

In 1916, Xiang Jingyu completed her study at Zhounan Girl's School and decided to return to her hometown and teach. At the time, however, the Xupu Girl's School existed in name only: the principal had long since resigned, school buildings had been swept away by floods, and teachers or pupils were nowhere to be found. Xiang Jingyu, then 20 years old, took over as principal. With financial support from her family and other donations, she renovated the ruined school buildings and gave her schoolmates priority as teachers. She wrote decrees for the county government urging parents to send their daughters to school and traveled into remote mountain areas to enlist female pupils. She also succeeded in liberating most of the girls in the area from the monstrous practice of foot-binding. The school was re-established, and the following year an exhibition featuring the school's achievements was held in the county town, making a strong impression on the community. Many of the school's pupils went on to higher education. Still, during this time, feudalism prevailed in China, and, among other things, conflicts arose because the school was not teaching classical Chinese literature. More embarrassing, the commander of the local garrison tried everything possible to marry her, although he was repeatedly refused. Unable to continue her career in Xupu, Xiang Jingyu heard of a work-study program in France. For this purpose, she traveled to Beijing, then returned to Changsha and organized the French work-study program in Hunan province.

On the ship sailing to France, she met Cai Hesun. Like Mao Zedong, Cai was also a well-known student leader in Hunan province and would later be one of the founders of the Chinese Communist party. Though both Xiang and Cai were known for their belief in celibacy, they fell in love and were married in France several months later. Called the

''Xiang-Cai alliance,'' the marriage attracted much attention, as it represented the combination of two famous and influential persons. Since Xiang Jingyu's beliefs were greatly influenced by her husband, she now turned from democracy to Marxism. She no longer believed that China could be saved through cultural and educational methods, but that political struggle should be waged and that women could be liberated only through the complete reform of society. Thus, in France, she became a revolutionary.

In 1922, Xiang Jingyu returned to China and became the head of the women's department of the Chinese Communists. Based in Shanghai, she threw herself into the women's movement both in the south and north. With the help of women's rights organizations throughout the country, she actively encouraged women's participation in politics, girls enlistment in schools, the employment of women, the prevention of prostitution, and the protection of women worker's interests, etc. She saw the women's movement as more than a women's rights campaign, pointing out that in a country which had no universal human and civil rights, the women's movement did not mean wringing some rights out of men while ignoring the basic problems posed by a lack of civil rights.

Xiang Jingyu set a clear course for the women's movement in China. Believing that educated women were the backbone of the women's movement, she emphasized the importance of mingling with female students in colleges and universities to cultivate leaders for the women's movement. She also believed that the massive force of laboring women should form the nucleus of the women's movement, so she set up public schools for girls and night schools for working women. In addition, she led several women workers' strikes. Through her strenuous efforts, the women's movement in China changed its image; it ceased to be a movement for Christian women or privileged women of the upper classes and became instead a powerful, large scale movement that included all strata of Chinese society. In 1924, cooperation between Nationalists and Communists offered conditions for a united women's movement in China, and Xiang Jingyu became the head this movement in Shanghai. In November of that year, Dr. Sun Yat-sen went to Beijing and appealed to the government to hold the national assembly to formulate a constitution; soon thereafter, a movement appeared all over the country demanding the convening of the national assembly. This proved an opportunity for the energetic development of the women's movement. With the leadership of Xiang Jingyu, a Women's Federation for the Convening of National Assembly was established in Shanghai and similar acts were followed by women's organizations in all corners of the country. Xiang Jingyu proposed the formation of a united national women's organization, and the China Women's Federation declared its founding in 1925, signifying that the women's civil rights movement had taken on a nationwide scale.

In 1925, Xiang Jingyu and Cai Hesun's marriage began to falter and would soon be dissolved. That same year, the Communists dispatched her to study in Moscow. Returning in 1927, she was assigned to work in Wuhan. But in July, when the cooperation between the Nationalists and Com-

munists collapsed, the Nationalists launched a massacre of Communists and left-wing Nationalists. Xiang Jingyu, who persisted in working under dangerous circumstances, was eventually arrested and killed the following year. She was 33.

Further Reading

Biography Research Association of CPC Personages. *Biographies of CPC Personages.* Vol 6. Shanxi People's Publishing House, September 1982.

Women's Movement History Research Office of All-China Women's Federation. *History Materials on Chinese Women Movement (1921-1927).* People's Publishing House, 1981.

Haozhi, He. *Biography of Xiang Jinyu.* Shanghai People's Publishing House, 1990. □

Xu Guangqi

Xu Guangqi (1562–1633) was a Chinese scholar-official, who rose to one of the highest government positions in the Ming dynasty, pioneered in the introduction of Western science and technology into China, and became one of the "Three Pillars of the Catholic Religion in China" in the 17th century.

Xu Guangqi was born in Shanghai in 1562. At the age of 19, he passed the first stage of the Chinese civil service examination system, receiving the *shengyuan* (bachelor) degree. He did not, however, pass the second stage *juren* (master) degree examination until 1597, and even at that late date his success was something of a miracle. When the chief examiner Chiao Hung (1541-1620), concerned that he could not find an outstanding candidate for the ''Number One Graduate'' position, began to review some of the rejected exam papers, he was surprised to find the excellent essays of Xu Guangqi. Quickly elevated from the ''failed grade'' to the ''Number One Position,'' Xu became well-known. But it took him another two attempts over a seven-year span before he passed the third stage *jin-shi (chin-shih;* doctorate) exam in 1604. At the age of 42, he was finally qualified for higher government positions.

Xu was born into a family whose finances were in disarray. Although his grandfather had amassed a small fortune through commercial dealings, the Xu family estate had been plundered by the Japanese pirates who had raided the Shanghai area from 1551 to 1557. Division of family properties with relatives led to further impoverishment. Xu's father engaged in both farming and teaching to make ends meet, while his grandmother and mother augmented income with spinning and weaving. Out of sheer necessity, Xu combined his preparations for the civil service examinations with jobs in farming and handicraft. Rumors of renewed Japanese pirate raids also drove him to pay attention to military affairs and to study the problems of maritime defense. He became aware that the Ming dynasty was ten times weaker militarily than the Song (Sung or Soong) dynasty (960-1279) which had been conquered by the Mongols. The question of how to make the dynasty prosperous and strong absorbed a great deal of his thinking. Influenced by traditional Chinese theories, he became convinced by the year 1597 that it was only through emphasis on agriculture that China could be prosperous, and it was only through a properly trained and equipped military force that the Ming dynasty could be strong.

According to his only son, Xu Guangqi harbored a deep sense of patriotism toward the Chinese nation. With his interest in agriculture, handicraft, technology, and military arts, he gradually developed a scientific spirit and innovative attitude. His son says that Xu Guangqi regularly "investigated ancient records and evaluated contemporary sources concerning the national economy," and that he "took voluminous notes and gathered various information on economic matters."

By the early 17th century, the Ming dynasty was not only economically and militarily weak, but also politically corrupt. The abilities of the emperors degenerated and the eunuchs steadily gained power. Chinese scholar officials who were concerned about the fate of the nation became restless. Some of them formed partisan groups to advocate needed reforms. Some sought escapes through their interest in Buddhism and Taoism. Others searched for new answers to the old problem of dynastic decline. Thus, the new knowledge about a distant Great West (i.e., Europe), which the Jesuit missionary Matteo Ricci (1552-1610) and his companions brought to China from 1583 onward, attracted the attention of a number of enlightened and patriotic Confucian scholar officials. It was in such a political and intellectual climate that Xu Guangqi was converted to the Roman Catholic faith.

There were several factors involved in Xu's conversion. Firstly, the new knowledge concerning a well-governed Europe attracted his deep interest. By 1603, Xu believed that the Catholic religion could supplement Confucianism, replace Buddhism, and facilitate "good government." He was convinced that the new religion could make the heart of each Chinese sincere and honorable, thus recreating a noble society in China. Secondly, Xu admired the lifestyle of the Jesuit missionaries such as Ricci, Lazare Cattaneo (1560-1640), and Joao de Rocha (1566-1623). He asserted that the saintly lifestyle of the Jesuits was comparable to that of the sages idealized in Confucian literature through the centuries. Thirdly, Xu was searching for the meaning of life and death, and he found that the existence of a personal Christian God allowed him peace of mind. Fourthly, Xu was fascinated by European science and technology which the Jesuits brought to China. He was interested particularly in Western geography, mathematics, astronomy, mechanics, hydraulics, and military arts. In each of the fields, China had its own achievements, but was falling behind.

Fifthly, the Jesuit missionaries, under the leadership of Ricci, had adopted a policy of cultural accommodation vis-a-vis Confucianism. This policy had grown out of a respect for the Chinese tradition and the Sinocentric view of the world. Realizing that the Europeanization policy adopted elsewhere had no future in China, the accommodation pol-icy allowed for the use of traditional Chinese terminology to express the religious ideas of Christianity. It permitted the Chinese converts to continue their participation in the performance of traditional Confucian civic rites. This policy impressed the Chinese intellectuals that Catholicism and Confucianism were complementary. According to Xu, the coming of the Jesuits was prompted by the fact that they "realized that Confucianism also teaches the doctrine of service for Heaven and the cultivation of the individual mind." In China, a Confucian scholar official could adhere to any religious faith so long as he fulfilled his social and political obligations to the emperor and the state. The cultural accommodation policy thus made it possible for Chinese scholar officials, such as Xu Guangqi, Li Zhizao (1565-1630), Yang Tingyun (1557-1627), to make necessary changes within the Chinese tradition.

Last, but most important, the conversion of Xu Guangqi was made possible because it occurred at a time when the Chinese did not possess any first-hand knowledge of Europe. Neither did they know anything about the Portuguese *Padroado* (Patronage) which was, according to George H. Dunne, the "union between the mission and colonial imperialism" insisted on by the kings of Portugal. Being an idealist, Xu was more or less convinced that a utopia existed in Europe. He had no knowledge about the Protestant Reformation then taking place.

The conversion of Xu Guangqi to the Roman Catholic faith was, nevertheless, an important chapter in the history of Sino-Western cultural contacts. In the past, Catholic writers in China and in the West have generally glorified this unusual event. But some modern Chinese writers tend to downgrade its significance and prefer to stress Xu's preeminence as a scientist and authority on agriculture. During his lifetime, Xu himself seemed to have succeeded in compartmentalizing his own religious acculturation. That is, in religious matters, he accepted the Roman Catholic faith and followed the instructions of the Jesuit fathers. But in the field of political and social obligations to the state, he acted like a typical Confucian scholar official in his loyal service to the dynasty.

In political activities, Xu was a member of two important offices of the Ming imperial court from 1604 to 1621: the Hanlin Academy, which provided literary service to the court, and the Supervisorate of Imperial Instruction, which directed the education of the heir apparent to the throne. These positions gave him knowledge of the inner workings of the court; they also insulated him from the factional strife which became frequent as the dynasty weakened. He probably knew that he was not without sympathy in the court when he defended the Jesuits against unjustified accusations in 1616. Although he had to observe the mandatory three-year mourning period from 1607 to 1610 after the death of his father in 1607, his positions in these offices would be resumed in 1611 with regular promotions. He would also be assigned a few special duties: in 1611, he would be asked to teach Confucian classics to the eunuchs; in 1613, he would serve as a co-examiner for the *jin-shi* examination; and in 1617 he would be dispatched to the province of Ningxia (Ninghsia) to bestow imperial investiture on a member of the imperial family.

Before returning to Shanghai in 1607 to observe the mourning period, Xu received instructions in mathematics, astronomy, and Christian theology from Matteo Ricci. A lasting result of their joint efforts was the preparation of a Chinese translation of the first six chapters of Euclid's *Elements of Geometry* which was published in May of 1607. This translation was based on the Latin version of Euclid produced by Christopher Clavius, a famous Jesuit mathematician and Ricci's professor in Rome. It became the first Western scientific book rendered into the Chinese language. Following this, they also produced a Chinese translation of a work on trigonometry. In addition, Xu wrote a postscript for a book on Christian teaching written by Ricci. Xu wrote two booklets on the surveying method as well.

On his way to Shanghai via Nanjing (Nanking), Xu also invited Father Cattaneo to establish a Catholic church in his hometown. This church eventually developed into a major Catholic center in Shanghai by the early 20th century. Meanwhile, Xu used the mourning period to engage in agricultural enterprises. He planted sweet potatoes, which were then introduced into China from America, and advocated their widespread planting in order to deal with drought and flood emergencies. He promoted the seeding of turnips for food as well. Recognizing that the willow trees which dotted the countryside had only aesthetical appeal, he advised the farmers to plant a special evergreen tree and bamboo tree as both had real economic values. Moreover, by discarding ancient myth, he proved beyond doubt that cotton could be planted in North China and that the textile industry could be gainfully established there as well. When news of Matteo Ricci's death reached him, Xu made preparations for his return to Beijing (Peking) and was there when Ricci's sealed coffin was buried on November 1st, 1611, on All Saints' Day.

From 1611 onward, Xu continued to introduce Western scientific and technological knowledge into China. With the help of the Jesuits, he published in 1612 a work on the Western system of water conservation and irrigation. At that time, he also made an unsuccessful bid to have the Ming court employ Jesuits to reform the Chinese lunar calendar on which many of the farm activities were based. In 1613, securing a sick leave, he went to the area of Tianjin (Tientsin), about 100 miles from Beijing, to establish a 120-acre (800 *mou*) experimental farm. While there, he tried new methods of reclamation, irrigation, and flood control. He also experimented with the utilization of fertilizers and the planting of rice, beans, mulberry trees in the northern climate.

In July of 1616, Xu was quickly recalled to the capital. It was at that time that a conservative official in Nanjing initiated the persecution and deportation of the Jesuits. Private church services and rapid conversions had fostered suspicions of secret aims. Xu boldly defended the missionaries, offering to receive punishment himself should there be any truth in the false charges. His petition to the throne, the *Pien-hsüeh chang-su* (*Memorial on Western Teachings*), is the most important document in the early history of the Chinese Catholic Church. Eventually Xu, together with Li Zhizao and Yang Tingyun, were able to protect those Jesuits who were not involved in the Nanjing episode.

While in the north in the 1610s, Xu had worried about the safety of his son's family when he heard rumors of renewed designs on Shanghai by Japanese pirates. The rumors were false, however, and no attack occurred. Then the Manchu-Qing tribes began to threaten the Ming dynasty's mandate to rule China. Although Xu used every effort to propose measures to deal with the Manchu challenge, he was unable to alter the gradual decay of the Ming rule, especially after the notorious eunuch Wei Zhongxian (Wei Chung-hsien; 1568-1627) gained control of the government from 1621 to 1627. As a consequence, Xu was forced to retire to his hometown in Shanghai, and he returned to his agricultural studies. It was during those years that he compiled the *Nung-cheng chuan-shu* (Complete Treatise on Agriculture) which became one of the five most important works on agriculture in Chinese history. He also published his recollections concerning the throne, and its dealings with the Manchu threat, under the title *Hsü-shih pao-yen* (Xu's Private Thoughts). Copies of this book were later destroyed during the literary inquisition ordered by the Manchu Emperor Qianlong (Ch'ien-lung; r. 1736-96). Fortunately, a rare copy was kept in the French Bibliotheque Nationale in Paris and was reprinted in 1933 to commemorate the 350th anniversary of the death of Xu Guangqi.

Xu ended his years of forced retirement in 1628 after the Chong Zhen emperor, the last Ming ruler, ascended the throne. In five years, Xu rose from the post of vice minister in the Ministry of Rites to grand secretary in the imperial cabinet and concurrently the Minister of Rites. Though he achieved great prestige and additional recognition, other grand secretaries with seniority in the imperial cabinet monopolized the political power. Xu decided to concentrate his efforts in the Calendrical Bureau for which he was also the head. In completing the reform of the Chinese calendar from 1629 until his death in 1633, he earned the perpetual gratitude of the Chinese people. In that task, he brought in the Jesuits to help. He not only safeguarded their positions in China but also paved the way for the German Jesuit Johann Adam Schall von Bell (1591-1666) to become influential in the early Manchu dynasty. Under Xu's direction, the Jesuits and their Chinese co-workers translated Western books on astronomy into Chinese, designed new astronomical instruments, calculated the movements of the celestial bodies, and produced a new system of Chinese lunar calendar which was in use officially from the mid-17th to the early years of the 20th century. Unofficially, this calendar is still referred to today when Chinese people everywhere in the world celebrate the annual lunar New Year's Day.

Xu again urged the use of Western cannons and firearms to cope with the Manchu threat. He also suggested the training of new armies and the enlistment of Portuguese soldiers. Due to official inertia, factional rivalries, and financial stringency, all of his appeals came to naught. The fall of the Ming dynasty could be partially traced to the fact that such measures as proposed by Xu were not implemented. Xu also recommended that the Calendrical Bureau be transformed into a sort of Science Academy, this also was not accepted by the imperial court. Had this proposal been acted upon, Chinese science nd technology would not have been so behind the Western world when the Opium War broke out in 1839.

In early 1628, however, Xu was overjoyed to see the publication of the *T'ien-hsueh ch'u-han* (*Books Related to the Lord of Heaven Religion—First Collection*). "Heaven Religion" meant Catholicism. This work, which consisted of 20 previously published titles written by the Jesuit missionaries and their Chinese collaborators, deals with various religious and scientific subjects. It stands out as a great landmark in the history of Sino-Western relations and a permanent tribute not only to Matteo Ricci and his Jesuit companions, but also to learned Chinese Catholics of the early 17th century.

Xu died on November 8th, 1633. His descendants continued to be active in the Catholic Church in China. A distant relative of the 11th generation was Madame Chiang Kai-shek (Song Meiling).

Further Reading

Kuang-ch'i, Hsü (Collected Writings of Xu Guangqi). Edited by Wang Chung-min. Shanghai: Chung-hua Book Co., 1963.

"Kuang-ch'i, Hsü" in A. H. Hummel, ed., *Emminent Chinese of the Ch'ing Period.* Library of Congress, 1943-44, pp. 316-19.

Kuang-ch'i nien-p'u, Hsü (Chronological Biography of Xu Guangqi). Edited by Liang Chia-mien. Shanghai: Classics Publishing Co., 1981.

Chen, Min-sun. "Hsü Kuang-ch'i (1562-1633) and His Image of the West," in Cyriac K. Pullapilly and Edwin J. Van Kley, eds. *Asia and the West.* Notre Dame, Indiana: Cross Cultural Publications, 1986.

Dunne, George H. S. J. *Generation of Giants.* University of Notre Dame Press, 1962.

Trigault, Nicolas. *China in the Sixteenth Century: The Journals of Matthew Ricci, 1583-1610.* Translated by Louis J. Gallagher, S. J. Random House, 1953.

Ronan, Charles E., S. J. Oh, and Bonnie B. C. Oh, eds. *East Meets West: the Jesuits in China, 1582-1773.* Loyola University Press, 1988. □

Y

Abu Yusuf Yakub al-Mansur

Abu Yusuf Yakub al-Mansur (reigned 1184-1199) was the third caliph of the Almohad dynasty and the victor against the Spanish Christians at the battle of Alarcos.

Abu Yusuf served as vizier of the Almohad empire during the reign of his father, Abu Yakub Yusuf (1162-1184), and at his death was chosen as his successor as Yakub I. Having gained considerable practical experience as an administrator in the vizierate, Yakub kept firm control of the state in his own hands, continuing the Almohad tradition of active leadership in religious affairs and vigorous military campaigns against the enemies of the state.

The first part of Yakub's reign was spent in repelling an offensive against Almohad territory in North Africa launched by the Banu Ghaniya, the Sanhaja Berbers who had continued Berber rule on the Balearic Islands. The attack came in 1185 against the eastern holdings of the Almohads on the Algerian coast and resulted in the capture of Bougie, Algiers, and other towns. The Almohad army sent by Yakub regained the Algerian possessions in 1186, and the Banu Ghaniya retreated into Ifrikiya (Tunisia). Yakub himself led an army into Ifrikiya and in 1187 defeated the Banu Ghaniya, temporarily restoring the area to the Almohad Empire. However, upon his withdrawal to Morocco and the diversion of his efforts to Spain, the Banu Ghaniya soon succeeded in challenging Almohad sovereignty in the east, which was too far removed from the seat of Almohad power to keep under permanent control without a large army of occupation.

In Spain, Yakub's military success was equally spectacular and equally ephemeral; here, as in North Africa, the Almohad campaign was a response to the invasion of their territory, though in Spain the response amounted to holy war since the invaders were Christians, led by Alfonso VIII of Castile. Between 1190—when Yakub crossed into Spain—and 1195, the fighting was inconclusive and was checked by a loose armistice agreement. But in 1195 the great battle for which Yakub is famous in Islamic history took place at Alarcos, where he won a stunning victory over the Christians and temporarily halted their advance into Moslem Spain. This battle was followed by forays led by Yakub into Christian territory, which were ended by a two-year truce when he withdrew to Morocco.

Yakub sponsored religious activities, both scholarly and popular, and built many civil and religious edifices in Spain and Morocco. In the last year of his life, weakened from an illness which had befallen him on a trip to Spain, he devoted himself wholly to piety, leaving the affairs of state to his son whom he appointed as his successor.

Further Reading

There is no detailed biographical study of Yakub. His role in Almohad history is discussed in Henri Terrasse, *History of Morocco* (2 vol., 1949-1950; trans., 1 vol., 1952). There are also chapters on the Almohads in Eleanor Hoffman, *Realm of the Evening Star: A History of Morocco and the Lands of the Moors* (1965), and in Nevill Barbour, *Morocco*, (1965). In English, the standard comprehensive work on Arabic history is Philip K. Hitti, *History of the Arabs: From the Earliest Times to the Present* (1937; 8th ed. 1963). For works that discuss Yakub in relation to Spanish history see S. M. Imamuddin, *A Political History of Muslim Spain* (1961), and W. Montgomery Watt, *A History of Islamic Spain* (1965). □

426

Rosalyn S. Yalow

The American physicist Rosalyn S.Yalow (born 1921) made her most outstanding contribution to modern medicine in developing radioimmunoassay (RIA), for which she received a Nobel Prize in physiology/ medicine (1977).

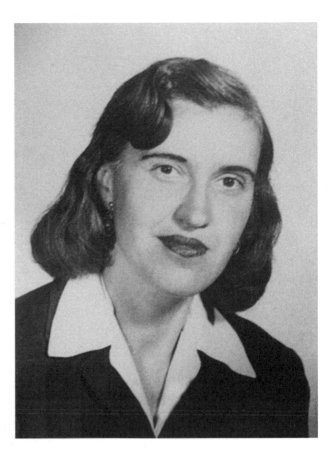

Rosalyn S.Yalow was born in New York City on July 19, 1921, the second child and only daughter of Simon Sussman and Clara Zipper. Her mother came to America from Germany at the age of four. Her father was born on the Lower East Side of New York. In her early childhood she was already an avid reader. Having no books at home, she took weekly trips to the public library with her brother, Alexander.

As she recalled, mathematics fascinated her while in the seventh grade. Later, at Walton High School, she was attracted to chemistry by an outstanding teacher, Mr. Mondzak. Her interest in physics developed at Hunter College, where two of her professors, Herbert N. Otis and Duane Roller, played a vital role.

Looking back to the end of the 1930s, Yalow recollected physics, particularly nuclear physics, as the most exciting field in the world. Madame Marie Curie's biography, written by her daughter Eve, had just been published. Yalow believed that this book ought to be read by every young aspiring woman scientist. Enrico Fermi's colloquium on the discovery of nuclear fission in January 1939 remained another highlight for her.

Yalow was convinced her career would be in physics. Her family thought the position of elementary school teacher might be more appropriate. She prevailed due to encouragement from her physics professors. On her graduation (A.B. in physics and chemistry) from Hunter College in January 1941, she went to business school, but only for a short time. In mid-February 1941 an offer came to be an assistant in physics at the University of Illinois in Champaign-Urbana. When she arrived there in September 1941, the faculty of the College of Engineering was composed of 400 members. She discovered she was the only woman and the first since 1917.

On the first day of graduate school she met Aaron Yalow. He had come to Illinois to start graduate study in physics. They married on June 6, 1943. They had two children: Benjamin, a systems programmer, and Elanna, an educational psychologist.

Yalow received an M.S. in physics in 1942 and a Ph.D. in nuclear physics in January 1945, both from the University of Illinois. She had been an instructor there in 1944 and 1945. Her thesis director, Maurice Goldhaber, later became director of Brookhaven National Laboratories. Yalow acknowledged the support and encouragement that he and his wife, Gertrude Goldhaber, herself a distinguished physicist, gave to her.

In January 1945 she went back to New York as an assistant engineer at the Federal Telecommunications Laboratory. In this ITT research laboratory she was the only woman engineer.

In 1946 she returned to Hunter College as a lecturer and temporary assistant professor in physics and stayed there until the spring semester of 1950. In this women's college (now part of the City University of New York) she taught physics not to women, but to veterans in a pre-engineering program. In December 1947 she joined the Bronx Veterans Administration (VA) Hospital as a part-time consultant. She equipped and developed the Radioisotope Service. She started research projects together with Bernard Roswit, chief of the Radiotherapy Service, and with other physicians in various clinical fields. The Bronx VA's Radioisotope Service was one of the first supported by the VA under a new national plan of development.

In January 1950 Yalow decided to renounce teaching and stay with the VA on a full-time basis. In the spring of 1950 she met Solomon (Sol) A. Berson, then completing his residency in internal medicine. In July 1950 Berson joined her service, and they began a close collaboration which lasted 22 years until his death on April 11, 1972. As Yalow wrote in 1979, "A multidisciplinary approach is necessary to weave the tools and concepts of physics into medicine. Maximal effectiveness is achieved only when each member of an interdisciplinary team makes a commitment to at least on-the-job training in the discipline of the other(s). . . . I learned medicine and [Berson] showed a remarkable talent for physics and mathematics. We learned to talk the same hybrid language—a major factor in our success as a research team."

In 1968 Berson became chairman of the Department of Medicine at the Mount Sinai School of Medicine. Had Berson lived longer, as Yalow noted, he would have shared the Nobel Prize. As a memorial tribute, Yalow requested her laboratory to be designated the Solomon A. Berson Research Laboratory so that his name would appear in her articles as long as she published.

Their investigations dealt with the application of radio-isotopes to blood volume determination, clinical diagnosis of thyroid diseases, and the kinetics of iodine metabolism. They extended these techniques to the study of the distribution of globin (because of its possible use as a plasma expander), serum proteins, and smaller peptides, the hormones. The most readily available highly purified hormone was insulin. On the basis of the delayed rate of insulin disappearance from the circulation of insulin-treated subjects, they deduced that these patients develop antibodies to the animal insulins. While studying the reaction of insulin with antibodies they realized they had a potential tool for measuring circulating insulin. Several additional years of work were necessary to achieve the practical measurement of plasma insulin in humans. Yalow considered that the era of radioimmunoassay genuinely opened in 1959. By the mid-1980s RIA was used to measure hundreds of substances of biological interest in thousands of laboratories in all parts of the world.

In 1977 Yalow was awarded the Nobel Prize in medicine/physiology. From 1974 to mid-1985, 37 honorary degrees were conferred upon her. The honors bestowed upon her included membership in the National Academy of Sciences (1975) and the American Academy of Arts and Sciences (1979). She was also a foreign associate of the French Academy of Medicine (1981). Beginning in 1972 Yalow was the senior medical investigator at the VA, and beginning in 1973 she was director of the Solomon A. Berson Research Laboratory at the VA Hospital in the Bronx.

In 1995 Yalow was one of fourteen eminent scientists and six Nobel laureates who joined the American Medical Association and the California Medical Association in filing briefs with the California Supreme Court stating they could find no link between electric and magnetic fields (EMF) from power lines and cancer. The briefs were filed in a homeowner's suit against San Diego Gas & Electric, charging that nearby power lines had devalued luxury homes. She was still at the Mt. Sinai School of Medicine. Her report stated "no scientifically documented health risk has been associated with the usually occurring levels of electromagnetic fields."

Further Reading

Yalow is listed in *Who's Who of American Women* (14th edition, 1985-1986) and in *Who's Who in America* (43rd edition, 1984-1985). An autobiographical sketch was published by the Nobel Foundation under the title *Les Prix Nobels/The Nobel Prizes 1977* (1978). For Yalow's vision on women and science and the future of humanity, see her Nobel address. She gave a detailed account of her researches and discoveries in "A physicist in biomedical investigation," in *Physics Today*, 32 (October 1979). □

Aritomo Yamagata

Aritomo Yamagata (1838-1922) was a Japanese general and a member of the oligarchy which dominated Meiji Japan. He was instrumental in building a modern army, strengthening the power of the civil and military bureaucracy, and checking the development of popular influences on the government.

Aritomo Yamagata was born the son of a low-ranking samurai family on April 22, 1838, in Hagi, the castle town of Choshu domain. Like Hirobumi Ito Yamagata studied at the private academy of Shoin Yoshida, who advocated revolt against unworthy rulers and severely criticized the shogunate's weak response to the Western nations. Not surprisingly, Yamagata became an active participant in the imperial loyalist movement in Choshu. As an officer of the Kiheitai, a militia force made up of both peasants and samurai, he fought under the leadership of Shinsaku Takasagi in engagements with the Westerners at shimonoseki, in the Choshu civil war, and in the wars of the restoration.

During the 1870s Yamagata became the main force behind the organization of a national army. He was the chief architect of the military conscription law of 1873, which created an army recruited from the peasantry and other commoners as well as from the former samurai class. He also introduced in 1879 the German model of a general-staff system of military administration, which made the army independent of civilian control. He held high-ranking positions in the army until his death, exercising considerable influence on military planning and policy, and his proteges dominated the military high command down to the early 1920s.

Although Yamagata was radical in his military innovations, he was a thoroughgoing conservative in civilian politics. As minister of home affairs from 1883 to 1888, he built up a strong centrally controlled police force, drafted laws suppressing political opposition, and reorganized the local government system in order to strengthen the power of local officials to maintain local order. He wished to keep political power in the hands of a responsible, dedicated bureaucracy, free of self-interest and backed by the more stable propertied elements in the countryside.

Yamagata grudgingly supported the constitutional system devised by Hirobumi Ito, serving twice as premier (1889-1891, 1898-1900). Yamagata remained a firm believer in "transcendental government", free from control or interference by the popularly elected house of the Diet. As genro, or senior statesman, he bent every effort to keep political party leaders from organizing cabinets and maneuvered to put his own followers in the premiership. Only in 1918 did he finally consent to the idea of party rule.

Yamagata was an advocate of a strong foreign policy, based on the need to extend Japan's defense perimeter to Korea and the Asian mainland. He supported enthusiastically the decision to fight China in 1894, and subsequently

he urged an anti-Russian policy, which led to war and victory in 1905. He continually sought to buttress Japan's military position and political influence on the Asian mainland.

At his death on Feb. 22, 1922, Yamagata had long been one of the most powerful figures on the political scene. But because of his opposition to popular government and his cold and aloof personality, he was also one of the least popular.

Further Reading

Roger F. Hackett, *Yamagata Aritomo in the Rise of Modern Japan, 1838-1922* (1971), is an able and scholarly biography based on Japanese sources. Both Josef Washington Hall, *Eminent Asians: Six Great Personalities of the New East* (1930), and Marius B. Jansen, ed., *Changing Japanese Attitudes toward Modernization* (1965), devote a chapter to Yamagata and his work. An interesting contemporary study is Rikitaro Fujisawa, *The Recent Aims and Political Development of Japan* (1923). For general background see Hugh Borton, *Japan's Modern Century, from Perry to 1970* (1955; rev. ed. 1970); George M. Beckmann, *The Modernization of China and Japan* (1962); Joseph Pittau, *Political Thought in Early Meiji Japan, 1868-1889* (1967); and Robert E. Ward, ed., *Political Development in Modern Japan* (1968). □

Isoroku Yamamoto

Yamamoto Isoroku (1884–1943) was Commander-in-chief of combined Japanese fleet, who was Japan's greatest naval strategist in World War II.

Yamamoto Isoroku, "the Nelson of the Japanese navy," was originally born Takano Isoroku, sixth son of an impoverished schoolteacher, Takano Teikichi, and his second wife Mineko, on April 4, 1884. Isoroku belonged to the Echigo clan, an old tough warrior people who had resisted the unification of Japan under the Meiji emperor. His father gave him the name *Isoroku* (meaning 56 in Japanese) as he was that age when his son was born in the small village of Kushigun Sonshomura on a bleak northern island that produced many Japanese sailors. Soon after his birth, his father became headmaster of the primary school in the nearby market town of Nagaoka.

At age 16, after taking competitive examinations, Isoroku enrolled in the Naval Academy at Etajima, off the shore of Hiroshima. There he spent three years, combining study with rigorous physical training. After that, he spent a year on a square-rigged windjammer. Graduating in 1904 as seventh in his class, he fought against Russia's Baltic Fleet at Tsushima, a strait between Japan and Korea, in an engagement recognized by historians as "one of the most decisive naval actions in history." As an ensign on the cruiser *Nisshin,* part of the protective screen for Admiral

Togo Heihachiro's flagship *Mikasa,* Isoroku saw closeup the tactics of one of the world's greatest admirals. From Togo, he learned one thing above all: the need for surprise in battle. In a letter to his family, the young seaman described a major mishap:

> When the shells began to fly above me I found I was not afraid. The ship was damaged by shells and many were killed. At 6:15 in the evening a shell hit the *Nisshin* and knocked me unconscious. When I recovered I found I was wounded in the right leg and two fingers of my left hand were missing. But the Russian ships were completely defeated and many wounded and dead were floating on the sea.

Between 1904 and the outbreak of World War I, Isoroku went on training cruises to Korea and China, traveled to the west coast of the United States, and toured every major port in Australia. In 1913, he was sent to the Naval Staff College at Tsukiji, a prerequisite for high command. Upon graduation in 1916, he was appointed to the staff of the Second Battle Squadron.

That same year, at age 30, Isoroku—now a lieutenant commander—was adopted by the wealthy and socially prestigious Yamamoto family. Such adoptions were a common practice in Japan: families lacking a male heir sought to keep the lineage from dying out. As Isoroku's parents had died several years earlier, he felt he could accept the Yamamoto's generous invitation. At a formal ceremony in a Buddhist temple, he took on the family name, which means "Base of the Mountain."

At age 30, Yamamoto married Reiko Mihashi, daughter of a dairy farmer from his own province and a woman who bore him four children. Although he engaged in intensive Buddhist meditation, he made no secret of his relationships with "ladies of the night." A talented calligrapher, he would decorate the geisha houses of his past and current mistresses, and lived far beyond his means, earning a second income from his skill at bridge and poker. He once said, "If I can keep 5,000 ideographs in my mind, it is not hard to keep in mind 52 cards."

In April of 1919, Yamamoto began two years of study at Harvard University, where he concentrated on the oil industry—the lifeblood of any modern navy. Returning with the rank of commander in July of 1921, he was appointed instructor at the naval staff college in Tokyo. In June of 1923, he became captain of the cruiser *Fuji.*

Yamamoto received his first major command when in September of 1924 he was sent to the new air-training center at Kasumigaura, 60 miles northeast of Tokyo, where at age 40 he took flying lessons. Within three months, he was director of studies. Yamamoto's handpicked pilots became an élite corps, the most sought-after arm of the Japanese navy. From January of 1926 to March of 1928, he was naval attaché to the Japanese embassy in Washington, there to investigate America's military might.

Historian Gordon W. Prange describes Yamamoto at the height of his powers as:

a man short even by Japanese standards (five feet three inches), with broad shoulders accentuated by massive epaulets and a thick chest crowded with orders and medals. But a strong, commanding face dominates and subdues all the trappings. The angular jaw slants sharply to an emphatic chin. The lips are full, cleancut, under a straight, prominent nose; the large, well-spaced eyes, their expression at once direct and veiled, harbor potential amusement or the quick threat of thunder.

The year 1928 saw him briefly serving with the naval general staff and commanding the light cruiser *Isuzu* and the carrier *Akagi.* He was then appointed to the navy ministry's naval affairs bureau, where he was an innovator concerning air safety and navigation. In 1930, Yamamoto served as a special assistant to the Japanese delegation to the London Naval Conference; made rear admiral, he was instrumental in raising the Japanese quota level for light cruisers to 70 percent of American and British forces. From December of 1930 to October of 1933, he headed the technical section of the navy's aviation bureau, and from December of 1935 to December of 1936, he was chief of the bureau itself. Here he directed the entire naval air program—carriers, seaplanes, and land-based craft.

All this time, Yamamoto fought for naval parity with the other great sea powers. For example in 1934, when another naval conference was held in London, Yamamoto—now vice admiral and chief delegate—firmly rejected any further extension of the 5-5-3 ratio. This quota, established at the Washington Conference of 1921-22, had limited Japanese building of heavy warships to 60 percent of American and British construction. Calling the existing ratio a "national degradation," he demanded full equality, using the analogy of a diplomatic dinner party: "I was never told there that being much shorter than the others I ought to eat only three-fifths of the food on my plate. I ate as much as I needed."

During the attempted putsch of February 26, 1936, an effort to topple Japan's parliamentary government in favor of direct military rule, junior officers at the admiralty asked Yamamoto to join the rebels. He immediately ordered them to return to their desks, to which they responded without a murmur.

In December of 1936, Yamamoto was made vice minister of the Japanese navy and hence was firmly placed in Japan's policymaking élite. He accepted the post reluctantly, for he loved air command and hated politics. In office, he did the expected: promoted the development of aircraft carriers. At the same time, he vainly opposed the construction of new battleships, claiming that they could be sunk by torpedo planes. Yamamoto quoted an old Japanese proverb, "The fiercest serpent may be overcome by a swarm of ants," then elaborated: "These [battle]ships are like elaborate religious scrolls which old people hung up in their homes. They are of no proved worth. They are purely a matter of faith—not reality."

While in office, he took several courageous stands. He opposed army desires for an alliance with Germany, fearing that such an agreement would lead to war with the United

States and Britain, the world's two strongest naval powers, and possibly the Soviet Union. Moreover, he noted, the Imperial Navy and indeed the entire Japanese economy depended on imports of raw materials from the United States. In 1937, he opposed Japan's invasion of China, telling a friend, "The stupid army has started again." On December 12, 1937, Japanese planes bombed the U.S. gunboat *Panay,* cruising China's Yangtse River. Three Americans were killed, and 43 were injured. Yamamoto personally apologized to U.S. Ambassador Joseph C. Grew, saying, "The Navy can only hang its head."

Such views made Yamamoto unpopular and like Admiral Yonai Mitsumasa, Japan's navy minister, he became a target for extremist attacks. The atmosphere became so hostile that tanks and machine guns were installed in the Navy Ministry. Supposedly, extreme rightists offered 100,000 yen as reward for his assassination.

On August 30, 1939, two days before Hitler invaded Poland, Yamamoto was appointed commander-in-chief of the combined fleet. Holding the rank of full admiral, he was operational head of Japan's entire navy; it was the highest honor the Japanese fleet could bestow. In addition, Yonai later said, "It was the only way to save his life—send him off to sea."

When on September 27, 1940, Japan signed the Tripartite Pact with Germany and Italy, Yamamoto warned Premier Konoye Fumimaro concerning possible war with the United States:

If I am told to fight regardless of the consequences, I shall run wild for the first six months or a year, but I have utterly no confidence for the second or third year. The Tripartite Pact has been concluded and we cannot help it. Now that the situation has come to this pass, I hope you will endeavor to avoid a Japanese-American war.

That October, he privately described the nature of the next war by saying:

As I see it, naval operations of the future will consist of capturing an island, then building an airfield in as short a time as possible—within a week or so—moving up air units, and using them to gain air and surface control over the next stretch of the ocean. Do you think we have the kind of industrial capacity to do that?

Already Yamamoto was thinking in terms of bold, almost reckless, strikes. During fleet maneuvers in the spring of 1940, in noting the achievements of carrier-based planes, he thought that an attack on the American fleet, stationed at Pearl Harbor, Hawaii, might be possible, and immediately presented his plan to Fukudome Shigeru, chief of staff of the combined fleet. At the end of July of 1941, Yamamoto said to the commander of the submarine fleet: "If we fight both Britain and America we will be defeated. . . . If war comes, our only chance is to destroy the fleet at Pearl Harbor and send submarines to the west coast of America."

On July 25, 1941, U.S. President Franklin D. Roosevelt froze Japanese assets in retaliation for its occupation of

southern Indochina, a move that severed all trade between the two nations. Now Japan's ever-precious supply of oil was cut off, causing it to seek domination of the petroleum-rich Dutch East Indies and to risk war with the United States and Britain. In late September, Yamamoto visited Admiral Nagano Osami, chief of the naval general staff, to dissuade him from pursuing military plans made on September 6 to fight the United States. If war, however, was truly inevitable, Japan—Yamamoto said—should scrap traditional plans centering on lying in wait for the American battle fleet and ambushing it near Japan itself. Rather than allow a U.S. build-up, Japan must make a preemptive strike, crippling the American navy at the outset of the conflict. Such a move could shift the strategic balance in Japan's favor, protect the all-important southern flank in southeast Asia, and hopefully lead to a negotiated peace.

Yamamoto's plan eventually called for a massive air strike involving all six large carriers of the First Air Fleet; they had to approach within 200 miles of Hawaii without being discovered. Writes his biographer John Dean Potter:

The plan was his—and his alone. . . . He had supervised the smallest detail, perfected it, fought single-handed past the opposition of every senior admiral, offered to lead it personally from the bridge of the leading carrier—and finally threatened to resign if it were not approved.

In October 1941, Nagano gave his reluctant approval. On December 1, Japan's highest decision-making body, the Imperial Conference, decided upon war with the United States, Britain, and the Netherlands. Emperor Hirohito personally issued the orders to Yamamoto: "You must be determined to meet our expectations by exalting our force and authority throughout the world by annihilating the enemy." Aboard his flagship *Yamato,* stationed in Japan's Inland Sea, Yamamoto gave the coded attack orders to his strike force: "Climb Mount Niitaka," a reference to a peak in Formosa that was the highest point in the Japanese empire.

On December 7, the greatest air operation the world had yet seen took place—Yamamoto's famous strike on Pearl Harbor. In a single blow, 353 planes from six aircraft carriers almost completely destroyed the U.S. Pacific Fleet; 18 American ships were sunk or disabled as were nearly 200 planes; 2,335 servicemen and 68 civilians were killed. Commander Genda Minoru recommended a second strike, seeking to hit two American aircraft carriers and undamaged fuel tanks on Oahu. Admiral Nagumo Chuichi, the task force's leader, refused. A second strike, he reasoned, would be pressing one's luck and furthermore the Japanese carriers were needed for major offensives in Southeast Asia. Nagumo was a torpedo expert and lacked the needed imagination for such an operation; he had only been given carrier command because he was a senior admiral.

Rear Admiral Kuroshima Kameto immediately sought to overrule Nagumo by ordering a search for the American carriers, but Yamamoto replied: "[Nagumo] may have information we do not have. He must fight his own battle. I have complete faith in him." When his operations officer wanted to transfer Nagumo, Yamamoto responded: "How can I? He is an old-fashioned *samurai* type. If I move him he will commit hari-kiri because he will consider it such a disgrace."

Because of such restraint, Rear Admiral Edwin T. Layton, a leading U.S. staff officer, can write: "Pearl Harbor may have been a disaster, but it was a long way from being the knockout blow that Yamamoto had intended." Furthermore, by sinking so many battleships and thereby forcing the United States to adopt carrier warfare, Yamamoto had inadvertently contributed to American victory.

Yamamoto was always uneasy about his success, ever possessing a curious fatalism. He wrote a friend: "The fact that we have had a small success at Pearl Harbor is nothing. . . . Personally I do not think it is a good thing to whip up propaganda to encourage the nation. People should think things over and realize how serious the situation is." To win, he warned, "We would have to march into Washington and sign the treaty in the White House."

On February 27-28, 1942, the battle of Java Sea took place. Fought on both sides entirely by cruisers, it was the biggest surface engagement since Jutland. The Japanese defeated a combined force of Dutch, British, and American ships, thereby enabling Japan to seize oil-rich Java. Yamamoto now had sufficient oil to keep his fleet afloat in the foreseeable future.

Yamamoto anticipated that the United States might attempt a carrier raid on Tokyo. Believing that it was his foremost duty to protect the Imperial City, and the emperor in particular, he established a picketboat line extending over a 1,000-mile front some 600 to 700 miles east of Japan. He also ordered naval aircraft to engage in long-range patrols. On April 18, 1942, some 700 miles from Japan, 16 B-25 bombers from the U.S. carrier *Hornet* headed for Tokyo. Soon Lieutenant Colonel James H. Doolittle was bombing the Japanese capital as well as such neighboring cities as Yokohama, Kawasaki, and Yokosuka. Although the damage was relatively slight, Yamamoto was shocked, regarding it as a mortifying personal defeat. Writes biographer Potter, noting how impulsive the admiral suddenly became: "There can be no doubt however that his normally clear judgment was warped by the Doolittle raid."

From May 4-8, 1942, the world's first major carrier engagement took place in the Coral Sea. Entirely fought by aircraft, it was the first sea battle in history in which no warship of either side ever saw an enemy craft. The Japanese sought to take Port Moresby in New Guinea, thereby cutting off Australia from Allied aid. Tactically, the battle was a Japanese victory, for they had sunk the carrier *Lexington* and two smaller warships. Yet Japan lost the carrier *Shoho,* saw severe damage to the carrier *Shokaku,* and experienced the loss of most of the *Zuikaku's* planes. The Japanese commander, Vice Admiral Inouye Shigeyoshi, deprived of most of his striking power in aircraft, withdrew. His failure to pursue the damaged *Yorktown* drew Yamamoto's ire, though Inouye had little choice. Strategically, the Coral Sea marked a U.S. victory because the Japanese abandoned plans to occupy Port Moresby and attack Australia. Furthermore, Yamamoto was served notice

that despite U.S. numerical inferiority, the Japanese fleet was not invincible.

Seeking retribution for the Doolittle raid, Yamamoto decided to draw out what was left of the U.S. Pacific Fleet in a decisive battle. The capture of Midway Island, a coral atoll six miles in diameter and a U.S. base just 1,136 miles from Hawaii, would give Japan an advanced outpost for air and submarine patrols. Furthermore, so Yamamoto believed, the strike would draw out the fullest strength of the U.S. Pacific Fleet. He would establish a lethal ambush, one that would destroy the carriers that had escaped him at Pearl Harbor. Once Midway was seized, Hawaii would be invaded, forcing the U.S. to sue for peace. Conversely, Yamamoto believed that if Japan did not soon engage in a decisive sea battle, its defeat was simply a matter of time. In a sense, Midway was his last chance.

Yamamoto assembled the largest fleet in the history of Japanese naval warfare—some 260 ships, among them 11 battleships, 8 carriers, 22 cruisers, 65 destroyers, and 21 submarines. Also involved were some 700 planes and 100,000 naval personnel.

On the surface, Yamamoto's strategy was extremely sophisticated, perhaps too much so. He divided his fleet into widely separated groups. A northern force, including two carriers, would capture Kiska and Attu, islands at the western end of the Aleutians. This strike would not only divert attention from the main target, Midway, it would keep American forces from using the islands as stepping stones to Japan. (He planned to withdraw Japanese forces from the islands before the grueling winter). The bombing of Dutch Harbor would cause even further diversion. An advance force of Japanese submarines, patrolling west of Hawaii, would warn of any U.S. craft in the vicinity, sinking such ships before they could defend Midway. Twenty-four hours after the Aleutian strike, Admiral Nagumo's striking force of four large carriers would hit Midway from the northwest, followed the next day by Vice Admiral Kondo Nobutake's second fleet of two battleships, a small aircraft carrier, half a dozen heavy cruisers, and an invasion convoy. As the main strength of the American fleet lay in Hawaiian or Australian waters (so the Japanese believed), the strike on Midway would be a complete surprise.

Once Midway was captured, the remnants of the U.S. fleet would be forced to attempt its rescue. But by then the Japanese would have the advantage of position as well as at least a 2:1 advantage in carriers and four to five times the number of screening vessels. At that point, Yamamoto himself would lead the combined fleet's main force, a powerful unit of seven battleships that included the two largest in the world then or since: his flagship *Yamato* and her sister ship, the *Musashi*. While he would be shutting the jaws of a gigantic trap, the northern force would come from the Aleutians to cut off the U.S. line of retreat. Notes Layton:

> His intricate battle choreography also required that his opponents move according to predicted positions; one false step or foreknowledge of the plan could throw the entire operation into disarray.

In the battle, which took place from June 4 to 6, 1942, Yamamoto operated under many disadvantages. Thanks to American cryptographers, the Japanese sailed into a trap. Some Japanese ships had even mentioned their destination by name, and on May 20 a lengthy order of Yamamoto himself was intercepted. By the last week of May, the United States knew the date, place, and time of operation, as well as the composition of the Japanese forces. Yamamoto's submarines were ordered to report on the presence of American carriers, but they arrived on station 25 minutes too late to do so. Yamamoto's operations officer had information pointing to the presence of a powerful U.S. carrier force, but failed to inform Admiral Nagumo. By maintaining radio silence on his flagship, Yamamoto was unable to give instructions when needed. Not a single senior admiral had been fully briefed; all were drawn into combat on the shortest of notice. Nagumo failed to order an immediate attack once he learned of U.S. ships in the vicinity, thereby dooming his force to destruction.

In the ensuing battle, no surface ships sighted each other or exchanged gunfire. The devastating exchanges were carried out entirely by aircraft at long ranges. Three American carriers unexpectedly appeared, the *Enterprise, Hornet,* and *Yorktown*—the last ship fresh from hasty repairs. Within ten minutes, they sank three Japanese carriers—*Kaga, Akagi,* and *Soryu*— that comprised close to half of Japan's entire carrier tonnage. The remaining Japanese carrier *Hiryu* successfully sunk the *Yorktown,* but later in the day it was hit by the *Enterprise.*

A particularly crucial turning point took place when Nagumo, having learned that his initial air strike did not succeed in critically damaging Midway, decided to use his reserve planes in a second strike. While his carrier crews were in the act of changing from torpedoes to bombs, his force found itself suddenly exposed to the carrier-based planes of the U.S. Pacific Fleet.

Yamamoto himself took no part in the battle until it was too late. He wanted to engage the Americans with his battleships, and in a desperate move sought the daylight bombing of Midway. Yet not being able to bring his scattered groups together on time, he feared further losses and withdrew. Only 307 Americans died compared to 3,500 Japanese. Henceforth, Japan fought on the defensive. Writes military historian Ronald H. Spector: "For the Japanese, Midway was an ill-conceived, sloppily executed operation." One commentator finds it the most decisive battle since Trafalgar, another the Stalingrad of the Pacific.

Even if conquered by Japan, Midway would have been difficult to hold. It would remain an exposed salient (line of defense), subject to frequent bombing. Although the Japanese were able to conquer Kiska and Attu without real opposition, neither island possessed strategic value. The loss of an undamaged Zeke-Zero fighter in a feint on Dutch Harbor enabled the United States to design the sturdier and more powerful F6F Hellcat.

Yamamoto never fully recovered from the shock of this defeat, although he soon commanded air offensive in the Solomons campaign. Noting the strategic importance of Guadalcanal, he realized that the establishment of an American base there challenged his domination of the South Pacific. Engaging in a war of attrition to dislodge U.S. marines who started landing on August 7, 1942, Yamamoto's fleet suffered huge losses of aircraft and pilots. After major efforts, he realized that his destroyer transports, called the "Tokyo Express," could not remove the Americans. Finally, on January 4, 1943, he ordered the evacuation of that island's 13,000 Japanese troops; doing so was one of the great tactical successes of the war. He confessed to an old classmate: "I do not know what to do next."

In an effort to build morale, Yamamoto decided to make inspection trips throughout the South Pacific. In particular, he wanted to thank troops recovering from their ordeal on Guadalcanal. At age 59, he was tired, weary of war, and of life itself: "I have killed quite a few of the enemy, and many of my own men have been killed. So I believe the time has come for me to die too." During the Guadalcanal conflict, his hair had turned snowy-white.

In April 1943, U.S. intelligence intercepted advance reports of Yamamoto's tour. Eighteen American Lightning planes were waiting for the first attempt in history to ambush an enemy commander-in-chief in the air. On the 18th, his aircraft, under the escort of nine zeroes, was shot down by a P-38 near Kahili in southern Bougainville. On June 5, the admiral's ashes were honored in Tokyo in full state ceremony, a tribute accorded only once before—on the exact same day in 1934 to Admiral Togo.

Further Reading

Agawa, Hiroyuli. *The Reluctant Admiral: Yamamoto and the Imperial Navy.* Translated by John Bester. Kodansha International, 1979.

Hoyt, Edwin B. *Yamamoto: The Man Who Planned Pearl Harbor.* McGraw-Hill, 1990.

Potter, John Dean. *Yamamoto: The Man Who Menaced America.* Viking, 1965.

Evans, David C., ed. and trans. *The Japanese Navy in World War II: In the Words of Former Naval Officers.* Naval Institute Press, 1986.

Prange, Gordon W., Donald M. Goldstein, and Katherine V. Dillon. *At Dawn We Slept: The Untold Secret of Pearl Harbor.* McGraw-Hill, 1981.

———. *Miracle at Midway.* McGraw-Hill, 1982.

Spector, Ronald H. *Eagle Against the Sun: The American War with Japan.* Free Press, 1985.

Toland, John. *The Rising Sun: The Decline and Fall of the Japanese Empire, 1936-1945.* Random House, 1970. □

Ahmed Zaki Yamani

Sheik Ahmed Zaki Yamani (born 1930) was a Saudi Arabian lawyer and minister of petroleum and mineral resources from 1962 to 1986. A major architect of the energy policies of his country, he served as an influential spokesman for Saudi Arabia and for the Organization of Petroleum Exporting Countries (OPEC).

Ahmed Zaki Yamani was born in Mecca, Saudi Arabia, in 1930. His father, Hassan Yamani, was a scholar of Islamic law and a qadhi, or religious judge, whose patience, wisdom, and quiet sense of humor inspired his son as he grew up in Islam's holiest city, one of three children.

The young Yamani earned a bachelor's degree in law at Cairo University in 1951 and a master's degree in law at New York University in 1955. He graduated from Harvard law school in 1956. He later was awarded honorary degrees from institutions around the world, including Nihon University in Japan (1969), Osmania University in India (1975), Leobon University in Austria (1979), and the American Graduate School of Business in Arizona (1979).

Yamani's first job was as a legal adviser to the Oil and Tax departments of the Saudi Ministry of Finance from 1956 to 1958. At the same time, he established one of the first private law offices in Jeddah. He maintained his private practice throughout his public career. From 1958 to 1960 he was a legal adviser to the Council of Ministers, becoming a minister of state and member of the Council of Ministers in 1959.

OPEC Spokesman

The Saudi royal family soon recognized Yamani's potential. Yamani was one of the first of the capable, English-speaking, Western-educated young Saudi technocrats equipped to deal effectively with the Americans and Europeans who were eager to secure access to the lucrative and

strategically important oil of the Arabian Gulf. While oil revenues were needed for development, Saudi leaders were also concerned about the effects of rapid economic change on the values of a conservative Muslim society. Crown Prince Faisal, who was virtually running the Saudi government administration under his older brother King Saud even before he was crowned king in 1965, was a strong supporter of Yamani. In March 1962 the royal family named Yamani to the key post of minister of petroleum and mineral resources, a position he would hold for 24 years.

Saudi Arabia needed young Saudis with the education and technical expertise to run its own oil industry. Yamani envisioned a local institution that would provide such training for Saudis and for students from other developing nations of the region. He was instrumental in founding the University of Petroleum and Minerals at Dhahran in 1964; it soon became a major science and engineering school.

As minister of petroleum, Yamani took his place as a director of the Arabian American Oil Company (ARAMCO), originally a consortium of four American oil companies operating in Saudi Arabia under a concession agreement. Beginning in 1963 he also served as chairman of the board of directors of the General Petroleum and Minerals Organization (PETROMIN), the Saudi government agency responsible for management of energy and mineral resources in the kingdom. He became president of the Supreme Consultative Council for Petroleum and Mineral Resources in 1975. His department promoted the development of solar technology and other alternate energy sources. Yamani was made chairman of the board of the Saudi Arabian Fertilizer Company (SAFCO) in 1966. He was also chairman of the Saudi Arabian/Sudanese Joint Commission for Exploitation of Red Sea Resources beginning in 1974.

Within the Organization of Petroleum Exporting Countries (OPEC), Yamani worked for price stability, energy conservation, and an orderly international oil market. He was secretary-general of OPEC in 1968-1969. In the 1970s member countries took control of their own natural resources. Saudi Arabia negotiated the nationalization of the assets of foreign companies while retaining their cooperation and expertise. Yamani mediated among the opposing interests of the commercial companies and the oil-producing developing nations. His negotiating style was patient but dogged, punctuated occasionally by outbursts of frustration.

Yamani masterminded the 1973 oil embargo, which sent worldwide oil prices soaring to record levels and caused economic shock waves worldwide. Eloquent and shrewd, he was the primary spokesman of the political objectives of the embargo. The severe product shortages which resulted were intended as a clear demonstration of the strategic importance of Arab resources. With the oil embargo, Yamani had the world's attention, and he held it for the next 13 years as "he came to embody Arab oil power," in the words of John Tagliabue of the *New York Times* (October 30, 1986). "For more than two decades, Ahmed Zaki Yamani's commands boosted or battered personal pocketbooks and national economies around the world," wrote Pamela Sherrid in *U.S News & World Report* (February 15, 1988).

Volatile Times

In March 1975 Yamani witnessed the assassination of King Faisal, his mentor and friend, at the hands of the king's nephew. In December 1975 he was taken hostage by pro-Palestinian terrorists, along with several other OPEC ministers, during a conference at OPEC's Vienna headquarters. They were released unharmed after two days aboard an aircraft. Despite these incidents, Yamani remained unaffected by politics. "I'm a very pragmatic man," he said. "I know little about ideologies."

Yamani had eight children and three marriages. He spent his spare time composing poetry in Arabic. He was a devout Muslim. For his OPEC work, Faisal rewarded him with gifts of land, but Yamani insisted he never profited from oil. Yamani owned homes in Switzerland, England, and Saudi Arabia, dressed in expensive Western suits, was driven to meetings in Rolls Royce limousines, and made frequent trips to Europe to shop for jewelry and clothes while negotiating oil contracts. He was a salaried minister and chairman of several Saudi corporations, and his law firm did work for many Saudi government agencies.

After the major oil price adjustments of 1973, which shifted the patterns of worldwide economic development and planning, Yamani chaired OPEC's Long-Term Strategy Committee in its attempts to devise a unified policy to support oil prices and stabilize international markets. This proved to be a difficult task. In the 1980s world demand began to fall and production contracted. The petroleum market remained volatile, subject to the influence of a variety of political and economic factors. Between 1980 and 1984 the Saudi share of oil production among non-Communist nations dropped from 16.5 percent to 7.6 percent, and Yamani was criticized at home for not fighting for unrestrained production before other OPEC countries were able to increase their market share.

In 1985 Saudi oil production plummeted to two million barrels of oil a day, its lowest level in 20 years. Yamani responded with a policy of unrestrained OPEC oil production, which caused a rapid drop in oil prices and a budget crisis at home. On October 29, 1986, the Saudi government suddenly dismissed Yamani from all his positions with no explanation, replacing him with Hisham Nazer. Yamani heard the news on the radio.

Yamani moved his principal residence to the Swiss ski town of Crans-sur-Sierre and in 1988 made an aborted attempt to take over Vacheron Constantin, a prestigious maker of luxury watches. In 1989 he formed the Centre for Global Energy Studies in London, a forum for OPEC oil ministers, oil company leaders, and representatives of governments and consumers. In the 1990s, as director of that think tank, he spent most of his time in London and continued to be a respected commentator and consultant on global oil policies.

Further Reading

Yamani is the author of *Islamic Law and Contemporary Issues* (1980), published in both English and Arabic. For additional information on Yamani and his public service see Ragaei El Mallakh, editor, *OPEC: Twenty Years and Beyond* (1982) and Ragaei and Dorothy H. El Mallakh, editors, *Saudi Arabia, Energy, Development Planning, and Industry* (1982). □

Tomoyuki Yamashita

The Japanese general Tomoyuki Yamashita (1885-1946) distinguished himself as the "Tiger of Malaya" during World War II. After the war he surrendered in the Philippines, where he was tried for war crimes and executed by the Allies.

Tomoyuki Yamashita was born on Nov. 8, 1885, in Shikoku, son of a medical doctor, who started the child in a military career. At the military academy he was a year junior to his lifetime rival, Hideki Tojo, and graduated at the head of his class. By 1932, when only 47, he became section chief of military affairs in the War Ministry and was earmarked as an eventual war minister or even premier. He was one of the generals admired by a fanatical group of radical young officers, called the Imperial Way faction, who carried out an abortive coup d'etat on Feb. 26, 1936. Although Yamashita, then a major general, refused to go along with the plot, he came under such a cloud of suspicion that he almost retired but instead took an assignment in Korea. This actually put him in an advantageous position when the China incident of July 1937 broke out, and he distinguished himself in action so well that he was promoted to lieutenant general and placed in charge of North Korea.

Meanwhile, Gen. Tojo, whose control faction had benefited from the Imperial Way faction's demise, again began to fear Yamashita's revived popularity and finally got him transferred to an isolated Manchurian outpost in 1941. But when Japan entered the war against the Allies, Yamashita was placed in charge of the 25th Army and dramatically took Singapore by a surprise attack through Malaya. The British commander, Lt. Gen. Percival, surrendered to him in February 1942, and Yamashita was made a full general.

Jealous of Yamashita's fame, Tojo quickly transferred him to the quiet Manchurian border until October 1944, when Yamashita took full command of all the Imperial forces in the Philippines, as the Allies relentlessly moved in. On Sept. 2, 1945, he surrendered his sword at Bagio to the representatives of the Allied forces, among whom was Gen. Percival. By direction of Gen. Douglas MacArthur, Yamashita was almost immediately put on trial as the one responsible for the last-minute wild massacres by Japanese troops in Manila, establishing a principle of responsibility the implications of which frightened a number of American officers. Yamashita was hanged on Feb. 23, 1946.

Gen. Yamashita is remembered in Japan as a military leader whose personal career was victimized by that very factionalism in the military that had so much to do with dragging Japan into the euphoria of war and the humiliation and suffering of defeat. His honorary pen name was Hobun.

Further Reading

An intimate picture of Yamashita, based on an account by his chief of staff and on notes by American Army psychiatrists, is in the book by his defense lawyer, Adolf F. Reel, *The Case of General Yamashita* (1949), although most of the book is concerned with the trial and its implications. Another biography, focusing on the Malayan campaign but also relating his life, is in Arthur Swinson, *Four Samurai* (1968), one of whom is Yamashita; it contains the most up-to-date bibliography. A more detailed account of the Malayan campaign is by the pro-Tojo former colonel Masanobu Tsuji, *Singapore: The Japanese Version*, edited by H. V. Howe and translated by Margaret E. Lake (1960).

Additional Sources

Hoyt, Edwin Palmer, *Three military leaders: Heihachiro Togo, Isoroku Yamamoto, Tomoyuki Yamashita*, Tokyo; New York: Kodansha International, 1993. □

William Lowndes Yancey

U.S. congressman William Lowndes Yancey (1814-1863) was known for his unexcelled oratorical abilities as a spokesman of Southern interests.

William Yancey was born in Warren County, Ga., on Aug. 10, 1814, the son of an attorney who died in 1817. A few years later Yancey's mother married a clergyman, and the family moved to Troy, N.Y. Yancey attended Williams College, but left in 1833 without graduating and entered the law office of a strong unionist in Greenville, S.C.

Yancey became editor of the *Greenville Mountaineer*, a unionist paper. In 1837 he moved to Alabama, bought a sizeable plantation, and purchased two newspapers. Between 1836 and 1840 Yancey moved from ardent unionism to an equally zealous states'-rights position. He was elected to the Alabama Legislature in 1841 and 1843. Twice elected to the U.S. Congress, he served from 1844 until 1846, when he resigned out of disgust at party politics. A powerful speaker, he was occasionally intemperate in his oratory, resulting in a number of duels.

In 1848 Yancey devised resolutions that were adopted by the Alabama Democratic Convention, announcing the extreme demand that slavery be permitted into the territories and be protected by Federal law. He worked to arouse the South to realize the dangers of abolition and to promote concerted action among Southern states. He believed that Southern unity could come only with the disintegration of existing parties and the submergence of partisan hatreds in the face of a common threat. Yancey encouraged the formation of local Southern rights associations and agitated to reopen the African slave trade to spread slavery's blessings to poor white Southerners. Preaching the notion of

secession more convincingly than any contemporary, he was later called the "orator of secession."

At the national Democratic convention in 1860, Yancey delivered his finest statement of the Southern position. The Southern delegates' subsequent withdrawal split the Democratic party and assured the election of Republican Abraham Lincoln. Yancey became the spokesman of the Constitutional Democratic party.

After Lincoln's election Yancey dominated the Alabama secessionist convention and drafted the ordinance of secession. In March 1861 he went to England and France as a commissioner from the Confederate States of America. His mission was ineffective, perhaps because of his passionate defense of slavery, which both countries hated. Upon his return in 1862, he was elected to the Confederate Senate. In 1863, in a noisy debate, Benjamin H. Hill, a senator from Georgia, threw an inkstand at Yancey, hitting him in the face and splattering blood and ink. On July 27 Yancey died near Montgomery, Ala., and Hill's enemies falsely accused him of having indirectly caused Yancey's death.

Further Reading

There has been little recent work on Yancey. John W. DuBose, *The Life and Times of William Lowndes Yancey* (2 vols., 1892; repr. 1942), is a well-researched study striving for objectivity, but occasionally the author's pro-Southern bias shows. Also useful is Austin L. Venable, *The Role of William Yancey in the Secession Movement* (1945). □

Chen Ning Yang

The Chinese-born American physicist Chen Ning Yang (born 1922) codiscovered the nonconservation of parity in weak interactions.

Academically inclined from childhood Chen Yang was born September 22, 1922, in Hotei, Anhwei, in China, enjoying what he later categorized as "a tranquil childhood that was unfortunately denied most of the Chinese of my generation." His father was a professor of mathematics at Tsinghua University, where Yang came to do post-graduate study after earning his bachelor's degree in 1942.

In 1944 Yang completed his master's degree, after which he taught in a Chinese high school for a time and then traveled to the United States on a fellowship. Determined to benefit from direct contact with Enrico Fermi (the 1938 Nobel laureate who later built the world's first nuclear reactor), Yang enrolled at the University of Chicago in 1946. He completed his doctoral degree in less than two years, his thesis being supervised by Edward Teller.

Soaring to the Top

Yang remained a year at the University of Chicago as instructor in physics, and in 1949 went to the Institute for Advanced Study in Princeton; in 1955 he became one of the

very small number of professors on the institute's permanent staff. In 1950 he married Chih Li Tu, a former student of his in China, who was studying in Princeton. The Yangs had two sons and one daughter.

Although Yang consistently made very significant contributions to statistical mechanics and symmetry principles, he is best known for his and Lee's joint work demonstrating the limitations of the principle of conservation of parity. This principle, although tacitly assumed for centuries to be valid, took on entirely new significance with the birth of relativity, with an empirical rule discovered by O. Laporte in 1924, the advent of quantum mechanics, and E.P. Wigner's 1927 proof that Laporte's rule follows from the "right-left symmetry" of the electromagnetic forces in the atom. Conservation of parity, along with, for example, conservation of energy and momentum, seemed to be a general law of nature. Indeed, its consequences—for example, that the same experiment carried out on an object and its mirror image should yield the same result—seemed to be so obviously true that its universal validity was unquestioned.

Lee and Yang came to feel otherwise in the course of their attempts to understand what was known as the "theta-tau puzzle"; two particles, the theta meson and the tau meson, having the same mass and lifetime, would ordinarily have been considered to be one and the same particle, except that while the former decayed into two pions ("even parity"), the latter decayed into three ("odd parity")—and the *same* particle decaying into two states of *different* parity would constitute a violation of conservation of parity. Only after intensive study and an extensive survey of the relevant

experimental evidence did Lee and Yang conclude in early 1956 that for interactions like the ones described—the so-called "weak interactions," in contrast to the "strong" nuclear interactions, the electromagnetic interactions, and the gravitational interactions—there was absolutely no conclusive experimental basis for conservation of parity. This astonishing fact had escaped all their contemporaries. Indeed, in the words of O.B. Klein, it had been revealed to Lee and Yang only as a consequence of their "consistent and unprejudiced thinking."

But nonconservation of parity in weak interactions was still only a hypothesis. Lee and Yang therefore suggested a number of specific experimental tests for it, all of which yielded positive results. Perhaps the most famous of the tests was the cobalt-60 beta-decay experiment carried out by Madame C.S. Wu of Columbia University and her National Bureau of Standards collaborators. Since Lee and Yang's discovery led to a reexamination of all of the conservation laws, it shook the very foundations of physics, opening up entirely new and unanticipated vistas. For it, they received a number of honors, the highest of which was their shared Nobel Prize for 1957.

A New Life at Stony Brook

In the summer on 1965 Yang was invited, as he often was, to spend a summer worrking at the Brookhaven National Laboratory near the new Stony Brook-based State University of New York. He met many of the physics faculty there, and the following year he was appointed Albert Einstein Professor of Physics and Director of the Institute of Theoretical Physics, which was established especially to attract other top physicists who wished to work with Professor Yang.

By 1997 Yang had been at Stony Brook for 31 years. A man with a strong moral conscience, he had done whatever he could to promote friendship between his adopted homeland and his native China. In 1971 he beecame the first President of the National Association of Chinese Americans, following up with encouragement in every possible quarter to establish the diplomatic relationship between the two countries that finally came to pass in 1979. He also raises an ongoing fund of money, that allows scholars from China to visit the Stony Brook campus for study purposes. Most of them are aware of his many trailblazine papers, which were collected together in a book called *Selected Papers 1945-1980*, published in 1983 by W.H.Freeman. In honor of Professor Yang's 70th birthday, another volume, *Chen Ning Yang: A Great Physicist of the Twentieth Century,* was produced by several former students. Obviously, all of them have great respect and affection for him. As many of the pieces in the book note, it is Yang's warmth and sensitivity as much as his reputation which have elevated the Physics Department of the State University of New York to great heights in the world of scientific research.

Further Reading

Yang discussed his and Lee's discovery in his Nobel lecture, reprinted in Nobel Foundation, *Nobel Lectures in Physics,*

vol. 3 (1967). A detailed account of the discovery is also in Jeremy Bernstein, *A Comprehensible World* (1967).

Additional Sources

Selected Papers 1945-1980 W. H. Freeman, 1983.
Liu, C. S., ed. *Chen Ning Yang: A Great Physicist of the Twentieth Century.* □

Mary Alexander Yard

Mary Alexander Yard (born c. 1912) was a feminist, a political organizer, and a social activist. She served as president of the National Organization for Women (NOW), 1987-1991.

Mary Alexander Yard, who preferred to be called Molly, was born sometime around 1912 in Chengtu, the capital of Szechwan Province in China. Her father, James Maxon Yard, was a Methodist missionary, and the Yard family lived in China until she was 13 years old. Yard was the third of her parents' children—all girls. When she was born, Chinese friends gave her father an ornate brass bowl as a consolation gift, to show their sympathy that his wife had given birth to yet another daughter. She later said that living in a country where women were so discriminated against made her a feminist almost from birth.

From her parents Yard inherited a sense of the importance of social activism. As a student at Swarthmore College in the early 1930s she protested and demonstrated against the sorority and fraternity system when a Jewish student was refused admission. Her campaign was successful. Fraternities and sororities were abolished at Swarthmore.

She graduated from college in 1933 at the peak of the Great Depression. She worked briefly as a social worker, but found the work unrewarding and frustrating. As a social worker she wasn't expected to change things, and she was too militant for that. She turned to activism in the trade union movement, as well as in early civil rights organizations.

Yard became active in the American Student Union, and served first as the national organizational secretary and then as chairperson. The ASU was critical of Franklin Roosevelt's administration and the New Deal. They felt that the government wasn't doing enough to create jobs, especially for young people. It was through her position in the ASU that Yard met Eleanor Roosevelt. She considered herself Eleanor Roosevelt's spiritual heir and as president of the National Organization for Women, spoke of her often. During her years in the ASU she worked in campaigns against Reserve Officers Training Corps (ROTC) programs and in support of the Spanish Republic during that nation's civil war.

In 1938 Yard married Sylvester Garrett, a labor arbitrator. She kept her own name, but found that other forms of independence were difficult to maintain in the 1940s and 1950s. For example, when she and her husband tried to

open a joint bank account using both their names they were told it was impossible unless they stopped claiming to be married and admitted that she was Garrett's mistress instead.

Through the 1940s, while caring for her three young children, Yard was actively involved in Pennsylvania Democratic politics. She and her husband moved briefly to California in 1950, and after her return to Pennsylvania, she served in the administration of Philadelphia Mayor Joseph Clark. When Clark ran for the United States Senate in 1956 she worked in his campaign, and again in 1962. In 1964 she ran for her own seat in the state legislature. Although she won the Democratic primary, she lost in the general election.

Throughout the 1960s Yard was active in a variety of political and social movements. She was much aware of the tensions and the excitement of the times. She was an organizer in western Pennsylvania for the 1963 Civil Rights March on Washington. In 1964 she led a march on the Pittsburgh Post Office delivering thousands of letters to senators and congressmen urging passage of the Civil Rights Act.

She continued her active involvement with Democratic state politics, but she was growing increasingly frustrated at the exclusion of women from higher circles of decision making. She became active in the local chapter of NOW and met Eleanor Smeal, who was then head of Pennsylvania NOW. After Smeal was elected national president of the National Organization for Women in 1977, Yard followed

her to Washington to work on the campaign for the passage of the Equal Rights Amendment (ERA). She led the fight for ratification of the amendment in several key states including Florida, Oklahoma, North Carolina, and Virginia.

After the failure to ratify the Equal Rights Amendment, Yard continued her involvement in NOW's political campaigns. She served on the Political Action Committee (PAC) staff from 1978 to 1984 and from 1985 to 1987 she was NOW's political director.

She ran for president of national NOW in 1987 against Noreen Connell, the New York State NOW president. Connell felt that the organization should concentrate on strengthening its local chapters, but Yard instead called for large scale national actions to focus attention on the fight for women's rights. Yard won and immediately called for the impeachment of President Reagan and joined in the successful efforts to block the nomination of Robert H. Bork, an abortion rights opponent, to the Supreme Court.

Yard also pledged support for women candidates at every level of government and for a renewed fight for ERA. Under her leadership, NOW and other women's rights organizations organized massive demonstrations in Washington in April and November of 1989.

Yard was a strident leader of NOW and antagonized many members of the organization as well as nonmembers. She was a radical feminist at a time when many NOW members were concerned that women who lead traditional lives felt excluded from the women's movement and from NOW.

In late 1989, when Yard called for the formation of a third party, many leaders of women's organizations opposed her suggestion, feeling that it was much more important to concentrate efforts on supporting women within the two national parties. She was embroiled in continuous controversy from the day of her election, when her refusal to tell her age was the subject of numerous news articles. She was the first grandmother to head a major women's organization, and she was certainly the most radical. Yard was succeeded by Patricia Ireland on December 15, 1991. After serving as NOW's president, Yard continued to actively support the organization with appearances and speeches. In a column appearing in *The Advocate* (1991), she addressed the issue of lesbian concerns and NOW's agenda. Yard shared her dreams for women throughout the world in a 1994 interview appearing in *Anima*.

Further Reading

There are many articles about NOW in the years of Molly Yard's presidency, including the *National NOW Times*, which is available in many libraries. Ellen Hawkes' book *Feminism on Trial: The Ginny Foat Case and the Future of the Women's Movement* (1986) describes the controversies that NOW faced when Yard was elected. Other books discuss the ERA campaign, in which Yard was deeply involved. A few titles are *Why ERA Failed* (1986) by Mary Frances Berry and *The Equal Rights Amendment: the History and the Movement* (1984) by Sharon Whitney. Her article on lesbian concerns and NOW's agenda was published in *The Advocate* (March 26, 1991). A special interview with Yard appeared in *Anima* (fall 1994). ☐

Minoru Yasui

Minoru Yasui (1917–1987)was a lawyer who fought for the civil rights of Japanese Americans during World War II, most notably he argued about the unconstitutionality of the internment camps.

D uring the early 1900s, many Japanese people moved to the United States because of better opportunity for advancement. Due to historical racism against Asians, however, they often found only backbreaking labor open to them. Many of the Japanese labored in the lumber mills and fruit orchards. Employers doubted that these slender laborers could endure hard work, and so the Japanese worked twice as hard to prove their abilities. For example, logging companies cut down thousands of acres of forest, leaving only stumps and brush behind. Up to 600 Japanese laborers were hired each season to clear the stumps with hoes and dynamite. There might be as many as 100 stumps per acre, and often it took several days to clear one stump.

Settle in America

Many of the Japanese immigrants came to America intending to earn their fortune and return home to Japan. Minoru's father, Masuo Yasui, however, intended to settle in America. In Japan, Masuo learned English and converted to Christianity, following his father and brothers to America in 1903. In 1908, when he was twenty-one years old, he moved to Hood River, Oregon, a town with a large Japanese population. With the help of his brother Renichi, Masuo established a merchandising business called the "Yasui Brothers Company." The store sold Japanese goods such as soy sauce, imported rice, and toys. Renichi worked the counter, talking to customers and running the register, while Masuo kept track of the accounts and the bills. Together they built a small and successful business. Masuo gained recognition in Hood River as a key businessman and leader, eventually expanding his business to include contract labor and selling insurance.

Minoru's mother, Shidzuyo Miyake, finished college in Japan and worked as a teacher before coming to America. This was unusual because at that time, most Japanese women were uneducated. She and Masuo met briefly as children and exchanged letters and photographs while Masuo lived in Hood River. When Masuo proposed marriage in a letter, Shidzuyo accepted and moved to America to live with her new husband.

Shidzuyo traveled by ship to the United States to marry Masuo, breathing stale air, eating hard rice and sleeping in bunk beds. Ship toilets consisted of mere holes in the floor; the women could see the sea water rushing below. After three long weeks, Shidzuyo arrived in Hood River in 1912.

Childhood

In time, Shidzuyo and Masuo had eight children— Minoru was the third son in a wealthy family. His parents

encouraged their children to become Americanized and expected them to succeed in church and school. Minoru, a small, wiry boy with a quick wit and love for challenge, excelled. Independent and confident, Min, as he was called, set high academic goals for himself and performed well. He and his older brothers, Kay and Chop, were the first Japanese Americans to attend school in Hood River and the first to enroll in the Methodist Sunday school and Boy Scouts.

Children born in America to Japanese immigrants were called *nisei*, meaning "second generation." The *nisei* acquired both Japanese and American identities. Parents expected their *nisei* children to respect customary Japanese values such as authority, yet at the same time, the *nisei*, born and raised in the United States, displayed American characteristics such as independence. But nisei children were not totally accepted by others. The community viewed them as foreigners because they looked Japanese and spoke both languages.

Despite their success in school, Kay, Chop, and Min found childhood difficult as *nisei*. Due to their Japanese background, they made few friends during their school years. Isolated, Kay, Chop, and Min played with one another, fishing, hunting, and exploring the Oregon countryside.

Tragedy

As the oldest son, Kay held considerable power and authority within the family. His parents, however, expected Kay not only to be a role model for the younger children but also to represent the family within the community. Despite Kay's excellence in school and status as a budding poet, Masuo, a very strict father, disciplined Kay more harshly than the other children. On February 27, 1931, Shidzuyo told Kay to wake Minoru. Instead, Kay played a joke on Minoru by painting his face black. When Minoru awoke, both Minoru and his father yelled at Kay, shaming him tremendously. When a person is shamed in Japanese culture, they bring shame not only upon themselves but upon the entire family. Perhaps the combination of shame and pressure from his school and family grew too much for Kay to endure. Nobody knows exactly why, but Kay poisoned himself that evening, drinking water mixed with strychnine, a rat poison. He died that night.

Stricken with grief by the suicide, the family spoke little about the circumstances, simply informing the community that Kay died. Few people, including Minoru's younger bothers and sisters, knew that Kay had killed himself. The loss affected both Minoru and his father immensely, and Masuo blamed them both. He wrote Minoru: "Yourself and father are directly responsible for the loss of our dearest one. Your feeling and thought of the 27 of February meet exactly mine. You will surely feel very keenly toward your responsibility. . . . There lies our common sorrow and great point which we must suffer for the rest of our lives."

School

In 1933, at the age of sixteen, Minoru left Hood River to attend the University of Oregon in Eugene. He continued scoring high marks, rising quickly to the top of his class by making the honor roll every quarter and performing well in debates. Participating in the Reserve Officers Training Corps (ROTC), he was promoted to commanding officer by the end of his junior year. Minoru's classmates also elected him as secretary/treasurer of the dormitory and president of the school's international organization.

Despite his obvious talents, Minoru continued to experience prejudice due to his Japanese background. The fraternity clubs excluded him, for example, because membership was reserved for white males only.

After graduating, Minoru entered the University of Oregon's law school. He found his studies uninteresting but worked hard and at the end of his first year became the first Japanese American member of the Phi Beta Kappa honor society. In 1941 Minoru Yasui became the first nisei to graduate this law school. He passed the Oregon bar exam that summer.

Career move

Yasui tried to set up a law practice in Portland, but few people had money due to the Great Depression. So he took a job with the Japanese Consulate in Chicago. Meanwhile, prejudice against the Japanese grew. Other Americans believed that the Japanese filled jobs that did not belong to them, noting that the Japanese worked hard and became successful businessmen who competed with whites. Some whites, afraid the Japanese would take over the country if they could buy land, sought to limit land ownership to U.S. citizens only. In California, angry whites passed a 1913 act forbidding aliens to own land.

World War II and Pearl Harbor

By 1941 the Allied powers of Great Britain, France and Russia had fought for several years against Germany and the Axis powers. The United States, however, refrained from entering the war until December 7, 1941, when Japan bombed Pearl Harbor in Hawaii. The decision to declare war against Japan, Germany, Italy, and the other Axis powers greatly affected the Japanese Americans. Most Japanese immigrants lived on the West Coast, and the U.S. government began to fear that Japan had spies among the immigrant and nisei populations. Encouraged by anti-Asian groups, the government questioned the loyalty of the Japanese and Japanese Americans, assuming that they would side with Japan because of their ethnic background. The government, in fact, accused Japanese Americans of disloyalty to the United States and arrested many people on suspicion of spying or conspiracy. The frightened victims went to great lengths to prove that they were loyal Americans. In California, for example, a Japanese group bought the U.S. government a $50,000 antiaircraft weapon to show their support for the war.

Effects of prejudice

Yasui resigned his position at the Japanese Consulate the day of the Pearl Harbor attack. Later that week, the government informed Yasui that his father had been taken into custody on suspicion of spying. Yasui, it said, had to report to Fort Vancouver in Washington to fulfill his duty as a commanding officer in the U.S. Army.

When Yasui arrived at Fort Vancouver on January 19, 1942, the army would not let him report for duty. They turned him away because they did not understand how somebody who looked Japanese could fight for the United States in a war against Japan. Yasui repeatedly tried to report for duty, but the army refused each time and, after some debate, eventually classified him as not eligible for service.

Yasui traveled to Fort Missoula to attend his father's trial. At the trial, Yasui saw his father, a man who gave up his homeland to work and raise his children in the United States, accused as a spy and a traitor. Helpless, Yasui returned to Portland and set up a small office to help Japanese immigrants and their children deal with new legal problems caused by the war, such as the mounds of paperwork the government required of all people with Japanese ancestry.

Minoru's arrest

On February 19, 1942, President Franklin Delano Roosevelt signed Executive Order 9066, designating some areas as sensitive military zones from which any or all persons might be removed as the military saw fit. Yasui realized that this was directed at the Japanese.

The U.S. Constitution states that all citizens are equal under the law, and Yasui, recognizing the order as a violation of this ideal, prepared to fight a legal battle. "It is my belief that no military authority has the right to subject any United States citizen to any requirement that does not equally apply to all other U.S. citizens," Yasui declared.

In order to test the constitutionality of a law, the law must first be broken. Yasui decided to fight the first discriminatory order against the Japanese that resulted from Executive Order 9066. On March 24, 1942, General John L. DeWitt issued a curfew for all German, Italian, and Japanese nationals, as well as for citizens of Japanese descent. Yasui believed this violated his basic constitutional right as a citizen to equal and fair treatment. He aimed to challenge "special treatment" of persons based on race alone.

On March 28, 1942, at 6:00 Yasui calmly told his secretary to inform the police that a Japanese man was illegally out after curfew. He walked out the front door, down the street and waited for the police to come. They never showed. He kept walking and eventually found a policeman standing on the street. Yasui told the policeman to arrest him since he was obviously of Japanese ancestry and was therefore breaking the law by walking around after dark. The policeman told Yasui to run along because he would only get himself into trouble. Finally, about 11:00 Yasui walked into the police station and demanded to be arrested. The police sergeant threw him into the drunk tank, where he stayed until Monday morning when his bond was posted.

The fight begins

After his arrest, Yasui began an intense letter-writing campaign to Japanese associations and to General DeWitt. To drum up support, he circulated petitions protesting the discriminatory treatment of the Japanese. Yasui contacted various Japanese organizations, including the Japanese American Citizens League (JACL). But the JACL chose not to support Yasui because it did not want to support a constitutional challenge. Eager to demonstrate loyalty to the United States, many Japanese believed it was best to comply with governmental requests. The JACL supported this philosophy and actually tried to put a stop to Minoru's case. Still, Yasui held fast to the idea that loyalty to the United States meant abiding by its Constitution. If the nation strayed from the basic rights outlined in the Constitution, Yasui believed that it was his duty as a citizen of the nation to correct the error.

The war increased hostility against the Japanese. The attack on Pearl Harbor had created an atmosphere of fear and suspicion. Many citizens, including some military persons, feared a Japanese attack on the West Coast. Japanese submarines sank several American ships in the Pacific in late December 1941, causing an uproar among the nation's leaders. They were positive that Japan had spies in the United States and suspected all Japanese Americans as capable of betrayal. From February to March 1942, people of Japanese descent were encouraged to move from the West Coast to other areas of the country. But it was difficult to find any other area where they were welcome. And often reloca-

tion was not possible because the Japanese had no money or connections.

Arrest

On March 26, 1942, the military posted a notice in West Coast newspapers stating, "All Japanese and Japanese Americans residing in military area number One, comprising the western parts of Washington, Oregon, California and southern Arizona will be forbidden to leave the area after Sunday, the Western Defense Command announced tonight." It was the last chance to leave voluntarily. In May 1942, the military posted a final order forcing the Japanese to evacuate. They had to leave their homes and relocate to special centers designed to keep them in one place and under control. Yasui notified the army that he would evacuate only if they arrested him. On May 12, the military arrested and escorted him to the Portland detainment center, which he dubbed the "North Portland Pigpen."

Minoru's case and constitutional debate

In June 1942, the case *United States of America* v. *Minoru Yasui* was brought before the U.S. District Court in Portland. The case was important to the government because the outcome could confirm that its wartime policies towards the Japanese were legal. The government argued that Japanese characteristics naturally prompted these people to betray the United States, and therefore all Japanese were potential spies for Japan. The government realized, however, that this would be difficult to prove and intended to use "judicial notice." Under "judicial notice," lawyers do not have to prove facts that are deemed self-evident. The government wanted to establish the genetic tendency of Japanese towards treachery as self-evident.

Yasui and his lawyer Earl Bernard argued that it was unconstitutional for the government to single out one group of citizens based on ancestry. The Fourteenth and Fifth Amendments guaranteed the civil rights of citizens to equal protection and due process of law. Everybody agreed that these rights were absolute during times of peace and that internment constituted a violation of these rights. During wartime, however, the government has special authority. At stake was whether General DeWitt had the power, during a time of war, to single out U.S. citizens based on their race and strip them of these rights.

The verdict

The verdict was not reached until November. Judge Alger Fee referred to a decision set in 1866 called *Ex Parte Milligan*. In this case, the courts ruled that while Congress could authorize the president to suspend *habeas corpus* (which protects citizens from illegal or unjust imprisonment) and declare martial or military law, martial law could not exist unless civil courts ceased to function. Judge Fee noted that in Minoru's case, the president and Congress had not declared martial law, nor suspended *habeas corpus*. He declared that holding citizens was undeclared martial law and was not constitutional due to the Fifth and Fourteenth Amendments. Aliens, however, could be detained. Judge Fee then ruled that because Yasui had worked with the

Japanese Consulate, he had renounced his desire to be a U.S. citizen. He stripped Yasui of his citizenship and pronounced Yasui guilty, as an alien, sentencing him to one year in jail. Although Yasui immediately instructed his attorney to begin the appeals process, he spent nine months in solitary confinement. He was allowed neither to exercise nor shower.

The Supreme Court

In May 1943, Minoru's appeal reached the Supreme Court, the highest body of law in the country. The government restated its position that the Constitution allowed the government special "war powers" for the protection of the people and that the Japanese were dangerous. The Fifth and Fourteenth Amendments, it said, must give way to the decision-making of the military during wartime. The government argued that the order was a military necessity and proceeded to describe the supposedly forthcoming Japanese invasion on the West Coast as reason enough to detain the Japanese Americans.

The justices considered the case for months, finally reversing Judge Fee's decision. They referred to the recent case of *United States* v. *Hirabayashi*. In this case, the Court determined that special governmental powers, outlined in Articles I and II of the Constitution, such as "provide for the Common Defense" and "make all Laws which shall be necessary and proper," override individual rights during wartime. General DeWitt's actions were, in fact, constitutional during a time of war. Also, the Supreme Court ruled that Minoru's citizenship had nothing to do with the issues at hand. It returned his citizenship, and Yasui, as a Japanese American, was sent to the Minidoka Relocation Center in southern Idaho.

Life in the internment camps

When the Japanese received their orders to evacuate, many were given less than forty-eight hours to leave their homes. Two-thirds of these people were United States citizens by birth. They left their homes, their possessions and their businesses, often selling them for less money than they were worth. The government froze Japanese bank accounts, and bandits either stole or destroyed most of the possessions left behind. People sometimes threatened the Japanese physically.

Most of the internment or concentration camps contained numerous barracks with no furniture. Located in remote desert regions, the camps were filled with dusty air. Inmates lacked hot water and privacy. People ate together, slept together and bathed together. Camp life shattered family solidarity, an important characteristic in Japanese culture. Fathers had little power over their family, and mothers lost control over their children. Parents ate in huge mess halls, often separated from children and relatives. Some Japanese died in the camps, while many found the conditions hard to bear: "The thing that really hit most of us was the lack of privacy. There was no privacy whatsoever. . . . No closets. Just a potbelly stove for each family in one room. I really felt sorry for some of the teenagers, especially the shy

ones. Some couldn't take it. I recall one girl that lost her mind."

Months passed, and the internment camps slowly came to resemble life in the outside world. Some developed recreation facilities, libraries, social halls, and playing fields. Each center housed several thousand children, so schools opened in 1942. They were woefully lacking in desks, chairs, and most importantly, teachers. To pass the time, women organized arts and crafts classes, such as flower arranging and gardening. Cut off from the outside world, the interns lived a ghostlike existence. One intern expressed a feeling of being forgotten: "It seems that since evacuation, I have gradually lost contact with my friends outside. You see, when one is enclosed in the narrow confines of a camp, strange things happen. Time and the life of the world outside simply pass by without touching us."

By November 1, 1942, almost 112,000 evacuees were in temporary or permanent centers, even though during this time there was not one proven case of spying or sabotage by a Japanese American. Italian and German Americans, whose families came from other Axis countries, were not bothered.

Postwar life

Japanese internment officially ended on December 17, 1944, towards the end of World War II. Many people spent as long as two years in the camps and afterward faced new problems. A great number did not have anything to return to, having lost their homes and businesses due to the move to the camps. Yet Japanese Americans continued to face fear and prejudice. There were instances of racial terrorism and refusals to let them buy supplies or apply for desperately needed jobs. Movie theaters refused to sell them tickets, and barbers would not cut their hair. In many towns, businesses posted signs stating, "NO JAPS ALLOWED."

Released from Minidoka in 1944, Yasui moved to Colorado, passed the state bar exam, and set up a law practice. In 1946 he married True Shibata, with whom he had three daughters. Despite Minoru's talents, the family remained poor for many years. Yasui did a great deal of volunteer work, founding a City League and the first interracial Boy Scout Troop. During the 1950s he quit law. Yasui labored for the next twenty-four years on Denver's Commission on Community Relations to set up programs for the city's minorities. In time, the city recognized him as an outstanding citizen, established a monthly service award in his honor, and proclaimed Minoru Yasui Recognition Day.

Continued protests

Yasui continued his protests against the federal government for the rest of his life. In the 1970s, he led the JACL in a fight to right the wrongs done to the Japanese during WWII. He believed the government should admit its mistake by publicly apologizing to the Japanese Americans and paying compensation to those who suffered internment. In 1980 Congress funded a committee to report on the internment camp situation, and in 1983 the committee recommended that the government apologize. The committee also suggested $1.5 billion (about $20,000 per person interned) as compensation. Yasui meanwhile fought the government to clear his name, as his 1942 conviction still held. The government refused to reverse its decision, and when he died of cancer in 1986, the Supreme Court closed the case. Yasui died fighting.

On August 10, 1988, President Ronald Reagan signed the Civil Liberties Act of 1988, which provided each survivor of internment with the proposed $20,000. He also issued a formal apology, admitting the United States had wronged its citizens: "What is important in this bill has less to do with property than with honor, for here we admit to wrong. Here, we reaffirm our commitment as a nation to equal justice under the law."

Although Yasui was no longer alive, his children heard the message. It had taken over forty years for the United States to formally recognize its mistake. But, in the end, the government had reaffirmed the constitutional right of all of its citizens to be treated as equals. Yasui, in his long series of legal battles, played an important role in launching the struggle that led to this just verdict.

Further Reading

Fukei, Budd, *The Japanese American Story,* Minneapolis: Dillon Press, Inc., 1976.

Hopkinson, Lynall, *Nothing to Forgive,* Trafalgar: Chatto and Windus, 1990.

Kessler, Lauren, *Stubborn Twig,* New York: Random House, 1993.

Leathers, Noel L., *The Japanese in America,* Minneapolis: Lerner Publications Company, 1967. □

Chuck Yeager

Charles E. Yeager (born 1923), a test pilot for the United States Air Force, was the first person to fly a plane faster than the speed of sound.

Charles ("Chuck") E. Yeager was born in Myra, West Virginia on February 13, 1923. His father was a driller for natural gas in the West Virginia coal fields. As the United States began mobilizing for World War II, Yeager enlisted in the Army Air Force in 1941 at the age of 18. In 1943 he became a flight officer, a non-commissioned officer who could pilot aircraft. He went to England where he flew fighter planes over France and Germany during the last two years of the war.

In his first eight missions, at the age of 20, Yeager shot down two German fighters. On his ninth mission he was shot down over German-occupied France, suffering flak wounds. He bailed out of the plane and was rescued by members of the French resistance who smuggled him across the Pyrenees Mountains into Spain. In Spain he was jailed briefly but made his way back to England where he flew fighter planes in support of the Allied invasion of Normandy.

On October 12, 1944, Yeager took on and shot down five German fighter planes in succession. On November 6, flying a propeller-driven P-51 Mustang, he shot down one of the new jet fighters the Germans had developed, the Messerschmidt-262, and damaged two more. On November 20 he shot down four FW-190s. By the end of the war, at which time he was 22 years old, he was credited with having shot down 13.5 German planes (one was also claimed by another pilot).

In 1946 and 1947 Yeager was trained as a test pilot at Wright Field in Dayton, Ohio. He showed great talent for stunt-team flying and was chosen to go to Muroc Field in California, later to become Edwards Air Force Base, to work on the top-secret XS-1 project. At the end of the war, the U.S. Army had found that the Germans had not only developed the world's first jet fighter but also a rocket plane that had tested at speeds as fast as 596 miles an hour. Just after the war, a British jet, the Gloster Meteor, had raised the official world speed record to 606 miles per hour. The next record to be broken was to attain the speed of sound, Mach 1, which was what the XS-1 project was designed to do.

The measurement for the speed of sound was named after the German scientist Ernst Mach, who had discovered that sound traveled at different speeds at different altitudes, temperatures, and wind speeds. On a calm day at 60°F at sea level it was about 760 miles an hour. This speed decreased at higher altitudes. Airplane pilots who had come close to the speed of sound in dives reported that their controls froze and the structure of the plane shook uncontrollably. A British test plane disintegrated as it approached

the speed of sound. Because of these experiences, Mach 1 became known as the "sound barrier."

The Army had developed an experimental plane called the X-1 to break the barrier. Built by the Bell Aircraft Corporation, it was a rocket shaped like a bullet that was launched from another plane once they were airborne. The idea was to send up the X-1 on a number of flights, each time getting a little closer to Mach 1. A top commercial test pilot had been making these flights and had reached .8 Mach, where the plane shook violently. The pilot demanded a large bonus to fly the plane up to Mach 1. The Army refused to pay the bonus, and Yeager was given the job of piloting the X-1 at his usual salary.

In his test flights Yeager was able to get the plane to fly at .9 Mach and still keep control of the plane. It was his personal belief that the heavy vibration of the plane would actually calm down after reaching Mach 1. The date of October 14, 1947 was set for breaking the "sound barrier." On the night of October 12, Yeager went horseback riding and fell off the horse. The next day his right side was in a great deal of pain. Afraid of being taken off the flight, he drove to a local town and saw the doctor there who told him that he had broken two ribs.

Yeager went ahead with the flight without telling anyone of his injury. Because of his injury, he was unable to close the plane's right side door, but he solved the problem by taking the handle of a broomstick with him and using it to close the door with his left hand. Early on the morning of October 14, Yeager went up in the B-29 bomber that carried the X-1. He entered the X-1 and locked himself in at 7,000 feet. The B-29 released the X-1 at 26,000 feet. At .87 Mach the violent vibrations began, but Yeager continued to push the aircraft faster. Just as he had predicted, at .96 Mach the aircraft steadied and he passed Mach 1. At that moment a giant roar was heard on the desert at the experimental test site—the first man-made sonic boom. Yeager reached Mach 1.05 and stayed above Mach 1 for seven minutes. On his way back to the field he performed victory rolls and wing-over-wing stunts.

As soon as Yeager landed safely, the results were telephoned to the head of Army aviation, who ordered the base not to give out any information about the flight. Rumors of the flight appeared in the aviation press in December 1947, but the Air Force (as the Army Air Force became) did not confirm it and release Yeager's name until June 1948.

Yeager continued to test planes at Edwards Air Force Base. In December 1953 he set a new record by flying the X-1A to Mach 2.4. He left Edwards in 1954 and then went to Okinawa where he flew Soviet planes captured in the Korean War in order to test their performance. He returned to the United States in 1957 to lead an air squadron, and flew on training operations and readiness maneuvers at Air Force bases in the United States and abroad. In 1961 he was appointed director of test flight operations at Edwards Air Force Base and the following year was made commandant of the Aerospace Research Pilot School at Edwards.

In 1963 Yeager tested an experimental plane designed for high altitude flying, the NF-104, to see if it could beat the record set by a Soviet military plane of 113,890 feet. Yeager reached 108,000 feet when the plane spun out of control, and he was forced to eject from the plane. He was severely burned on the left side of his face and left hand. He spent a month in the hospital but was able to return to flying duties and as head of the experimental test pilot school.

Yeager was promoted to brigadier general in 1969, by which time he had flown more than one hundred missions in Southeast Asia in B-57 tactical bombers. Yeager had become the most famous pilot in the United States, and the Air Force called upon him increasingly for its public relations and recruiting efforts. He served in a variety of Air Force positions until his retirement in 1975. He is the recipient of numerous military awards and was awarded the Presidential Medal of Freedom in 1985.

Further Reading

Yeager has written two autobiographies. The first was entitled simply *Yeager* and published in New York by Bantam Books in 1985. This was followed by *Press On: Further Adventures of the Good Life*, Bantam Books, 1988. An interesting account of Yeager's life was written by William Lundgren and published as *Across the High Frontier* (New York: Morrow, 1955; paperback edition, New York: Bantam Books, 1987). There is an exciting retelling of Yeager's flights in the X-1 in Tom Wolfe, *The Right Stuff* (New York: Farrar, Straus & Giroux, 1979; paperback edition, New York: Bantam, 1980). Wolfe's book was later made into a movie (Warner Brothers, 1983), with Sam Shepard playing the role of Yeager. □

William Butler Yeats

The Irish poet and dramatist William Butler Yeats (1865-1939) was perhaps the greatest poet of the 20th century. He won the Nobel Prize for literature in 1923 and was the leader of the Irish Literary Renaissance.

The work of William Butler Yeats forms a bridge between the romantic and often decadent poetry of the fin de siècle and the hard clear language of modern poetry. Under his leadership the Abbey Theatre Company of Dublin contributed several major dramatists to the modern theater.

Yeats was born on June 13, 1865, in Dublin. He was the oldest of four children of John Butler Yeats, a noted portrait artist of the Pre-Raphaelite school, who supplemented William's formal schooling at the Godolphin School in Hammersmith, England, with lessons at home that gave him an enduring taste for the classics. The effect of John Yeats's forceful personality and his personal philosophy—a blend of estheticism and atheism—upon William were felt much later, in the mature poet's abiding interest in magic and the occult sciences and in his highly original system of esthetics. During his holidays each year in Country Sligo (the "Yeats Country" of modern tourism), the mysterious wildness and beauty of western Ireland made a deep impression.

At the age of 19, Yeats enrolled in the Metropolitan School of Art in Dublin, intending to become a painter. Here he formed a lifelong friendship with the poet "AE" (George Russell), and a year later they founded the Dublin Hermetic Society. In 1887 Yeats joined the Theosophical Society of London and also became literary correspondent for two American newspapers. Among his acquaintances at this time were his father's artist and writer friends, including William Morris, William Ernest Henley, George Bernard Shaw, and Oscar Wilde.

Important Friendships

In 1889 the Fenian party leader, John O'Leary, introduced Yeats to the woman who became the greatest single influence on his life and poetry, Maud Gonne. A passionate and beautiful woman, fiercely involved in the politics of Irish independence, she was Yeats's first and deepest love. She admired his poetry but rejected his repeated offers of marriage, choosing instead to marry Maj. John MacBride, later executed by the British government for his part in the Easter Rebellion of 1916. Maud Gonne came to represent for Yeats the ideal of feminine beauty (she appears as Helen of Troy in several of his poems), but a beauty disfigured and wasted by what Yeats considered an unsuitable marriage and her involvement in a hopeless political cause.

Always an organizer of artists and a joiner of groups, Yeats became a founding member of the Rhymers' Club in London in 1891 and of the Irish Literary Society of Dublin in 1892. During this period he formed some of the most important friendships of his life. Mrs. Olivia Shakespear, whom he

met in 1894, became his confidante; John Millington Synge, to whom he was introduced in 1896, later shared the codirectorship of the Abbey Theatre with Yeats; and Lady Augusta Gregory, whom he met in 1896, completed the feminine trinity of friendships of which Yeats later wrote in the poem "Friends": "Three women that have wrought/ What joy is in my days." For 20 years Yeats spent his summers as Lady Gregory's quest at Coole Park, her home in Galway. Her son, Maj. Robert Gregory, a young painter who died in World War I, and her nephew, Hugh Lane, an art collector, both figured prominently in the poems of Yeats's later period.

The young American poet Ezra Pound, the instigator of the imagist and vorticist movements in modern poetry, came to London expressly to meet Yeats in 1909. Pound later married Mrs. Shakespear's daughter Dorothy, and he served as Yeats's secretary off and on between 1912 and 1916. Pound introduced Yeats to the Japanese No drama, which gave a distinctive discipline and mood—ceremonial formality and symbolism—to Yeats's verse dramas. His poetry during this period began to show the hardness, brevity, and conciseness that characterize the best poems of his final period.

The death of Maud Gonne's husband seemed to offer promise that she might now accept Yeats's proposal of marriage. Upon her final refusal in 1917, he proposed to her daughter, Iseult MacBride, only to be rejected by her too. That same year he married Miss George Hyde-Less, daughter of an aristocratic Anglo-Irish family. Soon after their wedding, his wife developed the power of automatic writing and began to utter phrases of a strange doctrine, seemingly dictated by spirits from another world, in her sleep. Yeats copied down these fragments and incorporated them into his occult esthetic system, published as *A Vision* in 1925. A daughter, Anne Butler Yeats, was born in 1919, and a son, William Michael, 2 years later.

Poet and Dramatist

Yeats's first book of poems, *The Wanderings of Oisin and Other Poems,* was published in 1889. In the long title poem, he began his celebration of the ancient Irish heroes Oisin, Finn, Aengus, and St. Patrick. This interest was evident also in his collection of Irish folklore: *Fairy and Folk Tales* (1888). His long verse drama, *The Countess Cathleen* (1892), drew criticism because of its unorthodox theology, but it represents a successful fusion in dramatic form of ancient beliefs with modern Irish history. His collection of romantic tales and mood sketches, *The Celtic Twilight* (1893), attracted the attention of folklore collectors, among them Lady Gregory, who dated her interest in Yeats from her reading of this volume.

Yeats's *The Secret Rose* (1897) includes poems that he called personal, occult, and Irish, and it contains his rose and tree symbols based on Rosicrucian and Cabalistic doctrines. More figures from ancient Irish history and legend appeared in this volume: King Fergus, Conchubar the Red Branch King, and Yeats's most powerful hero, Cuchulain. *The Wind among the Reeds* (1899) won the Royal Academy Prize as the best book of poems published that year.

An important milestone in the history of the modern theater occurred in 1902, when Yeats, Maud Gonne, Douglas Hyde, and George Russell founded the Irish National Theatre Society, out of which grew the Abbey Theatre Company in 1904. Yeats's experience with the theater gave to his volume of poems *In the Seven Woods* (1907) a new style—less elaborate, less romantic, and more matter-of-fact in language and imagery. These changes were less noticeable in the play contained in this volume, *On Baile's Strand*. His play *The Green Helmet,* contained in a volume of poems published in 1910 by his sister's press, still exhibited his preoccupation with ancient royalty and "half-forgotten things," but his poetry was unmistakably new. Yeats's play *At the Hawk's Well,* written and produced in 1915, showed the influence of Japanese No drama in its use of masks and in its dances by a Japanese choreographer.

From 1918 to 1923 Yeats and his wife lived in a restored tower at Ballylee (Galway), of which the poet said, "I declare this tower is my symbol." Signifying restored tradition, ancient yet modern, nobility, aristocracy, and masculinity, the tower became a prominent symbol in his best poems, notably in those that make up *The Tower* (1928).

Because Yeats based his esthetic on the principle of opposites, his personal life was made complete when he officially became the "smiling public man" of his poem "Among School Children" through two events: he was elected an Irish senator in 1922, a post he filled conscientiously until his retirement in 1928; and he received the Nobel Prize for literature in 1923. His acceptance of the role and its responsibilities had been foreshadowed in his poems *Responsibilities* (1914). The outbreak of civil war in Ireland in 1922 had heightened his conviction that the artist must lead the way through art, rather than through politics, to a harmonious ordering of chaos.

Esthetic Theories and Systems

Yeats devised his doctrine of the mask as a means of presenting very personal thoughts and experiences to the world without danger of sentimentality or that kind of "confessional poetry" that is often a subtle form of self-pity. By discovering the kind of man who would be his exact opposite, Yeats believed he could then put on the mask of this ideal "anti-self" and thus produce art from the synthesis of opposing natures. For this reason his poetry is often structured on paired opposites, as in "Sailing to Byzantium," in which oppositions work against each other creatively to form a single unity, the poem itself.

Yeats turned to magic for the nonlogical system that would oppose and complete his art. He drew upon theosophy, Hermetic writings, and Buddhism, as well as upon Jewish and Christian apocryphal books (for example, the Cabala). To explain his theories he invented "a lunar parable": the sun and moon, day and night, and seasonal cycles became for him symbols of the harmonious synthesis of opposites, a means of capturing "in a single thought reality and justice." He illustrated his theory with cubist drawings of the gyres (interpenetrating cones) to show how antithetical elements in life (solarlunar, moral-esthetic, objective-subjective) interact. By assigning a different type of personality to each of the 28 phases of the moon (arranged like spokes on a "Great Wheel"), he attempted to show how one could find his exact opposite and at the same time discover his place in the scheme of universal order. Yeats believed that history was cyclic and that every 2,000 years a new cycle begins, which is the opposite of the cycle that has preceded it. In his poem "The Second Coming," the birth of Christ begins one cycle, which ends, as the poem ends, with a "rough beast," mysterious and menacing, who "slouches towards Bethlehem to be born."

Last Works

Yeats's last plays, *Purgatory* (1938) and *The Death of Cuchulain* (1938), also presaged his own death, which occurred on Jan. 28, 1939, in Roquebrune, France, where ill health had forced him into semiretirement. His final volumes of poems were *The Winding Stair* (1933), *A Full Moon in March* (1935), and *New Poems* (1938). His *Last Poems* (1940) brought Cuchulain from the grave into a realm beyond death, and this volume included Yeats's last poem, "Under Ben Bulben," in which he dictated the epitaph that adorns the headstone of his grave in Drumcliffe Churchyard (Sligo): "Cast a cold eye on life on death. Horseman, pass by!"

Further Reading

The only biography of Yeats is Joseph M. Hone, *W. B. Yeats, 1865-1939* (1943; 2d ed. 1962); but additional biographical information is in Alexander Norman Jeffares, *W. B. Yeats: Man and Poet* (1949). The best studies of Yeats's poetry are Richard Ellmann, *Yeats: The Man and the Masks* (1948) and *The Identity of Yeats* (1954); Donald A. Stauffer, *The Golden Nightingale* (1949); Thomas R. Henn, *The Lonely Tower: Studies in the Poetry of W. B. Yeats* (1950; 2d ed. 1965); and John Unterecker's indispensable *A Reader's Guide to William Butler Yeats* (1959). An excellent short study of Yeats is William York Tindall's pamphlet, *W. B. Yeats* (1966).

On Yeats as a dramatist, particularly useful are Helen H. Vendler, *Yeats's Vision and the Later Plays* (1963), and Leonard Nathan, *Figures in a Dance: William Butler Yeats' Development as a Tragic Dramatist, 1884-1939* (1965). Two excellent collections of essays by various critics are James Hall and Martin Steinman, eds., *The Permanence of Yeats: Selected Criticism* (1950), and John Unterecker, ed., *Yeats: A Collection of Critical Essays* (1963). Recommended for general background on the period are Ernest Boyd, *Ireland's Literary Renaissance* (1916); Dorothy Macardle, *The Irish Republic* (1937); William York Tindall, *Forces in Modern British Literature, 1885-1956* (1965); and Donald Connery, *The Irish* (1968). □

Yeh-lü Ch'u-ts'ai

Yeh-lü Ch'u-ts'ai (1189-1243), secretary-astrologer to Genghis Khan and chief of the Secretariat under his son Ögödei, was famous for his administrative reforms introduced in North China during the early years of the Mongol conquest.

The son of a Sinicized Khitan noble serving the Jürchen-Chin dynasty (1115-1234), Yeh-lü Ch'uts'ai was born in the Chin capital Chung-tu (modern Peking). He began the study of Chinese classics at the age of 12. Placing first in the degree examination, he was appointed a district vice-prefect in modern Hopei (1213); when the Chin emperor transferred his court to Pien-ching (K'ai-feng) in 1214, Yeh-lü returned to the old capital to become an auxiliary secretary in the Secretariat Council. He stayed to witness the fall of Peking to the Mongol forces in 1215.

Meanwhile, Yeh-lü had developed an interest in Buddhism and lived in seclusion as a lay disciple until he was summoned by Genghis Khan to Mongolia in April 1218. When Genghis set out for central Asia on his expedition against the Khwarezmian empire (in Russian Turkistan) the following year, Yeh-lü accompanied him as secretary-astrologer. He is said to have invoked the legend of the unicorn to dissuade the Great Khan from prolonging his futile campaign against Khwarezm. Yeh-lü was also credited with persuading Genghis to invite the famed Chinese Taoist Chiu Ch'iu-chi to the Mongol quarters to advise on government and religious matters. Genghis retreated with his forces in 1222, but Yeh-lü delayed his return to Peking until 1227.

In September 1229 Ögödei was elected Khan by the Mongol assembly in succession to Genghis, who had died in 1227. Ögödei was faced with a double task in North China: to annihilate the Chin and to consolidate the Mongol rule and devise effective means of exploiting the conquered territory. While the first task presented little problem, the second was beset by serious difficulties. The conservative faction of the Mongol court favored the complete annihilation of the native population and the turning of the entire occupied territory into pasture land. Opposing this radical suggestion, Yeh-lü proposed a more rational alternative for exploiting the country. He won and was put in charge of the taxation program; meanwhile, he presented to the Emperor an 18-point plan for dealing with the state of chaos in North China.

Administration of Conquered Territories

Yeh-lü's chief concern was to restore order and create a strong, centralized government, a prerequisite for a systematic and effective exploitation of the country. This was impossible when the conquered areas were under the control of the military commanders, who were virtually independent of the court; hence Yeh-lü insisted on a strict separation between the military and civil authority. He divided the country into 10 principal administrative units and established in each of these centers a tax collection bureau administered by civil officials to replace the arbitrary collection of levies by the local military officials. His fiscal reforms of 1229-1230 represented the first step toward transforming these confused fiscal practices into a rational system on Chinese lines.

Yeh-lü introduced a land tax on a household basis, a poll tax on all adults, a tax on commerce, and the traditional Chinese duties on liquor and vinegar, salt, iron smelters,

and mining products. He also curbed the excess privileges of the clergy by rescinding some of their exemption from levies granted by Genghis Khan. To implement his program, Yeh-lü began to build up a network of civil officials, but he gained little headway, as the Mongols resented the appointment of Chinese nationals to positions of responsibility.

These fiscal reforms bore the first fruit in September 1231 as the amount of revenue collected in Yün-chung (in modern Shansi) tallied with the figure Yeh-lü had projected. Ögödei was so pleased that he appointed Yeh-lü chief of the secretariat. He ran into difficulty when he wanted to carry out his reforms on a wider scale, because of the displacement of the population owing to war and famine and the impossibility of taxing the privileged non-Chinese residents of North China (Mongols, central Asians, and others).

Upon Yeh-lü's recommendation, a national census was ordered in 1234 and was completed 2 years later. He was in favor of the census for administrative reasons, but the Mongol nobles supported it as the basis of appropriating a larger share of land in the conquered areas.

Much against Yeh-lü's advice, Ögödei divided North China into a series of appanages and distributed them among the Mongol nobles and other dignitaries. This measure further weakened the central authority and presented a serious obstacle to Yeh-lü's reform programs. Meanwhile, Yeh-lü also encountered much difficulty in attempting to reorganize the civil service. In 1237 Ögödei consented to Yeh-lü's proposal of selecting Chinese for office through competitive examinations. Examinations were held, but the successful candidates only served in an advisory capacity on local administrative matters to their Mongol or central Asian superiors. This system was abolished after 1238.

Yeh-lü's Loss of Power

Yeh-lü's failure to reintroduce the traditional examination system coincides with the decline of his power at the Mongol court. Several factors contributed to this: Ögödei's withdrawal of support after 1235, the growing anti-Chinese feeling at court, the rise of central Asian merchants as tax collectors, and Yeh-lü's conflicts with his colleagues in the Secretariat.

Having lost out in his contest of power to the pro-Moslem faction of the court, Yeh-lü remained only as the titular head of the Secretariat after 1240 and ceased to play a decisive part in government affairs. Following Ögödei's death in 1241 and the succession of his widow Töregene as regent of the empire, Yeh-lü's position became more precarious. His support of the election of Siremün, the successor designated by Ögödei, to the khanate against the wishes of Töregene, who favored the candidacy of Ögödei's son Güyüg (who was finally elected in 1246), must have further jeopardized Yeh-lü's relationship with the Mongol ruling oligarchy. Yeh-lü died in 1243 and was buried near Peking.

Besides being a vigorous administrator, Yeh-lü was also a man of letters in the Confucian tradition. His collected works, in 14 chapters, were published after 1236. The record of his journey to central Asia, entitled *Hsi-Yu lu*, was written in 1228 and published in 1229.

Further Reading

An English translation of Yeh-lü's record of travel in central Asia is in Emil V. Bretshneider, *Mediaeval Researches from Eastern Asiatic Sources,* vol. 1 (1888; repr. 1967). Another translation, with annotations by Igor de Rachewiltz, is in *Monumenta Sinica,* vol. 21 (1962). There is no book-length biography of Yeh-lü in English. The authoritative essay on his life and career is Igor de Rachewiltz's "Yeh-lü Ch'u-ts'ai (1189-1243): Buddhist Idealist and Confucian Statesman" in Arthur F. Wright and Denis Twitchett, eds., *Confucian Personalities* (1962). Recommended for general historical background are Michael Charol (pseudonym of Michael Prawdin), *The Mongol Empire: Its Rise and Legacy,* translated by Eden and Cedar Paul (1940), and René Grousset, *The Rise and Splendour of the Chinese Empire* (trans. 1952). □

Yekuno Amlak

The Ethiopian king Yekuno Amlak (reigned ca. 1268-1283) restored the Solomonic dynasty to the throne of Ethiopia after it had been held by the Zagwe dynasty for about 300 years.

Almost everything that has been written about Yekuno Amlak pertains to a single, central event in his life: his restoration of the Solomonic dynasty to the Ethiopian throne. The official royal chronicles were begun about this time, but until the next century these chronicles record little more than lists of names and tell us little about Yekuno Amlak's life. Much of what has been written about the restoration of the Solomonic dynasty was in fact written several centuries later and is largely apocryphal.

According to traditions in manuscripts written after the 13th century, the Solomonic kings, whose ancestry was traced back to Solomon and Sheba, had been ousted by a northern dynasty known as the Zagwe about the 10th century. However, the Solomonic kings managed to maintain their dynasty in the Shoa Province of central Ethiopia while the Zagwe ruled from Lasta in the north. Naakuto Laab, the successor of the most famous Zagwe king, Lalibela, was said to have been convinced by Takla Haymanot, head of the Ethiopian Church, that Zagwe rule could never be "purged from the stain and crime of usurpation." Naakuto Laab was then supposed to have voluntarily relinquished this throne to Yekuno Amlak, who was ruling Shoa as the last survivor of the Solomonic line.

This story of peaceful transfer of power is of course highly suspicious. Naakuto Laab and his heirs were to retain a sort of quasi-independence in a small section of Lasta; the Church was to receive for its efforts a third of the land in the entire country. Regardless of the exact details of these events, it is clear that the Church grew greatly in wealth and power from this time until the 16th century.

Little else is known about Yekuno Amlak's reign. He established his capital in Tegulet in Shoa and thus continued the historical movement of the center of the Ethiopian state to the south, while touching off what has been called the era of "roving capitals." By this time Amharic had replaced Geez, or Old Ethiopic, as the court language, though Geez continued to be used in the Church much like Latin in the Western Church. Friction with the neighboring Islamic states, which had kept Ethiopia isolated for almost 6 centuries, was growing, and Yekuno Amlak mounted some military campaigns against them. However, the main conflicts came much later.

Yekuno Amlak was succeeded by Yagbea Sion, who ruled from about 1283 or 1285 to 1294; and his grandson, Amda Sion (reigned 1314-1344), who finally consolidated the empire and began a period of major expansion.

Further Reading

Since nothing has been written specifically on the life of Yekuno Amlak, students must rely on general histories for information. Good surveys include Estelle S. Pankhurst, *Ethiopia: A Cultural History* (1955); Edward Ullendorff, *The Ethiopians* (1960; 2d ed. 1965); and Richard K.P. Pankhurst, *An Introduction to the Economic History of Ethiopia, from Early Times to 1800* (1961). A rare but important traveler's account is the source of much of what modern historians have written on Yekuno: James Bruce, *Travels to Discover the Source of the Nile* (5 vols., 1790); volume 1 contains a discussion of Ethiopian history based on what were then contemporary traditions. □

Boris Nikolaevich Yeltsin

Boris Nikolaevich Yeltsin (born 1931), who became president of Russia in 1991, was one of the most complex and enigmatic political leaders of his time. A long-time Communist Party leader in Sverdlovsk (Ekaterinburg) and later Moscow, he was an important leader in the reform movements of the late 1980s and 1990s. Yeltsin was perceived at varying times as a folk hero, as a symbol of Russia's struggle to establish a democracy, and as a dictatorial figure.

Boris Nikolaevich Yeltsin was born into a Russian working-class family on February 1, 1931, in the small Siberian village of Butko. Yeltsin lived and worked in Siberia for most of his life. His early life, like that of most of his countrymen in the 1930s and 1940s, was marked by hardship, and as the oldest child Boris had numerous responsibilities at home. Only a month older than Mikhail Sergeevich Gorbachev, their lives and careers have many similarities and some differences. Both men came from rural worker and peasant families (Gorbachev lived in the village of Privolnoe in the Stavropol district) and succeeded in a society that paid lip service to workers and peasants but in reality was run by an elitist bureaucracy that disdained provincials.

A strong-willed child, Boris twice stood up to the educational system. At his elementary school graduation he criticized his homeroom teacher's abusive and arbitrary behavior, resulting in his expulsion. He appealed the decision and, after an investigation, the teacher was dismissed. During his last year in high school Yeltsin was stricken with typhoid fever and forced to study at home. Denied the right to take final examinations because he had not attended school, he appealed and won. His actions were extraordinary in the repressive climate of the Stalin period but help explain the mature Yeltsin. In July 1990 he walked to the podium at the 28th Congress of the Communist Party of the Soviet Union (CPSU) and submitted his resignation.

Trained as an engineer, Yeltsin graduated from the Ural Polytechnic Institute. He married his wife Naina at a young age; they had two daughters. The family is believed to be closely knit.

Yeltsin initially worked as an engineer in the construction industry in Sverdlovsk, moved into management of the industry, and later went to a career in the Communist Party, eventually becoming first secretary of the party in Sverdlovsk. Yeltsin joined the CPSU at age 30, relatively late for a man with political aspirations.

A Party Leader in Moscow

In 1985 Mikhail S. Gorbachev, the new general secretary of the CPSU, brought Yeltsin to Moscow to serve as secretary for the construction industry. Within a year he was appointed head of the Communist Party of Moscow. The 18 months that followed were a time of achievement and frustration, culminating in his dismissal as a Candidate member

of the Politburo and first secretary of the Moscow Party ("the Yeltsin affair").

Yeltsin did not like Moscow at first and criticized the privileges of the city's political elite as extravagant compared with life in Sverdlovsk. In a letter to Gorbachev, written in late summer 1987, Yeltsin asked to be relieved of his responsibilities in the Politburo. Initially he did not receive a response, but a disagreement on policy issues led to the confrontation in the Central Committee in October 1987. Yeltsin criticized the pace of the reforms known as *perestroika* and the behavior of some Politburo members. Yeltsin was removed as secretary of the Moscow party and his resignation from the Politburo was accepted. Yeltsin remained a party member, and Gorbachev appointed him a deputy minister in the construction industry, an area in which he had decades of experience.

As a political leader in Sverdlovsk and Moscow, Yeltsin was described as both a populist and an autocrat in his management style. At times preemptory in his action and approach, he often traveled to work on public transportation and mingled with ordinary people, unusual behavior among the Soviet elite, accustomed to travel in curtained limousines.

In the late 1980s, after Yeltsin criticized *perestroika,* his personal relationship with Gorbachev deteriorated. Publicly Gorbachev was reticent, but from 1987 to 1991 Yeltsin faced opposition at every step as he attempted to rebuild his political career. In the 1989 elections for the newly created Congress of People's Deputies (the new parliament), Yeltsin ran for a seat in Moscow against the nominee of the Communist Party, who managed the prestigious ZIL automobile factory. Yeltsin surprised the party by receiving 90 percent of the vote and, with great difficulty, was subsequently elected by the deputies to the smaller, more important, parliamentary body, the Supreme Soviet. Gorbachev was elected (chairman) president of the U.S.S.R. by the new parliament.

During 1989-1990 Yeltsin's populist views made him a folk hero in Moscow, where crowds chanting "Yeltsin, Yeltsin" were a frequent sight. In the Supreme Soviet he served on the steering committee of the interregional coalition of deputies with Andrei Sakharov. Yeltsin was also elected to the Russian parliament, which in May 1990 selected him as chairman (president) of the Russian Republic.

Yeltsin and Gorbachev never again achieved a sustained close working relationship, although at times they cooperated during the last 18 months of the Soviet Union. At the CPSU's 28th Congress in 1990 Yeltsin and other reformers within the party supported Gorbachev's leadership against the conservatives, led by Y.K. Ligachev. Although the Congress favored the conservatives, Ligachev was forced into retirement. Yeltsin had the last word when, late in the Congress, he publicly resigned from the party.

In June 1991 the Russian Republic held its first popularly contested election for president, and Yeltsin defeated six opponents to win the presidency. As president he declared the Russian Republic autonomous of the U.S.S.R. and offered to cooperate with the Baltic Republics, which were seeking freedom from the U.S.S.R. Such movements contributed to Gorbachev's decision to negotiate with the 15 Soviet republics to discuss ways to enhance their self government. The result was a draft treaty scheduled for signing in late August 1991.

President of the Republic of Russia

Yeltsin as president of the Russian Republic (RSFSR) and Gorbachev as president of the U.S.S.R. agreed to cooperate on economic reform, a reversal of their estrangement since 1987. However, on August 19, 1991, eight conservative party and government leaders perpetrated a coup against the vacationing Gorbachev. Yeltsin led the dramatic struggle on the ramparts of the Russian parliament (the "White House") in Moscow that defeated the coup and secured Gorbachev's return to Moscow.

In the aftermath of Gorbachev's rescue, Yeltsin consolidated his own power. Arguing the complicity of some of their leaders in the coup, Yeltsin led the movement to dissolve the Russian parliament and outlaw the Communist Party on Russian soil. These acts further weakened Gorbachev's power base. The draft treaty of the republics was never signed. In the fall of 1991 Yeltsin and other republic leaders declared the independence of their respective republics, and in December the presidents of Russia, Ukraine, and Belarus (Belorussia) formed the Commonwealth of Independent States (CIS), declaring they would no longer recognize the U.S.S.R. as of January 1, 1992. Eight other republics joined the CIS, while four republics became completely independent. Gorbachev resigned before year's end, and as of January 1, 1992, there was no more U.S.S.R. Yeltsin, who in 1987 had been dismissed from the Soviet leadership, became the head of post-Soviet Russia, the largest of the Soviet successor states. This was a political comeback unprecedented in Soviet history.

Yeltsin began a new chapter in 1992 as president of independent Russia. He undertook an ambitious program of economic reform known as "shock therapy," which accelerated the pace of privatization and allowed prices to float as a strategy to move quickly toward a market economy. The results were mixed. Privatization progressed but at the price of skyrocketing inflation and currency devaluation without increased production. Yeltsin's policies were frequently challenged during 1992, culminating in a major showdown with the Russian parliament in December 1992. Acting Prime Minister Yegor Gaidar, an advocate of shock therapy, was forced out, although within a year he returned to Yeltsin's cabinet. Viktor Chernomyrdin, a compromise candidate, became prime minister. Yeltsin's relationship with the parliament further deteriorated in 1993, and some of his 1991 political allies on the ramparts of the White House led the parliamentary opposition. Yeltsin dissolved parliament in September 1993, a sit-in ensued, and in early October 1993, a confrontation occurred, resulting in hundreds of deaths and injuries as well as considerable damage to the White House and other Moscow landmarks. The sit-in was eventually routed.

Yeltsin survived the political crisis, but his prestige and reputation suffered. The democratic Yeltsin who protested in the streets of Moscow in the late 1980s was forgotten, and a dictatorial image of Yeltsin emerged. In December 1993 Yeltsin suffered a further setback in the parliamentary elections, which he had called. Prominent reformers ran in rival parties, thus weakening their overall impact. The radical right, led by Vladimir Zhirinovsky, and the neo-Communists consequently made a better showing in the elections than they might have done if reformers had been united.

Yeltsin remained at the helm of Russian politics, but as a less heroic figure than the Yeltsin of 1991. Although reelected in 1996, Yeltsin's future was clouded by Russia's economic crisis and the failure of his reform program, combined with the bitter aftertaste of Yeltsin's confrontation with parliament. More importantly, after the 1996 elections it became clear that he had deceived the Russian people about his health. In fact, he had suffered a heart attack prior to elections, and was not well. In *The Nation* Daniel Singer wrote, "The Russians would not have voted for Yeltsin had they known he was such an invalid. Only extraordinarily tight government control over television enabled the stage managers to conceal his heart attack." Although he continued as president, there was much speculation within the international and Russian community as to who his successor would be. In May 1997 *World Press Review* observed, "Considering that most recent Russian leaders have been sickly, it is odd that the Russian constitution seems to presuppose a vigorous leader." The problem left many more than a little uneasy.

Despite his poor health, Yeltsin met with President Clinton in Helsinki in March 1997. Among the important issues addressed, Yeltsin approved a new Russian role in NATO, despite his opposition to NATO expansion. In essence, President Clinton assured the Russians a seat on NATO councils, stating they would "have a voice, not a veto." But it was clear that Yeltsin expected a right to override actions Russia found unacceptable. In exchange for this new position within NATO, Yeltsin implied the Russians would cease their opposition to NATO expansion.

In his new term, Yeltsin continued to face domestic problems in 1997. The Russian financial picture continued to grow grim: the gross national product fell another 6 percent in 1996, industrial production was off even more, and even the life expectancy dropped drastically, by 6 years. Of the 1997 Russian financial picture, Singer pointed out, "Barter, debt-swapping and hidden financial transactions are replacing normal exchange. Fiscal fraud has reached epidemic proportions." Indeed, in 1997, employees frequently waited as long as three months for payment. Despite such a grim financial picture, President Yeltsin was a resilient politician with keen political insights who rebounded from defeat after defeat.

Further Reading

A number of books treat Yeltsin the politician and the man. Considerable insights can be gained from his two autobiographies—*Against the Grain,* written as a diary about his political life, with flashbacks into his early life and career; and *The Struggle for Russia* (1994), in which he describes his role in both attempted coups, and profiles friends and adversaries in Russia and abroad. Other biographers include John Morrison, whose *Boris Yeltsin* (1991) portrays Yeltsin the politician in the context of Soviet politics. His relationship with Gorbachev and the "Yeltsin affair" are described in Seweryn Bialer's *Inside Gorbachev's Russia* (1989). The preclude to Yeltsin's rule is described by Robert Daniels in *The End of the Communist Revolution* (1993). An excellent article on Yeltsin and Russia can be found in *The Nation* (March 31, 1997). □

Yen Fu

Yen Fu (1853-1921) was a Chinese translator and scholar. His translations and annotations were enormously influential in introducing European thought regarding political theory and sociology to China.

Born in Fukien Province to a scholar-gentry family, Yen Fu was early exposed to China's traditional learning. This education, which would have led to competition in the civil service examinations and an official career, was aborted when his father died in 1866, leaving the family in straitened circumstances. Young Yen then continued his education as a student in the school of the Foochow Shipyard. There he learned English and studied Western science. He also traveled extensively, visiting Singapore and Japan, and in 1877 went to England, where he studied at the Greenwich Naval College. Thus at the age of 26 he was, among Chinese, one of the best-informed about the Western world.

Throughout most of the ensuing years, until 1906, Yen served as superintendent of the Tientsin Naval Academy. But even before his trip to England in 1877, he had become obsessed with the weakness and humiliation of China, and he devoted most of his mature years searching for the secret that had brought wealth and power to Europe generally and to Great Britain in particular. Having read widely in English, Yen almost completely rejected his Chinese intellectual heritage. He developed a strong aversion for Confucianism and all those elements of traditional China that seemed to obstruct China's progress to wealth and power. This rejection of traditional values placed Yen in stark contrast to nearly all his contemporaries, who at this time still hoped that they could preserve China's traditional culture by adopting minimal increments of the West's material technology.

The strongest influence upon Yen's intellectual development was Herbert Spencer, whose concepts of evolution, struggle, and dynamic individualism Yen eagerly accepted. He became convinced that Great Britain had become strong because the people possessed freedom, as a consequence of which the driving, creative energies of individuals were released. These energies had, in turn, led to the development and strength of knowledge, industry, and military force in the Western nations.

After the devastating defeat of China in the Sino-Japanese War of 1894-1895, Yen determined to make his insights regarding the sources of wealth and power known to his fellow countrymen. He wrote some essays, but his most effective medium was through the translation of important Western works. Between 1895 and 1908 he translated eight major pieces, among which were T. H. Huxley's *Evolution and Ethics* (1896), John Stuart Mill's *On Liberty* (1899), Adam Smith's *Wealth of Nations* (1900), *Spencer's Study of Sociology* (1903), and Montesquieu's *The Spirit of the Laws* (1905).

Yen's concept of gradual, evolutionary progress caused him to oppose the revolutionaries who ultimately overthrew the Manchu dynasty in 1912. After the revolution, he progressively retreated from the "radical" ideas of his earlier years. He lent his reputation and advice to the unsavory regime of Yüan Shih-k'ai. And, as a result of the butchery of World War I, Yen became utterly disillusioned with the West and concluded that the nondynamic values of traditional China were of greater benefit to human welfare than were the Promethean drives of the Europeans. He died in 1921, completely pessimistic regarding the effects of historical evolution on China.

Further Reading

The only study of Yen Fu in English is Benjamin I. Schwartz, *In Search of Wealth and Power: Yen Fu and the West* (1964). This work is an intellectual biography that treats Yen's life only sketchily; it does, however, offer deep insights into the nature of the cultural conflicts that occurred when China was confronted with the challenge of the West. □

Yen Hsi-shan

The Chinese warlord Yen Hsi-shan (1883-1960) ruled Shansi Province in northwest China from 1911 to 1949. Because of his program of reforms, Shansi was dubbed the "model province."

Yen Hsi-shan was born in the village of Ho-pien not far from the provincial capital of Taiyüan. His father was a small banker, an occupation in which Shansiers had traditionally been famous, and Yen served as apprentice while studying the classics. In 1901 the bank's failure forced Yen to leave home and enroll in the government-supported military college in Taiyüan. He continued his military education in Japan under a government scholarship; there he joined the revolutionary T'ung-meng hui, of which Sun Yat-sen was a prominent leader. Following his return home, Yen rose to the rank of colonel in the New Shansi Army.

Hearing of the Wuchang revolt in October 1911, Yen declared Shansi independent of the Manchu government, but only the abdication of the Manchu emperor saved Yen's outnumbered troops from a crushing defeat. President Yüan Shih-k'ai appointed Yen military governor of the province. In July 1917 Yen seized full powers and became Shansi's one-man ruler.

During the next decade, Yen proved himself a master of the complicated game of warlord politics. Dealing from a position of weakness, he maximized his leverage to determine the balance of power. On June 5, 1927, he threw in his

lot with the Nationalist forces and was appointed commander in chief of the revolutionary armies in the North. On June 8, 1928, he occupied Peking. The new government at Nanking appointed him governor of Shansi and rewarded him with other high posts in the Kuomintang military and party structure.

Estranged from Chiang Kai-shek over the issue of troop disbandment, Yen refused to help Chiang put down a rebellion by Feng Yü-hsiang in 1929. In February 1930 he joined Fang in the "northern coalition" against Chiang, a movement that received military support from the Kwangsi clique and political encouragement from Wang Ching-wei's Reorganizationist faction. However, Chiang's offensive of August 1930, followed by the intervention on Chiang's side by Manchurian warlord Chang Hsüeh-liang, forced Yen to send his army back to Shansi and retire to Dairen.

Japan's attack on Manchuria on Sept. 18, 1931, led to Yen's return to Shansi. In 1932 he was appointed pacification commissioner of Shansi and Suiyuan. In 1934 he initiated a 10-year development plan to fortify the province against Japanese and Communist threats. He curtailed the power of the local gentry; fostered woman's rights, and encouraged public education. However, at the beginning of the Second Sino-Japanese War, most of Shansi was occupied either by Japanese or by Communists. Yen finally cooperated with the foreign invader against his domestic foes and, after the Japanese surrender of August 1945, used Japanese troops against the Communists.

Yen could not prevail against the Communist tide. In March 1949 he fled to Nanking, and on April 24 his army surrendered. In June, Yen became president of the Executive Yüan and minister of national defense. On December 8 he fled to Taiwan, where he served briefly as premier of the exiled Nationalist government. But Yen was nothing without Shansi. During the last decade of his life his political role was an advisory one only. He died on May 24, 1960.

Further Reading

A good, up-to-date biography of Yen Hsi-shan is Donald G. Gillin, *Warlord: Yen Hsi-shan in Shansi Province, 1911-1949* (1967). Doak Barnett, *China on the Eve of Communist Takeover* (1961), deals with the period and the causes leading up to the takeover and includes extensive information on Yen as well as a short biography. Also useful is F.F. Liu, *A Military History of Modern China* (1956). □

Yen Li-pen

The Chinese painter Yen Li-pen (died 673) was the greatest master of the early T'ang dynasty. He was primarily a figure painter, and his style expresses the confident, expansive air of his age.

Yen Li-pen was born in the late 6th century in Wannien, Yung-chou (modern Shensi Province). His father, Yen P'i, was a court painter and official under the Northern Chou and Sui dynasties; and his older brother, Yen Li-te, was also a painter who rose to the position of minister of the Board of Works. Yen Li-pen succeeded him in this post in 656, and in 668 he became one of two ministers of state. Despite his high offices in government, he was regarded primarily as a painter and summoned to perform at the Emperor's whim. In consequence, Yen Li-pen is said to have discouraged his son from becoming a painter.

Yen Li-pen's art typifies the grand imperial spirit of the early T'ang period. His greatest predecessor, Ku K'aichih, had developed a style featuring a fine brush line "like silken thread," that was well suited to an intimate, humanistic expression. Yen Li-pen's brushwork is described as "iron-wire line," a thin, hard, even lineament used with heavy shading and bold color, which is better suited to a powerful, monumental art.

The most impressive painting surviving under Yen's name is the *Scroll of the Emperors* in Boston, portraying 13 emperors from the 2d century B.C. to the 7th century. Each monarch is depicted with attendants and is effectively characterized as an individual, as we know from accounts of their personalities in dynastic annals. The overriding impression, however, is one of majesty and remote dignity, quite different from the gentler, more personal art of Ku K'aichih. A similar work in Peking, representing Emperor T'aitsung receiving a foreign ambassador, reinforces this image, though it is a somewhat later copy. Several of Yen Li-pen's portraits of meritorious officials, painted at imperial command in 643, have been preserved as rubbings made from engravings on stone cut in 1090.

A quite different style is seen in a lovely handscroll also in Boston. *Scholars of the Northern Ch'i Dynasty Collating Texts* has been attributed to Yen Li-pen at least since the beginning of the 12th century and is among the most remarkable of all early Chinese figure paintings. As in the works mentioned above, the figures are placed against a plain background, without setting, and the brushwork is fine and even. However, the color is pale and transparent, there is relatively little shading, and each figure is individually conceived in the most sensitive manner. The interaction between members of the group is also striking. If the work is truly related to Yen Li-pen, then it reveals a more penetrating and personal master than his other works suggest.

After his death in 673, Yen Li-pen was honored by the Emperor with the posthumous title *Wen-chen* (Cultured and True). His art became a classical ideal to later masters.

Further Reading

There is no monograph on Yen Li-pen. The best source in English is Oswald Siren, *Chinese Painting: Leading Masters and Principles* (7 vols., 1956-1958). See also the passages on Yen in Eli Lancman, *Chinese Portraiture* (1966). □

Robert Mearns Yerkes

Robert Mearns Yerkes (1876-1956), American psychologist, played a leading role in the development of psychology in America by laying the groundwork for important new areas of both research and practice.

Robert Yerkes was born in Bucks County, Pa., on May 26, 1876. He graduated from Ursinus College in 1892. Financial problems and the offer of a fellowship in zoology at Harvard deflected him from a long-held wish to study medicine. At Harvard he shifted gradually from zoology to animal psychology and received his doctorate in 1902. He remained at Harvard to teach and do research for the next 15 years. In 1916 he was elected president of the American Psychological Association.

As chief of the Psychology Division in the Surgeon General's Office during World War I, Yerkes organized the first large-scale utilization of psychologists in a professional capacity. He developed the Army Alpha Testing Program. This mental screening device, used on 1.7 million recruits, established the value of applying psychological methods to solving human problems and was a major factor in the development of psychology as an independent profession in America. Yerkes's books that resulted from this work, *Army Mental Tests* (1920) and *Psychological Examining in the U.S. Army* (1921), were models for the further expansion of intelligence testing as a field in psychology and are still in use today.

Yerkes also devised basic methodological tools for studying learning in animals and enunciated an important law relating the effect of fear on learning. Even more important was his pioneering effort to promote research on primates and the scientific study of sex. From 1921 until 1947 Yerkes served as chairman of the National Research Council Committee for Research on Problems of Sex, which sponsored projects that led to such studies as the Kinsey Report.

Yerkes's classic studies *The Great Apes: A Study of Anthropoid Life* (1919), coauthored with his wife, and *Chimpanzees: A Laboratory Colony* (1943) established the significance of studying the almost-human primate behavior. While a professor of psychology at Yale from 1924 to 1944, Yerkes established the first experimental primate breeding colony in America at Orange Park, Fla. It was renamed the Yerkes Laboratory of Comparative Psychobiology after his death.

Although sidetracked from pursuing a medical career directly, Yerkes realized his concern with medicine in his efforts toward making psychology one of the helping professions. He viewed his scientific studies of behavior as part of a basic science fundamental to the care of human problems. He died on Feb. 3, 1956.

Further Reading

Yerkes's autobiography appears in *A History of Psychology in Autobiography,* edited by Carl Murchison (1961). The most extensive review of Yerkes is Earnest R. Hilgard's "Robert Mearns Yerkes" in *National Academy of Sciences Biographical Memoirs,* vol. 38 (1965), which includes a complete bibliography of Yerkes's writings. See also E. G. Boring's "Robert Mearns Yerkes (1876-1956)" in the 1936 *Yearbook* of the American Philosophical Society, published in 1956. □

Yevgeny Alexandrovich Yevtushenko

Yevgeny Alexandrovich Yevtushenko (born 1933), the most popular of contemporary Soviet poets, was the leading literary spokesman for the generation of Russians who grew to maturity after Stalin's death in 1953.

Yevgeny Yevtushenko was born on July 18, 1933, in Zima, Siberia, into a peasant family of mixed Ukrainian, Russian, and Tatar stock. His father, a geologist, and his mother, a geologist and singer, were divorced in the early 1940s, and Yevgeny spent his early childhood in Moscow with his mother and sister, Yelena.

During World War II Yevtushenko was evacuated to Zima, returning to Moscow in 1944. Expelled from school on a false charge, he ran away to Kazakhstan; he joined his father on geological expeditions there and to the Altai, later returning to Moscow. As a youth, Yevtushenko was an athlete; his favorite sports were cycling, table tennis, and soccer.

Early Poems

Yevtushenko published his first poem in 1949 in a Soviet sports magazine and thereafter became a regular contributor to *Komsomolskaya Pravda, Literaturnaya Gazeta, Novy Mir,* and other important Soviet publications. As a result of the success of his first book of poetry, *The Prospectors of the Future* (1952), he joined the Soviet Writers' Union and began studying at the Gorky Literary Institute, which he left after several years without graduating.

After Stalin's death in 1953, Yevtushenko abandoned his pro-Stalinist themes and began writing love poetry. The following year he married Bella Akhmadulina, a poet (they were later divorced). *Third Snow* (1955), his second book of poems, was heavily attacked by official critics, and he became famous. Other volumes of verse were published in 1956 and 1957. "Zima Junction," his finest poem, relates a visit to his hometown in 1953 and reflects the confusion and search for values of a young man in post-Stalinist Russia. The rebellious attitudes characteristic of the poems of these years provoked attacks by the more orthodox Soviet writers and critics, but Yevtushenko's fame continued to grow. His themes, both personal and social, were marked by an unconformist attitude and conveyed a strong feeling of human sympathy.

Later Poems

Longbow and Lyre (1959) contained poems about Georgia and translations from the Georgian language. *Po-*

ems *of Several Years* (1959), a retrospective anthology, contained most of Yevtushenko's best shorter poems. *The Apple* (1960) marked a distinct falling-off in his work, but his next book, *A Sweep of an Arm* (1962), contained some of his most powerful poems.

Beginning in 1961, Yevtushenko traveled extensively outside the Soviet Union. He made trips to Bulgaria, France, Ghana, Cuba, the United States, and Great Britain. Everywhere he was received as an unofficial representative of post-Stalinist Russia. Reading his poems before large audiences, he received widespread adulation. Westerners were entranced, as Marc Slonim (1964) wrote, by "this tall, handsome, outgoing Siberian, an athletic, devil-may-care fellow, who personified youth and poetry."

Bratsk Station (1965) is a collection of poems that presents a panoramic view of Russian history and celebrates the creative efforts of the Soviet builders of communism. A 5,000-line, 35-poem cycle, it commemorates the construction of a vast hydroelectric power complex in Siberia; the poet contrasts it as a symbol of faith and human progress to an Egyptian pyramid. The work was not entirely successful, and Slonim argued that Yevtushenko "simply does not have enough breadth and power to make large compositions poetically convincing—despite the sonority, catching rhythm and verbal dynamism of numerous separate passages. It could be argued that, in general, he shows more talent for lyrical stanzas than for narrative poetry or vociferous political verse."

The Immortal *Babiy Yar*

Perhaps Yevtushenko's most famous poem is "Babiy Yar," written in 1961 and later revised. It memorializes some 96,000 Jews massacred by the Nazis in a ravine near Kiev during World War II. Until the publication of this poem, the Soviet government had not acknowledged that most of the victims of the Babiy Yar massacres were Jews. The poem strongly indicts continuing anti-Semitism in the Soviet Union, concluding with the lines: "No Jewish blood runs among my blood,/ but I am as bitterly and hardly hated/ by every anti-Semite/as if I were a Jew. By this/ I am a Russian." The poem was rapturously received by a Russian public, and was even defended by Nikita Khrushchev, who allowed it to be published in the leading newspaper, *Pravda*.

An Unpopular Stance

But Khrushchev was not so liberal in 1962, when Yevtushenko dared to publish an uncensored and unscrutinized autobiography in the West. *A Precocious Autobiography* first serialized in *Stern* included a frank discussion on the tragic flaws in Soviet society, laid the blame for many of them at the late Joseph Stalin's door, and announced the author's intention of trying to work for social improvement. The result was immediate. Yevtushenko was publicly denounced by Khrushchev for cheap sensationalism, and vilified for his sentiments and even for his literary technique.

Khrushchev himself was under the gun, and in fact, was ousted in October 1964, and replaced by the unyielding, intensely conservative Leonid Brezhnev. Like other literary figures, Yevtushenko began to chafe under the scrupulously observed new restrictions, and was allowed neither to travel nor to give his usual poetry readings.

He lived in relative obscurity until 1966, when his name surfaced again in connection with the trial of Yuli Daniel and Andrei Sinyavsky, two writers who had been caught after smuggling supposedly anti-Soviet books to the West for clandestine publication under pen names. Along with several other writers, Yevtushenko protested the trial, and was almost stopped from traveling to America that same year. Permitted to go only because his passport had already been issued, he later claimed to have been told by Senator Robert Kennedy that America's Central Intelligence Agency had been the agency responsible for getting the writers into trouble. Supposedly, they had contacted their Russian counterparts and told them about Sinyavsky and Daniel and their ploy for publication, in order to deflect attention away from criticism against the Vietnam War.

Interviewed in 1987 by *Time* magazine, he commented on why he felt it imperative to support these writers despite the danger to his own reputation. Using the expression *glasnost*, the Russian word for "openness", that will forever be associated with Mikhail Gorbachev, the Soviet Union's democratic leader of the 1980s, Yevtushenko looked back on the Daniel/Sinyavsky trial and remarked: "*Glasnost* is us. We fought for it for many years past."

Fresh Fields to Conquer

In 1991, a collection of his work called *Fatal Half Measures*, was published by Random House. Centered around the themes of *glasnost* and *perestroika*, the book contained excerpts from several earlier works, all supporting Yevtushenko's strong political convictions. His concerns about the rising racism and increasing desperation of Russian society came strongly to the fore, as they have done in many other works. In the essay "A Nation Begins with Women", Yevtushenko entreated that Russian women at last be treated with long-overdue respect, paid salaries on a par with those earned by men doing the same jobs, and offered opportunities to hold positions of authority in an economy long monopolized by men. Perhaps his most telling comment is the one concluding this piece: "Can a nation be respected if it does not respect its women?"

Yevtushenko had also been trying his wings in new fields. His first novel, *Wild Berries* was published in 1984, to a lukewarm reception, and after several others, *Don't Die Before You're Dead* (1995) received favorable attention from most major reviewers. Dealing with the attempted coup that took place in Russia in 1991, the book detailed the fortunes of several actual people (Yeltsin, Gorbachev) as well as fictional ones, designed to show a panorama of Russian society.

Yevtushenko also ventured into photography, with *Divided Twins: Siberia and Alaska* and *Invisible Threads* . Even films offered him a world of novelty worthy of exploration. In 1995 a movie he co-directed, called *I Am Cuba*, found an audience, though judgmental, generally labelling it, in the words of *The Nation* "a film that has still not found its historical moment." This was certainly no deterrent to the vigorous Yevtushenko, who had always regarded the possibility of improvement as a zestful challenge.

By 1996 he was back in New York, teaching Russian poetry and literature at Queens College. He chose to live among his students in Queens, rather than in Manhattan, with the majority of his more prosperous colleagues because he enjoyed the wide ethnic mix that Queens had always offered.

Further Reading

All of Yevtushenko's major works are available in English translation, in several versions of varying quality. *Bratsk Station, and Other New Poems,* translated by Tina Tupikina-Glaessner, Geoffrey Dutton, and Igor Mezhakoff-Koriakin, is a brilliant translation of Yevtushenko's major work. Another good source on Yevtushenko is his *A Precocious Autobiography,* translated by Andrew R. MacAndrew (1963). For critical commentary, see Marc Slonim's, *Soviet Russian Literature: Writers and Problems* (1964), and Olga Carlisle's, *Poets on Street Corners: Portraits of Fifteen Russian Poets* (1969).

Additional Sources

Fatal Half Measures, Random House, 1991.
Atlantic Monthly, October, 1995.
New York Times, November 12, 1995; February 7 1996.
The Nation, March 20, 1995.
Time, February 9, 1987. □

Yi Hwang

Yi Hwang (1501-1570), Yi-dynasty philosopher, poet, scholar, and educator, was one of the greatest Korean Confucian philosophers, famous for his comprehensive studies of the great Sung Neo-Confucian philosopher Chu Hsi.

Yi Hwang, whose literary appellation was T'oegye (Stream Hermit), was the youngest son of scholar Yi Sik, who died seven months after Yi Hwang's birth. The family was plunged into "honest" poverty because of the loss of the father's government stipend. When Yi was 12, he began his studies in preparation for the government entrance examinations, a basic feature of the Confucian bureaucracy. He studied the *Analects* of Confucius with his uncle Yi U. Yi Hwang attracted the attention of his elders by his precocity. He is said to have loved the poetry of T'ao Yuan-ming, the outstanding post-Han era nature poet of China.

When Yi was 17, he began his study of the Confucian commentaries of the Sung Neo-Confucian philosopher Chu Hsi which was to bring him lasting fame. About his twentieth birthday Yi was initiated into the mysteries of the *Book of Changes* (*I ching*) and is said to have injured his health and even neglected his meals pondering the philosophy of change.

Yi married when he was 21, and his first son was born two years later. In 1527 he passed the Kyngsang provincial qualifying examination and passed the metropolitan examination the next spring, placing second and earning his literary licentiate degree. His wife died only a few months before his success. In 1530 he remarried, and another son was born the following year. In 1534 Yi placed in the higher government examination and was appointed to office in the Royal Secretariat. He was prevented from advancing in his career by a faction led by Kim Anno despite his aristocratic background.

Yi held various minor posts until his mother died when he was 37. In accordance with Confucian custom, he left the government for an extended period of mourning. Near the end of this mourning period Kim Anno's faction fell from power, and there were no further major political obstacles in Yi's official career. He was given a post in the very powerful Office of Special Counselors and simultaneously in the prestigious Office of Royal Lectures. At 43 he was appointed assistant headmaster of the National Academy, but he left office shortly thereafter and returned to his home, turning his back on court politics to devote himself to his philosophic studies.

Five years later Yi was made headman of Tanyang county, a position which provided him with a stipend away from the factional tensions of court; however, his elder brother, Duke Taehn, was made chief magistrate of the province, obligating Yi to request a transfer for the sake of propriety. He was transferred to P'unggi county in Kyngsang Province to serve as headman there. The next year he pe-

titioned the chief magistrate to relieve him from duty, and his request was granted the following year. He retired to the west bank of T'oegye Stream and devoted himself to philosophical studies.

At the age of 52 Yi was recalled to the capital to be the headmaster of the National Academy. He repeatedly requested to be relieved because of his failing health; however, he served as minister of works, minister of rites, and chancellor of the Office of Royal Decrees. In 1569 he returned to his home in Andong in poor health. The next year he passed away. The Tosan Academy in Kyngsang Province was established in his honor five years after his death. The following year the King conferred the posthumous title of Mun Sun (Pure Word) upon him.

Chu Hsi and Neo-Confucianism

In the late 12th century Chu Hsi became the leader of the Sung philosophical School of Principle, and his commentaries on the Confucian canon and his interpretations of Confucian principles became the orthodoxy of the Yi-dynasty Confucianists in Korea under the influence of Yi Hwang (T'oegye), Yi I (Yulgok), and others. Even in China, the Chu Hsi interpretation stood as the standard for government examinations with only occasional challenges by new interpretations from philosophers such as Wang Yang-ming and Lu Hsiang-shan. Self-improvement, polishing of one's virtues, was the ideal and objective of the true adherents of Neo-Confucianism.

Two major Confucian schools in Korea were the Yngnam school, led by Yi at Andong in North Kyngsang Province, and the Kiho school, led by Yi's contemporary Yi I, the only other Korean philosopher of T'oegye's stature. Both schools were factions of the Korean School of Nature and Law, but they differed substantially in interpretation. A third contemporary, S Kyngdok, evolved a monistic emphasis in his cosmology; Yi T'oegye, a dualistic emphasis; and Yi Yulgok's group, a middle ground.

"Twelve Songs of Tosan"

Yi wrote a large corpus of poetry in Chinese in traditional Chinese forms. He also composed a famous cycle of *sijo*, three-line poems, in Korean titled the *Twelve Songs of Tosan*. They sing of the beauties of Mt. To, yet each incorporates a didactic Confucian lesson, such as the eleventh song of the cycle: "The ancients see me not, nor I, the ancients,/ Though I see the ancients not, the Way they trod is before me,/ Their Way before me, can I but follow?" Yi also wrote *Tosan Records,* a diary of his recollections at Tosan.

Further Reading

There are no major studies of Yi Hwang's life or works in Western languages. For background see Evelyn McCune, *Korea: Its Land and People and Culture of All Ages* (Seoul, 1960; rev. ed. 1963) and *The Arts of Korea: An Illustrated History* (1962), and Peter H. Lee, *Korean Literature: Topics and Themes* (1965). □

Yi Sng-gye

Yi Sng-gye (1335-1408) was the founder of the Yi dynasty, which lasted until 1910. An able military leader, he unified Korea under Chinese suzerainty.

Yi Sng-gye was born in modern Ynghung, the second son of Yi Chach'un. Yi's family, originally said to be of Chnju in the south, moved to the northeast in the second half of the 13th century. This migration was undertaken by Yi's great-great-grandfather, who later held a Mongol office. Yi's father is mentioned in the official annals for the first time in 1355, when he arrived in the capital to pay homage to King Kongmin. Later, when the King initiated a campaign to free himself from the Mongol occupation and to regain Korean territories in the north, Yi Chach'un received royal orders and participated in the successful campaign.

Thus Yi Sng-gye's ancestors were Kory nationals who had served the Mongols in the northeast. Because of geographical proximity, they were in contact not only with the Mongols but with the Jürchen tribes and were familiar with their manners and customs. Raised in such surroundings, Yi excelled in equestrian archery from his boyhood.

Military Career

Yi held his first office in 1361; in December he repulsed the Red Turbans, recapturing the capital from these Chinese rebels. In 1362 he annihilated the forces of the Mongol general on the plain of Hamhung and in 1364 suppressed the rebellion of a Kory traitor who fled to the Mongols. In 1370, as the general of the northeast, he marched north to destroy the Mongol garrisons and to sever relations with the Northern Yüan. His troops went deep into the enemy territory, to the right bank of the T'ung-chia River, and captured the enemy stronghold. As a consequence of these campaigns, his name was dreaded by the Mongols and Jürchen alike.

His military genius was equally manifested in his campaigns against the Japanese pirates in the south. The coastal raids of the Japanese, begun in 1232, became more frequent and disastrous under the reign of the third-last ruler of Kory. There were a series of successful campaigns in 1371, 1377, and 1378; but the most famous was that in 1380, when Yi Sng-gye attacked the pirates, cornered them at Mt. Hwang, and annihilated them. After filling a number of important posts, Yi was promoted in 1388 to vice-chancellor, and his name and fame were firmly established at court and abroad.

Dramatic Decision

Perhaps the most dramatic decision taken by Yi before his enthronement was his refusal to march north to drive out Ming garrisons in Liaotung (1388). Instead, he and his army turned back from Wihwa Island, thus inflicting a deadly blow on the waning Kory dynasty and its pro-Mongol faction. It was the culmination of a chain of events begun in 1374.

Although Sino-Korean relations immediately after the founding of Ming were friendly, two events that took place in 1374 overshadowed these relations: the assassination of King Kongmin by eunuchs (October 19), and the murder of the returning Ming envoy by a Korean escort (December 28). These events caused the Ming founder to be suspicious of Korean sincerity, and he prohibited receiving Korean envoys. Those sent on numerous occasions were turned back at Liaotung (1374-1378), and those who managed to reach Nanking were banished or imprisoned. Despite the Emperor's ill-treatment of envoys and his exorbitant demand of tribute horses, Kory continued to demonstrate its goodwill.

However, the Chinese emperor continued to make unreasonable demands, such as the purchase of 5,000 Korean horses, and the drawing of the Ming-Korean border far below the Yalu, on the border of modern Kangwn and Hamgyng provinces. The latter proposal particularly disturbed the Korean court, which decided to march to Liaotung to destroy Ming garrisons there. Upon recrossing the Yalu and marching back to the capital, Yi Snggye banished the war advocates and took the helm of state affairs.

Leader of a Revolution

Yi's progressive pro-Ming party, comprising mainly students of Neo-Confucianism, set out to remove the sources of future worries. Since the two rulers from the last dynasty were descendants of an evil monk and hence not of the legitimate royal line, Yi and his supporters had them banished and later executed. King Kong-yang was installed in their place (1389). They then enforced a land reform in 1389 and burned the land registers of the old Kory nobility in the following year. The last step was the assassination of the Kory loyalist Chng Mong-ju on the night of April 26, 1392, thus removing the last obstacle to final victory. On July 31 the last Kory king was sent into exile, and five days later Yi ascended the throne.

New Dynasty

Yi's enthronement meant the victory of the pro-Ming and anti-Buddhist party, whose members were mostly supporters of the newly imported Neo-Confucianism. The new dynasty, therefore, rejected Buddhism, which had been the state religion for over 800 years, as subversive of public morality and adopted Neo-Confucianism as its official political philosophy. It also adopted the Confucian concept of the "heavenly mandate" as a means of emphasizing the legitimacy of the dynasty.

The "meritorious subjects," who had assisted in the revolution and framed and executed the new policy, set out to compose eulogies to win the minds of men. Such poems praised not only the cultural and military accomplishments of the founder but also the beauty of the new capital, Seoul. In 1396 city walls were constructed around the capital. Yi and his ministers remodeled political and cultural institutions and reinstated and perfected the civil service examination system. In order to legalize new institutions, a set of codes and statutes was compiled. Envoys from the Liu-ch'iu

Islands (1392, 1394, 1397) and from Siam (1393) arrived to pledge their allegiance.

Foreign Relations

Soon after his ascension of the throne, Yi sent envoys to Nanking informing the Ming of the dynastic change. He also requested the Ming founder to select the new name for Korea. Thereupon, the Emperor chose Chosn ("brightness of the morning sun"), a most beautiful and fitting name for Korea, which was adopted on March 27, 1393.

However, owing to matters concerning Korean-Jürched relations and yearly tribute, friendly relations were not easily established. The Ming emperor accused Korea of influencing Ming border officials, of enticing the Jürchen to cross the Yalu and violate Ming territory, and of sending weak horses as tribute. Several missions sent to exculpate Korea of these charges were unsuccessful, until Yi's third son went to Nanking (1394). Sino-Korean relations were, however, normalized only in 1401, when Ming envoys brought investiture and the golden seal of the "King of Korea."

When the investiture belatedly came (1401), Yi had already abdicated in favor of his second son, who was in turn succeeded by Yi's third son. Yi died on June 18, 1408. He had eight sons and five daughters.

Further Reading

A forthcoming English publication by Peter H. Lee will be titled *Songs of Flying Dragons*, a critical study of the eulogy cycle compiled to praise the founding of the Yi dynasty. For background on Yi Sng-gye's life and reign see Takashi Hatada, *A History of Korea* (1951; trans. 1969), and Edwin O. Reischauer and John K. Fairbank, *A History of East Asian Civilization*, vol. 1: *East Asia: The Great Tradition* (1958). □

Yi Sunsin

Yi Sunsin (1545-1598) was a Korean military strategist and naval hero. His victories during the Japanese invasions of Korea are remembered by modern Koreans as among the most heroic feats in their history.

Yi Sunsin was born in Seoul on April 18, 1545, the son of a gentry family of moderate means. Although in his early education he aimed for a civil career, he decided, when 21 years old, to become a military officer. After passing the military examinations in 1576, he served in a variety of posts, both on the northern frontier against the Jürchen tribesmen and on the southern coast as the commander of a small naval station. In all his assignments he demonstrated his competence and courage and also a narrow insistence on doing everything according to regulations. His attention to correct procedure was at the root of his later organizational successes, but it also marked him as a man difficult to get along with.

In his early career Yi was rather unpopular, and his successes earned him more jealousy than praise. In time,

however, he began to attract attention in high places, and from 1589, when he served on the staff of the Chŏlla provincial military inspector, his reputation rose steadily. In 1591 he was appointed, over many senior officers, commander of the Left Chŏlla Fleet (Korea's two southernmost provinces, Kyŏngsang on the east and Chŏlla on the west, were each divided into Left and Right naval districts).

Turtle Ships

When Yi reached his post, in the town now known as Yŏsu, the Japanese invasion was still 14 months away. The Korean court had had hints of the Japanese plans as early as 1590, but it was deeply divided over the meaning of the threat. The Japanese dictator Toyotomi Hideyoshi had said plainly that he intended to invade Ming China and required transit through Korea, but few believed he would attempt a land invasion, and even these had little idea how massive it would be.

Yi, however, believed war would come and began preparations from his arrival at Yŏsu. He strengthened the fortifications and enforced discipline with an awesome sternness. But most of his attention was given to the development of the famous "turtle ships." These vessels had a curved covering deck which resembled a turtle carapace. The deck and sides were ironclad and bristled with spikes to prevent boarding. On the prow was a fierce-looking dragon head in which was mounted a medium gun; along the sides were 12 gunports with heavy pieces which could fire missiles, spears, or buckshot. On the high seas the ships moved by sail power; in action the sails and masts were removed and oars were used. Vessels resembling the turtle ships had been known earlier in both China and Korea, but it was Yi who perfected the design and, more importantly, developed the tactics by which they could be most effective. He used the turtle ships as attack vessels; they would move directly into the enemy force and disrupt it and then go after the bigger ships, either ramming them or broadsiding them with the heavy cannons.

First Successes

The Japanese invasion force landed at Pusan on May 25, 1592. The first Korean naval encounter proved disastrous: under the timid commander of the Right Kyŏngsang Fleet, Wŏn Kyun, nearly the whole Kyŏngsang fleet was lost or scuttled. Yi boldly decided not to wait for an attack but to go on the offensive immediately. On June 13 he left Yŏsu with a fleet of 85 ships; 24 of these were armed warships (not including the turtle ships, which were not yet ready), the rest communication and supply ships. When he returned a week later, he could claim a total of 42 enemy ships destroyed or taken, all but 2 of these being large or medium vessels. He himself had suffered no losses.

In the months afterward Yi led three more expeditions from Yŏsu, now adding the powerful turtle ships to his squadron. These proved spectacularly successful in a major battle off Hansan Island on August 14, when Yi met a force of 73 Japanese ships and sank or took 59 of them; his own losses were minimal. Four such expeditions made in the summer and fall netted 375 Japanese ships.

The reasons for Yi's conspicuous success lay in his general aggressiveness, his total knowledge of the notoriously tricky Korean coastal tides, and his mastery of engagement tactics, whereby he was able to lure the enemy out to the open sea, where he could maneuver with greater freedom. The Japanese later learned to avoid these encounters, but at the cost of keeping themselves bottled up in the coves and inlets.

The strategic effect of Yi's early victories was considerable. By keeping the enemy from the Chŏlla coasts, he ensured the safety of his own bases. He made the Japanese land occupation of Chŏlla Province impossible, thus retaining its major rice and manpower resources. Finally, he kept the Japanese navy completely away from the west coast of the peninsula and away from the major cities of the north, thus weakening the Japanese land positions near P'yŏngyang and contributing to the eventual loss of the positions.

Defeat by Intrigue

In mid-1593 the war had reached a stalemate: the Japanese had been forced back to their coastal strongholds near Pusan, where the Koreans and their Chinese allies had the power to hold them but were unable to expel them. At this juncture peace talks began between the Chinese and Japanese generals. The Koreans did not join these talks and, in fact, fought a limited number of battles during 1593 and 1594, but in general they were forced to go along with the truce. Yi moved his headquarters eastward to Hansan Island—closer to the main Japanese base at Pusan—and assumed the post of commander of the Unified Triprovincial Fleet, a title created especially for him which in effect gave him command of the entire Korean navy (July 1593). But this period was for him one of enforced idleness, frustrating and unpleasant.

When the peace talks collapsed in 1596, Toyotomi Hideyoshi began to ready a second invasion. Having been unable to eliminate Yi in combat, the Japanese resorted now to intrigue and exploited Korean factionalism and their own. On the one hand, Yi's steady successes had reaped the jealousy of his court enemies, who backed the incompetent Wŏn Kyun. On the other, there was a deep rift between the two principal Japanese generals, Konishi Yukinaga and Kato Kiyomasa. Through a double agent, Korean officials were persuaded that Konishi wanted to kill Kato and, to accomplish this, would tell Yi the date and place of Kato's crossing from Japan. Yi recognized the obvious trap and refused to obey the court's instructions to join the plot. For this insubordination his enemies had him arrested and brought to Seoul. Here he was tried and sentenced to death, but his supporters were able to have this commuted to banishment in custody of the army. Stripped of his rank and titles, Yi joined the headquarters of the Chŏlla army on July 17, 1597.

Return to Action

Yi's vindication was not long in coming. No sooner had Wŏn Kyun assumed Yi's former commands than he led over 200 ships into a disastrous defeat (Aug. 27, 1597). With Wŏn Kyun dead and only a handful of ships left and the base at Hansan Island untenable, the survivors burned their naval stores and retreated to the Chŏlla coast. The humiliated court was now forced to return command to Yi. Reappointed on September 13, he reached his ragged fleet 2 weeks later to find he had only 12 ships, none of them turtle ships, and only a handful of demoralized men. He had no supplies, and his base at Yŏsu was unusable. Moreover, the Japanese were now sweeping through the major inland Chŏlla cities and massing their ships for a decisive blow at the remaining Korean naval force.

But Yi, combining his meager resources with courage and a thorough knowledge of his native waters, produced his greatest victory, the battle of Myŏngnyang (Oct. 26. 1597). Allowing his tiny group to be sighted by the Japanese force of 133 ships, he lured them into the Myŏngnyang Strait, between the mainland and the large island of Chindo. While the narrow space provided sufficient maneuverability for Yi's 12 ships, most of the enemy vessels were put out of the battle for lack of room—"one man on a narrow mountain path can terrorize a thousand," as Yi remarked in his diary. After the tide shifted in his favor, he pursued the enemy, and when the day was over, 31 of the retreating Japanese ships had been sunk while Yi had lost none.

The Japanese advance collapsed, and by the end of 1597 they were forced once more to cling to their narrow strip of coastline. Chinese reinforcements streamed into Korea, including a naval force under the admiral Ch'en Lin, who joined Yi at his southern headquarters in August 1598. The two began an uneasy but fruitful relationship. To his other skills Yi now added those of the diplomat in order to contain his vain and temperamental Chinese colleague.

Death in Battle

In October 1598, after a Chinese offensive against the coastal strongholds had failed and it looked as if another long standoff was in prospect, Toyotomi Hideyoshi suddenly died, leaving behind a deathbed order to bring all troops home from Korea. Most of the Japanese were able to buy off their besiegers and evacuate their fortifications without difficulty, but Konishi Yukinaga, held in his bastion near Sunch'on, found himself opposed by a strong Sino-Korean fleet and an unbribable Yi. On December 14-15 a massive Japanese fleet came to Konishi's rescue. The furious fight that followed, known as the battle of Noryang, was the bloodiest of the war. Konishi escaped, but the Japanese lost some 200 ships and thousands of men. However, the Koreans and Chinese sustained heavy casualties. The greatest loss was Yi himself, hit in the neck by a bullet as he stood beside his signalman at the height of the battle. His last order was to keep his death a secret until the battle was over, lest the news adversely affect the outcome.

Yi is Korea's greatest hero and one of the outstanding naval commanders of world history. His battles, well documented in his diary and reports, bear careful study by modern naval historians, and his courage and patriotism are still models for modern Koreans of all persuasions, who find in him a powerful symbol of national resistance against foreign powers, particularly the Japanese.

Further Reading

There is no biography of Yi Sunsin in English. Some details of his life and achievements can be found in standard survey histories, such as Takashi Hatada, *A History of Korea,* translated and edited by Warren W. Smith and Benjamin H. Hazard (1969); and Woo-keun Han, *The History of Korea,* translated by Kyung-sik Lee and edited by Grafton Mintz (1970).

Additional Sources

Park, Yune-hee, *Admiral Yi Sun-shin and his turtleboat armada,* Seoul, Korea: Hanjin Pub. Co., 1978. □

Yngjo

Yngjo (1694-1776) was a Korean king who ruled from 1724 to 1776. His reign was the longest and one of the most brilliant of the Yi dynasty.

The formal name of Yngjo was Yi Kum; in the years before acceding to the throne he was known as Prince Yning. His first posthumous name was Yngjong, but this was changed to Yngjo in 1889. Born on Oct. 31, 1694, he was the fourth son of King Sukchong (reigned 1674-1720) and the younger half brother of King Kyngjong (1720-1724). From his childhood, it was evident that Yngjo was the most intelligent and capable of Sukchong's sons. Kyngjong's four-year reign was torn by constant political crises. Because he was childless, Yngjo was made his heir in 1720; later he became in addition prince regent, sharing authority with the dowager queen. He became king on Oct. 16, 1724, five days after Kyngjong's suspiciously sudden death.

His Achievement

Yngjo's greatest achievement was the restoration of political order, and it was accomplished early in his reign. Political factionalism had been endemic to Korean life since the end of the 16th century, but it had raged with particular intensity since the 1690s, when certain court officials had split over a number of issues into factions called the Noron and the Soron. The Soron had protected the interests of Kyngjong, but when he came to the throne in 1720, the Noron occupied the chief ministerial positions. The Noron succeeded in having Yngjo designated heir and prince regent.

Once on the throne, Yngjo was determined to end the Noron-Soron struggle. Early in 1725 he proclaimed his famous policy of "broad equity," whereby worthy men of both groups were to be given key government positions. He, however, grew increasingly cool toward the Soron, and they soon lapsed into a dormant, if still live, political force.

Yngjo's achievements during his long reign were typical of those which traditional eastern Asian historians expected in a "vigorous ruler." He restored order, revised legal codes, built up military strength (emphasizing the capital rather than the frontiers, which were not threatened in his lifetime), refurbished buildings, expanded Seoul's sewer system, reformed the corvée labor system, encouraged agriculture, rationalized taxation practices, forbade certain cruel punishments, elaborated channels for the communication of popular grievances, promoted scholarship and education, reformed court ritual and music, supported printing and publishing, and in general presided actively over a state then enjoying its most prosperous age.

In spite of these very real achievements, there were flaws in Yngjo's character that contradict the historical stereotype and at the same time render his personality somewhat mysterious. He was arbitrary and capricious in many of his decisions, and he was given to sudden outbursts of uncontrollable rage. Certainly his terrible unpredictability was a factor in the control in which he constantly held his officials. His vanity knew no bounds. But in his calmer moments he was solicitous of his officials and generous with subordinates, and he showed a genuine concern for the welfare of the common people. He was strict and firm in his decisions, worked long and hard at his duties, and was always intimately familiar with governmental affairs.

Death of His Son

In one matter only was Yngjo disappointed: the arrangement of a smooth succession. His first son, Prince Hyojang, had died in 1728. In 1735 one of Yngjo's consorts produced a son, Prince Sado. Yngjo made him crown prince in 1736 and spared no effort in his upbringing and education. But eventually something went wrong in their relationship; the early hope turned into bitterness and hatred and ended, in 1762, in filicide. The reasons are unclear, mostly as a result of the expurgation of historical records. But judging from what has survived, and other clues scattered through unofficial sources, it is apparent that officials sympathetic to the Soron cause had attached themselves to the crown prince. They may have suggested to Sado that his father was responsible for the death of Kyngjong.

Through the 1750s the political tension grew. Yngjo frequently reprimanded his son for both his personal behavior and his princely decisions. The final crisis in the affair began in October 1761. Yngjo discovered that Sado had taken a pleasure trip in May without reporting it to his father; this was an extremely serious breach of filial piety and court protocol. Yngjo nominally forgave Sado this indiscretion, but he had certainly not forgotten it when, in June 1762, a palace employee submitted a memorial charging Sado with "unspeakable" crimes. To the end Sado denied all the charges. On July 4 Yngjo demanded Sado's suicide. Sado attempted to hang himself but was courageously released from the rope by his own loyal retainers. Yngjo next stripped Sado of his rank and offices, decreed him a commoner, and locked him in a box, where he died eight days later from starvation. Immediately after his son's death, Yngjo forgave Sado, restored his rank and titles, and gave him the name by which he has since been known—Sado Seja, which, according to the conventions often used in interpreting posthumous names, can mean "Contritely Lamented Prince." The bizarre method of execution, strange even in consideration of the traditional Korean prohibition against the shedding of royal blood, and the tardy and oddly sudden remorse combine to suggest Yngjo's disturbed personality.

Yngjo lived for nearly 14 years after Sado's death, and some of his most famous enactments date from this period. Yngjo died on April 22, 1776, in Kynghui Palace in Seoul.

Further Reading

There is no biography of Yngjo in English. The events of his reign can be perused in survey histories such as Takashi Hatada, *A History of Korea,* translated and edited by Warren W. Smith and Benjamin H. Hazard (1969), and Woo-keun Han, *The History of Korea,* translated by Kyung-sik Lee and edited by Grafton Mintz (1970). Much of interest concerning the reigns of both Yngjo and Kyngjong can be found in Chao-ying Fang, *The Asmai Library* (1969). □

Yo Fei

The Chinese general Yo Fei (1103-1141), also known as Yo P'eng-chü, led the Chinese army against the Chin invaders, the Jürchen Tatars. He is a symbol of national resistance against foreign aggression.

Yo Fei was of a peasant family in T'ang-yin, Honan. Legend has it that at his birth a bird called *p'eng* (a symbol of greatness) soared over the house; hence his personal name was associated with the *p'eng*. He lost his father in his early years and was devoted to his mother. Largely self-taught, he read Sun Wu's *Art of War* (an ancient military classic) and practiced archery.

Yo lived in an age of political chaos and foreign invasion. He joined the army early and distinguished himself as a great soldier. His statement—"Civil officials should not be greedy of money; nor should military officers be afraid of death"—has been the first principle of Chinese government. Yo's military campaign consisted of two stages: extermination of the puppet regime of Liu Yü, who, with the Tatars' support, set himself up as emperor in 1130; and recovery of the North occupied by the Tatar forces under Wu-shu, the Chin commander in chief.

In 1133 Liu Yü led his troops south and occupied several important cities south of the Yellow River. Yo expelled Liu Yü's forces and in the following years recaptured a large area from insurgent leaders.

In 1136 Yo's vanguard had advanced to the Yellow River, and he sought approval to push the battle to the North. However, Ch'in kuei, the prime minister, was in favor of peace and opposed the plan.

Meanwhile, Wu-shu, having dropped Liu Yü, proceeded to the conquest of the Sung empire. In 1140 the Tatar troops pushing south pursued the Sung armies in Shun-chang (Anhwei) and Fufeng (Shensi). Then Yo led his army across the Yellow River and made straight for Yen-cheng (Honan), where Wu-shu summoned his nomad cavalry, called *Kuei-tzu Ma* (that is, three mailed horses linked together to form a battle unit). Yo's army, too strongly en-

trenched to be pushed back, repeatedly crushed the onslaughts of the Tatar cavalry. "It is easy to move a mountain, but difficult to shatter the Yo soldiers" was the comment of the Tatars. Just when Yo was within an ace of recapturing Pien-liang (K'ai-feng, the former capital), Emperor Kao Tsung, on the advice of Ch'in Kuei, ordered a withdrawal.

In 1141 Ch'in Kuei divested Yo of his command, then had him imprisoned on a fictitious accusation, and finally arranged for him and his son Yo Yün to be executed. But in 1162 Emperor Hsiao Tsung designated Yo a Hero of Loyalty and ennobled him as the Prince of Yo; in 1179 the Emperor canonized Yo as the Saint of War. A temple bearing his name at Lin-an (Hangchow, the capital), where he was buried, was built in his honor.

Further Reading

Yo Fei is the subject of an essay in Arthur F. Wright and Denis Twitchett, eds., *Confucian Personalities* (1962). □

Yogananda

Yogananda (1893-1952) was an Indian yogi who came to the United States in 1920 to spend over 30 years working with Americans interested in the practice of yoga or God-realization.

Yogananda was born Mukunda Lal Ghose in 1893 in Gorakhpur, India. Both of his parents were disciples of Lahiri Mahasaya, and his father was an executive of the Bengal-Nagpur Railway. Mukunda's name was changed to Yogananda in 1914 when he entered the Swami Order (an ancient monastic order founded by the Indian philosopher Sankara), and his guru Sri Yukteswar bestowed the further religious title Paramahansa in 1935. Yogananda means bliss through yoga or union with God, while Paramahansa means highest swan. The sacred swan was thought to have the power to extract milk from a mixture of milk and water and is therefore a symbol of spiritual discrimination.

The Spiritual Quest

Even as a child Yogananda was endowed with psychic powers and with a deep fascination for Indian holy men. His *Autobiography of a Yogi* depicts his search for God-realization and for a spiritual teacher who could guide him to that goal. It describes his encounter with numerous Indian holy men, most of whom possessed supranormal powers. He lived in a world in which he encountered healings through photographs and physical contact with yogis, a vision which predicted the death of his mother, the materialization of an amulet, the ability to materialize an extra body, the miraculous restoration of a severed arm, clairvoyant knowledge of the future, and the ability to levitate.

None of these occurrences was considered strange and none was seen to contradict natural law. Such happenings were perceived as the result of subtle laws that govern hidden spiritual planes and are discernable through the science of yoga. Human ills are the result of a violation of some law of nature. But the bad karma effected by such violations can be minimized through prayer, yoga, astrology, and consultation with holy men. The specific method for God-realization was kriya yoga. The method was never described in books, since it had to be learned from an authorized practitioner.

Yogananda was also interested in education, founding his first school for boys in Bengal at the age of 24. A year later, the Maharajah of Kasimbazar donated his palace and 25 acres of land in Bihar for this school, which was named Yogoda Satsanga Vidyalaya. The curriculum included not only standard subjects but also yoga concentration, meditation, and a special set of energization exercises for health. Yogananda founded the Yogoda Satsanga Society of India. Its counterpart in the United States is the Self-Realization Fellowship. The Yogoda Satsanga Society of India also supports a college, a girl's school, a kindergarten, a music school, an arts and crafts school, a medical dispensary, and a college of homeopathic medicine. Yogananda saw yoga, physical exercise, and scientific study as interrelated.

The American Missionary

As numerous other Indian gurus who came to the United States in the 20th century, Yogananda came as a result of an order from his guru Sri Yukteswar, who told him to "spread to all peoples the knowledge of the self-liberating yoga techniques." He began that mission in 1920 when he addressed the International Congress of Religious Liberals in Boston on the topic "The Science of Religion." He was well-received and travelled extensively throughout the United States giving lectures and classes in most major American cities. Self-Realization Fellowship centers were also established in major cities. The headquarters and buildings for resident monastics were built on a beautiful 12-acre estate on Mount Washington in Los Angeles. Yogananda also founded an ashram on a 23-acre estate in Encinitas, California, overlooking the Pacific Ocean. Temples were built in Hollywood (1942), San Diego (1943), and Long Beach (1947). Both the international and the Indian headquarters have printing facilities which produce magazines, study guides, and the works of Yogananda. In 1950, two years before his death, an impressive Lake Shrine was established at Pacific Palisades, California.

Yogananda was convinced that the yoga that he taught could be found in all scriptures and was the essence of all religions. The Ten Commandments were seen as the first step of Patanjali's yoga. Yogananda also used his understanding of yoga to interpret the sayings of Jesus and Paul, being convinced that both Jesus and Paul were yoga masters. He was certain that a Western Christian would find nothing contradictory in adopting his kriya yoga once both Christianity and yoga were properly understood. He found it equally comfortable to quote from the Old and New Testaments as from Indian religious texts.

A yogi consciously exits from the body at the appropriate time. Yogananda's "exit" was on March 7, 1952. It was reported that 20 days after his death his body showed no signs of deterioration. The Self-Realization Fellowship quoted from a notarized letter from the mortuary director of Forest Lawn Memorial Park in support of this remarkable phenomenon. The report received considerable publicity in newspapers and magazines.

Further Reading

The most important source for the life of Yogananda is his *Autobiography of a Yogi,* a 572-page account of his life published by the Self-Realization Fellowship (SRF) in 1946. After that one can proceed to some of the works of Yogananda also published by the SRF. Those works are *The Science of Religion* (1953), *Scientific Healing Affirmations* (1958), *Cosmic Chants* (1938, 1943), *Metaphysical Meditations* (n.d.), *Whispers from Eternity* (1959), and *Songs of the Soul* (1983).

Additional Sources

Ghosh, Sananda Lal, *Mejda: the family and early life of Paramahansa Yogananda,* Los Angeles, Calif.: Self-Realization Fellowship, 1980.
Yogananda, Paramhansa, *Autobiography of a Yogi,* Los Angeles, Calif.: Self-Realization Fellowship, 1981. □

Minamoto Yoritomo

The Japanese warrior chieftain Minamoto Yoritomo (1147-1199) founded Japan's first military government, or shogunate, in 1185 and thereby inaugurated the medieval period of Japanese history, which lasted until 1573.

In the 12th century, Japan was still ruled by the government of the imperial court in Kyoto and in particular by the courtier family of Fujiwara, which held the office of imperial regent and many other high ministerial positions at court. However, by regarding the provinces merely as a source of revenue from their private landed estates and by concerning themselves almost exclusively with life and affairs in the capital, the Kyoto courtiers sadly neglected provincial administration. The rise of a warrior class from about the 10th century stemmed directly from the need to provide order and control in the provinces.

By the 12th century, this emergent warrior class was dominated by two great clans, the Minamoto and the Taira, both of which traced their descent from the imperial family itself—that is, from former princes who had gone out to the provinces and had settled there. During the late 11th and the early 12th centuries, chieftains of the Minamoto and Taira increasingly came to participate in the politics of the court, and as the result of two armed conflicts in Kyoto, in 1156 and 1159, the Taira succeeded in supplanting the Fujiwara as the most powerful ministerial family in the land.

Period of Taira Dominance

Yoritomo was only 12 years old at the time of the 1159 conflict, in which the Taira decisively defeated the

Minamoto, who were commanded by his father, Yoshitomo. Although his father was killed, Yoritomo's life was spared, and he was sent into exile in the eastern provinces of Japan by Kiyomori, the Taira leader.

During the next 20 years Kiyomori and his kinsmen, following the Fujiwara practice of marrying their daughters into the imperial family, were the unrivaled masters of the court at Kyoto. But they did little to improve provincial administration or to provide for the needs of the new warrior class in general. Beginning in 1180, several prominent Minamoto leaders, including Yoritomo, were encouraged by growing signs of discontent with the rule of the Taira in Kyoto to rise in arms against them.

Overthrow of the Taira

The war between the Minamoto and the Taira lasted from 1180 until 1185. In the early years of fighting Yoritomo devoted his attention mainly to the assertion of his leadership over the various branches of the Minamoto clan and to the consolidation of his position as warrior hegemon in the eastern provinces. Even during the period from 1183 to 1185, when Minamoto armies drove the Taira from Kyoto to final destruction at the battle of Dannoura in the Shimonoseki Strait, Yoritomo himself remained in the eastern provinces to supervise the overall strategy of victory and to establish governing offices to exercise the powers that he had acquired.

Kamakura Shogunate

Yoritomo established his new warrior regime at Kamakura, a small coastal village south of present-day Tokyo, where the Minamoto had long been influential. From the time of his first rising, in 1180 (when he had received a decree to destroy the Taira from a prince who, owing to Taira interference, had been passed over in the line of succession to the throne), Yoritomo had sought to "legitimize" all of his actions and to avoid being cast in the role of rebel by the throne. Among the titles he received from the Emperor after victory over the Taira, the most important was that of shogun, or "generalissimo." On the basis of this, the government Yoritomo founded, which lasted from 1185 until 1333, is known as the Kamakura shogunate.

The strength of Yoritomo's rulership lay in the feudal-type, lord-vassal relationships he established with his followers. In return for allegiance and military service, Yoritomo provided his vassals with protection, confirmed them in their existing landholdings, and bestowed new lands upon them.

Yoritomo's authority, which was restricted chiefly to the provinces of eastern Japan during the war with the Taira, was made national in scope in 1185, when he received permission from the throne to appoint his vassals as stewards to various private estates throughout the country and as constables or protectors in each province. Although the steward-constable system of the Kamakura period never fully displaced the old imperial administration in the provinces, and although many estates remained immune from all outside interference or control, the Kamakura shogunate

nevertheless decisively replaced the imperial court at Kyoto as the effective central government of Japan.

Yoritomo's Death

Probably the greatest shortcoming of Yoritomo as a ruler was his failure to provide for effective succession to the office of shogun. Fearful that they might challenge his own position, Yoritomo had liquidated several of his brothers and other close relatives, and when he himself died at the age of 52, in 1199, his two young sons, who became the second and third shoguns, were unable to sustain the power of the Minamoto. Before long the Hojo family, who were related to Yoritomo by marriage, assumed control of the government at Kamakura as shogunate regents. To legitimize their position, the Hojo installed Fujiwara courtiers and, later, imperial princes as figurehead shoguns.

In contrast to Yoritomo, who had ruled in a generally autocratic fashion, the Hojo regents established a council of state at Kamakura that gave other warrior chieftains of the east the opportunity to participate more directly in the decision-making process of the shogunate.

Further Reading

An excellent book on Yoritomo and his times is Minoru Shinoda, *The Founding of the Kamakura Shogunate, 1180-1185* (1960). For a more general treatment of the growth of a warrior class in Japan and the rise of Yoritomo to power see Sir George Sansom, *A History of Japan,* vol. 1 (1958). □

Shigeru Yoshida

Shigeru Yoshida (1878-1967), Japanese diplomat and prime minister, led his country through a difficult period of postwar recovery.

Shigeru Yoshida was born on Sept. 22, 1878, in Tokyo, the fifth son of Tsuna Takenouchi, a prominent politician from Tosa on the island of Shikoku. He was subsequently adopted by a family acquaintance, Kenso Yoshida, who wanted a son to carry on his family name and prosperous silk business.

Early Career

Following his graduation from Tokyo Imperial University in 1906, Yoshida embarked upon a distinguished diplomatic career that was greatly favored by his marriage to the eldest daughter of Count Nobuaki Makino, who became lord privy seal and a close adviser of the Emperor. After appointment to various consular posts in China and Manchuria, Yoshida served in London and Washington, and in 1919 he was a member of the Japanese delegation at the Paris Peace Conference. He was named vice-minister of foreign affairs in the Giichi Tanaka Cabinet and served successively as ambassador to Italy and to Great Britain.

Yoshida was recalled from his post in London and retired from the Foreign Service in March 1939. Reportedly, he had been considered for the position of foreign minister in the Koki Hirota Cabinet in 1936 but was vetoed by the military because of its dislike for his father-in-law. In any case, it proved fortunate for Yoshida that he was in private life during the war years.

Service as Prime Minister

Untainted by association with the military leadership and possessing the added advantage of having been arrested during the war by the military police and briefly jailed, Yoshida was one of the comparatively few prominent prewar political figures who were not purged by the Occupation. In September 1945 he was appointed foreign minister in the first postwar Cabinet.

In the 1946 House of Representatives election, the Liberal party won a plurality, and the party president, Ichiro Hatoyama, seemed assured the premiership. But the Occupation found him unacceptable, and Yoshida was persuaded to take his place as party president and prime minister of Japan, a position he held (except for a 16-month interval in 1947-1948) until the end of 1954. Yoshida's tough, pragmatic, anti-Communist attitudes suited the Occupation authorities. On the whole, he worked harmoniously with Gen. Douglas MacArthur, and together they presided over an era of revolutionary changes in Japanese society.

Yoshida built up a strong personal following, composed mostly of former bureaucrats, in the Diet, and he ruled in an autocratic fashion rare in Japanese politics. With

the end of the Occupation in 1952, purged party leaders began to return to politics, undermining Liberal party unity and eroding Yoshida's strength. Conservative opposition to him gradually coalesced about Hatoyama, who unseated Yoshida in 1954.

Yoshida continued after his resignation to be an influential elder statesman and adviser. He died on Oct. 20, 1967, in his seaside estate at Oiso. Representatives of 74 countries attended his funeral, the first state funeral in Japan since the war.

Further Reading

Yoshida's recollections of his postwar leadership are in his *The Yoshida Memoirs* (1962). A general account of the Occupation is Kazuo Kawai, *Japan's American Interlude* (1960). For a close analysis of the workings of Japanese politics in the Yoshida era see Donald C. Hellmann, *Japanese Foreign Policy and Domestic Politics* (1969).

Additional Sources

Dower, John W., *Empire and aftermath: Yoshida Shigeru and the Japanese experience, 1878-1954,* Cambridge, Mass.: Council on East Asian Studies, Harvard University: Distributed by Harvard University Press, 1988. □

Tokugawa Yoshimune

Tokugawa Yoshimune (1684-1751) was a Japanese ruler, or shogun. He attempted most energetically to revitalize the Tokugawa shogunate after it began to encounter economic and other difficulties in the late 17th and early 18th centuries.

Established in the early 17th century by Tokugawa Ieyasu at Edo (present-day Tokyo), the Tokugawa shogunate was based on a form of government that has been described as "centralized feudalism." Beginning with Ieyasu, the Tokugawa shoguns exercised hegemony over some 260 daimyos, or regional barons, who in turn ruled their own virtually autonomous domains. The chief means by which the Tokugawa were able to maintain this hegemony was the policy of national seclusion that they instituted in the 1630s. According to this policy, only the Dutch and the Chinese were permitted to trade on a limited scale at the single port of Nagasaki.

When the seventh shogun died without an heir in 1716, he was succeeded by Tokugawa Yoshimune, the daimyo of a branch family of the Tokugawa. Yoshimune had been a successful administrator and reformer in his own domain, and he now sought to apply his ideas on the national level. His reforms included a restressing of the martial arts among the country's ruling warrior (samurai) class, the reclamation of agricultural lands, and the reminting of coins to correct the periodic debasements engaged in by his predecessors.

Scholars are in disagreement about the success of Yoshimune's reforms, many of which were highly reactionary. But he was responsible for at least one measure that was unquestionably of great importance for the future. On the advice of his aides, Yoshimune lifted the ban on the importation of foreign books that had been imposed at the time of adoption of the national seclusion policy. So long as they did not deal with Christianity, which the Tokugawa regime regarded as a dangerously subversive creed, books from China and the West could henceforth (from 1725) be brought into Japan through Nagasaki. It was through these books that a small but crucial number of Japanese scholars were able to acquire a basic knowledge of advancements in Western technology that proved invaluable to their country when it was forced to abandon its seclusion policy and to enter the modern world in the mid-19th century.

Yoshimune abdicated the office of shogun in favor of his son in 1745. He died 6 years later.

Further Reading

A general account of Tokugawa Yoshimune's period is in George Sansom, *A History of Japan, 1615-1867* (1963). Conrad Totman, *Politics in the Tokugawa Bakufu 1600-1843* (1967), deals specifically with the political developments of the age. ☐

Fulbert Youlou

Fulbert Youlou (1917-1972) was a Congolese priest who became a political leader and rose to the presidency of the Republic of the Congo.

Fulbert Youlou was born on July 9, 1917, near Brazzaville, a member of the Balali tribe, largest of the three major subgroups of the Bakongo people. He studied for the priesthood and was ordained on his thirty-second birthday, becoming a parish priest in Brazzaville in 1949. His relations with his superiors were stormy, and his growing interest for politics led to disciplinary action against him. By the end of 1955, the diminutive priest had made up his mind to enter politics on a full-time basis, although he continued to wear priestly garments long after he had been enjoined from performing any pastoral duties.

Prior to 1956, politics in the (then) French Congo had been monopolized by Félix Tchicaya's Parti Progressiste Congolais (PPC), based in Pointe Noire and the neighboring Kouilou-Niari region, and by Jacques Opangault, leader of the Mbochi tribe of middle Congo, with the Balali (the dominant group in the city of Brazzaville) remaining on the sidelines. In the 1956 election, however, Youlou managed almost overnight to unfreeze this bloc of votes and to canalize latent Balali militancy, thus transforming a bipolar party system into a triangular one. Within a few months, by skillfully maximizing his newfound support, utilizing the prestige of his habit, and exploiting internal divisions among his adversaries, he not only organized a new party, the Union Démocratique pour la Défense des Intérêts Africains

(UDDIA), but also won upset victories in the November 1956 municipal elections in Brazzaville (of which he became mayor) and Pointe Noire. The PPC collapsed almost entirely at that point, leaving only Youlou and Opangault as contenders in the 1957 election, which resulted in a stalemate. The tug-of-war between the two factions, only briefly interrupted by the collapse of the Fourth French Republic and the introduction of the Franco-African Community (which both leaders endorsed), continued unabated during 1957 and 1958. Through a number of dubious maneuvers, Youlou eventually managed to undermine Opangault's position and was elected prime minister in November 1958 as the opposition walked out. Antagonism between the Balali and the Mbochi culminated in serious riots in Brazzaville (February 1959), which had to be put down by the French army and which the wily Youlou utilized to clamp down on the opposition. After new elections, characterized by unabashed gerrymandering, his party gained 84 percent of the seats with only 58 percent of the vote (April 1959); and by the time the Congo became independent (August 1960), a chastened Opangault agreed to serve under Youlou in a largely symbolic position.

Youlou, who had previously extended his assistance to Joseph Kasavubu before the latter had become president of the former Belgian Congo, now became deeply embroiled in the politics of that neighboring country. He first offered Kasavubu logistical support in eliminating prime minister Patrice Lumumba from power; then, possibly under the influence of right-wing members of his French entourage, he championed the cause of Katanga's secessionist leader Moïse Tshombe among the states of former French Africa, which came to be known as the "Brazzaville group" after the December 1960 conference held in Youlou's bailiwick.

Domestically, Youlou consolidated his position by introducing a presidential system of government and by having himself elevated to the presidency through an election in which he was the only candidate (March 1961). In August 1962 he announced his intention to move toward a single-party system, and during the next 12 months he concentrated his efforts on eliminating his opponents (rather than coopting them into the system as he had done previously).

Increasing opposition on the part of labor unions during the spring of 1963 escalated into a full-blown conflict, and on Aug. 13-15, 1963, widespread rioting in the capital city resulted in Youlou's overthrow and imprisonment. The new government had to contend with his Balali supporters, but the danger of a pro-Youlou counter-revolution really became serious when Tshombe returned to Kinshasa as premier. After one of several plots allegedly engineered by Tshombe, Youlou escaped to Kinshasa (February 1965), where he pursued his oppositional activities until Tshombe's fall from power. Hamstrung by the Joseph Mobutu regime, Youlou slipped out of Kinshasa in early 1966 and, after having been refused entry into France, settled in Madrid, where he died on May 5, 1972.

Further Reading

For information on Youlou see Virginia Thompson and Richard Adloff, *The Emerging States of French Equatorial Africa*

(1960), and John A. Ballard's "Four Equatorial States" in Gwendolen M. Carter, ed., *National Unity and Regionalism in Eight African States* (1966). □

Andrew Jackson Young Jr.

Andrew Jackson Young, Jr. (born 1932) was a preacher, civil rights activist, and politician who served as a leader of the Southern Christian Leadership Conference, as a U.S. congressman, as U.S. ambassador to the United Nations, and as mayor of Atlanta, Georgia.

Andrew Jackson Young, Jr. was born in New Orleans, Louisiana, on March 12, 1932, the grandson of a prosperous "bayou entrepreneur" and the eldest of two sons comfortably reared by Andrew J. Young, a dentist, and Daisy (Fuller) Young, a teacher. He and his brother grew up as the only African American children in a white, middle-class neighborhood in New Orleans. In 1947 he graduated from Gilbert Academy, a private high school, and entered Dillard University. Intending to become a dentist, he transferred to Howard University the following year.

After graduating with a pre-medical B.S. degree in 1951, however, Young decided on the ministry and enrolled in the Hartford Theological Seminary in Connecticut. He completed his B.D. degree four years later, and, strongly influenced by his study of the teachings of Mohandas Gandhi, Young resolved to "change this country without violence."

Civil Rights Activist

In 1955 Young was ordained a minister in the socially liberal and predominantly white United Church of Christ. He pastored African American Congregational churches in Marion, Alabama, and the southern Georgia small towns of Thomasville and Beachton, before becoming the associate director of the Department of Youth Work for the National Council of Churches in 1957. As a part of his duties there he administered a voter education and registration project funded by the Field Foundation, and this brought him into contact with Martin Luther King, Jr. and the Southern Christian Leadership Conference (SCLC). In the summer of 1961 Young joined that organization and rapidly became an able administrative assistant and confidant of King.

Worldly in matters of finance and organizational techniques and conversant in the language of the white establishment as well as the *patois* of the uneducated rural African Americans, Young excelled as a fund-raiser and strategist and was SCLC's principal negotiator. While others became newsworthy by getting arrested and beaten, Young worked quietly behind the scene to persuade the white power structure of the futility of resistance to the African American civil rights movement. He helped direct the massive campaign against racial segregation in Birmingham, Alabama, in 1963, and his success at the negotiating table in

winning important gains for Birmingham African Americans led to the selection of Young as executive director of SCLC in 1964.

Young marched at King's side in St. Augustine, Florida, in 1964; Selma, Alabama, in 1965; Chicago in 1966; and Memphis in 1968 and was at the motel in Memphis when the civil rights leader was shot and killed on April 4, 1968. Young remained with the SCLC as its executive vice-president for two more years, but increasingly articulated the view the movement would have to shift from protest to political action.

Congressman, U.N. Ambassador, and Mayor

In 1970 Young resigned from the SCLC to seek election to the United States House of Representatives from Georgia's nearly two-thirds white Fifth Congressional District in Atlanta. Young lost the congressional race to a conservative white Republican incumbent, but ran strongly enough to pre-empt the Democratic field for a rematch two years later. In 1972, with the Fifth Congressional District having been redistricted by court order to increase the proportion of African American votes to nearly 45 percent, Young put together a coalition of African Americans and white liberals to defeat his Republican opponent by a vote of 72,289 to 64,495, becoming the first African American to be elected to Congress from the Deep South since the Reconstruction Era.

Mastering the art of the negotiating style of politics and of de-racializing what he called "people" issues, Young quickly became an influential Democrat in the House and was returned to Congress in landslide victories of 72 percent in 1974 and 80 percent in 1976. He consistently voted against increased military expenditures and in favor of legislation to assist the poor, but his readiness to compromise and conciliate made him remarkably acceptable to all factions of the Democratic Party. In 1976, believing former Georgia Governor Jimmy Carter was the only Democratic candidate who could deliver the South and win in November, Young was the first nationally known elected official to publicly endorse him. Throughout the year Young campaigned on Carter's behalf and was generally credited with mustering the heavy support from African American voters which proved decisive to Carter's victories in key primaries and in the general election. On December 16, 1976, President-elect Carter nominated Young for the position of America's ambassador and chief delegate to the United Nations.

During his brief and stormy career at the United Nations Young was the most outspoken and influential of all Carter's many African American appointees, playing an important diplomatic role which transcended the traditional activities of a U.N. ambassador. He emerged as a leading architect and spokesman for American relations with African and Third World nations. A storm of protest from Israeli and American Jewish leaders following Young's violation of the government's prohibition against meeting with representatives of the Palestine Liberation Organization (PLO), however, forced the ambassador to resign on August 15, 1979.

In October 1981 Young was elected mayor of Atlanta after a hard-fought general campaign against six other aspirants and a runoff election against Sidney Marcus, a white state representative. Receiving 55 percent of the vote, the 49-year old preacher, civil rights activist, and politician became Atlanta's second African American mayor. He took office at a time of reduced federal spending to help cities and a shrinking local tax base caused by the movement of white residents and businesses to the suburbs. He also faced the challenge of governing a predominantly African American city in which most of the economic power was in the hands of whites.

Some critics doubted Young's ability to deal with the Atlanta's problems. He was seen as antibusiness, a weak administrator, and too much of an activist to "bridge the racial gap," as one Georgia politician put it in the New Republic. Young quickly proved his critics wrong. By 1984, Ebony reported, the city had been so successful at attracting new businesses that it was experiencing "a major growth spurt," and by 1988, U.S. News and World Report noted, a survey of 385 executives showed that Atlanta was "their overwhelming first choice to locate a business." In addition, the crime rate had dropped sharply.

Though African Americans dominated the city's politics and whites dominated its economy, both groups seemed willing to work together. "My job," Young told Esquire's Art Harris in 1985, "is to see that whites get some of the power and blacks get some of the money." Some

black leaders accused Young of catering exclusively to the white business establishment and neglecting the black poor, but he garnered the support of Atlanta's growing black middle class and was reelected decisively in 1985.

Limited by law to two terms as mayor, Young decided to run for governor of Georgia in 1990. "It's something I have to do," he told Robin Toner of the New York Times. "If I don't get elected I think I'd probably say 'Free at last.' But I have to give it my best possible shot." Young ran primarily on his record of presiding over Atlanta's economic boom; he was criticized, however, for not being a "hands-on" mayor, and was blamed for Atlanta's crime rate, which had risen again after falling during the early years of his administration.

There was also the issue of race. Though Young was popular with younger, suburban whites, many rural and small-town white Georgians still hesitated to vote for a black man. Young made it through the first stage of the primary, but was defeated by Lieutenant Governor Zell Miller in a runoff that featured a low black turnout.

The loss left Young free to concentrate on another project—preparing Atlanta to host the 1996 Olympic games. As chairman of the Atlanta Organizing Committee, he was, according to Black Enterprise's Alfred Edmond, Jr., "the reason Atlanta was able to capture and hold the attention of the IOC (International Olympic Committee)." Young's diplomatic experience was important in Atlanta's winning the bid over such contenders as Athens, Greece and Melbourne, Australia: "I knew government officials and business people in almost every country represented in the IOC," he told Edmond. "Our approach was intensely personal."

As of the early 1990s, Young had announced no career plans beyond his involvement in the Olympics, political or otherwise. He has remained, observed Joseph Lelyveld in the New York Times, "a preacher and a moralist." Young described himself in the New Republic as "a reformer . . . an advocate of change." But his biographer, Carl Gardner, doubted that Young was ever much of a long-range planner of his own life. "That wasn't his style," Gardner wrote. "He always let things happen. He just naturally evolved."

In June of 1997 Young told Emerge magazine the younger son of Martin Luther King Jr. had asked him to form a commission to investigate King's 1968 assassination. Young said Dexter King, head of the King Center in Atlanta, wanted him to set up "something like a truth commission in South Africa. He's saying, 'Let's declare an amnesty (for confessed King assassin James Earl Ray). Then let's go back and look at the assassination,'" Young said in the interview, published in the magazine's July-August issue.

Further Reading

Good background for Young's role in SCLC are David L. Lewis, King: A Critical Biography (1970) and Paul Good, The Trouble I've Seen (1975). For his political views in the 1970s see Roger M. Williams, "The Making of Andrew Young," Saturday Review (October 16, 1976).

Additional Sources

Discovering Biography, Gale Research (1997).
Jones, Bartlett C., *Flawed Triumphs: Andy Young at the United Nations* (1996).
Simpson, Janice Clair, *Andy Young: A Matter of Choice* (1978).
Young, Andrew, *An Easy Burden: The Civil Rights Movement and the Transformation of America* (1996). □

Brigham Young

Brigham Young (1801-1877), American colonizer and second president of the Church of Jesus Christ of Latter Day Saints, led the Mormons to Utah, colonized it, and served as official and unofficial governor of Oregon Territory.

Brigham Young was born at Whitingham, Vt., on June 1, 1801. When he was three, the family moved to an area of New York where religious mysticism and revivalism were strong. He had only two months of formal education, for the family was poor and rootless. He became a house painter and glazier, and, at the age of 22, a Methodist. He married Miriam Works, and they settled at Mendon, N.Y., in 1829.

In 1832, after studying Joseph Smith's *Book of Mormon* for two years, Young was baptized into the new Church and became very active in it. The following year he moved to Kirtland, Ohio, to form a Mormon church. He traveled through the eastern United States seeking converts, as well as joining "Zion's Army," a militant Mormon branch.

Rise in the Church

In February 1835, when the Quorum of Twelve Apostles was established as an administrative aid to Prophet Joseph Smith, Young was third in rank. By 1838, when the Mormons were expelled from Missouri, he was senior member of this body and directed the removal to Nauvoo, Ill. In 1839 he went to England on a successful mission, returning to Illinois in 1841 to become the Church's leading fiscal agent. By 1844 he had contracted three polygamous marriages.

In 1844 Smith determined to run for president of the United States, and Young left on a speaking tour in support of this. In Boston that July he heard of Smith's murder two weeks earlier. He returned to Nauvoo to find the membership in panic and virtually leaderless. He rallied the members, defeated Sidney Rigdon for leadership, and began searching for a new location for the Mormons, who were again being persecuted.

Colonizer of Utah

After studying government documents and talking with travelers, Young sent agents to various parts of the West to look for the new Zion. He selected the Great Salt Lake region in the hope that there the believers would not be bothered again by outsiders. The move was accomplished under his leadership in 1846-1847, financed by funds from foreign missions and by the salaries of a battalion of men he sent to serve the U.S. Army during the Mexican War. On Dec. 5, 1847, at Salt Lake City, Young was elected president of the Quorum of Twelve Apostles, a position he held until his death.

Young planned a grand city at Salt Lake; the Church retained complete control through prior appropriation of available water, and irrigated farming became the backbone of the colony. He sent colonists to establish Mormon communities at strategic locations in the Great Basin area, some 357 towns in all, and sent missionaries all over the world to seek recruits. To assist the approximately 70,000 converts who came from Europe, he established the Perpetual Emigration Fund to extend loans which, when repaid, would assist still more to come. When funds were low, he directed the immigrants to come from St. Louis, pushing their goods in handcarts, but this advice was somewhat discredited when one group died in a snowstorm at Sweetwater River, Wyo., in 1856.

To keep money in the territory, Young urged development of home industries, the Zion's Cooperative Mercantile Institution. Also, he preached the necessity of hard work and thrift, and he forbade the faithful to engage in mining, fearing the discovery of gold would bring in large numbers of non-Mormons.

Young was a pragmatic leader who sought to strengthen the Church by cooperative means. He loved dancing, singing, and the theater, so these were acceptable;

he forbade liquor, tobacco, all stimulants, gambling, and cardplaying. He encouraged polygamy because it was hated by non-Mormons; thus its practice insured Mormon unity against outsiders. Young himself had an estimated 19 to 27 wives and 56 children. He also urged a good educational system, and he established the University of Deseret (now the University of Utah) in 1850.

Political Leader

The Mexican War brought Utah into American hands, so Young gathered a constitutional convention to petition for statehood under the name Deseret. Congress refused, naming it the Territory of Utah, but Young became governor. In 1857 opposition to the Mormons became so strong from Federal officials that he was removed as governor. When he refused to be ousted, a Federal army under Gen. Albert Sidney Johnston was sent to expel him. The so-called "Mormon War" ended in 1858 by compromise; Young gave way to a non-Mormon governor but continued to govern unofficially through his position in the Church until his death in Salt Lake City on Aug. 29, 1877. A domineering tyrant in public, privately Young had been genial and benevolent.

Further Reading

Works on Young include Frank J. Cannon and George L. Knapp, *Brigham Young and His Mormon Empire* (1913), a hostile treatment; M. R. Werner, *Brigham Young* (1925); Susa Young Gates and Lead D. Widtsoe, *The Life Story of Brigham Young* (1930), which contains excellent material on his family life; Milton R. Hunter, *Brigham Young: The Colonizer* (1940; 2d ed. 1941); Ray B. West, *Kingdom of the Saints: The Story of Brigham Young and the Mormons* (1957); and Stanley P. Hirshson's unfavorable portrait, *The Lion of the Lord: A Biography of Brigham Young* (1969). The last is less a biography than an account of Mormon history, emphasizing the more sensational aspects of Young's life. A good, overall picture of Young and his work is in Thomas F. O'Dea, *The Mormons* (1957). □

Coleman Alexander Young

Coleman Alexander Young (born 1918) was elected Detroit's first African American mayor in 1973 and served until 1993, longer than any other Detroit mayor.

Born in Tuscaloosa, AL, on May 24, 1918, Coleman Young was the oldest of five children born to Coleman and Ida Reese (Jones) Young. His family moved to Detroit's "Black Bottom" neighborhood when he was five. "Black Bottom" was the center of African American culture and politics in segregated Detroit in the era before World War II. Young's father set up a tailor shop and also worked for the post office. Young attended a Catholic elementary school and Eastern High School, graduating with honors. Working on the assembly line for the Ford Motor

Company, Young took part in the sitdown strikes of 1937. He served in World War II as a second lieutenant and bombadier-navigator. During the postwar period Young worked as a union organizer for the Congress of Industrial Organizations, but was fired because he clashed with union leader Walter Reuther.

In 1951 Young was executive secretary of the National Negro Labor Council, which the Truman administration labeled "subversive." In the McCarthy era, Young was investigated by federal authorities as a suspected Communist sympathizer. In the 1950s, Young worked in a laundry and a butcher shop, ran his own cleaning service, drove a taxi, and sold insurance. In 1960, he plunged into politics, winning a seat as a delegate to the Michigan Constitutional Convention. He was elected to the Michigan Senate in 1964, and became a Democratic floor leader during his nine years there.

Detroit's First Black Mayor

When Young first ran for mayor in 1973, Detroit's population was about 50 percent African American. Young, getting an estimated 92 percent of the African American vote, narrowly beat a white Detroit police chief, John F. Nichols, who got 91 percent of the white vote. Nichols ran a "law-and-order" campaign, playing on fears of unrest that remained from Detroit's destructive 1967 riots, while Young attacked the police force, and particularly its special tactical crime unit STRESS, as a racist organization. After his victory, Young, the first African American to be mayor of Detroit, took a harder line on crime, hoping to blunt Detroit's repu-

tation as the murder capital of the nation. He told a prayer breakfast meeting: "I issue an open warning now to all dope pushers, to all rip-off artists, to all muggers. It's time to leave Detroit. I don't give a damn if you are black or white . . . hit the road!"

Often profane and always blunt, Young was one of the first African American big-city mayors to achieve national prominence. One of his major goals was to transform the police department from one dominated by whites into an institution more closely reflecting the racial makeup of the city, which was becoming increasingly African American. He blistered white police officers who lived in the suburbs, saying they were like an "army of occupation" and charging: "They don't give a damn about the city. They come in and kick some ass and go back" to their suburban homes. Young suspended police living outside the city, demoted others, promoted a large number of African Americans through use of the quota system, recruited women and minorities for police work, and disbanded STRESS. The mayor cited better police-community relations and the integration of the police force and other institutions as his administration's proudest achievements.

Young was re-elected in 1977, 1981, 1985 and 1989 by sizable majorities, with little more than token opposition. In Detroit's African American community, Young was a heroic figure. He created a formidable political machine and raised millions for his campaign war chest. He imposed a ban on city workers speaking to reporters and he became famous for his obscenity-laced attacks on political opponents. Young became a force in state and national politics, trying to get assistance for Detroit's daunting urban problems during an era of decreasing aid to cities from the federal and state government. In Michigan, he became a symbol of the state's deep racial divisions, despised by many white suburbanites and praised by African Americans and liberal whites.

Abandoned in the decades after the 1967 civil disturbances by most of the city's white, middle-class residents and most of its businesses and investors, Detroit in the 1970s and 1980s was reeling from the rapid decline of the domestic auto industry, which had made Detroit world-famous as the Motor City. With almost all its auto factories closed, Detroit struggled with massive unemployment, abandoned housing, poor schools, lack of public transit and rampant crime. Young was saddled with these deep-rooted problems during an era where urban issues moved from near the top of the national agenda to near the bottom. His major strategy to reverse Detroit's decline was to court business leaders in efforts to rebuild downtown, hoping to recapture businesses and jobs. He forged solid relationships with top automotive and financial leaders and tried to promote Detroit as a "renaissance city." Young pointed to the building of the Renaissance Center, an office-hotel tower on the Riverfront, as the first step to a downtown revival which never lived up to expectations.

An important fight which defined Young's priorities was his deal to bring a new General Motors assembly plant to an area known as Poletown. The city, state, and business leaders devised a plan to raze an old but relatively stable mixed-ethnic community to clear land for the plant, touting the promise of thousands of jobs. Community activists opposed the destruction of the neighborhood. Young prevailed, touting the new GM plant as a symbol of the city's revival, but the economic spin-off promised never materialized, and fewer than half the promised jobs were created after the plant opened.

In his last three terms as mayor, Young's administration was plagued by allegations of fraud, bribery, and mismanagement. The mayor remained blunt and unapologetic, and his combative relations with the press worsened. During Young's last term, his police chief was indicted in a financial scandal amid allegations that Young had operated a slush fund from his campaign war chest. Young was plagued by poor health and seemed ever farther removed from the everyday problems of the city. A growing number of critics, including a younger generation of African American politicians and other community leaders, attacked the Young administration for neglecting the city's neighborhoods, not tearing down abandoned houses, allowing basic city services to decline, and failing to stem crime.

Undaunted, Young remained until the end of his tenure an outspoken booster of Detroit and a critic of his many political opponents. In his 20 years in office, he transformed Detroit from a city run by whites to a city led by African Americans, in government, the police department, the schools, and business. But he failed to make much headway against the daunting social problems that plagued a city abandoned by its major industry and the owners of its wealth. In 1993, Young retired and a new mayor, Dennis Archer, was elected. Archer immediately adopted a more conciliatory attitude toward suburbanites. After his retirement, Young remained outspoken on issues such as the 1995-1997 Detroit newspaper strike and his political machine continued to be a major factor in Detroit politics.

Further Reading

For the political life of Mayor Young see Chicago *Tribune* (April 17, 1977), Detroit *Free Press* (May 9, 1974) and *New York Times* (April 8, 1983). See also *The Biographical Dictionary of American Mayors, 1820-1980* (1981); Melvin G. Holli, *Detroit* (1975); *African American Biographies* (1992); and *African American Almanac* (1994). □

Lester Willis Young

The American musician Lester Willis ("Prez") Young (1909-1959) was one of jazz's premier stylists, a startlingly innovative tenor saxophonist whose approach was marked by finesse and relaxation rather than power and passion.

On and off the bandstand, Lester "Prez" (for "President") Young was unique. His musical genius is well documented on recordings, but his eccentricities of speech and attire survive only in anecdotes and photographs and in the memory of those who knew him. Many jazz slang locutions, whose origins have since been obscured, were coined by Young (for example, "I feel a draft" for "I sense hostility"); his wide-brimmed porkpie hat was one of several sartorial trademarks, paralleled by such linguistic oddities as his habit of addressing everyone, man or woman, as "Lady"—followed by the person's last name. (Count Basie, then, would become "Lady Basie.") Unfortunately, this buoyant, creative genius was traumatized, and ultimately destroyed, by his experiences during World War II.

The eldest of three children, Lester Willis Young was born on August 27, 1909, in Woodville, Mississippi, and shortly after his birth the family moved to Algiers, Louisiana, just across the river from New Orleans. The father, Willis H. Young, who had studied at Tuskegee Institute, musically tutored Lester, Lester's brother Lee (later a professional jazz drummer), and their sister Irma. Lester was taught trumpet, alto saxophone, violin, and drums.

Young's parents divorced in 1919, and the father moved with the children to Minneapolis in 1920; there he married a woman saxophonist and formed a family band, in which Young played alto sax and drums as the band toured the larger Midwestern cities. But Young, unwilling to tour the South, left the band in 1927. For the next five years he worked with a variety of Midwestern bands, including the Original Blue Devils and King Oliver's Band. In 1934 he replaced Coleman Hawkins, the reigning tenor saxophone king, with the famous Fletcher Henderson band, but his lightness of tone on the instrument was ridiculed as

"wrong" by the band's other musicians, and after a few months the sensitive Young quit the band.

Joins Count Basie Band

In 1936 Young petitioned Count Basie for a place in his band and was hired; his early recordings with a small Basie unit as well as with the full orchestra provided Lester with solo spots on "Lady Be Good," "Shoe Shine Boy," and "Taxi War Dance" and heralded the arrival of a distinctively new instrumental voice. The band's other superb tenor saxophonist, Herschel Evans, had a heavier, Coleman Hawkins-influenced approach to the instrument, and the contrast produced a friendly rivalry between the two that generated tremendous excitement for audience and record buyers. Evans' death (of heart disease) in 1939 depressed Young severely and was an important reason for his leaving Basie in 1940.

For the next several years Young worked as a "single," playing on both coasts but living chiefly in California. He was now a star, but was drinking heavily and his morale was low, a condition that was ameliorated in 1944 by his rejoining Basie's band. Shortly thereafter, however, he was ambushed one night by an FBI man posing as a jazz fan, who arranged an Army induction for Young on the following day. He was immediately inducted despite his obvious unsuitability for military service: he was a chronic alcoholic and a long-time marijuana smoker, was pathologically afraid of needles, and had tested positive for syphilis.

Stationed in Alabama, he was plagued by racism, and he was not allowed to play music (his horn was confiscated), which exacerbated his need for alcohol and narcotic pills. Shortly into his service, pills were found in his possession, and a court-martial resulted in dishonorable discharge, but the Alabama military court prolonged his agony by committing him to a year of hard labor at Fort Gordon, Georgia.

The profound effects of this disastrous experience were not immediately apparent. Young returned to civilian life in the midst of a jazz revolution called bebop; he participated in Jazz at the Philharmonic (JATP), a concert tour that mixed the young rebels with the Old Guard players, and Young fared better at these concerts than his great rival Coleman Hawkins. His style was more adaptive to the new harmonics—in fact, he had been a primary inspiration for the new music. The sadness that had begun to enter Young's playing, however, is evident on a 1952 recording session with the Oscar Peterson Quartet, although his melodic inventiveness compensates somewhat for the loss of power.

Further signs of a crushed spirit gradually emerged, and the 1950s was not a productive decade for Young. Symbolic of the decline, perhaps, was the quirky angle at which Young held his horn while playing: earlier it had been a 45 degree angle, but by the 1950s the rakish tilt had vanished. Always a shy, sensitive man, Young was unable to rebound from the brutal humiliation officialdom had inflicted upon him; his playing in those final years, despite bursts of brilliance, seemed to lack conviction and grew increasingly mechanical and spiritless.

In the last dozen years of his life Young had long spells of poor health, undergoing hospital treatment on four separate occasions—in 1947, in 1955, in 1957, and in 1958. Finally, that year, he moved into New York's Alvin Hotel, leaving his wife and son in their home in Queens, New York. A day after returning from a one-month Paris engagement, on March 15, 1959, he died at the hotel of a heart attack brought on by esophageal varicosity and severe internal bleeding.

The Young Music

When Young arrived on the major jazz scene in the mid-1930s the commanding presence of Coleman Hawkins dictated tenor saxophone style. Hawkins played with fierce intensity, investing every chorus (virtually every bar) with power and passion—the quintessential romantic. Young, on the other hand, was all light and air, velvety of tone, buoyantly disregarding bar lines, floating the rhythm effortlessly, attacking the melody obliquely, subtly rather than head-on. The difference between the two sensibilities is voluminously documented, but nowhere more clearly than on the original 1937 recording of Basie's theme, "One O'Clock Jump," on which Herschel Evans, a Hawkins disciple, leads off with a thrilling, hard-edged chorus and Lester later responds with an equally thrilling, marshmallow-toned solo. Thus was the Hawkins monolith toppled and replaced by the twin towers of Hawkins and Young—the two essential styles of jazz performance, hot and cool.

Examples of Young's genius abound. One of the earliest was a 1935 series of Billie Holiday sessions on which she's accompanied by a Teddy Wilson-led unit; it remains a classic record date, not only for Billie's excellence and the uniformly high quality of the musicianship, but also for the extraordinary musical understanding between Young and Billie, a model of symbiosis. The two sustained a 25-year friendship (she labeled him "the President" or "Prez"; he dubbed her "Lady Day"—nicknames that have endured), and ironically they died the same year.

From 1935 to 1946 Young was unfailingly at the top of his form; among his many sterling features with Basie were "Louisiana," "Easy Does It," "Every Tub," "Broadway," "Lester Leaps in," "Jumpin' at the Woodside," "Dickie's Dream," "I Never Knew," and his own composition, "Tickle Toe." His excellent work on clarinet, in evidence on a number of small Basie units (the Kansas City 5), can also be heard in the big band context of Basie's classic "Blue and Sentimental." Even more noteworthy were his small group tenor saxophone outings of the early-mid-1940s, because those smaller units allowed more "stretching out" (that is, longer solos); a 1942 trio session with pianist Nat Cole and bassist Red Callender produced masterful versions of "Tea for Two," "Indiana," "I Can't Get Started," and the ballad apotheosized by Coleman Hawkins, "Body and Soul." *Lester Young: The Complete Savoy Recordings* includes perhaps a half dozen masterpieces: "Blue Lester," "These Foolish Things," and two versions each of "Indiana" and "Ghost of a Chance." A 1945 session with trombonist Vic Dickenson and a rhythm section anchored by pianist Dodo Marmarosa has two as-

tounding tracks, "D.B. Blues" and another version of "These Foolish Things." Young's greatest recorded live performance is probably the 1946 JATP concert, at which he was co-featured with bebop genius Charlie Parker; his long solos on "Lady Be Good" and "After You've Gone" are a perfect meld of high excitement and artistic integrity.

In the 1970s some West Coast jazzmen formed a midsized band (variably eight or nine pieces) called Prez Conference, the sole purpose of which was to perform in full ensemble transcriptions of Young's great solos. His legacy is further perpetuated by WKCR, Columbia University's FM radio station, which every Presidents' Day weekend plays exclusively the music of Lester "President" Young.

Further Reading

There are many good articles on Lester Young, but none better than pianist Bobby Scott's insightful "The House in the Heart" in Gene Lees' Jazzletter (September 1983). There are a number of biographies, American and European: Luc Delannoy's *Lester Young. Profession: Président* (Paris:1987); Vittorio Franchini's *Lester Young* (Milan: 1961); Dave Gelly's *Lester Young* (England: 1984); Lewis Porter's *Lester Young* (1985); and probably the most definitive, Frank Buchmann Moller's *You Just Fight for Your Life: The Story of Lester Young* (1990, translated from the Danish by John Irons). John Clellon Holmes' 1959 novel *The Horn,* a fictionalized biography of Lester in his last years, offers an intimate and moving look at a man in despair.

Additional Sources

Delannoy, Luc, *Pres: the story of Lester Young,* Fayetteville: University of Arkansas Press, 1993.
Gelly, Dave, *Lester Young,* Tunbridge Wells: Spellmount; New York: Hippocrene Books, 1984.
Porter, Lewis, *Lester Young,* Boston, Mass.: Twayne Publishers, 1985. □

Owen D. Young

Owen D. Young (1874-1962), American industrialist and monetary authority, authored financial plans for Germany after World War I.

Owen D. Young was born Oct. 27, 1874, on a farm near Van Hornsdale, N.Y. At the age of 16 he entered St. Lawrence University and in 1896 took his law degree *cum laude* from the Boston University Law School. Starting as a clerk in the firm of Charles H. Tyler, in 1907 Young became a partner. He also lectured at the Boston Law School. In 1898 he married Josephine Edmonds, who bore him four sons.

Young specialized in public utility securities law. The Panic of 1893 and the ensuing depression required reorganization of many utility companies, mainly because of the demise of their major supplier, General Electric (GE).

In 1913 Young's handling of a case against a GE subsidiary brought an invitation to become GE's general counsel. By 1922 he had become chairman of the board. Always interested in the problems of the laboring man, he pushed for the adoption of employee stock option plans and the use of unemployment insurance.

Young's participation in President Woodrow Wilson's Second Industrial Conference following World War I marked the beginning of his counseling of five U.S. presidents. In 1924 he coauthored the Dawes Plan, which provided for a reduction in the annual amount of German reparations, a loan to stabilize the German currency, and the French evacuation of the Ruhr Valley. The Dawes Plan worked, primarily because of American loans and investments. In the late 1920s investments fell, and Germany again defaulted on its payments. In 1929 a new international body met to consider a program for the final release of German obligations. Young acted as chairman. Germany's total reparations were reduced and spread over 59 annual payments. The Young Plan, which also reduced Allied war debts to the United States, collapsed with the coming of the Great Depression.

During the 1920s Young organized the Radio Corporation of America and acted as its board chairman until 1929, when he became chairman of the executive committee. In 1939 he retired to the family farm, where he began dairy farming. More than 20 colleges awarded him honorary degrees. Long interested in education, he served as a New York State regent and in 1949 labored on the state commission that recommended the present system of higher education. His donations to the New York Public Library were valued at over $1,000,000. He died on July 11, 1962.

Further Reading

For further details on Young see Ida M. Tarbell, *Owen D. Young: A New Type of Industrial Leader* (1932), and the section on him in Ray Thomas Tucker, *The Mirrors of 1932* (1931).

Additional Sources

Case, Josephine Young, *Owen D. Young and American enterprise: a biography,* Boston: D.R. Godine, 1982. □

Stark Young

Stark Young (1881-1963) was a drama critic, editor, translator, painter, playwright, and novelist.

Stark Young was born in Como, Mississippi, on October 11, 1881, the son of a physician in a family which traced its ancestry in the United States back to 1795. Young received his Bachelor's degree from the University of Mississippi in 1901 and his Master's degree in English from Columbia University in 1902. For the next six months he lived in a hut in the North Carolina mountains studying Dante and other classic poets and writing poems. In 1903 he accepted a position teaching at a military school in Water Valley, Mississippi. In 1905 he accepted a position in the English Department at the University of Mississippi.

Young published his first volume of poetry, *The Blind Man at the Window,* and his verse play *Guenevere* in 1906. A year later he left the University of Mississippi to accept a position at the University of Texas, where he founded the Curtain Club in 1909. In 1912 he published a collection of short plays, *Addio, Madretto and Other Plays,* and translated Jean Regnard's *Le legataire universal.* While still at the University of Texas Young founded the *Texas Review* (1915), which later became the *Southwest Review* when it was transferred to Southern Methodist University. From 1915 to 1920 Young was professor of English at Amherst College. During this time he published his first articles in the *New Republic.* In 1922 he became an editor for *Theatre Arts Magazine,* drama critic for the *New Republic,* and member of the editorial board of the *New Republic,* a magazine with which he would be connected until 1947.

In 1923 Young's first book of theatre criticism, *The Flower in Drama,* was published. He resigned from the *New Republic* to become drama critic for the *New York Times* in 1924, but a year later returned to the *New Republic* as drama critic and editor. In 1927 Young's most famous collection of critical essays, *The Theatre,* was published. For the next ten years he devoted himself to writing of all kinds, publishing essays, novels, collections of short stories, and plays. In 1938 Young translated Chekhov's *The Sea Gull* for an Alfred Lunt and Lynn Fontanne production. Eventually, Young translated four Chekhov plays (*The Sea Gull, The Cherry Orchard, The Three Sisters,* and *Uncle Vanya*), all of which were produced in New York City by the 4th Street Theatre in 1955-1956 and appeared in the collection *Best Plays of Chekhov* (1956).

Young lectured frequently, and during 1925-1928 was a lecturer at the New School for Social Research in New York City. In 1931 he delivered the Westinghouse Lectures before leading Italian literary and philosophical societies in Rome, Florence, and Milan to acquaint students with American culture and ideals. For this he was made a commander of the Order of the Crown in Italy. He subsequently gave lectures at Cornell and Yale universities, the University of Mississippi, Wellesley College, and the Carnegie Institute of Technology. In 1958 he was the Theodore Spector Lecturer at Harvard University. In recognition of his contributions to the arts, he was awarded the Brandeis University Medal in 1958 and the Southern Theatre Association Award in 1959. A memorial room was established in his name at the University of Texas. He was a member of Sigma Chi, Sigma Upsilon, and Phi Beta Kappa. Stark Young died in New York City on January 6, 1963. He never married.

Young was a prolific letter writer. His letters, collected and edited into two volumes by John Pilkington, were published by Louisiana State University Press. Pilkington, in his introduction to Young's *Letters,* said of Young that

> on both the scholarly and practical levels, Stark Young brought to his dramatic criticism an exhaustive knowledge of all the components required for the effective production of a play. . . . Young always had in mind a standard of excellence to which the particular component should conform. His knowledge of the parts, moreover, extended to a concept of the whole. . . . The public liked his forthrightness, while

the actors, directors and designers learned professionally from his sharp remarks and thanked him for his advice.

Further Reading

In addition to the poetry, plays, and translations cited in the text, Young wrote a well-regarded historical novel, *So Red the Rose* (1934). His criticisms and essays reveal something of his persona, but probably the most information is contained in the two volumes of *Letters* (1975), edited by John Pilkington.

Additional Sources

Pilkington, John, *Stark Young,* Boston: Twayne, 1985. □

Thomas Young

The English physicist Thomas Young (1773-1829) is best known for his double-slit interference experiment which validated the wave theory of light and for the elastic modulus named for him.

Concerning Thomas Young, the noted physicist Sir Humphry Davy wrote: "He was a most amiable and good tempered man . . . of universal erudition, and almost universal accomplishments. Had he limited himself to any one department of knowledge, he must have been the first in that department. But as a mathematician, a scholar, a hieroglyphist, he was eminent, and he knew so much it was difficult to say what he did not know."

Young was born in Milverton near Taunton on June 16, 1773, of Quaker parentage. A child prodigy, he had read through the Bible twice by the age of four and was reading and writing Latin at six. By the time he was 14 he had a knowledge of at least five languages, and eventually his repertoire grew to 12.

Young chose medicine as a career and trained at the universities of London, Edinburgh, Göttingen, and finally Cambridge (1797-1799). In 1808 he began practice in London, but because of his blunt truthfulness and his distrust of the practices of purging and bleeding then common he was not popular with his patients. In 1811 he joined the staff of St. George's Hospital. He died in his London home on May 10, 1829.

In 1793 Young explained the process of accommodation in the human eye. In 1801 he presented a paper on the nature of visual astigmatism and gave the constants of the eye; this paper is considered by ophthalmologists to be his most brilliant contribution. The following year he gave his theory of color vision, a notable advance in physiological optics.

In a lecture on the proper construction of arches Young casually pointed out that within wide limits the ratio of stress to strain was for most materials a constant. This characteristic constant for stretching is called Young's modulus of the substance. Turning to a completely different field, he "penetrated the obscurity that had veiled for ages the hiero-

glyphics of Egypt'' through his deciphering of the Rosetta Stone.

Young's famous two-volume *Lectures on Natural Philosophy* (1807) contained the 60 lectures he gave at the Royal Institution while he was professor of natural philosophy there (1801-1803). The first volume contains the lectures and almost 600 drawings; the second volume includes several of his papers and about 20,000 references to the literature, many annotated.

Further Reading

A particularly good book on Young is by Frank Oldham, *Thomas Young: F.R.S. Philosopher and Physician* (1933). See also Alexander Wood, *Thomas Young: Natural Philosopher, 1773-1829* (1954). A good, brief discussion of him is in James Gerald Crowther, *Scientific Types* (1970).

Additional Sources

Kline, Daniel Louis, *Thomas Young, forgotten genius: an annotated narrative biography,* Cincinnati, Ohio: Vidan Press, 1993. ☐

Whitney Moore Young Jr.

Whitney Moore Young, Jr. (1921-1971), black American civil rights leader and social work administra-

tor, was one of America's most influential civil rights leaders during the 1960s.

W hitney Young, Jr., was born on July 31, 1921, in Lincoln Ridge, Ky. He received a bachelor of science degree from Kentucky State College in 1941 and a master of arts degree from the University of Minnesota in 1947. He served in several capacities for local Urban League chapters in St. Paul, Minn., and Omaha, Nebr., and then became dean of the School of Social Work of Atlanta University in 1954.

After studying at Harvard University during 1960-1961, Young became executive director of the National Urban League. At this time the League was largely a northern-based social welfare agency concerned mainly with helping black migrants from the South find jobs and adjust to their new northern industrial urban environment. Young, however, transformed it into a major civil rights organization. In 1963 he suggested that preferential treatment be given black Americans in jobs, educational facilities, and housing. He reasoned that it was not enough for the United States to merely erase barriers to equal opportunity; rather, in order to overcome centuries of deliberately depriving black people, it was necessary to begin a deliberate, positive program of uplift. He called for a ''Domestic Marshall Plan''—an all-out crash program to eliminate poverty and deprivation in the same manner that the Marshall Plan had been launched to rehabilitate war-torn Europe after World War II.

Young saw his role as one of trying to maintain contacts and liaison between increasingly polarizing white and black groups in American society. He admonished black civil rights protesters against violence and at the same time warned white decision makers that, unless substantial gains were made, violence from blacks could be expected, if not condoned. Under Young's leadership, the National Urban League received grants from government and private sources to work on such projects as job training, open housing, minority executive recruitment, and "street academies" (schools in ghetto communities for students who have dropped out of regular school).

Young served on several presidential commissions. In 1967 President Lyndon Johnson appointed him a member of an American team to observe elections in Vietnam.

On Jan. 2, 1944, Young married Margaret Buchner and they had two daughters. He received the Medal of Freedom in 1969 from President Richard Nixon. His programs for integration are outlined in *To Be Equal* (1964) and *Beyond Racism* (1969). He died on March 11, 1971, in Lagos, Nigeria; he received posthumous honorary degrees.

Further Reading

Elton C. Fox, *Contemporary Black Leaders* (1970), and George R. Metcalf, *Black Profiles* (1970), contain chapters on Young. A biographical sketch of him is in *Historical Negro Biographies* of the *International Library of Negro Life and History,* edited by Wilhelmena S. Robinson (1968). For commentary on Young's role in the civil rights movement see August Meier and Elliot Rudwick, eds., *Black Protest in the Sixties* (1970). □

Sir Francis Edward Younghusband

Sir Francis Edward Younghusband (1863-1942) was an English soldier, explorer, leader of an expedition to Lhasa, and the founder of the World Fellowship of Faiths.

Born into a family with strong military and Indian connections, Francis Younghusband duly entered the army and was posted to India in 1882. The lure of exploration in mountainous frontiers of strategic importance took him, on leave in 1886, across central Asia from Manchuria through Inner Mongolia and Sinkiang—regions where Russian interest was evident—to Kashmir, which he entered by the exacting Mustagh Pass. Accepted into the Foreign Service of the Indian government, he reconnoitered Russian activities in Hunza, where he crossed the extremely difficult, unexplored Saltoro Pass.

In 1891 Younghusband again encountered the Russians in the Pamir, and he was arrested and deported from territory claimed by them. On leave in 1895, he covered for the *London Times* the relief, from attack by local tribesmen, of the northwestern outpost of Chitral. When stationed there

earlier, Younghusband had met George Curzon, traveling privately in Asia.

In 1903 Curzon, then viceroy of India, chose Younghusband to lead a mission to negotiate with the Tibetans, who were encouraging Russian overtures while contumeliously rejecting neighborly relations with India. Progress was inhibited by disagreement between the clear-sighted viceroy and the vacillating Balfour ministry in London; but, after prolonged Tibetan obstruction on the chilly Himalayan border, approval was given for a military expedition through unmapped mountain tracks and eventually to Lhasa itself.

In difficulty and danger Younghusband was a self-possessed, resolute, and fearless leader, but his humane nature was saddened by the losses inflicted on the illmatched Tibetans before they were overcome in two sharp engagements. Reaching Lhasa in August 1904, he was urged to conclude a treaty speedily and withdraw before winter. Slow communications with London precluded an exchange of views, and the favorable response of the Tibetans to Younghusband's generous integrity led him to include in the final terms two conditions advantageous to India but which went beyond his brief. They were reversed by London; and, through the animosity of the secretary of state for India, St. John Brodrick, who suspected he had flouted orders at Curzon's instigation, Younghusband though awarded a knighthood was also officially reprimanded. That injustice to a remarkable achievement was only redressed 17 years later by a subsequent administration. Meanwhile, showing no bitterness, Younghusband enjoyed four years as the Resident in Kashmir before retiring at the age of 47.

Thereafter, as president of the Royal Geographical Society, Younghusband, characteristically, promoted expeditions to Mt. Everest. But the dominant interest in the remaining years of his long life was a mystical idealism, present at all times, that inspired him to lead with vigorous but benign enthusiasm a crusade for worldwide religious unity. Younghusband was married and had one son and one daughter.

Further Reading

Younghusband's life and character are sensitively depicted in George Seaver, *Francis Younghusband: Explorer and Mystic* (1952). Peter Fleming, *Bayonets to Lhasa* (1961), gives a brilliant account of the Tibetan expedition. Both books contain lists of Younghusband's own published works.

Additional Sources

French, Patrick, *Younghusband: the last great imperial adventurer,* London: HarperCollins, 1994. □

Marguerite Yourcenar

French novelist, poet, essayist, dramatist, world traveller, and translator Marguerite Yourcenar (1903-

1987) was the first woman elected to the French Academy.

Marguerite Yourcenar was born on June 8, 1903, and baptized Marguerite Antoinette Ghislaine. Her father, Michel de Crayencour, was a native of Lille and a restless traveller, and it was by chance that she was born during her family's brief sojourn in Brussels. Her mother, Frenande de Cartier de Marchienne, a Belgian, died ten days after the birth of her daughter of puerperal fever. As a young girl Marguerite lived frequently with an aunt in Belgium and with family friends in northern France until 1912 when she and her father settled in Paris. She was educated by a professional teacher, but she was in large measure self-educated by visits to museums, the classical theaters, and extensive reading.

Her first trip beyond the continent was to England in 1914 where she spent a year learning English and visiting famous museums and historical sites. The remaining years of World War I she passed in Paris with her father, who began her instruction in ancient Greek, or in Provence where her father after suffering serious financial losses, attempted to recover his fortune by gambling at Monte Carlo and elsewhere. She continued her education with various private tutors and received a Baccalaureate degree in 1919. At this point her formal education ended.

Between the ages of 19 and 23 she began writing and, with a subsidy from her father, published two books of poems: *Le Jardin des Chimères* (1921) and *Les Dieux ne sont pas morts* (1922). Equally with the aid of her father she worked out the anagram that became Yourcenar, her pen-name, which became her legal name in 1947. She composed several hundred pages of manuscript during her early years, threw most of them away, yet preserved fragments that she would turn into complete books 30 or more years later. The lucubrations of her youth were seedbeds for her fertile, restless imagination. So were certain events: a visit to the Villa Adriana was the inspiration for her most famous novel, *Mémoires d'Hadrien,* which was not completed until 1951.

The 1920s were years of continuous travel. In Italy she witnessed Mussolini's march on Rome. Her knowledge of fascism derived from her acquaintance with Italian life and conversations with Italian intellectuals exiled in Switzerland and southern France. From these experiences she published her novel *Denier du rêve* (1934), revised in 1959. For Yourcenar, a republication became the occasion for re-writing her text, so a new edition was frequently a new book. She travelled extensively in Switzerland, Germany, and Eastern Europe where political transformations were having a degrading effect on the classical culture that had formed the basis of her education. She published several articles in prominent reviews deploring the decline of European culture; she also published several short stories, mostly in the classical style. However, her reading now included contemporary authors as well as the theories of socialism and anarchy, with the result that her outlook assumed a leftward orientation. She even published a story, thanks to Henri Barbusse, in *L'Humanité,* the French Communist Party's newspaper.

Politics, however, rarely made up the substance of her compositions. In these years she wrote a story—*Alexis ou le traité du vain combat* (1929)—about a young musician, married and father of a child, who renounced his family in order to follow his bent toward homosexuality. In the 1920s this was a delicate subject, also taken up by André Gide. Its use in fiction was still unusual and provoked perhaps more outrage than her novel *Denier du rêve* about a failed plot to assassinate Mussolini. Il Duce had many backers in France.

Yourcenar was remarkably prolific, finding time to think, read, and write while travelling extensively in Greece where she wrote the manuscript of *Feux,* a series of aphorisms and personal impressions on the subject of passion— above all, carnal passion. A visit to London in 1937 led her to Virginia Woolf, whose novel *The Waves* she translated into French. Two years later she translated *What Maisie Knew* by Henry James. Back in Paris she made the acquaintance of an American, Grace Frick, who became a life-time friend and the translator of her major novels. In September 1938 she left for the United States, settled in New Haven where Grace lived, and came to love New England. She also travelled extensively in the upper South, became aware of the condition of the African American population, and began collecting and translating African American spirituals in an anthology which she later published under the appropriate title *Fleuve profond, sombre rivière* (1964).

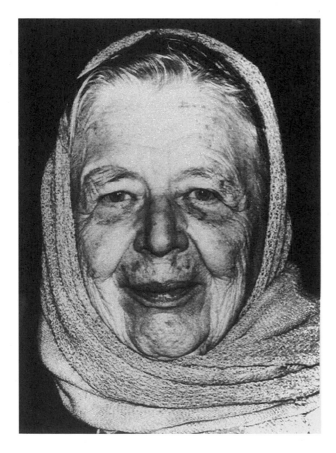

In 1938 she settled in a villa on the Isle of Capri where she composed *Le Coup de Grâce* (1939), a novel based on an event that occurred during the civil war in Russia between the Reds and the Whites. She continued her travels in Europe, returning to the United States when war broke out. She established a residence there for 11 years, meanwhile travelling to Chicago and the Mid-West to lecture and accepting a part-time teaching job at Sarah Lawrence College from 1942 to 1949.

She undertook extensive reading in the libraries of Yale University and other research centers to expand her knowledge of classical antiquity and finally completed the original manuscript of *Hadrian's Memoires,* first sketched in 1937-1938 and published in 1951. Her second historical novel, *L'Oeuvre au noir* (1968), came to dominate the historical novel school in France. About her family's origins she published *Souvenirs pieux* (1974) and *Archives du Nord* (1977). Her writings represent a form of modern classicism. Her language shows a "favorable inclination toward the soft, fluid French of the century of Versailles that gives to the least word the retarded grace of a dead language."

Yourcenar was the recipient of many awards, including the Prix Femina-Vacaresco (1952) for *Mémoires d'Hadrien,* for which she was also honored by the French Academy; the page one award of the Newspaper Guild of New York in 1955 for Frick's translation of *Hadrian's Memoires;* the Prix Combat for *Sous bénéfice d'inventaire* in 1962; the Prix Femina for *Oeuvre au noir* in 1968; Legion of Honor and officer of the Order of Leopold of Belgium in 1971; the Grand prix national de la Culture in 1974; and the Grand prix de l'Académie Française and the Grande Médaille de Vermeil of the City of Paris in 1977. She received honorary doctorates from Smith College, Colby College, and Harvard University and was a member of the Belgian Academie Royale de Langue et de Littérature Française (1979), the Académie Française (1980), and the American Academy of Arts and Letters (1982).

Yourcenar died December 17, 1987, at Mount Desert Island Hospital of complications following a stroke. French premier Jacques Chirac said, "French letters has just lost an exceptional woman."

Further Reading

The best English language introduction to the writings of Yourcenar is Frederic Farrell, *Marguerite Yourcenar: Criticism and Interpretations* (1983). The following sources are all in French: M. Yourcenar, *Oeuvres romanesques* (Gallimard, 1982), which provides a chronology of events in her life; J. Blot, *Marguerite Yourcenar* (Seghers, 1971), a useful biographical portrait; R. de Rosbo, *Entretiens radiophoniques avec Marguerite Yourcenar* (Mercure de France, 1972), an extensive interview; and B. Vercier and J. Lecarme, editors, *La Littérature Française depuis 1968* (Bordas, 1982), which is the best study of her writings and her place in French classical literature.

Additional Sources

Savigneau, Josyane, *Marguerite Yourcenar: inventing a life,* Chicago: The University of Chicago Press, 1993.

Yourcenar, Marguerite, *Dear departed,* New York: Farrar Straus Giroux, 1991. □

Yüan Mei

Yüan Mei (1716-1798), Chinese author, was one of the great poets of the Ch'ing dynasty. He is especially noted for his cultivation of naturalness and individuality in his poetry and criticism as well as in his life.

A native of Hangchow, Chekiang, Yüan Mei was a precocious boy who earned his *hsiu-ts'ai* degree at the age of eleven. He received his *chin-shih,* the highest academic degree, at 23 and was retained in the imperial Hanlin Academy. But failing to pass the examination on the Manchu language, which was his assigned subject of study, he was released from the academy in 1742 and successively appointed to several districts in Kiangsu province as magistrate.

In 1748 Yüan retired from government service and in the next year moved to his newly acquired garden in Nanking known as Sui-yüan, the "Garden of Contentment." The garden was once owned by the wealthy Ts'ao family, and the novelist Ts'ao family, and the novelist Ts'ao Hsüehch'in, Yüan Mei's contemporary, wrote about it in his novel *Hunglou meng* (*Dream of the Red Chamber*). By 1755 Yüan had abandoned all thoughts of an official career and moved his large family to his garden. He commanded high fees for such things as funerary inscriptions and thus lived in comfort and style. After the age of 60 he made journeys to various provinces and scenic spots in China and came to be known as a leading poet of his time.

Yüan Mei was a hedonist and something of a romantic, and with all his wide-ranging learning and curiosity, he celebrated in his poetry and prose primarily the joy of being alive and being receptive to all the sensuous pleasures. Arthur Waley, his biographer in the Western world, has aptly described him as "a writer of poetry that even at its lightest always had an undertone of deep feeling and at its saddest may at any moment light a sudden spark of fun." Yüan was above all an individualist and the reverse of a Confucian didacticist, believing that it is the poet's business to express his nature and feelings and these could be shared by all.

For a student of Chinese literature, Yüan Mei's poetic criticism is perhaps even more important than his poetry because it represents a full-bodied affirmation of what one could call the individualist view of poetry as self-expression. "Poetry Talks" (*shih-hua*) had been written by Chinese poets since the Sung dynasty; most of these are short collections of random observations and anecdotes. Yüan Mei's jottings, entitled *Sui-yüan shih-hua,* are bulkier than most and also far more unified in expressing a consistent point of view.

Among Yüan Mei's voluminous writings are a book of ghost stories and a cookbook entitled *Sui-yüan shih-tan*

(*Sui-yüan's Menu*). The latter interest indicates a Chinese hedonist's unashamed delight in good food. Similarly, Yüan Mei was fond of female company, and in his old age he was surrounded by female disciples. Though he courted notoriety in his time by his sponsorship of female poetic talent, he was a humane person who believed that women as well as men should develop their sensibility and intellect to the full for the enrichment of society and culture.

Further Reading

The standard biography in English is Arthur Waley, *Yüan Mei: Eighteenth Century Chinese Poet* (1956), which contains many examples of Yüan's poetry and prose in translation. James J. Y. Liu, *The Art of Chinese Poetry* (1962), gives a good exposition of Yüan Mei's poetic theories. □

Yüan Shih-k'ai

Yüan Shih-k'ai (1859-1916), an outstanding Chinese military leader, held the balance of power when the Revolution of 1911 broke out and used it to secure the presidency. He became increasingly dictatorial but failed to establish himself as emperor of a new dynasty.

Yüan Shih-k'ai came from a family of Honan officials who had gained prominence in fighting the Nien rebels during the 1850s and 1860s. Though educated in the classics, he preferred the strenuous life. Having failed twice to obtain the *chü-jen* degree (the second level of the traditional examination system), he purchased a title and used family connections to acquire a post with a maritime defense unit in Shantung Province.

Sino-Japanese War

Yüan's opportunity to prove his abilities came as a result of the Sino-Japanese rivalry in Korea. In 1882, when an uprising provided Japan with an opportunity to consolidate its position, Yüan played a leading role in the successful Chinese intervention. During the turbulent years leading up to the Sino-Japanese War of 1894-1895, he remained on duty in Korea.

Yüan's energy and resourcefulness won the attention of Li Hung-chang, and in 1885 Yüan was named commissioner of commerce and Chinese Resident in Korea. In this capacity, he developed a reputation as a skillful diplomat, a master of political intrigue, and a masterful military organizer. As a response to the xenophobic Tunghak uprising, he urged the launching of the Chinese military expedition that helped to precipitate the Sino-Japanese War. Returning to China just before the outbreak of hostilities, he won further recognition from high Manchu officials for his skillful organization of Chinese logistical operations.

China's defeat underscored the necessity of military reform. As commander of the Newly Created Army (a linear descendant of Li Hung-chang's Anhwei Army), Yüan, aided by German officers, introduced Western principles of training and organization. The army was financed by the central government but developed a personal loyalty to its commander. Yüan deftly overcame criticism of hostile officials and temporarily succeeded in keeping powerful friends at court while also developing a favorable reputation among reformers. However, during the Hundred Days Reform of 1898, Yüan had to choose between these increasingly polarized elements. Asked to support a palace coup against the empress dowager, he refused and, according to most accounts, betrayed the conspirators to the conservative leader, Jung Lu.

Military Strong Man

In December 1899 Yüan was appointed governor of Shantung and charged with handling the Boxer Rebellion. Yüan resisted pressure from the court, where a controlling faction was sympathetic to these antiforeign zealots. Refusing to commit his troops to battle, he used the emergency to augment his forces. He thereby emerged as the strongest military leader in North China and, equally important, a man in the good graces of the foreign powers. In November 1901 he succeeded the late Li Hung-chang as governor general of the metropolitan province of Chihli and as high commissioner of military and foreign affairs in North China.

In accordance with the court's newly found enthusiasm for reform, Yüan carried out policies of educational, economic, and military modernization. Now assured of ample political and financial support, he extended the network of personal relationships that provided the foundations of the

Peiyang military clique. Yüan's increasing power caused acute apprehension among his enemies, and by August 1907 hostile forces in the court had deprived him of his high positions and transferred from his command four of his six army divisions. The death of the empress dowager in November 1908 removed his strongest supporter, and on Jan. 2, 1909, he was forced into retirement.

Rise to the Presidency

The Wuchang uprising of Oct. 10, 1911, gave Yüan opportunity for revenge. Imperiled by the wildfire spread of revolt through South China, the desperate court begged him to save the dynasty. Instead he used his leverage to act as power broker between the court and the revolutionists. In Peking, the infant emperor was forced to abdicate in favor of a republic, and in Nanking, Sun Yat-sen was persuaded to resign the provisional presidency in favor of Yüan Shih-k'ai.

Following his inauguration on March 12, 1912, Yüan interpreted the provisional constitution to enhance his personal power and to thwart the desire of those who favored a Western-style republic. By June 1912 even his premier and protégé, T'ang Shao-yi, had resigned in protest; the Cabinet became a pliant tool of President Yüan. For a time Yüan managed to work with Sun Yat-sen and Huang Hsing, leaders of the revolutionary T'ung-meng hui, but Sung Chiao-jen, who reorganized this body into the Kuomintang, steadfastly opposed his autocratic rule.

On March 20, 1913, Sung was assassinated shortly after he had led his party to victory in the National Assembly elections. Strengthened by a £125 million loan from a foreign consortium, Yüan went on to ban the Kuomintang and seize the provinces under its control. Resistance to this move, the so-called "second revolution," was brief and ineffectual. On Oct. 10, 1913, Yüan was installed as full-fledged president of the republic. Exactly three months later, he dissolved the National Assembly and replaced it with a "political council," which drafted a "constitutional compact" granting dictatorial powers to the president. Yüan was made president for life.

Yüan's domestic triumphs soon were overshadowed by threats from abroad. The outbreak of World War I in 1914 preoccupied the European powers and left Japan a free hand in China. Japan lost no time in seizing the German concessions in Shantung and in presenting Yüan with the Twenty-one Demands, which would turn China into a protectorate. Yüan stalled as long as he dared but finally capitulated to all but the most severe of the demands.

With the encouragement of high-ranking advisers, including Professor Frank Goodnow of Columbia University and a number of Japanese, Yüan now moved decisively toward the throne. On Jan. 1, 1916, Yüan Shin-k'ai became the Hung-hsien emperor. However, the carefully planned revival of Confucian institutions and the generation of favorable "public opinion" provided weak bulwarks against the massive protest that accompanied this move. Even Yüan's staunchest supporters found it difficult to accept his imperial pretensions. Following a series of revolts in southwestern China, Yüan set aside the throne. His reign had lasted 83 days.

The reestablishment of the republic failed to restore Yüan's power. His lieutenants, who had become independent regional satraps, refused to rally behind their discredited leader. When Yüan succumbed to uremia on June 6, 1916, many said he had "died of a broken heart." In a sense, this may indeed have been true.

Further Reading

The principal Western-language work on Yüan is Jerome Ch'en, *Yüan Shih-k'ai, 1859-1916* (1961). Another major source is Ralph L. Powell, *The Rise of Chinese Military Power, 1895-1912* (1955). Useful background material is in Li Chien-nung, *The Political History of China, 1840-1928* (1956), and O. Edmund Clubb, *20th Century China* (1964). □

Hideki Yukawa

The Japanese physicist Hideki Yukawa (1907-1981) was one of the world's most highly-respected theoretical physicists. His most visible contributions to science were in the field of particle physics.

Hideki Yukawa was born in Tokyo on Jan. 23, 1907. His father was a professor of geology at Kyoto University, and Yukawa grew up in an academically-oriented household which focused his attention on science from his early years. He entered Kyoto University in 1926, and, showing his intelligence early, graduated only three years later with a master's degree. Setting out on the long journey to academic achievement, Yukawa spent the next ten years continuing his education and teaching. First came three years of research, which was followed by a 1934 appointment as a physics lecturer at Kyoto University. Next, there was a move to a lecturer's post at Osaka University, where Yukawa completed his doctorate in physics in 1938.

Scientific Achievements

By this time, Yukawa was already immersed in the study of sub-atomic particles that be his focus for the rest of his life. His first paper, "On the Interaction of Elementary Particles," met with a lukewarm reception when he presented it in Osaka at the 1934 meeting of the Physico-Mathematical Society. Nevertheless, he chose to publish it the following year, in the Society's *Proceedings,* Yukawa's paper postulated that, as an analogy to the way in which a particle of light may be exchanged between two charged particles in the "electromagnetic interaction," a new particle (later termed the meson) might be exchanged between two nucleons in the "nuclear interaction." The meson was envisioned by Yukawa to be a particle providing the "glue" for holding together the various other particles making up the nucleus of the atom.

The theory caused great interest in scientific circles, especially after such a particle was discovered in cosmic radiation by Carl Anderson, a 1936 Nobel laureate from the California Institute of Technology. Used together by researchers, the work of Yukawa and Anderson provided a

noteworthy overture to the 1939 discovery of nuclear fission. Now an eminent scientist, Yukawa took his place in 1939 as Professor of Physics at Kyoto University. He taught there during World War II, which ended abruptly for Japan in 1945 with the shattering atomic destruction of Hiroshima and Nagasaki.

The Scientist's Real Responsibility

In 1948 he was invited to spend a year at Princeton University's Institute for Advanced Study. It was here that Yukawa met Albert Einstein, with whom he remained friendly for the rest of the older scientist's life. Quoted in Yukawa's own obituary in *The Bulletin of the Atomic Scientists* was an excerpt from his graceful epitaph for Einstein: "I feel very strongly that we have to take up his search and striving for world peace," a mission which Yukawa himself took extremely seriously.

His feeling that at least some of the responsibility for preventing war must rest with the scientists who produce its technology was strongly expressed once again in 1962, at the Kyoto Conference of Scientists. "The results of physics are inevitably connected with the problems of humanity through their application to human society," he warned. In 1975, at the 25th Pugwash International Symposium held in Kyoto, he took this theme even further. "Usually it has been thought that, particularly in pure science, it is desirable for its progress not to include any value criterion other than true-or-false. We physicists, by experience, have realized that the advent of nuclear weapons dealt a great blow to the above-mentioned way of thinking," he noted.

Yukawa's strong feelings on science's duty to humanity had begun to crystallize by 1949, when he won the Nobel Prize. He chose to donate most of his award money to several institutions in Japan, including the Research Institute for Fundamental Physics at Kyoto University, to which he returned in 1953 after three years at Columbia University. It was time, he said, to return to Japan to train "new faces." He remained there until 1970, when he retired.

Yukawa died at his home in Kyoto in 1981.

Further Reading

Yukawa discussed his contributions to meson theory in his Nobel lecture, reprinted in *Nobel Lectures in Physics,* vol. 3 (1964). Niels H. deV. Heathcote, *Nobel Prize Winners, 1901-1950* (1953), contains important biographical material. For additional insights into his work see Rudolf Ernst Peierl's, *The Laws of Nature* (1956); Richard M. Harbeck and Lloyd K. Johnson's, *Physical Science* (1965); and Samuel A. Morantz's, *Physics* (1969).

Additional Sources

Bulletin of the Atomic Scientists, October 1982.
New York Times, September 10, 1981. □

Yung-lo

Yung-lo (1360-1424) was the third emperor of the Ming dynasty of China, and in his reign the dynasty reached the height of its power owing to his military prowess and civil reforms.

A favorite son of Hung-wu, Chu Ti, whose reign title was Yung-lo, was made the prince of Yen in 1370, at the age of 10, and received the fief of Peking in 1380. Growing up to be a brave and intelligent campaigner, he was given command of expeditions against the Mongols. Ambitious and self-willed, he was rather disappointed that when Hung-wu's eldest son, Chu Piao, died in 1392, the Emperor named his grandson Chu Yu-wen as the heir designate. Chu Ti began to plot to usurp the throne.

Chu Ti allied himself with the imperial officials in the North and the court eunuchs and began his rebellion shortly after the ascension of his nephew in June 1398. After some hard fighting during which sections of the North were devastated, Chu Ti captured Nanking, the capital, in July 1403 and declared himself emperor in August. The deposed emperor is said to have burnt himself alive, but report also had it that he fled the capital in disguise.

During his 20 years of rule, Yung-lo brought the Ming dynasty to the zenith of its power. He initiated several institutional innovations designed to strengthen his authority. The major change was the transfer of the imperial seat to Peking, which formally became the capital in 1421. The government agencies in Nanking were not abolished but were made subordinate to those in Peking. He also inaugurated the rule of allowing Hanlin scholars to participate in the deliberation of state affairs, but he had them counterchecked by the eunuchs, who began to rise in political importance.

Several construction works were undertaken during Yung-lo's rule, the most important ones being the dredging of the Grand Canal (1411) and the rebuilding of Peking (1417-1420). The compilation of the *Yung-lo tatien* (1403-1408) under imperial order marked a monumental literary undertaking. Its 22,937 chapters in 11,915 volumes contained excerpts and entire works pertaining to all subjects; about 800 chapters have survived.

In foreign affairs, Yung-lo pursued a vigorous policy. He renewed offensive operations against the Mongol tribes, who had retreated from China, and took personal command of five expeditions. Annam was made a Chinese province in 1407. Japan under Ashikaga Yoshimitsu paid tribute. Several embassies were sent to central Asia with satisfactory results. For a while China regained control of the caravan route into Sinkiang, and Sultan Shahrukh Bahadur, Tamerlane's fourth son, who ruled at Herat in central Asia, sent an embassy to the Ming court.

Beginning in 1405, Yung-lo commanded the eunuch Cheng Ho to head several expeditions to the South Seas, visiting as far off as Aden and the Somali coast of Africa. Under Yung-lo, China reasserted its claim to universal sovereignty over the neighboring states and reestablished the traditional tributary system. The Emperor died at Yü-much'uan, in southern Jehol, returning from an expedition against a Mongol tribe, on Aug. 2, 1424, and was succeeded by his son Chu Kao-chih (Emperor Hunghsi, 1424-1425).

Further Reading

There is no book-length biography of Yung-lo in a Western language. A translation of his biography in the Chinese official history of the Ming dynasty, *Ming-shih,* is included in Lewis C. Arlington and William Lewisohn, *In Search of Old Peking* (1935), which also contains useful information on Yung-lo's rule. Recommended for general historical background are K. S. Latourette, *The Chinese: Their History and Culture* (1934; 4th ed. rev. 1964); L. Carrington Goodrich, *A Short History of the Chinese People* (1943; rev. ed. 1959); and Edwin O. Reischauer and John K. Fairbank, *A History of East Asian Civilization,* vol. 1: *East Asia: The Great Tradition* (1958). □

Yun Sondo

Yun Sondo (1587-1671) was a major Korean sijo poet who captured the Korean spirit in native terms.

Yun Sondo, whose literary names were Kosan (Lonely Mountain) and Haeong (Old Man of the Sea), was born in July 1587 in Seoul to Yun Yusim, an official of the third rank. He was adopted and educated by his uncle Yun Yugi, a childless official of the first rank. In 1612 Yun Sondo passed the licentiate degree, but he chose not to enter public service. In 1616 he memorialized the throne concerning official corruption under Minister Yi Ich'om and earned a reputation for honesty and courage. Subsequently he was forced into exile until Yi's death.

In 1618, during his exile, Yun wrote *Songs upon Gloom (Kyonhoe-yo)* at Kyoongwon. These poems, his earliest, are in the *sijo* form, which reached its maturity in his hands. The form, which evolved in the 14th century, consists of a three-line stanza with 14 or 15 syllables per line. Generally, each line has a major caesura in sense and rhythm. *Sijo* permits great flexibility in structure and subject.

In 1628 Yun placed first in a higher government examination and took office as tutor to the heir apparent (who later became King Hyojong). Yun held various offices until he again fell victim to court intrigue in 1635, was demoted, and sent to Haenam. In 1638 he was offered office but declined, again exposing himself to attack. He was sent into exile but was freed shortly thereafter. In 1642 he went to Kumsoe Valley and wrote a series of poems titled *New Songs among the Mountains.*

Yun's former pupil ascended the throne as King Hyojong in 1649; however, Yun, a member of the weak Southerners faction, was prevented from being recalled. In 1651 he wrote his most famous poems, *The Fisherman's Songs of the Four Seasons,* a cycle of 40 *sijo.* They were reflections on a scholar's life in retirement. He was finally recalled by the King and given high office, but the powerful Westerners faction prevented Yun from assuming and active role in government. He fell ill and retired. Later that year he was elevated to third minister of rites and returned only to see his appointment canceled. He was eventually exiled again in another factional dispute and one of his memorials burned. He remained in exile until shortly before his death in 1671. He spent a total of 14 years in official exile.

Yun's poetry was diverse in method and mood, unique and varied in rhythm. He gave a new beauty and dignity to the Korean language and contributed greatly to the popularization of the vernacular.

Further Reading

For general background and information on Yun see Peter H. Lee, *Korean Literature: Topics and Themes* (1965). □

Z

Ossip Joselyn Zadkine

Ossip Joselyn Zadkine (1890-1967), a Russian sculptor and teacher, was one of the most adventurous and inventive cubist sculptors.

Ossip Zadkine was born in Smolensk, where his father was a professor of ancient languages. When he was 16, Zadkine went to London to study art. Three years later he went to Paris to study at the École des Beaux-Arts, but, disenchanted with its rigidly academic approach, he left and opened his own studio. He served in the French army during World War I.

Zadkine's first one-man show took place in Brussels in 1919. The following year he married, and in 1921 he became a French citizen. By 1924 he had acquired an international reputation. In 1932 he received an important commission to carve relief panels for public buildings in Poissy, Paris, and Brussels.

Zadkine lived in New York City from 1941 to 1945, teaching at the Art Students' League. He participated in the influential 1942 Artists in Exile exhibition. On his return to Paris he established a studio and took students. In 1947 Zadkine received one of his most important commissions: the city of Rotterdam ordered a monument to commemorate its near destruction by the Germans during World War II. His memorial, *For a Devastated City,* completed and installed in 1953, depicts an agonized, mutilated giant whose abstracted limbs bend and quake, suggesting the extremes of inner torment and physical pain. In 1950 he received the Grand Prize at the Venice Biennale.

In 1962 Zadkine gave a series of lectures at the École des Beaux-Arts. Just a week before his death in Paris, a large retrospective exhibition of his sculpture opened at the Bibliothèque Nationale.

The early sculpture of Zadkine reveals his great admiration for the expressive power of primitive art; he adapted its boldness, formality, and stark simplicity to his own work. In his cubist sculptures, he translated the abstract character of cubist painting into shifting flat planes, angularity, and contrasts of convex and concave areas, as in *Mother and Child* (ca. 1920). Much of his art after 1930 contains neoclassic elements. Many pieces recall the art of Giorgio de Chirico, but Zadkine's figures are usually more frenetic. He favored nervous contours and surprising syncopations. He was given to hollowing out limbs of figures and to inscribing features by drawing them on a flat or gently curved surface rather than modeling them in the round.

Zadkine's work is novel, distinctive, and full of derring-do, but its fundamental eclectic character deprives it of force. His late work employs the formal language of the earlier sculpture, but it is more complex, elaborate, and virtuosic.

Further Reading

Ionel Jianou, *Zadkine* (1964), which contains a good selection of fine plates, is scholarly and yet readable. Abraham M. Hammacher, *Zadkine* (1959), is also recommended. Zadkine is discussed in two excellent histories of modern sculpture: Michel Seuphor, *Sculpture of This Century* (1960), and Abraham M. Hammacher, *The Evolution of Modern Sculpture* (1969). □

Saad Zaghlul Pasha

Saad Zaghlul Pasha (1859-1927), Egyptian political leader, founded the country's most important political party, the Wafd.

S aad Zaghlul was born in Ibyana, a village in the province of Gharbiyyah in the Egyptian Delta, of pure Egyptian parents of modest means. At Azhar University he specialized in Islamic law, philosophy, and theology and came under the strong influence of the Islamic reformers Jamal al-Din al-Afghani and Muhammad Abduh. Zaghlul's subsequent career reflected the imprint of these reformers, and he championed the internal reform of Egyptian social, educational, and political institutions till the end of his eventful life.

Zaghlul's first appointment was as assistant editor of the Arabic section of the Egyptian *Official Journal,* which was edited by Muhammad Abduh. His insight and commitment to educational reforms soon began to be reflected in the various essays either written or inspired by Zaghlul that were highly critical of the low state of Egyptian education and institutions. With the outbreak of the first Egyptian revolution (1879-1882), commonly referred to as the Arabi Rebellion, the Egyptian political scene became complex, and most reformers of the time were implicated in that rebellion.

Rise in the Bureaucracy

Zaghlul experienced his first detention. Upon his release, he practiced law and distinguished himself; amassed some independent means, which enabled him to participate in Egyptian politics, then dominated by the struggle-moderate and extreme—against British occupation; and effected useful and permanent links with different factions of Egyptian nationalists. He became close to Princess Nazli, and his contacts with the Egyptian upper class led to his marriage to the daughter of the Egyptian prime minister Mustafa Pasha Fahmi, whose friendship with Lord Cromer, then the effective ruler of Egypt, accounts in part for the eventual acceptability of Zaghlul to the British occupation. In succession Zaghlul was appointed judge, minister of education (1906-1908), minister of justice (1910-1912); in 1913 he became vice president of the Legislative Assembly.

In all his ministerial positions Zaghlul undertook certain measures of reform that were acceptable to both Egyptian nationalists and the British occupation. Throughout this period, he kept himself outside extreme Egyptian nationalist factions, and though he was acceptable to the British occupation, he was not thereby compromised in the eyes of his Egyptian compatriots. The relationship between Britain and Egypt continued to deteriorate during and after World War I.

Leader of a Revolution

Egyptian insistence on, and British refusal to grant, independence ultimately led to the outbreak of the second Egyptian revolution, in 1919. Leading the revolution was Zaghlul, who as the head of the Egyptian delegation (Wafd) presented the demands for Egyptian independence to the British high commissioner. Zaghlul was arrested and in March deported to Malta. Upon his release in April, he went first to Paris to try to present to the Peace Conference the Egyptian demand for independence; was refused a hearing; in June 1920 traveled to London to negotiate with the Colonial Office; and returned empty-handed to Egypt in March 1921.

Zaghlul continued his disruptive activities, and the British once more imprisoned him and deported him later in 1921, first to Aden, then to the Seychelles, and finally to Gibraltar. He was finally released in March 1923 and was permitted to return to Egypt. The Egyptian delegation which he had initially led was transformed into the Wafd party, the largest and most effective political party ever formed in Egypt. He was called upon to form the first Cabinet of the independent kingdom of Egypt (January-November 1924).

For the next three years Zaghlul was the effective national leader of Egypt without, however, occupying any official position. He tried, unsuccessfully, to check the autocratic tendencies of King Fuad I and to increase the effectiveness of the Cabinet and the Parliament. Zaghlul died on Aug. 23, 1927. He is remembered by all Egyptian elements for his educational, judicial, and social reforms; for his skilled political and leadership qualities; and ultimately as the father of Egyptian independence. His house became known as the "House of the Nation," where future leaders of Egypt received their first lessons in Egyptian politics.

Further Reading

Information on Zaghlul Pasha is in Lord Cromer, *Modern Egypt* (2 vols., 1908); Jamal M. Ahmed, *The Intellectual Origins of Egyptian Nationalism* (1960); Albert H. Hourani, *Arabic Thought in the Liberal Age, 1798-1939* (1962); and Afaf Lutfi al-Sayyid, *Egypt and Cromer: A Study in Anglo-Egyptian Relations* (1968). □

Peterson Zah

Peterson Zah (born 1937) has devoted his life to the service of the Navajo people. He has been active in the field of education, in legal matters, in attempts to reconcile disputes with the Hopi, and in efforts to resolve the issues of depletion of natural resources on the reservation. In 1990, he was elected as the first president of the Navajo Nation. He also received the Humanitarian Award from the City of Albuquerque and an honorary doctorate from Santa Fe College.

Zah was born December 2, 1937, in Low Mountain, Arizona, the disputed joint-use area. Henry and Mae (Multine) Zah raised their son to respect his heritage. Considering his mother his best teacher, Zah often quotes her sayings in his addresses. She speaks no English and is one of the 125,000 who are still fluent in the Navajo language which he, as educator, is attempting to restore on the reservation. A striking illustration of the binding force of the old language came from his assertion that his mother had always told him to use his culture "as a canoe with which to stay afloat." The metaphor, so inappropriate in a desert setting, is over six centuries old and refers to the Athapaskan ancestors who migrated from the North to New Mexico perhaps 1,000 years ago. Zah attended Phoenix Indian School until 1960, then went to Arizona State University on a basketball scholarship; he graduated with a bachelor's degree in education in 1963.

From 1963 to 1964, he worked for the Arizona Vocational Education Department in Phoenix as a journeyman carpenter instructing adults in employable skills. He then participated in the domestic peace corps known as Volunteers in Service to America (VISTA). Zah served as field coordinator of the training center at Arizona State University at Tempe from 1965 to 1967. This assignment enabled him to utilize his considerable gifts of cultural mediation, since his job was to teach cultural sensitivity to those volunteers who would work on Indian reservations. From 1967 to 1981, Zah was executive director of the people's legal services at Window Rock. This nonprofit organization, chartered by the state of Arizona, was called DNA—Dinebeuna Nahiilna Be Agaditiahe or "Lawyers Who Contribute to the Economic Revitalization of the People." During his decade directing DNA, Zah was in charge of more than 100 employees at nine reservation offices, and 33 tribal court advocates, as well as 34 attorneys. He suc-

ceeded in having several cases reach the U.S. Supreme Court, which established Indian sovereignty, and in winning some landmark cases. This grassroots legal aid system offered hope to impoverished Native Americans who would have otherwise had no recourse to the law courts.

Teaches Navajo Language and Culture

Misguided educational policies have hindered the Navajo for decades. Ever since the conquest, in 1868, reservation agents have tried to send children away to Bureau of Indian Affairs (BIA) boarding schools to speed their assimilation. Competing institutions were the mission schools run by various religious denominations, or public schools in towns neighboring the reservations. By 1946, only one in four Navajo children was enrolled in any of these schools. The Window Rock Public School District compiled the evidence that led to significant changes, more relevant curriculum and parental involvement led to increased enrollment.

Zah was elected in 1972 to the first all-Navajo school board at Window Rock, and assumed its presidency in 1973. In this capacity, he hired more Navajo teachers, installed a Navajo curriculum, developed Navajo textbooks, renewed religious ceremonies, and restored knowledge of tribal history. Zah believed that to preserve the language, it must be taught in all classes, including science and math, before the introduction of English, because it conveys concepts that cannot be translated. The ecological wisdom of the elders who sought to preserve the harmony of the natural world is retained in the earth-derived vocabulary; to live as a good Navajo, for example, one must "speak the language of the earth."

Under the guidelines of Public Law 93-638, school boards made up of local community people set up contract schools; under the control of the Navajo Tribal Council, these institutions flourished. Materials were created in a Navajo spelling system devised by Oliver LaFarge and John Peabody Harrington. Medicine men were invited into classrooms to lecture. Students set up a local television station, and published a Navajo newspaper. One of the Rock Point graduates, Rex Lee Jim, went on to Princeton, and then returned to the reservation to compose a libretto for the first Navajo opera and to try to found a school for the performing arts on the reservation. By the 1990s, there were twice as many applicants for college-level professional training as could be accommodated by the tribal scholarship funds.

Zah also began fundraising in 1987 for a group soliciting scholarships for worthy Navajo students from the private sector. The Navajo Education and Scholarship Foundation enabled many impoverished young people to attend school. In 1989, Zah founded the Native American Consulting Services to obtain congressional assistance for constructing new schools on the reservation. From 1989 to 1990, he was director of the western regional office of the Save the Children Federation.

Becomes Tribal Chair

From 1983 to 1987, Zah served as chairman of the Navajo Tribal Council at Window Rock. This site was selected as a capital by John Collier who began its construction under federal work programs in the 1930s. The council meets in an eight-sided stone building modeled after a traditional hogan. There, the elected delegates govern the largest reservation in the United States—about 24,000 square miles or close to 16 million acres in Arizona, New Mexico, and southeastern Utah. These desiccated and badly-eroded lands house over 200,000 Navajo whose population is increasing at the rate of more than two percent per year. Zah invested his energies in reforming education as one way of coping with the intractable troubles of poverty.

Elected President of the Navajo Nation

From 1990 to 1994, Zah was the first elected president in the history of the Navajo Nation. His childhood friend and classmate, Ivan Sidney, became the tribal leader of the Hopi, with whom Zah tried to work out the difficulties of government-imposed relocation. A film, *Broken Rainbow*, was made about this Hopi-Navajo land dispute. Underneath this disputed land is coal; and each year, the Peabody Coal Company extracts seven million tons from this area, ruining the landscape and sullying the air. The two longtime friends worked to resolve hostilities generated by their predecessors, Peter MacDonald and Abbot Sekaquptewa, by ordering a suspension of all lawsuits over land in April of 1983, and by pledging cooperation in all areas of mutual concern including negotiations of future contracts with mining companies.

Zah's administration has been grievously tested. Just as plans had been drawn up and sites approved for the construction of six sorely needed hospital facilities, the government announced a 30 percent cut in health services. While Zah was in Washington, D.C., attempting to reverse this measure, an outbreak of hanta virus afflicted his people. Epidemiologists from the Centers for Disease Control worked frantically to find the causes of the mysterious deaths occurring on the reservation. Also, an extraordinary number of miners who had worked for Kerr-McGee extracting uranium have died of anaplastic cancer of the lungs. The Atomic Energy Commission, who bought the uranium ore, refused to clean up the radioactive tailings which are blown by the winds over the reservation, and seep into the drinking water. Drilling for petroleum and gas by Mobil, Standard Oil, and Exxon has poisoned the ground, desecrated sacred sites, and polluted the air. The stripmining of coal subjects the Navajo to a perpetual fallout of toxic fumes from the power plants. According to Stephen Trimble, Zah has tried to warn his people to think of the future when these nonrenewable energy sources have been depleted: "Someday the coal, oil, and gas are going to be gone. What's going to happen to the Navajo children then? Pete Zah won't be around then . . . you have to think about the future."

Zah lives at the capital, Window Rock, with his wife, Rosalind (Begay), and his children, Elaine, Eileen, and Keeyonnie.

Further Reading

Mattheissen, Peter, "Four Corners," in *Indian Country*, New York, Penguin, 1984.
"Navajo Education," in *Handbook of North American Indians; Southwest,* Volume 10, edited by Alfonso Ortiz, Washington, D.C., Smithsonian Institution, 1983.
Tome, Marshall, "The Navajo Nation Today," in *Handbook of North American Indians, Southwest,* Volume 10, edited by Alfonso Ortiz, Washington, D.C., Smithsonian Institution, 1983.
Trimble, Stephen, "The Navajo," in *The People,* Santa Fe, New Mexico, School of American Research Press, 1993; 121-194.
"Proceedings of the First National Conference on Cancer in Native Americans," *American Indian Culture and Research Journal,* 16:3, 1992.
Trebay, Guy, "Bad Medicine: Illness as Metaphor in Navajoland," *Village Voice,* August 3, 1993; 39-43. □

Mildred Didrikson Zaharias

Called "the athlete phenomenon of our time, man or woman," Mildred "Babe" Didrikson Zaharias (1913-1956) participated in almost every sport. She excelled as an Olympic athlete and as a golfer.

Mildred Didrikson, known throughout her life as Babe, was born June 26, 1913, at Port Authur, Texas. She always credited her father for her interest in sports. Babe first came to national attention when the Dallas-based basketball team for which she played forward won the national AAU (Amateur Athletic Union) championship. Her outstanding play earned her an All-American award in 1929. In 1932 she entered the tryouts for the Olympic games at the national AAU's women's track and field championship. Of the eight events that she entered, she won five—shot put, baseball throw, long jump, javelin, and 80-meter hurdles. In a single afternoon she set four world records, scoring an incredible 30 points. The second place finisher, with only 22 points, was an entire women's athletic club.

Later that year she competed in the Olympic games held at Los Angeles. She won gold medals in two events—hurdles and javelin—and set world records in both. For her performance the Associated Press (AP) named Babe the Woman Athlete of the Year. She would win that award five more times. Later, in 1950, she was named AP's Woman Athlete of the First Half of the Twentieth Century.

Meanwhile, Babe took up other sports—football, boxing, baseball. She played for the touring baseball team of the House of David and pitched an inning for the then Brooklyn Dodgers and in an exhibition game for the St. Louis Cardinals. She even managed to strike out the equally famous Joe DiMaggio. It was for such all-around skills that sports writer Grantland Rice called her "the athlete phenomenon of our time."

After the 1932 Olympics Babe turned to golf and in 1934 won her first tournament. Due to a technicality, she

was declared ineligible to compete as an amateur and as a result played as a professional until she was reinstated as an amateur in 1944. In 1938 Babe married former professional wrestler George Zaharias, who became her biggest supporter. She won 17 straight amateur tournaments, and in 1947 she became the first American to win the prestigious British Women's Amateur Championship.

She then gave up her amateur standing and, with Patty Berg, founded the Ladies Professional Golf Association. She won the Women's Open in 1948 and 1950 and the Tampa Open in 1951. In 1953 she contracted cancer, but after an operation she returned to win the Women's Open in 1954 and received yet another AP Woman Athlete of the Year Award. The cancer, however, proved to be terminal, and Babe died on September 27, 1956. She was 43.

Further Reading

To relive the excitement that Babe Didrickson Zaharias created, a reading of contemporary newspaper accounts, particularly those of Grantland Rice, are a must. The definitive biography is William O. Johnson's *Whatta-gal: The Babe Didrikson Story* (1977). Younger readers might enjoy Gene Schoor's *Babe Didrikson, the World's Greatest Athlete* (1978). ☐

Israel Zangwill

The Jewish author and philosopher Israel Zangwill (1864-1926) was an influential leader of English Jewry and a Zionist activist.

I srael Zangwill was born in London. His family, Russian Jews, lived in London's east side in the Jewish quarter of White-chapel. After receiving both an English and a Jewish education, he studied philosophy, history, and the sciences at the University of London. At the same time he taught at the Free Jewish School of London. Having left teaching for a career in journalism, he generated much popular interest as a writer and a literary editor. Even in his first articles he showed a keen sensitivity to tragic and comic themes alike and succeeded in combining powers of realistic description with a fertile imagination.

Zangwill's *Children of the Ghetto* was published in 1892. The work had considerable impact in the non-Jewish world, giving the English reader a jarring glimpse of the poverty-stricken life of London's Jewish quarter. His success encouraged him both to continue his literary work and to deal with the themes of ghetto life. Thus he published *Ghetto Tragedies* in 1894 and *Dreams of the Ghetto* in 1898. His stories and novels are not merely peopled with Jewish characters but are permeated by a sense of the Jewish life-style and its values. It is in this pervading quality that the uniqueness of Zangwill's contribution to English literature lies.

Zangwill's productivity ranged over many literary genres. He wrote a number of unsuccessful plays. In 1908 he published a volume of poetry, *Blind Children*, followed by another, *Italian Phantasies*, in 1910. He translated into

English a selection of religious poetry by the Jewish medieval poet Solomon in Cabirol, which he published in *Selected Religious Poems* (1903).

In the early 1890s Zangwill had joined the Lovers of Zion movement in England. In 1897 he participated in the "pilgrimage" of English Jews to Palestine. That year he also joined Theodor Herzl in founding the World Zionist Organization and later took part in the first seven Zionist congresses. Zangwill was renowned as an orator, and his impassioned speeches made deep impressions upon the delegates to the Zionist congress. He advocated the plan for Jewish settlement in Uganda, and after this plan was rejected by the Seventh Zionist Congress (1905), he with Max Mandelstamm, founded the Jewish Territorial Organization. This organization investigated sites for the establishment of a Jewish nation in Canada, Argentina, Australia, and Africa.

When the prospects of Jewish settlement in Palestine became more clearly defined at the end of World War I, Zangwill returned to the Zionist effort and took active part in soliciting the Balfour Declaration, proclaiming the right of a Jewish national homeland in Palestine.

Further Reading

The most complete study of Zangwill in English is Maurice Wohlgelernter, *Israel Zangwill: A Study* (1964). Other biographies are Harry Schneiderman's short and laudatory *Israel Zangwill* (1928) and Joseph Leftwich's largely anecdotal *Israel Zangwill* (1957).

Additional Sources

Udelson, Joseph H., *Dreamer of the ghetto: the life and works of Israel Zangwill,* Tuscaloosa: University of Alabama Press, 1990. ☐

Emiliano Zapata

Emiliano Zapata (ca. 1879-1919), Mexican agrarian leader and guerrilla fighter, was the symbol of the agrarian revolution.

Emiliano Zapata was born in Anenecuilco, Morelos, to a landless, but not poor, family which dealt in livestock. Orphaned at 16, he sharecropped and traded horses in his birth-place. During the closing years of the Porfirio Diaz dictatorship Zapata took part in local opposition politics, with a 6-month interruption while he served as a soldier.

In September 1909 Zapata was elected president of the group in Anenecuilco designated to reclaim the community's ejidal lands. He backed the unsuccessful opposition gubernatorial candidacy of Patricio Leyva. In March 1911, after several months of contact with the *maderistas,* Zapata joined the rebellion against Diaz. The major effort of the *zapatistas* was an attack on Cuautla.

With the fall of the Diaz regime Zapata initiated his recurring demands—land for the peasants, removal of federal troops from Morelos, and designation of an acceptable commander of state forces. The efforts of the interim De la Barra regime, endorsed by Francisco Madero, to discharge the revolutionary forces irritated Zapata, who became incensed when during the Madero's pacification efforts Francisco de la Barra ordered Victoriano Huerta to march into Morelos in August 1911.

Zapata's view of revolutionary goals was quite parochial, and he was unwilling to await patiently the results of Madero's dreamed-of democratic processes to effect land reform. Nineteen days after Madero assumed the presidency, Zapata revolted under the Plan of Ayala. Waging guerrilla warfare, as he had before and would again, Zapata began distribution of ejidal lands in Puebla in April 1912 and followed with other distributions in Morelos and Tlaxcala. Agricultural students were employed in the formation of agrarian commissions. Program and strategy for the moustached and almost illiterate Zapata were formulated by a group of intellectuals, including Antonio Diaz Soto y Gama and schoolteacher Otilio Montaño.

After Madero's death, Zapata joined with Pancho Villa and Venustiano Carranza in an uneasy alliance to defeat Huerta. However, it was the *carrancistas* who occupied Mexico City, and the First Chief (Carranza) sought to control the situation through the Convention of Generals. *Villista* and *zapatista* opposition forced removal of the gathering to Aguascalientes, where the representatives of Zapata had the first public and national hearing of their cause.

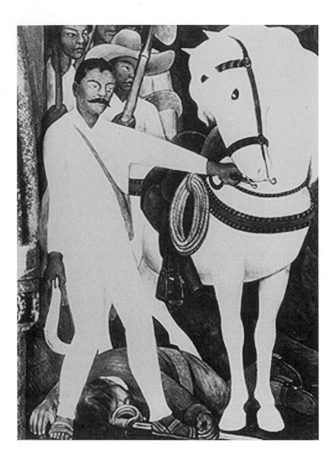

The Plan of Ayala was accepted in principle, and the convention government was established, resting on the armed support of Villa and Zapata. Their joint armies occupied the Mexican capital in December 1914. However, cooperation in subsequent military operations was another matter. As Álvaro Obregón led his Constitutionalist army back toward Mexico City, Villa withdrew to the north and Zapata turned back southward into Morelos.

From 1915 on Zapata waged defensive guerrilla warfare against the Constitutionalist. Forces under Gen. Pablo González sought, as others before, to wipe out the *zapatistas* without success. Finally, González sent Col. Jesús Guajardo to trick Zapata into receiving him as an ally. Zapata was ambushed and killed at Chinameca on April 10, 1919. However, there were those who insisted that he was not dead, that he had been seen riding his horse in the sierra watching out for his peasants. A little more than a year later the demands of the *zapatistas* were being met by the Obregón government.

Further Reading

The excellent, scholarly work by John Womack, *Zapata and the Mexican Revolution* (1969), catches the essence of Zapata and the spirit of *zapatismo*. Edgecumb Pinchon, *Zapata: The Unconquerable* (1941), is a romanticized study, and H. H. Dunn, *The Crimson Jester: Zapata of Mexico* (1933), is a more sketchy and less sympathetic account. Ronald Atkin's competent review of the factors that contributed to the uprising, *Revolution: Mexico, 1910-20* (1970), contains a good portrait of Zapata and of other major figures of the time. Robert P.

Millon, *Zapata: The Ideology of a Peasant Revolutionary* (1969), is a Marxist interpretation. Also useful are Frank Tannenbaum, *The Mexican Agrarian Revolution* (1929), and Eyler N. Simpson, *The Ejido* (1937). □

Gioseffo Zarlino

The Italian music theorist and composer Gioseffo Zarlino (1517-1590) wrote the most lucid and comprehensive exposition of 16th-century counterpoint.

Born in Chioggia near Venice, Gioseffo Zarlino received his initial training in religion and music from Franciscans, whose order he entered as early as 1537. Although a promising priest and theologian at the age of 24, he nevertheless abandoned this calling in 1541 to study music with the world-famous Adrian Willaert, *maestro di cappella* of St. Mark's in Venice. Among his fellow students was Cipriano de Rore, who succeeded Willaert at the Cathedral. In 1565 Rore relinquished the post to Zarlino, who held it until his death.

Because of his position in one of the most important churches of Christendom, Zarlino wrote many Masses and motets for liturgical and devotional purposes. But he was also known for his numerous madrigals and secular music to celebrate political events, such as the brilliant naval victory of Lepanto (1571). Zarlino esteemed and emulated Willaert, crediting him with having the restored music to a level previously enjoyed only in classical times. Like his teacher, Zarlino wrote imitative polyphony in diatonic movement, with chromaticism reserved largely for the madrigals.

Although 16th-century opinion considered Zarlino a talented composer, his main significance then and now lies with his three contributions to music theory: *Le istitutioni harmoniche* (1558), *Dimostrationi harmoniche* (1571), and *Sopplimenti musicali* (1588). The first treatise probably contains his most valuable thinking. For the first time among theorists, Zarlino considered the triad rather than the interval as the basic entity of musical composition. His rules for the proper placement of text are still followed by editors of Renaissance music. The prominent place accorded the Ionian mode on C and the Aeolian on A in part IV of the *Istitutioni harmoniche* not only stressed the importance of these modes but also anticipated their supremacy in the 18th century. While vigorously opposed by his own student Vincenzo Galilei, he favored the Ptolemaic rather than the older Pytheagorean intonation. In his third treatise, *Sopplimenti musicali,* written in part as a reply to Galilei's attacks, he proposed for the fretted lute a form of equal temperament, commonly accepted only 2 centuries later.

Even while, or perhaps because, Zarlino was a conservative composer, he wrote the best critique of the music of his time and the age that led up to it. His insights and views had far-reaching results in later years, even though he took little part in the musical revolution inaugurated under his eyes by his own student and most formidable opponent, Galilei.

Further Reading

Part III of Zarlino's *Le istitutioni harmoniche* was translated by Guy A. Marco and Claude V. Palisca as *The Art of Counterpoint* (1968). Sections from parts III and IV of the same treatise are also translated in William Oliver Strunk, ed., *Source Readings in Music History* (1950). For a study of Zarlino's position in 16th-century music and music theory see Gustave Reese, *Music in the Renaissance* (1954; rev. ed. 1959); Hugo Riemann, *History of Music Theory, Books I and II* (trans. 1962); and Friedrich Blume, *Renaissance and Baroque Music* (trans. 1967). □

Shaykh Zayid bin Sultan Al-Nahyan

Shaykh Zayid bin Sultan Al-Nahyan (born 1923) served for 18 years as the governor of the Buraimi Oasis and for five years as the ruler of the emirate of Abu Dhabi, one of the Trucial States, before becoming president of the United Arab Emirates (U.A.E.) upon its formation in 1971.

Shaykh (Sheik) Zayid bin Sultan Al-Nahyan was the president of the United Arab Emirates (U.A.E.), a federation of the seven former shaykhdoms, or states, of Abu Dhabi, Dubai, Sharjah, Ajman, Umm al-Qaiwain, Fujairah, and Ras al-Khaimah (the states are sometimes called "trucial," from a truce made with Great Britain). The federation was formed in December 1971, on the day before Great Britain terminated all of its treaty relations in the Persian Gulf. On December 8, 1971, the U.A.E. joined the Arab League and it became a member of the United Nations.

But even before the rise of the U.A.E., Shaykh Zayid was a noted figure in the emirate of Abu Dhabi: he had served for 18 years as the energetic governor of Buraimi Oasis. In August 1966 Shaykh Shakhbut bin Sultan, who had ruled Abu Dhabi since 1928, was deposed by members of his family (with British encouragement) and replaced by his younger brother, Shaykh Zayid. The new ruler therefore brought with him considerable experience in administration and an affinity he had established with the tribes of the country.

The peaceful transfer of power of Shaykh Zayid opened the possibility of growth and development, quickly changing the prevalent attitude toward progress from that of threat to one of opportunity.

With the increase of oil production in the late 1960s, Shaykh Zayid embarked on a program of reform and development. His great success in Abu Dhabi, together with his contributions to the development of neighboring emirates, increased his popularity in the Arab Gulf region. Moreover,

Shaykh Zayid extended help in education to the other emirates in the lower Gulf; Abu Dhabi began to build schools and employ teachers, particularly in Ajman, Umm al-Qaiwain, and Ras al-Khaimah.

Modernization and urbanization brought about profound changes in political outlook and thinking. The construction of highways and modern airports and communication systems within the emirates themselves and the provision of links with both the Arab world and the outside put an end to the isolation experienced in that part of the Gulf.

It was in the late 1960s and early 1970s that Abu Dhabi emerged as the leading emirate among the seven Trucial States. This achievement was attributable to both its oil wealth and Shaykh Zayid's prominent role in cementing relationships between rival and competing, sometimes quarreling, rulers. It was here that he asserted himself as a great leader and statesman, seeking a true unity of the Trucial States.

Three factors—an unsettled Gulf situation, the Arab regional environment, and the British decision to withdraw from the Gulf—together induced him to sponsor the creation of a federation of the competing city-states. The rulers of the various lower shaykhdoms had, since the early part of 1962, been seeking some kind of cooperation for mutual security. The small size of their population, along with their strategic location and new found oil wealth, made them particularly vulnerable to outside threats. Their rulers were especially concerned with the threat of "radical" nationalist movements then active in the Federation of South Arabia which was due to become independent of Great Britain in January 1968. (It did become independent as the Marxist state of South Yemen, later a part of a united Yemen). It was fear of such "radical" movements that prompted Shaykh Zayid of Abu Dhabi to call for cooperation and unity of the shaykhdoms on the heels of the British announcement of withdrawal.

But it is to be remembered that the former Trucial States have more in common than a history of treaty relations with Great Britain. Their social structure and their social, geographical, and political characteristics all combine to link them together. The first time all the rulers of the Trucial Coast gathered together was in 1905, when Zayid bin Khalifah called a meeting in Abu Dhabi in order to solve outstanding territorial disputes. The meeting was not successful. But in 1968, with British announcement of complete withdrawal from the Gulf by the end of 1971, the need for unity became urgent. On February 18, 1968, Shaykh Zayid bin Sultan and Shaykh Rashid bin Said of Dubai met and the two rulers announced a union which they invited the other Shaykh of the Trucial States and the rulers of Qatar and Bahrain to join. But when, on December 2, 1971, the U.A.E. was proclaimed with Shaykh Zayid as president neither Qatar nor Bahrain were willing to join. On August 14, 1971, Bahrain declared its independence, and on September 1 of the same year, Qatar followed suit.

The document that was signed on February 11, 1972, by the seven Trucial States was entitled "Provisional Constitution of the United Arab Emirates." It was to be valid for five years only, during which period a permanent constitution was to be prepared. However, the initial constitution is still is force today.

In that constitution five central authorities are outlined: the Supreme Council of the union; the president of the union and his deputy; the Council of Ministers of the union; the National Assembly of the union; and the judiciary of the union. The Supreme Council is the highest political authority in the emirates: its members are the rulers of the seven emirates. It is vested with legislative as well as executive powers. Its executive power is to exercise supreme control over the affairs of the union in general. The constitution stipulates that procedural matters of the council shall be decided by majority vote. Should most members of the Supreme Council feel strongly about a particular issue, no decision would be taken without the agreement of the rulers of Abu Dhabi and Dubai.

The Council of Ministers is described as the executive authority of the union, and under the supreme control of the president of the union, it is responsible for all domestic and foreign affairs. As for the National Assembly of the union, the constitution stipulates that it is neither the exclusive nor the most prominent legislative authority in the union, but in reality has a predominantly consultative character. It may not initiate bills, but it discusses those which are submitted by the cabinet.

The members of the National Assembly do not have to be elected by popular vote: the nature of the tribal societies in each of the seven emirates and the absence of widespread formal education at the time, limited the choice of suitable representatives to the small number of leading families. The assembly's main role as a key link in strengthening the federation does not prevent it from developing certain characteristics of other assemblies and voicing the opinions of a progressively intellectual elite that is the backbone of the union.

When Iraq invaded Kuwait August 2, 1990, the U.A.E. joined in the United Nations coalition to oust Saddam Hussein's army from Kuwait. Under the leadership of Zayid, the U.A.E. continued to make serious efforts to develop alternatives to oil industries during the 1990s. Progress was made in land reclamation, development of industries and in development of ports into centers of trade. Zayid also focused on health and education with the U.A.E. enjoying a health care system better than many western countries and a compulsory school attendance for all children. In 1995 the U.A.E. received international attention when a Philippine maid, Sarah Balabagan, was found guilty of murdering her former employee and sentenced to death by an Islamic court. In an appeal, Balagagan's death sentence was reduced to 100 lashes and one year in jail.

Shaykh Zayid was the principal force behind the rise of the U.A.E. Personal reputation and kinship still play the legitimizing role in the union, but the setting is quite new. His authority is no longer just traditional or charismatic, it is also becoming increasingly legal-rational. Zayid is respected for his Bedouin (nomadic Arab) virtues of impressive generosity and strength of character; he has taken care to observe the conciliar ancient custom of tribal govern-

ment, consulting with tribal notables and making himself accessible to ordinary people.

Further Reading

Additional information on Shaykh Zayid bin Sultan can be found in Wilfred Thesiger, *Arabian Sands* (1959); J.B. Kelly, *Eastern Arabian Frontiers* (1964); Frauk Heard-Bey, *From Trucial States to United Arab Emirates* (1982); Muhammad Morsy Abdullah, *The United Arab Emirates: A Modern History* (1978); Michael C. Hudson, *Arab Politics: The Search for Legitimacy* (1977); Rosemarie Said Zahlan, *The Origins of the United Arab Emirates: A Political and Social History of the Trucial States* (1978) and *The Making of the Modern Gulf States* (1989); and Ali Mohammed Khalifa, *The United Arab Emirates: Unity in Fragmentation* (1979). Information on the U.A.E. and Zayid can be found in the *Enclopaedia Arabica* ☐

Kanze Zeami

Kanze Zeami (1364-1444), also called Zeami Motokiyo, was a Japanese actor, playwright, and critic. His theoretical works on the art of the No are as justly celebrated as his dramas.

I t was the great esthete, statesman, and patron of the fine arts, the shogun Ashikaga Yoshimitsu, who discovered Zeami and his father, Kannami, a brilliant No actor. At a command performance of *Okina,* Kannami appeared before the Shogun and impressed him so favorably that he was at once named knight companion to Yoshimitsu, a considerable distinction. Kannami died in 1384 on tour. Zeami always spoke of his father in the most adulatory and respectful terms as a great actor, playwright, composer, and choreographer, for talent in all these capacities is required in the creation of a No drama.

Zeami first appeared before Shogun Yoshimitsu in a performance at the Imakumano Shrine in 1374. Before he reached his majority at 20, Zeami was considered an accomplished and polished performer. Upon the death of his father Zeami became the head of the troupe. Sometime in his early 20s Zeami entered the awkward age, when he was neither a charming youth nor yet the great artiste he was to become at the height of his fame.

Resolved to suffer the embarrassments of the awkward age, Zeami blossomed forth in his mid-20s as a serious actor of note. Zeami was not spoiled by his new success, for he realized that only with the passing of years and the coming of wisdom was the actor's true "flower" achieved. Perseverance and a life devoted to art were keys to the formula of his success.

Writings on No

Zeami wrote extensively on the art of the No in *Kadensho* (1400; *On Transmitting the Flower*); *Shikadosho* (1420; *On the Way of the Highest Flower*); and *Nosakusho* (1423; *On the Composition of No*). The No drama is a combination of many elements, rather like opera. It is a mixture of singing, dancing, orchestral accompaniment, and usually a dramatic theme expressed in poetry of a very high order. The actors are clothed in gorgeous brocaded robes and wear masks. One No play usually takes about an hour to perform. The play is constructed in three parts: *jo,* or introduction; *ha,* or development, an increase of the dramatic rhythm; and *Kyu,* the climax, in which there is usually a spirited dance.

There are five types of plays. A program might have one of each to present variety: god plays, hero plays, lady plays, contemporary or variety plays, and demon plays. Of all the different ingredients of the No play, it was the art of acting that Zeami wrote about in great detail, giving us a glimpse of the ideals and the reality of the life of the stage 600 years ago.

In the *Kadensho* Zeami is at pains to describe the virtuosity of his father so that later generations might know what a great and original actor he was. In this critical work Zeami stressed the importance of *yugen* as the most fundamental element of No. *Yugen,* which means elegance or grace, also means a special quality more real than apparent which transforms something common into art.

Zeami in his essays on acting expressed the opinion that a young actor, even eleven years old, has a certain charming quality which enhances his performance. His youthful appearance and voice help him to offset any criticism of his lack of finesse. If this emphasis on youth seems inconsistent with Zeami's insistence on the maturity and virtuosity of the accomplished actor, it must be noted that the Shogun himself was only a few years older than Zeami and was surrounded by a youthful entourage of samurai. Zeami was favored and cultivated by many because of his intimacy with the Shogun.

Height and Decline of His Career

In addition to being assigned the authorship of some of the best-known dramas, such as *Matsukaze, Eguchi,* and *Sotoba Komachi,* Zeami is also credited with the No dance, *kusemai,* an important addition to the structure of a No play. Zeami was once assumed to have been the author of about half of the known repertory. Modern scholarship has now left him with about 25 of the finest, most artistic examples of Japan's classical drama.

Zeami reached the height of his fame when he appeared at Yoshimitsu's villa at Kitayama in a performance in honor of Emperor Go-komatsu in 1408. Within a few weeks Yoshimitsu had died of an illness, and the No had lost its most important patron. The next shogun showered his patronage on a rival actor. For some years after this Zeami seems to have fallen out of favor and to have spent his time composing dramas and writing criticism on the actor's art. In 1422 Zeami retired from the world into Holy Orders, leaving to his son the leadership of his troupe.

In later years both Zeami and his son Motomasa experienced the hostility of Shogun Yoshinori, while Zeami's nephew was shown preference. Father and son were not bidden to the palace of the Shogun and later were excluded from performing before the retired emperor. When Motomasa died in seclusion in the country, Zeami was

inconsolable. His grief blighted the remaining years of his life.

The leadership of Zeami's school of the No passed to his son-in-law Komparu Zenchiku. In 1434 Zeami was banished to the remote island of Sado in the Sea of Japan. He remained there until the assassination of Yoshinori resulted in a general amnesty in 1441. Zeami then returned to Kyoto.

Further Reading

There is little on Zeami in English. For useful background see Arthur Waley, *The No Plays of Japan* (1921); Ezra Pound and Ernest Fenollosa, *The Classic Noh Theatre of Japan* (1959); and Donald Keene, with photos by Kaneko Hiroshi, *No: The Classical Theatre of Japan* (1966). □

Ernesto Zedillo Ponce de Leon

On March 29, 1994, Mexico's ruling Institutional Revolutionary Party (PRI) named Ernesto Zedillo Ponce de Leon (born 1951) as its candidate for president after the party's original nominee, Luis Donaldo Colosio Murrieta, was assassinated. Zedillo was elected president of Mexico on August 21, 1994.

The selection of Colosio's successor sparked dissent within the PRI, which had governed the country since 1929. Old-guard activists, the so-called "dinosaurs" who inhabited the party's labor and peasant sectors, voiced dismay over the professorial Zedillo, 42, who had earned M.A. and Ph.D. degrees in economics from Yale and enjoyed a meteoric rise in his nation's financial bureaucracy. Rather than a cosmopolitan "egg-head," PRI's traditional bosses wanted as their candidate a back-slapping, savvy operative in tune with grassroots politics. After two Ivy League-educated chief executives, they longed for someone who appreciated patronage and payola more than econometric models and floating exchange rates. Their favorite was party chairman Fernando Ortiz Arana.

Unfortunately, Ortiz Arana bowed out of the contest, paving the way for incumbent chief executive Carlos Salinas de Gortari to name the individual whom he believed would best serve Mexico's interests. For Salinas it was more important to convince financial decision makers in New York, London, and Tokyo that Mexico would not veer from a liberal trade policy and market-focused reforms than to propitiate ward-heelers in Mexico City, Chihuahua, and Oaxaca.

Zedillo was just the man to calm nervous investors and continue Mexico's version of *perestroika,* launched in the mid-1980s. Not only were his academic credentials impeccable, but he won praise as research director of Mexico's highly regarded central bank and as head of the FICORCA program that helped private Mexican companies restructure

their foreign debt. He also performed brilliantly as Salinas' secretary of planning and budget (1988-1992). In this sensitive position, he emerged as a major architect of Mexico's economic liberalization. He helped convert a 20 percent federal government deficit into a surplus—the equivalent of 4.5 Gramm-Rudman-Hollings agreements in the United States. Along the way he deftly salved the bruised egos of losers in the budget process, while sharply boosting outlays for the antipoverty Solidarity initiative and other social ventures. Moreover, he played a key role in crafting the anti-inflation plan that pivoted on a wage-and price-control pact among government, unions, and the private sector. This scheme slashed price increases from 159.2 percent in 1987, the year before Salinas took office, to 8 percent in 1993—with a further reduction anticipated in 1994.

More ambiguous was Zedillo's record as education secretary (1992-1993). He raised hackles by producing an expensive new grade school text that revised the acutely nationalist interpretation of his country's history. The book, for example, implicated the Mexican Army in the killing of hundreds of protestors in Mexico City in 1968. Such entries, combined with alleged factual errors, led both to the recall of the volume and the decline in Zedillo's political stock. To his credit, the youthful cabinet member bounced back by decentralizing the nation's underfunded, extremely politicized educational system. This move forced the aggressive, strike-prone, 800,000-member teachers' union to hammer out separate accords with 31 different state governments in lieu of negotiating a nationwide contract.

Zedillo began his quest for the presidency by wrapping himself in the mantle of Colosio, whose campaign he had managed. He employed the slain leader's name 35 times in his 20-minute speech accepting the PRI nomination. ''Luis Donaldo Colosio was the best man for Mexico,'' he told a gathering of party leaders. ''Let us continue the work that Luis Donaldo Colosio took on.''

Zedillo needed to capitalize on the outpouring of sympathy for the martyred Colosio, the popularity of Salinas and Solidarity, a conservative electorate, and the PRI's well-financed electoral machine. The Mexican public, for whom he began the campaign as an unknown quantity, liked the fact that the unpretentious candidate grew up in a lower-middle-class family in Mexicali. As a child, he even sold old cans to scrap dealers. He made it to the top through brains and hard work, not a political pedigree and door-opening contacts.

Although not brimming with enthusiasm, most old-line Priistas climbed aboard Zedillo's bandwagon. He may not have been their first choice, but they realized that party loyalty was a prerequisite for legislative nominations, city council seats, bureaucratic posts, and favorable labor management decisions. Besides, PRI veterans loathed Cuauhtémoc Cárdenas, nominee of the left-nationalist Democratic Revolutionary Party and Zedillo's strongest opponent. They regarded Cárdenas, a former governor and son of a beloved, late president, as a Judas. After all, he bolted the PRI in 1987 and challenged Salinas for the presidency a year later. He also sought to make political capital out of the Indian-focused rebellion that erupted in southern Chiapas state on January 1, 1994.

Presidential Administration

After winning the presidential election in 1994, Zedillo began the tough job that lay ahead. It was clear that Mexico's next president needed to gradually marginalize dinosaur politicians, while broadening access to the political process for elements of the business community. Professionals, women, young people, shantytown dwellers, and small farmers all saw the departing regime as representing repression, rigged elections, and corruption. At the same time, Zedillo worked to convince dirt-poor Chiapan peasants and other ''have nots'' that their country's foreign-educated mandarins cared about their plight, as Salinas attempted to do through Solidarity.

In keeping with his plans for change, in 1995 Zedillo surprised everyone—including his fellow party members—when he announced reforms within the PRI. One change that ultimately failed was Zedillo's decision to draw the Mexican military into the drug war. Within months of appointing General Jesus Gutierrez Rebollo to head the federal drug agency, he was forced to dismiss him when he was discovered to have been collaborating with a notorious drug lord. Nevertheless, U.S. President Bill Clinton said that the dismissal proved Mexico was intent on fighting drug trafficking, and certified to Congress Mexico's cooperation in the drug war. Many in Congress, including Senator Dianne Feinstein of California, were displeased with Clinton's certification of Mexico, and moved to reverse the certification.

Such turmoil in the first years of Zedillo's administration only further undermined PRI's flagging influence in Mexico. The PRI hardliners of 1994 did not pack the political wallop they had a generation previously, a trend more fully observed in July 1997 when the National Action opposition party won control of the Congress, as well as many other key positions throughout Mexico. The Mexico City mayorship was lost to National Action politician, Cuauhtemoc Cardenas, and two of six governor's races were also lost to the rival party. Zedillo might well be the first Mexican president since 1913 to face an opposition legislature. The shift in power was regarded positively both within Mexico and abroad. President Clinton said of the change, "Anything that adds to Mexico as a democracy is good for our common future." Financial markets approved of the electoral results, as well; the peso gained against the dollar, the stock market rose, and Mexico's bonds rallied.

Born on December 27, 1951, in Mexico City, Zedillo married Nilda Patricia Velasco, an economist. The couple had five children. Although a workaholic, Zedillo was an avid cyclist sometimes seen at cycling events around Mexico City.

Further Reading

For more information on Zedillo, see a major newspaper for results of both the 1994 election, as well as the July 1997 election. □

José Santos Zelaya

The Nicaraguan president José Santos Zelaya (1853-1919) instituted improvements in education and transportation which, unfortunately, were accompanied by tyrannical methods. His ambition to dominate Central America and his conflicts with United States policy contributed to his downfall.

José Santos Zelaya was born on Oct. 31, 1853, in Managua to a wealthy coffee planter, José Maria Zelaya, and Juana López. After attending school in Granada, Nicaragua, young José and his brother went to France for advanced study. Returning home in 1876, Zelaya participated in many conspiracies against the Conservative administrations of the "Thirty Years" (1863-1893) and once was exiled for such activity.

When the Conservative regime of Roberto Sacasa was ousted because of division within his party, there followed political confusion from which Zelaya, heading a Liberal group, emerged as president in July 1893. Through manipulated elections and ability to play one faction against another, Zelaya retained power for 16 years. During his administration he created new schools, provided new school furniture and instructional material, increased teachers' pay, and established an office of inspector of public education. He built roads, extended the railway system and steamer service on Nicaraguan lakes, improved agriculture, and started transformation of Managua from a village to the nation's first city.

While some of Zelaya's policies were progressive, others were repressive. He and his associates used their positions for enrichment by selling concessions and demanding tribute from persons doing business in Nicaragua. Zelaya often exiled or imprisoned enemies and confiscated their property.

Desirous of dominating Central America, Zelaya supported a Central American union under his leadership and frequently interfered in neighboring countries. In 1907, after he had encouraged an unsuccessful revolutionary attack on the Honduran government, Nicaraguan troops defeated the Honduran army, along with a force from El Salvador, and occupied Tegucigalpa. A general Central American war threatened, for which the U.S. State Department blamed Zelaya. Mexico and the United States through the Central American Conference in Washington (1907) supported treaties which aimed at stabilizing Central America. Despite the treaties, Zelaya's meddling continued.

In October 1909 a revolution against Zelaya broke out on Nicaragua's east coast. After two Americans aiding the revolutionists were captured and executed on Zelaya's orders, the United States broke relations with Nicaragua. Facing insurmountable odds, Zelaya resigned on Dec. 16, 1909, and went into exile in Mexico.

Zelaya eventually went to Spain and in 1913 came to the United States. When charges were brought against him for murdering two Americans many years earlier, he spent 8

days in jail. After charges were dropped, he went back to Spain but returned to New York in 1916, where he died on May 17, 1919.

Further Reading

There is no biography of Zelaya in English. Dana G. Munro's *The Five Republics of Central America* (1918; repr. 1967) and Munro's *Intervention and Dollar Diplomacy in the Caribbean, 1900-1921* (1964) give good brief accounts of Zelaya.

☐

Samuel Zemurray

Samuel Zemurray (1877-1961), a Russian-born U.S. fruit importer, in a classic "rags to riches" career built the United Fruit Company into a powerful international corporation. The economic power of his banana companies dwarfed the Central American states where they operated and allowed him to play a major economic and political role there in the mid-20th century.

S amuel Zemurray was born in Kishinev, Bessarabia, Russia, on January 18, 1877, to poor Jewish parents, David and Sarah (Blausman) Zmuri. In 1892 he emigrated to Selma, Alabama, and worked at several low-paying jobs that enabled him to help the rest of his family come to Alabama by the time he was 19. In 1895 he entered the banana business, buying carloads of "ripes" in Mobile and peddling them to small-town grocers along the railway. He expanded this trade to New Orleans, getting a contract from the United Fruit Company (UFCO) to sell to small dealers and peddlers bananas too ripe to ship into the interior. Grocers called him "Sam the Banana Man," a name that stuck throughout his career. Within three years he had $100,000 in the bank.

In 1905 he and a partner, Ashbel Hubbard of Mobile, bought a bankrupt steamship line with UFCO supplying 60 percent of the capital. Zemurray went to Honduras to purchase bananas along the Cuyamel River. Although heavily in debt, he developed a profitable business. UFCO sold its interest in 1907, and in 1910 Zemurray became president of Cuyamel Fruit Company. He then financed a revolution by Manuel Bonilla who, upon becoming president of Honduras in 1912, rewarded Zemurray with concessions that were highly important to Cuyamel's success and to stopping UFCO's bid for monopoly. Zemurray acquired land for banana plantations, built railroads, and began extensive irrigation, pest control, and agricultural research. By 1916 he was out of debt and prospering. Fiercely competitive with the giant UFCO, Zemurray expanded into other parts of Central America and in 1922 acquired the Bluefields Fruit & Steamship Company in Nicaragua from his father-in-law, Jake Weinberger of New Orleans.

The energetic Zemurray developed a deep affection and understanding for the people of Central America that gave him a distinct advantage over UFCO. He became involved in Honduran politics in order to achieve favorable business concessions. He earned a reputation for direct, bold, and decisive actions. Unlike UFCO executives, who stayed in their Boston offices, Zemurray worked actively in the mosquito-infested Central American lowlands, learned Spanish, and personally supervised Cuyamel's tropical production. His methods included the hiring of soldiers-of-fortune such as Lee Christmas and Guy "Machine Gun" Molony to support revolutionary factions favorable to Zemurray interests, exploiting border disputes among the Central American states, and aiding political parties that promised friendly treatment.

Zemurray retired from active management of the banana industry in 1929 when he sold Cuyamel to UFCO for 300,000 shares of the latter, making him the largest stockholder. He became a director of UFCO, but for the moment devoted himself primarily to affairs in Louisiana, including actively opposing Huey Long with his money and influence. During the Depression UFCO's stock dropped by 90 percent, so in 1932 Zemurray went to Boston and took over the company. As "the fish who swallowed the whale," he became managing director of operations and rapidly reversed UFCO's declining fortunes by providing aggressive leadership in its tropical operations and bringing into the company's management seasoned veterans of Cuyamel. President of the company from 1938 to 1948, he stepped down briefly to attend to private interests in Louisiana, but resumed the UFCO presidency from 1948 to 1951 and continued as chairman of the executive committee and as a director of UFCO until his retirement in 1957. Although flamboyant, he was at the same time modest and shy in his personal relationships and was more comfortable with the ordinary "banana cowboys" in the company's tropical operations than with the aristocratic company directors in Boston.

Under Zemurray's leadership the United Fruit Company expanded to other parts of the world, but it was in Central America that the company's role was most dominant. He faced and overcame with research and bold experimentation a near-disastrous epidemic of sigatoka and other tropical diseases. UFCO had a near monopoly on steamship and rail transportation, radio communications, and the export of bananas and other tropical crops. Zemurray's close relationships with the leaders of these states caused some to regard them as lackeys of "Yankee imperialism" and engendered resentment from nationalists. Critics considered Zemurray to be the most powerful man in Central America. Zemurray began to address the problem of UFCO's unfavorable image in Central America. He launched major public relations efforts to emphasize the company's development of the tropical lowlands, crop diversification, research toward eradicating human and plant diseases, and the higher wages and educational and health benefits received by its employees. He also engaged in major philanthropic enterprises to develop educational, human, and cultural resources in Central America and in the United States. This included restoration of Mayan ruins, major donations to Central American and tropical medicine research at Tulane University, and development of botanical gardens and the School of Pan-American Agriculture in Honduras. His personal philanthropy extended over a much wider range of projects.

A strong supporter of Franklin Roosevelt and the New Deal, Zemurray helped frame the Agricultural Adjustment Administration industry codes, and during World War II, as an adviser to the Board of Economic Welfare, he cooperated closely with the war effort. UFCO chartered ships to the government and concentrated on production of rubber, hemp, quinine, rotenone, soybeans, and other strategic tropical crops in Central America. Zemurray was still influential within UFCO during the company's involvement with the CIA-backed 1954 overthrow of the Guatemalan government. He was a leading figure in the campaign to alarm the U.S. government and public of the "communist" threat in Guatemala, although he was never publicly identified with the CIA plot.

Without Zemurray's active leadership UFCO was in serious decline by the mid-1950s. Recognizing this, and seriously ill from Parkinson's disease, Zemurray divested himself of all UFCO stock. He died in New Orleans on November 30, 1961.

Further Reading

A detailed biographical article on Zemurray is Stephen Whitfield, "Strange Fruit: The Career of Samuel Zemurray," *American Jewish History* 73 (March 1984). Favorable accounts of his contribution to United Fruit are also found in Charles Wilson, *Empire in Green and Gold* (1947); Stacy May and Galo Plaza, *The United Fruit Company in Latin America* (1958); and

Thomas McCann, *An American Company, the Tragedy of United Fruit* (1976). More critical is Charles Kepner, Jr. and Jay Soothill, *The Banana Empire* (1935). Useful for his descriptions of Zemurray's relationships with others in the industry is Thomas Karnes, *Tropical Enterprise, The Standard Fruit and Steamship Company in Latin America* (1978). Stephen Schlesinger and Stephen Kinzer, *Bitter Fruit* (1982) provides detail on Zemurray and the 1954 overthrow of the Guatemalan government. □

John Peter Zenger

John Peter Zenger (1697-1746), American printer, was selected to print a weekly newspaper by a faction of influential men opposed to a governor of New York. Zenger was charged with libel and acquitted. The case has forever associated his name with the cause of freedom of speech and of the press in America.

John Peter Zenger was born in a part of the Rhine country of Germany called the Palatinate. This area was a prime source of emigration to America because the country had been impoverished by a succession of wars and the extravagance of the local rulers. In 1710, 3,000 Palatinate refugees were sent by Queen Anne of England in order to establish the production of naval stores in New York. In return for seven years of labor, the emigrants were promised grants of land. Bad fortune began when a fourth of their number died during a disastrous voyage; the scheme led to bitter experiences even for those who survived. Among the dead was the father of 13-year-old John Peter Zenger, whose mother arrived in the New World with three children to care for.

Apprentice Years

In 1711 Zenger was apprenticed for 8 years to William Bradford, one of the pioneers of American printing. When he completed his apprenticeship, Zenger moved to Chestertown, Md., to make his own living. Though he was named to print the session laws of the legislature, he apparently did not prosper there and in 1722 returned to New York. For a short time he entered a partnership with Bradford, then in 1726 again started his own business. Much of what he printed was in Dutch; little was important, except for the first arithmetic printed in New York. He was neither thriving nor influential. His first wife had died, and in 1722 he had married again.

The colony of New York was faction-ridden. A brief period of internal peace ended with the arrival in 1732 of the new governor, William Cosby, who wished to use the post to enhance his own fortunes. Cosby's high-handedness and greed conflicted with the self-esteem and greed of other New Yorkers. When, in the middle of a rather squalid financial case, Cosby summarily removed the chief justice, Lewis Morris, Morris assembled a faction of powerful men whose economic goals were being thwarted by the gover-

John Peter Zenger (center)

nor. The Morris group gained considerable popular support in the city of New York. There followed a period of intense party warfare. The government controlled the only newspaper, the *Gazette,* which happened to be printed by Zenger's old master, William Bradford.

New York Political Squabbles

The Morris faction, needing a newspaper for its barbs against the government, selected Zenger as their printer. On Nov. 5, 1733, the first issue of the *New-York Weekly Journal* appeared. It was not printed well, and Zenger's command of English was poor. But most of the writing was done by the Morris group, particularly by the brilliant James Alexander. The paper soon attracted a popular following with its sharp criticism of the government. Besides articles on Cosby's policies, there were poems making fun of the governor. Since the opposition faction had to be concerned about freedom of speech, Alexander's essays took a much more advanced position on this issue than would be common in America for many years. Bradford's *Gazette,* on the other hand, took the more usual position that governments depended on the unflagging loyalty of their subjects.

Zenger Case

As publisher, Zenger was by law responsible for what appeared in the *Journal.* Cosby decided the paper must be suppressed, though early efforts were unsuccessful. On Nov. 17, 1734, Zenger was arrested for printing seditious and libelous material. In another of the government's high-handed actions, Alexander and another lawyer, who were to defend Zenger, were swiftly disbarred. But Alexander obtained the services of Andrew Hamilton, a prominent Philadelphian who had no reason to fear New York intrigues.

Hamilton made an eloquent and dramatic presentation to the jury. He argued for an enlarged role for the jury, as opposed to the judges, in libel cases. He also insisted that the truth of the charges was crucial in deciding whether or not what had been said was unlawful. Both of these arguments contradicted established legal practice. Customarily, judges instructed juries as to the law, and harsh attacks on the government were seditious even if they were true. But Hamilton carried the day. Zenger, who had been in jail for nearly ten months, was freed.

Zenger's paper had continued to appear during his imprisonment. His wife was acknowledged as the printer, as she would be again after his death in 1746. In prison Zenger had been a useful martyr for the Morris forces. With the political compromises that followed the trial, he received a good deal of patronage printing. Throughout, he had managed to remain obscure. But the trial that bore his name became synonymous with freedom of the press.

Significance of the Case

Actually the case had little effect on freedom for printers afterward. It was a fluke in colonial law. It did not limit the power of legislatures to suppress printers. Not until the end of the 18th century would there be many consistent advocates of freedom of expression.

In a way, the Zenger case was an isolated episode in the political infighting of one colony. In other ways, it did foreshadow future developments in the freedoms of Americans. Alexander used the case to give voice to some of the most advanced thoughts about liberty that an educated man of his time could encounter. And the decision of the jury, ignoring the demands of English law, revealed the way in which new situations in America might transform old beliefs and old loyalties.

Further Reading

A good introduction to the case which made Zenger famous was written by his contemporary James Alexander, *A Brief Narrative of the Case and Trial of John Peter Zenger* (1736). It was reprinted with a helpful introduction by the editor Stanley Nider Katz (1963). Also important for understanding the Zenger case is Leonard W. Levy, *Legacy of Suppression: Freedom of Speech and Press in Early American History* (1960). Levy straightens out much of the confusion surrounding the meaning of the case. Biographies of Zenger are Livingston Rutherford, *John Peter Zenger* (1904), and Irving G. Cheslaw, *John Peter Zenger and "The New-York Weekly Journal"* (1952). □

Zeno of Citium

The Greek philosopher Zeno of Citium (335-263 B.C.) was the founder of Stoicism. His teachings had a profound influence throughout the ancient world and in important respects helped pave the way for Christianity.

Zeno the son of Mnaseas, was born in the Cypriot town of Citium and may have been part Semitic. His education, however, was thoroughly Greek, and he went to Athens about 313 B.C., where he attended the lectures of various philosophers, including Crates the Cynic, Stilpo, Xenocrates, and Polemo. Crates was his most important early master, and his first book, the *Republic*, was Cynic in inspiration and viewpoint. He took what he thought was the best of his masters' teachings and developed a complete philosophical system of his own. His followers were at first called Zenonians, but the name Stoics, which derived from the Stoa Poikile where Zeno taught, proved more popular. He was greatly respected at Athens and was honored by the Athenians with a golden crown and a bronze statue. He was also on good terms with the king of Macedon, Antigonus Gonatas, and was invited to live at the court in Pella. He declined the offer, although he did send two of his followers. Diogenes Laertius, who wrote a biography of Zeno in the 3d century A.D., preserves the titles of several of his works, although all have perished. In addition to the *Repub-*

lic, these include *Life according to Nature, On Appetite* (or *The Nature of Man*), *On Becoming, On the Doctrines of the Pythagoreans, On Problems Relating to Homer, On Art, Memorabilia,* and the *Ethics of Crates.*

His Philosophy

Zeno's philosophical system embraced physics, logic, and ethics. Its greatest strength lay not in the elaborate but false theories set forth as explanations for the make-up of the universe, but in the almost evangelical message of its ethics. Man, in Zeno's view, had the key to true happiness within himself. He must identify with Nature (or Zeus or Providence or the Cosmos, for all were used interchangeably) and strive for self-sufficiency, which meant the rejection of all the external goods and values men traditionally cherished. In place of these, the divine reason given to every person must be cultivated toward the understanding and acceptance of God's universe. Social position was unimportant, and it was possible for the pauper or the king to strive toward the Stoic goal. The true Stoic sage was aware of the laws of Nature and followed them willingly because a beneficent Providence was guiding events. Individual suffering and misfortunes were subsumed under a larger and more important good. The ultimate goal was *apathia,* a state in which a person was completely indifferent to all but his own divinely given understanding of things. Virtue was defined as knowledge and vice as ignorance. The path to virtue was not easy, however. It demanded tough discipline and strict control over natural feelings and reactions such as pleasure, lust, anxiety, and fear. It also demanded a great deal of study of both theory and practical science, for only through complete awareness of the truth of the material world could the Stoic sage come to that understanding which gave him happiness.

Stoic physics and logic followed Heraclitus, Aristotle, and the two Socratic thinkers Antisthenes and Diodorus. It was an eclectic system which mixed a corporeal universe with an ultimate divine reason. God, the divine and beneficent reason behind all things, was originally one and the same with Fire, the basis of the physical universe. Through an elaborate process of separation, God willed Himself apart from corporeality and caused the chain of events which we know as the history of the universe. At some specific moment in the future, He will take corporeality back unto Himself in a mighty conflagration. This process will repeat itself infinitely and history will repeat itself exactly an endless number of times. Man's freedom in such a totally predetermined chain of causation is possible only through the independence of his mind, which bears the same relationship to his body as does God to the corporeal universe. Through reason man may come to an understanding and acceptance of the way things are and may willingly comply with Nature. Ignorance of the truth leads to vain hopes and expectations, and the ignorant man is condemned to a life of blindness. It can be readily seen from the Stoic view of a beneficent God at work in a completely preordained universe that Stoicism was among the first philosophical systems to claim that this is the best of all possible worlds.

Zeno's successors as leaders of the Stoa were Cleanthes, Chrysippus, Zeno of Tarsus, Diogenes the Babylonian, Panaetius of Rhodes, Posidonius, and Hecaton. The Stoic system, with its emphasis on fortitude and discipline, appealed to the Romans and became the most widely accepted Greek philosophy among the Roman ruling classes. Greek and Roman writers in imperial times came to identify the good Roman emperors, such as Trajan, Hadrian, Antoninus Pius, and Marcus Aurelius, with the Stoic king, and the evil emperors, such as Caligula, Nero, and Domitian, with the depraved tyrant. Marcus Aurelius was the emperor who most obviously accepted Stoicism as a way of life, and his collection of personal memoirs bears eloquent witness to the appeal which Zeno's system had to a fine and sensitive mind.

With the demise of the city-states and the concomitant failure of the older and simpler religious views to satisfy men's new spiritual needs in a time of changing values, Zeno's philosophical teachings imparted a sense of worth and dignity to the lives of great numbers of men. The striking similarities between Stoicism and Christianity made it one of the important precursors of that religion in antiquity.

Further Reading

An excellent introduction to Zeno and the Stoic school is in Moses Hadas, ed., *Essential Works of Stoicism* (1961). A more critical summary of Stoic theory and teachings is in Eduard Zeller, *Outlines of the History of Greek Philosophy,* revised by Wilhelm Nestle and translated by L. R. Palmer (1955). Briefer treatments of Zeno are in the surveys of ancient philosophy, such as Gordon H. Clark, ed., *Selections from Hellenistic Philosophy* (1940), and Arthur H. Armstrong, *An Introduction to Ancient Philosophy* (1947; 4th ed. 1965). □

Zeno of Elea

Zeno of Elea (born ca. 490 B.C.) was a Greek philosopher and logician. A member of the Eleatic school of philosophy, he was famous throughout antiquity for the rigorously logical and devastating arguments which he used to show the absurdities and contradictions of his opponents.

Zeno was born in the southern Italian city of Elea. Plato says that Zeno and Parmenides visited Athens about 449 B.C., where the young Socrates made their acquaintance and where Zeno made a striking impression. Ancient authorities asserted that, like Parmenides, Zeno was a Pythagorean, that he engaged in political activity in his native city, and that he was put to death for plotting against a tyrant. An oft-repeated story tells of his bravery under torture and the painful death which he endured.

It is possible that Zeno wrote more than one work, but he is best known for a single volume of *epicheiremata* (attacks) on the postulates of Parmenides's opponents. Only fragments of this work have survived, but a fairly clear idea of his methods may be found in the summaries given by

Aristotle and the 6th-century A.D. Neoplatonist Simplicius. Zeno seems to have had no constructive theories of his own to set forth, and some of his destructive arguments seem to apply equally well to the conclusions drawn by Parmenides.

Zeno's original contribution to thought was the method of deduction which he developed to work out two sets of contradictory conclusions from a given postulate. From his argument against the pluralists, the following example is typical. Let it be postulated that everything has developed from an originally plural source (as opposed to Parmenides's One). If things are many, then they are finite since they are the number that they are. But if things are many, they are infinite since there must always be other things between them, and others between those ad infinitum.

From Zeno's arguments on motion comes the famous example which shows the impossibility of ever reaching the end of a given line. A moving body cannot reach the end because it must constantly reach the midpoint, and then another midpoint, again ad infinitum. It is unclear from the available evidence if Zeno's purpose was to offer a serious defense of the One or if he simply wanted to show that other arguments were no better. Aristotle called him the inventor of dialectic, and Zeno was undoubtedly one of the important early Greek logicians.

Further Reading

Selected passages from Zeno's work in English translation and with commentary are in Geoffrey S. Kirk and John E. Raven, *The Presocratic Philosophers: A Critical History with a Selection of Texts* (1957). Excellent discussions of Zeno's importance and place in the development of Greek thought are in John Burnet, *Early Greek Philosophy* (1892; 4th ed. 1930), and Kathleen Freeman, *The Pre-Socratic Philosophers: A Companion to Diels, Fragmente der Vorsokratiker* (1940; 3d ed. 1953). More generalized discussions of the Pre-Socratics and their place in Greek literature and thought appear in the standard histories of Greek literature, such as that by Albin Lesky, *A History of Greek Literature* (1958; trans. 1966). □

Zenobia

Zenobia, a Palmyrene warrior queen, daringly declared independence from Rome and sought to establish her own united kingdom in the East.

Great physical strength, tremendous beauty, respected intellect and chastity, all overlaid with the suspicion of murder and betrayal, have come to stand for the third-century warrior queen of Palmyra. The scarcity of detail concerning all but five historic years of her life has not helped to demystify her image nor shed light upon her true character. Even the course of her five ruling years differs enormously from one account to another, and the majority of these accounts come from the pens of those whom she ambitiously opposed, the Romans. The *Scriptores Historiae Augustae,* a collection of biographies attributed to the fourth century, details the Roman emperors from 117 to 284, and most existing information concerning Zenobia can be traced to this source. Though the *Scriptores* was apparently authored by six, only two, Trebellius Pollio and Flavius Vopiscus, are credited with the period of the queen's rule. The discrepancies between these two accounts alone point to the impossibility of separating Zenobia from the legend that surrounds her.

Where most contemporary historians have resisted the urge to fill in missing details, the Eastern nomads of Zenobia's day did not show comparable discretion. One popular story told of her great desert-chief father who was blessed with numerous wives and sons. Though from time to time he needed a daughter to seal contracts with neighboring tribes, Zenobia's arrival in the family was not one such occasion. When her father tried to dispose of her, she was hidden away and grew up with the household's many boys, thus accounting for what were considered her manly talents of hunting, shooting for the kill, and enduring physical hardships. This scenario, however, does less to provide a credible summation of the queen's childhood than it does to illuminate the tradition of ascribing a powerful woman's strength to masculine influences.

Under whatever conditions she was raised, and by whom, Zenobia's native tongue was Aramaic. She was most likely of Arabic descent, though Pollio wrote that she "claimed to be of the family of the Cleopatras and the Ptolemies." But if her ancestry remains uncertain, at least she can be accurately placed in history.

Following the death of Severus Alexander in 235, the Roman power center was losing its capacity to control a far-flung empire extending from the Cadiz to the Euphrates and from Britain and the Danube to Libya and Egypt. Though Emperor Alexander had fully committed his armies in an attempt to maintain law and order throughout the kingdom, his death heralded a period of great disturbance; one short-lived emperor followed the next. Consequently, in the north of Syria, the people of Palmyra realized that they would be unable to rely on the Empire for protection, and as the safest caravan route in the region ran through their city, along an avenue lined with more than 375 Corinthian columns, lack of such protection could greatly jeopardize their wealth. Thus, the Palmyrenes both strengthened their local army and took charge of their own political administrative affairs, which actions seem to have well-suited the decentralized Empire.

As Palmyra became increasingly autonomous, Septimius Odainat emerged as the city's uncrowned king. When Roman Emperor Valerian was held captive and killed by Sapur I of Persia, Odainat aligned himself with the Empire in a war against Persia which lasted eight years until the Palmyrenes defeated King Sapur in 260. Having preserved the Empire's eastern frontier and reconquered Mesopotamia for Rome, Odainat was rewarded by the incoming emperor Gallienus in 262 with a title hitherto born only by emperors, *Restitutor totius Orientis, Corrector of all the East.*

However, there was another title Odainat desired. Taking on the Persian style, he deemed himself "King of Kings." Because the Empire had been busy on other fronts and Odainat had shown such loyalty in driving back the Persians, Rome did not object to such grand displays of autonomy. As it was, no one turned a wary eye toward Palmyra until 267, the year Odainat was murdered along with his son and assumed heir Hairan. Though the murder was attributed to Odainat's nephew Maeonis, many did not believe him responsible and blamed instead someone they thought a more likely candidate, his wife, Bat Zabbai—better known as Queen Zenobia. Whether she was suspected because her son Vaballath became heir in her stepson's stead, or because she was actually guilty, will never be known. History has neither relieved nor condemned her.

Whereas Emperor Gallienus recognized the boy-king Vaballath as heir to the throne, and Zenobia his regent, in 268 Gallienus's successor Claudius set aside the decision. Claudius's actions could not have pleased the queen, who was busy assembling a court known both for its material riches and intellectual prowess. The Greek philosopher Cassius Longinus became her most trusted advisor and would serve in such capacity until his death; it is likely that he tutored Vaballath while assisting Zenobia in her study of Greek and Roman authors. Though she is known to have most often used Arabic or Greek in conversation, the queen was versed in five languages including Aramaic, Egyptian, and Latin. Another trusted advisor was her chief general Zabdas and two other names appear to figure prominently in her court, the historian Callinicus Dutorius and one Nicomachus.

Following her husband's death, Zenobia was preparing to continue Odainat's course of action by extending the limits of Palmyra further north and south, when Emperor Claudius died and was replaced by Emperor Aurelian who Vopiscus describes as a "comely man . . . rather tall . . . very strong in muscles . . . endowed with manly grace . . . a little too fond of wine and food." Regardless of these rumored excesses, he managed to strike commendable blows against the Goths who plagued the Empire in northern Italy; and, with such successes to his name, he began pulling the crumbling Roman power center back together again. Where Palmyra was concerned, Aurelian recognized Vaballath, conferring Odainat's titles upon him and allowing him to rule a small Armenian province. Most significantly, he ordered coins struck, bearing Vaballath's portrait on one side, and on the other, his own.

Though undoubtedly relieved to see Vaballath recognized, Zenobia intended that she, not Aurelian, command the east with her son. Thus, in 269, to the shock of the existing world, she sent Zabdas to invade one of the wealthiest provinces in the Roman Empire—Egypt. She had already acquired most of Syria which had simply been annexed to the Palmyrene kingdom. The following year, Egypt was hers. One key point of attack was the little-resisting Antioch in the north. There, the queen ordered the mints to halt production of coins in the name of Claudius. Instead, coins were issued bearing her name and the name of her son. The severity of such an insult to the Empire cannot be underestimated; it was, in fact, equivalent to a declaration of war. Twice during her reign, the Palmyrenes consulted oracles to discover if their good fortune would see them through. In Syria, their offering to the Venus Aphacitis floated on the surface of the goddess's cistern, indicating that she had rejected them. The Apollo Sapedonius at Seleucia was more succinct:

Accursed race! avoid my sacred fane Whose treach'rous deeds the angry gods disdain.

But the queen was not deterred. Not only had Palmyra's borders extended south and north, but the city was declared independent of Rome, and Aurelian was so occupied with internal unrest that he could not yet send his soldiers against her. When the arrogant woman could be ignored no longer, he sent his general Probus to take any necessary steps in order that Lower Egypt be restored to Rome. By autumn of 271, his orders had been carried out, and Aurelian headed across the Straits in pursuit of the infamous queen about whom he'd undoubtedly heard many rumors. She was said to walk for miles alongside her troops, rather than ride in her chariot. She wore a helmet, Pollio wrote, "girt with a purple fillet, which had gems hanging from the lower edge, while its center was fastened with the jewel called chochlis, used instead of the brooch worn by women, and her arms were frequently bare." She could drink with the best of men, but was said to do so only to get the better of them. Then, as Pollio confirms, there was the matter of her rumored chastity: "Such was her continence, it is said, that she would not know her own husband save for the purpose of conception." Also detailed by Pollio was the queen's well-known beauty:

Her face was dark and of a swarthy hue, her eyes were black and powerful beyond the usual wont, her spirit divinely great, and her beauty incredible. So white were her teeth that many thought that she had pearls in place of teeth. Her voice was clear and like that of a man. Her sternness, when necessity demanded, was that of a tyrant, her clemency . . . that of a good emperor.

As Aurelian pursued Zenobia through the east, he met little opposition until reaching the city of Tyana which, under orders from Zenobia, bolted its gates against him. "In this city," cried Aurelian, "I will not leave even a dog alive." However, according to Vopiscus, Tyana's famous mystic, Apollonius, visited Aurelian's tent in ghostly form the night he took Tyana. Meanwhile, Zenobia passed through the city and was making her way to Antioch where she would be able to choose her battleground and make her stand. Vopiscus provides a narration of Apollonius's terrifying visitation which some have since ascribed to the queen's ingenuity:

Aurelian, if you wish to conquer, there is no reason why you should plan the death of my fellow-citizens. Aurelian, if you wish to rule, abstain from the blood of the innocent. Aurelian, act with mercy if you wish to live long.

According to legend, when the emperor announced his decision the following day to spare the city, his soldiers were so indignant that they reminded him of his threat not to leave even a single dog alive. Said Aurelian, "Well, then, kill all the dogs." And, as Vopiscus remarks:

Notable, indeed, were the prince's words but more notable still was the deed of the soldiers; for the entire army, just as though it were gaining riches thereby, took up the prince's jest, by which both booty was denied them and the city preserved intact.

Zenobia reached Antioch considerably ahead of Aurelian, in time to convince the populace that she and Zabdas could defend the city against the Romans. Aurelian approached from the east, and Zenobia's troops fell back on the line of the Orontes River, just outside Antioch, and there the two armies faced each other. Despite the desert heat, the queen's horses and men were weighted down with chain armor. Soon, in a reversal of his usual strategy, Aurelian sent his infantry across the river first, followed by his cavalry which, rather than engaging the enemy, feigned fright and retreated. Zabdas pursued the Romans some 30 miles near the village of Immae. With the enemy forces suitably exhausted beneath their heavy armor, Aurelian ordered his cavalry to attack and easily defeated them.

Escaping back to Antioch, Zabdas and the survivors convinced the citizens that they had conquered the Romans by parading a man resembling Aurelian through the streets. Their ploy was successful. Zenobia and her general withdrew under the cover of darkness before the people of Antioch could awake to find themselves without protection. However, again Apollonius's ghost is said to have appeared to Aurelian, convincing him to spare the city. His men then tracked the queen to Emesa where, on the bank of the Orontes, Zenobia's last battle took place. Though some sources say she had by then a force of 70,000 men, Zosimus, a fifth-century Greek, reports that the slaughter inflicted upon her troops was "promiscuous" (unrestricted).

Zenobia and Zabdas escaped the massacre and headed the approximately 100 miles back to Palmyra. Aurelian followed and set up camp outside the city's walls. Thanks at least in part to Palmyra's famous sharpshooters and archers, the siege dragged on and on. Tired of watching their comrades picked off by Zenobia's arrows, many of Aurelian's soldiers rebelled and were replaced by slaves. But Aurelian had heard reports of the food and water shortages increasing within the walls. Ordering the siege suspended for two days, he forwarded the following letter, penned in Greek and later recorded by Vopiscus, to Palmyra's queen:

> From Aurelian, Emperor of the Roman world and recoverer of the East, to Zenobia and all others who are bound to her by alliance in war. You should have done of your own free will what I now command in my letter. For I bid you surrender, promising that your lives shall be spared, and with the condition that you, Zenobia, together with your children shall dwell wherever I, acting in accordance with the wish of the most noble Senate, shall appoint a place. Your jewels, your gold, your silver, your silks, your horses, your camels, you shall . . . hand over to the Roman treasury. As for the people of Palmyra, their rights shall be preserved.

Zenobia's response, according to Vopiscus, was written by Nicomachus in Aramaic as dictated by Zenobia, then translated into Greek; however, the authorship of this historic letter has been the subject of great controversy with some believing it was actually inspired by Longinus, others believing he tried to dissuade the queen from ever sending it.

> From Zenobia, Queen of the East, to Aurelian Augustus. None save yourself has ever demanded by letter what you now demand. Whatever must be accomplished in matters of war must be done by valour alone. You demand my surrender as though you were not aware that Cleopatra preferred to die a Queen rather than remain alive, however high her rank. . . . If [the forces] we are expecting from every side, shall arrive, you will, of a surety, lay aside that arrogance with which you now command my surrender.

The siege was renewed, and Zenobia went to work securing aid from the Persians with whom the Palmyrenes had a common enemy in Rome. On a female camel, known for their fast flight, Zenobia set off for Persia. It is unclear when or how Aurelian learned of her escape, but as she was heading into a boat to cross the Euphrates, his men overtook and captured her. Once the citizens of Palmyra discovered their queen had fallen into Aurelian's hands, their defense crumbled.

A trial of Zenobia and her chiefs was held in Emesa where her life and that of Zabdas were spared. Longinus and Nicomachus, however, were not so fortunate. Zenobia has been accused of betrayal by faulting them for the proud letter sent to Aurelian. Some have gone so far as to say that she placed the entire blame for her uprising against the Empire on Longinus. Others, on the contrary, maintain she would not have turned against her councillors. Regardless, at Emesa, Aurelian ordered them beheaded. "But the woman," wrote Vopiscus, "he saved for his triumph."

Aurelian had to return to Palmyra to quell another revolt in which Sandarion, the governor he'd left behind, had been killed along with his 600 bodyguards. Evidently when the emperor reached the city, he gave his men free reign as is evident by a letter to his deputy Bassus:

> The swords of the soldiers should not proceed further. . . . We have not spared the women, we have slain the children, we have butchered the old men, we have destroyed the peasants.

Upon his return to Rome, Aurelian was granted the highest honor the Roman Senators could grant, a triumphal entry through the imperial gates in which his army, booty, and prisoners would be displayed. "It was," wrote Vopiscus, "a most brilliant spectacle." Chariots, wild beasts, tigers, leopards, elephants, prisoners, and gladiators paraded through the streets. Each group was labeled with a placard identifying captives and booty from 16 conquered nations for the spectators. One placard identified Odainat's chariot, another that of Zenobia. But, as she had often walked with her soldiers on foot, Zenobia did not ride that fateful day. Rather, she walked, without a placard, though the expectant crowd had no trouble recognizing her, "adorned with gems so huge that she labored under the weight of her ornaments." Pollio continues:

> This woman, courageous though she was, halted very frequently, saying that she could not endure the load of the gems. Furthermore, her feet were bound with shackles of gold and her hands with golden fetters, and even on her neck she wore a chain of gold, the weight of which was borne by a Persian buffoon.

Aurelian later returned yet again to Palmyra, putting down another rebellion; eventually, repeated plundering and a shift in the trade routes put an end to Palmyrene civilization. How long Vaballath survived after his mother's capture will never be known. It is popularly believed that Zenobia's life was spared by her adversary, and that, adapting remarkably well to her new circumstances, she married a Roman senator, living in the manner of a Roman matron on a Tibur estate presented to her by the very Empire against which she'd so daringly risen.

Further Reading

Browning, Iain. *Palmyra*. Chatto & Windus, 1979.
Fraser, Antonia. *Boadicea's Chariot*. Weidenfeld and Nicolson, 1988.
Vaughan, Agnes Carr. *Zenobia of Palmyra*. Doubleday, 1967.
Stoneman, Richard. "The Syrian Cuckoo," in *History Today*. December 1988. □

Clara Zetkin

German political activist Clara Zetkin (1857-1933) was a prominent member of socialist and communist organizations in Europe in the nineteenth and twentieth centuries. As a longtime supporter of the German Social Democratic Party, she argued that equality of women could only be accomplished through a class revolution that overthrew the capitalist system. She later was a founder of the German Communist Party and became a respected political ally of Vladimir Lenin in the Soviet Union.

C lara Zetkin was a distinguished member of Socialist and Communist organizations in Europe in the late 1800s and early 1900s. Throughout her political career, she focused on the liberation of women in society through Marxist reforms of the capitalist system. For many years she promoted her radical thought as the editor of *Die Gleichheit,* the women's journal of the German Social Democratic Party. In her later years, Zetkin served as both a representative of the German Communist Party in the Reichstag legislative body and as an associate of Vladimir Ilich Lenin in the Soviet Union.

Zetkin was born Clara Eissner on July 5, 1857, in Wiederau, near Leipzig, Germany. She was the oldest of the three children of Gottfried Eissner, a schoolteacher and church organist, and Josephine Vitale Eissner, Gottfried's second wife, who was the widow of a local doctor. Josephine Eissner was active in women's education societies and a believer in equal rights and economic power for women. Her work was inspired by feminist organizations, including the German Women's Association and the Federation of German Women's Associations, led by women's rights activists such as Auguste Schmidt and Luise Otto. When Eissner was 15, her father retired and the family moved to Leipzig, where she was enrolled at Schmidt and Otto's Van Steyber Institute in 1875. She studied there until 1878, and her activities during these years included reading socialist newspapers and books and attending meetings of the Leipzig Women's Education Society and the National Association of German Women. These areas of feminist and socialist thought became the focus of her lifelong political activities.

Joined German Social Democrats

In 1878, Zetkin befriended some students from Russia, who introduced her to the political ideals of the German Social Democratic Party, or SPD. One of her new associates was Ossip Zetkin, a native of Odessa, Russia. Ossip Zetkin acted as a political mentor, teaching her about the writings of Karl Marx and Friedrich Engels and the ideas of scientific socialism. At his suggestion, she began to attend meetings of the Leipzig Workers' Education Society and reject her bourgeois lifestyle, which ultimately led to a split with her family and her feminist mentor, Auguste Schmidt. In 1879, Zetkin

traveled to Russia to observe the activities of Marxist groups there.

These experiences gave Zetkin a strong sympathy for the proletariat struggle and she decided to devote her life to the Marxist reform of society. Due to a German law forbidding women to join political parties, she could not become an official member of the SPD, but she spent all her energies supporting its cause. After the passage of the 1878 Anti-Socialist Law in Germany, Ossip Zetkin was forced to leave the country, and Zetkin decided to leave as well. She first traveled to Linz, Austria, where she worked as a tutor of factory workers. She joined a group of SPD members in Zurich in 1882 to write propaganda to sneak into Germany. In November of that year, she was reunited with Ossip Zetkin in Paris. The two lived together and eventually had two sons, Maxim and Konstantine, but were never officially married because Zetkin did not want to give up her German citizenship. She did, however, adopt his surname, and remained Ossip's companion until the end of his life.

Linked Women's Rights to Social Revolution

In Paris, Zetkin began to concentrate on combining her interests in socialism and feminism in an attempt to accomplish equality for working women in the proletariat movement. Her return to feminist issues also led her to reestablish ties with her family, who came to her assistance after Zetkin contracted tuberculosis due to her impoverished conditions in Paris. Her family took her into their home at Leipzig while she recovered, and it was in Leipzig that she gave her first public speech on the liberation of women and all workers through a class revolution. She believed that once class equality was established in a Marxist society, the economic and social oppression of women would naturally come to an end. Because of this line of thought, for many years she fought against special provisions and laws to protect women in the workplace; her thought was that becoming satisfied with such measures would detract from the focus on a total restructuring of the class system. After her convalescence, Zetkin returned to Paris to nurse Ossip, who was suffering from spinal tuberculosis. He never recovered and died in January of 1889.

Zetkin overcame her grief at her partner's death by immersing herself in her political work. Her preoccupation with the socialist cause was so great, in fact, that rearing her two sons constituted her only personal considerations for many years. She would later be married to the painter Georg Friedrich Zundel, a man 18 years her junior. The marriage, which began in 1899, began to disintegrate during World War I and ended in divorce in 1927, primarily due to Zetkin's overwhelming commitment to her work. She became one of the leading women in the socialist movement and in July of 1889 served as one of the eight women delegates who attended the Second International Congress in Paris. She was there as a representative of the working class women of Berlin, Germany, and in a speech before the Congress, she clearly outlined the ideas in support of women's equality that she had been developing. Her speech, later published as *Working Women and the Con-*

temporary *Women Question,* reiterated her belief that she and her comrades should not focus on winning specific rights for women, such as education or economic equality, but should instead concentrate on ending the capitalist system that oppressed women and all workers. In a move that foreshadowed her growing differences with her fellow socialists, the Congress did not support her extremism, voting in favor of equal pay for equal work by women and voicing opposition to hazardous labor by women. This stance did not undermine Zetkin's role in the party, however. She was selected during the Congress to help lead recruiting and education efforts for the SPD in Berlin; she and six other women returned to Germany to found the Berlin Agitation Committee.

Edited Socialist Journal for Women

With the expiration of the Anti-Socialist Law in 1890, SPD members were allowed to return to Germany. Zetkin received another assignment from the party at this time, editing an SPD journal for women. The first issue of *Die Gleichheit* appeared in January of 1892, and under Zetkin's guidance, the journal set an agenda reflecting her beliefs in spreading socialist and Marxist thought among women and fighting the kind of feminist legal reforms supported by bourgeois women's groups. Still forbidden by law from direct membership in the SPD, Zetkin became active in a less direct method of advocating socialism and recruiting women—trade unionism. She helped to link unions in Germany with international organizations and organized strike funds in addition to giving hundreds of speeches. Her involvement with working people helped to moderate some of her views. At an 1896 SPD conference, she gave her support to measures protecting working mothers and advocating women's right to vote.

In general though, Zetkin refused to compromise her rigid adherence to Marxist ideology. After 1900, other members of the SPD were increasingly drawn to a revisionist interpretation of Marx's thought that proposed working within the legal system to accomplish reform. Revisionists saw Zetkin as too theoretical in her journal, and she was instructed to modify *Die Gleichheit* to reach a more general audience, including housewives and children. But although many complained about Zetkin, she was well established in the party and was in no danger of being removed. In 1895 she had become the first woman in the SPD governing body and in 1906 she was named to the central committee on education.

In 1908, women in Germany were given the right to join political parties. Zetkin felt that bringing women into the SPD would result in them being voiceless in an organization run by men, so she worked to form a separate women's group within the party. To this end, she participated in the first International Women's Conferences in 1907 and 1910 and became secretary of the International Women's Bureau, a group which adopted *Die Gleichheit* as its official publication. But her work in this area did not erase the tensions between her and the revisionists. World War I brought the conflict to the forefront. Zetkin, along with other radicals in the party, such as Rosa Luxemburg,

wanted the SPD to condemn the imperialist stance of Germany and its military activities. When the party voted to support the government, Zetkin opposed the move in a series of writings in *Die Gleichheit,* resulting in her removal from the post of editor in 1917. Zetkin left the party to join antiwar socialists in the Independent Social-Democratic Party. Later she and three other radical socialists formed the Gruppe Internationale, also known as the Sparticus League, which became the German Communist Party, or KPD, in November of 1918.

Active in Communist Party

Although her political affiliation had changed, Zetkin's goals remained the same. At the 1919 Third International Congress, she gave a speech emphasizing the importance of having educated women as an active force in the international Communist struggle. In 1920 she was elected the international secretary for Communist women, a post in which she continued to argue that women's issues could only be addressed through reforms for all workers. In the years after World War I, her active role in Communist politics took her to the Soviet Union frequently. There she was an important ally of Soviet Communist leader Vladimir Lenin. She also held a post in the German Reichstag as a member of the KPD. As its oldest member, she was given the honor of convening the legislative body in 1932, and she used to occasion to speak out against Nazi leader Adolf Hitler and his Fascist policies.

Zetkin suffered from poor health in her later years, and she died outside of Moscow in the Soviet Union on June 20, 1933. She was honored with an elaborate funeral and buried in the Kremlin wall. The services were attended by leading Communists from across Europe, including Joseph Stalin and Nadezhda Krupskaya, the widow of Lenin. The presence of such luminaries demonstrated the importance of the life and work of Zetkin to supporters of Communism throughout the world.

Further Reading

Boxer, Marilyn J., and Jean H. Quataert, editors, *Socialist Women: European Socialist Feminism in the Nineteenth and Early Twentieth Centuries,* Elsevier, 1978.

Evans, Richard J., "Theory and Practice in German Social Democracy, 1880-1914: Clara Zetkin and the Socialist Theory of Women's Emancipation," *History of Political Thought,* summer, 1982, pp. 285-304.

Pore, Renate, *A Conflict of Interest: Women in German Social Democracy, 1919-1933,* Greenwood Press, 1981.

Zetkin, Clara, *Clara Zetkin: Selected Writings,* edited by Philip S. Foner, translated by Kai Schoenhals and Angela Y. Davis, International Publishers, 1984. □

Zhao Kuang-yin

Founder of the Song Dynasty, Zhao Kuang-yin (927-976) ended the practice of frequent military coups, which had exhausted China for more than half a

century, and successfully re-established the "civilian empire."

Zhao Kuang- yin, known to history as Song Tai Zu (implying grand progenitor), was the first emperor (960-976) of the Song Dynasty, which was to last over 300 years. During this era of transformation, China became more prosperous than under the rule of any previous dynasty. The population reached 100 million, and the prominent achievements made in economy, technology, and culture placed China in the forefront of the world. At that time, the use of paper money prevailed; both internal and external trade flourished; the civil service system was perfected; and philosophic thinking was permitted to proceed in a relatively free political environment. Zhao Kuang-yin founded the magnificent Song dynasty, which oversaw these years of institutional and cultural growth.

Before becoming emperor, Zhao was a chief-general in the service of the preceding dynasty, Hou Zhuo. As had most of the dynasty founders before him, he usurped the throne by military force; however, unlike those who'd come before him, Zhao was neither an aristocrat nor a minority leader. He was, rather, from an army officer's family and was himself a professional army man. Interestingly, his usurpation in 960 would prove the last in Chinese history.

Zhao Kuang- yin was born in Lo-yang in central China. It was said that when his mother gave birth to him the whole house suddenly filled with golden light and the smell of

incense. He grew into a tall teenager and valiant fighter. Fighting in the north and south with his father and brothers, he was no stranger to military accomplishments and excelled in martial skills.

In his youth, Zhao Kuang-yin watched the country suffer painful disunity and tangled warfare. The Chinese world had relapsed into anarchy for half a century (called the Five Dynasties period), and, taking advantage of the civil war, army commanders became founders of several isolated regimes. The imperial domain was reduced to merely some provinces in the north, whereas nine provincial kingdoms appeared in south China and another in the northwest. During 53 years, 14 monarchies from eight royal families were replaced successively, forming five short-lived dynasties in central China. Zhao Kuang-yin was trusted by the astute Emperor Shi Zong of Hou Zhou, the last dynasty, and was appointed the chief commander of the capital armies.

In 959, Shi Zong died, leaving a seven-year-old son as his heir. Both the officials and the masses were duly alarmed by the turbulent situation, and it seemed necessary for a strong man to take power. Thus, Zhao Kuang-yin prepared to take over the empire with the assistance of his brothers, friends, and consultants.

In the beginning of 960, it was rumored that the Khitan, a northern minority regime, was going to invade Hou Zhou. Hastily, the chief chancellors of Hou Zhou assigned Zhao Kuang-yin to direct the counterattack. Commanding crack troops, Zhao Kuang-yin then left the capital for the frontier border; by evening, when the troops stopped at a place called Chen Qiao Yi, about ten miles away from the capital, the plan behind Zhao Kuang-yin's usurpation was in full swing. The next morning at dawn, the troops were stirred. Instigated by Zhao Kuang-yin's brother Zhao Kuang-yi and his secretary Zhao Pu, hundreds of soldiers surrounded Zhao Kuang-yin's tent. Shouting and cheering, they dressed him in an imperial yellow robe and declared him their emperor.

In the middle of his troops, Zhao Kuang-yin addressed the soldiers: "Don't do harm to the empress dowager and the little emperor. Don't bully the ministers and other officials. And don't loot inside or outside the capital. . . . If you obey me, you will get a handsome reward; but if you fail me, I shall not spare you." Bowing submissively, the soldiers promised to obey his orders.

The troops then marched in perfect order back toward Kai Feng, the capital. Zhao's friends inside the city opened the city gate, and Zhao Kuang-yin went to the palace where he forced the boy emperor from the throne while assuring him that he and his mother would be safe. Thus, Zhao Kuang-yin ascended to the throne without bloodshed. As China's new emperor was previously a regional commander at the Song prefecture, he named his new dynasty "Song."

Immediately upon the establishment of the Song administration, Zhao Kuang-yin faced two urgent problems: how to unify the disintegrated country and how to strengthen the centralization of authority to eliminate the chance of future usurpation. Addressing the problem as to how to unify China, Zhao Kuang-yin repeatedly consulted with his ministers and generals. Evidently, on a snowy night, he went out with his brother Kuang-yi to his adviser Zhao Pu's house. Surprised by the unexpected visit, Zhao Pu asked if there was an urgent matter to be discussed. "I simply cannot fall asleep," the Emperor replied, "I feel that there are so many other people sleeping soundly around my bed. . . . Our territory is too small. . . . It is time to reunite China." Military operations were carefully discussed until Zhao Kuang- yin finally designed a strategy to subjugate the various kingdoms one by one, beginning in the south, which was rich in production but weak in forces.

In order to request tolerance and recognition, the wealthy states in the south sent priceless treasures to the Song Court. Zhao Kuang-yin responded to such efforts with both hard and soft tactics. For instance, when the king of the Wu Yue state came to the capital to pay respects to Zhao Kuang-yin, most of the Song officials asked permission to arrest him so that he would surrender his territory. Zhao Kuang-yin, however, ignored their suggestions and let the king return to his land with a small present—a brocade bag. Opening the bag on his way back, the king found the requests submitted by the Song officials, asking for his arrest. Impressed by the emperor's largesse, the king soon pledged his allegiance.

Nan Tang, another small state, hurried to prepare a defensive war against Song. Simultaneously, the king of Nan Tang sent an envoy to Kai Feng, imploring the emperor to show mercy. Drawing his sword, Zhao Kuang-yin replied in a stern voice: "The whole China should be integrated. It is unbearable for me that somebody else acts as ruler nearby!"

Song's troops went from victory to victory in the south. During the 16 years of his reign, Zhao Kuang-yin eliminated all the challenges to Song authority and brought the south back into the imperial domain. Most notably, the majority of these conquests were accompanied by no violence towards the civilian population. From then on, the rich south became more prosperous, contributing to the national economy.

In addition to his interest in unifying China, Zhao Kuang-yin took steps to ensure that never again would someone claim power as he had, ascending to the throne by *coup d'etat*. Taking a series of measures to centralize authority, he established bureaucracy loyal to the Song house and formed a national army directly controlled by the emperor. After decades of political and military chaos, it was unimaginable how difficult recentralization would be; yet, through some flexible and pragmatic policies, Zhao Kuang-yin showed his wisdom in coping with the oncoming problems.

His former comrades did not know what the emperor had in mind when he invited them to a palace banquet. The high-ranking generals had a bit to drink before Zhao Kuang-yin let the attendants go and poured out his feelings: "It is too hard," he said, "to be an emperor. . . . I would rather be a governor." His chief officers did not understand. "In this world," Zhao Kuang-yin continued, "everybody wants to be an emperor." Shocked, the generals paled. "Your Majesty," they cried, going down on their knees, "you are the only son of the heaven. Who dares raise an objection?"

Zhao Kuang-yin went on: "Though you do not want to challenge the throne, how about your subjects? They might put the imperial yellow robe on you!" Seized with terror, the chiefs could say no more. Zhao Kuang-yin then persuaded them to renounce their military positions and return to their hometowns and enjoy their lives. In exchange, he promised to reward them with lands and riches.

The next day, all the leading generals asked for sick leave and returned to their homes. From then on, the army was directly controlled by the emperor's hand, while the local governors lost military power. In this way, Zhao Kuang-yin assured the central government's control over military power and eliminated the warlordism that had splintered China for more than half a century.

Under Zhao Kuang-yin, the administration of the whole empire was more thoroughly centralized than ever before in Chinese history. He strove for a more workable administrative structure and set up a series of organs over which he had direct, personal control. The chief-councilor's power was limited by the appointment of a vice-councilor, military commissioners, and finance commissioners, all of whom were responsible directly to the emperor. He developed the supervisory system and assigned well-behaved officials as executive censors whose power included the ability to criticize and impeach officials, including high-ranking ones. Further, he encouraged officers, and even the masses, to expose the abuse of power. When an officer disclosed information regarding some illegal acts committed by his adviser Zhao Pu, for example, Zhao Kuang-yin immediately dismissed Zhao Pu in rage.

Though Zhao Kuang-yin was not a scholar, he held intellectuals in high esteem, telling his court that "the councilor should be a scholar." In order to choose eligible civil officials, he presided over the "palace examination" in person. As a result, all the civil servants who passed the examination felt directly grateful to the emperor.

Unlike other emperors in Chinese history, who often lived secluded lives, Zhao Kuang-yin ventured from his palace as a common man, without the imperial robe. It was said that the curtains in his house were never made of silk and satins but only grey cotton. He once turned down a suggestion to decorate his sedan with gold, replying: "I can even inlay my palace with gold. But of course I cannot squander money in that way, simply because I am managing the economic life of the whole country." He often exhorted the empresses and princesses to keep away from luxury and had the reputation of usually treating his subjects with kindness and sincerity, while punishing corrupt officials severely.

The measures employed by Zhao Kuang-yin for centralization solidified the Song Dynasty and primarily put an end to the previous situation of separatist rules that had lasted for 200 years. To his successors in the Song Dynasty, his reign was considered a model. Against the historical background of his time, Zhao Kuang- yin worked to guard against internal disorder and strife, exerting a deep influence on the history of both the Song Dynasty and of China.

Further Reading

Guang-ming, Deng, ed. *History of Liao, Song, Xia, and Jin.* Chinese Encyclopedia Press, 1988: pp. 292-293.

Tuo, Tuo, ed. *The Song History.* Vol. 1-3. Zhong Hua Publishing House, 1963: pp. 1-51.

Jia-ju, Zhang. *Biography of Zhao Kuang-yin.* Jian Su: People's Publishing House, 1959.

Tang, Li. *Song Tai Zu.* Tai Bei: He Luo Press, 1978. □

Zhao Ziyang

The Chinese politician Zhao Ziyang (Zhao Xiusheng; born 1919) was premier of the People's Republic of China from 1980 to 1989 and general secretary of the Chinese Communist Party from 1987 to 1989. He championed a number of political and economic reforms but was ousted for his role in creating conditions which led to the student pro-democracy movement.

Born into a family of landlords in Huaxian County, Henan Province, in China, in 1919, Zhao Ziyang attended elementary school in his hometown and middle schools first in Kaifeng and later in Wuhan. He was married to Liang Bogi and had four sons and one daughter. Zhao joined the Communist Youth League in 1932 and became a member of the Chinese Communist Party (CCP) in 1938. During the War of Resistance Against Japan (World War II) and the civil war against the Kuomingtang (KMT), Zhao served as a local party leader at the country and prefectural levels in central China, primarily engaged in land reform.

After the CCP took over power from the KMT of Chiang Kai-shek in 1949, Zhao was transferred to South China where he served as a member of the standing committee of the South China subbureau in the Central-South China Bureau of the CCP Central Committee (1950), secretary-general of the same subbureau (1952), director of the Rural Work Department in the same subbureau (1953), and third secretary in the same subbureau (1954). In 1955 he was elected a member of the People's Council of Guangdong Province and appointed deputy party secretary of Guangdong Province. In April 1965 he became the first party secretary of Guangdong Province. Under his leadership, Guangdong was among the first provinces to return to guaranteed private plots, free rural markets, and contracting output to households after the disastrous Great Leap Forward campaign of Mao Tse-Tung.

During the Cultural Revolution spearheaded by the Red Guards, Zhao was persecuted and exiled to a factory as a laborer because of his support for "revisionist" policies. In 1971 he reappeared in China's political arena and became the party secretary of the Inner Mongolia Autonomous Region. One year later he served concurrently as chairman of the Revolutionary Committee of Inner Mongolia Autonomous Region.

In April 1972 Zhao returned to Guangdong where he was appointed vice-chairman of the Revolutionary Committee. In 1974 he was promoted to the first party secretary and chairman of the Revolutionary Committee of Guangdong Province. In Guangdong, Zhao reportedly played a crucial role in the release of Li Yi Zhe, the pseudonym of three dissident Red Guards who wrote wall posters that repudiated the theoretical justification of Mao's Cultural Revolution.

In 1976 Zhao was transferred and reassigned as first party secretary and chairman of the Revolutionary Committee of Szechwan Province, and first political commissar of Chengtu Military Region. In Szechwan, China's most populous province (more than 100 million people), Zhao championed the so called "household production responsibility system," which related peasants' performance with their remuneration and provided them with incentive for production, resulting in a big increase in grain supply.

His successful rural reform and other reform measures in Szechwan boosted his political career enormously, as he was co-opted by Deng Xiaoping into the reform camp. Zhao was elected an alternate member of the Politburo in the CCP 11th Congress in August 1977 and became a full member of the Politburo two years later. He was promoted to be vice premier in April 1980 and premier in September of the same year. After Hu Yaobang's ouster in the wake of student demonstrations in 1987, Zhao replaced Hu as CCP general secretary. As premier, Zhao traveled in numerous countries, including the United States in 1984. Two years later, like his predecessor, he was ousted for having sympathy for the students' prodemocracy movement, which reached a climax with the military assault on the students in Tiananmen Square on June 4, 1989.

Zhao was widely considered a major architect of China's economic and political reforms as well as an outstanding administrator. In addition to the household production responsibility system, a highly successful reform measure which contributed largely to the economic growth in China's rural areas, Zhao initiated and implemented the following major reform programs: decentralization of power to local governments and to state enterprises; introduction of a market-oriented economy; and relaxation of the CCP's rigid control over the government, society, mass media, mass organizations, and people.

Although Zhao's political and economic reforms gave the Chinese people more freedom and democracy and significantly improved their living standard, these measures also brought about many problems. Among them were an unprecedented skyrocketing inflation, abuse of power in local governments and enterprises, "official racketeering," corruption, and bribery. These side effects of the reforms contributed to people's widespread dissatisfaction at the government, which in turn gave rise to the pro-democracy movement in the spring of 1989. Zhao was involved in an intra-CCP power struggle and chose to support the protest movement. "At this critical juncture involving the destiny of the party and state," Zhao was accused by Premier Li Peng, his major political enemy, of having "made the mistake of supporting the turmoil and splitting the party." Because of "his unshirkable responsibilities for the development of the turmoil" and of "the serious nature and consequences of his mistake," on June 24, 1989, the 13th CCP Central Committee, decided to "dismiss him as general secretary of the Central Committee, member of the Political Bureau of the Central Committee, and first vice chairman of the Military Commission of the CCP Committee, and decided to look further into his case."

After Tiananmen Square, Zhao was replaced by Jiang Zemin as head of the Chinese Communist Party. Bao Tong, Zhao's right-hand man, was sentenced to seven years in jail for inciting counter-revolutionary activities. Zhao was officially disgraced and placed in retirement and rehabilitation (house arrest). In 1997 Tong was released from prison and Zhao, while still being rehabilitated, was reported well and playing golf regularly while under guard.

Further Reading

Additional information on Zhao Ziyang can be found in David L. Shambaugh's *The Making of a Premier: Zhao Ziyang's Provincial Career* (1984). For information on the student movement in the context of today's China see Lee Feigon's *China Rising: The Meaning of Tiananmen* (1990), and By Yi and Mark V. Thompson, *Crisis at Tiananmen: Reform and Reality in Modern China* (1990). Accounts of Ziyang during his rehabilitation can be found in *Asia Week* and similar news sources. □

Vladimir Volfovich Zhirinovsky

Vladimir Volfovich Zhirinovsky (born 1946) led the extreme nationalist Liberal Democratic Party of Russia to surprising success in the Russian parliamentary elections of December 1993.

Zhirinovsky proved himself a master of the media available to Russian politicians in the December 1993 elections. A gifted demagogue, his message of extreme nationalism struck a chord among Russians suffering and fearing the hardships and uncertainties brought about by the collapse of the Soviet empire and the transformation from a planned economy to a market economy. He won support from those most vulnerable in the transformation, and from people who wanted to make an emphatic protest of the course Russia was following. His populist style and the simple solutions he proposed came in contrast to the professorial style and approaches of many of his reformist opponents. The unexpected success of Zhirinovsky's party, the Liberal Democratic Party of Russia, was regarded by many observers inside and outside Russia as a sign that reform was unraveling.

Zhirinovsky was given to extreme positions expressed vividly, vigorously, and often outrageously. For example, he once proposed that nuclear waste be buried along the borders of the Baltic countries to poison their inhabitants. He favored a strong, even authoritarian, president for Russia and advocated a return to Russia's "natural borders," which would mean the incorporation of parts of the former Soviet Union in the Russian Federation. In his autobiography, *Last Thrust to the South,* he argues for a division of the world by the great powers that would allow Russia to acquire Iran, Turkey, and Afghanistan. Russian soldiers, he wrote, would "wash their boots in the warm water of the Indian Ocean." Many of the ills that afflicted Russia, he believed, came from the southern regions of the former Soviet Union and the countries that extend southward to the Indian Ocean. Making them a part of Russia would make Russia peaceful, prosperous, and void of ethnic conflict.

Zhirinovsky was born in 1946 in Almaty, the capital of Kazakhstan. His father, who was Jewish, died in an automobile accident before Zhirinovsky was a year old. His mother was left alone to raise Zhirinovsky and his five older brothers and sisters. He attended a Russian school in Almaty, a mostly Russian city in a republic where Russians formed a minority. He grew up resenting both his poverty and the discrimination he saw favoring the Kazakhs, whom he believed were favored over Russians in everything from grades in school to political appointments.

He went to Moscow to study Turkish at the Institute of Oriental Languages and earned a diploma with distinction. He proved to have a talent for languages and learned English, French, and German as well as Turkish. While in his final year at the university, Zhirinovsky spent eight months in Turkey as an interpreter for a delegation of engineers. But

Nikolai Ryzhkov, the chairman of Gorbachev's Council of Ministers. This was a surprising result for someone previously unknown.

He immediately declared his intention to run again and kept himself in the public eye through his sometimes incendiary remarks. In 1993 he participated in drafting the new constitution that was approved through a referendum held at the same time as the new legislature was elected.

In the December 1993 elections to the new legislature, the Federal Assembly, the Liberal Democratic Party won almost a quarter of the vote for the half of the lower house elected according to party lists, but did less well in the other half of the State Duma, which was elected by district. The party thus gained 63 of the 450 seats in the State Duma, enough to become a significant force allied to the Communist Party of Russia and other conservative forces. Zhirinovsky sought to become the speaker of the Duma, but was denied the post. Despite his strong showing in 1993, Zhirinovsky's often boorish behavior alienated him from many of his supporters. After the LDPR lost 13 seats in the 1995 parliamentary elections Zhirinovsky himself placed only fifth in a field of ten contenders in the preliminary elections for president in 1996. Questioning the fairness of the existing election processes, Zhirinovsky, refused, to vote for any candidate that year indicating they were unsuitable for the task. He then vowed to run again, and win, future elections.

Further Reading

Zhirinovsky's autobiography, (*The Final March South*) has not yet been published in English however, David Remnick's *Lenin's Tomb* (1993) provides a vivid description of the Soviet Union as it collapsed. John Dunlop's *The Rise of Russia and the Fall of the Soviet Empire* (1993) is a well-researched account of the Soviet collapse that deals specifically with the rise of nationalist movements. Vladimir Kartsen's *!Zhirinovsky! An insider's account of Yeltsin's chief rival* (1995) provides a first hand look at the man himself. Authoritative and accessible analyses of recent events in Russia and Russian foreign policy can be found in the research reports of Radio Free Europe/ Radio Liberty (RFE/RL). Among the many press reports see "Comrade Zhirinovsky's Shadowy Past" in *Parade Magazine* (January 30, 1994), Lee Hockstader's "How Russia's Zhirinovsky Rose" in *The Washington Post* (March 6, 1994), Michael Specter's "Zhirinovsky and the Motherland" in *New York Times Magazine* (June 19, 1994), Arshad Mohammed, "Zhirinovsky calls polls unfair vows return," *Reuters* (July 7, 1997) and George Zarycky's, "A primer on Russian elections," *Freedom Review* (May 1, 1996). □

he left after the police arrested him for distributing badges with Soviet symbols. This was his second trip abroad, his first outside the Soviet bloc.

Following graduation Zhirinovsky served for two years in the army as a political officer in Tbilisi, Georgia. He then returned to Moscow to work in the International Relations Section of the Soviet Committee for the Defense of Peace. In 1975 he began to work with foreign students at the Higher School of the Trade Union Movement in the office of the dean. Both jobs gave him the opportunity to work extensively with foreigners who came to Moscow.

After he earned a law degree by taking evening courses at the Law Faculty of Moscow State University, he worked at the Foreign Law Collegium under the Moscow City Bar and then as a legal consultant at the Mir Publishing House. He also served as a legal adviser to Shalom, a Jewish cultural organization sponsored by the Soviet Government.

His political career began in 1987 with membership in the informal group Fakel. In December 1989 he joined the Democratic Union, a radical group given to staging demonstrations and challenging the authorities. He and others left to found the Liberal Democratic Party in March 1990. The following April the Liberal Democratic Party became the first political party to be officially registered after the constitution of the U.S.S.R. was amended to end the monopoly enjoyed by the Communist Party.

He ran for president of Russia in June 1991 and received 6.2 million votes, almost 8 percent of the total, which made him third in the race, behind Boris Yeltsin and

Todor Zhivkov

Todor Zhivkov (born 1911) was the leader of the Bulgarian Communist Party and the head of the Bulgarian government for 35 years, from 1954 to 1989.

odor Zhivkov was born on September 7, 1911, in the village of Pravets, 40 miles northeast of Sofia, in the Balkan mountains of Bulgaria. His father, a poor peasant, was a leather worker in Gabrovo. Zhivkov became a printer's apprentice at the State Printing Office in Sofia, attending its trade school from 1929 to 1932. The printing office was a traditional stronghold of socialist-minded workers, and Georgi Dimitrov, a leader of the Bulgarian Communist Party, had begun his career as a labor organizer there. Zhivkov fell in with the Communists, becoming a member of the party's youth league in 1930. He joined the party itself in 1932. In the next two years he rose to secretary of the party's committee for the Third Urban District of Sofia.

After an aborted uprising in 1923, the Communist Party had gone underground and its leaders, including Dimitrov, Vasil Kolarov, and others fled to the Soviet Union. The Bulgarian party was marked by inner turmoil, and Zhivkov joined a faction known as the Left Sectarians, who rejected the Soviet-sanctioned policies of the party's exiled leaders. When the Left Sectarians were purged in 1935 by emissaries from Moscow, Zhivkov was one of the victims. He remained on the political sidelines through the 1930s, serving as a conscript in the paramilitary Labor Service. He married Mara Maleeva, a physician and fellow activist, and kept active in public reading clubs (*chitalishta*) wherever they lived, occasionally directing plays and acting in them.

Rise to Power

The German invasion of the Soviet Union in 1941 brought unity among Communists worldwide. Zhivkov re-

turned to his job as the party's district secretary in Sofia. As Soviet troops beat back the Germans and began advancing westward, the party hoped to engineer an uprising when the Red Army came to Bulgaria's borders. Zhivkov was dispatched by party insurgent commanders to his native mountainous area to spur on the partisan movement there. He led a detachment called Chavdar (after a 16th-century Bulgarian hero who fought the Turks), which grew in size as the Red Army came closer. In April 1944 the party proclaimed itself the First Bulgarian Partisan Brigade, with Zhivkov as its political commissar, communicating with the command in Sofia. The Chavdar brigade became the main arm of the party leaders in Sofia for sabotage, raids, and intimidation around the capital.

When the time came to seize power, Zhivkov was put in charge of the operation in Sofia. During the night of September 8, 1944, he led the partisans in capturing, without bloodshed, the Ministry of War, arresting the ministers and seizing the communications system. As the partisans became the new militia, Zhivkov was appointed its political chief of staff and directed the round-up and execution of thousands of enemies of Communism in Bulgaria. According to official figures, 12,000 people were delivered to people's tribunals, while untold numbers disappeared without a trial.

Zhivkov was rewarded by being named a non-voting member of the party's central committee in 1945. In 1948 he became first secretary of the party's committee for Sofia, equivalent to mayor, and a full member of the central committee. He became a member of the Politboro, the party's ruling group, in 1950. Zhivkov's rise was helped by the removal and execution in 1949 of the party's chief secretary, Traicho Kostov, on charges, later declared false, of conspiring with party enemies abroad.

The emergence of Nikita Khrushchev as the leader of the Soviet Union, replacing Joseph Stalin, also helped Zhivkov reach the top in Bulgaria. More pragmatic than dogmatic, Zhivkov adapted more readily than his rivals to the new, more moderate line from Moscow. In 1954 he became first secretary, the top post in the leadership, and in April 1956 he ousted the arch-Stalinist Vulko Chervenkov from the premiership and charted a Khrushchev-like policy known as the April Line. However, the new premier, Anton Iugov, emerged as the leader of a faction seeking to make the Council of Ministers, rather than the party secretariat, the center of authority. Zhivkov eliminated the threat in 1962 by ousting Iugov and his faction and making himself head of the government as well as of the party.

Follower of Soviets

During his lengthy reign, Zhivkov's main policy was to follow the Soviet model. He often stated that loyalty to the Soviet Union was the test of a Bulgarian's patriotism. He pursued increasing integration with the Soviet economy and resisted the economic experimentation of neighboring Hungary. In cultural affairs he bought off the creative intelligentsia to head off dissent. There were few major crises during his time in power except for one military plot, several instances of terrorism, and occasional outbursts of dissent.

Opposition to Zhivkov and his policies existed but rarely surfaced openly until the late 1980s. Zhivkov's major innovation was the Council of State, established by the new constitution of 1971 to formulate all policy. At that time he resigned as premier to become president of that council.

By 1985 Bulgaria was conducting 57 percent of its foreign trade with the Soviet Union, mainly sending grain, and it owed the Soviets $7.5 billion. When Mikhail Gorbachev took power in the Soviet Union and instituted the reforms known as *perestroika,* Zhivkov followed suit in Bulgaria, loosening the hold of government on the economy and smoothing the way for joint ventures with foreign companies.

In 1984 Zhivkov launched a ruthless campaign to force Bulgarian's Turks, an ethnic minority of one million people, to change their names. In May 1989, Zhivkov encouraged a mass exodus of Turks, and about 310,000 fled before Turkey closed its border. The loss of so many people infuriated Peter Mladenov, Bulgaria's foreign minister, and in October he resigned, accusing Zhivkov of ruining Bulgaria's reputation and its economy. After a trip to Moscow, Mladenov returned. On the same day the Berlin Wall fell, symbolizing the end of the Cold War, Mladenov won a vote at a Bulgarian Politburo meeting, forcing Zhivkov to resign in a bloodless coup. Mladenov became party leader. In elections in 1990, the Communist Party, renamed the Bulgarian Socialist Party, remained in power.

Zhivkov was charged with corruption and embezzlement and placed under house arrest in Sofia. He denied responsibility for any purges or crimes committed under his rule. In an interview with the *New York Times* in 1990, Zhivkov stated that Bulgaria should embrace capitalism and the United States. The staunch Soviet hard-liner said: "If I had to do it all over again, I would not even be a Communist."

Further Reading

The official biography issued by the party is *Todor Zhivkov: biografichen ocherk* (Sofia, 1981). There is a short biography in English in *Leaders of the Communist World,* edited by R. Swearingen (1971). *Todor Zhivkov: Statesman and Builder of New Bulgaria* (1982) in the "Leaders of the World" series of Pergamon Press contains, in addition to his speeches and statements, a short autobiography, chronology of his life, and list of his works in various languages. G. Markov, *The Truth That Killed* (1984), offers rare personal observations. Useful for the context is J. D. Bell, *The Bulgarian Communist Party from Blagoev to Zhivkov* (1985). □

Georgi Konstantinovich Zhukov

Georgi Konstantinovich Zhukov (1896-1974) was the Soviet Union's most prominent military leader during World War II. In the 1950s he played a crucial role in Bolshevik party politics.

Georgi Zhukov was born to a peasant family in Kaluga Province, where he was appapprenticed in the fur trade at the age of eleven. Then, in 1915, he was conscripted into the Imperial Army, serving well enough to merit a promotion to the rank of noncommissioned officer. Nevertheless, he was cautious enough to change sides as soon as the Russian Revolution ended, entering the Red Army in 1918, and the Communist Party the following year.

A zealous student of military history and tactics, he distinguished himself during the Russian Civil War (1918-1920), and continued to carry out his responsibilities with the same conscientiousness after he was posted to the Belorussian Military District during the 1920s. Having proved himself to be an impressive officer, he was sent to the Frunze Military Academy, from which he graduated in 1931. Thereafter, when sent back to the Belorussian Military District, he advanced rapidly under the sponsorship of Gen. Semyon K. Timoshenko, under whom he had served in the civil war. Stalin's purges of military leaders in 1937-1938 passed Zhukov by, and he was sent to the Far East, where he acquitted himself well in border skirmishes with sizable Japanese forces.

Zhukov's skill impressed Joseph Stalin, and he was chosen over several senior generals in early 1941 to become chief of the general staff. When the Germans invaded the Soviet Union that year, Zhukov quickly proved his merit, first racing to Leningrad in September to halt the German threat and then returning to save Moscow from almost certain German capture. He was promoted to first deputy commander in chief, an office second only to Stalin's, then, in 1943 he was named a marshal of the Soviet Union.

It was generally agreed that Zhukov was a difficult leader. Many of his fellow generals found him arrogant and high-handed, and ruthless enough to sacrifice thousands of military lives to achieve success. However, everyone acknowledged that his military feats were astounding. In 1943, with the success of his armor battle at Kursk, even the German military effort was blunted. Despite the rivalry of other marshals, notably Ivan Konev, Zhukov kept the confidence of Stalin, who assigned him the task of seizing Berlin. He reluctantly summoned assistance from Konev when German resistance stiffened, but on May 8, 1945, he reached the pinnacle of his military career when he accepted the German surrender.

The showers of praise that Zhukov received from a grateful Russian public infuriated Stalin, who swiftly set out to claim all military victories as his own by cutting the General down to size. Starting in 1946, Zhukov received a series of demotions culminating in an obscure command in the Urals Military District.

However, this exile proved to be a relatively short one. Within 24 hours of Stalin's death in March 1953, Zhukov began a new political ascendancy. He was appointed Deputy Minister of Defense, and soon afterward he took his place as a full member of the Central Committee. Here he earned even greater prominence, especially after Russians realized that he had been instrumental in the arrest of

Lavrenty Beria, the secret-police chief who was executed shortly after Stalin's death in punishment for the thousands of political executions he had performed.

In 1955 Zhukov became Minister of Defense, and he attended the summit meeting that year in Geneva. In February 1956, at the Twentieth Party Congress, Zhukov's popularity and power were obvious—perhaps too obvious—and all factions openly courted him. There is considerable reason to believe that it was his insistence that forced Russian military intervention in Hungary in November 1956, and it is certain that his support enabled Nikita Khrushchev to withstand the challenge of the "antiparty" faction of Georgi Malenkov and Vyacheslav Molotov in 1957.

Once that challenge was met, Zhukov's power became a matter of concern to the party leadership. In October 1957, while he was on a goodwill tour of Albania, he was removed from office and publicly denounced by his own subordinates and by presumed supporters, for "anti-Leninist acts." He was forced to retire, living by turns in a small Moscow apartment and a little countryside dacha, although the Soviet leadership allowed him an occasional public appearance, such as at the twentieth anniversary of the Nazi surrender in May 1965.

By this time, however, the tide was beginning to turn in Zhukov's favor yet again. Krushchev himself was forced to retire, and now lived in a little apartment in the same building as Zhukov. So he was not on hand, in 1966, to watch as Zhukov was feted at the 25th anniversary of the victory against the Germans at Moscow.

It was a great celebration, and he enjoyed it as a fast-aging man who now spent most of his time writing his memoirs. In 1971, after intense scrutiny by Party officials, they were published in the West. Just three years later Zhukov died at age 77, receiving the accolade of a highly complimentary obituary signed by Leonid I. Brezhnev, Aleksei Kosygin and Nikolai Podgorny.

Further Reading

The *Memoirs of Marshal Zhukov* (1969; trans. 1971) is available. Portions of his memoirs were published as *Marshal Zhukov's Greatest Battles,* edited and introduced by Harrison E. Salisbury (trans. 1969). Otto Preston Chaney, Jr., *Zhukov* (1971), is an excellent study, and the bibliography is indispensable for those interested in Soviet military history. A good treatment of Zhukov is the biographical essay by Seweryn Bialer in George W. Simmonds, ed., *Soviet Leaders* (1967). Zhukov also figures prominently in Alexander Werth, *Russia at War, 1941-45* (1964), and Roman Kolkowicz, *The Soviet Military and the Communist Party* (1967). *New York Times Biographical Edition* (June, 1974). □

Mohammad Zia ul-Haq

Mohammad Zia ul-Haq (1924-1988), an army officer, was president of Pakistan from 1978 until his death in an air crash that was a suspected assassina-tion. **He sustained a military government while strengthening Islamic institutions and practices.**

Mohammad Zia ul-Hag was born into a middle-class family on August 12, 1924, at Jullunder in East Pubjab, India. After completing his early education at home, he enrolled at St. Stephen's College in New Delhi, India. Choosing a career in the British army, he joined the Royal Indian Military Academy in Dehra Dun and then served with British troops in Burma, Malaysia and Indonesia during the latter part of World War II.

After the partition of India into India and Pakistan in 1947, Zia joined the Pakistani army. In 1955 he graduated from the Command Staff College in Quetta, where he later served as an instructor. He attended two military schools in the United States, first at Fort Knox, KY, in 1959, and then the U.S. Command and General Staff School at Fort Leavenworth, KS, in 1963. Zia was on active duty in Kashmir during the 1965 war between India and Pakistan, and after it he was promoted to colonel. In 1969 he was made a brigadier, and for two years he was adviser to the Royal Jordanian Army in their conflict with Palestinian guerrillas.

Leader of Coup

Under the government of Prime Minister Z.A. Bhutto, Zia advanced rapidly within the army ranks. In 1975 he was promoted to lieutenant-general and in 1976 was appointed

as army chief of staff, chosen over several more senior officers. Because the military had been so prominent in Pakistan's politics, Bhutto apparently wanted a less qualified officer with little political ambition as chief of staff. But Bhutto underestimated Zia. Accusations by opposition leaders that the prime minister's party had manipulated the results of the March 1977 parliamentary elections led to widespread public demonstrations and violence. The military, headed by Zia, stepped in on July 5, 1977, to impose martial law and deposed Bhutto in a bloodless coup.

Zia took office as chief martial law administrator and said his sole purpose was to hold "free and fair" elections as early as possible. Instead, he suspended the 1973 constitution, dissolved the National Assembly, and banned political activity. Declaring himself president in 1978, Zia abandoned his plan for elections for fear that Bhutto would return to power and seek revenge. Zia instead began a purge of politicians associated with Bhutto's Pakistan People's Party. Bhutto was implicated in a case concerning the assassination of a political opponent's father, and in April 1979, despite international protests, Zia had him executed.

Islamic Policies

Bhutto's execution made Zia unpopular, the economy was in trouble, and in November 1979 Islamic extremists burned the American embassy in Islamabad. Zia's days seemed numbered, but on Christmas Eve 1979 the Soviet Union invaded Afghanistan, and the United States reversed its long opposition to Pakistan and began aiding Zia's regime to help it fend off Soviet agression.

Zia continued to suppress political activity, saying the country was not ready to return to democracy. He embarked on a program of strengthening Pakistan's economy and reforming social, economic, and political institutions in accordance with Islamic precepts. His government encouraged foreign and domestic investment that had been frightened off by nationalization and threats of government takeovers during the Bhutto years. Islamic penal and fiscal injunctions were incorporated into the legal system. Zia's Islamization program won him the backing of an important fundamentalist party and tempered criticism of his military regime. Zia skillfully coopted and suppressed a divided opposition and outmaneuvered potential challengers within the military. He had hundreds of dissidents arrested and imprisoned. Many were publicly flogged in accord with Islamic law.

Soviet intervention in Afghanistan resulted in a revival of U.S. strategic interests in the region and in an economic and military aid package of $3.2 billion to Pakistan. During the conflict, Zia helped smuggle U.S. supplies to the Soviet-backed Afghan rebels and allowed them to operate training bases in Pakistan. He offered shelter to three million Afghan refugees. But the influx of Afghans exacerbated ethnic and regional conflicts and placed serious new burdens on the economy.

Zia strived to maintain Pakistan's good relations with other Arab countries and China. He assumed a conciliatory stance towards India, proposing normalized relations and a non-aggression pact to end decades of hostility. But in the

mid-1980s Indian President Rajiv Gandhi accused Zia of stirring up unrest among Sikhs, a religious sect pushing for independence in the Indian state of Punjab, bordering Pakistan.

In December 1984 Zia abruptly called for a referendum to determine support for his Islamization policies. He declared that public criticism or advocacy of a boycott of the referendum was a punishable offense. The referendum passed overwhelmingly, and Zia considered it a mandate to remain as president for another five years. in March 1985, elections for a national assembly took place, but major political parties were not allowed to participate. Announced as a step towards returning the country to civilian rule, the elections served mainly to legitimize Zia's government. Zia had engineered constitutional changes which increased his presidential powers and permitted him to dissolve the National Assembly at his discretion. Zia also assumed the authority to appoint a prime minister from among the assembly's elected members.

Return of Opposition

In 1986 Benazir Bhutto, daughter of the executed president, returned to Pakistan after two years of self-imposed exile and started to organize the opposition. Prime Minister Mohammed Khan Junejo led efforts to exert more civilian control over the military. In May 1988, Zia fired Junejo and his 33-member cabinet and dissolved the National Assembly. Bhutto declared that her Pakistan People's Party was "ready to go to the people."

On August 17, 1988, Zia was on a secret mission to a desert area in eastern Pakistan, meeting U.S. Ambassador Arnold Raphel for a demonstration of the M-1 Abrams tank. With an American military attache and 27 Pakistani advisors, Zia and Raphel boarded a C-130 plane to return to the capital. Within minutes after takeoff, it exploded, killing everyone aboard. The crash was suspicious. But Pakistani and American investigators failed to confirm the plane had been bombed. Experts speculated about which of Zia's many enemies might have assassinated him. The Soviet Union, the government of India, Bhutto's People Party and Zia's own military all came under suspicion, but no culprit was ever found. After Zia's death, democracy was restored to Pakistan and Benazir Bhutto, the daughter of the leader whom Zia had executed, was elected prime minister in November 1988.

Further Reading

Contemporary Pakistan: Politics, Economy and Society (1980), edited by Manzooruddin Ahmed, provides an overview of the 1977 coup and Zia's government. "Pakistan in 1982: Holding On" by Marvin G. Weinbaum and Stephen P. Cohen in *Asian Survey* (February 1983) describes the martial law system and Zia's handling of the government opposition and the economy. *The Pakistan Army* (1984) by Stephen P. Cohen offers a comprehensive analysis of Zia's policies and the problems confronting him. "Pakistan in 1984: Digging In" by William Richter in *Asian Survey* (February 1985) provides a useful discussion of Zia's policies. "Islamization and Social Policy in Pakistan: The Constitutional Crisis and the Status of Women" by J. Henry Korson and Michelle Mashielle in *Asian Survey*

(June 1985) is helpful in understanding Zia's Islamization policies and their implications. "Death in the Skies" by Michael Serrill in *Time* (August 29, 1988) discusses Zia's death and possible suspects. ☐

Ziaur Rahman

Bangladesh president Ziaur Rahman, popularly known as Zia (1936-1981), succeeded to a significant extent in bringing political and economic stability to the new nation following a period of great disruption.

Mansur Rahman, father of Ziaur Rahman, was a chemist working for the government of India stationed in Calcutta. Ziaur Rahman was born there January 19, 1936. When Calcutta became the target of Japanese air strikes in 1940, like many urban Bengali families with rural links Mansur Rahman sent his family to his ancestral home in the small town of Bogra in northern Bengal. After Germany surrendered and the Japanese threat to Calcutta diminished, Mansur Rahman brought his family back and enrolled Zia in one of the leading boys schools of Calcutta—Hare School—where Zia studied until the independence and partition of India in 1947. On August 14, 1947, Mansur Rahman, like many Muslims working for the old British government of India, exercised his option to work for the new state of Pakistan and moved to Karachi, the first capital of Pakistan.

Zia's character and style as one of the most effective leaders in the underdeveloped world was largely shaped by the issues, attitudes, and events during his years at Hare School. Subhas Bose, a former president of the All-India Congress Party, and Mohandas K. Gandhi were the two charismatic leaders of India whose lives baffled the young students. For trying to use the Japanese to force the British out of India, Bose was regarded a hero by the students, but the British and their supporters in India considered him a traitor for his collaboration with the Japanese. To most of the Hare School boys treason and patriotism did not seem to make much sense. Nor did Gandhi's open support of India's involvement in British war efforts clarify the appropriate role of India's leaders. What dismayed many students, particularly Ziaur Rahman, most was the inability of the authority figures—teachers, parents, and leaders—to clarify the issues or to help achieve a consensus in regard to what was a just policy.

After the war the political situation became even more amorphous. Gandhi's Congress Party and Muhammad A. Jinnah's Muslim League Party, representing the two main communities of India—Hindu and Muslim—failed to come to an agreement about sharing power in the future independent republic of India. When Syed Ahmed's two-nation theory became a reality after the referenda of 1946 which ensured the division of India the life of Muslim boys in Hare School became almost intolerable. Having lost faith in mutual cooperation and sharing as means to diffuse tension

and resolve conflicts, Zia took it upon himself to justify the impending creation of Pakistan and, in the process, often became engaged in fist fights. An otherwise reserved and somewhat introverted boy of 11 often took on older school bullies and beat them.

The Making of a Reformer

Communal conflicts, political uncertainty, and family dislocation convinced Zia of the need for changes which the leaders seemed to be unable to bring about. During his later schooling in Karachi's D.J. College and the Pakistan Military Academy at Kakul he was struck by the economic disparities between the Bengali East Pakistan and non-Bengali West Pakistan that resulted in inequities and deprivations being suffered by East Pakistani Bengalis.

Graduating from the Pakistan Military Academy in 1955 in the top ten percent of his class, Zia went to East Pakistan on a short visit and was amazed by the negative attitude of the Bengali middle class towards the military, which consumed a large chunk of the country's resources. The low representation of the Bengalis in the military was largely due to discrimination, but Zia felt that the Bengali attitude towards the military perhaps prevented promising young Bengalis from seeking military careers. As a Bengali army officer he became a staunch advocate of military careers for Bengali youth. Zia argued that Bengali attitudes would change when they were in a position to share the resources and power of the military which was traditionally enjoyed by West Pakistanis, particularly those from the Punjab and Northwest Frontier provinces. Ayub Khan's highly successful military rule from 1958 to 1968 further convinced Zia of the need for a fundamental change in the Bengali attitude towards the military. During that period Zia offered a role model for Bengali youth, excelling in his army career both as a field commander in the Indo-Pakistani War of 1965 and later as an instructor of the Pakistan Military Academy. He was instrumental in raising two battalions manned largely by Bengalis, called the 8th and 9th Bengals. In the late 1960s he was promoted to major. After serving in Pakistani military intelligence he was posted as second-in-command of the 8th Bengal battalion in Jaidebpur, near Dhaka, and later moved to Chittagong with his battalion.

Bangladesh Becomes Independent

In late March 1971 Zia became aware of the resolve of the Pakistani military to crush the nascent Bengali autonomy movement, starting with disarming and selectively eliminating Bengali officers and men of the armed forces in East Pakistan. On March 24 he preempted the Pakistani military move in Chittagong and three days later unilaterally declared the independence of East Pakistan as the new nation of Bangladesh. A nine month war followed until independence was fully established on December 16, 1971. Sheik Mujibur Rahman returned from a Pakistani jail to take over the new government. Zia was appointed deputy chief of staff of the army, making an officer who was junior to him (same class) his boss. Quietly but determinately Zia bided time.

The opportunity came when Sheik Mujib was over-thrown and killed in 1975 by a handful of junior officers who immediately chose Zia as the new chief of staff. Within three months two more coups took place, one by right-wing military officers headed by Brigadier Khaled Moshar-raf and the other by privates who had received support from the Jatio Samaj Tantrik Dal—a leftist political party (which Zia later suppressed). Uninvolved in both coups, Zia emerged as the most dependable military leader and one who could perhaps bring stability to an unstable nation. With most potential opposition dissipated, Zia took over the government of Bangladesh.

Zia succeeded to a great extent in ushering in political and economic stability to Bangladesh through three stages. First, he used moderate and left-leaning groups and their leaders to neutralize the strength of the radicals who were insisting on bringing about fundamental changes to Bengali society through revolution, if necessary. Second, he legiti-mized his power through a referendum (1977), local elec-tions (1977), a presidential election (1978), and a parliamentary election (1979). Except in the local elections of 1977, Zia and the candidates of his newly created politi-cal party—Bangladesh Nationalist Party—won landslide electoral victories.

By 1980 Zia made a complete transformation from a military man to a charismatic, populist political leader, en-joying the full confidence of the vast majority of Bangla-deshis. During this time he embarked on the last stage of bringing about national stability. His three-pronged peace-ful revolution to achieve self-sufficiency in food, full liter-acy, and zero population growth signalled an era of hope for the new nation. He instinctively realized that without global cooperation his peaceful revolution could be replaced by a bloody revolution. Perhaps for this reason Zia continuously sought cooperation not only from developed countries, through the North-South dialogue, but also from other less developed countries through the non-aligned movement. In fact, it was Zia who first conceptualized a possible regional cooperation among seven countries of South Asia and took the initiative to formally propose a plan for the South Asia Regional Cooperation in 1980, which culminated as a co-operation movement through an agreement between the seven countries in 1983.

Through Zia's "open arms" policy the traditional factionalism of Bengali politics was contained and a bal-ance between opposing views and camps in civilian and military vested interests was struck, at least for the time being. But personal rivalries coupled with the perception of injustice by one of his trusted lieutenants, Major General Abul Manzoor, abruptly ended Zia's presidency. On the early morning of May 31, 1981, in the city of Cittagong, Zia was assassinated in a coup led by Manzoor. After several months of turmoil General Hossain Mohammad Ershad (born 1930) took over the government.

Further Reading

Baxter, Craig *Bangladesh: A New Nation in an Old Setting* (1984) and Zillur R. Khan, *Leadership in the Least Developed Nation:*

Bangladesh (1983) provide additional information on Zia as the leader of Bangladesh. □

Florenz Ziegfeld

Florenz Ziegfeld (1869-1932) developed the Ameri-can musical revue and became a dominant force in musical theater in the early 20th century.

F
lorenz Ziegfeld was born in Chicago, Ill., on March 21, 1869. His father was a German musician of the old school who eventually became president of the Chicago Musical College. Young "Flo" found this dignified life too quiet. In his first venture into show business he managed Sandow, the strong man of the World's Colum-bian Exposition, in 1893. He next turned to theatrical man-agement. In London in the 1890s he met the French beauty Anna Held and placed her under contract. Recognizing the American public's insatiable urge to know about the private lives of stars, he promoted Held into national attention with press releases describing her milk baths. He married her in 1897; they were divorced in 1913.

Ziegfeld's early musical productions enjoyed modest success; more important, he was perfecting his style. In 1906 *The Parisian Model* featured the beautiful girls and intricate though precise musical numbers that made him famous. That summer he visited Paris, and the Folies-Bergère became the model for his annual *Ziegfeld Follies*. Recognizing that the risqué elements of the Folies would be unacceptable in the United States, Ziegfeld substituted more displays of beautiful girls.

Few realized the future of the *Ziegfeld Follies* when it first opened in July 1907. Presented on the New York The-ater roof, the *Follies* was an immediate success, and in Sep-tember Ziegfeld moved it indoors. By 1910 others were beginning to copy his format, but no other revues had the precision, discipline, and homogeneity of the *Ziegfeld Follies*.

In 1915 Ziegfeld added an important element when he hired Joseph Urban as designer. Urban's sense of spectacle was perfectly suited to the Ziegfeld idea—beautiful girls, intricate numbers, lavish and artistic design. The Ziegfeld pattern was completed with stars: Fannie Brice, Marilyn Miller, Bert Williams, W. C. Fields, Eddie Cantor, Gilda Grey, Gallagher and Shean, and Will Rogers were under contract at one time or another. Ziegfeld had a sharp eye for talent. The first *Follies* had cost only $13,000 to produce; the preproduction costs of the 1927 *Follies* totaled nearly $300,000.

While continuing the *Follies,* Ziegfeld returned to mu-sical comedy in 1920. Among his hits were *Sally* (1920), *Show Boat* and *Rio Rita* (both 1927), and *Bitter Sweet* (1929). Ziegfeld abandoned the *Follies* in 1927; by the time he returned to it in 1931, the magic was gone. He had lost some of his touch, and the mood of the country, deep in the

Great Depression, had changed. He died on July 22, 1932, in Hollywood, Calif.

Further Reading

No definitive work on Ziegfeld has appeared, but Cecil Smith, *Musical Comedy in America* (1950), contains information about his career.

Additional Sources

Ziegfeld, Richard E., *The Ziegfeld touch: the life and times of Florenz Ziegfeld, Jr.,* New York: H.N. Abrams, 1993. □

Bernd Alois Zimmermann

The German composer Bernd Alois Zimmermann (1918-1970) was one of the few musicians to remain independent of various 20th-century musical doctrines and to establish an individual style of composition.

Bernd Alois Zimmermann was born in Bliesheim, near Cologne, just as World War I was ending in 1918. His Catholic, classical education was interrupted when he was conscripted into the German army during World War II. In a private, unpublished letter written during this period he stated that he had never actually discharged a weapon at another person all the time he was a soldier. Wounded early in the war, he was able to resume his education in 1942. While a student, Zimmermann supported himself by playing in dance bands. In Darmstadt in 1949-1950 he abandoned a musicological dissertation on the use of the fugue in modern music in order to pursue a career as a composer.

Throughout his adult career Zimmermann earned his livelihood as a professor of composition and wrote, in addition to his art music, many commercial scores for radio, film, and the stage. His academic employment afforded him the means to live but interfered with his creative work. Indeed, Zimmermann's most productive periods as a composer occurred when he was able to obtain sabbaticals from his academic appointments. His relative independence from such fashionable, avant-garde approaches to composition as serialism and aleatory music contributed to his inability to become independently established as a composer. In fact, Zimmermann's work was known only to musicians until after his death, when a larger general audience for his music began to grow.

Zimmermann's Catholic education and Christian faith were influential in his compositions and led to the use of ecclesiastical references and concepts in his music. Like St. Augustine, Zimmermann believed in the simultaneity of past, present, and future as an eternal moment in the mind of God. Therefore, he developed a technique of quoting past masters in his own modern compositions: his favorites included Bach, Mozart, and Debussy. These quotations are always notated in Zimmermann's scores but may not be noticeable to the listener because Zimmermann so changed both the quotations and the contexts in which they were used. These quotations were meant to register Zimmermann's participation in an eternally present music, even though the material from the past, a melody or rhythm or some other musical structure, might be seamlessly woven into Zimmermann's own more expressionistic or chromatic or atonal context. Zimmermann's methods of quotation developed into a form of collage, that technique used in the visual arts whereby a seemingly random group of images and objects is combined. The composer would put together elements from different periods in music history and from different musical cultures and make them a part of his own unified musical compositions.

Zimmermann's compositions are at once starkly original and profoundly involved with music history. He assimilated music of the past with music of the present and non-European musics of the past with Western art-music. His music can be very compressed: for example, in *Stille und Umkehr* (1970) only four or five instruments in a 42-piece ensemble ever play simultaneously. At other times his music can seem quite spontaneous. His associates saw these opposite tendencies as the expression of the composer's complex personality, which seemed to combine both monastic and Dionysian traits.

Despite his religious faith and his discipline, Zimmermann wrote music which expressed a deep unhappiness. His pacifism and view of the world wars characteristic of his times are reflected in his opera *Die Soldaten,* often considered to be the most significant German work in that genre since those by Alban Berg. In 1967-1969, troubled by poor eyesight and preoccupied with death, Zimmermann composed *Requiem für einen jungen Dichter,* which recapitulated European history during the composer's lifetime, incorporating excerpts from political speeches and the writings of poets who had committed suicide. Zimmermann himself committed suicide in Königsberg in 1970. Since that time a number of conductors and performers have presented his music to a general audience that continues to grow and to develop an interest in the composer's work.

Further Reading

Articles on Bernd Zimmermann appear in *The New Grove Dictionary of Music and Musicians* (London, 1980) and in *Baker's Biographical Dictionary,* 6th edition (1978). Zimmermann himself was the author of *Intervall und Zeit* (1974). The composer has been the subject of the following articles and books: A. Porter, "Musical events," *The New Yorker* (February 12, 1979); W. Gruhn, "Integrale Komposition: zu Bernd Alois Zimmermanns Pluralismus-Begriff," in *Archiv für Musikwissenschaft* (1983); *The New Yorker* (March 28, 1983); Andreas von Imhoff, *Untersuchungen zum Klavierwerk Bernd Alois Zimmermanns* (Regensburg, 1976); and Clemens Kühn, Die *Orchesterwerke Bernd Alois Zimmermanns* (Hamburg, 1978). □

Johann Baptist and Domenikus Zimmermann

The work of the German stuccoworker and painter Johann Baptist Zimmermann (1680-1758) and his architect brother, Domenikus Zimmermann (1685-1766), epitomizes the Bavarian rococo style. Their masterpiece is the church of Die Wies.

Both the Zimmermann brothers were born at Gaispoint near Wessobrun, Johann Baptist on Jan. 3, 1680, and Domenikus on June 30, 1685. The region was famous for its artisans who worked in colored stucco made in imitation of marble (*Stuckmarmor* or *stucco lustro*), and the brothers were trained in this craft at the abbey of Wessobrun. Domenikus also became a master mason, while Johann Baptist became a fresco painter after studying in Augsburg, the leading center for artistic training of the day. They practiced extensively as stucco designers and stuccoworkers, although after 1724 Domenikus dedicated himself almost exclusively to architecture and Johann Baptist concentrated more and more on fresco painting.

Outstanding among the churches designed by Domenikus are the pilgrimage churches at Steinhausen (1727-1731) and Günzburg (1736-1741), where he worked on the perennial problem of combining a central-plan church with a longitudinal one. He executed an oval nave surrounded by arcades that provide an ambulatory in the one; the choir extends beyond the nave in the form of a transverse oval in the other. These churches were designed so that the processions of devout pilgrims could move around without interference. At Steinhausen the pale pastel interior is brilliantly lighted by large windows and is richly, but sparingly, decorated with rocaille ornament of supreme craftsmanship and fantastic inventiveness. The whole nave is topped with a brightly colored fresco by Johann Baptist.

The collaboration of the Zimmermanns culminated in the church of Die Wies (1745-1754), an isolated little pilgrimage church in the middle of a forest clearing not far from Steingaden in Upper Bavaria. It is one of the greatest achievements of the Bavarian rococo. There Domenikus used, amalgamated into a dazzling unity, the ideas he had worked out in his other two oval churches. The white nave with its touches of gold, the richly colored sanctuary, and particularly the fantastic ornament and the gaily colored ceiling fresco (1750) by Johann Baptist make Die Wies an unforgettable experience. It is Domenikus's masterpiece, from which he apparently could not tear himself away, for he lived at Wies for the rest of his life and died there on Nov. 16, 1766.

Johann Baptist also produced many works independently. After his appointment to the court at Munich in 1720, he worked with the court architects Joseph Effner and François Cuvilliés on the fresco decoration of the palace at Schleissheim and in 1726 at Nymphenburg and in the Residenz, Munich. From 1734 on he worked under Cuvilliés at the Amalienburg, creating some of his finest stucco ornament for its interior. Johann Baptist also produced frescoes for the churches at Vilgertshofen (1734), Berg am Laim (1739-1744), and Dietramszell (1744). He decorated the church of St. Peter, Munich (1753-1756); the churches at Andechs (1754) and Schäftlarn (1754-1756); the ceiling of the Residenz Theater (1752-1753; the only part of the theater destroyed in World War II); and the ceiling of the Great Hall at Nymphenburg Palace (1756-1757), where he also designed some of his most effervescent ornament. He died in February 1758 in Munich.

Further Reading

The Zimmermann brothers are dealt with directly in Henry-Russell Hitchcock, *German Rococo: The Zimmermann Brothers* (1968). They figure in the major surveys of the period: Nicholas Powell, *From Baroque to Rococo* (1959); John Bourke, *Baroque Churches of Central Europe* (1962); Eberhard Hempel, *Baroque Art and Architecture in Central Europe* (1965); and Henry-Russell Hitchcock, *Rococo Architecture in Southern Germany* (1968). □

Zine el Abidine Ben Ali

A member of the struggle for Tunisian independence, Zine el Abidine Ben Ali (born 1936) held many posts in the new government, rising to the position of prime minister in 1987. On November 7, 1987, he removed the aging and infirm President Habib Bourguiba from office, assuming the position of president.

On November 7, 1987, Zine el Abidine Ben Ali, prime minister of Tunisia, announced on state television that he had assumed the duties of president. He had removed the aged, ill Habib Bourguiba from the presidency, citing mental infirmity as the main reason for his action. Bourguiba had been the chief architect of Tunisian independence from France in 1956 and had led the moderate Arab state as its president since that time. However, the Tunisian ship of state seemed to flounder as Bourguiba aged and lost control of the governmental and political mechanisms which made Tunisia a respected Arab nation. There appeared to be no real successor to Bourguiba, and the party which had guided Tunisia's destiny since independence had atrophied. Tunisia was being swept along with North African and Middle Eastern events. Into this void stepped Zine Ben Ali.

Zine el Abidine Ben Ali was born on September 3, 1936, in the village of Hamman-Sousse in the Sahel, only a few kilometers from the city of Sousse, near the eastern coast. Coming from a modest but respected family, Zine Ben Ali had the opportunity to attend school in Sousse, where he engaged in anti-French, pro-independence activity. Basically, he acted as a runner between local Neo-Destour (Destour was a liberal, constitutional political party) activists in Sousse and members of guerrilla bands operating nearby. When his Neo Destour activities came to the attention of the French colonial administration, Zine Ben Ali was expelled from school and denied admittance to any French-administered school in the colony. After independence in 1956, he was rewarded for his support of the now victorious Neo-Destour Party by being selected for advanced education. There was never any question about Zine Ben Ali's intelligence or his great interest in military matters. Ironically, Zine Ben Ali was selected to go to France, the former colonizer, to study at the difficult, respected InterArms School at Saint-Cyr.

After attending Saint-Cyr, Zine Ben Ali was chosen to attend the well-known French artillery school at ChÉlons-sur-Marne, and then attended various military courses in the United States. Known as an electronic engineer, he began his rise within the structure of the Tunisian government. Zine Ben Ali organized and administered the Tunisian Military Security Department from 1964 until 1974.

This was an important step in his rise to prominence in that it served to make Zine Ben Ali aware of the many internal problems faced by Tunisia as part of the North African and Arab Islamic world. He also gained great insights into the workings of Tunisian politics at the local level, and he became acquainted with those party officials, civil servants, and army officers who would be important in November 1987.

In 1977 Zine Ben Ali was appointed as the director general of national security, a post which he held for three years. It was during this three-year tenure that he became aware of the deteriorating conditions within the Tunisian government and of the outside forces which were threatening Tunisian internal security. There was increasing interest in the charismatic, troublesome Libyan strongman Muammar Qaddaffi (Gaddafi), whose anti-Western, anti-Israeli posturing attracted the attention of many Tunisian youth. There was a rising tide of feeling in support of the Palestinian cause as many Palestinians migrated to Tunisia. Zine Ben Ali tended to interpret his own support for the Palestinian homeland in the light of his anti-colonialist activities prior to Tunisian independence. He became very much aware of the strength of Islamic revivalism in Tunisia, which, in reality, was little different from other Arab states. As the national security chief for Tunisia, Zine Ben Ali was able to see that there were many problems pressing in on a state which appeared to have less and less direction from the top.

From 1980 to 1984 Zine served in an important post as Tunisian ambassador to Poland, and in 1984 he was recalled to Tunis to assume the post of head of national security. One year later, Zine Ben Ali became the minister of national security, and in 1986 he took over the vitally important portfolio of the Interior Ministry. Between 1986 and November of 1987, Zine consolidated his political power, and in October 1987 he became prime minister as well as the secretary general of the PSD, the Destourian Socialist Party. As prime minister he replaced Muhammad Mzali, the man who had been designated to replace the now failing Bourguiba. Mzali had come to the prime ministership with high hopes, but found that external pressures and internal economic, political, and religious discord kept Tunisia from developing viable programs. Bourguiba's health was at a point where he could no longer make rational decisions on a continual basis, and on November 7, 1987, Zine Ben Ali simply removed the old man, placing him under house arrest. Mzali and a few supporters fled to France, but there were few violent reactions to the change of government.

A severe drought in 1988, followed by a locust invasion, resulted in major crop damage and widespread food shortages. Zine took steps to deal with the crisis and ensured domestic order without resorting to massive police or army intervention or repression. In 1989 the French Center for Political and Society Studies gave to Zine Ben Ali the "Man of the Year" award for his work in promoting human rights in Tunisia. The following year, the U.S. State Department asked Congress for authorization to increase funds for assistance to Tunisia for fiscal year 1990. The American perception, as expressed by official opinion, was that Zine Ben Ali was trying to revitalize a nation that had been in serious trouble.

From 1990 to 1992 President Zine emphasized Tunisia's stand against extremism and terrorism. In what he described as measures "beyond simple considerations of security", he used swift and effective police actions to deal a defeating blow to militiant Islamic groups, sending their leaders into exile. In 1994 Zine was re-elected president in an unopposed election.

For his long time support of youth sports and promotion of olympic values, Zine was presented the Olympic Merit Award in 1996 by the Association of National Olympic Committees. During the same year he welcomed the visiting Pope John Paul II to Tunisia and also received the "Health for All" Gold Medal from the World Health Organization.

During a speech on the 9th anniversary of his accession to the presidency, Zine announced the creation of a political academy thay would help increase popular participation in national domestic issues. In a speech to dedicate the academy, President Zine said; "Accomplishing the tasks ahead, ensuring the success of the comprehensive upgrading of the national economy, and meeting the challenges imposed by competition are all goals that can only be achieved if the political forces assume their mobilizing role."

Further Reading

There have been a few articles which bear upon him, including L.B. Ware, "Ben Ali's Constitutional Coup in Tunisia," and Dirk Vandewalle," From the New State to the New Era: Toward a Second Republic in Tunisia," both in *The Middle East Journal* (Fall 1988), and "Ben Ali Tackles Reforms in Post-Bourguiba Tunisia," *Africa Report* (January-February 1988). Information on Zine and Tunisia can be found in the *Encyclopaedia Arabica*. □

Howard Zinn

American political scientist and historian Howard Zinn (born 1922) was a leading exponent of the New Left perspective in scholarship and a political radical known for his activity in the civil rights and peace movements.

Howard Zinn was born on August 24, 1922, in New York City. During World War II, he served from 1943 to 1945 as a second lieutenant in the United States Army Air Force and participated in bombing missions in Europe. He was awarded an Air Medal and several battle stars. After his discharge from the service he attended New York University and received his bachelor's degree in 1951. He did graduate work in political science at Columbia University, completing his masters degree in 1952 and his Ph.D. in 1958. During this time he was an instructor at Upsala College in East Orange, NJ, from 1953 to 1956.

Zinn's doctoral dissertation on New York Mayor Fiorello LaGuardia's congressional career was published in 1959 as *LaGuardia in Congress.* Zinn portrayed LaGuardia as a feisty liberal Republican who fought for pro-labor legislation and criticized the upper-class bias of his party's economic policies. Although LaGuardia would remain one of his heroes, Zinn's own political views grew much more radical. In Zinn's introduction to his anthology *New Deal Thought* (1965), he argued that President Franklin D. Roosevelt and his leading advisers thwarted a possible American social revolution by pursuing the modest goal of restoring the American middle class to prosperity and rejecting more radical social reform.

Civil Rights Activist

Events in the late 1950s and early 1960s reinforced Zinn's disillusionment with American liberalism. In 1956 he moved to Atlanta, GA, to accept a post as chairman of the department of history and social science at Spelman College, an African-American women's school. During the seven years he taught there, Zinn saw and participated in some of the key events of the civil rights movement. He was shocked by the violence directed at African-Americans and dismayed by the federal government's failure to defend their rights more vigorously. Zinn was critical of President John Kennedy's administration. Though it was regarded as liberal by many Americans, it seemed to Zinn to be weak in response to demands for equality.

Zinn's study of one of the major civil rights organizations, the Student Nonviolent Coordinating Committee, was published as *SNCC: The New Abolitionists* (1964). The book was both an impassioned first-hand description of the civil rights struggle and a cogent historical analysis of the modern movement's links with pre-Civil War abolitionism.

Anti-War Activist

Zinn joined Boston University's Government Department in 1964 and remained a professor of political science there the rest of his career. He became well known in New Left circles for his opposition to United States military involvement in Vietnam. In his book *Vietnam: The Logic of Withdrawal* (1967), he made a powerful case for reversing the Lyndon Johnson administration's policy of escalation. Zinn's role in the peace movement was not limited to his scholarly writings. Throughout the mid-1960s he was active in the American Mobilization Committee's national drive to bring an end to the United States intervention. In February 1968, he travelled to North Vietnam with the radical priest, Father Daniel Berrigan, to secure the release of three American bomber pilots shot down on air raids. As he had done earlier with his experiences in the civil rights movement, Zinn wrote articles that offered a first-hand account of his trip to Hanoi.

Traditional academics scolded Zinn for being partisan about his subject matter. In a collection of his essays, *The Politics of History* (1970), Zinn rejected the view that historical scholarship was objective. He argued that all historical writing was political and that historians should align themselves with humane values. To fail to speak out against evil, he warned, was to be irrelevant and irresponsible. Zinn sought to illustrate the usefulness of a politically engaged approach to history in his essays on World War II, the civil rights movement, and the Vietnam War. They provided examples of how his historical approach worked in practice.

People's Historian

When critics charged that the New Left historians' work was deficient because radical scholars had not produced a full-scale synthesis of American history, Zinn set to work to prove them wrong. Zinn's *A People's History of the United States* (1980), surveyed all of American history from the point of view of the working classes and minority groups. He documented the history of race, sex, and class; the history of civil disobedience; how hopes for a more egalitarian society had been frustrated, and how a small, upper-class elite had retained its hold on power and wealth. "Zinn admits his bias candidly," noted reviewer Luther Spoehr in

Saturday Review "insisting that 'we need some counter force to avoid being crushed into submission.'" Eric Foner, in the *New York Times Book Review,* said the book could be considered "a step toward a coherent new version of American history." In 1984, the book was abridged and updated and republished as *The Twentieth Century: A People's History.*

Zinn remained active in leftist politics and contributed to scholarly journals and popular publications, including *Harper's, Saturday Review* and *The Nation.* With his wife Roslyn, he had two children. He became a professor emeritus at Boston University in 1988. In 1985, he published a play, *Daughter of Venus,* which was first performed at New York's Theatre for New City. In 1990, his book *Declarations of Independence* continued his populist approach to American history.

Further Reading

A brief sketch of Zinn's career appears in Nelson Lichtenstein, editor, *Political Profiles: The Johnson Years* (1976). See also the references cited in the text for Zinn's "personal" approach to current history. Reviews of his major books are in the *New York Times Book Review* (June 4, 1967; February 16, 1969; September 20, 1970; March 2, 1980; July 22, 1984). ☐

Grigori Evseevich Zinoviev

The Soviet politician Grigori Evseevich Zinoviev (1883-1936) served the Russian Communist party in several high positions between 1901 and 1927. Opposed by Stalin, he was executed after a dramatic purge trial.

Although he did not possess Lenin's decisive leadership abilities and strong will, Grigori Zinoviev was a man of intense ambition. An indefatigable and brilliant public speaker, he used his skills in collaboration with V. I. Lenin throughout the prerevolutionary era. To a large extent his senior position within the party elite rested on his reputation as Lenin's closest supporter during the dark and hungry days after the failure of the Revolution of 1905 and before the outbreak of the Revolution of 1917.

Zinoviev, whose real family name was Radomyslsky, was born in the southern Russian town of Elizavetgrad (Kirovgrad). His parents were middle-class Jews able to provide him with an exceptionally good education as well as a financial headstart. In spite of this, as early as 1901 he made his first contacts with the illegal Russian Social Democratic Workers' party. By 1903 he had become a close disciple of Lenin. From that time until the Revolution of 1917, Zinoviev is generally believed to have followed Lenin more closely than any other member of the Bolshevik political leadership.

Early Career

As a consequence of his close affiliation with Lenin and other leading Bolsheviks, Zinoviev was at the center of decision making during the Revolution of 1917. For example, together with Leon Trotsky, Joseph Stalin, and others, he was a member of the first Politburo of the Communist party. As the political position of the Bolsheviks improved during the fall of 1917, plans were laid for a seizure of power. Zinoviev argued forcefully against such plans. When his pleas went unheeded, he made a public appeal which had the effect of betraying the previously secret insurrection to the provisional government. For this, Zinoviev was to be haunted throughout the remainder of his political life with Lenin's epithet of "strikebreaker" of the Revolution.

Immediately following the successful revolution, Zinoviev clashed with Lenin again. At issue was whether the new Bolshevik government could or should survive as a one-party government, as Lenin wanted, or whether it should be a coalition government, including the major leftist parties. Failing to secure their point with the Politburo and the party's Central Committee, several proponents of the coalition government resigned their posts in government and party. Prominent among these was Zinoviev.

A third political crisis which arose at this time concerned the means of concluding Russia's continuing role in the world war. The Soviet leadership was split over whether to go on fighting this costly, losing war or to sue for peace on terms extremely unfavorable to the Revolutionary government. In this issue, Lenin supported the option for peace at virtually any price—a breathing space, as it were, for the Bolshevik government. Zinoviev supported Lenin strongly in this position and was thus able to reestablish close relations with him. From this time until 1925, Zinoviev, as chairman of the Petrograd Soviet, member of both the Politburo and the Executive of the Communist International (Comintern) played a highly visible and authoritative role in Soviet politics.

Struggle for Power

In 1923 Lenin was incapacitated by a cerebral hemorrhage. The Politburo, and later a small group within the Politburo, began making the day-to-day high-level decisions of government in Lenin's absence. Gradually, a triumvirate, consisting of Zinoviev, Lev Kamenev, and Stalin, emerged from the Politburo as a whole, with Zinoviev being recognized as the senior member of this group. As later events were to show, the emergence and maintenance of the triumvirate is to be principally explained by two crucial factors: first, Zinoviev and Kamenev tended to reflect Lenin's attitudes, ideological prejudices, and interests closely, and they were known for this throughout the party; second, all three members were strongly antagonistic to Trotsky and his ambitions to become Lenin's successor. As long as common enemies threatened the interests of the triumvirate, it tended to function cohesively. Difficulties arose, however, when Trotsky was isolated and removed from his position as commissar of war in 1925. Soon, Zinoviev found it increasingly difficult to maintain his position of seniority in the triumvirate. In part this directly resulted from the fact that there was no longer a common enemy against whom Zinoviev, Kamenev, and Stalin could cooperate. In addition, however, it resulted from the fact that Stalin was now cooperating with new allies against Zinoviev and Kamenev.

In the spring of 1926 Zinoviev and his old enemy, Trotsky, found it expedient to stand together against Stalin in a "Joint Opposition." By this time, however, Stalin had deprived both men of their bases of authority within the government and party. Although the Joint Opposition remained a notable force in Soviet politics for a year and a half (spring 1926 to fall 1927), it suffered a decisive defeat within the Communist party apparatus at the Central Committee meeting of July 14-23, 1926. Defeated within the party, the Joint Opposition appealed to the public in Leningrad and Moscow, only to be met with indifference or the hostility of well-organized Stalinist mobs. At a joint meeting of the party's Central Control Commission and the Central Committee (Nov. 14, 1927), Zinoviev and Trotsky were expelled from the party. Shortly thereafter Zinoviev publicly recanted his position and was later readmitted to the party until 1932, when Stalin again found it possible to expel him. This time he was not readmitted until 1933.

Trial and Execution

In December 1934 Sergei Kirov, a close collaborator with Stalin in arranging the downfall of Zinoviev, was assassinated. Almost immediately Zinoviev was expelled again from the party and this time arrested, tried, and sentenced to imprisonment for complicity in the assassination. In 1936 Zinoviev was removed from prison long enough to be tried again for treason in one of the most famous purge trials conducted by Andrei Vishinsky under Stalin's direction. Having admitted to the most humiliating and demeaning acts against the Soviet state and the party, Zinoviev was condemned and executed.

Further Reading

As is the case with most of the old Bolsheviks (except Trotsky), there is little book-length material in English on Zinoviev's life. Lewis Chester and others, *The Zinoviev Letter* (1968), deals with an episode in diplomatic history which has little more than passing significance in Zinoviev's life. His early career and his role in the struggle for power is covered in Isaac Deutscher's works *The Prophet Armed: Trotsky, 1879-1921* (1954) and *The Prophet Unarmed: Trotsky, 1921-1929* (1959). Additional material on Zinoviev and the historical background is in Leonard B. Schapiro, *The Communist Party of the Soviet Union* (1960), and Edward Hallett Carr, *A History of Soviet Russia* (9 vols., 1951-1969). ☐

Count Nikolaus Ludwig von Zinzendorf

Count Nikolaus Ludwig von Zinzendorf (1700-1760), a German-born clergyman of the Moravian denomination, tried to unite the German religious groups in Pennsylvania into one spiritual community.

Nikolaus Ludwig von Zinzendorf was born in Dresden on May 26, 1700. He was a godson of Philipp Jacob Spener, the founder of German Pietism. Zinzendorf was brought up under strong Pietistic influences. As a student at the University of Halle, he joined in organizing the Order of the Grain of Mustard Seed, whose members were pledged to the Pietistic ideal of a life of religious devotion and Christian service instead of belief in a creed.

In loyalty to this pledge, in 1722 Zinzendorf opened his estate at Berthelsdorf to a company of Moravian and Lutheran exiles who became the nucleus of the community of Herrnhut, which was one of the most active centers of missionary activity in the world in its time. After a period of harmony, Zinzendorf was accused of harboring views contrary to those of the Lutheran Church and in 1736 was exiled for ten years. Henceforth he identified himself with the Moravians.

In 1741 Zinzendorf went to America. He arrived in disguise under the name Domine de Thurstein at the Moravian settlement in Bethlehem, Pa. This settlement had formerly been located in Georgia but, through the courtesy of William Penn, had moved into the territory close to settlements of other Pietistic groups: Lutherans, Reformed, Dunk-

ers, Ephrataites, Quakers, Mennonites, and Schwenkfelders. It was Zinzendorf's hope that all these groups could be united in what he called the "Church of God in the Spirit."

Zinzendorf labored diligently and in 1741 called a series of seven synods, in which ministers and representative laymen from each of the sects met to find the fundamental agreements as to the nature of God and the ideals of the Christian life they all shared. This was a noble conception which might have had a chance 2 centuries later, but in 1741 sectarian differences were still too important to these groups for any general basis of unity to be possible. Ardent sectarians in several groups misunderstood Zinzendorf to be attempting an organic union which would have authority over the various sects. Though his ideal was spiritual only, it was too early for such an ideal to be understood, and he finally gave up the project.

Subsequently Zinzendorf explored Indian territory and established Indian missions, several of which were notable among America's earliest attempts to Christianize the Indians. In 1749 he returned to Herrnhut, Germany, and continued to direct the affairs of Nazareth and Bethlehem in Pennsylvania. He died on May 6, 1760.

Further Reading

John Rudolph Weinlick, *Count Zinzendorf* (1956), is a biography. Studies of Zinzendorf are Henry Herman Meyer, *Child Nature and Nurture according to Nicolaus Ludwig von Zinzendorf* (1928), and Arthur James Lewis, *Zinzendorf: The Ecumenical Pioneer* (1962). See also Jacob John Sessler, *Communal Pietism among Early American Moravians* (1933), and Ruth Rouse and Stephen Charles Neill, *A History of the Ecumenical Movement* (1954; 2d ed. 1967), for background. ☐

Florian Znaniecki

Florian Znaniecki (1882-1958) was a Polish-American sociologist and educator who helped to develop concern for a responsible emphasis on subjective aspects of social behavior.

Florian Znaniecki was born near Swiatniki, Poland. After a childhood of broad exposure to foreign languages, he developed an interest in philosophy, which he studied at the universities of Warsaw and Geneva, among others. He received the doctorate at the University of Cracow (1909) and published extensively in Polish during the next five years. While working as director of the Polish Emigrants Protective Association, he was invited by W. I. Thomas to come to the United States and collaborate on a project dealing with Polish migrants. The result was their monumental *The Polish Peasant in Europe and America* (1918-1920).

After World War I, Znaniecki returned to Poland to teach sociology at the University of Poznan, where he founded the *Polish Sociological Review* and the Polish Sociological Institute. He was a visiting professor at Columbia University in 1932-1934 and again in 1939. In 1940 he began a final and happy tenure at the University of Illinois until his retirement in 1950. In 1953 he was elected president of the American Sociological Society.

Znaniecki's first works in English—*Cultural Reality* (1919), *The Laws of Social Psychology* (1925), *The Method of Sociology* (1934), and *Social Actions* (1936)—shared the basic objective of forging a viable connection between sociology and social psychology. In *Cultural Reality,* he emphasized the importance of values as components of social action. This was further developed in *The Polish Peasant,* but he analyzed changes in values, attitudes, and behavior as emergents from the process of social interaction in *Laws of Social Psychology.* Znaniecki then identified the strategy of sociology as seeking patterns in human valuation in four related phenomena—single actions, social relations, social roles of given individuals, and specified social groups. Focusing on social action as the most basic unit, he distinguished the structure of social action into a set of key values: those dealing with other persons, with methods of influence, with responses of others, and with self-evaluation.

Turning from actions to social roles, Znaniecki developed a detailed theory of the origins and specialization of roles around circles of common interest in *The Social Role of the Man of Knowledge* (1940). He illustrated his general theory in accounting for modern nations as cultural units in *Modern Nationalities* (1952).

Znaniecki's most ambitious work, *Cultural Sciences* (1952), tried to combine basic methodology and a general theoretical orientation for sociology. Essentially, he regarded sociology as the study of actions propelled by different kinds of attitudes or tendencies, though he was specially interested in creative or innovative action, which he took to be difficult to explain in causal terms. However, he was unable to complete a complementary volume on his revised systematic theory of social roles. His incomplete manuscript was posthumously published in 1965 as *Social Relations and Social Roles.*

Further Reading

Extended discussions of Znaniecki's work are not available, apart from an unpublished doctoral dissertation by Hyman Frankel, *The Sociological Theory of Florian Znaniecki* (University of Illinois, 1959). A critical summary of *Cultural Sciences* is in Pitirim A. Sorokin, *Sociological Theories of Today* (1966), and a more general summary of his work is in Alvin Boskoff, *Theory in American Sociology* (1969). Znaniecki's daughter, Helen Lopata, appended a biographical sketch to his posthumous work, *Social Relations and Social Roles* (1965).

Additional Sources

Dulczewski, Zygmunt, *Florian Znaniecki: life and work,* Poznan: Wydawn. Poznanskie, 1992. □

Zoë

The Byzantine empress Zoë (ca. 978-1050) and her sister, the last living members of the great Macedonian dynasty, prolonged their house through marriages and independent rule. The frivolities of their court, however, helped hasten the empire's rapid decline.

Zoë was the second of three daughters of Emperor Constantine VIII (reigned 1025-1028), younger brother and unworthy successor to the great Basil II (reigned 976-1025). Little is known of her early life. She remained unmarried until her father lay dying and, with no son to continue the dynasty, sought a son-in-law. Zoë's elder sister, scarred by disease, had become a nun, while her younger sister, Theodora, was unattractive and uninterested in marriage. Zoë herself, still lovely despite her 50 years, eagerly accepted long-delayed conjugality. Her husband, the vain and incompetent aristocrat Romanus III Argyrus, soon tired of her, and his neglect drove her ardently to various lovers.

After Romanus's murder in 1034, Zoë arranged to make one of her lovers his successor as emperor and husband. This replacement, Michael IV the Paphlagonian (reigned 1034-1041), was not without ability and dedication, but he was also of poor health and, in his guilt and remorse, likewise came to neglect Zoë. Kept under careful watch this time, she grudgingly accepted her eclipse and then acquiesced in the succession of his nephew Michael V Calaphates (the Caulker, reigned 1041-1042).

The new emperor, misjudging his position, decided to dispense with this unpredictable old lady and had her bundled off into exile. But he reckoned without the irrational but profound love in which the populace held Zoë, as the last representative of the beloved dynasty. Ferocious rioting staggered Michael V's regime, and he tried the maneuver of bringing Zoë back. But it was too late: driven from the palace, he was murdered by the mobs. Meanwhile, Theodora had been brought out from the confinement into which her jealous sister had placed her, and she was set on the throne by one governmental faction. The two women confronted each other, reconciled, and agreed to rule together. But Zoë was frivolous and irresponsible, while Theodora was dour and aloof; despite some positive efforts, their disagreements prompted the desire within a month for another man at the helm. Theodora again declined marriage, but Zoë, though in her mid-60s, readily accepted a third husband in June 1042. The new choice was another docile aristocrat, a puppet of the civil bureaucrats: Constantine IX Monomachus (reigned 1042-1055), previously one of Zoë's lovers.

Genuinely well-meaning and not unintelligent, but imprudent, prodigal, and disastrously unperceptive as a sovereign, Constantine was Zoë's worst failure among her husbands. No more than politely fond of her, he longed desperately for his beloved mistress, Sclerina, and he soon arranged to bring her to court, installing her openly as his consort. Her ardor perhaps on the wane at last, Zoë accepted this public sharing of her husband and yielded herself to religious ecstasies or to her hobby of making perfumes in her apartments; while Theodora—theoretically also sharing power—settled into the background and devoted herself to hoarding money. After Sclerina died, Constantine replaced her with a new mistress, an Alan princess, who was likewise complacently accepted.

In this appropriately inane court setting, Zoë died in 1050. Constantine mourned her genuinely but consoled himself and reigned on disastrously for some 5 more years. At his death (January 1055) Theodora was left to rule alone, as sovereign in her own exclusive right, for 18 months, until her death in 1056 ended the Macedonian dynasty definitively.

Further Reading

Zoë figures prominently and vividly in the court memoirs of the contemporary scholar and official Michael Psellus, *The Chronographia,* which was translated into English by E. R. A. Sewter (1953). An illuminating commentary on this account by J. B. Bury, "Roman Emperors from Basil II to Isaac Komnenos," is reprinted in his *Selected Essays,* edited by Harold Temperley (1930). A lively sketch of Zoë is in Charles Diehl, *Byzantine Empresses* (trans. 1963), and she is also described in Joseph McCabe, *The Empresses of Constantinople* (1913). For the political context of her career see *The Cambridge Medieval History,* vol. 4 (1923), and the second edition, pt. 1 (1966); George Ostrogorsky, *History of the Byzantine State* (trans. 1956; rev. ed. 1969); and Romilly Jenkins, *Byzantium: The Imperial Centuries* (1966). □

Zog I

Zog I (1895–1961) was an Albanian ruler who fought to defend Albanian autonomy.

Ahmed Bey Zog, originally Zogolli (Zogu), son of the most powerful Muslim chieftain in northern Albania, the head of the Mati tribe, was born in the village of Burgayet. His formal Ottoman education was limited to three years of study, first at the Galata-Serail Lyceum for notables and later at a military school in Bitola (Monastir). Following his training, Zog resided briefly in Constantinople. In 1911 he was called back to Albania to lead his tribe in a revolt against the increasing authority of the Young Turks. The following year he distinguished himself in a campaign against the invading Serbian army. During that conflict Zog fought in defense of Albanian autonomy, and when Albania's independence was proclaimed in the marketplace of Vlorë on November 28, 1912, Zog was among the eighty-some notables present.

Zog was one of the first supporters of the new Albanian state. In March 1914 a German Prince, William of Wied, was selected by the Great Powers as Albania's ruler. Despite Zog's considerable military backing, Prince William was not able to suppress an Italian-sponsored rebellion against his government and he thus fled Albania in September 1914. Having returned to their northern district, Zog and his tribesmen joined the Austrians who penetrated Albania during the early stages of the First World War. Initially the

Austrians awarded Zog with the title of Imperial and Royal Colonel and the Order of Francis Joseph, but later, suspecting him of plotting to restore Albanian independence, they interned him in Vienna until the end of the war. Zog returned to Albania in November 1918 to discover a country overwhelmed by crisis. The nation had been physically devastated by the preceding conflict, central authority was non-existent, and most of Albania was under foreign occupation. In February 1920 an Albanian provisional government was formed in order to organize resistance against the French, Greek, Italian, and Yugoslav plans for the partition of Albania. Zog was appointed interior minister and commander-in-chief of the Albanian armed forces. Due to international diplomatic conditions, and in no small part to Zog's military leadership, Albania succeeded in preserving its territorial integrity, and by November 1921, all foreign occupation forces had withdrawn from Albania.

Taking advantage of his countrymen's admiration of his organizational skills and his proven determination to rid Albania of foreign troops, Zog pursued parliamentary politics as a means to promote his ambitions. In the politically unstable period from 1921 to 1924 Zog advanced his influence at every opportunity through the Albanian military and the Legislative Assembly. After exploiting a number of political crises as his pretext, Zog entered the capital of Tirana at the head of the army in December 1921 and proclaimed martial law. During the following year Zog attempted to crush his opponents which condemned him for governing as a dictator, but opposition to his regime expanded under the leadership of his former parliamentary ally, Fan Stylian Noli. Nevertheless, Zog became prime minister in December 1922. That same month Noli and his supporters left Zog's Popular party to organize an opposition bloc in parliament. After a series of electoral crises, mounting parliamentary and popular opposition, and an assassination attempt against him, Zog resigned from the premiership in February 1924. A new government was formed without Zog, but it was made up of his cronies and it was apparent that Zog continued to rule using the government as his front. Dissatisfaction with Zog's policies was great enough to produce a rebellion against his government. On June 10, 1924, Zog fled to Yugoslavia as insurgents entered Tirana. Zog's rival, Noli, took command of the state and formed a new liberal government. However, in December 1924, with the military backing of the Yugoslavs, Zog returned to Albania and forced Noli into exile.

With the overthrow of the Noli government and the emergence of Zog as Albania's dominant political personality, prospects for the survival of a democratic parliamentary system dimmed. A newly convened parliament under Zog's control proclaimed him president at the close of January 1925. In March of that same year a new constitution was approved which invested the president with virtually dictatorial powers. Despite at least five different uprisings, Zog continued to solidify his authority. On September 1, 1928, Zog realized his ultimate ambition-the parliament unanimously proclaimed Albania a hereditary monarchy and Zog assumed the title of "Zog I, King of the Albanians." Zog's royal dictatorship was characterized by a combination of despotism and Western reform. Although Zog continued to practice oppressive policies, his regime enacted a substantial number of reforms. Western-style civil, commercial, and penal codes were adopted while some modern facilities and technology were introduced into Albania for the first time. A major land-tenure. reform law was approved in 1930, but was never effectively implemented.

Although Zog succeeded in centralizing his regime's political authority, he was incapable of developing Albania's primitive economy with the domestic resources at his disposal-his policies in this sphere eventually led to his downfall. Zog turned to Italy for assistance. Accordingly, in March 1925 Rome and Tirana concluded a far-reaching economic agreement which quickly drew both countries closer together politically as well. By 1927 Italian economic and political influence so dominated Albania that Rome had assumed responsibility for the training and equipping of the Albanian army. During the 1930s Zog attempted on several occasions to lessen Rome's tightening grip on Albania. However, in April 1939, angered by Zog's refusal to transform Albania into an Italian protectorate, Mussolini's forces invaded Albania. The Italian army was met with little resistance, and Zog fled to Greece on April 8, 1939, to join his wife, Geraldine Apponyi of Hungary, whom he had married a year earlier, and his newborn son, Leka. Zog's monarchy came to a formal end on April 12, 1939, when the Albanian parliament abolished the 1928 constitution and proclaimed Albania's union with Rome by offering the crown to the Italian monarch, Victor Emmanuel III. Zog's wartime attempts to gain allied recognition, organize a provisional government, and lead an Albanian resistance movement against the axis from abroad ended unsuccessfully. Until his death outside Paris in 1961, Zog spent most of his very private years in exile in Britain, Egypt, and France. Although Zog's regime ended in failure, it was significant for having established the foundations for a cohesive and centralized Albanian state.

Further Reading

See *King Zog and the Struggle for Stability in Albania*, Bernd Jurgen Fischer (1984). □

Émile Zola

The French novelist Émile Zola (1840-1902) was the foremost proponent of the doctrine of naturalism in literature. He illustrated this doctrine chiefly in a series of 20 novels published between 1871 and 1893 under the general title "Les Rougon-Macquart."

Shortly after his birth in Paris on April 2, 1840, Émile Zola was taken to the south of France by his father, a gifted engineer of Venetian extraction, who had formed a company to supply Aix-en-Provence with a source of fresh water. He died before the project had been completed, leaving his widow to struggle with an increasingly difficult financial situation. Despite this, Émile's boyhood and schooling at Aix were, on the whole, a happy period of his life. He retained a lasting affection for the sunbaked countryside of this part of France. One of his closest friends at school and his companion on many a summer's ramble was Paul Cézanne, the future painter.

Early Years in Paris

In 1858 Zola and his mother moved to Paris, where he completed his rather sketchy education. He never succeeded in passing his *baccalauréat* examinations. For a few years after leaving school, he led a life of poverty verging on destitution. Finally, in 1862, he was given a job in the publishing firm of Hachette, which he kept for 4 years. Here he learned much about the business and promotional sides of publishing and met several distinguished writers, among them the philosopher and literary historian Hippolyte Taine, whose ideas strongly influenced the development of Zola's thought. It was one of Taine's sayings ("Vice and virtue are chemical products like vitriol and sugar") that Zola took as the epigraph of his early novel *Thérèse Raquin* (1867). The formula was well suited to the uncompromising materialism that imbues this macabre story of adultery, murder, and suicide.

"Les Rougon-Macquart"

About 1868-1869, when Zola was working as a freelance journalist, he conceived the idea of writing a series of interlinked novels tracing the lives of various members of a single family whose fortunes were to counterpoint the rise

and fall of the Second Empire (1852-1870). He proposed in particular to demonstrate how the forces of heredity might influence the character and development of each individual descendant of a common ancestress. The scheme enabled him to apportion to each novel the analysis of a particular section of society, ranging from the upper stratum of high finance and ministerial authority down to the suffering masses starving in the slums or toiling in the mines. *Les Rougon-Macquart* was originally planned in ten volumes; but the design was so obviously promising that Zola eventually extended it to twice that number. The volumes were designed as social documents rather than as pure works of fiction, but his powerfully emotive imagination and primitive symbolism conferred on the best of them, nonetheless, many of the qualities of expressionistic prose poetry.

The first six volumes were largely ignored by the critics, although they included some powerful pieces of social satire. For example, *La Curée* (1872) dealt with real estate speculation; *Le Ventre de Paris* (1873) attacked the pusillanimous conservatism of the small-shopkeeper class; and *Son Excellence Eugène Rougon* (1876) was an exposure of political jobbery. Only with the seventh, *L'Assommoir* (1877), did Zola finally produce a best seller that made him one of the most talked of writers in France and one of the most bitterly assailed. The plot of this novel is almost nonexistent. He contented himself with tracing the life story of a simpleminded, good-hearted laundress who lived in a working-class district in the north of Paris. By dint of hard work she achieves at first a modest prosperity, until her husband's increasing fecklessness and addiction to drink drag her down to utter destitution. For the title of his novel Zola used a contemporary slang word for a liquor store. The problem of alcoholism among the poor looms large in the book, as do the related problems of overcrowded housing conditions, prostitution, and the risk of starvation during the periods of prolonged unemployment. Though in no sense a work of propaganda, *L'Assommoir* succeeded in drawing attention to the wretched conditions in which the urban proletariat had been living throughout the 19th century.

Succeeding volumes of the *Rougon-Macquart* cycle included many others that were universally read, even though savagely condemned by conservative critics. *Nana* (1880) dealt with the lives of the demi-mondaines and their wealthy, dissipated clients. The heroine's career was modeled on the careers of a number of successful courtesans of the heyday of the Second Empire. *Germinal* (1885), doubtless Zola's masterpiece, narrated the preliminaries, outbreak, and aftermath of a coal miners' strike in northeast France; it was the first novel in which the possibility of a social revolution launched by the proletariat against the middle classes was seriously mooted. In his descriptions of the dangerous daily labor in the pits and of the rioting of the exasperated strikers, Zola achieved effects of agony and terror of a kind never before realized in literature. *La Terre* (1887) represents his attempt to do for the farm laborer what he had done for the miner in *Germinal*. The picture of rural life he offered was anything but idyllic, rape and murder being shown as the inevitable concomitants of the narrowness of the peasant's horizons and his atavistic land hunger. Finally, *La Débâcle* (1892) gave an epic dignity to the story of France's calamitous defeat at the hands of the Prussians in 1870.

Naturalism in Theory and Practice

The immense sales of his works enabled Zola, by 1878, to purchase a property outside Paris, at Médan, a hamlet where he lived quietly for most of the year, occasionally entertaining the younger writers who made up the vanguard of the short-lived naturalist school. Five of them collaborated with him in the production of a volume of short stories issued in 1880 under the title *Soirées de Médan*. Of these five, the two most talented, Guy de Maupassant and Joris Karl Huysmans, forswore their allegiance shortly afterward. Zola did, however, have important disciples outside France: Giovanni Verga in Italy, Eça de Queiros in Portugal, George Moore in England, and Frank Norris and Stephen Crane in the United States.

Zola set out his fundamental theoretical beliefs in *Le Roman expérimental* (1880), but even he adhered very loosely to them in practice. Naturalism embraced many of the tenets of the older realist movement, such as an interest in average types rather than above-average individuals, the cultivation of a pessimistic and disillusioned outlook, a studious avoidance of surprising incident, and a strict obedience to consequential logic in plot development. The special innovation of naturalism lay in its attempt to fuse science with literature. This meant, in practice, that human behavior had to be interpreted along strictly materialistic or physiological lines ("the soul being absent," as Zola put it) and that the individual was to be shown as totally at the mercy of twin external forces, heredity and environment. The emphasis placed on environment accounts for the immense pains that Zola took to document the setting he proposed to use in any particular novel.

Last Years

Zola's private life was not free of strains. He married in 1870, but this union was childless. Then, in 1888, he set up a second home with a young seamstress, who bore him two children. This unexpected blossoming of domestic happiness probably accounts for the sunnier tone of the books he wrote after the completion of *Les Rougon-Macquart*. They included a trilogy—*Lourdes, Rome,* and *Paris* (1894-1898)—dealing with the conflict between science and religion, and a tetralogy of utopian novels, *Les Quatre Évangiles,* of which only the first three were completed.

Zola's dramatic intervention on behalf of Alfred Dreyfus carried his name even further than had his literary work. Dreyfus, a Jewish officer in the French army, had been wrongfully condemned for espionage in 1894, and with much courage and recklessness of consequences Zola challenged the findings of the court-martial in an open letter to the President of the Republic (*J'accuse,* Jan. 13, 1898). Since his statement charged certain highranking army officers with falsification of evidence, Zola was put on trial. He lost his case, spent a year in hiding in England, and returned to France on June 5, 1899. His sudden death in Paris on Sept. 29, 1902, from carbon monoxide poisoning may not have been accidental as the inquest found. There is reason to believe that he was the victim of an assassination plot engineered by a few of the more fanatical of his political enemies.

Further Reading

The most detailed and authoritative study of Zola's life and work is F. W. J. Hemmings, *Émile Zola* (1953; 2d rev. ed. 1966). Other good general studies are Angus Wilson, *Émile Zola: An Introductory Study of His Novels* (1952), and Elliott M. Grant, *Émile Zola* (1966). John C. Lapp, *Zola before the "Rougon-Macquart"* (1964), is a highly suggestive study of Zola's early writings. An excellent brief account of the different aspects of Zola's literary method, with illustrative extracts, is Philip D. Walker, *Émile Zola* (1968). □

William Zorach

William Zorach (1887-1966), American sculptor and painter, sought to vitalize the traditional figurative sculpture by turning to African, Egyptian, and Near Eastern art for inspiration. He pioneered in carving directly in wood and stone.

William Zorach was born in Eurberg, Lithuania. His father emigrated to America in the hope of bettering his condition. The Zorachs settled in Ohio, and William attended the public schools. In 1903 he went to Cleveland to learn a trade and attended art school at night. He studied painting at the National Academy of Design in New York City (1907-1910) and then went to Paris. There he saw his first modern art and was particularly attracted to cubism. Before long Zorach was painting abstractly. In 1911 he returned to America. Two of his paintings were accepted for the famous 1913 Armory Show in New York.

In 1917 Zorach made his first sculpture. Though it was done merely as a diversion, he was soon devoting himself entirely to carving. One of his early works, *Two Children* (a mahogany, 1922), was successful enough to convince him to make sculpture a full-time occupation. In 1924 he executed his first piece in stone: a portrait head of his wife.

Though Zorach was completely self-taught as a sculptor, he knew what he wanted. "Real sculpture," he said in 1925, "is something monumental, something hewn from solid mass, something with repose, with inner and outer form, with strength and power." Such qualities are seen in *Child with Cat* (1926). Carved from Tennessee marble, it is compact and simple. The quality of the stone as a hard, resisting material is not violated—that is, not made to suggest flesh, fur, hair, or any other substance.

Zorach had his first one-man show in 1924. In 1929 he accepted a post at the Art Students' League, where he taught for more than 30 years. He received national attention with his *Mother and Child* (1931), a monumental marble. He began receiving commissions for monumental pieces, among them *Benjamin Franklin* (1937) for the Post Office

Building, Washington, D.C. His basreliefs for the Mayo Clinic, Rochester, Minn. (1952-1953), are considered among his best efforts in architectural decoration.

During the 1940s Zorach did a series of heads of a monumental character. Best known is his *Head of Christ* (1940). Christ is represented unconventionally as being like a peasant, a tough yet beautiful man. He often returned to favored themes, such as the mother and child in the *Future Generation* (1942-1947) and the lovers in *Youth* (1936) and *Lovers* (1958). Critics found Zorach's later pieces sentimental and less inventive than earlier work.

Further Reading

Zorach's own writings are *Zorach Explains Sculpture* (1947) and *Art Is My Life: The Autobiography of William Zorach* (1967), essential reading for the Zorach scholar. Recommended studies are Paul S. Wingert, *The Sculpture of William Zorach* (1938), and John I. H. Baur, *William Zorach* (1959). □

Zoroaster

Zoroaster (active 1st millennium B.C.) was a prophet of ancient Iran and the founder of the Iranian national religion. Zoroastrianism is ranked with Judaism, Christianity, and Islam among the higher religions originating in the Middle East.

The dates given for Zoroaster by ancient and modern writers differ considerably. The more sober authors have placed him between 1000 and 600 B.C. The latter date conforms to the tradition of the Zoroastrians themselves, who regard Zoroaster as having revealed his religion 258 years before Alexander the Great conquered Iran in 331 B.C. The main sources for the life and career of Zoroaster are the *Avesta,* the sacred book of the Zoroastrians, the oldest and most reliable source; later Zoroastrian literature, among which *Denkart,* an encyclopedic work in Middle Persian, stands out; and non-Zoroastrian works, which include Persian, Arabic, Armenian, and classical histories.

Zoroaster was known among the classic writers chiefly as the initiator of the Magian belief and was regarded as a great sage. The Magians were a priestly class of ancient Iran and were the repository of Persian religious lore and learning. Zoroaster is first mentioned by a Lydian historian of the 5th century B.C. Plato mentions Zoroaster in *Alcibiades* in connection with Magian teachings, and Plutarch gives a summary of Zoroaster's religious doctrine and cosmology.

Only the earliest part of the *Avesta* was composed by the prophet himself. This portion is called *Gathas* (Hymns). The other parts, which include hymns, prayers, litanies, and religious law, were written over a period of perhaps several centuries. The dialect of the *Gathas* is slightly different from the rest of the *Avesta* and somewhat more archaic. The language of the *Avesta* has long been dead. Ambiguities in a number of Avestan passages have given rise to differences of

interpretation and have made some aspects of the prophet's life the subject of heated controversy.

Zoroaster's Career

A brief sketch of the prophet's career, however, may be gleaned from the *Gathas*. In these metrical preachings Zoroaster appears as a human and plausible figure, devoid of many of the mythical and legendary details found in later literature. According to the *Gathas*, Zarathushtra (as Zoroaster is called in the *Avesta*), son of Pourushaspa and from the house of Spitama, is a preacher inspired by and in communion with his Lord, Ahura Mazda. He is distressed at the spread of wickedness and the neglect of truth. He tries to awaken his people to the importance of righteousness and warns them against following false leaders practicing animal sacrifice, mistreating the cattle, and permitting the drinking of *homa* (an intoxicating drink) in the ritual. His exhortations, however, are not heeded. He meets with the indifference of his people and the opposition of the communities' religious leaders. He puts his trust in his Lord, with whom he holds a number of discourses. He seeks the active help and guidance of Ahura Mazda and eventually succeeds in converting King Vishtaspa, who then accords him protection and support.

In later Zoroastrian literature, Zoroaster's life becomes wrapped in marvels and miraculous events. In these sources he is presented as a native of Media in western Iran. Through Doghdova, his mother, he inherits *farnah*, the Divine Glory, without which no Persian king or prophet could succeed. According to the seventh book of the *Denkart*, which gives an account of the miraculous birth and life of the prophet, Ahura Mazda himself intervenes in the selection of the essence of Zoroaster's body and soul from celestial spheres.

Sorcerers and demons, perceiving Zoroaster as a threat to their interests, make several attempts on his life, but he is protected by Ahura Mazda and his aides, the Holy Immortals, who reveal to him the "Good Religion." Harassed by his opponents, he flees to eastern Iran, where he converts the Kianid king, Vishtaspa, to his religion. He marries the daughter of Vishtaspa's good vizier, Frashaoshtra, and gives his own daughter in marriage to Jamaspa, another good vizier of the King. A series of battles against the neighboring infidel tribes follows King Vishtaspa's conversion, and Zoroaster is killed at an altar during one of these battles.

Time and Place of Zoroaster

Agathius (6th century A.D.) was already facing the difficulty of determining the time of Zoroaster when he observed that the Persians said that Zoroaster lived under Hystaspes (Vishtaspa), but that it was not clear whether they meant Darius's father or another Hystaspes. This question has continued into our own day. Whereas Samuel Nyberg placed Zoroaster in a remote period and among primitive people, Ernst Herzfeld (1947) insisted that he was related to the house of the Median kings and that his protector, Vishtaspa, was none other than Darius's father. However, one must follow the convincing argument of W. B. Henning (1951), who upholds the authenticity of the Zoroastrian tradition and places Zoroaster in the court of a king of eastern Iran whose domain was eventually absorbed into the Achaemenid empire. This makes Zoroaster a contemporary of Buddha and Confucius.

As to the native land of the prophet, all the evidence in the *Avesta*, including geographical names, points to eastern Iran as the scene of Zoroaster's activities. It is most probable that his alleged Median origin was a fabrication of the Magi.

Zoroaster's Message

The Zoroastrian religion has gone through different phases, attracting in the course of time many elements from different sources. Among these sources are the pre-Zoroastrian religion of the Iranians and the ritualistic cult of the Magi, but the central element remains the message of Zoroaster himself. It was this message which shaped the new religion and afforded the Iranians spiritual comfort and cohesion for many centuries.

The most characteristic aspect of Zoroaster's faith is belief in dualism. He conceived of two primeval powers active in the universe, Good and Evil. Our world is the scene of their conflict and admixture. The outcome of this conflict, upon which depends the destiny of man, is decided as much by man's choice as by any other factor. The choice is between siding with Ahura Mazda and following the path of truth, or uniting with Angra Mainyu (Ahriman) and following the way of falsehood. In the fateful struggle between Ahura Mazda and Angra Mainyu, it is man and his deeds which hold the balance. It is through the good thoughts, good words, and good deeds of pious men and women that e forces of Good eventually triumph. There will be a day of reckoning when those who have resisted the temptations of Angra Mainyu and have followed the dictates of the "Good Religion" will be blessed.

In assigning this choice to man, Zoroaster raises him to an exalted rank in the scheme of creation. Man's noble position and his positive contribution to the triumph of righteousness is the second important characteristic of Zoroaster's message. His religion is not affected by a notion of original sin or by ascetic tendencies. The raising of children and the planting of trees are stressed as meritorious deeds. Zoroaster's kingdom of God is not necessarily a vision to be realized only in the hereafter.

Zoroaster, who seems to have reacted against a form of monotheism, reveals a striking and original way of thinking. From the *Gathas* we gain the impression of an impassioned preacher who strives for the material and spiritual well-being of his people. The success of his faith bears witness to the pertinence of his message for his people.

Further Reading

An English translation of the Gathas is in Jacques Duchesne-Guillemin, *The Hymns of Zarathustra,* translated from the French by M. Henning (1925), and of the *Avesta* in *The Zend Avesta,* translated by James Darmstetter (2d ed. 1895). A. V. Williams Jackson, *Zoroaster: The Prophet of Ancient Iran* (1899), is still the most comprehensive work on the life of Zoroaster. Also useful is Ernst Herzfeld, *Zoroaster and His World* (2 vols., 1947). For a discussion and critique of various opinions on Zoroaster's time and place, the best source is W. B. Henning, *Zoroaster* (1951). A general discussion of Zoroastrianism is Robert C. Zaehner, *The Dawn and Twilight of Zoroastrianism* (1961), which contains useful bibliographies. □

Juan Zorrilla de San Martin

Juan Zorrilla de San Martin (1855-1931), Uruguayan poet and newspaperman, was declared his country's national poet. His work is characterized by patriotic passion and vigor and by great sentiment for a romanticized past.

Juan Zorrilla was born in Montevideo on Dec. 28, 1855. His parents were natives of Spain and very devout Catholics; he maintained both loyalties throughout his life. He studied in the *colegio* (grade school) of the Jesuit order in Santa Fé, Argentina, and the school of the Bayon Fathers in Montevideo. His father sent him to study law at the National University in Santiago, Chile, because the anti-Catholic atmosphere of Montevideo at that time offended his family.

Zorrilla began writing nationalist and patriotic poetry and prose while in Santiago. His first prose epic, *Ituzaingó* (1874), commemorated a battle of that name, fought in 1828, which was vital to Uruguayan independence. He and other students wrote for a literary journal, *Estrella de Chile,* which appeared infrequently. Zorrilla's first collection of Poems, *Notas de un himno* (1876), met with critical acclaim.

In 1877 Zorrilla received his law degree. The following year he returned to Montevideo and was appointed a justice of the peace, a post he held for 6 months. He founded and became the editor of *El Bien Público,* a proclerical newspaper, which he used partially as a base from which to attack the dictatorship of Máximo Santos. Zorrilla's *La leyenda pátria* (1879) is a lyrical poem in praise of his nation, and *Jesuitas* (1879) is a collection of essays in support of that religious order. In 1880 he won the chair of general literature in the University of Montevideo by a *concurso* (competitive application), and he also became an instructor of natural law in the Liceo Universitario of the city. Santos eventually ordered Zorrilla removed from his teaching posts and harassed him; he fled to Buenos Aires in 1885 and remained there until 1887 when Santos resigned.

Zorrilla spent seven years working on *Tabaré* (1888), an epic poem in three books. This major piece, published in Paris, relates the struggle for survival of the region's indigenous way of life and its eventual extermination. It established him in the Spanish literary world as a major writer; the legend later was retold in operatic from by the Spanish composer Tomás Bretón. Zorrilla was elected to the Academia de la Lengua of Madrid as an individual correspondent.

Zorrilla's career in public affairs began at this time. He served briefly in the Chamber of Deputies after being elected in 1888. In 1891 he was appointed minister plenipotentiary to Spain; while in Madrid he took an active part

in the city's intellectual life and in the 400th anniversary of Columbus's discovery of the Americas. Zorrilla traveled widely in Europe and served briefly as chargé d'affaires in Paris.

In 1898 Zorrilla returned to Montevideo, resumed the editorship of *El Bien Público,* and won the chair of international and public law in the university. In 1903 he acted briefly as chief of the Office of Emission of Currency in the Banco de la República. The year 1910 was the centennial of José Artigas's declaration of Uruguay independence; on commission from the government, Zorrilla published *La epopeya de Artigas.*

Late in life, Zorrilla was honored by the Pope for service and loyalty to the Church and for his Catholic activities. While president of the Club Católico Oriental in Montevideo, Zorrilla also maintained his deeply pro-Spanish attitudes. Having been twice widowed, he left 13 living children on his death in Montevideo on Nov. 4, 1931.

Zorrilla's work was acclaimed widely for its lyricism, dedication to the values of Catholic Hispanism, and patriotic fervor. His work was not abstractly romantic but sought to recount the glories of an era of heroism and idealism. He blended history and creativity in the form of legend and became a principal spokesman for conservative and traditional standards against the populist and modernizing standards that swept the country during his lifetime.

Further Reading

Zorrilla's *Tabaré: An Indian Legend of Uruguay* (trans. 1956) has an introduction and biographical foreword by Enrique Anderson-Imbert. Anderson-Imbert's *Spanish-American Literature: A History* (1954; trans. 1963; 2d ed., 2 vols., 1969) also discusses Zorrilla and is recommended for general historical background. □

Zoser

Zoser (active ca. 2686 B.C.) was the first king of the Third Dynasty, which ushered in Egypt's first golden age, the Old Kingdom.

Zoser is always described on his monuments as the "Horus Neteryerkhet." In the so-called Turin Canon of Kings, a hieratic papyrus dating from about the reign of Ramses II, his importance as the founder of a new epoch (Third Dynasty, 2686-2613 B.C.) is noted by the exceptional use of red ink in writing his name. According to the Turin list, he reigned for 19 years, but this period seems much too short for the erection of his vast monument, the Step Pyramid. The Ptolemaic historian Manetho allots him a reign of 29 years.

Zoser's main claim to fame is his Step Pyramid at Saqqara, overlooking the ancient capital city of Memphis. The man responsible for its conception and construction was Zoser's architect Imhotep. Known to the Greeks as Imouthes, he became a legendary figure to later generations

of Egyptians, who looked upon him not only as an architect but also as a learned physician and astronomer. In the Saite period (663-525 B.C.) he was deified and he was identified by the Greeks with their own god of medicine, Asklepios (Aesculapius).

The Step Pyramid was the dominant edifice of a large complex of stone buildings and courtyards which were intended for various ceremonies in connection with the afterlife of Zoser. Its base measurements were approximately 411 feet from east to west and 358 feet from north to south. In its final form it rose in six unequal stages to a height of 204 feet. The substructure of the pyramid consists of a deep shaft which gives access to a maze of corridors and rooms without parallel in other pyramids of the Old Kingdom.

The pyramid and the related complex of buildings were enclosed by a massive stone wall, covering an area approximately 597 yards from north to south and 304 yards from east to west. Limestone from the Tura quarries on the east side of the Nile was used for the outer facing of the buildings, and local stone for the inner cores.

A large brick mastaba at Bêt Khallâf in Upper Egypt may also have been constructed for Zoser, possibly as a cenotaph. At Wadi Maghâra in the Sinai Peninsula is a relief depicting Zoser smiting the Bedouin of the region. A lengthy rock inscription of Ptolemaic date on the island of Sehêl in the First Cataract of the Nile recounts how, through the counsel of Imhotep, Zoser brought to an end a seven-year famine which had afflicted Egypt by presenting to the ram-headed god Khnum of Elephantine, who controlled the Nile inundation, the stretch of territory in Lower Nubia known in Greek as the Dodekaschoinos. The historical accuracy of this inscription is a matter of debate.

Further Reading

The development and main features of the Step Pyramid complex are discussed by Earl Baldwin Smith, *Egyptian Architecture as Cultural Expression* (1938). On Imhotep and his career see Jamieson B. Hurry, *Imhotep: The Vizier and Physician of King Zoser* (1928). The mastaba at Bêt Khallâf is described by the excavator, John Garstang, *Mahasna and Bêt Khallâf* (1903). □

Juan de Zumárraga

The Spanish churchman Juan de Zumárraga (ca. 1468-1548), first bishop and first archbishop of Mexico, was an outstanding representative of a group of 16th-century Spanish clergy in America who combined missionary zeal, a sensitive social conscience, and love of learning.

Juan de Zumárraga was born in Tavira de Durango, Vizcaya. Entering the Franciscan order as a youth, he rose in its ranks and in 1527 was appointed first bishop of Mexico. Soon after his arrival in Mexico in 1528, he clashed with the *audiencia* (a court with executive functions) which Charles V had appointed to govern Mexico in place of Hernan Cortés. The judges proved to be greedy and corrupt men whose main concern was to enrich themselves at the expense of the Indians and the Cortés faction. Since Zumárraga combined with his episcopal office that of protector of the Indians, he attempted to put an end to the abuses committed against the natives by the *audiencia,* but in vain.

The quarrel between Zumárraga and the judges reached such a pitch that he excommunicated the offenders and placed Mexico City under interdict. Summoned to Spain in 1532 to justify his action, he did so with entire success. The first *audiencia,* meanwhile, had been removed and replaced with able and conscientious judges with whom Zumárraga maintained excellent relations.

Despite his concern for Indian welfare, Zumárraga did not oppose the *encomienda* (the assignment to a Spanish colonist of a group of Indians who were to serve him with tribute and labor). He believed that this system, properly regulated, could be beneficial to both Spaniards and Indians.

From 1535 to 1543 Zumárraga served as inquisitor in Mexico. He was extremely active in the pursuit of heresy and other offenses against orthodoxy. The high point of his inquisitorial career was the trial for heresy of the Indian cacique of Texcoco, Don Carlos, whom Zumárraga condemned to death by burning. This excessive severity brought a rebuke from Spain and his removal from the post of inquisitor. Despite the earnest efforts of his principal biographer to clear Zumárraga of the charge of destroying pre-Conquest codices, there is no doubt that he was responsible for the destruction of these and other relics of the Indian past.

Zumárraga made important contributions to the education of Indian youth and to Mexican culture in general. With the aid of Viceroy Antonio de Mendoza he established the famous Colegio de Santa Cruz de Tlatelolco in 1536 to train the sons of Indian chiefs. Before this school began to decline in the second half of the 16th century, it had produced a generation of Indian scholars who assisted Spanish friars in the writing of important works on the history, religion, and customs of the ancient Mexicans. Zumárraga also built hospitals for both races, introduced the printing press to Mexico in 1539, and wrote and published books for the religious instruction of the Indians.

Zumárraga was appointed the first archbishop of Mexico in 1547. He died on June 3, 1548, in Mexico City. Strongly influenced by the Christian humanism of Erasmus and Thomas More, Zumárraga drew heavily on Erasmus's books for the preparation of his own writings, but selectively, using only that material which was clearly orthodox. His thought was a fusion of medieval and Renaissance elements, but the medieval friar in him was certainly dominant.

Further Reading

The classic biography of Zumárraga is in Spanish. Richard E. Greenleaf's excellent *Zumárraga and the Mexican Inquisition, 1536-1543* (1962) covers briefly, but soundly, various

aspects of his career. See also the sections on Zumárraga in Lesley Byrd Simpson, *Many Mexicos* (1941; new ed. 1966), and R. C. Padden, *The Hummingbird and the Hawk: Conquest and Sovereignty in the Valley of Mexico, 1503-1541* (1967). □

Elmo Russell Zumwalt Jr.

Elmo Russell Zumwalt, Jr. (born 1920) was a career Navy officer who became the youngest chief of naval operations in U.S. history. As commander of U.S. naval forces in Vietnam, he ordered the use of the chemical Agent Orange to defoliate the Mekong Delta. His son, who patrolled Vietnamese rivers for the Navy, died from the apparent effects of Agent Orange in 1988.

Elmo Russell (Bud) Zumwalt, Jr., the son of two physicians, Elmo Russell and Frances Zumwalt, was born at Tulare, CA, in the San Joaquin Valley, on November 29, 1920. He had a brother and two sisters. Zumwalt was educated at Tulare High School, where he was a top student, played football, and graduated in 1938. He went to Rutherford Preparatory School (1938-1939), considered a career as an Army physician, then entered the United States Naval Academy. Academically, he was in the top five percent of his class and in the top two percent militarily. His disregard for meaningless regulations placed him near the bottom in conduct. His later reforms as chief of naval operations seemed to reflect his desire to see "common sense" prevail in the Navy.

War and Peacetime Service

Zumwalt graduated in 1942 and went to sea on the destroyer *USS Phelps.* He later served aboard the *USS Robinson.* He rose to full lieutenant, third in command. While on destroyer duty in the Pacific Ocean in World War II, Zumwalt engaged in the battles of Savo Island and Suriago Strait, and the landings on Attu and Kiska. He was awarded the Bronze Star.

At the close of the war Zumwalt took a gunboat seized from the Japanese, *HIJMS Ataka,* with a crew of 20, into Shanghai. They were among the first Americans to arrive. There he met Mouza Coutelais-du-Roche, a woman of Franco-Russian descent. They married and had two sons and a daughter.

After the war Zumwalt was accepted to both medical and law school, but chose a naval career, because he wanted to defend the United States against the threat posed by the Soviet Union. His career from 1945 to 1952 was built around sea service. He served as executive officer on the *USS Saufley* and the *USS Zellars.* Later, he was assistant professor of naval science at the University of North Carolina-Chapel Hill from 1948 to 1950. He returned to the sea as commanding oficer of the destroyer escort *USS Tills,* 1950-1951, and then as navigator on the battleship *USS*

Wisconsin, 1951-1952, in Korean waters during the Korean War.

Zumwalt served in the Navy Department from 1953 to 1955 and from 1957 to 1959, where he gained personnel experience. He commanded the *USS Arnold J. Isbell,* 1955-1957, and the *USS Dewey,* 1959- 1961. He was promoted to captain in 1961 and attended the National War College (1961-1962). There, his lecture on Soviet leaders came to the attention of Paul Nitze, then assistant secretary of the Navy. After completing his War College studies, Zumwalt spent a year in the Office of the Secretary of Defense and then joined Nitze's staff, staying with him when Nitze became secretary of the Navy in 1963.

As executive assistant to Nitze, Zumwalt handled North Atlantic Treaty Organization (NATO) affairs and details of the blockade of Cuba. He was awarded the Legion of Merit and promoted to rear admiral, then left the Pentagon in 1965 to command Cruiser-Destroyer Flotilla Seven. He earned a Gold Star, then returned to the Pentagon to set up the Division of Systems Analysis in the Office of the Chief of Naval Operations (CNO). He frequently went to Capitol Hill on behalf of the CNO, receiving the Distinguished Service Medal (DSM) for his work there.

Vietnam Naval Chief

In September 1968 Zumwalt assumed command of US Naval Forces in Vietnam and the duties of chief, Naval Advisory Group. In October 1968 he was promoted to vice admiral and led the river forces, the "brown-water navy," in

which his son, Elmo Zumwalt 3rd, was a lieutenant. In order to allow better air surveillance of the Mekong Delta, Vice-Admiral Zumwalt ordered the widespread use of the chemical Agent Orange to defoliate the jungles around the delta.

Zumwalt remained as Navy leader in Vietnam until he was selected as Chief of Naval Operations (CNO) in July 1970. At the Pentagon, he became famous for his "Z-grams," directives for implementing reforms in living conditions, terms of leave, and the dress code. He developed grievance systems and ombudsmen for enlisted personel. He also encouraged the development of new vessels, such as surface effect craft and gas turbine gunboats.

Zumwalt soon became alienated from President Richard Nixon's administration. He opposed the administration's cuts in naval spending and its stance on the SALT (Strategic Arms Limitation Treaty) talks with the Soviets. In 1974, Zumwalt accepted an offer to appear on the television program "Meet the Press" to discuss his views on SALT. Nixon ordered James Schlesinger, the secretary of defense, to fire Zumwalt and to court-martial him if he appeared on the show. Schlesinger refused to carry out the order, and Zumwalt retired. Schlesinger spoke at the retirement ceremony and awarded Zumwalt a Gold Star, contrary to White House instructions, according to Zumwalt's memoirs.

Zumwalt's successors as chief of naval operations kept most of his reforms in place. After retirement Zumwalt published his memoirs, in 1976. That year, he ran for the Democratic nomination for U.S. senator from Virginia, but lost. Zumwalt joined numerous corporate boards, continued to act as a spokesman for defense and the Navy, spent a year as a visiting professor at several colleges and universities, and in 1979 opened a consulting firm, Admiral Zumwalt and Associates, Inc.

Agent Orange Legacy

In the 1980s, the slow-acting effects of Agent Orange on thousands of American personnel began to be more noticed, and the controversy over its use became a public issue. Veterans said the highly toxic chemical dioxin in Agent Orange caused cancer and other illnesses, miscarriages and birth defects in their children. In 1983, Elmo Zumwalt 3rd, then a practicing lawyer, was diagnosed with cancer. In an article in the August 24, 1986, *New York Times,* Zumwalt 3d said he was convinced that Agent Orange "is the cause of all the medical problems—nervous disorders, cancer and skin problems—reported by Vietnam veterans" as well as their children's birth defects. Zumwalt's own son, Elmo Russell Zumwalt 4th, suffered from a birth defect that confused his senses. "I realize that what I am saying may imply that my father is responsible for my illness and Russell's disability," Zumwalt 3rd said. "I do not doubt that the saving of American lives was always his first priority. Certainly thousands, perhaps even myself, are alive today because of his decision to use Agent Orange." In the same article, Admiral Zumwalt said: "We checked with the Army and Air Force about the possible injurious effects on humans of Agent Orange, which had been used in other defoliation efforts. We were told there were none. . . . Knowing what I know now, I still would have ordered the defoliation to achieve the objectives it did, of reducing casualties. But that does not ease the sorrow I feel for Elmo, or the anguish his illness, and Russell's disability, give me." In 1986, the Zumwalts wrote a book, *My Father, My Son*, and it was made into a television movie with the same title.

On June 30, 1988, the U.S. Supreme Court let stand a $240 million settlement between Vietnam veterans and the manufacturers of Agent Orange. On August 13, 1988, Elmo Zumwalt 3rd died of cancer at his home in Fayetteville, North Carolina.

Further Reading

Zumwalt is listed in Roger J. Spiller, editor, *Dictionary of American Military Biography* (1984), Vol. 111. His memoirs, a controversial work, is the principal source for his views on his tour as chief of naval operations: Elmo R. Zumwalt, Jr., *On Watch: A Memoir* (1976). Also of interest is Admiral Elmo Zumwalt, Jr., and Lieutenant Elmo Zumwalt, III, with John Pekkanen, *My Father, My Son* (1986). □

Leopold Zunz

The German-born Jewish scholar Leopold Zunz (1794-1886) was the founder of modern historical and philological study of Judaism.

Leopold Zunz was born at Lippe, Detmold, on Aug. 10, 1794. Educated in Wolfenbüttel at the Samson Free School, he went on to study classics and history at Berlin University. Initially (1824-1831) he earned his livelihood as the editor of a newspaper (*Hande-Spenersche Zeitung*). Then he became teacher and school principal at the Jewish Teachers Seminary, Berlin (1840-1850). In later years he devoted most of his time to historical research and scientific writings.

Zunz was a direct product of the "Century of Lights," the 18th century, and of the civil and intellectual enlightenment and enfranchisement which Moses Mendelssohn and others made possible. Indeed, Zunz did for the history and the literature of Judaism what Mendelssohn had done for Jewish theology and philosophy. Both applied a cultured and liberally educated mind to the ancient heritage of Judaism and rabbinic literature and theology. Zunz and Mendelssohn were only two of a group of writers and thinkers in the 19th and 18th centuries who fought for a greater liberalism within Judaism and between Judaism and Christianity. It was all part of the Enlightenment headed by the French *encyclopédistes* and fomented by Gotthold Ephraim Lessing (his *Nathan der Weise* was published in 1779), the Prussian C. W. von Duhm, and others in France, England, and Austria.

Before Zunz's time, Jewish writings and literary works had never been subjected to "modern" methods of historical and literary criticism and research. For this reason, it had been thought that the main body of Jewish thought was of a static character with little or no relation to the changing social and cultural circumstances of each new era. Jewish orthodox traditionalism helped to confirm this view. Zunz's studies changed this. He proceeded on the principle that what was essential in Judaism must and does remain inviolate but that continual reform and renewal must take place. Zunz achieved his purpose through a series of published studies. In 1832 he published *Die Gottesdienstlichen Vorträge der Juden*. This was a study of the inner development of Hebrew literature against the background of concrete historical events. His method was new; the wealth of historical and philological details brought to bear on Hebrew literature was new. He followed this with his German translation of the Hebrew Bible (1837).

In 1845 Zunz published *Zur Geschichte und Literatur*. In this he not only located medieval Jewish literary works within the general context of European literature; he successfully demonstrated the inner relationships and mutual influences exercised between the various phases of Jewish religious speculation and thought throughout the different literary types: Talmud, synagogal poetry, Cabala, and so on. Zunz took up synagogal poetry in three subsequent works analyzing the poems as a literary genre and relating them to other Hebrew forms, to European forms, and to historical events. Zunz's other works were published in three volumes as *Gesammelte Schriften* (1875-1876). He died in Berlin on March 18, 1886.

Further Reading

Some information on Zunz appears in Heinrich H. Graetz, *History of the Jews* (6 vols., 1891-1898), and Solomon Schecter, *Studies in Judaism, Series III* (1924). □

Francisco de Zurbarán

Francisco de Zurbarán (1598-1644), a Spanish painter in the baroque style, was among the foremost artists of Spain's Golden Century.

Francisco de Zurbarán was born in Fuentes de Cantos, Badajoz Province (Estremadura), and baptized on Nov. 7, 1598. His father was a prosperous shopkeeper of Basque descent. In 1614 Zurbarán was in Seville, apprenticed to a mediocre painter of images, Pedro Díaz de Villanueva. Zurbarán opened a workshop in Llerena in 1617 and married an heiress older than himself. She died after having three children. He contracted a second marriage with a widow in 1623.

During his 11 years in Llerena, Zurbarán's piety was influenced by Spanish Quietism, a religious movement that taught inner withdrawal, the discovery of God in humbly submissive silence, and the use of penitential exercises to subdue the senses and calm the intellect. Although this influence had a profound effect upon his art, it in no way limited his artistic activities. The contracts for this period are so numerous that he would have been obliged to assign many of them to assistants. In addition, he was commuting to Seville (a 2-day trip) to execute works for the Dominican, Trinitarian, Mercedarian, and Franciscan monasteries.

In 1629 the Seville Town Council persuaded Zurbarán to move his workshop to their city. He arrived with his wife, children, and eight servants. The following year the painters' Guild of St. Luke ordered him to submit to an examination; he refused, and the town council supported him. His patrons continued to be mostly monasteries: the Capuchins, Carthusians, and Jeronymites were added to the list.

In April 1634 the painter Diego Velázquez, who was in charge of the decorations for the new Royal Palace in Madrid, commissioned Zurbarán to execute for the Hall of Realms two battle scenes, which were to belong to a series that included Velázquez's *Surrender of Breda,* and ten Labors of Hercules. (All the paintings, except one battle scene lost in a fire, are now in the Prado.) Zurbarán returned to Seville in November with the honorary title of Painter to the King and the happy memory that Philip IV had called him the king of painters.

Zurbarán was at a peak of creativity and felicity in 1639, when his wife died. His art production declined markedly and his style became more grave. He married for the third time, in 1644, but his artistic star was descending as the popularity of the young Bartolomé Esteban Murillo rose. Lacking sufficient commissions at home, Zurbarán was obliged to produce the majority of his works for South America, particularly Lima and Buenos Aires. With four more children born of his new marriage, he even sold

Flemish landscapes and paints and brushes to the South American market. He continued to produce mostly for South America until 1658, when he decided to try to change his luck in Madrid. His art, however, was little appreciated there, and he died destitute on Aug. 27, 1664.

Zurbarán's art is an anomaly which causes some art historians to dismiss him as second-rate and others to praise him unrestrainedly. This is caused seemingly by a complexity of factors. It all stems, one surmises, from the basic paradox that Zurbarán was essentially a provincial profoundly involved with the infinite. This duality caused his art to be tense with opposites: sophisticated technique and ingenuous primitivism, precise exactitude and transcendent dissimilitude, accurate realism and ineffable mysticism, emphatic corporeality and divine immanence. His rigorous materiality is vibrated by stillness and silence, producing a tremolo audible to the ear of the soul. His saints wear no halos; they mysteriously exhale the breath of divine grace. There is an unabashed frankness in this holy deportment that may disconcert the unready observer. This there's-more-to-me-than-meets-the-eye halo is present even in his still lifes. Martin Soria (1953) was moved to quote Deuteronomy to express the transcendence of *Still Life with Oranges* (1633).

Fundamentally and almost exclusively, Zurbarán was a painter of religious subjects by his own free choice. He has a vast repertoire of monastic canvases. Of his extant works, approximately two-thirds were painted in the 1630s; the other third is about equally divided before and after that decade.

St. Serapion (1628) is an excellent example of Zurbarán's almost reverential fidelity to the physical while achieving his primary objective of expressing imperturbable sanctity. He had a singular preference for representing the Virgin Mary as a young child, and he invented a unique hagiography for individual, standing, female saints who are modishly dressed in 17th-century costumes, for example, *St. Dorothy*. He was an admirable portraitist with the ability to create an impact by a sense of immediacy or presence, as exemplified in *Doctor of Salamanca. St. Luke Painting the Crucifixion* (ca. 1639-1640) is believed to be a self-portrait. St. Luke is shown in half-length in front of his canvas in such a way that he appears to be actually standing beneath the cross at Golgotha. His right hand holds a long-handled brush against his chest; in his left, he holds the palette; his head is turned in profile, raised toward Christ. The attitude is one appropriate to Quietism, humble and contemplative.

Further Reading

The majority of sources on Zurbarán are in Spanish. A major study in English is Martin S. Soria, *The Paintings of Zurbarán* (1955). Jacques Lassaigne, *Spanish Painting* (2 vols., 1952), has a good discussion of Zurbarán and is recommended for general background.

Additional Sources

Zurbarán, Francisco, *Zurbarán, 1598-1664,* New York: Rizzoli, 1977. □

Ellen Taaffe Zwilich

Ellen Taaffe Zwilich (born 1939) was a highly regarded American composer who received the Pulitzer Prize for Music in 1983 for her *Symphony No. 1* (*Three Movements for Orchestra*). Her style of composition is lyrical, well-constructed, and appealing, combining modern tonal language with older compositional devices.

Zwilich was born in Miami, Florida, in 1939 and began writing music when she was ten years old. She received her B.M. in 1956 and her M.M. in 1962 from Florida State University and then went to New York to attend the Juilliard School. While there she studied under Elliot Carter and Roger Sessions and in 1970 was the first woman to receive a doctorate in composition from the school. She also studied the violin under Richard Burgin and Ivan Galamian, and her ability as a violinist earned her a place in the American Symphony Orchestra under Leopold Stokowski. This experience as an orchestral player affected her attitude toward composition. As she said, "Ultimately, the player is the life-blood of the music, and when I write, I think instrumentally. I never write a piece unless I am dying to write for that particular combination, and if I am writing for orchestra, I want to exploit it. There's a whole stage full of virtuosos! I have great respect for instruments and performers."

In recognition of her talents she received many awards, grants, and commissions and was able to live on her earnings as a composer without the necessity of teaching or performing. She received the Marion Freschl Prize three times while she was studying at Juilliard, the Elizabeth Sprague Coolidge Chamber Music Prize in 1974, the National Endowment for the Arts composer fellowship grant in 1976 for a concerto for violin, the International Composition Competition "J.B. Viotti" Gold Medal in 1975, and a Martha Baird Rockefeller Fund for Music grant to record the String Quartet in 1977. In 1983 she became the first woman to receive the Pulitzer Prize for Music. Later she received a Guggenheim fellowship.

Orchestral Works

The piece for which Ellen Zwilich received the Pulitzer Prize—*Symphony No. 1* (*Three Movements for Orchestra*)—illustrates how her style of composition, although influenced by Stravinsky, Bartók, and Shostakovich, was independent of any one source of inspiration. "I live in a time of enormous variety," she said, "where I have access to music of all kinds and places and times. The idea of influence was more germane when there was a monolithic art world, but there is too much available now to speak of 'direction' in music." In her *Symphony No. 1* Zwilich created a piece with long lyrical lines and simple motivic ideas which, though reminiscent of late romantic music, is thoroughly modern and reflective of her personal style.

She completed *Symposium for Orchestra* in 1972, and it was first performed by the Juilliard Orchestra under Pierre Boulez in 1975. This piece was chosen to be the official U.S. entry in the International Society for Contemporary Music World Music Days in Paris, France. It is a one movement piece for orchestra in which the symposium consists of discussion of a musical topic by various instruments of the orchestra. Thus an opening statement is presented and varied, elaborated, and treated to rather abstract permutations. It is immediately accessible at the first hearing, the structure being lucidly presented, thus allowing the imaginative interplay of the orchestra to be foremost in the audience's mind.

The *Prologue and Variations for String Orchestra* (1983) is a short piece, built on the interval of a minor second. For all its brevity, it is richly expressive. The Indianapolis Symphony Orchestra commissioned Zwilich to write *Celebration for Orchestra* (1984) for the inaugural concerts of the Circle Theatre in Indianapolis. Zwilich included in the piece the musical image of bells as evocative of celebration. In addition, she viewed the work as a kind of test piece for the new hall, creating a wide range of sonority and volume within the composition. The *Symphony No. 2* (*Cello Symphony*) (1985) was written on commission for the San Francisco Symphony. In 1987 Zwilich wrote *Images for Two Pianos and Orchestra* on commission for the opening of the National Museum for Women in the Arts in Washington, D.C. It conveyed the moods of the works of five artists—Alice Bailly, Suzanne Valadon, Alma Thomas, Elaine de Kooning, and Helen Frankenthaler.

Chamber Music

The large number of compositions she has written for chamber groups attests to her ability to explore the different sounds possible in small groups. She had a close relationship with the Boston Musica Viva chamber ensemble directed by Richard Pittman. They commissioned several works, one of which was the *Chamber Symphony,* which they played on their European tour in 1981 and was written shortly after the sudden death of the violinist Joseph Zwilich, husband of the composer. It is written for flute, violin, viola, cello, and piano and projects an elegiac quality throughout. Earlier, she composed a *Sonata in Three Movements* (1973) for violin and piano for her husband, which he recorded. In 1974 she wrote a *String Quartet* which Andrew Frank characterized as "brimming with wonderfully musical ideas. The writing for the four instruments is masterly, idiomatic, and resourceful, while happily avoiding cliches so commonly found in much of the contemporary string quartet literature." The *Clarino Quartet* (1977) was performed first by the Minnesota Orchestra trumpet section in St. Paul and also at the 1979 Festival of Contemporary Music at Tanglewood. It is written for B-flat piccolo and D, C, and B-flat trumpets and is divided into three movements: Maestoso/allegro vivo, Largo, and Veloce. It also lends itself to performance by a clarinet quartet. The writing is virtuosic and varied so that the timbres of the different instruments are blended with imagination.

The *String Trio* (1982) is in three movements that contain the same musical idea—a regular pulsation underlying a melodic theme. The use of cyclic themes and the consequent variations are characteristic of much of Zwilich's writing. In her own words, she had "been developing techniques that combine modern principles of continuous variation with other (but still immensely satisfying) principles, such as melodic and pitch recurrence and clearly defined areas of contrast. Thus, while the *String Trio* is in three movements of differing character (Vivace, Adagio, Presto [Lento]) the whole piece is generated by the same musical material and the cyclical quality of the work will perhaps be recognizable on first hearing, even before the epilogue which emphasizes it." The *Divertimento for Flute, Clarinet, Violin and Cello* (1983), commissioned by the New York State Music Teachers Association, is a light piece in four movements. The *Fantasy for Harpsichord* (1983) was commissioned by Linda Kobler for her debut at Carnegie Hall.

Intrada (1983) was commissioned by the DaCapo Chamber Players with funds provided by Chamber Music America. It was conceived as an overture to an evenings' program of music, and it serves to present the instruments—in this case flute/piccolo, clarinet, violin, cello, and piano—in a vivid way to the audience. The Chamber Music Society of Lincoln Center commissioned the *Double Quartet for Strings* (1984), which combines and contrasts the two groups of instruments. In the first and last movements, they are presented as a unit, but in the second and third, the divisions between the instruments surface. *New York Times* critic Donal Henahan wrote of the quartet ". . . throughout her piece Mrs. Zwilich displayed clear-eyed maturity and a

rare sense of balance. She writes music that pleases the ear and yet has spine." A National Endowment for the Arts Consortium Commission enabled Zwilich to write the *Chamber Concerto for Trumpet and 5 Players,* which was performed in several American cities.

Vocal Music

Zwilich's vocal works use a variety of texts. Poems by Sandor Petöfi provide the text for the songs *Érik a Gabona* (1976) and *Emlékezet* (1978). The second of the two songs was commissioned by the Hungarian singer Terézia Csajbók and is written for soprano and piano. In addition, Zwilich wrote two works based on poems by Hermann Hesse, *Einsame Nacht* (1971) and *Im Nebel* (1972). The first piece is a song cycle for baritone and piano and the second for contralto and piano. *Trompeten* (1974) is based on a text by Georg Trakl which Zwilich translated and set to music for soprano and piano. *Passages* (1981) is a work for soprano and chamber ensemble which sets to music the poems of A. R. Ammons. It was performed frequently in the United States and abroad in this version and also in an orchestral one.

Zwilich's wide ranging musical interests and creative talents were evident in her 1995 *American Concerto* for trumpet and orchestra. The work was created for Doc Severinsen, who premiered the jazz styled concerto with the Buffalo Philharmonic. Zwilich described Severinsen as a "killer trumpet player." A long time fan of the Peanuts comic strip, she composed *Peanuts Gallery* (1997) with the blessings of Charles Schultz, the strips' creator. After a world premiere at New York City's Carnegie Hall, it was reported that both 5-year-olds and adults were cheering.

Further Reading

Zwilich was at the beginning of her career as a composer in 1985, and there are no books yet written about her or about her music. Some of her works have been recorded by Northeastern, Cambridge, and New World records and are good recordings, well worth listening to. Reviews of premieres and performances of her compositions can be found in general publications such as *Time* and *Newsweek.* Reviews of recordings of her works by various orchestras can be found in the *American Record Guide.* □

Huldreich Zwingli

The Swiss Protestant reformer Huldreich Zwingli (1484-1531) paved the way for the Swiss Reformation. His influence on the church-state relations of the cantons that became Protestant was profound and durable.

An exact contemporary of Martin Luther, Huldreich Zwingli experienced and contributed to the profound changes in religious and intellectual life that, arising in the early 1500s, permanently affected Western civilization. He was born on Jan. 1, 1484, in the village of Wildhaus, one of ten children. His experience with ecclesiastical traditions came early, through an uncle who was a priest. Huldreich was destined by his parents for the priesthood.

Early Years and Education

Zwingli's education was markedly humanistic. In 1494 he was sent to school at Basel and in 1498 to Bern, where a famous classicist, Heinrich Wölflin, fired a love in him for ancient writers, including the pagans, that he never lost. In 1500 Zwingli entered the University of Vienna to study philosophy, and there too the ideals of humanism were nurtured and deepened in him, for at that time the university boasted the presence of Conradus Celtes, one of the leading scholars of the humanistic tradition. Zwingli also acquired a deep appreciation and understanding of music and learned to play several instruments.

At the age of 18 Zwingli was again in Basel, where he studied theology. In 1506 he received his master's degree and was ordained a priest by the bishop of Constance. After celebrating his first Mass at Wildhaus, he was elected parish priest of Glarus a few miles away. He spent ten years in Glarus, a decade that in several important respects formed the most decisive period of his life. He developed his character as a reformer, his knowledge and love of Greek, his admiration for the great humanist Erasmus, and his bitterness at the corruption in the Church. Zwingli became so enamored of Homer, Pindar, Democritus, and Julius Caesar that he refused to believe that they and other great pagans were unredeemed because they had not known Christ.

By 1516, when Zwingli moved to Einsiedeln in the canton of Schwyz, he was already arriving at doctrinal opinions divergent from those of Rome. He not only attacked such abuses as the sale of indulgences and the proliferation of false relics but also began to speak openly of a religion based only on the Bible. Independently of Luther, Zwingli concluded that the papacy was unfounded in Scriptures and that Church tradition did not have equal weight with the Bible as a source of Christian truth.

Reformation in Zurich

Zwingli's preaching was so impressive that he was asked to become the vicar, or people's priest, of the Grossmünster in Zurich. This city bristled with intellectual activity, and on Dec. 10, 1518, he eagerly accepted the offer. At Zurich, under his leadership, the Swiss Reformation began. He preached against the excessive veneration of saints, the celibacy of the priesthood, and fasting. When his parishioners were accused of eating meat during Lent, he defended them before the city council and wrote a forceful tract on the subject. His stand against the celibacy of the clergy brought down the wrath of the bishop of Constance upon him. In 1523 Zwingli admirably defended his position on this topic with 67 theses presented in a public disputation. The city council not only found itself in accord with him but also voted to sever the canton from the bishop's jurisdiction. Thus Zurich adopted the Reformation.

During the 1520s Zwingli wrote much; not all of his writings were theological. Unlike Luther and John Calvin, the Swiss reformer possessed a profound patriotic element, a quality that caused him to inveigh heavily against the pernicious practice of hiring out soldiers to fight as mercenaries in the wars of other nations. In 1521 he convinced Zurich to abolish this policy.

Zwingli's Theology

The doctrinal matter that set Zwingli apart from Luther on the one hand and Roman Catholicism on the other was that of the Eucharist. Zwingli denied the real presence of Christ in the Host and insisted that the Eucharist was not the repetition of Christ's sacrifice but only a respectful remembrance.

Since Jesus was God as well as man one performance of the act of redemption was enough. Moreover, the Scriptures contain all Christian truth and what cannot be found therein must be ruthlessly cast from the true Church. Thus the concept of purgatory, the hierarchy, the veneration of relics and images, the primacy of the pope, and canon law must all be cast aside. Zwingli expressed these views in the 67 theses of 1523 and in the tract *De vera et falsa religione* of 1525. In general, his theology was absorbed in and superseded by that of Calvin.

Zwingli's disagreement with Luther was fundamental, and after the two reformers met at Marburg in 1529 and had a profitless discussion, it became clear that no unification of their movements could result. Zwingli was also unsuccessful in winning over all of Switzerland to his cause. Uri, Schwyz, Unterwalden, Lucerne, and Zug—the conservative forest cantons—remained faithful to Roman Catholicism and formed a league to fight Protestant movements.

Tensions grew, and civil war threatened in 1529 and then broke out in 1531. Zwingli counseled the war and entered the fray as chaplain at the side of the citizens of Zurich and their allies. He was slain at the battle of Kappel on Oct. 11, 1531. His body was abused by the victorious Catholics, who quartered it and burnt it on a heap of manure.

Further Reading

Studies of Zwingli are S. M. Jackson, *Huldreich Zwingli* (1901), and Oskar Farner, *Zwingli, the Reformer: His Life and Work* (trans. 1952). The clearest exposition of Zwingli's doctrines is in Philip Schaff, *The Swiss Reformation* (1892). Roland H. Bainton, *The Reformation of the Sixteenth Century* (1953), is brief but very helpful. For a charmingly written general account see Preserved Smith, *The Age of the Reformation* (1920).

Additional Sources

Gabler, Ulrich, *Huldrych Zwingli: his life and work,* Philadelphia: Fortress Press, 1986.
Swengel, Jean, *Threads of time,* Shippensburg, PA: Treasure House, 1994. □

Vladimir Kosma Zworykin

The Russian-American physicist and radio engineer Vladimir Kosma Zworykin (1889-1982) made important contributions to the development of television, as well as to the newer field of electronics.

Vladimir Zworykin was born in Mourom, Russia, on July 30, 1889. He is best known for his pioneering work in the development of television.

Early Education and Career

Zworykin received a degree in electrical engineering from the St. Petersburg Institute of Technology in 1912 and a doctorate in physics in 1926 from the University of Pittsburgh. Like many European intellectuals of the 20th century, Zworykin was driven to the United States by the recurrent religious persecution and political repression which rocked Europe and Russia. He came to America in 1920, 3 years after the Russian Revolution, and joined the research staff of Westinghouse Electric and Manufacturing Company in Pittsburgh. In 1930 he went to the Radio Corporation of America (RCA), where he was made director of the electronics research laboratory.

The Race for Television

Zworykin was one of the earliest pioneers in the development of television. Before he left the St. Petersburg laboratory of Boris Rosing in 1919, he had the germ of an idea for an improved television system. When he joined Westinghouse in 1920, he hoped to be able to continue his work but soon discovered that firm was interested only in radio research. He left Pittsburgh to join a small development company in Kansas but returned to Westinghouse in 1923, this time with the agreement that he could continue work on television. According to an interview conducted for the *RCA Engineers Collection,* July 4, 1975, Zworykin details early developments with primitive geometric pictures generated as early as 1923. In that year he applied for a patent on his "Iconoscope," a device which transmitted television images quickly and sharply. It was perhaps the single most important breakthrough in the history of television development. When Westinghouse transferred most of its radio research work to RCA in 1930, he moved over too and continued its development. A PBS documentary series, *The American Experience* titled "Who is Philo T. Farnsworth?" (researched by Alison Trinkl and David Dugan and based partly on the book *Tube: The Invention of Television* by David E. Fisher and Marshal John Fisher) details the race to create a working television. According to the documentary, at the time of Zworykin's transfer to RCA, he met with fellow television pioneer Philo T. Farnsworth. Under the guise of a fellow-researcher, Zworykin spent three days in Farnsworth's lab, and was given almost total access to Farnsworth's technology. After his return to New York, Zworykin's work incorporated many of the innovations that he'd seen at Farnsworth's lab. Zworykin and Farnsworth battled in court for many years before patents were awarded

to both men in the 1930's. But RCA had the marketing might and money to prevail. In 1929, David Sarnoff, Chairman of RCA asked Zworykin how much he thought it would cost to develop a workable system, and Zworykin estimated "$100,000." It ended up costing RCA $40,000,000 before they began turning a profit. Television broadcasts were available in limited areas, at limited times in Berlin, London, Russia and the US prior to World War II. Commercial television was authorized in the United States in 1940, but its growth was held up by World War II. Ironically, Zworykin was unimpressed by the television programming available, terming it in a 1981 interview as "awful."

After Television

During the war Zworykin, like many scientists who specialized in electronics, played an important role in developing new weapons for the military. He served on the Scientific Advisory Board to the Commanding General of the U.S. Army Air Force, as well as on the Ordnance Advisory Committee on Guided Missiles. At the same time he personally directed important research work and served on three subcommittees of the National Defense Research Committee.

After the war Zworykin continued his electronics work and made important contributions to the development of the electron microscope. He was also instrumental in the development of the electric eye used in security systems and automatic door openers, a device to read print to the blind, and electronically controlled missiles and automobiles. In 1952 he was awarded the Edison Medal of the American

Institute of Electrical Engineers for "outstanding contributions to the concept and development of electronic components and systems."

In 1947 he became a vice president of RCA and technical consultant to the RCA Laboratories Division, positions he held until 1954. While most of his career was spent developing television and its electrical components, Zworykin spent his time after retirement from RCA in 1954 as Director of Medical Research at the Medical Electronics Center at the Rockefeller Institute for Medical Research (now Rockefeller University) until 1962.

Personal Information

Zworykin married Tatiana Vasilieff around 1915 and had two children. He emigrated with his family to the United States in 1919, becoming a US citizen in 1924. He was divorced from Vasilieff and married Katherine Polevitsky in 1951. He died on July 29, 1982, one day short of his 93rd birthday.

Further Reading

There is no biography of Zworykin. Some of his work on television is described in John Jewkes, David Sawers, and Richard Stillerman's, *The Sources of Invention* (1958; 2d ed. 1969). The standard book on radio development is W. Rupert MacLaurin's, *Invention and Innovation in the Radio Industry* (1949). The Zworykin interview noted above, a part of the *RCA Engineers Collection* is available on the World Wide Web (circa 1997) at http://www.ieee.org/history_center/oral_histories/abstracts/zworykin21_abstract.html and http://www.ieee.org/history_center/oral_histories/transcripts/zworykin21.html. Additional World Wide Web sites to visit (circa 1997) http://trfn.clpgh.org/nmb/nmbzwkn.htm, and http://www.invent.org/book/book-text/111.html. □